BEST OF
EUROPE

2013

CONTENTS

Germany, Austria & Switzerland

Neustrelitz

POLAND

uruppin

CHSENHAUSEN

Tegel
Berlin   Frankfurt an der Oder
A-10   Potsdam   Schönefeld
andenburg
SANSSOUCI PALACE
A-9
A-13
Rzepin
A-12

ssau   Wittenberg
Elbe
Cottbus   Zary

Ostrow Wielkopolski

Lauchhammer
A-15
Bolesławiec   Legnica   Wrocław

de   Leipzig   MORITZBURG
A-13
Bautzen   Görlitz
Brzeg
Meissen   A-4   Zgorzelec
SILESIA
SAXONY   Dresden   Bad Schandau   Zittau
Opole

auchau   A-4   Chemnitz   Seiffen   Děčín
Nysa

A-72
Plauen
Ústí nad Labem
Litoměřice
TEREZÍN
Náchod
Ruzyně
Hradec Králové

Karlovy Vary   Prague
Lichkov
Cheb
Kutná Hora   CZECH
Olomouc   Štramberk
Mariánské Lázně   E-50   KARLŠTEJN CASTLE
REPUBLIC
Marktredwitz
Plzeň
E-50   E-65   MORAVIA
Kroměříz

A-93
Česká Kubice
BOHEMIA   Tabor
Telč   Brno   Zlín
Furth
Veselí nad Lužnicí
Slavonice   Břeclav
Regensburg
České Budějovice   České Velenice   Gmund
Kuty
Ober-traubling
Český Krumlov
SLOVAKIA

93
Passau   Summerau
WACHAU   Krems
Danube   Durnstein   Danube   Grinzing   Vienna
A-92
Linz
MAUTHAUSEN   Melk   SCHÖNBRUNN PALACE   Bratislava
A
St. Valentin
Puchberg   Eisenstadt   M-1

HERREN-CHIEMSEE   Chiemsee
Attnang-Puchheim   A-1
SCHNEEBERG   A-2
Sopron
senheim
A-8   Salzburg   Bad Ischl
AUSTRIA
ESTERHÁZY PALACE
Berchtesgaden   Hallstatt   Selzthal
Kufstein   Hallein   SALZKAMMERGUT
Szombathely
A-12
Wörgl   Zell am See
Stainach Irdning
Bruck an der Mur
Leoben
INTERHORNALM
Kitzbühel   Piber   Graz
ll
Badgastein
HUNGARY
ENNER
'ASS
GROSS-GLOCKNER PASS
A-10
A-9
Dobbiaco   Lienz   Spittal
Klagenfurt   Spielfeld
ALPE DI SIUSI   Cortina
Villach   Maribor   Nagykanizsa
Tarvisio   VRŠIČ PASS   Jesenice   Bled/Lesce
SLOVENIA   CROATIA

England

LEGEND

═══A24═══	Freeway/Motorway
──	Major Rail Line
✈	Airport
♠	National Park/ Natural Wonder
■	Ruin, Museum, Other Point of Interest
⬛	Castle/Monument/Palace

0 km	50 km	100 km

0 miles		50 miles

Berwick-upon-Tweed
Holy Island
BAMBURGH CASTLE
Alnwick
Newcastle-upon-Tyne
AMISH SEUM
Durham
A1
Middlesbrough
YORK SHIRE LES
Staithes
Grosmont
NORTH YORK MOORS
Whitby
Robin Hood's Bay
EVAULX ABBEY
Thirsk
Hutton-le-Hole
Goathland
CASTLE HOWARD
EDEN CAMP
Pickering
Scarborough
York
Doncaster
Bridlington
ads
Sheffield
M1
Kingston-upon-Hull
Grimsby

North Sea

LAND

MIDLANDS

erby
Lincoln
Newark
Skegness
Nottingham
Boston
The Wash
M1
icester
Stamford
Cromer
Coventry
Peterborough
King's Lynn
Norwich
Great Yarmouth
Warwick
tratford
LDS oreton
Northampton
Ely
EAST
Cambridge
ANGLIA
Oxford
M1
Luton
NHEIM ACE
dcot
Hertford
Stansted
M11
Ipswich
Harwich
M40
Reading
Thames
Windsor
London
City
Greenwich
Colchester
Southend-on-Sea
Heathrow
M3
M23
M20
M2
Whitstable
Ramsgate
Winchester
Gatwick
SISSINGHURST GARDENS
Canterbury
Ostende
Bruges
KENT
Ashford
Folkestone
WHITE CLIFFS OF DOVER
Dover
outhampton
Portsmouth
ARUNDEL
Battle
Rye
Calais
Dunkerque
E40
BELGIUM
E17
FISHBOURNE ROMAN PALACE
Brighton
Hastings
Pevensey
wport le of ight
Newhaven
Alfriston
Beachy Head
Eastbourne
Channel
FRANCE
Lille
E42
A16
A26

Channel

To Esbjerg, Denmark
To Amsterdam, Netherlands
To Hoek van Holland, Netherlands

To Cherbourg France
To Ouistreham, France
To Dieppe, France
To Paris
To Paris
To Brussels

Rick Steves'

BEST OF
EUROPE
2013

AVALON
TRAVEL

INTRODUCTION

Big Ben, the Eiffel Tower, and the Roman Colosseum. Yodeling in the Alps, biking down cobblestone paths, and taking a canal ride under the stars. Michelangelo's *David* and "Mad" King Ludwig's castles. Sunny Riviera beaches, medieval German towns, and Spanish streets that teem with people at night. Pasta and bratwurst, strudel and scones, Parisian crêpes and Tuscan grapes....

Europe offers a rich smorgasbord of cultures. To wrestle it down to a manageable size, this book breaks Europe into its top destinations. It then gives you all the information and opinions necessary to wring the maximum value out of your limited time and money in each location. If you plan to stay for two months or less in Europe, this book is all you need for a blitz trip.

Experiencing Europe's culture, people, and natural wonders economically and hassle-free has been my goal for more than 30 years of traveling, tour guiding, and travel writing. With this book, I pass on to you the lessons I've learned, updated for 2013.

Rick Steves' Best of Europe is the crème de la crème of places featured in my country guidebooks. It's balanced to include a comfortable mix of exciting cities and cozy towns: from Paris, London, and Rome to traffic-free Italian Riviera ports, alpine villages, and mom-and-pop châteaux. It covers the predictable biggies and mixes in a healthy dose of Back Door intimacy. Along with Leonardo in the Louvre, you'll enjoy Caterina in her cantina. I've been selective. For example, rather than listing countless medieval towns, I recommend only the best.

The best is, of course, only my opinion. But after three decades of travel research, I've developed a sixth sense for what travelers enjoy.

Key to This Book

Updates

This book is updated every year, but things change. For the latest, visit www.ricksteves.com/update. For a valuable list of reports and experiences—good and bad—from fellow travelers, check www.ricksteves.com/feedback.

Abbreviations and Times

I use the following symbols and abbreviations in this book:

Sights are rated:

▲▲▲	**Don't miss**
▲▲	**Try hard to see**
▲	**Worthwhile if you can make it**
No rating	**Worth knowing about**

Tourist information offices are abbreviated as **TI,** and bathrooms are **WC**s. To categorize accommodations, I use a **Sleep Code** (described on page 15).

Like Europe, this book uses the **24-hour clock** for schedules. It's the same through 12:00 noon, then keep going: 13:00, 14:00, and so on. For anything over 12, subtract 12 and add p.m. (14:00 is 2:00 p.m.).

When giving **opening times,** I include both peak season and off-season hours if they differ. So, if a museum is listed as "May–Oct daily 9:00–16:00," it should be open from 9 a.m. until 4 p.m. from the first day of May until the last day of October (but expect exceptions).

For **transit** or **tour departures,** I first list the frequency, then the duration. So, a train connection listed as "2/hour, 1.5 hours" departs twice each hour, and the journey lasts an hour and a half.

About This Book

This book is organized by destinations. Each destination is a mini-vacation on its own, filled with exciting sights, strollable neighborhoods, affordable places to stay, and memorable places to eat. In each chapter, you'll find these sections:

Planning Your Time suggests a schedule for how to best use your limited time.

Orientation includes specifics on public transportation, helpful hints, local tour options, easy-to-read maps, and tourist information.

Sights describes the top attractions and includes their cost and hours.

Sleeping describes my favorite hotels, from good-value deals to cushy splurges.

Eating serves up a range of options, from inexpensive eateries to fancy restaurants.

Map Legend

🔭	Viewpoint	✈	Airport	Tunnel	
↑	Entrance	ⓣ	Taxi Stand	Pedestrian Zone	
❸	Tourist Info	🇹	Tram Stop	Railway	
WC	Restroom	🇲	Metro Stop	Ferry/Boat Route	
🏰	Castle	⊖	Tube	Tram	
▪	Statue/Point of Interest	🇻	Vaporetto Stop	Stairs	
🏛	Church	🇹	Traghetto Crossing	Walk/Tour Route	
	Mosque	🇬	Gondola Station	Trail	
	Synagogue	🇦	Alilaguna Stop	Funicular	
◎	Fountain	Ⓑ	Bus Stop	Mtn. Lift	
▲	Mountain Peak	🇵	Parking	Mtn. Rail	
	Park	Ⓢ	S-Tog Station	Cable Car	
	Mtn. Pass	🚌	Harbor Bus	Gondola	
		⛴	Boat Stop		

Use this legend to help you navigate the maps in this book.

Connections outlines your options for traveling to destinations by train, bus, and plane.

The **appendix** has transportation basics, a calling chart, a hotel reservation form, and information on US embassies for the countries in this book.

Browse through this book, choose your favorite destinations, and link them up. Then have a great trip! Traveling like a temporary local and taking advantage of the information here, you'll get the absolute most out of every mile, minute, and dollar. I'm happy you'll be visiting places I know and love, and meeting some of my favorite people.

Planning

This section will help you get started on planning your trip—with advice on trip costs, when to go, and what you should know before you take off.

Travel Smart

Your trip to Europe is like a complex play—easier to follow and to fully appreciate on a second viewing. While no one does the same trip twice to gain that advantage, reading this book's chapters on your intended destinations before your trip accomplishes much the same thing.

Design an itinerary that enables you to visit sights at the best possible times. Note holidays, festivals, specifics on sights, and days when sights are closed. For example, many sights in Florence are closed on Mondays; Tuesdays are bad in Paris. Museums and sights, especially large ones, usually stop admitting people 30–60 minutes before closing time.

Sundays have the same pros and cons as they do for travelers in the US (special events, limited hours, banks and many shops closed, limited public transportation, no rush hour). Saturdays are virtually weekdays, with earlier closing hours and no rush hour. Popular destinations are even more popular on weekends; book ahead for Fridays and Saturdays.

Be sure to mix intense and relaxed periods in your itinerary. To maximize rootedness, minimize one-night stands. It's worth a long drive (or train ride) after dinner to be settled into a town for two nights. Hotels are also more likely to give a good price to someone staying more than one night. Every trip—and every traveler—needs at least a few slack days (for picnics, laundry, people-watching, and so on). Pace yourself. Assume you will return.

Reread this book as you travel, and visit local TIs. Upon arrival in a new town, lay the groundwork for a smooth departure; get the schedule for the train, bus, or boat that you'll take when you depart.

Get online at Internet cafés or your hotel, and buy a phone card or carry a mobile phone: You can find out tourist information, learn the latest on sights (special events, English tour schedule, etc.), book tickets and tours, make reservations, reconfirm hotels, research transportation connections, and keep in touch with your loved ones.

Enjoy the friendliness of the local people. Slow down and ask questions—most locals are eager to point you in their idea of the right direction. Keep a notepad in your pocket to organize your thoughts, note directions, and confirm prices with vendors. Wear your money belt, and figure out how to estimate prices in dollars. Those who expect to travel smart, do.

Trip Costs

Five components make up your trip cost: airfare, surface transportation, room and board, sightseeing and entertainment, and shopping and miscellany.

Airfare: A basic round-trip US-to-Europe flight costs around $700–1,500, depending on where you fly from and when (cheaper in winter), plus another $300–500 in taxes, fuel surcharges, and other fees. Consider saving time and money in Europe by flying into one city and out of another—for example, into London and out of Rome.

Best of Europe Itinerary

300 Miles
500 Kilometers

START
London
Amst.
U
Berlin
Bruges
END
RHINE
Roth.
BAVARIA
Salzburg
Paris
SWISS
ALPS
Vienna
PROVENCE
Venice
Florence
Barcelona
Nice
CINQUE
TERRE
Rome

Surface Transportation: Your best mode of travel depends on the length and scope of your trip. For many, the best option is a Eurail Pass. Train passes are normally available only outside of Europe, though you may save money by simply buying tickets as you go (for more information, see page 1310 of the appendix).

Drivers can figure about $375 per person per week (based on two people splitting the cost of the car, tolls, gas, and insurance). Car rental is cheapest to arrange from the US; for trips of three weeks or more, look into leasing.

Room and Board: You can easily manage in Europe in 2013 on an overall average of $120 a day per person for room and board (more for cities, less for towns). A $120-a-day budget allows an average of $15 for lunch, $5 for a snack, $25 for dinner, and $75 for lodging (based on two people splitting the cost of a $150 double room that includes breakfast). Students and tightwads can enjoy Europe for as little as $60 a day ($30 per hostel bed, $30 for meals and snacks).

Sightseeing and Entertainment: In big cities, figure $10–20 per major sight, $5–10 for minor ones, and $30 for splurge experiences (e.g., tours, concerts, gelato binges). An overall average of $30 a day works for most. Don't skimp here. After all, this category is the driving force behind your trip—you came to sightsee, enjoy,

INTRODUCTION

and experience Europe.

Shopping and Miscellany: Figure $2 per postcard, $3 per coffee and ice-cream cone, and $6 per beer. Shopping can vary in cost from nearly nothing to a small fortune. Good budget travelers find that this category has little to do with assembling a trip full of lifelong and wonderful memories.

Sightseeing Priorities

Only have a week to "see" Europe? You can't, of course, but if you're organized and energetic, you can see the two art-filled cultural capitals of London and Paris plus Europe's most magnificent landscape—the Swiss Alps.

Whether you have just a week, or longer, here are my recommended priorities. These itineraries are fast-paced, but doable by car or train, and each allows about two nights in each spot (I've taken geographical proximity into account). Most work best if you fly in and out of different cities (e.g., into London and out of Vienna).

If you have...

5 days:	Paris, Swiss Alps
7 days, add:	London
10 days, add:	Rome
14 days, add:	Rhine, Amsterdam, Haarlem
18 days, add:	Venice, Florence
24 days, add:	Cinque Terre, Rothenburg, Bavaria
27 days, add:	Salzburg, Hallstatt
33 days, add:	Nice, Provence, Barcelona
38 days, add:	Vienna, Berlin
40 days, add:	Bruges

When to Go

May, June, September, and October are the best travel months. Peak season, July and August, offers the sunniest weather and the most exciting slate of activities—but the worst crowds. During this busy time, it's best to reserve rooms well in advance, particularly in big cities.

During the off-season, October through April, expect generally shorter hours at attractions, more closures for lunchtime (especially at smaller sights), fewer activities, and fewer—if any—guided tours in English. Especially off-season, be sure to confirm opening hours for sights at local tourist information offices.

As a general rule any time of year, the climate north of the Alps is mild (like Seattle), while south of the Alps it's like Arizona. For specifics, see www.worldclimate.com. If you wilt in the heat, avoid the Mediterranean in summer. If you want blue skies in the Alps and Britain, travel during the height of summer.

Rick Steves' Free Audio Europe

If you're bringing a mobile device, be sure to check out **Rick Steves Audio Europe,** where you can download free audio tours and hours of travel interviews (via the Rick Steves Audio Europe smartphone app, www.ricksteves.com/audioeurope, or iTunes).

My self-guided **audio tours** are user-friendly, easy-to-follow, fun, and informative and cover the major sights and neighborhoods in:

Vienna: St. Stephen's Cathedral, Vienna City Walk, and Ringstrasse Tram Tour

Salzburg: Salzburg Town Walk

Paris: Historic Paris Walk, Louvre, Orsay, and Versailles Palace

Rhine: Rhine Castles

London: British Museum, British Library, St. Paul's Cathedral, Westminster Walk, and The City of London Walk

Rome: Colosseum, Forum, Pantheon, St. Peter's Basilica, Sistine Chapel, Trastevere, Jewish Ghetto, and Ostia Antica

Venice: Grand Canal, St. Mark's Square, St. Mark's Basilica, and Frari Church

Florence: Renaissance Walk, Uffizi Gallery, and Accademia

Plan your itinerary to meet your needs. To beat the heat, start in the south in the spring and work your way north. To moderate culture shock, start in Britain and travel south and east.

Know Before You Go

Your trip is more likely to go smoothly if you plan ahead. Check this list of things to arrange while you're still at home.

You need a **passport**—but no visa or shots—to travel to any of the countries in this book. You may be denied entry into certain European countries if your passport is due to expire within three to six months of your ticketed date of return. Get it renewed if you'll be cutting it close. It can take up to six weeks to get or renew a passport (for more on passports, see www.travel.state.gov). Pack a photocopy of your passport in your luggage in case the original is lost or stolen.

Book your rooms well in advance if you'll be traveling during peak season or any major **holidays or festivals** (the lists at www .ricksteves.com/festivals include most national holidays and major festivals, but www.whatsonwhen.com lists more festivals).

Call your **debit- and credit-card companies** to let them know the countries you'll be visiting, to ask about fees, and more (see "Money," later).

Do your homework if you want to buy **travel insurance.** Compare the cost of the insurance to the likelihood of your using it and your potential loss if something goes wrong. Also, check whether your existing insurance (health, homeowners, or renters) covers you and your possessions overseas. For more tips, see www.ricksteves.com/insurance.

If you're planning on **renting a car** in Europe, you'll need your driver's license. In addition, an International Driving Permit is required in Austria, Italy, and Spain. They're available at your local AAA office ($15 plus the cost of two passport-type photos, see www.aaa.com). For information on car-rental insurance, check www.ricksteves.com/cdw. Confirm pick-up hours—many car-rental offices close Saturday afternoon and all day Sunday.

Because **airline carry-on restrictions** are always changing, visit the Transportation Security Administration's website (www.tsa.gov/travelers) for an up-to-date list of what you can bring on the plane with you...and what you must check. Some airlines may restrict you to only one carry-on (no extras like a purse or day-pack); check with your airline.

Practicalities

Emergency and Medical Help: If you get sick, do as many Europeans do and go to a pharmacist for advice. Or ask at your hotel for help—they'll know the nearest medical and emergency services.

Theft or Loss: To replace a passport, you'll need to go in person to an embassy or consulate (see page 1307). If your credit and debit cards disappear, cancel and replace them (see "Damage Control for Lost Cards" on page 12). File a police report, either on the spot or within a day or two; it's required to submit an insurance claim for lost or stolen railpasses or travel gear, and can help with replacing your passport or credit and debit cards. For more information, see www.ricksteves.com/help. Precautionary measures can minimize the effects of loss: Back up photos and other files frequently, and use passwords to protect any sensitive data on your electronic devices.

Time Zones: Most of continental Europe is generally six/nine hours ahead of the East/West Coasts of the US. Britain, which is one hour earlier than most of continental Europe, is five/eight hours ahead of the East/West Coasts. For a handy online time converter, try www.timeanddate.com/worldclock.

Watt's Up? Europe's electrical system is 220 volts, instead of North America's 110 volts. Most newer electronics (such as laptops, battery chargers, and hair dryers) convert automatically, so you won't need a converter, but you will need an adapter plug with two round prongs (or three square prongs in Britain), sold inexpensively at travel stores in the US. Avoid bringing older appliances that don't automatically convert voltage; instead, buy a cheap replacement in Europe.

Discounts: While discounts are not listed in this book, seniors (age 60 and over), students with International Student Identification Cards, teachers with proper identification, and youths under 18 often get discounts—but you have to ask. To get a teacher or student ID card, visit www.statravel.com or www.isic.org.

Additional Online Resources: Shoppers can check on VAT refunds (www.ricksteves.com/vat) and custom rules and duty rates (www.cbp.gov; click on "Travel," then "Know Before You Go"). For information on making calls, see www.ricksteves.com/phoning. For sightseeing tips and museum strategies, check www.ricksteves.com/sights.

Money

This section offers advice on how to pay for purchases on your trip (including getting cash from ATMs and paying with plastic), dealing with lost or stolen cards, and tipping.

What to Bring

Bring both a credit card and a debit card. You'll use the debit card at cash machines (ATMs) to withdraw cash for most purchases, and the credit card to pay for larger items.

For an emergency reserve, bring several hundred dollars in hard cash (in easy-to-exchange $20 bills). Avoid using currency exchange booths (lousy rates and/or outrageous fees); if you have foreign currency to exchange, take it to a bank. (But if you're in France, you'll have to use currency booths—banks won't take dollars.) Don't use traveler's checks—they're not worth the fees or long waits at slow banks.

Cash

Cash is just as desirable in Europe as it is at home. Small businesses (hotels, restaurants, and shops) prefer that you pay your bills with cash. Some vendors will charge you extra for using a credit card, and some won't take credit cards at all. Cash is the best—and sometimes only—way to pay for bus fares, taxis, and local guides.

Throughout Europe, cash machines (ATMs) are the standard way for travelers to get cash. Most ATMs in Europe are located outside of a bank. Try to use the ATM when the branch is open; if your card is munched by a machine, you can immediately go inside for help.

Exchange Rates

1 euro (€) = about $1.40. To roughly convert prices in euros to dollars, add 40 percent: €20 is about $28.

1 British pound (£1) = about $1.60. To convert prices in pounds to dollars, add 60 percent.

1 Swiss franc (SF) = about $1.10. To easily convert prices in Swiss francs to dollars, add 10 percent.

To withdraw money from an ATM, you'll need a debit card (ideally with a Visa or MasterCard logo for maximum usability), plus a PIN code. Know your PIN code in numbers; there are only numbers—no letters—on European keypads. For security, it's best to shield the keypad when entering your PIN at an ATM. Although you can use a credit card for ATM transactions, it's generally more expensive because it's considered a cash advance rather than a withdrawal.

When using an ATM, try to withdraw large sums of money to reduce the number of per-transaction bank fees you'll pay. If the machine refuses your request, try again and select a smaller amount (some cash machines limit the amount you can withdraw—don't take it personally). If that doesn't work, try a different machine. (Be aware that some ATMS will tell you to take your cash within 30 seconds, and if you aren't fast enough, your cash may be sucked back into the machine...and you'll have a hassle trying to get it from the bank.)

It's easier to pay for purchases with smaller bills; if the ATM gives you big bills, try to break them at a major museum or larger store.

Even in Europe, you'll need to keep your cash safe. Use a money belt—a pouch with a strap that you buckle around your waist like a belt and wear under your clothes. Pickpockets target tourists. A money belt provides peace of mind, allowing you to safely carry your passport, credit cards, and lots of cash. Don't waste time every few days tracking down a cash machine—withdraw a week's worth of money, stuff it in your money belt, and travel!

Credit and Debit Cards

For purchases, Visa and MasterCard are more commonly accepted than American Express. Just like at home, credit or debit cards work easily at larger hotels, restaurants, and shops. I typically use my debit card to withdraw cash to pay for most purchases. I use my credit card only in a few specific situations: to book hotel reservations by phone, to cover major expenses (such as car rentals, plane tickets, and long hotel stays), and to pay for things near the end of my trip (to avoid another visit to the ATM). While you could use a debit card to make most large purchases, using a credit card offers a greater degree of fraud protection (because debit cards draw funds directly from your account).

Ask Your Credit- or Debit-Card Company: Before your trip, contact the company that issued your debit or credit cards.

• Confirm your card will work overseas, and alert them that you'll be using it in Europe; otherwise, they may deny transactions if they perceive unusual spending patterns.

• Ask for the specifics on transaction **fees.** When you use your credit or debit card—either for purchases or ATM withdrawals— you'll often be charged additional "international transaction" fees of up to 3 percent (1 percent is normal) plus $5 per transaction. If your fees are too high, consider getting a card just for your trip: Capital One (credit cards only, www.capitalone.com) and most credit unions have low-to-no international fees.

• If you plan to withdraw cash from ATMs, confirm your daily **withdrawal limit,** and if necessary, ask your bank to adjust it (withdrawal limits are set by your bank, but foreign banks or ATMs often also set withdrawal amounts—usually a maximum of about €300 in the Eurozone and £300 in the UK). Some travelers prefer a high limit that allows them to take out more cash at each ATM stop, while others prefer to set a lower limit in case their card is stolen.

• Ask for your credit card's **PIN** in case you encounter Europe's chip-and-PIN system; the bank will not reveal your PIN over the phone, so allow time for it to reach you by mail.

Chip and PIN: If your card is declined for a purchase in Europe, it may be because of chip and PIN, which requires cardholders to punch in a PIN code instead of signing a receipt. Much of Northern Europe (including Great Britain, Ireland, France, Belgium, the Netherlands, and Scandinavia) is adopting this system. The good news is that you're unlikely to have a problem at businesses (stores, restaurants, and hotels), because most cashiers can swipe your card and print a receipt for you to sign instead; if not, pay cash.

You're most likely to encounter problems with chip and PIN at automated payment machines (e.g., for train and subway tickets, luggage lockers, bike-rental kiosks, toll roads, parking garages, and self-serve pumps at gas stations). If a machine won't take your card, try entering your PIN code, see if a cashier is nearby who can process your transaction, or check if one of the machines takes cash.

You can avoid potential hassles by getting your own chip-and-PIN card just for your trip, but so far your options are limited and pricey. Major US banks are beginning to offer these credit cards for a hefty annual fee. Travelex's chip-and-PIN cash card ("Cash

Passport") is sold at many airports, preloaded with euros or pounds (at a bad rate), and accepted only at places that take MasterCard. These cards probably aren't worth it unless you're staying for several weeks in a country that's adopted chip-and-PIN cards.

Dynamic Currency Conversion: If merchants offer to convert your purchase price into dollars (called dynamic currency conversion, or "DCC"), refuse this "service." You'll pay even more in fees for the expensive convenience of seeing your charge in dollars.

Damage Control for Lost Cards

If you lose your credit, debit, or ATM card, you can stop people from using it by reporting the loss immediately to the respective global customer-assistance centers. Call these 24-hour US numbers collect: Visa (tel. 410/581-9994), MasterCard (tel. 636/722-7111), and American Express (tel. 623/492-8427).

At a minimum, you'll need to know the name of the financial institution that issued you the card, along with the type of card (classic, platinum, or whatever). Providing the following information will allow for a quicker cancellation of your missing card: full card number, whether you are the primary or secondary cardholder, the cardholder's name exactly as printed on the card, billing address, home phone number, circumstances of the loss or theft, and identification verification (your birth date, your mother's maiden name, or your Social Security number—memorize this, don't carry a copy). If you are the secondary cardholder, you'll also need to provide the primary cardholder's identification-verification details. You can generally receive a temporary card within two or three business days in Europe.

If you promptly report your card lost or stolen, you typically won't be responsible for any unauthorized transactions on your account, although many banks charge a liability fee of $50.

Tips on Tipping

Tipping in Europe isn't as automatic and generous as it is in the US—but for special service, tips are appreciated, if not expected. Here are some general guidelines.

Restaurants: Virtually anywhere in Europe, you can do as the Europeans do, and if you're pleased with the service, round up a euro or two. In most places, 5 percent is adequate and 10 percent is considered a big tip. Please believe me—tipping 15–20 percent in Europe is unnecessary, if not culturally insensitive. Tipping is expected only at restaurants with wait staff; skip the tip if you order food at a counter (in a pub, for example). Servers prefer to be tipped in cash even if you pay with your credit card (otherwise the tip may never reach your server).

Taxis: For a typical ride, round up about 5–10 percent (to pay a €4.50 fare, give €5; for a €28 fare, give €30). If the cabbie hauls your bags and zips you to the airport to help you catch your flight, you might want to toss in a little more. But if you feel like you're being driven in circles or otherwise ripped off, skip the tip.

Special Services: Tour guides at public sights often hold out their hands for tips after they give their spiel. If I've already paid for the tour, I don't tip extra unless they've really impressed me. At hotels, if you let porters carry your luggage, it's polite to give them a euro per bag (another reason to pack light). If you tip maids, leave a euro per overnight at the end of your stay.

In general, if someone in the service industry does a super job for you, a tip of a euro or two is appropriate...but not required.

When in doubt, ask. If you're not sure whether (or how much) to tip for a service, ask your hotelier or the TI; they'll fill you in on how it's done on their turf.

Sleeping

I favor accommodations (and restaurants) that are handy to your sightseeing activities. Rather than list lodgings scattered throughout a city, I choose two or three favorite neighborhoods and recommend the best accommodations values in each, from dorm beds to fancy doubles with all the comforts.

A major feature of this book is its extensive listing of good-value rooms. I like places that are clean, central, relatively quiet at night, reasonably priced, friendly, small enough to have a hands-on owner and stable staff, run with a respect for European traditions, and not listed in other guidebooks. (In Europe, for me, six out of these eight criteria means it's a keeper.)

Rates and Deals

I've described my recommended accommodations using a Sleep Code (see the sidebar). Prices listed are for one-night stays in peak season, include breakfast unless otherwise noted, and assume you're booking directly (not through a TI or online hotel-booking engine).

As you look over the listings in this book, you'll notice that some accommodations promise special discounts to my readers who book direct (without using a room-finding service or hotel-booking website, which take a commission). To get these discounts, you must mention this book when you reserve, and then show the book upon arrival.

In general, prices can soften if you do any of the following: offer to pay cash, stay at least three nights, or mention this book. You can also try asking for a cheaper room or a discount, or offer to skip breakfast.

Types of Accommodations
Hotels

Double rooms in hotels listed in this book will range from about $50 (very simple, toilet and shower down the hall) to $450 (maximum plumbing and more), with most clustering at about $150 (with private bathrooms). Prices are higher in big cities and heavily touristed cities, and lower off the beaten path.

Hoteliers can be a great help and source of advice. Most know their city well and can assist you with everything from public transit and airport connections to finding a good restaurant, the nearest Internet café, or launderette. But even at the best places, mechanical breakdowns occur: Air-conditioning malfunctions, sinks leak, hot water turns cold, and toilets gurgle and smell. Report your concerns clearly and calmly at the front desk. For more complicated problems, don't expect instant results.

If you suspect night noise will be a problem, ask for a quiet room in the back or on an upper floor. To guard against theft in your room, keep valuables out of sight. Some rooms come with a safe, and others have safes at the front desk. Use them if you're concerned.

Checkout can pose problems if surprise charges pop up on your bill. If you settle up your bill the day before you leave, you'll have time to discuss and address any points of contention (before 19:00, when the night shift usually arrives).

Bed-and-Breakfasts and Pensions

Between hotels and hostels in price and style is a special class of accommodations: bed-and-breakfasts (B&Bs) and pensions. These are small, warm, and family-run, and offer a personal touch at a budget price—about $40–60 per person. Each country has these friendly accommodations in varying degrees of abundance, facilities, and service. Some include breakfast; some don't. They have different names from country to country—they're called *Gasthäuser* in Germany, *chambre d'hôte* in France, *affitta camere* in Italy, and *casa particulare* in Spain—but all have one thing in common: They satisfy the need for a place to stay that gives you the privacy of a hotel and the comforts of home at an affordable price.

Hostels

You'll pay about $25–30 per bed to stay at a hostel. Travelers of any age are welcome if they don't mind dorm-style accommodations or meeting other travelers. Cheap meals are sometimes available. Most hostels offer kitchen facilities, Internet access, Wi-Fi, a self-service laundry, and rental sheets (or bring your own sleep sack). Family and private rooms are sometimes available on request, but it's basically boys' dorms and girls' dorms. You usually can't check

Sleep Code

To help you sort easily through my hotel listings, I've divided the accommodations into three categories based on the price for a standard double room with bath during high season:

$$$ **Higher Priced**
$$ **Moderately Priced**
$ **Lower Priced**

I always rate hostels as $, whether or not they have double rooms, because they have the cheapest beds in town. Prices can change without notice; verify the hotel's current rates online or by email.

To give maximum information in a minimum of space, I use the following code to describe accommodations in this book. Prices are listed per room, not per person. When a price range is given for a type of room, it means the price fluctuates with the season, size of room, or length of stay; expect to pay the upper end for peak-season stays.

S = Single room (or price for one person in a double).

D = Double or twin room. "Double beds" can be two twins sheeted together and are usually big enough for nonromantic couples.

T = Triple (generally a double bed with a single).

Q = Quad (usually two double beds; adding an extra child's bed to a T is usually cheaper).

b = Private bathroom with toilet and shower or tub.

s = Private shower or tub only (the toilet is down the hall).

According to this code, a couple staying at a "Db-€140" hotel in would pay a total of €140 (about $200) for a double room with a private bathroom. Unless otherwise noted, breakfast is included, hotel staff speak basic English, and credit cards are accepted.

If I mention "Internet access" in a listing, there's a public terminal in the lobby for guests to use. If I specify "Wi-Fi," you can generally access it in public areas and often (though not always) in your room, but only if you have your own laptop or other Wi-Fi device.

in before 17:00 and must be out by 10:00. There is often a late-night curfew.

Making Reservations

Given the good value of the accommodations I've found for this book, I'd recommend that you reserve your rooms in advance, particularly if you'll be traveling during peak season. Note that some national holidays and major festivals jam things up (check www.ricksteves.com/festivals and www.whatsonwhen.com).

Requesting a Reservation: To make a reservation, contact hotels and B&Bs directly by email, phone, or fax. Or you can go straight to the hotel website; many have secure online reservation forms and can instantly inform you of availability and any special deals.

The hotelier wants to know these key pieces of information (also included in the sample request form in the appendix):

- number and type of rooms
- number of nights
- date of arrival
- date of departure
- any special needs (e.g., bathroom in the room or down the hall, twin beds vs. double bed, air-conditioning, quiet, view, ground floor, etc.)

When you request a room, use the European style for writing dates: day/month/year. For example, for a two-night stay in July 2013, I would request "2 nights, arrive 16/07/13, depart 18/07/13." Consider in advance how long you'll stay; don't assume you can tack on extra days once you arrive. Make sure you mention any discounts offered—for Rick Steves readers or otherwise—when you make the reservation.

Confirming a Reservation: If the hotel's response includes its room availability and rates, it's not a confirmation. You must tell them that you want that room at the given rate. Many hoteliers will request your credit-card number for a one-night deposit to hold the room. While you can email your credit-card information (I do), it's safer to share that confidential info via phone call, fax, split between two emails, or via a secure online reservation form (if the hotel has one on its website).

Canceling a Reservation: If you must cancel your reservation, it's courteous to do so with as much advance notice as possible—at least three days. Simply make a quick phone call or send an email. Hotels in larger cities such as London sometimes have strict cancellation policies. For example, you might lose a deposit if you cancel within two weeks of your reserved stay, or you might be billed for the entire visit if you leave early. Internet deals may require prepayment, with no refunds for cancellations. Ask about cancellation policies before you book.

Reconfirm a Reservation: Always call to reconfirm your room reservation a day or two in advance from the road. On the small chance that a hotel loses track of your reservation, bring along a hard copy of your emailed or faxed confirmation.

Reserving Rooms as You Travel: You can make reservations as you travel, calling hotels or B&Bs a few days to a week before your arrival. If you'd rather travel without any reservations at all,

How Was Your Trip?

Were your travels fun, smooth, and meaningful? If you'd like to share your tips, concerns, and discoveries, please fill out the survey at www.ricksteves.com/feedback. I value your feedback. Thanks in advance—it helps a lot.

you'll have greater success snaring rooms if you arrive at your destination early in the day. When you anticipate crowds (weekends are worst), call hotels at about 9:00 or 10:00 on the day you plan to arrive, when the hotel clerk knows who'll be checking out and just which rooms will be available.

Traveling As a Temporary Local

We travel all the way to Europe to enjoy differences—to become temporary locals. You'll experience frustrations. Certain truths that we find "God-given" or "self-evident," like cold beer, ice in drinks, bottomless cups of coffee, hot showers, and bigger being better, are suddenly not so true. One of the benefits of travel is the eye-opening realization that there are logical, civil, and even better alternatives. A willingness to go local ensures that you'll enjoy a full dose of European hospitality.

Europeans generally like Americans. But if there is a negative aspect to the European image of Americans, it's that we are big, loud, aggressive, impolite, rich, and a bit naive.

My European friends place a high value on speaking quietly in public places. Listen while on the bus or in a restaurant—the place can be packed, but the decibel level is low. Try to adjust your volume accordingly to show respect for the culture.

While Europeans look bemusedly at some of our Yankee excesses—and worriedly at others—they nearly always afford us individual travelers all the warmth we deserve.

Judging from all the positive comments I receive from travelers who have used this book, it's safe to assume you'll enjoy a great, affordable vacation—with the finesse of an experienced, independent traveler. Thanks, and happy travels!

Back Door Travel Philosophy
From *Rick Steves' Europe Through the Back Door*

Travel is intensified living—maximum thrills per minute and one of the last great sources of legal adventure. Travel is freedom. It's recess, and we need it.

Experiencing the real Europe requires catching it by surprise, going casual..."Through the Back Door."

Affording travel is a matter of priorities. (Make do with the old car.) You can eat and sleep—simply, safely, and enjoyably—anywhere in Europe for $120 a day plus transportation costs (allow more for bigger cities). In many ways, spending more money only builds a thicker wall between you and what you traveled so far to see. Europe is a cultural carnival, and time after time, you'll find that its best acts are free and the best seats are the cheap ones.

A tight budget forces you to travel close to the ground, meeting and communicating with the people. Never sacrifice sleep, nutrition, safety, or cleanliness to save money. Simply enjoy the local-style alternatives to expensive hotels and restaurants.

Connecting with people carbonates your experience. Extroverts have more fun. If your trip is low on magic moments, kick yourself and make things happen. If you don't enjoy a place, maybe you don't know enough about it. Seek the truth. Recognize tourist traps. Give a culture the benefit of your open mind. See things as different, but not better or worse. Any culture has plenty to share.

Of course, travel, like the world, is a series of hills and valleys. Be fanatically positive and militantly optimistic. If something's not to your liking, change your liking.

Travel can make you a happier American, as well as a citizen of the world. Our Earth is home to seven billion equally precious people. It's humbling to travel and find that other people don't have the "American Dream"—they have their own dreams. Europeans like us, but with all due respect, they wouldn't trade passports.

Thoughtful travel engages us with the world. In tough economic times, it reminds us what is truly important. By broadening perspectives, travel teaches new ways to measure quality of life.

Globetrotting destroys ethnocentricity, helping us understand and appreciate other cultures. Rather than fear the diversity on this planet, celebrate it. Among your most prized souvenirs will be the strands of different cultures you choose to knit into your own character. The world is a cultural yarn shop, and Back Door travelers are weaving the ultimate tapestry. Join in!

AUSTRIA

VIENNA

Wien

Vienna is the capital of Austria, the cradle of classical music, the home of the rich Habsburg heritage, and one of Europe's most livable cities. The city center is skyscraper-free, pedestrian-friendly, dotted with quiet parks, and traversed by quaint electric trams. Many buildings still reflect 18th- and 19th-century elegance, when the city was at the forefront of the arts and sciences. Compared with most modern European urban centers, the pace of life is slow.

Vienna (*Wien* in German—pronounced "veen") has always been considered the easternmost city of the West. For 640 years, Vienna was the capital of the enormous Austrian Empire (a.k.a. the Austro-Hungarian Empire, a.k.a. the Habsburg Empire). Stretching from the Alps of northern Italy to the rugged Carpathians of Romania, and from the banks of the Danube to sunny Dubrovnik, this multiethnic empire was arguably the most powerful European entity since Rome. And yet, of its 60 million people, only eight million were Austrian; Vienna was a kind of Eastern European melting pot. Today, the truly Viennese person is not Austrian, but a second-generation Habsburg cocktail, with grandparents from the distant corners of the old empire—Hungary, the Czech Republic, Slovakia, Poland, Slovenia, Croatia, Bosnia-Herzegovina, Serbia, Romania, and Italy.

Vienna reached its peak in the 19th century. Politically, it hosted European diplomats at the 1814 Congress of Vienna, which reaffirmed Europe's conservative monarchy after the French Revolution and Napoleon. Vienna became one of Europe's cultural capitals, home to groundbreaking composers (Beethoven, Mozart, Brahms, Strauss), scientists (Doppler, Boltzmann), philosophers

(Freud, Husserl, Schlick, Gödel, Steiner), architects (Wagner, Loos), and painters (Klimt, Schiele, Kokoschka). In 1900, Vienna's 2.2 million inhabitants made it the world's fifth-largest city—after New York, London, Paris, and Berlin. By the turn of the 20th century, Vienna sat on the cusp between stuffy Old World monarchy and subversive modern trends.

However, after starting and losing World War I, the Habsburgs lost their far-flung holdings. Then came World War II: While Vienna's old walls had long held out would-be invaders— Germanic barbarians (in Roman times), marauding Magyars (today's Hungarians, 10th century), Mongol hordes (13th century), Ottoman Turks (the sieges of 1529 and 1683)—they were no match for WWII bombs, which destroyed nearly a quarter of the city's buildings. In the Cold War, neutral Austria took a big bite out of the USSR's Warsaw Pact buffer zone—and Vienna became, for a time, a den of spies.

Today Vienna has settled down into a somewhat sleepy, pleasant place where culture is still king. Classical music is everywhere. People nurse a pastry and coffee over the daily paper at small cafés. It's a city of world-class museums, big and small. Anyone with an interest in painting, music, architecture, beautiful objects, or Sacher-Torte with whipped cream will feel right at home.

From a practical standpoint, Vienna serves as a prime "gateway" city. The location is central and convenient to most major Eastern European destinations. Actually farther east than Prague, Ljubljana, and Zagreb, and just upstream on the Danube from Budapest and Bratislava, Vienna is an ideal launchpad for a journey into the East.

Planning Your Time

For a big city, Vienna is pleasant and laid-back. Packed with sights, it's worth two days and two nights on even the speediest trip. To be grand-tour efficient, you could sleep on the train on your way in and out—Prague, Kraków, Warsaw, Berlin, Venice, Rome, the Swiss Alps (via Zürich), and the Rhine Valley are each handy night trains away.

Palace Choices: The Hofburg and Schönbrunn are both world-class palaces, but seeing both is redundant—with limited time or money, I'd choose just one. The Hofburg comes with the popular Sisi Museum and is right in the town center, making for an easy visit. With more time, a visit to Schönbrunn—set outside town amid a grand and regal garden—is also a great experience.

Vienna in One to Four Days

Below is a suggested itinerary for how to spend your time. I've left the **evenings** open for your choice of activities. The best options are taking in a concert, opera, or other musical event; enjoying a leisurely dinner (and people-watching) in the stately old town or atmospheric Spittelberg Quarter; heading out to the *Heuriger* wine pubs in the foothills of the Vienna Woods; or touring the Haus der Musik interactive music museum (open nightly until 22:00). Plan your evenings based on the schedule of musical events while you're in town.

Day 1

9:00	Take the 1.5-hour Red Bus City Tour, or circle the Ringstrasse by tram, to get your bearings.
10:30	Drop by the TI for planning and ticket needs.
11:00	Enjoy the Albertina Museum.
13:00	Take the Opera tour (buy tickets at 12:40).
14:00	Follow my Vienna City Walk, including Kaisergruft

VIENNA

visit and St. Stephen's Cathedral Tour (nave closes at 16:30, or 17:30 June-Aug).

Day 2

9:00 Browse the colorful Naschmarkt, or shop along Mariahilfer Strasse.

11:00 Tour the Kunsthistorisches Museum.

14:00 After a short break (and maybe a picnic) in the Burggarten, tour the Hofburg Palace Imperial Apartments and Treasury; if time, interest, and energy hold out, dip into the New Palace museums.

Day 3

Choose from among the following sights: Belvedere Palace, with its fine collection of Viennese art and great city views; the engaging Karlsplatz sights (Karlskirche, Wien Museum, Academy of Fine Arts, and The Secession); or a wide range of honorable mentions (Natural History Museum, Liechtenstein Museum, Kunst-HausWien and Hundertwasserhaus, Museum of Applied Art, Imperial Furniture Collection, Sigmund Freud Museum, Jewish sights, and so on).

If you need a break, linger in a classic Viennese café.

Or, to get out of town, tromp through the Vienna Woods, ending at the *Heuriger* wine pubs for dinner.

Day 4

9:00 Head out to Schönbrunn Palace to enjoy the royal apartments and grounds.

12:00 If the weather's good, picnic at Schönbrunn (on the lawn in front of the Gloriette), then return to downtown.

13:00 Rent a bike and head out to the modern Danube City "downtown" sector, Danube Island (for fun people-watching), and the Prater amusement park.

Orientation to Vienna

(area code: 01)

Vienna sits between the Vienna Woods (Wienerwald) and the Danube (Donau). To the southeast is industrial sprawl. The Alps, which arc across Europe from Marseille, end at Vienna's wooded hills, providing a popular playground for walking and sipping new wine. This greenery's momentum carries on into the city. More than half of Vienna is parkland, filled with ponds, gardens, trees, and statue-maker memories of Austria's glory days.

VIENNA

Vienna's City Center

VIENNA

1. Shakespeare & Co. Bookstore
2. The British Bookshop
3. Internet Cafés (2)
4. Ruefa Travel Agency
5. Royal Tours
6. Pedal Power Bike Rental
7. Red Bus City Tours Start Point
8. Opera Tour Entrance
9. Opera Museum

Think of the city map as a target with concentric sections: The bull's-eye is St. Stephen's Cathedral, the towering cathedral south of the Danube. Surrounding that is the old town, bound tightly by the circular road known as the Ringstrasse, marking what used to be the city wall. The Gürtel, a broader ring road, contains the rest of downtown. Outside the Gürtel lies the uninteresting sprawl of modern Vienna.

Addresses start with the district, or *Bezirk,* followed by the street and building number. The Ringstrasse (a.k.a. the Ring) circles the first *Bezirk.* Any address higher than the ninth *Bezirk* is beyond the Gürtel, far from the center.

Much of Vienna's sightseeing—and most of my recommended restaurants—are located in the old town (inside the Ringstrasse). Walking across this circular district takes about 30 minutes. St. Stephen's Cathedral sits in the center, at the intersection of the two main (pedestrian-only) streets: Kärntner Strasse runs north-south and Graben runs east-west. To the northwest of the cathedral is the "Bermuda Triangle" of pubs and cafés for nightlife.

Several sights sit along, or just beyond, the Ringstrasse: to the southwest are the Hofburg and related Habsburg sights, and the Kunsthistorisches Museum; to the south is a cluster of intriguing sights near Karlsplatz; to the southeast is Belvedere Palace. A branch of the Danube River (*Donau* in German, DOH-now) borders the Ring to the north. As a tourist, concern yourself only with this compact old center. When you do, sprawling Vienna suddenly becomes manageable.

Arrival in Vienna
By Train
Vienna's train stations will be in disarray for the next few years, as a central train station (Hauptbahnhof) is built in the former Südbahnhof location that will handle most of the traffic. Until this is done (likely in 2013), trains to different destinations depart from various stations around the city. As these departure points are prone to change, confirm carefully which station your train uses. As the stations themselves are also in flux (the main ones are all being renovated), the details I've listed below for each one are also subject to change. From most stations, the handiest connection to the city center is usually the U-Bahn (subway) system; line numbers and stop names are noted below. The latter two stations also have a handy tram connection to the center.

Westbahnhof (West Station): In the midst of a massive renovation, this station (at the west end of Mariahilfer Strasse, on the U-3 and U-6 lines) serves trains to/from many points in **Austria** (including Hallstatt and Salzburg), as well as **Germany,**

Switzerland, and **Hungary.** The Reisebüro am Bahnhof office sells maps, books hotels (for a pricey fee), and answers questions (Mon-Fri 8:00-19:00, Sat 8:00-13:00, closed Sun). During the ongoing construction, this station's many services are scattered throughout a provisional hall—including a train ticket office (daily 5:30-22:45), grocery store (daily 5:30-23:00), ATMs, change offices, a post office, and luggage lockers (€2-3.50). To reach airport buses and taxis, from the platforms, head outside and to the left. For the city center, ride the U-3 line (buy your ticket or transit pass from a machine, then follow *U-3* signs to the tracks; direction: Simmering). If your hotel is along Mariahilfer Strasse, your stop is on this line. If you're sleeping in the center—or just can't wait to start sightseeing—ride five stops to Stephansplatz, at the very center of town. From there, the TI is a five-minute stroll down pedestrian Kärntner Strasse.

VIENNA

Wien-Meidling Bahnhof: This temporary "main station" (a mile and a half southeast of Schönbrunn Palace, at the Philadelphiabrücke stop on the U-6 subway line and tram #62) serves most international trains, including southbound trains to/from **Italy, Slovenia,** and **Croatia,** as well as northbound trains to/from the **Czech Republic** and **Poland.** The once-small suburban station has been souped up to accommodate the traffic that formerly passed through the Südbahnhof. It has train info desks (near track 1 and underground, near track 4), ATMs (near tracks 1 and 6), luggage lockers (underground, near track 7), and airport bus services. To reach the hotels on Mariahilfer Strasse, or to head to Stephansplatz, take the U-Bahn on the U-6 line (direction: Floridsdorf) to the Westbahnhof, then change to the U-3 line (see "Westbahnhof," above). If you're staying near the Opera, catch the direct tram #62 (direction: Karlsplatz). For Schwedenplatz, take the U-6 (direction: Floridsdorf) two stops to Längenfeldgasse, then change to the U-4 (direction: Heiligenstadt).

Ostbahnhof (East Station), a.k.a. Südbahnhof (South Station): The temporary Ostbahnhof (just south of Belvedere Palace) is near the former Südbahnhof, and is in the midst of the massive construction zone for the brand-new Hauptbahnhof (Main Station)—so, confusingly, it goes by any of these three names. For now, this station serves trains to/from **Bratislava,** Slovakia. To reach the city center, take tram #D to the Ring; to reach Mariahilfer Strasse, hop on bus #13A (U-1: Südtiroler Platz is also nearby).

By Plane

For information on nearby airports, see "Vienna Connections," at the end of this chapter.

VIENNA

Tourist Information

Vienna's one real TI is a block behind the Opera at Albertinaplatz (daily 9:00-19:00, tel. 01/211-140, www.vienna.info). At the TI, confirm your sightseeing plans, and pick up the free and essential city map with a list of museums and hours (also available at most hotels), the monthly program of concerts (called *Wien-Programm*) and the *Vienna from A to Z* booklet (both described below), and the annual city guide (called *Vienna Journal*). Ask about their program of guided walks (€14 each). The TI also books rooms for a €3 fee. While hotel and ticket-booking agencies at the train station and airport can answer questions and give out maps and brochures, I'd rely on the official TI if possible.

Wien-Programm: This monthly entertainment guide is particularly important, listing all of the events, including music, walks, expositions, and evening museum hours. Note the key for abbreviations on the inside cover, which helps make this dense booklet useful even for non-German speakers.

Vienna from A to Z: Consider this handy booklet, sold by TIs for €3.60. Every major building in Vienna sports a numbered flag banner that keys into this booklet and into the TI's city map—useful for finding your way if you get turned around.

Vienna Card: The much-promoted €18.50 Vienna Card is not worth the mental overhead for most travelers. It gives you a 72-hour transit pass (worth €13.60) and discounts of 10-40 percent at the city's museums. It might save the busy sightseer a few euros (though seniors and students will do better with their own discounts).

Helpful Hints

Sisi Ticket: This €23.50 ticket covers the Royal Imperial Apartments at the Hofburg (including the Sisi Museum and Imperial Porcelain and Silver Collection—but *not* the Hofburg Treasury), Schönbrunn Palace's Grand Tour, and the Imperial Furniture Collection; the ticket saves €0.50 off the combined cost of the Hofburg apartments and Schönbrunn, making the good Furniture Collection effectively free (sold at any participating sight).

Teens Sightsee Free: Those under 19 get in free to state-run museums and sights.

Music Sightseeing Priorities: Be wary of Vienna's various music sights. Many "homes of composers" are pretty disappointing. My advice to music-lovers is to concentrate on these activities: Take in a concert, tour the Opera house, snare cheap standing-room tickets to see an opera there (even just part of a performance), enjoy the Haus der Musik, and scour the wonderful Collection of Ancient Musical Instruments in the Hofburg's

New Palace. If in town on a Sunday, don't miss the glorious music at the Augustinian Church Mass (see page 58).

Internet Access: The TI has a list of Internet cafés. **Surfland Internet Café** is near the Opera (€6/hour, daily 10:00-23:00, Krugerstrasse 10, tel. 01/512-7701).

Post Offices: The main post office is near Schwedenplatz at Fleischmarkt 19 (Mon-Fri 7:00-22:00, Sat-Sun 9:00-22:00). Branch offices are at the Westbahnhof (Mon-Fri 7:00-22:00, Sat-Sun 9:00-20:00), near the Opera (Mon-Fri 7:00-19:00, closed Sat-Sun, Krugerstrasse 13), and scattered throughout town.

English Bookstore: Stop by the woody and cool Shakespeare & Co. (Mon-Sat 9:00-19:00 and sometimes later, generally closed Sun, north of Hoher Markt at Sterngasse 2, tel. 01/535-5053). Also inside the Ring is The British Bookshop (Mon-Fri 9:30-18:30, Sat 9:30-18:00, closed Sun, between Franziskaner Platz and the Ring at Weihburggasse 24, tel. 01/512-194-522).

Keeping Up with the News: Don't buy newspapers. Read them for free in Vienna's marvelous coffeehouses. It's much classier.

Travel Agency: Conveniently located just off the Graben, **Ruefa** sells tickets for flights, trains, and boats to Bratislava. They'll waive the service charge for train tickets for my readers (Mon-Fri 9:00-18:00, Sat 10:00-13:00, closed Sun, Spiegelgasse 15, tel. 01/513-4000).

Getting Around Vienna

By Public Transportation: Take full advantage of Vienna's simple, cheap, and super-efficient transit system, which includes trams (a.k.a. streetcars), buses, U-Bahn (subway), and S-Bahn (faster suburban trains). The smooth, modern trams are Porsche-designed, with "backpack technology" that locates the engines and mechanical hardware on the roofs for a lower ride and easier entry. I generally stick to the tram to zip around the Ring and take the U-Bahn to outlying sights or hotels. Trams #1, #2, and #D all travel partway around the Ring.

The free Vienna map, available at TIs and hotels, includes a smaller schematic map of the major public transit lines, making the too-big €2.50 transit map unnecessary. (Transit maps are also posted conveniently on U-Bahn station walls.) As you study the map, note that tram lines are marked with numbers or letters (such as #38 or #D). Buses have numbers followed by an *A* or *B* (such as #38A); three-digit numbers are for buses into the outskirts. Night buses, which start with *N* (such as #N38), run after other public transit stops running. U-Bahn lines begin with U (e.g., U-1), and the directions are designated by the end-of-the-line stops. Blue

VIENNA

lines are the speedier S-Bahns. Transit info: tel. 01/790-9100, www.wienerlinien.at.

Trams, buses, the U-Bahn, and the S-Bahn all use the same tickets. Buy tickets from *Tabak-Trafik* shops, station machines, marked *Vorverkauf* offices in the station, or—for trams or buses only—on board (tickets only, more expensive). You have lots of choices:

- Single tickets (€2, €2.20 if bought on tram or bus, good for one journey with necessary transfers)
- 24-hour transit pass (€6.70)
- 48-hour transit pass (€11.70)
- 72-hour transit pass (€14.50)
- 7-day transit pass (*Wochenkarte,* €15—but the catch is that it starts on Monday, even if you buy it on a Saturday)
- 8-day "Climate Ticket" *(Acht-Tage-Klimakarte,* €33.80, can be shared—for example, 4 people for 2 days each). With a per-person cost of about €4.25/day (compared to €6.70/day for a 24-hour pass), this can be a real saver for groups.

Kids under 15 travel free on Sundays and holidays; kids under 6 always travel free.

Stamp a time on your ticket as you enter the Metro system, tram, or bus (stamp it only the first time for a multiple-use pass). Cheaters pay a stiff €100 fine, plus the cost of the ticket. Rookies miss stops because they fail to open the door. Push buttons, pull latches—do whatever it takes. Before you exit a U-Bahn station, study the wall-mounted street map. Choosing the right exit—signposted from the moment you step off the train—saves lots of walking.

Cute little electric buses wind through the tangled old center. Bus #1A is best for a joyride—hop on and see where it takes you.

By Car: Vienna's comfortable, civilized, and easy-to-flag-down **taxis** start at €2.50. You'll pay about €10 to go from the Opera to the Westbahnhof. Pay only what's on the meter—any surcharges (other than the €2 fee for calling a cab or €10 fee for the airport) are just crude cabbie rip-offs. Rates are legitimately higher at night.

Consider the luxury of having your own **car and driver.** Johann (a.k.a. John) Lichtl is a kind, honest, English-speaking cabbie who can take up to four passengers in his car (€27/1 hour, €25/hour for 2 hours or more, €27 to or from airport, mobile 0676-670-6750). Consider hiring gentle Johann for a day trip to the Danube Valley (€160, up to 8 hours) or to drive you to Salzburg with Danube sightseeing en route (€350, up to 14 hours; other trips can be arranged). These special prices are valid with this book in 2013 and 2014.

By Bike: Vienna is a great city for biking. The bike path along the Ring is wonderfully entertaining. Your best sightseeing by bike is around the Ring, through the City Park, across the Danube Island, and out to the modern "Donau City" business district and nearby beach.

Borrowing a Free/Cheap Bike: Citybike Wien lets you borrow bikes from public racks all over town (toll tel. 0810-500-500, www.citybikewien.at). The bikes are heavy, clunky, and difficult to maneuver—with a solid wheel, single gear, basket, built-in lock, and ads on the side—but they're perfect for a short, practical joyride in the center (such as around the Ringstrasse).

While bike programs in other European cities are difficult for tourists to take advantage of, Vienna's system is easy to use. Bikes are locked into more than 50 stalls scattered through the city center. To borrow a bike, use the computer terminal at any rack to register: Press the credit card button, insert and pull out your card, register your name and address, and select a username and password for future rentals (you can also register online at www.citybikewien.at). Then punch in the number of the bike that you want to use to unlock it. Registration costs €1 (first time only), and they'll place a refundable €20 hold on your card while you're using the bike (only one bike per credit card—couples must use two different cards). Since the bikes are designed for short-term use, it costs more per hour the longer you keep it (first hour free, second hour €1, third hour €2, €4/hour after that). To avoid registering at a machine, you can also get a Citybike Tourist Card (sold for €2/day at Royal Tours, near the Hofburg at Herrengasse 1-3)—but this extra step isn't worth the trouble. When you're done, drop off your bike at any stall, and make sure it's fully locked into the rack to avoid getting charged for more time.

Renting a Higher-Quality Bike: If you want to ride beyond the town center—or you simply want a better set of wheels—check out **Pedal Power,** with a handy central location near the Opera house. The local authority on bike touring both in town and from here to points along the Danube, Pedal Power rents bikes and provides good biking info (€5/hour, €17/4 hours, €27/24 hours, daily 8:30-18:00, Elisabethstrasse 13 at the corner of Eschenbachgasse). They can also deliver a bike to your hotel and pick it up when you're done (€32/day including delivery, tel. 01/729-7234, www.pedalpower.at), and they organize bike tours (described later). **Crazy Chicken** bike rental, a short tram ride from the Westbahnhof, is less convenient but a lot cheaper (€3/hour, €12/day, daily 8:30-19:00, near recommended Pension Fünfhaus at Sperrgasse 12—see page 98 for directions, tel. 01/892-2134, mobile 0664-421-4789, www.crazychicken.at).

Tours in Vienna

To sightsee on your own, download my series of free **audio tours** that illuminate some of Vienna's top sights: St. Stephen's Cathedral, my Vienna City Walk, and the Ringstrasse Tram Tour (see sidebar on page 7 for details).

Walking Tours—The TI's *Walks in Vienna* brochure describes the city's many guided walks. The basic 1.5-hour "Vienna at First Glance" introductory walk is offered daily throughout the summer (€14, leaves at 14:00 from near the Opera, in both English and German, just show up, tel. 01/876-7111, mobile 0664-260-4388, www.wienguide.at). Various specialized tours go once a week and are listed on their website.

Bike Tours—Several companies offer city tours. **Pedal Power** runs two different three-hour tours daily from May to September (€26/tour includes bike, €44 for both tours, €14 extra to keep the bike for the day, departs at 9:45 and 14:15 in front of Opera at corner of Operngasse and the Kärntner Ring, also rents bikes, tel. 01/729-7234, www.pedalpower.at). **Wolfgang Höfler** leads bike tours as well as walking tours (€140/2 hours, mobile 0676-304-4940, www.vienna-aktivtours.com, office@vienna-aktivtours.com; also listed later, under "Local Guides").

Bus Tours—**Red Bus City Tours'** convertible buses do a 1.5-hour loop, hitting the highlights of the city with a 20-minute shopping break in the middle. It covers the main first-district attractions as well as a big bus can, along with the entire Ringstrasse. But the most interesting part of the tour is outside the center—zipping through Prater Park, over the Danube for a glimpse of the city's Danube Island playground, and into the "Donau City" skyscraper zone. If the weather's good, the bus goes topless and offers great opportunities for photos (€14, departs hourly April-Oct 10:00-18:00, less frequently off-season, tours start one block behind the Opera at Lobkowitzplatz 1, pretty good recorded narration in any language, your own earbuds are better than the beat-up headphones they provide, tel. 01/512-4030, www.redbuscitytours.at). The boss, Gabriel, gives those with this book a free cold drink from the shop where you buy your tickets.

Vienna Sightseeing offers a longer, three-hour city tour, including a tour of Schönbrunn Palace (€39, 3/day April-Oct, 2/day Nov-March). They also run hop-on, hop-off bus tours with recorded commentary. The schedule is posted curbside (three different routes, €13/1 hour, €16/2 hours, €20/all day, departs from the Opera 4/hour July-Aug 10:00-20:00, runs less frequently and stops earlier off-season, tel. 01/7124-6830, www.viennasightseeing.at). Given the city's excellent public transportation and this outfit's meager frequency, I'd skip this tour; if you just want a quick, guided city tour, take the Red Bus tours recommended above.

Ring Tram Tour—One of Europe's great streets, the Ringstrasse is lined with many of the city's top sights. Take a tram ride around the ring with my free audio tour (see page 7), which gives you a fun orientation and a ridiculously quick glimpse of some major sights as you glide by. Neither tram #1 nor #2 makes the entire loop around the Ring, but you can see it all by making one transfer between them (at the Schwedenplatz stop). A single transit ticket (€2, or €2.20 if bought on tram) can be used to cover the whole route, including the transfer, though you're not allowed to interrupt your trip except to transfer. For more on riding Vienna's trams, see page 29.

The **Vienna Ring Tram**, a made-for-tourists streetcar, is an easier though pricier option, running clockwise along the entire Ringstrasse (€6 for one 30-minute loop, €9 for 24-hour hop-on, hop-off privileges, 2/hour 10:00-18:00, July-Aug until 19:00, recorded narration). The tour starts at the top and bottom of each hour on the Opera side of the Ring at Kärntner Ring. At each stop, you'll see an ad for this tram tour (look for *VRT Ring-Rund Sightseeing*). The schedule clearly notes the next departure time.

Horse-and-Buggy Tour—These traditional horse-and-buggies, called *Fiakers*, take rich romantics on clip-clop tours lasting 20 minutes (€40-old town), 40 minutes (€65-old town and the Ring), or one hour (€95-all of the above, but more thorough). You can share the ride and cost with up to five people. Because it's a kind of guided tour, talk to a few drivers before choosing a carriage, and pick someone who's fun and speaks English (tel. 01/401-060).

Local Guides—You'll pay about €140 for two hours. Get a group of six or more together and call it a party. The tourist board's website (www.vienna.info) has a long list of local guides with their specialties and contact information. **Lisa Zeiler** is an excellent guide (tel. 01/402-3688, lisa.zeiler@gmx.at). **Wolfgang Höfler,** a generalist with a knack for having psychoanalytical fun with history, enjoys the big changes of the 19th and 20th centuries (€135/2 hours, mobile 0676-304-4940, www.vienna-aktivtours.com, office @vienna-aktivtours.com, also leads bike tours—described earlier). If Lisa and Wolfgang are booked, they work with other good guides and can set you up.

Self-Guided Walk

Vienna City Walk

This walk connects the top three sights in Vienna's old center: the Opera, St. Stephen's Cathedral, and the Hofburg Palace. Along the way, you'll see sights covered elsewhere in this chapter (to find the full descriptions, flip to "Sights in Vienna," later), and get an

VIENNA

Vienna City Walk

1. Opera
2. Café Sacher
3. Albertinaplatz
4. Monument Against War & Fascism
5. Café Tirolerhof
6. Kärntner Strasse
7. Kaisergruft
8. Neuer Markt
9. Stephansplatz
10. Haas Haus
11. Graben
12. Plague Column
13. St. Peter's Church
14. Loos' Loos (Public WCs)
15. Kohlmarkt
16. Demel Bakery & Manz Bookstore
17. Michaelerplatz & Hofburg Entrance
18. Imperial Apartments
19. Spanish Riding School
20. Treasury & Imperial Music Chapel
21. Heldenplatz

overview of Vienna's past and present. Allow one hour, and more time if you plan to stop into any of the major sights along the way. You can download a free Rick Steves **audio tour** of this walk; see page 7.

• Begin at the square outside Vienna's landmark Opera house. (The Opera's entrance faces the Ringstrasse; we're starting at the busy pedestrian square that's to the right of the entrance as you're facing it.)

Opera

If Vienna is the world capital of classical music, this building is its throne room, one of the planet's premier houses of music. It's typical of Vienna's 19th-century buildings in that it features a revival style—Neo-Renaissance—with arched windows, half-columns, and the sloping, copper mansard roof typical of French Renaissance châteaux. Since the structure was built in 1869, almost all of the opera world's luminaries have passed through here. Its former musical directors include Gustav Mahler, Herbert von Karajan, and Richard Strauss. Luciano Pavarotti, Maria Callas, Placido Domingo, and many other greats have sung from its stage.

In the pavement along the side of the Opera (and all along Kärntner Strasse, the bustling shopping street we'll visit shortly), you'll find star plaques forming a Hollywood-style walk of fame. These represent the stars of classical music—famous composers, singers, musicians, and conductors.

Looking up at the Opera, notice the giant outdoor screen onto which some live performances are projected (as noted in the posted schedules).

If you're a fan, take a guided tour of the Opera. If you're not, you still might consider springing for an evening performance (standing-room tickets are surprisingly cheap; see page 85). Regular opera tickets are sold at various points near here: The closest one is the small ticket office just below the screen, while the main one is across from the opposite side of the Opera, on Operngasse. For information about other entertainment options during your visit, check in at the Wien Ticket kiosk in the booth on this square.

The Opera marks a busy intersection in Vienna, where Kärntner Strasse meets the Ring. The Karlsplatz U-Bahn station in front of the Opera is an underground shopping mall with fast food, newsstands, lots of pickpockets, and even a Vienna Opera Toilet experience (€0.60, *mit Musik*).

• *Walk behind the Opera and across the street toward the dark-red awning to find the famous...*

Café Sacher

This is the home of the world's classiest chocolate cake, the Sacher-Torte: two layers of cake separated by apricot jam and covered in dark-chocolate icing, usually served with whipped cream. It was invented in a fit of improvisation in 1832 by Franz Sacher, dessert chef to Prince Metternich (the mastermind diplomat who redrew the map of post-Napoleon Europe). The cake became world-famous when the inventor's son served it next door at his hotel (you may have noticed the fancy doormen). Many locals complain that the cakes here have gone downhill, and many tourists are surprised by how dry they are—you really need that dollop of *Schlagobers*. Still, coffee and a slice of cake here can be €8 well invested for the historic ambience alone. While the café itself is grotesquely touristy, the adjacent Sacher Stube has ambience and natives to spare (same prices). For maximum elegance, sit inside.

• *Continue past Hotel Sacher. At the end of the street is a small, triangular, cobbled square adorned with modern sculptures.*

Albertinaplatz

As you enter the square, to the right you'll find the **TI.** On your left, the tan-and-white Neoclassical building with the statue alcoves marks the tip of the Hofburg Palace—the sprawling complex of buildings that was long the seat of Habsburg power (we'll end this walk at the palace's center). The balustraded terrace up top was originally part of Vienna's defensive rampart. Later, it was the balcony of Empress Maria Theresa's daughter Maria Christina, who lived at this end of the palace. Today, her home houses the **Albertina Museum,** topped by a sleek, controversial titanium canopy (called the "diving board" by critics). The museum's plush, 19th-century rooms are hung with facsimiles of its graphic collection, and an entire floor is dedicated to the Batliner collection, covering each artistic stage from Impressionism to the present day.

Albertinaplatz itself is filled with statues that make up the powerful, thought-provoking **Monument Against War and Fascism,** which commemorates the dark years when Austria came under Nazi rule (1938-1945).

The statue group has four parts. The split white monument, *The Gates of Violence,* remembers victims of all wars and violence. Standing directly in front of it, you're at the gates of a concentration camp. Then, as you explore the statues, you step into a montage of wartime images: clubs and WWI gas masks, a dying woman birthing a future soldier, and chained slave laborers sitting on a pedestal of granite cut from the infamous quarry at Mauthausen concentration camp, not far up the Danube from here. The hunched-over figure on the ground behind is a Jew forced to scrub anti-Nazi graffiti off a street with a toothbrush. Of Vienna's 200,000 Jews, more than 65,000 died in Nazi concentration camps. The statue with its head buried in the stone is Orpheus entering the underworld, meant to remind Austrians (and the rest of us) of the victims of Nazism...and the consequences of not keeping our governments on track. Behind that, the 1945 declaration that established Austria's second republic—and enshrined human rights—is cut into the stone.

Viewing this monument gains even more emotional impact when you realize what happened on this spot: During a WWII bombing attack, several hundred people were buried alive when the cellar they were using as shelter was demolished.

Austria was led into World War II by Germany, which

annexed the country in 1938, saying Austrians were wannabe Germans anyway. But Austrians are not Germans—never were, never will be. They're quick to proudly tell you that Austria was founded in the 10th century, whereas Germany wasn't born until 1870. For seven years, just before and during World War II (1938-1945), there was no Austria. In 1955, after 10 years of joint occupation by the victorious Allies, Austria regained total independence on the condition that it would be forever neutral (and never join NATO or the Warsaw Pact). To this day, Austria is outside of NATO (and Germany).

VIENNA

Behind the monument is **Café Tirolerhof,** a classic Viennese café full of things that time has passed by: chandeliers, marble tables, upholstered booths, waiters in tuxes, and newspapers. For more on Vienna's cafés, see page 79.

Often parked on the same square are the Red Bus City Tour buses, offering a handy way to get a quick overview of the city (see "Tours in Vienna," earlier).

• *From the café, turn right on Führichsgasse, passing the recommended cafeteria-style Rosenberger Markt Restaurant. Walk one block until you hit...*

Kärntner Strasse

This grand, mall-like street (traffic-free since 1974) is the people-watching delight of this in-love-with-life city. Today's Kärntner Strasse (KAYRNT-ner SHTRAH-seh) is mostly a crass commercial pedestrian mall—its famed elegant shops are long gone. But locals know it's the same road Crusaders marched down as they headed off from St. Stephen's Cathedral for the Holy Land in the 12th century. Its name indicates that it leads south, toward the region of Kärnten (Carinthia, a province divided between Austria and Slovenia). Today it's full of shoppers and street musicians.

Where Führichsgasse meets Kärntner Strasse, note the city **Casino** (across the street and a half-block to your right, at #41)—once venerable, now tacky, it exemplifies the worst of the street's evolution. Turn left to head up Kärntner Strasse, going away from the Opera. As you walk along, be sure to look up, above the modern storefronts, for glimpses of the street's former glory. Near the end of the block, on the left at #26, **J & L Lobmeyr Crystal** ("Founded in 1823") still has its impressive brown storefront with gold trim, statues, and the Habsburg double-eagle. In the market for some $400 napkin rings? Lobmeyr's your place. Inside, breathe in the classic Old World ambience as you climb up to the glass museum (free entry, Mon-Fri 10:00-19:00, Sat 10:00-18:00, closed Sun).

• *At the end of the block, turn left on Marco d'Aviano Gasse (passing the fragrant flower stall) to make a short detour to the square called Neuer*

Markt. Straight ahead is an orange-ish church with a triangular roof and cross, the Cappuccin Church. In its basement is the...

Kaisergruft

Under the church sits the Imperial Crypt, filled with what's left of Austria's emperors, empresses, and other Habsburg royalty. For centuries, Vienna was the heart of a vast empire ruled by the Habsburg family, and here is where they lie buried in their fancy pewter coffins. You'll find all the Habsburg greats, including Maria Theresa, her son Josef II (Mozart's patron), Franz Josef, and Empress Sisi. Before moving on, consider paying your respects here.

• *Stretching north from the Kaisergruft is the square called...*

Neuer Markt

A block farther down, in the center of Neuer Markt, is the **four rivers fountain** showing Lady Providence surrounded by figures symbolizing the rivers that flow into the Danube. The sexy statues offended Empress Maria Theresa, who actually organized "Chastity Commissions" to defend her capital city's moral standards. The modern buildings around you were rebuilt after World War II. Half of the city's inner center was intentionally destroyed by Churchill to demoralize the Viennese, who were disconcertingly enthusiastic about the Nazis.

• *Lady Providence's one bare breast points back to Kärntner Strasse (50 yards away). Before you head back to the busy shopping street, you could stop for a sweet treat at the heavenly, recommended Kurkonditorei Oberlaa (to get there, disobey the McDonald's arrows—it's at the far-left corner of the square).*

Leave the square and return to Kärntner Strasse. Turn left and continue down Kärntner Strasse. As you approach the cathedral, you're likely to first see it as a reflection in the round-glass windows of the modern Haas Haus. Pass the U-Bahn station (which has WCs) where the street spills into Vienna's main square...

Stephansplatz

The cathedral's frilly spire looms overhead, worshippers and tourists pour inside the church, and shoppers and top-notch street entertainers buzz around the outside. You're at the center of Vienna.

The Gothic **St. Stephen's Cathedral** (c. 1300-1450) is known for its 450-foot south tower, its colorful roof, and its place in Viennese history. When it was built, it was a huge church for what was then a tiny town, and it helped put the fledgling city on the map. At this point, you may want to take a break from the walk to tour the church (see my self-guided tour on page 47).

Where Kärntner Strasse hits Stephansplatz, the grand, soot-covered building with red columns is the **Equitable Building** (filled with lawyers, bankers, and insurance brokers). It's a fine example of Neoclassicism from the turn of the 20th century—look up and imagine how slick Vienna must have felt in 1900.

Facing St. Stephen's is the sleek concrete-and-glass **Haas Haus,** a postmodern building by noted Austrian architect Hans Hollein (finished in 1990). The curved facade is supposed to echo the Roman fortress of Vindobona (its ruins were found near here). Although the Viennese initially protested having this stark modern tower right next to their beloved cathedral, since then, it's become a fixture of Vienna's main square. Notice how the smooth, rounded glass reflects St. Stephen's pointy architecture, providing a great photo opportunity—especially at twilight.

• *Exit the square with your back to the cathedral. Walk past the Haas Haus, and bear right down the street called...*

Graben

This was once a *Graben*, or ditch—originally the moat for the Roman military camp. Back during Vienna's 19th-century heyday, there were nearly 200,000 people packed into the city's inner center (inside the Ringstrasse), walking through dirt streets. Today this area houses 20,000. Graben was a busy street with three lanes of traffic until the 1970s, when it was turned into one of Europe's first pedestrian-only zones. Take a moment to absorb the scene—you're standing in an area surrounded by history, postwar rebuilding, grand architecture, fine cafés, and people enjoying life...for me, quintessential Europe.

Two blocks after leaving Stephansplatz, you reach Doro-theergasse, on your left, which leads (after two more long blocks) to the **Dorotheum** auction house. Consider poking your nose in here later for some fancy window-shopping. Also along this street are two recommended eateries: the sandwich shop Buffet Trześniewski—one of my favorite places for lunch—and the classic Café Hawelka (both described later).

In the middle of this pedestrian zone is the extravagantly blobby **Holy Trinity plague column** *(Pestsäule)*. The 60-foot pillar of clouds sprouts angels and cherubs, with the wonderfully gilded Father, Son, and Holy Ghost at the top (all protected by an anti-pigeon net).

In 1679, Vienna was hit by a massive epidemic of bubonic plague. Around 75,000 Viennese died—about a third of the city. Emperor Leopold I dropped to his knees (something emperors never did in public) and begged God to save the city. (Find Leopold about a quarter of the way up the monument, just above the brown banner. Hint: The inbreeding typical of royal families left him with a gaping underbite.) His prayer was heard by Lady Faith (the statue below Leopold, carrying a cross). With the help of a heartless little cupid, she tosses an old naked woman—symbolizing the plague—into the abyss and saves the city. In gratitude, Leopold vowed to erect this monument, which became a model for other cities ravaged by the same plague.

• *Thirty yards past the plague monument, look down the short street to the right, which frames a Baroque church with a stately green dome.*

St. Peter's Church
Leopold I ordered this church to be built as a thank-you for surviving the 1679 plague. The church stands on the site of a much older church that may have been Vienna's first (or second) Christian church. Inside, St. Peter's shows Vienna at its Baroque best. Note that the church offers free organ concerts (Mon-Fri at 15:00, Sat-Sun at 20:00).

• *Continue west on Graben, where you'll immediately find some stairs leading underground to...*

Loos' Loos
In about 1900, a local chemical-maker needed a publicity stunt to prove that his chemicals really got things clean. He purchased two wine cellars under Graben and had them turned into classy WCs in the Modernist style (designed by Adolf Loos—Vienna's answer to Frank Lloyd Wright), complete with chandeliers and finely crafted mahogany. While the chandeliers are gone, the restrooms remain a relatively appealing place to do your business—in fact, they're so inviting that they're used for poetry readings. Locals and tourists happily pay €0.50 for a quick visit.

• *Graben dead-ends at the aristocratic supermarket Julius Meinl am Graben. From here, turn left. In the distance is the big green and gold dome of the Hofburg, where we'll end this walk. The street leading up to the Hofburg is...*

Kohlmarkt
This is Vienna's most elegant and unaffordable shopping street, lined with Cartier, Armani, Gucci, Tiffany, and the emperor's palace at the end. Strolling Kohlmarkt, daydream about the edible window displays at **Demel,** the ultimate Viennese chocolate shop (#14, daily 10:00-19:00). The room is filled with Art Nouveau boxes of Empress Sisi's choco-dreams come true: *Kandierte Veilchen* (candied violet petals), *Katzenzungen* (cats' tongues), and so on. The cakes here are moist (compared to the dry Sacher-Tortes). The enticing window displays change monthly, reflecting current happenings in Vienna. Inside, there's an impressive cancan of Vienna's most beloved cakes—displayed to tempt visitors into springing

for the €10 cake-and-coffee deal (point to the cake you want). You can sit inside, with a view of the cake-making, or outside, with the street action (upstairs is less crowded). Shops like this boast "K.u.K."—signifying that during the Habsburgs' heyday, it was patronized by the *König und Kaiser* (king and emperor—same guy). If you happen to be looking through Demel's window at exactly 19:01, just after closing, you can witness one of the great tragedies of modern Europe: the daily dumping of its unsold cakes.

Next to Demel, the **Manz Bookstore** has a Loos-designed facade.

• *Kohlmarkt ends at the square called...*

Michaelerplatz

This square is dominated by the **Hofburg Palace.** Study the grand Neo-Baroque facade, dating from about 1900. The four heroic giants illustrate Hercules wrestling with his great challenges (Emperor Franz Josef, who commissioned the gate, felt he could relate).

In the center of this square, a scant bit of **Roman Vienna** lies exposed just beneath street level.

Do a slow, clockwise pan to get your bearings, starting (over your left shoulder as you face the Hofburg) with **St. Michael's Church,** which offers fascinating tours of its crypt. To the right of that is the fancy **Loden-Plankl shop,** with traditional Austrian formalwear, including dirndls. Farther to the right, across Augustinerstrasse, is the wing of the palace that houses the **Spanish Riding School** and its famous white Lipizzaner stallions. Farther down this street lies **Josefsplatz,** with the Augustinian Church, and the Dorotheum auction house. At the end of the street are Albertinaplatz and the Opera (where we started this walk).

Continue your spin: Two buildings over from the Hofburg (to the right), the modern **Loos House** (now a bank) has a facade featuring a perfectly geometrical grid of square columns and windows. Although the Loos House might seem boring today, in its time, it was considered to be Vienna's first "modern" building—with a trapezoidal footprint that makes no attempt to hide the awkwardly shaped street corner it stands on. Windows lack the customary cornice framing the top—a "house without eyebrows." Compared to the Neo-Rococo facade of the Hofburg, the stern Modernism of the Loos House appears to be from an entirely different age. And yet, both of these—as well as the Eiffel Tower and Mad Ludwig's fairy-tale Neuschwanstein Castle—were built in the same generation, roughly around 1900. In many ways, this jarring juxtaposition exemplifies the architectural turmoil of the turn of the 20th century, and represents the passing of the torch from Europe's age of divine monarchs to the modern era.

VIENNA

• *We'll finish up our tour where Austria's glorious history began—at the...*

Hofburg

This is the complex of palaces where the Habsburg emperors lived (except in summer, when they lived out at Schönbrunn Palace). Enter the Hofburg through the gate, where you immediately find yourself beneath a big rotunda (the netting is there to keep birds from perching). The doorway on the right is the entrance to the **Imperial Apartments,** where the Habsburg emperors once lived in chandeliered elegance. Today you can tour its lavish rooms, as well as a museum on Empress Sisi, and a porcelain and silver collection. To the left is the ticket office for the **Spanish Riding School.**

Continuing on, you emerge from the rotunda into the main courtyard of the Hofburg, called **In der Burg.** The Caesar-like statue is of Habsburg Emperor Franz II (1768-1835), grandson of Maria Theresa, grandfather of Franz Josef, and father-in-law of Napoleon. Behind him is a tower with three kinds of clocks (the yellow disc shows the phase of the moon tonight). To the right of Franz are the Imperial Apartments, and to the left are the offices of Austria's mostly ceremonial president (the more powerful chancellor lives in a building just behind this courtyard).

Franz Josef faces the oldest part of the palace. The colorful red, black, and gold gateway (behind you), which used to have a drawbridge, leads over the moat and into the 13th-century Swiss Court (Schweizerhof), named for the Swiss mercenary guards once stationed there. As you enter, you're passing into the historic core of the palace, the site of the first fortress, and, historically, the place of last refuge. Here you'll find the **Treasury** (Schatzkammer) and the **Imperial Music Chapel** (Hofmusikkapelle), where the Boys' Choir sings the Mass.

Back at In der Burg, face Franz and turn left, passing through the **tunnel,** with a few tourist shops and restaurants.

The tunnel spills out into spacious **Heldenplatz** (Heroes' Square). On the left is the impressive curved facade of the **New Palace** (Neue Burg). This vast wing was built in the early 1900s to be the new Habsburg living quarters (and was meant to have a matching building facing it). But in 1914, the heir to the throne, Archduke Franz Ferdinand—while waiting politely for his long-lived uncle, Emperor Franz Josef, to die—was assassinated in Sarajevo. The archduke's death sparked World War I and the eventual end of eight centuries of Habsburg rule.

This impressive building saw even sadder days a few decades later, when Adolf Hitler addressed adoring throngs from the New Palace balcony in 1938, after Austria had been annexed.

Today the building houses the **New Palace museums,** an

eclectic collection of weaponry, suits of armor, musical instruments, and ancient Greek statues. The two equestrian statues depict Prince Eugene of Savoy (1663-1736), who battled the Ottoman Turks, and Archduke Charles (1771-1847), who battled Napoleon. Eugene gazes toward the far distance at the prickly spires of Vienna's City Hall.

The Hofburg's **Burggarten** (with its much-photographed Mozart statue) is not visible from here, but it's just behind the New Palace. If you continued on through the Greek-columned passageway (the Äussere Burgtor), you'd reach the Ringstrasse, the Kunsthistorisches Museum, and the MuseumsQuartier.

• *Our walk is finished. You're in the heart of Viennese sightseeing. The Hofburg contains some of Vienna's best sights and museums. From the Opera to the Hofburg, from chocolate to churches, from St. Stephen's to Sacher-Tortes—Vienna waits for you.*

Sights in Vienna

In the Old Town, Within the Ring

These sights are listed roughly from south to north. For a self-guided walk connecting many of central Vienna's top sights—including some of the ones below—see my "Vienna City Walk," earlier.

▲▲▲**Opera (Staatsoper)**—The Opera, facing the Ring and near the TI, is a central point for any visitor. Vienna remains one of the world's great cities for classical music, and this building still belts out some of the finest opera, both classic and cutting-edge. While the critical reception of the building 130 years ago led the architect to commit suicide, and though it's been rebuilt since its destruction by WWII bombs, it's still a sumptuous place. The interior has a chandeliered lobby and carpeted staircases perfect for making the scene. The theater itself features five wrap-around balconies, gold and red decor, and a bracelet-like chandelier.

Depending on your level of tolerance for opera, you can simply admire the Neo-Renaissance building from the outside, take a guided tour of the lavish interior, visit the Opera Museum, or attend a performance.

Performances: For information on buying tickets and attending a performance, see page 85.

Tours: You can only enter the Opera if you're attending a performance or if you join a guided 45-minute tour in English (€6.50, ticket covers modest Opera Museum, described below; tours run July-Aug generally daily at the top of each hour 10:00-16:00; Sept-June fewer tours, afternoons only, and none on Sun; buy tickets 20 minutes before tour departs—ticket office is around the left side, as you face the main entrance; tcl. 01/514-442-606). Note that tour times are often changed or canceled due to rehearsals and performances. Schedules with daily listings for each month (including tour times) are posted all around the building; you can also pick up the monthly *Prolog* program, which includes the schedule for tours.

Opera Museum: Included in your opera tour ticket (whether you like it or not), this museum is a let-down. The permanent exhibit chronologically traces the illustrious history of the Vienna State Opera, highlighting the most famous singers, directors (including Gustav Mahler and Herbert von Karajan), and performances. It also features old posters, costumes, and lots of photographs (main topics in English, but most descriptions in German only). With luck, you may find something more interesting amid the special exhibits (€3, or included in the Opera tour ticket; Tue-Sun 10:00-18:00, closed Mon; across the street and a block away from the Opera toward the Hofburg, tucked down a courtyard at Hanuschgasse 3, near Albertina Museum, tel. 01/514-442-100).

▲▲**Haus der Musik**—Vienna's "House of Music" is a high-tech experience that celebrates this hometown specialty. The museum is unique for its effective use of interactive touch-screen computers and headphones to explore the physics of sound. Really experiencing the place takes time. It's open late and makes a good evening activity. The first floor features a small exhibit on the Vienna Philharmonic Orchestra, including the batons of prominent conductors and Leonard Bernstein's tux. On the second floor, wander through the "sonosphere" and marvel at the amazing acoustics. Spend some time at the well-presented, interactive headphone stations to learn about the nature of sound and music; I could actually hear what I thought only a piano tuner could discern. The third floor features fine audiovisual exhibits on each of the famous hometown boys (Haydn, Mozart, Beethoven, Schubert, Strauss, and Mahler). Before leaving, pick up a virtual baton to conduct the Vienna Philharmonic. Each time you screw up, the musicians put their instruments down and ridicule you; make it through the piece, and you'll get a rousing round of applause.

Cost and Hours: €11, includes audioguide for third floor only, half-price Tue after 17:30, €17 combo-ticket with Mozarthaus, daily 10:00-22:00, last entry one hour before closing, 2 blocks from the Opera at Seilerstätte 30, tel. 01/513-4850, www.hdm.at.

▲**The Dorotheum: Vienna's Auction House**—For an aristocrat's flea market, drop by Austria's answer to Sotheby's. The ground floor has shops, an info desk with a schedule of upcoming auctions, and a few auction items. Some items are available for immediate sale (marked *VKP*, for *Verkaufpreis*—"sales price"), while others are up for auction (marked *DIFF. RUF*). Labels on each item predict the auction value.

The three upstairs floors have antique furniture and fancy

knickknacks (some for immediate sale, others for auction), many brought in by people who've inherited old things and don't have room. Wandering through here, you feel like you're touring a museum with exhibits you can buy (Mon-Fri 10:00-18:00, Sat 9:00-17:00, closed Sun, classy little café on second floor, between the Graben pedestrian street and Hofburg at Dorotheergasse 17, tel. 01/51560, www.dorotheum.com).

Afterwards, you can continue your hunt for the perfect curio on the streets around the Dorotheum, lined with many fine antique shops.

VIENNA

▲**St. Peter's Church (Peterskirche)**—Baroque Vienna is at its best in this gem, tucked away a few steps from the Graben. Admire the rose-and-gold, oval-shaped Baroque interior, topped with a ceiling fresco of Mary kneeling to be crowned by Jesus and the Father, while the dove of the Holy Spirit floats way up in the lantern. Taken together, the church's elements—especially the organ, altar painting, pulpit, and coat of arms (in the base of the dome) of church founder Leopold I—make St. Peter's one of the city's most beautiful and ornate churches.

To the right of the altar, a dramatic golden statue shows the martyrdom of St. John Nepomuk (c. 1340-1393). The Czech saint defied the heretical King Wenceslas, so he was tossed to his death off the Charles Bridge in Prague. In true Baroque style, we see the dramatic peak of his fall, when John has just passed the point of no return. The Virgin Mary floats overhead in a silver cloud.

The present church (from 1733) stands atop earlier churches dating back 1,600 years. On either side of the nave are glass cases containing skeletons of Christian martyrs from Roman times. Above the relic on the left is a painting of the modern saint Josemaría Escrivá, founder of the conservative Catholic organization Opus Dei, of *Da Vinci Code* notoriety.

Cost and Hours: Free, Mon-Fri 7:00-19:00, Sat-Sun 9:00-19:00; free organ concerts Mon-Fri at 15:00, Sat-Sun at 20:00; just off the Graben between the Plague Monument and Kohlmarkt, tel. 01/533-6433.

Mozarthaus Vienna—Opened in 2006 to commemorate Wolfgang's 250th birthday, this museum is easy to get excited about, but it disappoints. Exhibits fill the only surviving Mozart residence in Vienna, where he lived from 1784 to 1787, when he had lots of money (and produced some of his most famous works, including *The Marriage of Figaro* and *Don Giovanni*). While the museum might be worth the time and money for enthusiasts, I much prefer the Haus der Musik (described earlier).

Cost and Hours: €10, includes audioguide, €17 combo-ticket with Haus der Musik, daily 10:00-19:00, last entry 30 minutes before closing, a block behind the cathedral, go through arcade at #5a and walk 50 yards to Domgasse 5, tel. 01/512-1791, www .mozarthausvienna.at.

Judenplatz Memorial and Museum—The classy square called Judenplatz marks the location of Vienna's 15th-century Jewish community, one of Europe's largest at the time. The square, once filled with a long-gone synagogue, is now dominated by a blocky **memorial** to the 65,000 Viennese Jews killed by the Nazis. The memorial—a library turned inside out—symbolizes Jews as "people of the book" and causes viewers to ponder the huge loss of culture, knowledge, and humanity that took place between 1938 and 1945.

The **Judenplatz Museum,** while sparse and overpriced, has displays on medieval Jewish life and a well-done video re-creating the ghetto as it looked five centuries ago. Wander the scant remains of the medieval synagogue below street level—discovered during the construction of the Holocaust memorial. This was the scene of a medieval massacre. Since Christians weren't allowed to lend money, Jews were Europe's moneylenders. As so often happened in Europe, when Viennese Christians fell too deeply into debt, they found a convenient excuse to wipe out the local ghetto—and their debts at the same time. In 1421, 200 of Vienna's Jews were burned at the stake. Others who refused a forced conversion committed mass suicide in the synagogue (€10 ticket also covers a different Jewish Museum on Dorotheergasse; alternatively, consider €15 "Vienna Museum Melange" combo-ticket with either Haus der Musik, Hundertwasser's KunstHausWien, or Mozarthaus; Sun-Thu 10:00-18:00, Fri 10:00-14:00, closed Sat, Judenplatz 8, tel. 01/535-0431, www.jmw.at).

▲▲▲St. Stephen's Cathedral (Stephansdom)

This massive church is the Gothic needle around which Vienna spins. According to the medieval vision of its creators, it stands like a giant jeweled reliquary, offering praise to God from the center of the city. The church and its towers, especially the 450-foot south tower, give the city its most iconic image. (Check your pockets for €0.10 coins; ones minted in Austria feature the south tower on the back.) The cathedral has survived Vienna's many wars and today symbolizes the city's spirit and love of freedom.

Cost: It's free to enter the back part and north aisle of the church, but it costs €3.50 to get into the main nave, where most of the interesting items are located (more for special exhibits). Going up the towers costs €3.50 (by stairs, south tower) or €4.50 (by elevator, north tower). The €14.50 combo-ticket—covering entry, audioguide, both towers, and the catacombs tour—is overkill for most visitors.

Hours: The church doors are open daily 7:00-22:00, but the main nave is open for tourists Mon-Sat 9:00-11:30 & 13:00-16:30,

Sun 13:00-16:30, until 17:30 June-Aug. During services, you can't enter the main nave (unless you're attending Mass) or access the north tower elevator or catacombs, but you can go into the back of the church.

Information: Tel. 01/515-523-526, www.stephanskirche.at.

Tours: The €4.50 **tours** in English are entertaining (daily at 15:45, check information board inside entry to confirm schedule, price includes main nave entry). The €1 **audioguide** is helpful. You can download a free Rick Steves **audio tour** of St. Stephen's; see page 7.

۞ Self-Guided Tour: This tour will give you a good look at the cathedral, inside and out.

Cathedral Exterior: Before we go inside, let's circle around the cathedral for a look at its impressive exterior.

• *As you face the church's main entry, go to the right across the little square, and find the old-time photos next to the door marked* 3a Stephansplatz. *From here, you can take in the sheer magnitude of this massive church, with its skyscraping spire.*

The church we see today is the third one on this spot. It dates mainly from 1300-1450, when builders expanded on an earlier structure and added two huge **towers** at the end of each transept. The impressive 450-foot south tower—capped with a golden orb and cross—took two generations to build (65 years) and was finished in 1433. The tower is a rarity among medieval churches in that it was completed before the Gothic style—and the age of faith—petered out. The half-size north tower (223 feet), around the other side of the church, was meant to be a matching steeple. But around 1500, it was abandoned in mid-construction, when the money was used to defend the country against the Ottomans rather than to build church towers. You can ascend both towers (stairs to the south tower, an elevator to the north tower); for details, see the end of this tour.

The cathedral was heavily damaged at the end of World War II. Near where you are standing are **old photos** showing the destruction. In 1945, Vienna was caught in the chaos between the occupying Nazis and the approaching Soviets. Allied bombs sparked fires in nearby buildings. The embers leapt to the cathedral rooftop. The original timbered Gothic roof burned, the cathedral's huge bell crashed to the ground, and the fire raged for two days. Civic pride prompted a financial outpouring, and the roof was rebuilt to its original splendor by 1952—doubly impressive considering the bombed-out state of the country at that time.

• *Circle the church exterior counterclockwise, passing the entrance to the south tower. If you're up for climbing the 343 stairs to the top, you could do it now, but it's better to wait until the end of this tour (tower climb described at the end of this tour).*

As you hook around behind the church, look for the cathedral book-shop (Dombuchhandlung) at the end of the block. Pause in front of that shop and look toward the cathedral.

Just above street level, notice the marble **pulpit** under the golden starburst. The priest would stand here, stoking public opinion against the Ottomans to crowds far bigger than could fit into the church. Above the pulpit (in a scene from around 1700), a saint stands victoriously atop a vanquished Turk.

To your right, notice the entrance to the forlorn **Cathedral Museum.** This pricey, skippable sight provides a close-up look at piles of religious paintings, statues, stained-glass windows, illuminated manuscripts, and a treasury (€7, Tue-Sat 10:00-17:00, closed Sun-Mon, Stephansplatz 6, tel. 01/515-523-689).

• *Continue circling the church, passing a line of horse carriages waiting to take tourists for a ride. Go all the way around to the west facade.*

The Romanesque-style **main entrance** is the oldest part of the church (c. 1240—part of a church that stood here before). Right behind you is the site of Vindobona, a Roman garrison town. Before the Romans converted to Christianity, there was a pagan temple here, and this entrance pays homage to that ancient heritage. Roman-era statues are embedded in the facade, and the two **octagonal towers** flanking the main doorway are dubbed the "heathen towers" because they're built with a few recycled Roman stones (flipped over to hide the pagan inscriptions and expose the smooth sides).

• *Step inside.*

Cathedral Interior: Find a spot to peer through the gate down the immense **nave**—more than a football field long and nine stories tall. Stylistically, the nave is Gothic with a Baroque overlay. The nave's columns are richly populated with 77 life-size stone statues, making a saintly parade to the high altar.

To the right as you enter, in a gold-and-silver sunburst frame, is a crude Byzantine-style **Maria Pócs Icon** (Pötscher Madonna), brought here from a humble Hungarian village church. The picture of Mary and Child is said to have wept real tears in 1697, as Central Europe was once again being threatened by the Turks.

Along the left side of the nave is the **gift shop.** Step in to marvel at the 14th-century statuary decorating its wall—some of the finest carvings in the church.

To the left of the gift shop is the gated entrance to the **Chapel of Prince Eugene of Savoy.** Prince Eugene (1663-1736), a teenage seminary student from France, arrived in Vienna in 1683 as the city was about to be overrun by the Ottoman Turks. He volunteered for the army and helped save the city, launching a brilliant career as a military man for the Habsburgs. His specialty was conquering the Ottomans. When he died, the grateful Austrians buried him here, under this chapel, marked by a tomb hatch in the floor.

• *To access the main nave of the church, you'll have to pay admission. Once through the ticket line, start down the nave toward the altar.*

At the second pillar on the left is the Gothic sandstone **pulpit** (c. 1500), a masterpiece carved from three separate blocks (see if you can find the seams). A spiral stairway winds up to the lectern, surrounded and supported by the four church "fathers," whose writings influenced early Catholic dogma. The pulpit is as crammed with religious meaning as it is with beautifully realistic carvings. The top of the stairway's railing swarms with lizards (animals of light), and toads (animals of darkness). The "Dog of the Lord" stands at the top, making sure none of those toads pollutes the sermon. Below the toads, wheels with three parts (the Trinity) roll up, while wheels with four spokes (the four seasons and the four cardinal directions, symbolizing mortal life) roll down.

Find the guy peeking out from under the stairs. This may be a **self-portrait** of the sculptor. In medieval times, art was done for the glory of God, and artists worked anonymously. But this pulpit was carved as humanist Renaissance ideals were creeping in from Italy—and individual artists were becoming famous. So the artist included what may be a rare self-portrait bust in his work.

• *Continue up to the main altar.*

During World War II, many of the city's top art treasures were stowed safely in cellars and salt mines—hidden by both the Nazi occupiers (to protect against war damage) and by citizens (to protect against Nazi looters). The **stained-glass windows** behind the high altar were meticulously dismantled and packed away. The pulpit was encased in a shell of brick. As the war was drawing to a close, it appeared St. Stephen's would escape major damage. But as the Nazis were fleeing, the bitter Nazi commander in charge of the city ordered that the church be destroyed. Fortunately, his underlings disobeyed. Unfortunately, the church accidentally caught fire during Allied bombing shortly thereafter, and the wooden roof collapsed onto the stone vaults of the ceiling. The Tupperware-colored glass on either side of the nave dates from the 1950s. Before the fire, the church was lit mostly with clear Baroque-era windows.

To the right of the main altar is the **tomb of Frederick III.** This imposing, red-marble tomb is like a big king-size-bed coffin with an effigy of Frederick lying on top (not visible—but there's a photo of the effigy on the left). The top of the tomb is decorated with his coats of arms, representing the many territories he ruled over. Frederick III (1415-1493) is considered the "father" of Vienna for turning the small village into a royal town with a cosmopolitan feel.

• *After exploring the nave, consider three more church-related sights: touring the catacombs, and ascending either one of the two towers.*

Catacombs (Katakomben): The catacombs (viewable by guided tour only) hold the bodies—or at least the innards—of 72 Habsburgs, including that of Rudolf IV, the man who began building the south tower. This is where Austria's rulers were buried before the Kaisergruft was built (see page 60), and where later Habsburgs' entrails were entombed. The copper urns preserve the imperial organs in alcohol. I touched Maria Theresa's urn...and it wobbled (€4.50, daily 10:00-11:30 & 13:30-16:30, until 17:30 June-Aug, tours depart about every 30 minutes and are in German and English). Just be at the stairs in the left/north transept to meet the guide.

Ascending the North Tower: This tower, reached from inside the church (look for the *Aufzug zur Pummerin* sign), holds the famous "Pummerin" bell—cast from captured Ottoman cannons, this bell rings in the New Year. This tower is easier to ascend than the south tower (described next), but it's much shorter and not as exciting, with lesser views (€4.50, daily 9:00-11:30 & 13:00-16:30, until 17:30 in June-Aug, entrance inside the church on the left/north side of the nave; you can access this elevator without buying a ticket for the main nave).

Climbing the South Tower: The iconic south tower offers a far better view than the north one, but you'll earn it by climbing 343 tightly wound steps up the spiral staircase (€3.50, daily 9:00-17:30; this hike burns about one Sacher-Torte of calories). To reach the entrance, exit the church and make a U-turn to the left. This tower, once key to the city's defense as a lookout point, is still dear to Viennese hearts. (It's long been affectionately nicknamed "Steffl," Viennese for "Stevie.") No church spire in (what was) the Austro-Hungarian Empire is taller—by Habsburg decree. From the top, use your city map to locate the famous sights.

The Hofburg Palace

The complex, confusing, and imposing Imperial Palace, with 640 years of architecture, demands your attention. This first Habsburg residence grew with the family empire from the 13th century until 1913, when the last "new wing" opened. The winter residence of the Habsburg rulers until 1918, it's still the home of the Austrian president's office, 5,000 government workers, and several important museums. For an overview of the palace layout, see map opposite.

Planning Your Time: Don't get confused by the Hofburg's myriad courtyards and many museums. Focus on three sights: the Imperial Apartments, Treasury, and the museums at the New Palace (Neue Burg). With more time, consider the Hofburg's many other sights, covering virtually all facets of the imperial lifestyle.

Eating at the Hofburg: Down the tunnel to Heroes' Square is

Vienna's Hofburg Palace

SCHAUFLERGASSE
LOOS HOUSE
CAFÉ DEMEL
KOHLMARKT
Ballhaus-platz
Volksgarten
Michaeler-platz
ROMAN RUINS
ST. MICHAEL'S
❾
EMPEROR FRANZ I STATUE
IMPERIAL APARTMENTS
In der Burg
❷
❺
REITSCHUL
❶
WC
ARCHDUKE KARL STATUE
Schweizer-hof
❸
❿
GASSE
❺
EMPEROR JOSEF II STATUE
DOROTHEUM
TREASURY ENTRANCE
Josefsplatz
AUGUSTINERSTRASSE
Heldenplatz (Heroes' Square)
PRINCE EUGENE STATUE
❼
SPIEGELGASSE
BURGTOR
❻
NEW PALACE
❹
❽
To Kaisergruft
❶❶
ALBERTINA MUSEUM
MUSEUM ENTRANCE
MUSEUM ENTRANCE
BURGRING
Burg-garten
Albertina-platz
KUNST-HISTORISCHES MUSEUM
Burgring
MOZART STATUE
GOETHEGASSE
OPERA MUSEUM
OPERNGASSE
OPERA
BABENBERGERSTR.
OPERNRING
To Mariahilfer-strasse
GOETHE STATUE
50 Meters
50 Yards

- ❶ In der Burg Square
- ❷ Imperial Apartments
- ❸ Schweizerhof (Entrances to Treasury & Imperial Music Chapel)
- ❹ New Palace Museums
- ❺ Spanish Riding School Tickets (2 Locations)
- ❻ Augustinian Church
- ❼ National Library & Soho Kantine
- ❽ Butterfly House
- ❾ Rest. zum Alten Hofkeller
- ❿ Hofburg Stüberl (Snacks)
- ❶❶ Café Restaurant Palmenhaus

VIENNA

a tiny but handy sandwich bar called **Hofburg Stüberl.** It's ideal for a cool, quiet sit and a drink or snack (same €3 sandwich price whether you sit or go, Mon-Fri 7:00-18:00, Sat-Sun 10:00-16:00). For a cheap, quick meal, duck into the mod and efficient, cafeteria-style **Restaurant zum Alten Hofkeller** in a cellar under the palace (€5 plates, Mon-Fri 7:30-13:30, closed Sat-Sun and in Aug, on the street that runs along the right side of the Hofburg as you face the main entry, on the left-hand side at Schauflergasse 7). The **Soho Kantine,** in the basement of the National Library, is a cheap-but-not-cheery option (described on page 106).

▲▲▲Hofburg Imperial Apartments (Kaiserappartements)

These lavish, Versailles-type, "wish-I-were-God" royal rooms are the downtown version of the grander Schönbrunn Palace. If you're rushed and have time for only one palace, make it this one. Palace visits are a one-way romp through three separate exhibits: a porcelain and silver collection, a museum dedicated to the enigmatic and troubled Empress Sisi, and the luxurious apartments themselves.

The Imperial Apartments are a mix of Old World luxury and modern 19th-century conveniences. Here, Emperor Franz Josef I lived and worked along with his wife Elisabeth, known as Sisi. The Sisi Museum traces the development of her legend, analyzing how her fabulous but tragic life created a 19th-century Princess Diana. You'll read bits of her poetic writing, see exact copies of her now-lost jewelry, and learn about her escapes, dieting mania, and chocolate bills.

Cost and Hours: €10.50, includes well-done audioguide, also covered by €23.50 Sisi Ticket (see page 28), daily July-Aug 9:00-18:00, Sept-June 9:00-17:30, last entry one hour before closing, enter from courtyard through St. Michael's Gate—just off Michaelerplatz, tel. 01/533-7570, www.hofburg-wien.at.

Information: With the included audioguide and the self-guided tour below, you won't need the €8 *Imperial Apartments/Sisi Museum/Silver Collection* guidebook. If you listen to the entire audioguide, allow 40 minutes for the silver collection, 30 minutes for the Sisi Museum, and 40 minutes for the apartments.

❷ Self-Guided Tour: Your visit (and the excellent audioguide) starts on the ground floor.

Imperial Porcelain and Silver Collection: Here you'll see the Habsburg court's vast tableware collection, which the audioguide actually manages to make fairly interesting. Browse the collection to gawk at the opulence and to take in some colorful Habsburg trivia. (Who'd have thunk that the court had an official way to fold a napkin—and that the technique remains a closely guarded secret?)

Once you're through all those rooms of dishes, climb the stairs—the same staircase used by the emperors and empresses who lived here. At the top is a timeline of Sisi's life. Swipe your ticket to pass through the turnstile, consider the WC, and enter the room with the **Model of the Hofburg.** Circle to the far side to find where you're standing right now, near the smallest of the Hofburg's three domes. The Hofburg was the epicenter of one of Europe's great political powers—600 years of Habsburgs lived here. The Hofburg started as a 13th-century medieval castle (near where you are right now) and expanded over the centuries to today's 240,000-square-meter (60-acre) complex, now owned by the state. To the left of the dome (as you face the facade) is the steeple of the

Augustinian Church. It was there, in 1854, that Franz Josef married 16-year-old Elisabeth of Bavaria, and their story began.

Sisi Museum: Empress Elisabeth (1837-1898)—a.k.a. "Sisi" (SEE-see)—was Franz Josef's mysterious, beautiful, and narcissistic wife. This museum traces her fabulous but tragic life. The exhibit starts where her life ended and her legend began (see her death mask and pictures of her funeral procession). You'll read bits of her poetic writing, see exact copies of her now-lost jewelry, and learn about her escapes, dieting mania, and chocolate bills. Admire Sisi's hard-earned thin waist (20 inches at age 16, 21 inches at age 50...after giving birth to four children). The black statue in the dark room represents the empress after the suicide of her son—aloof, thin, in black, with her back to the world. At the end, ponder the crude, knife-like file that an Italian anarchist used to murder Sisi in Geneva in 1898.

Imperial Apartments: After the Sisi Museum, a one-way route takes you through a series of royal rooms. The first room— as if to make clear that there was more to the Habsburgs than Sisi—shows a family tree tracing the Habsburgs from 1273 to their messy WWI demise. From here, enter the private apartments of the royal family (Franz Josef's first, then Sisi's).

Franz Josef's apartments illustrate the lifestyle of the last great Habsburg ruler. In these rooms, he presided over defeats and liberal inroads as the world was changing and the monarchy becoming obsolete. Here he met with advisors and welcomed foreign dignitaries, hosted lavish, white-gloved balls and stuffy formal dinners, and raised three children. He slept (alone) on his austere bed while his beloved wife Sisi retreated to her own rooms. He suffered through the assassination of his brother, the suicide of his son and heir, the murder of his wife, and the assassination of his nephew, Archduke Ferdinand, which sparked World War I and spelled the end of the Habsburg monarchy.

Among the Franz Josef rooms you'll see is the **audience room,** where Franz Josef received commoners from around the empire. They came from far and wide to show gratitude or to make a request. Imagine you've traveled for days to have your say before the emperor. You're wearing your new fancy suit—Franz Josef required that men coming before him wear a tailcoat, women a black gown with a train. You've rehearsed what you want to say. You hope your hair looks good. Suddenly, you're face-to-face with the emp himself. (The portrait on the easel shows Franz Josef in 1915, when he was more than 80 years old.) Despite your efforts, you probably weren't in this room long. He'd stand at the high table (far left) as the visiting commoners had their say. (Standing kept things moving.) You'd hear a brief response from him (quite likely the same he'd given all day), and then you'd back out of the room while bowing (also required). On the table is a partial list of 56 appointments he had on January 3, 1910 (three columns: family name, meeting topic, and *Anmerkung*—the emperor's "action log").

Franz Josef's **bedroom** shows off his spartan lifestyle. Notice his no-frills iron bed. He typically rose at 3:30 and started his day in prayer, kneeling at the prayer stool against the far wall. While he had a typical emperor's share of mistresses, his dresser was always well-stocked with photos of Sisi.

Sisi's Rooms include her exercise/dressing room, where servants worked three hours a day on the empress' famous hair. She'd exercise on the wooden structure and on the rings suspended from the doorway to the left. Afterward, she'd get a massage on the red-covered bed. In Sisi's main bathroom, you'll see her huge copper tub (with the original wall coverings behind it), where servants washed her hair—an all-day affair. Sisi was the first Habsburg to have running water in her bathroom (notice the hot and cold faucets). In the small salon, the portrait is of Crown Prince Rudolf, Franz Josef and Sisi's only son. On the morning of January 30, 1889, the 30-year-old Rudolf and a beautiful baroness were found shot dead in an apparent murder-suicide in his hunting lodge in Mayerling. The scandal shocked the empire and tainted the Habsburgs; Sisi retreated further into her fantasy world, and Franz Josef carried on stoically with a broken heart.

The tour ends in the **dining room.** It's dinnertime, and Franz Josef has called his extended family together. The settings are modest...just silver. Gold was saved for formal state dinners. Next to each name card was a menu listing the chef responsible for each dish. (Talk about pressure.) While the Hofburg had tableware for 4,000, feeding 3,000 was a typical day. The cellar was stocked with 60,000 bottles of wine. The kitchen was huge—50 birds could be roasted at once on the hand-driven spits. Franz Josef enforced strict protocol at mealtime: No one could speak without being spoken to by the emperor, and no one could eat after he was done. While the rest of Europe was growing democracy and expanding personal freedoms, the Habsburgs preserved their ossified worldview to the bitter end.

In 1918, World War I ended, Austria was created as a modern nation-state, the Habsburgs were tossed out...and Hofburg Palace was destined to become a museum.

▲▲▲Hofburg Treasury (Weltliche und Geistliche Schatzkammer)

One of the world's most stunning collections of royal regalia, the Hofburg Treasury shows off sparkling crowns, jewels, gowns, and assorted Habsburg bling in 21 darkened rooms. The treasures, well-explained by an audioguide, include the crown of the Holy

Roman Emperor, Charlemagne's saber, a "unicorn horn," and more precious gems than you can shake a scepter at.

Cost and Hours: €12, €18 combo-ticket with Kunsthistorisches Museum and New Palace museums, Wed-Mon 10:00-18:00, closed Tue; from the Hofburg's central courtyard pass through the black, red, and gold gate, then follow *Schatzkammer* signs to the Schweizerhof; tel. 01/525-240, www.khm.at.

Audioguide Tours: A basic audioguide covering the top 11 jewels is included with your ticket. Or, for €2, you can rent an audioguide programmed to describe the top 100 stops—well worth it to get the most out of this dazzling collection.

❍ Self-Guided Tour: Here's a rundown of the highlights (the audioguide is much more complete).

Room 2: The personal crown of Rudolf II has survived since 1602—it was considered too well-crafted to cannibalize for other crowns. It's a big deal because it's the adopted crown of the Austrian Empire, established in 1806 after Napoleon dissolved the Holy Roman Empire (an alliance of Germanic kingdoms so named because it wanted to be considered the continuation of the Roman Empire). Pressured by Napoleon, the Austrian Francis II—who had been Holy Roman Emperor—became Francis I, Emperor of Austria (the stern guy on the wall, near where you entered). Look at the crown. Its design symbolically merges a bishop's miter ("Holy"), the arch across the top of a Roman emperor's helmet ("Roman"), and the typical medieval king's crown ("Emperor").

Rooms 3 and 4: These rooms contain some of the **coronation vestments and regalia** needed for the new Austrian (not Holy Roman) Emperor. There was a different one for each of the emperor's subsidiary titles, e.g., King of Hungary or King of Lombardy. So many crowns and kingdoms in the Habsburgs' vast empire!

Room 5: Ponder the **Cradle of the King of Rome,** once occupied by Napoleon's son, who was born in 1811 and made King of Rome. While pledging allegiance to democracy, Napoleon in fact crowned himself Emperor of France and hobnobbed with Europe's royalty. When his wife, Josephine, could not bear him a male heir, Napoleon divorced her and married into the Habsburg family. With the birth of the baby King of Rome, Napoleon and his new wife, Marie Louise, were poised to start a new dynasty of European rulers...but then Napoleon met his Waterloo, and the Habsburgs remained in power.

Room 6: For Divine Right kings, even child-rearing was a sacred ritual that needed elaborate regalia for public ceremonies. The 23-pound **gold basin and pitcher** were used to baptize noble children, who were dressed in the **hooded baptismal dresses** displayed nearby.

Room 7: These jewels are the true "treasures," a cabinet of wonders used by Habsburgs to impress their relatives (or to hock when funds got low).

Room 8: The eight-foot-tall, 500-year-old **"unicorn horn"** (a narwhal tusk), was considered to have magical healing powers bestowed from on high. This one was owned by the Holy Roman Emperor—clearly a divine monarch.

Religious Rooms: The next several rooms contain **religious objects**—crucifixes, chalices, mini-altarpieces, reliquaries, and bishops' vestments. Habsburg rulers mixed the institutions of church and state, so these precious religious accoutrements were also part of their display of secular power.

Room 10: The big red-silk and gold-thread **mantle,** nearly 900 years old, was worn by Holy Roman Emperors at their coronation.

Room 11: The collection's highlight is the 10th-century **crown of the Holy Roman Emperor.** It was probably made for Otto I (c. 960), the first king to call himself Holy Roman Emperor. The Imperial Crown swirls with symbolism "proving" that the emperor was both holy and Roman: The cross on top says the HRE ruled as Christ's representative on earth, and the jeweled arch over the top is reminiscent of the parade helmet of ancient Romans. The jewels themselves allude to the wearer's kinghood in the here and now. Imagine the impression this priceless, glittering crown must have made on the emperor's medieval subjects.

Nearby is the 11th-century **Imperial Cross** that preceded the emperor in ceremonies. Encrusted with jewels, it had a hollow compartment (its core is wood) that carried substantial chunks thought to be from *the* **cross** on which Jesus was crucified and *the* **Holy Lance** used to pierce his side (both pieces are displayed in the same glass case). Holy Roman Emperors actually carried the lance into battle in the 10th century. Look behind the cross to see how it was a box that could be clipped open and shut, used for holding holy relics. You can see bits of the "true cross" anywhere, but this is a prime piece—with the actual nail hole.

Room 12: Now picture all this regalia used together. The **painting** shows the coronation of Maria Theresa's son Josef II as Holy Roman Emperor in 1764. Set in a church in Frankfurt (filled with the bigwigs—literally—of the day), Josef is wearing the same crown and royal garb that you've just seen.

Room 12 also displays the **leather cases** used to store and transport the crowns, crosses, and other objects. Another glass case contains **relics**—such as a fragment of Jesus' manger, a piece of Christ's loincloth, and a shred of the Last Supper tablecloth.

The Rest of the Treasury: Rooms 13-15 have (among other things) **portraits of important Habsburgs,** such as Maximilian I and Mary of Burgundy. Room 16 contains the **royal vestments** (15th century), which display perhaps the most exquisite workmanship in the entire Treasury. Look closely—they're "painted" with gold and silver threads. But after seeing so much bling, by the time you view these vestments, they can seem downright understated— just another example of the pomp and circumstance of the majestic Habsburgs.

More Hofburg Sights

▲▲Hofburg New Palace Museums—The New Palace (Neue Burg) houses three separate collections (covered by a single ticket): The **Arms and Armor Collection** displays weaponry and body armor from all over the vast Habsburg Empire, including exotic Turkish suits of armor. The **Ancient Musical Instruments Collection** shows instruments through the ages, especially the rapid evolution from harpsichord to piano. Admire Beethoven's (supposed) clarinet, Leopold Mozart's violin, a keyboard perhaps played by Wolfgang Mozart, and Brahms' piano. The **Ephesus Museum** has artifacts from the bustling ancient Roman city of 300,000 people (located in modern-day Turkey, near Kuşadası on the southwestern coast). The *Bronze Statue of an Athlete* is a jigsaw of 234 shattered pieces meticulously put back together. The *Statue of Artemis,* representing a pagan fertility goddess, is draped with sexy round objects—which may have symbolized breasts, eggs, or bulls' testicles. The included audioguide brings the exhibits to life and lets you hear the collection's fascinating old instruments being played. An added bonus is the chance to wander alone among the royal Habsburg halls, stairways, and painted ceilings.

Cost and Hours: €12, ticket covers all three collections and the Kunsthistorisches Museum across the Ring, €18 combo-ticket also includes the Hofburg Treasury, Wed-Sun 10:00-18:00, closed Mon-Tue, last entry 30 minutes before closing, almost no tourists, tel. 01/525-240, www.khm.at.

▲Spanish Riding School—This stately 300-year-old Baroque Hall at the Hofburg Palace is the home of the renowned Lipizzaner stallions. The magnificent building was an impressive expanse in its day. Built without pillars, it offers clear views of the prancing horses under lavish chandeliers, with a grand statue of Emperor Charles VI on horseback at the head of the hall.

Lipizzaner stallions were a creation of horse-loving Habsburg Archduke Charles, who wanted to breed the perfect animal. He imported Andalusian horses from his homeland of Spain, then mated them with a local line to produce an extremely intelligent and easily trainable breed. Italian and Arabian bloodlines were later added to tweak various characteristics. Lipizzaner stallions are known for their noble gait and Baroque profile. These regal horses have changed shape with the tenor of the times: They were bred strong and stout during wars, and frilly and slender in more cultured eras. But they're always born black, fade to gray, and turn a distinctive white in adulthood.

The school offers three options for seeing the horses:

Performances: The Lipizzaner stallions put on great 80-minute shows in spring and fall (late Aug-late June Sun at 11:00 and either Sat at 11:00 or Fri at 19:00, fewer shows in Jan-Feb, none late June-late Aug, tel. 01/533-9031, www.srs.at). The formal emcee thoughtfully introduces each number in German and English as horses do their choreographed moves to jaunty recorded Viennese classical music (in 4:4 meter rather than 3:4—I guess the horses don't waltz). The pricey seats book up months in advance, but standing room is usually available the same day, and there's not a bad view in the house (seats: €47-173, standing room: €23-31; box office opens at 9:00 and is located inside the Hofburg—go through the main Hofburg entryway from Michaelerplatz, then turn left into the first passage).

Training Sessions: Luckily for the masses, training sessions with music take place in the same hall and are open to the public. Don't have high expectations, as the horses often do little more than trot and warm up (€14 at the door, roughly early Aug-late June Tue-Fri 10:00-12:00—but only when the horses are in town). Tourists line up early at Josefsplatz (the large courtyard between Michaelerplatz and Albertinaplatz), at the door marked *Spanische Hofreitschule*. But there's no need to show up when the doors open at 10:00, since tickets never really "sell out." Only the horses stay for the full two hours. As people leave, new tickets are printed, so you can just prance in with no wait at all. You can also buy tickets for the training sessions at the box office.

Stables: Any time of day, you can see the horses in their stalls and view videos of them prancing in the Reitschulgasse corridor. Guided one-hour tours of stalls are given daily (€16; tours at 14:00, 15:00, and 16:00; in English and German, reserve by calling 01/533-9031).

▲**Augustinian Church (Augustinerkirche)**—This is the Gothic and Neo-Gothic church where the Habsburgs got latched (weddings took place here), then dispatched (the royal hearts are in the vault—not open to the public). Don't miss the exquisite, tomb-like Canova memorial (Neoclassical, 1805) to Maria Theresa's favorite daughter, Maria Christina, with its incredibly sad white-marble procession. The church's 11:00 Sunday Mass is a hit with music-lovers—both a Mass and a concert, often with an orchestra accompanying the choir (acoustics are best in front). Pay by contributing to the offering plate and buying a CD afterwards. Programs are posted by the entry (church open long hours daily, Augustinerstrasse 3—facing Josefsplatz, with its statue of the great reform emperor Josef II and the imperial library next door).

Austrian National Library—Next to the Augustinian Church, this was once the library of the Habsburgs. Wandering through this impressive temple of learning—with a statue of Charles VI in the center—you find yourself whispering. The setting takes you back to 1730 and gives you the sense that, in imperial times, knowledge of the world was for the elite—and with that knowledge, the elite had power (€7, Tue-Sun 10:00-18:00, Thu until 21:00, closed Mon, recommended Soho Kantine in the basement good for a cheap lunch).

Burggarten (Palace Garden) and Butterfly House—This greenbelt, once the backyard of the Hofburg and now a people's park, welcomes visitors to loiter on the grass. On nice days, it's lively with office workers enjoying a break. The statue of Mozart facing the Ringstrasse is popular. The iron-and-glass pavilion now houses the recommended Café Restaurant Palmenhaus and a small but fluttery butterfly exhibit (€5.50; April-Oct Mon-Fri 10:00-16:45, Sat-Sun 10:00-18:15; Nov-March daily 10:00-15:45).

▲▲Albertina Museum—This building, at the southern tip of the Hofburg complex (near the Opera), was the residence of Maria Theresa's favorite daughter, Maria Christina, who was the only one allowed to marry for love rather than political strategy. Her many sisters were jealous. (Marie-Antoinette had to marry the French king...and lost her head over it.)

Maria Christina's husband, Albert of Saxony, was a great collector of original drawings and amassed an enormous assortment of works by Dürer, Rembrandt, Rubens, Schiele, and others. Today, reproductions of some of these works hang in the Albertina's elegant French-Classicist–style **state rooms** (*Prunkräume*). Head to these rooms first for a great opportunity to wander freely under the chandeliers of a Habsburg palace, with its pure 19th-century imperial splendor unconstrained by velvet ropes.

Then follow signs for *Meisterwerke der Moderne* (*Die Sammlung Batliner*, on the top floor). These modern galleries hold a wonderful rotating exhibit from the museum's **Batliner collection** of modern art (from Impressionism to Abstract Expressionism, with minor works by major artists—Monet, Picasso, Chagall, Matisse), along with temporary exhibits.

To understand both the imperial apartments and the wonderful Batliner works, invest in the €4 **audioguide,** which makes this collection a luxurious lesson in modern art appreciation—from Monet to today.

Cost and Hours: €11, generally meaningless without €4 audioguide, daily 10:00-18:00, Wed until 21:00, overlooking Albertinaplatz across from the TI and Opera, tel. 01/534-830, www.albertina.at.

Church Crypts near the Hofburg

Two churches near the Hofburg offer starkly different looks at dearly departed Viennese: the Habsburg coffins in the Kaisergruft, and the commoners' graves in St. Michael's Church.

▲▲Kaisergruft: The Remains of the Habsburgs—Visiting the imperial remains is not as easy as you might imagine. These original organ donors left their bodies—about 150 in all—in the unassuming Kaisergruft (the Imperial Crypt at the Cappuccin Church), their hearts in the Augustinian Church (vaults closed to public), and their entrails in the crypt below St. Stephen's Cathedral (described on page 50). Don't tripe.

Cost and Hours: €5, daily 10:00-18:00, last entry at 17:40, behind the Opera on Neuer Markt, tel. 01/512-6853.

Highlights: As you enter, be sure to buy the €0.50 map with a Habsburg family tree and a chart locating each coffin.

Find the pewter double-coffin under the dome. This tomb of **Maria Theresa** (1717-1780) and her husband, **Franz I** (1708-1765), is worth a close look for its artwork. Maria Theresa outlived her husband by 15 years—which she spent in mourning. Old and fat, she installed a special lift enabling her to get down into the crypt to be with her dear, departed Franz (even though he had been far from faithful). The couple reclines—Etruscan-style—atop a fancy lead coffin. At each corner are the crowns of the Habsburgs—the Holy Roman Empire, Hungary, Bohemia, and Jerusalem. Notice the contrast between the Rococo splendor of Maria Theresa's tomb and the simple box holding her more modest son, **Josef II** (at his parents' feet). This understated tomb is in keeping with his enlightened politics.

Nearby, find the appropriately austere military tomb of **Franz Josef** (1830-1916) in the more brightly lit modern section. Flanking Franz Josef are the tombs of his son, the archduke **Rudolf,** and Empress Elisabeth. Rudolf and his teenage mistress supposedly committed suicide together in 1889 at Mayerling hunting lodge and—since the Church figured he forced her to take her own life and was therefore a murderer—it took considerable legal hairsplitting to win Rudolf this spot (after examining his brain, it was determined that he was mentally disabled and therefore incapable of knowingly killing himself and his girl). *Kaiserin* Elisabeth (1837-1898), a.k.a. **Sisi,** always gets the "Most Flowers" award.

In front of those three are the two most recent Habsburg tombs. **Empress Zita** was laid to rest here in 1989, followed by her son, **Karl Ludwig,** in 2007. The funeral procession for Karl, the fourth son of the last Austrian emperor, was probably the last such Old Regime event in European history. The monarchy died hard in Austria. Today there are about 700 living Habsburg royals, mostly living in exile. When they die, they get buried in their countries of exile.

Body parts and ornate tombs aside, the real legacy of the Habsburgs is the magnificence of this city. Step outside. Pan up. Watch the clouds glide by the ornate gables of Vienna.

▲**St. Michael's Church Crypt**—St. Michael's Church, which faces the Hofburg on Michaelerplatz, offers a striking contrast to the imperial crypt. Regular tours take visitors underground to see a typical church crypt—filled with the rotting wooden coffins of well-to-do commoners.

Climbing below the church, you'll see about a hundred 18th-century coffins and stand on three feet of debris, surrounded by niches filled with stacked lumber from decayed coffins and countless bones. You'll meet a 1769 mummy in lederhosen and a wig, along with a woman clutching a cross with flowers painted on her high heels. You'll learn about death in those times—from how the wealthy didn't want to end up in standard shallow graves, instead paying to be laid to rest below the church, to how, in 1780, the enlightened emperor Josef II ended the practice of cemetery burials in cities but allowed the rich to become the stinking rich in crypts under churches. You'll also discover why many were buried with their chins strapped shut (because when the muscles rot, your jaw falls open and you get that ghostly skeleton look that nobody wants).

Cost and Hours: €5 for 45-minute tour, Mon-Sat at 11:00 and 13:30, mostly in German but with enough English, wait at the sign that advertises the tour at the church entrance and pay the guide directly.

Kunsthistorisches Museum and Nearby

▲▲▲**Kunsthistorisches Museum**—This exciting museum, across the Ring from the Hofburg Palace, showcases the grandeur and opulence of the Habsburgs' collected artwork in a grand building (purpose-built in 1888 to display these works). While there's little Viennese art here, you will find world-class European masterpieces galore (including canvases by Raphael, Caravaggio, Velázquez, Dürer, Rubens, Vermeer, Rembrandt, and a particularly exquisite roomful of Bruegels), all well-hung on one glorious floor, plus a fine display of Egyptian, classical, and applied arts.

Cost and Hours: €12, also includes New Palace museums across the Ring; free for kids under 18, €18 combo-ticket also includes the Hofburg Treasury, Tue-Sun 10:00-18:00, Thu until 21:00, closed Mon, on the Ringstrasse at Maria-Theresien-Platz, U-2 or U-3: Volkstheater/Museumsplatz (exit toward *Burgring*), tel. 01/525-240, www.khm.at.

Audioguide Tours: You can rent an audioguide at the desk in the atrium. The free "Highlights" audioguide covers a selection of 20 pieces (including just 13 paintings). The €3 "Total" audio-guide is far more comprehensive, covering 560 items (worth it if you want an in-depth tour).

⊙ **Self-Guided Tour:** The Kunsthistorwhateveritis Museum—let's just say "Koonst"—houses some of the most beautiful, sexy, and fun art from two centuries (c. 1450-1650). The collection reflects the joie de vivre of Austria's luxury-loving Habsburg rulers. At their peak of power in the 1500s, the Habsburgs ruled Austria, Germany, northern Italy, the Netherlands, and Spain—and you'll see a wide variety of art from all these places and beyond.

VIENNA

If you're short on time, focus on the Painting Gallery *(Gemäldegalerie)* on the first floor. Climb the main staircase, featuring Antonio Canova's statue of *Theseus Clubbing the Centaur.* Italian, Spanish, and French art is in the right half of the building (as you face Theseus), and Northern European art to the left. Notice that the museum labels the largest rooms with Roman numerals (Saal I, II, III), and the smaller rooms around the perimeter with Arabic (Rooms 1, 2, 3).

Italian, Spanish, and French Art: Saals I-III cover the Venetian renaissance. The first spans the long career of **Titian,** who painted portraits, Christian Madonnas, and sexy Venuses with equal ease. Next comes Paolo **Veronese,** whose colorful works reflect the wealth of Venice, the funnel through which luxury goods from the exotic East flowed into northern Europe. And **Tintoretto**'s many portraits give us a peek at the movers and shakers of the Venetian Empire.

Rooms 1-4 hold some of the museum's most important works: **Mantegna**'s *St. Sebastian,* **Correggio**'s *Jupiter and Io,* and **Raphael**'s *Madonna of the Meadow (Die Madonna im Grünen),* a geometrically perfect masterpiece of the High Renaissance, painted when Raphael was just 22.

Farther along, through the small rooms along the far end of this wing (likely Room 7, or possibly out on loan), find the cleverly deceptive portraits by Giuseppe **Arcimboldo.** With a pickle nose, pear chin, and corn-husk ears, Arcimboldo's subject literally is what he eats.

Caravaggio (in Saal V) shocked the art world with brutally honest reality. Compared with Raphael's super-sweet *Madonna of the Meadow,* Caravaggio's *Madonna of the Rosary* (*Die Rosenkranzmadonna,* the biggest canvas in the room) looks perfectly ordinary, and the saints kneeling around her have dirty feet. In *David with the Head of Goliath (David mit dem Haupt des Goliath)* Caravaggio turns a third-degree-interrogation light on a familiar Bible story. David shoves the dripping head of the slain giant—the artist's self portrait—right in our noses.

When the Habsburgs ruled both Austria and Spain, cous-

Kunsthistorisches Museum

To Opera

VAN DER WEYDEN & VAN EYCK

DÜRER   BOSCH

EARLY NORTHERN ART

COREGGIO & PARMIGIANINO

MANTEGNA

RAPHAEL

17   16   14

HOLBEIN

SNYDERS

Saal XI   Saal X   Saal IX

BRUEGEL

WC   WC

THESEUS STATUE

TITIAN Saal I

1   2   3   4

VERONESE Saal II

TINTO-RETTO

Saal III

NORTHERN EUROPEAN ART

TOUR BEGINS

ITALIAN, SPANISH & FRENCH ART

RINGSTRASSE

MORE NORTHERN ART

MAIN STAIRCASE

CAFÉ

MORE ITALIAN ART

ARCIMBOLDO

RUBENS

Saal XIII   Saal XIV   Saal XV

CANALETTO Saal VII

BAROQUE Saal VI

CARA-VAGGIO Saal V

7

21   22   VERMEER   23

VELÁZQUEZ 10

TOUR ENDS

REMBRANDT

Not to Scale

ENTRANCE (on ground level)

MARIA-THERESIEN-PLATZ

VIENNA

ins kept in touch through portraits of themselves and their kids. Diego **Velázquez** (in Room 10) was the greatest of Spain's "photojournalist" painters: heavily influenced by Caravaggio's realism, capturing his subjects without passing judgment, flattering, or glorifying them.

Northern European Art: The other half of this floor features works of the "Northern Renaissance," which was more secular and Protestant than Catholic-funded Italian art (that means fewer Madonnas, saints, and Greek gods and more peasants, landscapes, and food). Paintings are smaller and darker, full of down-to-earth objects. Northern artists sweated the details, encouraging the patient viewer to appreciate the beauty in everyday things.

The undisputed master of the slice-of-life village scene was Pieter **Bruegel** the Elder—the Norman Rockwell of the 16th century. Saal X contains the largest collection of Bruegels in captivity. Despite his many rural paintings, Bruegel was actually a cultivated urbanite who liked to wear peasants' clothing to observe country folk at play (a trans-fest-ite?). He celebrated their simple life, but he also skewered their weaknesses—not to single them out as hicks, but as universal examples of human folly. *The Peasant Wedding (Bauernhochzeit),* Bruegel's most famous work, is less about the wedding than the food. It's a farmers' feeding frenzy, as the barnful of wedding guests scrambles to get their share of free eats. *Bruegel's Peasant Dance (Bauerntanz)* shows a celebration at the consecration of a village church. The three Bruegel landscape paintings are part of an original series of six "calendar" paintings, depicting the seasons of the year.

Also in this section, don't miss **Rubens**' large, lush canvases (including *The Little Fur/Das Pelzchen,* depicting his much younger, dimpled bride); **Vermeer**'s *The Art of Painting (Die Malkunst),* showing the painter at work in his studio, with a painstaking attention to detail; and **Rembrandt**'s frank self-portraits—one as a defiant young artist, the other as a broken old man.

▲**Natural History Museum**—In the twin building facing the Kunsthistorisches Museum, you'll find moon rocks, dinosaur stuff, and the fist-sized *Venus of Willendorf*—at 25,000 years old, the world's oldest sex symbol. This four-inch-tall, chubby stone statuette, found in the Danube Valley, is a generic female (no face or feet) resting her hands on her ample breasts. The statue's purpose is unknown, but she may have been a symbol of fertility for our mammoth-hunting ancestors. Even though the museum is not glitzy or high-tech, it's a hit with children and scientifically curious grown-ups. Of the museum's 20 million objects, you're sure to find something interesting.

Cost and Hours: €10, Wed-Mon 9:00-18:30, Wed until 21:00, closed Tue, on the Ringstrasse at Maria-Theresien-Platz, U-2 or U-3: Volkstheater/Museumsplatz, tel. 01/521-770, www .nhm-wien.ac.at.

MuseumsQuartier—The vast grounds of the former imperial stables now corral a cutting-edge cultural center for contemporary arts and design, including several impressive museums; the best are the Leopold Museum and the Museum of Modern Art.

Walk into the complex from the Hofburg side, where the main entrance (with visitors center, shop, and ticket office) leads to a big courtyard with cafés, fountains, and ever-changing "installation lounge furniture," all surrounded by the quarter's various museums. At the visitors center, various **combo-tickets** are available for those interested in more than just the Leopold and Modern Art museums. You can also rent a €4 **audioguide** that explains the complex (behind Kunsthistorisches Museum, U-2 or U-3: Volkstheater/Museumsplatz, tel. 01/525-5881, www.mqw.at).

The **Leopold Museum** features several temporary exhibits of modern Austrian art. The top floor holds the largest collection of works by Egon Schiele (1890-1918; these works make some people uncomfortable—Schiele's nudes are *really* nude) and a few paintings by Gustav Klimt, Kolo Moser, and Oskar Kokoschka. While this is a great collection, you can see even better works from these artists in the Belvedere Palace, described later (€11, €3 audio-guide—worth it only for enthusiasts; June-Aug daily 10:00-18:00, Thu until 21:00; Sept-May Wed-Mon 10:00-18:00, Thu until 21:00, closed Tue; tel. 01/525-700, www.leopoldmuseum.org).

The **Museum of Modern Art** (Museum Moderner Kunst Stiftung Ludwig, a.k.a. "MUMOK") is Austria's leading gallery for international modern and contemporary art. It's the striking lava-paneled building—three stories tall and four stories deep, offering seven floors of far-out art that's hard for most visitors to appreciate. This huge, state-of-the-art museum owns works by "classical" modernists (Paul Klee, Pablo Picasso, Pop artists) and shows off up-to-the-minute contemporary art in revolving exhibits (€9, €3 audioguide has more than you probably want to hear, daily 10:00-18:00, Thu until 21:00, tel. 01/52500, www.mumok.at).

Rounding out the sprawling MuseumsQuartier are an architecture center, Electronic Avenue, design forum, children's museum, "Quartier 21" (with gallery space and shops), and the **Kunsthalle Wien**—an exhibition center for contemporary art (two halls with different exhibitions, €8.50 for one, €7 for the other, €11.50 for both; daily 10:00-19:00, Thu until 22:00, tel. 01/521-8933, www.kunsthallewien.at).

Karlsplatz and Nearby

These sights cluster around Karlsplatz, just southeast of the Ringstrasse (U-1, U-2, or U-4: Karlsplatz). From the U-Bahn station's passageway, it's a 30-minute walk around the sights on Karlsplatz: the Karlskirche, Secession, and Naschmarkt (allow more time to actually visit these sights).

Karlsplatz—This picnic-friendly square, with its Henry Moore sculpture in the pond, is ringed with sights. The massive, domed Karlskirche and its twin spiral columns dominate the square. The small green, white, and gold pavilions that line the street across the square from the church are from the late-19th-century municipal train system *(Stadtbahn)*. One of Europe's first subway systems, this precursor to today's U-Bahn was built with a military purpose in mind: to move troops quickly in times of civil unrest—specifically, out to Schönbrunn Palace. With curvy iron frames, decorative marble slabs, and painted gold trim, these are pioneering works in the *Jugendstil* (Art Nouveau) style, designed by Otto Wagner, who influenced Klimt and the Secessionists. One of the pavilions has an exhibit on **Otto Wagner** (€2, April-Oct Tue-Sun 10:00-18:00, closed Mon and Nov-March, near the Ringstrasse, tel. 01/5058-7478-5173).

▲**Karlskirche (St. Charles' Church)**—Charles Borromeo, a 16th-century bishop from Milan, was an inspiration during plague times. This "votive church" was dedicated to him in 1713, when an epidemic spared Vienna. The church offers the best Baroque in Vienna, with a unique combination of columns (showing scenes from the life of Charles Borromeo, à la Trajan's Column in Rome), a classic pediment, and an elliptical dome. The dome's color-ful 13,500-square-foot fresco—painted in the 1730s by Johann Michael Rottmayr—shows Signor Borromeo (in red-and-white bishops' robes) gazing up into heaven, spreading his arms wide, and pleading with Christ to spare Vienna from the plague.

The church is especially worthwhile for the chance to ride an **elevator** (installed for renovation work) up into the cupola. While the restoration of the interior is complete, work on the exterior will likely continue into 2013; when it's finished, the scaffolding and elevator will likely be taken down. Until that happens, the indus-trial lift takes you to a platform at the base of the 235-foot dome (if you're even slightly afraid of heights, skip this trip). Consider that the church was built and decorated with a scaffolding system essen-tially the same as this one. Once up top, you'll climb stairs to the steamy lantern at the extreme top of the church. At that dizzying height, you're in the clouds with cupids and angels. Many details that appear smooth and beautiful from ground level—such as gold leaf, paintings, and fake marble—look rough and sloppy up close. It's surreal to observe the 3-D figures from an unintended angle—check out Christ's leg, which looks dwarf-sized up close. Give yourself a minute to take it in: Faith, Hope, and Charity triumph and inspire. Borromeo lobbies heaven for plague relief. Meanwhile, a Protestant's Lutheran Bible is put to the torch by angels. At the very top, you'll see the tiny dove representing the Holy Ghost, sur-rounded by a cheering squad of nipple-lipped cupids.

Cost and Hours: €6, ticket covers church interior, elevator ride, and skippable one-room museum; audioguide-€2; Mon-Sat 9:00-18:00, Sun 13:00-18:00, last entry 30 minutes before closing; elevator runs until 17:30, last ascent at 17:00. The entry fee may seem steep, but remember that it funds the restoration.

Wien Museum Karlsplatz—This underappreciated city history museum, worth ▲ for those intrigued by Vienna's illustrious past, walks you through the story of Vienna with well-presented arti-facts. Work your way up chronologically. The ground floor exhibits prehistoric and Roman fragments, along with some original stat-ues from St. Stephen's Cathedral (c. 1350). The first floor focuses on the Renaissance and Baroque eras, including suits of armor, old city maps, booty from an Ottoman siege, and an 1850 city model showing the town just before the wall was replaced by the Ring. Finally, the second floor displays a city model from 1898 (with the new Ringstrasse), sentimental Biedermeier paintings and objets d'art, and early 20th-century paintings (including four by Klimt, as well as works by Schiele, Kokoschka, and other Secessionists).

Cost and Hours: €6, free first Sun of the month, open Tue-Sun 10:00-18:00, closed Mon, tel. 01/505-8747, www.wien museum.at.

▲**Academy of Fine Arts (Akademie der Bildenden Künste)**—Recently refurbished, this museum features a small but impressive collection of works by big-name artists, including quick, sketchy cartoons Rubens used to create his giant canvases; a Venice series by Guardi; a self-portrait by a 15-year-old Van Dyck; and a round Botticelli canvas, recently cleaned to show off its vivid colors, depicting the Madonna tenderly embracing the Baby Jesus. The collection's highlight is the captivating, harrowing *Last Judgment* triptych by Hieronymus Bosch (c. 1482, with some details added by Lucas Cranach). Read the altarpiece from left to right, following the pessimistically medieval narrative about humankind's fall from God's graces: In the left panel, at the bottom, God pulls Eve from Adam's rib in the Garden of Eden. Just above that, we see a female representing the serpent hold out the forbidden fruit to tempt Eve. Above that, Adam and Eve are being shooed away by an angel. At the top of this panel, God sits on his cloud, evicting the fallen angels (who turn into insect-like monsters). In the middle panel, Christ holds court over the living and the dead. Notice the jarring contrast between Christ's serene expression and the grotesque scene playing out beneath him. These disturbing images crescendo in the final (right) panel, showing an unspeakably horrific vision of hell that few artists have managed to top in the more than half-millennium since Bosch.

The collection is magnificently lit and well-described by the €2 audioguide, and comes with comfy chairs. The fact that it's housed upstairs in a working art academy gives it a certain authenticity. As you wander the halls of the academy, ponder how history might have been different if Hitler—who applied to study architecture here but was rejected—had been accepted as a student. Before leaving, peek into the ground floor's central hall—textbook Historicism, the Ringstrasse style of the late 1800s.

Cost and Hours: €8, audioguide-€2; Tue-Sun 10:00-18:00, closed Mon, 3 blocks from the Opera at Schillerplatz 3; once inside, go up two floors, following signs for *Gemäldegalerie;* tel. 01/588-162-201, www.akademiegalerie.at.

▲**The Secession**—This little building, strategically located behind the Academy of Fine Arts, was created by the Vienna Secession movement, a group of nonconformist artists led by Gustav Klimt, Otto Wagner, and friends.

The young trees carved into the walls and the building's bushy "golden cabbage" rooftop are symbolic of a renewal cycle. The Secessionist motto, under the cabbage, reads: "To each age its art, and to art its liberty." Today, the Secession continues to showcase cutting-edge art, as well as one of Gustav Klimt's most famous works.

VIENNA

VIENNA

250 Meters

250 Yards

While the staff hopes you take a look at the temporary exhibits (and they're included in the ticket price whether you like it or not), most tourists head directly for the basement, home to the museum's highlight: Klimt's classic *Beethoven Frieze* (a.k.a. the "Searching Souls"). One of the masterpieces of Viennese Art Nouveau, this 105-foot-long fresco was the multimedia centerpiece of a 1902 exhibition honoring Ludwig van Beethoven. Read the free flier, which explains Klimt's still-powerful work, inspired by Beethoven's Ninth Symphony. Klimt embellished the work with painted-on gold (his brother and colleague was a goldsmith), and by gluing on reflecting glass and mother-of-pearl for the ladies' dresses and jewelry.

Cost and Hours: €5, as high as €8.50 during special exhibits, Tue-Sun 10:00-18:00, closed Mon, Friedrichstrasse 12, tel. 01/587-5307, www.secession.at.

▲**Naschmarkt**—In 1898, the city decided to cover up its Vienna River. The long, wide square they created was filled with a lively produce market that still bustles most days (closed Sun). It's long been known as *the* place to get exotic faraway foods. In fact, locals say, "From here start the Balkans."

From near the Opera, the Naschmarkt (roughly, "Munchies Market") stretches along Wienzeile street. This "Belly of Vienna" comes with two parallel lanes—one lined with fun and reasonable eateries, and the other featuring the town's top-end produce and gourmet goodies. This is where top chefs like to get their ingredients. At the gourmet vinegar stall, you sample the vinegar—like perfume—with a drop on your wrist. Farther from the center, the Naschmarkt becomes likeably seedy and surrounded by sausage stands, Turkish *Döner Kebab* stalls, cafés, and theaters. At the market's far end is a line of buildings with fine Art Nouveau facades. Each Saturday, the Naschmarkt is infested by a huge flea market where, in olden days, locals would come to hire a monkey to pick little critters out of their hair.

Hours and Location: Mon-Fri 6:00-18:30, Sat 6:00-17:00, closed Sun, closes earlier in winter; U-1, U-2, or U-4: Karlsplatz. For a picnic in the park, pick up your grub here and walk over to Karlsplatz (described earlier).

More Sights Beyond the Ring
South of the Ring

▲▲**Belvedere Palace (Schloss Belvedere)**—This is the elegant palace of Prince Eugene of Savoy (1663-1736), the still-much-appreciated conqueror of the Ottomans. Today you can tour Eugene's lavish palace, see sweeping views of the gardens and the Vienna skyline, and enjoy world-class art starring Gustav Klimt, French Impressionism, and a grab-bag of other 19th- and early-

20th-century artists. While Vienna's other art collections show off works by masters from around Europe, this has the city's best collection of homegrown artists.

Cost and Hours: €11 for Upper Belvedere Palace only, €16 for Upper and Lower palaces—generally not worth it, gardens are free except for privy garden—included in big ticket, audioguide-€4 or €6/2 people, daily 10:00-18:00, Lower Palace only open Wed until 21:00, grounds open until dusk, no photos allowed inside, entrance at Prinz-Eugen-Strasse 27, tel. 01/7955-7134, www.belvedere.at.

Getting There: The palace is a 15-minute walk south of the Ring. To get there from the center, catch tram #D at the Opera (direction: Südbahnhof). Get off at the Schloss Belvedere stop (just below the Upper Palace gate), cross the street, walk uphill one block, and look for the gate on your right.

⊙ Self-Guided Tour: The Belvedere Palace is actually two grand buildings—the Upper Palace and Lower Palace—separated by a fine garden. For our purposes, the Upper Palace is what matters. Buy your ticket at the office behind the palace, then go around to the front to enter. Once inside, the palace's eclectic collection is tailor-made for browsing. It's organized roughly chronologically as you go up.

Ground Floor: The main floor displays a collection of Austrian Baroque (on the left) and medieval art (on the right). The Baroque section includes a fascinating room of grotesquely grimacing heads by **Franz Xaver Messerschmidt** (1736-1783), a quirky 18th-century Habsburg court sculptor who left the imperial life to follow his own, somewhat deranged muse. After his promising career was cut short by mental illness, Messerschmidt relocated to Bratislava and spent the rest of his days sculpting a series of eerily lifelike "character heads" *(Kopfstücke)*. Their most unusual faces are contorted by extreme emotions.

• *From the entrance, climb the staircase to the first floor and enter the grand red-and-gold, chandeliered...*

Marble Hall (First Floor): This was Prince Eugene's party room. *Belvedere* means "beautiful view," and the view from the Marble Hall is especially spectacular.

• *To the right is the...*

East Wing (First Floor): Alongside Renoir's ladies, Monet's landscapes, and Van Gogh's rough brushstrokes are similar works by their lesser-known Austrian counterparts. Around 1900, Austrian artists come to the fore, soaking up Symbolism, Expressionism, and other Modernist trends.

In the two rooms full of sumptuous paintings by **Gustav Klimt,** you can get caught up in his fascination with the beauty and danger he saw in women. To Klimt, all art was erotic art. He painted during the turn of the century, when Vienna was a splendid laboratory of hedonism. The famous painting of *Judith I* (1901) shows no biblical heroine—Klimt paints her as a high-society Vienna woman with an ostentatious dog-collar necklace. With half-closed eyes and slightly parted lips, she's dismissive... yet mysterious and bewitching. Holding the head of her biblical victim, she's the modern femme fatale. In what is perhaps Klimt's best-known painting, *The Kiss,* two lovers are wrapped up in the colorful gold-and-jeweled cloak of bliss. Klimt's woman is no longer dominating, but submissive, abandoning herself to her man in a fertile field and a vast universe. In a glow emanating from a radiance of desire, the body she presses against is a self-portrait of the artist himself.

Klimt nurtured the next generation of artists, especially **Egon Schiele.** While Klimt's works are mystical and otherworldly, Schiele's tend to be darker and gloomier. One of Schiele's most recognizable works, *The Embrace,* shows a couple engaged in an erotically charged, rippling moment of passion. Striking a darker tone is *The Family,* which depicts a crouching couple. This family portrait from 1918 is especially poignant because his wife died while he was still working on it.

The Rest of the Upper Palace: The Belvedere's collection goes through the whole range of 19th- and 20th-century art: Historicism, Romanticism, Impressionism, Realism, tired tourism, Expressionism, Art Nouveau, and early Modernism.

Grounds and Gardens: The delightfully manicured grounds are free and fun to explore. The only area with an entry fee is the **privy garden,** along the left side of the Lower Palace (and accessed through that palace).

Lower Palace: Covered by a separate ticket, this is the home where Prince Eugene actually hung his helmet. Today it contains a small stretch of three of his private apartments (relatively uninteresting compared to the sumptuous Habsburg apartments elsewhere in town). The Lower Palace also houses some generally good special exhibits, as well as the entrance to the privy garden, orangerie, and stables (until 12:00). If the special exhibits intrigue you, it's worth buying the combo-ticket to get in here; otherwise, I wouldn't bother to visit.

East of the Ring
Museum of Applied Art (Österreichisches Museum für Angewandte Kunst)—Facing the old town from across the Ring, the MAK, as it's called, is Vienna's answer to London's Victoria and Albert Museum. The MAK is more than just another grand building on the Ringstrasse. It was built to provide models of historic design for Ringstrasse architects and is a delightful space in itself (many locals stop in to enjoy a coffee on the plush couches

in the main lobby). The relatively sparse collection shows off the fancies of local aristocratic society, including fine *Jugendstil* pieces (among them Klimt designs for a palace in Brussels). Each wing is dedicated to a different era. Exhibits, well-described in English (borrow the captions in each room), come with a playful modern flair—notable modern designers were assigned various spaces. The unique gift shop also makes for a fun diversion.

Cost and Hours: €8, €10 includes a hefty English guidebook, free on Sat, open Tue-Sun 10:00-18:00, Tue until 24:00, closed Mon, Stubenring 5, tel. 01/711-360, www.mak.at.

Eating at the MAK: The beautiful lobby hosts an inviting **café.** The **Restaurant Österreicher im MAK,** in the same building, is named for Chef Helmut Österreicher, who's renowned for his classic and modern Viennese cuisine. Classy and mod, it's trendy for locals (€9-23 plates, daily 8:30-1:00 in the morning, reserve for evening, tel. 01/714-0121).

▲**KunstHausWien: Hundertwasser Museum**—This "make yourself at home" museum and nearby apartment complex are a hit with lovers of modern art, mixing the work and philosophy of local painter/environmentalist Friedensreich Hundertwasser (1928-2000). Stand in front of the colorful checkerboard building and consider Hundertwasser's style. He was against "window racism": Neighboring houses allow only one kind of window, but 100H_2O's windows are each different—and he encouraged residents in the Hundertwasserhaus (a 5-10 minute walk away, described below) to personalize them. He recognized "tree tenants" as well as human tenants. His buildings are spritzed with a forest and topped with dirt and grassy little parks—close to nature and good for the soul.

Floors and sidewalks are irregular—to "stimulate the brain" (although current residents complain it just causes wobbly furniture and sprained ankles). Thus 100H_2O waged a one-man fight—during the 1950s and 1960s, when concrete and glass ruled—to save the human soul from the city. (Hundertwasser claimed that "straight lines are godless.")

Inside the museum, start with his interesting biography. His fun paintings are half psychedelic *Jugendstil* and half just kids' stuff. Notice the photographs from his 1950s days as part of Vienna's bohemian scene. Throughout the museum, keep an eye out for the fun philosophical quotes from an artist who believed, "If man is creative, he comes nearer to his creator."

Cost and Hours: €9 for Hundertwasser Museum, €12 combo-ticket includes special exhibitions, half-price on Mon, open daily 10:00-19:00, extremely fragrant and colorful garden café, tel. 01/712-0491, www.kunsthauswien.com.

Getting There: It's located at Untere Weissgerberstrasse 13 (tram #1: Radetzkyplatz or U-3: Landstrasse). Note that the tram stop is much closer than the U-Bahn stop. From the Landstrasse U-Bahn stop, walk 10 minutes downhill (north) along Untere Viaduktgasse (a block east of the station), or ride tram #0 three stops to Radetzkyplatz; from there signs point to the museum.

Hundertwasserhaus: The KunstHausWien provides by far the best look at Hundertwasser, but for an actual lived-in apartment complex by the green master, walk five minutes to the one-with-nature Hundertwasserhaus (at Löwengasse and Kegelgasse). This complex of 50 apartments, subsidized by the government to provide affordable housing, was built in the 1980s as a breath of architectural fresh air in a city of boring, blocky apartment complexes. While not open to visitors, it's worth visiting for its fun and colorful patchwork exterior and the Hundertwasser festival of shops across the street. Don't miss the view from Kegelgasse to see the "tree tenants" and the internal winter garden that residents enjoy.

Hundertwasser detractors—of which there are many—remind visitors that 100H$_2$O was a painter, not an architect. They describe the Hundertwasserhaus as a "1950s house built in the 1980s" that was colorfully painted with no real concern for the environment, communal living, or even practical comfort. Almost all of the original inhabitants got fed up with the novelty and moved out.

North of the Ring

▲**Liechtenstein Museum**—The noble Liechtenstein family (who own only a tiny country, but whose friendship with the Habsburgs goes back generations) amassed an incredible private art collection. Their palace was long a treasure for Vienna art-lovers. Then, in 1938—knowing Hitler was intent on plundering artwork to create an immense "Führer Museum"—the family fled to their pint-size homeland with their best art. Since the museum reopened in 2004, attendance has been disappointing, but the problem is its location (and perhaps its steep price)...not its worthiness. The Liechtensteins' "world of Baroque pleasures" includes the family's rare "Golden Carriage," which was used for their grand entry into Paris in 1738. It was carted to the edge of town and assembled there. It's a rare example of the French Rococo style, as nearly all such carriages were destroyed in the French Revolution. The museum also has a plush Baroque library, an inviting English Garden, and an impressive collection of paintings, including a complete cycle of early Rubens.

Cost and Hours: €10 on Fri-Sat and Mon-Tue, more for temporary exhibits; €30 on Sun—when ticket includes permanent and temporary exhibits, lunch, and concerts at 11:00 and 15:00; gardens are free but aren't worth the trip on their own; audioguide-€1; Fri-Tue 10:00-17:00, last entry 30 minutes before closing, closed

Wed-Thu, gardens open until 20:30; Fürstengasse 1—take tram #D to Bauernfeldplatz/Porzellangasse, tel. 01/319-5767-252, www .liechtensteinmuseum.at.

Sigmund Freud Museum—Freud enthusiasts enjoy seeing the humble apartment and workplace of the man who fundamentally changed our understanding of the human psyche. Dr. Sigmund Freud (1856-1939), a graduate of Vienna University, established his practice here in 1891. For the next 47 years, he received troubled patients who hoped to find peace by telling him their dreams, life traumas, and secret urges. It was here that he wrote his influential works, including the landmark *Interpretation of Dreams* (1899). Today, you can walk through his three-room office (but not the apartments next door, where Freud lived with his large family). The rooms are tiny and disappointingly bare. Freud, who was Jewish, fled Vienna when the Nazis came to power. He took most of his furniture with him, including the famous couch that patients reclined on (now in a London museum). All in all, the museum is quite old-fashioned—tediously described in a three-ring binder loaned to visitors, which complements the more general audio-guide.

Cost and Hours: €7, audioguide-€2, daily July-Sept 9:00-18:00, Oct-June 9:00-17:00, cool shop, half a block downhill from the Schlickgasse tram #D stop, Berggasse 19, tel. 01/319-1596, www.freud-museum.at.

West of the Ring, on Mariahilfer Strasse

▲Imperial Furniture Collection (Hofmobiliendepot)—Bizarre, sensuous, eccentric, or precious, this collection is your peek at the Habsburgs' furniture—from grandma's wheelchair to the emperor's spittoon—all thoughtfully described in English. The Habsburgs had many palaces, but only the Hofburg was permanently furnished. The rest were done on the fly—set up and taken down by a gang of royal roadies called the "Depot of Court Movables" (Hofmobiliendepot). When the monarchy was dissolved in 1918, the state of Austria took possession of the Hofmobiliendepot's inventory—165,000 items. Now this royal storehouse is open to the public in a fine and sprawling museum. Don't go here for the *Jugendstil* furnishings. The older Baroque, Rococo, and Biedermeier pieces are the most impressive and tied most intimately to the royals. Combine a visit to this museum with a stroll down the lively shopping boulevard, Mariahilfer Strasse.

Cost and Hours: €7.90, covered by €23.50 Sisi Ticket (see page 28), Tue-Sun 10:00-18:00, closed Mon, Mariahilfer Strasse 88, main entrance around the corner at Andreasgasse 7, U-3: Zieglergasse, tel. 01/5243-3570, www.hofmobiliendepot.at.

▲▲▲Schönbrunn Palace (Schloss Schönbrunn)

Among Europe's palaces, only Schönbrunn rivals Versailles. This former summer residence of the Habsburgs is big, with 1,441 rooms. But don't worry—only 40 rooms are shown to the public. Of the plethora of sights at the palace, the highlight is a tour of the Royal Apartments—the chandeliered rooms where the Habsburg nobles lived. You can also stroll the gardens, tour the coach museum, and visit a handful of lesser sights nearby.

Getting There: While on the outskirts of Vienna, Schönbrunn is an easy 10-minute subway ride from downtown. Take U-4 to Schönbrunn and follow signs for *Schloss Schönbrunn*. Exit bearing right, then cross the busy road and continue to the right along the yellow building to the main entry courtyard, which will be on your left.

▲▲▲Royal Apartments—While the palace's exterior is Baroque, the interior was finished under Maria Theresa in let-them-eat-cake Rococo. As with the similar apartments at the Hofburg (the Habsburgs' winter home), these apartments give you a sense of the quirky, larger-than-life personalities who lived here—especially Franz Josef (r. 1848-1916) and Sisi. Your tour of the apartments, accompanied by an audioguide, covers one small section of the palace's grand interior on a clearly signed route. You have two tour options: Imperial (shorter and cheaper) or Grand (longer and more expensive). Both follow the same route at first, but after a certain point the Imperial group is politely excused while the Grand gang continues on to see a few more rooms.

Moving from room to room, you're immersed in imperial splendor. The chandeliers are made either of Bohemian crystal or hand-carved wood with gold-leaf gilding. Highlights include Franz Josef's study and bedroom (and the bed he actually died in). The Mirrored Room was where six-year-old Wolfie Mozart performed his first concert. The opulent, chandeliered Great Gallery—with its mirrored walls and dramatically frescoed ceilings—was the site of a famous 1961 summit between John F. Kennedy and Nikita Khrushchev.

Fortunately, the palace managed to escape destruction when WWII bombs rained on the city and the palace grounds. The palace itself took only one direct hit. Thankfully, that bomb, which crashed through three floors—including the sumptuous central ballroom—was a dud. Most of the public rooms are decorated in Neo-Baroque, as they were under Franz Josef and Sisi. The rest of the palace was converted to simple apartments and rented to the families of 260 civil servants, who enjoy rent control and governmental protections so they can't be evicted.

Cost: The 22-room **Imperial Tour** (€10.50, 35 minutes, Grand Palace rooms plus apartments of Franz Josef and Sisi—

mostly 19th-century and therefore least interesting) or the 40-room **Grand Tour** (€13.50, one hour, includes Imperial Tour plus Maria Theresa's apartments—18th-century Rococo). If venturing beyond the apartments, consider one of two combo-tickets: The **Schönbrunn Classic Pass Light** includes the Grand Tour, as well as other sights on the grounds—the Gloriette viewing terrace, maze, and privy garden (€16.50, available April-Oct only). The **Schönbrunn Classic Pass** includes all of the above, plus the court bakery (complete with *Apfelstrudel* demo and tasting; €19.50). However, none of these extra sights is really worth the cost of entry, so I'd skip them and just do the Grand Tour, followed by a mosey through the impressive grounds (which are free).

Hours: Daily July-Aug 8:30-18:00, April-June and Sept-Oct 8:30-17:00, Nov-March 8:30-16:30.

Crowd-Beating Tips: Schönbrunn suffers from crowds. It can be a jam-packed sauna in the summer. It's busiest from 9:30 to 11:30, especially on weekends and in July and August; it's least crowded after 14:00, when there are no groups. To avoid the long delays in summer, make a reservation by telephone for no extra charge a few days in advance (tel. 01/8111-3239, answered daily 8:00-17:00, wait through the long message for the operator). You can also book online with a credit card at www.schoenbrunn .at. You'll get an appointment time and a ticket number. Check in at least 30 minutes early. Upon arrival, go to the "Group and Reservations" desk, give your number, pick up your ticket, and jump in ahead of the masses (the reservations desk has long been located immediately inside the gate on the left at the gate house— far before the actual palace; but by the time you visit, it may have moved to a new visitors center). If you have time to kill, spend it exploring the gardens or Coach Museum.

▲▲**Palace Gardens**—Unlike the gardens of Versailles, meant to shut out the real world, Schönbrunn's park was opened to the public in 1779 while the monarchy was in full swing. It was part of Maria Theresa's reform policy, making the garden a celebration of the evolution of civilization from autocracy into real democracy. Today it's a delightful, sprawling place to wander—especially on a sunny day. You can spend hours here, enjoying the views and the people-watching. And most of the park is free, as it has been for more than two centuries (open daily sunrise to dusk, entrance on either side of the palace).

The large, manicured grounds are laid out on angled, tree-lined axes that gradually incline, offering dramatic views back to the palace. The small side gardens flanking the palace are the most elaborate. As you face the back of the palace, to the right is the **privy garden** (*Kronprinzengarten*, €2); to the left are the free **Sisi Gardens**. Better yet, just explore, using a map (pick one up at the palace) to locate several whimsical **fountains;** a kid-friendly **maze** *(Irrgarten)* and playground area (€2.90); and the **Gloriette,** a purely decorative monument celebrating an obscure Austrian military victory and offering a fine city view (pay for a pricey drink in the café or shell out €2 to hike up to the viewing terrace—or skip the whole thing, as views are about as good from the lawn in front; included in Schönbrunn Passes described earlier, daily April-Sept 9:00-18:00, July-Aug until 19:00, Oct 9:00-17:00, closed Nov-March).

At the west end of the grounds is Europe's oldest **zoo** *(Tiergarten),* built by Maria Theresa's husband for the entertainment and education of the court in 1752 (€14, €20 combo-ticket with desert and palm house, daily April-Sept 9:00-18:30, closes earlier off-season, tel. 01/877-9294). Nearby are two skippable sights: The **palm house** *(Palmenhaus;* €4, €6 combo-ticket with desert house, €20 combo-ticket also includes zoo, daily May-Sept 9:30-18:00, Oct-April 9:30-17:00, last entry 30 minutes before closing) and the **Desert Experience House** *(Wüstenhaus;* €4, same combo-tickets and hours as palm house).

A **tourist train** makes the rounds all day, connecting Schönbrunn's many attractions (€6, 2/hour in peak season, none Nov-mid-March, one-hour circuit). Unfortunately, there's no bike rental nearby.

▲**Coach Museum Wagenburg**—The Schönbrunn coach museum is a 19th-century traffic jam of 50 impressive royal carriages and sleighs. Highlights include silly sedan chairs, the death-black hearse carriage (used for Franz Josef in 1916, and most recently for Empress Zita in 1989), and an extravagantly gilded imperial carriage pulled by eight Cinderella horses. This was rarely used other than for the coronation of Holy Roman Emperors, when it was disassembled and taken to Frankfurt for the big event. You'll also get a look at one of Sisi's impossibly narrow-waisted gowns, and (upstairs) Sisi's "Riding Chapel," with portraits of her 25 favorite horses.

Cost and Hours: €6, audioguide-€2, daily April-Oct 9:00-18:00, Nov-March 10:00-16:00, last entry 15 minutes before closing, 200 yards from palace, walk through right arch as you face palace, tel. 01/525-24-3470.

East of the Danube Canal

▲**Prater**—Since the 1780s, when the reformist Emperor Josef II gave his hunting grounds to the people of Vienna as a public park, this place has been Vienna's playground. While tired and a bit run-down these days, Vienna's sprawling amusement park still tempts visitors with its huge 220-foot-tall, famous, and lazy Ferris wheel *(Riesenrad),* roller coaster, bumper cars, Lilliputian railroad, and endless eateries. Especially if you're traveling with kids, this is a fun, goofy place to share the evening with thousands of Viennese (rides run May-Sept 9:00-24:00—but quiet after 22:00, March-April and Oct 10:00-22:00, Nov-Dec 10:00-20:00, grounds always open, U-1: Praterstern, www.prater.at). For a local-style family dinner, eat at Schweizerhaus (good food, great Czech Budvar—the original "Budweiser"—beer, classic conviviality).

Donauinsel (Danube Island)—In the 1970s, the city dug a canal parallel to the mighty Danube River, creating both a flood barrier and a much-loved island escape from the city (easy U-Bahn access on U-1 to Donauinsel). This skinny, 12-mile-long island provides a natural wonderland. All along the traffic-free, grassy park, you'll find locals—both Viennese, and especially immigrants and those who can't afford their own cabin or fancy vacation—at play. The swimming comes tough, though, with rocky entries rather than sand. The best activity here is a bike ride. If you venture far from the crowds, you're likely to encounter nudists on inline skates.

"Donau City"—This modern part of town, just beyond the Donauinsel, is the skyscraping "Manhattan" of Austria. A business, residential, and shopping zone surrounded by inviting parkland, this corner of the city is likely to grow as Vienna expands. Its centerpiece is the futuristic UNO City, a major outpost of offices for the United Nations. While it lacks the Old World character, charm, and elegance of the rest of Vienna, Donau City may interest travelers who are into contemporary glass-and-steel architecture (U-1: Kaisermühlen VIC).

Experiences in Vienna

Vienna's Café Culture

In Vienna, the living room is down the street at the neighborhood coffeehouse. This tradition is just another example of Viennese expertise in good living. Each of Vienna's many long-established (and sometimes even legendary) coffeehouses has its individual character (and characters). Today these classic cafés can be a bit tired, with a shabby patina and famously grumpy waiters who treat you like an uninvited guest invading their living room. Yet these spaces somehow also feel welcoming, offering newspapers, pastries, sofas, quick and light workers' lunches, elegant ambience, and "take all the time you want" charm for the price of a cup of coffee. Rather than buy the *International Herald Tribune* ahead of time, spend the money on a cup of coffee and read the paper for free, Vienna-style, in a café.

As in Italy and France, Viennese coffee drinks are espresso-based. Obviously, *Kaffee* means coffee and *Milch* is milk; *Obers* is cream, while *Schlagobers* is whipped cream. Americans who ask for a "latte" are mistaken for Italians and given a cup of hot milk.

Cafés

These are some of my favorite Viennese cafés. All of them, except for Café Sperl, are located inside the Ring (see map on page 101).

VIENNA

Café Hawelka has a dark, "brooding Trotsky" atmosphere, paintings by struggling artists who couldn't pay for coffee, a saloon-wood flavor, chalkboard menu, smoked velvet couches, an international selection of newspapers, and a phone that rings for regulars. Frau Hawelka died just a couple weeks after Pope John Paul II. Locals suspect the pontiff wanted her much-loved *Buchteln* (marmalade-filled doughnuts) in heaven. Herr Hawelka, now alone and understandably a bit forlorn, still oversees the action (Wed-Mon 8:00-2:00 in the morning, Sun from 10:00, closed Tue, just off the Graben, Dorotheergasse 6, U-1 or U-3: Stephansplatz, tel. 01/512-8230).

Café Central, while a bit touristy, remains a classic place, lavish under Neo-Gothic columns. They serve fancy coffees (€4-6) and two-course lunches (€10), as well as entertain guests with live piano each evening from 17:00-22:00 (daily 7:30-22:00, corner of Herrengasse and Strauchgasse, U-3: Herrengasse, tel. 01/533-3764).

Café Sperl dates from 1880 and is still furnished identically to the day it opened—from the coat tree to the chairs (Mon-Sat 7:00-23:00, Sun 11:00-20:00 except closed Sun July-Aug, just off Naschmarkt near Mariahilfer Strasse, Gumpendorfer 11, U-2: Museumsquartier, tel. 01/586-4158; see map on page 95).

Café Bräunerhof, between the Hofburg and the Graben, offers classic ambience with no tourists and live music on weekends (light classics, no cover, Sat-Sun 15:00-18:00), along with a practical menu with daily specials (open long hours daily, Stallburgasse 2, U-1 or U-3: Stephansplatz, tel. 01/512-3893).

Other Classics in the Old Center: All of these places are open long hours daily: **Café Pruckel** (at Dr.-Karl-Lueger-Platz, across from Stadtpark at Stubenring 24); **Café Tirolerhof** (2 blocks from the Opera, behind the TI on Tegetthoffstrasse, at Führichgasse 8); and **Café Landtmann** (directly across from the City Hall on the Ringstrasse at Dr.-Karl-Lueger-Ring 4). The Landtmann is unique, as it's the only grand café built along the Ring with all the other grand buildings. **Café Sacher** (see page 35) and **Demel** (see page 40) are famous for their cakes, but they also serve good coffee drinks.

Wein in Wien: Vienna's Wine Gardens

The *Heuriger* (HOY-rih-gur) is a uniquely Viennese institution. When the Habsburgs let Vienna's vintners sell their own new wine (called *Sturm*) tax-free, several hundred families opened *Heurigen* (HOY-rih-gehn)—wine-garden restaurants clustered around the edge of town. A tradition was born. Today, they do their best to maintain the old-village atmosphere, serving their homemade wine (the most recent vintage, until November 11, when a new vintage year begins) with small meals and strolling musicians. Most *Heurigen* are decorated with enormous antique presses from their vineyards. Wine gardens might be closed on any given day; call ahead to confirm if you have your heart set on a particular place. (For a near-*Heuriger* experience in downtown Vienna, drop by Gigerl Stadtheuriger—see page 102.)

I've listed three good *Heuriger* neighborhoods—all on the outskirts of Vienna (see the map on page 21). I've listed them in order from east to west, and from least to most touristy. To reach the neighborhoods from downtown Vienna, it's best to use public transportation (cheap, 30 minutes, runs late in the evening, directions given per listing below), or you can take a 15-minute taxi ride from the Ring (about €15-20).

Planning Your Time: While there are some "destination" *Heurigen*, it can be disappointing to seek out a particular place, as the ambience can change depending with that evening's clientele (i.e., locals vs. tour groups). I've described a few neighborhoods that are worth exploring; wander around one or two of them, then choose the *Heuriger* with the best atmosphere. It's easiest to stick to one *Heuriger* neighborhood, though it's potentially more fun to hop from area to area; the handy bus #38A (described below) connects Heiligenstadt, Grinzing, and (with a transfer to tram #D) Nussdorf.

Getting Around the *Heurigen*: The three neighborhoods I list are relatively close to each other—within a few minutes' bus ride or about a half-hour walk. The handiest public-transit connections are these:

Tram #D runs from the Ring to Nussdorf, the least touristy *Heuriger* neighborhood. On the way, it passes the Grinzinger Strasse stop, where you can catch bus #38A (toward the other two neighborhoods). Tram #D runs every 5-10 minutes (fewer trams after 23:00, last tram around 24:30).

Bus #38A connects the Heiligenstadt U-Bahn station (U-4 line) with the *Heurigen* in Heiligenstadt (Fernsprechamt/Heiligenstadt stop), and then Grinzing (Grinzing or Himmelstrasse stops). Bus #38A runs frequently into the evening (8/hour until 19:00, then 6/hour until 22:00, then 4/hour until 24:00; last bus around midnight).

Tram #38 starts on the Ring at the Schottentor stop and goes to Grinzing (roughly the same hours as Tram #D).

Taxis stand by in touristy Grinzing; from the other places, you might need to ask the *Heuriger* to call one for you (figure about €15-20 between the *Heurigen* and the Ring or any hotel I list).

Nussdorf—An untouristy district, characteristic and popular with the Viennese, Nussdorf has plenty of *Heuriger* ambience. This area feels more real than the other two—with a working-class vibe, streets lined with local shops, and characteristic *Heurigen* that feel a little bit rougher around the edges. Right at the last stop on tram #D's route (Beethovengang), you'll find three long and skinny places side by side. Of these, **Schübel-Auer Heuriger** is my favorite—bigger, classier, and with the most user-friendly buffet (many dishes are labeled, and the patient staff speaks English). Its rustic ambience can be enjoyed indoors or out (Tue-Sat 16:00-24:00, closed Sun-Mon, Kahlenberger Strasse 22, tel. 01/370-2222). The other two are also worth considering: **Heuriger Kierlinger** has a particularly rollicking, woody room around its buffet (daily 15:30-24:00, Kahlenberger Strasse 20, tel. 01/370-2264). **Steinschaden** feels a bit more like a traditional restaurant. Though it has a typical *Heuriger* buffet, it also has menus and table service (daily 15:00-24:00, Kahlenberger Strasse 18, tel. 01/370-1375).

Getting to the Nussdorf *Heurigen*: Take tram #D from the Ringstrasse (stops include the Opera, Hofburg/Kunsthistorisches Museum, and City Hall) to its endpoint (the stop labeled *Nussdorf* isn't the end—stay on for one more stop to Beethovengang). Exit the tram, cross the tracks, bear right down the street, and look for the *Heurigen* on your left.

Heiligenstadt (Pfarrplatz)—Between Nussdorf and Grinzing, hiding just above the unappealing main road, is Pfarrplatz, which feels like a charming village square watched over by a church. Beethoven lived—and began work on his Ninth Symphony—here in 1817; he'd previously written his Sixth Symphony *(Pastorale)* while staying in this then-rural district. He hoped the local spa would cure his worsening deafness. (Confusingly, the name "Heiligenstadt" is used for two different locations: this little neighborhood, and the big train and U-Bahn station near the river.) Right next to the church, **Mayer am Pfarrplatz** (a.k.a. Beethovenhaus) is famous, touristy, and feels more polished—almost trendy—compared to the other *Heurigen* I list. This place has a charming inner courtyard under cozy vines with an accordion player, along with a sprawling backyard with a big children's play zone (Mon-Fri 16:00-24:00, Sat-Sun 11:00-24:00, Pfarrplatz 2, tel. 01/370-1287). **Weingut and Heuriger Werner Welser** is a block uphill (go up Probusgasse). It's big (serving large tour groups) and traditional, with dirndled waitresses and lederhosened waiters. It feels a bit crank-'em-out, but it's still lots of fun, with music nightly from 19:00 (open daily 15:30-24:00, Probusgasse 12, tel. 01/318-9797).

Getting to the Heiligenstadt *Heurigen*: Take the U-4 line to its last station, Heiligenstadt, then transfer to bus #38A. Get off at Fernsprechamt/Heiligenstadt, walk uphill, and take the first right onto Nestelbachgasse, which leads to Pfarrplatz and the Beethovenhaus. Bus #38A also runs uphill from here, past the Grinzing *Heurigen*, to the Kahlenberg viewpoint (described later).

Grinzing—Of the many *Heuriger* suburbs, Grinzing is the most famous, lively...and touristy. If you're looking to avoid tour groups, head elsewhere. But it's the easiest, most accessible zone that I list. You can't walk down the street without stumbling over great, interchangeably touristy options—so much so, in fact, that I won't bother pointing you to a specific place. Just find your favorite ambience. (Since this isn't exactly fine wine anyway, the difference in quality is negligible.) The district is also simply pretty. Like the other two, it feels like a charming town all its own, with an onion-domed church and carefully manicured streetscape.

Getting to the Grinzing *Heurigen*: Take tram #38 from the Schottentor stop on the Ring to its endpoint. If you are coming from the other *Heurigen* neighborhoods, bus #38A makes two stops in this district: The Grinzing stop is at the bottom of town (and just across the street from the stop for tram #38); the next stop is Himmelstrasse, a bit uphill (and easier for strolling down past your options). If you get off at the Grinzing stop, follow Himmelgasse uphill toward the green onion-top dome. You'll pass plenty of wine gardens—and tour buses—on your way up. Just past the dome, you'll find the heart of the Heurigen.

Entertainment in Vienna

Vienna—the birthplace of what we call classical music—still thrives as Europe's music capital. On any given evening, you'll have your choice of opera, Strauss waltzes, Mozart chamber concerts, and lighthearted musicals. The Vienna Boys' Choir lives up to its worldwide reputation. If techno or rock are more your scene, you'll find plenty in the pubs and clubs of the "Bermuda Triangle" neighborhood near St. Stephen's Cathedral and along the Gürtel.

Besides music, you can spend an evening enjoying art, watching a classic film, or sipping Viennese wine in a village wine garden. Save some energy for Vienna after dark.

Music

As far back as the 12th century, Vienna was a mecca for musicians—both sacred and secular (troubadours). The Habsburg emperors of the 17th and 18th centuries were not only generous supporters of music, but fine musicians and composers themselves. (Maria Theresa played a mean double bass.) Composers such as Haydn, Mozart, Beethoven, Schubert, Brahms, and Mahler gravitated to this music-friendly environment. They taught each other, jammed together, and spent a lot of time in Habsburg palaces. Beethoven was a famous figure, walking—lost in musical thought—through the Vienna Woods. In the city's 19th-century belle époque, "Waltz King" Johann Strauss and his brothers kept Vienna's 300 ballrooms spinning.

This musical tradition continues into modern times, leaving some prestigious Viennese institutions for today's tourists to enjoy: the Opera, the Boys' Choir, and the great Baroque halls and churches, all busy with classical and waltz concerts. As you poke into churches and palaces, you may hear groups practicing. You're welcome to sit and listen.

The best-known entertainment venues are the Staatsoper (a.k.a., "the Opera"), the Volksoper (for musicals and operettas), the Theater an der Wien (newly reopened, opera and other performances), the Wiener Musikverein (home of the Vienna Philharmonic Orchestra), and the Wiener Konzerthaus (various events). These events are listed in the monthly *Wien-Programm* (available at TI).

In Vienna, it's music *con brio* from October through June, reaching a symphonic climax during the Vienna Festival each May and June. Sadly, in summer (generally July and August), the Boys' Choir, Opera, and many other serious music companies are—like you—on vacation. But Vienna hums year-round with live classical music; touristy, crowd-pleasing shows are always available.

Buying Tickets: Most tickets run from €40 to €55 (plus a stiff booking fee when booked in advance or through a box office like the one at the TI). A few venues charge as little as €25; look around if you're not set on any particular concert. While it's easy to book tickets online long in advance, spontaneity is also workable, as there are invariably people selling their extra tickets at face value or less outside the door before concert time. If you call a concert hall directly, they can advise you on the availability of (cheaper) tickets at the door. Vienna takes care of its starving artists (and tourists) by offering cheap standing-room tickets to top-notch music and opera (generally an hour before each performance).

Vienna Boys' Choir (Wiener Sängerknaben)—The boys sing (from a high balcony, heard but not seen) at the 9:15 Sunday Mass from September through June in the Hofburg's Imperial Music Chapel (Hofmusikkapelle). The entrance is at Schweizerhof; you can get there from In der Burg square or go through the tunnel from Josefsplatz.

Reserved seats must be booked two months in advance (€5-29; reserve by fax, email, or mail: fax from the US 011-431-533-992-775, whmk@chello.at, or write Hofmusikkapelle,

Hofburg-Schweizerhof, 1010 Wien; call 01/533-9927 for information only—they can't book tickets at this number).

Much easier, standing room inside is free and open to the first 60 who line up. Even better, rather than line up early, you can simply swing by and stand in the narthex just outside, where you can hear the boys and see the Mass on a TV monitor.

Boys' Choir concerts are also given Fridays at 16:00 in late April, May, June, September, and October on stage at the Musikverein, near the Opera and Karlsplatz (€36-56, around 30 standing-room tickets go on sale at 15:30 for €15, Karlsplatz 6; U-1, U-2, or U-4: Karlsplatz; tel. 01/5880-4173).

They're talented kids, but, for my taste, not worth all the commotion. Remember, many churches have great music during Sunday Mass. Just 200 yards from the Boys' Choir chapel, the Augustinian Church has a glorious 11:00 service each Sunday (see page 58).

The Opera—The Vienna State Opera (Staatsoper), featuring Vienna Philharmonic Orchestra musicians in the pit, is one of the world's top opera houses. They put on 300 performances a year, but in July and August the singers rest their voices (or go on tour). Since there are different operas nearly nightly, you'll see big trucks out back and constant action backstage—all the sets need to be switched each day. Even though the expensive seats normally sell out long in advance, the opera is perpetually in the red and subsidized by the state. The excellent "electronic libretto" translation screens help make the experience worthwhile for opera newbies. (Press the button to turn yours on; press again for English.)

Opera Tickets: Seats range from €8 to €168. You can book tickets in advance by phone (tel. 01/513-1513, phone answered daily 10:00-21:00) or online (www.wiener-staatsoper.at); you'll give them your credit-card number, then pick up your tickets at the box office just before show time. If you want to inquire about tickets in person, head to the theater's box office, which is open from 9:00 until one hour before each performance. The Opera has two ticket offices. The main one is on the west side of the building, across Operngasse and facing the Opera. A smaller one is just under the big screen on the east side of the Opera (facing Kärntner Strasse).

Unless Placido Domingo is in town, it's easy to get one of 567 **standing-room tickets** (*Stehplätze*, €3 up top or €4 downstairs). While the front doors open one hour before the show starts, a side door (middle of building, on the Operngasse side) opens 80 minutes before curtain time, giving those in the know an early grab at standing-room tickets (tickets sold until 20 minutes after curtain time). Just walk straight in, then head right until you see the ticket booth marked *Stehplatze*. If fewer than 567 people are in line, there's no need to line up early. If you're one of the first 160 in line, try for the "Parterre" section and you'll end up dead-center at stage level, directly under the Emperor's Box (otherwise, you can choose between the third floor—*Balkon,* or the fourth floor—*Galerie*). Dress is casual (but do your best) at the standing-room bar. Locals save their spot along the rail by tying a scarf to it.

Rick's Crude Tips: For me, three hours is a lot of opera. But just to see and hear the Opera in action for half an hour is a treat. You can buy a standing-room spot and drop in for part of the show. Ending time is posted in the lobby—you could stop by for just the finale. If you go at the start or finish, you'll get the added entertainment of seeing Vienna all dressed up. Of the 567 people with cheap standing-room tickets, invariably many will not stand through the entire performance. If you drop by after showtime, you can wait for people to leave and bum their tickets off them—be sure to ask them for clear directions to your spot. (While it's perfectly legal to swap standing-room spots, be discreet if finding your spot mid-performance—try to look like you know where you're going.) Even those with standing-room tickets are considered "ticket-holders," and are welcome to explore the building. As you leave, wander around the first floor (fun if skipping out early, when halls are empty) to enjoy the sumptuous halls (with prints of famous stage sets and performers) and the grand entry staircase. The last resort (and worst option) is to drop into the Café Oper Vienna and watch the performance live on TV screens (inside the Opera, reasonable menu and drinks).

"Live Opera on the Square": Demonstrating its commitment to bringing opera to the masses, each summer the Vienna Opera projects several performances live on a huge screen on its building, and even puts out chairs for the public to enjoy…and it's all free (these projected performances are noted as *Oper live am Platz* in the official Opera schedule—posted all around the Opera building; they are also listed in the *Wien-Programm* brochure).

Vienna Volksoper—For less-serious operettas and musicals, try Vienna's other opera house, located along the Gürtel, west of the city center (see *Wien-Programm* brochure or ask at TI for schedule, Währinger Strasse 78, tel. 01/5144-4360, www.volksoper.at).

Theater an der Wien—Considered the oldest theater in Vienna, this venue was designed in 1801 for Mozart operas—intimate, with just a thousand seats. Reopened in 2006 for Mozart's 250th birthday, it treats Vienna's music-lovers to a different opera every month—generally Mozart with a contemporary setting and modern interpretation—with the excellent Vienna Radio Orchestra in the pit. With the reopening of Theater an der Wien, Vienna now supports three opera companies; this one is the only company playing through the summer. They also feature occasional ballet, operetta, and other performances (facing the Naschmarkt at Linke Wienzeile 6, tel. 01/5883-0660 for information, tickets available at www.theater-wien.at).

Touristy Mozart and Strauss Concerts—If the music comes to you, it's touristy—designed for flash-in-the-pan Mozart fans. Powdered-wig orchestra performances are given almost nightly in grand traditional settings (€25-50). Pesky wigged-and-powdered Mozarts peddle tickets in the streets. They rave about the quality of the musicians, but you'll get second-rate chamber orchestras, clad in historic costumes, performing the greatest hits of Mozart and Strauss. These are casual, easygoing concerts with lots of tour groups. While there's not a Viennese person in the audience, the tourists generally enjoy the evening.

To sort through your options, check with the ticket office in the TI (same price as on the street, but with all venues to choose from). Savvy locals suggest getting the cheapest tickets, as no one seems to care if cheapskates move up to fill unsold pricier seats. Critics explain that the musicians are actually very good (often Hungarians, Poles, and Russians working a season here to fund an entire year of music studies back home), but that they haven't performed much together so aren't "tight."

Of the many fine venues, the **Mozarthaus** might be my favorite. Intimate chamber-music concerts take place in a small room richly decorated in Venetian Renaissance style (€35-42, Thu-Fri at 19:30, Sat at 18:00, near St. Stephen's Cathedral at Singerstrasse 7, tel. 01/911-9077).

Strauss Concerts in the Kursalon—For years, Strauss concerts have been held in the Kursalon, where the "Waltz King" himself directed wildly popular concerts 100 years ago (€39-56, concerts nightly generally at 20:15, tel. 01/512-5790 to reserve). Shows last two hours and are a mix of ballet, waltzes, and a 15-piece orchestra. It's touristy—tour guides holding up banners with group numbers wait out front after the show. Even so, the performance is playful, visually fun, fine quality for most, and with a tried-and-tested, crowd-pleasing format. The conductor welcomes the crowd in German (with a wink) and English; after that...it's English only.

Musicals—The Wien Ticket pavilion next to the Opera (near Kärntner Strasse) sells tickets to contemporary American and British musicals performed in German (€10-109). Same-day tickets are available at a 24 percent discount from 14:00 until 18:00 (ticket pavilion open daily 10:00-19:00). Or you can reserve (full-price) tickets for the musicals by phone (call Wien Ticket at tel. 01/58885).

Films of Concerts—To see free films of great concerts in a lively, outdoor setting near City Hall, see "Nightlife in Vienna," next.

Ballroom Dancing—If you like to dance (waltz and ballroom), or watch people who are really good at it, consider the Dance Evening at the Tanz Café in the Volksgarten (€5-6, May-Aug Sun from 18:00, www.volksgarten.at).

Organ Concerts—St. Peter's Church puts on free organ concerts weekdays at 15:00 and weekends at 20:00 (see page 45).

Classical Music to Go—To bring home Beethoven, Strauss, or the Wiener Philharmonic on a top-quality CD, shop at Gramola on the Graben or EMI on Kärntner Strasse.

VIENNA

Nightlife in Vienna

If powdered wigs and opera singers in Viking helmets aren't your thing, Vienna has plenty of alternatives. For an up-to-date run-down on fun after dark, check www.viennahype.at.

City Hall Open-Air Classical-Music Cinema and Food Circus—A thriving people scene erupts each evening in summer (mid-July-mid-Sept) at the park in front of City Hall (Rathaus, on the Ringstrasse). Thousands of people keep a food circus of 24 simple stalls busy. There's not a plastic cup anywhere, just real plates and glasses—Vienna wants the quality of food to be as high as the music that's about to begin. About 3,000 folding chairs face a 60-foot-wide screen up against the City Hall's Neo-Gothic facade. When darkness falls, an announcer explains the program, and then the music starts. The program is different every night—mostly movies of opera and classical concerts, with some films. The TI has the schedule (programs generally last about 2 hours, starting when it's dark—between 21:30 in July and 20:30 in Aug and early Sept).

Since 1991, the city has paid for 60 of these summer event nights each year. Why? To promote culture. Officials know that the City Hall Music Festival is mostly a "meat market" where young people come to hook up. But they believe many of these people will develop a little appreciation of classical music and high culture on the side.

Bermuda Triangle (Bermuda Dreieck)—The area known as the "Bermuda Triangle"—north of St. Stephen's Cathedral, between Rotenturmstrasse and Judengasse—is the hot nightspot in the old town. You'll find lots of music clubs and classy pubs, or *Beisl* (such as Krah Krah, Salzamt, Bermuda Bräu, and First Floor—for cocktails with a view of live fish). The serious-looking guards have nothing to do with the bar scene—they're guarding the synagogue nearby.

Gürtel—The Gürtel is Vienna's outer ring road. The arches of a lumbering viaduct (which carries a train track) are now filled with trendy bars, sports bars, dance clubs, strip clubs, antique shops, and restaurants. To experience—or simply see—the latest scene in town, head out here. The people-watching—the trendiest kids on the block—makes the trip fun even if you're looking for exercise rather than a drink. Ride U-6 to Nussdorfer Strasse or Thaliastrasse and hike along the viaduct.

English Cinema—Several great theaters offer three or four screens of English movies nightly (€6-9): **Burg Kino,** a block from the Opera, facing the Ring (see below); **English Cinema Haydn,** near my recommended hotels on Mariahilfer Strasse (Mariahilfer Strasse 57, tel. 01/587-2262, www.haydnkino.at); and **Artis International Cinema,** right in the town center a few minutes from the cathedral (Schultergasse 5, tel. 01/535-6570).

The Third Man at Burg Kino—This movie, voted the best British film ever by the British Film Institute, takes place in 1949 Vienna—when it was divided, like Berlin, between the four victorious Allies. With a dramatic Vienna cemetery scene, coffeehouse culture surviving amid the rubble, and Orson Welles being chased through the sewers, the tale of a divided city about to fall under Soviet rule and rife with smuggling is an enjoyable two-hour experience while in Vienna (€8, in English; 3-4 showings weekly—usually Friday evening, Sunday afternoon, and Tuesday early evening; Opernring 19, tel. 01/587-8406, www.burgkino.at).

Sleeping in Vienna

As you move out from the center, hotel prices drop. My listings are in the old center (figure at least €100 for a decent double), along the likeable Mariahilfer Strasse (about €90), and near the Westbahnhof (about €70).

Book ahead for Vienna if you can, particularly for holidays. Business hotels have their highest rates in September and October, when it's peak convention time. Prices are also high right around New Year's Eve. Steer clear of Internet booking sites—hotels lose big and you pay more. Book direct by phone, fax, or email.

While few accommodations in Vienna are air-conditioned, you can generally get fans on request. Places with elevators often have a few stairs to climb, too. Viennese elevators can be confusing: In most of Europe, 0 is the ground floor, and 1 is the first floor up (our "second floor"). But in Vienna, elevators can also have floors P, U, M, and A before getting to 1—so floor 1 can actually be what we'd call the fifth floor.

For tips on reaching your hotel upon arrival in Vienna, see "Vienna Connections" at the end of this chapter.

Sleep Code

(€1 = about $1.40, country code: 43, area code: 01)
S = Single, **D** = Double/Twin, **T** = Triple, **Q** = Quad, **b** = bathroom, **s** = shower only. Unless otherwise noted, credit cards are accepted, and breakfast is included. Everyone listed here speaks English.

To help you easily sort through these listings, I've divided the accommodations into three categories, based on the price for a double room with bath during high season:

$$$ Higher Priced—Most rooms €120 or more.
  $$ Moderately Priced—Most rooms between €75-120.
    $ Lower Priced—Most rooms €75 or less.

Prices can change without notice; verify the hotel's current rates online or by email. For other updates, see www.ricksteves.com/update.

Within the Ring, in the Old City Center

You'll pay extra to sleep in the atmospheric old center, but if you can afford it, staying here gives you the best classy Vienna experience.

$$$ Hotel am Stephansplatz is a four-star business hotel with 56 rooms. It's plush but not over-the-top, and reasonably priced for its sleek comfort and incredible location facing the cathedral. Every detail is modern and quality; breakfast is superb, with a view of the city waking up around the cathedral; and the staff is always ready with a friendly welcome (Sb-€160-180, Db-€210-250, prices vary with season and room size, prices shoot up during conventions—most often in Sept-Oct; generally less Fri-Sun, July-Aug, and in winter; extra bed-€50, children stay for free or very cheap, air-con, free Internet access and Wi-Fi, gym and sauna, elevator, Stephansplatz 9, U-1 or U-3: Stephansplatz, tel. 01/534-050, fax 01/5340-5710, www.hotelamstephansplatz.at, office@hotelamstephansplatz.at).

$$$ Hotel Pertschy, circling an old courtyard, is big and hotelesque. Its 56 huge rooms are elegantly creaky, with chandeliers and Baroque touches. Those on the courtyard are quietest (Sb-€95-114, Db-€139-169 depending on room size, €20-30 cheaper off-season, extra bed-€36, non-smoking rooms, free Internet access and Wi-Fi, elevator, Habsburgergasse 5, U-1 or U-3: Stephansplatz, tel. 01/534-490, fax 01/534-4949, www.pertschy.com, pertschy@pertschy.com).

$$$ Pension Aviano is another peaceful, family-run place. It has 17 comfortable rooms with flowery carpet and other Baroque frills, all on the fourth floor above lots of old-center action

Hotels in Central Vienna

VIENNA

1 Hotel am Stephansplatz
2 Hotel Pertschy
3 Pension Aviano
4 Hotel Schweizerhof
5 Hotel zur Wiener Staatsoper
6 Pension A und A
7 Pension Nossek
8 Pension Suzanne
9 Schweizer Pension
10 Pension Neuer Markt
11 Pension Dr. Geissler

(Sb-€104, Db-€148-169 depending on size, roughly €20-30 cheaper per room in July-Aug and Nov-March, 5 percent discount if you book direct and mention Rick Steves, extra bed-€25-33, non-smoking, fans, free Internet access and Wi-Fi, elevator, between Neuer Markt and Kärntner Strasse at Marco d'Avianogasse 1, tel. 01/512-8330, fax 01/5128-3306, www.secrethomes.at, aviano @secrethomes.at).

$$$ Hotel Schweizerhof is classy, with 55 big rooms, all the comforts, shiny public spaces, and a formal ambience. It's centrally located midway between St. Stephen's Cathedral and the Danube Canal (Sb-€85-95, Db-€120-140, low prices are for July-Aug and slow times, with cash and this book get your best price and then claim a 10 percent discount, extra bed-€35, grand breakfast, free Wi-Fi, elevator, Bauernmarkt 22, U-1 or U-3: Stephansplatz, tel. 01/533-1931, fax 01/533-0214, www.schweizerhof.at, office @schweizerhof.at). Since this is in the "Bermuda Triangle" night-club area, it can be noisy on weekends (Thu-Sat). If you'll be here then, ask for a quiet room when you reserve.

$$$ Hotel zur Wiener Staatsoper, the Schweizerhof's sister hotel, is quiet, with a more traditional elegance. Its 22 tidy rooms come with high ceilings, chandeliers, and fancy carpets on parquet floors (tiny Sb-€80-100, Db-€115-150, Tb-€135-175, rates depend on demand, cheaper prices are for July-Aug and Dec-March, extra bed-€22, fans on request, elevator, free Wi-Fi, a block from the Opera at Krugerstrasse 11; U-1, U-2, or U-4: Karlsplatz; tel. 01/513-1274, fax 01/513-127-415, www.zurwienerstaatsoper.at, office@zurwienerstaatsoper.at, manager Claudia).

$$$ Pension A und A, a friendly eight-room B&B run by Andreas and Andrea, offers a sleek, mod break from crusty old Vienna. This pricey place, wonderfully located just off the Graben, replaces Baroque doilies with contemporary style and blinding-white minimalist public spaces (Sb-€98-128 depending on sea-son; Db-€149 in May-Aug, €179 in Sept-Oct, €129 in Nov-Feb; includes breakfast, air-con, free Wi-Fi, Habsburgergasse 3, floor M, tel. 01/890-5128, www.aunda.at, office@aunda.at).

$$ At Pension Nossek, an elevator takes you above any street noise into Frau Bernad and Frau Gundolf's world, where the chil-dren seem to be placed among the lace and flowers by an interior designer. With 32 rooms right on the wonderful Graben, this is a particularly good value (S-€52-60, Ss-€62, Sb-€76-80, Db-€120, €30 extra for sprawling suites, extra bed-€35, cash only, air-con, elevator, pay Internet access and Wi-Fi, Graben 17, U-1 or U-3: Stephansplatz, tel. 01/5337-0410, fax 01/535-3646, www.pension -nossek.at, reservation@pension-nossek.at).

$$ Pension Suzanne, as Baroque and doily as you'll find in this price range, is wonderfully located a few yards from the Opera.

It's small, but run with the class of a bigger hotel. The 25 rooms are packed with properly Viennese antique furnishings and paintings (Sb-€82, Db-€106-127 depending on size, 4 percent discount with this book and cash, extra bed-€25, spacious apartment for up to 6 also available, discounts in winter, fans on request, elevator, free Internet access and Wi-Fi, Walfischgasse 4; U-1, U-2, or U-4: Karlsplatz and follow signs for Opera exit; tel. 01/513-2507, fax 01/513-2500, www.pension-suzanne.at, info@pension-suzanne.at, manager Michael).

$$ Schweizer Pension has been family-owned for four generations. Anita and her son Gerald offer lots of tourist info and 11 homey rooms for a great price, with parquet floors. True to its name, it feels very Swiss—tidy and well-run (S-€46-55, big Sb-€68-81, D-€68-79, Db-€89-98, Tb-€109-125, prices depend on season and room size, cash only, entirely non-smoking, elevator, free Wi-Fi, laundry-€18/load, Heinrichsgasse 2, U-2 or U-4: Schottenring, tel. 01/533-8156, fax 01/535-6469, www.schweizer pension.com, schweizer.pension@chello.at). They also rent a quad with bath (€129-139—too small for 4 adults but great for a family of 2 adults/2 kids under age 15).

$$ Pension Neuer Markt is family-run, with 37 comfy but faded rooms in a perfectly central locale. Its hallways have the ambience of a cheap cruise ship (Ss-€70-80, Sb-€90-110, smaller Ds-€80-90, Db-€90-135, prices vary with season and room size, extra bed-€20, request a quiet room when you reserve, fans, elevator, free Internet access and Wi-Fi, Seilergasse 9, tel. 01/512-2316, fax 01/513-9105, www.hotelpension.at/neuermarkt, neuermarkt @hotelpension.at).

$$ Pension Dr. Geissler has 23 plain-but-comfortable rooms in a modern, nondescript apartment building about 10 blocks northeast of St. Stephen's, near the canal (S-€48, Ss-€68, Sb-€76, D-€65, Ds-€77, Db-€95, 20 percent less in winter, elevator, Postgasse 14, U-1 or U-4: Schwedenplatz—Postgasse is to the left as you face Hotel Capricorno, tel. 01/533-2803, fax 01/533-2635, www.hotelpension.at/dr-geissler, dr.geissler@hotelpension.at).

On or near Mariahilfer Strasse

Lively Mariahilfer Strasse connects the Westbahnhof (West Station) and the city center. The U-3 line, starting at the Westbahnhof, goes down Mariahilfer Strasse to the cathedral. This tourist-friendly, vibrant area is filled with shopping malls, simpler storefronts, and cafés. Its smaller hotels and private rooms are generally run by people from the non-German-speaking part of the former Habsburg Empire (i.e., Eastern Europe). Most hotels are within a few steps of an U-Bahn stop, just one or two stops from the Westbahnhof (direction from the station: Simmering).

VIENNA

100 Meters
100 Yards

Hotels & Restaurants Outside the Ring

VIENNA

1. Hotel NH Atterseehaus
2. Hotel NH Wien
3. Hotel Pension Corvinus, Haydn Hotel & Cinema
4. Hotel Pension Mariahilf
5. K&T Boardinghouse (2)
6. Hotel Kugel
7. Hotel Admiral
8. Pension Hargita
9. Pension Lindenhof
10. Hotel Mercure Wien Europaplatz
11. Hotel Ibis Wien
12. To Pension Fünfhaus & Hostel Ruthensteiner
13. Jugendherberge Myrthengasse
14. Westend City Hostel
15. MOjOvie Hostel
16. Wombat's City Hostels (3)
17. Amerlingbeisl Restaurant
18. Zu Ebener Erde und Erster Stock Rest.
19. Witwe Bolte Restaurant
20. Plutzer Bräu Restaurant
21. Buffet Trześniewski
22. Schnitzelwirt Restaurant
23. Naschmarkt
24. Akakiko Sushi
25. Café Sperl
26. Launderette
27. Internet Café

The nearest place to do laundry is **Schnell & Sauber Waschcenter** (wash-€4.50 for small load or €9 for large load, plus a few euros to dry, daily 6:00-23:00, a few blocks north of Westbahnhof on the east side of Urban-Loritz-Platz).

$$$ NH Hotels, a Spanish chain, runs two stern, stylish-but-passionless business hotels a few blocks apart on Mariahilfer Strasse. Both rent ideal-for-families suites, each with a living room, two TVs, bathroom, desk, and kitchenette (rack rate: Db suite-€99-200, going rate usually closer to €110-125, €17/person for optional breakfast, apartments for 2-3 adults, 1 kid under 12 free, non-smoking rooms, elevator, pay Wi-Fi). The 73-room **NH Atterseehaus** is at Mariahilfer Strasse 78 (U-3: Zieglergasse, tel. 01/524-5600, fax 01/524-560-015, nhatterseehaus@nh-hotels .com), and **NH Wien** has 105 rooms at Mariahilfer Strasse 32 (U-3: Neubaugasse—follow *Stiftgasse* signs to exit and turn left from top of escalator; from Mariahilfer Strasse, enter through shop passageway between Nordsee and Tchibo—or from Lindengasse 9, tel. 01/521-720, fax 01/521-7215, nhwien@nh-hotels.com). The website for both is www.nh-hotels.com.

$$ Hotel Pension Corvinus is bright, modern, and proudly and warmly run by a Hungarian family: Miklós, Judit, Anthony, and Zoltan. Its 12 comfortable rooms are spacious, and some are downright sumptuous (Sb-€69-79, Db-€99-109, Tb-€119-129, get these special Rick Steves prices with this book, extra bed-€26, also has apartments with kitchens, most rooms non-smoking, air-con, elevator, free Internet access and Wi-Fi, parking garage-€17/ day, on the third floor at Mariahilfer Strasse 57-59, U-3: Neubaugasse, tel. 01/587-7239, fax 01/587-723-920, www.corvinus.at, hotel @corvinus.at).

$$ Hotel Pension Mariahilf's 12 rooms are clean, well-priced, and good-sized (if outmoded), with a slight Art Deco flair (Sb-€60-75, twin Db-€78-98, Db-€88-109, Tb-€99-139, 5-6-person apartment with kitchen-€129-169, lower prices are for Nov-Feb or longer stays, book direct and ask about a Rick Steves discount, elevator, free Wi-Fi, parking-€18, Mariahilfer Strasse 49, U-3: Neubaugasse, tel. 01/586-1781, fax 01/586-178-122, www .mariahilf-hotel.at, office@mariahilf-hotel.at).

$$ K&T Boardinghouse rents spacious, comfortable, good-value rooms in two locations. The first has three bright and airy rooms three flights above lively Mariahilfer Strasse (no elevator). The second location, just across the street, has five units on the first floor (Db-€79, Tb-€99, Qb-€119, 2-night minimum, no breakfast, air-con-€10/day, cash only but reserve with credit card, non-smoking, free Internet access and Wi-Fi, coffee in rooms; first location: Mariahilfer Strasse 72, second location: Chwallagasse 2; for either, get off at U-3: Neubaugasse; tel. 01/523-2989,

mobile 0676-553-6063, fax 01/522-0345, www.ktboardinghouse
.at, k.t@chello.at, Tina). To reach the Chwallagasse location
from Mariahilfer Strasse, turn left at Café Ritter and walk down
Schadekgasse one short block; tiny Chwallagasse is the first right.

$$ Haydn Hotel is big and formal, with masculine public
spaces and 50 spacious rooms (Sb-€80-90, Db-€110-120, suites
and family apartments, ask about 10 percent Rick Steves discount,
extra bed-€30, all rooms non-smoking, air-con, elevator, free
Internet access, pay Wi-Fi, parking-€15/day, Mariahilfer Strasse
57-59, U-3: Neubaugasse, tel. 01/5874-4140, fax 01/586-1950, www
.haydn-hotel.at, info@haydn-hotel.at, Nouri).

$$ Hotel Kugel is run with pride and attitude. "Simple quality and good value" is the motto of the hands-on owner, Johannes
Roller. It's a big 32-room hotel with simple Old World charm, offering a fine value (Db-€85, supreme Db with canopy beds-€105-115,
cash only, completely non-smoking, free Internet access, free cable
Internet in some rooms, some tram noise, Siebensterngasse 43,
at corner with Neubaugasse, U-3: Neubaugasse, tel. 01/523-3355,
fax 01/5233-3555, www.hotelkugel.at, office@hotelkugel.at). Herr
Roller also offers several cheaper basic rooms for backpackers.

$$ Hotel Admiral is huge and practical, with 80 large,
workable rooms. This last resort is on a dreary street across from
a rowdy nightclub (request a quiet room), and lacks the charm
and personality of my other listings (Sb-€70, Db-€94, mention
this book for these special prices, cheaper in winter, extra bed-
€25, breakfast-€6/person, free Internet access and Wi-Fi; limited
free parking is first-come, first-served—otherwise €10/day; a block
off Mariahilfer Strasse at Karl-Schweighofer-Gasse 7, U-2 or U-3:
Volkstheater, tel. 01/521-410, fax 01/521-4116, www.admiral.co.at,
hotel@admiral.co.at).

$ Pension Hargita rents 19 generally small, bright, and tidy
rooms (mostly twins) with Hungarian woody-village decor. While
the pension is directly on bustling Mariahilfer Strasse, its win-
dows block noise well. This spick-and-span, well-located place is a
great value (S-€40, Ss-€47, Sb-€57, D-€54, Ds-€60, tiny Db-€65,
Db-€68, Ts-€75, Tb-€82, Qb-€112, reserve with credit card but
pay with cash to get these rates, extra bed-€12, breakfast-€5, com-
pletely non-smoking, lots of stairs and no elevator, free Internet
access, pay Wi-Fi in some rooms, corner of Mariahilfer Strasse
and Andreasgasse, Andreasgasse 1, U-3: Zieglergasse, tel. 01/526-
1928, fax 01/526-0492, www.hargita.at, pension@hargita.at, Erika
and Tibor).

$ Pension Lindenhof rents 19 very basic, very worn but clean
rooms. It's a dark and mysteriously dated time warp filled with
plants (and a fun guest-generated postcard wall); the stark rooms
have outrageously high ceilings and teeny bathrooms (S-€32,

Sb-€40, D-€54, Db-€72, T-€81, Tb-€108, Q-€108, Qb-€144, cheaper during slow times, hall shower-€2, cash only, elevator, next door to a harmless strip bar at Lindengasse 4, U-3: Neubaugasse, tel. 01/523-0498, fax 01/523-7362, www.pensionlindenhof.at, pension lindenhof@yahoo.com, run by Gebrael family; Zara, Keram, and his father George speak English).

Near the Westbahnhof (West Station)

$$$ Hotel Mercure Wien Europaplatz offers high-rise modern efficiency and comfort in 211 air-conditioned rooms, directly across from the Westbahnhof (Db-€130-170 depending on season, online deals as cheap as Db-€69 if you book well in advance, breakfast-€15, free Internet access and Wi-Fi in lobby, pay Wi-Fi in rooms, elevator, parking-€15/day, Matrosengasse 6, U-3: Westbahnhof, tel. 01/5990-1181, fax 01/597-6900, www.mercure .com, h1707@accor.com).

$$ Hotel Ibis Wien, a modern high-rise hotel with American charm, is ideal for anyone tired of quaint old Europe. Its 340 cookie-cutter rooms are bright, comfortable, and modern, with all the conveniences (Sb-€69-75, Db-€87-93, Tb-€106, breakfast-€10, air-con, elevator, free Internet access and Wi-Fi in lobby, parking garage-€12/day; exit Westbahnhof to the right and walk 400 yards, Mariahilfer Gürtel 22-24, U-3: Westbahnhof; tel. 01/59998, fax 01/597-9090, www.ibishotel.com, h0796@accor.com).

$ Pension Fünfhaus is big, plain, clean, and bare-bones—almost institutional—with tile floors. The neighborhood is run-down (with a few ladies loitering late at night), but this 47-room pension offers the best doubles you'll find for under €60 (S-€34, Sb-€43, D-€49, Db-€58, Tb-€84-92, 4-person apartment-€98-104, cash only, closed mid-Nov-Feb, includes basic breakfast, Sperrgasse 12, U-3: Westbahnhof, tel. 01/892-3545 or 01/892-0286, fax 01/892-0460, www.pension5haus.at, vienna@pension5haus.at, Frau Susi Tersch). Half the rooms are in the main building and half are in the annex, which has good rooms but is near the train tracks and a bit scary on the street at night. From the station, ride tram #52 or #58 two stops down Mariahilfer Strasse away from center, and ask for Sperrgasse. Crazy Chicken bike rental, listed on page 31, is just a block farther down Sperrgasse.

Cheap Dorms and Hostels near Mariahilfer Strasse

$ Jugendherberge Myrthengasse is your classic huge and well-run HI youth hostel, with 280 beds (€17-21/person in 2- to 6-bed rooms, price depends on season, includes sheets and breakfast, non-members pay €3.50 extra, pay Internet access, free Wi-Fi in lobby, always open, no curfew, lockers and lots of facilities, coin-op laundry, Myrthengasse 7, tel. 01/523-6316, fax 01/523-5849, hostel@chello.at).

$ Westend City Hostel, just a block from the Westbahnhof and Mariahilfer Strasse, is well-run and well-located, with 180 beds in 4- to 12-bed dorms (€22-29/person depending on how many in the room, Db-€66-92, rates vary by season, cheaper Nov-mid-March—except around New Year's; includes sheets, breakfast, and locker; cash only, pay Internet access, free Wi-Fi, laundry-€7, Fügergasse 3, tel. 01/597-6729, fax 01/597-672-927, www.westend hostel.at, info@westendhostel.at).

$ MOjOvie is a creative "little neighbourette," combining a residential apartment feel with a hostel vibe. This network of apartments offers dorm beds as well as private units sleeping two to four (dorm bed-€20, €23-26/person in a private room with shared bathroom, €35-45/person for apartment with private bathroom, includes sheets and towels, cash only for charges under €100, free Wi-Fi, laundry service, shared kitchen, reception open 8:00-23:00, Kaiserstrasse 77, tram #5 or a 10-minute walk from Westbahnhof, mobile 0699-1155-5505, www.mymojovie.at, accommodation@my mojovie.at).

$ *More Hostels:* Other hostels with €17-20 beds and €50 doubles near Mariahilfer Strasse are **Wombat's City Hostel** (3 locations: one near tracks behind the station at Grangasse 6, another even closer to station at Mariahilfer Strasse 137, and a new one near the Naschmarkt at Rechte Wienzeile 35; tel. 01/897-2336, www.wombats-hostels.com, office@wombats-vienna.at) and **Hostel Ruthensteiner** (smoke-free; leave the Westbahnhof to the right and follow Mariahilfer Strasse behind the station, then left on Haidmannsgasse for a block, then turn right and find Robert-Hamerling-Gasse 24; tel. 01/893-4202, www.hostelruthensteiner .com, info@hostelruthensteiner.com).

Eating in Vienna

The Viennese appreciate the fine points of life, and right up there with waltzing is eating. The city has many atmospheric restaurants (and many offer a *"menu,"* a fixed-price bargain meal, at lunch-time). As you ponder the Eastern European specialties on menus, remember that Vienna's diverse empire may be no more, but its flavors linger.

While cuisines are routinely named for countries, Vienna claims to be the only *city* with a cuisine of its own: Vienna soups come with fillings (semolina dumpling, liver dumpling, or pancake slices). *Gulasch* is a beef ragout based on a traditional Hungarian shepherd's soup (spiced with onion and paprika). Of course, Wiener schnitzel is traditionally a breaded and fried veal cutlet

VIENNA

1. Gigerl Stadtheuriger
2. Zu den Drei Hacken
3. Buffet Trześniewski
4. Reinthaler's Beisl & Café Hawelka
5. Plachutta Rest.
6. Cantinetta La Norma
7. Gyros
8. Akakiko Sushi (3)
9. Zanoni & Zanoni Gelateria (2)
10. Zum Schwarzen Kameel Rest. & Wine Bar
11. Rest. Ofenloch
12. Brezel-Gwölb
13. Beisl zum Scherer
14. Biobar von Antun Vegetarian Rest.
15. Esterhazykeller
16. Melker Stiftskeller
17. Julius Meinl am Graben Deli

VIENNA

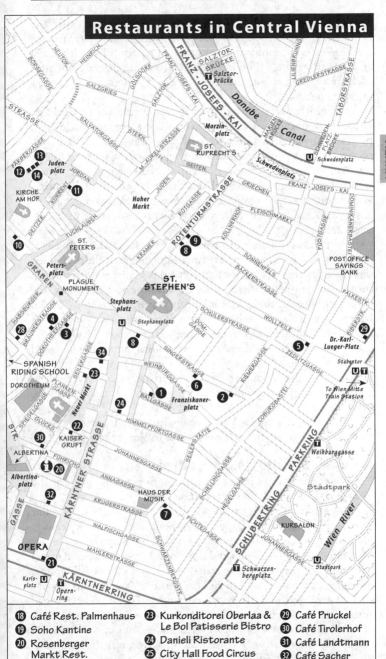

Restaurants in Central Vienna

18 Café Rest. Palmenhaus
19 Soho Kantine
20 Rosenberger Markt Rest.
21 Ruckenbauer (in Underpass)
22 Lucky Chinese Rest.

23 Kurkonditorei Oberlaa & Le Bol Patisserie Bistro
24 Danieli Ristorante
25 City Hall Food Circus
26 Justizcafe
27 Café Central
28 Café Braunerhof

29 Café Pruckel
30 Café Tirolerhof
31 Café Landtmann
32 Café Sacher
33 Café Demel
34 American Bar

(though pork is more common these days). Another meat specialty is boiled beef *(Tafelspitz)*. While you're sure to have *Apfelstrudel,* try *Topfenstrudel,* too (wafer-thin strudel pastry filled with sweet cheese and raisins). The *dag* you see in some prices stands for "dekagram" (10 grams). Therefore, *10 dag* is 100 grams, or about a quarter-pound.

On nearly every corner, you can find a colorful *Beisl* (BYE-zul). These uniquely Viennese taverns are a characteristic cross between an English pub and a French brasserie—filled with poetry teachers and their students, couples loving without touching, housewives on their way home from cello lessons, and waiters who enjoy serving hearty food and drinks at an affordable price. Ask at your hotel for a good *Beisl.* (Beware: Despite non-smoking laws, *Beisls* may still be quite smoky; fortunately, most have outdoor seating.)

For hardcore Viennese cuisine, drop by a *Würstelstand.* The local hot-dog stand is a fixture on city squares throughout the old center, serving a variety of hot dogs and pickled side dishes with a warm corner-meeting-place atmosphere. Be adventurous: Generally, the darker the weenie, the spicier it is. Key words: *Weisswurst*—boiled white sausage; *Bosna*—with onions and curry; *Käsekrainer*—with melted cheese inside; *Debreziner*—spicy Hungarian; *Frankfurter*—our weenie; *frische*—fresh; *Kren*—horseradish; and *Senf*—mustard (ask for *süss*—sweet, or *scharf*—sharp). Only a tourist puts the sausage in a bun like a hot dog. Munch alternately between the meat and the bread ("that's why you have two hands"), and you'll look like a native.

Two other don't-miss Viennese institutions, its cafés and wine gardens, are covered under "Experiences in Vienna" on page 79.

Near St. Stephen's Cathedral

Each of these eateries is within about a five-minute walk of the cathedral (U-1 or U-3: Stephansplatz).

Gigerl Stadtheuriger offers a fun, near-*Heuriger* wine cellar experience (described on page 80), without leaving the city center. Just point to what looks good. Food is sold by the piece or weight; 100 grams *(10 dag)* is about a quarter-pound (cheese and cold meats cost about €3 per 100 grams, salads are about €2 per 100 grams; price sheet posted on wall to right of buffet line). The *Karree* pork with herbs is particularly tasty and tender. They also have menu entrées, spinach strudel, quiche, *Apfelstrudel,* and, of course, casks of new and local wines (sold by the *Achtel,* about 4 oz). Meals run €7-12, and there's often accordion or live music on weekends (daily 15:00-24:00, indoor/outdoor seating, behind cathedral, a block off Kärntner Strasse, a few cobbles off Rauhensteingasse on Blumenstock, tel. 01/513-4431).

Zu den Drei Hacken, another fun and typical *Weinstube*, is famous for its local specialties (€10 plates, Mon-Sat 11:00-23:00, closed Sun, indoor/outdoor seating, Singerstrasse 28, tel. 01/512-5895).

Buffet Trześniewski is an institution—justly famous for its elegant and cheap finger sandwiches and small beers (€1 each). Three different sandwiches and a *kleines Bier (Pfiff)* make a fun, light lunch. Point to whichever delights look tasty (or grab the English translation sheet and take time to study your 22 sandwich options). The classic favorites are *Geflügelleber* (chicken liver), *Matjes mit Zwiebel* (herring with onions), and *Speck mit Ei* (bacon and eggs). Pay for your sandwiches and a drink. Take your drink tokens to the lady on the right. Sit on the bench and scoot over to a tiny table when a spot opens up. Trześniewski has been a Vienna favorite for more than a century...and many of its regulars seem to have been here for the grand opening (Mon-Fri 8:30-19:30, Sat 9:00-17:00, closed Sun; 50 yards off the Graben, nearly across from brooding Café Hawelka, Dorotheergasse 2; tel. 01/512-3291). In the fall, this is a good opportunity to try the fancy grape juices—*Most* or *Traubenmost*. Their other location, at Mariahilfer Strasse 95 (near many recommended hotels), serves the same sandwiches with the same menu in the same ambience (Mon-Fri 8:30-19:00, Sat 9:00-18:00, closed Sun, U-3: Zieglergasse, tel. 01/596-4291).

Reinthaler's Beisl is a time warp that serves simple, traditional *Beisl* fare all day. It's handy for its location (a block off the Graben, across the street from Buffet Trześniewski) and because it's a rare restaurant in the center that's open on Sunday. Its fun, classic interior winds way back (use the handwritten daily menu rather than the printed English one, €6-12 plates, daily 11:00-22:30, at Dorotheergasse 4, tel. 01/513-1249).

Plachutta Restaurant, with a stylish green-and-cream, elegant-but-comfy interior and breezy covered terrace, is famous for the best beef in town. You'll find an enticing menu with all the classic Viennese beef dishes, fine desserts, attentive service, and an enthusiastic and sophisticated local clientele. They've developed the art of beef to the point of producing popular cookbooks. Their specialty is a page-long list of *Tafelspitz*—a traditional copper pot of boiled beef with broth and vegetables. Treat the broth as your soup course. A chart on the menu lets you choose your favorite cut. Make a reservation for this high-energy Vienna favorite (€16-21/pot, daily 12:00-22:30, 10-minute walk from St. Stephen's Cathedral to Wollzeile 38, U-3: Stubentor, tel. 01/512-1577).

Cantinetta La Norma, a short walk from the cathedral, serves fresh, excellent Italian dishes amid a cozy yet energetic ambience. Even on weeknights the small dining area is abuzz with chatter among its multinational, loyal regulars (€8 pizzas and pastas,

€7-18 entrées, lunch specials, daily 11:00-24:00, outdoor seating, Franziskaner Platz 3, tel. 01/512-8665, run by friendly Paco).

Gyros is a humble little Greek/Turkish joint run by Yilmaz, a fun-loving Turk from Izmir. He simply loves to feed people—the food is great, the prices are decent, and you almost feel like you took a quick trip to Istanbul (€8-12 plates, Mon-Sat 10:00-24:00, Sun 10:00-18:00, a long block off Kärntner Strasse at corner of Fichtegasse and Seilerstätte, mobile 0699-1016-3726).

Akakiko Sushi is a small chain of Japanese restaurants with an easy pan-Asian menu that's worth considering if you're just schnitzeled out. They serve sushi, of course, but also noodles, stir-fry, and other meals. The €11 bento box meals are a decent value. There are several convenient locations: Singerstrasse 4 (a block off Kärntner Strasse near the cathedral), Rotenturmgasse 6 (also near the cathedral), Heidenschuss 3 (near other recommended eateries just off Am Hof, U-3: Herrengasse), and Mariahilfer Strasse 42-48 (fifth floor of Kaufhaus Gerngross, near many recommended hotels, U-3: Neubaugasse). Though they lack charm, these are fast and reasonable (€8-11 meals, all open daily 10:30-23:30).

Ice Cream!: **Zanoni & Zanoni** is a very Italian *gelateria* run by an Italian family. They're mobbed by happy Viennese hungry for their huge €2 cones to go. Or, to relax and watch the thriving people scene, lick your gelato in their fun outdoor area (daily 7:00-24:00, 2 blocks up Rotenturmstrasse from cathedral at Lugeck 7, tel. 01/512-7979). There's another location behind the Kunsthistorisches Museum, facing the Ring (at Burgring 1, U-2 or U-3: Volkstheater/Museumsplatz).

Near Am Hof Square

The square called Am Hof (U-3: Herrengasse) is surrounded by a maze of atmospheric medieval lanes; the following eateries are all within a block of the square.

Zum Schwarzen Kameel Wine Bar ("The Black Camel") is filled with a professional local crowd enjoying small plates from the same kitchen as their fancy restaurant, but at a better price. This is *the* place for horseradish and thin-sliced ham (*Beinschinken mit Kren*, €8.50 a plate, *Achtung*—the horseradish is *hot*). I'd order their *Vorspeisenteller* (a great antipasti dish that comes with ham and horseradish) or *Tafelspitz* (€16). Stand, grab a stool, find a table on the street, or sit anywhere you can—it's customary to share tables in the wine-bar section. Fine Austrian wines are sold by the *Achtel* (eighth-liter glass) and listed on the board; Aussie bartender Karl can help you choose. They also have a buffet of tiny €1-2 sandwiches. For a splurge, the **Zum Schwarzen Kameel Restaurant** is a tiny, elegant alternative. The dark-wood, 12-table, Art Nouveau restaurant serves fine gourmet Viennese cuisine (three-course lunch-€40, three-course dinner-€65 plus pricey wine, both open Mon-Sat 8:30-24:00, closed Sun, Bognergasse 5, tel. 01/533-8125).

Restaurant Ofenloch serves good, old-fashioned Viennese cuisine with formal service, both indoors and out. This 300-year-old eatery, with great traditional ambience, is dressy (with white tablecloths) but intimate and woodsy (€10 lunch specials, €13-19 main courses, Mon-Sat 11:00-22:30, closed Sun, Kurrentgasse 8, tel. 01/533-8844).

Brezel-Gwölb, a Tolkienesque wine cellar with outdoor dining on a quiet square, serves forgettable food in an unforgettable atmosphere. It's ideal for a romantic late-night glass of wine (daily 11:30-23:30; leave Am Hof on Drahtgasse, then take first left to Ledererhof 9; tel. 01/533-8811).

Beisl zum Scherer, around the corner, is untouristy and serves traditional plates for €8-15. Sitting outside, you'll face a stern Holocaust memorial. Inside comes with a soothing woody atmosphere and intriguing decor. Let friendly Sakis explain the daily specials—which don't show up on the English menu (Mon-Sat 11:30-22:00, closed Sun, Judenplatz 7, tel. 01/533-5164).

Biobar von Antun Vegetarian Restaurant is a cheery and earthy little place with a €7 lunch special and hearty €10 salads, plenty of vegan options, and the fancy juices you'd expect (daily 12:00-23:00, on Judenplatz at Drahtgasse 3, tel. 01/968-9351).

Esterhazykeller, both ancient and popular, has traditional fare deep underground. For a cheap and sloppy buffet, climb down to the lowest cellar. For table service on a pleasant square, sit outside (Mon-Sat 11:00-23:00, Sun 16:00-23:00, may close for lunch in Aug-Sept and/or in bad weather, just below Am Hof at Haarhof 1, tel. 01/533-3482).

Melker Stiftskeller is an untouristy *Stadtheuriger* in a deep and rustic circa-1626 cellar with hearty, inexpensive meals and new wine. Avoid this place when it's hot out, as there's no outdoor seating (Tue-Sat 17:00-24:00, closed Sun-Mon and mid-July-mid-Aug, between Am Hof Square and Schottentor U-Bahn stop at Schottengasse 3, tel. 01/533-5530).

Julius Meinl am Graben, a posh supermarket with two floors of temptations right on the Graben, has been famous since 1862 as a top-end delicatessen with all the gourmet fancies. Assemble a meal from the picnic fixings on the shelves. There's also a café, with light meals and great outdoor seating; a stuffy and pricey restaurant upstairs; and a take-away counter with good benches for people-watching while you munch (shop open Mon-Fri 8:00-19:30, Sat 9:00-18:00, closed Sun; restaurant open Mon-Sat until 24:00, closed Sun; Am Graben 19, tel. 01/532-3334).

Near the Opera

These eateries are within easy walking distance of the Opera (U-1, U-2, or U-4: Karlsplatz).

Café Restaurant Palmenhaus overlooks the Palace Garden (Burggarten—see page 59). Tucked away in a green and peaceful corner two blocks behind the Opera in the Hofburg's backyard, this is a world apart. If you want to eat modern Austrian cuisine surrounded by palm trees rather than tourists, this is the place. And, since it's at the edge of a huge park, it's great for families. Their fresh fish with generous vegetables specials are on the board (€8.50 lunch plates available Mon-Fri, €15-18 entrées, open daily 10:00-24:00, serious vegetarian dishes, fish, extensive wine list, indoors in greenhouse or outdoors, Burggarten 1, tel. 01/533-1033).

Soho Kantine is a grim, government-subsidized cantina serving the National Library and offering the best cheap, sit-down lunches in the Hofburg. Pay for your meal—your choice of bland meat or bland vegetarian—and a drink at the bar, take your token to the kitchen, and then sit down and eat with the locals (€6 two-course lunch, Mon-Fri 11:30-15:00, closed Sat-Sun and Aug, hard to find on ground floor of library—opposite the butterflies in a forlorn little square with no sign, Burggarten, Josefsplatz 1, tel. 01/532-8566, mobile 0676-309-5161).

Rosenberger Markt Restaurant is mobbed with tour groups. Still, if you don't mind a freeway-cafeteria ambience in the center of the German-speaking world's classiest city, this self-service eatery is fast and easy. It's just a block toward the cathedral from the Opera. The best cheap meal here is a small salad or veggie plate stacked high (daily 10:30-23:00, lots of fruits, veggies, fresh-squeezed juices, addictive banana milk, ride the glass elevator downstairs, Maysedergasse 2, tel. 01/512-3458).

Ruckenbauer, a favorite for a quick bite, is a fast-food kiosk in a transit underpass under the street in front of the Opera, between the entryways marked *U2/U4* and *U1*. Their €1.60 *Tramezzini* sandwiches and fine pastries make a classy, quick picnic lunch or dinner before the Opera, just 100 yards away (Mon-Fri 6:00-20:00, Sat-Sun 9:00-20:00).

Lucky Chinese Restaurant is simply a good, modern, and well-located option for Chinese food. The inside is fresh and air-conditioned, the outside seating is on a great square, and the service is friendly (€10-15 plates, daily 11:30-23:00, Neuer Markt 8, tel. 01/512-3428).

Kurkonditorei Oberlaa may not have the royal and plush fame of Demel (see page 40), but this is where Viennese connoisseurs serious about the quality of their pastries go to get fat. With outdoor seating on Neuer Markt, it's particularly nice on a hot summer day. Upstairs has more temptations and good seating (€10 daily three-course lunches, great selection of cakes, daily 8:00-20:00, Neuer Markt 16, other locations about town, including the Naschmarkt, tel. 01/5132-9360).

Le Bol Patisserie Bistro (next to Oberlaa) satisfies your need for something French. The staff speaks to you in French, serving fine €8 salads, baguette sandwiches, and fresh croissants (Mon-Sat 8:00-22:00, Sun 10:00-20:00, Neuer Markt 14).

Danieli Ristorante is your best classy Italian bet in the old town. White-tablecloth dressy, but not stuffy, it has reasonable prices. Dine in their elegant back room or on the street (€13-18 pizzas and pastas, €18-25 main courses, fresh fish specialties, daily 10:00-24:00, 30 yards off Kärntner Strasse opposite Neuer Markt at Himmelpfortgasse 3, tel. 01/513-7913).

City Hall Food Circus

During the summer, scores of outdoor food stands and hundreds of picnic tables are set up in the park in front of the City Hall (Rathausplatz). Local mobs enjoy mostly ethnic meals for decent-but-not-cheap prices and classical entertainment on a big screen. The fun thing here is the energy of the crowd and a feeling that you're truly eating as the Viennese do...not schnitzel and quaint traditions, but trendy "world food" with young people out having fun in a fine Vienna park setting (mid-July-mid-Sept daily from 11:00 until late, in front of City Hall on the Ringstrasse, U-2: Rathaus).

Just West of the Ring

Justizcafe, the cafeteria serving Austria's Supreme Court of Justice, offers a fine view, great prices, and a memorable lunchtime experience—even if the food is somewhat bland. Enter the Palace of Justice through its grand front door, pass through tight security, say "wow" to the Historicist architecture in the courtyard, and ride the elevator to the rooftop. You can sit behind the windows inside or dine outside on the roof, enjoying one of the best views of Vienna while surrounded by legal beagles (€8-12 main dishes, Mon-Fri 11:00-14:30, closed Sat-Sun, Schmerlingplatz 10, U-2 or U-3: Volkstheater/Museumsplatz, mobile 0676-755-6100).

Spittelberg Quarter

A charming cobbled grid of traffic-free lanes and Biedermeier apartments has become a favorite neighborhood for Viennese wanting a little dining charm between the MuseumsQuartier and Mariahilfer Strasse (handy to many recommended hotels; take Stiftgasse from Mariahilfer Strasse, or wander over here after you close down the Kunsthistorisches Museum; U-2 or U-3: Volkstheater/Museumsplatz). Tables tumble down sidewalks and into breezy courtyards filled with appreciative natives enjoying dinner or a relaxing drink. It's only worth the trip on a balmy summer evening, as it's dead in bad weather. Stroll Spittelberggasse, Schrankgasse, and Gutenberggasse, then pick your favorite. Don't miss the vine-strewn wine garden at Schrankgasse 1. To locate these restaurants, see the map on page 94.

Amerlingbeisl, with a charming, casual atmosphere both on the cobbled street and in its vine-covered courtyard, is a great value, serving a mix of traditional Austrian and international dishes (always a €5 vegetarian daily special, other specials for €6-10, €9-14 dinners, daily 9:00-2:00 in the morning, Stiftgasse 8, tel. 01/526-1660).

Zu Ebener Erde und Erster Stock ("Downstairs, Upstairs") is a charming little restaurant with a near-gourmet menu. True to its name, it has two distinct eating zones (with the same menu): a casual, woody bistro downstairs (traditionally the quarters of the poor); and a fancy Biedermeier-style dining room with red-velvet chairs and violet tablecloths upstairs (where the wealthy convened). There are also a few al fresco tables out front. Reservations are smart (€10-19 main dishes, €25 traditional three-course fixed-price meal, seasonal specials, Mon-Fri 7:30-21:30, last seating at 20:00, closed Sat-Sun, Burggasse 13, tel. 01/523-6254).

Witwe Bolte is classy and a good choice for uninspired Viennese cuisine with tablecloths. The interior is tight, but its tiny square has wonderful leafy ambience (€11-17 main dishes, daily 11:30-23:30 except closed 15:00-17:30 mid-Jan-mid-March, Gutenberggasse 13, tel. 01/523-1450).

Plutzer Bräu, next door to Amerlingbeisl, feels a bit more touristy. It's a big, sprawling, impersonal brewpub serving stick-to-your-ribs pub grub (€7-9 vegetarian dishes, €9-20 meals, ribs, burgers, traditional dishes, Tirolean beer from the keg, also brew their own, daily 11:00-2:00 in the morning, food until 24:00, Schrankgasse 4, tel. 01/526-1215).

Near Mariahilfer Strasse

Mariahilfer Strasse (see map on page 94) is filled with reasonable cafés serving all types of cuisine. For a quick yet traditional bite, consider the venerable **Buffet Trześniewski** sandwich bar at Mariahilfer Strasse 95.

Schnitzelwirt is an old classic with a 1950s patina and a clientele to match. In this smoky, working-class place, no one finishes their schnitzel ("to-go" for the dog is wrapped in newspaper, "to-go" for you is wrapped in foil). You'll find no tourists, just cheap €6-11 schnitzel meals (Mon-Sat 10:00-23:00, closed Sun, Neubaugasse 52, U-3: Neubaugasse, tel. 01/523-3771).

The **Naschmarkt** (described on page 70) is Vienna's best Old

World market, with plenty of fresh produce, cheap local-style eateries, cafés, *Döner Kebab* and sausage stands, and the best-value sushi in town (Mon-Fri 6:00-18:30, Sat 6:00-17:00, closed Sun, closes earlier in winter; U-1, U-2, or U-4: Karlsplatz, follow *Karlsplatz* signs out of the station). Survey the lane of eateries at the end of the market nearest the Opera. The circa-1900 pub is inviting. Picnickers can buy supplies at the market and eat on nearby Karlsplatz (plenty of chairs facing the Karlskirche).

Vienna Connections

By Train

Remember, Vienna has several train stations, the biggest of which are undergoing an extensive renovation. Be sure you know which station your train departs from; see page 26 for the basic run-down, but always confirm locally. For general train information in Austria, call 051-717 (to get an operator, dial 2, then 2), or visit www.oebb.at.

From Vienna by Train to: **Budapest** (every 2 hours direct, 3 hours; more with transfers), **Prague** (5/day direct, 4.75 hours; more with 1 change, 5-6 hours; 1 night train, 8 hours), **Kraków** (3 decent daytime options, 6.25 hours direct or 7-8.5 hours with 1-3 changes, plus a night train), **Ljubljana** (1 convenient early-morning direct train, 6 hours; otherwise 6/day with change in Villach, Maribor, or Graz, 6-7 hours), **Salzburg** (almost hourly, 2.5-3 hours), **Hallstatt** (hourly, 4 hours, change in Attnang-Puchheim), **Innsbruck** (almost hourly, 5 hours), **Munich** (6/day direct, 4.25 hours; otherwise about hourly, 5-5.75 hours, transfer in Salzburg), **Berlin** (8/day, most with 1 change, 9.5 hours, some via Czech Republic; longer on night train), **Zürich** (nearly hourly, 9-10 hours, 1 with changes in Innsbruck and Feldkirch, night train), **Rome** (3/day, 12-13 hours, plus several overnight options), **Venice** (3/day, 8-9.5 hours with changes—some may involve bus connection; plus 1 direct night train, 12 hours), **Frankfurt** (6/day direct, 7 hours; plus 1 direct night train, 10 hours), **Paris** (7/day, 12-17 hours, 1-3 changes), **Amsterdam** (3/day, 11.5-12.5 hours, 1-2 changes, longer night-train options involve change in Germany).

By Plane

Vienna International Airport, 12 miles from the center, has easy connections to Vienna's various train stations (airport tel. 01/700-722-233, www.viennaairport.com).

Two different trains transport airport passengers into Vienna. Both go to the same point in the city center: the Wien-Mitte Bahnhof, on the east side of the Ring (adjacent to the Landstrasse U-Bahn stop, with a handy connection to Mariahilfer Strasse hotels and other accommodations neighborhoods). The main differences between them are time and cost. The **S-Bahn** commuter train (S-7 yellow line) works just fine and is plenty fast (€3.60, 2/hour, 24 minutes, buy 2-zone ticket from machines on the platform, price includes any bus or S- or U-Bahn transfers). The fast **CAT** (City Airport Train) takes a third less time but costs nearly triple (€10, €11.50 includes a ride to your final destination on Vienna's transit system, 2/hour, usually departs at :05 and :35, 16 minutes, www.cityairporttrain.com).

Convenient express airport **buses** go to various points in Vienna: the Schwedenplatz U-Bahn station (for city-center hotels), Westbahnhof (for Mariahilfer Strasse hotels), and Wien-Meidling Bahnhof (while this train station is acting as Vienna's main station during construction). To reach these buses from the arrivals hall, go outside and to your left (note destination and times on curbside TV monitors; €6, 2-3/hour, generally 20-30 minutes, buy ticket from driver, tel. 0810-222-333 for timetable info, www.postbus.at).

The 30-minute ride into town by **taxi** costs about €35-40 (including the €11 airport surcharge).

Bratislava Airport (Letisko Bratislava)

Bratislava Airport is six miles northeast of downtown Bratislava (www.letiskobratislava.sk). The airport offers budget flights on low-cost carriers Ryanair (www.ryanair.com) and Danube Wings (www.danubewings.eu). Some airlines market it as "Vienna-Bratislava," thanks to its proximity to both capitals. To reach Vienna, you can take a Eurolines bus to the Erdberg stop of Vienna's U-3 subway line. A taxi directly to Vienna costs €60-90 (depending on whether you use a cheaper Slovak or more expensive Austrian cab).

SALZBURG

Salzburg, just over the Austrian border, makes a fun day trip from Munich (1.5-2 hours by direct train). Thanks to its charmingly preserved old town), splendid gardens, Baroque churches, and Europe's largest intact medieval fortress, Salzburg feels made for tourism. As a musical mecca, the city puts on a huge annual festival, as well as constant concerts, and its residents—or at least its tourism industry—are forever smiling to the tunes of Mozart and *The Sound of Music*. It's a city with class. Vagabonds wish they had nicer clothes.

Planning Your Time

While Salzburg's sights are, frankly, mediocre, the town itself is a Baroque museum of cobbled streets and elegant buildings—simply a touristy stroller's delight. Even if your time is short, consider allowing half a day for the *Sound of Music* tour. The *S.O.M.* tour kills a nest of sightseeing birds with one ticket (city overview, *S.O.M.* sights, and a fine drive by the lakes).

You'd probably enjoy at least two nights in Salzburg—nights are important for swilling beer in atmospheric local gardens and attending concerts in Baroque halls and chapels. Seriously consider one of Salzburg's many evening musical events (a few are free, some are as cheap as €12, and most average €30-40). To get away from it all, bike down the river or hike across the Mönchsberg cliffs that rise directly from the middle of town.

Salzburg

Even without Mozart and the von Trapps, Salzburg is steeped in history. In about A.D. 700, Bavaria gave Salzburg to Bishop Rupert in return for his promise to Christianize the area. Salzburg remained an independent city (belonging to no state) until Napoleon came in the early 1800s. Thanks in part to its formidable fortress, Salzburg managed to avoid the ravages of war for 1,200 years...until World War II. Much of the city was destroyed by WWII bombs (mostly around the train station), but the historic old town survived.

Eight million tourists crawl its cobbles each year. That's a lot of Mozart balls—and all that popularity has led to a glut of businesses hoping to catch the tourist dollar. Still, Salzburg is both a must and a joy.

Orientation to Salzburg

(country code: 43, area code: 0662)

Salzburg, a city of 150,000 (Austria's fourth-largest), is divided into old and new. The old town, sitting between the Salzach River and its mini-mountain (Mönchsberg), holds nearly all the charm and most of the tourists. The new town, across the river, has its own share of sights and museums, plus some good accommodations.

Tourist Information

Salzburg has three helpful TIs (main tel. 0662/889-870, www .salzburg.info): at the **train station** (daily June-Aug 8:15-19:30, Sept-May 8:45-18:00, tel. 0662/8898-7340); on **Mozartplatz** in the old center (daily 9:00-18:00, July-mid-Sept until 19:00, closed Sun mid-Jan-Easter and Oct-mid-Nov, tel. 0662/889-870); and at the **Salzburg Süd park-and-ride** (generally open daily July-Aug 10:00-16:30 but sometimes longer hours, May-June Thu-Sat 10:00-16:30, Sept Mon-Sat 10:00-16:30, closed in winter, tel. 0662/8898-7360).

At any TI, you can pick up a free city-center map (the €0.70 map has a broader coverage and more information on sights, but probably isn't necessary), the Salzburg Card brochure (listing sights with current hours and prices), and a bimonthly events guide. Book a concert upon arrival. The TIs also book rooms (€2.20 fee and 10 percent deposit).

Salzburg Card: The TIs sell the Salzburg Card, which covers all your public transportation (including the Mönchsberg elevator and funicular to the fortress) and admission to all the city sights (including Hellbrunn Castle and a river cruise). The card is pricey, but if you'd like to pop into all the sights, it can save money and enhance your experience (€25/24 hours, €34/48 hours, €40/72 hours, cheaper Nov-April). To analyze your potential savings, here are the major sights and what you'd pay without the card: Hohensalzburg Fortress and funicular-€10.50; Mozart's Birthplace and Residence-€12; Hellbrunn Castle-€9.50; Salzburg Panorama 1829-€2; Salzach River cruise-€13; 24-hour transit pass-€4.20. Busy sightseers can save plenty. Get this card, feel the financial pain once, and the city will be all yours.

Arrival in Salzburg

By Train: The Salzburg station is undergoing a huge renovation, so during your visit its services will likely be operating out of temporary structures in the parking lot. Still, you'll find it all here: train information, tourist information, luggage lockers, and so on.

Getting downtown couldn't be easier, as immediately in front of the station a bus stop labeled *Zentrum-Altstadt* has **buses** lined up and leaving every two minutes. Buses #1, #3, #5, #6, and #25 all do the same route into the city center before diverging at the far end of town. For most sights and city-center hotels, get off just after the bridge. For my recommended hotels in the new town, get off at Makartplatz, just before the bridge. (Buses to and from the airport use the *Flughafen* stop in front of the train station.) **Taxis** charge about €8 (plus €1/bag) to take you to your hotel.

To **walk** downtown (15 minutes), turn left as you leave the station, and walk straight down Rainerstrasse, which leads under the tracks past Mirabellplatz, turning into Dreifaltigkeitsgasse. From here, you can turn left onto Linzergasse for many of my recommended hotels, or cross the Staatsbrücke bridge for the old town (and more hotels). For a slightly longer but more dramatic approach, leave the station the same way but follow the tracks to the river, turn left, and walk the riverside path toward the fortress.

By Car: Coming on A-8 from Munich, cross the border into Austria. Take A-10 toward Hallein, and then take the next exit (Salzburg Süd) in the direction of Anif. First, you'll pass Hellbrunn Castle (and zoo), then the Salzburg Süd TI and a park-and-ride lot—a smart place to park while visiting Salzburg. Park your car (€5/24 hours), get sightseeing information and transit tickets from the TI, and catch the shuttle bus into town (€1.90 single-ride ticket, covered by €4.20 *Tageskarte* day pass, both sold at the TI, more expensive if you buy tickets on board, every 5 minutes; bus #3, #8, or #28). If traveling with more than one other person, take advantage of a park-and-ride combo-ticket: For €13 (€10 July-Aug), you get 24 hours of parking and a round-trip on the shuttle bus for up to five people.

Mozart never drove in the old town, and neither should you.

SALZBURG

Salzburg

SALZBURG

1. Bob's Special Tours
   (Sound of Music by Minibus)
2. Panorama Tours
   (Sound of Music by Big Bus)
3. Fräulein Maria Tours
   (Sound of Music by Bike)
4. Start of Steingasse Stroll
5. Start of Mönchsberg Walk
6. Salzburg Museum &
   Panorama 1829 Exhibit
7. Alm River Canal Exhibit
8. City Cruise Line
9. Bike Rentals (2)

SALZBURG

But if you don't believe in park-and-rides, the easiest, cheapest, most central parking lot is the 1,500-car Altstadt lot in the tunnel under the Mönchsberg (€14/day, note your slot number and which of the twin lots you're in, tel. 0662/846-434). Your hotel may provide discounted parking passes.

Helpful Hints

Recommendations Skewed by Kickbacks: Salzburg is addicted to the tourist dollar, and it can never get enough. Virtually all hotels are on the take when it comes to concert and tour recommendations, influenced more by their potential kickback than by what's best for you. Take any advice with a grain of salt.

Music Festival: The Salzburg Festival (Salzburger Festspiele) runs each year from late July to the end of August (see page 139).

Internet Access: Two Internet cafés at the bottom of the cliff, between Getreidegasse and the Mönchsberg lift, have good prices and long hours (€2/hour, daily 10:00-22:00). Across the river, there's a big, handy Internet café on Theatergasse (near Mozart's Residence, €2/hour, daily 9:00-23:00). Travelers with this book can get online free for a few minutes (long enough to check email) at the Panorama Tours terminal on Mirabellplatz (daily 8:00-18:00).

Post Office: A full-service post office is located in the heart of town, in the New Residenz (Mon-Fri 8:00-18:00, Sat 9:00-12:00, closed Sun).

Laundry: A handy launderette is at the corner of Paris-Lodron-Strasse and Wolf-Dietrich-Strasse, near my recommended Linzergasse hotels (€10 self-service, €15 same-day full-service, Mon-Fri 7:30-18:00, Sat 8:00-12:00, closed Sun, tel. 0662/876-381).

Cinema: Das Kino is an art-house movie theater that plays films in their original language (a block off the river and Linzergasse on Steingasse, tel. 0662/873-100).

Getting Around Salzburg

By Bus: Single-ride tickets for central Salzburg *(Einzelkarte-Kernzone)* are sold on the bus for €2.10. At machines and *Tabak/Trafik* shops, you can buy €1.90 single-ride tickets or a €4.20 day pass *(Tageskarte,* good for 24 hours; €5 if you buy it on the bus). To get from the old town to the station, catch bus #1 from Hanuschplatz; or, from the other side of the river, catch #1, #3, #5, or #6 at Theatergasse, near Mirabell Gardens. Bus info: tel. 800-660-660.

By Bike: Salzburg is great fun for cyclists. The following two bike-rental shops offer 20 percent off to anyone with this book—

ask for it. **Top Bike** rents bikes on the river next to the Staatsbrücke (€6/2 hours, €10/4 hours, €15/24 hours, usually daily April-June and Sept-Oct 10:00-17:00, July-Aug 9:00-19:00, closed Nov-March, free helmets with this book, tel. 06272/4656, mobile 0676-476-7259, www.topbike.at, Sabine). **A'Velo Radladen** rents bikes in the old town, just outside the TI on Mozartplatz (€4.50/1 hour, €10/2 hours, €16/24 hours; electric or mountain bike-€6/hour, €22/24 hours; daily 9:00-18:00, until 19:00 July-Aug, but hours unreliable, shorter hours off-season and in bad weather, passport number for security deposit, mobile 0676-435-5950). Some of my recommended hotels and pensions also rent bikes, and several of the B&Bs on Moosstrasse have free loaner bikes for guests.

By Funicular and Elevator: The old town is connected to the top of the Mönchsberg mountain (and great views) via funicular and elevator. The **funicular** *(Festungsbahn)* whisks you up to the imposing Hohensalzburg Fortress (included in castle admission, goes every few minutes—for details, see page 131). The **elevator** *(MönchsbergAufzug)* on the east side of the old town propels you to the recommended Gasthaus Stadtalm café and hostel, the Museum of Modern Art, wooded paths, and more great views (€2 one-way, €3.20 round-trip, daily 8:30-19:00, Wed until 21:00, July-Aug daily until 1:00 in the morning, May-Sept starts running at 8:00).

By Taxi: Meters start at about €3 (from train station to your hotel, allow about €8). Small groups can taxi for about the same price as riding the bus.

By Buggy: The horse buggies *(Fiaker)* that congregate at Residenzplatz charge €36 for a 25-minute trot around the old town (www.fiaker-salzburg.at).

Tours in Salzburg

Walking Tours—On any day of the week, you can take a two-language, one-hour guided walk of the old town without a reservation—just show up at the TI on Mozartplatz and pay the guide. The tours are informative, but you'll likely be listening to everything in both German and English (€9, daily at 12:15 and 14:00, tours split into two single-language groups when turnout is sufficiently high, tel. 0662/8898-7330). To save money (and avoid all that German), you can easily do it on your own using this chapter's self-guided walk. You can also download a free Rick Steves audio tour of my walk (see page 7).

Local Guides—Salzburg is home to over a hundred licensed guides. I recommend two hardworking young guides in particular. **Christiana Schneeweiss** ("Snow White") has been instrumental in both my guidebook research and my TV production in Salzburg

(€135/2 hours, €150/3 hours, tel. 0664/340-1757, www.kultur -tourismus.com, info@kultur-tourismus.com); check her website for bike tours, private minibus tours, and more. **Sabine Rath** also knows her city well, and is a joy to learn from (€140/2 hours, €180/4 hours, €270/8 hours, tel. 0664/201-6492, www.tourguide -salzburg.com, info@tourguide-salzburg.com). Salzburg has many other good guides (to book, call 0662/840-406).

Boat Tours—City Cruise Line (a.k.a. Stadt Schiff-Fahrt) runs a basic 40-minute round-trip river cruise with recorded commentary (€13, 9/day July-Aug, 7/day May-June, fewer Sept-Oct and April, no boats Nov-March). For a longer cruise, ride to Hellbrunn and return by bus (€16, 1-2/day April-Oct). Boats leave from the old-town side of the river just downstream of the Makartsteg bridge (tel. 0662/825-858, www.salzburgschifffahrt.at). While views can be cramped, passengers are treated to a fun finale just before docking, when the captain twirls a fun "waltz."

▲▲*The Sound of Music* **Tour**—I took this tour skeptically (as part of my research)—and liked it. It includes a quick but good general city tour, hits the *S.O.M.* spots (including the stately home used in the movie, flirtatious gazebo, and grand wedding church), and shows you a lovely stretch of the Salzkammergut Lake District. This is worthwhile for *S.O.M.* fans and those who won't otherwise be going into the Salzkammergut. Warning: Many think rolling through the Austrian countryside with 30 Americans singing "Doe, a deer..." is pretty schmaltzy. Local Austrians don't understand all the commotion, and the audience is mostly native English speakers.

Of the many companies doing the tour, consider Bob's Special Tours (usually uses a minibus) and Panorama Tours (more typical and professional, big 50-seat bus). Each one provides essentially the same tour (in English with a live guide, 4 hours) for essentially the same price: €37 for Panorama, €45 for Bob's. You'll get a €5 discount from either if you book direct, mention Rick Steves, pay cash, and bring this book along (you'll need to show them this book to get the deal). Getting a spot is simple—just call and make a reservation (calling Bob's a week or two in advance is smart). Note: Your hotel will be eager to call to reserve for you—to get their commission—but if you let them do it, you won't get the discount I've negotiated.

Minibus Option: Most of **Bob's Special Tours** use an eight-seat minibus (and occasionally a 20-seat bus) and therefore have good access to old-town sights, promote a more casual feel, and spend less time waiting to load and unload. Calling well in advance increases your chances of getting a seat (€45 for adults, €5 discount with this book if you pay cash and book direct, €40 for kids and students with ID, €35 for kids in car seats, daily at 9:00 and 14:00 year-round, they'll pick you up at your hotel for the morning tour, afternoon tours leave from Bob's office along the river just east of Mozartplatz at Rudolfskai 38, tel. 0662/849-511, mobile 0664-541-7492, www.bobstours.com). Nearly all of Bob's tours stop for a fun summer luge ride when the weather is dry (mountain bobsled-€4.30 extra, generally April-Oct, confirm beforehand). They'll pick you up at your hotel (morning only), or you can meet the bus at their office. Bob's guides get mixed reviews (some of them can be gruff), and they sometimes cancel at the last minute if not enough people sign up. A different minibus tour company is **Kultur Tourismus** (€45, tel. 0664/340-1757, www.kultur-tourismus.com, info@kultur-tourismus.com).

Big-Bus Option: Panorama Tours depart from their smart kiosk at Mirabellplatz daily at 9:30 and 14:00 year-round (€37, €5 discount with this book if you book direct and pay cash, book by calling 0662/874-029 or 0662/883-2110, or online at www.panoramatours.com). Many travelers appreciate their more businesslike feel, roomier buses, and slightly higher vantage point.

Bike Option: For some exercise with your tour, you can meet **Fräulein Maria** at the Mirabell Gardens (at Mirabellplatz 4, 50 yards to the left of palace entry) for a *S.O.M.* bike tour. The main attractions that you'll pass during the seven-mile pedal include the Mirabell Gardens, the horse pond, St. Peter's Cemetery, Nonnberg Abbey, Leopoldskron Palace, and, of course, the gazebo (€24 includes bike, €2 discount with this book, €15 for kids 6-15, €10 for kids under 6, daily May-Sept at 9:30, June-Aug also at 16:30, allow 3.5 hours, family-friendly, reservations required only for afternoon tours, tel. 0650/342-6297, www.mariasbicycletours.com). For €8 extra, you're welcome to keep the bike all day.

Beyond Salzburg

Both Bob's and Panorama Tours also offer an extensive array of other day trips from Salzburg (e.g., Berchtesgaden/Eagle's Nest, salt mines, and Salzkammergut lakes and mountains).

Bob's Special Tours offers two particularly well-designed day tours (both depart daily at 9:00; either one costs €90 with a €10 discount if you show this book and book direct, does not include entrance fees). Their *Sound of Music*/**Hallstatt Tour** first covers everything in the standard four-hour *Sound of Music* tour, then continues for a four-hour look at the scenic, lake-speckled Salzkammergut (with free time to explore charming Hallstatt). Bob's **Bavarian Mountain Tour** covers the main things you'd want to do in and around Berchtesgaden (Königssee cruise, Hitler's mountaintop Eagle's Nest, salt mine tour).

Self-Guided Walk

▲▲▲Salzburg's Old Town

I've linked the best sights in the old town into this handy self-guided orientation walk. You can download a free Rick Steves **audio tour** of this walk; see page 7.

• *Begin in the heart of town, just up from the river, near the TI on...*

❶ Mozartplatz

All the happy tourists around you probably wouldn't be here if not for the man honored by this statue—Wolfgang Amadeus Mozart (erected in 1842; locals consider the statue a terrible likeness). Mozart spent much of his first 25 years (1756-1777) in Salzburg, the greatest Baroque city north of the Alps. But the city itself is much older: The Mozart statue sits on bits of Roman Salzburg, and the pink Church of St. Michael that overlooks the square dates from A.D. 800. The first Salzburgers settled right around here. Near you is the TI (with a concert box office), and just around the downhill corner is a pedestrian bridge leading over the Salzach River to the quiet and most medieval street in town, Steingasse (described on page 136).

• *Walk toward the cathedral and into the big square with the huge fountain.*

❷ Residenzplatz

Important buildings have long ringed this square. Salzburg's energetic Prince Archbishop Wolf Dietrich von Raitenau (who ruled 1587-1612) was raised in Rome, was a cousin of the influential Florentine Medici family, and had grandiose Italian ambitions for Salzburg. After a convenient fire destroyed the town's cathedral, Wolf Dietrich set about building the "Rome of the North." This square, with his new cathedral and palace, was the centerpiece of his Baroque dream city. A series of interconnecting squares—like you'll see nowhere else—make a grand processional way, leading from here through the old town. As we enjoy this heart and soul of historic Salzburg, notice how easily we slip from noisy commercial streets to peaceful, reflective courtyards. Also notice the two dominant kinds of stone around town: a creamy red marble and a chunky conglomerate, both quarried nearby.

For centuries, Salzburg's leaders were both important church officials *and* princes of the Holy Roman Empire, hence the title "prince archbishop"—mixing sacred and secular authority. But Wolf Dietrich misplayed his hand, losing power and spending his last five years imprisoned in the Hohensalzburg Fortress. (It's a complicated story—basically, the pope counted on Salzburg to hold the line against the Protestants for several generations fol-

Salzburg Old Town Walk

1. Mozartplatz
2. Residenzplatz
3. New Residenz & Glockenspiel
4. Old Residenz
5. Salzburg Cathedral
6. Kapitelplatz
7. St. Peter's Cemetery
8. St. Peter's Church
9. Toscanini Hof
10. Universitätsplatz
11. Getreidegasse
12. Mozart's Birthplace
13. Alter Markt

lowing the Reformation. Wolf Dietrich was a good Catholic, as were most Salzburgers. But the town's important businessmen and the region's salt miners were Protestant, and for Salzburg's financial good, Wolf Dietrich dealt with them in a tolerant and pragmatic way. So the pope—who couldn't allow any tolerance for Protestants in those heady Counter-Reformation days—had Wolf Dietrich locked up and replaced.)

The fountain is as Italian as can be, with a Triton matching Bernini's famous Triton Fountain in Rome. Situated on a busy trade route to the south, Salzburg was well aware of the exciting things going on in Italy. Things Italian were respected (as in colonial America, when a bumpkin would "stick a feather in his cap and call it macaroni"). Local artists even Italianized their names in order to raise their rates.

• *Along the left side of Residenzplatz (as you face the cathedral) is the...*

❸ New (Neue) Residenz and Glockenspiel

This former palace, long a government administration building, now houses the central post office, the **Heimatwerk** (a fine shop showing off all the best local handicrafts, Mon-Fri 9:00-18:00, Sat 9:00-17:00, closed Sun), and two worthwhile sights: the fascinating **Salzburg Panorama 1829** exhibit (definitely worth the entry fee); and the **Salzburg Museum,** which offers the best peek at the history of this one-of-a-kind city (both sights described on page 129).

The famous **glockenspiel** rings atop the New Residenz. This bell tower has a carillon of 35 17th-century bells (cast in Antwerp) that chimes throughout the day and plays tunes (appropriate to the month) at 7:00, 11:00, and 18:00. A big barrel with adjustable tabs turns like a giant music-box mechanism, pulling the right bells in the appropriate rhythm. Notice the ornamental top: an upside-down heart in flames surrounding the solar system (symbolizing that God loves all of creation). Seasonal twice-weekly tours let you get up close to watch the glockenspiel action (€3, April-Oct Thu at 17:30 and Fri at 10:30, no tours Nov-March, meet in Salzburg Panorama 1829, just show up).

Look back, past Mozart's statue, to the 4,220-foot-high **Gaisberg**—the forested hill with the television tower. A road leads to the top for a commanding view. Its summit is a favorite destination for local nature-lovers and strong bikers.

• *Head to the opposite end of the square. This building is the...*

❹ Old (Alte) Residenz

Across from the New Residenz is Wolf Dietrich's palace, the Old Residenz, which is connected to the cathedral by a skyway. Its series of ornately decorated rooms is well-described in an included audioguide, which gives you a good feel for the wealth and power of the prince archbishop. Walking through 15 fancy state rooms (all on one floor), you'll see Renaissance, Baroque, and Classicist styles—200 years of let-them-eat-cake splendor.

Cost and Hours: €8.50, daily 10:00-17:00, tel. 0662/8042-2690.

• *Walk under the prince archbishop's skyway and step into Domplatz (Cathedral Square), where you'll find...*

❺ Salzburg Cathedral (Salzburger Dom)

This cathedral, rated ▲▲, was one of the first Baroque buildings north of the Alps. It was consecrated in 1628, during the Thirty Years' War. (Pitting Roman Catholics against Protestants, this war devastated much of Europe and brought most grand construction projects to a halt.) Experts differ on what motivated the builders: to emphasize Salzburg's commitment to the Roman Catholic cause and the power of the Church here, or to show that there could be a peaceful alternative to the religious strife that was racking Europe at the time. Salzburg's archbishop was technically the top papal official north of the Alps, but the city managed to steer clear of the war. With its rich salt production, it had enough money to stay out of the conflict and carefully maintain its independence from the warring sides, earning it the nickname "Fortified Island of Peace."

Domplatz is surrounded by the prince archbishop's secular administration buildings. The **statue of Mary** (1771) is looking away from the church, welcoming visitors. If you stand in the rear of the square, immediately under the middle arch, you'll see that she's positioned to be crowned by the two angels on the church facade.

The dates on the iron gates refer to milestones in the church's history: In 774, the previous church (long since destroyed) was founded by St. Virgil, to be replaced in 1628 by the church you see today. In 1959, a partial reconstruction was completed, made necessary by a WWII bomb that had blown through the dome.

Cost and Hours: Free, but donation requested; Easter-Oct Mon-Sat 9:00-18:00, Sun 13:00-18:00; Nov-Easter Mon-Sat 10:00-17:00, Sun 13:00-17:00.

Visiting the Cathedral: Enter the cathedral as if part of a festival procession—drawn toward the resurrected Christ by the brightly lit area under the dome, and cheered on by ceiling paintings of the Passion.

Built in just 14 years (1614-1628), the church boasts harmonious architecture. When Pope John Paul II visited in 1998, some 5,000 people filled the cathedral (330 feet long and 230 feet tall). The baptismal font (dark bronze, left of the entry) is from the previous cathedral (basin from about 1320, although the lid is modern). Mozart was baptized here (Amadeus means "beloved by God"). Concert and Mass schedules are posted at the entrance; the Sunday Mass at 10:00 is famous for its music.

The **paintings** lining the nave, showing events leading up to Christ's death, are relatively dark. But the Old Testament themes that foreshadow Jesus' resurrection, and the Resurrection scene painted at the altar, are well-lit. The church has never had stained glass—just clear windows to let light power the message.

The stucco, by a Milanese artist, is exceptional. Sit under the **dome**—surrounded by the tombs of 10 archbishops from the 17th century—and imagine all four organs playing, each balcony filled with musicians...glorious surround-sound. Mozart, who was the organist here for two years, would advise you that the acoustics are best in pews immediately under the dome. Study the symbolism of the decor all around you—intellectual, complex, and cohesive. Think of the altar in Baroque terms, as the center of a stage, with sunrays as spotlights in this dramatic and sacred theater.

In the left transept, stairs lead down into the **crypt** *(Krypta)*, where you can see foundations of the earlier church, more tombs, and a tourist-free chapel (reserved for prayer) directly under the dome.

Other Cathedral Sights: The **Cathedral Excavations Museum** (outside the church on Residenzplatz and down the stairs) offers a chance to see the foundations of the medieval church, some Roman engineering, and a few Roman mosaics from Roman street level. It has the charm of an old basement garage; unless you've never seen anything Roman, I'd skip it (€2.50, July-Aug daily 9:00-17:00, closed Sept-June).

The **Cathedral Museum** (Dom Museum) has a rich collection of church art (entry at portico, €6, mid-May-Oct Mon-Sat 10:00-17:00, Sun 11:00-18:00, closed Nov-mid-May except during Advent, tel. 0662/8047-1870).

• *From the cathedral, exit left and walk toward the fortress into the next square.*

❻ Kapitelplatz

Head past the underground public WCs (€0.50) to the giant **chessboard.** It's just under the golden orb topped by a man gazing up at the castle, trying to decide whether to walk up or shell out €10.50 for the funicular. Every year since 2002, a foundation has commissioned a different artist to create a new work of public art somewhere in the city; this is the piece from 2007. A small road leads uphill to the fortress (and fortress funicular; see arrow pointing to the *Stieglkeller*).

Keep going across the square to the pond. This was a **horse bath,** the 18th-century equivalent of a car wash. Notice the puzzle above it—the artist wove the date of the structure into a phrase. It says, "Leopold the Prince Built Me," using the letters LLDVICMXVXI, which total 1732 (add it up...it works)—the year it was built. With your back to the cathedral, leave the square through a gate in the right corner that reads *zum Peterskeller*. It leads to a waterfall and St. Peter's Cemetery (described later).

The **waterwheel** is part of a clever canal system that has brought water into Salzburg from Berchtesgaden, 15 miles away, since the 13th century. Climb uphill a few steps to feel the medieval water power. The stream was divided into smaller canals and channeled through town to provide fire protection, to flush out the streets (Thursday morning was flood-the-streets day), and to power factories (there were more than 100 watermill-powered firms as late as the 19th century). Because of its water-powered hygiene (relatively good for the standards of the time), Salzburg never suffered from a plague—it's probably the only Austrian town you'll see with no plague monument. For more on the canal system, check out the **Alm River Canal exhibit** (at the exit of the funicular, described on page 133).

Before leaving, drop into the fragrant and traditional **bakery** at the waterfall, which sells various fresh rolls—both sweet and not, explained on the wall, for less than €1 (Thu-Tue 7:00-17:30, Sat until 13:00, closed Wed). There's a good view of the funicular climbing up to the castle from here.

• *Now find the* Katakomben *sign and step into...*

❼ St. Peter's Cemetery

This collection of lovingly tended mini-gardens abuts the Mönchberg's rock wall. Walk in about 50 yards to the intersection of lanes at the base of the cliff marked by a stone ball. You're surrounded by three churches, each founded in the early Middle Ages atop a pagan Celtic holy site. St. Peter's Church is closest to the stone ball. Notice the fine Romanesque stonework on the apse of the chapel nearest you, and the rich guys' fancy Renaissance-style tombs decorating its walls.

Wealthy as those guys were, they ran out of caring relatives. The graves surrounding you are tended by descendants of the deceased. In Austria, gravesites are rented, not owned. Rent bills are sent out every 10 years. If no one cares enough to make the payment, your tombstone is removed.

While the cemetery where the von Trapp family hid out in *The Sound of Music* was a Hollywood set, it was inspired by this one.

Look up the cliff. Legendary medieval hermit monks are said to have lived in the hillside—but "catacombs" they're not. You can climb lots of steps to see a few old caves, a chapel, and some fine views.

Cost and Hours: Cemetery—free, silence is requested, daily April-Sept 6:30-19:00, Oct-March 6:30-18:00; caves—€1, May-Sept Tue-Sun 10:30-17:00, closed Mon, shorter hours Oct-April.

Nearby: To enjoy a peaceful side-trip, stroll past the stark Gothic funeral chapel (c. 1491) to the uphill corner of the cemetery, and return along the high lane to see the finer tombs in the arcade. Tomb #XXXI belongs to the cathedral's architect—forever facing his creation. Tomb #LIV, at the catacomb entry, is a chapel carved into the hillside, holding the tombs of Mozart's sister and Joseph Haydn's younger brother Michael, also a composer of great note.

• Continue downhill through the cemetery and out the opposite end. Just outside, hook right and drop into...

❽ St. Peter's Church

Just inside, enjoy a carved Romanesque welcome. Over the inner doorway, a fine tympanum shows Jesus on a rainbow flanked by Peter and Paul over a stylized Tree of Life and under a Latin inscription reading, "I am the door to life, and only through me can you find eternal life." Enter the nave and notice how the once purely Romanesque vaulting has since been iced with a sugary Rococo finish. Salzburg's only Rococo interior feels Bavarian (because it is—the fancy stucco work was done by Bavarian artists). Up the right side aisle is the tomb of St. Rupert, with a painting showing Salzburg in 1750 (one bridge, salt ships sailing the river, and angels hoisting barrels of salt to heaven as St. Rupert prays for his city). If you're here during the town's Ruperti-Kirtag festival in late September, you'll see candles and fresh flowers, honoring the city's not-forgotten saint. On pillars farther up the aisle are faded bits of 13th-century Romanesque frescoes. Similar frescoes hide under Rococo whitewash throughout the church.

Cost and Hours: Free, long hours daily.

*• Leaving the church, notice on the left the recommended **Stiftskeller St. Peter** restaurant—known for its Mozart Dinner Concert. Charlemagne ate here in A.D. 803, allowing locals to claim that it's the oldest restaurant in Europe. Opposite where you entered the square (look through the arch), you'll see St. Rupert waving you into the next square. Once there, you're surrounded by early 20th-century Bauhaus-style dorms for student monks. Notice the modern crucifix (1926) painted on the far wall. Here's a good place to see the two locally quarried stones (marble and conglomerate) so prevalent in all the town's buildings.*

Walk through the archway under the crucifix into...

❾ Toscanini Hof

This square faces the 1925 **Festival Hall.** The hall's three theaters seat 5,000. This is where Captain von Trapp nervously waited before walking onstage (in the movie, he sang "Edelweiss"), just before he escaped with his family. On the left is the city's 1,500-space, inside-the-mountain parking lot; ahead, behind the *Felsenkeller* sign, is a tunnel (generally closed) leading to the actual concert hall; and to the right is the backstage of a smaller hall where carpenters are often building stage sets (door open on hot days). The stairway leads a few flights up to a picnic perch with a fine view, and then up to the top of the cliff and the recommended Stadtalm Café and hostel.

Walk downhill to **Max-Reinhardt-Platz.** Pause here to survey the line of Salzburg Festival concert halls. As the festival was started in the austere 1920s, the city remodeled existing buildings (e.g., the prince archbishop's stables and riding school) for venues.

• *Continue straight—passing the big church on your left, along with lots of popular wurst stands and a public WC—into...*

❿ Universitätsplatz

This square hosts an **open-air produce market**—Salzburg's liveliest (mornings Mon-Sat, best on Sat). Salzburgers are happy to pay more here for the reliably fresh and top-quality produce. (These days, half of Austria's produce is grown organically.) The market really bustles on Saturday mornings, when the farmers are in town. Public marketplaces have fountains for washing fruit and vegetables. The fountain here—a part of the medieval water system—plummets down a hole and to the river. The sundial (over the water hole) is accurate (except for the daylight savings hour) and two-dimensional, showing both the time (obvious) and the date (less obvious). The fanciest facade overlooking the square (the yellow one) is the backside of Mozart's Birthplace (we'll see the front soon).

• *Continue past the fountain to the end of the square, passing several characteristic and nicely arcaded medieval tunnels (on right) that connect the square to Getreidegasse (described next). Just for fun, weave between this street and Getreidegasse several times, following these "through houses" as you work your way toward the cliff face. For a look at the giant horse troughs, adjacent to the prince's stables, cross the big road (looking left at the string of Salzburg Festival halls again). Paintings show the various breeds and temperaments of horses in his stable. Like Vienna, Salzburg had a passion for the equestrian arts.*

Turn right (passing a courtyard on your left that once housed a hospital for the poor, and now houses a toy museum and a museum of historic musical instruments), and then right again, which brings you to the start of a long and colorful pedestrian street.

⓫ Getreidegasse

This street, rated ▲▲, was old Salzburg's busy, colorful main drag. It's been a center of trade since Roman times (third century). It's lined with *Schmuck* (jewelry) shops and other businesses. This is the burgher's (businessman's) Salzburg. The buildings, most of which date from the 15th century, are tall for that age, and narrow, and densely packed. Space was tight here because so little land was available between the natural fortifications provided by the mountain and the river, and much of what was available was used up by the Church. Famous for its old wrought-iron signs (best viewed from this end), the architecture on the street still looks much as it did in Mozart's day—though its former elegance is now mostly gone, replaced by chain outlets.

As you walk away from the cliffs, look up and enjoy the traditional signs indicating what each shop made or sold: Watch for spirits, bookmakers, a horn (indicating a place for the postal coach), brewery (the star for the name of the beer, Sternbräu—"Star Brew"), glazier (window-maker), locksmith, hamburgers, pastries, tailor, baker (the pretzel), pharmacy, and a hatter.

On the right at #39, **Sporer** serves up homemade spirits (€1.50/shot, open 8:30-17:00). This has been a family-run show for a century—fun-loving, proud, and English-speaking. *Nuss* is nut, *Marille* is apricot (typical of this region), the *Kletzen* cocktail is like a super-thick Baileys with pear, and *Edle Brande* are the stronger schnapps. The many homemade firewaters are in jugs at the end of the bar.

Continue down Getreidegasse, noticing the old doorbells—one per floor. At #40, **Eisgrotte** serves good ice cream. Across from Eisgrotte, a tunnel leads to the recommended **Balkan Grill** (signed as *Bosna Grill*), the local choice for the very best wurst in town. At #28, Herr Wieber, the iron- and locksmith, welcomes the curious. Farther along, you'll pass McDonald's (required to keep its arches Baroque and low-key).

The knot of excited tourists and salesmen hawking goofy gimmicks marks the home of Salzburg's most famous resident. **Mozart's Birthplace** (*Geburtshaus*, ⑫ on map)—the house where Mozart was born, and where he composed many of his early works—is worth a visit for his true fans (described on page 130). But for most, his **Residence,** across the river, is more interesting (described on page 135).

At #3, dip into the passage and walk under a whalebone, likely once used to advertise the wares of an exotic import shop. Look up at the arcaded interior. On the right, at the venerable **Schatz Konditorei,** you can enjoy coffee under the vaults with your choice of top-end cakes and pastries (Mon-Fri 8:30-18:30, Sat 8:00-17:00, closed Sun).

Leaving the pastry shop, go straight ahead through the passage to Sigmund-Haffner-Gasse. Before heading right, look left to see the tower of the old City Hall at the end. The blue-and-white ball halfway up is an 18th-century moon clock. It still tells the phase of the moon.

• *Go right, then take your first left to....*

⑬ Alter Markt

Here in Salzburg's old marketplace, you'll find a sausage stand, the recommended **Café Tomaselli,** a fun **candy shop** at #7, and, next door, the beautifully old-fashioned **Alte F.E. Hofapotheke** pharmacy—duck in discreetly to peek at the Baroque shelves and containers (be polite—the people in line are here for medicine, no photography).

• *Our walk is finished. From here, you can circle back to some of the old-town sights (such as those in the New Residenz, described next); head up to the Hohensalzburg Fortress on the cliffs over the old town (see page 131); or continue to some of the sights across the river. To reach those sights, head for the river, jog left (past the fast-food fish restaurant and free WCs), climb to the top of the Makartsteg pedestrian bridge, and turn to page 134.*

Sights in Salzburg

In the Old Town

In the New (Neue) Residenz

▲▲**Salzburg Museum**—This two-floor exhibit is the best in town for history. The included audioguide wonderfully describes the great artifacts in the lavish prince archbishop's residence.

The Salzburg Personalities exhibit fills the first floor with a charming look at Salzburg's greatest historic characters—mostly artists, scientists, musicians, and writers who would otherwise be forgotten. And upstairs is the real reason to come: lavish ceremonial rooms filled with an exhibit called The Salzburg Myth, which traces the city's proud history, art, and culture since early modern times. The focus is on its quirky absolutist prince archbishop and its long-standing reputation as a fairy-tale "Alpine Arcadia." The *Kunsthalle* in the basement shows off special exhibits.

From the Salzburg Museum, the Panorama Passage (clearly marked from the entry) leads underground to the Salzburg Panorama (described next). This passage is lined with archaeological finds (Roman and early medieval), helping you trace the development of Salzburg from its Roman roots until today.

Cost and Hours: €7, €8 combo-ticket with Salzburg Panorama, includes audioguide, Tue-Sun 9:00-17:00, Thu until 20:00, closed Mon, tel. 0662/620-8080, www.smca.at.

▲**Salzburg Panorama 1829**—In the early 19th century, before the advent of photography, 360-degree "panorama" paintings of great cities or events were popular. These creations were even taken on extended road trips. When this one was created, the 1815 Treaty of Vienna had just divvied up post-Napoleonic Europe, and Salzburg had become part of the Habsburg realm. This photo-realistic painting served as a town portrait done at the emperor's request. The circular view, painted by Johann Michael Sattler, shows the city as seen from the top of its castle. When complete, it spent 10 years touring the great cities of Europe, showing off Salzburg's breathtaking setting.

Today, the exquisitely restored painting offers a fascinating look at the city in 1829. The river was slower and had beaches. The old town looks essentially as it does today, and Moosstrasse still leads into idyllic farm country. Paintings from that era of other great cities around the world are hung around the outside wall with numbers but without labels, as a kind of quiz game. A flier gives the cities' names on one side, and keys them to the numbers. See how many 19th-century cities you can identify.

Cost and Hours: €2, €8 combo-ticket with Salzburg Museum, open daily 9:00-17:00, Thu until 20:00, Residenzplatz 9.

▲Mozart's Birthplace (Geburtshaus)

Mozart was born here in 1756. It was in this building that he composed most of his boy-genius works. Today it's the most popular Mozart sight in town—for fans, it's almost a pilgrimage. American artist Robert Wilson was hired to spiff up the exhibit, to make it feel more conceptual and less like a museum. Even so, I was unimpressed. If you're tackling just one Mozart sight, skip this one. Instead, walk 10 minutes from here to Mozart's Residence (described later), which provides a more informative visit. But if you want to max out on Mozart, a visit here is worthwhile.

Shuffling through with all the crowds, you'll peruse three floors of rooms with old-school exhibits displaying paintings, letters, personal items, and lots of facsimiles, all attempting to bring life to the Mozart story (and all explained in English). A period living room shows what Wolfgang's world likely looked like, and portraits introduce you to the family. A particular highlight is an old clavichord he supposedly composed on. (A predecessor of the more complicated piano, the clavichord's keys hit the strings with a simple teeter-totter motion that allowed you to play very softly—ideal for composers living in tight apartment quarters.) At the end, there's a room of dioramas dedicated to Mozart's operas.

Cost and Hours: €7, €12 for combo-ticket includes Mozart's Residence, daily 9:00-17:30, July-Aug until 20:00, last entry 30 minutes before closing, only the shop has air-con, Getreidegasse 9, tel. 0662/844-313.

Atop the Cliffs Above the Old Town

The main "sight" above town is the Hohensalzburg Fortress. But if you just want to enjoy the sweeping views over Salzburg, you have a couple of cheaper options: Head up to the castle grounds on foot, take the elevator up the cliffs of Mönchsberg (explained in "Getting Around Salzburg" on page 117), or visit the castle in the evening on a night when they're hosting a concert (about 300 nights a year). This is the only time you can buy a funicular ticket without paying for the castle entrance—since the castle museums are closed, but the funicular still runs to bring up concert-goers.

▲▲Hohensalzburg Fortress (Festung)

Construction of Hohensalzburg Fortress was begun by Archbishop Gebhard of Salzburg as a show of the Catholic Church's power. Built on a rock (called Festungsberg) 400 feet above the Salzach River, this fortress was never really used. That's the idea. It was a good investment—so foreboding, nobody attacked the town for 1,000 years. The city was never taken by force, but when Napoleon stopped by, Salzburg wisely surrendered. After a stint as a military barracks, the fortress was opened to the public in the 1860s by Habsburg Emperor Franz Josef. Today, it remains one of Europe's mightiest castles, dominating Salzburg's skyline and offering incredible views.

Cost: Your daytime funicular ticket includes admission to the fortress grounds and all the museums inside—whether you want to see them or not (€10.50, €24.30 family ticket). Save a few euros by walking up—the climb is much easier than it looks, and the views are fantastic. At the top, you'll pay €7.40 to enter (includes grounds and museums). If you'd rather take the funicular but want to skip the museums, head up the hill in the evening: Within one hour of the museums' closing time, the funicular and entry to the castle grounds cost €6.20 one-way/€7.60 round-trip; on concert nights and in summer, after the museums have closed, the funicular is just €3.80 round-trip.

Hours: The complex is open daily year-round (May-Sept 9:00-19:00, Oct-April 9:30-17:00, last entry 30 minutes before closing, tel. 0662/8424-3011). On nights when there's a concert, and nightly in July and August, the castle grounds are free and open from after the museums close until 22:00.

Concerts: The fortress also serves as a venue for evening concerts (Festungskonzerte). For details, see "Concerts at Hohensalzburg Fortress" on page 140.

Café: The café between the funicular station and the castle entry is a great place to nibble on apple strudel while taking in the jaw-dropping view.

Orientation: The fortress visit has three parts: a relatively dull courtyard with some fine views from its various ramparts; the fortress itself (with a required and escorted 45-minute audio tour); and the palace museum (by far the best exhibit of the lot). At the bottom of the funicular, you'll pass through an interesting little exhibit on the town's canal system (free).

● Self-Guided Tour: From the top of the funicular, head to your right and down the stairs to bask in the **view,** either from the café or the view terrace a little farther along.

Once you're done snapping photos, walk through to the castle grounds and go left, following the path up and around to reach the inner courtyard (labeled *Inneres Schloß*). Immediately inside, circling to the right (clockwise), you'll encounter cannons (still poised to defend Salzburg against an Ottoman invasion), a marionette exhibit, the palace museum, the Kuenburg Bastion, scant ruins of a Romanesque church, the courtyard (with path down for those walking), toilets, shops, a restaurant, and the fortress tour.

• *Begin at the...*

Marionette Exhibit: Several fun rooms show off this local tradition, with three videos playing continuously: two with peeks at Salzburg's ever-enchanting Marionette Theater performances of Mozart classics (described under "Music in Salzburg," later) and one with a behind-the-scenes look at the action. Give the hands-on marionette a whirl.

• *Hiking through the former palace, you'll find the best exhibits at the...*

Palace Museum (Festungsmuseum Carolino Augusteum): The second floor has exhibits on castle life, from music to torture. The top floor shows off fancy royal apartments, a sneak preview of the room used for the nightly fortress concerts, and the Rainer Regiments Museum, dedicated to the Salzburg soldiers who fought in both world wars.

Castle Courtyard: The courtyard was the main square for the castle's 1,000-some medieval residents, who could be self-sufficient when necessary. The square was ringed by the shops of craftsmen, blacksmiths, bakers, and so on. The well dipped into a rain-fed cistern. The church is dedicated to St. George, the protector of horses (logical for an army church) and decorated by fine red marble reliefs (c. 1502). Behind the church is the top of the old lift that helped supply the fortress. (From near here, steps lead back into the city, or to the mountaintop "Mönchsberg Walk," described later.) You'll also see the remains of a Romanesque chapel, which are well-described.

• *Near the chapel, turn left into the Kuenburg Bastion (once a garden) for fine city and castle views.*

Kuenburg Bastion: Notice how the castle has three parts: the original castle inside the courtyard, the vast whitewashed walls (built when the castle was a residence), and the lower, beefed-up fortifications (added for extra defense against the expected Ottoman invasion). Survey Salzburg from here and think about fortifying an important city by using nature. Mönchsberg (the cliffs to the left) and Festungsberg (the little mountain you're on) naturally cradle the old town, with just a small gate between the ridge and the river needed to bottle up the place. The new town across the river needed a bit of a wall arcing from the river to its hill. Back then, only one bridge crossed the Salzach into town, and it had a fortified gate.

• *Back inside the castle courtyard, continue your circle. The Round Tower (1497) helps you visualize the inner original castle.*

Fortress Interior: Tourists are allowed in this part of the fortified palace only with an escort. (They say that's for security, though while touring it, you wonder what they're protecting.) A crowd assembles at the turnstile, and every quarter-hour 40 people are issued their audioguides and let in for the escorted walk. You'll go one room at a time, listening to a 45-minute commentary. While the interior furnishings are mostly gone—taken by Napoleon—the rooms survived as well as they did because no one wanted to live here after 1500, so the building was never modernized. Your tour includes a room dedicated to the art of "excruciating questioning" ("softening up" prisoners, in American military jargon)—filled with tools of that gruesome trade. The highlight is the commanding city view from the top of a tower.

• *After seeing the fortress, consider hiking down to the old town, or along the top of Mönchsberg (see "Mönchsberg Walk," below). If you take the funicular down, don't miss (at the bottom of the lift) the...*

Alm River Canal Exhibit: At the base of the funicular, below the castle, is this fine little exhibit on how the river was broken into five smaller streams—powering the city until steam took up the energy-supply baton. Pretend it's the year 1200 and follow (by video) the flow of the water from the river through the canals, into the mills, and as it's finally dumped into the Salzach River. (The exhibit technically requires a funicular ticket—but you can see it by slipping through the exit at the back of the amber shop, just uphill from the funicular terminal.)

Mönchsberg Sights

▲**Mönchsberg Walk**—For a great 30-minute hike, exit the fortress by taking the steep lane down from the castle courtyard. At the first intersection, right leads into the old town, and left leads across the Mönchsberg. The lane leads 20 minutes through the woods high above the city (stick to the high lanes, or you'll end up back in town), taking you to the recommended Gasthaus Stadtalm café (light meals, cheap beds). From the Stadtalm, pass under the medieval wall and walk left along the wall to a tableau showing how it once looked. Take the switchback to the right and follow the lane downhill to the Museum of Modern Art (described next), where the *MönchsbergAufzug* elevator zips you back into town (€2 one-way, €3.20 round-trip, daily 8:00-19:00, Wed and July-Aug until 21:00). If you stay on the lane past the elevator, you eventually pass the Augustine church that marks the rollicking, recommended Augustiner Bräustübl beer garden.

In 1669, a huge Mönchsberg landslide killed more than 200

townspeople. Since then the cliffs have been carefully checked each spring and fall. Even today, you might see crews on the cliff, monitoring its stability.

Museum of Modern Art on Mönchsberg—The modern-art museum on top of Mönchsberg was built in 2004. While the collection is not worth climbing a mountain for, the M32 restaurant has some of the best views in town.

  Cost and Hours: €8, €9.70 including elevator ticket, Tue-Sun 10:00-18:00, Wed until 20:00, closed Mon except during festival; restaurant open Tue-Sat 9:00-24:00, closed Mon except during festival; at top of Mönchsberg elevator, tel. 0662/842-220-403, www.museumdermoderne.at.

In the New Town, North of the River

The following sights are across the river from the old town. I've connected them with walking instructions.

• *Begin at the Makartsteg pedestrian bridge, where you can survey the...*

Salzach River

Salzburg's river is called "salt river" not because it's salty, but because of the precious cargo it once carried—the salt mines of Hallein are just nine miles upstream. Salt could be transported from here all the way to the Danube, and on to the Mediterranean via the Black Sea. The riverbanks and roads were built when the river was regulated in the 1850s. Before that, the Salzach was much wider and slower moving. Houses opposite the old town fronted the river with docks and "garages" for boats. The grand buildings just past the bridge (with their elegant promenades and cafés) were built on reclaimed land in the late 19th century.

  Scan the cityscape. Notice all the churches. Salzburg, nicknamed the "Rome of the North," has 38 Catholic churches (plus two Protestant churches and a synagogue). Find the five streams gushing into the river. These date from the 13th century, when the river was split into five canals running through the town to power its mills. The Stein Hotel (upstream, just left of next bridge) has a popular roof-terrace café (see page 137). Downstream, notice the Museum of Modern Art atop Mönchsberg, with a view restaurant and a faux castle (actually a water reservoir). The Romanesque bell tower with the green copper dome in the distance is the Augustine church, site of the best beer hall in town (the recommended Augustiner Bräustübl).

• *Cross the bridge, pass the recommended Café Bazar (a fine place for a drink), walk two blocks inland, and take a left past the heroic statues into...*

▲Mirabell Gardens and Palace (Schloss)

The bubbly gardens laid out in 1730 for the prince archbishop have been open to the public since 1850 (thanks to Emperor Franz Josef, who was rattled by the popular revolutions of 1848). The gardens are free and open until dusk. The palace is open only as a concert venue (explained later). The statues and the arbor (far left) were featured in *The Sound of Music*. Walk through the gardens to the palace. Look back, enjoy the garden/cathedral/castle view, and imagine how the prince archbishop must have reveled in a vista that reminded him of all his secular and religious power. Then go around to the river side of the palace and find the horse.

The rearing **Pegasus statue** (rare and very well-balanced) is the site of a famous *Sound of Music* scene where the kids all danced before lining up on the stairs (with Maria 30 yards farther along). The steps lead to a small mound in the park (made of rubble from a former theater, and today a rendezvous point for Salzburg's gay community).

Nearest the horse, stairs lead between two lions to a pair of tough dwarfs (early volleyball players with spiked mittens) welcoming you to Salzburg's **Dwarf Park.** Cross the elevated walk (noticing the city's fortified walls) to meet statues of a dozen dwarfs who served the prince archbishop—modeled after real people with real fashions in about 1600. This was Mannerist art, from the hyper-realistic age that followed the Renaissance.

There's plenty of **music** here, both in the park and in the palace. A brass band plays free park concerts (May-Aug Sun at 10:30 and Wed with lighted fountains at 20:30, unless it's raining). To properly enjoy the lavish Mirabell Palace—once the prince archbishop's summer palace and now the seat of the mayor—get a ticket to a Schlosskonzerte (my favorite venue for a classical concert—see page 140).

• *To visit Salzburg's best Mozart sight, go a long block southeast to Makartplatz, where, opposite the big and bright Hotel Bristol, you'll find...*

▲Mozart's Residence (Wohnhaus)

This reconstruction of Mozart's second home (his family moved here when he was 17) is more informative than the exhibits at his birthplace, with an interesting film that provides insight into Mozart's life and music.

In the main hall—used by the Mozarts to entertain Salzburg's high society—notice the family portrait (c. 1780) on the wall, showing Mozart with his sister Nannerl, their father, and their mother—who'd died two years earlier in Paris. Mozart also had silly crude bull's-eyes made for the pop-gun game popular at the time (licking an "arse," Wolfgang showed his disdain for the rigors of high society). Later rooms feature real artifacts that explore his loves, his intellectual pursuits, his travels, and more.

Cost and Hours: €7, €12 combo-ticket includes Mozart's Birthplace in the old town, daily 9:00-17:30, July-Aug until 20:00, last entry 30 minutes before closing, allow at least one hour for visit, Makartplatz 8, tel. 0662/8742-2740.

• *From here, you can walk a few blocks back to the main bridge (Staatsbrücke), where you'll find the Platzl, a square once used as a hay market. Pause to enjoy the kid-pleasing little fountain. Near the fountain (with your back to the river), Steingasse leads darkly to the right.*

▲Steingasse Stroll

This street, a block in from the river, was part of the only road in the Middle Ages going south over the Alps to Venice (this was the first stop north of the Alps). Today, it's wonderfully tranquil and free of Salzburg's touristy crush. Inviting cocktail bars along here come alive at night (see "Steingasse Pub Crawl" on page 156).

At #9, a plaque (of questionable veracity) shows where Joseph Mohr, who wrote the words to "Silent Night," was born—poor and illegitimate—in 1792. There is no doubt, however, that the popular Christmas carol was composed and first sung in the village of Oberndorf, just outside of Salzburg, in 1818. Stairs lead from near here up to a 17th-century Cappuccin monastery.

On the next corner, the wall is gouged out. This scar was left even after the building was restored, to serve as a reminder of the American GI who tried to get a tank down this road during a visit to the town brothel—two blocks farther up Steingasse.

At #19, find the carvings on the old door. Some say these are notices from beggars to the begging community (more numerous after post-Reformation religious wars, which forced many people out of their homes and towns)—a kind of "hobo code" indicating whether the residents would give or not. Trace the wires of the old-fashioned doorbells to the highest floors.

Farther on, you'll find a commanding Salzburg view across the river. Notice the red dome marking the oldest nunnery in the German-speaking world (established in 712) under the fortress and to the left. The real Maria, who inspired *The Sound of Music*, taught in this nunnery's school. In 1927, she and Captain von Trapp were married in the church you see here (not the church filmed in the movie). He was 47. She was 22. Hmmmm.

From here look back, above the arch you just passed through, at part of the town's medieval fortification. The coat of arms on the arch is of the prince archbishop who paid Bavaria a huge ransom to stay out of the Thirty Years' War (smart move). He then built this fortification (in 1634) in anticipation of rampaging armies from both sides.

Today, this street is for making love, not war. The Maison de Plaisir (a few doors down, at #24) has for centuries been a Salzburg brothel. But the climax of this walk is more touristic.

• *For a grand view, head back to the Platzl and the bridge, enter the Stein Hotel (left corner, overlooking the river), and ride the elevator to...*

Stein Terrasse

This café offers perhaps the best views in town (aside from the castle). Hidden from the tourist crush, it's a trendy, professional, local scene. You can discreetly peek at the view, or enjoy a drink or light meal (small snacks, indoor/outdoor seating, Sun-Thu 9:00-24:00, Fri-Sat 9:00-1:00 in the morning).

• *Back at the Platzl and the bridge, you can head straight up Linzergasse (away from the river) into a neighborhood packed with recommended accommodations, as well as our final new-town sight, the...*

▲St. Sebastian Cemetery

Wander through this quiet oasis. Mozart is buried in Vienna, his mom's in Paris, and his sister is in Salzburg's old town (St. Peter's)—but Wolfgang's wife Constanze ("Constantia") and his father Leopold are buried here (from the black iron gate entrance on Linzergasse, walk 17 paces and look left). When Prince Archbishop Wolf Dietrich had the cemetery moved from around the cathedral and put here, across the river, people didn't like it. To help popularize it, he had his own mausoleum built as its centerpiece. Continue straight past the Mozart tomb to this circular building (English description at door). In the corner to the left of the entrance is the tomb of the Renaissance scientist and physician Paracelsus, best known for developing laudanum as a pain-killer.

Cost and Hours: Free, daily April-Oct 9:00-18:30, Nov-March 9:00-16:00, entry at Linzergasse 43 in summer; in winter go around the corner to the right, through the arch at #37, and around the building to the doorway under the blue seal.

Near Salzburg

▲Hellbrunn Castle—About the year 1610, Prince Archbishop Sittikus (after meditating on stewardship and Christ-like values) decided he needed a lavish palace with a vast and ornate garden purely for pleasure. He built this and just loved inviting his VIP guests out for fun with his trick fountains. Today, the visit is worthwhile for the Baroque garden, one of the oldest in Europe. More notably, it's full of clever fountains...and tour guides getting sadistic joy from soaking tourists. (Hint: When you see a wet

Greater Salzburg

1. Hotel Rosenvilla
2. Brigitte Lenglachner Rooms
3. Pension Bloberger Hof
4. Haus Reichl
5. Frau Ballwein Rooms
6. Helga Bankhammer Rooms

place, cover your camera.) After buying your ticket, you must wait for the English tour and laugh and scramble through the entertaining 40-minute trick-water-toy tour, and are then free to tour the forgettable palace with an included audioguide.

While it can be fun—especially on a hot day or with kids—for many, it's a lot of trouble for a few water tricks. *Sound of Music* fans not taking an *S.O.M.* tour, however, may want to visit just to see the "Sixteen Going on Seventeen" gazebo, now located in the gardens.

Cost and Hours: €9.50, daily May-Sept 9:00-17:30, July-Aug until 21:00—but tours from 18:00 on don't include the castle, mid-March-April and Oct 9:00-16:30, these are last tour times, closed Nov-mid-March, tel. 0662/820-3720, www.hellbrunn.at.

Getting There: Hellbrunn is nearly four miles south of Salzburg (bus #25 from station or from Staatsbrücke bridge, 2-3/hour, 20 minutes). In good weather, it makes a pleasant 30-minute bike excursion along the riverbank from Salzburg (described next).

▲▲**Riverside or Meadow Bike Ride**—The Salzach River has smooth, flat, and scenic bike lanes along each side (thanks to medieval tow paths—cargo boats would float downstream and be dragged back up by horses). On a sunny day, I can think of no more shout-worthy escape from the city. The nearly four-mile path upstream to Hellbrunn Castle is easy, with a worthy destination (leave Salzburg on castle side). Perhaps the most pristine, meadow-filled farm-country route is the four-mile Hellbrunner Allee from Akademiestrasse. Even a quickie ride across town is a great Salzburg experience. In the evening, the riverbanks are a world of floodlit spires.

Music in Salzburg

▲▲Salzburg Festival (Salzburger Festspiele)

Each summer, from late July to the end of August, Salzburg hosts its famous Salzburg Festival, founded in 1920 to employ Vienna's musicians in the summer. This fun and festive time is crowded, but there are usually plenty of beds (except for a few August weekends). Events take place primarily in three big halls: the Opera and Orchestra venues in the Festival House, and the Landes Theater, where German-language plays are performed. Tickets for the big festival events are generally expensive (€50-600) and sell out well in advance (bookable from January). Most tourists think they're "going to the Salzburg Festival" by seeing smaller non-festival events that go on during the festival weeks. For these lesser events, same-day tickets are normally available (the ticket office on Mozartplatz, in the TI, prints a daily list of concerts and charges a 30 percent fee to book them). For specifics on this year's festival schedule and tickets, visit www.salzburgfestival.at, or contact the Austrian National Tourist Office in the United States (tel. 212/944-6880, fax 212/730-4568, www.austria.info, travel @austria.info).

▲▲Musical Events Year-Round

Salzburg is busy throughout the year, with 2,000 classical performances in its palaces and churches annually. Pick up the events calendar at the TI (free, bimonthly). I've never planned in advance, and I've enjoyed great concerts with every visit. Whenever you visit, you'll have a number of concerts (generally small chamber groups) to choose from. Here are some of the more accessible events:

SALZBURG

Concerts at Hohensalzburg Fortress (Festungskonzerte)— Nearly nightly concerts—Mozart's greatest hits for beginners—are held atop Festungsberg, in the "prince's chamber" of the fortress, featuring small chamber groups (open seating after the first six more expensive rows, €31 or €38 plus €3.80 for the funicular; at 19:30, 20:00, or 20:30; doors open 30 minutes early, tel. 0662/825-858 to reserve, pick up tickets at the door). The medieval-feeling chamber has windows overlooking the city, and the concert gives you a chance to enjoy the grand city view and a stroll through the castle courtyard. (The funicular ticket costs €3.80 within an hour of the show—ideal for people who just want to ascend for the view.) For €51, you can combine the concert with a four-course dinner (starts 2 hours before concert).

Concerts at the Mirabell Palace (Schlosskonzerte)—The nearly nightly chamber music concerts at the Mirabell Palace are performed in a lavish Baroque setting. They come with more sophisticated programs and better musicians than the fortress concerts. Baroque music flying around a Baroque hall is a happy bird in the right cage (open seating after the first five pricier rows, €29-35, usually at 20:00—but check flier for times, doors open one hour ahead, tel. 0662/848-586, www.salzburger-schlosskonzerte.at).

"Five O'Clock Concerts" (5-Uhr-Konzerte)—These concerts—next to St. Peter's in the old town—are cheaper, since they feature young artists. While the series is formally named after the brother of Joseph Haydn, it offers music from various masters (€12-15, July-Sept Tue and Thu at 17:00, no concerts Oct-June, 45-60 minutes, tel. 0662/8445-7619, www.5-uhr-konzerte.com).

Mozart Piano Sonatas—St. Peter's Abbey hosts these concerts each weekend. This short (45-minute) and inexpensive concert is ideal for families (€18, €9 for children, €45 for a family of four, Fri and Sat at 19:00 year-round, in the abbey's Romanesque Hall—a.k.a. Romanischer Saal, tel. 0664/423-5645).

Marionette Theater—Salzburg's much-loved marionette theater offers operas with spellbinding marionettes and recorded music. Adults and kids alike are mesmerized by the little people on stage (€18-35, June-Sept nearly nightly at 17:00 or 19:30, none on Sun, also 3-4/week in May, some 14:00 matinees, box office open Mon-Sat 9:00-13:00 and 2 hours before shows, near the Mirabell Gardens and Mozart's Residence at Schwarzstrasse 24, tel. 0662/872-406, www.marionetten.at). For a sneak preview, check out the videos playing at the marionette exhibit up in the fortress.

Mozart Dinner Concert—For those who'd like some classical music but would rather not sit through a concert, the recommended Stiftskeller St. Peter restaurant offers a traditional candlelit meal with Mozart's greatest hits performed by a string quartet and singers in historic costumes gavotting among the tables. In this elegant Baroque setting, tourists clap between movements and get three courses of food (from Mozart-era recipes) mixed with three 20-minute courses of crowd-pleasing music (€51, Mozart-lovers with this guidebook pay €42 when booking direct, almost nightly at 20:00, dress is "smart casual," call to reserve at 0662/828-695, www.mozartdinnerconcert.com).

Sound of Salzburg Dinner Show—The show at the recommended Sternbräu Inn is Broadway in a dirndl with tired food. But it's a fun show, and *Sound of Music* fans leave with hands red from clapping. A piano player and a hardworking quartet of singers wearing historical costumes perform an entertaining mix of *S.O.M.* hits and traditional folk songs (€46 for dinner, begins at 19:30). You can also come by at 20:30, pay €32, skip the dinner, and get the show and a drink. Those who book direct (not through a hotel) and pay cash get a 10 percent discount with this book (nightly mid-May-mid-Oct, Griesgasse 23, tel. 0662/826-617, www.soundofsalzburgshow.com).

Music at Mass—Each Sunday morning, three great churches offer a Mass, generally with glorious music. The Salzburg Cathedral is likely your best bet for fine music to worship by (10:00). The Franciscan church—the locals' choice—is enthusiastic about its musical Masses (at 9:00). St. Peter's Church also has music (10:30). See the Salzburg events guide (available at TIs) for details.

Free Brass Band Concert—A traditional brass band plays in the Mirabell Gardens (May-Aug Sun at 10:30 and Wed with lighted fountains at 20:30).

Sleeping in Salzburg

Finding a room in Salzburg, even during its music festival (mid-July-Aug), is usually easy. Rates rise significantly (20-30 percent) during the music festival, and sometimes around Easter and Christmas; these higher prices do not appear in the ranges I've listed. Many places charge 10 percent extra for a one-night stay.

In the New Town, North of the River

These listings, clustering around Linzergasse, are in a pleasant neighborhood (with easy parking) a 15-minute walk from the train station (for directions, see "Arrival in Salzburg," earlier) and a 10-minute walk to the old town. If you're coming from the old town, simply cross the main bridge (Staatsbrücke) to the mostly traffic-free Linzergasse. If driving, exit the highway at Salzburg-Nord, follow Vogelweiderstrasse straight to its end, and turn right.

$$$ Altstadthotel Wolf-Dietrich, around the corner from Linzergasse on pedestrians-only Wolf-Dietrich-Strasse, is well-located (half its rooms overlook St. Sebastian Cemetery). With

SALZBURG

27 tastefully plush rooms, it's a good value for a big, stylish hotel (Sb-€80, Db-€120, price depends on size, family deals, €20-40 more during festival, complex pricing but readers of this book get a 10 percent discount on prevailing price—insist on this discount deducted from whatever price is offered that day, elevator, free Internet access and Wi-Fi, pool with loaner swimsuits, sauna, free DVD library, Wolf-Dietrich-Strasse 7, tel. 0662/871-275, fax 0662/871-2759, www.salzburg-hotel.at, office@salzburg-hotel.at). Their annex across the street has 14 equally comfortable rooms (€20 less, no elevator).

$$$ Hotel Trumer Stube, well-located three blocks from the river just off Linzergasse, has 20 clean rooms and is warmly run by the Hirschbichler family (official rates: Sb-€65, Db-€105, Tb-€128, Qb-€147—email and ask for the best Rick Steves cash-only rate; buffet breakfast-€7, non-smoking, elevator, free Wi-Fi, easy parking, Bergstrasse 6, tel. 0662/874-776, fax 0662/874-326, www.trumer-stube.at, info@trumer-stube.at; the mom and daughter, both named Marianne, may charm you into extending your Salzburg stay).

$$$ Hotel Goldene Krone, about five blocks from the river, is plain and basic, with 20 big, quiet, creaky, and well-kept rooms. Stay a while in their pleasant cliffside garden (Sb-€69, Db-€119, Tb-€159, Qb-€189, claim your 15 percent discount off these prices with this book, dim lights, elevator, free Wi-Fi, parking-€12/day, Linzergasse 48, tel. 0662/872-300, fax 0662/8723-0066, www.hotel-goldenekrone.com, office@hotel-goldenekrone.com, Günther Hausknost). Günther offers tours (€10/person, 2 hours,

5 people minimum) and a "Rick Steves Two Nights in Salzburg" deal, which covers your room, a 24-hour Salzburg Card, a concert in Mirabell Palace, and a tour with Günther (Sb-€171, Db-€304, Tb-€429, Qb-€532; book on the hotel's website).

$$ Hotel Schwarzes Rössl is a university dorm that becomes a student-run hotel each July, August, and September. The location couldn't be handier. It looks like a normal hotel from the outside, and its 50 rooms, while a bit spartan, are as comfortable as a hotel on the inside (S-€50, Sb-€60, D-€80, Db-€100, Tb-€132, good breakfast, Internet access and Wi-Fi, no rooms rented Oct-June, just off Linzergasse at Priesterhausgasse 6, tel. 0662/874-426, www.academiahotels.at, schwarzes.roessl@academiahotels.at).

$$ Institute St. Sebastian is in a somewhat sterile but very clean historic building next to St. Sebastian Cemetery. From October through June, the institute houses female students from various Salzburg colleges and also rents 40 beds for travelers (men and women). From July through September, the students are gone, and they rent all 100 beds (including 20 twin rooms) to travelers. The building has spacious public areas, a roof garden, a piano that guests are welcome to play, and some of the best rooms and dorm beds in town for the money. The immaculate doubles come with modern baths and head-to-toe twin beds (S-€36, Sb-€44, D-€55, Db-€70, Tb-€84, Qb-€98, includes simple breakfast, elevator, self-service laundry-€4/load; reception open daily July-Sept 7:30-12:00 & 13:00-21:30, Oct-June 8:00-12:00 & 16:00-21:00; Linzergasse 41, enter through arch at #37, tel. 0662/871-386, fax 0662/8713-8685, www.st-sebastian-salzburg.at, office@st-sebastian-salzburg.at). Students like the €21 bunks in 4- to 10-bed dorms (€2 less if you have sheets, no lockout, free lockers, free showers). You'll find self-service kitchens on each floor (fridge space is free; request a key). If you need parking, request it well in advance.

Pensions on Rupertgasse: These two hotels are about five blocks farther from the river on Rupertgasse, a breeze for drivers but with more street noise than the places on Linzergasse. They're both modern and well-run—good values if you don't mind being a bit away from the old town. **$$$ Bergland Hotel** is charming and classy, with comfortable neo-rustic rooms. It's a modern building and therefore spacious and solid (Sb-€65, Db-€100, Tb-€125, Qb-€155, elevator, pay Internet access, free Wi-Fi, English library, bike rental-€6/day, Rupertgasse 15, tel. 0662/872-318, fax 0662/872-3188, www.berglandhotel.at, office@berglandhotel.at, Kuhn family). The similar, boutique-like **$$$ Hotel-Pension Jedermann,** a few doors down, is tastefully done and comfortable, with an artsy painted-concrete ambience and a backyard garden (Sb-€65, Db-€95, Tb-€120, Qb-€160, much more during festival, elevator, free Internet access and Wi-Fi, Rupertgasse 25, tel.

Salzburg Hotels

SALZBURG

TRAIN STATION

1 Altstadthotel Wolf-Dietrich
2 Hotel Trumer Stube
3 Hotel Goldene Krone
4 Hotel Schwarzes Rössl
5 Institute St. Sebastian
6 Bergland Hotel
7 Hotel-Pension Jedermann
8 Gasthaus zur Goldenen Ente & Hotel am Dom
9 Hotel Weisse Taube
10 Gasthaus Stadtalm
11 Jugendgästehaus Salzburg
12 Pension Adlerhof
13 International Youth Hotel
14 To Hotel Rosenvilla
15 Haus Arenberg
16 To Brigitte Lenglachner Rooms
17 To Moosstrasse Accommodations
18 Launderette

To A-1 Freeway (Salzburg Nord Exit) & Vienna

VOGELWEIDER.

BREITENFELDER STRASSE

LASTENSTRASSE

WEISERHOF STRASSE

MERIANSTRASSE

PARACELSUSSTR.

PH.-HARPFF-STR.

BAYERHAMMERSTRASSE

STR.

GABELSBERGERSTRASSE

STERNECKSTR.

LASSER.

PARACELSUSSTR.

HAYDNSTR.

STELZHAMMERSTR.

AUERSPERGSTRASSE

STRASSE

RUPERTGASSE

ARNOGASSE

VIRGILGASSE

JOSEF-

NENGASSE

WOLF-DIETRICH-STR.

VIERTHALER-STRASSE

GLOCKENGASSE

LODRON-STR.

18 1

ST. SEBASTIAN CEMETERY

5

2

STR.

LINZER GASSE

3

4

MONASTERY

STEINGASSE

Kapuzinerberg

GISELAKAI

IMBERGSTRASSE

ARENBERGSTRASSE

ARENBERGSTR.

PAUSINGERSTRASSE

15

JUDENGASSE

TOWN

MOZART-STEG

RUDOLFSKAI

River

Dr.-Franz-Rehrl-Platz

BÜRGLSTEINSTRASSE

8

Mozart-platz

Residenz-platz

9

NEUE RESIDENZ

BASTEIGASSE

NONNTALER BRÜCKE

To 14

CATHEDRAL

Kapitel-platz

KAIGASSE

KAJETAN CHURCH

Rudolfs-platz

IGNAZ-RIEDER-KAI

HERRENGASSE

Kajetaner-platz

NONNBERG ABBEY

FRANZ-HINTERHOLZER-KAI

FUNICULAR

HOHEN-SALZBURG FORTRESS

NONNTALER HAUPTSTRASSE

PETERSBRUNNSTRASSE

ERZABT-KLOTZ-STR.

JOSEF-PREIS-ALLEE

HELLBRUNNER STRASSE

To Hallein

berg

BRUNNHAUSGASSE

To Hellbrunn Castle

11

To A-10 freeway (Salzburg Süd Exit), Hallein & Berchtesgaden

0662/873-2410, fax 0662/873-2419, www.hotel-jedermann.com, office@hotel-jedermann.com, Herr und Frau Gmachl).

In or Above the Old Town

Most of these hotels are near Residenzplatz. While this area is car-restricted, you're allowed to drive your car in to unload, pick up a map and parking instructions, and head for the €14-per-day garage in the mountain.

$$$ Gasthaus zur Goldenen Ente is in a 600-year-old building with medieval stone arches and narrow stairs. Located above a good restaurant, it's as central as you can be on a pedestrian street in old Salzburg. The 22 rooms are modern and newly renovated, and include classy amenities. While the advertised rates are too high, travelers with this book get 10 percent off (except in July-Aug), and prices may dip lower according to demand. Ulrike, Franziska, and Anita run a tight ship for the absentee owners (most of the year: Sb-€85, Db-€125; late July-Aug and Dec: Sb-€95, Db-€160; extra person-€40, firm mattresses, elevator, free Internet access, Goldgasse 10, tel. 0662/845-622, fax 0662/845-6229, www.ente.at, hotel@ente.at).

$$$ Hotel Weisse Taube has 30 comfortable rooms in a quiet dark-wood 14th-century building, well-located about a block off Mozartplatz (Sb-€69-88, Db with shower-€98-139, bigger Db with bath-€119-172, 10 percent discount with this book if you reserve direct and pay cash, elevator, pay Internet access and Wi-Fi, tel. 0662/842-404, fax 0662/841-783, Kaigasse 9, www.weissetaube.at, hotel@weissetaube.at).

$$$ Hotel am Dom is perfectly located—on Goldgasse a few steps from the cathedral—and offers 15 chic rooms, some with their original wood-beam ceilings (twin Db-€90-160, standard Db-€130-240, "superior" Db-€150-290, air-con, non-smoking, free Internet access and Wi-Fi, Goldgasse 17, tel. 0662/842-765, fax 0662/8427-6555, www.hotelamdom.at, office@hotelamdom.at).

Hostels

For another hostel (on the other side of the river), see the International Youth Hotel listed later, in "Near the Train Station."

$ Gasthaus Stadtalm (a.k.a. the *Naturfreundehaus*) is a local version of a mountaineer's hut and a great budget alternative. Snuggled in a forest on the remains of a 15th-century castle wall atop the little mountain overlooking Salzburg, it has magnificent town and mountain views. While the 22 beds are designed-for-backpackers basic, the price and view are the best in town—with the right attitude, it's a fine experience (€18.50/person in 4- and 6-bed dorms, same price for room with double bed; includes breakfast, sheets, and shower; lockers, 2 minutes from top of €2

Mönchsberg elevator, Mönchsberg 19C, tel. & fax 0662/841-729, www.diestadtalm.com, info@diestadtalm.com, Peter). Once you've dropped your bags here, it's a five-minute walk down the cliffside stairs into Toscanini Hof, in the middle of the old town (path always lit).

$ Jugendgästehaus Salzburg, just steps from the old town center, is nevertheless removed from the bustle. While its dorm rooms are the standard crammed-with-beds variety—and the hallways will bring back high-school memories—the doubles and family rooms are modern, roomy, and bright, and the public spaces are quite pleasant (bed in 8-person dorm-€23; Db, Tb, and Qb available at much higher prices; includes breakfast and sheets, pay Internet access, free Wi-Fi, *The Sound of Music* plays daily, bike rental-€10/day or €6/half-day, free parking, just around the east side of the castle hill at Josef-Preis-Allee 18; from train station, take bus #5 or #25 to the Justizgebäude stop, then head left one block along the bushy wall, cross Petersbrunnstrasse, find shady Josefs-Preis-Alle, and walk a few minutes to the end—the hostel is the big orange/green building on the right; tel. 0662/842-670, fax 0662/841-101, www.jufa.at/salzburg, salzburg@jufa.at). The hotel at the back of the hostel isn't as cheap, but does offer more standard hotel amenities, such as TVs (Db-€110 depending on season, includes breakfast).

Near the Train Station

$$ Pension Adlerhof, a plain and decent old pension, is two blocks in front of the train station (left off Kaiserschutzenstrasse), but a 15-minute walk from the sightseeing action. It has a quirky staff, a boring location, and 30 stodgy-but-spacious rooms (Sb-€56, Db-€80, Tb-€115, Qb-€130, price varies a bit with the season and size of room, cash only, elevator, pay Internet access and free Wi-Fi, limited free parking, Elisabethstrasse 25, tel. 0662/875-236, fax 0662/873-663, www.gosalzburg.com, adlerhof@pension-adlerhof.at).

$ International Youth Hotel, a.k.a. the "Yo-Ho," is the most lively, handy, and American of Salzburg's hostels. This backpacker haven is a youthful and easygoing place that speaks English first; has cheap meals, 186 beds, lockers, tour discounts, and no curfew; plays *The Sound of Music* free daily at 10:30; runs a lively bar; and welcomes anyone of any age. The noisy atmosphere and lack of a curfew can make it hard to sleep (€18-19/person in 4- to 8-bed dorms, €21-22 in dorms with bathrooms, D-€55, Ds-€65, Q-€72, Qs-€81, includes sheets, cheap breakfast, pay Internet access, free Wi-Fi, laundry-€4 wash and dry, 6 blocks from station toward Linzergasse and 6 blocks from river at Paracelsusstrasse 9, tel. 0662/879-649, fax 0662/878-810, www.yoho.at, officc@yoho.at).

Four-Star Hotels in Residential Neighborhoods away from the Center

If you want plush furnishings, spacious public spaces, generous balconies, gardens, and free parking, consider the following places. These two modern hotels in nondescript residential neighborhoods are a fine value if you don't mind the 15-minute walk from the old town. While not ideal for train travelers, drivers in need of no-stress comfort for a home base should consider these (see map on page 144).

$$$ Hotel Rosenvilla, close to the river, offers 16 rooms with bright furnishings, surrounded by a leafy garden (Sb-€79-108, Db-€135-165, bigger Db-€145-199, Db suite-€168-255, at least €30 more during festival, free Wi-Fi, Höfelgasse 4, tel. 0662/621-765, fax 0662/625-2308, www.rosenvilla.com, hotel@rosenvilla.com).

$$$ Haus Arenberg, higher up opposite the old town, rents 17 big, breezy rooms—most with generous balconies—in a quiet garden setting (Sb-€85-105, Db-€129-165, Tb-€149-176, Qb-€158-185, higher prices are during festival, Blumensteinstrasse 8, tel. 0662/640-097, fax 0662/640-0973, www.arenberg-salzburg.at, info@arenberg-salzburg.at, family Leobacher).

Private Rooms *(Privatzimmer)*

These are generally roomy and comfortable, and come with a good breakfast, easy parking, and tourist information. Off-season, competition softens prices. While they are a bus ride from town, with a €4.20 transit day pass *(Tageskarte)* and the frequent service, this shouldn't keep you away (see map on page 138). In fact, most homeowners will happily pick you up at the train station if you simply telephone them and ask. Most will also do laundry for a small fee for those staying at least two nights. I've listed prices for two nights or more—if staying only one night, expect a 10 percent surcharge. Most push tours and concerts to make money on the side. As they are earning a commission, if you go through them, you'll probably lose the discount I've negotiated for my readers who go direct.

Beyond the Train Station

$ Brigitte Lenglachner rents eight basic, well-cared-for rooms in her home in a quiet suburban-feeling neighborhood that's a 25-minute walk, 10-minute bike ride, or easy bus ride away from the center. Frau Lenglachner serves breakfast in the garden (in good weather) and happily provides plenty of local information and advice (S-€25, D-€40, Db-€49, Tb-€68, Qb-€96, 5b-€113; apartment with kitchen—Db-€56, Tb-€95, Qb-€110; apartment requires minimum 3-night stay, easy and free parking, Scheibenweg

8, tel. & fax 0662/438-044, www.bei-brigitte.at, bedandbreakfast
4u@yahoo.de). It's a 10-minute walk from the station: Head for the
river, cross the pedestrian Pioneer Bridge (Pioniersteg), turn right,
and walk along the river to the third street (Scheibenweg). Turn
left, and it's halfway down on the right.

On Moosstrasse

The busy street called Moosstrasse, which runs southwest of
Mönchsberg (behind the mountain and away from the old town
center), is lined with farmhouses offering rooms. Handy bus #21
connects Moosstrasse to the center frequently (Mon-Fri 4/hour
until 19:00, Sat 4/hour until 17:00, evenings and Sun 2/hour,
20 minutes). To get to these pensions from the train station,
take bus #1, #5, #6, or #25 to Makartplatz, where you'll change
to #21. If you're coming from the old town, catch bus #21 from
Hanuschplatz, just downstream of the Staatsbrücke bridge near the
Tabak kiosk. Buy a €1.90 *Einzelkarte-Kernzone* ticket (for one trip)
or a €4.20 *Tageskarte* (day pass, good for 24 hours) from the streetside machine and punch it when you board the bus. The bus stop
you use for each place is included in the following listings. If you're
driving from the center, go through the tunnel, continue straight
on Neutorstrasse, and take the fourth left onto Moosstrasse.
Drivers exit the autobahn at *Süd* and then head in the direction of
Grodig. Each place can recommend a favorite Moosstrasse eatery
(Reiterhof, at #151, is particularly popular).

$$ Pension Bloberger Hof, while more a hotel than a pen-
sion, is comfortable and friendly, with a peaceful, rural location
and 20 farmer-plush, good-value rooms. It's the farthest out, but
reached by the same bus #21 from the center. Inge and her daugh-
ter Sylvia offer a 10 percent discount to those who have this book,
reserve direct, and pay cash (Sb-€55-70, Db-€75-80, big new Db
with balcony-€95-100, Db suite-€120, extra bed-€20, 10 percent
extra for one-night stays, family apartment with kitchen, non-
smoking, free Internet access and Wi-Fi, restaurant for guests, free
loaner bikes, free station pickup if staying 3 nights, Hammerauer
Strasse 4, bus stop: Hammerauer Strasse, tel. 0662/830-227, fax
0662/827-061, www.blobergerhof.at, office@blobergerhof.at).

$$ Haus Reichl, with three good rooms at the end of a long
lane, feels the most remote. Franziska offers free loaner bikes for
guests (20-minute pedal to the center) and bakes fresh cakes most
days (Sb-€36-45, Db-€58-64, Tb-€75-84, Qb-€92-104, cash preferred, doubles and triples have balcony and view, all have in-room
tea/coffee, non-smoking, between Ballwein and Bankhammer
B&Bs, 200 yards down Reiterweg to #52, bus stop: Gsengerweg,
tel. & fax 0662/826-248, www.privatzimmer.at/haus-reichl, haus
.reichl@telering.at).

$ Frau Ballwein offers four cozy, charming, and fresh rooms in two buildings, some with intoxicating-view balconies (Sb-€35-45, Db-€53-64, Tb-€75-85, Qb-€80-95, 2-bedroom apartment for up to 5 people-€95-110, prices depend on season, family deals, cash only, farm-fresh breakfasts amid her hanging teapot collection, non-smoking, small pool, 2 free loaner bikes, free parking, Moosstrasse 69-A, bus stop: Gsengerweg, tel. & fax 0662/824-029, www.haus-ballwein.at, haus.ballwein@gmx.net).

$ Helga Bankhammer rents four nondescript rooms in a farmhouse, with a real dairy farm out back (D-€44, Db-€55, no surcharge for one-night stays, family deals, non-smoking, laundry about €6/load, Moosstrasse 77, bus stop: Marienbad, tel. & fax 0662/830-067, www.privatzimmer.at/helga.bankhammer, bankhammer@aon.at).

Eating in Salzburg

In the Old Town

Salzburg boasts many inexpensive, fun, and atmospheric eateries. Most of these restaurants are centrally located in the old town, famous with visitors but also enjoyed by locals.

Gasthaus zum Wilden Mann is *the* place if the weather's bad and you're in the mood for *Hofbräu* atmosphere and a hearty, cheap meal at a shared table in one small, smoky, well-antlered room. Notice the 1899 flood photo on the wall. For a quick lunch, get the *Bauernschmaus,* a mountain of dumplings, kraut, and peasant's meats (€11.50). While they have a few outdoor tables, the atmosphere is all indoors, and the menu is not great for hot-weather food. Owner Robert—who runs the restaurant with Schwarzenegger-like energy—enjoys fostering a convivial ambience (you'll share tables with strangers) and serving fresh traditional cuisine at great prices. I simply love this place (€8.50 two-course lunch specials, €10-12 daily specials posted on the wall, kitchen open Mon-Sat 11:00-21:00, closed Sun, 2 minutes from Mozart's Birthplace, enter from Getreidegasse 22 or Griesgasse 17, tel. 0662/841-787).

Stiftskeller St. Peter has been in business for more than 1,000 years—it was mentioned in the biography of Charlemagne. It's classy and high-end touristy, serving uninspired traditional Austrian cuisine. Through the centuries, they've learned to charge for each piece of bread and don't serve free tap water (€10-27 meals, daily 11:30-22:30, indoor/outdoor seating, next to St. Peter's Church at foot of Mönchsberg, restaurant tel. 0662/841-268). They host the Mozart Dinner Concert described on page 140.

St. Paul's Stub'n Beer Garden is tucked secretly away under the castle with a decidedly untouristy atmosphere. The food is better than a beer hall, and a young, bohemian-chic clientele fills its

SALZBURG

two troll-like rooms and its idyllic tree-shaded garden. *Kasnock'n* is a tasty mountaineers' pasta with cheese served in an iron pan with a side salad for €9—it's enough for two (€6-12 daily specials, €7-15 plates, Mon-Sat 17:00-22:30, open later for drinks only, closed Sun, Herrengasse 16, tel. 0662/843-220).

Zirkelwirt serves modern Mediterranean, Italian, and Austrian dishes, a daily fish special, and always a good vegetarian option. It's an old *Gasthaus* dining room with a medieval tiki-hut terrace a block off Mozartplatz, yet a world away from the tourism of the old town. While the waitstaff, music, and vibe feel young, it attracts Salzburgers of all ages (€9-15 plates, cheese dumplings and daily fish special, nightly 17:00-24:00, Pfeifergasse 14, tel. 0662/843-472).

Fisch Krieg Restaurant, on the river where the fishermen used to sell their catch, is a great value. They serve fast, fresh, and inexpensive fish in a casual dining room—where trees grow through the ceiling—as well as great riverside seating (€2 fishwiches to go, self-serve €7 meals, salad bar, Mon-Fri 8:30-18:30, Sat 8:30-13:00, closed Sun, Hanuschplatz 4, tel. 0662/843-732).

Sternbräu Inn, a sloppy, touristy Austrian food circus, is a sprawling complex of popular eateries (traditional, Italian, self-serve, and vegetarian) in a cheery garden setting. Explore both courtyards before choosing a seat (Bürgerstube is classic, most restaurants open daily 9:00-24:00 with food served until 23:00, enter from Getreidegasse 34, tel. 0662/842-140). One fancy, air-conditioned room hosts the Sound of Salzburg dinner show (described on page 141).

Café Tomaselli (with its Kiosk annex and terrace seating across the way) has long been Salzburg's top place to see and be seen. While pricey, it is good for lingering and people-watching. Tomaselli serves light meals and lots of drinks, keeps long hours daily, and has fine seating on the square, a view terrace upstairs, and indoor tables. Despite its fancy inlaid wood paneling, 19th-century portraits, and chandeliers, it's surprisingly low-key (€3-7 light meals, daily 7:00-21:00, until 24:00 during music festival, Alter Markt 9, tel. 0662/844-488).

Saran Essbar is the product of hardworking Mr. Saran (from the Punjab), who cooks and serves with his heart. This delightful little eatery casts a rich orange glow under medieval vaults. Its fun menu is small (Mr. Saran is committed to both freshness and value), mixing Austrian (great schnitzel and strudel), Italian, and Asian vegetarian, and always offering salads (€10-15 meals, cash only, daily 11:00-22:00, often open later, a block off Mozartplatz at Judengasse 10, tel. 0662/846-628).

Bar Club Café Republic, a hip hangout for local young people near the end of Getreidegasse, feels like a theater lobby during

Salzburg Restaurants

SALZBURG

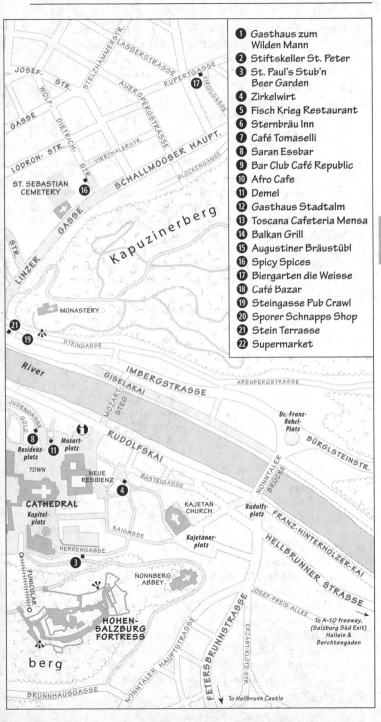

1 Gasthaus zum Wilden Mann
2 Stiftskeller St. Peter
3 St. Paul's Stub'n Beer Garden
4 Zirkelwirt
5 Fisch Krieg Restaurant
6 Sternbräu Inn
7 Café Tomaselli
8 Saran Essbar
9 Bar Club Café Republic
10 Afro Cafe
11 Demel
12 Gasthaus Stadtalm
13 Toscana Cafeteria Mensa
14 Balkan Grill
15 Augustiner Bräustübl
16 Spicy Spices
17 Biergarten die Weisse
18 Café Bazar
19 Steingasse Pub Crawl
20 Sporer Schnapps Shop
21 Stein Terrasse
22 Supermarket

SALZBURG

intermission. It serves good food with smoky indoor and outdoor seating. It's ideal if you want something mod, untouristy, and un-wursty (trendy breakfasts 8:00-18:00, Asian and international menu, €9-15 plates, lots of hard drinks, daily until late, music with a DJ Fri and Sat from 23:00, salsa dance club Tue night from 21:00, no cover, Anton Neumayr Platz 2, tel. 0662/841-613).

Afro Cafe, between Getreidegasse and the Mönchsberg lift, is a hit with local students. Its agenda: to put a fun spin on African cuisine (adapted to European tastes). It serves tea, coffee, cocktails, and tasty food with a dose of '70s funk and a healthy sense of humor. The menu includes pan-African specialties—try the spicy chicken couscous—as well as standard soups and salads (€9-13 main courses, Mon-Fri 9:00-24:00, closed Sun, between Getreidegasse and cliff face at Bürgerspitalplatz 5, tel. 0662/844-888).

Demel, an outpost of Vienna's famed chocolatier, is a wonderland of desserts that are as beautiful as they are delectable. Sink into the pink couches upstairs, or have them box up a treat for later (daily 9:00-19:00, near TI and cathedral at Mozartplatz 2, tel. 0662/840-358).

On the Cliffs Above the Old Town: **Gasthaus Stadtalm,** Salzburg's mountaineers' hut, sits high above the old town on the edge of the cliff with cheap prices, good food, and great views. If hiking across Mönchsberg, make this your goal (traditional food, salads, cliffside garden seating or cozy-mountain-hut indoor seating—one indoor view table is booked for a decade of New Year's celebrations, daily 10:00-18:00, July-Aug until 23:00, 2 minutes from top of €3.20 round-trip Mönchsberg elevator, also reachable by stairs from Toscanini Hof, Mönchsberg 19C, tel. 0662/841-729, Peter). For the location, see map on page 152.

Eating Cheaply in the Old Town

Toscana Cafeteria Mensa is the students' lunch canteen, fast and cheap—with indoor seating and a great courtyard for sitting outside with students and teachers instead of tourists. They serve a daily soup-and-main course special for €5 (Mon-Fri 8:30-18:00, hot meals served 11:00-13:30 only, closed Sat-Sun, behind the Old Residenz, in the courtyard opposite Sigmund-Haffner-Gasse 16).

Sausage stands *(Würstelstände)* serve the town's favorite "fast food." The best stands (like those on Universitätsplatz) use the same boiling water all day, which gives the weenies more flavor. The Salzburgers' favorite spicy sausage is sold at the 60-year-old **Balkan Grill,** run by chatty Frau Ebner (€3; survey the five spicy options—described in English—and choose a number; takeaway only, steady and sturdy local crowd, daily 11:00-19:00, hours vary with demand, hiding down the tunnel at Getreidegasse 33 across from Eisgrotte).

Picnickers will appreciate the bustling morning **produce market** (daily except Sun) on Universitätsplatz behind Mozart's Birthplace, as well as the well-stocked **Billa supermarket** (Mon-Fri 7:15-19:30, Sat 7:15-18:00, closed Sun), just across the street from the recommended Fisch Krieg Restaurant on Griesgasse.

Away from the Center

Augustiner Bräustübl, a huge 1,000-seat beer garden within a monk-run brewery in the Kloster Mülln, is rustic and raw. On busy nights, it's like a Munich beer hall with no music but the volume turned up. When it's cool outside, you'll enjoy a historic setting inside beer-sloshed and smoke-stained halls. On balmy evenings, it's like a Renoir painting—but with beer breath—under chestnut trees. Local students mix with tourists eating hearty slabs of schnitzel with their fingers or cold meals from the self-serve picnic counter, while children frolic on the playground kegs. For your beer: Pick up a half-liter or full-liter mug, pay the lady (*schank* means self-serve price, *bedienung* is the price with waiter service), wash your mug, give Mr. Keg your receipt and empty mug, and you will be made happy. Waiters only bring beer; they don't bring food—instead, go up the stairs, survey the hallway of deli counters, and assemble your own meal (or, as long as you buy a drink, you can bring in a picnic). Classic pretzels from the bakery and spiraled, salty radishes make great beer even better. For dessert—after a visit to the strudel kiosk—enjoy the incomparable floodlit view of old Salzburg from the nearby Müllnersteg pedestrian bridge and a riverside stroll home (open daily 15:00-23:00, Augustinergasse 4, tel. 0662/431-246).

Getting There: It's about a 15-minute walk along the river (with the river on your right) from the Staatsbrücke bridge. After passing the pedestrian Müllnersteg bridge, just after Café am Kai, follow the stairs up to a busy street, and cross it. From here, either continue up more stairs into the trees and around the small church (for a scenic approach to the monastery), or stick to the sidewalk as it curves around to Augustinergasse. Either way, your goal is the huge yellow building. Don't be fooled by second-rate gardens serving the same beer nearby.

North of the River, near Recommended Linzergasse Hotels

Spicy Spices is a trippy vegetarian-Indian restaurant where Suresh Syal (a.k.a. "Mr. Spicy") serves tasty curry and rice, samosas, organic salads, vegan soups, and fresh juices. It's a *namaste* kind of place, where everything's proudly organic (€6.50 specials, Mon-Fri 10:30-21:30, Sat-Sun 12:00-21:30, takeout available, Wolf-Dietrich-Strasse 1, tel. 0662/870-712).

Biergarten die Weisse, close to the hotels on Rupertgasse and away from the tourists, is a longtime hit with the natives. If a beer hall can be happening, this one—modern yet with antlers—is it. Their famously good beer is made right there; favorites include their fizzy wheat beer *(Weisse)* and their seasonal beers (on request). Enjoy the beer with their good, cheap traditional food in the great garden seating, or in the wide variety of indoor rooms—sports bar, young and noisy, or older and more elegant (daily specials, Mon-Sat 10:00-24:00, closed Sun, Rupertgasse 10, east of Bayerhamerstrasse, tel. 0662/872-246).

Café Bazar, overlooking the river between Mirabell Gardens and the Staatsbrücke bridge, is as close as you'll get to a Vienna coffee house in Salzburg. It's *the* venerable spot for a classy drink with an old-town-and-castle view (light meals, Mon-Sat 7:30-23:00, Sun 9:00-18:00, Schwarzstrasse 3, tel. 0662/874-278).

Steingasse Pub Crawl

For a fun post-concert activity, crawl through medieval Steingasse's trendy pubs (all open until the wee hours). This is a local and hip scene, but accessible to older tourists: dark bars filled with well-dressed Salzburgers lazily smoking cigarettes and talking philosophy as avant-garde Euro-pop throbs on the soundtrack. Most of the pubs are in cellar-like caves...extremely atmospheric. (For more on Steingasse, see page 136.) These four pubs are all within about 100 yards of each other. Start at the Linzergasse end of Steingasse. As they are quite different, survey all before choosing your spot.

Pepe Cocktail Bar, with Mexican decor and Latin music, serves Mexican snacks *con* cocktails (nightly 19:00-3:00 in the morning, live DJs Fri-Sat from 19:00, Steingasse 3, tel. 0662/873-662).

Shrimps Bar-Restaurant, next door and less claustrophobic, is more a restaurant than a bar, serving creative international dishes (spicy shrimp sandwiches and salads, Mon-Sat 17:30-24:00, closed Sun, Steingasse 5, tel. 0662/874-484).

Saiten Sprung wins the "Best Atmosphere" award. The door is kept closed to keep out the crude and rowdy. Ring the bell and enter its hellish interior—lots of stone and red decor, with mountains of melted wax beneath age-old candlesticks and a classic soul music ambience. Stelios, who speaks English with Greek charm, serves cocktails, fine wine, and wine-friendly Italian antipasti (nightly 21:00-4:00 in the morning, Steingasse 11, tel. 0662/881-377).

Fridrich, just next door, is an intimate little place under an 11th-century vault, with lots of mirrors and a silver ceiling fan. Bernd Fridrich is famous for his martinis and passionate about Austrian wines, and has a tattered collection of vinyl that seems to keep the 1970s alive. He serves little dishes to complement the focus, which is socializing and drinking (€5-12 small dishes, Thu-Mon from 18:00 in summer, from 17:00 in winter, closed Tue-Wed, Steingasse 15, tel. 0662/876-218).

Salzburg Connections

By train, Salzburg is the first stop over the German-Austrian border. This means that if Salzburg is your only stop in Austria, and you're using a railpass that covers Germany but not Austria, you don't have to pay extra or add Austria to your pass to get here.

From Salzburg by Train to: Füssen (roughly hourly, 4 hours, 1-2 changes), **Reutte** (hourly, 5 hours, change either in Munich and Kempten, or in Innsbruck and Garmisch), **Nürnberg** (hourly with change in Munich, 3 hours), **Hallstatt** (hourly, 50 minutes to Attnang Puchheim, 20-minute wait, then 1.5 hours to Hallstatt), **Vienna** (2/hour, 2.5-3 hours), **Ljubljana** (every 2 hours, 4.25-5 hours, some with change in Villach), **Interlaken** (7/day, 7.5-8 hours, 2-3 changes), **Florence** (4/day, 8-8.5 hours, 2 changes, 1 overnight option via Villach). Austrian train info: Austrian tel. 051-717 (to get an operator, dial 2, then 2), www.oebb.at.

SALZBURG

HALLSTATT
and the SALZKAMMERGUT

Commune with nature in the Salzkammergut, Austria's Lake District. "The hills are alive," and you're surrounded by the loveliness that has turned on everyone from Emperor Franz Josef to Julie Andrews. This is *Sound of Music* country. Idyllic and majestic, but not rugged, it's a gentle land of lakes, forested mountains, and storybook villages, rich in hiking opportunities and inexpensive lodging. Settle down in the postcard-pretty, lake-cuddling town of Hallstatt.

Planning Your Time

While there are plenty of lakes and charming villages in the Salzkammergut, Hallstatt is really the only one that matters. One night and a few hours to browse are all you'll need to fall in love. To relax or take a hike in the surroundings, give it two nights and a day. It's a relaxing break between Vienna and Salzburg.

Orientation to Hallstatt

(area code: 06134)

Lovable Hallstatt (HAHL-shtaht) is a tiny town bullied onto a ledge between a selfish mountain and a swan-ruled lake, with a waterfall ripping furiously through its middle. It can be toured on foot in about 15 minutes. Salt veins in the mountain rock drew people here centuries before Christ. The symbol of Hallstatt, which you'll see all over town, consists of two adjacent spirals—a design based on jewelry found in Bronze Age Celtic graves high in the nearby mountains.

Hallstatt has two parts: the tightly packed medieval town center (which locals call the Markt) and the newer, more car-friendly Lahn, a few minutes' walk to the south. A lakeside promenade connects the old center to the Lahn. The tiny "main" boat dock (a.k.a. Market Dock), where boats from the train station arrive, is in the old center of town. Another boat dock is in the Lahn, next to Hallstatt's bus stop and grocery store.

The charms of Hallstatt are the village and its lakeside setting. Come here to relax, nibble, wander, and paddle. While tourist crowds can trample much of Hallstatt's charm in August, the place is almost dead in the off-season. The lake is famous for its good fishing and pure water.

Tourist Information

At the helpful TI, Claudia and her staff can explain hikes and excursions, and find you a room (July-Aug Mon-Fri 9:00-17:00, Sat 10:00-14:00, closed Sun; Sept-June Mon-Fri 9:00-12:00 & 14:00-17:00, closed Sat-Sun; one block from Market Square, across from museum at Seestrasse 169, tel. 06134/8208, www.dachstein -salzkammergut.at).

In the summer, the TI offers 1.5-hour **walking tours** of the town in English and German (€4, mid-May-Sept Sat at 10:00). They can arrange private tours for €75.

Arrival in Hallstatt

By Train: If you're coming on the main train line that runs between Salzburg and Vienna, you'll change trains at Attnang-Puchheim to get to Hallstatt (you won't see Hallstatt on the schedules, but any train to Ebensee and Bad Ischl will stop at Hallstatt). Daytrippers can check their bags at the Attnang-Puchheim station (follow signs for *Schliessfächer,* coin-op lockers are at the street, curbside near track 1, €2.50/24 hours, a ticket serves as your key). Note: Connections can be fast—check the TV monitor.

Hallstatt's train station is a wide spot on the tracks across the lake from town. *Stefanie* (a boat) meets you at the station and glides scenically across the lake to the old town center (€2.20, meets each train until 18:48—don't arrive after that, www.hallstattschifffahrt .at). The last departing boat-train connection leaves Hallstatt at 18:15, and the first boat goes in the morning at 6:50 (8:50 Sat-Sun).

Once in Hallstatt, walk left from the boat dock for the TI; you're steps away from the hotels in the old center, and a 15-minute walk from accommodations in the Lahn.

By Bus: Hallstatt's bus stop is by the boat dock in the Lahn. It takes 15 minutes to walk from the bus stop into the old center along the lakeside path.

By Car: The main road skirts Hallstatt via a long tunnel above the town. Gates close off traffic to the old center, but if you have

HALLSTATT

HALLSTATT CENTER

TUNNEL

To Bad Ischl & Salzburg

100 Meters
100 Yards

N

BONE CHAPEL

BOAT RENTAL

CATHOLIC CHURCH & CEMETERY

Market Dock

To Salzbergwerk Hallstatt (Salt Mine)

PROTESTANT CHURCH

KIRCHEN WEG

Market Square

P P1

MUSEUM

DR. MORTON WEG

SEESTRASSE

AM HOF

BOAT RENTAL

Hallstätter See

BOAT RENTAL

1 Heritage Hotel
2 Hotel/Rest. Grüner Baum
3 Bräugasthof Hallstatt
4 Gasthof Zauner
5 Gasthof Simony
6 Pension Sarstein
7 Gasthof Pension Grüner Anger
8 Helga Lenz Rooms
9 Haus Trausner
10 Herta Höll Rooms
11 Gasthaus zur Mühle Hostel & Pizza
12 Strand Café
13 Ruth Zimmerman Pub
14 Internet Access
15 Campground (Laundry Service)

ECHERNTAL

ECHERNTALWEG

a hotel reservation, the guard will let you drive into town to drop your bags. Ask your hotel for parking suggestions. There are numbered parking areas outside the center (P1 through P5). Parking there is free with a guest card (available from your hotel), and it's a laid-back system—just show your card later. The problem is that the lots are often full, especially P1 (in the tunnel above town); try P2 or P3, in the Lahn, a lovely 15- to 20-minute lakeside walk from the old center. Without a guest card, per-day parking is still quite reasonable (lot P1: €4.20/day, lot P2: €6/day; less after 14:00). Off-season (Nov-April), parking is free and easy. All of the accommodations I recommend in the Lahn have free parking.

Helpful Hints

Internet Access: Try **Hallstatt Umbrella Bar** (€4/hour, summers only, weather permitting—since it's literally under a big umbrella, halfway between the old center and the Lahn along the lake at Seestrasse 145). For free Wi-Fi, drop by the café at the recommended **Heritage Hotel.**

Laundry: The staff of the **campground** in the Lahn will wash and dry (but not fold) your clothes for €8/load (drop off mid-April-mid-Oct daily 8:00-10:00 & 16:00-18:00, pick up in afternoon or next morning, closed off-season, tel. 06134/83224). In the center, the recommended **Hotel Grüner Baum** does laundry for non-guests (€13/load, on Market Square).

Boat Rental: Two places rent electric boats; both rent from two locations in high season. **Riedler** is next to the main boat dock, and 75 yards past Bräugasthof (€13/hour, tel. 06134/20619). **Hemetsberger** is near Gasthof Simony, and by the Lahn boat dock (€12/hour, tel. 06134/8228). Both are open daily until 19:00 in peak season and in good weather. Boats have two speeds: slow and stop. Spending an extra €3/hour gets you a faster, 500-watt boat. Both places also rent rowboats and paddleboats (slightly cheaper).

Parks and Swimming: Green and peaceful lakeside parks line the south end of Lake Hallstatt. If you walk 15 minutes south of the old center to the Lahn, you'll find a grassy public park, playground, mini-golf, and swimming area *(Badestrand)* with the fun Badeinsel play-island.

Views: For a great view over Hallstatt, hike above the recommended Helga Lenz B&B as far as you like, or climb any path leading up the hill. The 40-minute steep hike down from the salt-mine tour gives the best views (see "Sights in Hallstatt," later). While most visitors stroll the lakeside drag between the old and new parts of town, make a point to do the trip once by taking the more higgledy-piggledy high lane called Dr.-Morton-Weg.

Self-Guided Walk

Welcome to Hallstatt

• *This short walk starts at the dock.*

Boat Landing: There was a Hallstatt before there was a Rome. In fact, because of the importance of salt mining here, an entire epoch—the Hallstatt Era, from 800 to 400 B.C.—is named for this important spot. Through the centuries, salt was traded and people came and went by boat. You'll still see the traditional *Fuhr* boats, designed to carry heavy loads in shallow water.

Towering above the town is the **Catholic church.** Its faded St. Christopher—patron saint of travelers, with his cane and baby Jesus on his shoulder—watched over those sailing in and out. Until 1875, the town was extremely remote...then came a real road and the train. The good ship *Stefanie* shuttles travelers back and forth from here to the Hallstatt train station, immediately across the lake. The *Bootverleih* sign advertises boat rentals. By the way, *Schmuck* is not an insult...it means "jewelry."

Notice the one-lane road out of town (below the church). Until 1966, when a bigger tunnel was built above Hallstatt, all the traffic crept single-file right through the town.

Look down the shore at the huge homes. Several families lived in each of these houses, back when Hallstatt's population was about double its present 1,000. Today, the population continues to shrink, and many of these generally underused houses rent rooms to visitors.

Parking is tight here in the tourist season. Locals and hotels have cards getting them into the prime town-center lot. From November through April, the barricade is lifted and anyone can park here. Hallstatt gets about three months of snow each winter, but the lake hasn't frozen over since 1981.

See any swans? They've patrolled the lake like they own it since the 1860s, when Emperor Franz Josef and Empress Sisi—the Princess Diana of her day—made this region their annual holiday retreat. Sisi loved swans, so locals made sure she'd see them here. During this period, the Romantics discovered Hallstatt, many top painters worked here, and the town got its first hotel (now the Heritage Hotel).

Tiny Hallstatt has two big churches: Protestant (bordering the square on the left, with a grassy lakeside playground) and Catholic (up above, with its fascinating bone chapel).

• *Walk over the town's stream, and pop into the...*

Protestant Church: The Catholic Counter-Reformation was very strong in Austria, but pockets of Protestantism survived, especially in mining towns like Hallstatt. In 1860, Emperor Franz Josef finally allowed non-Catholic Christians to build churches. Before that, they were allowed to worship only in low-key "houses of prayer." In 1863, Hallstatt's miners pooled their humble resources and built this fine church. Step inside (free and often open). It's very plain, emphasizing the pulpit and organ rather than fancy art and saints. Check out the portraits: Martin Luther (left of altar), the town in about 1865 with its new church (left wall), and a century of pastors.

• *Continue past the church to the...*

Market Square (Marktplatz): In 1750, a fire leveled this part of town. The buildings you see now are all late 18th-century structures built of stone rather than flammable wood. The three big buildings on the left are government-subsidized housing (mostly for seniors and people with health problems). Take a close look at the two-dimensional, up-against-the-wall pear tree (it likes the sun-warmed wall). The statue features the Holy Trinity.

• *Continue a block past Gasthof Simony. At the first corner, just before the Gemeindeamt (City Hall), jog left across the little square and then right down the tiny lane marked Am Hof, which leads through an intimate bit of domestic town architecture, boat houses, lots of firewood, and maybe a couple of swans hanging out. The lane circles back to the main drag and the...*

Museum Square: Because 20th-century Hallstatt was of no industrial importance, it was untouched by World War II. But once upon a time, its salt was worth defending. High above, peeking out of the trees, is Rudolfsturm (Rudolf's Tower). Originally a 13th-century watchtower protecting the salt mines, and later the mansion of a salt-mine boss, it's now a restaurant with a great view. A zigzag trail connects the town with Rudolfsturm and the salt mines just beyond. The big, white houses by the waterfall were water-powered mills that once ground Hallstatt's grain. (If you hike up a few blocks, you'll see the river raging through town.)

Around you are the town's TI, post office, museum, City Hall, and Dachstein Sport Shop (described later). A statue recalls the mine manager who excavated prehistoric graves in about 1850. Much of the *Schmuck* sold locally is inspired by the jewelry found in the area's Bronze Age tombs.

The memorial wooden stairs in front of the museum are a copy of those found in Hallstatt's prehistoric mine—the original stairs are more than 2,500 years old. For thousands of years, people have been leaching salt out of this mountain. A brine spring sprung here, attracting Bronze Age people in about 1600 B.C. Later, they dug tunnels to mine the rock (which was 70 percent salt), dissolved it into a brine, and distilled out the salt—precious for preserving meat. For a look at early salt-mining implements and the town's story, visit the museum (described later).

Across from the TI, Pension Hallberg has a quirky hallway full of Nazi paraphernalia and other stuff found on the lake bed (€1). Only recently did local divers realize that, for centuries, the lake had been Hallstatt's garbage can. If something was *kaputt*, locals would just toss it into the lake. In 1945, Nazi medals decorating German and Austrian war heroes suddenly became dangerous to own. Throughout the former Third Reich, hard-earned medals floated down to lonely lake beds, including Hallstatt's.

Under the TI is the "Post Partner"—a government-funded attempt to turn inefficient post offices into something more viable (selling souvenirs, renting bikes, and employing people with disabilities who otherwise wouldn't work). The *Fischerei* provides the town with its cherished fresh lake fish. The county allows two commercial fishermen on the lake. They spread their nets each morning and sell their catch here to town restaurants, or to any locals cooking up a special dinner (Mon-Fri 9:00-12:00, closed Sat-Sun).

• *Nearby, still on Museum Square, find the...*

Dachstein Sport Shop: During a renovation project, the builders dug down and hit a Celtic and ancient Roman settlement. Peek through the glass pavement on the covered porch to see where the Roman street level was. If the shop is open, pop in and go downstairs (free). You'll walk on Roman flagstones and see the small gutter that channeled water to power an ancient hammer mill (used to pound iron into usable shapes). In prehistoric times, people lived near the mines. Romans were the first Hallstatt lakeside settlers. The store's owners are committed to sharing Hallstatt's fascinating history, and often display old town paintings and folk art.

• *From this square, the first right (after the bank) leads up a few stairs to...*

Dr.-Morton-Weg: House #26A dates from 1597. Follow the lane uphill to the left past more old houses. Until 1890, this was the town's main drag, and the lake lapped at the lower doors of these houses. Therefore, many main entrances were via the attic, from this level. Enjoy this back-street view of town. Just after the arch, near #133, check out the old tools hanging outside the workshop, and the piece of wooden piping. It's a section taken from the 25-mile wooden pipeline that carried salt brine from Hallstatt to Ebensee. This was in place from 1595 until the last generation, when the last stretch of wood was replaced by plastic piping. At the pipe, enjoy the lake view and climb down the stairs. From lake level, look back up at the striking traditional architecture (the fine woodwork on the left was recently rebuilt after a fire; parts of the old house on the right date to medieval times).

• *Your tour is finished. From here, you have boat rentals, the salt-mine*

*tour, the town museum, and the Catholic church (with its bone chapel)
all within a few minutes' walk.*

Sights in Hallstatt

▲▲**Catholic Church and Bone Chapel**—Hallstatt's Catholic
church overlooks the town from above. From near the main boat
dock, hike up the covered wooden stairway and follow the *Kath.
Kirche* signs. The lovely church has twin altars. The one on the left
was made by town artists in 1897. The one on the right is more
historic—dedicated in 1515 to Mary, who's flanked by St. Barbara
(on right, patron of miners) and St. Catherine (on left, patron of
foresters—a lot of wood was needed to fortify the many miles of
tunnels, and to boil the brine to distill the salt).

Behind the church, in the well-tended graveyard, is the 12th-
century Chapel of St. Michael (even older than the church). Its
bone chapel—or charnel house *(Beinhaus)*—contains more than
600 painted skulls. Each skull has been lovingly named, dated,
and decorated (skulls with dark, thick garlands are oldest—18th
century; those with flowers are more recent—19th century). Space
was so limited in this cemetery that bones had only 12 peaceful, buried years here before making way for the freshly dead.
Many of the dug-up bones and skulls ended up in this chapel.
They stopped this practice in the 1960s, about the same time the
Catholic Church began permitting cremation. But one woman
(who died in 1983) managed to sneak her skull in later (dated 1995,
under the cross, with the gold tooth). The skulls on the books are
those of priests.

Cost and Hours: €1.50, free English flier, daily May-Sept
10:00-18:00, Oct 10:00-16:00, closed Nov-April, tel. 06134/8279.

▲**Hallstatt Museum**—This pricey but high-quality museum tells
the story of Hallstatt. It focuses on the Hallstatt Era (800-400
B.C.), when this village was the salt-mining hub of a culture that
spread from France to the Balkans. Back then, Celtic tribes dug
for precious salt, and Hallstatt was, as its name means, the "place
of salt." While its treasures are the countless artifacts excavated
from prehistoric gravesites around the mine, you'll get the whole
gamut—with 26 displays on everything from the region's flora and
fauna to local artists and the surge in Hallstatt tourism during
the Romantic Age. Everything is labeled in English, and the ring
binders have translations of the longer texts.

Cost and Hours: €7.50, May-Sept daily 10:00-18:00, shorter
hours off-season, closed Mon-Tue Nov-March, adjacent to TI at
Seestrasse 56, tel. 06134/828-015, www.museum-hallstatt.at. On
Thursdays in summer, when candlelit boats run, the museum stays
open until 20:00 (see "Nightlife in Hallstatt," later).

▲**Lake Trip**—For a quick boat trip, you can ride the *Stefanie* across the lake and back for €4.40. It stops at the tiny Hallstatt train station for 30 minutes (note return time in the boat's window), giving you time to walk to a hanging bridge (ask the captain to point you to the *Hängebrücke*—HENG-eh-brick-eh—a 10-minute lakeside stroll to the left). Longer lake tours are also available (€8/50 minutes, €9.50/75 minutes, sporadic schedules—especially off-season—so check chalkboards by boat docks for today's times). Those into relaxation can rent a sleepy electric motorboat to enjoy town views from the water.

▲**Salt-Mine Tour**—If you have yet to tour a salt mine, consider visiting Hallstatt's, which claims to be the oldest in the world. To get to the mine, take the funicular railway, which starts in the Lahn, close to the bus stop and Lahn boat dock.

After riding the funicular above town, you'll hike 10 minutes to the mine (past excavation sites of many prehistoric tombs and a glass case with 2,500-year-old bones—but there's little to actually see). Report back 10 minutes before the tour time on your ticket, check your bag, and put on old miners' clothes. Then hike 200 yards higher in your funny outfit to meet your guide, who escorts your group down a tunnel dug in 1719. Inside the mountain, you'll watch a slide show, follow your guide through several caverns as you learn about mining techniques over the last 7,000 years, see a silly laser show on a glassy subterranean lake, peek at a few waxy cavemen with pickaxes, and ride the train out. The highlight for most is sliding down two banisters (the second one is longer and ends with a flash for an automatic souvenir photo that clocks your speed—see how you did compared to the rest of your group after the tour).

The presentation is very low-tech, as the mining company owns all three mine tours in the area and sees little reason to invest in the experience when they can simply mine the tourists. While the tour is mostly in German, the guide is required to speak English if you ask...so ask. Be sure to dress for the constant 47-degree temperature.

Cost and Hours: €24 combo-ticket includes mine and funicular round-trip, €18 for mine tour only, buy all tickets at funicular station—note the time and tour number on your ticket, daily May-mid-Sept 9:00-16:00, mid-Sept-Oct 9:00-14:30, later funicular departures miss the last tour of the day, closed Nov-April, no children under age 4, arrive early or late to avoid summer crowds, tel. 06132/200-2400, www.salzwelten.at.

Funicular: You can also just take the funicular without going on the mine tour (€7 one-way, €12 round-trip, 4/hour, daily May-mid-Sept 9:00-18:00, mid-Sept-Oct 9:00-16:30, closed Nov-April).

Salzkammergut

HALLSTATT

Returning to Hallstatt: If you skip the funicular down, the scenic 40-minute hike back into town is (with strong knees) a joy. At the base of the funicular, notice the train tracks leading to the Erbstollen tunnel entrance. This lowest of the salt tunnels goes many miles into the mountain, where a shaft connects it to the tunnels you just explored. Today, the salty brine from these tunnels flows 25 miles through the world's oldest pipeline—made of wood until quite recently—to the huge modern salt works (next to the highway) at Ebensee.

▲**Local Hikes**—Mountain-lovers, hikers, and spelunkers who use Hallstatt as their home base keep busy for days (ask the TI for ideas). A good, short, and easy walk is the two-hour round-trip up the Echern Valley to the Waldbachstrub waterfall and back: From the parking lot, follow signs to the salt mines, then follow the little wooden signs marked *Echerntalweg*. With a car, consider hiking around nearby Altaussee (flat, 3-hour hike) or along Grundlsee to Toplitzsee. Regular buses connect Hallstatt with Gosausee for a pleasant hour-long walk around that lake. Or consider walking nine miles halfway around Lake Hallstatt via the town of Steeg (boat to train station, walk left along lake and past idyllic farmsteads, returning to Hallstatt along the old salt trail, *Soleleitungsweg*); for a shorter hike, walk to Steeg along either side of the lake, and catch the train from Steeg back to Hallstatt's station. The TI can also recommend a great two-day hike with an overnight in a nearby mountain hut.

Biking—The best two bike rides take nearly the same routes as the hikes listed previously: up the Echern Valley, and around the lake (bikers do better going via Obertraun along the new lakeside bike path—start with a ride on the *Stefanie*). There's no public bike rental in Hallstatt, but some hotels have loaner bikes for guests.

Near Hallstatt

▲▲Dachstein Mountain Cable Car and Caves

From Obertraun, three miles beyond Hallstatt on the main road (or directly across the lake as the crow flies), a cable car glides up to the Dachstein Plateau. Along the way, you can hop off to tour two different caves: the refreshingly chilly Giant Ice Caves and the less-impressive Mammoth Caves.

Getting to Obertraun: The cable car to Dachstein leaves from the outskirts of Obertraun. To reach the cable car from Hallstatt, the handiest and cheapest option is the bus (€1.70, 5-6/day, leaves from Lahn boat dock, drops you directly at cable-car station). Romantics can take the boat from Hallstatt's main boat dock to Obertraun (€5.50, 5/day July-Aug, 3/day in June and Sept, 30 minutes, www.hallstattschifffahrt.at)—but it's a 40-minute hike from there to the lift station. The impatient can consider hitching a ride—virtually all cars leaving Hallstatt to the south will pass through Obertraun in a few minutes.

Returning to Hallstatt: Plan to leave by midafternoon. The last bus from the cable-car station back to Hallstatt (at 17:05 in summer) inconveniently leaves before the last cable car down—if you miss the bus, try getting a ride from a fellow cable-car passenger. Otherwise, you can either call a taxi (€13, ask cable-car staff for help), or simply walk back along the lakefront (about one hour).

Dachstein Cable Car—From Obertraun, this mighty gondola goes in three stages high up the Dachstein Plateau—crowned by Dachstein, the highest mountain in the Salzkammergut (9,800 ft). The first segment stops at **Schönbergalm** (4,500 ft, runs May-late Oct), which has a mountain restaurant and two huge caves (described next). The second segment goes to the summit of

Krippenstein (6,600 ft, runs mid-May-late Oct). The third segment descends to **Gjaidalm** (5,800 ft, runs mid-June-late Oct), where several hikes begin. For a quick high-country experience, Krippenstein is better than Gjaidalm.

From **Krippenstein**, you'll survey a scrubby, limestone, karstic landscape (which absorbs, through its many cracks, the rainfall that ultimately carves all those caves), with 360-degree views of the surrounding mountains.

Cost and Hours: Round-trip cable-car ride to Schönbergalm and the caves-€17, to Krippenstein and Gjaidalm-€25; cheaper family rates available, last cable car back down usually at about 17:00, tel. 06131/50140, www.dachstein-salzkammergut.com.

Combo-Ticket Tips: The several combo-tickets available for the cable car and caves generally won't save you any money over buying individual tickets. But if you're gung-ho enough to want to visit one or both caves, and plan to ride the cable car farther up the mountain, the €35 same-day combo-ticket makes sense (covers the cable car all the way to Gjaidalm and back, as well as entry to both caves).

Giant Ice Caves (Riesen-Eishöhle)—Located near the Schönbergalm cable-car stop (4,500 ft), these caves were discovered in 1910. Today, guides lead tours in German and English on an hour-long, half-mile hike through an eerie, icy, subterranean world, passing limestone canyons the size of subway stations.

At the Schönbergalm lift station, report to the ticket window to get your cave appointment. Drop by the little free museum near the lift station—in a local-style wood cabin designed to support 200 tons of snow—to see the cave-system model, exhibits about its exploration, and info about life in the caves. Then hike 10 minutes from the station up to the cave entry. The temperature is just above freezing, and although the 700 steps help keep you warm, you'll want to bring a sweater. The limestone caverns, carved by rushing water, are named for scenes from Wagner's operas—the favorite of the mountaineers who first came here. If you're nervous, note that the iron oxide covering the ceiling takes 5,000 years to form. Things are very stable. Allow 1.5 hours total from the station.

Cost and Hours: €27, €32 combo-ticket with Mammoth Caves, €35 combo-ticket covers the cable car up to Gjaidalm and entry to both caves, open May-late Oct, hour-long tours start at 9:20, last tour at 15:30, stay in front and assert yourself to get English information, tel. 06131/51310.

Mammoth Caves (Mammuthöhle)—While huge and well-promoted, these are much less interesting than the ice caves and—for most—not worth the time. Of the 30-mile limestone labyrinth excavated so far, you'll walk a half-mile with a German-speaking guide.

Cost and Hours: €27, €32 combo-ticket with ice caves, €35 combo-ticket covers the cable car up to Gjaidalm and entry to both caves, open May-late Oct, hour-long tours in English and German 10:15-14:30, entrance a 10-minute hike from lift station.

Summer Luge Rides (Sommerrodelbahnen) on the Hallstatt-Salzburg Road

If you're driving between Salzburg and Hallstatt, you'll pass two luge rides operated by the same company (www.rodelbahnen.at). Each is a ski lift that drags you backward up the hill as you sit on your go-cart. At the top, you ride the cart down the winding metal course. It's easy: Push to go, pull to stop, take your hands off your stick and you get hurt.

Each course is just off the road with easy parking. The ride up and down takes about 15 minutes. The one in **Fuschl am See** (closest to Salzburg, look for *Sommerrodelbahn* sign) is half as long and cheaper (€4.30/ride, 1,970 ft, tel. 06226/8452). The one in **Strobl** near Wolfgangsee (look for *Riesenschutzbahn* sign) is a double course, more scenic with grand lake views (€6.40/ride, €43/10 rides, 4,265 ft, each track is the same speed, tel. 06137/7085). Courses are open May through October from 10:00 to 18:00—but generally closed in bad weather.

Nightlife in Hallstatt

Locals would laugh at the thought. But if you want some action after dinner, you do have a few options: **Gasthaus zur Mühle** is a youth hostel with a rustic sports-bar ambience in its restaurant when drinks replace the food (open late, closed Tue Sept-mid-May, run by Ferdinand). Or, for your late-night drink, savor the Market Square from the trendy little pub called **Ruth Zimmermann,** where locals congregate with soft music, a good selection of drinks, two small rooms, and tables on the square (daily May-Sept 10:00-2:00 in the morning, Oct-April 11:00-2:00, mobile 0664/501-5631). From late July to late August, **candlelit boat rides** leave at 20:30 on Thursday evenings (€13.50, €16 combo-ticket with Hallstatt Museum).

Sleeping in Hallstatt

Hallstatt's TI can almost always find you a room (either in town or at B&Bs and small hotels outside of town—which are more likely to have rooms available and come with easy parking). Drivers, remember to ask if your hotel has in-town parking when you book your room.

Mid-July and August can be tight. Early August is worst.

Sleep Code

(€1 = about $1.40, country code: 43, area code: 06134)
S = Single, **D** = Double/Twin, **T** = Triple, **Q** = Quad, **b** = bathroom, **s** = shower only. Unless otherwise noted, credit cards are accepted, English is spoken, and breakfast is included.

To help you sort easily through these listings, I've divided the rooms into three categories, based on the price for a standard double room with bath:

$$$ Higher Priced—Most rooms €90 or more.
 $$ Moderately Priced—Most rooms between €60-90.
  $ Lower Priced—Most rooms €60 or less.

Prices can change without notice; verify the hotel's current rates online or by email. For other updates, see www.ricksteves.com/update.

Hallstatt is not the place to splurge—some of the best rooms are *Gästezimmer,* just as nice and modern as rooms in bigger hotels, at half the cost. In summer, a double bed in a private home costs about €50 with breakfast. It's hard to get a one-night advance reservation (try calling the TI for help). But if you drop in and they have a spot, one-nighters are welcome. Prices include breakfast, lots of stairs, and a silent night. *"Zimmer mit Aussicht?"* (TSIMmer mit OWS-zeekt) means "Room with view?"—worth asking for. Unlike many businesses in town, the cheaper places don't take credit cards.

As most rooms here are in old buildings with well-cared-for wooden interiors, dripping laundry is a no-no at Hallstatt pensions. Be especially considerate when hanging laundry over anything but tile—if you must wash larger clothing items here, ask your host about using their clothesline.

$$$ Heritage Hotel, next to the main boat dock, is the town's fanciest place to stay. It has 34 rooms with modern furnishings in a lakeside main building with an elevator; uphill are another 20 rooms in two separate buildings for those willing to climb stairs for better views (Sb-€90, Db-€150, show this book and ask for best Rick Steves price, free sauna, free cable Internet in rooms and Wi-Fi in lobby, laundry service-€13, parking-€10/day, Landungsplatz 120, tel. 06134/20036, fax 06134/20042, www.heritagehotel.at, info@heritagehotel.at).

$$$ Hotel Grüner Baum, on the other side of the church from the main boat dock, has a great location, fronting Market Square and overlooking the lake in back. The owner, Monika, moved here from Vienna and renovated this stately   but still a bit creaky—old hotel with urban taste. Its 22 rooms are huge, each with a separate living area and ancient hardwood floors, but you may not need so much space and the high price that comes with it (suite-like Db-€140-210, price depends on view, discount with this book, family rooms, Internet access in restaurant, laundry service-€13, closed in Nov, 20 yards from boat dock, tel. 06134/82630, fax 06134/826-344, www.gruenerbaum.cc, contact@gruener baum.cc).

$$$ Bräugasthof Hallstatt is like a museum filled with antique furniture and ancient family portraits. This former brewery, now a good restaurant, rents eight clean, cozy upstairs rooms. It's run by Virena and her daughter, Virena. Six of the rooms have gorgeous little lakeview balconies (Sb-€55, Db-€98, Tb-€140, free parking, just past TI along lake at Seestrasse 120, tel. 06134/8221, fax 06134/82214, www.brauhaus-lobisser.com, info@brauhaus -lobisser.com, Lobisser family).

$$$ Gasthof Zauner is run by a friendly mountaineer, Herr Zauner, whose family has owned it since 1893. The 13 pricey, pine-flavored rooms near the inland end of Market Square are decorated with sturdy alpine-inspired furniture (sealed not with lacquer but with beeswax, to let the wood breathe out its calming scent). Lederhosen-clad Herr Zauner recounts tales of local mountaineering lore, including his own impressive ascents (Sb-€60, Db-€107, lakeview Db-€112, cheaper mid-Oct-April, Internet access in office, closed Nov-early Dec, Marktplatz 51, tel. 06134/8246, fax 06134/82468, www.zauner.hallstatt.net, zauner@hallstatt.at).

$$$ Gasthof Simony is a well-worn, grandmotherly, 12-room place on the square, with a lake view, balconies, ancient beds, creaky wood floors, slippery rag rugs, antique furniture, and a lakefront garden for swimming. Reserve in advance, and call if arriving late (S-€35, D-€55, Ds-€65, Db-€95, third person-€30-35 extra, cash only, kayaks for guests, Marktplatz 105, tel. & fax 06134/8231, www.gasthof-simony.at, info@gasthof-simony .at, Susanna Scheutz and family).

$$ Pension Sarstein is a big, flower-bedecked house right on the water on the edge of the old center. Its seven renovated rooms are bright, and all have lakeview balconies. You can swim from its plush and inviting lakeside garden (D-€50, Db-€65, Tb-€85; apartments with kitchen: Db-€65, Tb-€75, Qb-€85, apartment prices don't include breakfast; €3 extra per person for 1-night stay, cash only, pay Internet access, 200 yards to the right of the main boat dock at Gosaumühlstrasse 83, tel. 06134/8217, www.pension -sarstein.at.tf, pension.sarstein@aon.at, helpful Isabelle and Klaus Fischer).

$$ Gasthof Pension Grüner Anger, in the Lahn near the bus station and base of the funicular, is practical and modern.

It's big and quiet, with 11 rooms and no creaks or squeaks. There are mountain views, but none of the lake (Sb-€43-48, Db-€76-86, third person-€15, price depends on season, non-smoking, free Internet access and Wi-Fi, free loaner bikes, free parking, Lahn 10, tel. 06134/8397, fax 06134/83974, www.anger.hallstatt.net, anger @aon.at, Sulzbacher family). If arriving by train, have the boat captain call Herr Sulzbacher, who will pick you up at the dock. They run a good-value restaurant, too, with discounts for guests.

$ **Helga Lenz** rents two fine *Gästezimmer* a steep five-minute climb above Dr.-Morton-Weg (look for the green *Zimmer* sign). This large, sprawling, woodsy house has a nifty garden perch, wins the "Best View" award, and is ideal for those who sleep well in tree houses and don't mind the steps up from town (Db-€50, Tb-€75, €2 more per person for one-night stay, cash only, family room, closed Nov-March, Hallberg 17, tel. 06134/8508, www.hallstatt .net/lenz, haus-lenz@aon.at).

$ Two *Gästezimmer* are a few minutes' stroll south of the center, just past the bus stop/parking lot and over the bridge. **Haus Trausner** has three clean, bright, new-feeling rooms adjacent to the Trausner family home (Ds/Db-€50, 2-night minimum for reservations, cash only, breakfast comes to your room, free parking, Lahnstrasse 27, tel. 06134/8710, trausner1@aon.at, charming Maria Trausner makes you want to settle right in). **Herta Höll** rents out three spacious, modern rooms on the ground floor of her riverside house crawling with kids (Db-€50, apartment for up to five-€60-90, €2 more per person for one-night stay, cash only, free parking, free cable Internet, Salzbergstrasse 45, tel. 06134/8531, fax 06134/825-533, frank.hoell@aon.at).

$ *Hostel:* **Gasthaus zur Mühle Jugendherberge,** below the waterfall and along the gushing town stream, has 46 of the cheapest good beds in town (bed in 3- to 8-bed coed dorms-€14, twin D-€28, family quads, sheets-€4 extra, breakfast-€5, big lockers with a €15 deposit, closed Nov, reception closed Tue Sept-mid-May—so arrange in advance if arriving on Tue, below P1 tunnel parking lot, Kirchenweg 36, tel. & fax 06134/8318, toeroe-f @hallstatturlaub.at, Ferdinand Törö). It's also popular for its great, inexpensive pizza (described below).

Eating in Hallstatt

In this town, when someone is happy to see you, they'll often say, "Can I cook you a fish?" While everyone cooks the typical Austrian fare, fish is your best bet here. *Reinanke* (whitefish) is caught wild out of Lake Hallstatt and served the same day. *Saibling* (lake trout) is also tasty and costs less. You can enjoy good food inexpensively, with delightful lakeside settings. Restaurants in Hallstatt tend to have unreliable hours and close early on slow nights, so don't wait too long to get dinner. Most of the eateries listed here are run by recommended hotels.

Restaurant Bräugasthof, on the edge of the old center, is a good value. The indoor dining room is cozy in cool weather. On a balmy evening, its great lakeside tables offer the best ambience in town—you can feed the swans while your trout is being cooked (€10-14 three-course daily specials, daily May-Oct 11:30-late, closed Nov-April, Seestrasse 120, tel. 06134/8221).

Hotel Grüner Baum is a more upscale option, with elegant service at tables overlooking the lake inside and out (€15-21 main dishes, daily Dec-Oct 8:00-22:00, closed Nov, at bottom of Market Square, tel. 06134/8263).

Gasthof Simony's Restaurant am See serves Austrian cuisine on yet another gorgeous lakeside terrace, as well as indoors (€12-16 main courses, Thu-Tue 11:30-20:00, until 21:00 June-Sept and on winter weekends, closed Wed, tel. 06134/20646).

Gasthaus zur Mühle serves the best pizza in town. Chow down cheap and hearty here with fun-loving locals and the youth-hostel crowd (€7 pizza, lots of Italian, some Austrian, Wed-Mon in summer 16:00-21:00, closed Tue, Kirchenweg 36, tel. 06134/8318, Ferdinand).

Strand Café, a local favorite, is in the Lahn, near Badeinsel, the town beach (€8-15 main courses, plenty of alcohol, Tue-Sun April-mid-Sept 10:00-21:00, mid-Sept-Oct 11:30-20:00, closed Mon and Nov-March, great garden setting on the lake, Seelände 102, tel. 06134/8234).

Picnics and Cheap Eats: The **Zauner** bakery/butcher/grocer, great for picnickers, makes fresh sandwiches to go (Tue-Fri 7:00-12:00 & 15:00-18:00, Sat and Mon 7:00-12:00, closed Sun, uphill to the left from Market Square). The only **supermarket** is Konsum, in the Lahn at the bus stop (Mon-Fri 7:30-12:00 & 15:00-18:00, Sat 7:30-12:00, closed Sun, July-Aug no midday break and until 17:00 on Sat, Sept-April closed Wed). **Snack stands** near the main boat dock and the Lahn boat dock sell *Döner Kebab* and so on for €3 (tables and fine lakeside picnic options nearby).

Hallstatt Connections

By Public Transportation
From Hallstatt by Train: Most travelers leaving Hallstatt are going to Salzburg or Vienna. In either case, you need to catch the shuttle boat (€2.20, departs 15 minutes before every train) to the little Hallstatt train station across the lake, and then ride 1.5 hours to **Attnang-Puchheim** (hourly from about 7:00 to 18:00). Trains are synchronized, so after a short wait in Attnang-Puchheim,

you'll catch your onward connection to **Salzburg** (50 minutes) or **Vienna** (2.5 hours). The Hallstatt station has no staff or ticket machines, but you can buy tickets from the conductor without a penalty. In town, your hotel or the TI can help you find schedule information, or check www.oebb.at. Train info: tel. 051-717 (to get an operator, dial 2, then 2).

By Bus: The bus ride from Hallstatt to **Salzburg** is cheaper and more scenic than the train, and only slightly slower. You can still start off from Hallstatt by rail, taking the boat across the lake to the station and then the train toward Attnang-Puchheim—but get off after about 20 minutes in **Bad Ischl,** where you catch bus #150 to Salzburg (€8.80, Mon-Fri almost hourly, less Sat-Sun).

Alternatively, you can reach Bad Ischl by bus from the Hallstatt bus stop (€4.20, change in Gosaumühle), and then catch bus #150 to Salzburg. The Hallstatt TI has a schedule. In Salzburg, bus #150 stops at Hofwirt and Mirabellplatz (convenient to Linzergasse hotels) before ending at the Salzburg train station.

HALLSTATT

BELGIUM

BRUGES

With pointy gilded architecture, stay-a-while cafés, vivid time-tunnel art, and dreamy canals dotted with swans, Bruges is a heavy-weight sightseeing destination, as well as a joy. Where else can you ride a bike along a canal, munch mussels and wash them down with the world's best beer, savor heavenly chocolate, and see Flemish Primitives and a Michelangelo, all within 300 yards of a bell tower that jingles every 15 minutes? And do it all without worrying about a language barrier?

The town is Brugge (BROO-ghah) in Flemish, and Bruges (broozh) in French and English. Its name comes from the Viking word for wharf. Right from the start, Bruges was a trading center. In the 11th century, the city grew wealthy on the cloth trade.

By the 14th century, Bruges' population was 35,000, as large as London's. As the middleman in the sea trade between northern and southern Europe, it was one of the biggest cities in the world and an economic powerhouse. In addition, Bruges had become the most important cloth market in northern Europe.

In the 15th century, while England and France were slugging it out in the Hundred Years' War, Bruges was the favored residence of the powerful Dukes of Burgundy—and at peace. Commerce and the arts boomed. The artists Jan van Eyck and Hans Memling had studios here.

But by the 16th century, the harbor had silted up and the economy had collapsed. The Burgundian court left, Belgium became a minor Habsburg possession, and Bruges' Golden Age abruptly ended. For generations, Bruges was known as a mysterious and dead city. In the 19th century, a new port, Zeebrugge, brought renewed vitality to the area. And in the 20th century, tourists discovered the town.

Today, Bruges prospers because of tourism: It's a uniquely well-preserved Gothic city and a handy gateway to Europe. It's no secret, but even with the crowds, it's the kind of place where you don't mind being a tourist.

Bruges' ultimate sight is the town itself, and the best way to enjoy it is to get lost on the back streets, away from the lace shops and ice-cream stands.

Planning Your Time

Bruges needs at least two nights and a full, well-organized day. Even non-shoppers enjoy browsing here, and the Belgian love of life makes a hectic itinerary seem a little senseless. With one day—other than a Monday, when the three museums are closed—the speedy visitor could do the Bruges blitz described below:

9:30	Climb the bell tower on the Markt (Market Square).
10:00	Tour the sights on Burg Square.
11:30	Tour the Groeninge Museum.
13:00	Eat lunch and buy chocolates.
14:00	Take a short canal cruise.
14:30	Visit the Church of Our Lady and see Michelangelo's *Madonna and Child*.
15:00	Tour the Memling Museum.
16:00	Catch the De Halve Maan Brewery tour (note that their last tour runs at 15:00 in winter on weekdays).
17:00	Relax in the Begijnhof courtyard.
18:00	Ride a bike around the quiet back streets of town or take a horse-and-buggy tour.
20:00	Lose the tourists and find dinner.

If this schedule seems insane, skip the bell tower and the brewery—or stay another day.

Orientation to Bruges

The tourist's Bruges—and you'll be sharing it—is less than one square mile, contained within a canal (the former moat). Nearly everything of interest and importance is within a convenient cobbled swath between the train station and the Markt (Market Square; a 20-minute walk). Many of my quiet, charming, recommended accommodations lie just beyond the Markt.

Tourist Information

The main tourist office, called **In&Uit** ("In and Out"), is in the big, red concert hall on the square called 't Zand (daily 10:00-18:00, take a number from the touch-screen machines and wait, 't Zand 34, tel. 050-444-646, www.bruggc.bc). The other TI is at the train

BRUGES

Bruges

SEE HOTEL & RESTAURANT
DETAIL MAPS

BRUGES

Sights & Services

1 In&Uit Tourist Info
(in Concert Hall)
2 De Halve Maan
Brewery Tour
3 Dumon Chocolate
4 The Chocolate Line
5 Confiserie De Clerck
6 Choco-Story: The
Chocolate Museum
7 Friet Museum
8 Internet Café
9 Bike Rentals (5)
10 City Minibus Tours

Accommodations & Restaurants

11 Hotel Egmond
12 Hotel 't Keizershof
13 To Waterside B&B
14 To B&B AM/PM
15 Snuffel Backpacker Hostel
16 Bistro de Bekoring

P PARKING
B BOAT TOURS
B BUS
⚓ VIEW

TO
OSTENDE

'T
ZAND

CONCERT
HALL

TO
OSTENDE

TO
OSTENDE
VIA
FREEWAY

R-30

¼ MILE

400 METERS

STATIONS-
PLEIN

TRAIN STATION

TO
BRUSSELS

station (Mon-Fri 10:00-17:00, Sat-Sun 10:00-14:00).

The TIs sell the €2.50 *Love Bruges Visitors' Guide,* which comes with a map (costs €0.50 if bought separately), a few well-described self-guided walking tours, and listings of all the sights and services (free with Brugge City Card). You can also pick up a free monthly English-language program called *events@brugge* and a free, fun map/guide "made by locals for young travelers." The TIs have information on train schedules and tours (see "Tours in Bruges," later). Many hotels give out free maps with more detail than the map the TIs sell.

Arrival in Bruges

By Train: Coming in by train, you'll see the bell tower that marks the main square (Markt, the center of town). Upon arrival, stop by the train station TI to pick up the *Love Bruges Visitors' Guide* (with map). The station has ATMs and lockers (€3-4).

The best way to get to the town center is by **bus.** Buses #1-9, #11-17, and #25 go to the Markt (all marked *Centrum*). Simply hop on, pay €1.60 (€1.20 if you buy in advance at Lijnwinkel shop just outside the train station), and in four minutes, you're there (get off at third stop—either Markt or Wollestraat). Buses #4 and #14 continue to the northeast part of town (to the windmills and recommended accommodations on and near Carmersstraat, stop: Gouden Handstraat). If you arrive after 20:30, when the daytime bus routes end, you can still take the bus, but the "evening line" buses run much less frequently (buses marked *Avondlijn Centrum, Avondlijn Noord*—#91, *Avondlijn Oost*—#92, and *Avondlijn Zuid*—#93 all go to the Markt).

The **taxi** fare from the train station to most hotels is about €8.

It's a 20-minute **walk** from the station to the center—no fun with your luggage. If you want to walk to the Markt, cross the busy street and canal in front of the station, head up Oostmeers, and turn right on Zwidzandstraat. You can rent a **bike** at the station for the duration of your stay, but other bike rental shops are closer to the center (see "Helpful Hints," below).

By Car: Park in front of the train station in the handy two-story garage for just €2.50 for 24 hours. The parking fee includes a round-trip bus ticket into town and back for everyone in your car. There are pricier underground parking garages at the square called 't Zand and around town (€9/day, all of them well-marked). Paid parking on the street in Bruges is limited to four hours. Driving in town is very complicated because of the one-way system. The best plan for drivers: Park at the train station, visit the TI at the station, and rent a bike or catch a bus into town.

Helpful Hints

Blue Monday: In Bruges, nearly all museums are open Tuesday through Sunday year-round from 9:30 to 17:00 and are closed on Monday. If you're in Bruges on a Monday, you can still enjoy a bell-tower climb on the Markt, Begijnhof, Church of Our Lady, the De Halve Maan Brewery Tour, Basilica of the Holy Blood, City Hall's Gothic Room, and chocolate shops and museum. You can also join a boat, bus, or walking tour, or rent a bike and pedal into the countryside.

Museum Passes: The 't Zand TI and city museums sell a **museum combo-ticket** (any five museums for €15, valid for 3 days). Because the Groeninge and Memling museums cost €8 each, art lovers will save money with this pass.

    The **Brugge City Card** is a more extensive pass covering entry to 22 museums, including all the major sights (€34/48 hours, €39/72 hours, sold at TIs and many hotels). If you'll be doing some serious sightseeing, this card can save you money. Its long list of bonuses and discounts includes a free canal boat ride (March-Nov), a visitors' guide, and discounts on bike rental, parking, and some performances.

Market Days: Bruges hosts markets on Wednesday morning (on the Markt) and Saturday morning ('t Zand). On good-weather Saturdays, Sundays, and public holidays, a flea market hops along Dijver in front of the Groeninge Museum. The Fish Market sells souvenirs and seafood Tuesday through Saturday mornings until 13:00.

Shopping: Shops are generally open from 10:00 to 18:00. Grocery stores are usually closed on Sunday. The main shopping street, Steenstraat, stretches from the Markt to 't Zand Square. The **Hema** department store is at Steenstraat 73 (Mon-Sat 9:00-18:00, closed Sun).

Internet Access: Punjeb Internet Shop, just a block off the Markt, is the most central of the city's many "telephone shops" offering Internet access (€1.50/30 minutes, €2.50/hour, daily 9:00-20:00, Philipstockstraat 4). **Bean Around the World** is a cozy coffeehouse with imported Yankee snacks and free Wi-Fi for customers (€1/15 minutes on their computers, Thu-Mon 10:00-19:00, Wed 11:30-19:00, closed Tue, Genthof 5, tel. 050-703-572, run by American expat Olene).

Post Office: It's on the Markt near the bell tower (Mon-Fri 9:00-18:00, Sat 9:30-15:00, closed Sun, tel. 050-331-411).

Laundry: Bruges has three self-service launderettes, each a five-minute walk from the center; ask your hotelier for the nearest one.

Bike Rental: Bruges Bike Rental is central and cheap, with friendly service and long hours (€3.50/hour, €5/2 hours, €7/4

BRUGES

hours, €10/day, show this book to get student rate, no deposit required—just ID, daily 10:00-22:00, free city maps and child seats, behind the far-out iron facade at Niklaas Desparsstraat 17, tel. 050-616-108, Bilal). **Fietsen Popelier Bike Rental** is also good (€4/hour, €8/4 hours, €12/day, 24-hour day is OK if your hotel has a safe place to store bike, no deposit required, daily 10:00-19:00, sometimes open later in summer, free Damme map, Mariastraat 26, tel. 050-343-262). **Koffieboontje Bike Rental** is just under the bell tower on the Markt (€4/hour, €9/day, €20/day for tandem, confirm that you're getting Rick Steves price, daily 9:00-22:00, free city maps and child seats, Hallestraat 4, tel. 050-338-027).

Other rental places include the less-central **De Ketting** (cheap at €6/day, Mon-Fri 9:00-12:15 & 13:30-18:30 except Mon opens at 10:00, Sat 9:30-12:15, closed Sun, Gentpoortstraat 23, tel. 050-344-196, www.deketting.be) and **Fietspunt Brugge** at the train station (€9.50/day, €6.50/half-day after 14:00, €13 deposit, Mon-Fri 7:00-19:30, closed Sat-Sun, just outside the station and to the left as you exit, tel. 050-302-329).

Best Town View: The bell tower overlooking the Markt rewards those who climb it with the ultimate town view.

Getting Around Bruges

Most of the city is easily walkable, but you may want to take the bus or taxi between the train station and the city center at the Markt (especially if you have heavy luggage).

By Bus: A bus ticket is good for an hour (€1.20 if you buy in advance at Lijnwinkel shop just outside the train station, or €1.60 on the bus). While you can buy various day passes, there's really no need to buy one for your visit. Nearly all city buses go directly from the train station to the Markt and fan out from there; they then return to the Markt and go back to the train station. Note that buses returning to the train station from the Markt also leave from the library bus stop, a block off the square on nearby Kuiperstraat (every 5 minutes). Your key: Use buses that say either *Station* or *Centrum*.

By Taxi: You'll find taxi stands at the station and on the Markt (€8/first 2 km; to get a cab in the center, call 050-334-444 or 050-333-881).

Tours in Bruges

Bruges by Boat—The most relaxing and scenic (though not informative) way to see this city of canals is by boat, with the captain narrating. The city carefully controls this standard tourist activity, so the many companies all offer essentially the same thing: a 30-minute route (roughly 4/hour, daily 10:00-17:00), a price of €7 (cash only), and narration in three or four languages. Qualitative differences are because of individual guides, not companies. Always let them know you speak English to ensure you'll understand the spiel. Two companies give the group-rate discount to individuals with this book: Boten Stael (just over the canal from Memling Museum at Katelijnestraat 4, tel. 050-332-771) and Gruuthuse (Nieuwstraat 11, opposite Groeninge Museum, tel. 050-333-393).

Bruges by Bike—QuasiMundo Bike Tours leads daily five-mile English-language bike tours around the city (€25, discount with this book, 2.5 hours, departs March-Oct at 10:00, in Nov only with good weather, no tours Dec-Feb). For more details and contact info, see their listing under "Near Bruges," later.

City Minibus Tour—City Tour Bruges gives a rolling overview of the town in an 18-seat, two-skylight minibus with dial-a-language headsets and video support (€14.50, 50 minutes, pay driver). The tour leaves hourly from the Markt (10:00-20:00 in summer, until 19:00 in spring, until 18:00 in fall, less in winter, tel. 050-355-024, www.citytour.be). The narration, while clear, is slow-moving and a bit boring. But the tour is a lazy way to cruise past virtually every sight in Bruges.

Walking Tour—Local guides walk small groups through the core of town (€9, 2 hours, daily July-Aug, Sat-Sun only mid-April-June and Sept-Oct, depart from TI on 't Zand Square at 14:30—just drop in a few minutes early and buy tickets at the TI desk). Though earnest, the tours are heavy on history and given in two languages, so they may be less than peppy. Still, to propel you beyond the pretty gables and canal swans of Bruges, they're good medicine. In the off-season, "winter walks" leave from the same TI four evenings a week (€9, Nov-Feb Sat-Mon and Wed at 17:00).

Local Guide—A private two-hour guided tour costs €50 (reserve at least one week in advance through TI, tel. 050-448-686). Or contact Christian Scharlé and Daniëlle Janssens, who give two-hour walks for €70, three-hour guided drives for €150, and full-day tours of Bruges and Brussels for €200 (Christian's mobile 0475-659-507, Daniëlle's mobile 0476-493-203, www.tourmanagement belgium.be, tmb@skynet.be).

Horse-and-Buggy Tour—The buggies around town can take you on a clip-clop tour (€36, 35 minutes; price is per carriage, not per person; buggies gather in Minnewater, near entrance to Begijnhof). When divided among four or five people, this can be a good value.

Near Bruges

Popular tour destinations from Bruges are Flanders Fields (famous WWI sites about 40 miles to the southwest) and the picturesque town of Damme (4 easy-to-bike miles to the northeast).

Quasimodo Countryside Tours—This company offers those with extra time two entertaining, all-day, English-only bus tours through the rarely visited Flemish countryside. The "Flanders Fields" tour concentrates on WWI battlefields, trenches, memorials, and poppy-splattered fields (Tue-Sun at 9:15, no tours Mon or in Jan, 8 hours, visit to In Flanders Fields Museum not included). The other tour, "Triple Treat," focuses on Flanders' medieval past and rich culture, with tastes of chocolate, waffles, and beer (departs Mon, Wed, and Fri at 9:15, 8 hours). Be ready for lots of walking.

Tours cost €60, or €50 if you're under 26 (cash preferred, €10 discount on second tour if you've taken the other, includes sandwich lunch, 9- or 30-seat bus depending on demand, non-smoking, reservations required—call 050-370-470, www.quasimodo.be). After making a few big-hotel pickups, the buses leave town from the Park Hotel on 't Zand Square (arrange for pickup when you reserve).

Flanders Fields Battlefield Daytours by Nathan—Nathan (or his right-hand man Karl) leads small groups on minibus day trips to the WWI sights between here and Ypres (Ieper). While pricier than Quasimodo's tour (listed above), Nathan's are more intimate: eight travelers on a minibus rather than a big busload (allowing your guide to tailor the tours to passengers' interests and nationalities); pickup from any hotel or B&B (because the small bus is allowed in the town center); and an included restaurant lunch instead of a picnic. Nathan's tours also include free time at the excellent museums in Ypres and Passchendaele (€65, discount when booked direct using this book, price includes admissions, cash only, departs Tue-Sun around 8:45 from your hotel or B&B, 8.5 hours, call 050-346-060 or toll-free 0800-99133 to reserve, www.visitbruges.org, info@visitbruges.org). In the evening, Nathan offers a shorter **Last Post Evening Tour,** with a stop at Tyne Cot Cemetery en route to the moving 20:00 bugle call at the Menin Gate in Ypres (€40, no discounts, departs Tue-Sun around 18:15 from your B&B/hotel, returns to Bruges around 21:15).

Bike Tours—**QuasiMundo Bike Tours,** which runs bike tours around Bruges (listed earlier) also offers a daily "Border by Bike" tour through the nearby countryside to Damme (€25, discount with this book, March-Oct, departs at 13:00, 15 miles, 4 hours, tel. 050-330-775, www.quasimundo.com). Both their city and border tours include bike rental, a light raincoat (if necessary), water, and a drink in a local café. Meet at the metal "car wash" fountain on Burg Square 10 minutes before departure. If you already have a bike, you're welcome to join either tour for €15. Jos, who leads most departures, is a high-energy and entertaining guide.

Charming Mieke of **Pink Bear Bike Tours** takes small groups on an easy and delightful 3.5-hour guided pedal along a canal to the historic town of Damme and back, finishing with a brief tour of Bruges. English tours go daily through peak season and nearly daily the rest of the year (€22, discount with this book, €15 if you already have a bike, meet at 10:25 under bell tower on the Markt, tel. 050-616-686, mobile 0476-744-525, www.pinkbear.freeservers .com).

For bike rental shops in Bruges, see "Helpful Hints," earlier.

Sights in Bruges

These sights are listed in walking order, from the Markt, to Burg Square, to the cluster of museums around the Church of Our Lady, to the Begijnhof (10-minute walk from beginning to end, without stops).

▲**Markt (Market Square)**—Ringed by a bank, the post office, lots of restaurant terraces, great old gabled buildings, and the iconic bell tower, this square is the modern heart of the city (most city buses run from near here to the train station—it's a block down Kuiperstraat at the library bus stop). Under the bell tower are two great Belgian-style french-fry stands, a quadrilingual Braille description of the old town, and a metal model of the tower. In Bruges' heyday as a trading center, a canal came right up to this square. Geldmuntstraat, just off the square, is a delightful street with many fun and practical shops and eateries.

▲▲**Bell Tower (Belfort)**—Most of this bell tower has presided over the Markt since 1300, serenading passersby with carillon music. The octagonal lantern was added in 1486, making it 290 feet high—that's 366 steps. The view is worth the climb and probably even the pricey admission.

Cost and Hours: €8, daily 9:30-17:00, 16:15 last-entry time strictly enforced—best to show up before 16:00, €0.30 WC in courtyard.

▲▲**Burg Square**—This opulent square is Bruges' civic center, the historic birthplace of Bruges, and the site of the ninth-century castle of the first count of Flanders. Today, it's an atmospheric place to take in an outdoor concert while surrounded by six centuries of architecture.

▲**Basilica of the Holy Blood**—Originally the Chapel of Saint Basil, this church is famous for its relic of the blood of Christ, which, according to tradition, was brought to Bruges in 1150 after the Second Crusade. The lower chapel is dark and solid—a fine example of Romanesque style. The upper chapel (separate

BRUGES

entrance, climb the stairs) is decorated Gothic. An interesting treasury museum is next to the upper chapel.

Cost and Hours: Treasury-€1.50; April-Sept daily 9:30-12:00 & 14:00-17:00; Oct-March Thu-Tue 10:00-12:00 & 14:00-17:00, Wed 10:00-11:45 only; Burg Square, tel. 050-336-792, www.holy blood.com.

▲**City Hall**—This complex houses several interesting sights. Your €2 ticket includes an audioguide; access to a room full of old town maps and paintings; the grand, beautifully restored **Gothic Room** from 1400, starring a painted and carved wooden ceiling adorned with hanging arches (daily 9:30-17:00, last entry 30 minutes before closing, Burg 12); and the less impressive **Renaissance Hall** (Brugse Vrije), basically just one ornate room with a Renaissance chimney (same hours, separate entrance—in corner of square at Burg 11a).

▲▲▲**Groeninge Museum**—This recently renovated museum has one of the world's best collections of the art produced in the city and surrounding area, from Memling to Magritte. In the 1400s, Bruges was northern Europe's richest, most cosmopolitan, and most cultured city. Beautiful paintings were an affordable luxury, like fancy clothes or furniture. Internationally known artists set up studios in Bruges, producing portraits and altarpieces for wealthy merchants from all over Europe.

While there's plenty of worthwhile modern art, the Groeninge's highlights are the vivid and pristine Flemish Primitives. ("Primitive" here means "before the Renaissance.") This early Flemish style, though less appreciated and understood today than the Italian Renaissance art produced a century later, is subtle, technically advanced, and beautiful. Flemish art is shaped by its love of detail, its merchant patrons' egos, and the power of the Church. Lose yourself in the halls of Groeninge: Gaze across 15th-century canals, into the eyes of reassuring Marys, and through town squares littered with leotards, lace, and lopped-off heads.

Cost and Hours: €8, more for special exhibits, audioguide for some special exhibits-€4, Tue-Sun 9:30-17:00, closed Mon, Dijver 12, tel. 050-448-711, www.brugge.be.

Gruuthuse Museum—Once a wealthy brewer's home, this 15th-century mansion is a sprawling smattering of everything from medieval bedpans to a guillotine (though extensive restoration efforts may close parts of it through the end of 2012).

Cost and Hours: €6, Tue-Sun 9:30-17:00, closed Mon, Dijver 17, Bruges museums tel. 050-448-711, www.brugge.be.

▲▲**Church of Our Lady (Onthaalkerk Onze-Lieve-Vrouw)**—The church stands as a memorial to the power and wealth of Bruges in its heyday. A delicate *Madonna and Child* by Michelangelo is near the apse (to the right if you're facing the altar). It's said to be the only Michelangelo statue to leave Italy in his lifetime (thanks to the wealth generated by Bruges' cloth trade). If you like tombs and church art, pay to wander through the apse.

Cost and Hours: Michelangelo viewing is free, art-filled apse-€4; church open Mon-Fri 9:30-17:00, Sat 9:30-16:45, Sun 13:30-17:00; last entry 30 minutes before closing, Mariastraat, www.brugge.be.

▲▲**Memling Museum/St. John's Hospital (Sint Janshospitaal)**—The former monastery/hospital complex has a fine museum in what was once the monks' church. The museum offers a glimpse into medieval medicine, displaying surgical instruments, documents, and visual aids as you work your way to the museum's climax: several of Hans Memling's glowing masterpieces. Memling's art was the culmination of Bruges' Flemish Primitive style. His serene, soft-focus, motionless scenes capture a medieval piety that was quickly fading. The popular style made Memling (c. 1430-1494) one of Bruges' wealthiest citizens, and his work was gobbled up by visiting Italian merchants, who took it home with them, cross-pollinating European art. His *Mystical Wedding of St. Catherine* triptych is a highlight, as is the miniature, gilded-oak shrine to St. Ursula.

Cost and Hours: €8, includes fine audioguide, Tue-Sun 9:30-17:00, closed Mon, last entry 30 minutes before closing, across the street from the Church of Our Lady, Mariastraat 38, Bruges museums tel. 050-448-743, www.brugge.be.

▲▲**Begijnhof**—Inhabited by Benedictine nuns, the Begijnhof courtyard (free, daily 6:30-18:30) almost makes you want to don a habit and fold your hands as you walk under its wispy trees and whisper past its frugal little homes. For a good slice of Begijnhof life, walk through the simple museum, the Beguine's House museum (€2, Mon-Sat 10:00-17:00, Sun 14:30-17:00, shorter hours off-season, English explanations, museum is left of entry gate).

Minnewater—Just south of the Begijnhof is Minnewater, an idyllic world of flower boxes, canals, and swans.

Almshouses—As you walk from the Begijnhof back to the town center, you might detour along Nieuwe Gentweg to visit one of about 20 almshouses in the city. At #8, go through the door marked *Godshuis de Meulenaere 1613* into the peaceful courtyard (free). This was a medieval form of housing for the poor. The rich would pay for someone's tiny room here in return for lots of prayers.

Bruges Experiences: Beer, Chocolate, Windmills, and Biking

▲▲**De Halve Maan Brewery Tour**—Belgians are Europe's beer connoisseurs, and this handy tour is a great way to pay your respects. The brewery makes the only beers brewed in Bruges:

BRUGES

Brugse Zot ("Fool from Bruges") and Straffe Hendrik ("Strong Henry"). The happy gang at this working-family brewery gives entertaining and informative, 45-minute tours in three languages. Avoid crowds by visiting at 11:00.

Cost and Hours: €6.50 includes a beer, lots of very steep steps, great rooftop panorama; tours run April-Oct daily on the hour 11:00-16:00, Sat until 17:00; Nov-March Mon-Fri 11:00 and 15:00 only, Sat on the hour 11:00-17:00, Sun until 16:00; Walplein 26, tel. 050-444-222, www.halvemaan.be.

▲**Chocolate Shops**—Bruggians are connoisseurs of fine chocolate. You'll be tempted by chocolate-filled display windows all over town. While Godiva is the best big-factory/high-price/high-quality brand, there are plenty of smaller, family-run places in Bruges that offer exquisite handmade chocolates. All three of the following chocolatiers are proud of their creative varieties, generous with their samples, and welcome you to assemble a 100-gram assortment of five or six chocolates.

Dumon: Perhaps Bruges' smoothest and creamiest chocolates are at Dumon (€2.20/100 grams). Madame Dumon and her children (Stefaan, Natale, and Christophe) make their top-notch chocolate daily and sell it fresh just off the Markt (Thu-Tue 10:00-18:00 except closes Sun at 17:00, occasionally open Wed, old chocolate molds on display in basement, Eiermarkt 6, tel. 050-346-282; two other Dumon shops around town offer the same chocolate, but not the same experience). The Dumons don't provide English labels because they believe it's best to describe their chocolates in person—and they do it with an evangelical fervor. Try a small mix-and-match box to sample a few out-of-this-world flavors, and come back for more of your favorites.

The Chocolate Line: Locals and tourists alike flock to The Chocolate Line (pricey at €5/100 grams) to taste the *gastronomique* varieties concocted by Dominique Person—the mad scientist of chocolate. His unique creations mix chocolate with various, mostly savory flavors. Even those that sound gross can be surprisingly good (be adventurous). Options include Havana cigar (marinated in rum, cognac, and Cuban tobacco leaves—so therefore technically illegal in the US), lemongrass, lavender, ginger (shaped like a Buddha), saffron curry, spicy chili, Moroccan mint, Pop Rocks/cola chocolate, wine vinegar, fried onions, bay leaf, sake, lime/vodka/passionfruit, wasabi, and tomatoes/olives/basil. The kitchen—busy whipping up 80 varieties—is on display in the back. Enjoy the window display, renewed monthly (daily 9:30-18:00 except Sun-Mon opens at 10:30, between Church of Our Lady and the Markt at Simon Stevinplein 19, tel. 050-341-090).

Confiserie De Clerck: Third-generation chocolate maker Jan sells his handmade chocolates for just €1.20/100 grams, making this one of the best deals in town. Some locals claim his chocolate's just as good as at pricier places—taste it and decide for yourself. The time-warp candy shop itself is so delightfully old-school, you'll want to visit no matter what (Mon-Wed and Fri-Sat 10:00-19:00, closed Sun and Thu, Academiestraat 19, tel. 050-345-338).

Choco-Story: The Chocolate Museum—This museum is rated ▲ for chocoholics. The Chocolate Fairy leads you through 2,600 years of chocolate history—explaining why, in the ancient Mexican world of the Mayas and the Aztecs, chocolate was considered the drink of the gods, and cocoa beans were used as a means of payment. With lots of artifacts well-described in English, the museum fills you in on the production of truffles, bonbons, hollow figures, and solid bars of chocolate. Then you'll view a delicious little video (8 minutes long, repeating continuously, alternating Flemish, French, and then English; peek into the theater to check the schedule. If you have time before the next English showing, visit the exhibits in the top room). Your finale is in the "demonstration room," where—after a 10-minute cooking demo—you get a taste.

Cost and Hours: €7, €11 combo-ticket includes nearby Friet Museum, daily 10:00-17:00; where Wijnzakstraat meets Sint Jansstraat at Sint Jansplein, 3-minute walk from the Markt; tel. 050-612-237, www.choco-story.be. The Chocolate Museum is adjacent to (and offers a combo-ticket with) a lamp museum that's very skippable, unless you're a hard-core lamp enthusiast (in that case, boy, are you in luck).

Friet Museum—It's the only place in the world that enthusiastically tells the story of french fries, which, of course, aren't even French—they're Belgian.

Cost and Hours: Not worth €6, €11 combo-ticket includes Chocolate Museum, daily 10:00-17:00, Vlamingstraat 33, tel. 050-340-150, www.frietmuseum.be.

Windmills and Lace by the Moat—A 15-minute walk from the center to the northeast end of town (faster by bike) brings you to four windmills strung along a pleasant grassy setting on the "big moat" canal. The St. Janshuys **windmill** is open to visitors (€2; May-Aug Tue-Sun 9:30-12:30 & 13:30-17:00, closed Mon, last entry at 16:30; Sept same hours but open Sat-Sun only; closed Oct-April; go to the end of Carmersstraat and hang a right).

The **Folklore Museum,** in the same neighborhood, is cute but forgettable (€2, Tue-Sun 9:30-17:00, last entry at 16:30, closed Mon, Balstraat 43, tel. 050-448-764). To find it, ask for the Jerusalem Church. On the same street is a lace shop with a good reputation, 't **Apostelientje** (Tue 13:00-17:00, Wed-Sat 9:30-12:15 & 13:15-17:00, Sun 10:00-13:00, closed Mon, Balstraat 11, tel. 050-337-860, mobile 0495-562-420).

BRUGES

▲▲Biking—The Flemish word for bike is *fiets* (pronounced "feets"). While Bruges' sights are close enough for easy walking, the town is a treat for bikers, and a bike quickly gets you into dreamy back lanes without a hint of tourism. Take a peaceful evening ride through the town's nooks and crannies and around the outer canal. Consider keeping a bike for the duration of your stay—it's the way the locals get around in Bruges. Along the canal that circles the town is a park with a delightful bike lane. Rental shops have maps and ideas (see "Helpful Hints," earlier, for more info).

Nightlife in Bruges

Herberg Vlissinghe and **De Garre,** listed under "Eating in Bruges," later, are great places to just nurse a beer and enjoy new friends.

Charlie Rockets is an American-style bar—lively and central—with foosball games, darts, and five pool tables (€9/hour) in the inviting back room. It also runs a youth hostel upstairs and therefore is filled with a young, international crowd (a block off the Markt at Hoogstraat 19). It's open nightly until 3:00 in the morning with non-stop rock 'n' roll.

Nighttime Bike Ride: Great as these pubs are, my favorite way to spend a late-summer evening in Bruges is in the twilight on a rental bike, savoring the cobbled wonders of its back streets, far from the touristic commotion.

Evening Carillon Concerts: The tiny courtyard behind the bell tower has a few benches where people can enjoy the free carillon concerts (generally Mon, Wed, and Sat at 21:00 in the summer; schedule posted on courtyard wall).

Sleeping in Bruges

Bruges is a great place to sleep, with Gothic spires out your window, no traffic noise, and the cheerily out-of-tune carillon heralding each new day at 8:00 sharp. (Thankfully, the bell tower is silent from 22:00 to 8:00.) Most Bruges accommodations are located between the train station and the old center, with the most distant (and best) being a few blocks to the north and east of the Markt (Market Square).

B&Bs offer the best value. All are on quiet streets and (with a few exceptions) keep the same prices throughout the year.

Bruges is most crowded Friday and Saturday evenings from Easter through October, with July and August weekends being the worst. Many hotels charge a bit more on Friday and Saturday, and won't let you stay just one night if it's a Saturday.

Sleep Code

(€1 = about $1.40, country code: 32)
S = Single, **D** = Double/Twin, **T** = Triple, **Q** = Quad, **b** = bathroom,
s = shower only. Everyone speaks English. Unless otherwise
noted, breakfast is included and credit cards are accepted.

To help you easily sort through these listings, I've divided
the accommodations into three categories, based on the price
for a standard double room with bath:

$$$ **Higher Priced**—Most rooms €125 or more.
$$ **Moderately Priced**—Most rooms between €80-125.
$ **Lower Priced**—Most rooms €80 or less.

Prices can change without notice; verify the hotel's
current rates online or by email. For other updates, see www
.ricksteves.com/update.

Hotels

$$$ Hotel Heritage offers 24 rooms, with chandeliers that seem
hung especially for you, in a solid and completely modernized old
building with luxurious public spaces. Tastefully decorated and
offering all the amenities, it's one of those places that does every-
thing just right yet still feels warm and inviting—if you can afford
it (Db-€170, superior Db-€218, deluxe Db-€270, extra bed-€60,
wonderful buffet breakfast-€21/person, continental breakfast-€11/
person, air-con, elevator, free Internet access and Wi-Fi, sauna,
tanning bed, fitness room, bike rental, free 2-hour guided city tour,
parking-€22/day, Niklaas Desparsstraat 11, a block north of the
Markt, tel. 050-444-444, fax 050-444-440, www.hotel-heritage
.com, info@hotel-heritage.com). It's run by cheery and hardwork-
ing Johan and Isabelle Creytens.

$$$ Hotel Adornes is small and classy—a great value situ-
ated in the most charming part of town. This 17th-century canal-
side house has 20 rooms with full modern bathrooms, free parking
(reserve in advance), free loaner bikes, and a cellar lounge with
games and videos (small Db-€120, larger Db-€140-150, Tb-€175,
Qb-€180, elevator, free Wi-Fi in lobby, some street noise, near
Carmersstraat at St. Annarei 26, tel. 050-341-336, fax 050-342-
085, www.adornes.be, info@adornes.be). Nathalie runs the family
business.

$$ Hotel Patritius, family-run and centrally located, is a
grand, circa-1830, Neoclassical mansion with hardwood oak floors
in its 16 stately, high-ceilinged rooms. It features a plush lounge,
a chandeliered breakfast room, and a courtyard garden. This

BRUGES

Bruges Accommodations near the Center

1 Hotels Heritage & Nicolas
2 Hotel Adornes
3 Hotel Patritius
4 Hotel Botaniek
5 Hotel ter Reien
6 Walwyck Cool Down Hotel
7 Hotel Cordoeanier
8 Hotel Cavalier
9 To Hotel de Pauw
10 Hotel Imperial & Passage Hostel
11 Hotel Notre Dame
12 Absoluut Verhulst B&B
13 Gastenhuis Sint-Andriescruyse
14 B&B Gheeraert
15 B&B Setola
16 Dieltiens B&B
17 To Debruyne B&B
18 't Geerwijn B&B
19 Royal Stewart B&B
20 Charlie Rockets Hostel
21 To Snuffel Backpacker Hostel

is the best value in its price range (Db-€100-130, Tb-€140-155, Qb-€165-180, cheaper in off-season, rates depend on room size and demand—check site for best price, extra bed-€25, air-con, elevator, pay Internet access, free Wi-Fi on ground floor, coin-op laundry, parking-€8, garage parking-€14, Riddersstraat 11, tel. 050-338-454, fax 050-339-634, www.hotelpatritius.be, info@hotelpatritius .be, Garrett and Elvi Spaey).

$$ **Hotel Egmond** is a creaky mansion located in the middle of the quietly idyllic Minnewater. Its eight 18th-century rooms are plain, with small modern baths shoehorned in, and the guests-only garden is just waiting for a tea party. This hotel is ideal for romantics who want a countryside setting—where you sleep surrounded by a park, not a city (Sb-€95, small twin Db-€105, larger Db-€115, Tb-€150, cheaper in winter, free Wi-Fi, parking-€10, Minnewater 15, tel. 050-341-445, fax 050-342-940, www.egmond .be, info@egmond.be, Steven).

$$ **Hotel Botaniek,** quietly located a block from Astrid Park, is a fine, pint-sized hotel with a comfy lounge, renting nine rooms—some of them quite big (Db-€95 weekday special for my readers, €99 Fri-Sat; Tb-€130 on weekdays, €140 Fri-Sat; Qb-€145, €149 Fri-Sat; less for longer and off-season stays, free museum-discount card, elevator, Waalsestraat 23, tel. 050-341-424, fax 050-345-939, www.botaniek.be, info@botaniek.be, Andy).

$$ **Hotel ter Reien** is big and basic, with 26 rooms overlooking a canal in the town center (Db-€80-110, Tb-€110-130, Qb-€140-160, rates vary widely with demand—check their website for best prices; cheapest rates for weekdays, stays of at least 3 nights, rooms without canal views; extra bed-€24-29, pay Internet access and Wi-Fi, Langestraat 1, tel. 050-349-100, fax 050-340-048, www.hotelterreien.be, info@hotelterreien.be, owned by Diederik and Stephanie Pille-Maes).

$$ **Walwyck Cool Down Hotel**—a bit of modern comfort, chic design, and English verbiage in a medieval shell—is a nicely located hotel with 18 spacious rooms (small Db-€90, standard Db-€100, "superior" Db-€120, Tb-€135, family room-€155, "superior" family room-€180, Internet access, free Wi-Fi, Leeuwstraat 8, tel. 050-616-360, fax 050-616-560, www.walwyck.com, rooms@walwyck.com).

$$ **Hotel Cordoeanier,** a charming family-run hotel, rents 22 simple, fresh, hardwood-floor rooms on a quiet street two blocks off the Markt. It's one of the best deals in town (Sb-€70-95, Db-€75-100, twin Db-€85-100, Tb-€95-110, Qb-€125, Quint/b-€145, for best price pay cash and show this book, breakfast buffet served in their pleasant Café Rose Red, no elevator, pay Internet access, free Wi-Fi, patio, Cordoeanierstraat 16-18, tel. 050-339-051, fax 050-346-111, www.cordoeanier.be, info@cordoeanier.be, Kris).

$ Hotel Cavalier, with more stairs than character, rents eight decent rooms and serves a hearty buffet breakfast in a once-royal setting (Sb-€55, Db-€70, Tb-€90, Qb-€100, two lofty en-suite "back-packers' doubles" on fourth floor-€45-50, book direct and mention this book for special Rick Steves price, pay Wi-Fi, Kuipersstraat 25, tel. 050-330-207, fax 050-347-199, www.hotel cavalier.be, info@hotelcavalier.be, run by friendly Viviane De Clerck).

$ Hotel de Pauw is tall, skinny, flower-bedecked, and family-run, with eight straightforward rooms on a quiet street next to a church (Sb-€65-75, Db-€70-85, no elevator, free and easy street parking, Sint Gilliskerkhof 8, tel. 050-337-118, fax 050-345-140, www.hoteldepauw.be, info@hoteldepauw.be, Philippe and Hilde).

$ Hotel 't Keizershof is a dollhouse of a hotel that lives by its motto, "Spend a night...not a fortune." (Its other motto: "When you're asleep, we look just like those big fancy hotels.") It's simple and tidy, with seven small, cheery, old-time rooms split between two floors, with a shower and toilet on each (S-€30-45, D-€45, T-€66, Q-€84, cash only, free Wi-Fi, free and easy parking, laundry service-€7.50, Oostmeers 126, a block in front of station, tel. 050-338-728, www.hotelkeizershof.be, info@hotelkeizershof.be). The hotel is run by Stefaan and Hilde, with decor by their children, Lorie and Fien; it's situated in a pleasant area near the train station and Minnewater, a 15 minute-walk from the Markt.

$ Hotel Nicolas feels like an old-time boarding house that missed Bruges' affluence bandwagon. Its 14 big, plain rooms are a good value, and the location is ideal—on a quiet street a block off the Markt (Sb-€55, Db-€63, Tb-€75, elevator, pay Wi-Fi, TV on request, closed in Jan, Niklaas Desparsstraat 9, tel. 050-335-502, fax 050-343-544, www.hotelnicolas.be, hotel.nicolas@telenet.be, Yi-Ling and Thomas).

$ Hotel Imperial is an old-school hotel with seven old-school rooms. It's simple and well-run in a charming building on a handy, quiet street (Db-€70-90, cash only, no elevator, pay Wi-Fi, Dweersstraat 24, tel. 050-339-014, www.hotelimperial.be, info @hotelimperial.be, Paul Bernolet and Hilde).

$ Hotel Notre Dame is a humble and blocky little budget option, renting 12 worn rooms in the busy thick of things (Db-€70-75, free Internet access and Wi-Fi, Mariastraat 3, tel. 050-333-193, fax 050-337-608, www.hotelnotredame.be, info@hotelnotre dame.be).

Bed-and-Breakfasts

These B&Bs, run by people who enjoy their work, offer a better value than hotels. Most families rent out their entire top floor—generally three rooms and a small sitting area. And most are mod

Bruges Accommodations away from the Center

P Parking
B Boat Tours
B Bus

1/4 MILE
400 METERS

TO LACE CENTER & WINDMILLS

BRUGES

① Hotel Egmond
② Hotel 't Keizershof
③ To Waterside B&B
④ To B&B AM/PM
⑤ Bistro de Bekoring

and stylish—they're just in medieval shells. Each is central, with lots of stairs and €70 doubles you'd pay €100 for in a hotel. Most places charge €10 extra for one-night stays. It's possible to find parking on the street in the evening (pay 9:00-19:00, 2-hour maximum for metered parking during the day, free overnight).

$$ Absoluut Verhulst is a great, modern-feeling B&B with three rooms in a 400-year-old house, run by friendly Frieda and Benno (Db-€95; huge and lofty suite-€130 for 2, €160 for 3, €180 for 4; €10 more for one-night stays, cash only, non-smoking, free Wi-Fi, 5-minute walk east of the Markt at Verbrand Nieuwland 1, tel. 050-334-515, www.b-bverhulst.com, b-b.verhulst @pandora.be).

$$ Gastenhuis Sint-Andriescruyse offers warmly decorated rooms with high ceilings in a spacious, cheerfully red canalside house a short walk from the Old Town action. Owners Luc and Christiane treat guests like long-lost family (S-€75, D/Db-€100, T-€125, Q-€150, family room for up to 5 comes with board games, cash only, free soft drinks, free Internet access, free pick-up at station, Verversdijk 15A, tel. 050-789-168, mobile 0477-973-933, www.gastenhuisst-andriescruyse.be, luc.cloet@telenet.be).

$$ B&B Gheeraert is a Neoclassical mansion where Inne rents three huge, bright, comfy rooms (Sb-€75, Db-€85, Tb-€95, two-night minimum stay required, cash only, personal check required for first-night's deposit, strictly non-smoking, fridges in rooms, free Internet access and Wi-Fi, Riddersstraat 9, 5-minute walk east of the Markt, tel. 050-335-627, fax 050-345-201, www .bb-bruges.be, bb-bruges@skynet.be).

$ B&B Setola, run by Lut and Bruno Setola, offers three expansive rooms and a spacious breakfast/living room on the top floor of their house. Wooden ceiling beams give the modern rooms a touch of Old World flair, and the family room has a fun loft (Sb-€60, Db-€70, €20 per extra person, €10 more for one-night stays, free Wi-Fi, 5-minute walk from the Markt, Sint Walburgastraat 12, tel. 050-334-977, fax 050-332-551, www.bedandbreakfast -bruges.com, setola@bedandbreakfast-bruges.com).

$ Koen and Annemie Dieltiens are a friendly couple who enjoy getting to know their guests while sharing a wealth of information on Bruges. You'll eat a hearty breakfast around a big table in their comfortable house (Sb-€60, Db-€70, Tb-€90, €10 more for one-night stays, cash only, free Internet access and Wi-Fi, Waalsestraat 40, three blocks southeast of Burg Square, tel. 050-334-294, www.bedandbreakfastbruges.be, dieltiens@bedand breakfastbruges.be).

$ Debruyne B&B, run by Marie-Rose and her architect husband, Ronny, offers three rooms with artsy, modern decor (check out the elephant-size white doors—Ronny's design) and genuine warmth (Sb-€60, Db-€65, Tb-€85, €10 more for one-night stays, cash only, Internet access, free Wi-Fi, 7-minute walk north of the Markt, two blocks from the little church at Lange Raamstraat 18, tel. 050-347-606, www.bedandbreakfastbruges.com, mietje debruyne@yahoo.co.uk).

$ 't Geerwijn B&B, run by Chris de Loof, offers homey rooms in the old center. Check out the fun, lofty A-frame room upstairs (Ds/Db-€75-80 depending on season, Tb-€85-90, cash only, pleasant breakfast room and royal lounge, free Wi-Fi, Geerwijnstraat 14, tel. 050-340-544, fax 050-343-721, www.geerwijn .be, info@geerwijn.be). Chris also rents an apartment that sleeps five.

$ Royal Stewart B&B, run by Scottish Maggie and her husband, Gilbert, has three thoughtfully decorated rooms in a quiet, almost cloistered 17th-century house that was inhabited by nuns until 1953 (S-€48, D/Db-€65, Tb-€85, cash only, pleasant breakfast room, Genthof 25-27, 5-minute walk from the Markt, tel. 050-337-918, fax 050-337-918, www.royalstewart.be, r.stewart @pandora.be).

$ Waterside B&B has two fresh, Zen-like rooms, one floor above a peaceful canal south of the town center (D-€75, €5 more on Sat, continental breakfast, free Wi-Fi, 15-minute walk from Burg Square at Kazernevest 88, tel. & fax 050-616-686, mobile 0476-744-525, www.waterside.be, waterside@telenet.be, run by Mieke of recommended Pink Bear Bike Tours).

$ B&B AM/PM sports three ultramodern rooms in a residential neighborhood just west of the Old Town (Db-€70, Tb-€90, €10 more for one-night stay, cash only, free Internet access—mornings only, free Wi-Fi, 5-minute walk from 't Zand at Singel 10, mobile 0485-071-003, www.bruges-bedandbreakfast.com, info @bruges-bedandbreakfast.com, artsy young couple Tiny and Kevin). From the train station, head left down busy Buiten Begijnevest to the roundabout. Stay to the left, take the pedestrian underpass, then follow the busy road (now on your left). Just before the next bridge, turn right onto the footpath called Buiten Boeverievest, then turn left onto Singel; the B&B is at #10.

Hostels

Bruges has several good hostels offering beds for around €15 in two- to eight-bed rooms. Breakfast is about €3 extra. The American-style **$ Charlie Rockets** hostel (and bar), a backpacker dive, is the liveliest and most central. The ground floor feels like a 19th-century sports bar, with a foosball-and-movie-posters party ambience. Upstairs is an industrial-strength pile of hostel dorms (90 beds, €18/bed with sheets, €20/bed with sheets and breakfast, 4-6 beds/room, D-€50 includes breakfast, lockers, pay Internet

access, Hoogstraat 19, tel. 050-330-660, www.charlierockets.com).
Other small and loose places are the minimal, funky, and central
$ Passage (€15/bed with sheets, 4-7 beds/room, D-€50, Db-€65,
Dweerstraat 26, tel. 050-340-232, www.passagebruges.com, info
@passagebruges.com) and **$ Snuffel Backpacker Hostel,** which
is less central and pretty grungy, but friendly and laid-back (60
beds, €15-19/bed includes sheets and breakfast, 4-14 beds/room,
Ezelstraat 47, tel. 050-333-133, www.snuffel.be).

Eating in Bruges

Bruges' specialties include mussels cooked a variety of ways (one
order can feed two), fish dishes, grilled meats, and french fries.
The town's two indigenous beers are the prizewinning Brugse Zot
(Bruges Fool), a golden ale, and Straffe Hendrik, a potent, bitter
triple ale.

You'll find plenty of affordable, touristy restaurants on floodlit
squares and along dreamy canals. Bruges feeds 3.5 million tourists
a year, and most are seduced by a high-profile location. These can
be fine experiences for the magical setting and views, but the quality of food and service will likely be low. I wouldn't blame you for
eating at one of these places, but I won't recommend any. I prefer
the candle-cool bistros that flicker on back streets.

Restaurants

Rock Fort is a chic spot with a modern, fresh coziness and a high-
powered respect for good food. Two young chefs, Peter Laloo and
Hermes Vanliefde, give their French cuisine a creative and gourmet
twist. At the bar, they serve a separate tapas menu. Reservations
are required for dinner and recommended for lunch. This place is
a winner (€6-12 tapas, great pastas and salads, €15 Mon-Fri lunch
special, beautifully presented €19-34 dinner plates, €40 five-tapas
special, fancy €50 fixed-price four-course meal, open Mon-Fri
12:00-14:30 & 18:30-23:00, closed Sat-Sun, Langestraat 15, tel.
050-334-113).

Bistro de Bekoring, cute, candlelit, and Gothic, fills two
almshouses and a delightful terrace with people thankful for good
food. Rotund and friendly Chef Roland and his wife, Gerda, love
to tempt the hungry—as the name of their bistro implies. They
serve traditional Flemish food (especially eel and beer-soaked
stew) from a small menu to people who like holding hands as they
dine. Reservations are smart (€15 weekday lunch, €30 fixed-price
dinners, €42 with wine, Wed-Sat 11:45-13:45 & 18:30-21:00, closed
Sun evening and Mon-Tue; out past the Begijnhof at Arsenaalstraat
53, for location see map on page 199, tel. 050-344-157).

Bistro in den Wittenkop, very Flemish, is a stylishly small,

Bruges Restaurants

N

¼ MILE
400 METERS

P PARKING
B BOAT TOURS

DCH

BRUGES

1. Rock Fort Restaurant
2. Bistro in den Wittenkop
3. Bistro den Amand & Medard Brasserie
4. The Flemish Pot
5. Lotus Vegetarian Restaurant
6. De Hobbit
7. Rest. de Koetse
8. Carlito's
9. Restaurant Sint-Barbe
10. Café-Brasserie Craenenburg
11. 't Brugs Beertje Pub
12. De Garre Pub
13. Café Terrastje
14. Herberg Vlissinghe Pub
15. L'Estaminet Restaurant
16. Pub 't Gezelleke
17. Frituur Stands
18. 't Brugsch Friethuys
19. Laurenzino Waffles
20. Gelateria Da Vinci & Grocery
21. Tom's Diner

laid-back, old-time place specializing in the local favorites. It's a classy spot to enjoy hand-cut fries, which go particularly well with Straffe Hendrik beer (€37-40 three-course meal, €20-25 plates, Tue-Sat 18:00-21:30, closed Sun-Mon, reserve ahead, terrace in back in summer, Sint Jakobsstraat 14, tel. 050-332-059).

Bistro den Amand, with a plain interior and a few outdoor tables, exudes unpretentious quality the moment you step in. In this mussels-free zone, Chef An is enthusiastic about vegetables, as her busy wok and fun salads prove. The creative dishes—some with a hint of Asian influence—are a welcome departure from Bruges' mostly predictable traditional restaurants. It's on a bustling pedestrian lane a half-block off the Markt (€33-35 three-course meal, €20 plates; Mon-Tue and Thu-Sat 12:00-14:00 & 18:00-21:00, closed Wed and Sun; Sint-Amandstraat 4, tel. 050-340-122, An Vissers and Arnout Beyaert). Reservations are smart for dinner.

The Flemish Pot (a.k.a. The Little Pancake House) is a hardworking eatery serving up traditional peasant-style meals. They crank out pancakes (savory and sweet) and homemade *wafels* for lunch. Then, at 18:00, enthusiastic chefs Mario and Rik stow their waffle irons and pull out a traditional menu of vintage Flemish specialties served in little iron pots and skillets. Seating is tight and cluttered. You'll enjoy huge portions, refills from the hovering "fries angel," and a good selection of local beers (€26-30 three-course meals, €16-24 plates, Wed-Sun 12:00-22:00, closed Mon-Tue, reservations smart, family-friendly, just off Geldmuntstraat at Helmstraat 3, tel. 050-340-086).

Lotus Vegetarian Restaurant serves serious lunch plates (€10 *plat du jour* offered daily), salads, and homemade chocolate cake in a pleasantly small, bustling, and upscale setting without a trace of tie-dye. To keep carnivorous companions happy, they also serve several very good, organic meat dishes (Mon-Fri from 11:45, last orders at 14:00, closed Sat-Sun, cash only, just north of Burg Square at Wapenmakersstraat 5, tel. 050-331-078).

De Hobbit, featuring an entertaining menu, is always busy with happy eaters. For a swinging deal, try the all-you-can-eat spareribs with bread and salad for €18.50. It's nothing fancy, just good, basic food served in a fun, crowded, traditional grill house (daily 18:00-23:00, Fri-Sat until 23:30, family-friendly, Kemelstraat 8-10, reservations smart, tel. 050-335-520).

Tom's Diner is a trendy, cozy little candlelit bistro in a quiet, cobbled residential area a 10-minute walk from the center. Young chef Tom gives traditional dishes a delightful modern twist. If you want to flee the tourists and experience a popular neighborhood joint, this is it—the locals love it (€15-20 plates, Wed-Mon 18:00-24:00, closed Tue, north of the Markt near Sint-Gilliskerk at West-Gistelhof 23, tel. 050-333-382).

Restaurant de Koetse is a fine bet for central, good-quality, local-style food. The feeling is traditional, a bit formal (stuffy even), and dressy, yet accessible. The cuisine is Belgian and French, with an emphasis on grilled meat, seafood, and mussels (€30 three-course meals, €20-30 plates include vegetables and a salad, Fri-Wed 12:00-14:30 & 18:00-22:00, closed Thu, non-smoking section, Oude Burg 31, tel. 050-337-680, Piet).

Carlito's is a good choice for basic Italian fare. Their informal space, with whitewashed walls and tea-light candles, is two blocks from Burg Square (€8-13 pizzas and pastas, daily 12:00-14:00 & 18:00-22:30, patio seating in back, Hoogstraat 21, tel. 050-490-075).

Restaurant Sint-Barbe, on the eastern edge of town, serves classy Flemish dishes made from local ingredients in a fresh, modern space on two floors. Their €12 soup-and-main lunch is a great deal (€14-25 main courses, Thu-Mon 11:30-14:30 & 18:00-22:00, closed Tue-Wed, food served until 21:00, St. Annaplein 29, tel. 050-330-999, Evi).

Restaurants on the Markt: Most tourists seem to be eating on the Markt with the bell tower high overhead and horse carriages clip-clopping by. The square is ringed by tourist traps with aggressive waiters expert at getting you to consume more than you intended. Still, if you order smartly, you can have a memorable meal or drink here on one of the finest squares in Europe at a reasonable price. Consider **Café-Brasserie Craenenburg,** with a straightforward menu, where you can get pasta and beer for €15 and spend all the time you want ogling the magic of Bruges (daily 7:30-23:00, Markt 16, tel. 050-333-402).

Cheap Eats: **Medard Brasserie,** just a block off the Markt, serves the cheapest hot meal in town—hearty meat spaghetti (big plate-€3, huge plate-€5.50, sit inside or out, Fri-Wed 11:00-20:30 except opens on Sun at 12:30, closed Thu, Sint Amandstraat 18, tel. 050-348-684).

Bars Offering Light Meals, Beer, and Ambience

My best budget-eating tip for Bruges: Stop into one of the city's atmospheric bars for a simple meal and a couple of world-class beers with great Bruges ambience. The last three pubs listed are in the wonderfully *gezellig* (cozy) quarter, northeast of the Markt.

The **'t Brugs Beertje** is young and convivial. While any pub or restaurant carries the basic beers, you'll find a selection here of more than 300 types, including brews to suit any season. They serve light meals, including pâté, spaghetti, toasted sandwiches, and a traditional cheese plate. You're welcome to sit at the bar and talk with the staff (five cheeses, bread, and salad for €11; Thu-Tue

16:00-24:00, closed Wed, Kemelstraat 5, tel. 050-339-616, run by fun-loving manager Daisy).

De Garre is another good place to gain an appreciation of the Belgian beer culture. Rather than a noisy pub scene, it has a dressy, sit-down-and-focus-on-your-friend-and-the-fine-beer vibe. It's mature and cozy with tables, light meals (cold cuts, pâtés, and toasted sandwiches), and a selection of 150 beers (daily 12:00-24:00, additional seating up tiny staircase, off Breidelstraat between Burg and Markt, on tiny Garre alley, tel. 050-341-029).

Café Terrastje is a cozy pub serving light meals. Experience the grown-up ambience inside, or relax on the front terrace overlooking the canal and heart of the *gezellig* district (€6-8 sandwiches, €10-18 dishes; food served Fri-Mon 12:00-21:00, open until 23:30; Tue 12:00-18:00; closed Wed-Thu; corner of Genthof and Langerei, tel. 050-330-919, Ian and Patricia).

Herberg Vlissinghe is the oldest pub in town (1515). Bruno keeps things simple and laid-back, serving simple plates (lasagna, grilled cheese sandwiches, and famous €8 angel-hair spaghetti) and great beer in the best old-time tavern atmosphere in town. This must have been the Dutch Masters' rec room. The garden outside comes with a *boules* court—free for guests to watch or play (Wed-Sat 11:00-24:00, Sun 11:00-19:00, closed Mon-Tue, Blekersstraat 2, tel. 050-343-737).

L'Estaminet is a youthful, jazz-filled eatery, similar to one of Amsterdam's brown cafés. Don't be intimidated by its lack of tourists. Local students flock here for the Tolkien-chic ambience, hearty €9 spaghetti, and big dinner salads. Since this is Belgium, it serves more beer than wine. For outdoor dining under an all-weather canopy, enjoy the relaxed patio facing peaceful Astrid Park (Fri-Wed 11:30-24:00, Thu 16:00-24:00, Park 5, tel. 050-330-916).

Pub 't Gezelleke lacks the mystique of the Vlissinghe, but it's a true neighborhood pub offering quality fare and a fine chance to drink with locals. Its name is an appropriate play on the word for cozy and the name of a great local poet (Mon-Fri 11:00-24:00, closed Sat-Sun, Carmersstraat 15, tel. 050-338-381, Zena).

Fries, Fast Food, and Picnics

Local french fries *(frites)* are a treat. Proud and traditional *frituur*s serve tubs of fries and various local-style shish kebabs. Belgians dip their *frites* in mayonnaise, but ketchup is there for the Yankees (along with spicier sauces). For a quick, cheap, hot, and scenic snack, hit a *frituur* and sit on the steps or benches overlooking the Markt (convenience benches are about 50 yards past the post office).

Markt Frituurs: Twin, take-away fry carts are on the Markt

BRUGES

at the base of the bell tower (daily 10:00-24:00). Skip the ketchup and have a sauce adventure. I find the cart on the left more user-friendly.

't Brugsch Friethuys, a block off the Markt, is handy for sit-down fries. Its forte is greasy, fast, deep-fried Flemish fast food. The €11 "menu 1" comes with three traditional gut bombs: shrimp, *frikandel* minced-meat sausage, and "gypsy stick" sausage (daily 11:00-late, at the corner of Geldmuntstraat and Sint Jakobstraat).

Delhaize-Proxy Supermarket is ideal for picnics. Its push-button produce pricer lets you buy as little as one mushroom (Mon-Sat 9:00-19:00, closed Sun, 3 blocks off the Markt on Geldmuntstraat). For midnight snacks, you'll find Indian-run corner grocery stores scattered around town.

Belgian Waffles and Ice Cream

You'll see waffles sold at restaurants and take-away stands. **Laurenzino** is particularly good, and a favorite with Bruges' teens when they get the waffle munchies. Their classic waffle with chocolate costs €2.50 (daily in summer 10:00-22:00, until 23:00 Fri-Sat; winter 10:00-20:00, until 22:00 Fri-Sat; across from Gelateria Da Vinci at Noordzandstraat 1, tel. 050-333-213).

Gelateria Da Vinci, the local favorite for homemade ice cream, has creative flavors and a lively atmosphere. As you approach, you'll see a line of happy lickers. Before ordering, ask to sample the Ferrero Rocher (chocolate, nuts, and crunchy cookie) and plain yogurt (daily 10:00-22:00, until 24:00 April-Sept and in good-weather off-season, Geldmuntstraat 34, run by Sylvia from Austria).

Bruges Connections

From Bruges by Train to: Brussels (2/hour, usually at :31 and :58, 1 hour, €12.90), **Brussels Airport** (2/hour, 1.5 hours, transfer at Brussels Nord), **Delft** (hourly, 3 hours, change in Ghent, Antwerp, and Rotterdam), **Paris** (roughly hourly via Brussels, 2.5 hours on fast Thalys trains—it's best to book by 20:00 the day before), **Amsterdam** (hourly, 3.25-3.75 hours, transfer at Ghent and Antwerp Central or Brussels Midi; transfer can be tight—be alert and check with conductor; some trips via Thalys train, which requires supplement), **Amsterdam's Schiphol Airport** (hourly, 3.5 hours, change in Ghent and/or Antwerp; less frequent connections via Brussels with Thalys save 30 minutes), **Haarlem** (hourly, 3.5 hours, 2-3 changes—avoid Thalys if traveling with a railpass), **Bacharach** (at least every 2 hours, 5.5 hours, some via Thalys trains, 3 changes), **Köln** (nearly hourly, 3.25 hours, some via Thalys, 3 changes). Train info: tel. 050/302-424.

BRUGES

Trains from London: Bruges is an ideal "Welcome to Europe" stop after London. Take the Eurostar train from London to Brussels (10/day, 2.5 hours), then transfer, backtracking to Bruges (2/hour, 1 hour, entire trip just a few dollars more with Eurostar ticket; see Eurostar details on page 757).

Trains to London: Eurostar trains to London leave from tracks 1 and 2 at Brussels' Midi/Zuid/South Station. Arrive 30 minutes early to get your ticket validated and your luggage and passport checked by British authorities (similar to airport check-in for an international flight).

By Bus to: London (cost can vary, but generally €35 one-way, €70 round-trip, about 9 hours, Eurolines tel. 02-203-0707 in Brussels, www.eurolines.com).

BRUGES

FRANCE

PARIS

Paris—the City of Light—has been a beacon of culture for centuries. As a world capital of art, fashion, food, literature, and ideas, it stands as a symbol of all the fine things human civilization can offer. Come prepared to celebrate this, rather than judge our cultural differences, and you'll capture the romance and *joie de vivre* that this city exudes.

Paris offers sweeping boulevards, chatty crêpe stands, chic boutiques, and world-class art galleries. Sip decaf with deconstructionists at a sidewalk café, then step into an Impressionist painting in a tree-lined park. Climb Notre-Dame and rub shoulders with the gargoyles. Cruise the Seine, zip up the Eiffel Tower, and saunter down avenue des Champs-Elysées. Master the Louvre and Orsay museums. Save some after-dark energy for one of the world's most romantic cities.

Planning Your Time

For up to five very busy but doable days in Paris, I've listed sights in descending order of importance in the planning sections below. Therefore, if you have only one day, just do Day 1; for two days, add Day 2; and so on. When planning where to plug in Versailles, keep in mind that the Château is closed on Mondays and especially crowded on Sundays and Tuesdays—try to avoid these days.

Day 1
Morning: Follow this chapter's Historic Paris Walk, featuring Ile de la Cité, Notre-Dame, the Latin Quarter, and Sainte-Chapelle.
Afternoon: Tour the Louvre.

Evening: Enjoy the Trocadéro scene and a twilight ride up the Eiffel Tower.

Day 2

Morning: Wander the Champs-Elysées from the Arc de Triomphe down the grand avenue des Champs-Elysées to the Tuileries Garden.

Afternoon: Cross the pedestrian bridge from the Tuileries Garden, then tour the Orsay Museum.

Evening: Take one of the tours by bus, taxi, or retro-chic Deux Chevaux car. (If you're staying more than two days, save this for your last-night finale.)

Day 3

Morning: Catch the RER suburban train by 8:00 to arrive early at Versailles (before it opens at 9:00) and tour the palace's interior. (If you get a later start, reverse today's plan by doing the gardens first and the château's interior later in the afternoon).

Midday: Have lunch in the gardens at Versailles.

Afternoon: Spend the afternoon touring the gardens, the Trianon Palaces, and Domaine de Marie-Antoinette.

Evening: Have dinner in Versailles town or return to Paris. For dessert, cruise the Seine River.

Day 4

Morning: Visit Montmartre and the Sacré-Cœur Basilica. Have lunch on Montmartre.

Afternoon: Continue your Impressionist theme by touring the Orangerie and the Rodin Museum, or change themes entirely and tour the Army Museum and Napoleon's Tomb.

Evening: Enjoy dinner on Ile St. Louis, then a floodlit walk by Notre-Dame.

Day 5

Morning: Ride scenic bus #69 to the Marais and tour this neighborhood, including the Pompidou Center.

Afternoon: Tour the Opéra Garnier (English tours available), and end your day enjoying the glorious rooftop views at the Galeries Lafayette and Printemps department stores.

Evening: Stroll the Champs-Elysées at night.

Orientation to Paris

Paris (population of city center: 2,234,000) is split in half by the Seine River, divided into 20 arrondissements (proud and independent governmental jurisdictions), circled by a ring-road freeway (the *périphérique*), and speckled with Métro stations. You'll find Paris easier to navigate if you know which side of the river you're on, which arrondissement you're in, and which Métro stop you're closest to. If you're north of the river (the top half of any city map), you're on the Right Bank (Rive Droite). If you're south of it, you're on the Left Bank (Rive Gauche). The bull's-eye of your Paris map is Notre-Dame, which sits on an island in the middle of the Seine. Most of your sightseeing will take place within five blocks of the river.

Arrondissements are numbered, starting at the Louvre and moving in a clockwise spiral out to the ring road. The last two digits in a Parisian zip code indicate the arrondissement number. The abbreviation for "Métro stop" is "Mo." In Parisian jargon, the Eiffel Tower is on *la Rive Gauche* (the Left Bank) in the *7ème* (7th arrondissement), zip code 75007, Mo: Trocadéro.

Paris Arrondissements

Paris Métro stops are used as a standard aid in giving directions, even for those not taking the Métro. As you're tracking down addresses, these words and pronunciations will help: Métro (may-troh), *place* (plahs; square), *rue* (roo; road), *avenue* (ah-vuh-noo), *boulevard* (boo-luh-var), and *pont* (pohn; bridge).

Tourist Information

Paris' TIs have long lines, offer little information, and may charge for maps. All you really need are this book and one of the freebie maps available at any hotel. On the plus side, TIs sell individual tickets to sights (see "Avoiding Lines with Advance Tickets" under "Helpful Hints," later) as well as Paris Museum Passes, but if you plan to get a Museum Pass, it's quicker to buy these at participating sights.

If you must visit a TI, you can do so at several locations, including **Pyramides** (daily May-Oct 9:00-19:00, Nov-April 10:00-19:00, at Pyramides Métro stop between the Louvre and Opéra), **Gare de Lyon** (Mon-Sat 8:00-18:00, closed Sun), **Gare du Nord** (daily 8:00-18:00), and **Montmartre** (two branches, both with focus on Montmartre: one on place du Tertre, daily 10:00-19:00, tel. 01 42 62 21 21, and the other above the Anvers Métro stop, daily 10:00-18:00). In summer, small TI kiosks may pop up in the squares in front of Notre-Dame and Hôtel de Ville. Pick up

Paris Neighborhoods

the free *Paris for You!* booklet. The official website for Paris' TIs is www.parisinfo.com. Both **airports** have handy information offices (called ADP) with long hours and short lines.

Pariscope: The weekly €0.40 *Pariscope* magazine (or one of its clones, available at any newsstand) lists museum hours, art exhibits, concerts, festivals, plays, movies, and nightclubs. Smart sightseers rely on this for the latest listings.

Other Publications: *L'Officiel des Spectacles* (€0.35), which is similar to *Pariscope,* also lists goings-on around town (in French). The *Paris Voice,* with snappy reviews of concerts, plays, and current events, is available only online at www.parisvoice.com. For a schedule of museum hours and English museum tours, get the free *Musées, Monuments Historiques, et Expositions* booklet at any museum.

Helpful Websites: These websites come highly recommended for local events in Paris: www.gogoparis.com, www.secretsofparis.com, and www.bonjourparis.com.

American Church and Franco-American Center: This interdenominational church—in the rue Cler neighborhood, facing the river between the Eiffel Tower and Orsay Museum—is a nerve center for the American expat community. Worship services are held every Sunday (traditional services at 9:00 and 11:00, contemporary service at 13:30); the coffee hour after church and the free Sunday concerts (generally Sept-June at 17:00—but not every week and not in Dec) are a good way to get a taste of émigré life in Paris (reception open Mon-Sat 9:00-12:00 & 13:00-22:00, Sun

14:30-19:00, 65 quai d'Orsay, Mo: Invalides, tel. 01 40 62 05 00, www.acparis.org). It's also a handy place to pick up free copies of *France-USA Contacts* (an advertisement paper with info on housing and employment for the 50,000 Americans living in Paris, www.fusac.fr).

Arrival in Paris

For a comprehensive rundown of the city's train stations and airports, see "Paris Connections" on page 340. For information on parking a car, see page 216.

Helpful Hints

Theft Alert: Troublesome thieves thrive near famous monuments and on Métro and RER lines that serve high-profile tourist sights. Beware of pickpockets working busy lines (e.g., at ticket windows at train stations). Pay attention when it's your turn and your back is to the crowd—keep your bag firmly gripped in front of you.

In general, it's smart to wear a money belt, put your wallet in your front pocket, loop your day bag over your shoulders, and keep a tight grip on your purse or shopping bag. Muggings are rare, but they do occur. If you're out late, avoid the dark riverfront embankments and any place where the lighting is dim and pedestrian activity is minimal.

Paris is taking action to combat crime by stationing police at monuments, on streets, and on the Métro, as well as security cameras at key sights. You'll go through quick and reassuring airport-like security checks at many major attractions.

Tourist Scams: Be aware of the latest scams, including these current favorites. The "found ring" scam involves an innocent-looking person who picks up a ring off the ground and asks if you dropped it. When you say no, the person examines the ring more closely, then shows you a mark "proving" that it's pure gold. He offers to sell it to you for a good price—several times more than he paid for it before dropping it on the sidewalk.

In the "friendship bracelet" scam, a vendor approaches you and asks if you'll help him with a demonstration. He proceeds to make a friendship bracelet right on your arm. When finished, he asks you to pay for the bracelet he created just for you. And since you can't easily take it off on the spot, he counts on your feeling obliged to pay up.

Distractions by a stranger—often a "salesman," or someone asking you to sign a petition, or posing as a deaf person to show you a small note to read—can all be tricks that function as a smokescreen for theft. As you try to wriggle away from the pushy stranger, an accomplice picks your pocket.

In popular tourist spots (such as in front of Notre-Dame) young ladies ask if you speak English, then pretend to beg for money while actually angling to get your wallet.

To all these scammers, simply say "no" firmly, don't apologize, don't smile, and step away purposefully.

Street Safety: Parisian drivers are notorious for ignoring pedestrians. Look both ways (many streets are one-way) and be careful of seemingly quiet bus/taxi lanes. Don't assume you have the right of way, even in a crosswalk. When crossing a street, keep your pace constant and don't stop suddenly. By law, drivers are allowed to miss pedestrians by up to just one meter—a little more than three feet (1.5 meters in the countryside). Drivers calculate your speed so they won't hit you, provided you don't alter your route or pace.

Watch out for bicyclists. This popular and silent transportation may come at you from unexpected places and directions—cyclists have a right to use lanes reserved for buses and taxis. Also, bikes commonly go against traffic, as many bike paths are on one-way streets. Again, always look both ways.

Museum Strategies: The worthwhile Paris Museum Pass, covering most sights in the city, is sold at TIs, museums, FNAC stores, and monuments. For detailed information, see "Paris Museum Pass" on page 240.

Avoiding Lines with Advance Tickets: Throughout Paris, TIs and FNAC department stores sell individual *"coupe-file"* tickets, which allow you to use the Museum Pass entrance at sights and thereby skip ticket lines. TIs sell these tickets for no extra fee, but FNAC stores add a surcharge of 10-20 percent (possibly worth it, given the convenience of FNAC's many locations). For sights that can otherwise have long waits (such as the Arc de Triomphe, Opéra Garnier, and Versailles), these tickets are a good idea. (Note that Versailles and the Arc de Triomphe are also covered by the Paris Museum Pass, which allows you to skip lines—and are also sold, without surcharge, at TIs and FNAC stores.)

You can also buy Paris Museum Passes and tickets for several major sights online without a surcharge (no more than three weeks in advance, http://en.parisinfo.com/express-booking/). You'll have to print vouchers and redeem them in person at a Paris TI for the actual passes or tickets (or pay to have them shipped to you); you can't use the vouchers to get directly into museums.

Bookstores: Paris has many English-language bookstores, where you can pick up guidebooks (at nearly double their American prices). Most carry Rick Steves titles.

PARIS

My favorite is the friendly **Red Wheelbarrow Bookstore** in the Marais neighborhood, run by mellow Penelope. She sells most of my guidebooks at good prices, and carries a great collection of other books about Paris and France for both adults and children (Mon 10:00-18:00, Tue-Sat 10:00-19:00, Sun 14:00-18:00, 22 rue St. Paul, Mo: St. Paul, tel. 01 48 04 75 08).

Other options include the following:

Shakespeare and Company (some used travel books, Mon-Fri 10:00-23:00, Sat-Sun 11:00-23:00, 37 rue de la Bûcherie, across the river from Notre-Dame, Mo: St. Michel, tel. 01 43 25 40 93);

W. H. Smith (Mon-Sat 9:00-19:00, Sun 12:30-19:00, 248 rue de Rivoli, Mo: Concorde, tel. 01 44 77 88 99);

Village Voice (Mon 14:00-19:30, Tue-Sat 10:00-19:30, Sun 12:00-18:00, near St. Sulpice Church at 6 rue Princesse, Mo: Mabillon, tel. 01 46 33 36 47); and

San Francisco Book Company (Mon-Sat 11:00-21:00, Sun 14:00-19:30, 17 rue Monsieur le Prince, Mo: Odéon, tel. 01 43 29 15 70).

Public WCs: Public toilets are free (though it's polite to leave a small tip of €0.20-0.50 if there's an attendant). Modern, sanitary street-booth toilets provide both relief and a memory (don't leave small children inside unattended). The restrooms in museums are free and the best you'll find. Or walk into any sidewalk café like you own the place, and find the toilet in the back. If you have to buy something, your cheapest option is to order a shot of espresso *(un express)* standing at the bar. Keep toilet paper or tissues with you, as some WCs are poorly supplied.

Parking: Street parking is generally free at night (19:00 to 9:00), all day Sunday, and anytime in August, when many Parisians are on vacation. To pay for streetside parking, you must go to a *tabac* and buy a parking card *(une carte de stationnement)*, sold in €10, €20, and €30 denominations. Insert the card into the meter (chip-side in) and punch the desired amount of time (generally €1-2/hour), then take the receipt and display it in your windshield. Meters limit street parking to a maximum of two hours. For a longer stay, park for less at an airport (about €10/day) and take public transport or a taxi into the city. Underground lots are numerous in Paris—you'll find them under Ecole Militaire, St. Sulpice Church, Les Invalides, the Bastille, and the Panthéon; all charge about €27-36/day (€58/3 days, €10/day more after that, for locations see www.vincipark.com). Some hotels offer parking for less—ask your hotelier.

Tobacco Stands *(Tabacs):* These little kiosks—usually just a counter inside a café—sell cards for parking meters, some public-transit tickets, postage stamps (though not all sell international postage—to mail something home, use two domestic stamps, or go to a post office), prepaid phone cards, and...oh yeah, cigarettes. To find one anywhere in Paris, just look for a *Tabac* sign and the red cylinder-shaped symbol above certain cafés.

Winter Activities: The City of Light sparkles year-round. For background on what to do and see here in winter months, see www.ricksteves.com/pariswinter.

Getting Around Paris

Paris is easy to navigate. Your basic choices are Métro (in-city subway), RER (suburban rail tied into the Métro system), public bus, and taxi. (Also consider the hop-on, hop-off bus and boat tours, described under "Tours in Paris," page 223.) You can buy tickets and passes at Métro stations and at many tobacco stands *(tabacs)*. Staffed ticket windows in stations are gradually being phased out in favor of ticket machines, so expect some stations to have machines only—be sure to carry coins or small bills of €20 or less (not all machines take bills and none take American credit cards). If a ticket machine is out of order or if you're out of change, buy tickets at a *tabac*.

Public-Transit Tickets: The Métro, RER, and buses all work on the same tickets. You can make as many transfers as you need on a single ticket, except when transferring between the Métro/RER system and the bus system, which requires using an additional ticket. A **single ticket** costs €1.70. To save money, buy a *carnet* (kar-nay) of 10 tickets for €12.50 (cheaper for ages 4-10). *Carnets* can be shared among travelers.

Passes: You can buy a chip-embedded card, called the **Passe Navigo** (though for most tourists, *carnets* are a better deal). You pay a one-time €5 fee for the Navigo card itself (which also requires a postage stamp-size photo of yourself—bring your own, print a color photo, or use the €4 photo booths in major Métro stations). For a weekly *(hebdomadaire)* version, you'll pay €23.85 (includes €5 card fee), which gives you free run of the bus, Métro, and non-suburban RER system from Monday to Sunday (expiring on Sunday, even if you buy it on Friday). A monthly version is also available.

To use the Navigo, whether at a Métro turnstile or on the bus, touch the card to the purple pad, wait for the green validation light and the "ding," and you're on your way. The basic pass covers only central Paris, not regional destinations such as Versailles.

Navigo or *Carnet*? It's hard to beat the *carnet.* Two 10-packs of *carnets*—enough for most travelers staying a week—cost €25, are shareable, and don't expire until they're used. The Passe Navigo only becomes worthwhile for visitors who stay a full week or more and use the system a lot.

Other Passes: A handy one-day bus/Métro pass (called **Mobilis**) is available for €6.30. The overpriced **Paris Visite** passes are poorly designed for tourists, and offer minor reductions at minor sights (1 day/€9.30, 2 days/€15.20, 3 days/€20.70, 5 days/€29.90).

By Métro

In Paris, you're never more than a 10-minute walk from a Métro station. Europe's best subway system allows you to hop from sight to sight quickly and cheaply (runs daily 5:30-24:30 in the morning, Fri-Sat until 2:00 in the morning, www.ratp.fr). Learn to use it. Color Métro maps are free at Métro stations and included on freebie Paris maps at your hotel.

How the Métro Works: To get to your destination, determine the closest "Mo" stop and which line or lines will get you there. The lines are color-coded and numbered, and you can tell their direction by their end-of-the-line stops. For example, the La Défense/Château de Vincennes line, also known as line 1 (yellow), runs between La Défense, on its west end, and Vincennes on its east end. Once in the Métro station, you'll see the color-coded line numbers and/or blue-and-white signs directing you to the train going in your direction (e.g., *direction: La Défense*). Insert your ticket in the automatic turnstile, reclaim your ticket, pass through, and keep it until you exit the system (some stations require you to pass your ticket through a turnstile to exit). As mentioned earlier, the smallest stations are unstaffed and have ticket machines (coins are essential).

Be warned that fare inspectors regularly check for cheaters and accept absolutely no excuses—keep that ticket or pay a minimum fine of €25.

Be prepared to walk significant distances within Métro stations (especially when you transfer). Transfers are free and can be made wherever lines cross, provided you do so within 1.5 hours. When you transfer, follow the appropriately colored line number for your next train, or find orange *correspondance* (connection) signs that lead to your next line.

When you reach your destination, look for the blue-and-white *sortie* signs pointing you to the exit. Before leaving the station, check the helpful *plan du quartier* (map of the neighborhood) to get your bearings. At stops with several *sorties*, you can save time by choosing the best exit.

After you exit the system, toss or tear your used ticket so you don't confuse it with unused tickets—they look almost identical.

Beware of Pickpockets: Thieves dig the Métro and RER. Be on guard. For example, if your pocket is picked as you pass

PARIS

through a turnstile, you end up stuck on the wrong side (after the turnstile bar has closed behind you) while the thief gets away. Stand away from Métro doors to avoid being a target for a theft-and-run just before the doors close. Any jostling or commotion—especially when boarding or leaving trains—is likely the sign of a thief or a team of thieves in action. See page 214 for tips on keeping your bag close. Make any fare inspector show proof of identity (ask locals for help if you're not certain). Never show anyone your wallet.

By RER

The RER (Réseau Express Régionale; air-ay-air) is the suburban arm of the Métro, serving outlying destinations such as Versailles, Disneyland Paris, and the airports. These routes are indicated by thick lines on your subway map and identified by the letters A, B, C, and so on.

Within the city center, the RER works like the Métro and can be speedier if it serves your destination directly, because it makes fewer stops. Métro tickets and the Passe Navigo card are good on the RER when traveling in the city center. You can transfer between the Métro and RER systems with the same ticket. But to travel outside the city (to Versailles or the airport, for example), you'll need a separate, more expensive ticket. Unlike the Métro, not every train stops at every station along the way; check the sign over the platform to see if your destination is listed as a stop (*"toutes les gares"* means it makes all stops along the way), or confirm with a local before you board. For RER trains, you may need to insert your ticket in a turnstile to exit the system.

By City Bus

Paris' excellent bus system is worth figuring out. Buses don't seem as romantic as the famous Métro and are subject to traffic jams, but savvy travelers know that buses can have you swinging through the city like Tarzan in an urban jungle. Buses require less walking and fewer stairways than the Métro, and you can see Paris unfold as you travel.

Bus stops are everywhere, and every stop comes with all the information you need: a good city bus map, route maps showing exactly where each bus that uses this stop goes, a frequency chart and schedule, a *plan du quartier* map of the immediate neighborhood, and a *soirées* map explaining night service, if available (www.ratp.fr).

Just like with the Métro, every bus stop has a name, and every bus is headed to one end-of-the-line stop or the other. First, find your stop on the chart, then find your destination stop. Now, find out exactly where to catch the bus going in that direction. (On the maps showing the bus route, notice the triangle-shaped arrows pointing in the direction the bus is headed. With so many one-way streets in Paris, it's easy to get on the bus in the wrong direction.) When the bus pulls up, double-check that the sign on the front of the bus has the end-of-the-line stop going in your direction.

Buses use the same tickets and passes as the Métro and RER. One Zone 1 ticket buys you a bus ride anywhere in central Paris within the freeway ring road *(le périphérique)*. Use your Métro ticket or buy one on board for €0.20 more. (The ticket system has a few quirks—see "More Bus Tips," below.)

Board your bus through the front door (or on long buses, push the green button by the other doors to open them). If you already have a ticket, validate it in the yellow machine (and then remember to reclaim it). If you have a Passe Navigo, scan it on the purple touchpad. Otherwise, buy a ticket from the driver. Keep track of what stop is coming up next by following the on-board diagram or listening to recorded announcements. When you're ready to get off, push the red button to signal you want a stop, then exit through the rear door. Even if you're not certain you've figured out the system, do some joyriding.

More Bus Tips: Avoid rush hour (Mon-Fri 8:00-9:30 & 17:30-19:30), when buses are jammed and traffic doesn't move. Not all city buses are air-conditioned, so they can become rolling greenhouses on summer days. You can transfer from one bus to another on the same ticket (within 1.5 hours, re-validate your ticket in the next bus's yellow machine), but you can't do a round-trip or hop on and off on the same line. Neither can you transfer between the bus and the Métro/RER systems on a single ticket. Also, you can't transfer between buses with a ticket bought on board—go figure.

Handy bus-system maps *(plans des autobus)* are available in any Métro station (and in the €6 *Paris Pratique* map book sold at newsstands). For longer stays, consider buying the €6 *Le Bus* book of bus routes. While the Métro shuts down at about 24:30 in the morning, some buses continue much later (called *Noctilien* lines, www.noctilien.fr).

I've listed the handiest bus routes for each recommended hotel neighborhood under "Sleeping in Paris," later.

By Taxi

Parisian taxis are reasonable, especially for couples and families. The meters are tamper-proof. Fares and supplements (listed in English on the windows) are straightforward and tightly regulated.

A taxi can fit three people comfortably, and a fourth for €3 extra. (Cabbies are legally required to accept four passengers, though they don't always like it.) Groups of up to five can use a larger vehicle, which can sometimes be found at taxi stands but can more reliably be booked in advance (€3/person extra for over 3 people)—ask your hotelier to call. For a sample taxi tour of the city at night, see page 286.

Rates: All Parisian taxis start with €2.30 on the meter, and have a minimum charge of €6.20. A 20-minute ride (e.g., Bastille to the Eiffel Tower) costs about €20 (versus €1.25/person to get anywhere in town using a *carnet* ticket on the Métro or bus). Drivers charge higher rates at rush hour, at night, all day Sunday, and to any of the airports. Each piece of luggage you put in the trunk is €1 extra (though it won't appear on the meter, it is a legitimate charge). To tip, round up to the next euro (at least €0.50).

How to Catch *un Taxi:* You can try waving down a taxi, but it's often easier to ask someone for the nearest taxi stand (*"Où est une station de taxi?";* oo ay ewn stah-see-ohn duh "taxi"). Taxi stands are indicated by a circled "T" on good city maps, and on many maps in this chapter. To order a taxi in English, call 01 41 27 66 99, or ask your hotelier for help. When you summon a taxi by phone, the meter starts running as soon as the call is received, often adding €6 or more to the bill.

Taxis are tough to find during rush hour, when it's raining, on weekend nights, or on any night after the Métro closes (Sun-Thu at 24:30 in the morning, Fri-Sat at 2:00 in the morning). If you need to catch a train or flight early in the morning, book a taxi the day before (especially for weekday departures). Some taxi companies require a €5 reservation fee by credit card for weekday morning rush-hour departures (7:00-10:00) and only have a limited number of reservation spots.

By Bike

Paris is surprisingly easy by bicycle. The city is flat, and riders have access to more than 370 miles of bike lanes and the many priority lanes for buses and taxis (though be careful on these). I biked along the river from Notre-Dame to the Eiffel Tower in 15 wonderfully scenic minutes. Since the inauguration of the Vélib' bike program in 2007 (see "'Bike Freedom' for Parisians," next page), Parisian drivers have become accustomed to sharing the road with bicycles.

Urban bikers will find Paris a breeze. First-timers will get the hang of it quickly enough by following some simple rules. Always stay to the right in your lane, bike single-file, stay off sidewalks, watch out for opening doors on parked cars, signal with your arm before making turns, and use bike paths when available. Obey the traffic laws as if you were driving a car. Parisians use the same road rules as Americans, with two exceptions: When passing vehicles or other bikes, always pass on the left (it's illegal to ever pass on the right); and where there is no stoplight, always yield to traffic merging from the right, even if you're on a major road and the merging driver is on a side street. You'll find a bell on your bike; use it like a horn to warn pedestrians who don't see you.

The TIs have a helpful "Paris à Vélo" map, which shows all the dedicated bike paths. Many other versions are available for sale at newsstand kiosks, some bookstores, and department stores.

Both bike companies listed below rent bikes at good rates, sell maps, and also offer organized tours by bike (listed under "Tours in Paris," later).

Bike About Tours is your best bet for bike rental. Their bikes are also foldable, which allows you to collapse your bike and jump on the Métro if the weather turns bad or if you get tired (€15/day during office hours, €20/24 hours; includes locks, helmets, and comfy gel seats; daily mid-Feb-mid-April 9:00-11:30, mid-April-Sept 9:00-11:30 & 13:30-16:00, closed Oct-mid-Feb; shop located near Hôtel de Ville at 4 rue de Lobau in Vinci parking garage—see map on page 229, Mo: Hôtel de Ville, www.bikeabouttours.com, info@bikeabouttours.com). They sell detailed maps for €6 (free for Rick Steves readers with bike rental) and are full of advice for routes and things to see.

Fat Tire Bike Tours has some bikes for rent—call ahead to check availability (€4/hour, €25/24 hours, includes helmets and locks, credit-card imprint required for deposit; ask about discounts with this book; office open daily 9:00-18:30, May-Aug bike rental only after 11:30 as priority is given to those taking a tour, ask for their map of suggested routes, 24 rue Edgar Faure—see map on page 256, Mo: Dupleix, tel. 01 56 58 10 54, www.fattirebiketours paris.com).

"Bike Freedom" for Parisians: The high-tech bike racks you see all over town are part of the city's innovative **Vélib'** program, which gives those with a Vélib' card access to more than 20,000 bikes around the city for just €30 per year (rides of up to 30 minutes are free). These bikes are geared mainly for residents to rent (the machines take chip-embedded European credit cards, and American Express cards—but no other American cards; though you can order online with US credit cards at http://en.velib.paris .fr/). The plus side of the popular, highly touted Vélib' program is that it has prompted the city to add more bike paths, and has helped Parisian drivers learn to share the road with bicycles.

By Scooter

Left Bank Scooters will deliver and pick up rental scooters to daring travelers over 20 years old with a valid driver's license (€80-100/day, price depends on size of the scooter and how long you keep it, mobile 06 78 12 04 24, www.leftbankscooters.com).

Tours in Paris

To sightsee on your own, download my series of **free audio tours** that illuminate some of Paris' top sights and neighborhoods: my Historic Paris Walk, the Louvre, the Orsay, and the palace at Versailles (see sidebar on page 7 for details).

By Bus

Bus Tours—**Paris Vision** (also called Cityrama) offers bus tours of Paris, day and night (advertised in hotel lobbies). I'd consider a Paris Vision tour only for their nighttime tour (see page 285). During the day, the hop-on, hop-off bus tours and the Batobus (both described in this section) are a better value, providing transportation between sights as well as commentary.

Hop-on, Hop-off Bus Tours—Double-decker buses connect Paris' main sights, allowing you to hop on and off along the way. You get a disposable set of ear plugs to listen to a basic running commentary (dial English for the so-so narration). You can get off at any stop, tour a sight, then catch a later bus. These are best in good weather, when you can sit up top. There are two companies: L'Open Tours and Les Cars Rouges (pick up their brochures showing routes and stops from any TI or on their buses). You can start either tour at just about any of the major sights, such as the Eiffel Tower.

   L'Open Tours uses bright yellow buses and provides more extensive coverage (and slightly better commentary) on four different routes, rolling by most of the important sights in Paris. Their Paris Grand Tour (the green route) offers the best introduction. The same ticket gets you on any of their routes within the validity period. Buy your tickets from the driver (1 day-€29, 2 days-€32, kids 4-11 pay €15 for 1 or 2 days, allow 2 hours per tour). Two to four buses depart hourly from about 10:00 to 18:00; expect to wait 10-15 minutes at each stop (stops can be tricky to find—look for yellow signs; tel. 01 42 66 56 56, www.parislopentour.com). A combo-ticket covers both the Batobus boats (described later) and L'Open Tours buses (€44, kids under 12 pay €20, valid 3 days).

   Les Cars Rouges' bright red buses offer largely the same service, with only one route and just nine stops, for less (recorded narration, adult-€26, kids 4-12 pay €13, good for 2 days, 10 percent cheaper when booked online, tel. 01 53 95 39 53, www.carsrouges .com).

By Boat

Seine Cruises—Several companies run one-hour boat cruises on the Seine. For the best experience, cruise at twilight or after dark.

PARIS

(To dine while you cruise, see "Dinner Cruises" on page 340.) Two of the companies—Bateaux-Mouches and Bateaux Parisiens—are convenient to the rue Cler hotels, and both run daily year-round (April-Oct 10:00-22:30, 2-3/hour; Nov-March shorter hours, runs hourly). Some offer discounts for early online bookings.

Bateaux-Mouches, the oldest boat company in Paris, departs from pont de l'Alma's right bank, and has the biggest open-top, double-decker boats (higher up means better views). But this company often has too many tour groups, causing these boats to get packed (€11, kids 4-12 pay €5.50, tel. 01 42 25 96 10, www.bateaux-mouches.fr).

Bateaux Parisiens has smaller covered boats with handheld audioguides, fewer crowds, and only one deck. It leaves from right in front of the Eiffel Tower. From April to October, they usually have a second departure point on the quai de Montebello near Notre-Dame (€12, kids 3-12 pay €5, half-price if you have a valid France or France-Switzerland railpass—does not use up a day of a flexipass, tel. 01 76 64 14 45 or toll 08 25 01 01 01, www.bateauxparisiens.com).

Vedettes du Pont Neuf offers essentially the same one-hour tour as the other companies, but starts and ends at pont Neuf, closer to recommended hotels in the Marais and Luxembourg Garden neighborhoods. The boats feature a live guide whose delivery (in English and French) is as stiff as a recorded narration—and as hard to understand, given the quality of their sound system (€13, ask about discount if you book direct with this book, kids 4-12 pay €6, tip requested, check for online advance-purchase discounts, nearly 2/hour, daily 10:30-22:30, tel. 01 46 33 98 38, www.vedettesdupontneuf.com).

Hop-on, Hop-Off Boat Tour—**Batobus** allows you to get on and off as often as you like at any of eight popular stops along the Seine. The boats, which make a continuous circuit, stop in this order: Eiffel Tower, the Orsay, St. Germain-des-Prés, Notre-Dame, Jardin des Plantes, Hôtel de Ville, the Louvre, and pont Alexandre III—near the Champs-Elysées (1 day-€14, 2 days-€18, 5 days-€21, boats run June-Aug 10:00-21:30, mid-March-May and Sept-Oct 10:00-19:00, Nov-early Jan and Feb-mid-March 10:30-16:30, no service last three weeks in Jan, every 15-20 minutes, 45 minutes one-way, 1.5-hour round-trip, worthless narration, www.batobus.com). If you use this for getting around—sort of a scenic, floating alternative to the Métro—it can be worthwhile, especially with a 5-day pass. But if you just want a guided boat tour, Batobus is not as good a value as the regular tour boats described previously.

Low-Key Cruise on a Tranquil Canal—**Canauxrama** runs a lazy 2.5-hour cruise on a peaceful canal out of sight of the Seine.

Tours start from place de la Bastille and end at Bassin de la Villette (near Mo: Stalingrad). During the first segment of your trip, you'll pass through a long tunnel (built at the order of Napoleon in the early 19th century, when canal boats were vital for industrial transport). Once outside, you glide—not much faster than you can walk—through sleepy Parisian neighborhoods and slowly climb through four double locks as a guide narrates the trip in French and English (€16, check online for discounts for advance booking, departs at 9:45 and 14:30 across from Opéra Bastille, just below boulevard de la Bastille, opposite #50—where the canal meets place de la Bastille, tel. 01 42 39 15 00, www.canauxrama.com). The same tour also goes in the opposite direction, from Bassin de la Villette to place de la Bastille (departs at 9:45 and 14:45). It's OK to bring a picnic on board.

On Foot

Paris Walks—This company offers a variety of two-hour walks, led by British and American guides. Tours are thoughtfully prepared and entertaining. Don't hesitate to stand close to the guide to hear (€12-15, generally 2/day—morning and afternoon, private tours available, family guides and Louvre tours a specialty, call tel. 01 48 09 21 40 for schedule in English, or check printable online schedule at www.paris-walks.com). Tours focus on the Marais (4/week), Montmartre (3/week), medieval Latin Quarter (Mon), Ile de la Cité/Notre-Dame (Mon), the "Two Islands" (Ile de la Cité and Ile St. Louis, Wed), the Revolution (Tue), and Hemingway's Paris (Fri). Call a day or two ahead to hear the current schedule and starting point. Most tours don't require reservations, but specialty tours (such as the Louvre, Fashion, or Chocolate tour) require advance reservations and prepayment with credit card (not refundable if you cancel less than two days in advance).

Context Paris—These "intellectual by design" walking tours, geared for serious learners, are led by docents (historians, architects, and academics). They cover both museums and specific neighborhoods, and range from traditional topics such as French art history in the Louvre and the Gothic architecture of Notre-Dame to more thematic explorations like immigration and the changing face of Paris, jazz in the Latin Quarter, and the history of the baguette. It's best to book in advance—groups are limited to six participants and can fill up fast (€40-90/person, admission to sights extra, generally 3 hours, tel. 01 72 81 36 35, US tel. 800-691-6036, www.contextparis.com). They also offer private tours and excursions outside Paris.

Classic Walks—The antithesis of Context Paris' walks, these lowbrow, low-information, but high-fun walking tours are run by Fat Tire Bike Tours. Their 3.5-hour "Classic Walk" covers most major sights (€20, March-Oct, daily at 10:00, meet at their office—see their listing under "By Bike," below). They also do two-hour walks on various themes and neighborhoods: Montmartre, French Revolution, World War II, and Latin Quarter (€12-20, ask about discount with this book, leaves several times a week—see website for details and ask about their new "Skip the Line" tours of individual monuments and sights, 24 rue Edgar Faure, Mo: Dupleix, tel. 01 56 58 10 54, www.classicwalksparis.com).

Local Guides—For many, Paris merits hiring a Parisian as a personal guide. **Arnaud Servignat** is an excellent licensed guide (€190/half-day, also does car tours of the countryside around Paris for a little more, mobile 06 68 80 29 05, www.french-guide.com, arnotour@me.com). **Thierry Gauduchon** is a terrific guide well worth his fee (€180/half-day, €350/day, tel. 01 56 98 10 82, mobile 06 19 07 30 77, tgauduchon@aol.com). **Elisabeth Van Hest** is another likeable and capable guide (€190/half-day, tel. 01 43 41 47 31, elisa.guide@gmail.com).

Food Tours—Friendly Canadian **Rosa Jackson** designs personalized "Edible Paris" itineraries based on your interests, and three-hour "food-guru" tours of Paris led by her or one of her two colleagues (non-guided itineraries from €125, €300 guided tours for up to 3, mobile 06 81 67 41 22, www.edible-paris.com, rosa @rosajackson.com).

By Bike

Paris is terrific by bike (see "Getting Around Paris—By Bike," page 221) and made easier by a bike tour. Both companies below sell bottled water and bike maps of Paris, and can give advice on biking routes of the city. Their tour routes cover different areas of the city, so avid cyclists could do both without much repetition.

Bike About Tours—Run by Christian (American) and Paul (New Zealander), this company offers easygoing tours with a focus on the eastern half of the city. Their four-hour tours run daily year-round at 10:00 (also at 15:00 June-Sept). You'll meet at the statue of Charlemagne in front of Notre-Dame. The tour includes a good back-street visit of the Marais, Rive Gauche outdoor sculpture park, Ile de la Cité, heart of the Latin Quarter (with a lunch break), Louvre, Les Halles, and Pompidou Center. Group tours have a 12-person maximum—reserve online to guarantee a spot, or show up and take your chances (€30, ask about discount with this book, maximum 2 discounts per book, 15 percent discount for families, includes helmets upon request, private tours available, see listing on page 222 for contact info).

Fat Tire Bike Tours—A hardworking gang of young American expats operates an extensive program of bike, Segway, and walking tours.

Their high-energy guides run four-hour bike tours of Paris, by day and by night. Reservations aren't necessary—just show up. Tours cost €28; show this book and ask for a discount (maximum 2 discounts per book).

On the day tour, you'll pedal with a pack of 10-20 riders with a lunch stop in the Tuileries Garden (tours leave daily rain or shine at 11:00, April-Oct at 15:00 as well). Night tours follow a route past floodlit monuments, are livelier, and include a boat cruise on the Seine (April-Oct daily at 19:00, March daily at 18:00, end of Feb and all of Nov Tue, Thu, and Sat-Sun at 18:00, no night tours Dec-mid-Feb). Both tours meet at the south pillar of the Eiffel Tower (for contact info see listing on page 222). They also run bike tours to Versailles and Giverny (reservations required, see website for details). Their office has Internet access with English keyboards.

Fat Tire's pricey four-hour **City Segway Tours**—on stand-up motorized scooters—are novel in that you learn to ride a Segway while exploring Paris (you'll get the hang of it after about half an hour). These tours take no more than eight people at a time, so reservations are required (€75, daily at 9:30, April-Oct also at 14:00 and 18:30, March and Nov also at 14:00, tel. 01 56 58 10 54, www.citysegwaytours.com).

Weekend Tour Packages for Students in Paris

Andy Steves (Rick's son) runs **Weekend Student Adventures**, offering experiential three-day weekend tours for €250 designed for American students studying abroad (see www.wsaeurope.com for details on tours of Paris and other great European cities).

Excursions from Paris

Most of the local guides listed earlier will do excursion tours from Paris using your rental car. Or consider these companies, which provide transportation:

Paris Webservices, a reliable outfit, offers many services, including day trips with English-speaking chauffeur-guides in cushy minivans for private groups (figure €90-120/person for groups of 4 or more, use promo code "RSteves 77" and show current edition of this book for a discount; see contact info in listing on page 346).

Many companies offer bus tours to regional sights. **Paris Vision** (tel. 01 42 60 30 01, www.parisvision.com) runs uninspired minivan and bus tours to several popular regional destinations, including the Loire Valley, Champagne region, D-Day beaches, and Mont St. Michel. Minivan tours are pricier, but more personal and given in English, and most offer convenient pickup at your hotel (half-day tour about €80/person, day tour about €190/person). Their Cityrama full-size bus tours are multilingual,

PARIS

mass-marketed, and nothing special, but cheaper than the mini-van tours—worthwhile for some travelers simply for the ease of transportation to the sights (about €70-150, destinations include Versailles, Giverny, and more, www.pariscityrama.fr).

Self-Guided Walk

Historic Paris Walk

(This information is distilled from the Historic Paris Walk chapter in *Rick Steves' Paris,* by Rick Steves, Steve Smith, and Gene Openshaw. You can download a free Rick Steves audio tour of this neighborhood; see page 7.)

Allow four hours to do justice to this three-mile walk; just follow the gray line on the "Historic Paris Walk" map. Start where the city did—on the Ile de la Cité, the island in the Seine River and the physical and historic bull's-eye of your Paris map. The closest Métro stops are Cité, Hôtel de Ville, and St. Michel, each a short walk away.

• *On the square in front of Notre-Dame Cathedral, stand far enough back to take in the whole facade. View it from the bronze plaque on the ground marked "Point Zero" (30 yards from the central doorway). You're standing at the center of France, the point from which all distances in France are measured. Find the circular window in the center of the cathedral's facade.*

▲▲▲Notre-Dame Cathedral

This 700-year-old cathedral is packed with history and tourists. Study its sculpture and windows, take in a Mass, eavesdrop on guides, and walk all around the outside.

Cost and Hours: Free, cathedral open daily 8:00-18:45, Sat-Sun until 19:15; Treasury-€3, not covered by Museum Pass, daily 9:30-18:00, Sat-Sun until 18:30; audioguide-€5, free English tours—normally Wed and Thu at 14:00, Sat at 14:30; Mo: Cité, Hôtel de Ville, or St. Michel; tel. 01 42 34 56 10, www.notredame deparis.fr. The international Mass is held Sun at 11:30, with an organ concert at 16:30. Call or check the website for a full schedule. On Good Friday and the first Friday of the month at 15:00, the (physically underwhelming) relic known as Jesus' Crown of Thorns goes on display.

Tower: You can climb to the top of the facade between the towers, and then to the top of the south tower, 400 steps total, for a grand view (€8, covered by Museum Pass but no bypass line for passholders, daily April-Sept 10:00-18:30, June-Aug Sat-Sun until 23:00, Oct-March 10:00-17:30, last entry 45 minutes before closing, arrive before 10:00 or after 17:00 to avoid long lines, tel. 01 53 10 07 00, www.notre-dame-de-paris.monuments-nationaux.fr).

Historic Paris Walk

RIGHT BANK

TO LES HALLES

TO LOUVRE

QUAI DU LOUVRE

PONT NEUF

RUE DE SEBAST.

CHATELET (+R)

TOUR ST. JACQUES

BLVD SEBAST.

RIVOLI

TO POMPIDOU

RENARD

TO PLACE BASTILLE

HOTEL DE VILLE

FINISH 9

BOATS

PONT NEUF

SEINE

QUAI DE L'HORLOGE

CHANGE 10

NOTRE DAME

QUAI DE L'HOTEL DE VILLE

PALAIS DE JUSTICE 8

6

CITÉ

MKT. 7

TO ORSAY & PONT DES ARTS

SAINTE-CHAPELLE

5

WC

RUE DE LUTECE

HOTEL DIEU HOSPITAL

QUAI D'ARCOLE

START

PLACE ST. MICHEL

RUE ST. ANDRE-DES-ARTS

4

CRYPT

PLACE PARVIS 1

NOTRE-DAME

3

PLACE ST. ANDRE-DES-ARTS

R

M

HUCHETTE

SHAKESPEARE & BOOKS

B

2

ODEON M

BLVD.

ST. MICHEL

R. HARPE

R. ST. SEVERIN

RUE DE LA

HUCHETTE

JACQUES

GALANDE

LA GRANGE

QUAI TOURNELLE

TO ST. SULPICE

CLUNY

CLUNY MUSEUM

ST.

MAUBERT MUTUALITE M

GERMAIN

R. MONGE

LEFT BANK

TO SORBONNE & LUXEMBOURG GARDEN

TO RUE MOUFFETARD

200 YARDS
200 METERS

➡ WALKING TOUR ROUTE

Ⓜ METRO STATION   Ⓑ BATOBUS BOAT STOP

Ⓡ RER STOP   ⚲ VIEW

DCH

❶ Point Zero & Notre-Dame
❷ Deportation Memorial
❸ Ile St. Louis
❹ Latin Quarter
❺ Sainte-Chapelle
❻ Palais de Justice

❼ Cité Métro Stop & Flower Market
❽ Conciergerie
❾ Pont Neuf
❿ Paris Plages Center

PARIS

Affording Paris' Sights

Paris is an expensive city for tourists, with lots of pricey sights, but—fortunately—lots of freebies, too. Smart, budget-minded travelers begin by buying and getting the most out of a **Paris Museum Pass** (see page 240), then considering these frugal sightseeing options.

Free Museums: Museums that are always free (with the possible exception of special exhibits) include the Carnavalet, Petit Palais, Victor Hugo's House, and Fragonard Perfume Museum. Many of Paris' most famous museums offer free entry on the first Sunday of the month, including the Louvre, Orsay, Rodin, Cluny, Pompidou Center, Quai Branly, and Delacroix museums. These sights are free on the first Sunday of off-season months: the Arc de Triomphe (Oct-March) and Versailles (Nov-March). Expect big crowds on free days. You can also visit the Orsay Museum for free at 17:00 (or Thu at 21:00), an hour before the museum closes. One of the best everyday values is the Rodin Museum's garden, where it costs just €1 to experience many of Rodin's finest works in a lovely outdoor setting.

Other Freebies: Many worthwhile sights don't charge entry, including the Notre-Dame Cathedral, Père Lachaise Cemetery, Deportation Memorial, Holocaust Memorial, Paris Plages (summers only), Sacré-Cœur Basilica, St. Sulpice Church (with organ recital), and La Défense.

Paris' glorious, entertaining parks are free, of course. These include Luxembourg Garden, Champ de Mars (under the Eiffel Tower), Tuileries Garden (between the Louvre and place de la Concorde), Palais Royal Courtyards, Jardin des Plantes, Parc Monceau, the Promenade Plantée walk, and Versailles' gardens (except when the fountains perform on Tue late May-late June and weekends April-Oct).

Reduced Price: Several museums offer a discount if you enter later in the day, including the Orsay (Fri-Wed after 16:15 and Thu after 18:00) and the Army Museum and Napoleon's

● **Self-Guided Tour:** The **cathedral facade** is worth a close look. The church is dedicated to "Our Lady" *(Notre Dame)*. Mary is center stage—cradling God, right in the heart of the facade, surrounded by the halo of the rose window. Adam is on the left and Eve is on the right.

Below Mary and above the arches is a row of 28 statues known as the Kings of Judah. During the French Revolution, these biblical kings were mistaken for the hated French kings, and Notre-Dame represented the oppressive Catholic hierarchy. The citizens stormed the church, crying, "Off with their heads!" All were decapitated, but have since been recapitated.

Speaking of decapitation, look at the carving to the left of

Tomb (after 16:00).

Free Concerts: Venues offering free or cheap (€6-8) concerts include the American Church, Hôtel des Invalides, St. Sulpice Church, La Madeleine Church, and Notre-Dame Cathedral. For a listing of free concerts, check *Pariscope* magazine (under the "Musique" section) and look for events marked *entrée libre*.

Self-Guided Bus Tours: Instead of paying €25 for a tour company to give you an overview of Paris, ride city bus #69 for the cost of a Métro ticket. This scenic route crosses the city east-west, running between the Eiffel Tower and Père Lachaise Cemetery, and passing these great monuments and neighborhoods: Eiffel Tower, Ecole Militaire, rue Cler, Les Invalides (Army Museum and Napoleon's Tomb), Louvre Museum, Ile de la Cité, Ile St. Louis, Hôtel de Ville, Pompidou Center, Marais, Bastille, and Père Lachaise.

You can board daily until 22:30 (last departure from Eiffel Tour stop). It's best to avoid weekday rush hours (8:00-9:30 & 17:30-19:30) and hot days (no air-con). Sundays are quietest, and it's easy to get a window seat. Evening bus rides are magical from fall through spring (roughly Sept-April), when it gets dark early enough to see the floodlit monuments before the bus stops running. In the rue Cler area, eastbound line #69 leaves from the Eiffel Tower on avenue Joseph Bouvard (the first stop is at the southwestern end of the avenue; the second stop is at the eastern end (just before avenue de la Bourdonnais).

Good-Value Tours: At €12-15, Paris Walks' tours are a good value. The €11-14 Seine River cruises, best after dark, are also worthwhile.

Pricey...but worth it? Certain big-ticket items—primarily the Eiffel Tower, Louvre, and Versailles—are expensive and crowded, but offer once-in-a-lifetime experiences. All together they amount to less than a ticket to Disneyland—only these are real.

PARIS

the doorway on the left. The man with his head in his hands is St. Denis. Back when there was a Roman temple on this spot, Christianity began making converts. The fourth-century bishop of Roman Paris, Denis was beheaded as a warning to those forsaking the Roman gods. But those early Christians were hard to keep down. The man who would become St. Denis got up, tucked his head under his arm, headed north, paused at a fountain to wash it off, and continued until he found just the right place to meet his maker: Montmartre. (Although the name "Montmartre" comes from the Roman "Mount of Mars," later generations—thinking of their beheaded patron, St. Denis—preferred a less pagan version, "Mount of Martyrs.") The Parisians were convinced by this miracle, Christianity gained ground, and a church soon replaced the pagan temple.

Medieval art was OK if it embellished the house of God and told biblical stories. For a fine example, move to the base of the central column (at the foot of Mary, about where the head of St. Denis could spit if he were really good). Working around from the left, find God telling a barely created Eve, "Have fun, but no apples." Next, the sexiest serpent I've ever seen makes apples à la mode. Finally, Adam and Eve, now ashamed of their nakedness, are expelled by an angel. This is a tiny example in a church covered with meaning.

Step **inside.** You'll be routed around the ambulatory, in much the same way medieval pilgrims were. Notre-Dame has the typical basilica floor plan shared by so many Catholic churches: a long central nave lined with columns and flanked by side aisles. It's designed in the shape of a cross, with the altar placed where the crossbeam intersects. The church can hold up to 10,000 faithful, and it's probably buzzing with visitors now, just as it was 600 years ago. The quiet, deserted churches we see elsewhere are in stark contrast to the busy, center-of-life places they were in the Middle Ages. Don't miss the **rose windows** that fill each of the transepts. Just past the altar is the "**choir,**" enclosed with carved-wood walls, where more intimate services can be held in this spacious building. Circle the choir—the back side of the choir walls features **scenes of the resurrected Jesus** (c. 1350). Just ahead on the right is the **Treasury.** It contains lavish robes, golden reliquaries, and the humble tunic of King (and St.) Louis IX, but it probably isn't worth the €3 entry fee.

Back outside, walk around the church through the park on the riverside for a close look at the **flying buttresses.** The Neo-Gothic 300-foot **spire** is a product of the 1860 reconstruction of the dilapidated old church. Around its base (visible as you approach the back end of the church) are apostles and evangelists (the green men) as well as Eugène-Emmanuel Viollet-le-Duc, the architect in charge of the work. The apostles look outward, blessing the city, while the architect (at top) looks up the spire, marveling at his fine work.

Nearby: The **archaeological crypt** is a worthwhile 15-minute stop if you have a Paris Museum Pass (€4 without Museum Pass, Tue-Sun 10:00-18:00, last entry 30 minutes before closing, closed Mon, enter 100 yards in front of cathedral). You'll see remains of the many structures that have stood on this spot in the center of Paris: Roman buildings that surrounded a temple of Jupiter; a wall that didn't keep the Franks out; the main medieval road that once led grandly up the square to Notre-Dame; and even (wow) a 19th-century sewer.

• *Behind Notre-Dame, cross the street and enter through the iron gate*

*into the park at the tip of the island. Look for the stairs and head down
to reach the...*

▲Deportation Memorial
(Mémorial de la Déportation)

This memorial to the 200,000 French victims of the Nazi concentration camps (1940-1945) draws you into their experience. France was quickly overrun by Nazi Germany, and Paris spent the war years under Nazi occupation. Jews and dissidents were rounded up and deported—many never returned.

As you descend the steps, the city around you disappears. Surrounded by walls, you have become a prisoner. Your only freedom is your view of the sky and the tiny glimpse of the river below. Enter the dark, single-file chamber up ahead. Inside, the circular plaque in the floor reads, "They went to the end of the earth and did not return."

The hallway stretching in front of you is lined with 200,000 lighted crystals, one for each French citizen who died. Flickering at the far end is the eternal flame of hope. The tomb of the unknown deportee lies at your feet. Above, the inscription reads, "Dedicated to the living memory of the 200,000 French deportees shrouded by the night and the fog, exterminated in the Nazi concentration camps." The side rooms are filled with triangles—reminiscent of the identification patches inmates were forced to wear—each bearing the name of a concentration camp. Above the exit as you leave is the message you'll find at many other Holocaust sites: "Forgive, but never forget."

Cost and Hours: Free, April-Sept Tue-Sun 10:00-19:00, Oct-March Tue-Sun 10:00-18:00, closed Mon year-round. It's at the east tip of the island named Ile de la Cité, behind Notre-Dame and near Ile St. Louis (Mo: Cité, mobile 06 14 67 54 98).

• *Back on street level, look across the river (north) to the island called...*

Ile St. Louis

If Ile de la Cité is a tugboat laden with the history of Paris, it's towing this classy little residential dinghy, laden only with high-rent apartments, boutiques, characteristic restaurants (see page 331), and famous ice-cream shops.

Ile St. Louis wasn't developed until much later than Ile de la Cité (17th century). What was a swampy mess is now harmonious Parisian architecture and one of Paris' most exclusive neighborhoods. If you won't have time to return here for an evening stroll (see page 283), consider taking a brief detour across the pedestrian bridge, Pont St. Louis. It connects the two islands, leading right to rue St. Louis-en-l'Ile. This spine of the island is lined with interesting shops and reasonably priced restaurants. A short stroll takes

Ile St. Louis

☆ VIEW
Ⓜ METRO STATION
Ⓑ BATOBUS BOAT STOP

❶ Berthillon Ice Cream
❷ Amorino Gelati
❸ Good Picnic Spot
❹ Grocery Store

you to the famous Berthillon ice cream parlor at #31. Gelato-lovers head instead to Amorino Gelati at 47 rue St. Louis-en-l'Ile. When you're finished exploring, loop back to the pedestrian bridge along the parklike quays (walk north to the river and turn left). This walk is about as peaceful and romantic as Paris gets.

• *From the Deportation Memorial, cross the bridge onto the Left Bank and turn right (west). Walk along the river, toward the front end of Notre-Dame. Stairs detour down to the riverbank if you need a place to picnic. This side view of the church from across the river is one of Europe's great sights and is best from river level.*

After passing the pont au Double (the bridge leading to the facade of Notre-Dame), watch on your left for **Shakespeare and Company,** *an atmospheric reincarnation of the original 1920s bookshop and a good spot to page through books (37 rue de la Bûcherie; see page 216). Before returning to the island, walk a block behind Shakespeare and Company, and take a spin through...*

▲The Latin Quarter

This area's touristy fame relates to its intriguing, artsy, bohemian character. This was perhaps Europe's leading university district in the Middle Ages, when Latin was the language of higher education.

The neighborhood's main boulevards (St. Michel and St.

Germain) are lined with cafés—once the haunts of great poets and philosophers, now the hangouts of tired tourists. Though still youthful and artsy, much of this area has become a tourist ghetto filled with cheap North African eateries. Exploring a few blocks up or downriver from here gives you a better chance of feeling the pulse of what survives of Paris' classic Left Bank. For colorful wandering and café-sitting, afternoons and evenings are best.

Walking along rue St. Séverin, you can still see the shadow of the medieval sewer system. The street slopes into a central channel of bricks. In the days before plumbing and toilets, when people still went to the river or neighborhood wells for their water, flushing meant throwing it out the window. At certain times of day, maids on the fourth floor would holler, *"Garde de l'eau!"* ("Watch out for the water!") and heave it into the streets, where it would eventually wash down into the Seine.

Consider a visit to the **Cluny Museum** for its medieval art and unicorn tapestries (see page 261). The **Sorbonne**—the University of Paris' humanities department—is also nearby; visitors can ogle at the famous dome, but they are not allowed to enter the building (two blocks south of the river on boulevard St. Michel).

Be sure to see **place St. Michel.** This square (facing the pont St. Michel) is the traditional core of the Left Bank's artsy, liberal, hippie, bohemian district of poets, philosophers, and winos. In less commercial times, place St. Michel was a gathering point for the city's malcontents and misfits. In 1830, 1848, and again in 1871, the citizens took the streets from the government troops, set up barricades *Les Miz*-style, and fought against royalist oppression. During World War II, the locals rose up against their Nazi oppressors (read the plaques under the dragons at the foot of the St. Michel fountain). Even today, whenever there's a student demonstration, it starts here.

• *From place St. Michel, look across the river and find the prickly steeple of the Sainte-Chapelle church. Head toward it. Cross the river on pont St. Michel and continue north along the boulevard du Palais. On your left, you'll see the doorway to Sainte-Chapelle.*

You'll need to pass through a strict security checkpoint to get into the Sainte-Chapelle complex. (This is more than a tourist attraction— France's Supreme Court meets to the right of Sainte-Chapelle.) Bags are screened, and sharp objects (e.g., Swiss army knives) will be confiscated. Past security, you'll enter the courtyard outside Sainte-Chapelle, where you'll find WCs and information about upcoming church concerts (for concert details, see page 282).

The ticket-buying line into the church may be long. If you have a Museum Pass or a Conciergerie combo-ticket, you may be able to skip some of the security line (look for signs), and can certainly bypass the ticket-buying line. You can also bypass it by buying your ticket or

Museum Pass from the tabac *shop across the street from the security entrance.*

Enter the humble ground floor.

▲▲▲Sainte-Chapelle

This triumph of Gothic church architecture is a cathedral of glass like no other. It was speedily built between 1242 and 1248 for King Louis IX—the only French king who is now a saint—to house the supposed Crown of Thorns. Its architectural harmony is due to the fact that it was completed under the direction of one architect and in only six years—unheard of in Gothic times. In contrast, Notre-Dame took over 200 years.

Cost and Hours: €8, under 18 free, €11 combo-ticket with Conciergerie, covered by Museum Pass; March-Oct daily 9:30-18:00, Wed until 21:30 mid-May-mid-Sept; Nov-Feb daily 9:00-17:00; last entry 30 minutes before closing, English tours most days at 10:45 and 14:45, evening concerts—see page 282, 4 boulevard du Palais, Mo: Cité, tel. 01 53 40 60 80, www.sainte-chapelle.monuments-nationaux.fr.

Visiting the Church: Inside, the layout clearly shows an *ancien régime* approach to worship. The low-ceilinged **basement** was for staff and other common folks—worshipping under a sky filled with painted fleurs-de-lis, a symbol of the king. Royal Christians worshipped upstairs. The paint job, a 19th-century restoration, helps you imagine how grand this small, painted, jeweled chapel was. (Imagine Notre-Dame painted like this...) Each capital is playfully carved with a different plant's leaves.

Climb the spiral staircase to the **Chapelle Haute.** Fill the place with choral music, crank up the sunshine, face the top of the altar, and really believe that the Crown of Thorns is there, and this becomes one awesome space.

Fiat lux. "Let there be light." From the first page of the Bible, it's clear: Light is divine. Light shines through stained glass like God's grace shining down to earth. Gothic architects used their new technology to turn dark stone buildings into lanterns of light. The glory of Gothic shines brighter here than in any other church.

There are 15 separate panels of stained glass (6,500 square feet—two thirds of it 13th-century original), with more than 1,100 different scenes, mostly from the Bible. These cover the entire Christian history of the world, from the Creation in Genesis (first window on the left, as you face the altar), to the coming of Christ (over the altar), to the end of the world (the round "rose"-shaped window at the rear of the church). Each individual scene is interesting, and the whole effect is overwhelming.

The altar was raised up high to better display the Crown of Thorns, the relic around which this chapel was built. The supposed

Sainte-Chapelle

20 METERS

20 YARDS

DCH

JESUS'
PASSION SCENES

TO
COURTYARD
ENTRANCE
& SECURITY
CHECK

ALTAR

CAMPAIGN OF
HOLOFERNES

ST.
LOUIS'
PEEK-A-
BOO
WINDOW

MORE MOSES

LIFE OF MOSES

CAIN CLUBBING
ABEL

HELENA IN
JERUSALEM

ROSE
WINDOW

SPIRAL
STAIRCASE

SPIRAL
STAIRCASE

TO
WC

STAINED
GLASS

BUTTRESSES

ENTER BELOW
(INTO LOWER CHAPEL)

crown cost King Louis three times as much as this church. Today, it is kept by the Notre-Dame Treasury (though it's occasionally brought out for display).

• *Exit Sainte-Chapelle. Back outside, as you walk around the church exterior, look down to see the foundation and take note of how much Paris has risen in the 750 years since Sainte-Chapelle was built.*

Next door to Sainte-Chapelle is the...

Palais de Justice

Sainte-Chapelle sits within a huge complex of buildings that has housed the local government since ancient Roman times. It was the site of the original Gothic palace of the early kings of France. The only surviving medieval parts are Sainte-Chapelle and the Conciergerie prison.

Most of the site is now covered by the giant Palais de Justice, built in 1776, home of the French Supreme Court. The motto

Liberté, Egalité, Fraternité over the doors is a reminder that this was also the headquarters of the Revolutionary government. Here they doled out justice, condemning many to imprisonment in the Conciergerie downstairs or to the guillotine.

• *Now pass through the big iron gate to the noisy boulevard du Palais. Cross the street to the wide, pedestrian-only rue de Lutèce and walk about halfway down.*

Cité "Metropolitain" Métro Stop

Of the 141 original early-20th-century subway entrances, this is one of only a few survivors—now preserved as a national art treasure. (New York's Museum of Modern Art even exhibits one.) It marks Paris at its peak in 1900—on the cutting edge of Modernism, but with an eye for beauty. The curvy, plantlike ironwork is a textbook example of Art Nouveau, the style that rebelled against the erector-set squareness of the Industrial Age. Other similar Métro stations in Paris are Abbesses and Porte Dauphine.

The flower and plant market on place Louis Lépine is a pleasant detour. On Sundays this square flutters with a busy bird market. And across the way is the Préfecture de Police, where Inspector Clouseau of *Pink Panther* fame used to work, and where the local resistance fighters took the first building from the Nazis in August of 1944, leading to the Allied liberation of Paris a week later.

• *Pause here to admire the view. Sainte-Chapelle is a pearl in an ugly architectural oyster. Double back to the Palais de Justice, turn right onto boulevard du Palais, and enter the...*

▲Conciergerie

Though pretty barren inside, this former prison echoes with history (and is free with the Museum Pass—remember that passholders can skip the ticket-buying line). Positioned next to the courthouse, the Conciergerie was the gloomy prison famous as the last stop for 2,780 victims of the guillotine, including France's last *ancien régime* queen, Marie-Antoinette. Before then, kings had used the building to torture and execute failed assassins. (One of its towers along the river was called "The Babbler," named for the pain-induced sounds that leaked from it.) When the Revolution (1789) toppled the king, the building kept its same function, but without the torture. The progressive Revolutionaries proudly unveiled a modern and more humane way to execute people—the guillotine.

Inside, pick up a free map and breeze through the one-way circuit. It's well-described in English. See the spacious, low-ceilinged Hall of Men-at-Arms (Room 1), used as the guards' dining room, with four large fireplaces (look up the chimneys). This big room gives a feel for the grandeur of the Great Hall (upstairs, not open to visitors), where the Revolutionary tribunals grilled scared prisoners on their political correctness. You'll also see a re-creation of Marie-Antoinette's cell, which houses a collection of her mementos. In another room, a list of those made "a foot shorter at the top" by the "national razor" includes ex-King Louis XVI, Charlotte Corday (who murdered the Revolutionary writer Jean-Paul Marat in his bathtub), and—oh, the irony—Maximilien de Robespierre, the head of the Revolution, the man who sent so many to the guillotine.

Cost and Hours: €7, €11 combo-ticket with Sainte-Chapelle, covered by Museum Pass, daily March-Oct 9:30-18:00, Nov-Feb 9:00-17:00, last entry 30 minutes before closing, 2 boulevard du Palais, Mo: Cité, tel. 01 53 40 60 80, www.conciergerie.monuments -nationaux.fr.

• *Back outside, turn left on boulevard du Palais and head north. On the corner is the city's oldest public clock. The mechanism of the present clock is from 1334, and even though the case is Baroque, it keeps on ticking.*

Turn left onto quai de l'Horloge and walk west along the river, past "The Babbler" tower. The bridge up ahead is the pont Neuf, where we'll end this walk. At the first corner, veer left into a sleepy triangular square called place Dauphine. Marvel at how such coziness could be lodged in the midst of such greatness. At the equestrian statue of Henry IV, turn right onto the old bridge and take refuge in one of the nooks on the Eiffel Tower side; or continue through the park to the end of the island (the departure point for Seine river cruises offered by Vedettes du Pont Neuf, described under "By Boat," page 223).

Pont Neuf

This "new bridge" is now Paris' oldest. Built during Henry IV's reign (about 1600), its arches span the widest part of the river. Unlike other bridges, this one never had houses or buildings growing on it. The turrets were originally for vendors and street entertainers. In the days of Henry IV, who promised his peasants "a chicken in every pot every Sunday," this would have been a lively scene. From the bridge, look downstream (west) to see the next bridge, the pedestrian-only pont des Arts. Ahead on the Right Bank is the long Louvre Museum. Beyond that, on the Left Bank, is the Orsay. And what's that tall black tower in the distance?

• *Our walk is finished. From here, you can tour the Seine by boat, continue to the Louvre, or (if it's summer) head to the...*

Paris Plages (Paris Beaches)

The Riviera it's not, but this string of fanciful faux beaches—assembled in summer along a one-mile stretch of the Right Bank of the Seine (roughly between pont des Arts and pont de Sully)—is a fun place to stroll, play, and people-watch on a sunny day. Each summer since 2002, the Paris city government has closed the embankment's highway and trucked in potted palm trees, hammocks, lounge chairs, and 2,000 tons of sand to create colorful urban beaches. You'll also find "beach cafés," climbing walls, prefab pools, trampolines, *boules,* a library, beach volleyball, badminton, and Frisbee areas.

Cost and Hours: Free, mid-July-mid-Aug daily 8:00-24:00, no beach off-season; on Right Bank of Seine, just north of Ile de la Cité, between pont des Arts and pont de Sully, http://parisplages .paris.fr/en.

Sights in Paris

Paris Museum Pass

In Paris, there are two classes of sightseers—those with a Paris Museum Pass, and those who stand in line. The pass admits you to many of Paris' most popular sights, allowing you to skip ticket-buying lines. You'll save time and money by getting this pass.

Buying the Pass

The pass pays for itself with four key admissions in two days (for example, the Louvre, Orsay, Sainte-Chapelle, and Versailles), and lets you skip the ticket line at most sights (2 days/€39, 4 days/€54, 6 days/€69, no youth or senior discount). It's sold at participating museums, monuments, FNAC department stores, and TIs (even at airports). Try to avoid buying the pass at a major museum (such as the Louvre), where the supply can be spotty and lines long. For more info, visit www.parismuseumpass.com or call 01 44 61 96 60.

If you want to make sure the pass is a good value for your trip, tally up what you want to see from the list on the next page—and remember, an advantage of the pass is that you skip to the front of most lines, which can save hours of waiting, especially in summer. At a few sights (including the Louvre, Sainte-Chapelle, Notre-Dame's tower, and the Château de Versailles), everyone has to shuffle through the slow-moving baggage-check lines for security—but you still save time by avoiding the ticket line. Most lines at sights are for people without passes. Don't be shy—even if it feels rude, always walk to the front of the line and show your pass to avoid waiting (Sainte-Chapelle and the Arc de Triomphe are places where passholders often wait needlessly).

Families: The pass isn't worth buying for children and teens, as most museums are free or discounted for those under 18 (teenagers may need to show ID as proof of age). Kids can usually skip ticket lines if you have a Museum Pass, although a few places (such as the Arc de Triomphe and Army Museum) require you to stand in line to collect your child's free ticket. Of the few museums that charge for children, some allow kids in for free if their parents have a Museum Pass, while others charge admission, depending on age (the cutoff age varies from 5 to 18). The free directory that comes with your pass lists the current hours of sights, phone numbers, and the price that kids pay.

What the Paris Museum Pass Covers

Most of the sights listed in this chapter are covered by the pass. Notable exceptions are: the Eiffel Tower, Montparnasse Tower, Marmottan Museum, Opéra Garnier, Notre-Dame Treasury, Jacquemart-André Museum, Grand Palais, Catacombs, Montmartre Museum, Sacré-Cœur's dome, Dalí Museum, Museum of Erotic Art, and the ladies of Pigalle.

Here's a list of key included sights and their admission prices without the pass:

Louvre (€10)	Notre-Dame Tower (€8)
Orsay Museum (€8)	Paris Archaeological Crypt (€4)
Orangerie Museum (€7.50)	Paris Sewer Tour (€4.30)
Sainte-Chapelle (€8)	Cluny Museum (€8)
Arc de Triomphe (€9.50)	Pompidou Center (€10-12)
Rodin Museum (€6)	Jewish Art and History Museum (€7)
Army Museum (€9)	National Maritime Museum (€7)
Conciergerie (€7)	Delacroix Museum (€5)
Panthéon (€8)	Quai Branly Museum (€8.50)

Architecture and Monuments Museum (€8)
Versailles (€25 total—€15 for Château, €10 for Trianon Palaces and Domaine de Marie-Antoinette)

Activating and Using the Pass

The pass is activated the first time you use it (write the starting date on the pass), so validate it only when you're ready to tackle the covered sights on consecutive days. Plan carefully to make the most of your pass—make sure the sights you want to visit will be open (many museums are closed Mondays or Tuesdays). The Paris Museum Pass even covers Versailles' two major sights—worth €25 alone. Keep in mind that sights such as the Arc de Triomphe and Pompidou Center are open later in the evening, and that the Notre-Dame Tower, Sainte-Chapelle, Louvre, Orsay, and Army Museum and Napoleon's Tomb have late hours on selected evenings, allowing you to stretch the day for your Paris Museum Pass. On days that you don't have pass coverage, plan to visit free sights as well as those not covered by the pass (see page 230 for a list of free sights).

To use your pass at sights, boldly walk to the front of the ticket line (after going through security if necessary), hold up your pass, and ask the ticket-taker: *"Entrez, pass?"* (ahn-tray pahs). You'll

PARIS

Paris Sights

To LA DÉFENSE &
LA GRANDE ARCHE

JACQUEMART-
ANDRÉ MUSEUM

BLVD.

GALLERIES
LAFAYETTE

CHAMPS-
ELYSEES

OPERA
GARNIER

8

MADELEINE

16

AVE KLEBER

ARC
DE
TRIOMPHE

PLACE
DE LA
CONCORDE

PLACE
VENDOME

GRAND
PALAIS

TO
MARMOTTAN
MUSEUM

ARCHITECTURE &
MONUMENTS MUSEUM

RIVER
CRUISES

PETIT
PALAIS

RUE

ORANGERIE
TUILERIES
GDN.

S E I N E

1

TROCA-
DERO

CAFÉ CARLU

RIVER
CRUISES

SEWER
TOUR
ST.

R.

MARITIME
MUSEUM

QUAI
BRANLY
MUSEUM

RUE

DOMINIQUE

BLVD.

ORSAY

EIFFEL
TOWER

7

RUE
CLER

ARMY MUSEUM
& NAPOLEON'S
TOMB

ST GERMAIN

PARC DU

QUAI

CHAMP
DE MARS

RODIN
MUSEUM

BLVD

RASPAIL

RER RAIL TO
VERSAILLES

15

ECOLE
MILITAIRE

6

TO MONTPARNASSE
TOWER
& CATACOMBS

VIEW   PARIS PLAGES

GRAY NUMBERS INDICATE
ARRONDISSEMENTS (DISTRICTS)

DCH

PARIS

either be allowed to enter at that point or you'll be directed to a special entrance. For major sights, such as the Louvre and Orsay museums, I've identified passholder entrances on the maps in this chapter.

With the pass, you can pop into sights as you're walking by (even for a few minutes) that otherwise might not be worth the expense (e.g., the Conciergerie or Paris Archaeological Crypt).

Major Museums Neighborhood

Paris' grandest park, the Tuileries Garden, was once the private property of kings and queens. Today it links the Louvre, Orangerie, Jeu de Paume, and Orsay museums. And across from the Louvre are the tranquil, historic courtyards of the Palais Royal.

▲▲▲Louvre (Musée du Louvre)

This is Europe's oldest, biggest, greatest, and second-most-crowded museum (after the Vatican). Housed in a U-shaped, 16th-century palace (accentuated by a 20th-century glass pyramid), the Louvre is Paris' top museum and one of its key landmarks. It's home to *Mona Lisa, Venus de Milo,* and hall after hall of Greek and Roman masterpieces, medieval jewels, Michelangelo statues, and paintings by the greatest artists from the Renaissance to the Romantics (mid-1800s).

Touring the Louvre can be overwhelming, so be selective. Focus on the Denon wing (south, along the river), with Greek sculptures, Italian paintings (by Raphael and da Vinci), and—of course—French paintings (Neoclassical and Romantic). For extra

Major Museums Neighborhood

PARIS

credit, tackle the Richelieu wing (north, away from the river), displaying works from ancient Mesopotamia (today's Iraq), as well as French, Dutch, and Northern art; or the Sully wing (connecting the other two wings), with Egyptian artifacts and more French paintings. You'll find my self-guided tour of the Louvre's highlights on page 247.

Expect Changes: The sprawling Louvre is constantly in flux. Rooms are periodically closed for renovation, and pieces are removed from display if they're being restored or loaned to other museums. An exciting new Islamic art wing in the Cour Visconti should be open by the time of your visit, but various galleries devoted to decorative arts are in flux until spring 2013. If you don't find the artwork you're looking for, ask the nearest guard for its new location.

Cost: €10, free on first Sun of month, covered by Museum

Pass. Tickets good all day; reentry allowed.

Hours: Wed-Mon 9:00-18:00, until 21:45 on Wed and Fri (except on holidays), closed Tue. Galleries start shutting down 30 minutes early. The last entry is 45 minutes before closing.

When to Go: Crowds are worst on Sun, Mon, Wed, and mornings. Evening visits are peaceful, and the glass pyramid glows after dark.

Getting There: You have a variety of options:

By Métro: The Métro stop Palais Royal-Musée du Louvre is closer to the entrance than the stop called Louvre-Rivoli. From the Palais Royal-Musée du Louvre stop, you can stay underground to enter the museum, or exit above ground if you want to go in through the pyramid (more details below).

By Bus: Handy bus #69 runs every 10-20 minutes. Buses headed west from the Marais drop off passengers next to the Palais Royal-Musée du Louvre Métro stop on rue de Rivoli. Buses headed east from rue Cler drop off along the Seine River (at quai François Mitterand).

By Taxi: You'll find a taxi stand on rue de Rivoli, next to the Palais Royal-Musée du Louvre Métro station.

Getting In: Enter through the pyramid, or opt for shorter lines elsewhere.

Main Pyramid Entrance: There is no grander entry than through the main entrance at the pyramid in the central courtyard, but metal detectors (not ticket-buyers) can create a long line.

Museum Pass/Group Entrance: Museum Pass-holders can use the group entrance in the pedestrian passageway (labeled *Pavilion Richelieu*) between the pyramid and rue de Rivoli. It's under the arches, a few steps north of the pyramid; find the uniformed guard at the security checkpoint entrance, at the down escalator.

Underground Mall Entrance: You can enter the Louvre from its less crowded underground entrance, accessed through the Carrousel du Louvre shopping mall. Enter the mall at 99 rue de Rivoli (the door with the red awning) or directly from the Métro stop Palais Royal-Musée du Louvre (stepping off the train, exit at the end of the platform, following signs to *Musée du Louvre-Le Carrousel du Louvre*). Once inside the underground mall, continue to the Louvre's security entrance. Museum Pass-holders can skip to the head of the security line.

Information: Pick up the free *Plan/Information* in English at the information desk under the pyramid as you enter. Tel. 01 40 20 53 17, recorded info tel. 01 40 20 51 51, www.louvre.fr.

Buying Tickets: Self-serve ticket machines located under the pyramid are faster to use than the ticket windows (machines accept euro notes, coins, and Visa cards). The *tabac* in the underground mall at the Louvre sells tickets to the Louvre, Orsay, and

PARIS

The Louvre

RIGHT **BANK**

PALAIS ROYAL

Palais Royale
Musée du Louvre

RUE DE RIVOLI

RICHELIEU

NEAR EASTERN

PEDESTRIAN PASSAGEWAY

FRENCH

LOUVRE-RIVOLI

ARC DU CARROUSEL

MAIN ENTRANCE

PYRAMID

COUR CARREE

SULLY

FORMER TUILERIES PALACE

Louis XIV

ITALIAN + FRENCH

GREEK

RUE L'AMIRAL DE COLIGNY

DENON

WINGED VICTORY

CAFES

TUILERIES GARDEN

AXIS VIEW

QUAI

F. MITTERAND

PONT ROYAL

PONT CARROUSEL

SEINE RIVER

PONT DES ARTS

DCH

QUAI VOLTAIRE

TO ORSAY MUSEUM (15 MIN. WALK)

LEFT **BANK**

TO LATIN QUARTER (15 MIN. WALK)

Ⓜ METRO STATION Ⓑ BUS #69 STOP 🅱 BATOBUS BOAT STOP

Ⓣ TAXI STAND → ONE-WAY STREET

❶ Museum Pass/Group Entrance (in passageway)
❷ Underground Mall Entrance
❸ Café le Nemours
❹ Le Fumoir

PARIS

Versailles, plus Museum Passes, for no extra charge (cash only).

Tours: Ninety-minute English-language **guided tours** leave twice daily (except the first Sunday of the month) from the *Accueil des Groupes* area, under the pyramid between the Sully and Denon wings (normally at 11:00 and 14:00, sometimes more often in summer; €9 plus your entry ticket, tour tel. 01 40 20 52 63). Digital **audioguides** provide eager students with commentary on about 130 masterpieces (€6, available at entries to the three wings, at the top of the escalators). You can download a free Rick Steves **audio tour** of the Louvre; see page 7. You'll also find English explanations throughout the museum.

Baggage Check: The free *bagagerie* is under the pyramid, to the right of the Denon wing entrance (it is signed *visiteurs individuels*). Large bags must be checked, and you can also check small bags to lighten your load. Coats cannot be left at the *bagagerie* unless they're stuffed into bags. (The coat check, or *Vestiaire*, is near the Richelieu wing.) The baggage-claim clerk might ask you in French, "Does your bag contain anything of value?" You can't check cameras, money, passports, or other valuables.

Services: WCs are located under the pyramid, behind the escalators to the Denon and Richelieu wings. Once you're in the galleries, WCs are scarce.

Photography: Photography without a flash is allowed. (Flash photography damages paintings and distracts viewers.)

● **Self-Guided Tour:** Start in the Denon Wing and visit the highlights, in the following order (thanks to Gene Openshaw for his help writing this tour).

Look for the famous *Venus de Milo (Aphrodite)* statue. You'll find her not far from another famous statue, the *Winged Victory of Samothrace*. This goddess of love (c. 100 B.C., from the Greek island of Melos) created a sensation when she was discovered in 1820. Most "Greek" statues are actually later Roman copies, but *Venus* is a rare Greek original. She, like Golden Age Greeks, epitomizes stability, beauty, and balance. After viewing *Venus,* wander through the **ancient Greek and Roman works** to see the Parthenon frieze (stone fragments that once decorated the exterior of the greatest Athenian temple), mosaics from Pompeii, Etruscan sarcophagi, and Roman portrait busts.

Later Greek art was Hellenistic, adding motion and drama. For a good example, see the exciting *Winged Victory of Samothrace* (*Victoire de Samothrace,* on the landing). This statue of a woman with wings, poised on the prow of a ship, once stood on a hilltop to commemorate a naval victory. This is the *Venus de Milo* gone Hellenistic.

The **Italian collection** is on the other side of the *Winged Victory* in the Grand Gallery. In painting, the Renaissance meant realism, and for the Italians, realism was spelled "3-D." Painters were inspired by the realism and balanced beauty of Greek sculpture. Painting a 3-D world on a 2-D surface is tough, and after a millennium of Dark Ages, artists were rusty. Living in a religious age, they painted mostly altarpieces full of saints, angels, Madonnas-and-bambinos, and crucifixes floating in an ethereal gold-leaf heaven. Gradually, though, they brought these otherworldly scenes down to earth. (The Italian collection—including the *Mona Lisa*—are scattered throughout the rooms of the long Grand Gallery—look for **two Botticelli frescoes** as you enter.)

Two masters of the Italian High Renaissance (1500-1600) were Raphael (see his *La Belle Jardinière,* showing the Madonna, Child, and John the Baptist) and Leonardo da Vinci. The Louvre has the greatest collection of Leonardos in the world—five of them, including the exquisite *Virgin, Child, and St. Anne;* the neighboring *Virgin of the Rocks;* and the androgynous *John the Baptist.* His most

PARIS

famous, of course, is the *Mona Lisa*.

The *Mona Lisa* (*La Joconde* in French) is in the Salle des Etats, midway down the Grand Gallery, on the right. After several years and a €5 million renovation, Mona is alone behind glass on her own false wall. Leonardo was already an old man when François I invited him to France. Determined to pack light, he took only a few paintings with him. One was a portrait of a Lisa del Giocondo, the wife of a wealthy Florentine merchant. When Leonardo arrived, François immediately fell in love with the painting, making it the centerpiece of the small collection of Italian masterpieces that would, in three centuries, become the Louvre museum. He called it *La Gioconda (La Joconde* in French)—both her last name and a play on the Italian word for "happy woman." We know it as a contraction of the Italian for "my lady Lisa"—*Mona Lisa*. Warning: François was impressed, but *Mona* may disappoint you. She's smaller than you'd expect, darker, engulfed in a huge room, and hidden behind a glaring pane of glass.

The huge canvas opposite *Mona* is Paolo Veronese's **The Marriage at Cana,** showing the Renaissance love of beautiful things gone hog-wild. Venetian artists like Veronese painted the good life of rich, happy-go-lucky Venetian merchants.

Now for something **Neoclassical.** Exit behind *Mona Lisa* and turn right into the Salle Daru to find *The Coronation of Napoleon* by Jacques-Louis David. Neoclassicism, once the rage in France (1780-1850), usually features Greek subjects, patriotic sentiment, and a clean, simple style. After Napoleon quickly conquered most of Europe, he insisted on being made emperor (not merely king) of this "New Rome." He staged an elaborate coronation ceremony in Paris, and rather than let the pope crown him, he crowned himself. The setting was Notre-Dame Cathedral, with Greek columns and Roman arches thrown in for effect. Napoleon's mom was also added, since she couldn't make it to the ceremony. A key on the frame describes who's who in the picture.

The **Romantic** collection, in an adjacent room (Salle Mollien), has works by Théodore Géricault (*The Raft of the Medusa*—one of my favorites) and Eugène Delacroix *(Liberty Leading the People)*. Romanticism, with an emphasis on motion and emotion, is the flip side of cool, balanced Neoclassicism, though they both flourished in the early 1800s. Delacroix's *Liberty,* commemorating the stirrings of democracy in France, is also an appropriate tribute to the Louvre, the first museum ever opened to the common rabble of humanity. The good things in life don't belong only to a small, wealthy part of society, but to everyone. The motto of France is *Liberté, Egalité, Fraternité*—liberty, equality, and the brotherhood of all.

Exit the room at the far end (past the Café Mollien) and go downstairs, where you'll bump into the bum of a large, twisting male nude looking like he's just waking up after a thousand-year nap. The two *Slaves* (1513-1515) by Michelangelo are a fitting end to this museum—works that bridge the ancient and modern worlds. Michelangelo, like his fellow Renaissance artists, learned from the Greeks. The perfect anatomy, twisting poses, and idealized faces appear as if they could have been created 2,000 years earlier. Michelangelo said that his purpose was to carve away the marble to reveal the figures God put inside. The *Rebellious Slave,* fighting against his bondage, shows the agony of that process and the ecstasy of the result.

Although this makes for a good first tour, there's so much more. After a break (or on a second visit), consider a stroll through a few rooms of the Richelieu wing, which contain some of the Louvre's oldest and biggest pieces. Bible students, amateur archaeologists, and Iraq War vets may find the collection especially interesting.

Palais Royal Courtyards

Across from the Louvre are the lovely courtyards of the stately Palais Royal. Although the palace is closed to the public, the courtyards are open. Enter through a whimsical (locals say tacky) courtyard filled with stubby, striped columns and playful fountains (with fun, reflective metal balls). Next, you'll pass into a perfectly Parisian garden. This is where in-the-know Parisians come to take a quiet break, walk their poodles and kids, or enjoy a rendezvous—amid flowers and surrounded by a serene arcade. Bring a picnic and create your own quiet break, or have a drink at one of the outdoor cafés at the courtyard's northern end. This is Paris.

Exiting the courtyard at the side facing away from the Seine brings you to the Galeries Colbert and Vivienne, good examples of shopping arcades from the early 1900s and worth a look.

Cost and Hours: Courtyards are free and always open. The Palais Royal is directly north of the Louvre on rue de Rivoli (Mo: Palais Royal-Musée du Louvre).

▲▲Orangerie Museum (Musée de l'Orangerie)

Step out of the tree-lined, sun-dappled Impressionist painting that is the Tuileries Garden, and into the Orangerie (oh-rahn-zheh-ree), a little bijou of select works by Claude Monet and his contemporaries. Start with the museum's claim to fame: Monet's water lilies. These eight mammoth-scale paintings are displayed exactly as Monet intended them—surrounding you in oval-shaped rooms—so you feel as though you're immersed in his garden at Giverny.

Working from his home there, Monet built a special studio with skylights and wheeled easels to accommodate the canvases—1,950 square feet in all. Each canvas features a different part of the pond, painted from varying angles at distinct times of day—but the true subject of these works is the play of reflected light off the surface of the pond. The Monet rooms are considered the first art installation, and the blurry canvases signaled the abstract art to come.

Downstairs you'll see artists that bridge the Impressionist and Modernist worlds—Renoir, Cézanne, Utrillo, Matisse, and Picasso. Together they provide a snapshot of what was hot in the world of art collecting, circa 1920.

Cost and Hours: €7.50, under 18 free, €13 combo-ticket with Orsay Museum (valid four days, one visit per sight), covered by Museum Pass, audioguide-€5, Wed-Mon 9:00-18:00, closed Tue, free English tours usually offered Mon and Thu at 14:30, located in Tuileries Garden near place de la Concorde, Mo: Concorde, tel. 01 44 77 80 07, www.musee-orangerie.fr.

▲▲▲Orsay Museum (Musée d'Orsay)

The Musée d'Orsay (mew-zay dor-say) houses French art of the 1800s and early 1900s (specifically, 1848-1914), picking up where the Louvre's art collection leaves off. For us, that means Impressionism, the art of sun-dappled fields, bright colors, and crowded Parisian cafés. The Orsay houses the best general collection anywhere of Manet, Monet, Renoir, Degas, Van Gogh, Cézanne, and Gauguin.

Cost: €8, €5.50 Fri-Wed after 16:15 and Thu after 18:00, free first Sun of month, covered by Museum Pass. Combo-tickets are available with the Orangerie Museum (€13) or Rodin Museum (€12); both are valid four days, with one visit per sight. You can scoot in free of charge Tue-Wed and Fri-Sun at 17:00 or Thu at 21:00 for a fast look at the Impressionist galleries. Advance tickets can be purchased in person at FNAC department stores and TIs, or online for pick-up in Paris; see www.musee-orsay.fr.

Hours: Tue-Sun 9:30-18:00, Thu until 21:45, closed Mon, last entry one hour before closing. The top-floor Impressionist galleries begin closing 45 minutes early.

Getting There: The museum sits above the RER-C stop called Musée d'Orsay. The Solférino Métro stop is three blocks southeast of the Orsay. Handy bus #69 also serves the museum. The museum is at 1 rue de la Légion d'Honneur. A taxi stand is in front of the entrance on quai Anatole France. The Batobus boat also makes a stop here (see page 224).

Getting In: As you face the front of the museum from rue de la Légion d'Honneur (with the river on your left), passholders and ticket-holders enter on the right side of the museum (Entrance C). Ticket-purchasers enter closer to the river (Entrance A).

Orsay Museum—Ground Floor

TO LOUVRE (15 MIN. WALK)

BUS #69 FROM RUE CLER TO LOUVRE & MARAIS

PONT ← ROYAL

Ⓑ

← RUE DU BAC →

SEINE RIVER

Ⓑ

Ⓑ

QUAI ANATOLE FRANCE

ESCALATOR UP TO **IMPRESSIONISM**

MANET

REALISM

CONSERVATIVE ART

START

BOOKSTORE

BOOKS

SECURITY

VESTIAIRE (BAGGAGE CHECK)

BUS #69 FROM MARAIS TO RUE CLER & EIFFEL TOWER

Ⓑ

Ⓣ

MUSÉE D'ORSAY

Ⓡ

ENTRANCE ← ADVANCE TICKET PASS HOLDERS

TICKET PURCHASERS

DCH

SOLFERINO PED. BRIDGE

← TO ORANGERIE

RUE DE LA LÉGION D'HONNEUR

RUE DE BELLECHASSE →

TO Ⓜ SOLFERINO (5 MIN. WALK) & RODIN MUSEUM

Ⓑ Bus #69 Stop   Ⓡ RER Stop   Ⓣ Taxi Stand
Ⓜ Metro Station   Ⓑ Batobus Boat Stop   → One-Way Street

PARIS

Information: The booth inside the entrance provides free floor plans in English. Tel. 01 40 49 48 14, www.musee-orsay.fr. Photography is forbidden.

Tours: Audioguides cost €6. English guided tours usually run daily at 11:30 (€7.50/1.5 hours, none on Sun, may run at other times—inquire when you arrive). You can download a free Rick Steves **audio tour** of the Orsay; see page 7.

Background: Here's a primer on Impressionism: The camera threatened to make pictoral artists obsolete. Now a machine could capture a better likeness faster than you could say "Etch-a-Sketch."

But true art is more than just painting reality. It gives us reality from the artist's point of view, with the artist's personal impressions of the scene. Impressions are often fleeting, so working quickly is essential.

The Impressionist painters rejected camera-like detail for a quick style more suited to capturing the passing moment. Feeling stifled by the rigid rules and stuffy atmosphere of the Academy, the Impressionists took as their motto, "Out of the studio, into the open air." They grabbed their berets and scarves and went on excursions to the country, where they set up their easels (and newly invented tubes of premixed paint) on riverbanks and hillsides, or they sketched in cafés and dance halls. Gods, goddesses, nymphs, and fantasy scenes were out; common people and rural landscapes were in.

The quick style and everyday subjects were ridiculed and called childish by the "experts." Rejected by the Salon, the Impressionists staged their own exhibition in 1874. They brashly took their name from an insult thrown at them by a critic who laughed at one of Monet's "impressions" of a sunrise. During the next decade, they exhibited their own work independently. The public, opposed at first, was slowly won over by the simplicity, the color, and the vibrancy of Impressionist art.

Visiting the Museum: The museum shows art that is also both old and new, conservative and revolutionary. You'll start on the ground floor with the Conservatives and the early rebels (like Manet and Gustave Courbet) who paved the way for the Impressionists. Here, sappy soft-focus Venuses (popular with the 18th-century bourgeoisie) are displayed alongside the grittier work of the Realists. For most visitors, the most important part of the museum is the Impressionist collection on the top floor—this is where you can study many pictures you've probably seen in books, such as Renoir's *Dance at the Moulin de la Galette,* Monet's *Cathedral of Rouen,* Degas' *The Dance Class,* James Abbott McNeill Whistler's *Portrait of the Artist's Mother,* Van Gogh's *The Church at Auvers-sur-Oise,* Cézanne's *The Card Players,* and Henri de Toulouse-Lautrec's *Jane Avril Dancing.* You'll also see Primitive works by Gauguin and Henri Rousseau. As you approach these beautiful, easy-to-enjoy paintings, remember that there is more to this art than meets the eye.

Eiffel Tower and Nearby
▲▲▲**Eiffel Tower (La Tour Eiffel)**—It's crowded, expensive, and there are probably better views in Paris, but visiting this 1,000-foot-tall ornament is worth the trouble. Visitors to Paris

may find *Mona Lisa* to be less than expected, but the Eiffel Tower rarely disappoints, even in an era of skyscrapers.

Cost: There are three observation levels; the higher you go, the more you pay. It costs €13.40 for an elevator ride all the way to the top, or €8.20 if you're only going up to the two lower levels (not covered by Museum Pass). You can save some time in line by climbing the stairs to the first and second level for €4.70, or €3.70 if you're under 25. (Elevators and stairs are both free going down.) Once inside the tower, you can buy your way to the top with no penalty—ticket booths and machines on the first and second levels sell supplements for €5 (walkers need to climb to second level to ride elevator up).

Hours: Daily mid-June-Aug 9:00-24:00, last ascent to top at 23:00 and to lower levels at 23:30; Sept-mid-June 9:30-23:00, last ascent to top at 22:00 and to lower levels at 22:30 (elevator) or 18:00 (stairs). During windy weather, the top level may close to tourists.

Reservations: Frankly, you'd be crazy to show up without a reservation. At www.tour-eiffel.fr, you can book an entry time (for example, June 12 at 16:30) and skip the line—at no extra cost. Book well in advance, as soon as you know when you'll be in Paris. Just pay online with a credit card and print your own ticket (or have a confirmation sent to your mobile phone). Arrive at the tower 10 minutes before your entry time and look for either of the two entrances marked *Visitors with Reservation,* where attendants scan your ticket and put you on the first available elevator. Even with a reservation, when you want to get from the second level to the summit, you'll still have to wait in line like everybody else (and show your ticket again).

The website is easy, but here are a few tips: First, when you "Choose a ticket," make sure you select "Lift entrance ticket with access to the summit" in order to go all the way to the top. For "Type of ticket," it doesn't really matter whether you pick "Group" or "Individual"; a "Group" ticket just gives you one piece of paper covering everyone in your party. You must enter a mobile phone number for identification purposes, so if you don't have one, make one up—and jot it down so you won't forget it (French mobile phone numbers begin with 06 or 07). To print the ticket, follow their specifications carefully (white paper, blank on both sides, etc.). If you're on the road without a printer, try forwarding your email confirmation notice to your hotel reception. They can click on a link to the website, where you can enter your information and print out your ticket.

When to Go: For the best of all worlds, arrive with enough light to see the views, then stay as it gets dark to see the lights. The views are grand whether you ascend or not. At the top of the hour,

PARIS

a five-minute display features thousands of sparkling lights (best viewed from place du Trocadéro or the grassy park below).

Avoiding Lines: Crowds overwhelm this place much of the year, with one- to two-hour waits to get in (unless it's raining, when lines can evaporate). Weekends and holidays are worst, but prepare for ridiculous crowds almost any time. The best solution is to make an online reservation (see above). If you don't have a reservation, go early; get in line 30 minutes before the tower opens. Going later is the next-best bet (after 19:00 May-Aug, after 17:00 off-season; see "Hours," earlier, for last-ascent times). If you're in line to buy tickets, estimate about 20 minutes for every 100 yards, plus 30 minutes more after you reach the security check near the ticket booths. When you buy tickets, all members of your party must be with you; you can't buy tickets in advance for people not present. To get reduced prices for kids, bring proof of ID. You can bypass some (but not all) lines if you have a reservation at either of the tower's view restaurants or hike the stairs (shorter lines).

Planning Your Time: Budget three hours to wait in line, get to the top, and sightsee your way back down. With online reservations and/or no crowds, figure 1.5 hours to the top and back (with time for sightseeing). If you don't want to miss a single level, here's a plan for getting the most out of your visit: Ride the elevator to the second level, then immediately line up for the elevator to the top. Enjoy the views on top, then ride back down to the second level. Frolic there for a while and take in some more views. When you're ready, head to the first level by taking the stairs (no line) or lining up for the elevator (before boarding, confirm that elevator will stop on first level—not all do). Explore the shops and exhibits on the first level and have a snack. Once you're ready to leave, you can line up for the elevator, but it's quickest and most memorable to take the stairs back down to earth.

Getting There: The tower is about a 10-minute walk from the Métro (Bir-Hakeim or Trocadéro stops) or train (Champ de Mars-Tour Eiffel RER stop). The Ecole Militaire Métro stop in the rue Cler area is 20 minutes away. Buses #69 and #87 stop nearby on avenue Joseph Bouvard in the Champ de Mars park.

Nearby: Before or after your tower visit, you can catch the Bateaux Parisiens boat for a Seine cruise (near the base of Eiffel Tower, see "By Boat," page 223).

Information: An Eiffel Tower information office is between the north and east pillars. Each level on the tower has displays pointing out the landmarks and monuments visible below. Tel. 01 44 11 23 23, www.tour-eiffel.fr.

Pickpockets: Beware. Street thieves plunder awestruck visitors gawking below the tower. And tourists in crowded elevators are like fish in a barrel for predatory pickpockets. *En garde.* There's a police station at the Jules Verne pillar.

Security Check: Bags larger than 19 × 8 × 12 inches are not allowed, but there is no baggage check. All bags are subject to a security search. No knives, glass bottles, or cans are permitted.

Services: Free WCs are at the base of the tower, behind the east pillar. Inside the tower itself, WCs are on all levels, but they're small, with long lines.

Photography: All photos and videos are allowed.

Best Views: The best place to view the tower is from place du Trocadéro to the north. It's a 10-minute walk across the river, a happening scene at night, and especially fun for kids. Consider arriving at the Trocadéro Métro stop for the view, then walking toward the tower. Another delightful viewpoint is from the Champ de Mars park to the south. However impressive it may be by day, the tower is an awesome thing to see at twilight, when it becomes engorged with light, and virile Paris lies back and lets night be on top. When darkness fully envelops the city, the tower seems to climax with a spectacular light show at the top of each hour...for five minutes.

Background: Built on the 100th anniversary of the French Revolution (and in the spirit of the Industrial Revolution), the tower was the centerpiece of a World Expo designed simply to show off what people could build in 1889. Bridge-builder Gustave Eiffel (1832-1923) won the contest to build the fair's centerpiece by beating out rival proposals such as a giant guillotine. To a generation hooked on technology, the tower was the marvel of the age, a symbol of progress and human ingenuity. Not all were so impressed, however; many found it a monstrosity. The writer Guy de Maupassant (1850-1893) routinely ate lunch in the tower just so he wouldn't have to look at it.

Touring *La Tour*: Delicate and graceful when seen from afar, the Eiffel Tower is massive—even a bit scary—close up. You don't appreciate its size until you walk toward it; like a mountain, it seems so close but takes forever to reach. Despite the tower's 7,300 tons of metal and 60 tons of paint, it is so well-engineered that it weighs no more per square inch at its base than a linebacker on tiptoes.

There are three observation platforms, at 200, 400, and 900 feet. To get to the top, you need to change elevators at the second level. A separate elevator—with another line—shuttles between the second level and the top. (Note: Whether you have a ticket for the top or just for the second level, elevators going up do not stop at the first level. You can see the first level on the way back down; from the second level, either take the stairs down to the first level, or make sure the elevator will stop at the first level.) Although being on the windy top of the Eiffel Tower is a thrill

Eiffel Tower & Nearby

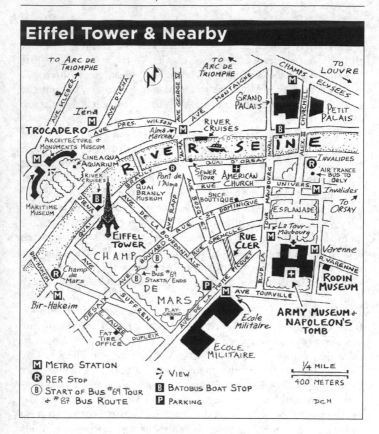

TO ARC DE TRIOMPHE
TO ARC DE TRIOMPHE
CHAMPS-ELYSEES
TO LOUVRE

Iéna M
TROCADERO
Architecture & Monuments Museum
Cineaqua Aquarium
River Cruises
MARITIME MUSEUM

PRES. WILSON
Alma Marceau M
GRAND PALAIS
PETIT PALAIS

RIVER CRUISES
RIVER   SEINE

Pont de l'Alma
Quai Branly Museum

Sewer Tour
Quai D'ORSAY
AMERICAN CHURCH
SNCF BOUTIQUE
RUE CLER

INVALIDES
AIR FRANCE BUS TO ORLY
Invalides
TO ORSAY
ESPLANADE

EIFFEL TOWER
CHAMP

Bus #69 Starts/Ends

DE
MARS
PLAYGROUND

La Tour-Maubourg M
Varenne M
R. VARENNE
RODIN MUSEUM

Bir-Hakeim
Champ de Mars
FAT TIRE OFFICE
DUPLEIX

Ecole Militaire
AVE TOURVILLE

ECOLE MILITAIRE

ARMY MUSEUM & NAPOLEON'S TOMB

M Metro Station
R RER Stop
B Start of Bus #69 Tour & #87 Bus Route

View
B Batobus Boat Stop
P Parking

¼ MILE
400 METERS

DCH

you'll never forget, the view is better from the second level, where you can actually see Paris' monuments. The stairs—yes, you can walk up to the first and second levels—are next to the entrance to the pricey Jules Verne restaurant. As you ascend through the metal beams, imagine being a worker, perched high above nothing, riveting this thing together.

The **top level,** called *le sommet,* is tiny. (It can close temporarily without warning when it reaches capacity.) All you'll find here are wind and grand, sweeping views. The city lies before you (pick out sights with the help of the panoramic maps). On a good day, you can see for 40 miles.

The **second level** (400 feet) has the best views because you're closer to the sights and the monuments are more recognizable. (While the best views are up the short stairway, on the platform without the wire-cage barriers, at busy times much of that zone is taken up by people waiting for the elevator to the top.) This level has souvenir shops, public telephones to call home, and a small stand-up café. While you'll save no money, consider taking the elevator up and the stairs down (five minutes from second level to first, five minutes more to ground) for good exercise and views.

The **first level** (200 feet) has more great views, all well-described by the tower's panoramic displays. There are a number of photo exhibits on the tower's history, WCs, a conference hall (closed to tourists), an ATM, and souvenirs. A small café sells pizza and sandwiches (outdoor tables in summer). The 58 Tour Eiffel restaurant (listed on page 322) has more accessible prices than the Jules Verne Restaurant and is also run by Alain Ducasse (for Jules Verne, allow €200/person for dinner or weekend lunch at the restaurant, €85 for weekday lunch, reserve three months in advance). In winter, part of the first level is set up for winter activities (most recently as an ice-skating rink).

Climb the stairs to Cineiffel for a small gallery and theater. A tired eight-minute video shows continuously, and features clips of the tower's construction, its paint job, its place in pop culture, and the millennium fireworks.

▲**Architecture and Monuments Museum (Cité de l'Architecture et du Patrimoine)**—This museum, on the east side of place du Trocadéro, brilliantly displays casts and models of some of France's most cherished monuments and offers a dazzling exhibition of modern architecture. Gaze into the eyes of medieval statues and wander under doorways, tympanums, and arches from the abbey of Cluny, Chartres Cathedral, Château de Chambord, and much more. You'll discover how colorfully painted the chapels were in Romanesque churches. There's also a vast array of models from modern projects, including a great display upstairs of the sky-high Millau Bridge (Viaduc de Millau) in southern France—the world's highest. The views from the upper rooms to the Eiffel Tower are sensational, as are those from the terrace of the on-site café, Café Carlu.

Cost and Hours: €8, covered by Museum Pass, audio-guide-€3, Wed-Mon 11:00-19:00, Thu until 21:00, closed Tue, excellent English explanations, café open to public, 1 place du Trocadéro, Mo: Trocadéro, RER: Champ de Mars-Tour Eiffel, tel. 01 58 51 52 00, www.citechaillot.fr.

Quai Branly Museum (Musée du Quai Branly)—This is the best collection I've seen anywhere of so-called Primitive Art from Africa, Polynesia, Asia, and America. It's presented in a wild, organic, and strikingly modern building that caused a stir in Paris when it opened in 2006. Masks, statuettes, musical instruments, clothes, voodoo dolls, and a variety of temporary exhibitions and activities are artfully presented and exquisitely lit. It's not, how-ever, accompanied by much printed English information—to really appreciate the exhibit, use the €5 audioguide. It's a 10-minute walk east (upriver) of the Eiffel Tower, along the river. Even if you skip the museum, drop by its peaceful garden café for its fine Eiffel Tower views (closes 30 minutes before museum) and enjoy the intriguing gardens. The pedestrian bridge that crosses the river and runs up to the museum has terrific views of the Eiffel Tower.

Cost and Hours: €8.50, free on first Sun of the month, covered by Museum Pass; museum—Tue-Sun 11:00-19:00, Thu-Sat until 21:00, closed Mon; gardens—Tue-Sun 9:15-19:30, Thu-Sat until 21:15, closed Mon; 37 quai Branly, RER: Champ de Mars-Tour Eiffel or Pont de l'Alma, tel. 01 56 61 70 00, www.quai branly.fr.

National Maritime Museum (Musée National de la Marine)—This extensive museum houses an amazing collection of ship models, submarines, torpedoes, cannonballs, *beaucoup* bowsprits, and naval you-name-it, including a small boat made for Napoleon. Don't miss the model and story of how the obelisk on place de la Concorde was delivered from Egypt to Paris entirely by waterways (behind stairs leading down to special exhibits space). Take advantage of the audioguide that explains key exhibits and adds important context to your visit. Kids love it, too.

Cost and Hours: Adults-€7, under 26 free, covered by Museum Pass, audioguide-€2 for passholders—otherwise free, Mon and Wed-Thu 11:00-18:00, Fri 11:00-21:30, Sat-Sun 11:00-19:00, closed Tue, on left side of place du Trocadéro with your back to Eiffel Tower, tel. 01 53 65 69 69, www.musee-marine.fr.

▲Paris Sewer Tour (Les Egouts de Paris)—Discover what happens after you flush. This quick, interesting, and slightly stinky visit (a perfumed hanky helps) takes you along a few hundred yards of water tunnels in the world's first underground sewer system. Pick up the helpful English self-guided tour, then drop down into Jean Valjean's world of tunnels, rats, and manhole covers. (Victor Hugo was friends with the sewer inspector when he wrote *Les Misérables*.) You'll pass well-organized displays with helpful English information explaining the history of water distribution in Paris, from Roman times to the present. The evolution of this amazing network of sewers is surprisingly fascinating. More than 1,500 miles of tunnels carry 317 million gallons of water daily through this underworld. It's the world's longest sewer system—so long, they say, that if it was laid out straight, it would stretch from Paris all the way to Istanbul.

Ask about the slideshow in the gift shop and occasional tours in English. The WCs are just beyond the gift shop.

Cost and Hours: €4.30, covered by Museum Pass, Sat-Wed May-Sept 11:00-17:00, Oct-April 11:00-16:00, closed Thu-Fri, located where pont de l'Alma greets the Left Bank—on the right side of the bridge as you face the river, Mo: Alma-Marceau, RER: Pont de l'Alma, tel. 01 53 68 27 81.

▲▲**Army Museum and Napoleon's Tomb (Musée de l'Armée)**—The Hôtel des Invalides, a former veterans' hospital topped by a golden dome, houses Napoleon's over-the-top-ornate tomb, as well as Europe's greatest military museum. Visiting the Army Museum's different sections, you can watch the art of war unfold from stone axes to Axis powers.

At the center of the complex, Napoleon Bonaparte lies majestically dead inside several coffins under a grand dome—a goose-bumping pilgrimage for historians. Your visit continues through an impressive range of museums filled with medieval armor, cannons and muskets, Louis XIV-era uniforms and weapons, and Napoleon's horse—stuffed and mounted.

The best section is dedicated to the two World Wars. Walk chronologically through displays on the trench warfare of World War I, France's horrendous losses, the victory parades, and the humiliating Treaty of Versailles that led to World War II. The WWII rooms use black-and-white photos, maps, videos, and a few artifacts to trace Hitler's rise, the Blitzkrieg that overran France, the concentration camps, America's entry into the war, D-Day, the atomic bomb, and the eventual Allied victory. There's special insight into France's role (the French Resistance), and how it was Charles de Gaulle that actually won the war.

Cost: €9, €7 after 16:00, free for military personnel in uniform, free for kids but they must wait in line for ticket, covered by Museum Pass. Admission includes Napoleon's Tomb and all of the museums within the Les Invalides complex.

Hours: Daily April-Sept 10:00-18:00, Sun until 18:30 and Tue until 21:00, July-Aug tomb stays open until 19:00; daily Oct-March 10:00-17:00, Sun until 17:30; last tickets sold 30 minutes before closing; Oct-June closed first Mon of every month, Charles de Gaulle Museum (within the complex) closed Mon year-round.

Location: The Hôtel des Invalides is at 129 rue de Grenelle; Mo: La Tour Maubourg, Varenne, or Invalides, tel. 01 44 42 38 77 or toll tel. 08 10 11 33 99, www.invalides.org.

▲▲**Rodin Museum (Musée Rodin)**—This user-friendly museum is filled with passionate works by the greatest sculptor since Michelangelo. Auguste Rodin (1840-1917) sculpted human figures on an epic scale, revealing through their bodies his deepest thoughts and feelings. The museum is currently undergoing renovation, and rooms will be opened one by one as they're finished. The project won't be completed until 2014, but the gardens will remain open throughout the renovation.

Like many of Michelangelo's unfinished works, Rodin's statues rise from the raw stone around them, driven by the life force. With missing limbs and scarred skin, these are prefab classics, making ugliness noble. Rodin's people are always moving

PARIS

restlessly. Even the famous *Thinker* is moving. While he's plopped down solidly, his mind is a million miles away.

Rodin worked with many materials—he chiseled marble (though not often), modeled clay, cast bronze, worked plaster, painted, and sketched. He often created different versions of the same subject in different media.

Rodin lived and worked in this mansion, renting rooms alongside Henri Matisse, the poet Rainer Maria Rilke (Rodin's secretary), and the dancer Isadora Duncan. The well-displayed exhibits trace Rodin's artistic development, explain how his bronze statues were cast, and show some of the studies he created to work up to his masterpiece (the unfinished *Gates of Hell*). Learn about Rodin's tumultuous relationship with his apprentice and lover, Camille Claudel. Mull over what makes his sculptures some of the most evocative since the Renaissance. And stroll the gardens, packed with many of his greatest works (including *The Thinker, Balzac,* the *Burghers of Calais,* and the *Gates of Hell*). The beautiful gardens are ideal for artistic reflection.

Cost and Hours: €6, under 18 free, free on first Sun of the month, €12 combo-ticket with Orsay Museum (valid four days, one visit per sight), covered by Museum Pass. It costs €1 to get into the gardens only—which may be Paris' best deal, as many works are on display there (also covered by Museum Pass). Audioguides are €4, and baggage check is mandatory. Open Tue-Sun 10:00-17:45, closed Mon, gardens close at 18:00, Oct-March at 17:00, last entry 30 minutes before closing, near the Army Museum and Napoleon's Tomb, 79 rue de Varenne, Mo: Varenne, tel. 01 44 18 61 10, www.musee-rodin.fr.

▲▲**Marmottan Museum (Musée Marmottan Monet)**—This intimate, less-touristed mansion on the southwest fringe of urban Paris has the best collection of works by the father of Impressionism, Claude Monet (1840-1926). Fiercely independent and dedicated to his craft, Monet gave courage to the other Impressionists in the face of harsh criticism.

Though the museum is not arranged chronologically, you can trace his life. You'll see black-and-white sketches from his youth, his discovery of open-air painting, and the canvas—*Impression: Sunrise*—that gave Impressionism its name. There are portraits of his wives and kids, and his well-known "series" paintings (done at different times of day) of London, Gare St. Lazare, and the Cathedral of Rouen. The museum's highlight is scenes from his garden at Giverny—the rose trellis, the Japanese bridge, and the larger-than-life water lilies.

In addition, the Marmottan features a world-class collection of works by Berthe Morisot and other Impressionists; an eclectic collection of non-Monet objects (furniture, illuminated manuscript drawings); and temporary exhibits.

Cost and Hours: €10, not covered by Museum Pass, Tue-Sun 10:00-18:00, Thu until 20:00, closed Mon, last entry 30 minutes before closing, 2 rue Louis-Boilly, bus #32 or Mo: La Muette, tel. 01 44 96 50 33, www.marmottan.com.

Left Bank

Opposite Notre-Dame, on the left bank of the Seine, is the Latin Quarter.

▲▲**Cluny Museum (Musée National du Moyen Age)**—This treasure trove of Middle Ages (Moyen Age) art fills old Roman baths, offering close-up looks at stained glass, Notre-Dame carvings, fine goldsmithing and jewelry, and rooms of tapestries. The highlights are several original stained-glass windows from Sainte-Chapelle, and the exquisite *Lady and the Unicorn* series of six tapestries: A delicate, as-medieval-as-can-be noble lady introduces a delighted unicorn to the senses of taste, hearing, sight, smell, and touch. This museum helps put the Middle Ages in perspective, reflecting a time when Europe was awakening from a thousand-year slumber and Paris was emerging on the world stage. Trade was booming, people actually owned chairs, and the Renaissance was moving in like a warm front from Italy.

Cost and Hours: €8, free on first Sun of month, covered by Museum Pass, Wed-Mon 9:15-17:45, closed Tue, last entry at 17:15, near corner of boulevards St. Michel and St. Germain at 6 place Paul Painlevé; Mo: Cluny-La Sorbonne, St. Michel, or Odéon; tel. 01 53 73 78 16, www.musee-moyenage.fr.

St. Germain-des-Prés—A church was first built on this site in A.D. 558. The church you see today was constructed in 1163 and is all that's left of a once sprawling and influential monastery. The colorful interior reminds us that medieval churches were originally painted in bright colors. The surrounding area hops at night with venerable cafés, fire-eaters, mimes, and scads of artists.

Cost and Hours: Free, daily 8:00-20:00, Mo: St. Germain-des-Prés.

▲**St. Sulpice Church and Organ Concert**—Since it was featured in *The Da Vinci Code*, this grand church has become a trendy stop for the book's many fans. But the real reason to visit is to see and hear its intimately accessible organ. For pipe-organ enthusiasts, this is one of Europe's great musical treats. The Grand Orgue at St. Sulpice Church has a rich history, with a succession of 12 world-class organists—including Charles-Marie Widor and Marcel Dupré—that goes back 300 years. Widor started the tradition of opening the loft to visitors after the 10:30 service

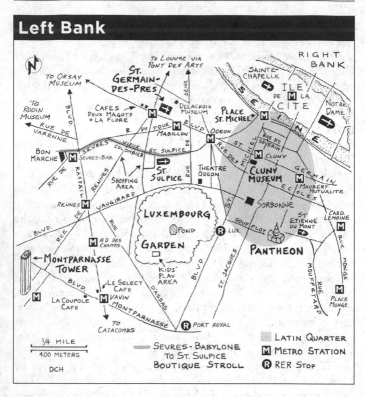

Left Bank

Map labels:

RIGHT BANK

To LOUVRE via PONT DES ARTS

St. GERMAIN-DES-PRES

Sainte-CHAPELLE

To ORSAY MUSEUM

ILE DE LA CITE

To RODIN MUSEUM

CAFES DEUX MAGOTS & LA FLORE

DELACROIX MUSEUM

NOTRE DAME

RUE DE VARENNE

BLVD. RASPAIL

FOUR MABILLON

PLACE St. MICHEL

RUE ST. SEVERIN

BON MARCHE

Sevres-Bab.

VIEUX COLOMBIER

ST. SULPICE

Odeon

Cluny

SEINE

SHOPPING AREA

St. SULPICE

THEATRE Odeon

CLUNY MUSEUM

Maubert Mutualite

RUE DE RENNES

VAUGIRARD

LUXEMBOURG

Sorbonne

Pond

St. ETIENNE DU MONT

CARD. LEMOINE

N.D. DES CHAMPS

GARDEN

SOUFFLOT

LUX.

RER

PANTHEON

MONTPARNASSE TOWER

KIDS' PLAY AREA

BLVD.

St. JACQUES

RUE MONGE

Le SELECT CAFE

VAVIN

DASSAS

RUE MOUFFETARD

La COUPOLE CAFE

MONTPARNASSE

PLACE MONGE

To CATACOMBS

PORT ROYAL

1/4 MILE

400 METERS

DCH

SEVRES-BABYLONE TO ST. SULPICE BOUTIQUE STROLL

LATIN QUARTER

M METRO STATION

R RER STOP

---

on Sundays. Daniel Roth (or his understudy) continues to welcome guests in three languages while playing five keyboards. (See www.stsulpice.com for concerts.)

The 10:30-11:30 Sunday Mass (come appropriately dressed) is followed by a high-powered 25-minute recital. Then, at noon, the small, unmarked door is opened (left of entry as you face the rear). Visitors scamper like sixteenth notes up spiral stairs, past the 19th-century StairMasters that five men once pumped to fill the bellows, into a world of 7,000 pipes. You can see the organ and visit with Daniel (or his substitute, who might not speak English). Space is tight—only 15 people are allowed in at a time, and only a few can gather around the organist at once—you need to be quick to allow others a chance to meet him. You'll likely have about 20 minutes to kill before watching the master play during the next Mass (church views are great and there's a small lounge to wait in); you can leave at any time. If you're late or rushed, show up around 12:30 and wait at the little door (last entry is at 13:00). As someone leaves, you can slip in, climb up, and catch the rest of the performance. Tempting boutiques surround the church, and Luxembourg Garden is nearby.

Cost and Hours: Free, church open daily 7:30-19:30, Mo: St. Sulpice or Mabillon.

Delacroix Museum (Musée National Eugène Delacroix)—This museum for Eugène Delacroix (1798-1863) was once his home and studio. A friend of bohemian artistic greats—including George Sand and Frédéric Chopin—Delacroix is most famous for the flag-waving painting *Liberty Leading the People,* which is displayed at the Louvre, not here.

Cost and Hours: €5, free on first Sun of the month, covered by Museum Pass, Wed-Mon 9:30-17:00, Sat-Sun until 17:30 in summer, closed Tue, last entry 30 minutes before closing, 6 rue de Furstenberg, Mo: St. Germain-des-Prés, tel. 01 44 41 86 50, www.musee-delacroix.fr.

▲Luxembourg Garden (Jardin du Luxembourg)—Paris' most beautiful, interesting, and enjoyable garden/park/recreational area, le Jardin du Luxembourg, is a great place to watch Parisians at rest and play. These 60-acre gardens, dotted with fountains and statues, are the property of the French Senate, which meets here in the Luxembourg Palace. Luxembourg Garden has special rules governing its use (for example, where cards can be played, where dogs can be walked, where joggers can run, and when and where music can be played). The brilliant flower beds are completely changed three times a year, and the boxed trees are brought out of the orangerie in May. Children enjoy the rentable toy sailboats. The park hosts marionette shows (Les Guignols, in French, Wed, Sat, Sun) and pony rides may be available in summer. Challenge the card and chess players to a game (near the tennis courts), or find a free chair near the main pond and take a well-deserved break.

Cost and Hours: Park free and open daily dawn until dusk, Mo: Odéon, RER: Luxembourg.

Nearby: The grand Neoclassical-domed Panthéon, now a mausoleum housing the tombs of great French notables, is three blocks away (see next listing).

Other Parks: If you enjoy Luxembourg Garden and want to see more green spaces, you could visit the more elegant **Parc Monceau** (Mo: Monceau), the colorful **Jardin des Plantes** (Mo: Jussieu or Gare d'Austerlitz, RER: Gare d'Austerlitz), or the hilly and bigger **Parc des Buttes-Chaumont** (Mo: Buttes-Chaumont).

▲Panthéon—This state-capitol-style Neoclassical monument celebrates France's illustrious history and people, balances Foucault's pendulum, and is the final home of many French VIPs.

Inside the vast building (360' by 280' by 270') are monuments tracing the celebrated struggles of the French people: a beheaded St. Denis (painting on left wall of nave), St. Geneviève saving the fledgling city from Attila the Hun, and scenes of Joan of Arc (left transept).

Foucault's pendulum swings gracefully at the end of a 220-foot cable suspended from the towering dome. It was here in 1851 that the scientist Léon Foucault first demonstrated the rotation of the earth. Stand a few minutes and watch the pendulum's arc (appear to) shift as you and the earth rotate beneath it.

Stairs in the back lead down to the crypt, where a pantheon of greats is buried. Rousseau is along the right wall as you enter, Voltaire faces him across the hall. Also buried here are scientist Marie Curie, Victor Hugo *(Les Misérables, The Hunchback of Notre-Dame)*, Alexandre Dumas *(The Three Musketeers, The Count of Monte Cristo)*, and Louis Braille, who invented the script for the blind.

From the main floor you can climb 206 steps to the dome gallery for fine views of the interior as well as the city (accessible only with an escort). Visits leave every hour until 17:30 from the bookshop near the entry—see schedule as you go in.

Cost and Hours: €8, under 18 free, covered by Museum Pass, daily 10:00-18:30 in summer, until 18:00 in winter, last entry 45 minutes before closing, Mo: Cardinal Lemoine, ask about occasional English tours or call ahead for schedule, tel. 01 44 32 18 00, www.pantheon.monuments-nationaux.fr.

Montparnasse Tower (La Tour Montparnasse)—This sadly out-of-place 59-story superscraper has one virtue: its sensational views are cheaper and far easier to access than the Eiffel Tower's. Come early in the day for clearest skies and be treated to views from a comfortable interior and from up on the rooftop. (Some say it's the very best view in Paris, as you can see the Eiffel Tower clearly...and you can't see the Montparnasse Tower at all.) Exit the elevator at the 56th floor, passing the eager photographer (they'll superimpose your group's image with the view) to views of *tout Paris*. Have a drink or a light lunch (OK prices) with a view, peruse the gift shop, and find good WCs. There may be plenty of dioramas identifying highlights of the star-studded vista, but the €3 "M-56" photo-guide makes a fun souvenir. Explore every corner of the floor for best views—from here it's easy to admire Haussmann's grand-boulevard scheme.

Enjoy fascinating historic black-and-white photos, and a plush little theater playing a worthwhile video that celebrates the big views of this grand city (free, 12 minutes, shows continuously). Climb to the open terrace on the 59th floor to enjoy the surreal scene of a lonely man in a box, and a helipad surrounded by the window-cleaner track. Here, 690 feet above Paris, you can scan the city with the wind in your hair, noticing the lush courtyards hiding behind grand street fronts.

Cost and Hours: €11.50, not covered by Museum Pass, daily April-Sept 9:30-23:30, Oct-March 9:30-22:30, Fri-Sat until 23:00, last entry 30 minutes before closing, sunset is great but views are disappointing after dark, entrance on rue de l'Arrivée, Mo: Montparnasse-Bienvenüe—from the Métro stay inside the station and follow the signs for *La Tour*, tel. 01 45 38 52 56, www.tour montparnasse56.com.

▲**Catacombs**—These underground tunnels contain the anonymous bones of six million permanent Parisians. In 1786, the citizens of Paris decided to relieve congestion and improve sanitary conditions by emptying the city cemeteries (which traditionally surrounded churches) into an official ossuary. They found the perfect locale in the many miles of underground tunnels from limestone quarries, which were, at that time, just outside the city. For decades, priests led ceremonial processions of black-veiled, bone-laden carts into the quarries, where the bones were stacked into piles five feet high and as much as 80 feet deep behind neat walls of skull-studded tibiae. Each transfer was completed by placing a plaque, indicating the church and district where the bones came from and the date that they arrived. Note to wannabe Hamlets: An attendant checks your bag at the exit for stolen souvenirs. A flashlight is handy. Being under 6'2" is helpful.

Cost and Hours: €8, not covered by Museum Pass, Tue-Sun 10:00-17:00, ticket booth closes at 16:00, closed Mon. Be warned that lines are long (figure an hour wait) and hard to avoid. Arrive no later than 14:30 or risk not getting in. Take the Métro to Denfert-Rochereau, then find the lion in the big traffic circle; if he looked left rather than right, he'd stare right at the green entrance to the Catacombs at 1 place Denfert-Rochereau. Tel. 01 43 22 47 63, www.catacombes-de-paris.fr.

Nearby: Enjoy the market street, rue Daguerre.

Champs-Elysées and Nearby

▲▲▲**Champs-Elysées**—This famous boulevard is Paris' backbone, with its greatest concentration of traffic. From the Arc de Triomphe down avenue des Champs-Elysées, all of France seems to converge on place de la Concorde, the city's largest square. And though the Champs-Elysées has become as international as it is Parisian, a walk here is still a must.

Background: In 1667, Louis XIV opened the first section of the street as a short extension of the Tuileries Garden. This year is considered the birth of Paris as a grand city. The Champs-Elysées soon became *the* place to cruise in your carriage. (It still is today; traffic can be gridlocked even at midnight.) A hundred years later, the café scene arrived. From the 1920s until the 1960s, this boulevard was pure elegance; Parisians actually dressed up to come here. It was mainly residences, rich hotels, and cafés. Then, in 1963, the government pumped up the neighborhood's commercial metabolism by bringing in the RER (commuter train). Suburbanites had

PARIS

Champs-Elysées & Nearby

easy access, and *pfft*—there went the neighborhood.

The *nouveau* Champs-Elysées, revitalized in 1994, has new benches and lamps, broader sidewalks, all-underground parking, and a fleet of green-suited workers who drive motorized street cleaners. Blink away the modern elements, and it's not hard to imagine the boulevard pre-1963, with only the finest structures lining both sides all the way to the palace gardens.

Strolling the Champs-Elysées: To reach the top of the Champs-Elysées, take the Métro to the Arc de Triomphe (Mo: Charles de Gaulle-Etoile) then saunter down the grand boulevard, following this commentary (Métro stops every few blocks, including Charles de Gaulle-Etoile, George V, and Franklin D. Roosevelt). If you plan to tour the Arc de Triomphe (see listing on page 267), do it before starting this walk.

Fancy car dealerships include **Peugeot,** at #136 (showing off its futuristic concept cars, often alongside the classic models), and **Mercedes-Benz,** a block down at #118, where you can pick up a Mercedes watch to go with your new car. In the 19th century, this was an area for horse stables; today, it's the district of garages, limo companies, and car dealerships. If you're serious about selling cars in France, you must have a showroom on the Champs-Elysées.

Next to Mercedes is the famous **Lido,** Paris' largest cabaret (and a multiplex cinema). You can walk all the way into the lobby. Paris still offers the kind of burlesque-type spectacles that have been performed here since the 19th century, combining music, comedy, and scantily clad women. Moviegoing on the Champs-Elysées provides another kind of fun, with theaters showing the very latest releases. Check to see if there are films you recognize, then look for the showings *(séances)*. A "v.o." *(version originale)* next to the time indicates the film will be shown in its original language.

The flagship store of leather-bag makers **Louis Vuitton** may be the largest single-brand luxury store in the world. Step inside. The store insists on providing enough salespeople to treat each customer royally—if there's a line, it means shoppers have over-whelmed the place.

Fouquet's café-restaurant (#99), under the red awning, is a popular spot among French celebrities, serving the most expen-sive shot of espresso I've found in downtown Paris (€8). Opened in 1899 as a coachman's bistro, Fouquet's gained fame as the hangout of France's WWI biplane fighter pilots—those who weren't shot down by Germany's infamous "Red Baron." It also served as James Joyce's dining room. Since the early 1900s, Fouquet's has been a favorite of French actors and actresses. The golden plaques at the entrance honor winners of France's Oscar-like film awards, the Césars (one is cut into the ground at the end of the red carpet). Look for the plaques for Gérard Depardieu, Catherine Deneuve, Roman Polanski, Juliette Binoche, and many famous Americans (but not Jerry Lewis). Recent winners are shown on the floor just inside. France's former first lady, Carla Bruni-Sarkozy, is often seen dining here.

Ladurée (two blocks downhill at #75, with green-and-purple awning) is a classic 19th-century tea salon/restaurant/*pâtisserie* with an interior out of the 1860s. Non-patrons can discreetly wander in through the door farthest downhill and peek into the cozy rooms upstairs (no photos). A coffee here is *très élégant* (only €3.50).

For much cheaper options, cross the boulevard and go down-hill a block to **La Brioche Dorée** and its next-door neighbor **Boulangerie Paul** (both have outdoor seating, Dorée also has WCs, air-con, and upstairs seating, 82 Champs-Elysées).

▲▲**Arc de Triomphe**—Napoleon had this magnificent arch com-missioned to commemorate his victory at the battle of Austerlitz. There's no triumphal arch bigger (165 feet high, 130 feet wide). And, with 12 converging boulevards, there's no traffic circle more thrilling to experience—either from behind the wheel or on foot (take the underpass).

The foot of the arch is a stage on which the last two centuries of Parisian history have played out—from the funeral of Napoleon to the goose-stepping arrival of the Nazis to the triumphant return of Charles de Gaulle after the Allied liberation. Examine the carvings on the pillars, featuring a mighty Napoleon and excitable Lady Liberty. Pay your respects at the Tomb of the Unknown Soldier. Then climb the 284 steps to the observation deck up top, with sweeping skyline panoramas and a mesmerizing view down onto the traffic that swirls around the arch.

Cost and Hours: Outside—free, always viewable. Interior—€9.50, under 18 free, free on first Sun of month Oct-March, covered by Museum Pass, daily April-Sept 10:00-23:00, Oct-March 10:00-22:30, last entry 30 minutes before closing, place Charles de Gaulle, use underpass to reach arch, Mo: Charles de Gaulle-Etoile, tel. 01 55 37 73 77, www.arc-de-triomphe.monuments-nationaux.fr.

▲**Opéra Garnier**—This gleaming grand theater of the belle époque was built for Napoleon III and finished in 1875. As you pass the bust of the architect, Monsieur Garnier, pay your respects and check out the bronze floorplan of the complex etched below. Notice how little space is given to seating. The building is huge—though the auditorium itself seats only 2,000. The real show was before and after the performance, when the elite of Paris—out to see and be seen—strutted their elegant stuff in the extravagant lobbies. Think of the grand marble stairway as a theater. As you wander the halls and gawk at the decor, imagine this place in its heyday, filled with beautiful people. The massive foundations straddle an underground lake (inspiring the mysterious world of the *Phantom of the Opera*). Visitors can peek from two boxes into the actual red-velvet performance hall to view Marc Chagall's colorful ceiling (1964) playfully dancing around the eight-ton chandelier (guided tours take you into the performance hall; you can't enter when they're changing out the stage). Note the box seats next to the stage—the most expensive in the house, with an obstructed view of the stage...but just right if you're here only to be seen.

The elitism of this place prompted President François Mitterrand to have an opera house built for the people in the 1980s, situated symbolically on place de la Bastille, where the French Revolution started in 1789. This left the Opéra Garnier home only to ballet and occasional concerts. The library/museum will interest opera buffs, but anyone will enjoy the second-floor grand foyer and Salon du Glacier, iced with decor typical of 1900.

Cost and Hours: €9, not covered by Museum Pass, erratic hours due to performances and rehearsals, but generally daily 10:00-17:00, mid-July-Aug until 18:00, last entry 30 minutes before closing, 8 rue Scribe, Mo: Opéra, RER: Auber.

Tours: English tours of the building run during summer and off-season on weekends and Wed, usually at 11:30 and 14:30—call to confirm schedule (€12.50, includes entry, 1.5 hours, tel. 01 40 01 17 89 or 08 25 05 44 05, press 2 for tours).

PARIS

Nearby: The Fragonard Perfume Museum (next) is on the left side of the Opéra, and the venerable Galeries Lafayette department store (marvelous views from roof terrace) is just behind. Across the street, the illustrious Café de la Paix has been a meeting spot for the local glitterati for generations. If you can afford the coffee, this spot offers a delightful break.

Fragonard Perfume Museum—Near Opéra Garnier, this perfume shop masquerades as a museum. Housed in a beautiful 19th-century mansion, it's the best-smelling museum in Paris—and you'll learn a little about how perfume is made, too (ask for the English handout).

Cost and Hours: Free, Mon-Sat 9:00-18:00, Sun 9:00-17:00, 9 rue Scribe, Mo: Opéra, RER: Auber, tel. 01 47 42 04 56, www.fragonard.com.

▲▲Jacquemart-André Museum (Musée Jacquemart-André)—This thoroughly enjoyable museum (with an elegant café) showcases the lavish home of a wealthy, art-loving, 19th-century Parisian couple. After wandering the grand boulevards, get inside for an intimate look at the lifestyles of the Parisian rich and fabulous. Edouard André and his wife Nélie Jacquemart—who had no children—spent their lives and fortunes designing, building, and then decorating this sumptuous mansion. What makes the visit so rewarding is the excellent audioguide tour (in English, free with admission, plan on spending an hour with the audioguide). The place is strewn with paintings by Rembrandt, Botticelli, Uccello, Mantegna, Bellini, Boucher, and Fragonard—enough to make a painting gallery famous.

Cost and Hours: €10, includes audioguide, not covered by Museum Pass, daily 10:00-18:00, Mon and Sat until 21:30 during special exhibits, 158 boulevard Haussmann, Mo: Miromesnil or St. Philippe-du-Roule, bus #80 makes a convenient connection to Ecole Militaire, tel. 01 45 62 11 59, www.musee-jacquemart-andre.com.

After Your Visit: Consider a break in the sumptuous museum tearoom, with delicious cakes and tea (daily 11:45-17:30). From here walk north on rue de Courcelles to see Paris' most beautiful park, Parc Monceau.

▲Petit Palais (and its Musée des Beaux-Arts)—This free museum displays a broad collection of paintings and sculptures from the 1600s to the 1900s. It's a museum of second-choice art, but the building itself is impressive, and there are a few 19th-century diamonds in the rough, including pieces by Courbet, Monet, the American painter Mary Cassatt, and other Impressionists. The Palais also has a pleasant garden courtyard and café.

Cost and Hours: Free, Tue-Sun 10:00-18:00, Thu until 20:00 for temporary exhibitions, closed Mon; across from Grand Palais on avenue Winston Churchill, a looooong block west of place de la Concorde; tel. 01 53 43 40 00, www.petitpalais.paris.fr.

Grand Palais—This grand exhibition hall, built for the 1900 World's Fair, is used for temporary exhibits. The building's Industrial Age, erector-set, iron-and-glass exterior is grand, but the steep entry price is only worthwhile if you're interested in any of the several different exhibitions (each with different hours and costs, located in various parts of the building). Many areas are undergoing renovations, which may still be under way during your visit. Get details on the current schedule from the TIs, in *Pariscope*, or from the website.

Cost and Hours: Admission prices and hours vary with each exhibition. Major exhibitions are usually €11 and not covered by Museum Pass. It's open daily (generally 10:00-20:00, Wed until 22:00), though some parts of the building are closed Mon, others are closed Tue, and the whole space is closed between exhibitions. Avenue Winston Churchill, Mo: Rond Point or Champs-Elysées, tel. 01 44 13 17 17, www.grandpalais.fr.

▲La Défense and La Grande Arche—Though Paris keeps its historic center classic and skyscraper-free, this district, nicknamed "le petit Manhattan," offers an impressive excursion into a side of Paris few tourists see: that of a modern-day economic super-power. La Défense was first conceived more than 60 years ago as a US-style forest of skyscrapers that would accommodate the business needs of the modern world. Today La Défense is a thriving commercial and shopping center, home to 150,000 employees and 55,000 residents.

For an interesting visit, take the Métro to the La Défense Grande Arche stop, follow *Sortie Grande Arche* signs, and climb the steps of La Grande Arche for distant city views. Then stroll gradually downhill among the glass buildings to the Esplanade de la Défense Métro station, and return home from there.

La Grande Arche de la Fraternité is the centerpiece of this ambitious complex. Inaugurated in 1989 on the 200th anniversary of the French Revolution, it was, like the Revolution, dedicated to human rights and brotherhood. The place is big—Notre-Dame Cathedral could fit under its arch. The "cloud"—a huge canvas canopy under the arch—is an attempt to cut down on the wind-tunnel effect this gigantic building creates.

Lunch on the Steps: Join the locals and picnic on the arch steps; good to-go places are plentiful (and cafés are nearby).

The Esplanade: La Défense is much more than its eye-catching arch. Survey the skyscraping scene from the top of the steps. Wander from the arch back toward the city center (and to the next Métro stop) along the Esplanade (a.k.a. "le Parvis")—a virtual open-air modern art gallery, sporting pieces by Joan Miró (blue, red, and yellow), Alexander Calder (red), and Yaacov Agam (the fountain with colorful stripes and rhythmically dancing spouts), among others. *La Défense de Paris*, the statue that gave the area its name, recalls the 1871 Franco-Prussian war—it's a rare bit of old Paris out here in the 'burbs.

As you descend the Esplanade, notice how the small gardens and *boules* courts (reddish dirt areas) are designed to integrate tradition into this celebration of modern commerce. Note also how the buildings decrease in height and increase in age—the Nexity Tower (closest to central Paris) looks old compared to the other skyscrapers. Dating from the 1960s, it was one of the first buildings at La Défense. Your walk ends at the amusing fountain of Bassin Takis, where you'll find the Esplanade de la Défense Métro station that zips you out of all this modernity and directly back into town.

Marais Neighborhood and Nearby

The Marais neighborhood extends along the Right Bank of the Seine, from the Pompidou Center to the Bastille. With more pre-Revolutionary lanes and buildings than anywhere else in town, the Marais is more atmospheric than touristy. It's medieval Paris, and the haunt of the old nobility. During the reign of Henry IV, this area—originally a swamp *(marais)*—became the hometown of the French aristocracy. In the 17th century, big shots built their private mansions *(hôtels)* close to Henry's stylish place des Vosges. With the Revolution, the aristocratic splendor of this quarter passed, and the Marais became a working-class quarter, filled with gritty shops, artisans, immigrants, and a Jewish community. Today this thriving, trendy, real community is a joy to explore. It looks the way much of the city did until the mid-1800s, when Napoleon III had Baron Georges-Eugène Haussmann blast out the narrow streets to construct broad boulevards (wide enough for the guns and tanks of the army, too wide for revolutionary barricades), thus creating modern Paris. When strolling the Marais, stick to the west-east axis formed by rue Ste. Croix de la Bretonnerie, rue des Rosiers (heart of Paris' Jewish community), and rue St. Antoine. On Sunday afternoons, this trendy area pulses with shoppers and café crowds.

Don't waste time looking for the **Bastille,** the prison of Revolution fame. It's Paris' most famous nonsight. The building is long gone; just the square remains.

▲**Place des Vosges**—Henry IV (r. 1589-1610) built this centerpiece of the Marais in 1605 and called it "place Royal." As he'd hoped, it turned the Marais into Paris' most exclusive neighborhood. Walk to the center, where Louis XIII, on horseback, gestures, "Look at this wonderful square my dad built." He's

Marais Neighborhood & Nearby

surrounded by locals enjoying their community park. You'll see children frolicking in the sandbox, lovers warming benches, and pigeons guarding their fountains while trees shade this escape from the glare of the big city (you can refill your water bottle in the center of the square).

Study the architecture: nine pavilions (houses) per side. The two highest—at the front and back—were for the king and queen (but were never used). Warm red brickwork—some real, some fake—is topped with sloped slate roofs, chimneys, and another quaint relic of a bygone era: TV antennas. The insightful writer **Victor Hugo** lived at #6—at the southeast corner of the square, marked by the French flag—from 1832 to 1848. This was when he wrote much of his most important work, including his biggest hit, *Les Misérables*. Inside you'll wander through eight plush rooms and enjoy a fine view of the square (free, optional special exhibits cost about €7—usually not worth paying for, audioguide-€5, Tue-Sun 10:00-18:00, closed Mon, last entry at 17:40, 6 place des Vosges; Mo: Bastille, St. Paul, or Chemin Vert; tel. 01 42 72 10 16, www.musee-hugo.paris.fr).

Leave the place des Vosges through the doorway at the southwest corner of the square and pass through the elegant **Hôtel de Sully** (great example of a Marais mansion, grand courtyard open daily 10:00-19:00, fine bookstore inside) to rue St. Antoine.

▲▲**Pompidou Center (Centre Pompidou)**—One of Europe's greatest collections of far-out modern art is housed in the Musée National d'Art Moderne, on the fourth and fifth floors of this colorful exhibition hall. The building itself is "exoskeletal" (like Notre-Dame or a crab), with its functional parts—the pipes, heating ducts, and escalator—on the outside, and the meaty art inside. It's the epitome of modern architecture, where "form follows function." Created ahead of its time, the 20th-century art in this collection is still waiting for the world to catch up.

Cost and Hours: €10-12 depending on current exhibits, free on first Sun of month, Museum Pass covers permanent collection and view escalators, Wed-Mon 11:00-21:00, closed Tue, ticket counters close at 20:00, Mo: Rambuteau or farther-away Hôtel de Ville, tel. 01 44 78 12 33, www.centrepompidou.fr.

Visiting the Museum: Buy your ticket on the ground floor, then ride up the escalator (or run up the down escalator to get in the proper mood). When you see the view, your opinion of the Pompidou's exterior should improve a good 15 percent. Find the permanent collection—the entrance is either on the fourth or fifth floor (it varies). Enter, show your ticket, and get the current floor plan *(plan du musée)*.

The 20th century—accelerated by technology and fragmented by war—was exciting and chaotic, and the art reflects the turbulence of that century of change. In this free-flowing and airy museum (with great views over Paris), you'll come face-to-face with works by Henri Matisse, Pablo Picasso, Marc Chagall, Salvador Dalí, Andy Warhol, Wassily Kandinsky, Max Ernst, Jackson Pollock, and many more. After so many Madonnas-and-children, a piano smashed to bits and glued to the wall is refreshing.

Nearby: The Pompidou Center and the square that fronts it are lively, with lots of people, street theater, and activity inside and out—a perpetual street fair. Kids of any age enjoy the fun, colorful fountain (called *Homage to Stravinsky*) next to the Pompidou Center.

▲**Jewish Art and History Museum (Musée d'Art et Histoire du Judaïsme)**—This fine museum, located in a beautifully restored Marais mansion, tells the story of Judaism in France and throughout Europe, from the Roman destruction of Jerusalem to the theft of famous artworks during World War II. Displays illustrate the cultural unity maintained by this continually dispersed population. You'll learn about the history of Jewish traditions, from bar mitzvahs to menorahs, and see the exquisite traditional

PARIS

costumes and objects central to daily life. The museum also displays paintings by famous Jewish artists, including Marc Chagall, Amedeo Modigliani, and Chaim Soutine. The English explanations posted in many rooms provide sufficient explanation for most; free audioguides provide greater detail.

Cost and Hours: €7, includes audioguide, covered by Museum Pass, Mon-Fri 11:00-18:00, Sun 10:00-18:00, closed Sat, last entry 45 minutes before closing, 71 rue du Temple; Mo: Rambuteau or Hôtel de Ville a few blocks farther away, RER: Châtelet-Les Halles; tel. 01 53 01 86 60, www.mahj.org.

Rue des Rosiers: Paris' Jewish Quarter—This tiny yet colorful Jewish district of the Marais was once considered the largest in Western Europe. Today, rue des Rosiers is lined with Jewish shops and kosher eateries, and the district is being squeezed by the trendy boutiques of modern Paris. Visit any day but Saturday, when most businesses are closed—it's best on Sunday. The intersection of rue des Rosiers and rue des Ecouffes marks the heart of the small neighborhood that Jews call the Pletzl ("little square"). Lively rue des Ecouffes, named for a bird of prey, is a derogatory nod to the moneychangers' shops that once lined this lane.

Eating: If you're visiting at lunchtime, you'll be tempted by kosher pizza and plenty of cheap fast-food joints selling falafel "to go" *(emporter)*. **L'As du Falafel,** with its bustling New York deli atmosphere, is terrific (at #34, sit-down or to go). The **Sacha Finkelsztajn** Yiddish bakery at #27 is also good (Polish and Russian cuisine, pop in for a tempting treat, sit for the same price as take-away). Nearby, the recommended **Chez Marianne** cooks up traditional Jewish meals and serves excellent falafel to go (at corner of rue des Rosiers and rue des Hospitalières-St-Germain; long hours daily).

Nearby: The Jewish Quarter is also home to the Holocaust Memorial (described next).

Holocaust Memorial (Mémorial de la Shoah)—Commemorating the lives of the more than 76,000 Jews deported from France in World War II, this memorial's focal point is underground, where victims' ashes are buried. Displaying original deportation records, the museum takes you through the history of Jews in Europe and France, from medieval pogroms to the Nazi era.

Cost and Hours: Free, Sun-Fri 10:00-18:00, Thu until 22:00, closed Sat and certain Jewish holidays, 17 rue Geoffroy l'Asnier, tel. 01 42 77 44 72, www.memorialdelashoah.org.

▲▲Picasso Museum (Musée Picasso)—This museum, closed for a major renovation until the summer of 2013, contains the world's largest collection of Picasso's paintings, sculptures, sketches, and ceramics, along with his small collection of Impressionist art.

Tucked into a corner of the Marais, it's worth ▲▲▲ if you're a Picasso fan. When the museum reopens, its exhibition space will be much larger; more than 500 of Picasso's works will be on view over four floors. Room-by-room English introductions will help make sense of Picasso's artwork—from the Toulouse-Lautrec–like portraits at the beginning of his career to his gray-brown Cubist period to his return-to-childhood, Salvador Dalí–like finish.

Cost and Hours: Reopens in 2013, entry about €7, likely covered by Museum Pass, additional fees for temporary exhibits, hours likely Wed–Mon 9:30–18:00, may be closed Tue, confirm cost and hours prior to your visit; 5 rue de Thorigny, Mo: St. Paul or Chemin Vert, tel. 01 42 71 25 21, www.musee-picasso.fr.

▲**Carnavalet Museum (Musée Carnavalet)**—At the Carnavalet Museum, French history unfolds in a series of stills—like a Ken Burns documentary, except you have to walk. The Revolution is the highlight, but you get a good overview of everything—from Louis XIV-period rooms to Napoleon to the belle époque.

The Revolution section is the best. No period of history is as charged with the full range of human drama: bloodshed, martyrdom, daring speeches, murdered priests, emancipated women, backstabbing former friends—all in the name of government "by, for, and of the people."

You'll see paintings of the Estates-General assembly that planted the seeds of democracy, then a model of the Bastille, the hated prison that was the symbol of oppression. Read the "Declaration of the Rights of Man." See pictures of the ill-fated King Louis XVI and Queen Marie-Antoinette, and the fate that awaited them—the guillotine. You'll see portraits of all the major players—Robespierre, Danton, Charlotte Corday—as well as the dashing general who would inherit democracy and turn it into dictatorship...Napoleon Bonaparte. Though explanations are in French only, many displays are fairly self-explanatory.

Cost and Hours: Free, audioguide-€5, Tue-Sun 10:00-18:00, closed Mon; avoid lunchtime (12:30-14:30), when many rooms may be closed; 23 rue de Sévigné, Mo: St. Paul, tel. 01 44 59 58 58, www.carnavalet.paris.fr.

Promenade Plantée Park (Viaduc des Arts)—This two-mile-long, narrow garden walk on an elevated viaduct was once used for train tracks and is now a fine place for a refreshing stroll or run. Botanists appreciate the well-maintained and varying vegetation. From west (near Opéra) to east, the first half of the path is elevated until the midway point, the pleasant Jardin de Reuilly (a good stopping point for most, near Mo: Dugommier), then it continues on street level—with separate paths for pedestrians and cyclists—out to Paris' ring road, the *périphérique*.

Cost and Hours: Free, opens Mon-Fri at 8:00, Sat-Sun at

9:00, closes at sunset (17:30 in winter, 20:30 in summer). It runs from place de la Bastille (Mo: Bastille) along avenue Daumesnil to St. Mandé (Mo: Michel Bizot or Porte Dorée), passing within a block of Gare de Lyon. From place de la Bastille (exit the Métro following *Sortie rue de Lyon* signs), walk a looooong block down rue de Lyon hugging the Opéra on your left. Find the low-key entry and steps up the red-brick wall a block after the Opéra.

▲Père Lachaise Cemetery (Cimetière du Père Lachaise)—Littered with the tombstones of many of the city's most illustrious dead, this is your best one-stop look at Paris' fascinating, romantic past residents. Enclosed by a massive wall and lined with 5,000 trees, the peaceful, car-free lanes and dirt paths of Père Lachaise cemetery encourage parklike meandering. Named for Father *(Père)* La Chaise, whose job was listening to Louis XIV's sins, the cemetery is relatively new, having opened in 1804 to accommodate Paris' expansion. Today, this city of the dead (pop. 70,000) still accepts new residents, but real estate prices are sky high (a 21-square-foot plot costs more than €11,000).

The 100-acre cemetery is big and confusing, with thousands of graves and tombs crammed every which way, and only a few pedestrian pathways to help you navigate. The maps available from any of the nearby florists will direct you to the graves of Frédéric Chopin, Molière, Edith Piaf, Oscar Wilde, Gertrude Stein, Jim Morrison, Héloïse and Abélard, and many more.

Cost and Hours: Free, Mon-Fri 8:00-18:00, Sat 8:30-18:00, Sun 9:00-18:00, closes at 17:30 in winter, last entry 15 minutes before closing. It's two blocks from Mo: Gambetta (not Mo: Père Lachaise) and two blocks from bus #69's last stop. Tel. 01 55 25 82 10, www.pere-lachaise.com.

Montmartre

Stroll along Paris' highest hilltop (420 feet) for a different perspective on the City of Light. Walk in the footsteps of the people who've lived here—monks stomping grapes (1200s), farmers grinding grain in windmills (1600s), dust-coated gypsum miners (1700s), Parisian liberals (1800s), Modernist painters (1900s), and all the struggling artists, poets, dreamers, and drunkards who came here for cheap rent, untaxed booze, rustic landscapes, and cabaret nightlife. With vineyards, wheat fields, windmills, animals, and a village tempo of life, it was the perfect escape from grimy Paris.

Getting There: You have several options. You can take the Métro to the Anvers stop (to avoid the stairs up to Sacré-Cœur Basilica, buy one more Métro ticket and ride the funicular, though it's sometimes closed for maintenance). The Abbesses stop is closer but less scenic. Or you can go to place Pigalle, then take the tiny electric Montmartrobus, which drops you right by place du Tertre, near Sacré-Cœur. A taxi to the top of the hill saves time and avoids sweat (about €13, €20 at night). For restaurant recommendations, see page 338.

▲▲**Sacré-Cœur**—The Sacré-Cœur (Sacred Heart) Basilica's exterior, with its onion domes and bleached-bone pallor, looks ancient, but was finished only a century ago by Parisians humiliated by German invaders. Otto von Bismarck's Prussian army laid siege to Paris for more than four months in 1870. Things got so bad for residents that urban hunting for dinner (to cook up dogs, cats, and finally rats) became accepted behavior. Convinced they were being punished for the country's liberal sins, France's Catholics raised money to build the church as a "praise the Lord anyway" gesture. The five-domed, Roman-Byzantine-looking basilica took 44 years to build (1875-1919). It stands on a foundation of 83 pillars sunk 130 feet deep, necessary because the ground beneath was honeycombed with gypsum mines. The exterior is laced with gypsum, which whitens with age.

Take a clockwise spin around the crowded interior to see impressive mosaics, and to give St. Peter's bronze foot a rub. For an unobstructed panoramic view of Paris, climb 260 feet (300 steps) up the tight and claustrophobic spiral stairs to the top of the dome (especially worthwhile if you have kids with excess energy).

Cost and Hours: Church free, open daily 6:00-22:30, last entry at 22:15, €5 to climb dome, not covered by Museum Pass, daily June-Sept 9:00-19:00, Oct-May 10:00-18:00.

The Heart of Montmartre—One block from the church, the **place du Tertre** was the haunt of Henri de Toulouse-Lautrec and the original bohemians. Today, it's mobbed with tourists and unoriginal bohemians, but it's still fun (to beat the crowds, go early in the morning). From here, follow rue des Saules (a block west, passing near the Dalí Museum—described next), and find Paris' lone vineyard and the **Montmartre Museum** (described below). Return uphill, then follow rue Lépic down to the old windmill, **Moulin de la Galette,** which once pressed monks' grapes and farmers' grain, and crushed gypsum rocks into powdery plaster of Paris (there were once 30 windmills on Montmartre). When the gypsum mines closed (c. 1850) and the vineyards sprouted apartments, this windmill turned into the ceremonial centerpiece of a popular outdoor dance hall. Farther down rue Lépic, you'll pass near the former homes of **Toulouse-Lautrec** (at rue Tourlaque—look for the brick-framed art-studio windows under the heavy mansard roof) and **Vincent van Gogh** (54 rue Lépic).

Dalí Museum (L'Espace Dalí)—This beautifully lit black gallery (well-described in English) offers a walk through statues, etchings, and paintings by the master of Surrealism. The Spaniard found

Montmartre

1 Sacré-Cœur Basilica
2 Place du Tertre
3 Dalí Museum
4 Montmartre Mus.
5 Au Lapin Agile Cabaret
6 Moulin de la Galette
7 Toulouse-Lautrec's House
8 Van Gogh's House
9 Moulin Rouge
10 Pigalle
11 Museum of Erotic Art

RUE

JUNOT

RUE

LEPIC

RUE CAULAINCOURT

R. THOLOZE

RUE

RUE DES ABBESSES

LEPIC

RUE

VERON

MOULIN ROUGE

RUE

BLVD.
Blanche M

DE

CLICHY

M METRO STATION
B BUS STOP
|||| STAIRS
i INFO KIOSK
⇗ VIEW

200 YARDS

200 METERS

DCH

RUE PIGALLE

PARIS

fame in Paris in the 1920s and '30s. He lived in Montmartre for a while, hung with the Surrealist crowd in Montparnasse, and shocked the world with his dreamscape paintings and experimental films. Don't miss the printed interview on the exit stairs.

Cost and Hours: €10, not covered by Museum Pass, audioguide-€3, daily 10:00-18:00, July-Aug until 20:00, 11 rue Poulbot, tel. 01 42 64 40 10, www.daliparis.com).

Montmartre Museum (Musée de Montmartre)—This 17th-century home re-creates the traditional cancan and cabaret Montmartre scene, with paintings, posters, photos, music, and memorabilia.

Cost and Hours: €8, includes good audioguide, not covered by Museum Pass, Tue-Sun 11:00-18:00, closed Mon, 12 rue Cortot, tel. 01 49 25 89 39, www.museedemontmartre.fr.

Pigalle—Paris' red light district, the infamous "Pig Alley," is at the foot of Butte Montmartre. *Ooh la la.* It's more racy than dangerous. Walk from place Pigalle to place Blanche, teasing desperate barkers and fast-talking temptresses. In bars, a €150 bottle of (what would otherwise be) cheap champagne comes with a friend. Stick to the bigger streets, hang on to your wallet, and exercise good judgment. Cancan can cost a fortune, as can con artists in topless bars. After dark, countless tour buses line the streets, reminding us that tour guides make big bucks by bringing their groups to touristy nightclubs like the famous Moulin Rouge (Mo: Pigalle or Abbesses).

Museum of Erotic Art (Musée de l'Erotisme)—Paris' sexy museum has five floors of risqué displays—mostly paintings and drawings—ranging from artistic to erotic to disgusting, with a few circa-1920 porn videos and a fascinating history of local brothels tossed in. It's in the center of the Pigalle red light district.

Cost and Hours: €9, €6 online, €6/person for groups of four or more, no...it's not covered by Museum Pass, daily 10:00-2:00 in the morning, 72 boulevard de Clichy, Mo: Blanche, tel. 01 42 58 28 73, www.musee-erotisme.com.

Entertainment in Paris

Paris is brilliant after dark. Save energy from your day's sightseeing and experience the City of Light lit. Whether it's a concert at Sainte-Chapelle, a boat ride on the Seine, a walk in Montmartre, a hike up the Arc de Triomphe, or a late-night café, you'll see Paris at its best. Night walks in Paris are wonderful.

The *Pariscope* magazine (€0.40 at any newsstand, in French) offers a complete weekly listing of music, cinema, theater, opera, and other special events. The *Paris Voice* website, in English, has a helpful monthly review of Paris entertainment (www.parisvoice.com).

Adjust your expectations to the changing times. Paris will always be the City of Light, but it shines a little dimmer these days. In an effort to go green and save money, Paris has toned down the lighting on several monuments, including the Arc de Triomphe and the Louvre's glass pyramid.

Music

Jazz and Blues Clubs—With a lively mix of American, French, and international musicians, Paris has been an internationally acclaimed jazz capital since World War II. You'll pay €12-25 to enter a jazz club (may include one drink; if not, expect to pay €5-10 per drink; beer is cheapest). See *Pariscope* magazine under "Musique" for listings, or, even better, the *Paris Voice* website for a good monthly review (www.parisvoice.com). You can also check each club's website (all have English versions), or drop by the clubs to check out the calendars posted on their front doors. Music starts after 21:00 in most clubs. Some offer dinner concerts from about 20:30 on. Here are several good bets:

Caveau de la Huchette, a characteristic old jazz/dance club, fills an ancient Latin Quarter cellar with live jazz and frenzied dancing every night (admission about €12 on weekdays, €14 on weekends, €6-8 drinks, daily 21:30-2:30 in the morning or later, 5 rue de la Huchette, Mo: St. Michel, recorded info tel. 01 43 26 65 05, www.caveaudelahuchette.fr).

For a spot teeming with late-night activity and jazz, go to the two-block-long rue des Lombards, at boulevard Sébastopol, midway between the river and the Pompidou Center (Mo: Châtelet). **Au Duc des Lombards** is one of the most popular and respected jazz clubs in Paris, with concerts nightly in a great, plush, 110-seat theater-like setting (admission €20-30, buy online and arrive early for best seats, cheap drinks, shows at 20:00 and 22:00, 42 rue des Lombards, tel. 01 42 33 22 88, www.ducdeslombards.fr). **Le Sunside,** run for 17 years by Stephane Portet, is just a block away. The club offers two little stages (ground floor and downstairs): "le Sunset" stage tends toward contemporary world jazz; "le Sunside" stage features more traditional and acoustic jazz (concerts range from free to €25, check their website; generally at 20:00, 21:00, and 22:00; 60 rue des Lombards, tel. 01 40 26 46 60, www.sunset -sunside.com).

For a less pricey—and less central—concert club, try **Utopia.** From the outside it's a hole in the wall, but inside it's filled with devoted fans of rock and folk blues. Though Utopia is officially a private club (and one that permits smoking), you can pay €3 to join for an evening, then pay a reasonable charge for the concert (usually €10 or under, concerts start about 22:00). It's located in the Montparnasse area (79 rue de l'Ouest, Mo: Perncty, tel. 01 43 22

79 66, www.utopia-cafeconcert.fr).

Old-Time Parisian Cabaret on Montmartre: Au Lapin Agile—This historic cabaret maintains the atmosphere of the heady days when bohemians would gather here to enjoy wine, song, and sexy jokes. For €24 (€17 for students) you gather with about 25 French people in a dark room for a drink and as many as 10 different performers—mostly singers with a piano. Performers range from sweet and innocent Amélie types to naughty Maurice Chevalier types. And though tourists are welcome, it's exclusively French, with no accommodation for English speakers (except on their website), so non-French-speakers will be lost. You sit at carved wooden tables in a dimly lit room, taste the traditional drink (brandy with cherries), and are immersed in a true Parisian ambience. The soirée covers traditional French standards, love ballads, sea chanteys, and more. The crowd sings along, as it has here for a century (€7 drinks, Tue-Sun 21:00-2:00 in the morning, closed Mon, best to reserve ahead, 22 rue des Saules, tel. 01 46 06 85 87, www.au-lapin-agile.com).

Classical Concerts—For classical music on any night, consult *Pariscope* magazine (check "Concerts Classiques" under "Musique" for listings), and look for posters at tourist-oriented churches.

From March through November, these churches regularly host concerts: St. Sulpice, St. Germain-des-Prés, La Madeleine, St. Eustache, St. Julien-le-Pauvre, and Sainte-Chapelle.

At **Sainte-Chapelle,** enjoy the pleasure of hearing Mozart, Bach, or Vivaldi, surrounded by 800 years of stained glass (unheated—bring a sweater). The acoustical quality is surprisingly good. There are usually two concerts per evening, at 19:00 and 20:30; specify which one you want when you buy or reserve your ticket. "Prestige" tickets get you a seat in the first seven rows; "normal" tickets are everything else. Seats are unassigned, so arrive at least 30 minutes early to snare a good view and to get through the security line. Two companies put on concerts—pick up schedules and tickets during the day at the small ticket booth to the left of the chapel entrance gate (€30 prestige, €25 normal; 4 boulevard du Palais, Mo: Cité; call 01 42 77 65 65 or 06 67 30 65 65 for schedules and reservations, you can leave your message in English—just speak clearly and spell your name; www.archetspf.asso.fr). Flavien from Euromusic offers discounts with this book (limit 2 discounted tickets per book, offer applies to Euromusic concerts and must be purchased with cash only at the Sainte-Chapelle ticket booth). The evening entrance is at 4 boulevard du Palais, between the gilded gate of the Palais de Justice and the Conciergerie. You'll enter through the law courts hall, directly into the royal upper chapel, just as St. Louis once did.

The **Salle Pleyel** hosts world-class artists, from string quartets and visiting orchestras to international opera stars. Tickets range from €10 to €150, depending on the artist and seats you choose, and are usually hard to come by, so it's best to order online in advance (252 rue du Faubourg St. Honoré, Mo: Ternes, tel. 01 42 56 13 13, www.sallepleyel.fr).

Look also for daytime concerts in parks, such as the Luxembourg Garden. Even the Galeries Lafayette department store offers concerts. Many of these concerts are free *(entrée libre),* such as the Sunday atelier concert sponsored by the American Church (generally Sept-June at 17:00 but not every week and not in Dec, 65 quai d'Orsay, Mo: Invalides, RER: Pont de l'Alma, tel. 01 40 62 05 00, www.acparis.org).

Opera—Paris is home to two well-respected opera venues. The **Opéra Bastille** is the massive modern opera house that dominates place de la Bastille. Come here for state-of-the-art special effects and modern interpretations of classic ballets and operas. In the spirit of this everyman's opera, unsold seats are available at a big discount to seniors and students 15 minutes before the show. Standing-room-only tickets for €15 are also sold for some performances (Mo: Bastille). The **Opéra Garnier,** Paris' first opera house, hosts opera and ballet performances. Come here for less expensive tickets and grand belle époque decor (Mo: Opéra). To get tickets for either opera house, it's easiest to reserve online at www.operadeparis.fr, or call 01 71 25 24 23 outside France or toll tel. 08 92 89 90 90 inside France. You can also go direct to the Opéra Bastille's ticket office (open daily 11:00-18:00).

Art in the Evening

Various museums are open late on different evenings, offering the opportunity for more relaxed, less crowded visits.

Night Walks

Go for an evening walk to best appreciate the City of Light. Break for ice cream, pause at a café, and enjoy the sidewalk entertainers as you join the post-dinner Parisian parade. Remember to avoid poorly lit areas and stick to main thoroughfares. Consider the following suggestions.

▲▲▲Trocadéro and Eiffel Tower—This is one of Paris' most spectacular views at night. Take the Métro to the Trocadéro stop and join the party on place du Trocadéro for a magnificent view of the glowing Eiffel Tower (see "Best Views" on page 255). It's a festival of hawkers, gawkers, drummers, and entertainers.

Walk down the stairs, passing the fountains and rollerbladers, then cross the river to the base of the tower, well worth the effort even if you don't go up (tower open daily mid-June-Aug until 24:00, Sept-mid-June until 23:00; see listing on page 252).

From the Eiffel Tower you can stroll through the Champ de Mars park past tourists and romantic couples, and take the Métro home (Ecole Militaire stop, across avenue de la Motte-Picquet from far southeast corner of park). Or there's a handy RER stop (Champ de Mars-Tour Eiffel) two blocks west of the Eiffel Tower on the river.

▲▲**Champs-Elysées and the Arc de Triomphe**—The avenue des Champs-Elysées glows after dark. Start at the Arc de Triomphe (observation deck open daily, April-Sept until 23:00, Oct-March until 22:30), then stroll down Paris' lively grand promenade. A right turn on avenue George V leads to the Bateaux-Mouches river cruises. A movie on the Champs-Elysées is a fun experience (weekly listings in *Pariscope* under "Cinéma"), and a drink or snack at Renault's futuristic car café is a kick (at #53, toll tel. 08 11 88 28 11).

▲**Ile St. Louis and Notre-Dame**—This stroll features floodlit views of Notre-Dame and a taste of the Latin Quarter. Take the Métro (line 7) to the Pont Marie stop, then cross pont Marie to Ile St. Louis. Turn right up rue St. Louis-en-l'Ile, stopping for dinner—or at least a Berthillon ice cream (at #31) or Amorino Gelati (at #47). At the end of Ile St. Louis, cross pont St. Louis to Ile de la Cité, with a great view of Notre-Dame. Wander to the Left Bank on quai de l'Archevêché, and drop down to the river for the best floodlit views. From May through September you'll find several permanently moored barges *(péniches)* that operate as bars. Although I wouldn't eat dinner on one of these barges, the atmosphere is great for a drink, often including live music on weekends (daily until 2:00 in the morning, closed Oct-April, live music often Thu-Sun from 21:00). End your walk on place du Parvis Notre-Dame in front of Notre-Dame (on Sat-Sun June-Aug, tower open until 23:00), or go back across the river to the Latin Quarter.

Open-Air Sculpture Garden—Day or night, this skinny river-front park dotted with modern art makes for a pleasant walk, but it's especially fun on balmy, sunny evenings in spring and summer, when it hosts open-air rock and salsa dancing (free, around 20:00, very weather-dependent, quai St. Bernard on Right Bank across from Ile St. Louis, park runs between pont d'Austerlitz/Arab World Institute and Jardin des Plantes—a Batobus stop, Mo: Cardinal Lemoine plus an 8-minute walk).

After-Dark Tours

Several companies offer evening tours of Paris. You can take a traditional, mass-produced bus tour for €24-25 per person, or for just a bit more (€90 for 3 people), take a vintage car tour with a student guide. Do-it-yourselfers can save money by hiring a cab for a private tour (€50 for one hour). All options are described below.

▲▲▲**Deux Chevaux Car Tours**—If rumbling around Paris, sticking your head out of the rolled-back top of a funky old 2CV car *à la* Inspector Clouseau sounds like your kind of fun, do this. Paris Authentic has assembled a veritable fleet of these "tin-can" cars (not made since 1985) for giving tourists tours of Paris day and night. Night is best. The student-guides are informal, speak English, and are passionate about showing you their city. The tours are flexible—you tell them where you'd like to go (use the taxi tour route described later). Trust your guide's detour suggestions and ask to get out as often as you like. Appreciate the simplicity of the vehicle you're in (France's version of the VW "bug"). Notice the bare-bones dashboard. Ask your guide to honk the horn, to run the silly little wipers, and to open and close the air vent—*c'est magnifique!* They'll pick you up and drop you at your hotel or wherever you choose (€80/hour for 1-2 person tour; €90/hour for 3 people, their 2-hour tour includes Montmartre and a bottle of champagne, 10 percent tip is appropriate, 23 rue Jean Jacques Rousseau, mobile 06 64 50 44 19, www.parisauthentic.com, infos@parisauthentic.com).

▲**Nighttime Bus Tours**—Below I've listed two different tours run by the same parent company (Paris Vision). Tickets are sold through your hotel (no booking fee, brochures in lobby) or directly at their office at 214 rue de Rivoli, across the street from the Tuileries Métro stop.

The nightly **Paris Vision** (also called **Cityrama**) tour connects all the great illuminated sights of Paris with a 100-minute bus tour in 12 languages. The double-decker buses have huge windows, but the most desirable front seats are sometimes reserved for customers who've bought tickets for the overrated Moulin Rouge. Left-side seats are better. Visibility is fine in the rain. These tours are not for everyone. You'll stampede on with a United Nations of tourists, get a set of headphones, dial up your language, and listen to a tape-recorded spiel (which is interesting, but includes an annoyingly bright TV screen and a pitch for the other, more expensive excursions). Uninspired as it is, the ride provides an entertaining overview of the city at its floodlit and scenic best. Bring your city map to stay oriented as you go. You're always on the bus, but the driver slows for photos at viewpoints (€24/person, kids under 12 ride free, 1.5 hours, departs from 2 rue des Pyramides at 19:00 Nov-March, at 22:00 April-Oct, reserve one day in advance, arrive 30 minutes early to wait in line for best seats, tel. 01 42 60 30 01, www.pariscityrama.fr. Skip the pricier minivan night tours.

L'Open Tour uses open-top, double-decker buses, and the guides don't hawk other packages (€25/person, departs from 2 rue des Pyramides at 22:00, 1.5 hours, June Fri-Sat only, daily July-Sept, closed Oct-May, must book in advance, tel. 01 42 66 56 56, www.parislopentour.com). If it's warm out, this is a great option.

▲▲▲**Do-It-Yourself Floodlit Paris Taxi Tour**—Seeing the City of Light floodlit is one of Europe's great travel experiences and a great finale to any day in Paris. Sunday is by far the best night to go, as there's less traffic—you'll get a better value for the time spent in a taxi. For less than the cost of two seats on a big bus tour, you can hire your own cab (maximum 4 passengers) and have a glorious hour of illuminated Paris on your terms and schedule. The downside: You don't have the high vantage point and big windows of a bus, and taxi drivers can be moody. The upside: It's cheaper, you go when and where you like, and you can jump out anywhere to get the best views and pictures. I recommend a loop trip that takes about an hour and connects these sights: the Louvre Museum, Hôtel de Ville, Notre-Dame, Ile St. Louis, the Orsay Museum, esplanade des Invalides, Champ de Mars park at place Jacques Rueff (five-minute stop), Eiffel Tower from place du Trocadéro (five-minute stop), Arc de Triomphe, Champs-Elysées, and place de la Concorde. The trip should cost you about €45 (taxis have a strict meter of €33/hour plus about €1/km).

Sleeping in Paris

I've focused most of my recommendations in four safe, handy, and colorful neighborhoods: the village-like rue Cler (near the Eiffel Tower), the artsy and trendy Marais (near place de la Bastille), a historic island in the Seine—Ile St. Louis (near Notre-Dame), and the lively and Latin yet classy Luxembourg Garden neighborhood (on the Left Bank). Before choosing a hotel, read the descriptions of the neighborhoods closely. Each offers different pros and cons: Your neighborhood is as important as your hotel for the success of your trip.

You'll also find recommendations for good budget accommodations in Montmartre and along lively rue Mouffetard, a few bed-and-breakfast and apartment-rental agencies, and suggestions for sleeping near Paris' airports.

Reserve ahead for Paris—the sooner, the better. In August and at other times when business is slower, some hotels offer lower rates to fill their rooms. Check hotel websites for the best deals.

If you're arriving early in the morning, your room probably won't be ready. You should be able to safely check your bag at the hotel and dive right into sightseeing.

Old, characteristic, budget Parisian hotels have always been cramped. Retrofitted with toilets, private showers, and elevators (as most are today), they are even more cramped. Hotels in France must charge a daily room tax *(taxe du séjour)* of about €1-2 per person per day. Some hotels include it in the price list, but most add

Sleep Code

(€1 = about $1.40, country code: 33)
S = Single, **D** = Double/Twin, **T** = Triple, **Q** = Quad, **b** = bathroom,
s = shower only, * = French hotel rating system (0-5 stars).

Unless otherwise noted, hotel staff speak basic English, credit cards are accepted, and breakfast is not included (but is usually optional). All hotels in these listings have elevators, air-conditioning, Internet access (a public terminal in the lobby for guests to use), and Wi-Fi for travelers with laptops or other wireless devices, unless otherwise noted. "Wi-Fi only" means there's no public computer available.

To help you easily sort through these listings, I've divided the accommodations into three categories based on the price for a standard double room with bath during high season:

$$$ Higher Priced—Most rooms €150 or more.
  $$ Moderately Priced—Most rooms between €100-150.
    $ Lower Priced—Most rooms €100 or less.

Prices can change without notice; verify the hotel's current rates online or by email. For other updates, see www.ricksteves.com/update.

it to your bill. Get suggestions from your hotelier for safe parking (for parking basics, see page 216).

In the Rue Cler Neighborhood
(7th arrondissement, Mo: Ecole Militaire, La Tour Maubourg, or Invalides)

Rue Cler, lined with open-air produce stands six days a week, is a safe, tidy, village-like pedestrian street. It's so French that when I step out of my hotel in the morning, I feel like I must have been a poodle in a previous life. How such coziness lodged itself between the high-powered government district, the Eiffel Tower, and Les Invalides, I'll never know. This is a neighborhood of wide, tree-lined boulevards, stately apartment buildings, and lots of Americans. The American Church and Franco-American Center (see page 213), American Library, American University, and many of my readers call this area home. Hotels here are a relatively good value, considering the elegance of the neighborhood and the higher prices of the more cramped hotels in other central areas. And for sightseeing, you're within walking distance of the Eiffel Tower, Army Museum, Quai Branly Museum, Seine River, Champs-Elysées, and Orsay and Rodin museums.

Become a local at a rue Cler café for breakfast, or join the afternoon crowd for *une bière pression* (a draft beer). On rue Cler

PARIS

Rue Cler Hotels

1. Hôtel Relais Bosquet
2. Hôtel du Cadran
3. Hôtel Valadon
4. Hôtel de la Motte Picquet
5. Hôtel Beaugency
6. Grand Hôtel Lévêque
7. Hôtel du Champ de Mars
8. Hôtel Duquesne Eiffel
9. Hôtel La Bourdonnais
10. Hôtel de France Invalides
11. Hôtel de Turenne
12. Hôtel de Londres Eiffel
13. Hôtel de la Tulipe
14. Hôtel de la Tour Eiffel
15. Hôtel Kensington
16. Hôtel Les Jardins d'Eiffel
17. Hôtel Tour Eiffel Invalides
18. Hôtel Muguet
19. Hôtel de l'Empereur
20. Hôtel 7 Eiffel
21. Hôtel Prince
22. Hôtel Royal Phare
23. Paris Home Studios
24. Paris Webservices
25. SNCF Boutique
26. Internet Café
27. Launderettes (3)

M Metro Station
B Bus Stop w/ Route #
P Parking
T Taxi Stand
Pedestrian Zone

PARIS

PARIS

you can eat and browse your way through a street full of cafés, pastry shops, delis, cheese shops, and colorful outdoor produce stalls. Afternoon *boules* (outdoor bowling) on the esplanade des Invalides is a relaxing spectator sport (look for the dirt area to the upper right as you face the front of Les Invalides). The manicured gardens behind the golden dome of the Army Museum are free, peaceful, and filled with flowers (at southwest corner of grounds, closes at about 19:00).

Though hardly a happening nightlife spot, rue Cler offers many low-impact after-dark activities. Take an evening stroll above the river through the parkway between pont de l'Alma and pont des Invalides. For an after-dinner cruise on the Seine, it's a 15-minute walk to the river and the Bateaux-Mouches (see page 340). For a post-dinner cruise on foot, saunter into the Champ de Mars park to admire the glowing Eiffel Tower. For more ideas on Paris after hours, see "Entertainment in Paris," earlier.

Services: There's a large **post office** at the end of rue Cler on avenue de la Motte-Picquet, and a handy **SNCF Boutique** at 80 rue St. Dominique (Mon-Sat 8:30-19:30, closed Sun, get there when it opens to avoid a long wait). At both of these offices, take a number and wait your turn. A smaller post office is closer to the Eiffel Tower on avenue Rapp, one block past rue St. Dominique toward the river.

Markets: Cross the Champ de Mars park to mix it up with bargain-hunters at the twice-weekly open-air market, **Marché Boulevard de Grenelle,** under the Métro, a few blocks southwest of the Champ de Mars park (Wed and Sun 7:00-12:30, between Mo: Dupleix and Mo: La Motte-Picquet-Grenelle). Two miniscule grocery stores, both on rue de Grenelle, are open until midnight: **Epicerie de la Tour** (at #197) and **Alimentation** (at corner with rue Cler). **Rue St. Dominique** is the area's boutique-browsing street and well worth a visit if shopping for clothes.

Internet Access: Com Avenue is good (about €5/hour, shareable and multi-use accounts, Mon-Sat 10:00-20:00, closed Sun, 24 rue du Champ de Mars, tel. 01 45 55 00 07).

Laundry: Launderettes are omnipresent; ask your hotel for the nearest. Here are three handy locations: on rue Augereau (between rue St. Dominique and rue de Grenelle), on rue Amélie (between rue St. Dominique and rue de Grenelle), and at the southeast corner of rue Valadon and rue de Grenelle.

Booking Agency: For help booking tickets to key sights, or assistance with hotels, transportation, or excursions, contact the helpful staff at **Paris Webservices** (Mon-Fri 9:00-21:00, Sat-Sun 9:00-18:00, 12 rue de l'Exposition, tel. 09 52 06 02 59 or 01 53 62 02 29, www.pariswebservices.com, contactpws@pariswebservices .com).

Métro Connections: Key Métro stops are Ecole Militaire, La Tour Maubourg, and Invalides. The useful RER-C line runs from the pont de l'Alma and Invalides stations, serving Versailles to the southwest; the Marmottan Museum to the northwest; and the Orsay Museum, Latin Quarter (St. Michel stop), and Austerlitz train station to the east.

Bus Routes: Smart travelers take advantage of these helpful bus routes (see "Rue Cler Hotels" map for stop locations):

Line #69 runs east-west along rue St. Dominique and serves Les Invalides, Orsay, Louvre, Marais, and Père Lachaise Cemetery.

Line #63 runs along the river (the quai d'Orsay), serving the Latin Quarter along boulevard St. Germain to the east (ending at Gare de Lyon), and Trocadéro and near the Marmottan Museum to the west.

Line #92 runs along avenue Bosquet, north to the Champs-Elysées and Arc de Triomphe (faster than the Métro) and south to the Montparnasse Tower and Gare Montparnasse.

Line #87 runs from avenue Joseph Bouvard in the Champ de Mars park up avenue de la Bourdonnais and serves the Sèvres-Babylone shopping area, St. Sulpice Church, Luxembourg Garden, the Bastille, and Gare de Lyon (also more convenient than Métro for these destinations).

Line #80 runs on avenue Bosquet, crosses the Champs-Elysées, and serves Gare St. Lazare.

Line #28 runs on boulevard de la Tour Maubourg and serves Gare St. Lazare.

Line #42 runs from avenue Joseph Bouvard in the Champs de Mars park (same stop as #87) to Gare du Nord—a long ride but less tiring than the Métro if you're carrying suitcases.

In the Heart of Rue Cler

Many of my readers stay in the rue Cler neighborhood. If you want to disappear into Paris, choose a hotel elsewhere. The first six hotels listed below are within Camembert-smelling distance of rue Cler; the others are within a 5- to 10-minute stroll.

$$$ Hôtel Relais Bosquet*** can be an excellent value, with generous public spaces and comfortable rooms that are large by local standards and feature effective darkness blinds. The staff are politely formal. Book well in advance for the best rates, which vary enormously based on demand (standard Db-€185-235, bigger Db-€225-285, book direct and ask about discount with this book, good €15 breakfast buffet with eggs and sausage, extra bed-€30, 19 rue du Champ de Mars, tel. 01 47 05 25 45, fax 01 45 55 08 24, www.hotel-paris-bosquet.com, hotel@relaisbosquet .com).

PARIS

$$$ Hôtel du Cadran***, perfectly located a *boule* toss from rue Cler, is daringly modern—with a *chocolat-et-macaron* shop/bar in the lobby, efficient staff, and stylish yet tight rooms featuring cool colors, mood lighting, and every comfort (Db-€250-280, discount and free, big breakfast when you use the code "RickSteves" and book by email or through their website, discount not valid on website promo rates which can be far better deals; 10 rue du Champ de Mars, tel. 01 40 62 67 00, fax 01 40 62 67 13, www.cadranhotel.com, resa@cadranhotel.com).

$$$ Hôtel Valadon***, almost across the street, is owned and operated by the Hôtel du Cadran (listed above), where you'll have breakfast. The Valadon's 12 cute-and-quiet rooms are slightly larger than those at the Cadran, with similar comfort, prices, and discounts (Db-€260, Tb-€290, 16 rue Valadon, tel. 01 47 53 89 85, www.hotelvaladon.com, info@hotelvaladon.com).

$$$ Hôtel de la Motte Picquet***, at the corner of rue Cler and avenue de la Motte-Picquet, is an intimate little place with narrow halls, comfortable but pricey rooms, and a terrific staff (Moe and Tina). Get a room off the street to avoid street noise (standard Db-€200, bigger Db-€250, Tb/Qb-€300, 30 avenue de la Motte-Picquet, tel. 01 47 05 09 57, fax 01 47 05 74 36, www.hotelmottepicquetparis.com, book@hotelmottepicquetparis.com).

$$ Hôtel Beaugency***, a good value on a quieter street a short block off rue Cler, has 30 small rooms with standard furnishings and a lobby you can stretch out in (Sb-€115-130, Db-€128-165, occasional discounts for Rick Steves readers—ask when you book, 21 rue Duvivier, tel. 01 47 05 01 63, fax 01 45 51 04 96, www.hotel-beaugency.com, infos@hotel-beaugency.com).

Warning: The next two hotels are super values, but very busy with my readers (reserve long in advance).

$$ Grand Hôtel Lévêque**, ideally located on rue Cler, is all about location. It's a busy, less personal place with a sliver-size elevator, a sleek breakfast room that doubles as a lounge, no real lobby, and so-so accommodations. Half the rooms (top floors) have been renovated and cost more, while others need new carpets. Those on rue Cler come with fun views but morning noise as the market sets up (S-€55-95, Db-€85-150, Tb-€110-185, 29 rue Cler, tel. 01 47 05 49 15, fax 01 45 50 49 36, www.hotel-leveque.com, info@hotel-leveque.com).

$ Hôtel du Champ de Mars**, with adorable rooms and serious owners Françoise and Stephane, is a cozy rue Cler option. This plush little hotel has a small-town feel from top to bottom. The rooms are snug but lovingly kept, and single rooms can work as tiny doubles. It's an excellent value despite the lack of air-conditioning (Sb-€95, Db-€100, 30 yards off rue Cler at 7 rue du Champ de

Mars, tel. 01 45 51 52 30, fax 01 45 51 64 36, www.hotelduchamp demars.com, reservation@hotelduchampdemars.com).

Near Rue Cler, Close to Ecole Militaire Métro Stop

The following listings are a five-minute walk from rue Cler, near Métro stop Ecole Militaire or RER: Pont de l'Alma.

$$$ Hôtel Duquesne Eiffel*,** a few blocks farther from the action, is calm, hospitable, and well-run. It features handsome rooms (some with terrific Eiffel Tower views for only €20 more), a welcoming lobby, and a big, hot breakfast for €13 (Db-€180-230, price grows with room size, Tb-€250, ask for discount with this book, check website for better deals, 23 avenue Duquesne, tel. 01 44 42 09 09, fax 01 44 42 09 08, www.hotel-duquesne-eiffel-paris .com, contact@hde.fr).

$$$ Hôtel La Bourdonnais*** is *très* Parisian, mixing an Old World feel with creaky, comfortable rooms and generous public spaces. Its mostly spacious rooms are traditionally decorated, and its bathrooms are due for an upgrade (Db-€180-210, Tb-€210, Qb-€235, ask about free breakfast with this book, check website for better deals, 111-113 avenue de la Bourdonnais, tel. 01 47 05 45 42, fax 01 45 55 75 54, www.hotellabourdonnais.fr, hlb@hotella bourdonnais.fr).

$$ Hôtel de France Invalides** is a good mid-range option away from most other hotels I list. It's well-run by a brother-sister team (Alain and Marie-Hélène) with a small bar/lounge and 60 fairly priced and well-maintained rooms, some with knockout views of Invalides' golden dome. Rooms on the courtyard are very quiet (Sb-€95, standard Db-€120, bigger Db-€140-170, Tb-€170, ask about discount with this book, connecting rooms possible for families, no air-con, 102 boulevard de la Tour Maubourg, tel. 01 47 05 40 49, fax 01 45 56 96 78, www.hoteldefrance.com, contact @hoteldefrance.com).

$ Hôtel de Turenne** is modest, with the cheapest air-conditioned rooms I've found and a lobby with windows on the world. Rooms are simple but comfortable, and the price is right. There are five true singles and several connecting rooms good for families (Sb-€70, Db-€85-107, Tb-€150, Wi-Fi only, 20 avenue de Tourville, tel. 01 47 05 99 92, fax 01 45 56 06 04, www.hotel -turenne-paris.com, info@hotel-turenne-paris.com).

Near Rue Cler, Closer to Rue St. Dominique (and the Seine)

$$$ Hôtel de Londres Eiffel*** is my closest listing to the Eiffel Tower and the Champ de Mars park. Here you get immaculate, warmly decorated rooms (several are connecting for families), snazzy public spaces, and a service-oriented staff. Some rooms are tight—request a bigger room. It's less convenient to the Métro (10-minute walk), but handy to buses #69, #80, #87, and #92, and to RER-C: Pont de l'Alma (Sb-€175, small Db-€190, bigger Db-€205, Db with Eiffel Tower view-€230, Tb-€270, 1 rue Augereau, tel. 01 45 51 63 02, fax 01 47 05 28 96, www.hotel-paris-londres-eiffel .com, info@londres-eiffel.com, helpful Cédric and Arnaud). The owners also run a good two-star hotel with similar comfort in the cheaper Montparnasse area, **$$ Hôtel Apollon Montparnasse** (Db-€120-150, look for Web deals, 91 rue de l'Ouest, Mo: Pernety, tel. 01 43 95 62 00, fax 01 43 95 62 10, www.apollon-montparnasse .com, info@apollon-montparnasse.com).

$$$ Hôtel de la Tulipe*,** three blocks from rue Cler toward the river, feels pricey but unique. The 20 small but artistically decorated rooms—each one different—come with stylish little bathrooms and surround a seductive, wood-beamed lounge and a peaceful, leafy courtyard. Ask about free breakfast with this book (Db-€165-185, Tb-€200, two-room suite for up to five people-€299, no air-con, no elevator, pay Wi-Fi, 33 rue Malar, tel. 01 45 51 67 21, fax 01 47 53 96 37, www.paris-hotel-tulipe.com, hoteldelatulipe@wanadoo.fr).

$ Hôtel de la Tour Eiffel** is a fair two-star value on a quiet street near several of my favorite restaurants. The rooms are well-designed but some have thin walls, and some could use new carpeting (snug Db-€89-105, bigger Db-€105-129, no air-con, no breakfast offered, Wi-Fi only, 17 rue de l'Exposition, tel. 01 47 05 14 75, fax 01 47 53 99 46, www.hotel-toureiffel.com, hte7@wanadoo.fr).

$ Hôtel Kensington** is a good budget value close to the Eiffel Tower and run by elegant, though formal, Daniele. It's an unpretentious place with mostly small, simple, but well-kept rooms (Sb-€63-73, Db-€80-97, big Db on back side-€96-115, Eiffel Tower views for those who ask, no air-con, pay Internet access, 79 avenue de la Bourdonnais, tel. 01 47 05 74 00, fax 01 47 05 25 81, www .hotel-kensington.com, hk@hotel-kensington.com).

Near La Tour Maubourg Métro Stop

The next four listings are within three blocks of the intersection of avenue de la Motte-Picquet and boulevard de la Tour Maubourg.

$$$ Hôtel Les Jardins d'Eiffel*,** on a quiet street, feels like the modern motel it is, with professional service, its own parking garage (€24/day), and a spacious lobby. Rooms are mostly spacious and peaceful (standard Db-€180-210, renovated Db-€215-240; ask about Rick Steves discount when you book direct, or check website for special discounts; 8 rue Amélie, tel. 01 47 05 46 21, fax 01 45 55 28 08, www.hoteljardinseiffel.com, reservations@hoteljardins eiffel.com).

$$$ Hôtel Tour Eiffel Invalides*** advertises its Best Western status proudly and offers a generous-size lobby with a small courtyard and good, traditionally decorated rooms with big beds but no firm prices (the Internet decides). Allow about €210 for a double but look for better rates on their website. Ask for a non-smoking room (35 boulevard de la Tour Maubourg, tel. 01 45 56 10 78, fax 01 47 05 65 08, www.timhotel.fr, invalides @timhotel.fr).

$$$ Hôtel Muguet***, a peaceful, stylish, immaculate refuge, gives you three-star comfort for a two-star price. This delightful spot offers 43 tasteful rooms, a greenhouse lounge, and a small garden courtyard. The hands-on owner, Catherine, gives her guests a restful and secure home in Paris (Sb-€120, Db-€160-210, Db with view-€185-215, Tb-€210, 11 rue Chevert, tel. 01 47 05 05 93, fax 01 45 50 25 37, www.hotelparismuguet.com, muguet@wanadoo.fr).

$$$ Hôtel de l'Empereur** is well-run and offers good service. It delivers smashing views of Invalides from most of its very comfortable and tastefully designed rooms. Fifth-floor rooms have small balconies, and all rooms have queen-size beds (Sb-€140, Db-€170-190, Tb-€215, two-room Qb-€370, 2 rue Chevert, tel. 01 45 55 88 02, fax 01 45 51 88 54, www.hotelempereurparis.com, contact@hotelempereur.com).

Lesser Values in the Rue Cler Area

Given how fine this area is, these are acceptable last choices.

$$$ Hôtel 7 Eiffel**** is an ultra-modern, high-design, four-star splurge, complete with bar and fireplace lounge in lobby, colorful rooftop terrace, room service, and all the usual comforts of a business hotel (Db-€270-370, check Web for deals, 17 bis rue Amélie, tel. 01 45 55 10 01, fax 01 47 05 28 68, www.7eiffel.com, reservation@7eiffel.com).

$$ Hôtel Prince**, across from the Ecole Militaire Métro stop, has a spartan lobby, drab halls, and plain-but-acceptable rooms for the price (Sb-€109, Db-€130, Tb-€150, ask about free breakfast with this book, Wi-Fi only, 66 avenue Bosquet, tel. 01 47 05 40 90, fax 01 47 53 06 62, www.hotelparisprince.com, paris @hotel-prince.com).

$ Hôtel Royal Phare**, facing the busy Ecole Militaire Métro stop, is a humble place. The 34 basic, pastel rooms are unimaginative but sleepable. Rooms on the courtyard are quietest, with peek-a-boo views of the Eiffel Tower from the fifth floor up (Sb-€84, Db with shower-€98, Db with tub-€108, Tb-€120, fridges in rooms, no air-con but fans, no Wi-Fi, 40 avenue de la Motte-Picquet, tel. 01 47 05 57 30, fax 01 45 51 64 41, www.hotel -royalphare-paris.com, hotel-royalphare@wanadoo.fr, friendly manager Hocin).

In the Marais Neighborhood
(4th arrondissement, Mo: Bastille, St. Paul, and Hôtel de Ville)
Those interested in a more SoHo/Greenwich Village-type locale should make the Marais their Parisian home. Once a forgotten Parisian backwater, the Marais—which runs from the Pompidou Center east to the Bastille (a 15-minute walk)—is now one of Paris' most popular residential, tourist, and shopping areas. This is jumbled, medieval Paris at its finest, where classy stone mansions sit alongside trendy bars, antiques shops, and fashion-conscious boutiques. The streets are a fascinating parade of artists, students, tourists, immigrants, and baguette-munching babies in strollers. The Marais is also known as a hub of the Parisian gay and lesbian scene. This area is *sans doute* livelier (and louder) than the rue Cler area.

In the Marais you have these major sights close at hand: the Carnavalet Museum, Victor Hugo's House, the Jewish Art and History Museum, the Pompidou Center, and the Picasso Museum (closed for a multiyear renovation). You're also a manageable walk from Paris' two islands (Ile St. Louis and Ile de la Cité), home to Notre-Dame and Sainte-Chapelle. The Opéra Bastille, Promenade Plantée park, place des Vosges (Paris' oldest square), Jewish Quarter (rue des Rosiers), the Latin Quarter, and nightlife-packed rue de Lappe are also walkable. Strolling home (day or night) from Notre-Dame along Ile St. Louis is marvelous. (For Marais sight descriptions, see page 271; for the Opéra, see page 283.)

Most of my recommended hotels are located a few blocks north of the Marais' main east-west drag, rue St. Antoine/rue de Rivoli.

Tourist Information: The nearest TI is in Gare de Lyon (Mon-Sat 8:00-18:00, closed Sun, www.parisinfo.com).

Services: Most banks and other services are on the main street, rue de Rivoli, which becomes rue St. Antoine. Marais **post offices** are on rue Castex and at the corner of rue Pavée and rue des Francs Bourgeois. There's a busy **SNCF Boutique** where you can take care of all train needs on rue St. Antoine at rue de Turenne (Mon-Fri 8:30-20:30, Sat 10:00-20:30, closed Sun). A quieter SNCF Boutique is nearer Gare de Lyon at 5 rue de Lyon (Mon-Sat 8:30-18:00, closed Sun).

Markets: The Marais has two good open-air markets: the sprawling **Marché de la Bastille,** along boulevard Richard Lenoir, on the north side of place de la Bastille (Thu and Sun until 14:30, arts market Sat 10:00-19:00); and the more intimate, untouristy **Marché d'Aligre** (Tue-Sat 8:00-13:00 and 16:00-19:30, closed Mon, cross place de la Bastille and walk about 10 blocks down rue du Faubourg St. Antoine, turn right at rue de Cotte to place d'Aligre; or, take Métro line 8 from Bastille in the direction of

Créteil-Préfecture, get off at the Ledru-Rollin stop, and walk a few blocks southeast). A small **grocery** is open until 23:00 on rue St. Antoine (near intersection with rue Castex). To shop at a Parisian Sears, find the **BHV** next to Hôtel de Ville. Paris' oldest covered market, **Marché des Enfants Rouges,** lies a 10-minute walk north of rue de Rivoli.

Bookstore: The Marais is home to the friendliest English-language bookstore in Paris, **Red Wheelbarrow** (see page 216).

Internet Access: Try **Paris CY** (Mon-Sat 10:00-20:00, Sun 13:00-20:00, 8 rue de Jouy, Mo: St. Paul, tel. 01 42 71 37 37).

Laundry: There are many launderettes; ask your hotelier for the nearest. Here are three you can count on: on impasse Guémenée (north of rue St. Antoine), on rue Ste. Croix de la Bretonnerie (just east of rue du Temple), and on rue du Petit Musc (south of rue St. Antoine).

Métro Connections: Key Métro stops in the Marais are, from east to west: Bastille, St. Paul, and Hôtel de Ville (Sully-Morland, Pont Marie, and Rambuteau stops are also handy). Métro connections are excellent, with direct service to the Louvre, Champs-Elysées, Arc de Triomphe, and La Défense (all on line 1); the rue Cler area and Opéra Garnier (line 8 from Bastille stop); and four major train stations: Gare de Lyon, Gare du Nord, Gare de l'Est, and Gare d'Austerlitz (all accessible from Bastille stop).

Bus Routes: For stop locations, see the "Marais Hotels" map.

Line #69 on rue St. Antoine takes you eastbound to Père Lachaise Cemetery and westbound to the Louvre, Orsay, and Rodin museums, plus the Army Museum, ending at the Eiffel Tower.

Line #86 runs down boulevard Henri IV, crossing Ile St. Louis and serving the Latin Quarter along boulevard St. Germain.

Line #87 follows a similar route, but also serves Gare de Lyon to the east and St. Sulpice Church/Luxembourg Garden, the Eiffel Tower, and the rue Cler neighborhood to the west.

Line #96 runs on rues Turenne and Rivoli, serves Ile de la Cité and St. Sulpice Church (near Luxembourg Garden), and ends at Gare Montparnasse.

Line #65 runs from Gare de Lyon up rue de Lyon, around place de la Bastille, and then up boulevard Beaumarchais to Gare de l'Est and Gare du Nord.

Taxis: You'll find taxi stands on place de la Bastille (where boulevard Richard Lenoir meets the square), on the south side of rue St. Antoine (in front of St. Paul Church), behind the Hôtel de Ville on rue du Lobau (where it meets rue de Rivoli), and a quieter one on the north side of rue St. Antoine (where it meets rue Castex).

PARIS

Marais Hotels

PARIS

1 Hôtel Castex
2 Hôtel Bastille Spéria
3 Hôtel du 7ème Art
4 Hôtel de la Place des Vosges
5 Grand Hôtel Jeanne d'Arc
6 Hôtel Lyon-Mulhouse
7 Hôtel Daval
8 Hôtel Sévigné

9 Hôtel du Sully
10 MIJE Hostels (3)
11 Hôtel Caron de Beaumarchais
12 Hôtel de la Bretonnerie
13 Hôtel Beaubourg
14 Hôtel de Nice

To MARCHE DES ENFANTS ROUGE + ⑰

LOT
TEMPLE
PERLE

PICASSO MUSEUM (CLOSED THROUGH 2013)

PLACE DE THORIGNY

200 YARDS
200 METERS

Ⓜ METRO STATION
Ⓣ TAXI STAND
Ⓟ PARKING
Ⓑ BUS STOP ᵂ/ ROUTE #

ELZEVIR
PARC ROYAL
PAYENNE
DES
SEVIGNE
DE TURENNE

CARNAVALET MUSEUM

FRANCS

POST

To MARCHE BASTILLE (THU + SUN A.M.)

Ⓑ #96

PLACE DES VOSGES

MAHLER
PLACE MARCHE S. CATH.
⑧
⑤
BOURGEOIS
B. RICH. LENOIR.

#69 Ⓑ
Ⓑ #96
⑱
RUE
⑨ ⑨ BIRAGUE ④
RUE ST. ANTOINE EXIT
#65 Ⓑ
BEAUMARCHAIS
Ⓑ #65
#65

ST. PAUL
RUE ST.
⑥
Ⓣ
⑦
ROQUETTE
RUE DE LAPPE

PAUL
㉑
⑳ ②
Ⓑ #65

③
CHARLES
BEAUTRELLIS
㉓
#69 Ⓑ
ANTOINE
Ⓟ
Ⓜ *Bastille*

PLACE DE LA BASTILLE
Ⓜ

Sully Morland
Ⓜ
RUE DE PETIT MUSC
CASTEX
POST
IV
Ⓣ
①
Ⓑ
Ⓜ ←*Bastille*

OPERA ←BASTILLE

BLVD. HENRI
Ⓑ
#86 +87
Ⓑ #69↓
Ⓜ

CANAUXRAMA BOAT DOCK ←

⑮ Hôtel Saint-Merry
⑯ Hôtel du Loiret
⑰ To Hôtel du Vieux Saule
⑱ SNCF Boutique
⑲ BHV Department Store

⑳ Late-Night Grocery
㉑ Red Wheelbarrow Books
㉒ Internet Café
㉓ Launderettes (3)

PARIS

Near Place des Vosges

$$$ Hôtel Castex*,** on a quiet street near place de la Bastille, is a well-located place with tile-floored rooms (that amplify noise). Their clever system of connecting rooms allows families total privacy between two rooms, each with its own bathroom. The 30 rooms are narrow (Sb-€140, Db-€170, Tb-€220, ask about free and filling buffet breakfast with this book, just off place de la Bastille and rue St. Antoine at 5 rue Castex, Mo: Bastille, tel. 01 42 72 31 52, fax 01 42 72 57 91, www.castexhotelparis.com, info @castexhotel.com).

$$$ Hôtel Bastille Spéria*,** a short block off place de la Bastille, offers business-type service in a great location. The 42 well-configured rooms are modern and comfortable, with big beds (Sb-€130-145, Db-€160-185, good buffet breakfast-€13, 1 rue de la Bastille, Mo: Bastille, tel. 01 42 72 04 01, fax 01 42 72 56 38, www .hotelsperia.com, info@hotelsperia.com).

$$ Hôtel du 7ème Art,** two blocks south of rue St. Antoine toward the river, is a young, carefree, Hollywood-nostalgia place with a full-service café-bar and Charlie Chaplin murals. Its 23 good-value rooms have brown 1970s decor, but are comfortable enough. Sadly, smoking is allowed in all rooms, so you might detect an odor. The large rooms are American-spacious (small Db-€100, standard Db-€115, large Db-€130-160, Tb-€150-180, extra bed-€20, no elevator, 20 rue St. Paul, Mo: St. Paul, tel. 01 44 54 85 00, fax 01 42 77 69 10, www.paris-hotel-7art.com, hotel7art @wanadoo.fr).

$$ Hôtel de la Place des Vosges** is a bare-bones place brilliantly located between rue St. Antoine and place des Vosges. Rooms are sparse, there's no air-conditioning, and the elevator skips floors five and six, but the price is right (Db-€107, 12 rue de Biraque, Mo: St. Paul, tel. 01 42 72 60 46, fax 01 42 72 02 64, www.hotelplacedesvosges.com, contact@hpdv.net).

$ Grand Hôtel Jeanne d'Arc,** a lovely little hotel with a stylish lobby and thoughtfully appointed rooms, is ideally located for (and very popular with) connoisseurs of the Marais. It's a fine value and worth booking way ahead (three months in advance, if possible). Sixth-floor rooms have views, and corner rooms are wonderfully bright in the City of Light. Rooms on the street can be noisy until the bars close (Sb-€64-92, Db-€92, larger twin Db-€118, Tb-€148, good Qb-€162, no air-con, Wi-Fi only—in lobby, 3 rue de Jarente, Mo: St. Paul, tel. 01 48 87 62 11, fax 01 48 87 37 31, www.hoteljeannedarc.com, information@hoteljeannedarc.com).

$ Hôtel Lyon-Mulhouse,** well-managed by gregarious Nathalia, is located on a busy street barely off place de la Bastille. Though less intimate than some, it is a solid deal, with pleasant, relatively large rooms—five are true singles with partial Eiffel

Tower views. (Sb-€74, Db-€100, Tb-€130, Qb-€150, 8 boulevard Beaumarchais, Mo: Bastille, tel. 01 47 00 91 50, fax 01 47 00 06 31, www.1-hotel-paris.com, hotelyonmulhouse@wanadoo.fr).

$ Hôtel Daval**, an unassuming place on the *wild side* of place de la Bastille, is ideal for night owls. The rooms are tiny and the halls are narrow, but the rates are good for an air-conditioned place. Ask for a quieter room on the courtyard side if sleep matters (Sb-€86, Db-€92-101, Tb-€112, Qb-€131, Wi-Fi only, 21 rue Daval, Mo: Bastille, tel. 01 47 00 51 23, fax 01 40 21 80 26, www .hoteldaval.com, info@hoteldaval.com, Didier).

$ Hôtel Sévigné**, run by straight-faced owner Monsieur Mercier, is a simple little hotel with 30 tidy, comfy rooms at good prices (Sb-€72, Db-€86-97, Tb-€100-117; one-night, no-refund policy for any cancellation; air-con turned off overnight, Wi-Fi only, 2 rue Malher, Mo: St. Paul, tel. 01 42 72 76 17, fax 01 42 78 68 26, www.le-sevigne.com, message.le-sevigne@wanadoo.fr).

$ Hôtel du Sully, sitting right on rue St. Antoine, is basic, cheap, central, and run by no-nonsense Monsieur Zeroual. The rooms are frumpy, dimly lit, and can smell of smoke, and the entry is narrow, but the hotel offers a fair deal (Db-€73, Tb-€86, Qb-€96, no elevator, no air-con, Wi-Fi only, 48 rue St. Antoine, Mo: St. Paul, tel. 01 42 78 49 32, fax 01 44 61 76 50, www.sully hotelparis.com, sullyhotel@orange.fr).

$ *MIJE Youth Hostels:* The Maison Internationale de la Jeunesse et des Etudiants (MIJE) runs three classy old residences, ideal for budget travelers. Each is well-maintained, with simple, clean, single-sex (unless your group takes a whole room), one- to four-bed rooms for travelers of any age. The hostels are **MIJE Fourcy** (biggest and loudest, €11 dinners available with a membership card, 6 rue de Fourcy, just south of rue de Rivoli), **MIJE Fauconnier** (no elevator, 11 rue du Fauconnier), and **MIJE Maubisson** (smallest and quietest, no outdoor terrace, 12 rue des Barres). None have double beds or air-conditioning; all have private showers in every room (all prices per person: Sb-€50, Db-€37, Tb-€33, Qb-€31, credit cards accepted, includes breakfast but not towels, required membership card-€2.50 extra/person, 7-day maximum stay, rooms locked 12:00-15:00, curfew at 1:00 in the morning). They all share the same contact information (tel. 01 42 74 23 45, fax 01 40 27 81 64, www.mije.com, info@mije.com) and Métro stop (St. Paul). Reservations are accepted (six weeks ahead online, 10 days ahead by phone)—though you must show up by noon, or call the morning of arrival to confirm a later arrival time.

PARIS

Near the Pompidou Center

These hotels are farther west, closer to the Pompidou Center than to place de la Bastille. The Hôtel de Ville Métro stop works well for all of these hotels, unless a closer stop is noted.

$$$ Hôtel Caron de Beaumarchais*,** on a busy corner, feels like a fluffy folk museum, with 20 pricey but cared-for and character-filled rooms. Its small lobby is cluttered with bits from an elegant 18th-century Marais house (small Db in back-€165, larger Db facing the front-€195, Wi-Fi only, 12 rue Vieille du Temple, tel. 01 42 72 34 12, fax 01 42 72 34 63, www.carondebeaumarchais.com, hotel@carondebeaumarchais.com).

$$ Hôtel de la Bretonnerie*,** three blocks from the Hôtel de Ville, makes a fine Marais home. It has a warm, welcoming lobby and 29 well-appointed, good-value rooms with an antique, open-beam warmth but no air-conditioning (standard "classic" Db-€145, bigger "charming" Db-€175, Db suite-€200, Tb/Qb-€225, Tb/Qb suite-€220, between rue Vieille du Temple and rue des Archives at 22 rue Ste. Croix de la Bretonnerie, tel. 01 48 87 77 63, fax 01 42 77 26 78, www.bretonnerie.com, hotel@bretonnerie.com).

$$ Hôtel Beaubourg*** is a solid three-star value on a small street in the shadow of the Pompidou Center. The lounge is inviting, and the 28 rooms are comfy, well-appointed, and quiet (standard Db-€140, bigger twin or king-size Db-€160 and worth the extra cost, rates vary wildly with availability, 11 rue Simon Le Franc, Mo: Rambuteau, tel. 01 42 74 34 24, fax 01 42 78 68 11, www.beaubourg-paris-hotel.com, reservation@hotelbeaubourg.com).

$$ Hôtel de Nice,** on the Marais' busy main drag, features a turquoise-and-fuchsia "Marie-Antoinette-does-tie-dye" decor. Its narrow halls are littered with paintings and layered with carpets, and its 23 Old World rooms have thoughtful touches and tight bathrooms. Twin rooms, which cost the same as doubles, are larger and on the street side—but have effective double-paned windows (Sb-€80-130, Db-€110-160, Tb-€135-170, reception on second floor, 42 bis rue de Rivoli, tel. 01 42 78 55 29, fax 01 42 78 36 07, www.hoteldenice.com, contact@hoteldenice.com, laissez-faire management).

$$ Hôtel Saint-Merry*** allows you to sleep in a Gothic church surrounded by carved wooden arches and trefoils. Located two blocks south of the Pompidou Center on a pedestrian street with bustling cafés, it features 12 unique and well-maintained rooms—but no elevator and only four rooms with air-conditioning. Corner rooms have good light but evening noise (Db-€130-160, deluxe Db-€200-230, suite Qb-€335, check online for special discounts, 78 rue de la Verrerie, tel. 01 42 78 14 15, fax 01 40 29 06 82, www.hotelmarais.com, hotelstmerry@wanadoo.fr).

$ Hôtel du Loiret* is a centrally located and rare Marais budget hotel. It's basic, but the rooms are surprisingly sharp, considering the price and location (Db-€70-90, Tb-€120, no air-con, pay

Internet access, no Wi-Fi, expect some noise, 8 rue des Mauvais Garçons, tel. 01 48 87 77 00, fax 01 48 04 96 56, www.hotel-du -loiret.fr, hotelduloiret@hotmail.com).

Near the Marché des Enfants Rouges

$$ Hôtel du Vieux Saule*** has 27 simple rooms in a great location. Rooms are tight but modern; the bathrooms have glass dividers instead of shower curtains. Avoid the smoking rooms on the first floor (Sb-€95-140, Db-€110-190, supérieure Db-€140-220, deluxe Db-€180-250, rates vary greatly with season, check online for best deals, small sauna free for guests, 6 rue de Picardie, Mo: Filles du Calvaire or Temple, tel. 01 42 72 01 14, fax 01 40 27 88 21, www.hotelvieuxsaule.com, reserv@hotelvieuxsaule.com).

On Ile St. Louis

(4th arrondissement; Mo: Pont Marie and Sully-Morland)
This area is smack-dab in the middle of the city, in the peaceful kernel of this busy metropolis. You won't find any budget values here, but the island's village ambience and proximity to the Marais, Notre-Dame, and the Latin Quarter help compensate for higher rates. For background on Ile St. Louis, see page 233 of the "Historic Paris Walk."

The residential character of this river-wrapped island, its brilliant location, and its homemade ice cream have drawn Americans for decades, allowing hotels to charge dearly. All of the following hotels are on the island's main drag, rue St. Louis-en-l'Ile, where I list several restaurants (see page 331). For nearby services, see the Marais neighborhood section on page 296.

$$$ Hôtel du Jeu de Paume**,** occupying a 17th-century tennis center, is the most expensive hotel I list in Paris. When you enter its magnificent lobby, you'll understand why. Greet Scoop, *le chien*, then take a spin in the glass elevator for a half-timbered-treehouse experience. The 30 rooms are carefully designed and tasteful, though quite small for the price (you're paying for the location and public spaces—check for deals on their website). Most rooms face a small garden; all are pin-drop peaceful (standard Db-€360, larger Db-€450, deluxe Db-€560, check for Web deals, €18 breakfast, 54 rue St. Louis-en-l'Ile, tel. 01 43 26 14 18, fax 01 40 46 02 76, www.jeudepaumehotel.com, info@jeudepaumehotel.com).

$$$ Hôtel de Lutèce*** charges top euro for its island address but comes with a sit-awhile wood-paneled lobby and a real fireplace. Rooms on lower floors have high ceilings. Twin rooms are larger and the same price as double rooms. Rooms with showers are on the louder street-side; baths are on the courtyard (Db-€210, Tb-€245, 65 rue St. Louis-en-l'Ile, tel. 01 43 26 23 52, fax 01 43 29 60 25, www.paris-hotel-lutece.com, info@hoteldelutece.com).

PARIS

Hotels & Restaurants on Ile St. Louis

▲ VIEW
M METRO STATION
B BATOBUS BOAT STOP

❶ Hôtel du Jeu de Paume
❷ Hôtel de Lutèce & Grocery
❸ Hôtel des Deux-Iles
❹ Hôtel Saint-Louis
❺ Le Tastevin Rest.
❻ Rests. La Taverne du Sergeant Recruteur & Nos Ancêtres les Gaulois
❼ La Brasserie de l'Ile St. Louis
❽ L'Orangerie & Auberge de la Reine Blanche
❾ Café Med
❿ Berthillon Ice Cream (3)
⓫ Amorino Gelati
⓬ Good Picnic Spot

$$$ Hôtel des Deux-Iles*** has the same owners as the Lutèce and similar prices with slightly more comfortable rooms (Db-€210, 59 rue St. Louis-en-l'Ile, tel. 01 43 26 13 35, fax 01 43 29 60 25, www.deuxiles-paris-hotel.com, info@hoteldesdeux iles.com).

$$$ Hôtel Saint-Louis*** has a classic feel with modern comforts. Rooms have white tile floors and exposed ceiling timbers. This place has reasonable rates...for the location (Db-€169-189, top-floor Db with micro-balcony-€239, Tb-€279, iPads available for guest in-room use, 75 rue St. Louis-en-l'Ile, tel. 01 46 34 04 80, fax 01 46 34 02 13, www.hotelsaintlouis.com, slouis @noos.fr).

In the Luxembourg Garden Area (St. Sulpice to Panthéon)

(5th and 6th arrondissements, Mo: St. Sulpice, Mabillon, Odéon, and Cluny-La Sorbonne; RER: Luxembourg)

This neighborhood revolves around Paris' loveliest park and

offers quick access to the city's best shopping streets and grandest café-hopping. Hotels in this central area are more expensive than those in the rue Cler area or Marais neighborhood, but a better value than accommodations on Ile St. Louis. Sleeping in the Luxembourg area offers a true Left Bank experience without a hint of the low-end commotion of the nearby Latin Quarter tourist ghetto. The Luxembourg Garden, boulevard St. Germain, Cluny Museum, and Latin Quarter are all at your doorstep. Here you get the best of both worlds: youthful Left Bank energy and the classic trappings that surround the monumental Panthéon and St. Sulpice Church.

Having the Luxembourg Garden as your backyard allows strolls through meticulously cared-for flowers, a great kids' play area, and a purifying escape from city traffic. Place St. Sulpice presents an elegant, pedestrian-friendly square and quick access to some of Paris' best boutiques. Sleeping in the Luxembourg area also puts several movie theaters at your fingertips (at Métro stop: Odéon), as well as lively cafés on boulevard St. Germain, rue de Buci, rue des Canettes, place de la Sorbonne, and place de la Contrescarpe, all of which buzz with action until late.

While it takes only 15 minutes to walk from one end of this neighborhood to the other, I've located the hotels by the key monument they are close to (St. Sulpice Church, the Odéon Theater, and the Panthéon). Most hotels are within a 5-minute walk of the Luxembourg Garden (and none is more than 15 minutes away).

Services: The nearest **TI** is across the river in Gare de Lyon (Mon-Sat 8:00-18:00, closed Sun). There are two useful **SNCF Boutiques** for easy train reservations and ticket purchase: at 79 rue de Rennes (Mon-Sat 10:00-19:00, closed Sun) and at 54 boulevard St. Michel (Tue-Sat 8:30-19:30, Mon 13:00-19:30, closed Sun).

Markets: The colorful street market at the south end of rue Mouffetard is a worthwhile 10- to 15-minute walk from these hotels (Tue-Sat 10:00-13:00 & 16:00-19:00, Sun 10:00-13:00, closed Mon, five blocks south of place de la Contrescarpe, Mo: Place Monge).

Bookstores: The **Village Voice** bookstore carries a full selection of English-language books (including mine), and is near St. Sulpice. Say hello to Michael but don't ask his opinion of *The Da Vinci Code* (Mon 14:00-19:30, Tue-Sat 10:00-19:30, Sun 12:00-18:00, 6 rue Princesse, tel. 01 46 33 36 47). **San Francisco Book Company** is a welcoming bookstore (Mon-Sat 11:00-21:00, Sun 14:00-19:30, 17 rue Monsieur le Prince, tel. 01 43 29 15 70).

Internet Access: You'll find it at **Le Milk** (always open, between the Luxembourg Garden and Panthéon at 13 rue Soufflot).

Métro Connections: Métro lines 10 and 4 serve this area (10 connects to the Austerlitz train station, and 4 runs to the

Hotels near Luxembourg Garden

1 Hôtel de l'Abbaye
2 Hôtel le Récamier
3 Hôtel Relais St. Sulpice
4 Hôtel la Perle
5 Hôtel Bonaparte
6 Hôtel Jean Bart
7 Hôtel Relais Médicis

8 Hôtel Michelet Odéon
9 Hôtel des Grandes Ecoles
10 Hôtel des 3 Collèges &
Hôtel Cujas Panthéon

PARIS

- ⑪ Hôtel Cluny Sorbonne
- ⑫ Hôtel des Mines
- ⑬ SNCF Boutiques (2)
- ⑭ Village Voice Books
- ⑮ San Francisco Book Company
- ⑯ Internet Café

Montparnasse, Est, and Nord train stations). Neighborhood stops are Cluny-La Sorbonne, Mabillon, Odéon, and St. Sulpice. RER-B (Luxembourg station is handiest) provides direct service to Charles de Gaulle airport and Gare du Nord trains, and access to Orly airport via the Orlybus (transfer at Denfert-Rochereau).

Bus Routes: Buses #86 and #87 run eastbound through this area on or near boulevard St. Germain, and westbound along rue des Ecoles, stopping on place St. Sulpice. Lines #63 and #87 provide a direct connection west to the rue Cler area. Line #63 also serves the Orsay and Marmottan museums to the west and Gare de Lyon to the east. Lines #86 and #87 run east to the Marais, and #87 continues to Gare de Lyon. Line #96 stops at place St. Sulpice southbound en route to Gare Montparnasse and runs north along rue de Rennes and boulevard St. Germain into the Marais.

Near St. Sulpice Church

These hotels are all within a block of St. Sulpice Church and two blocks from famous boulevard St. Germain. This is nirvana for boutique-minded shoppers—and you'll pay extra for the location. Métro stops St. Sulpice and Mabillon are equally close.

$$$ Hôtel de l'Abbaye**** is a lovely refuge just west of Luxembourg Garden; it's a find for well-heeled connoisseurs of this area. The hotel's four-star luxury includes refined lounges inside and out, with 44 sumptuous rooms and every amenity (standard Db-€246-266, bigger Db-€360-390, suites and apartments available for €550, includes breakfast, 10 rue Cassette, tel. 01 45 44 38 11, fax 01 45 48 07 86, www.hotelabbayeparis.com, hotel.abbaye@wanadoo.fr).

$$$ Hôtel le Récamier**, romantically tucked in the corner of place St. Sulpice, is high-end defined, with designer public spaces, elaborately appointed rooms, a courtyard tea salon, and professional service (classic Db-€260, deluxe Db-€300, traditional Db-€330, deluxe rooms offer best value, fitness room, 3 bis place St. Sulpice, tel. 01 43 26 04 89, fax 01 43 26 35 76, www.hotel recamier.com, contact@hotelrecamier.com).

$$$ Hôtel Relais St. Sulpice***, burrowed on the small street just behind St. Sulpice Church, is a high-priced boutique hotel with a cozy lounge and 26 dark, stylish rooms, most surrounding a leafy glass atrium. Top-floor rooms get more light and are worth requesting (Db-€213-260 depending on size, much less off-season, sauna free for guests, 3 rue Garancière, tel. 01 46 33 99 00, fax 01 46 33 00 10, www.relais-saint-sulpice.com, relaisstsulpice @wanadoo.fr).

$$$ Hôtel la Perle*** is a spendy pearl in the thick of the lively rue des Canettes, a block off place St. Sulpice. At this snappy, modern, business-class hotel, sliding glass doors open onto the traffic-free street, and you're greeted by a fun lobby built around a central bar and atrium (standard Db-€210, bigger Db-€225, luxury Db-€250, check website or call for last-minute deals within five days of your stay, includes breakfast, 14 rue des Canettes, tel. 01 43 29 10 10, fax 01 46 34 51 04, www.hotellaperle.com, frontdesk @hotellaperle.com).

$$ Hôtel Bonaparte, an unpretentious and welcoming place wedged between boutiques, is a few steps from place St. Sulpice. Although the 29 Old World rooms don't live up to the handsome entry, they're plenty comfortable and spacious by Paris standards, with big bathrooms, traditional decor, and molded ceilings (Sb-€107-132, Db-€140-163, big Db-€175, Tb-€182, 61 rue Bonaparte, tel. 01 43 26 97 37, fax 01 46 33 57 67, www.hotelbonaparte.fr, reservation@hotelbonaparte.fr; helpful Fréderic and owner Eric at reception).

West of Luxembourg Garden
$ Hôtel Jean Bart feels like it's from another era—prices included. Run by smiling Madame Lechopier, it's a rare budget hotel find in this neighborhood, one block from Luxembourg Garden. Beyond the dark, retirement home-like lobby, you'll find 33 simple, spotless rooms with creaking floors and tight bathrooms. The cheapest rooms share one shower on the first floor (S-€56, Sb-€75, D-€56, Db-€75, cash only, no air-con, 9 rue Jean-Bart, tel. 01 45 48 29 13, fax 01 45 48 10 79, hotel.jean.bart@gmail.com).

Near the Odéon Theater
These two hotels are between the Odéon Métro stop and Luxembourg Garden (five blocks east of St. Sulpice), and may have rooms when others don't. In addition to the Odéon Métro stop, the RER-B Luxembourg stop is a short walk away.

$$$ Hôtel Relais Médicis* is ideal if you've always wanted to live in a Monet painting and can afford it. A glassy entry hides 17 rooms surrounding a fragrant little garden courtyard and fountain, giving you a countryside break fit for a Medici in the heart of Paris. This delightful refuge is tastefully decorated with floral Old World charm, and is permeated with thoughtfulness (Sb-€172, Db-€208-228, deluxe Db-€258, Tb-€298, Qb-€348, €30 cheaper mid-July-Aug and Nov-March, includes extravagant continental breakfast, faces the Odéon Theater at 23 rue Racine, tel. 01 43 26 00 60, fax 01 40 46 83 39, www.relaismedicis.com, reservation @relaismedicis.com, kind Marie at reception).

$$ Hôtel Michelet Odéon sits in a corner of place de l'Odéon with big windows on the square. Though it lacks personality, it's a fair value in this pricey area, with 24 simple rooms with modern decor and views of the square (Db-€120-140, Tb-€170,

Qb-€190, no air-con, 6 place de l'Odéon, tel. 01 53 10 05 60, fax 01 46 34 55 35, www.hotelmicheletodeon.com, hotel@micheletodeon .com).

Near the Panthéon and Rue Mouffetard

$$ **Hôtel des Grandes Ecoles*** is idyllic. A private cobbled lane leads to three buildings that protect a flower-filled garden courtyard, preserving a sense of tranquility rare in this city. Its 51 rooms are French-countryside-pretty, simple, and reasonably spacious, but have no air-conditioning. This romantic spot is deservedly popular, so book ahead. Reservations are not accepted more than four months in advance; new openings become available on the 15th of each month (Db-€118-145 depending on size, extra bed-€20, no TVs in rooms, parking garage-€30, Wi-Fi only, 75 rue du Cardinal Lemoine, Mo: Cardinal Lemoine, tel. 01 43 26 79 23, fax 01 43 25 28 15, www.hotel-grandes-ecoles .com, hotel.grandes.ecoles@free.fr, mellow Marie speaks English, Mama does not).

$$ **Hôtel des 3 Collèges** greets clients with a bright lobby, narrow hallways, and unimaginative rooms...but fair rates (Sb-€85-110, Db-€106-150, Tb-€150-170, pay Wi-Fi only, 16 rue Cujas, tel. 01 43 54 67 30, fax 01 46 34 02 99, www.3colleges.com, hotel@3colleges.com).

$$ **Hôtel Cujas Panthéon** gives simple two-star comfort *sans* air-conditioning at relatively fair prices (Db-€120-135, Tb-€160-170, Wi-Fi only, 18 rue Cujas, tel. 01 43 54 58 10, fax 01 43 25 88 02, www.cujas-pantheon-paris-hotel.com, hotel-cujas -pantheon@wanadoo.fr).

$ **Hôtel Cluny Sorbonne** is a modest place located in the thick of things across from the famous university and below the Panthéon. Rooms are well-worn with thin walls (small Db-€100, really big Db/Tb/Qb-€160, check website for deals, no air-con, Wi-Fi only, 8 rue Victor Cousin, tel. 01 43 54 66 66, fax 01 43 29 68 07, www.hotel-cluny.fr, cluny@club-internet.fr).

South of Luxembourg Garden

$$$ **Hôtel des Mines** is less central, but its 50 well-maintained rooms are a fair value and come with updated bathrooms and an inviting lobby (Db-€165, Tb-€195, Qb-€225, less for last-minute bookings and stays of 3 nights or more, frequent Web deals, between Luxembourg and Port-Royal stations on the RER-B line, a 10-minute walk from Panthéon, one block past Luxembourg Garden at 125 boulevard St. Michel, tel. 01 43 54 32 78, fax 01 46 33 72 52, www.hoteldesminesparis.com, hotel@hoteldesmines paris.com).

Hotels & Restaurants near Rue Mouffetard

1 Young & Happy Hostel
2 Port-Royal-Hôtel
3 Hôtel de L'Espérance
4 Cave de Bourgogne

200 YARDS
200 METERS

M METRO STATION

Budget Accommodations Away from the Center

Acceptable budget accommodations in central neighborhoods are few and far between in Paris. I've listed the best I could find in the neighborhoods described earlier, most at about €100 for a double room. These are great (moderate) budget options, but if you want lower rates or greater selection, you need to look farther away from the river (prices drop proportionately with distance from the Seine). Below you'll find more budget listings in less-central, but still-appealing neighborhoods. You'll spend more time on the Métro or bus getting to sights, and save money by sleeping in these areas.

At the Bottom of Rue Mouffetard

These accommodations, away from the Seine and other tourists in an appealing workaday area, offer more room for your euro. Rue Mouffetard is the bohemian soul of this area. Two thousand years ago, it was the principal Roman road south to Italy. Today, this small, meandering street has a split personality. The lower half thrives in the daytime as a pedestrian shopping street. The upper half sleeps during the day, but comes alive after dark. Use Métro stop Censier Daubenton or Les Gobelins. A terrific Saturday market sprawls along boulevard Port Royal, just east of the Port Royal Métro stop.

$ Young & Happy Hostel is easygoing, well-run, and English-speaking, with Internet access, kitchen facilities, and acceptable hostel conditions. It sits dead-center in the rue Mouffetard action...which can be good or bad (all rates per person: bunk in 4- to 10-bed co-ed dorm-€23-30, in 3- to 5-bed female-only dorm-€28, in double room-€35, includes breakfast, sheet deposit-€5, towel-€1, credit cards accepted, no air-con, no lockers but safety box at reception, pay Wi-Fi, 11:00-16:00 lockout but reception stays open, no curfew, 80 rue Mouffetard, Mo: Place Monge, tel. 01 47 07 47 07, fax 01 47 07 22 24, www.youngand happy.fr, smile@youngandhappy.fr, friendly Alex at the helm).

$ Port-Royal-Hôtel* has only one star, but don't let that fool you. Its 46 rooms are polished top to bottom and have been well-run by the same proud family for 81 years. You could eat off the floors of its spotless, comfy rooms...but you won't find air-conditioning, Internet access, or Wi-Fi. Ask for a room away from the street (S-€42-56, D-€56, Db-€80-90 depending on size, big shower down the hall-€3, cash only, nonrefundable cash deposit required, on busy boulevard de Port-Royal at #8, Mo: Les Gobelins, tel. 01 43 31 70 06, fax 01 43 31 33 67, www.hotelportroyal.fr, portroyal hotel@wanadoo.fr).

$ Hôtel de L'Espérance** is a terrific two-star value. It's quiet and cushy, with soft rooms, canopy beds, and nice public spaces (Sb-€80-85, Db-€85-95, Tb-€120, 15 rue Pascal, Mo: Censier Daubenton, tel. 01 47 07 10 99, fax 01 43 37 56 19, www.hotelde lesperance.fr, hotel.esperance@wanadoo.fr).

Montmartre

Montmartre is surprisingly quiet once you get away from the touristy top of the hill. The neighborhood is young, trendy, and popular with the *bobo* crowd (*bourgeois bohemian*, French for "hipster"). Young and budget-minded travelers will find good deals on hotel rooms and a lively atmosphere, especially in the evenings when the terraces are full and tiny bars spill crowds onto the narrow streets.

Most of the action is centered around rue des Abbesses, starting at place des Abbesses, and stretching several blocks to rue Lépic. Rue Lépic is also lively, but the lower you go the seedier it gets: Scammers and shady characters swarm the base of the hill after hours (along boulevard Clichy and boulevard Rouchechouart, where you'll find what's left of Paris' red light district). For fun nightlife, explore the narrow streets uphill from rue des Abbesses around rue Durantin and rue des Trois Frères.

Métro line 12 is the handiest (use the Abbesses stop). Line 2 is also close, using the Blanche, Pigalle, or Anvers stops, but requires a four-block uphill walk to reach my recommended hotels. There's only one bus line here—the Montmartrobus electric bus—which connects Pigalle, Abbesses, and Place du Tertre in 10 minutes (4/hour). For restaurant suggestions, see page 338.

$$ Hôtel Regyn's Montmartre** is located directly on the lively Abbesses square, with 22 small but adequate rooms, no air-conditioning, and mediocre bathrooms. Rooms in the front come with pleasant views and noise from the square. Guests in fourth- and fifth-floor rooms can see all the way to the Eiffel Tower (Sb-€79-99, Db-€91-130, check website for specials, pay Wi-Fi, 18 place des Abbesses, tel. 01 42 54 45 21, fax 01 42 23 76 69, www.paris-hotels-montmartre.com, hrm18@club-internet.fr).

$ My Hôtel in France Montmartre, a chain hotel, has 41 small, basic-but-good-value rooms on six floors, with no elevator or air-conditioning. Twin rooms are larger than doubles for the same price. Continental breakfast and a sandwich lunch-box are included (Sb-€80-89, Db-€90-99, prices vary greatly depending on occupancy, 57 rue des Abbesses, tel. 01 42 51 50 00, fax 01 42 51 08 68, www.myhotelinfrance-montmartre.com, montmartre@my-hotel-in-france.com).

$ Plug-Inn Boutique Hostel is part hotel and part hostel, but with a hotel vibe. Half a block off of rue des Abbesses, it has a young clientele, bathrooms in all 30 rooms, free Wi-Fi, and several public computer terminals. Early arrivals can leave their luggage and take a shower. Not all rooms are available online, so book by phone or email (all prices per person: bunk in 4-bed dorm-€23-35, in 6-bed dorm-€22-28, private Db room-€35-45, female-only rooms available, includes breakfast, kitchen facilities, elevator, 24-hour front desk staff, no curfew, 7 rue Aristide Bruant, tel. 01 42 58 42 58, fax 01 42 23 93 88, www.plug-inn.fr, bonjour@plug-inn.fr).

$ Hôtel Bonséjour Montmartre, run by eager Michel and his family, is an old, worn, hostelesque place with dirt-cheap prices. All rooms have sinks, but share hallway toilets. Some rooms share one public shower on main floor, and others have oddly placed shower cabins right next to the bed (S-€35-50, D-€56-69, Tb-€80, higher price for private shower, breakfast-€6, no elevator, no air-con, 11 rue Burq, tel. 01 42 54 22 53, fax 01 42 54 25 92, www.hotel-bonsejour-montmartre.fr, hotel-bonsejour-montmartre@wanadoo.fr).

At or Near Paris' Airports

At Charles de Gaulle Airport

Both of these places are located outside the T-3 RER stop, and both have restaurants. For locations, see the map on page 345.

$$$ Novotel*** is a step up from cookie-cutter airport hotels (Db-€130-180, can rise to €280 for last-minute rooms, tel. 01 49 19

Hotels & Restaurants in Montmartre

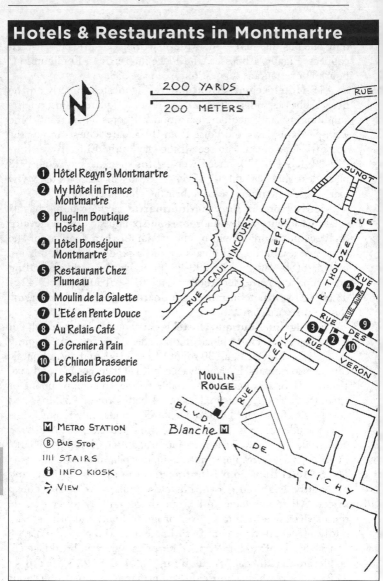

1 Hôtel Regyn's Montmartre

2 My Hôtel in France Montmartre

3 Plug-Inn Boutique Hostel

4 Hôtel Bonséjour Montmartre

5 Restaurant Chez Plumeau

6 Moulin de la Galette

7 L'Eté en Pente Douce

8 Au Relais Café

9 Le Grenier à Pain

10 Le Chinon Brasserie

11 Le Relais Gascon

M METRO STATION

B BUS STOP

IIII STAIRS

i INFO KIOSK

↗ VIEW

27 27, fax 01 49 19 27 99, www.novotel.com, h1014@accor.com).

$$ Hôtel Ibis CDG Airport** is huge and offers standard airport accommodations (Db-€95-130, tel. 01 49 19 19 19, fax 01 49 19 19 21, www.ibishotel.com, h1404@accor.com).

Near Charles de Gaulle Airport, in Roissy

The small village of **Roissy-en-France** (you'll see signs just before the airport as you come from Paris), which gave its name to the airport (Roissy Charles de Gaulle), has better-value chain hotels with free shuttle service to and from the airport (4/hour, 15 minutes, look for *navettes hôtels* signs to reach these hotels). Hotels have reasonably priced restaurants with long hours, though it's more pleasant to walk into the town, where you'll find a bakery, pizzeria, cafés, and a few restaurants. Most Roissy hotels list specials on their websites. These hotels are within walking distance of the town: **$ Hôtel Ibis CDG Paris Nord 2**** (Db-€75-90, usually cheaper than the Ibis right at the airport, 335 rue de la Belle Etoile, tel. 01 48 17 56 56, fax 01 48 17 56 51, www.ibishotel.com, h0815@accor.com), **$ Hôtel Campanile Roissy***** (Db-€75-100, allée des Vergers, tel. 01 34 29 80 40, fax 01 34 29 80 39, www.campanile-roissy.fr, roissy@campanile.fr), and **$$ Hôtel Golden Tulip Paris CDG***** (Db-€90-150, 11 allée des Vergers, tel. 01 34 29 00 00, fax 01 34 29 00 11, www.goldentulipcdgvillepinte.com, info@goldentulipcdgvillepinte.com). The cheapest option is **$ B&B Hôtel Roissy CDG***, where many flight attendants stay (Db-€55, rue du Verger, tel. 01 34 38 55 55, fax 01 34 38 55 00, www.hotelbb.com).

To avoid rush-hour traffic, drivers can consider sleeping north of Paris in either **Auvers-sur-Oise** (30 minutes west of airport) or in the pleasant medieval town of **Senlis** (15 minutes north of airport). **$ Hôtel Ibis Senlis**** is a few minutes from town (Db-€70-100, Wi-Fi, route nationale A1, tel. 03 44 53 70 50, fax 03 44 53 51 93, www.ibishotel.com, h0709@accor.com). If you don't have a car, sleep elsewhere.

Near Orly Airport

Two chain hotels, owned by the same company and very close to the Sud terminal, are your best option near Orly. Both have free shuttles *(navettes)* to the terminal.

$$$ Hôtel Mercure Paris Orly*** provides high comfort for a high price; check their website for discounts (Db-€130-200, book early for better rate, tel. 01 49 75 15 50, fax 01 49 75 15 51, www.accorhotel.com, h1246@accor.com).

$ Hôtel Ibis Orly Aéroport** is reasonable and basic (Db-€80-100, tel. 01 56 70 50 60, fax 01 56 70 50 70, www.ibishotel.com, h1413@accor.com).

Eating in Paris

The Parisian eating scene is kept at a rolling boil. Entire books (and lives) are dedicated to the subject. Paris is France's wine-and-cuisine melting pot. Though it lacks a style of its own (only French onion soup is truly Parisian; otherwise, there is no "Parisian cuisine" to speak of), it draws from the best of France. Paris could hold a gourmet Olympics and import nothing.

Budget Tips: If you plan to travel outside of Paris, save your splurges for the countryside, where you'll enjoy regional cooking for less money. To save piles of euros, go to a bakery for take-out, or stop at a café for lunch. Cafés and brasseries are happy to serve a

---

Restaurant Price Code

To help you choose among these listings, I've divided the restaurants into three categories, based on the price for a typical main course.

$$$ Higher Priced—Most main courses €25 or more.
$$ Moderately Priced—Most main courses €15-25.
$ Lower Priced—Most main courses €15 or less.

---

plat du jour (garnished plate of the day, about €12-18) or a chef-like salad (about €10-13) day or night. Many Parisian department stores have supermarkets in the basement, along with top-floor cafeterias offering not-really-cheap but low-risk, low-stress, what-you-see-is-what-you-get meals. To save even more, consider picnics (tasty take-out dishes available at charcuteries).

Good Picnic Spots: The Palais Royal (across place du Palais Royal from the Louvre) and place des Vosges in the Marais make exquisite spots for peaceful, royal picnics. For great river views, try the little triangular Henry IV park on the west tip of Ile de la Cité, the bench-equipped pedestrian pont des Arts bridge (across from the Louvre), or the grass parkway running along the Seine between Les Invalides and pont de l'Alma (near rue Cler). Parks, such as the Tuileries and Luxembourg Garden, make for ideal picnics—as do the gardens behind Les Invalides and the Champ de Mars park below the Eiffel Tower (eat at the sides of the park; the central area is off-limits). Be aware that parks, including the grassy area on place des Vosges, close at dusk. For an urban setting and terrific people-watching, try the Pompidou Center (by the *Homage to Stravinsky* fountains) or the courtyard around the pyramid of the Louvre. Hoteliers frown on in-room picnics.

Restaurants

My recommendations are centered on the same great neighborhoods listed in "Sleeping in Paris"; you can come home exhausted after a busy day of sightseeing and find a good selection of restaurants right around the corner. And evening is a fine time to explore any of these delightful neighborhoods, even if you're sleeping elsewhere.

Restaurants open for dinner at about 19:00, and small local favorites get crowded after 21:00. Linger longer over dinner—restaurants expect you to enjoy a full meal. Eat early with tourists or late with locals. Before choosing a seat outside, remember that smokers love outdoor tables.

Most restaurants I've listed have set-price *menus* between €15 and €35. In most cases, the few extra euros you pay are well-spent, and open up a variety of better choices. Remember that a service charge is included in the prices (so little or no tipping is expected). Most of the restaurants listed below accept credit cards.

In the Rue Cler Neighborhood

The rue Cler neighborhood caters to its residents. Its eateries, while not destination places, have an intimate charm. I've provided a full range of choices—from cozy ma-and-pa diners to small and trendy boutique restaurants to classic, big, boisterous bistros. For all restaurants listed in this area, use the Ecole Militaire Métro stop (unless another station is listed).

On Rue Cler

$ Café du Marché boasts the best seats, coffee, and prices on rue Cler. The owner's philosophy: Brasserie on speed—crank out good food at great prices to chic locals and savvy tourists. It's high-energy, with young waiters who barely have time to smile...*très* Parisian. This place is ideal if you don't mind a limited section and want to eat an inexpensive one-course meal among a commotion of people. The chalkboard lists your choices: good, hearty €10 salads or more filling €12 *plats du jour*. If coming for dinner, arrive before 19:30; it's packed at 21:00, and service can be slow (Mon-Sat 11:00-23:00, Sun 11:00-17:00, at the corner of rue Cler and rue du Champ de Mars, 38 rue Cler, tel. 01 47 05 51 27).

$ Tribeca Italian Restaurant, next door to Café du Marché, is run by the same people with essentially the same formula and an Italian accent. They offer similar value and more space, a calmer ambience, and more-patient service. This family-friendly eatery offers €13 pizzas and Italian *plats* (open daily).

$ Le Petit Cler is a locally popular, tiny café with long leather booths, a vintage interior, a handful of outdoor tables, and fine, inexpensive dishes (€9 omelets, €7 soup of the moment, €12 salads, €14 *plats*, mouthwatering *petit-pots* of chocolate or vanilla pudding, closed Mon, next to Grand Hôtel Lévêque at 29 rue Cler, tel. 01 45 50 17 50).

$ Crêperie Ulysée en Gaule offers cheap seats on rue Cler with crêpes to go. Readers of this book don't have to pay an extra charge to sit if they buy a drink. The family adores its Greek dishes, but their crêpes are your least expensive hot meal on this street (28 rue Cler, tel. 01 47 05 61 82).

$ Brasserie Aux PTT, a simple traditional café delivering fair-value fare, reminds Parisians of the old days on rue Cler. Rick Steves diners are promised a free *kir* with their dinner (closed Sun, 2-minute walk from most area hotels, opposite 53 rue Cler).

PARIS

Close to Ecole Militaire

$$ Le Florimond is fun for a special occasion. The setting is intimate and welcoming. Locals come for classic French cuisine at fair prices. Friendly English-speaking Laurent, whose playful ties change daily, gracefully serves one small room of tables and loves to give suggestions. The stuffed cabbage and the *confit de canard* are particularly tasty, and the house wine is wonderful (€36 *menu,* affordable wine selection, closed Sun, reservations smart, 19 avenue de la Motte-Picquet, tel. 01 45 55 40 38).

$$ Café le Bosquet is a modern Parisian brasserie with dressy waiters and your choice of a mod-elegant interior or tables on a broad sidewalk. Come here for a bowl of French onion soup or a *plat du jour* for about €12. Say *bonjour* to lanky owner Jean-François (a.k.a. Jeff). The escargots are tasty, and the house red wine is plenty good (€15-20 *plats,* continental breakfast for €6, free Wi-Fi, closed Sun, reservations smart Fri-Sat, corner of rue du Champ de Mars and avenue Bosquet, 46 avenue Bosquet, tel. 01 45 51 38 13).

$$ La Terrasse du 7ème is a sprawling, happening café with grand outdoor seating and a living room-like interior with comfy love seats. Located on a corner, it overlooks a busy intersection with a constant parade of people. Chairs are set up facing the street, as a meal here is like dinner theater—and the show is slice-of-life Paris (€15-20 *plats,* €16 daily *plats,* good €13 *salade niçoise,* no fixed-price *menu,* daily until at least 24:00 and sometimes until 2:00 in the morning, at Ecole Militaire Métro stop, tel. 01 45 55 00 02).

Between Rue de Grenelle and the River, East of Avenue Bosquet

$$ Le Petit Niçois celebrates fish from southern France. Come here for everything from bouillabaisse to bass to paella to mussels, and enjoy the area's top seafood at decent prices (a few meat dishes are available). Start with the delectable *escargot à la provençale,* dive into the *marmite du pêcheur*—a delicious version of bouillabaisse, sample the sinful puréed potatoes, and finish yourself off with the lemon twist finale *(citron confit givré aux frais)* or *café gourmand* desserts. The atmosphere is contemporary—warm though formal—and the welcome is genuine (€22 two-course *menu,* €32 three-course *menu;* better yet, ask the owner, caring Carlos, to give you the royal treatment—matching three courses with wine and apéritifs for €50; daily, 10 rue Amélie, Mo: La Tour Maubourg, tel. 01 45 51 83 65).

$$ L'Ami Jean offers top Basque specialties at palatable prices with tight but fun seating. Parisians detour long distances to savor the gregarious chef's cuisine and convivial atmosphere. Arrive by 19:30 or call ahead (€38 *menu,* closed Sun-Mon, 27 rue Malar, Mo: La Tour-Maubourg, tel. 01 47 05 86 89).

Rue Cler Restaurants

1. Café du Marché & Tribeca Italian Rest.
2. Le Petit Cler
3. Crêperie Ulysée en Gaule
4. Brasserie Aux PTT
5. Le Florimond
6. Café le Bosquet
7. La Terrasse du 7ème
8. Le Petit Niçois
9. L'Ami Jean
10. La Fontaine de Mars
11. Le P'tit Troquet
12. Billebaude Bistro
13. To Au Bon Accueil & Boulangerie-Pâtisserie de la Tour Eiffel
14. Le Royal Café
15. Gusto Italia
16. La Varangue
17. La Gourmandise Pizzeria
18. Le Violon d'Ingres, Café Constant & Les Cocottes
19. Late-Night Groceries (2)
20. Le Tourville & Café des Officiers
21. Café Roussillon
22. O'Brien's Pub

M METRO STATION
B BUS STOP w/ ROUTE #
P PARKING
T TAXI STAND
   PEDESTRIAN ZONE

TO SEINE RIVER

RUE

RAPP

AVENUE

D'ALMA

TO EIFFEL TOWER & 13

MONT.

AVENUE

R. VALENTIN

RUE LOGES

#80 & #92

BOSQUET

RUE

#80 & #92

R. DE L'EXPO.

AVE DE

TO EIFFEL TOWER

RUE

AUGER

LA

#87

#87 & #42

BOURDON

RUE

#87 & #42

CHAMP

DE

MARS

KIDS' PLAY AREA & PUPPETS

KIDS' PLAYGROUND

PARIS

Between Rue de Grenelle and the River, West of Avenue Bosquet

$$$ **58 Tour Eiffel,** on the tower's first level (about 300 feet up), is popular both for its incredible views and the cuisine of its famed French chef, Alain Ducasse. Dinner here is pricey (you must order a complete *menu*—€63-80) and requires a reservation (two seatings: 18:30 and 21:00; reserve long in advance, especially if you want a view, either by calling or going online; within France, dial toll tel. 08 25 56 66 62; from outside France, dial 01 76 64 14 64; www.restaurants-toureiffel.com). Lunch is easier (€20 *menu*, daily 11:30-16:00, no reservations possible, Mo: Bir-Hakeim or Trocadéro, RER: Champ de Mars-Tour Eiffel).

$$$ **La Fontaine de Mars,** a longtime favorite and neighborhood institution, draws Parisians who want to be seen. It's charmingly situated on a tiny, jumbled square with tables jammed together for the serious business of eating. Reserve in advance for a table on the ground floor or on the square, and enjoy the same meal Barack Obama did. Street-level seats come with the best ambience (€20-30 *plats du jour,* superb foie gras, superb-er desserts, 129 rue St. Dominique, tel. 01 47 05 46 44).

$$ **Le P'tit Troquet,** a petite eatery taking you back to the Paris of the 1920s, is gracefully and earnestly run by Dominique. The fragile elegance makes you want to hug a flapper. Dominique is particularly proud of her foie gras and lamb, and of her daughter Virginie's breads and pastries. The delicious three-course €33 *menu* comes with traditional choices. Delicate charm and gourmet flair make this restaurant a favorite of connoisseurs (opens at 18:00, closed Sun, reservations smart, 28 rue de l'Exposition, tel. 01 47 05 80 39).

$$ **Billebaude,** run by patient Pascal, is an authentic Parisian bistro popular with locals. The focus is on what's fresh, including catch-of-the-day fish and meats from the hunt (available in the fall and winter). Chef Sylvain, an avid hunter, is determined to deliver quality at a fair price (€33 *menu,* closed Sun-Mon, 29 rue de l'Exposition, tel. 01 45 55 20 96).

$$ **Au Bon Accueil,** a quiet, handsome place in the shadow of the Eiffel Tower, serves a small selection of delicious dishes at surprisingly affordable prices. You'll dine with a mostly local clientele (€9 *entrées,* €17 *plats,* €31 *menus,* closed Sun, 14 rue de Monttessuy, tel. 01 47 05 46 11).

$ **Le Royal** is a tiny neighborhood fixture. This time warp, with prices and decor from another era, comes from an age when cafés sold firewood and served food as an afterthought (€5 omelets, €9 *plats*, filling three-course *menu*-€13, closed Sat-Sun, 212 rue de Grenelle, tel. 01 47 53 92 90).

$ Gusto Italia serves up tasty, good-value Italian cuisine in a shoebox-size place with a few tables outside. Arrive early or plan to wait (€12 salads, €14 pasta, daily, 199 rue de Grenelle, tel. 01 45 55 00 43).

$ Boulangerie-Pâtisserie de la Tour Eiffel delivers inexpensive salads, quiches, and sandwiches. Enjoy the views of the Eiffel Tower (daily, outdoor and indoor seating, one block southeast of the tower at 21 avenue de la Bourdonnais, tel. 01 47 05 59 81).

$ La Varangue is an entertaining one-man show featuring English-speaking Philippe, who lives upstairs, and has found his niche serving a mostly American clientele. The food is cheap and basic, the tables are few, and he opens at 17:30. Norman Rockwell would dig his miniscule dining room—with the traditional kitchen sizzling just over the counter. Try his snails and chocolate cake (€12 *plats*, €18 *menu*, always a vegetarian option, closed Sun, 27 rue Augereau, tel. 01 47 05 51 22).

$ La Gourmandise is a kid-friendly, cheap pizzeria across from La Varangue (closed Sun, eat in or take out, 28 rue Augereau, tel. 01 45 55 45 16).

The Constant Lineup

Ever since leaving the venerable Hôtel Crillon, famed chef Christian Constant has made a career of taking the "snoot" out of French cuisine—and making it accessible to people like us. Today you'll find three of his restaurants strung along one block of rue St. Dominique between rue Augereau and rue de l'Exposition. Each is distinct, and offers a different experience and price range. None of these places is cheap, but they all deliver top-quality cuisine.

$$$ Le Violon d'Ingres, where Christian won his first Michelin star, makes for a good excuse to dress up and really dine finely in Paris. Glass doors open onto a lively and chic eating scene, service is formal yet helpful, and the cuisine is what made this restaurateur's reputation (€60-80 *menus*, daily, reservations essential, tel. 01 45 55 15 05, 135 rue St. Dominique).

$$ Café Constant is a cool, two-level place that feels more like a small bistro-wine bar than a café. Delicious and fairly priced dishes are served in a fun setting to a dedicated clientele. Arrive early to get a table (downstairs seating is better); the friendly staff speaks English (€11 *entrées*, €16 *plats*, €7 desserts, closed Sun-Mon, no reservations, corner of rue Augereau and rue St. Dominique, next to recommended Hôtel Londres Eiffel, tel. 01 47 53 73 34).

$$ Les Cocottes is a trendy, bar-stool-only place serving simple dishes in small iron pots to yuppie Parisians. France's president, Nicolas Sarkozy, brought a few of his buddies here last year (daily, 135 rue St. Dominique).

Picnicking near Rue Cler

Rue Cler is a festival of food. The street is lined with businesses run by people whose lives seem to be devoted to their specialty: polished produce, rotisserie chicken, crêpes, or cheese.

For a magical picnic dinner at the Eiffel Tower, assemble it in no fewer than five shops on rue Cler. Then lounge on the best grass in Paris, with the dogs, Frisbees, a floodlit tower, and a cool breeze in the Champ de Mars park (picnics are allowed off to the sides, but not in the central area, which is off-limits).

Asian delis (generically called *traiteurs asiatique*) provide tasty, low-stress, low-price take-out treats (€8 dinner plates; the one on rue Cler near rue du Champ de Mars has tables). **Crêperie Ulysée en Gaule,** the Greek restaurant on rue Cler across from Grand Hôtel Lévêque, sells take-away crêpes (see page 318). For the cheapest, easiest meals, consider getting sandwiches or döner kebabs, just beyond the cute zone a few steps past the Ecole Militaire Métro stop on avenue de Tourville. Small, **late-night groceries** are at 197 rue de Grenelle (open daily until midnight), as well as where rues Cler and Grenelle cross.

Breakfast on Rue Cler

Hotel breakfasts, though convenient, are generally not a good value. For a great rue Cler start to your day, drop by **Brasserie Aux PTT,** where Rick Steves readers are promised a *deux pour douze* breakfast special (2 "American" breakfasts—juice, a big coffee, croissant, bread, ham, and eggs—for €12; closed Sun, 53 rue Cler). For a continental breakfast for about €6, try nearby **Café Bosquet** (closed Sun, 46 avenue Bosquet).

Nightlife in Rue Cler

This sleepy neighborhood was not made for night owls, but there are a few notable exceptions. The focal point of before- and after-dinner posing occurs along the broad sidewalk at the intersection of avenues de la Motte-Picquet and Tourville (Mo: Ecole Militaire). **Le Tourville** and **Café des Officiers** gather a sea of outward-facing seats for the important business of people-watching—and fashion-model recruiting.

La Terrasse du 7ème, across the avenue, has a less-pretentious clientele (see listing, page 319). Nearby, **Café du Marché** (listed on page 318) attracts a Franco-American crowd until at least midnight, as does the younger **Café la Roussillon** (good French pub atmosphere, corner of rue de Grenelle and rue Cler). **O'Brien's Pub** is a relaxed Parisian rendition of an Irish pub, full of Anglophones (77 rue St. Dominique, Mo: La Tour Maubourg).

In the Marais Neighborhood

The trendy Marais is filled with diners enjoying good food in colorful and atmospheric eateries. The scene is competitive and changes all the time. I've listed an assortment of eateries—all handy to recommended hotels—that offer good food at decent prices, plus a memorable experience.

On Romantic Place des Vosges

This square offers Old World Marais elegance, a handful of eateries, and an ideal picnic site until dusk, when the park closes (use Bastille or St. Paul Métro stops). Strolling around the arcade after dark is more important than dining here—fanciful art galleries alternate with restaurants and cafés. Choose a restaurant that best fits your mood and budget; most have arcade seating and provide big space heaters to make outdoor dining during colder months an option. Also consider a drink or dessert on the square at Café Hugo or Carette after eating elsewhere.

$$$ **Ma Bourgogne** is a vintage eatery where you'll sit under warm arcades in a whirlpool of Frenchness, as bow-tied and black-aproned waiters serve you traditional French specialties: blood-red steak (try the *brochette de bœuf*), piles of fries, escargot, and good red wine. Monsieur Cougoureux (koo-goo-ruh) has commanded this ship since de Gaulle was sniveling at Americans. He offers anyone with this book a free *amuse-bouche* ("amusement for your mouth") of his homemade *steak tartare*. This is your chance to try this "raw spiced hamburger" delicacy without dedicating an entire meal to it (€40 *menu*, daily, cash only, at northwest corner at #19, tel. 01 42 78 44 64).

$$ **Carette** is a modern café serving good bistro fare under the arcades (€16 dinner salads, €20 *plats*, daily from 12:00, 28 place des Vosges, tel. 01 48 87 94 07).

$ **Café Hugo,** named for the square's most famous resident, is best for drinks only, as the cuisine does not live up to its setting (daily, 22 place des Vosges, tel. 01 42 72 64 04).

Near Place des Vosges

$$ **Royal Turenne**, a block off the square, is proudly Auvergnat (south-central France) in culture and serves up mostly meat-based dishes at good prices. Try the *marquise de bœuf* or the beefy salad topped with foie gras. Clients take their cue from the gregarious owner Philippe—don't come here for a romantic soirée. There's indoor and outdoor seating, live music on weekends, and lively crowds most evenings (daily, 24 rue de Turenne, tel. 01 42 72 04 53).

$$ **Les Bonnes Soeurs,** also a block from the square, blends modern and traditional fare with simple, contemporary ambience. Portions are big and inventive. The delicious and filling *pressé de*

Marais Restaurants

PARIS

1. Ma Bourgogne
2. Carette
3. Café Hugo
4. Royal Turenne
5. Les Bonnes Soeurs
6. Chez Janou
7. Café des Musées
8. Brasserie Bofinger
9. Au Temps des Cerises
10. Le Colimacon & La Droguerie Crêperie
11. Place du Marché Ste. Catherine Eateries
12. Robert et Louise Restaurant
13. Breizh Café
14. Le Bistrot des Compères
15. Chez Marianne

To MARCHE DES ENFANTS ROUGE

LOT

TEMPLE

PERLE

13

PICASSO MUSEUM (CLOSED UNTIL 2013)

PLACE DE THORIGNY

ELZEVIR
DES
PARC ROYAL
PAYENNE
SEVIGNÉ
TURENNE

7

16

FRANCS

MAHLER
RUE
DE

CARNAVALET MUSEUM

PLACE MARCHE S. CATH.

R. FOIN
DE
4
2
11
1

PLACE DES VOSGES

6
RUE R. VERLOMME
5
BOURGEOIS
3

TO MARCHE BASTILLE (THU + SUN A.M.)

BEAUMARCHAIS

BLVD. RICH. LENOIR

M METRO STATION

T TAXI STAND

P PARKING

200 YARDS
200 METERS

N

ST. PAUL
RUE ST.
PAUL
ST. CHARLES
BEAUTREILLIS
BIRAQUE
ANTOINE
POST

RUE ST. ANTOINE EXIT

T
P
8
M

T

R. ROQUETTE
RUE DE LAPPE

T

PLACE DE LA BASTILLE

M
9
RUE DU PETIT MUSC
CASTEX
HENRI IV
BLVD.
M

M

M

OPERA BASTILLE

CANAUXRAMA BOAT DOCK

16 Le Loir dans la Théière
17 L'As du Falafel
18 Au Bourguignon du Marais
19 L'Ebouillanté
20 Pizza Sant'Antonio

21 BHV Cafeteria
22 Au Petit Fer à Cheval & La Belle Hortense
23 La Perla Bar
24 Le Pick-Clops Bar Rest.

PARIS

chèvre starter (a hunk of goat cheese topped with tapenade and tomatoes) begs to be shared. Their hearty French hamburger comes with a salad and the best fries I've tasted in Paris (*plats* from €16, no *menu*, daily, 8 rue du pas de la Mule, tel. 01 42 74 55 80).

$$ Chez Janou, a Provençal bistro, tumbles out of its corner building and fills its broad sidewalk with happy eaters. At first glance, you know this is a find. Don't let the trendy and youthful crowd intimidate you: It's relaxed and charming, with helpful and patient service. The curbside tables are inviting, but I'd sit inside (with very tight seating) to immerse myself in the happy commotion. The style is French Mediterranean, with an emphasis on vegetables (€16-20 *plats du jour* that change with the season, daily from 19:45—book ahead or arrive when it opens, 2 blocks beyond place des Vosges at 2 rue Roger Verlomme, tel. 01 42 72 28 41). They're proud of their 81 varieties of *pastis* (licorice-flavored liqueur, €3.50 each, browse the list above the bar).

$ Café des Musées is an unspoiled, zinc-countered bistro serving traditional dishes with little fanfare and a €22 daily *menu* special that's hard to beat. The place is just far enough away to be overlooked by tourists, but packed with locals, so arrive early (daily, 49 rue de Turenne, tel. 01 42 72 96 17).

Near the Bastille

To reach these restaurants, use the Bastille Métro stop.

$$ Brasserie Bofinger, an institution for over a century, is famous for fish and traditional cuisine with Alsatian flair. You'll eat in a sprawling interior, surrounded by brisk, black-and-white-attired waiters. It's a high-energy feast for all the senses. Downstairs rooms are elaborately decorated and reminiscent of the Roaring Twenties, while upstairs rooms have traditional Alsatian decor. Eating under the grand 1919 *coupole* is a memorable treat (as is using the "historic" 1919 WC downstairs). Check out the boys shucking and stacking seafood platters out front before you enter. Their €28 two-course and €33 three-course *menus*, while not top cuisine, are a good value. If you've always wanted one of those picturesque seafood platters, this is a good place—you can take the standard platter or create one à la carte (open daily for lunch and for dinner, fun kids' menu, reasonably priced wines, 5 rue de la Bastille, don't be confused by the lesser "Petite" Bofinger across the street, tel. 01 42 72 87 82).

$ Au Temps des Cerises is a cozy little place serving wines by the glass and delicious meals with a smile. The woody 1950s atmosphere has tight seating and wads of character. Come for a glass of wine and move on, or, better yet, stay for a tasty dinner (€8 starters, €16 *plats*, cheap wine, daily, at rue du Petit Musc and rue de la Cerisaie, tel. 01 42 72 08 63).

In the Heart of the Marais

These are closest to the St. Paul Métro stop.

$$ Le Colimacon, named for its spiral steps that connect two trendy-but-cozy floors, is an intimate place. Not only are they passionate about wine, but they also serve tasty fare (€11 starters, €18-30 *plats*, daily, 44 rue Vieille du Temple, tel. 01 48 87 12 01).

$ Robert et Louise (now run by Pascal *et* François) crams tables into a tiny, rustic-as-it-gets interior, warmed by a fireplace grill. The food is red-meat good, well-priced, and popular with tourists (€7 starters, €18 *plats*, €6 desserts, closed Mon, 64 rue Vieille du Temple, tel. 01 42 78 55 89).

$ Breizh (Brittany) Café is a simple Breton place serving organic crêpes and small rolls made for dipping in rich sauces and salted butter. Try a sparkling cider, a Breton cola, or my favorite— *lait ribot*, a buttermilk-like drink (€7-12 dinner crêpes and *plats*, serves nonstop from 12:00 to late, closed Mon-Tue, 109 rue Vieille du Temple, tel. 01 42 72 13 77).

$ Le Bistrot des Compères has a privileged location on a quiet corner in the thick of the Marais, with a warm and welcoming feel whether you sit inside or out. The menu is non-traditional, the staff is relaxed, and the prices are fair (€7 starters, €15 *plats*, €7 desserts, closed Sun-Mon, 16 rue Charlemagne, tel. 01 42 72 14 16).

$ *On place du Marché Ste. Catherine:* ** This small, romantic square, just off rue St. Antoine, is an international food festival cloaked in extremely Parisian, leafy-square ambience. On a balmy evening, this is clearly a neighborhood favorite, with a handful of restaurants offering €20-30 three-course meals. Study the square, and you'll find three popular French bistros with similar features: **La Terrasse Ste. Catherine, **Le Marché**, and **Au Bistrot de la Place** (all open daily with €24 three-course *menus* on weekdays, must order à la carte on weekends, tight seating on flimsy chairs indoors and out). Other inviting eateries nearby serve a variety of international food. You'll eat under the trees, surrounded by a futuristic-in-1800 planned residential quarter.

$ Several hardworking **Asian fast-food eateries,** great for an €8 meal, line rue St. Antoine.

On Rue des Rosiers in the Jewish Quarter

These places line up along the same street in the heart of the Jewish Quarter.

$ Chez Marianne is a neighborhood fixture that blends delicious Jewish cuisine with Parisian *élan* and wonderful atmosphere. Choose from several indoor zones with a cluttered wine shop/deli feeling, or sit outside. You'll select from two dozen *Zakouski* elements to assemble your €12-16 *plat*. Vegetarians will find great options (€8 falafel sandwich—only €6 if you order it to go, long hours daily, corner of rue des Rosiers and rue des Hospitalières-St.-Gervais, tel. 01 42 72 18 86). For take-out, pay inside first and get a ticket before you order outside.

$ Le Loir dans la Théière ("The Dormouse in the Teapot") is a cozy, mellow teahouse offering a welcoming ambience for tired travelers. It's ideal for weekend brunch, baked goods, and hot drinks (Mon-Fri 12:00-19:00, Sat-Sun 10:00-19:00, 3 rue des Rosiers, tel. 01 42 72 90 61).

$ L'As du Falafel rules the falafel scene in the Jewish quarter. Monsieur Isaac, the "Ace of Falafel" here since 1979, brags, "I've got the biggest pita on the street...and I fill it up." (Apparently it's Lenny Kravitz's favorite, too.) Your inexpensive meal comes on plastic plates, in a bustling setting that seems to prove he's earned his success. The €7 "special falafel" is the big hit, but many Americans enjoy his lighter chicken version *(poulet grillé)* or the tasty and filling *assiette de falafel*. Their take-out service draws a constant crowd (long hours daily except closed Fri evening and all day Sat, air-con, 34 rue des Rosiers, tel. 01 48 87 63 60).

$ La Droguerie, an outdoor crêpe stand a few blocks farther down rue des Rosiers, is an option if falafels don't work for you, but cheap does (€5 dinner crêpes, closed Mon, 56 rue des Rosiers).

Near Hôtel de Ville

To reach these eateries, use the Hôtel de Ville Métro stop.

$$ Au Bourguignon du Marais is a handsome wine bar/bistro for Burgundy-lovers, where excellent wines (Burgundian only, available by the glass) blend with a good selection of well-designed dishes and efficient service. The *œufs en meurette* are mouthwatering, and the *bœuf bourguignon* could feed two (€10-14 starters, €17-22 *plats,* closed Sun-Mon, pleasing indoor and outdoor seating, 52 rue François Miron, tel. 01 48 87 15 40).

$ L'Ebouillanté is a breezy crêperie-café, romantically situated near the river on a broad, cobbled pedestrian lane behind a church. With great outdoor seating and an artsy, cozy interior, it's perfect for an inexpensive and relaxing tea, snack, or lunch—or for dinner on a warm evening. Their *Brick,* a Tunisian-inspired dish that looks like a stuffed omelet (several filling options), comes with a small salad; it left me stuffed (€13 *plats* and big salads, daily 12:00-21:30, closed Mon Nov-March, a block off the river at 6 rue des Barres, tel. 01 42 71 09 69).

$ Pizza Sant'Antonio is bustling and cheap, serving up €11 pizzas and salads on a fun Marais square (daily, barely off rue de Rivoli on place du Bourg Tibourg, 1 rue de la Verrerie).

$ BHV Department Store's fifth-floor cafeteria provides nice views, good prices, and no-brainer, point-and-shoot cafeteria cuisine (Mon-Sat 11:30-18:00, closed Sun, at intersection of rue du Temple and rue de la Verrerie, one block from Hôtel de Ville).

Picnicking in the Marais

Picnic at peaceful place des Vosges (closes at dusk) or on the Ile St. Louis *quais* (described later). Stretch your euros at the basement supermarket of the **Monoprix** department store (closed Sun, near place des Vosges on rue St. Antoine). You'll find small **groceries** open until 23:00 at 48 rue St. Antoine and on Ile St. Louis.

Nightlife in the Marais

Trendy cafés and bars—popular with gay men—cluster on rue des Archives and rue Ste. Croix de la Bretonnerie (closing at about 2:00 in the morning). There's also a line of bars and cafés providing front-row seats for the buff parade on rue Vieille du Temple, a block north of rue de Rivoli (the horseshoe-shaped **Au Petit Fer à Cheval** bar-restaurant and the atmospheric **La Belle Hortense** bookstore/wine bar are the focal points of the action). Nearby, rue des Rosiers bustles with youthful energy, but there are no cafés to observe from. **La Perla** dishes up inexpensive Tex-Mex and is stuffed with Parisian yuppies in search of the perfect margarita (26 rue François Miron).

$ Le Pick-Clops bar-restaurant is a happy peanuts-and-lots-of-cocktails diner with bright neon, loud colors, and a garish local crowd. It's perfect for immersing yourself in today's Marais world—a little boisterous, a little edgy, a little gay, fun-loving, easygoing... and no tourists. Sit inside on old-fashioned diner stools, or street-side to watch the constant Marais parade. The name means "Steal the Cigarettes"—but you'll pay €11 for your big salad (daily 7:00-24:00, 16 rue Vieille du Temple, tel. 01 40 29 02 18).

More Options: The best scene for hardcore clubbers is the dizzying array of wacky eateries, bars, and dance halls on **rue de Lappe.** Just east of the stately place de la Bastille, it's one of the wildest nightspots in Paris and not for everyone.

The most enjoyable peaceful evening may be simply mentally donning your floppy "three musketeers" hat and slowly strolling place des Vosges, window-shopping the art galleries.

On Ile St. Louis

This romantic and peaceful neighborhood is filled with promising and surprisingly inexpensive possibilities; it merits a trip for dinner even if your hotel is elsewhere. Cruise the island's main street for a variety of options, from cozy *crêperies* to Italian eateries to Alsatian brasseries and romantic bistros. After dinner, sample Paris' best ice cream and stroll across to Ile de la Cité to see a floodlit Notre-Dame. These recommended spots line the island's main drag, rue

St. Louis-en-l'Ile (see map on page 304; to get here use the Pont Marie Métro stop).

$$$ Le Tastevin is an intimate mother-and-son-run restaurant serving top-notch traditional French cuisine with white-tablecloth, candlelit, gourmet elegance under heavy wooden beams. The romantic setting (and the elegantly romantic Parisian couples enjoying the place) naturally makes you whisper. The *menus,* which start at €29 (two courses) and rise to €39-52 (three courses), offer a handful of classic choices that change with the season (daily, reserve for late-evening dining, fine wine list, 46 rue St. Louis-en-l'Ile, tel. 01 43 54 17 31, owner Madame Puisieux and her gentle son speak just enough English).

$$$ *Medieval Theme Restaurants:* La Taverne du Sergeant Recruteur, famous for its rowdy, medieval-cellar atmosphere, is ideal for hungry warriors and their wenches who like to swill hearty wine. They serve up a rustic all-you-can-eat buffet with straw baskets of raw veggies and bundles of sausage (cut whatever you like with your dagger), massive plates of pâté, a meat course, and all the wine you can stomach for €41. The food is just food; burping is encouraged. If you want to eat a lot, drink a lot of wine, be surrounded with tourists (mostly French), and holler at your friends while receiving smart-aleck buccaneer service, this food fest can be fun. And it comes with an historic twist: The "Sergeant Recruiter" used to get young Parisians drunk and stuffed here, then sign them into the army (daily from 19:00, 41 rue St. Louis-en-l'Ile, tel. 01 43 54 75 42). Next door, **Nos Ancêtres les Gaulois** is a bit goofier and grittier, and serves the same basic formula. As the name implies ("Our Ancestors the Gauls"), this place makes barbarians feel right at home (tel. 01 46 33 66 07). You might swing by both and choose the..."ambience" is not quite the right word... that fits your mood.

$$ La Brasserie de l'Ile St. Louis is situated at the prow of the island's ship as it faces Ile de la Cité, offering purely Alsatian cuisine (try the *choucroute garnie* or *coq au riesling* for €18), served in a vigorous, Teutonic setting with no-nonsense, slap-it-down service and wine-stained paper tablecloths. This is a good, balmy-evening perch for watching the Ile St. Louis promenade. If it's chilly, the interior is fun for a memorable night out (closed Wed, no reservations, 55 quai de Bourbon, tel. 01 43 54 02 59).

$ L'Orangerie is an inviting place with soft lighting and comfortable seating where diners speak in hushed voices so that everyone can appreciate the delicious cuisine and tasteful setting (€25 three-course *menu,* €20 two-course *menu,* Tue-Sun from 19:00, closed Mon, 28 rue St. Louis-en-l'Ile, tel. 01 46 33 93 98).

$ Auberge de la Reine Blanche welcomes diners willing to rub elbows with their neighbors under heaving beams. Energetic owner Michel serves traditional cuisine at reasonable prices. The giant goat-cheese salad is a beefy meal in itself (€20 two-course *menu*, €25 three-course *menu*, daily from 18:00, 30 rue St. Louis-en-l'Ile, tel. 01 46 33 07 87).

$ **Café Med,** near the pedestrian bridge to Notre-Dame, is a tiny, cheery *crêperie* with good-value salads, crêpes, and €11 *plats* (€14 and €20 *menus,* daily, limited wine list, 77 rue St. Louis-en-l'Ile, tel. 01 43 29 73 17). Two similar *crêperies* are just across the street.

Riverside Picnic for Impoverished Romantics
On sunny lunchtimes and balmy evenings, the *quai* on the Left Bank side of Ile St. Louis is lined with locals who have more class than money, spreading out tablecloths and even lighting candles for elegant picnics. And tourists can enjoy the same budget meal. A handy grocery store at #67 on the main drag (Wed-Mon until 22:00, closed Tue) has tabouli and other simple, cheap take-away dishes for your picnicking pleasure.

Ice-Cream Dessert
Half the people strolling Ile St. Louis are licking an ice-cream cone, because this is the home of *les glaces Berthillon* (now sold throughout Paris). The original **Berthillon** shop, at 31 rue St. Louis-en-l'Ile, is marked by the line of salivating customers (closed Mon-Tue). For a less famous but at least as satisfying treat, the homemade Italian gelato a block away at **Amorino Gelati** is giving Berthillon competition (no line, bigger portions, easier to see what you want, and they offer little tastes—Berthillon doesn't need to, 47 rue St. Louis-en-l'Ile, tel. 01 44 07 48 08). Having some of each is not a bad thing.

In the Luxembourg Garden Area
Sleeping in the Luxembourg neighborhood puts you near many appealing dining and after-hours options. Because my hotels in this area cluster near St. Sulpice Church and the Panthéon, I've organized restaurant listings the same way. Restaurants around St. Sulpice tend to be boisterous; those near the Panthéon are calmer; it's a short walk from one area to the other. Anyone sleeping in this area is close to the inexpensive eateries that line the always-bustling rue Mouffetard. You're also within a 15-minute walk of the *grands cafés* of St. Germain and Montparnasse (with Paris' first café and famous artist haunts).

Near St. Sulpice Church
The eateries in this section are served by the St. Sulpice, Mabillon, and St. Germain-des-Prés Métro stops. The streets between St.

Restaurants near Luxembourg Garden

① Lou Pescadou-Chez Julien

② Boucherie Rouliere & Santa Lucia

③ La Crêpe Rit du Clown

④ Chez Georges

⑤ Les Deux Magots & Le Café de Flore

⑥ Rue de Buci Eateries

⑦ To La Cigale Récamier

⑧ Brasserie Bouillon Racine

⑨ La Méditerranée Restaurant

10 Café de l'Odéon
11 Restaurant Polidor
12 Le Vin Qui Danse
13 Le Soufflot Café
14 Les Fontaines Café
15 Place de la Sorbonne Eateries
16 Le Pré Verre
17 Café Delmas

PARIS

Sulpice Church and boulevard St. Germain abound with restaurants, *crêperies,* wine bars, and jazz haunts (for this area, use Mo: St. Sulpice). Find rue des Canettes and rue Guisarde, and window-shop the many French and Italian eateries—most with similar prices, but each with a slightly different feel.

$$ Lou Pescadou-Chez Julien offers a comfortable atmosphere and above-average bistro fare in a zone where every restaurant looks the same (daily, some outdoor seating, 16 rue Mabillon, tel. 01 43 54 56 08).

$$ Boucherie Roulière has a dark interior crammed with locals in search of a thick steak or other meat dish (€7 *entrées,* €16 *plats,* €7 desserts, closed Mon, 24 rue des Canettes).

$ Santa Lucia draws positive reviews with wood-fired pizza, good pasta, and killer tiramisu (€12-14 pizza and pastas, €18 *plats,* closed Mon, 22 rue des Canettes, tel. 01 43 26 42 68).

$ La Crêpe Rit du Clown cooks up yummy crêpes (Mon-Sat 12:00-23:00, closed Sun, 6 rue des Canettes, tel. 01 46 34 01 02).

Chez Georges is a bohemian pub lined with black-and-white photos of the artsy and revolutionary French '60s. Have a drink as you sit in a cool little streetside table nook, or venture downstairs to find a hazy, drippy-candle, traditionally French world in the Edith Piaf-style dance cellar (cheap drinks from old-fashioned menu, Tue-Sat 14:00-2:00 in the morning, closed Sun-Mon and in Aug, 11 rue des Canettes, tel. 01 43 26 79 15).

Near Boulevard St. Germain: A five-minute walk from St. Sulpice Church, this venerable boulevard is home to some of Paris' most famous cafés and best pre- or post-dinner strolling. Consider a light dinner with a table facing the action at Hemingway's **Les Deux Magots** or at Sartre's **Le Café de Flore** (figure about €12 for an omelet and €18-28 for a salad or *plat*). A block north (toward the river), **rue de Buci** offers a lineup of bars, cafés, and bistros targeted to a young clientele who are more interested in how they look than how the food tastes. It's terrific theater for passersby.

$$ La Cigale Récamier, near the Sèvres-Babylone shopping area, is a classy place for a quiet meal at reasonable prices with appealing indoor and outdoor seating. It's about 10 minutes west of place St. Sulpice, on a short pedestrian square a block off rue de Sèvres (€20 *plats,* à la carte only, closed Sun, 4 rue Récamier, Mo: Sèvres-Babylone, tel. 01 46 48 86 58).

Near the Odéon Theater

To reach these, use the Odéon Métro stop. In this same neighborhood, you'll find the historic Café le Procope, Paris' more-than-300-year-old café.

$$ Brasserie Bouillon Racine takes you back to 1906 with an Art Nouveau carnival of carved wood, stained glass, and old-time

PARIS

lights reflected in beveled mirrors. The over-the-top decor and energetic waiters give it an inviting conviviality. Check upstairs before choosing a table. Their roast suckling pig (€19) is a house favorite. There's Belgian beer on tap and a fascinating history on the menu (€18-23 *plats*, €31 *menu*, a few fish options and lots of meat, daily, 3 rue Racine, tel. 01 44 32 15 60, Phillipe).

$$ La Méditerranée is all about seafood from the south served in a pastel and dressy setting...with similar clientele. The scene and the cuisine are sophisticated yet accessible, and the view of the Odéon is *formidable*. The sky-blue tablecloths and the lovingly presented dishes add to the romance (€27 two-course *menus*, €32 three-course *menus*, daily, reservations smart, facing the Odéon at 2 place de l'Odéon, tel. 01 43 26 02 30).

$ Café de l'Odéon offers a great chance to savor light meals with a classy crowd on a peaceful and elegant square in front of a venerable theater. Though limited, the menu is accessible and decently priced, and you'll feel like a winner eating so well and so reasonably in such a Parisian setting. From May to October, the café is outdoors-only and serves lunch and dinner—or just go for drinks (good €15 salads, salmon and steak tartare; open 12:00-23:00—weather permitting, no reservations, place de l'Odéon, tel. 01 44 85 41 30). In the winter (Nov-April) they serve lunch only, inside the palatial theater lobby.

$ Restaurant Polidor, a bare-bones neighborhood fixture since the 19th century, is much loved for its unpretentious quality cooking, fun old-Paris atmosphere, and fair value. Stepping inside, you know this is a winner—noisy, happy diners sit tightly at shared tables as waiters chop and serve fresh bread. The selection features classic bourgeois *plats* from every corner of France; their *menu fraîcheur* is designed for lighter summer eating (€12-15 *plats*, €20-30 three-course *menus*, daily 12:00-14:30 & 19:00-23:00, cash only, no reservations, 41 rue Monsieur-le-Prince, tel. 01 43 26 95 34).

Between the Panthéon and the Cluny Museum

$$ Le Vin Qui Danse is a warm little place serving a good selection of tasty dishes and well-matched wines to appreciative clients (€27 two-course *menu*, add €15 for three wines selected to complement your meal, daily, 4 rue des Fossés St. Jacques, tel. 01 43 54 80 81).

$ *On Rue Soufflot with Panthéon Views:* Facing each other are two cafés—**Le Soufflot** and **Les Fontaines**—that are well-positioned for afternoon sun and soft evening light. A block in front of the Panthéon, they deliver dynamite views of the inspiring dome. Both serve classic café food all day until late and are great for a pensive drink or a light meal—simply choose the one that appeals.

$ *Place de la Sorbonne:* This appealing little square surrounds a gurgling fountain and faces Sorbonne University, just a block

PARIS

from the Cluny Museum. It offers several opportunities for a good outdoor lunch or a pleasant-dining experience. At amiable Carole's tiny **Baker's Dozen,** you'll pay take-away prices for light fare you can sit down to eat (€5 salads and sandwiches, Mon-Fri until 15:30, closed Sun). **Café de l'Ecritoire** is a typical brasserie with salads, *plats du jour,* and good seating inside and out (daily, tel. 01 43 54 60 02). **Patios** serves basic Italian cuisine, including pizza, at decent prices (daily until late, tel. 01 45 38 71 19). **Le Bac de la Sorbonne** is a tad cheaper, but you get what you pay for…

$ **Le Pré Verre,** a block from the Cluny Museum, is a chic wine bistro—a refreshing alternative in a part of the Latin Quarter mostly known for low-quality, tourist-trapping eateries. Offering imaginative, modern cuisine at fair prices, the place is packed. The bargain lunch *menu* includes a starter, main course, glass of wine, and coffee for €14. The three-course dinner *menu* at €30 is worth every *centime.* They pride themselves equally on their small-producers' wine list, so follow your server's advice (closed Sun-Mon, 8 rue Thénard, reservations necessary, tel. 01 43 54 59 47).

On Rue Mouffetard

Several blocks behind the Panthéon, rue Mouffetard is a conveyer belt of comparison-shopping eaters with wall-to-wall budget options (fondue, crêpes, Italian, falafel, and Greek). Come here to sift through the crowds and eat cheaply. This street stays up late and likes to party (particularly around place de la Contrescarpe). The gauntlet begins on top, at thriving place de la Contrescarpe, and ends below where rue Mouffetard stops at St. Médard Church. Both ends offer fun cafés where you can watch the action. The upper stretch is pedestrian and touristy; the bottom stretch is purely Parisian. Anywhere between is no-man's land for consistent quality. Still, strolling with so many fun-seekers is enjoyable, whether you eat or not. To get here, use the Censier Daubenton or Place Monge Métro stop.

$$ **Café Delmas,** at the top of rue Mouffetard on picturesque place de la Contrescarpe, is *the* place to see and be seen. Come here for a before- or after-dinner drink on the terrace, typical but pricey café cuisine, or great chocolate ice cream (open daily).

$ **Cave de Bourgogne,** a young and local hangout, has reasonably priced café fare at the bottom of rue Mouffetard. The outside has picture-perfect tables on a raised terrace; the interior is warm and lively (€13-16 *plats,* specials listed on chalkboards, daily, 144 rue Mouffetard—see map on page 311).

In Montmartre

Much of Montmartre is extremely touristy, with mindless mobs following guides to cancan shows. But the ambience is undeniably fun, and an evening overlooking Paris is a quintessential experience in the City of Light. For locations, see the map on page 314.

Near Sacré-Cœur

The steps in front of Sacré-Cœur are perfect for a picnic with a view, though the spot comes with lots of company. Along the touristy main drag (near place du Tertre and just off it), several fun piano bars serve crêpes and great people-watching. The Anvers Métro stop works well if you're visiting Sacré-Cœur or Montmartre; I've listed the closest Métro stop in each restaurant listing.

$$ Restaurant Chez Plumeau, just off jam-packed place du Tertre, is touristy yet moderately priced, with formal service but great seating on a tiny, characteristic square (elaborate €17 salads, €18-22 *plats*, closed Tue Oct-April and Wed year-round, place du Calvaire, Mo: Abbesses, tel. 01 46 06 26 29).

$$ Moulin de la Galette lets you dine with Renoir under the historic windmill in a comfortable setting with good prices. Find the old photos scattered about the place (€17 two-course *menu*, €25 three-course *menu*, daily, 83 rue Lépic, Mo: Abbesses, tel. 01 46 06 84 77).

$ L'Eté en Pente Douce is a good Montmartre choice, hiding under the generous branches of street trees. Just downhill from the crowds on a classic neighborhood corner, it features cheery indoor and outdoor seating, €10 *plats du jour* and salads, vegetarian options, and good wines (daily, many steps below Sacré-Cœur to the left as you leave, down the stairs below the WC, 23 rue Muller, Mo: Anvers, tel. 01 42 64 02 67).

$ Au Relais, on the backside of Montmartre with no hint of tourists, is a neighborhood café, offering a two-course lunch *menu du jour* with a coffee for €11 and good-value dinners (daily, 48 rue Lamarck, at the intersection with rue Mont Cenis, outdoor seating, tel. 01 46 06 68 32). From place du Tertre, walk north on rue Mont Cenis, down two long staircases to rue Lamarck. If you don't want to brave the steps back up after you've finished your meal, head for the closest Métro stop, Lamarck-Caulaincourt (turn right out of the café).

On Rue des Abbesses

At the bottom of Montmartre, residents pile into a long lineup of brasseries and cafés along rue des Abbesses (Mo: Abbesses). The food is average; the atmosphere is anything but. Come here for a lively, tourist-free scene. The street is perfect for a picnic-gathering stroll with cheese shops, delis, wine stores, and bakeries. In fact, the baker at **Le Grenier à Pain** won the award for the Best Baguette in Paris in 2010 (Thu-Mon 7:30-20:00, closed Tue-Wed, 38 rue des Abbesses, tel. 01 42 23 85 36).

$ Le Chinon Brasserie offers good seating inside and out and is the best bet for café/wine bar ambience and food (daily, 49 rue des Abbesses, tel. 01 42 62 07 17).

$ Le Relais Gascon serves giant salads (€12) topped with their signature garlic *frites* and a selection of grilled meats (€12-15) in a narrow dining room on two floors (nonstop service daily 10:30-24:00, 6 rue des Abbesses, just after the post office as you leave place des Abbesses, tel. 01 42 58 58 22).

Dinner Cruises

The following companies all offer dinner cruises (reservations required). Bateaux-Mouches and Bateaux Parisiens have the best reputations and the highest prices. They offer multicourse meals and music in aircraft-carrier-size dining rooms with glass tops and good views. For both, proper dress is required—no denim, shorts, or sport shoes; Bateaux-Mouches requires a jacket and tie for men. The main difference between these companies is the music: Bateaux-Mouches offers violin and piano to entertain your romantic evening, whereas Bateaux Parisiens boasts a lively atmosphere with a singer, band, and dance floor.

Bateaux-Mouches, started in 1949, is hands-down the most famous. You can't miss its sparkling port on the north side of the river at Pont de l'Alma. The boats usually board 19:30-20:15, depart at 20:30, and return at 22:45 (€95-135/person, RER: Pont de l'Alma, tel. 01 42 25 96 10, www.bateaux-mouches.fr).

Bateaux Parisiens leaves from Port de la Bourdonnais, just east of the bridge under the Eiffel Tower. Begin boarding at 19:45, leave at 20:30, and return at 23:00 (€65-160/person, price depends on view seating and *menu* option, tel. 01 76 64 14 45, www.bateaux parisiens.com). The middle level is best. Pay the few extra euros to get seats next to the windows—it's more romantic and private, with sensational views.

Le Capitaine Fracasse offers the budget option (€50/person, €80 with wine or champagne; tables are first-come, first-serve, so get there early; boarding times vary by season and day of week, walk down stairs in the middle of Bir-Hakeim bridge near the Eiffel Tower to Iles aux Cygne, Mo: Bir-Hakeim or RER: Champ de Mars-Tour Eiffel, tel. 01 46 21 48 15, www.croisiere-paris .com).

Paris Connections

When leaving Paris, get to your departure point early to allow time for waiting in lines. Figure on 2-3 hours for an overseas flight; 1-2 hours for flights within Europe (particularly if flying with one of the budget airlines, which tend to have long check-in lines); and 40 minutes for a train trip or long-distance bus ride, if you're doing anything beyond simply boarding (Eurostar trains require you to check in at least 30 minutes early). Whether arriving or departing, always keep your luggage safely near you. Pickpockets prey on jet-lagged tourists on shuttle trains and buses.

Don't take an unauthorized taxi from cabbies greeting you on arrival. Official taxi stands are well-signed.

Trains

Paris is Europe's rail hub, with six major stations and one minor one, each serving different regions:
- Gare du Nord (northern France and Europe)
- Gare Montparnasse (northwestern France and TGV service to France's southwest)
- Gare de Lyon (southeastern France and Italy)
- Gare de l'Est (northeastern France and eastbound trains)
- Gare St. Lazare (northwestern France)
- Gare d'Austerlitz (southwestern France and Europe)
- Gare de Bercy (smaller station, regional trains to the south of France)

All six main train stations have banks or currency exchanges, ATMs, train information desks, telephones, cafés, newsstands, and clever pickpockets (pay attention in ticket lines—keep your bag firmly gripped in front of you). Because of security concerns, not all have baggage checks.

Any train station has schedule information, can make reservations, and can sell tickets for any destination. Buying tickets is handier from an SNCF neighborhood office.

Each station offers two types of rail service: long distance to other cities, called Grandes Lignes (major lines); and suburban service to nearby areas, called Banlieue, Transilien, or RER. You also may see ticket windows identified as *Ile de France*. These are for Transilien trains serving destinations outside Paris in the Ile de France region (usually no more than an hour from Paris).

Paris train stations can be intimidating, but if you slow down, take a deep breath, and ask for help, you'll find them manageable and efficient. Bring a pad of paper for clear communication at ticket/info windows. All stations have helpful information booths *(accueil)*; the bigger stations have roving helpers, usually wearing red or blue vests. They're capable of answering rail questions more quickly than the staff at the information desks or ticket windows. I make a habit of confirming my track number and departure time with these helpers.

PARIS

Paris' Train Stations

Métro and RER trains, as well as buses and taxis, are well-marked at every station. When arriving by Métro, follow signs for *Grandes Lignes-SNCF* to find the main tracks.

Gare du Nord

Key Destinations Served by Gare du Nord Grandes Lignes: Bruges (at least hourly, 2.5 hours, change in Brussels), **Amsterdam** (8-10/day, 3.5 hours direct), **Berlin** (6/day, 9 hours, 1-2 changes, via Belgium, better connections from Gare de l'Est), **Copenhagen** (7/day, 14-18 hours, two night trains), and **London** via Eurostar Chunnel train (12-15/day, 2.5 hours, toll tel. 08 36 35 35 39; for details, see "To Paris or Brussels via Eurostar Train" on page 757. Routes via **Brussels** (e.g., to Amsterdam and Bruges) require taking the pricey Thalys train; for details and tips, see "Amsterdam Connections" on page 1158.

By Banlieue/RER Lines: Charles de Gaulle Airport (4/hour, 30 minutes, runs 5:00-24:00, track 4).

Gare Montparnasse

Key Destinations Served by Gare Montparnasse: Chartres (10/day, 65 minutes), **Madrid** (3/day, 12-13 hours, expensive overnight trains from Gare d'Austerlitz), and **Lisbon** (1/day, 21.5 hours via Irun).

Gare de Lyon

Key Destinations Served by Gare de Lyon: Avignon (9/day in 2.5 hours to Avignon TGV Station, 5/day in 3.5 hours to Avignon Centre-Ville station, more connections with change—3-4 hours), **Arles** (11/day, 2 direct TGVs—4 hours, 9 with change in Avignon—5 hours), **Nice** (10/day, 6 hours, may require change, 11-hour night train possible out of Gare d'Austerlitz), **Venice** (3/day, 10-12 hours with change in Milan; 1 direct overnight, 13 hours, important to reserve ahead; 2 more night trains with changes), **Rome** (3/day, 13-16 hours, plus several overnight options, important to reserve ahead), **Interlaken** (7/day, 5-6.5 hours, 1-3 changes, 2 more from Gare de l'Est), and **Barcelona** (2/day, 7.5 hours, change in Figueres; night train possible from Gare d'Austerlitz).

Gare de Bercy

This smaller station handles regional trains to Lyon and the south of France (Mo: Bercy, one stop east of Gare de Lyon on line 14, exit the Métro station and it's across the street). Facilities are limited—just a WC and a sandwich-fare takeout café.

Paris Train Stations

Paris Train Stations & Destinations

❶ Gare du Nord: To London, Brussels, Amsterdam, Copenhagen & N. France (also Chantilly & Auvers-sur-Oise)

❷ Gare Montparnasse: To Spain, SW France (Languedoc & Dordogne), Loire Valley, Brittany & Mont St. Michel (also Chartres)

❸ Gare de Lyon: To Italy & SE France (Burgundy, Alps, Provence & Riviera; also Fontainebleau & Melun/Vaux-le-Vicomte)

❹ Gare de Bercy: Night trains to Italy

❺ Gare de l'Est: To NE France (Reims, Champagne & Alsace), Germany, Switzerland & Austria

❻ Gare St. Lazare: To Normandy (incl. Caen, Bayeux & Vernon/Giverny)

❼ Gare d'Austerlitz: To Spain, SW France & Loire Valley

Gare de l'Est

Key Destinations Served by Gare de l'Est: Interlaken (2/day, 6.5 hours, 2-3 changes, 7 more from Gare de Lyon), **Frankfurt** (4 direct/day, 4 hours; 4 more/day with change in Karlsruhe, 4.5 hours), **Vienna** (7/day, 12-17 hours, 1-3 changes, night train via Munich or Frankfurt), **Prague** (5/day, 12-18 hours, night train via Mannheim or Berlin), **Munich** (4/day, 6-7 hours, most with

1 change, 1 direct night train), and **Berlin** (6/day, 8-9 hours, 1-2 changes; 1 direct night train, 11.25 hours).

Gare St. Lazare
Key Destinations Served by Gare St. Lazare: Bayeux (9/day, 2.5 hours, some change in Caen), **Caen** (14/day, 2 hours), and **Pontorson/Mont St. Michel** (2/day, 4-5.5 hours, via Caen; more trains from Gare Montparnasse).

Gare d'Austerlitz
Key Destinations Served by Gare d'Austerlitz: Versailles (via RER line C, 4/hour, 35 minutes), **Barcelona** (1/night, 12.5 hours, make mandatory reservation at least 2 weeks ahead; day trains from Gare de Lyon), and **Madrid** (1 direct night train, 13 hours, make mandatory reservation at least 2 weeks ahead, 16 hours via Irun; day trains from Gare Montparnasse).

Airports
Charles de Gaulle Airport
Paris' primary airport has three terminals: T-1, T-2, and T-3 (see map). Most flights from the US use T-1 or T-2. To confirm which terminal serves your airline, check your ticket, or contact the airport (for flight info from French landlines dial 3950—€0.35/minute, from the US dial 011 33 1 70 36 39 50, www.adp.fr). T-1 and T-2 have airport information desks and tourist office desks (where you can buy the Paris Museum Pass).

Transportation Between Charles de Gaulle Airport and Paris
Three public-transportation routes, airport vans, and taxis link the airport's terminals with central Paris. If you're traveling with one or two companions, carrying lots of baggage, or are just plain tired, taxis are worth the extra cost (airport vans don't work well for arrivals, for reasons explained later in this section).

RER-B trains from the airport to Paris stop at T-2 and near T-3 (connections from T-1 via free CDGVAL shuttle train), then stop in central Paris at Gare du Nord, Châtelet-Les Halles, St. Michel, and Luxembourg (about €9, 4/hour, runs 5:00-24:00, 30 minutes to Gare du Nord). Follow *Paris by Train* signs, then *RER* signs. The RER station at T-2 mixes with a busy main train station, so pay attention—look for green *Paris/Ile de France* (Paris and Suburbs) ticket windows and expect lines. It's faster to buy tickets from the machines (coins required, break your bills at an airport shop), as lines can be long at ticket windows. The T-3 RER station is less crowded and just five minutes away by CDGVAL shuttle train.

Charles de Gaulle Airport

1 Novotel & Hôtel Ibis CDG Airport
2 To Roissy-en-France Hotels

TERMINAL 1

UNDERGROUND WALKWAYS

TERMINAL 3

CONTROL TOWER

TO LILLE & BRUSSELS

TERMINAL 2

TO ROISSY-EN-FRANCE, A-1 FREEWAY & PARIS

2 B 2 D 2 F

2 A 2 C 2 E

CONTROL TOWER

TRAIN STATION (TGV & R) & SHERATON HOTEL

TO DISNEYLAND PARIS, DIJON, LYON & AVIGNON

CDGVAL SHUTTLE TRAIN & STATION

R RER STOP

P PARKING

B AIR FRANCE/ROISSY BUS STOP

DCH

Roissy-Buses run to the Opéra Garnier (€9.40, 4/hour, runs 6:30-21:00, 50 minutes, buy ticket on bus). You'll arrive at a bus stop on rue Scribe on the left (west) side of the Opéra building. To get to the Métro entrance, turn left as you exit the bus and walk counterclockwise around the lavish Opéra building. The Métro station entrance faces the Opéra's front (in the center of the traffic circle). You can also take a taxi (about €12) to any of my listed hotels from behind the Opéra (go right as you exit the bus; the stand is in front of Galeries Lafayette department store, behind the Opéra).

"Les Cars" Air France buses serve central Paris (at least 2/hour, runs 5:45-23:00, toll tel. 08 92 35 08 20—€0.35/minute, www.lescarsairfrance.com). **Bus #2** runs from the airport to Porte Maillot (connections to Beauvais Airport—see page 348) and ends at the Arc de Triomphe (€15, 45 minutes). **Bus #4** runs to Gare de Lyon (45 minutes) and continues to the Montparnasse Tower/train station (€16.50, 1 hour). **Bus #3** connects Charles de Gaulle and Orly airports (€19, 1 hour). Buy tickets from the driver (10 percent cheaper online; round-trip tickets 20 percent cheaper than two one-way tickets). Here are the closest bus stops by terminal:

PARIS

T-1—door 34; T-2B and 2D—door B1; T-2A and 2C—door C2; T-2E and 2F—concourse level, exit 3. Buses to the airport stops at Etoile/Arc de Triomphe (on avenue Carnot—the non-Champs-Elysées side), Porte Maillot (on boulevard Gouvion-St-Cyr—right side of the Palais des Congres), Gare Montparnasse (on rue du Commandant Mouchotte—facing the station with the tower behind you, it's around the left side), and Gare de Lyon (in front of #20 boulevard Diderot—the main street in front of the station).

Taxis cost about €60 for up to three people with bags (more if traffic is bad). When returning to the airport, your hotel can call for a taxi: Specify that you want a real taxi *(un taxi normal)*, and not a limo service that costs €20 more (and gives your hotel a kickback). For weekday morning departures (7:00-10:00), reserve at least a day ahead (€5 reservation fee payable by credit card, expect to pay €1/bag handling fee). Groups of four or more are too big for a regular taxi and should pre-book a minivan taxi or consider an airport van, described next. For more on taxis in Paris, see page 220.

Airport vans work like those at home, packing in several passengers and making stops at multiple hotels. These work best for trips from your hotel to the airport. They don't work as well for trips from the airport—you must book a set pick-up time in advance, even though you don't know exactly when your flight will arrive, how long it will take to get your baggage, and so on (the exception is Paris Webservices, which meets you inside the terminal). Hotel-to-airport service takes longer than a taxi because you make several hotel stops, but is a particularly good deal for single travelers or big families. If your hotel doesn't work with a van service, reserve directly (book at least a day in advance—most hoteliers will make the call for you). Airport vans cost about €30 for one person, €43 for two, and €55 for three. Here are a couple of companies to consider: **Paris Shuttles Network** (tel. 01 45 26 01 58, www.shuttlesnetwork.com), **Airport Connection** (tel. 01 43 65 55 55, www.supershuttle.fr), and **Paris Webservices** (meets you inside the terminal, about €160-180 for up to 4 people round-trip, use promo code "RSteves77" and show current edition of this book for 10 percent discount, excursions available—see page 227, sells Museum Passes with no extra fee—order ahead, tel. 01 53 62 02 29, fax 01 53 01 35 84, www.pariswebservices.com, contactpws@pariswebservices.com). They also run vans from the rue Cler area to the airport (€30/one person, €44/2 people).

A Val d'Europe (VEA) **Disneyland shuttle bus** leaves from each terminal (€18, runs every 20 minutes daily 8:30-20:00ish, 30 minutes, www.vea-shuttle.co.uk). TGV trains also run to Disneyland from the airport in 10 minutes, but leave less frequently (hourly) and require shuttle buses at each end—take the shuttle van instead.

Orly Airport

This easy-to-navigate airport feels small, but Orly is good for rental-car pickup and drop-off, as it's closer to Paris and far easier to navigate than Charles de Gaulle Airport.

Transportation Between Orly Airport and Paris: Shuttle buses *(navettes)*, the RER, taxis, and airport vans connect Paris with either terminal.

"Les Cars" Air France bus #1 runs to Gare Montparnasse, Invalides, and Etoile Métro stops, all of which have connections to several Métro lines. Upon request, drivers will also stop at the Porte d'Orléans Métro stop. For the rue Cler neighborhood, take the bus to Invalides, then the Métro to La Tour Maubourg or Ecole Militaire. Buses depart from Ouest arrival level exit B-C or Sud exit L: Look for signs to *navettes* (€11.50 one-way, buy ticket from driver, 10 percent cheaper online, round-trip tickets 20 percent cheaper than two one-way tickets, 4/hour, 40 minutes to Invalides, www.lescarsairfrance.com).

The **Orlybus** goes directly to the Denfert-Rochereau Métro stop. From there, you can catch the Métro or RER-B to central Paris, including the Luxembourg area, Notre-Dame Cathedral, and Gare du Nord. The Orlybus departs from Ouest arrival level exit D and Sud exit H (€6.60, 3/hour, 30 minutes).

A different bus called **"Paris par le train"** takes you to the Pont d'Orly RER station, where you can catch the RER-C to Gare d'Austerlitz, St. Michel/Notre-Dame, Musée d'Orsay, Invalides (change here for rue Cler hotels), and Pont de l'Alma. Catch this bus at Ouest arrival level exit G or Sud exit F (€6.50 total, 4/hour, 40 minutes).

Taxis are outside Ouest arrival level exit B, and to the far right as you leave terminal Sud, at exit M. Allow €40-50 with bags for a taxi into central Paris.

Airport vans are good for single travelers or families of four or more (too many for most taxis) if going from Paris to the airport (see previous page; from Orly, figure about €23/1 person, €30/2 people, less per person for larger groups and kids).

Beauvais Airport

Budget airlines such as Ryanair use this small airport, offering dirt-cheap airfares but leaving you 50 miles north of Paris. Still, this airport has direct buses to Paris (see below), and is handy for travelers heading to Normandy or Belgium (car rental available; airport toll tel. 08 92 68 20 66—lines open daily 8:00-20:00, www.aeroport beauvais.com; Ryanair toll tel. 08 92 78 02 10—lines open Mon-Fri

9:00-19:00, Sat 10:00-17:00, Sun 11:00-17:00, www.ryanair.com).

Transportation Between Beauvais Airport and Paris: Buses depart from the airport when they're full (about 20 minutes after flights arrive) and take 1.5 hours to reach Paris. Buy your ticket (€15 one-way) at the little kiosk to the right as you exit the airport. Buses arrive at Porte Maillot on the west edge of Paris (on Métro line 1 and RER-C). The closest taxi stand is at Hôtel Concorde-Lafayette.

Buses heading to Beauvais Airport leave from Porte Maillot about 3.25 hours before scheduled flight departures. Catch the bus in the parking lot on boulevard Pershing next to Hôtel Concorde-Lafayette. Arrive with enough time to purchase your bus ticket before boarding (*parking* Pershing ticket booth tel. 01 58 05 08 45, airport ticket booth tel. 03 44 11 46 86).

Trains connect Beauvais' city center and Paris' Gare du Nord (20/day, 1.2 hours). To reach Beauvais' train station, take the Beauvais *navette* (€4, 6/day, 30 minutes) or local bus #12 (€1, 12/day, 30 minutes).

Taxis run from Beauvais Airport to Beauvais' train station or city center (€14) or central Paris (allow €125 and 1.25 hours).

The Val d'Europe (VEA) **shuttle bus to Disneyland** runs three times a day from Beauvais via Charles de Gaulle Airport to Disneyland (€30, 2.5 hours).

Versailles

If you've ever wondered why your American passport has French writing in it, you'll find the answer at Versailles (vehr-"sigh")—every king's dream palace. The powerful court of Louis XIV at Versailles set the standard of culture for all of Europe, right up to modern times. Today, if you're planning to visit just one palace in all of Europe, make it Versailles.

Versailles offers three blockbuster sights. The main attraction is the palace itself, called the **Château.** Here you walk through dozens of lavish, chandeliered rooms once inhabited by Louis XIV and his successors. Next come the expansive **Gardens** behind the palace, a landscaped wonderland dotted with statues and fountains. Finally, at the far end of the Gardens, is the pastoral area called the **Trianon Palaces and Domaine de Marie-Antoinette** (a.k.a. Trianon/Domaine), designed for frolicking blue bloods and featuring several small palaces and Marie's Hamlet—perfect for getting away from the mobs at the Château.

In general, allow 1.5 hours each for the Château, the Gardens, and the Trianon/Domaine. Add another two hours for round-trip transit, plus another hour for lunch, and you're looking at an eight-hour day—at the very least.

Visiting Versailles can seem daunting because of its size and hordes of visitors. But if you follow my tips, a trip here during even the busiest times is manageable.

Getting There

By Train: The town of Versailles is 35 minutes southwest of Paris. Take the **RER-C train** (4/hour, 35 minutes one-way, €6.20 round-trip) from any of these Paris RER stops: Gare d'Austerlitz, St. Michel, Musée d'Orsay, Invalides, Pont de l'Alma, or Champ de Mars. You can buy your train ticket at any Métro ticket window in Paris—for no extra cost it will include the connection from that Métro stop to the RER. At the RER station, catch any train listed as "Versailles R.G.," and ride to the last stop.

At the Versailles R.G. train station, exit through the turn-stiles by inserting your ticket. To reach the palace, just follow the crowds: Turn right out of the station, then left at the first boulevard, and walk 10 minutes. To return to Paris, all trains serve all downtown Paris RER stops on the C line.

Versailles has two other train stations—Rive Droite and Chantiers—that are not as useful to travelers (trains run from Paris' Gare St. Lazare to both of these stations).

By Taxi: The 30-minute ride (without traffic) between Versailles and Paris costs about €55.

By Car: Get on the *périphérique* freeway that circles Paris, and take the toll-free A13 autoroute toward Rouen. Exit at Versailles, follow signs to *Versailles Château*, and park in the huge pay lot at place d'Armes (€5.50/2 hours, €10/4 hours, €14.80/8 hours).

Orientation to Versailles

PARIS

Cost: Buy either a Paris Museum Pass or Versailles' "Le Passeport" Pass, both of which give you access to the most important parts of the complex (see "Passes," below).

If you don't get a pass, you can buy individual tickets for each of the three different sections:

• **The Château,** the main palace, costs €15 and includes an audioguide (under 18 free). Your Château ticket includes the famous Hall of Mirrors, the king and queen's living quarters, many lesser rooms, and any temporary exhibitions. For €1 more, you can get a guided tour of the Château—a great deal (see "Guided Tours," later). On the first Sunday of off-season months (Nov-March), entry is free.

• **The Trianon Palaces and Domaine de Marie-Antoinette** cost €10 (no audioguide available, under 18 free).

This ticket gives you access to the far corner of the Gardens, the small palaces called the Grand Trianon and Petit Trianon, the queen's Hamlet, and a smattering of nearby buildings. On the first Sunday of off-season months (Nov-March), entry is free.

• **The Gardens** are free, except when the fountains blast and the price is €8 (weekends April-Oct plus Tue late May-late June; see "Fountain Spectacles in the Gardens," later).

Passes: The following passes can save money and allow you to skip the long ticket-buying lines (though everyone must endure security checks before entering the palaces). Both cover the Château audioguide.

The **Paris Museum Pass** (see page 240) covers the Château and the Trianon/Domaine area (a €25 value) and is the best solution for most, but doesn't include the Gardens on Fountain Spectacle days (you'll have to buy an extra ticket for that).

The **Le Passeport** one-day pass covers your entrance to the Château, the Trianon/Domaine area, and the Gardens, including the weekend Fountain Spectacles. Le Passeport costs €18, or €25 on fountain days.

Buying Passes and Tickets: It's best to buy tickets or passes in advance. They're available at any Paris TI or FNAC department store (small fee), or online at www.chateauversailles.fr (print out your pass/ticket or pick it up near the entrance).

In Versailles, you can get them at the city TI (€2 fee; for TI details, see "Information," later). Your last option is to buy them at the Château ticket-sales office (to the left as you face the palace). Ticket windows may have long lines—avoid the wait by using the ticket machines at the back of the room (you'll need bills).

Hours: The **Château** is open Tue-Sun April-Oct 9:00-18:30, Nov-March 9:00-17:30; closed Mon year-round.

The **Trianon Palaces and Domaine de Marie-Antoinette** are open Tue-Sun April-Oct 12:00-18:30, Nov-March 12:00-17:30; closed Mon year-round (off-season only the two Trianon Palaces are open, not the Hamlet or other outlying buildings).

The **Gardens** are open April-Oct daily 9:00-20:30, but may close earlier for special events; Nov-March Tue-Sun 8:00-18:00, closed Mon.

Last entry to all areas is 30 minutes before closing.

Crowd-Beating Strategies: Versailles can be packed May-Sept 10:00-13:00. Avoid Tuesdays and Sundays, when the place is jammed from open to close. Lines to buy tickets and go through security can be long, and the Château is a slow shuffle of shoulder-to-shoulder tourists.

You can skip the ticket-buying line by using a Paris Museum Pass or Le Passeport, by buying tickets in advance, or by booking a guided tour (see below). Everyone—including holders of advance tickets and passes—must wait in line to go through security (longest lines 10:00-12:00). Before queuing up at the security entrance, check for signs that they might have opened up a special, shorter line for passholders (but don't count on it).

For fewer crowds, go early or late. If you go early, arrive by 9:00 (when the palace opens), and tour the Château first, then the Gardens. If you arrive later, tour the Gardens first (remembering that the Trianon/Domaine area doesn't open until noon), then visit the Château after 13:00 when crowds dissipate.

Pickpockets: Assume pickpockets are working the tourist crowds.

Information: Before you go, check their excellent website for updates and special events—www.chateauversailles.fr. The palace's general contact number is tel. 01 30 83 78 00. Versailles has two information offices. You'll pass the city TI on your walk from the RER station to the palace—it's just past the Pullman Hôtel (daily 9:00-19:00, tel. 01 39 24 88 88). The information office at the Château is on the left side of the courtyard as you face the Château (WCs, toll tel. 08 10 81 16 14). Pick up the free, useful map just inside the Château.

Guided Tours: The 1.5-hour English guided tour gives you access to a few extra rooms (the line-up varies) and lets you skip ticket-buying lines if you come *sans* pass. Ignore the tours hawked as you leave the train station. Book at the guided-tours office in the Château courtyard—it's to your right as you approach the palace (look for *Visites Conferences* signs). Reserve immediately upon arrival, since tours can sell out by 13:00 (€16 includes palace entry—just €1 more than entry alone, €7 if you have pass; tours run about every 45 minutes 9:00-15:00).

Audioguide Tours: A free audioguide to the Château is included in your admission (pick up just inside the palace, return as you leave).

You can download a free Rick Steves audio tour of Versailles; see page 7. Other podcasts and digital tours are available in the "multimedia" section at www.chateauversailles.fr.

The palace audioguide and Rick Steves' audio tour complement one another: Eager students can easily transfer earbuds between devices and listen to both tours as you shuffle through the lavish rooms.

Versailles

PARIS

500 METERS
500 YARDS

ROUTE DE ST CYR (N-10)

GRAND CANAL

PETIT CAN

BOAT RENTAL

REST.

WC

APOLLO BASIN

GAR DE

TAPIS VERT

ROADS & PATHS

SUGGESTED ROUTE

P PARKING

VIEW

COLONNADE

WC

WC & SNACK KIOSK

LATO BASI

ORANGERIE

GOLF-CART RENTAL

TRAM STOP

CHATEAU

KING'S VEGETABLE GARDEN

PLACE D'ARMES

AVE. ST

ST. LOUIS

SATORY

STABLES

AVE. DE GAULLE

AVE. SCEAUX

AVE. DE L'EUROPE

RER TRAIN STATION
(RIVE GAUCHE)

AVE. DE PARIS

TO PARIS

T

TRIANON PALACES +
DOMAINE DE
MARIE-
ANTOINETTE

WALL

AL

Grand
Trianon

French
Pavilion

MAIN
ENTRY

TRAM
STOPS

WC

Petit
Trianon

The
Hamlet

BIKE +
GOLF CART
RENTAL

AVE. DE Trianon

Temple
of Love

NS

BIKE
RENTAL

NAN

BLVD.

WALKING TIMES
Train Station to Château = 10 min.
Château to Grand Trianon = 30 min.
Grand Trianon to the Hamlet = 15 min.
Trianon/Domaine to Place du Marché = 40 min.

Neptune Basin

DE

CARNOT

PLACE
HOCHE

RUE DE LA PAROISSES

NOTRE DAME

LA

PLACE DU
MARCHE

CLOUD

O   W   N

REINE

Rive Droite Train Stn.

TO PARIS
(St. Lazare Stn.)

PARIS

Baggage Check: To enter the Château and the two Trianons, you must use the free baggage check if you have large bags or baby strollers (use a baby backpack or hire a babysitter for the day). You must retrieve your bags one hour before closing.

Services: Reminiscent of the days when dukes urinated behind the potted palm trees, WCs at the Château are tricky to find, and some come with long lines. There are WCs on either side of the Château courtyard (in the ticket-sales office and in the guided-tours office), immediately upon entering the Château (Entrance H), and near the exit from the Dauphin's Apartments. You'll also find WCs near the Grand Café d'Orléans, in the Gardens near the Latona Basin, at the Grand Canal, in the Grand Trianon and Petit Trianon, and at several other places scattered around the grounds. Any café generally has a WC.

Photography: Allowed, but no flash indoors.

Cuisine Art: To the left of the Château's golden Royal Gate entrance, the Grand Café d'Orléans has a restaurant (€13 salads, €20 *plats*) and a take-out bar (€5 sandwiches, great for picnicking in the Gardens). In the Gardens, you'll find several restaurants, cafés, and snack stands. Most are located near the Latona Fountain (less crowded) and in a delightful cluster at the Grand Canal (more crowds and more choices, including two restaurants).

In **town,** restaurants are on the street to the right of the parking lot (as you face the Château). Handy McDonald's and Starbucks (both with WCs) are across from the train station. The best choices are on the lively place du Marché Notre-Dame in the town center.

Fountain Spectacles in the Gardens: On spring and summer weekends, the Gardens charge a mandatory admission fee for these spectacles. Loud classical music fills the king's backyard, and the Gardens' fountains are in full squirt. Louis XIV had his engineers literally reroute a river to fuel these gushers. Even by today's standards, they are impressive.

The fountains run April-Oct Sat-Sun 11:00-12:00 & 15:30-17:30, with the finale 17:20-17:30. They also perform Tue late May-late June 11:00-12:00 & 14:30-16:00. On these "spray days," the Gardens cost €8. (Pay at the Gardens entrance; covered by Le Passeport but not Paris Museum Pass.) The calendar of spectacles also includes a few music-only days (on the rare Tue, €8) and elaborate sound-and-light displays on Sat June-Aug at 21:00 (€22). Check the Versailles website for what's happening during your visit.

Starring: Luxurious palaces, endless gardens, Louis XIV, Marie-Antoinette, and the *ancien régime.*

Overview

On this self-guided tour, we'll see the Château, the landscaped Gardens in the "backyard," and the Trianon Palaces and Domaine de Marie-Antoinette, located at the far end of the Gardens. If your time is limited or you don't enjoy walking, skip the Trianon/Domaine, which is a 40-minute hike from the Château.

In the Château, the highlights are the State Apartments of the King and Queen and the Hall of Mirrors.

Self-Guided Tour

This commentary, which leads you through the various attractions at Versailles, covers just the basics. For a detailed room-by-room rundown, consider *Rick Steves' Paris* (buy in the US or at any of the English-language bookstores in Paris listed earlier in this chapter) or the guidebook called *The Châteaux, the Gardens, and Trianon* (sold at Versailles).

Stand in the huge courtyard and face the palace, or Château. The original golden Royal Gate in the center of the courtyard, nearly 260 feet long and decorated with 100,000 gold leaves, is a recent replica of the original. The ticket-buying office is to the left; guided-tour sales are to the right. The entrance to the Château (once you have your ticket or pass) is through the modern concrete-and-glass security checkpoint, marked Entrance A.

After passing through security at Entrance A, you spill out into the open-air courtyard inside the golden Royal Gate. Enter the Château from the courtyard at Entrance H—the State Apartments. Once inside, there's an info desk (get a free map), WCs, and free audioguides.

The Château: The one-way walk through the palace leads you past the dazzling 700-seat **Royal Opera House;** by the intimate, two-tiered **Royal Chapel;** and through the glamorous **State Apartments.** In the **King's Wing** you'll see a billiard room, a royal make-out room, the Swiss bodyguard room, Louis' official bedroom, his grand throne room (the **Apollo Room**—with a 10-foot-tall canopied throne), and his war rooms.

Next you'll visit the magnificent **Hall of Mirrors**—250 feet long, with 17 arched mirrors matching 17 windows looking out upon royal garden views. The mirrors—a luxury at the time—reflect an age when beautiful people loved to look at themselves. In another age altogether, this was the room in which the Treaty of Versailles was signed, ending World War I.

You'll finish in the **Queen's Wing,** where you'll see the Queen's bedchamber, the guard room where Louis XVI and Marie-Antoinette surrendered to the Revolution, and Napoleon's coronation room.

Versailles Château—
Ground Floor & Entrances

GARDENS

■ 6

■ 5
← TO
ORANGERIE

TO
TRIANON
PALACES +
DOMAINE DE
MARIE-
ANTOINETTE

MESDAMES
APARTMENTS

TO
GARDENS
↑

■ 4

DAUPHIN'S
APARTMENTS
WC

● 3

INFO
DESK

Ⓗ

TO
FIRST FLOOR →

ROYAL

WC

WC

GRAND
CAFE
D'ORLEANS

COURTYARD

CHAPEL

ACCESS
TO
GARDENS

Ⓐ

TICKET
SALES   WC
ℹ   ● 1

← ROYAL GATE

CHATEAU
ENTRANCE

❷ GUIDED
TOURS
■ WC

↑
FROM TRAIN STATION

DCH

❶ Chateau Ticket & Pass Sales
❷ Guided-Tour Reservations
❸ Exit from State Apartments
❹ Fountain Spectacles Tickets
❺ Golf-Cart Rental
❻ Petit Train (Tram)

••• Self-Guided Tour

PARIS

Getting Around the Gardens: It's a 40-minute **walk** from the palace, down to the Grand Canal, past the two Trianon palaces, to the Hamlet at the far end of Domaine de Marie-Antoinette. Allow more time if you stop along the way. After enduring the slow Château shuffle, stretching your legs out here feels pretty good.

There's a **bike rental** station by the Grand Canal. A bike won't save you that much time (you can't take it inside the grounds of the Trianon/Domaine; park it near an entrance while you tour inside). Instead, simply enjoy pedaling around the greatest royal park in all of Europe (€6.50/hour or €15/half-day, kid-size bikes and tandems available).

The fast-looking, slow-moving *petit train* (tram) leaves from behind the Château (north side). It stops at the Grand Canal, and at the Grand and Petit Trianons (two of the entrance points to the Trianon/Domaine). You can hop on and off as you like (€7 day pass, €3.50 single trip, pay driver, free for kids under 11, 4/hour).

Another option is to rent a **golf cart** for a fun drive through the Gardens. You can't drive it in the Trianon/Domaine, but you can park it outside the entrance while you sightsee inside (€30/hour, rent down by the canal or at Orangerie side of palace).

Palace Gardens: The Gardens offer a world of royal amusements. The warmth from the Sun King was so great that he could even grow orange trees in chilly France. Louis XIV had a thousand of these to amaze his visitors. In winter they were kept in the greenhouses (beneath your feet) that surround the courtyard. On sunny days, they were wheeled out in their silver planters and scattered around the grounds.

With the palace behind you, it seems as if the grounds stretch out forever. Versailles was laid out along an eight-mile axis that included the grounds, the palace, and the town of Versailles itself, one of the first instances of urban planning since Roman times and a model for future capitals, such as Washington, D.C., and Brasilia. A promenade leads from the palace to the Grand Canal, where France's royalty floated up and down in imported Venetian gondolas.

Trianon Palaces and Domaine de Marie-Antoinette: Versailles began as an escape from the pressures of kingship. But in a short time, the Château had become as busy as Paris ever was. Louis XIV needed an escape from his escape and built a smaller palace out in the boonies. Later, his successors retreated still farther from the Château and French political life, ignoring the real world that was crumbling all around them. They expanded the Trianon area, building a fantasy world of palaces and pleasure gardens—the enclosure called Marie-Antoinette's Domaine.

The beautifully restored **Grand Trianon Palace** is as sumptuous as the main palace, but much smaller. With its pastel-pink colonnade and more human scale, this is a place you'd like to call home. Nearby are the **French Pavilion,** Marie-Antoinette's **Theater,** and the octagonal **Belvedere** palace.

You can almost see princesses bobbing gaily in the branches as you walk through the enchanting forest, past the white marble **Temple of Love** to the queen's fake-peasant **Hamlet** *(le Hameau).* Marie-Antoinette's happiest days were spent at the Hamlet, under a bonnet, tending her perfumed sheep and manicured gardens in a thatch-happy wonderland.

Despite her bad reputation with the public, Marie-Antoinette was a sweet girl from Vienna who never quite fit in with the fast, sophisticated crowd at Versailles. She made the **Petit Trianon,** a masterpiece of Neoclassical architecture, a place to get away and re-create the simple home life she remembered from her childhood. Here she played, while in the cafés of faraway Paris, revolutionaries plotted the end of the *ancien régime*.

PARIS

PROVENCE

This magnificent region is shaped like a giant wedge of quiche. From its sunburned crust, fanning out along the Mediterranean coast from the Camargue to Marseille, it stretches north along the Rhône Valley to Orange. The Romans were here in force and left many ruins—some of the best anywhere. Seven popes, artists such as Vincent van Gogh and Paul Cézanne, and author Peter Mayle all enjoyed their years in Provence. This destination features a splendid recipe of arid climate, oceans of vineyards, dramatic scenery, lively cities, and adorable hill-capping villages.

Explore France's greatest Roman ruin, the Pont du Gard aqueduct. Admire the skill of ball-tossing *boules* players in small squares in every Provençal village and city. Spend a few Van Gogh-inspired starry, starry nights in Arles. Youthful but classy Avignon bustles in the shadow of its brooding Palace of the Popes.

Planning Your Time

Make Arles or Avignon your sightseeing base—particularly if you have no car. Italophiles prefer smaller Arles, while poodles pick urban Avignon. Arles has a blue-collar quality; the entire city feels like Van Gogh's bedroom. Avignon—double the size of Arles—feels sophisticated, with more nightlife and shopping, and makes a good base for non-drivers thanks to its convenient public-transit options.

When budgeting your time, you'll want a full day for sightseeing in Arles (best on Wed or Sat, when it's market day); a half-day for Avignon; and a day or two for the villages and sights in the countryside. Pont du Gard is a 50-minute bus ride west of Avignon.

Public Transportation in Provence

RAIL
T.G.V. RAIL
BUS
BOAT
AIRPORTS (NOT ALL SHOWN)

TO LYON & PARIS

NOT TO SCALE

MONTELIMAR

NYONS

BUIS

VAISON LA ROMAINE

ORANGE

CHATEAUNEUF-DU-PAPE

PONT DU GARD

UZES

AVIGNON

ISLE-SUR-LA-SORGUE

ROUSSILLON

AVIGNON T.G.V.

CAV.

APT

NIMES

LUBERON

LOURMARIN

TARASCON

ST. REMY

TO MONTPELIER CARCASSONNE & BARCELONA (SPAIN)

LES BAUX

ARLES

CAMARGUE

AIX EN-PROVENCE

AIGUES MORTES

AIX T.G.V.

TO NICE

TOULON

STES MARIES

MARSEILLE

LA CIOTAT

LES CALANQUES

CASSIS

MEDITERRENEAN SEA

DCH

PROVENCE

Getting Around Provence

By Bus or Train: Public transit is good between cities and decent to some towns, but marginal at best to the smaller villages. Frequent trains link Avignon and Arles (no more than 30 minutes between each). From Avignon, you can bus to Pont du Gard.

By Car: The region is made to order for a car. The yellow Michelin maps #332 (Luberon and Côtes du Rhône) and #340 (Arles area) are worth considering; the larger-scale orange Michelin map #527 also includes the Riviera. Avignon (pop. 110,000) is a headache for drivers. Arles (pop. 52,000) is easier but still challenging. Be wary of thieves: Park only in well-monitored spaces and leave nothing valuable in your car.

Tours of Provence

Wine Safari—Dutchman Mike Rijken runs a one-man show, taking travelers through the region he adopted more than 20 years ago. Mike came to France to train as a chef, later became a wine steward, and has now found his calling as a driver/guide. His English is fluent, and though his focus is on wine and wine villages, Mike knows the region thoroughly and is a good teacher of its history (€60/half-day, €110/day, priced per person, group size varies from 2 to 6; pickups possible in Arles, Avignon, Lyon, Marseille, or Aix-en-Provence; tel. 04 90 35 59 21, mobile 06 19 29 50 81, www.winesafari.net, mikeswinesafari@wanadoo.fr).

Local Guides—**Celine Viany** is a retired wine sommelier turned charming tour guide. She's an easy-to-be-with expert on her region and its chief product (tel. 04 90 46 90 80, mobile 06 76 59 56 30, www.levinalabouche.com, contact@degustation-levinalabouche.com). Art historian **Daniela Wedel** eagerly shares her passion for the history, food, wine, and people of Avignon and the surrounding area (Aix-en-Provence, the Luberon, Arles, Marseille), and organizes personalized excursions for her clients (approximately €160/half-day, €270/day, price varies depending on itinerary and number of people, mobile 06 43 86 30 83, daniela@treasure-europe.com).

Avignon Wine Tour—For a playful and distinctly French perspective on wines of the Côtes du Rhône region, contact François Marcou, who runs his tours with passion and energy, offering different itineraries every day (€75/person for all-day wine tours that include 4-5 tastings, €350 for private groups, mobile 06 28 05 33 84, www.avignon-wine-tour.com, avignon.wine.tour@modulonet.fr).

Imagine Tours—Unlike most tour operators, this nonprofit organization focuses on cultural excursions, offering low-key, personalized tours that allow visitors to discover the "true heart of Provence and Occitania." The itineraries are adapted to your interests, and the guides will meet you at your hotel or the departure point of your choice (€170/half-day, €295/day, prices are for up to 4 people starting from the region around Avignon or Arles, mobile 06 89 22 19 87, fax 04 90 24 84 26, www.imagine-tours.net, imagine.tours@gmail.com). They are also happy to help you plan your itinerary, book hotel rooms, or address other traveler issues.

Wine Uncovered—Passionate and engaging Englishman Olivier Hickman takes small groups on focused tours of selected wineries in Châteauneuf-du-Pape and in the villages near Vaison la Romaine. Olivier is serious about French wine and knows his subject matter inside and out. His in-depth tastings include a half-day tour of two or three wineries—the Châteauneuf-du-Pape tour is especially popular. If you need transportation, he can help arrange

Provence

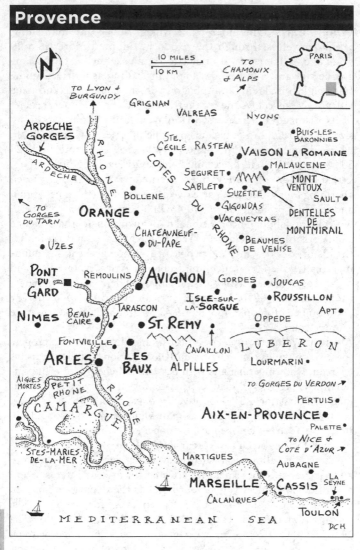

PROVENCE

it (€55/person, minimum 2 people, see website for full- and multiple-day rates, mobile 06 75 10 10 01, www.wine-uncovered.com, olivier.hickman@wine-uncovered.com).

Visit Provence—This company runs day tours from Avignon and Arles. Tours from Avignon run year-round and include a great variety of destinations; tours from Arles run April through September only and are more limited (check their website for current destinations). While these tours provide introductory commentary to what you'll see, there is no guiding at the actual sights.

They use eight-seat, air-conditioned minivans (about €60-80/half-day, €100-120/day; they'll pick you up at your hotel in Avignon or at the main TI in Arles). Ask about their cheaper big-bus excursions, or consider hiring a van and driver for your private use (plan on €220/half-day, €490/day, tel. 04 90 14 70 00, www.provence-reservation.com).

Madeleine's Culinary and Active Adventures—Madeleine Vedel, an effervescent American expat, plans small group tours from Avignon and Arles to visit food artisans and wineries. Madeleine also leads kid-friendly hikes in the countryside (€400/day for a full day with winery visits, less if no wineries, flat rate for 1-5 people; mobile 06 88 50 03 62, www.cuisineprovencale.com).

Arles

By helping Julius Caesar defeat Marseille, Arles (pronounced "arl") earned the imperial nod and was made an important port city. With the first bridge over the Rhône River, Arles was a key stop on the Roman road from Italy to Spain, the Via Domitia. After reigning as the seat of an important archbishop and a trading center for centuries, the city became a sleepy backwater of little importance in the 1700s. Vincent van Gogh settled here in the late 1800s, but left only a chunk of his ear (now long gone). American bombers destroyed much of Arles in World War II as the townsfolk hid out in its underground Roman galleries. But today Arles thrives again, with its evocative Roman ruins, an eclectic assortment of museums, made-for-ice-cream pedestrian zones, and squares that play hide-and-seek with visitors.

The city's unpolished streets and squares are not to everyone's taste. This workaday city has not sold out to tourism, so you won't see dolled-up lanes and perfectly preserved buildings. But to me, that's part of its charm.

Orientation to Arles

Arles faces the Mediterranean, turning its back on Paris. And though the town is built along the Rhône, it largely ignores the river. Landmarks hide in Arles' medieval tangle of narrow, winding streets. Virtually everything is close—but first-timers can walk forever to get there. Hotels have good, free city maps, and Arles provides helpful street-corner signs that point you toward sights and hotels. Speeding cars enjoy Arles' medieval lanes, turning sidewalks into tightropes and pedestrians into leaping targets.

PROVENCE

Arles

← Van Gogh Walking Tour

P Parking

B Bus Stop

◄ View

♙ Easel

100 YARDS

100 METERS

<u>Van Gogh Sights</u>

1 Place Lamartine (Easel)

2 Starry Night over the Rhône (Easel)

3 Place du Forum & Café at Night (Easel)

4 Espace Van Gogh (Easel)

5 Fondation Van Gogh

<u>Other</u>

6 Baggage Storage & Bike Rental

7 Launderette

8 To Avis Car Rental

9 Europcar Car Rental

10 Hertz Car Rental

11 Le Petit Train Departure Point

12 Bus #1 (to Ancient History Museum)

13 Cryptoporticos

TRINQUETAILLE BRIDGE

MARX

TRUCHET

QUAI

RUE

DR. FANTON

5 FOND. V.G.

RUE A. FRANCE

R. JOUVE   R. LIBERTE

TO ANCIENT HISTORY MUSEUM

ARLATEN FOLK MUSEUM (REOPENS IN 2013)

RUE GAMBETTA

REPUB-

ESPACE VAN GOGH

4

RUE   MOLIERE   R.

12 **B**

TO ANCIENT HISTORY MUSEUM ←   BLVD.

BUS STN.

DCH

TO
TRAIN
STATION
& ❽

TO LES BAUX,
FONTVIEILLE,
AVIGNON & ❾

AVE. STALIN.

MONOPRIX

❷

PLACE
LAMAR-
TINE ❶

PETANQUE

GATE

R H O N E

QUAI LAMARTINE

RUE JOUVEAU

RUE CAVALERIE

BLVD. JULES FERRY

BALZAC

EMILE COMBES

❻

R. L. BLUM

PLACE
VOLTAIRE

R. CONDORCET

REATTU
MUSEUM

DORMOY

RUE DU GRAND PRIEURE

RUE

SAUVAGE

RUE DE HOTEL DE VILLE

RUE DU QUATRE SEPT.

GRILLE

R. BARBES

R. AMPH.

RASPAIL

VOLTAIRE

R. TARDIEU

RUE PORTAGNEL

DU FOUR

R. REFUGE

❼

❿

SUISSES

BALE

FAURE

BAST.

ENTER

ROMAN
ARENA

NOTRE
DAME

PLACE
DU ❸
FORUM

RUE DES ARENES

R. NIC.

R. DIDEROT

R. BALZE

ST.
TROPHIME ❼

❶❸ ■WC

PLACE
REPUBL-
IQUE

LIQUE

ROTONDE

JAURES

RUE CALADE

DU CLOITRE

PORTE DE LAURE

ANCIENT
CITY
WALLS

EMILE COMBES

CLASSICAL
THEATER

CLOISTERS

RUE

JARDIN
D'ETE

MONTEE VAUBAN

BLVD.

V. HUGO

DES ❶❶

LICES

POST
& TAXIS

P

PLAYGROUND

R. E. FASSIN

TO LES AYLSCAMPS
CEMETERY

PROVENCE

Tourist Information

The **main TI** is on the ring road boulevard des Lices, at esplanade Charles de Gaulle (April-Sept daily 9:00-18:45; Oct-March Mon-Sat 9:00-16:45, Sun 10:00-13:00; tel. 04 90 18 41 20, www.arlestourisme.com). There's also a **train station TI** (Mon-Fri 9:00-13:30 & 14:30-16:45, closed Sat-Sun).

At either TI, pick up the city map, note the bus schedules (displayed in binders—ask for the schedule you need), and get English information on nearby destinations such as the Camargue wildlife area. Ask about "bullgames" (Provence's more humane version of bullfights—see page 374) and walking tours of Arles. Skip the useless €1 brochure describing several walks in Arles, including one that locates Van Gogh's "easels." Both TIs can help you reserve hotel rooms (credit card required for deposit).

Arrival in Arles

By Train: The train station is on the river, a 10-minute walk from the town center. Before heading into town, get what you need at the train station TI. There's no baggage storage at the station, but you can walk 10 minutes to stow it at Hôtel Régence (see "Helpful Hints," later).

To reach the town center, turn left out of the train station and walk 15 minutes; or wait for the free Navia bus at the shelter across the street (3/hour, Mon-Sat only). Taxis usually wait in front of the station, but if you don't see any, call the posted telephone numbers, or dial 04 89 73 36 00. If the train station TI is open, you can ask them to call. Taxi rates are fixed—allow about €10 to any of my recommended hotels.

By Bus: All buses stop at the Centre-Ville bus station, a few blocks below the main TI, on the ring road at 16-24 boulevard Georges Clemenceau.

By Car: Most hotels have parking nearby—ask for detailed directions (€1.50/hour at most meters, free 12:00-14:00 & 19:00-9:00). For most hotels, first follow signs to *Centre-Ville*, then *Gare SNCF* (train station). You'll come to a big roundabout (place Lamartine) with a Monoprix department store to the right. You can park along the city wall and find your hotel on foot; the hotels I list are no more than a 10-minute walk away (best not to park here overnight due to theft concerns and markets on Wed and Sat). Fearless drivers can plunge into the narrow streets between the two stumpy towers via rue de la Calade, and follow signs to their hotel. Again, theft is a problem—leave nothing in your car, and trust your hotelier's advice on where to park.

If you can't find parking near your hotel, Parking des Lices (Arles' only parking garage), near the TI on boulevard des Lices, is a good fallback (€3/hour, €9/24 hours).

Helpful Hints

Market Days: The big markets are on Wednesdays and Saturdays.

Crowds: An international photo event jams hotels the second weekend of July. The let-'er-rip, twice-yearly Féria draws crowds over Easter and in mid-September (see www.arles tourisme.com for dates).

Internet Access: Internet cafés in Arles change with the wind. Ask your hotelier or at the TI. You're most likely to find free Wi-Fi at the cafés near the main TI along boulevard des Lices.

Baggage Storage and Bike Rental: The recommended **Hôtel Régence** will store your bags for €3 (daily 7:30-22:00 mid-March-mid-Nov, closed in winter, 5 rue Marius Jouveau). They also rent bikes (€7/half-day, €14/day, one-way rentals within Provence possible, same hours as baggage storage) and may have electric bikes—ask.

Laundry: There's a launderette at 12 rue Portagnel (daily 7:00-21:30, you can stay later to finish if you're already inside, English instructions).

Car Rental: Avis is at the train station (tel. 04 90 96 82 42); **Europcar** and **Hertz** are downtown (Europcar is at 61 boulevard Stalingrad, tel. 04 90 93 23 24; Hertz is closer to place Lamartine at 10 boulevard Emile Combes, tel. 04 90 96 75 23).

Local Guide: Charming **Jacqueline Neujean,** an excellent guide, knows Arles and nearby sights intimately and loves her work (€90/2 hours, tel. & fax 04 90 98 47 51).

English Book Exchange: A small exchange is available at the recommended **Soleileis** ice-cream shop.

Public Pools: Arles has three public pools (indoor and outdoor). Ask at the TI or your hotel.

Boules: The local "*boul*ing alley" is by the river on place Lamartine. After their afternoon naps, the old boys congregate here for a game of *pétanque*.

Getting Around Arles

In this flat city, everything's within **walking** distance. Only the Ancient History Museum requires a healthy walk (or you can take a taxi or bus). The elevated riverside promenade provides Rhône views and a direct route to the Ancient History Museum (to the southwest) and the train station (to the northeast). Keep your head up for *Starry Night* memories, but eyes down for decorations by dogs with poorly trained owners.

Arles' **taxis** charge a set fee of about €10, but nothing except the Ancient History Museum is worth a taxi ride. To call a cab, dial 04 89 73 36 00 or 04 90 96 90 03.

The free **Navia minibus** circles the town (3/hour, Mon-Sat only), but is only useful for access to the train station.

Le Petit Train d'Arles, a typical tourist train, gives you the lay of the land—if you prefer sitting to walking (€7, 35 minutes, stops in front of the main TI and at the Roman Arena).

Sights in Arles

Most sights cost €3.50-7, and though any sight warrants a few minutes, many aren't worth their individual admission price. The TI sells two different monument passes (called Passeports). **Le Passeport Avantage** covers almost all of Arles' sights (€13.50, under 18-€12); **Le Passeport Liberté** (€9) lets you choose any five monuments (one must be a museum). Depending on your interests, the €9 Passeport is probably best.

Start at the Ancient History Museum (closed Tue) for a helpful overview (drivers should try to do this museum on their way into Arles), then dive into the city-center sights. Remember, many sights stop selling tickets 30-60 minutes before closing (both before lunch and at the end of the day).

▲▲Ancient History Museum (Musée de l'Arles et de la Provence Antiques)

Begin your town visit here, for Roman Arles 101. Located on the site of the Roman chariot racecourse (the arc of which is built into the parking lot), this air-conditioned, all-on-one-floor museum is just west of central Arles along the river. Models and original sculptures (with almost no posted English translations but a decent handout) re-create the Roman city, making workaday life and culture easier to imagine.

Cost and Hours: €6, Wed-Mon April-Oct 9:00-19:00, Nov-March 10:00-18:00, closed Tue year-round, presqu'île du Cirque Romain.

Information: Ask for the English booklet, which provides a helpful if not in-depth background on the collection, and inquire whether there are any free English tours (usually daily July-Sept at 17:00, 1.5 hours). Tel. 04 90 18 88 88, www.arles-antique.cg13.fr.

Getting There: To reach the museum on foot from the city center (a 20-minute **walk**), turn left at the river and take the riverside path to the big, blue, modern building. As you approach the museum, you'll pass the verdant Hortus Garden—designed to recall the Roman circus and chariot racecourse that were located here, and to give residents a place to gather and celebrate civic events. A **taxi** ride costs €10 (museum can call a taxi for your

PROVENCE

return). **Bus #1** gets you within a few minutes' walk (€0.80, 3/hour Mon-Sat, none Sun). Catch the bus in Arles (clockwise direction on boulevard des Lices), then get off at the Musée de l'Arles Antique stop (before the stop, you'll see the bright-blue museum ahead on the right). Turn left as you step off the bus, and follow the sidewalk. (To return to the city center, the bus stop is across the street from where you got off.)

◐ **Self-Guided Tour:** A huge **map** of the Roman Arles region greets visitors and shows the key Roman routes accessible to Arles. Find the impressive row of pagan and early-Christian **sarcophagi** (from the second to fifth centuries). These would have lined the Via Aurelia outside the town wall. In the early days of the Church, Jesus was often portrayed beardless and as the good shepherd, with a lamb over his shoulder.

Next you'll see **models** of every Roman structure in (and near) Arles. These are the highlight for me, as they breathe life into the buildings as they looked 2,000 years ago. Start with the model of Roman Arles, and imagine the city's splendor. Find the Forum—still the center of town today, though only two columns survive. Look at the space Romans devoted to their arena and huge racecourse—a reminder that an emphasis on sports is not unique to modern civilizations. The model also illustrates how little Arles seems to have changed over two millennia, with its houses still clustered around the city center, and warehouses still located on the opposite side of the river.

Look for individual models of the major buildings shown in the city model: the elaborately elegant forum; the floating bridge that gave Arles a strategic advantage (over the widest, and therefore slowest, part of the river); the theater (with its magnificent stage wall); the arena (with its movable stadium cover to shelter spectators from sun or rain); and the circus, or chariot racecourse. Part of the original racecourse was just outside the windows, and though long gone, it must have resembled Rome's Circus Maximus in its day—its obelisk is now the centerpiece of Arles' place de la République.

Finally, check out the model of the hydraulic mill of Barbegal, with its 16 waterwheels and eight grain mills cascading down a nearby hillside.

Other rooms in the museum display pottery, jewelry, metal and glass artifacts, and well-crafted mosaic floors that illustrate how Roman Arles was a city of art and culture. The many **statues** that you see are all original, except for the greatest—the *Venus of Arles*, which Louis XIV took a liking to and had moved to Versailles. It's now in the Louvre—and, as locals say, "When it's in Paris...bye-bye."

PROVENCE

In Central Arles

Ideally, visit these sights in the order listed below. I've included some walking directions to connect the dots (see the Arles map on page 364).

▲▲**Forum Square (Place du Forum)**—Named for the Roman forum that once stood here, place du Forum was the political and religious center of Roman Arles. Still lively, this café-crammed square is a local watering hole and popular for a *pastis* (anise-based apéritif). The bistros on the square, though no place for a fine dinner, can put together a good-enough salad or *plat du jour*—and when you sprinkle on the ambience, that's €12 well spent.

At the corner of Grand Hôtel Nord-Pinus (a favorite of Pablo Picasso), a plaque shows how the Romans built a foundation of galleries to make the main square level in order to compensate for Arles' slope down to the river. The two columns are all that survive from the upper story of the entry to the Forum. Steps leading to the entrance are buried—the Roman street level was about 20 feet below you (you can get a glimpse of it by peeking through the street-level openings under the Hôtel d'Arlatan, two blocks below place du Forum on rue du Sauvage). To see the underground arches, visit the Cryptoporticos (see next page).

The statue on the square is of **Frédéric Mistral** (1830-1914). This popular poet, who wrote in the local dialect rather than in French, was a champion of Provençal culture. After receiving the Nobel Prize in Literature in 1904, Mistral used his prize money to preserve and display the folk identity of Provence. He founded the regional folk museum (the Arlaten Folk Museum, described later) at a time when France was rapidly centralizing. (The local mistral wind—literally "master"—has nothing to do with his name.)

The **bright-yellow café**—called Café la Nuit—was the subject of one of Vincent van Gogh's most famous works in Arles. Although his painting showed the café in a brilliant yellow from the glow of gas lamps, the facade was bare limestone, just like the other cafés on this square. The café's current owners have painted it to match Van Gogh's version...and to cash in on the Vincent-crazed hordes who pay too much to eat or drink here.

• *Walk a block uphill (past Grand Hôtel Nord Pinus) and turn left. Walk through the Hôtel de Ville's vaulted entry (or take the next right if it's closed), and pop out onto the big...*

Republic Square (Place de la République)—This square used to be called "place Royale"...until the French Revolution. The obelisk was the former centerpiece of Arles' Roman Circus. The lions at its base are the symbol of the city, whose slogan is (roughly) "the gentle lion." Find a seat and watch the peasants—pilgrims, locals, and street musicians. There's nothing new about this scene.

• *Return to the Hôtel de Ville (where you came in) and look for the entrance to...*

Cryptoporticos (Cryptoportiques)—This dark, drippy underworld of Roman arches was constructed to support Forum Square. Two thousand years ago, most of this gallery of arches was at or above street level—modern Arles has buried about 20 feet of its history over the millennia. Pick up the minimalist English flier and read it before you descend into the dark.

Cost and Hours: €3.50, daily May-Sept 9:00-12:00 & 14:00-19:00, March-April and Oct 9:00-12:00 & 14:00-18:00, Nov-Feb 10:00-12:00 & 14:00-17:00.

• *Just outside the Hôtel de Ville, find...*

▲▲**St. Trophime Church**—Named after a third-century bishop of Arles, this church sports the finest Romanesque main entrance I've seen anywhere.

Cost and Hours: Church—free, daily April-Sept 9:00-12:00 & 14:00-18:30, Oct-March 9:00-12:00 & 14:00-17:00; cloisters—€3.50, daily March-Oct 9:00-18:00, Nov-Feb 10:00-17:00.

❂ **Self-Guided Tour:** Like a Roman triumphal arch, the church facade trumpets the promise of Judgment Day. The tympanum (the semicircular area above the door) is filled with Christian symbolism. Christ sits in majesty, surrounded by symbols of the four evangelists: Matthew (the winged man), Mark (the winged lion), Luke (the ox), and John (the eagle). The 12 apostles are lined up below Jesus. It's Judgment Day...some are saved and others aren't. Notice the condemned (on the right)—a chain gang doing a sad bunny-hop over the fires of hell. For them, the tune trumpeted by the three angels above Christ is not a happy one. Below the chain gang, St. Stephen is being stoned to death, with his soul leaving through his mouth and instantly being welcomed by angels. Ride the exquisite detail back to a simpler age. In an illiterate medieval world, long before the vivid images of our Technicolor time, this was a neon billboard over the town square.

Interior: Just inside the door on the right, a chart locates the interior highlights and helps explain the carvings you just saw on the tympanum.

Tour the church counterclockwise. The tall 12th-century Romanesque nave is decorated by a set of tapestries showing scenes from the life of Mary (17th century, from the French town of Aubusson). Amble around the Gothic apse. Two-thirds of the way around, find the relic chapel behind the ornate wrought iron gate, with its fine golden boxes that hold long-venerated bones of obscure saints. As you exit, look for the early-Christian sarcophagus from Roman Arles (dated about A.D. 300). The heads were lopped off during the French Revolution.

This church is a stop on the ancient pilgrimage route to

Santiago de Compostela in northwest Spain. For 800 years pilgrims on their way to Santiago have paused here...and they still do today. Notice the modern-day pilgrimages advertised on the far right near the church's entry.

Cloisters: Leaving the church, turn left, then left again through a courtyard to enter the adjacent cloisters.

The cloisters are worth a look only if you have a pass (big cleaning under way, enter at the far end of the courtyard). The many small columns were scavenged from the ancient Roman theater. Enjoy the sculpted capitals, the rounded 12th-century Romanesque arches, and the pointed 14th-century Gothic ones. The pretty vaulted hall exhibits 17th-century tapestries showing scenes from the First Crusade to the Holy Land. On the second floor, you'll walk along an angled rooftop designed to catch rainwater—notice the slanted gutter that channeled the water into a cistern and the heavy roof slabs covering the tapestry hall below.

• *Turn right out of the church cloisters, then take the first right on rue de la Calade to reach the...*

Classical Theater (Théâtre Antique)—This first-century B.C. Roman theater once seated 10,000. This theater was an elegant, 3-level structure with 27 arches radiating out to the street level. From the outside, it looked much like a halved version of Arles' Roman Arena.

Start with the video outside, which provides helpful background information and images that make it easier to put the scattered stones back in place (crouch in front to make out the small English subtitles). Next, walk to a center aisle and pull up a stone seat. To appreciate the theater's original size, look left (about 9:00) to the upper-left side of the tower and find the protrusion that supported the highest seating level. The structure required 33 rows of seats covering three levels to accommodate demand. During the Middle Ages, the old theater became a convenient town quarry— St. Trophime Church was built from theater rubble. Precious little of the original theater survives—though it still is used for events, with seating for 3,000 spectators.

Two lonely Corinthian columns are all that remain of a three-story stage wall that once featured more than 100 columns and statues painted in vibrant colors. The orchestra section is defined by a semicircular pattern in the stone in front of you. Stepping up onto the left side of the stage, look down to the slender channel that allowed the brilliant-red curtain to disappear below, like magic. The stage, which was built of wood, was about 160 feet across and 20 feet deep. The actors' changing rooms are backstage, down the steps.

Cost and Hours: €6, daily May-Sept 9:00-19:00, March-April and Oct 9:00-18:00, Nov-Feb 10:00-17:00. Budget travelers can peek over the fence from rue du Cloître and see just about everything for free.

• *A block uphill is the...*

▲▲▲**Roman Arena (Amphithéâtre)**—Nearly 2,000 years ago, gladiators fought wild animals here to the delight of 20,000 screaming fans. Today local daredevils still fight wild animals here—"bullgame" posters around the arena advertise upcoming spectacles (described later, under "Experiences in Arles"). A lengthy restoration process is well under way, giving the amphitheater an almost bleached-teeth whiteness.

In Roman times, games were free (sponsored by city bigwigs), and fans were seated by social class. The many exits allowed for rapid dispersal after the games—fights would break out among frenzied fans if they couldn't leave quickly. Through medieval times and until the early 1800s, the arches were bricked up and the stadium became a fortified town—with 200 humble homes crammed within its circular defenses. Three of the medieval towers survive (the one above the ticket booth is open and rewards those who climb it with terrific views). To see two still-sealed arches—complete with cute medieval window frames—turn right as you leave, walk to the Andaluz restaurant, and look back to the second floor.

Cost and Hours: €6, daily May-Sept 9:00-19:00, March-April and Oct 9:00-18:00, Nov-Feb 10:00-17:00.

• *The next three sights are back across town. The Arlaten Folk Museum (closed in 2012, reopens in 2014) and Fondation Van Gogh are close to place du Forum, and the Réattu Museum is near the river.*

▲**Arlaten Folk Museum (Musée Arlaten/Museon Arlaten)**—This museum, which explains the ins and outs of daily Provençal life, is closed for renovation until 2014. Ask at the TI or check the museum's website for the latest (www.museonarlaten.fr, French only).

▲**Fondation Van Gogh**—This small art gallery recently moved and should reopen in its new location in late 2012. The following description assumes the collection will stay intact.

The foundation offers a refreshing stop for modern-art-lovers and Van Gogh fans (but be warned that the collection contains no Van Gogh originals). Contemporary artists, including Roy Lichtenstein and Robert Rauschenberg, pay homage to Vincent through thought-provoking interpretations of his works. The black-and-white photographs (both art and shots of places that Vincent painted) complement the paintings.

Unfortunately, this collection is often on the road July through September, when non-Van Gogh material is displayed. A good variety of Van Gogh souvenirs, prints, and postcards is available in the gift shop.

Cost and Hours: Reopens in late 2012; when open, likely €6, April-June daily 10:00-18:00, July-Sept daily 10:00-19:00, Oct-March Tue-Sun 11:00-17:00, closed Mon, confirm cost and hours prior to your visit; a few blocks northwest of place du Forum at 35 rue du Dr. Fanton, tel. 04 90 49 94 04, www.fondationvangogh -arles.org.

Réattu Museum (Musée Réattu)—Housed in the former Grand Priory of the Knights of Malta, this modern-art collection is always changing. The permanent collection usually includes a series of works by homegrown Neoclassical artist Jacques Réattu, along with at least one Picasso painting and a roomful of his drawings (donated by the artist, some two-sided and all done in a flurry of creativity). The museum shuffles its large Picasso collection around regularly, as they have more works than space to display them. Most of the three-floor museum houses temporary exhibits of modern artists—check the website to see who's playing.

Cost and Hours: €7, Tue-Sun July-Sept 10:00-19:00, Oct-June 10:00-12:30 & 14:00-18:30, closed Mon year-round, last entry 30 minutes before closing for lunch or at end of day, 10 rue du Grand Prieuré, tel. 04 90 96 37 68, www.museereattu.arles.fr.

Experiences in Arles

▲▲Markets—On Wednesday and Saturday mornings, Arles' ring road erupts into an open-air festival of fish, flowers, produce...and you name it. The main event is on Saturday, with vendors jamming the ring road from boulevard Emile Combes to the east, along boulevard des Lices near the TI (the heart of the market), and continuing down boulevard Georges Clemenceau to the west. Wednesday's market runs only along boulevard Emile Combes, between place Lamartine and bis avenue Victor Hugo; the segment nearest place Lamartine is all about food, and the upper half features clothing, tablecloths, purses, and so on. On the first Wednesday of the month, a flea market doubles the size of the usual Wednesday market along boulevard des Lices near the main TI. Join in: Buy some flowers for your hotelier, try the olives, sample some wine, and swat a pickpocket. Both markets are open until 12:30.

▲▲Bullgames (Courses Camarguaises)—Occupy the same seats that fans have used for nearly 2,000 years, and take in Arles' most memorable experience—the *courses camarguaises* in the ancient arena. The nonviolent "bullgames" are more sporting than bloody bullfights (though traditional Spanish-style bullfights still take place on occasion). The bulls of Arles (who, locals stress, "die of old age") are promoted in posters even more boldly than their human foes. In the bullgame, a ribbon *(cocarde)* is laced between the bull's horns. The *razeteur,* with a special hook, has 15 minutes to snare the ribbon. Local businessmen encourage a *razeteur* (dressed in white with a red cummerbund) by shouting out how much money they'll pay for the *cocarde.* If the bull pulls a good stunt, the band plays the famous "Toreador" song from *Carmen.* The following day, newspapers report on the games, including how many *Carmens* the bull earned.

Three classes of bullgames—determined by the experience of the *razeteurs*—are advertised in posters: The *course de protection* is for rookies. The *trophée de l'Avenir* comes with more experience. And the *trophée des As* features top professionals. During Easter and the fall rice-harvest festival *(Féria du Riz),* the arena hosts traditional Spanish bullfights as it has for 150 years (look for *corrida*) with outfits, swords, spikes, and the whole gory shebang.

Don't pass on a chance to see *Toro Piscine,* a silly spectacle for warm summer evenings where the bull ends up in a swimming pool (uh-huh...get more details at TI). Nearby villages stage *courses camarguaises* in small wooden bullrings nearly every weekend; TIs have the latest schedule.

Cost and Hours: Bullgame tickets run €5-15; bullfights are pricier (€14-80). Schedules vary (usually July-Aug on Wed and Fri)—ask at the TI or check online at www.arenes-arles.com.

Sleeping in Arles

Hotels are a great value here—many are air-conditioned, though few have elevators. The Calendal, Musée, and Régence hotels offer exceptional value.

$$$ Hôtel le Calendal*** is a seductive place located between the Roman Arena and Classical Theater. Enter an expertly run hotel with airy lounges and a lovely palm-shaded courtyard. Enjoy the elaborate €12 buffet breakfast, have lunch in the courtyard or at the inexpensive sandwich bar (daily 12:00-15:00), and take advantage of their four free laptops for guests. You'll also find a Jacuzzi and a spa with a Turkish bath, hot pool, and massages at good rates. The comfortable rooms sport Provençal decor and come in all shapes and sizes (standard Db-€120-140, Db with balcony-€140-175, Tb-€135-175, Qb-€145-180, price depends on room size, air-con, Wi-Fi, reserve ahead for parking-€8, just above arena at 5 rue Porte de Laure, tel. 04 90 96 11 89, fax 04 90 96 05 84, www.lecalendal.com, contact@lecalendal.com). They also run the nearby, budget La Maison du Pelerin, described later.

$$$ Hôtel d'Arlatan***, built on the site of a Roman basilica, offers faded elegance in a classy shell. It has comfy public spaces, a tranquil terrace, a designer pool, and antique-filled rooms, many with high, wood-beamed ceilings and stone walls (a newer wing

PROVENCE

Sleep Code

(€1 = about $1.40, country code: 33)
S = Single, **D** = Double/Twin, **T** = Triple, **Q** = Quad, **b** = bathroom,
s = shower only, ***** = French hotel rating system (0-5 stars).
Unless otherwise noted, credit cards are accepted and English
is spoken.

To help you sort easily through these listings, I've divided
the accommodations into three categories based on the price
for a standard double room with bath:

$$$ Higher Priced—Most rooms €90 or more.
$$ Moderately Priced—Most rooms between €65-90.
$ Lower Priced—Most rooms €65 or less.

Prices can change without notice; verify the hotel's
current rates online or by email. For other updates, see www
.ricksteves.com/update.

has more modern rooms). In the lobby of this 15th-century building, a glass floor looks down into Roman ruins. Hallway carpets
are worn, and some rooms could use a little TLC, but the place
is still a fair value (standard Db-€137, bigger Db-€157, Db/Qb
suites-€180, apartments-€200-250, buffet breakfast-€15, air-con,
ice machines, elevator, Wi-Fi, parking garage-€14, closed Nov-
April, 1 block below place du Forum at 26 rue du Sauvage—tough
by car, tel. 04 90 93 56 66, fax 04 90 49 68 45, www.hotel-arlatan
.fr, hotel-arlatan@wanadoo.fr).

$$ Hôtel du Musée** is a quiet, affordable manor-home
hideaway tucked deep in Arles (difficult to find by car). This
delightful refuge comes with 28 air-conditioned and wood-floored
rooms, a flowery two-tiered courtyard, and comfortable lounges.
Lighthearted Claude and English-speaking Laurence, the gra-
cious owners, are eager to help (Sb-€50, Db-€65-80, Tb-€85-
95, Qb-€110-130, no elevator, Wi-Fi, laptop available for guests,
garage-€10, follow signs to *Réattu Museum* to 11 rue du Grand
Prieuré, tel. 04 90 93 88 88, fax 04 90 49 98 15, www.hoteldu
musee.com, contact@hoteldumusee.com).

$$ Hôtel de la Muette**, with reserved owners Brigitte and
Alain, is another good choice. Located in a quiet corner of Arles,
this low-key hotel is well kept, with stone walls, brown tones, and
a small terrace in front. You'll pay a bit more for the upgraded
rooms, but it's money well spent (most Db-€66, bigger Db-€75,
Tb-€77, Qb-€92, buffet breakfast-€8, air-con, no elevator, Wi-Fi,
private garage-€8, 15 rue des Suisses, tel. 04 90 96 15 39, fax 04 90
49 73 16, www.hotel-muette.com, hotel.muette@wanadoo.fr).

$ Hôtel Régence**, a top budget deal, has a riverfront location, immaculate and comfortable Provençal rooms, safe parking, and easy access to the train station (Db-€55-65, Tb-€70-75, Qb-€80-90, choose river view or quieter courtyard rooms, most rooms have showers, good buffet breakfast-€6, air-con, no elevator but only two floors, Internet access and Wi-Fi, garage-€6; from place Lamartine, turn right immediately after passing between towers to reach 5 rue Marius Jouveau; tel. 04 90 96 39 85, fax 04 90 96 67 64, www.hotel-regence.com, contact@hotel-regence.com). The gentle Nouvions speak some English.

$ Hôtel Acacias**, just off place Lamartine and inside the old city walls, is a modern hotel with less personality. The pretty pastel rooms are on the small side, but they're reasonably priced (standard Sb or Db-€53, larger Db-€64-78, extra bed-€15, breakfast-€6, air-con, elevator, Wi-Fi, 2 rue de la Cavalerie, tel. 04 90 96 37 88, fax 04 90 96 32 51, www.hotel-acacias.com, contact@hotel-acacias .com).

$ Hôtel Voltaire* rents 12 small, spartan rooms with ceiling fans and nifty balconies overlooking a fun square. A block below the arena, it's good for starving artists. Smiling owner "Mr." Ferran (fur-ran) loves the States, and hopes you'll add to his postcard collection (D-€30, Ds-€35, Db-€40, 1 place Voltaire, tel. 04 90 96 49 18, fax 04 90 96 45 49, levoltaire13@aol.com). They also serve a good-value lunch and dinner in their recommended restaurant.

$ La Maison du Pelerin offers spotless dorm rooms with three to six beds per room. It's a great value, just above the Roman Arena and Classical Theater, with a shared kitchen and homey living area. Book in advance by phone or email and get the door code. You can also check in next door at the recommended Hôtel le Calendal (they own the place) and get sheets if you need them (€25/person, shared bath, must pay in advance, 26 place Pomme, mobile 06 99 71 11 89, www.arles-pelerins.fr).

Eating in Arles

You can dine well in Arles on a modest budget—in fact, it's hard to blow a lot on dinner here (most of my listings have *menus* for under €25). The bad news is that restaurants change regularly, so double-check my suggestions. Before dinner, go local on place du Forum and enjoy a *pastis*. This anise-based apéritif is served straight in a glass with ice, plus a carafe of water—dilute to taste. Sunday is a quiet night for restaurants, though most eateries on place du Forum are open.

For **picnics,** a big, handy Monoprix supermarket/department store is on place Lamartine (Mon-Sat 8:30-19:25, closed Sun).

PROVENCE

Arles Hotels & Restaurants

← Van Gogh Walking Tour

P Parking

Ⓑ Bus Stop

⤜ View

🖼

100 YARDS

100 METERS

❶ Hôtel/Rest. le Calendal & La Maison du Pelerin

❷ Hôtel d'Arlatan

❸ Hôtel du Musée

❹ Hôtel de la Muette

❺ Hôtel Acacias

❻ Hôtel Régence

❼ Hôtel/Rest. Voltaire

❽ To La Peiriero & Domaine de Laforest

❾ To Mas du Petit Grava

❿ Rue du Dr. Fanton Eateries

⓫ Bistrot à Vins

⓬ La Cuisine de Comptoir

⓭ La Table d'L

⓮ La Pizza des Thermes

⓯ Café de la Major (Coffee/Tea)

⓰ Le Grillon Restaurant

⓱ Le Criquet Restaurant

⓲ L'Atelier & A Côté Restaurants

⓳ Soleileis Ice Cream

TRINQUETAILLE BRIDGE

R H

MARX

QUAI

RUE A. FRANCE

TRUCHET

DR. FANTON

⓬

TO ANCIENT HISTORY MUSEUM

R. JOUVE. R. LIBERTE

ARLATEN FOLK MUSEUM (CLOSED UNTIL 2013)

RUE GAMBETTA

REPUB-

ESPACE VAN GOGH

RUE

MOLIERE

R.

TO ANCIENT HISTORY MUSEUM ←

BLVD.

Ⓑ

BUS STN.

DCH

PROVENCE

On or near Place du Forum

Great atmosphere and mediocre food at fair prices await on place du Forum. By all accounts, the garish yellow Café la Nuit is worth avoiding. Most other cafés on the square deliver acceptable quality and terrific ambience. For better cuisine, wander away from the square.

On Rue du Dr. Fanton

A half-block below the Forum, on rue du Dr. Fanton, lies a terrific lineup of restaurants. Come here to peruse your options side by side. You can't go wrong—all offer good value and have appealing indoor and outdoor seating.

Le 16 is a warm, affordable place to enjoy a fresh salad (€10)—though it's almost too popular for its own good (€13 *plats*, €21 three-course *menu*, closed Sat-Sun, 16 rue du Dr. Fanton, tel. 04 90 93 77 36).

Le Gaboulet is a popular local spot, blending a cozy interior, classic French cuisine, and service with a smile (thanks to owner Frank). It's the most expensive of the places I list on this street, but it's still busy. If it's cold out, the huge chimney should be lit (€27 *menu,* great fries, closed Sun-Mon, 18 rue du Dr. Fanton, tel. 04 90 93 18 11).

Au Brin du Thym, next door, offers a reliable blend of traditional French and Provençal cuisine at very fair prices. Arrive early for an outdoor table or call ahead, and let hardworking and formal Monsieur and Madame Colombaud take care of you. Monsieur does *le cooking* while Madame does *le serving* (€19 three-course *menu;* excellent à la carte choices: €9 starters, €15 *plats;* closed Tue, 22 rue du Dr. Fanton, tel. 04 90 49 95 96).

Le Plaza, next to Au Brin, features delicious Provençal cuisine served in a fine setting at good prices (€22 *menu,* closed Wed, 28 rue du Dr. Fanton, tel. 04 90 96 33 15).

Bistrot à Vins suits wine-lovers who enjoy pairing food and drink, and those in search of a good glass of *vin*. Sit at a convivial counter or at one of five tables while listening to light jazz (book ahead for a table). Affable Ariane speaks enough English and offers a limited selection of simple, tasty dishes. Her savory tarts and fresh green salad make a great meal (€10-16), and the wines—many available by the glass—are well priced (indoor dining only from 18:30 to 22:00, closed Mon-Tue, 2 rue du Dr. Fanton, tel. 04 90 52 00 65).

Other Places near Place du Forum

At **La Cuisine de Comptoir,** a cool little bistro, locals of all ages abandon Provençal decor. Welcoming owners Alexandre and Vincent offer light *tartine* dinners—a delicious cross between pizza and bruschetta, served with soup or salad for just €10 (a swinging deal—the *brandada* is tasty and filling). Sit at the counter and watch *le chef* at work as you sip your €2 glass of rosé in fine glassware (closed Sun, mostly indoor dining, just off place du Forum's lower end at 10 rue de la Liberté, tel. 04 90 96 86 28).

La Table d'L has trendy decor, but is warmly run by eager-to-please waitress Ellie and chef Jay. New to Arles, Jay worked in a restaurant in New York for 17 years. The selection is limited but the quality is not. Jay loves her lamb and fish, and so will you (€15 starters, €23 *plats,* reasonably priced wine list, closed Mon, 1 bis rue Réattu, tel. 04 90 96 32 53).

La Pizza des Thermes is a welcoming eatery a few blocks north of place du Forum, serving good pizza and pasta for €9-12 (daily, 6 rue du Sauvage, tel. 04 90 49 60 64).

Café de la Major is *the* place to go to recharge with some serious coffee or tea (closed Sun, 7 bis rue Réattu, tel. 04 90 96 14 15).

Near the Roman Arena

For about the same price as on place du Forum, you can enjoy regional cuisine with a point-blank view of the arena. Because they change regularly, the handful of (mostly) outdoor eateries that overlook the arena are pretty indistinguishable.

Le Grillon, with the best view above the arena, offers friendly service and good-enough salads (the *camarguaise* is a riot of color), pizza and tasty *tartines* for €9 (including small salad), and *plats du jour* for €10-12 (closed all day Wed and Sun nights, at the top of the arena on rond-point des Arènes, tel. 04 90 96 70 97).

Le Criquet is a sweet little place serving Provençal classics at good prices two blocks above the arena (€19 three-course *menu,* indoor and outdoor dining, 21 rue Porte de Laure, tel. 04 90 96 80 51).

For details on the next two places, see their listings under "Sleeping in Arles," earlier. **Hôtel le Calendal** serves lunch in its lovely courtyard (€12-18, daily 12:00-15:00) or delicious little sandwiches for €2.50 each at its small café. **Hôtel Voltaire,** well-situated on a pleasing square, serves simple three-course lunches and dinners at honest prices to a loyal clientele (€13 *menus*; hearty *plats* and filling salads for €10—try the *salade fermière, salade Latine,* or the filling *assiette Provençale;* closed Sun evening).

A Gastronomic Dining Experience

One of France's most recognized chefs, Jean-Luc Rabanel, has created a sensation with two very different options 50 yards from place de la République (at 7 rue des Carmes). They sit side by side, both offering indoor and terrace seating.

L'Atelier is so intriguing that people travel great distances just

PROVENCE

for the experience. Diners fork over €100 (at lunch, you'll spoon out €60) and trust the chef to create a memorable meal...which he does. There is no menu, just an onslaught of delicious taste sensations served in artsy dishes. Don't plan on a quick dinner, and don't come for the setting—it's a contemporary, shoebox-shaped dining room, but several outdoor tables are also available. The get-to-know-your-neighbor atmosphere means you can't help but join the party. You'll probably spot the famous chef (hint: he has long brown hair), as he is very hands-on with his waitstaff (closed Mon-Tue, best to book ahead, friendly servers will hold your hand through this palate-widening experience, tel. 04 90 91 07 69, www .rabanel.com).

A Côté saddles up next door, offering a smart wine bar/bistro ambience and top-quality cuisine for far less. Here you can sample the famous chef's talents for as little as €18 (daily *plat*) or as much as €40 (three-course *menu*, smallish servings, reasonably priced wines, open daily, tel. 04 90 47 61 13).

And for Dessert...

Soleileis has Arles' best ice cream, with all-natural ingredients and unusual flavors such as *fadoli*—olive oil mixed with nougatine. There's also a shelf of English books for exchange (open daily 14:00-18:30, across from recommended Le 16 restaurant at 9 rue du Dr. Fanton).

Arles Connections

Some trains in and out of Arles require a **reservation**. These include connections with Nice to the east and Bordeaux to the west (including intermediary stops). Ask at the station.

From Arles by Train to: Paris (11/day, 2 direct TGVs—4 hours, 9 with transfer in Avignon—5 hours), **Avignon Centre-Ville** (roughly hourly, 20 minutes, less frequent in the afternoon), **Nîmes** (9/day, 30 minutes), **Marseille** (20/day, 1.5 hours), **Nice** (11/day, 3.75-4.5 hours, most require transfer in Marseille), **Barcelona** (2/day, 6 hours, transfer in Montpellier), **Italy** (3/day, transfer in Marseille and Nice; from Arles, it's 4.5 hours to Ventimiglia on the border, 8 hours to Milan, 9.5 hours to Cinque Terre, 11 hours to Florence, and 13 hours to Venice or Rome).

From Arles Train Station to Avignon TGV Station: If you're connecting from Arles to the TGV in Avignon, it's easiest to take the SNCF bus directly from Arles' train station to Avignon's TGV Station (10/day, 1 hour). Another option—which takes the same amount of time, but adds more walking—is to take the regular train from Arles to Avignon's Centre-Ville Station, then catch the *navette* (shuttle bus) to the TGV Station from there.

From Arles by Bus to: Nîmes (6/day, 1 hour). The bus station is at 16-24 boulevard Georges Clemenceau (2 blocks below main TI, next to Café le Wilson). Bus info: tel. 04 90 49 38 01 (unlikely to speak English).

Avignon

Famous for its nursery rhyme, medieval bridge, and brooding Palace of the Popes, contemporary Avignon (ah-veen-yohn) bustles and prospers behind its mighty walls. During the 94 years (1309-1403) that Avignon starred as the *Franco Vaticano* (the temporary residence of the popes) and hosted two antipopes, it grew from a quiet village into a thriving city. With its large student population and fashionable shops, today's Avignon is an intriguing blend of medieval history, youthful energy, and urban sophistication. Street performers entertain the international throngs who fill Avignon's ubiquitous cafés and trendy boutiques. If you're here in July, be prepared for big crowds and higher prices, thanks to the rollicking theater festival. (Reserve your hotel far in advance.) Clean, sharp, and popular with tourists, Avignon is more impressive for its outdoor ambience than for its museums and monuments.

Orientation to Avignon

The cours Jean Jaurès, which turns into rue de la République, runs straight from the Centre-Ville train station to place de l'Horloge and the Palace of the Popes, splitting Avignon in two. The larger eastern half is where the action is. Climb to the Jardin du Rochers des Doms for the town's best view, consider touring the pope's immense palace, lose yourself in Avignon's back streets (you can follow my "Discovering Avignon's Back Streets" self-guided walk), and find a shady square to call home. Avignon's shopping district fills the traffic-free streets near where rue de la République meets place de l'Horloge. As you wander through this energetic city, look for signs in Occitan—the language of the Occitania region; you might see the name of the city written as "Avinhon" or "Avignoun."

PROVENCE

Tourist Information

The **main TI** is between the Centre-Ville train station and the old town, at 41 cours Jean Jaurès (April-Oct Mon-Sat 9:00-18:00—until 19:00 in July, Sun 9:45-17:00; Nov-March Mon-Fri 9:00-18:00, Sat 9:00-17:00, Sun 10:00-12:00; tel. 04 32 74 32 74, www.avignon-tourisme.com). From April through mid-October,

Avignon

1. Start of Welcome to Avignon Walk
2. Start of Discovering Back Streets Walk (Hôtel La Mirande)
3. Best Views & Stairs to Tower
4. More Views
5. To Shakespeare Bookshop
6. Launderettes (2)
7. Carrefour City Grocery
8. Bike Rental
9. Shuttle Boat Stops (2)
10. Tourist Train Stop
11. TGV Shuttle Stop & Bus #11 Stop

200 YARDS
200 METERS

View
--- Ped. Path
P Parking
B Main Bus Stop
SELF-GUIDED WALKS

PROVENCE

LASSE

RIVER

Petit Palais Museum

TO 🅿,
& LYON
VIA
D-225
& A-7

BLVD. ST-LAZARE

JARDIN DU ROCHERS DES DOMS

POND

PALACE OF THE POPES

TO

R. INFIRM.

FERRUCE

RHONE

R. GROTTES

PALACE SQUARE

R. BALANCE

R. BANAS.

BERTRAND

ETIENNE

RUE

CITY HALL

PLACE DE L'HORLOGE

PEYROL

V. LEGAT

R. CROIX

CARNOT

ST. AGRICOL

RUE

ST. PIERRE

SYNAGOGUE

R. P. SAIN

MARCHANDS

PLACE CARN.

VIEUX PIE

PL. PIG.

JOSEPH

ROUG.

R. FOURB.

R. BONNETERIE

RUE

MARKET

THIERS

VERN.

R. ROI RENE

PLACE ST. DIDIER

R. DES LICES

R. TENTURIERS

FONDATION ANGLADON

R. 3 FAUC. CONS.

FABRE

RUE DES LICES

WATER-WHEEL

VERNET

R. ST. CHARLES

R. DE LA REPUBLIQUE

JAURES

ST.

PLACE DES CORPS-SAINTS

PORT. MAG.

BON-MART.

SORGUE RIVER

PERP.

MICHEL

OLD CITY WALLS

ST. MICHEL

Post

BOURSE

BLVD.

TASS.

Jean Jaures

COURS JFK

COURS

ST.

ROCH

BUS STN.

DCH

TRAIN STN. "CENTRE-VILLE"

TO ARLES & TGV TRAIN STN.

PROVENCE

branch TI offices are open inside the **St. Bénezet Bridge** entrance (daily 10:00-13:00 & 14:00-18:00) and inside **Les Halles market** (Fri-Sun 10:00-13:00, closed Mon-Thu). At any TI, get the helpful map. If you're staying awhile, pick up the free *Guide Pratique* (info on bike rentals, hotels, apartment rentals, events, and museums).

Sightseeing Pass: Everyone should pick up the free **Avignon Passion Pass** (valid 15 days, for up to five family members). Get the pass stamped when you pay full price at your first sight, and then receive reductions at the others (for example, €2 less at the Palace of the Popes and €3 less at the Petit Palais). The discounts add up—always show your Passion Pass when buying a ticket. The pass comes with the Avignon "Passion" map and guide, which includes several good (but tricky-to-follow) walking tours.

Arrival in Avignon

By Train

Avignon has two train stations: TGV (linked to downtown by frequent shuttle buses) and Centre-Ville. While most TGV trains serve only the TGV Station, some serve Centre-Ville—verify your station in advance.

TGV Station (Gare TGV): This shiny new station, on the outskirts of town, has no baggage storage (bags can be stored only at the Centre-Ville train station).

To get to the city center, take the *navette/*shuttle bus (marked *Navette/Avignon Centre;* €1.20, buy ticket from driver, 3/hour, 15 minutes). To find the bus stop, leave the station by the north exit *(sortie nord)*, walk down the stairs, and find the long bus shelter to the left. In downtown Avignon you'll arrive at a stop just inside the city walls, in front of the post office on cours Président Kennedy (see map on page 384). From here you're three blocks from the city's main TI and two blocks from the Centre-Ville train station. A **taxi** ride between the TGV Station and downtown Avignon costs about €20 (to find taxis, exit the TGV Station via *sortie nord).*

To pick up a **rental car** at the TGV Station, walk out the south exit *(sortie sud)* to find the *location de voitures* in the parking lot. If you're driving directly to Arles, leave the station, following signs to *Avignon Sud*, then *La Rocade.* You'll soon see exits to Arles.

If you're heading from the Avignon TGV Station to the **Arles train station,** catch the direct SNCF bus from the TGV Station's bus stop (10/day, 1 hour, schedule available at any information booth inside the TGV Station).

Centre-Ville Station (Gare Avignon Centre-Ville): All non-TGV trains (and a few TGV trains) serve the central station. You can stash your bags here—exit the station to the left and look for the *consignes* sign (confirm closing time when you leave your bag).

To reach the town center, cross the busy street in front of the station and walk through the city walls onto cours Jean Jaurès. The TI is three blocks down, at #41.

By Bus

The dingy bus station *(gare routière)* is 100 yards to the right as you leave the Centre-Ville train station, beyond and below Hôtel Ibis (info desk open Mon-Sat 8:00-19:30, closed Sun, tel. 04 90 82 07 35, staff speaks a little English).

By Car

Drivers entering Avignon follow *Centre-Ville* and *Gare SNCF* (train station) signs. You'll find central pay lots (about €10/half-day, €14/day) in the garage next to the Centre-Ville train station, at the Parking Jean Jaurès under the ramparts across from the station. Two less pricey options are the Parking Les Halles in the center of town, on place Pie ("pee"), and the Parking Palais des Papes. Hotels have advice for smart overnight parking, and some offer small discounts in the municipal parking garages.

Free or Cheap Parking: Two free lots have complimentary shuttle buses to the center (follow *P Gratuit* signs): One is just across Daladier Bridge (pont Daladier); the other is along the river past the Palace of the Popes, just northeast of the walls. Parking on the street is free in the *bleu* zones 12:00-14:00 and 19:00-9:00. It's €2 for 3 hours 9:00-12:00 and 14:00-19:00 (hint: if you put €2 in the meter after 19:00, it's good until 14:00 the next day). No matter where you park, leave nothing in your car.

Helpful Hints

Book Ahead for July: During the July theater festival, rooms are sparse—reserve very early, or stay in Arles.

Local Help: David at **Imagine Tours** (a nonprofit group whose goal is to promote this region) can help with hotel emergencies or tickets to special events (mobile 06 89 22 19 87, www .imagine-tours.net, imagine.tours@gmail.com). If you get no answer, leave a message.

Internet Access: The TI has a current list of Internet cafés, or you can ask your hotelier. The bigger cafés provide free Wi-Fi to anyone who buys a drink.

English Bookstore: Try **Shakespeare Bookshop** (Tue-Sat 9:30-12:00 & 14:00-18:30, closed Sun-Mon, 155 rue Carreterie, in Avignon's northeast corner, tel. 04 90 27 38 50).

Baggage Storage: You can leave your bags at Centre-Ville train station (see "Arrival in Avignon," earlier).

Laundry: The launderette at 66 place des Corps-Saints, where rue Agricol Perdiguier ends, has English instructions and is

PROVENCE

handy to most hotels (daily 7:00-20:00). Another is located at 9 rue Chapeau Rouge (behind place Pie).

Grocery Store: Carrefour City is central and has long hours (Mon-Sat 7:00-21:00, Sun 9:00-12:00, next to McDonald's, 2 blocks from the TI, toward place de l'Horloge on rue de la République).

Bike Rental: You'll see many **Vélopop** city bikes stationed at key points in Avignon, making one-way and short-term rental a breeze—if you can pay for them. Sadly, these machines only accept American Express and chip-and-PIN cards (described on page 11). Several rental options are near Centre-Ville Station: You can rent bikes at **Provence Bike** (7 avenue St. Ruf, tel. 04 90 27 92 61, www.provence-bike.com) and scooters at **Holiday Bikes** (52 boulevard St. Roch, tel. 04 90 27 92 61, holidaybikes84@gmail.com). You'll enjoy riding on the Ile de la Barthélasse.

Car Rental: The TGV Station has car-rental agencies (open long hours daily).

Shuttle Boat: A free shuttle boat, the *Navette Fluviale,* plies back and forth across the river (as it did in the days when the town had no functioning bridge) from near St. Bénezet Bridge (daily July-Aug 11:00-21:00, Sept-June roughly 10:00-12:30 & 14:00-18:00, 3/hour). It drops you on the peaceful Ile de la Barthélasse, with its recommended riverside restaurant, grassy walks, and bike rides with terrific city views. If you stay on the island for dinner, check the schedule for the last return boat—or be prepared for a taxi ride or a pleasant 25-minute walk back to town.

Commanding City Views: For great views of Avignon and the river, walk or drive across Daladier Bridge, or ferry across the Rhône on the *Navette Fluviale* (described above). I'd take the boat across the river, walk the view path to Daladier Bridge, and then cross back over the bridge (45-minute walk over mostly level ground). You can enjoy other impressive vistas from the top of the Jardin du Rochers des Doms, from the tower in the Palace of the Popes, from the end of the famous, broken St. Bénezet Bridge, and from the entrance to Fort St. André, across the river in Villeneuve-lès-Avignon.

Tours in Avignon

Walking Tours—On mid-season Mondays, the TI offers informative English walking tours of Avignon, which include a visit to the Palace of the Popes (€17, discounted with Avignon Passion Pass, April-June and Aug-Oct Mon at 10:30, no tours in July or Nov-March).

Tourist Trains—The little train leaves regularly from in front of the Palace of the Popes and offers a decent overview of the city, including the Jardin du Rochers des Doms and St. Bénezet Bridge (€7, 2/hour, 40 minutes, mid-March-mid-Oct daily 10:00-19:00, English commentary).

Guided Excursions—Several minivan tour companies based in Avignon offer transportation to destinations around Provence, including Pont du Gard (about €65-75/person for all-day tours). See "Tours of Provence" on page 361 (note that guides Madeleine Vedel, François Marcou, and Daniela Wedel, as well as Imagine Tours, are all based in Avignon).

Self-Guided Walks

For a fine overview of the city, combine these two walks. "Welcome to Avignon" covers the major sights, while "Discovering Avignon's Back Streets" leads you along the lanes less taken, delving beyond the surface of this historic city.

▲▲Welcome to Avignon

Before starting this walk—which connects the city's top sights—be sure to pick up the Avignon Passion Pass at the TI, then show it when entering each attraction to receive discounted admission (explained earlier, under "Tourist Information").

• *Start your tour where the Romans did, on place de l'Horloge, in front of City Hall (Hôtel de Ville).*

Place de l'Horloge

This café square was the town forum during Roman times and the market square through the Middle Ages. (Restaurants here offer good people-watching, but they also have less ambience and low-quality meals—you'll find better squares elsewhere to hang your beret in.) Named for a medieval clock tower mostly hidden behind City Hall (find plaque in English), this square's present popularity arrived with the trains in 1854. Walk a few steps to the center of the square, and look down the main drag, rue de la République. When the trains came to Avignon, proud city fathers wanted a direct, impressive way to link the new station to the heart of the city (just like in Paris)—so they plowed over homes to create rue de la République and widened place de l'Horloge. This main drag's Parisian feel is intentional—it was built not in the Provençal manner, but in the Haussmann style that is so dominant in Paris (characterized by broad, straight boulevards lined with stately buildings).

• *Walk uphill past the carousel (public WCs behind). Follow the golden statue of Mary, floating high above the buildings. Veer right at the street's end, and continue into...*

PROVENCE

Palace Square (Place du Palais)

This grand square is lined with the Palace of the Popes, the Petit Palais, and the cathedral. In the 1300s the entire headquarters of the Catholic Church was moved to Avignon. The Church bought Avignon and gave it a complete makeover. Along with clearing out vast spaces like this square and building this three-acre palace, the Church erected more than three miles of protective wall (with 39 towers), "appropriate" housing for cardinals (read: mansions), and residences for its entire bureaucracy. The city was Europe's largest construction zone. Avignon's population grew from 6,000 to 25,000 in short order. (Today, 13,000 people live within the walls.) The limits of pre-papal Avignon are outlined on city maps: Rues Joseph Vernet, Henri Fabre, des Lices, and Philonarde all follow the route of the city's earlier defensive wall.

The Petit Palais (Little Palace) seals the uphill end of the square and was built for a cardinal; today it houses medieval paintings (museum described later). The church just to the left of the Palace of the Popes is Avignon's cathedral. It predates the Church's purchase of Avignon by 200 years. Its small size reflects Avignon's modest, pre-papal population. The gilded Mary was added in 1854, when the Vatican established the doctrine of her Immaculate Conception. Mary is taller than the Palace of the Popes by design: The Vatican never accepted what it called the "Babylonian Captivity" and had a bad attitude about Avignon long after the pope was definitively back in Rome. There hasn't been a French pope since the Holy See returned to Rome—over 600 years ago. That's what I call a grudge.

Directly across the square from the palace's main entry stands a cardinal's residence, built in 1619 (now the Conservatoire National de Musique). Its fancy Baroque facade was a visual counterpoint to the stripped-down Huguenot aesthetic of the age. During this time, Provence was a hotbed of Protestantism—but, buried within this region, Avignon was a Catholic stronghold. Notice the stumps in front and nearby. Nicknamed *bites* (slang for the male anatomy), they effectively keep cars from double-parking in areas designed for people. Many of the metal ones slide up and down by remote control to let privileged cars come and go.

• *You can visit the massive* **Palace of the Popes** *(described on page 393) now, but it works better to visit that palace at the end of this walk, then continue directly to the "Discovering Avignon's Back Streets" walk, described later.*

Now is a good time to take in the...

Petit Palais Museum (Musée du Petit Palais)

This former cardinal's palace now displays the Church's collection of mostly medieval Italian painting (including one delightful

Botticelli) and sculpture. All 350 paintings deal with Christian themes. A visit here before going to the Palace of the Popes helps furnish and populate that otherwise barren building, and a quick peek into its courtyard (even if you don't tour the museum) shows the importance of cardinal housing.

Cost and Hours: €6, €3 English brochure, some English explanations posted; June-Sept Wed-Mon 10:00-13:00 & 14:00-18:00, closed Tue; Oct-May Wed-Mon 9:30-13:00 & 14:00-17:30, closed Tue; at north end of Palace Square, tel. 04 90 86 44 58.

• *From Palace Square we'll head up to the rocky hilltop where Avignon was first settled, then drop down to the river. With this short loop, you can enjoy a small park, hike to a grand river view, and visit Avignon's beloved broken bridge—an experience worth* ▲▲.

Start by climbing to the church level (you can fill your bottle with cold water here), then take the central switchback ramps up to...

▲▲Jardin du Rochers des Doms

Though the park itself is a delight—with a sweet little café (good prices for food and drinks) and public WCs—don't miss the climax: a panoramic view of the Rhône River Valley and the broken bridge. For the best views (and the favorite make-out spot for local teenagers later in the evening), find the terrace behind the odd zodiac display (across the grass from the pond-side park café, near the statue of Jean Althen). If the green fence is ruining it for you, stand on the short wall behind you, or detour a few minutes through the park (to the right, with the river on your left) to find a bigger terrace.

On a clear day, the tallest peak you see, with its white limestone cap, is Mont Ventoux ("Windy Mountain"). Below and just to the right, you'll spot free passenger ferries shuttling across the river (great views from path on other side of the river), and—tucked amidst the trees on the far side of the river—a fun, recommended restaurant, Le Bercail. The island in the river is the Ile de la Barthélasse, a nature preserve where Avignon can breathe.

Fort St. André (across the river on the hill; see the info plaque to the left) was built by the French in 1360, shortly after the pope moved to Avignon, to counter the papal incursion into this part of Europe. The castle was across the border, in the kingdom of France. Avignon's famous bridge was a key border crossing, with towers on either end—one was French, and the other was the pope's. The French one, across the river, is the Tower of Philip the Fair (described later, under "More Sights in Avignon").

Cost and Hours: Free, park gates open daily April-Sept 7:30-20:00, Oct-March 7:30-18:00.

• *From the smaller viewpoint (with the zodiac), take the stairs to the left (closed at night) down to the tower. You'll catch glimpses of the...*

PROVENCE

Ramparts

The only bit of the rampart you can walk on is accessed from St. Bénezet Bridge (pay to enter—see next). Just after the papacy took control of Avignon, the walls were extended to take in the convents and monasteries that had been outside the city. What you see today was restored in the 19th century.

• *When you come out of the tower on street level, take the right-side exit and walk left along the wall to the old bridge. Pass under the bridge to find its entrance shortly after.*

▲▲St. Bénezet Bridge (Pont St. Bénezet)

This bridge, whose construction and location were inspired by a shepherd's religious vision, is the "pont d'Avignon" of nursery-rhyme fame. The ditty (which you've probably been humming all day) dates back to the 15th century: *Sur le pont d'Avignon, on y danse, on y danse, sur le pont d'Avignon, on y danse tous en rond* ("On the bridge of Avignon, we will dance, we will dance, on the bridge of Avignon, we will dance all in a circle").

But the bridge was a big deal even outside of its kiddie-tune fame. Built between 1171 and 1185, it was the only bridge crossing the mighty Rhône in the Middle Ages—important to pilgrims, merchants, and armies. It was damaged several times by floods and subsequently rebuilt, until 1668, when most of it was knocked down by a disastrous icy flood. Lacking a government stimulus package, the townsfolk decided not to rebuild this time, and for more than a century, Avignon had no bridge across the Rhône. While only four arches survive today, the original bridge was huge: Imagine a 22-arch, 3,000-foot-long bridge extending from Vatican territory to the lonely Tower of Philip the Fair, which marked the beginning of France (see displays of the bridge's original length).

The ticket booth is housed in what was a medieval hospital for the poor (funded by bridge tolls). Admission includes a small room dedicated to the song of Avignon's bridge and your only chance to walk a bit of the ramparts (enter both from the tower). A Romanesque chapel on the bridge is dedicated to St. Bénezet. Though there's not much to see on the bridge, the audioguide included with your ticket tells a good enough story. It's also fun to be in the breezy middle of the river with a sweeping city view.

Cost and Hours: €4.50, €13 combo-ticket includes Palace of the Popes, same hours as the Palace of the Popes (next), tel. 04 90 27 51 16.

• *To get to the Palace of the Popes from here, exit left, then turn left again back into the walls. Walk to the end of the short street, then turn right following signs to* Palais des Papes. *Next, look for brown signs*

*leading left under the passageway. After a block of uphill walking, find
the stairs to the palace square.*

▲Palace of the Popes (Palais des Papes)

In 1309 a French pope was elected (Pope Clément V). At the
urging of the French king, His Holiness decided that dangerous
Italy was no place for a pope, so he moved the whole operation to
Avignon for a secure rule under a supportive king. The Catholic
Church literally bought Avignon (then a two-bit town), and popes
resided here until 1403. Meanwhile, Italians demanded a Roman
pope, so from 1378 on, there were twin popes—one in Rome and
one in Avignon—causing a schism in the Catholic Church that
wasn't fully resolved until 1417.

Cost and Hours: €10.50 (more for special exhibits), €13
combo-ticket includes St. Bénezet Bridge, daily mid-March-Oct
9:00-19:00, until 20:00 July and Sept, until 21:00 in Aug, Nov-
mid-March 9:30-17:45, last entry one hour before closing, tel. 04
90 27 50 74, www.palais-des-papes.com.

Visiting the Palace: A visit to the mighty yet barren papal
palace comes with an audioguide that leads you along a one-way
route and does an OK job of overcoming the complete lack of furnishings. It teaches the basic history while allowing you to tour at
your own pace. A small museum inside the palace also helps add
context. Still, touring the palace is pretty anticlimactic, given its
historic importance.

As you wander, ponder that this palace—the largest surviving
Gothic palace in Europe—was built to accommodate 500 people
as the administrative center of the Holy See and home of the pope.
This was the most fortified palace of the age (remember, the pope
left Rome to be more secure). Nine popes ruled from here, making this the center of Christianity for nearly 100 years. You'll walk
through the pope's personal quarters (frescoed with happy hunting scenes), see many models of how the various popes added to
the building, and learn about its state-of-the-art plumbing. The
rooms are huge. The "pope's chapel" is twice the size of the adjacent Avignon cathedral.

The last pope (or, technically, antipope, since by then Rome
also had its own rival pope) checked out in 1403 (escaping a siege),
but the Church owned Avignon until the French Revolution in
1789. During this interim period, the pope's "legate" (official representative, normally a nephew) ruled Avignon from this palace.
Avignon residents, many of whom had come from Rome, spoke
Italian for a century after the pope left, making it a linguistic
ghetto within France. In the Napoleonic age, the palace was a barracks, housing 1,800 soldiers. You can see cuts in the wall where
high ceilings gave way to floor beams. Climb the tower (Tour de la

PROVENCE

Gâche) for grand views and a rooftop café with surprisingly good food at very fair prices.

Wine Room: A room at the end of the tour (called *la boutellerie*) is dedicated to the region's wines, of which they claim the pope was a fan. Sniff "Le Nez du Vin"—a black box with 54 tiny bottles designed to develop your "nose." (Blind-test your travel partner.) The nearby village of Châteauneuf-du-Pape is where the pope summered in the 1320s. Its famous wine is a direct descendant of his wine. You're welcome to taste here (€6 for three to five fine wines and souvenir tasting cup). If it's only wine you want, go directly to the back entrance of the palace and enter the boutique.

• *You'll exit at the rear of the palace, where my "Back Streets" walking tour begins (described next). Or, to return to Palace Square, make two rights after exiting the palace.*

▲▲Discovering Avignon's Back Streets

Use the map in this chapter or the TI map to navigate this easy, level, 30-minute walk. This self-guided tour begins in the small square (place de la Mirande) behind the Palace of the Popes. If you've toured the palace, this is where you exit. Otherwise, from the front of the palace, follow the narrow, cobbled rue de la Peyrollerie—carved out of the rock—around the palace on the right side as you face it.

• *Our walk begins at the...*

Hôtel La Mirande: Located on the square, Avignon's finest hotel welcomes visitors. Find the atrium lounge and consider a coffee break amid the understated luxury (€13 afternoon tea served daily 15:00-18:00, includes a generous selection of pastries). Inspect the royal lounge and recommended dining room; cooking demos are offered in the basement below. Rooms start at about €400 in high season.

• *Turn left out of the hotel and left again on rue de la Peyrollerie ("Coppersmiths Street"), then take your first right on rue des Ciseaux d'Or. On the small square ahead you'll find the...*

Church of St. Pierre: The original chestnut doors were carved in 1551, when tales of New World discoveries raced across Europe. (Notice the Indian headdress, top center of left-side door.) The fine Annunciation (eye level on right-side door) shows Gabriel giving Mary the exciting news in impressive Renaissance 3-D. Now take 10 steps back from the door and look way up. The tiny statue breaking the skyline of the church is the pagan god Bacchus, with oodles of grapes. What's he doing sitting atop a Christian church? No one knows. The church's interior holds a beautiful Baroque altar. For recommended restaurants near the Church of St. Pierre, see "Eating in Avignon," later.

• *With your back to the church, follow the alley to the right, which was covered and turned into a tunnel during the town's population boom. It leads into...*

Place des Châtaignes: The cloister of St. Pierre is named for the chestnut *(châtaigne)* trees that once stood here (now replaced by plane trees). The practical atheists of the French Revolution destroyed the cloister, leaving only faint traces of the arches along the church side of the square.

• *Continue around the church and cross the busy street to the Banque Chaix. Across little rue des Fourbisseurs find the classy...*

15th-Century Building: With its original beamed eaves showing, this is a rare vestige from the Middle Ages. Notice how this building widens the higher it gets. A medieval loophole based taxes on ground-floor square footage—everything above was tax-free. Walking down rue des Fourbisseurs ("Street of the Animal Furriers"), notice how the top floors almost meet. Fire was a constant danger in the Middle Ages, as flames leapt easily from one home to the next. In fact, the lookout guard's primary responsibility was watching for fires, not the enemy. Virtually all of Avignon's medieval homes have been replaced by safer structures.

• *Turn left from rue des Fourbisseurs onto the traffic-free rue du Vieux Sextier ("Street of the Old Balance," for weighing items); another left under the first arch leads 10 yards to Avignon's...*

Synagogue: Jews first arrived in Avignon with the Diaspora (exile) of the first century. Avignon's Jews were nicknamed "the Pope's Jews" because of the protection that the Vatican offered to Jews expelled from France. Although the original synagogue dates from the 1220s, in the mid-19th century it was completely rebuilt in a Neoclassical Greek-temple style by a non-Jewish architect. This is the only synagogue under a rotunda that you'll see anywhere. It's an intimate, classy place dressed with white colonnades and walnut furnishings. To enter the synagogue, you'll have to email in advance of your visit (free, closed Sat-Sun, 2 place Jerusalem, tel. 04 90 55 21 24, rabinacia@hotmail.fr).

• *Retrace your steps to rue du Vieux Sextier and turn left, then continue to the big square and find the big, boxy...*

Market (Les Halles): In 1970, the town's open-air market was replaced by this modern one. The market's jungle-like green wall reflects the changes of seasons and helps mitigate its otherwise stark exterior (open Tue-Sun until 13:00, closed Mon, small TI inside open Fri-Sun). Step inside for a sensual experience of organic breads, olives, and festival-of-mold cheeses. The rue des Temptations cuts down the center. Cafés and cheese shops are on the right—as far as possible from the stinky fish stalls on the left. Follow your nose away from the fish and have a coffee with the locals.

• *Exit out the back door of Les Halles, turn left on rue de la Bonneterie*

("Street of Hosiery"), and track the street for five minutes to the plane trees, where it becomes...

Rue des Teinturiers: This "Street of the Dyers" is a tie-dyed, tree- and stream-lined lane, home to earthy cafés and galleries. This was the cloth industry's dyeing and textile center in the 1800s. The stream is a branch of the Sorgue River. Those stylish Provençal fabrics and patterns you see for sale everywhere were first made here, after a pattern imported from India.

About three small bridges down, you'll pass the Grey Penitents chapel on the right. The upper facade shows the GPs, who dressed up in robes and pointy hoods to do their anonymous good deeds back in the 13th century (long before the KKK dressed this way). As you stroll on, you'll see the work of amateur sculptors, who have carved whimsical car barriers out of limestone.

Trendy restaurants on this atmospheric street are recommended later, under "Eating in Avignon."

• *Farther down rue des Teinturiers, you'll come to the...*

Waterwheel: Standing here, imagine the Sorgue River—which hits the mighty Rhône in Avignon—being broken into several canals in order to turn 23 such wheels. In about 1800, waterwheels powered the town's industries. The little cogwheel above the big one could be shoved into place, kicking another machine into gear behind the wall.

• *To return to the real world, double back on rue des Teinturiers and turn left on rue des Lices, which traces the first medieval wall. (Lice is the no-man's-land along a wall.) After a long block you'll pass a striking four-story building that was a home for the poor in the 1600s, an army barracks in the 1800s, a fine-arts school in the 1900s, and is a deluxe condominium today (much of this neighborhood is going high-class residential). Eventually you'll return to rue de la République, Avignon's main drag.*

More Sights in Avignon

Most of Avignon's top sights are covered earlier by my self-guided walks. With more time, consider these options.

Fondation Angladon-Dubrujeaud—Visiting this museum is like being invited into the elegant home of a rich and passionate art collector. It mixes a small but enjoyable collection of art from Post-Impressionists to Cubists (including Paul Cézanne, Vincent van Gogh, Honoré Daumier, Edgar Degas, and Pablo Picasso) with re-created art studios and furnishings from many periods. It's a quiet place with a few superb paintings.

Cost and Hours: €6, Tue-Sun 13:00-18:00, closed Mon, 5 rue Laboureur, tel. 04 90 82 29 03, www.angladon.com.

Calvet Museum (Musée Calvet)—This fine-arts museum impressively displays its collection, highlighting French Baroque works. This museum goes ignored by most, but you'll find a few diamonds in the rough upstairs: Géricault, Soutine, and one painting each from Manet, Sisley, Bonnard, Dufy, and Vlaminck.

Cost and Hours: €6, includes audioguide, Wed-Mon 10:00-13:00 & 14:00-18:00, closed Tue, in the quieter western half of town at 65 rue Joseph Vernet, antiquities collection a few blocks away at 27 rue de la République—same hours and ticket, tel. 04 90 86 33 84, www.musee-calvet.org.

Near Avignon, in Villeneuve-lès-Avignon

▲Tower of Philip the Fair (Tour Philippe-le-Bel)—Built to protect access to St. Bénezet Bridge in 1307, this massive tower offers a terrific view over Avignon and the Rhône basin. It's best late in the day.

Cost and Hours: €2.10; April-Sept daily 10:00-12:30 & 14:00-18:30; Oct-Nov Tue-Sat 10:00-12:30 & 14:00-17:00, closed Sun-Mon; closed Dec-March.

Getting There: To reach the tower from Avignon, drive 5 minutes (cross Daladier Bridge, follow signs to *Villeneuve-lès-Avignon*), or take bus #11 (2/hour, catch bus in front of post office on cours Président Kennedy—see map on page 384).

Sleeping in Avignon

(€1 = about $1.40, country code: 33)
Hotel values are better in Arles, though I've found some good values in Avignon and have listed them below. Avignon is crazy during its July festival, when you must book long ahead (expect inflated prices). Drivers should ask about parking deals.

Near Avignon's Centre-Ville Station

These listings are a five- to ten-minute walk from the Centre-Ville train station.

$$$ Hôtel Bristol*** is a big, professionally run place on the main drag, offering predictable "American" comforts, including spacious public spaces, large rooms decorated in neutral tones, duvets on the beds, a big elevator, air-conditioning, and a generous buffet breakfast (standard Db-€88-103, bigger Db-€126, Tb/Qb-€153, breakfast-€12, parking-€12, 44 cours Jean Jaurès, tel. 04 90 16 48 48, fax 04 90 66 22 72, www.bristol-hotel-avignon.com, contact@bristol-avignon.com).

$$$ Hôtel Ibis Centre Gare** offers no surprises—just predictable two-star comfort at the central train and bus stations.

Avignon Hotels & Restaurants

1. Hôtel Bristol
2. Hôtel Ibis Centre Gare
3. Hôtel Colbert
4. Hôtel le Splendid
5. Hôtel Boquier
6. Hôtel d'Europe
7. Hôtel de l'Horloge
8. Hôtel Mercure Cité des Papes
9. Hôtel Pont d'Avignon
10. Hôtel Médiéval
11. Hôtel Danieli
12. Hôtel Kyriad Palais des Papes
13. Hôtel Mignon
14. La Banasterie Chambres
15. To Le Clos du Rempart & Lumani Chambres
16. To Auberge Bagatelle (Hostel) & Jardin de Bacchus Chambres
17. Church of St. Pierre Eateries
18. Place Crillon Eateries
19. Place des Corps-Saints Eateries
20. Restaurant Françoise
21. La Cave des Passages Wine Bar
22. To Restaurant Numéro 75
23. Restaurant Au Jardin de la Tour
24. L'Isle Sonnante Restaurant
25. Le Petit Bedon Restaurant
26. Le Caveau du Théâtre Rest.
27. Le Fou de Fa Fa Restaurant
28. Hôtel La Mirande Restaurant
29. L'Epice and Love Restaurant
30. Le Bercail Restaurant
31. Carrefour City Grocery

200 YARDS

200 METERS

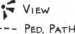 VIEW

- - - PED. PATH

P PARKING

B MAIN BUS STOP

This well-priced place offers generous public spaces, a café, and a bar (Db-€90, free Internet access and Wi-Fi, 42 boulevard St. Roch, tel. 04 90 85 38 38, fax 04 90 86 44 81, www.ibishotel.com, h0944@accor.com).

$$ Hôtel Colbert** is a solid two-star hotel and a good mid-range bet, with richly colored, comfortable rooms in many sizes. Your efficient hosts—Patrice, Annie, and *le chien* Brittany—care for this restored manor house, with its warm public spaces and sweet little patio. It's a popular place, so it's best to book in advance (Sb-€65, small Db-€78, bigger Db-€88, some tight bathrooms, no triples, rooms off the patio are a bit musty, creative homemade breakfast-€12, continental breakfast-€6.50, air-con, Wi-Fi, closed Nov-mid-March, turn right off cours Jean Jaurès on rue Agricol Perdiguier to #7, tel. 04 90 86 20 20, fax 04 90 85 97 00, www .lecolbert-hotel.com, contact@avignon-hotel-colbert.com).

$ Hôtel le Splendid* rents 17 acceptable rooms with faux-wood floors, most of which could use a little attention (Sb-€48, Db-€62, bigger Db with air-con-€72, Tb with air-con-€82, three Db apartments-€92, Internet access and Wi-Fi, turn right off cours Jean Jaurès on rue Agricol Perdiguier to #17, tel. 04 90 86 14 46, fax 04 90 85 38 55, www.avignon-splendid-hotel.com, splendid avignon@gmail.com).

$ Hôtel Boquier**,** run by engaging managers Madame Sendra and husband Pascal, has 12 quiet, good-value, and homey rooms under wood beams in a central location (small Db-€59, bigger Db-€70, Tb-€79, Qb-€90, air-con, Internet access and Wi-Fi, steep and narrow stairways to some rooms and no elevator, parking-€7, near the TI at 6 rue du portail Boquier, tel. 04 90 82 34 43, fax 04 90 86 14 07, www.hotel-boquier.com, contact@hotel -boquier.com).

In the Center, near Place de l'Horloge

$$$ Hôtel d'Europe***, with Avignon's most prestigious address, lets peasants sleep royally without losing their shirts—but only if you land one of the 10 surprisingly reasonable "standard" rooms. Enter a shady courtyard, linger in the lounges, and savor every comfort. The hotel is located on the handsome place Crillon, near the river (standard Db-€200, superior Db-€360, prestige Db-€495, breakfast-€17, elevator, Internet access, garage-€17, near Daladier Bridge at 12 place Crillon, tel. 04 90 14 76 76, fax 04 90 14 76 71, www.heurope.com, reservations@heurope.com). The hotel's restaurant is Michelin-rated (one star) and serves an upscale €48 *menu* in its formal dining room or front courtyard.

$$$ Hôtel de l'Horloge**, situated in the heart of town, offers 66 warmly colored rooms, some with terraces and panoramic views of the city and the Palace of the Popes (standard Db-€100-

120, bigger Db with terrace-€150-200, terrace rooms also work as Tb or Qb, rue Félicien David, tel. 04 90 16 42 00, fax 04 90 82 17 32, www.hotel-avignon-horloge.com, hotel.horloge@hotels-ocre -azur.com).

$$$ Hôtel Mercure Cité des Papes*** is a modern chain hotel within spitting distance of the Palace of the Popes. It has 89 small, smartly designed rooms (Sb-€135, Db-€145-180, promotional deals best if booked 15 days ahead, many rooms have views over place de l'Horloge, air-con, elevator, 1 rue Jean Vilar, tel. 04 90 80 93 00, fax 04 90 80 93 01, www.mercure.com, h1952@accor .com).

$$$ Hôtel Pont d'Avignon***, just inside the walls near St. Bénezet Bridge, is part of the same chain as the Hôtel Mercure Cité des Papes, with the same prices for its 87 rooms (direct access to a garage makes parking easier than at the other Mercure hotel, elevator, on rue Ferruce, tel. 04 90 80 93 93, fax 04 90 80 93 94, www.mercure.com, h0549@accor.com).

$$ Hôtel Médiéval** is burrowed deep a few blocks from the Church of St. Pierre. Built as a cardinal's home, this massive stone mansion has a small garden and 35 wood-paneled, air-conditioned, unimaginative rooms, with friendly-as-they-get Régis at the helm (Sb-€51, Db-€64-81, bigger Db or Tb-€88-95, kitchenettes available but require 3-night minimum stay, Wi-Fi, 5 blocks east of place de l'Horloge, behind Church of St. Pierre at 15 rue Petite Saunerie, tel. 04 90 86 11 06, fax 04 90 82 08 64, www.hotel medieval.com, hotel.medieval@wanadoo.fr).

Lesser-Value Hotels in the Center

If you're in a pinch, one of these central places may work as a port in a storm.

$$$ Hôtel Kyriad Palais des Papes**, a tall, skinny hotel on happening place de l'Horloge, lacks personality but offers modern comforts (Db-€90-110, 26 place de l'Horloge, tel. 04 90 82 21 45, www.kyriad-avignon.com, hotel@kyriad-avignon.com).

$$ Hôtel Danieli**, a basic two-star hotel on the main drag, is popular with groups (Db-€82-88, 17 rue de la République, tel. 04 90 86 46 82, www.hoteldanieli-avignon.com, hotel.danieli .avignon@gmail.com).

$ Hôtel Mignon* is an acceptable one-star place with basic comfort and no air-conditioning (Db-€55-75, 12 rue Joseph Vernet, tel. 04 90 82 17 30, www.hotel-mignon.com, contact@hotel -mignon.com).

Chambres d'Hôtes

$$$ La Banasterie, a well-located refuge in a historic building a block behind the Palace of the Popes, has five spacious rooms—

PROVENCE

two with decks—and welcoming owners (Db-€100-170, cash only, includes breakfast, air-con, 11 rue de la Banasterie, tel. 04 32 76 30 78, www.labanasterie.com).

$$$ At **Le Clos du Rempart,** a 10-minute walk from the center, Madame Assad rents two comfortable rooms and one apartment on a peaceful courtyard with Middle Eastern decor (Db-€120-160 depending on season and room size, 2-bedroom apartment for 4 with kitchen-€800-1,100/week, includes breakfast, cash only, air-con, Wi-Fi, 1 parking spot in garage, inside the walls east of the Palace of the Popes at 35-37 rue Crémade—call or check website for directions, tel. & fax 04 90 86 39 14, www.closdurempart.com, aida@closdurempart.com).

$$$ **Lumani** provides the ultimate urban refuge just inside the city walls, a 15-minute walk from the Palace of the Popes. In this graceful old manor house, gentle Elisabeth and Jean welcome guests to their art-gallery-cum-bed-and-breakfast that surrounds a fountain-filled courtyard with elbow room. She paints, he designs buildings, and both care about your experience in Avignon. The five rooms are decorated with flair; no two are alike, and all overlook the shady garden (small Db-€100, big Db-€140, Db suites-€170, extra person-€30, includes breakfast, credit cards OK except American Express, Internet access and Wi-Fi, music studio, parking-€10 or easy on street, 37 rue de Rempart St. Lazare, tel. 04 90 82 94 11, www.avignon-lumani.com, lux @avignon-lumani.com).

On the Outskirts of Town

$ **Auberge Bagatelle's hostel** offers dirt-cheap beds, lively atmosphere, café, grocery store, launderette, great views of Avignon, and campers for neighbors (D-€44, Ds-€48, T-€60, Ts-€67, Tb-€82, Q-€73, Qb-€100, dorm bed-€18, includes breakfast, across Daladier Bridge on Ile de la Barthélasse, bus #10 from main post office, tel. 04 90 86 71 31, fax 04 90 27 16 23, www.auberge bagatelle.fr, auberge.bagatelle@wanadoo.fr).

Near Avignon

$$$ At **Jardin de Bacchus,** just 15 minutes northwest of Avignon and convenient to Pont du Gard, enthusiastic and English-speaking Christine and Erik offer three rooms in their rural farmhouse, which overlooks the famous rosé vineyards of Tavel (Db-€90-120, €30 extra for one-night stays, includes breakfast, fine dinner possible, Wi-Fi, swimming pool, tel. 04 66 90 28 62, www.jardindebacchus.fr, jardindebacchus@free.fr). To learn about their small-group food and wine tours, check their website. For bus connections, see www.edgard-transport.fr.

PROVENCE

Eating in Avignon

Dining on a Square

Skip the overpriced, underwhelming restaurants on place de l'Horloge and find a more intimate location for your dinner. Avignon has many delightful squares filled with tables ready to seat you.

Near the Church of St. Pierre

The church stands between two enchanting squares: Quiet and intimate place St. Pierre (where L'Epicerie sits alone), and, just under the nearby arch, lively and enchanting place des Châtaignes, with a fun commotion of tables—peruse your options.

La Vache à Carreaux venerates cheese and wine (while offering a full range of cuisine). The colorful decor is as warm as the welcome, and the wine list is extensive and reasonable. This place is a hit with locals, who gather around outside, sipping €4 glasses of good wine, reluctant to leave (€12-18 *plats*, open daily, just off place des Châtaignes at 14 rue de la Peyrollerie, tel. 04 90 80 09 05).

L'Epicerie, homey inside and out, serves top cuisine with a focus on products from the south of France—expect lots of color and a dash of spice (€35 *menu*, €18-25 *plats*, closed Sun off-season, 10 place St. Pierre, tel. 04 90 82 74 22).

Other Place des Châtaignes Options: The **Crêperie du Cloître** makes mediocre dinner crêpes and salads (daily, cash only). Next door and across from La Vache à Carreaux is the family-run Vietnamese **Restaurant Nem** (*menus* from €12, cash only). **Pause Gourmande** is a small, lunch-only eatery with €9 *plats du jour*, and always has a veggie option (closed Sun, around the corner and behind the church).

Other Squares

Place Crillon: This more refined square, just off the river, attracts a stylish crowd and houses a variety of dining choices. Traditional French **Restaurant La Scène** (tel. 04 90 86 14 70) and *italiano* **La Piazza** (tel. 04 90 82 23 54) are both popular and in about the same price range (€11 lunch deals, €17 dinner *menus* with fine choices, open daily). **La Comédie** serves €9 crêpes and salads with mod seating (closed Sun).

Place des Corps-Saints: This untouristy yet welcoming square is my favorite place for simple outdoor dining in Avignon. You'll find several youthful and reasonable eateries with tables sprawling under big plane trees. **Bistrot à Tartines** specializes in—you guessed it—*tartines* (big slices of toast smothered with toppings), and has the coziest interior and best desserts on the square (€8 *tartines* and salads, €9 lunch *menu*, daily, tel. 04 90 85 58 70). **Zeste**

PROVENCE

is a friendly, modern deli offering fresh soups, pasta salads, wraps, smoothies, and more. Get it to go, or eat inside or on the scenic square—all at unbeatable prices (closed Sun, tel. 09 51 49 05 62).

By the Market (Les Halles)

Here you'll find a good selection of eateries with good prices. **Restaurant Françoise** is a pleasant café and tea salon, where fresh-baked tarts—savory and sweet—and a variety of salads and soups make a healthful meal, and vegetarian options are plentiful (€7-12 dishes, Mon-Sat 8:00-19:00, closed Sun, free Wi-Fi, 6 rue Général Leclerc, tel. 04 32 76 24 77).

Rue des Teinturiers

This "tie-dye" street has a wonderful concentration of eateries popular with the natives, and justifies the long walk. It's a trendy, youthful area, spiffed up with a canalside ambience and little hint of tourism.

La Cave des Passages makes a colorful pause before dinner. The owners enjoy serving you a fragrant and cheap glass of regional wine. Choose from the blackboard by the bar that lists all the bottles open today, then join the gang outside by the canal. In the evening, this place is a hit with the young local crowd for its wine and weekend concerts (Mon-Sat 10:00-15:00 & 18:00-1:00 in the morning, closed Sun, no food in evening, across from water-wheel at 41 rue des Teinturiers).

Restaurant Numéro 75 is worth the walk (just past where the cobbles end on rue des Teinturiers). It fills the Pernod mansion (of *pastis* liquor fame) and a large, romantic courtyard with outdoor tables. The menu is limited to Mediterranean cuisine, but everything's *très* tasty. It's best to go with the options offered by your young black-shirted server (€27 two-course lunch *menu* with wine and coffee, dinner *menus:* €34/appetizer and main course or main course and dessert, €43/three courses; Mon-Sat 12:00-14:00 & 20:00-22:00, closed Sun, 75 rue Guillaume Puy, tel. 04 90 27 16 00).

Elsewhere in Avignon

At **L'Isle Sonnante,** join chef Boris and wife Anne to dine intimately in their formal and charming one-room *bistrot.* You'll choose from a small selection offering only fresh products and be served by owners who care (*menus* from €30, closed Sun-Mon, 100 yards from the carousel on place de l'Horloge at 7 rue Racine, tel. 04 90 82 56 01, best to book ahead).

At **Le Petit Bedon** you can savor fine, gourmet Provençal cuisine served with elegance in a romantically snug setting. All 10 tables are inside (€28-40 *menus,* open daily, 70 rue Joseph Vernet, tel. 04 90 82 33 98).

PROVENCE

Le Caveau du Théâtre is a welcoming place where Richard invites diners to have a glass of wine or dinner at a sidewalk table, or inside in one of two carefree rooms (€13 *plats*, €18 *menus*, fun ambience for free, closed for lunch Sat and all day Sun, 16 rue des Trois Faucons, tel. 04 90 82 60 91).

Le Fou de Fa Fa sits across from Le Caveau du Théâtre. Its friendly British owners are making a splash with locals, serving top-notch crêpes and inexpensive dishes in a warm setting (closed Mon, 17 rue des Trois Faucons, tel. 04 32 76 35 13).

Hôtel La Mirande is the ultimate Avignon splurge. Reserve ahead here for understated elegance and Avignon's finest cuisine (€35 lunch *menu*, €115 dinner tasting *menu*; closed Tue-Wed— but for a price break, dine in the kitchen with the chef on these "closed" days for €110 including wine; behind Palace of the Popes, 4 place de la Mirande, tel. 04 90 14 20 20, www.la-mirande.fr).

At L'Epice and Love (the name is a fun French-English play on words, pronounced "lay peace and love"), English-speaking owner Marie creates a playful atmosphere in her inviting restaurant, where the few colorfully decorated tables (inside only) greet the hungry traveler. The small menu changes daily, and Marie cooks it all: tasty meat, fish, and vegetarian dishes, some with a North African touch, all served at good prices (€16 *menus*, closed Sun, 30 rue des Lices, tel. 04 90 82 45 96).

Restaurant Au Jardin de la Tour, tucked away on a little street, is well worth finding. Internationally renowned chef Jean-Marc Larrue transformed this old factory and its courtyard into one of the most popular and affordable gourmet destinations in Avignon (€20-60 *menus*, closed Sun-Mon, cooking classes available, 9 rue de la Tour, tel. 04 90 85 66 50, www.jardindelatour.fr).

Across the River

Le Bercail offers a fun opportunity to get out of town (barely) and take in *le fresh air* with a terrific riverfront view of Avignon, all while enjoying fun Provençal cooking served in big portions (*menus* from €25, serves late, daily April-Oct, tel. 04 90 82 20 22). Take the free shuttle boat (located near St. Bénezet Bridge) to the Ile de la Barthélasse, turn right, and walk five minutes. As the boat usually stops running at about 18:00 (except in July-Aug, when it runs until 21:00), you can either taxi home or walk 25 minutes along the pleasant riverside path and over Daladier Bridge.

Avignon Connections

By Train

Remember, there are two train stations in Avignon: the suburban TGV Station and the Centre-Ville Station in the city center (€1.20

shuttle buses connect to both stations, buy ticket from driver, 3/ hour, 15 minutes). TGV trains usually serve the TGV Station only, though a few depart from Centre-Ville Station (check your station). Only Centre-Ville has baggage storage (see "Arrival in Avignon," page 386). Car rental is available only at the TGV Station. Some cities are served by slower local trains from Centre-Ville Station as well as by faster TGV trains from the TGV Station; I've listed the most convenient stations for each trip.

From Avignon's Centre-Ville Station by Train to: Arles (11/ day, 20 minutes, less frequent in the afternoon), **Lyon** (10/day, 2 hours, also from TGV Station in 1 hour—see below), **Paris'** Gare de Lyon (4/day direct, 3.75 hours; more with change, 3-4 hours, also from TGV Station—see below), **Barcelona** (2/day, 6-9 hours, transfer in Montpellier).

From Avignon's TGV Station to: Arles (by SNCF bus, 10/ day, 1 hour), **Nice** (20/day, most by TGV, 4 hours, most require transfer in Marseille), **Marseille** (10/day, 35 minutes), **Lyon** (12/day, 1 hour, also from Centre-Ville Station—see above), **Paris'** Gare de Lyon (9/day direct, 2.5 hours; also from Centre-Ville Station—see above), **Paris'** Charles de Gaulle airport (7/day, 3 hours).

By Bus

The bus station *(gare routière)* is just past and below Hôtel Ibis, to the right as you exit the train station. Nearly all buses leave from this station (a few leave from the ring road outside the station—ask, buy tickets on bus, small bills only). The biggest exception is the SNCF bus service from the Avignon TGV Station to Arles (explained earlier). The Avignon TI has schedules. Service is reduced or nonexistent on Sundays and holidays. Check your departure time beforehand, and make sure to verify your destination with the driver.

From Avignon to Pont du Gard: Buses go to this famous old aqueduct (3-5/day, 40-50 minutes, departs from bus station, usually from stall #11); I'd also consider a taxi one-way and bus back.

PROVENCE

Pont du Gard

Throughout the ancient world, aqueducts were like flags of stone that heralded the greatness of Rome. A visit to this sight still works to proclaim the wonders of that age. This perfectly preserved Roman aqueduct was built in about 19 b.c. as the critical link of a 30-mile canal that, by dropping one inch for every 350 feet, supplied nine million gallons of water per day (about 100 gallons per second) to Nîmes—one of ancient Europe's largest cities. Though most of the aqueduct is on or below the ground, at Pont du Gard it spans a canyon on a massive bridge—one of the most remarkable surviving Roman ruins anywhere. Wear sturdy shoes if you want to climb around the aqueduct (footing is tricky), and bring swimwear and flip-flops if you plan to backstroke with views of the monument.

Getting to Pont du Gard

The famous aqueduct is between Remoulins and Vers-Pont du Gard on D-981, 13 miles from Avignon.

By Car: Pont du Gard is a 25-minute drive due west of Avignon (follow N-100 from Avignon, tracking signs to *Nîmes* and *Remoulins,* then *Pont du Gard* and *Rive Gauche*), and 45 minutes northwest of Arles (via Tarascon on D-15). While parking is available on the Rive Droite (Right Bank), it's farther away from the museum than parking on the Rive Gauche (Left Bank). If going

PROVENCE

to Arles from Pont du Gard, follow signs to *Nîmes* (not *Avignon*), then follow D-986 and then D-15 to Arles.

By Bus: Buses run to Pont du Gard (on the Rive Gauche side) from Avignon (3/day, 50 minutes), Nîmes, and Uzès. Consider this plan: Take a morning bus from Avignon's bus station (8:45 or 11:40), then hop on the early-afternoon (13:24) or evening (17:32) bus back to Avignon. (Confirm specific times locally.) Allow about two hours for visiting Pont du Gard.

Buses stop at the traffic roundabout 300 yards from the aqueduct (see Pont du Gard map). In summer and on weekends, however, buses usually drive into the Pont du Gard site and stop at the parking lot's ticket booth. Confirm where the bus stops at the parking booth inside the Pont du Gard site.

At the roundabout, the stop for buses coming from Avignon and Nîmes (and going to Uzès) is on the side opposite Pont du Gard; the stop for buses to Nîmes and to Avignon is on the same side as Pont du Gard (a block to your left as you exit Pont du Gard onto the main road). Make sure you're waiting for the bus on the correct side of the traffic circle (stops have schedules posted), and wave your hand to signal the bus to stop for you (otherwise, it'll chug on by). Buy your ticket when you get on and verify your destination with the driver.

By Taxi: From Avignon, it's about €50 for a taxi to Pont du Gard (allow €64 after 19:00 and on Sun). If you're staying in Avignon and only want to see Pont du Gard, consider splurging on a taxi to the aqueduct in the morning, then take the early-afternoon bus back.

Orientation to Pont du Gard

There are two riversides to Pont du Gard: the Left Bank (Rive Gauche) and Right Bank (Rive Droite). Park on the Rive Gauche, where you'll find the museums, ticket booth, ATM, cafeteria, WCs, and shops—all built into a modern plaza. You'll see the aqueduct in two parts: first the fine museum complex, then the actual river gorge spanned by the ancient bridge.

Cost and Hours: The aqueduct, museum, film, and outdoor *garrigue* nature area are all free, but parking is €15 per car (those arriving by bus or bike pay nothing). The museum is open daily May-Sept 9:00-19:00, Oct-April 9:00-17:00, closed two weeks in Jan. The aqueduct itself is open until 1:00 in the morning, as is the parking lot. The *garrigue* is always open. Toll tel. 08 20 90 33 30, www.pontdugard.fr.

Information: For an extra €6, you can rent an **audioguide** with detailed English explanations of the aqueduct. Call ahead or visit the website for information on **guided walks** on top of the aqueduct (€10). Consider the helpful €4 English **booklet** about the *garrigue*—the extensive nature area featuring historic crops and landscapes of the Mediterranean.

Canoe Rental: Floating under Pont du Gard by canoe is an experience you won't soon forget. Collias Canoes will pick you up at Pont du Gard (or elsewhere, if pre-arranged) and shuttle you to the town of Collias. You'll float down the river to the nearby town of Remoulins, where they'll pick you up and take you back to Pont du Gard (€21/person, €12/child under 12, usually 2 hours, though you can take as long as you like, good idea to reserve the day before in July-Aug, tel. 04 66 22 85 54).

Plan Ahead for Swimming and Hiking: Pont du Gard is perhaps best enjoyed on your back and in the water—bring along a swimsuit and flip-flops for the rocks. The best Pont du Gard viewpoints are up steep hills with uneven footing—bring good shoes.

Sights at Pont du Gard

▲**Museum**—In this state-of-the-art museum (well-presented in English), you'll enter to the sound of water and understand the critical role fresh water played in the Roman "art of living." You'll see examples of lead pipes, faucets, and siphons; walk through a mock rock quarry; and learn how they moved those huge rocks into place and how those massive arches were made. While actual artifacts from the aqueduct are few, the exhibit shows the immensity of the undertaking as well as the payoff. Imagine the excitement as this extravagant supply of water finally tumbled into Nîmes. A relaxing highlight is the scenic video of a helicopter ride along the entire 30-mile course of the structure, from its start at Uzès all the way to the Castellum in Nîmes.

Other Activities—Several additional attractions are designed to give the sight more meaning—and they do (but for most visitors, the museum is sufficient). A corny, romancing-the-aqueduct 25-minute film plays in the same building as the museum and offers good information in a flirtatious French-Mediterranean style...and a cool, entertaining, and cushy break. The nearby kids' museum, called *Ludo*, offers a scratch-and-sniff teaching experience (in English) of various aspects of Roman life and the importance of water. The extensive outdoor *garrigue* natural area, closer to the aqueduct, features historic crops and landscapes of the Mediterranean.

▲▲▲**Viewing the Aqueduct**—A park-like path leads to the aqueduct. Until a few years ago, this was an actual road—adjacent to the aqueduct—that had spanned the river since 1743. Before you cross the bridge, pass under it and hike about 300 feet along the riverbank for a grand viewpoint from which to study the world's second-highest standing Roman structure. (Rome's Colosseum is only 6 feet taller.)

This was the biggest bridge in the whole 30-mile-long aqueduct. It seems exceptional because it is: The arches are twice the width of standard aqueducts, and the main arch is the largest the Romans ever built—80 feet (so it wouldn't get its feet wet). The bridge is about 160 feet high and was originally about 1,100 feet long. Today, 12 arches are missing, reducing the length to 790 feet.

Though the distance from the source (in Uzès) to Nîmes was only 12 miles as the eagle flew, engineers chose the most economical route, winding and zigzagging 30 miles. The water made the trip in 24 hours with a drop of only 40 feet. Ninety percent of the aqueduct is on or under the ground, but a few river canyons like this required bridges. A stone lid hides a four-foot-wide, six-foot-tall chamber lined with waterproof mortar that carried the stream for more than 400 years. For 150 years, this system provided Nîmes with good drinking water. Expert as the Romans were, they miscalculated the backup caused by a downstream corner, and had to add the thin extra layer you can see just under the lid to make the channel deeper.

The bridge and the river below provide great fun for holiday-goers. While parents suntan on rocks, kids splash into the gorge from under the aqueduct. Some daredevils actually jump from the aqueduct's lower bridge—not knowing that crazy winds scrambled by the structure cause painful belly flops (and sometimes even accidental deaths). For the most refreshing view, float flat on your back underneath the structure.

The appearance of the entire gorge changed in 2002, when a huge flood flushed lots of greenery downstream. Those floodwaters put Roman provisions to the test. Notice the triangular-shaped buttresses at the lower level—designed to split and divert the force of any flood *around* the feet of the arches rather than *into* them. The 2002 floodwaters reached the top of those buttresses. Anxious park rangers winced at the sounds of trees crashing onto the ancient stones...but the arches stood strong.

The stones that jut out—giving the aqueduct a rough, unfinished appearance—supported the original scaffolding. The protuberances were left, rather than cut off, in anticipation of future repair needs. The lips under the arches supported wooden templates that allowed the stones in the round arches to rest on something until the all-important keystone was dropped into place. Each stone weighs four to six tons. The structure stands with no mortar—taking full advantage of the innovative Roman arch, made strong by gravity.

Hike over the bridge for a closer look and the best views. Steps lead up a high trail (marked *panorama*) to a superb viewpoint (go right at the top; best views are soon after the trail starts descending). You'll also see where the aqueduct meets a rock tunnel. Walk through the tunnel and continue for a bit, following a trail that meanders along the canal's path.

Back on the museum side, steps lead up to the Rive Gauche (parking lot) end of the aqueduct, where you can follow the canal path along a trail (marked with red-and-white horizontal lines) to find some remains of the Roman canal. You'll soon reach another *panorama* with great views of the aqueduct. Hikers can continue along the path, following the red-and-white markings that lead through a forest, after which you'll come across more remains of the canal (much of which are covered by vegetation). There's not much left to see because of medieval cannibalization—frugal builders couldn't resist the precut stones as they constructed area churches (stones along the canal were easier to retrieve than those high up on the aqueduct). The path continues for about 15 miles, but there's little reason to go farther. However, there is talk of opening the ancient quarry...someday.

NICE ON THE FRENCH RIVIERA

La Côte d'Azur

A hundred years ago, celebrities from London to Moscow flocked to the French Riviera to socialize, gamble, and escape the dreary weather at home. Today, budget vacationers and heat-seeking Europeans fill belle-époque resorts at France's most sought-after fun-in-the-sun destination.

Some of the Continent's most stunning scenery and intriguing museums lie along this strip of land—as do millions of sun-worshipping tourists. Evenings on the Riviera, a.k.a. La Côte d'Azur, were made for a promenade and outdoor dining.

My favorite (and the most convenient) home base is Nice, the region's capital and France's fifth-largest city. With easy train and bus connections to most regional sights, it's practical for train travelers. Urban Nice has a full palette of world-class museums, a splendid beachfront promenade, a seductive old town, and all the drawbacks of a major city (traffic, crime, pollution, and so on). Nice also has the best selection of hotels in all price ranges, and good nightlife options. A car is a headache in Nice, though it's easily stored at one of the many pricey parking garages or for free at an outer tram station.

Nice

Nice (sounds like "niece"), with its spectacular Alps-to-Mediterranean surroundings, is an enjoyable big-city highlight of the Riviera. Its traffic-free old city mixes Italian and French flavors to create a spicy Mediterranean dressing, while its big squares, broad seaside walkways, and long beaches invite lounging and people-watching. Nice may be nice, but it's hot and jammed in July and August—reserve ahead and get a room with air-conditioning *(une chambre avec climatisation)*. Everything you'll want to see in Nice is either within walking distance, or a short bus or tram ride away.

Orientation to Nice

The main points of interest lie between the beach and the train tracks (about 15 blocks apart). The city revolves around its grand place Masséna, where pedestrian-friendly avenue Jean Médecin meets Old Nice and the Albert 1er parkway (with quick access to the beaches). It's a 20-minute walk (or a €15 taxi ride) from the train station to the beach, and a 20-minute walk along the promenade from the fancy Hôtel Negresco to the heart of Old Nice.

A 10-minute ride on the smooth-as-silk tramway through the center of the city connects the train station, place Masséna, Old Nice, and the port (from nearby place Garibaldi). The tram and all city and regional buses cost only €1 per trip, making this one of the cheapest and easiest cities in France to get around in (see "Getting Around Nice," later).

Tourist Information

Nice's helpful TIs share a phone number and website (toll tel. 08 92 70 74 07—€0.34/minute, www.nicetourisme.com) and there are several locations: at the **airport** (desks in both terminals, typically quiet, daily 8:00-21:00, closed Sun off-season), next to the **train station** (busy, summer Mon-Sat 8:00-20:00, Sun 9:00-18:00; rest of year Mon-Sat 9:00-19:00, Sun 10:00-17:00); facing the **beach** at 5 promenade des Anglais (moderately busy, daily 9:00-18:00, until 20:00 July-Aug, closed Sun off-season); and in a kiosk at the south end of **place Masséna** (less busy, typically daily 10:00-19:00). Pick up the thorough *Practical Guide to Nice* and a free Nice map (or find a better one at your hotel), but skip the Riviera Pass. You can also get day-trip information at the TI.

Arrival in Nice

By Train: All trains stop at Nice's main station, Nice-Ville (baggage storage at the far right with your back to the tracks, lockers

NICE

The French Riviera

open daily 8:00–21:00). The station area is gritty and busy: Never leave your bags unattended and don't linger here longer than necessary.

Turn left out of the station to find a **TI** next door. Continue a few more blocks down avenue Jean Médecin for the Gare Thiers **tram stop** (this will take you to place Masséna, the old city, and the port). Board the tram heading toward the right, direction: Pont Michel (see "Getting Around Nice," later). You'll find many recommended hotels a 10- to 20-minute walk down the same street (listed under "Between Nice Etoile and the Sea" on page 438), though it's easier to take the tram to place Masséna and walk from there.

To walk to other recommended hotels (listed under "Between the Train Station and Nice Etoile" on page 434, and "Between Boulevard Victor Hugo and the Sea" on page 442), cross avenue Thiers in front of the station, go down the steps by Hôtel Interlaken, and continue walking down avenue Durante. Follow this same route for the fastest path from the station to the beach—avenue Durante turns into rue des Congrés. You'll soon reach the heart of Nice's beachfront promenade.

Taxis and **buses to the airport** (#23 and #99) wait in front of the train station. **Car rental** offices are to the right as you exit the station.

By Bus: Nice's bus station was recently demolished as part of a major project to expand Nice's central parkway. Most stops for bus routes important to travelers (those serving Antibes, the airport, Vence, Villefranche-sur-Mer, Monaco, and St-Jean-Cap-Ferrat) have been relocated between boulevard Jean Jaurès and avenue Félix Faure, near place Masséna (see maps on pages 416 and 440). Expect changes to bus stop locations as the parkway project evolves.

By Car: To reach the city center on the autoroute from the west, take the first Nice exit (for the airport—called Côte d'Azur, Central) and follow signs for *Nice Centre* and *Promenade des Anglais*. Try to avoid arriving at rush hour (usually Mon-Fri 8:00-9:30 & 17:00-19:30), when promenade des Anglais grinds to a halt. Hoteliers know where to park (allow €15-26/day; some hotels offer special deals but space is limited, so reserve ahead). The parking garage at the Nice Etoile shopping center on avenue Jean Médecin is pricey but near many recommended hotels (ticket booth on third floor, about €20/day, €11 from 20:00-8:00). The garage next to the recommended Hôtel Ibis at the train station has better rates. All on-street parking is metered (9:00-18:00 or 19:00), but usually free all day Sunday.

You can avoid driving in the center—and park for free during the day (no overnight parking)—by ditching your car at a parking lot at a remote tram stop (Las Planas is best) and taking the tram into town (€1, 15 minutes, 10/hour, don't leave anything in your car, tramway described later under "Getting Around Nice"). To find the Las Planas tram station from the A-8 autoroute, take the *Nice Nord* exit.

By Plane: For information on Nice's airport, see page 451.

Helpful Hints

Theft Alert: Nice has its share of pickpockets. Thieves target fanny packs: Have nothing important on or around your waist, unless it's in a money belt tucked out of sight. Don't leave things unattended on the beach while swimming, and stick to main streets in Old Nice after dark.

Medical Help: Riviera Medical Services has a list of English-speaking physicians all along the Riviera. They can help you

Nice

1/4 MILE
400 METERS

N

TO LAS PLANAS TRAM STOP, P & A-8 AUTOROUTE

AVE. MALAUSSENA

1. To High Corniche (sky-high route to Monaco)
2. To Middle Corniche (middle route, best for Monaco & Eze-le-Village)
3. To Low Corniche (low route to Villefranche-sur-Mer & Cap Ferrat)
4. Start of "Old Nice" Walk
5. To Fine Arts Museum
6. War Memorial
7. US Consulate
8. Trans Côte d'Azur Cruises
9. Le Grand Tour Bus Departure Point & Albert 1er Park

TO ENTRE-VAUX

CHEMINS DE FER TRAIN STN.

RUSSIAN CATH.

ELE-VATED AVE THIERS

i HI

DURANTE

GAMBETTA BLVD.

TRAIN STN.

BLVD CONGRES

Tram
P Parking

TO 5

R. DE FRANCE

MASSENA MUSEUM

HOTEL NEGRESCO

PROMENADE DES ANG

B E A C

TO AIRPORT

TO ANTIBES, CANNES & VENCE

DCH   MEDI

NICE

CIMIEZ

(B) #15 + #22

Matisse Museum

■ Roman Ruins

Archaeological Museum

BLVD. DE CIMIEZ

AVE. DES ARENES

(B) #17

Chagall Museum

TO PONT MICHEL TRAM STOP, P & A-8 AUTOROUTE

AVE. COMBOUL

(B) #15 + #22

DE CIMIEZ

TUNNEL

TUNNEL

RUE DES DIABLES BLEUS

TO ①

GHWAY

RAIMBALDI

DESAMBROIS

AVE. REPUBLIQUE

TO ②

JEAN MEDECIN

Notre-Dame P

DUBOUCHAGE

Modern Art Museum ■

RUE BARLA

CASSINI

HUGO

(B) #15 #17 + #22

AVE. FAURE

BLVD. JAURES

Place Gari-Baldi

TO ③

BLVD. CARNOT

RUE MASSENA

⑦ i

ⓘ

⑨

ℹ **Place Massena**

④ OLD NICE

COURS SALEYA

Castle Hill

QUAI DE LUNEL

PORT ⑧

LAIS

QUAI D. ETATS-UNIS

Elevator

⑥

H E S R

Tourist Train Pick-Up

Bellanda Tower

TO VILLEFRANCHE, MONACO & ITALY

TERRANEAN SEA

make an appointment or call an ambulance (tel. 04 93 26 12 70, www.rivieramedical.com).

Events: The Riviera is famous for staging major events. Unless you're actually taking part in the festivities, these occasions give you only hotel-room shortages and traffic jams. Here are the three biggies: **Nice Carnival** (mid-Feb-early March, www.nicecarnaval.com), **Grand Prix of Monaco** (late May, www.acm.mc), and Festival de Cannes, better known as the **Cannes Film Festival** (mid-May, www.festival-cannes.com).

Sightseeing Tips: Some Nice museums (Chagall, Matisse, Archaeological) are closed on Tuesdays, while others (Modern and Contemporary Art, Fine Arts) close on Mondays. City museums are free of charge, all of the sights in Nice—except the Chagall Museum and the Russian Cathedral (closed indefinitely)—cost zilch to enter, making rainy-day options a swinging deal here.

Internet Access: There's no shortage of places to get online. Almost all of the hotels I list have free Wi-Fi, and some have computers for guests. For other access points, ask at your hotel or look for one of these establishments, all with free Wi-Fi: **Quick Hamburger, Häagen Dazs,** and **McDonald's** (multiple locations), or the **Nice Etoile Shopping Center** and **Virgin Megastore** (on avenue Jean Médecin).

Laundry: You'll find launderettes everywhere in Nice—ask your hotelier for the nearest one.

Grocery Store: The big **Monoprix** on avenue Jean Médecin and rue Biscarra has it all, including deli counter, bakery, and cold drinks (Mon-Sat 8:30-21:00, closed Sun, see map on page 446). You'll also find many small grocery stores (some open Sun and/or until late hours) near my recommended hotels.

Boutique Shopping: The chic streets where rue Alphonse Karr meets rue de la Liberté and then rue de Paradis are known as the "Golden Square." If you need pricey stuff, shop here.

SNCF Boutique: There's a handy French rail ticket office a half-block west of avenue Jean Médecin at 2 rue de la Liberté (Mon-Sat 9:00-12:00 and 14:00-18:30, closed Sun).

Renting a Bike (and Other Wheels): Roller Station rents bikes (*vélos,* can be taken on trains, €5/hour, €10/half-day, €15/day), rollerblades, skateboards, and Razor-type scooters (*trotinettes,* €7/half-day, €9/day). You'll need to leave your ID as a deposit (daily April-June and Sept-Oct 10:00-20:00, July-Aug 10:00-24:00, Nov-March 10:00-18:00, next to yellow awnings of Pailin's Asian restaurant at 49 quai des Etats-Unis—see map on page 440, tel. 04 93 62 99 05, owner Eric). If you need more power, the TI has a list of places renting electric scooters.

You'll notice blue bikes **(Vélos Bleu)** stationed at various points in the city. A thousand of these bikes, available for locals to use when running errands, rent cheaply for short-term use (first 30 minutes free, requires European-style chip-and-PIN credit card).

Car Rental: Renting a car is easiest at Nice's airport, which has offices for all the major companies. You'll also find most companies represented at Nice's train station and near Albert 1er Park.

English Radio: Tune in to Riviera-Radio at FM 106.5.

Views: For panoramic views, climb Castle Hill (see page 427), or take a one-hour boat trip (described later, under "Tours in Nice").

Beach Gear: To make life tolerable on the rocks, swimmers should buy a pair of the cheap plastic beach shoes sold at many shops (flip-flops fall off in the water). **Go Sport** at #13 on place Masséna sells beach shoes, flip-flops, and cheap sunglasses (daily 10:00-19:00—see map on page 440).

Getting Around Nice

Although you can walk to most attractions in Nice, smart travelers make good use of the buses and tram. Both are covered by the same €1 single-ride ticket (good for 74 minutes in one direction, including transfers between bus and tram; can't be used for a round-trip). The **bus** is particularly handy for reaching the Chagall and Matisse museums and the Russian Cathedral (closed indefinitely). Pick up timetables at Nice's TIs (or view them online at www.lignesdazur .com) and buy tickets from the driver. Make sure to validate your ticket in the machine just behind the driver—watch locals do it and imitate.

The €4 all-day pass is valid on city buses and trams, as well as buses to some nearby destinations. The all-day ticket makes sense if you plan to take the bus to museums, use the tramway several times, or are going to the airport (you must validate your ticket on every trip). Express buses to and from the airport (#98 and #99) require the €4 all-day ticket, so savvy riders pack in other bus and/or tram rides on the day of their flight.

Nice's **tramway** makes an "L" along avenue Jean Médecin and boulevard Jean Jaurès, and connects the main train station (Gare Thiers stop), place Masséna (Masséna stop, near many regional bus stops and a few blocks' walk from the sea), Old Nice (Opéra-Vieille Ville, Cathédrale-Vieille Ville), and the Modern and Contemporary Art Museum and port (Place Garibaldi).

Boarding the tram in the direction of Pont Michel takes you from the train station toward the beach and Old Nice (direction: Las Planas goes the other way). Buy tickets at the machines on the platforms (coins only, no credit cards). Choose the English flag to

NICE

change the display language, turn the round knob and push the green button to select your ticket, press it twice at the end to get your ticket, or press the red button to cancel. Once you're on the tram, validate your ticket by inserting it into the top of the white box, then reclaiming it (http://tramway.nice.fr).

Taxis are useful for getting to Nice's less-central sights, and worth it if you're nowhere near a bus or tram stop (figure €15 from promenade des Anglais). Cabbies normally only pick up at taxi stands *(tête de station)*, or you can call 04 93 13 78 78.

The hokey **tourist train** gets you up Castle Hill (see "Tours in Nice," later).

Getting Around the Riviera

By Train and Bus: Nice is perfectly situated for exploring the Riviera by public transport. Monaco, Eze-le-Village, Villefranche-sur-Mer, Antibes, Vence, and St-Paul-de-Vence are all within about a one-hour bus or train ride. The train is pricier (fares range from €2 to nearby Villefranche-sur-Mer to €7.50 to farther-away Grasse) than the bus (€1 for most destinations), but will often save you time. You make the call—both modes of transportation work well.

All trains serving Nice arrive at and depart from the Nice-Ville station (www.sncf.com). Most regional buses stop near place Masséna, on or near boulevard Jean Jaurès, or near place Garibaldi (near Old Nice, see maps on pages 416 and 440 for stop locations, www.lignesdazur.com). For a summary of train and bus connections, see "Nice Connections" on page 450.

By Boat: From June to mid-September, Trans Côte d'Azur offers scenic trips from Nice to Monaco and Nice to St-Tropez. Boats leave in the morning and return in the evening, giving you all day to explore your destination. Drinks and WCs are available on board.

Boats to **Monaco** depart at 9:30 and 16:00, and return at 11:00 and 18:00 (€34 round-trip, €29 if you don't get off in Monaco, 45 minutes each way, June-Sept Tue, Thu, and Sat only).

Boats to **St-Tropez** depart at 9:00 and return at 19:00 (€57 round-trip, 2.5 hours each way; July-mid-Sept Tue-Sun, no boats Mon; June and late Sept Tue, Thu, and Sun only).

Reservations are required for both boats, and tickets for St-Tropez often sell out, so book a few days ahead (tel. 04 92 98 71 30 or 04 92 00 42 30, www.trans-cote-azur.com, croisieres @trans-cote-azur.com). The boats leave from Nice's port, bassin des Amiraux, just below Castle Hill—look for the blue ticket booth *(billeterie)* on quai de Lunel (see map on page 416). The same company also runs one-hour round-trip cruises along the coast to Cap Ferrat (see "Tours in Nice," next).

Public Transportation on the French Riviera

NOT TO SCALE

TO GRENOBLE

ITALY

FRANCE

VENTIMIGLIA

TO GENOA & CINQUE TERRE

ST. AUBAN

DIGNE

EZE-LE-VILLAGE

LA TURBIE

MENTON

TO AIX-EN-PROVENCE

EZE-BORD-DE-MER

MONACO

VENCE

CAP D'AIL

TOURETTES

NICE

BEAULIEU

BAR

ST. PAUL

CAP FERRAT

BIOT

VILLEFRANCHE

VALL.

ANTIBES

GRASSE

JUAN-LES-PINS

ST. RAPHAEL

CAP D'ANTIBES

TO MARSEILLE AVIGNON & PARIS

CANNES

RIVIERA

TO TOULON

ST. TROPEZ

—— RAIL

- - - BUS

•••• BOAT

✈ AIRPORTS (NOT ALL SHOWN)

MEDITERRANEAN SEA

DCH

Tours in Nice and the Riviera

Bus Tour—Le Grand Tour Bus provides a 14-stop, hop-on, hop-off service on an open-deck bus with headphone commentary (2/hour, 1.5-hour loop) that includes the promenade des Anglais, the old port, Cap de Nice, and the Chagall and Matisse museums on Cimiez Hill (€20/1-day pass, €23/2-day pass, cheaper for seniors and students, €10 for last tour of the day at about 18:00, some hotels offer small discounts, buy tickets on bus, main stop is near where promenade des Anglais and quai des Etats-Unis meet, across from the Plage Beau Rivage lounge, tel. 04 92 29 17 00, www.grayline.com—find Nice under "Our Destinations" tab). This tour is

NICE

a pricey way to get to the Chagall and Matisse museums, but it's an acceptable option if you also want a city overview. Check the schedule if you plan to use this bus to see the Russian Cathedral (closed indefinitely), as it may be faster to walk there.

Tourist Train—For €7 (€4 for children under age 9) you can spend 45 embarrassing minutes on the tourist train tooting along the promenade, through the old city, and up to Castle Hill. This is a sweat-free way to get to the top of the hill, but so is the elevator, which is much cheaper (every 30 minutes, daily 10:00-18:00, June-Aug until 19:00, recorded English commentary, meet train near Le Grand Tour Bus stop on quai des Etats-Unis, tel. 04 93 62 85 48, www.trainstouristiquesdenice.com).

▲**Boat Cruise**—Here's your chance to view Nice from the water. On this one-hour star-studded tour run by Trans Côte d'Azur, you'll cruise in a comfortable yacht-size vessel to Cap Ferrat and past Villefranche-sur-Mer, then return to Nice with a final lap along promenade des Anglais. It's a scenic trip; the best views are from the seats on top.

French (and sometimes English-speaking) guides play Robin Leach, pointing out mansions owned by some pretty famous people, including Elton John (just as you leave Nice, it's the soft-yellow square-shaped place right on the water), Sean Connery (on the hill above Elton, with rounded arches and tower), and Microsoft co-founder Paul Allen (in saddle of Cap Ferrat hill, above yellow-umbrella beach with sloping red-tile roof). I wonder if this gang ever hangs out together. Guides also like to point out the mansion where the Rolling Stones recorded *Exile on Main Street* (between Villefranche-sur-Mer and Cap Ferrat). (€16; April-Oct Tue-Sun 2/day, usually at 11:00 and 15:00, no boats Mon or in off-season; call ahead to verify schedule, arrive 30 minutes early to get best seats, drinks and WCs available.) For directions to the dock and contact information, see "Getting Around the Riviera—By Boat," earlier.

Walking Tours—The TI on promenade des Anglais organizes weekly walking tours of Old Nice in French and English (€12, May-Oct only, usually Sat morning at 9:30, 2.5 hours, reservations necessary, depart from TI, toll tel. 08 92 70 74 07). They also have evening art walks on Fridays at 19:00.

Minivan Tours—The TI and most hotels have information on minivan excursions from Nice (roughly €50-60/half-day, €80-110/day). **Revelation Tours** takes pride in its guides (tel. 04 93 53 69 85, www.revelation-tours.com). **Med-Tour** is one of many (tel. 04 93 82 92 58, mobile 06 73 82 04 10, www.med-tour.com); **Tour Azur** is another (tel. 04 93 44 88 77, www.tourazur.com). All also offer private tours by the day or half-day (check with them for their outrageous prices, about €90/hour).

Local Guides—Sylvie Di Cristo offers terrific full-day tours throughout the French Riviera in a car or minivan. She adores educating people about this area's culture and history, and loves adapting her tour to your interests, from overlooked hill towns to wine, cuisine, art, or perfume (€200/person for 2-3 people, €130-150/person for 4-6 people, €90/person for 7-8 people, 2-person minimum, mobile 06 09 88 83 83, www.frenchrivieraguides.net, dicristo sylvie@gmail.com). **Sofia Villavicencio** is a young, sweet guide with a passion for art (€135/half-day, €200/day, tel. 04 93 32 45 92, mobile 06 68 51 55 52, sofia.villavicencio@laposte.net). Lovely **Pascale Rucker** tailors her tours in Nice to your interests. Book in advance, though it's also worth a try on short notice (€179/half-day, €274/day, tel. & fax 04 93 87 77 89, mobile 06 16 24 29 52).

Les Petits Farcis Cooking Tour and Classes—Charming Canadian Francophile Rosa Jackson, a food journalist, Cordon Bleu-trained cook, and longtime resident of France, offers popular cooking classes in Old Nice. Her single-day classes include a morning trip to the open-air market on cours Saleya to pick up ingredients, and an afternoon session spent creating an authentic Niçois meal from your purchases (€195/person, mobile 06 81 67 41 22, www.petitsfarcis.com).

Self-Guided Walk

▲▲A Scratch-and-Sniff Walk Through Old Nice

• *See the map on page* 440, *and start at Nice's main market square...*

Cours Saleya (koor sah-lay-yuh): Named for its broad exposure to the sun *(soleil)*, this commotion of color, sights, smells, and people has been Nice's main market square since the Middle Ages (produce market held Tue-Sun until 13:00—on Mon, an antiques market takes center stage). Amazingly, part of this square was a parking lot until 1980, when the mayor of Nice had an underground garage built.

The first section is devoted to the Riviera's largest flower market (all day Tue-Sun and in operation since the 19th century). Here you'll find plants and flowers that grow effortlessly and ubiquitously in this climate, including the local favorites: carnations, roses, and jasmine. Not long ago, this region supplied all of France with its flowers; today, many are imported from Africa (the glorious orchids are from Kenya). Still, fresh flowers are perhaps the best value in this city.

The boisterous produce section trumpets the season with mushrooms, strawberries, white asparagus, zucchini flowers, and more—whatever's fresh gets top billing. Find your way down the center and buy something healthy.

NICE

The market opens up at place Pierre Gautier (also called Plassa dou Gouvernou—bilingual street signs include the old Niçoise language, an Italian dialect). This is where farmers set up stalls to sell their produce and herbs directly.

Continue down the center of cours Saleya, stopping when you see La Cambuse restaurant on your left. In front, hovering over the black-barrel fire with the paella-like pan on top, is the self-proclaimed **Queen of the Market,** Thérèse. She's cooking *socca,* Nice's chickpea crêpe specialty (until about 13:00). Spend €3 for a wad (careful—it's hot, but good). If Thérèse doesn't have a pan out, that means it's on its way (watch for the frequent scooter deliveries). Wait in line...or else it'll be all gone when you return.

• *Continue down cours Saleya. The fine golden building that seals the end of the square is where Henri Matisse spent 17 years with a brilliant view onto Nice's world. The **Café les Ponchettes** is perfectly positioned for a people-watching break. Turn at the café onto...*

Rue de la Poissonnerie: Look up at the first floor of the first building on your right. **Adam and Eve** are squaring off, each holding a zucchini-like gourd. This scene (post-apple) represents the annual rapprochement in Nice to make up for the sins of a too-much-fun Carnival (Mardi Gras, the pre-Lenten festival). Residents of Nice have partied hard during Carnival for more than 700 years.

A few steps away, check out the small **Baroque church** (Notre-Dame-de-l'Annonciation) dedicated to St. Rita, the patron saint of desperate causes. She holds a special place in locals' hearts, making this the most popular church in Nice.

• *Turn right on the next street, where you'll pass Old Nice's most happening café/bar **(Distilleries Ideales)**, with a lively happy hour (18:00-20:00) and a Pirates of the Caribbean-style interior. Now turn left on "Right" Street (rue Droite), and enter an area that feels like a Little Naples.*

Rue Droite: In the Middle Ages, this straight, skinny street provided the most direct route from wall to wall, or river to sea. Stop at **Esipuno's bakery** (at place du Jésus, closed Mon-Tue) and say *bonjour* to the friendly folks. Decades ago, this baker was voted the best in France—the trophies you see were earned for bread-making, not bowling. His son now runs the place. Notice the firewood stacked behind the oven. Try the house specialty, *tourte aux blettes*—a Swiss chard tart. It's traditionally made with jam (a sweet, tasty breakfast treat), but there's also a savory version, stuffed with pine nuts, raisins, and white beets (my favorite for lunch).

Farther along, at #28, Thérèse (whom you met earlier) cooks her *socca* in the wood-fired oven before she carts it to her barrel on cours Saleya. The balconies of the mansion in the next block mark the **Palais Lascaris** (c. 1647, gorgeous at night), a rare souvenir from one of Nice's most prestigious families. It's worth popping inside (handy WCs) for its Baroque Italian architecture and terrific collection of antique musical instruments—harps, guitars, violins, and violas (good English explanations). You'll also find elaborate tapestries and a few well-furnished rooms. The palace has four levels: The ground floor was used for storage, the first floor was devoted to reception rooms (and musical events), the owners lived a floor above that, and the servants lived at the top—with a good view but lots of stairs (free, Wed-Mon 10:00-18:00, closed Tue). Look up and make faces back at the guys under the balconies.

• *Turn left on rue de la Loge, then left again on rue Centrale, to reach...*

Place Rossetti: The most Italian of Nice's piazzas, place Rossetti feels more like Roma than Nice. Named for the man who donated his land to create this square, place Rossetti comes alive after dark. The recommended Fenocchio gelato shop is popular for its many flavors, ranging from classic to innovative.

Walk to the fountain and stare back at the church. This is the **Cathedral of St. Réparate**—an unassuming building for a major city's cathedral. It was relocated here in the 1500s, when Castle Hill was temporarily converted to military use only. The name comes from Nice's patron saint, a teenage virgin named Réparate whose martyred body floated to Nice in the fourth century accompanied by angels. The interior of the cathedral gushes Baroque, a response to the Protestant Reformation. With the Catholic Church's Counter-Reformation, the theatrical energy of churches was cranked up with re-energized, high-powered saints and eye-popping decor.

• *Our walk is over. Castle Hill is straight up the stepped lane opposite the cathedral.*

Sights in Nice

Walks and Beach Time

▲▲▲**Promenade des Anglais and Beach**—Welcome to the Riviera. There's something for everyone along this four-mile-long seafront circus. Watch Europeans at play, admire the azure Mediterranean, anchor yourself on a blue seat, and prop your feet up on the made-to-order guardrail. Later in the day, come back to join the evening parade of tans along the promenade.

The broad sidewalks of the promenade des Anglais ("walk-way of the English") were financed by upper-crust English tourists who wanted a secure and comfortable place to stroll and admire the view. The walk was done in marble in 1822 for aristocrats who didn't want to dirty their shoes or smell the fishy gravel.

Stroll like the belle-époque English aristocrats for whom the promenade was paved. Start at the pink-domed Hôtel Negresco, then cross to the sea and end your promenade at Castle Hill. The following sights are listed in the order you'll pass them. This walk is ideally done at sunset (as a pre-dinner stroll).

Hôtel Negresco—Nice's finest hotel is also a historic monument, offering up the city's most expensive beds (see "Sleeping in Nice," later) and a free "museum" interior (always open—provided you're dressed decently, absolutely no beach attire).

March straight through the lobby (as if you're staying here) into the exquisite **Salon Royal,** an elegant place for a drink and a frequent host to modern art exhibits (opens at 11:00). The chandelier hanging from the Eiffel-built dome is made of 16,000 pieces of crystal. It was built in France for the Russian czar's Moscow palace...but thanks to the Bolshevik Revolution in 1917, he couldn't take delivery (portraits of Czar Alexander III and his wife, Maria Feodorovna—who returned to her native Denmark after the revolution—are to the right, under the dome). Saunter around the perimeter counterclockwise. If the bar door is open (after about 15:00), wander up the marble steps for a look. Farther along, nip into the toilets for either an early 20th-century powder room or a Battle of Waterloo experience. The chairs nearby were typical of the age (cones of silence for an afternoon nap sitting up).

Bay of Angels (Baie des Anges)—Grab a blue chair and face the sea. The body of Nice's patron saint, Réparate, was supposedly escorted into this bay by angels in the fourth century. To your right is where you might have been escorted into France—Nice's airport, built on a massive landfill. On that tip of land way beyond the runway is Cap d'Antibes. Until 1860, Antibes and Nice were in different countries—Antibes was French, but Nice was a protectorate of the Italian kingdom of Savoy-Piedmont, a.k.a. the Kingdom of Sardinia. In 1850, the people here spoke Italian and ate pasta. As Italy was uniting, the region was given a choice: Join the new country of Italy or join good old France (which was enjoying good times under the rule of Napoleon III). The vast majority voted in 1860 to go French...and voilà!

The lower green hill to your left is Castle Hill (described later). Farther left lies Villefranche-sur-Mer (marked by the tower at land's end, and home to lots of millionaires), then Monaco (which you can't see, with more millionaires), then Italy (with lots of, uh, Italians). Behind you are the foothills of the Alps (Alpes-Maritimes), which trap threatening clouds, ensuring that the Côte d'Azur enjoys sunshine more than 300 days each year. While half a million people live here, pollution is carefully treated—the water is routinely tested and very clean.

Stroll the promenade with the sea starboard, and contemplate beach time on your way to the Albert 1er Park.

Beaches—Settle in on the smooth rocks or find a section with imported sand, and consider your options: You can play beach volleyball, table tennis, or *boules;* rent paddleboats, personal watercraft, or windsurfing equipment; explore ways to use your zoom lens and pretend you're a paparazzo; or snooze on a comfy beach bed.

To rent a spot on the beach, compare rates, as prices vary—beaches on the east end of the bay are usually cheaper (chair and mattress—*chaise longue* and *transat*—about €15, umbrella-€5, towel-€4). Some hotels have special deals with certain beaches for discounted rentals (check with your hotel for details). Have lunch in your bathing suit (€12 salads and pizzas in bars and restaurants all along the beach). Or, for a peaceful café au lait on the Mediterranean, stop here first thing in the morning before the crowds hit. *Plage Publique* signs explain the 15 beach no-nos (translated into English).

Albert 1er Park—The park is named for the Belgian king who enjoyed wintering here—these were his private gardens. While the English came first, the Belgians and Russians were also big fans of 19th-century Nice. That tall statue at the edge of the park commemorates the 100-year anniversary of Nice's union with France.

If you detour from the promenade into the park and continue down the center of the grassy strip, you'll be walking over Nice's river, the Paillon (covered since the 1800s). For centuries, this river was Nice's natural defense to the north and west (the sea protected the south, and Castle Hill defended the east). Imagine the fortified wall that ran along its length from the hills behind you to the sea. With the arrival of tourism in the 1800s, Nice expanded over and beyond the river.

▲Castle Hill (Colline du Château)—This hill—in an otherwise flat city center—offers sensational views over Nice, the port (to the east), the foothills of the Alps, and the Mediterranean. The views are best early or at sunset, or whenever the weather's clear (park closes at 20:00 in summer, earlier off-season). The city of Nice was first settled here by Greeks circa 400 B.C. In the Middle Ages, a massive castle stood here, with turrets, high walls, and soldiers at the ready. With the river guarding one side and the sea the other, this mountain fortress seemed strong—until Louis XIV leveled it in 1706. Nice's medieval seawall ran along the lineup of two-story buildings below. Today you'll find a waterfall, a playground, two cafés (with fair prices), and a cemetery—but no castle—on Castle Hill. Nice's port, where you'll find Trans Côte d'Azur's boat cruises (also described under "Tours in Nice"), is just below on the east edge of Castle Hill.

NICE

Getting There: You can get to the top of Castle Hill by foot, by elevator (€0.70 one-way, €1.10 round-trip, runs daily 10:00-19:00, until 20:00 in summer, next to beachfront Hôtel Suisse), or by pricey tourist train (described under "Tours in Nice," earlier).

Bike Routes—Meandering along Nice's seafront on foot or by bike is a must. To rev up the pace of your saunter, rent a bike and glide along the coast in either or both directions (about 30 minutes each way; for rental info see "Helpful Hints," earlier). Both of the following paths start along promenade des Anglais.

The path to the **west** stops just before the airport at perhaps the most scenic *boules* courts in France. Pause here to watch the old-timers while away the afternoon tossing shiny metal balls. If you take the path heading **east,** you'll round the hill—passing a scenic cape and the town's memorial to both world wars—to the harbor of Nice, with a chance to survey some fancy yachts. Pedal around the harbor and follow the coast past the Corsica ferry terminal (you'll need to carry your bike up a flight of steps). From there the path leads to an appealing tree-lined residential district.

Museums and Monuments

To bring culture to the masses, the city of Nice has nixed entry fees to all municipal museums—so it's free to enter all the following sights except the Chagall Museum and the Russian Cathedral (closed indefinitely). Cool.

The first two museums (Chagall and Matisse) are a long walk northeast of Nice's city center. Because they're in the same direction and served by the same bus line (buses #15 and #22 stop at both museums), it makes sense to visit them on the same trip. From place Masséna, the Chagall Museum is a 10-minute bus ride or a 30-minute walk, and the Matisse Museum is a 20-minute bus ride or a one-hour walk.

▲▲▲**Chagall Museum (Musée National Marc Chagall)**— Even if you're suspicious of modern art, this museum—with the world's largest collection of Marc Chagall's work in captivity—is a delight. After World War II, Chagall returned from the United States to settle in Vence, not far from Nice. Between 1954 and 1967 he painted a cycle of 17 large murals designed for, and donated to, this museum. These paintings, inspired by the biblical books of Genesis, Exodus, and the Song of Songs, make up the "nave," or core, of what Chagall called the "House of Brotherhood."

Each painting is a collage of images that draws from Chagall's Russian folk-village youth, his Jewish heritage, biblical themes, and his feeling that he existed somewhere between heaven and earth. He believed that the Bible was a synonym for nature, and that color and biblical themes were key for understanding God's love for his creation. Chagall's brilliant blues and reds celebrate nature, as do his spiritual and folk themes. Notice the focus on couples. To Chagall, humans loving each other mirrored God's love of creation.

NICE

Although Chagall would suggest that you explore his works without help, the free audioguide gives you detailed explanations of his works and covers temporary exhibits. The free *Plan du Musée* helps you locate the rooms, though you can do without, as the museum is pretty simple.

Cost and Hours: €7.50, €1-2 more with (frequent) special exhibits, free first Sun of the month (but crowded), open Wed-Mon 10:00-17:00, May-Oct until 18:00, closed Tue year-round, avenue Docteur Ménard, tel. 04 93 53 87 20, www.musee-chagall.fr.

Getting to the Chagall Museum: You can reach the museum, located on avenue Docteur Ménard, by bus or on foot.

Buses #15 and #22 serve the Chagall Museum from the Masséna Guitry stop, near place Masséna (5/hour Mon-Sat, 3/hour Sun, €1, immediately behind Galeries Lafayette department store—see map on page 440). The museum's bus stop (called Musée Chagall, shown on the bus shelter) is on boulevard de Cimiez (walk uphill from the stop to find the museum).

To **walk** from central Nice to the Chagall Museum (30 minutes), go to the train-station end of avenue Jean Médecin and turn right onto boulevard Raimbaldi. Walk four long blocks along the elevated road, then turn left onto avenue Raymond Comboul, and follow *Musée Chagall* signs.

Cuisine Art and WCs: An idyllic café (€10 salads and *plats*) awaits in the corner of the garden. A spick-and-span WC is next to the ticket desk (there's one inside, too).

Leaving the Museum: To take **buses** #15 or #22 back to downtown Nice, turn right out of the museum, then make another right down boulevard de Cimiez, and catch the bus heading downhill. To continue on to the Matisse Museum, catch buses #15 or #22 using the uphill stop located across the street. **Taxis** usually wait in front of the museum. It's about €12 for a ride to the city center.

To **walk** to the train station area from the museum (20 minutes), turn left out of the museum grounds on avenue Docteur Ménard, and follow the street to the left at the first intersection, continuing to hug the museum grounds. Where the street curves right (by #32), take the ramps and staircases down on your left, turn left at the bottom, cross under the freeway and the train tracks, then turn right on boulevard Raimbaldi to reach the station.

▲**Matisse Museum (Musée Matisse)**—This small museum contains a sampling of works from the various periods of Henri Matisse's long artistic career. The museum offers a painless introduction to the artist's many styles and materials, both shaped by Mediterranean light and by fellow Côte d'Azur artists Pablo Picasso and Pierre-Auguste Renoir. The collection is scattered throughout several rooms with a few worthwhile works, though it lacks a certain *je ne sais quoi* when compared to the Chagall Museum.

Matisse, the master of leaving things out, could suggest a woman's body with a single curvy line—letting the viewer's mind fill in the rest. Ignoring traditional 3-D perspective, he expressed his passion for life through simplified but recognizable scenes in which dark outlines and saturated, bright blocks of color create an overall decorative pattern. You don't look "through" a Matisse canvas, like a window; you look "at" it, like wallpaper.

Matisse understood how colors and shapes affect us emotionally. He could create either shocking, clashing works (early Fauvism) or geometrical, balanced, harmonious ones (later cutouts). Whereas other modern artists reveled in purely abstract design, Matisse (almost) always kept the subject matter at least vaguely recognizable. He used unreal colors and distorted lines not just to portray what an object looks like, but to express its inner nature (even inanimate objects). Meditating on his paintings helps you connect with life—or so Matisse hoped.

Cost and Hours: Free, Wed-Mon 10:00-18:00, closed Tue, 164 avenue des Arènes de Cimiez, tel. 04 93 81 08 08, www.musee-matisse-nice.org. The museum is housed in a beautiful Mediterranean mansion set in an olive grove amid the ruins of the ancient Roman city of Cemenelum.

Getting to the Matisse Museum: It's a long uphill walk from the city center. Take the bus (details follow) or a cab (€20 from promenade des Anglais). Once here, walk into the park to find the pink villa. **Buses #15, #17,** and **#22** offer regular service to the Matisse Museum from just off place Masséna on rue Sacha Guitry (Masséna Guitry stop, at the east end of the Galeries Lafayette department store—see map on page 440, 20 minutes; note that bus #17 does not stop at the Chagall Museum). **Bus #20** connects the port to the museum. On any bus, get off at the Arènes-Matisse bus stop (look for the crumbling Roman wall).

Leaving the Museum: When leaving the museum, find the stop for buses #15 and #22 (frequent service downtown and stops en route at the Chagall Museum): Turn left from the Matisse Museum into the park and keep straight on allée Barney Wilen, exiting the park at the Archeological Museum, then turn right. Pass the bus stop across the street (#17 goes to the city center but not the Chagall Museum, and #20 goes to the port), and walk to the small roundabout. Cross the roundabout to find the shelter (facing downhill) for buses #15 and #22 (see map on page 416).

▲Modern and Contemporary Art Museum (Musée d'Art Moderne et d'Art Contemporain)—This ultramodern museum features an explosively colorful, far-out, yet manageable collection focused on American and European-American artists from the 1960s and 1970s (Pop Art and New Realism styles are highlighted). The exhibits cover three floors and include a few works by Andy Warhol, Roy Lichtenstein, and Jean Tinguely, and small models of Christo's famous wrappings. You'll find rooms dedicated to Robert Indiana, Yves Klein, and Niki de Saint Phalle (my favorite). The temporary exhibits can be as appealing to modern-art lovers as the permanent collection: Check the museum website for what's playing. Don't leave without exploring the rooftop terrace.

Cost and Hours: Free, Tue-Sun 10:00-18:00, closed Mon, about a 15-minute walk from place Masséna, near Old Nice on promenade des Arts, tel. 04 93 62 61 62, www.mamac-nice.org.

Fine Arts Museum (Musée des Beaux-Arts)—Housed in a sumptuous Riviera villa with lovely gardens, this museum holds 6,000 artworks from the 17th to 20th centuries. Start on the first floor and work your way up to experience an appealing array of paintings by Monet, Sisley, Bonnard, and Raoul Dufy, as well as a few sculptures by Rodin and Carpeaux.

Cost and Hours: Free, Tue-Sun 10:00-18:00, closed Mon; inconveniently located at the western end of Nice, take bus #12 or #23 from the train station to the Rosa Bonheur stop and walk to 3 avenue des Baumettes; tel. 04 92 15 28 28, www.musee-beaux-arts -nice.org.

Molinard Perfume Museum—The Molinard family has been making perfume in Grasse (about an hour's drive from Nice) since 1849. Their Nice store has a small museum in the rear that illustrates the story of their industry. Back when people believed water spread the plague (Louis XIV supposedly bathed less than once a year), doctors advised people to rub fragrances into their skin and then powder their body. At that time, perfume was a necessity of everyday life.

The tiny first room shows photos of the local flowers, roots, and other plant parts used in perfume production. The second, main room explains the earliest (18th-century) production method. Petals were laid out in the sun on a bed of animal fat, which would absorb the essence of the flowers as they baked. For two months, the petals were replaced daily, until the fat was saturated. Models and old photos show the later distillation process (660 pounds of lavender produced only a quarter-gallon of essence). Perfume is "distilled like cognac and then aged like wine." The bottles on the tables demonstrate the role of the "blender" and the perfume mastermind called the "nose" (who knows best); clients are allowed to try their hand at mixing scents. Of the 150 real "noses" in the world, more than 100 are French. Notice the photos of these lab-coat-wearing perfectionists. You are welcome to enjoy the testing bottles.

Cost and Hours: Free, daily July-Aug 10:00-19:00, Sept-June 10:00-13:00 & 14:00-18:30, sometimes closed Mon off-season, just between beach and place Masséna at 20 rue St. François de Paule, see map on page 440, tel. 04 93 62 90 50, www.molinard.com.

▲**Russian Cathedral (Cathédrale Russe)**—Nice's Russian Orthodox church—claimed by some to be the finest outside Russia—recently closed to sightseers. In case it reopens, here is the background on the cathedral and a description of its interior.

Five hundred rich Russian families wintered in Nice in the late 19th century, and they needed a worthy Orthodox house of worship. Czar Nicholas I's widow provided the land (which required tearing down her house), and Czar Nicholas II gave this church to the Russian community in 1912. (A few years later, Russian comrades who *didn't* winter on the Riviera assassinated him.) Here in the land of olives and anchovies, these proud onion domes seem odd. But, I imagine, so did those old Russians.

The cathedral's one-room interior is filled with icons and candles, and old Russian music adds to the ambience. The wall of icons (iconostasis) divides things between the spiritual realm and the temporal world of the worshippers. Only the priest can walk between the two worlds, by using the "Royal Door." The items lining the front are interesting (described in order from left corner). The angel with red boots and wings—the protector of the Romanov family—stands over a symbolic tomb of Christ. The tall, black, hammered-copper cross commemorates the massacre of Nicholas II and his family in 1918. A Jesus icon is to the right of the Royal Door. According to a priest here, as worshippers meditate, staring deep into the eyes of Jesus, they enter a lake where they find their soul. Surrounded by incense, chanting, and your entire community...it could happen. Farther to the right, the icon of the unhappy-looking Virgin and Child is decorated with semiprecious stones from the Ural Mountains. Artists worked a triangle into each iconic face—symbolic of the Trinity.

Cost and Hours: Closed indefinitely to sightseers. Check its current status with TI. If it reopens, expect to pay admission (about €3) and dress modestly (no short shorts). It's at 17 boulevard du Tzarewitch (tel. 04 93 96 88 02, www.acor-nice.com). The park around the church stays open at lunch and makes a fine setting for picnics.

Getting to the Russian Cathedral: It's a 10-minute walk from the train station. Head west on avenue Thiers, turn right on avenue Gambetta, go under the freeway, and turn left following *Eglise Russe* signs. Or, from the station, take any bus heading west on avenue Thiers and get off at avenue Gambetta (then follow the previous directions).

Other Nice Museums

Both of these museums are acceptable rainy-day options, and free of charge.

Archaeological Museum (Musée Archéologique)—This museum displays various objects from the Romans' occupation of this region. It's convenient—just below the Matisse Museum—but has little of interest to anyone but ancient Rome aficionados. You also get access to the Roman bath ruins...which are, sadly, overgrown with weeds.

Cost and Hours: Free, very limited information in English, Wed-Mon 10:00-18:00, closed Tue, near Matisse Museum at 160 avenue des Arènes de Cimiez, tel. 04 93 81 59 57, www.musee -archeologique-nice.org.

Masséna Museum (Musée Masséna)—Like Nice's main square, this museum was named in honor of Jean-André Masséna, a highly regarded commander during France's Revolutionary and Napoleonic wars. The beachfront mansion is worth a gander for its lavish decor and lovely gardens alone (pick up your free ticket at the boutique just outside; no English information available).

There are three levels. The elaborate reception rooms on the ground floor host occasional exhibits and give the best feeling for aristocratic Nice at the turn of the 19th century (find Masséna's portrait to the right after entering). The first floor up, offering a folk-museum-like look at Nice through the years, deserves most of your time. Moving counterclockwise around the floor, you'll find Napoleonic paraphernalia, Josephine's impressive cape and tiara, and Napoleon's vest (I'd look good in it). Next, antique posters promote vacations in Nice—look for the model and photos of the long-gone La Jetée Promenade and its casino, Nice's first. You'll see paintings of Russian nobility who appreciated Nice's climate, images of the city before its river was covered over by place Masséna, and paintings honoring Italian patriot and Nice favorite Giuseppe Garibaldi. The top-floor painting gallery is devoted to the Riviera before World War II, with scenes of rural Villefranche-sur-Mer and other bucolic spots showing how the area looked before the tourist boom.

Cost and Hours: Free, daily 10:00-18:00, 35 promenade des Anglais, tel. 04 93 91 19 10.

Nightlife in Nice

Promenade des Anglais, cours Saleya, and rue Masséna are all worth an evening walk. Nice's bars play host to a happening late-night scene, filled with jazz, rock, and trolling singles. Most activity focuses on Old Nice. Rue de la Préfecture and place du Palais are ground zero for bar life, though place Rossetti and rue Droite are also good targets. **Distilleries Ideales** is a good place to start or end your evening, with a lively international crowd and a fun interior (where rues de la Poissonnerie and Barillerie meet, happy hour 18:00-20:00). **Wayne's Bar** is a happening spot for the younger, English-speaking backpacker crowd (15 rue Préfecture). Along the promenade des Anglais, the plush bar at **Hôtel Negresco** is fancy-cigar old English.

Plan on a cover charge or expensive drinks where music is involved. If you're out very late, avoid walking alone. Nice is well known for its lively after-dark action.

Sleeping in Nice

Don't look for charm in Nice. Go for modern and clean, with a central location and, in summer, air-conditioning. The rates listed here are for April through October. Prices generally drop €15-30 November through March, but go sky-high during the Nice Carnival, the Cannes Film Festival, and Monaco's Grand Prix. Between the film festival and the Grand Prix, the second half of May is very tight every year. Nice is also one of Europe's top convention cities, and June is convention month here. Reserve early if visiting from May through August, especially during these times. For parking, ask your hotelier (several hotels offer deals for stashing your car or have limited private parking; reserve early), or see "Arrival in Nice—By Car" on page 415.

I've divided my sleeping recommendations into three areas: between the train station and Nice Etoile shopping center (easy access to the train station and Old Nice via the tramway, 20-minute walk to promenade des Anglais); between Nice Etoile and the sea (east of avenue Jean Médecin, good access to Old Nice and the sea at quai des Etats-Unis); and between boulevard Victor Hugo and the sea (a somewhat classier and quieter area, offering better access to the promenade des Anglais but longer walks to the train station and Old Nice). I've also listed a hotel near the airport and a hostel on the outskirts. Before reserving, check hotel websites for deals (more common at larger hotels).

Between the Train Station and Nice Etoile

This area offers Nice's cheapest sleeps, though most hotels near the station ghetto are overrun, overpriced, and loud. The following hotels are the pleasant exceptions (most are near avenue Jean Médecin), and are listed in order of proximity to the train station, going toward the beach.

$$ Hôtel Ibis Nice Centre Gare**, 100 yards to the right as you leave the station, gives those in need of train station access a

---

Sleep Code

(€1 = about $1.40, country code: 33)
S = Single, **D** = Double/Twin, **T** = Triple, **Q** = Quad, **b** = bathroom,
s = shower only, ***** = French hotel rating (0-5 stars). Hoteliers
speak English; the hotels have elevators and accept credit
cards unless otherwise noted.

   To help you sort easily through these listings, I've divided
the accommodations into three categories based on the price
for a standard double room with bath:

   $$$ Higher Priced—Most rooms €200 or more.
   $$ Moderately Priced—Most rooms between €100-200.
    $ Lower Priced—Most rooms €100 or less.

   Prices can change without notice; verify the hotel's
current rates online or by email. For other updates, see www
.ricksteves.com/update.

---

secure refuge in this seedy area. It's big (200 rooms) and modern, but a good value with sharp rooms, a refreshing pool, and cheap €9 parking (Db-€93, big "Club" Db-€125, air-con, free Internet access and Wi-Fi, bar, café, 14 avenue Thiers, tel. 04 93 88 85 85, fax 04 93 88 58 00, www.ibishotel.com, h1396@accor.com).

   $$ At Hôtel Durante**, you know you're on the Mediterranean as soon as you enter this cheery, way-orange building with rooms wrapped around a flowery courtyard. Every one of its quiet rooms overlooks a spacious, well-maintained patio/garden with an American-style Jacuzzi. The rooms are good enough (mostly big beds), the price is right enough, and the parking (limited spaces) is free (Sb-€85-105, Db-€100-115, Tb-€150-175, Qb-€180-200, air-con, Wi-Fi, 16 avenue Durante, tel. 04 93 88 84 40, fax 04 93 87 77 76, www.hotel-durante.com, info@hotel-durante.com).

   $$ Hôtel St. Georges**, five blocks from the station toward the sea, is a basic place with reasonably clean, high-ceilinged rooms, orange tones, blue halls, fair rates, a backyard patio, and friendly Houssein at the reception (Sb-€95, Db-€115, Tb with 3 beds-€135, extra bed-€20, air-con, Wi-Fi, 7 avenue Georges Clemenceau, tel. 04 93 88 79 21, fax 04 93 16 22 85, www.hotelsaintgeorges.fr, contact@hotelsaintgeorges.fr).

   $ Hôtel Belle Meunière*, in a fine old mansion built for Napoleon III's mistress, offers cheap beds and private rooms a block below the train station. Lively and youth hostel-esque, this simple but well-kept place attracts budget-minded travelers of all ages with basic-but-adequate rooms and charismatic Mademoiselle Marie-Pierre presiding (with perfect English). Tables in the front

Nice Hotels

1. Hôtel Ibis Nice Centre Gare
2. Hôtel Durante
3. Hôtel St. Georges
4. Hôtel Belle Meunière
5. Auberge de Jeunesse les Camélias
6. B&B Nice Home Sweet Home
7. Hôtels la Perouse & Suisse
8. Hôtel Masséna
9. Hôtel Mercure Marché aux Fleurs
10. Hôtel Vendôme
11. Hôtel Lafayette

TO CHAGALL & MATISSE MUSEUMS

RUE MASSENA PEDEST. ZONE

TRAM W/ STOPS

¼ MILE

.5 KM

CIMIEZ

MODERN ART MUSEUM

TO PONT MICHEL TRAM STOP & A-8 AUTOROUTE

AVE. DESAMBROIS

RUE BARLA

DUBOUCHAGE

DEVOUCY

R. POSTES

DE LILLE

ST. JEAN

TO MIDDLE CORNICHE

BLACAS

PASTORELLI

ALBERTI

GUBERNATIS

HÔTEL GIOFFREDO

AVE.

PLACE GARIBALDI

PAROL

CASSINI

CATH. SEGURANE

⑩

⑪

⑧ B #15, #17 + #22

B #98 #98 B

FAURE

FELIX

BLVD. JEAN JAURES

#81, #82 + #112

TO LOW CORNICHE (VILLEFRANCHE)

DCH

B #200+ #400

B #100 + #81

AVE.

⑫

R. PREFECTURE

COLLET

ROS-SETTI

DROITE

OLD NICE

CASTLE HILL

R. ALEX MARI

ST. FRAN. PAULE

COURS SALEYA

R. PONCH

ELEVATOR

⑨

DES ETATS-UNIS

E S R

SEA

TO PORT LYMPIA

QUAI CAPEAU

⑦

⑫ Hôtel de la Mer
⑬ Hôtel Negresco
⑭ Hôtel West End
⑮ Hôtels Splendid & Gounod
⑯ Hôtel le Royal
⑰ Hôtel Massenet

⑱ Hôtel les Cigales
⑲ Hôtel Villa Victoria
⑳ To Villa Saint Exupéry & Chemins de Fer Station
㉑ SNCF Boutique

NICE

yard greet guests and provide opportunities to meet other travelers (bunk in 4-bed dorm-€22 with private bath, €18 with shared bath, Db-€68, Tb-€78, Qb-€108, includes breakfast, limited parking-€8, Wi-Fi, laundry service, 21 avenue Durante, tel. 04 93 88 66 15, fax 04 93 82 51 76, www.bellemeuniere.com, hotel.belle .meuniere@cegetel.net).

$ Auberge de Jeunesse les Camélias is a fun, laid-back youth hostel with a great location, modern facilities, and a fun evening atmosphere. Rooms accommodate between four and eight people of all ages in bunk beds (136 beds in all) and come with showers and sinks—WCs are down the hall. Reservations must be made on the website at least 3 days in advance. If you don't have a reservation, call by 10:00—or, better, try to snag a bunk in person. The place is popular but worth a try for last-minute availability (€26/bed, one-time €16 extra charge without hostel membership, includes breakfast, maximum 6-night stay, rooms closed 11:00-15:00 but can leave bags, Internet access, laundry, kitchen, safes, bar, 3 rue Spitalieri, tel. 04 93 62 15 54, www.hihostels.com, nice -camelias@fuaj.org).

$ B&B Nice Home Sweet Home is a great value. Gentle Genevieve (a.k.a. Jennifer) Levert rents out three large rooms and one small single in her home. Her rooms are simply decorated, with high ceilings, big windows, lots of light, and space to spread out. One room comes with private bath; otherwise, it's just like at home...down the hall (S-€35-44, D-€61-75, Db-€65-78, Tb-€75-85, Q-€80-110, includes breakfast, air-con units available in summer, elevator, one floor up, washer/dryer-€6, kitchen access, 35 rue Rossini at intersection with rue Auber, mobile 06 19 66 03 63, www.nicehomesweethome.com, glevert@free.fr).

Between Nice Etoile and the Sea

These hotels are either on the sea or within an easy walk of it, and are the closest to Old Nice. For locations, see the map on page 440.

$$$ Hôtel la Perouse****, built into the rock of Castle Hill at the east end of the bay, gets my vote for Nice's best splurge. This refuge-hotel is top-to-bottom flawless in every detail—from its elegant rooms (satin curtains, velour headboards) and attentive staff to its rooftop terrace with Jacuzzi, sleek pool, and lovely garden restaurant. Sleep here to be spoiled and escape the big city (garden view Db-€315, sea view Db-€466, good family options and Web deals, free Wi-Fi, 11 quai Rauba Capeu, tel. 04 93 62 34 63, fax 04 93 62 59 41, www.hotel-la-perouse.com, lp@hotel-la -perouse.com).

$$$ Hôtel Masséna***, in a classy building a few blocks from place Masséna, is a "professional" hotel (popular with tour groups) with 100 rooms at almost-reasonable rates and way-mod public spaces (small Db-€165, larger Db-€210, still larger Db-€310, skip the €20 breakfast, call same day for special rates—prices drop big time when hotel is not full, sixth-floor rooms have balconies, reserve parking ahead-€30/day, 58 rue Giofreddo, tel. 04 92 47 88 88, fax 04 92 47 88 89, www.hotel-massena-nice.com, info@hotel -massena-nice.com).

$$$ Hôtel Suisse***, below Castle Hill, has Nice's best ocean and city views for the money, and is surprisingly quiet given the busy street below. Rooms are quite comfortable, the decor is tasteful, and the staff helpful. There's no reason to sleep here if you don't land a view, so I've listed prices only for view rooms—many of which have balconies (Db-€170-220, extra bed-€36, breakfast-€15, Wi-Fi, 15 quai Rauba Capeu, tel. 04 92 17 39 00, fax 04 93 85 30 70, www.hotels-ocre-azur.com, hotel.suisse@hotels-ocre -azur.com).

$$ Hôtel Mercure Marché aux Fleurs*** is ideally situated across from the sea and behind cours Saleya. Rooms are tastefully designed and well maintained (some with beds in a loft). Prices are reasonable, though rates vary dramatically depending on demand—check their website for deals (standard Db-€170, superior Db-€200 and worth the extra euros, sea view-€50 extra, aircon, 91 quai des Etats-Unis, tel. 04 93 85 74 19, fax 04 93 13 90 94, www.hotelmercure.com, h0962@accor.com). Don't confuse this Mercure with the four others in Nice.

$$ Hôtel Vendôme*** gives you a whiff of the belle époque, with pink pastels, high ceilings, and grand staircases in a mansion set off the street. Its public spaces are delightful. The rooms are modern and come in all sizes; the best have balconies (on floors 4 and 5)—request *une chambre avec balcon* (Sb-€115-130, Db-€150-180, Tb-€180-200, prices vary with demand, check website for deals, air-con, Internet access and Wi-Fi, book ahead for limited parking-€13/day, 26 rue Pastorelli, tel. 04 93 62 00 77, fax 04 93 13 40 78, www.vendome-hotel-nice.com—useless except to book, contact@vendome-hotel-nice.com).

$$ Hôtel Lafayette***, in a handy location a block behind the Galeries Lafayette department store, is a great value. The hotel may look average from the outside, but inside it's comfortable and homey, with 18 well-designed, mostly spacious rooms, all one floor up from the street. It's family-run by Kirill, George, and young Victor. Rooms not overlooking rue de l'Hôtel des Postes are quieter and worth requesting (standard Db-€105-120, spacious Db-€115-130, preferential rates for Rick Steves readers, coffee service in rooms, air-con, no elevator, 32 rue de l'Hôtel des Postes, tel. 04 93 85 17 84, fax 04 93 80 47 56, www.hotellafayettenice.com, info@hotellafayettenice.com).

Old Nice Hotels & Restaurants

1. Hôtel la Perouse & Hôtel Suisse
2. Hôtel Masséna
3. Hôtel Mercure Marché aux Fleurs
4. To Hôtel Vendôme
5. To Hôtel Lafayette
6. Hôtel de la Mer
7. La Voglia Restaurant
8. La Cambuse Restaurant
9. La Festival de la Moule
10. Le Bistrot du Fromager
11. Oliviera Shop/Restaurant
12. Restaurant Castel

NICE

TO 3 CORNICHE ROADS

TO PLACE GARIBALDI

P PARKING

VIEW

TRAM w/ STOPS

JAURES

FRANCOIS

BOUCHERIE

CEMETERY

15

11

16

DROITE

LA LOGE

f

PLACE ROSSETTI

RUE ROSSETTI

STE. REPARATE

JESUS

ST. JACQUES

LESAGE

STE. REP.

RUE VIEILLE

10

13

LA PREFECTURE

POISSON.

16

MONTEE

CASTLE HILL

8

18

SALEYA

9

WC

20

RUE DES PONCHETTES

ETATS-

UNIS

PLAY FIELD

H

SEA

12

1

ELEVATOR & BELLANDA TOWER

⑬ L'Acchiardo Restaurant
⑭ Ville de Siena Restaurant
⑮ Lou Pilha Leva Restaurant
⑯ Fenocchio's Gelato (2)
⑰ Crema di Gelato

⑱ Distilleries Ideales
⑲ Wayne's Bar
⑳ Bike Rental
㉑ Go Sport
㉒ Start of "Old Nice Walk"

NICE

$$ Hôtel de la Mer** is a tiny place with an enviable position overlooking place Masséna, just steps from Old Nice (it's among the closest of my listings to the old town). Half of the rooms are smartly renovated and worth the higher price; the other half are "old school" and priced that way (older Db-€110, newer Db-€130, Tb-€155, air-con, Wi-Fi, 4 place Masséna, tel. 04 93 92 09 10, fax 04 93 85 00 64, www.hoteldelamernice.com, hotel.mer @wanadoo.fr).

Between Boulevard Victor Hugo and the Sea

These hotels are close to the promenade des Anglais (and far from Old Nice). The Negresco, West End, and le Royal are big, vintage Nice hotels that open onto the sea from the heart of the promenade des Anglais.

$$$ Hôtel Negresco**** owns Nice's most prestigious address on promenade des Anglais and knows it. Still, it's the kind of place that if you were to splurge just once in your life.... Rooms are opulent (see page 426 for more description), and tips are expected (viewless Db-€380, seaview Db-€490-600, view suite-€770-2,200, breakfast-€35, Old World bar, 37 promenade des Anglais, tel. 04 93 16 64 00, fax 04 93 88 35 68, www.hotel-negresco-nice.com, reservations@hotel-negresco.com).

$$$ Hôtel West End*** delivers formal service and décor, polished public spaces, and high prices. Its chic rooms come with effective blinds and all the comforts (viewless Db-€300, seaview Db-€340, check website for deals, Internet access and Wi-Fi, 31 promenade des Anglais, tel. 04 92 14 44 00, fax 04 93 88 85 07, www.hotel-westend.com, reception@westsend3ahotels.com).

$$$ Hôtel Splendid**** is a worthwhile splurge if you miss your Marriott. The panoramic rooftop pool, bar/restaurant, and breakfast room almost justify the cost...but throw in plush rooms (four of the six floors are non-smoking), a free gym, spa services, and air-conditioning, and you're as good as home (Db-€235— some with decks, deluxe Db with terrace-€280, suites-€360-410, breakfast-€16, better prices available on website, parking-€24/day, 50 boulevard Victor Hugo, tel. 04 93 16 41 00, fax 04 93 16 42 70, www.splendid-nice.com, info@splendid-nice.com).

$$ Hôtel le Royal*** is a relaxed resort hotel with 140 rooms, big lounges, and hallways that stretch forever. But the prices are reasonable considering the reliable air-conditioned comfort and terrific location—and sometimes they have rooms when others don't (viewless Db-€135-175, seaview Db-€175-195, bigger view room-€195-215 and worth it, extra person-€25, 23 promenade des Anglais, tel. 04 93 16 43 00, fax 04 93 16 43 02, www.hotel-royal -nice.cote.azur.fr, royal@vacancesbleues.com).

$$ Hôtel Massenet*** is tucked away a block off the promenade des Anglais in a pedestrian zone. A well-run place, it has 29 tidy rooms (love the shag carpet) at excellent rates (small Db-€90, standard Db-€130, larger Db-€150, some rooms with decks, parking-€10, 11 rue Massenet, tel. 04 93 87 11 31, fax 04 93 16 08 69, www.hotelmassenet.com, hotelmassenet@wanadoo.fr).

$$ Hôtel les Cigales***, a few blocks from the promenade des Anglais, is a smart little pastel place with tasteful decor, 19 sharp rooms (those with showers are a tad small, most have tub-showers and are standard size), air-conditioning, and a nifty upstairs terrace, all well managed by friendly Mr. Valentino, with Veronique and Elaine. Rick Steves readers who book directly through the hotel get a discount by typing this code: RICK (standard Db-€110-160, Tb-€130-180, free Wi-Fi, 16 rue Dalpozzo, tel. 04 97 03 10 70, fax 04 97 03 10 71, www.hotel-lescigales.com, info@hotel-lescigales.com).

$$ Hôtel Gounod*** is behind Hôtel Splendid. Because the two share the same owners, Gounod's guests are allowed free access to Splendid's pool, Jacuzzi, and other amenities. Don't let the lackluster lobby fool you—most rooms are comfortable, with high ceilings (Db-€170, palatial 4-person suites-€270, air-con, parking-€17/day, 3 rue Gounod, tel. 04 93 16 42 00, fax 04 93 88 23 84, www.gounod-nice.com, info@gounod-nice.com).

$$ Hôtel Villa Victoria*** is a fine place managed by cheery Marlena, who welcomes travelers into her spotless, classy old building with an open, attractive lobby overlooking a sprawling garden-courtyard. Rooms are traditional and well kept, with space to stretch out (streetside Db-€150, garden-side Db-€180, Tb-€160-185, suites-€210-235, breakfast-€15, air-con, minibar, Wi-Fi, parking-€18, 33 boulevard Victor Hugo, tel. 04 93 88 39 60, fax 04 93 88 07 98, www.villa-victoria.com, contact@villa-victoria.com).

Barely Beyond Nice

$ Villa Saint Exupéry, a service-oriented hostel (they answer the phone in English), is a haven two miles north of the city center. Its amenities and 60 comfortable, spick-and-span rooms create a friendly climate for budget-minded travelers of any age. Often filled with energetic youth, the place can be noisy. There are units for one, two, and up to six people. Many have private bathrooms and views of the Mediterranean—some come with balconies. You'll also find a laundry room, complete kitchen facilities, and a lively bar. There's easy Internet access with a wall of computers in the lobby and Wi-Fi in all the rooms (bed in dorm-€30/person, S-€50-70, Db-€60-90, Tb-€115, includes big breakfast, no curfew, 22 avenue Gravier, toll-free tel. 08 00 30 74 09, fax 04 92 09 82 94, www.vsaint.com, reservations@vsaint.com). To get there, take bus #23 from the airport or train station, take the tram—direction: Las Planas—to the Compte de Falicon stop and walk 10 minutes, or take the free shuttle from the Casino market by the tram stop (no service 12:00-17:00).

Near the Airport

Several airport hotels offer a handy and cheap port-in-the-storm for those with early flights or who are just stopping in for a single night: Etap Hôtel (the cheapest, www.etaphotel.com), Hôtel Première Classe (www.premiereclasse.com), and Hôtel Ibis Nice Aéroport (www.ibisnice.com). Free shuttles connect these hotels with both airport terminals.

You'll find greater comfort at the airport for a bit more (and free private shuttle vans) at these hotels: Novotel (www.novotel .com), Holiday Inn (www.holidayinn.com), and Campanile (www .campanile.fr).

Eating in Nice

Remember, you're in a resort. Seek ambience and fun, and lower your palate's standards. Italian is a low-risk and regional cuisine. The listed restaurants are concentrated in neighborhoods close to my recommended hotels. Several offer fixed-price, multi-course meals *(menus)*. Promenade des Anglais is ideal for picnic dinners on warm, languid evenings. Old Nice has the best and busiest dining atmosphere (and best range of choices), while the Nice Etoile area is more local, convenient, and also offers a good range of choices. To feast cheaply, eat on rue Droite in Old Nice, or explore the area around the train station. Allow yourself one dinner at a beachfront restaurant in Nice, and for terribly touristy trolling, wander the wall-to-wall eateries lining rue Masséna. Yuck.

In Old Nice

Nice's dinner scene converges on cours Saleya, which is entertaining enough in itself to make the generally mediocre food a good deal. It's a fun, festive spot to compare tans and mussels. Even if you're eating elsewhere, wander through here in the evening. For locations, see the map on page 440.

La Voglia has figured out a winning formula: Good food + ample servings + fair prices = good business. Come here early for top-value Italian cuisine, or plan on waiting for a table. There's fun seating inside and out (€12-14 pizza and pasta, €14-18 *plats*, open daily, at the western edge of cours Saleya at 2 rue St Francois de Paule, tel. 04 93 80 99 16).

La Cambuse sets a classy table...by cours Saleya standards. The tablecloths are real, the cuisine is Niçoise-Italian with an emphasis on Italy, and the service is attentive (€14 starters, €18-24 *plats*, good indoor/outdoor seating, 5 cours Saleya, tel. 04 93 80 82 40).

La Festival de la Moule is a simple, touristy place for lovers of mussels (or for just plain hungry folks). For €15 you get all-you-can-eat mussels (11 sauces possible) and fries in a youthful outdoor setting. Let twins Alex and Marc tempt you with their spicy and cream sauces—be daring and try several (other bistro fare available, across the square from La Cambuse, 20 cours Saleya, tel. 04 93 62 02 12).

Le Bistrot du Fromager's owner Hugo is crazy about cheese and wine. Come here to escape the heat and dine in cozy, cool, vaulted cellars surrounded by shelves of wine. All dishes use cheese as their base ingredient, although you'll also find pasta, ham, and salmon (with cheese, of course). This is a good choice for vegetarians (€10 entrees, €12-14 *plats*, €6 desserts, closed Sun, just off place de Gésu at 29 rue Benoit Bunico, tel. 04 93 13 07 83).

Oliviera venerates the French olive. This shop/restaurant sells a variety of oils, offers free tastings, and serves a menu of dishes paired with specific oils (think of a wine pairing). Welcoming owner Nadim, who speaks excellent English, knows all his producers and provides "Olive Oil 101" explanations with his tastings (best if you buy something afterward or have a meal). You'll learn how passionate he is about his products, and once you've had a taste, you'll want to stay and eat (allow €40 with wine, €16-24 main dishes, Tue-Sat 10:00-22:00, closed Sun-Mon, indoor seating only, 8 bis rue du Collet, tel. 04 93 13 06 45).

Restaurant Castel is a fine eat-on-the-beach option, thanks to its location at the very east end of Nice looking over the bay. You almost expect Don Ho to step up and grab a mic. Lose the city hustle and bustle by dropping down the steps below Castle Hill. The views are unforgettable even if the cuisine is not; you can even have lunch at your beach chair if you've rented one here (€10/half-day, €14/day). Dinner here is best: Arrive before sunset and find a waterfront table perfectly positioned to watch evening swimmers get in their last laps as the sky turns pink and city lights flicker on. Linger long enough to merit the few extra euros the place charges (€16 salads and pastas, €20-26 main courses, 8 quai des Etats-Unis, tel. 04 93 85 22 66).

Dining Cheap *à la Niçoise*

Try at least one of these places—not just because they're terrific budget options, but primarily because they offer authentic *niçoise* cuisine.

L'Acchiardo, hidden away in the heart of Old Nice, is a homey eatery that does a good job mixing a loyal clientele with

Nice Restaurants

1. Rue Biscarra Eateries
2. Bistrot les Viviers
3. L'Ovale Restaurant
4. Le Luna Rossa Restaurant
5. La Maison de Marie Restaurant
6. Villa d'Este Restaurant

NICE

TO CHAGALL & MATISSE MUSEUMS

RUE MASSENA
PEDEST. ZONE

TRAM w/ STOPS

1/4 MILE

.5 KM

CIMIEZ

AVE. DESAMBROIS

DEVOLUY

TO PONT MICHEL TRAM STOP & A-8 AUTOROUTE

MODERN ART MUSEUM

RUE BARLA

TO MIDDLE CORNICHE

DUBOUCHAGE

R. POSTES

DE LILLE

ST-JEAN

PLACE GARIBALDI

PASTORELLI

ALBERTI

DES

HOTEL

GUBERNATIS

GIOFFREDO

AVE. ST-JEAN

PAROL.

CASSINI

CATH. SEGURANE

TO LOW CORNICHE (VILLE-FRANCHE)

BLACAS

③

FAURE

FELIX

④ AVE.

B #15, #17 + #22

B #100 + #81

B #200 + #400

BLVD. JEAN JAURES

COLLET

#98 B #98 B

#81, #82 + #112 B

DCH

ROS-OSETTI

DROITE

R. PREFECTURE

R. ALEX MARI

ST. FRAN. DE PAULE

COURS SALEYA

POISS.

QUAI DES ETATS-UNIS

S E A

OLD NICE

CASTLE HILL

ELEVATOR

R. PONCH.

QUAI CAPEAU

TO PORT LYMPIA

⑦ Cave de l'Origine Wine Bar
⑧ Place Grimaldi Eateries
⑨ Chanterler Restaurant

⑩ Voyageur Nissart Restaurant
⑪ Zen Restaurant
⑫ Monoprix Grocery Store

hungry tourists. Its simple, hearty *niçoise* cuisine is served for fair prices by gentle Monsieur Acchiardo. The small plaque under the menu outside says it's been run by father and son since 1927 (€7 starters, €14 *plats*, €5 desserts, cash only, closed Sat-Sun, indoor seating only, 38 rue Droite, tel. 04 93 85 51 16).

Ville de Siena draws young travelers who dig this place for its big portions, fair prices, open kitchen, and raucous atmosphere with tables crammed on a narrow lane. The food is Italian and hearty (€12-17 *plats*, closed Sun, 10 rue St. Vincent, tel. 04 93 80 12 45).

Lou Pilha Leva delivers fun and cheap lunch or dinner options with *niçoise* specialties and always busy outdoor-only picnic-table dining (open daily, located where rues de la Loge and Centrale meet in Old Nice).

And for Dessert...

Gelato lovers should save room for the tempting ice-cream stands in Old Nice. **Fenocchio** is the city's favorite, with mouth-watering displays of 86 flavors ranging from tomato to lavender to avocado—all of which are surprisingly good (daily March-Nov until 24:00, two locations: 2 place Rossetti and 6 rue de la Poissonnerie). Gelato connoisseurs should head for **Crema di Gelato,** where the selection may be a fraction of Fenocchio's but the quality is superior (5 rue de la Préfecture, on place du Palais).

Eating near Nice Etoile

If you're not up for eating in Old Nice, try one of these spots around the Nice Etoile shopping mall.

On rue Biscarra: An appealing lineup of bistros overflowing with outdoor tables stretches along the broad sidewalk on traffic-free rue Biscarra (just east of avenue Jean Médecin behind Nice Etoile, all closed Sun). Come here to dine with area residents away from the tourists. These two places are both good choices, with good interior and exterior seating: **L'Authentic** has the most creative cuisine and comes with a memorable owner, burly Philippe (€23 two-course *menus,* €27 three-course *menus,* reasonable pasta dishes, tel. 04 93 62 48 88). **Le 20 sur Vin** is a neighborhood favorite with a cozy, wine-bar-meets-café ambience. It offers *(bien sûr)* good wines at fair prices, and basic bistro fare (tel. 04 93 92 93 20).

Bistrot les Viviers attracts those who require attentive service and authentic *niçoise* cuisine with a big emphasis on fish. This classy splurge offers two intimate settings as different as night and day: a soft, formal restaurant (€55 *menu,* €28-38 *plats*), and a relaxed *bistrot* next door (€25-32 *plats,* bouillabaisse-€44, bourride-€27, fish soup starter-€10). I'd reserve a table in the atmospheric *bistrot,* where some outdoor seating is available (restaurant closed Sun, *bistrot* open daily, 5-minute walk west of avenue Jean Médecin at

NICE

22 rue Alphonse Karr, tel. 04 93 16 00 48).

L'Ovale takes its name from the shape of a rugby ball, and is as local as it gets. This welcoming, well-run bistro has quality food at respectable prices, with an emphasis on the cuisine of south-western France. Say *bonsoir* to Jacqueline, David, and Johanna, and then dine inside on big *plats* for €10-13; consider their specialty, *cassoulet* (€17), or the *salade de manchons* with duck and walnuts (excellent €18 three-course *menu*, €13 big salads, daily, air-con, 29 rue Pastorelli, tel. 04 93 80 31 65).

Le Luna Rossa is *molto* Italian with a smart setting inside and out. It's also *molto* popular with locals, as prices are low and the quality high. Come early or book ahead (€10 starters, €14 *plats*, just north of the parkway at 3 rue Chauvain, tel. 04 93 85 55 66).

La Maison de Marie is a surprisingly good-quality refuge off touristy rue Masséna, where most other restaurants serve mediocre food to tired travelers. Enter through a deep-red arch to a bou-gainvillea-draped courtyard, and enjoy the fair prices and excellent cuisine that draw neighborhood regulars and out-of-towners alike. The interior tables are as appealing as those in the courtyard, but expect some smokers outside. The €22 *menu* is a terrific value (€10-15 starters and €15-30 *plats*, great fruit-salad dessert, open daily, look for the square red sign at 5 rue Masséna, tel. 04 93 82 15 93).

Villa d'Este has the same owners as the recommended La Voglia (listed earlier, under "In Old Nice"). The portions are big, the price is right, and the quality is tops (daily, on a busy pedes-trian street at 6 rue Masséna, tel. 04 93 82 47 77).

Near Promenade des Anglais

Worthwhile restaurants are few and far between in this area. Either head for Old Nice or try one of these good places.

Cave de l'Origine is a find, and would be even away from the tourist fray. Kind Isabelle and her English-speaking staff welcome you to their cozy wine shop/*bistrot*. Isabelle prepares fresh, home-made dishes and finds the perfect wine to match. She features original cuisine from many areas in France (especially the south-west), made with regional, fresh ingredients (€7-10 starters, €16-19 *plats,* open Tue-Sat for lunch and dinner, reservations smart, indoor seating only; wine shop open Tue-Sat 10:00-20:00, closed Sun-Mon; 3 rue Dalpozzo, tel. 04 83 50 09 60).

Place Grimaldi nurtures a lineup of appealing restaurants with good indoor and outdoor seating along a broad sidewalk under tall, leafy sycamore trees. **Crêperie Bretonne** is the only crêperie I list in Nice (€8 dinner crêpes, closed Sun, 3 place Grimaldi, tel. 04 93 82 28 47). **Le Grimaldi** is popular for its café fare (€12 pasta, €15-20 *plats*, closed Sun, 1 place Grimaldi, tel. 04 93 87 98 13).

Chantecler has Nice's most prestigious address—inside the

Hôtel Negresco. This is everything a luxury restaurant should be: elegant, soft, and top quality. If your trip is ending in Nice, call or email for reservations—you've earned this splurge (*menus* from €90, closed Mon-Tue, 37 promenade des Anglais, tel. 04 93 16 64 00, chantecler@lenegresco.com).

Near the Train Station

Both of the following restaurants, a block below the train station, provide good indoor and outdoor seating as well as excellent value.

Voyageur Nissart has blended good-value cuisine with cool Mediterranean ambience and friendly service since 1908. Current owner Max is a great host, and the quality of his cuisine makes this a good choice for travelers on any budget—try the wonderful €14 *filet de rouget à la niçoise* or the fine €8 *salade niçoise* (€16 three-course *menus*, good *plats* from €11, inexpensive wines, closed Mon, 19 rue d'Alsace-Lorraine, tel. 04 93 82 19 60).

Zen provides a Japanese break from French cuisine. Interior seating is arranged around the chef's stove, and the tasty specialties draw a strong following (€16 three-course *menu*, €8-13 sushi, open daily, 27 rue d'Angleterre, tel. 04 93 82 41 20).

Nice Connections

By Train and Bus

Note that most long-distance train connections to other French cities require a change in Marseille. The Grande Ligne train to Bordeaux (serving Antibes, Cannes, Toulon, Arles, Carcassonne, and other stops en route) requires a reservation. Remember that on regional buses (except on express airport buses), many one-way rides cost €1—regardless of length (the €1 ticket is good for up to 74 minutes of travel in one direction, including transfers).

From Nice by Train to: Cannes (2/hour, 30-40 minutes), **Antibes** (2/hour, 15-30 minutes), **Villefranche-sur-Mer** (2/hour, 10 minutes), **Eze-le-Village** (2/hour, 15 minutes to Eze-Bord-de-Mer, then bus #83 to Eze, 8/day), **Monaco** (2/hour, 20 minutes), **Menton** (2/hour, 25 minutes), **Grasse** (15/day, 1.25 hours), **Marseille** (18/day, 2.5 hours), **Arles** (11/day, 3.75-4.5 hours, most require transfer in Marseille or Avignon), **Avignon** (20/day, most by TGV, 4 hours, most require transfer in Marseille), **Paris'** Gare de Lyon (10/day, 6 hours, may require change; 11-hour night train goes to Paris' Gare d'Austerlitz), **Munich** (4/day, 12-13 hours with 2-4 transfers, night trains possible via Italy), **Interlaken** (5/day, 9-10 hours, 2-5 transfers), **Florence** (6/day, 7-9 hours, 1-3 transfers), **Venice** (5/day, 8-9 hours, all require transfers), **Barcelona** (1/day via Montpellier, 10.5 hours, more with multiple changes).

From Nice by Bus to: Cannes (#200, 2-4/hour, 1.5-1.75

NICE

hours), **Antibes** (#200, 2-4/hour, 1-1.5 hours), **Villefranche-sur-Mer** (#100, 3-4/hour, 15 minutes), **St-Jean-Cap-Ferrat** (#81, 2/hour, 30 minutes), **Eze-le-Village** (#82 or #112, 16/day, 25 minutes), **La Turbie** (4/day, 45 minutes), **Monaco** (#100, 3-4/hour, 45 minutes), **Menton** (#100, 4/hour, 1 hour), **St-Paul-de-Vence** (every 30 minutes, 45 minutes), **Vence** (every 30 minutes, 50 minutes), **Grasse** (every 30 minutes, 1.25 hours).

By Plane

Nice's easy-to-navigate airport (Aéroport de Nice Côte d'Azur) is on the Mediterranean, a 20- to 30-minute drive west of the city center. Planes leave roughly hourly for Paris (one-hour flight, about the same price as a train ticket, check www.easyjet.com for the cheapest flights to Paris' Orly airport). The two terminals (Terminal 1 and Terminal 2) are connected by frequent shuttle buses *(navettes)*. Both terminals have TIs, banks, ATMs, taxis, baggage storage (€6.50/day per piece, open daily 6:00-23:00), and buses to Nice (tel. 04 89 88 98 28, www.nice.aeroport.fr).

Getting from the Airport to the City Center

Taxis into the center are expensive considering the short distance (figure €35 to recommended hotels, 10 percent more 19:00-7:00 and all day Sun). Taxis stop outside door *(Porte)* A-1 at Terminal 1 and outside *Porte* A-3 at Terminal 2. Notorious for overcharging, Nice taxis are not always so nice. If your fare for a ride into town is much higher than €35 (or €40 at night or on Sun), refuse to pay the overage. If this doesn't work, tell the cabbie to call a *gendarme* (police officer). It's always a good idea to ask for a receipt *(reçu)*.

Airport shuttle vans work with some of my recommended hotels, but they only make sense when going *to* the airport, not when arriving on an international flight. Unlike taxis, shuttle vans offer a fixed price that doesn't rise on Sundays, early mornings, or evenings. Prices are best for groups (figure €30 for one person, and only a little more for additional people). **Nice Airport Shuttle** is one option (1-2 people-€32, additional person-€14, mobile 06 60 33 20 54, www.nice-airport-shuttle.com), or ask your hotelier for recommendations.

Three bus lines connect the airport with the city center, offering good alternatives to high-priced taxis. **Bus #99** (airport express) runs from both terminals to Nice's main train station (€4, 2/hour, 8:00-21:00, 30 minutes, drops you within a 10-minute walk of many recommended hotels). To take this bus *to* the airport, catch it right in front of the train station (departs on the half-hour). If your hotel is within walking distance of the station, #99 is a breeze.

Bus #98 serves both terminals, and runs along promenade des

Anglais to the edge of Old Nice (€4, 3/hour, from the airport 6:00-23:00, to the airport until 21:00, 30 minutes, see map on page 446 for stops). The slower, cheaper local **bus #23** serves only Terminal 1, and makes every stop between the airport and train station (€1, 5/hour, runs 6:00-20:00, 40 minutes, direction: St. Maurice).

For all buses, buy tickets in the information office just outside either terminal, or from the driver. To reach the bus information office and stops at Terminal 1, turn left after passing customs and exit the doors at the far end. Buses serving Terminal 2 stop across the street from the airport exit (information kiosk and ticket sales to the right as you exit).

If you take bus #98 or #99, hang on to your €4 ticket—it's good all day on any public bus and the tramway in Nice, and for buses between Nice and some nearby towns.

GERMANY

BAVARIA and TIROL

Füssen • King's Castles • Reutte, Austria

Two hours south of Munich, in Germany's Bavaria and Austria's Tirol, is a timeless land of fairy-tale castles, painted buildings shared by cows and farmers, and locals who still yodel when they're happy.

In Germany's Bavaria, tour "Mad" King Ludwig II's ornate Neuschwanstein Castle, Europe's most spectacular. Just over the border in Austria's Tirol, explore the ruined Ehrenberg Castle.

My favorite home base for exploring Bavaria's castles is actually in Austria, in the Tirolean town of Reutte. Reutte's hotels offer better value to those with a car. Füssen, in Germany, is more touristy, but a handier home base for train travelers.

Planning Your Time and Getting Around Bavaria

While Germans and Austrians vacation here for a week or two at a time, the typical speedy American traveler will find two days' worth of sightseeing. With a car and more time, you could enjoy three or four days.

By Public Transportation

Where you stay determines which sights you can see most easily. Train travelers use **Füssen** as a base, and bus or bike the three miles to Neuschwanstein and the Tegelberg luge or gondola. Although **Reutte** is the least convenient base if you're carless, travelers staying there can easily bike or hike to the Ehrenberg ruins, and can reach Neuschwanstein by bus (via Füssen), bike (1.5 hours), or taxi (€35 one-way); if you stay at the recommended Gutshof zum Schluxen hotel (between Reutte and Füssen, in Pinswang, Austria) it's a one-hour hike through the woods to Neuschwanstein. Those staying in **Füssen** can day-trip by bus to Reutte and the Ehrenberg ruins.

By Bike

This is great biking country. Many hotels loan bikes to guests, and shops in Reutte and at the Füssen train station rent bikes for €8-15 per day. The ride from Reutte to Neuschwanstein and the Tegelberg luge (1.5 hours) is a natural.

Füssen

Dramatically situated under a renovated castle on the lively Lech River, Füssen (FEW-sehn) is a handy home base for exploring the region. This town has been a strategic stop since ancient times. Its main street sits on the Via Claudia Augusta, which crossed the Alps (over the Brenner Pass) in Roman times. Going north, early traders could follow the Lech River downstream to the Danube, and then cross over to the Main and Rhine valleys—a route now known to modern travelers as the "Romantic Road." Today, while Füssen is overrun by tourists in the summer, few venture to the back streets...which is where you'll find the real charm. Apart from my self-guided walk and the Füssen Heritage Museum, there's little to do here. It's just a pleasant small town with a big history and lots of hardworking people in the tourist business.

Halfway between Füssen and the border (as you drive, or a woodsy walk from the town) is the **Lechfall,** a thunderous waterfall (with a handy WC).

Orientation to Füssen

(area code: 08362)
Füssen's train station is a few blocks from the TI, the town center (a cobbled shopping mall), and all my hotel listings.

Tourist Information

The TI is in the center of town (July-mid-Sept Mon-Fri 9:00-18:00, Sat 10:00-14:00, Sun 10:00-12:00; mid-Sept-June Mon-Fri 9:00-17:00, Sat 10:00-14:00, closed Sun; one free Internet terminal, 3 blocks down Bahnhofstrasse from station at Kaiser-Maximilian-Platz 1, tel. 08362/93850, www.fuessen.de). If necessary, the TI can help you find a room. After hours, the little self-service info pavilion near the front of the TI features an automated room-finding service with a phone to call hotels.

Füssen & Reutte Area

Arrival in Füssen

From the train station (lockers available, €2-3), exit to the left and walk a few blocks to reach the center of town and the TI. Buses to Neuschwanstein, Reutte, and elsewhere leave from a parking lot next to the station.

Helpful Hints

Internet Access: Beans & Bytes is the best place to get online, with fast terminals and good drink service (€2/2 hours, Wi-Fi, Skype, disc-burning, Mon-Sat 10:00-20:00, closed Sun except July-Aug, down the pedestrian alley off the main drag at Reichenstrasse 33, tel. 08362/926-8960).

Bike Rental: Bike Station, sitting right where the train tracks end, outfits sightseers with good bikes and tips on two-wheeled fun in the area (€8-10/24 hours, March-Oct Mon-Fri 9:00-12:00 & 14:00-18:00, Sat 9:00-13:00, Sun in good weather 9:00-12:00, closed Nov-Feb, tel. 08362/983-651, mobile 0176-2205-3080, www.ski-sport-luggi.de).

Car Rental: Peter Schlichtling, in the town center, rents cars for reasonable prices (€62/day, includes insurance, Mon-Fri 8:00-18:00, Sat 9:00-12:00, closed Sun, Kemptener Strasse 26, tel. 08362/922-122, www.schlichtling.de). **Auto Osterried/ Europcar** rents at similar prices, but is an €8 taxi ride away from the train station. Their cheapest car goes for about €59 per day (daily 8:00-19:00, past waterfall on road to Austria, Tiroler Strasse 65, tel. 08362/6381).

Local Guide: Silvia Beyer speaks English, knows the region very well, and can even drive you to sights that are hard to reach by train (€30/hour, silliby@web.de, mobile 0160-901-13431).

BAVARIA AND TIROL

Self-Guided Walk

Welcome to Füssen

For most, Füssen is just a home base for visiting Ludwig's famous castles. But the town has a rich history and hides some evocative corners, as you'll see when you follow this short orientation walk. Throughout the town, "City Tour" information plaques explain points of interest in English. Use them to supplement the information I've provided.

• *Begin at the square in front of the TI, three blocks from the train station.*

❶ **Kaiser-Maximilian-Platz:** The entertaining "Seven Stones" fountain on this square, by sculptor Christian Tobin, was built in 1995 to celebrate Füssen's 700th birthday. The stones symbolize community, groups of people gathering, conviviality... each is different, with "heads" nodding and talking. It's granite on granite. The moving heads are not connected, and nod only with waterpower. While frozen in winter, it's a popular and splashy play zone for kids on hot summer days.

• *Just half a block down the busy street stands...*

❷ **Hotel Hirsch and Medieval Towers:** Recent renovations have restored some of the original Art Nouveau flavor to Hotel Hirsch, which opened in 1904. In those days, aristocratic tourists came here to appreciate the castles and natural wonders of the Alps. Across the busy street stands one of two surviving towers from Füssen's medieval town wall (c. 1515), and next to it is a passageway into the old town.

• *Walk 50 yards farther down the street to another tower. Just before it, you'll see an information plaque and an archway where a small street called Klosterstrasse emerges through a surviving piece of the old town wall. Step through the smaller pedestrian archway, walk along Klosterstrasse for a few yards, and turn left through the gate into the...*

❸ **Historic Cemetery of St. Sebastian (Alter Friedhof):** This peaceful oasis of Füssen history, established in the 16th century, fills a corner between the town wall and the Franciscan monastery.

1. Hotel/Rest. Schlosskrone
2. Hotel Hirsch
3. Hotel Sonne
4. Altstadthotel zum Hechten & Rest. Ritterstub'n
5. Gästehaus Schöberl
6. Mein Lieber Schwan Apartments
7. House LA (2)
8. Youth Hostel
9. Gasthof Krone
10. Restaurant Aquila
11. Markthalle Food Court
12. Hohes Schloss Italian Ice Cream
13. Asian Eateries & Internet Café
14. Supermarket
15. Bike Rental
16. Car Rentals (2)

SELF-GUIDED WALK

A. Kaiser-Maximilian-Platz
B. Medieval Towers (2)
C. Historic Cemetery of St. Sebastian
D. Town View
E. Lech Riverbank
F. Church of the Holy Spirit, Bread Market & Lute-Makers
G. Benedictine Monastery
H. Füssen Heritage Museum
I. St. Magnus Basilica
J. High Castle

BAVARIA AND TIROL

It's technically full, and only members of great and venerable Füssen families (who already own plots here) can join those who are buried (free, daily April-Sept 7:30-19:00, Oct-March 8:00-17:00).

Just inside the gate (on the right) is the tomb of Dominic Quaglio, who painted the Romantic scenes decorating the walls of Hohenschwangau Castle in 1835. Over on the old city wall is the World War I memorial, listing all the names of men from this small town killed in that devastating conflict (along with each one's rank and place of death). A bit to the right, also along the old wall, is a statue of the hand of God holding a fetus—a place to remember babies who died before being born. And in the corner, farther to the right, are the simple wooden crosses of Franciscans who lived just over the wall in the monastery. Note the fine tomb art from many ages collected here, and the loving care this community gives its cemetery.

• *Exit on the far side, just past the dead Franciscans, and continue toward the big church.*

❶ Town View from Franciscan Monastery (Franziskaner-kloster): From the Franciscan Monastery (which still has big responsibilities, but only a handful of monks in residence), there's a fine view over the medieval town. The Church of St. Magnus and the High Castle (the summer residence of the Bishops of Augsburg) break the horizon. The chimney (c. 1886) and workers' housing on the left are reminders that when Ludwig built Neuschwanstein, the textile industry (linen and flax) was very big here. Walk all the way to the far end of the monastery chapel and peek around the corner, where you'll see a gate that proclaims the *Ende der romantischen Strasse* (end of the Romantic Road).

• *Now go down the stairway and turn left, through the medieval "Bleachers' Gate," to the riverbank.*

❷ Lech Riverbank: This low end of town, the flood zone, was the home of those whose work depended on the river—bleachers, rafters, and fishermen. In its heyday, the Lech River was an expressway to Augsburg (about 70 miles to the north). Around the year 1500, the rafters established the first professional guild in Füssen. As Füssen was on the Via Claudia, cargo from Italy passed here en route to big German cities farther north. Rafters would assemble rafts and pile them high with goods—or with people needing a lift. If the water was high, they could float all the way to Augsburg in as little as one day. There they'd disassemble their raft and sell off the lumber along with the goods they'd carried, then make their way home to raft again. Today you'll see no modern-day rafters here, as there's a hydroelectric plant just downstream.

• *Walk upstream a bit, and head inland immediately after crossing under the bridge.*

❻ Church of the Holy Spirit, Bread Market, and Lute-Makers: Climbing uphill, you pass the colorful Church of the Holy Spirit (Heilig-Geist-Spitalkirche) on the right. As this was the church of the rafters, their patron, St. Christopher, is prominent on the facade. Today it's the church of Füssen's old folks' home (it's adjacent—notice the easy-access skyway).

Farther up the hill on the right (almost opposite an archway into a big courtyard) is Bread Market Square (Brotmarkt), with a fountain honoring the famous 16th-century lute-making family, the Tieffenbruckers. In its day, Füssen was a huge center of violin- and lute-making, with about 200 workshops. Today only two survive.

• *Backtrack and go through the archway into the courtyard of the former...*

❼ Benedictine Monastery (Kloster St. Mang): From 1717 until secularization in 1802, this was the powerful center of town. Today the courtyard is popular for concerts, and the building houses the City Hall and Füssen Heritage Museum (and a public WC).

❽ Füssen Heritage Museum: This is Füssen's one must-see sight (€6, €7 combo-ticket includes painting gallery and castle tower; April-Oct Tue-Sun 11:00-17:00, closed Mon; Nov-March Fri-Sun 13:00-16:00, closed Mon-Thu; tel. 08362/903-146, www.fuessen.de). Pick up the loaner English translations and follow the one-way route. In the St. Anna Chapel, you'll see the famous *Dance of Death*. This was painted shortly after a plague devastated the community in 1590. It shows 20 social classes, each dancing with the Grim Reaper—starting with the pope and the emperor. The words above say, essentially, "You can say yes or you can say no, but you must ultimately dance with death."

Leaving the chapel, you walk over the metal lid of the crypt. Upstairs, exhibits illustrate the rafting trade and violin- and lute-making (with a complete workshop). The museum also includes an exquisite *Festsaal* (main festival hall), an old library, an exhibition on textile production, and a King Ludwig-style "castle dream room."

• *Leaving the courtyard, hook left around the old monastery and go uphill. The square tower marks...*

❾ St. Magnus Basilica (Basilika St. Mang): St. Mang (or Magnus) is Füssen's favorite saint. In the eighth century, he worked miracles all over the area with his holy rod. For centuries, pilgrims came from far and wide to enjoy art depicting the great works of St. Magnus. Above the altar dangles a glass cross containing his relics (including that holy stick). Just inside the door is a chapel remembering a much more modern saint—Franz Seelos (1819-1867), the local boy who went to America (Pittsburgh and New Orleans) and lived such a righteous life that in 2000 he was beatified by Pope John Paul II. If you're in need of a miracle, fill out a request card next to the candles.

• *From the church, a lane leads high above, into the courtyard of the...*

❶ **High Castle (Hohes Schloss):** This castle, long the summer residence of the Bishop of Augsburg, houses a painting gallery (the upper floor is labeled in English) and a tower with a view over the town and lake (included in the €7 Füssen Heritage Museum combo-ticket, otherwise €6, same hours as museum). Its courtyard is interesting for the striking perspective tricks painted onto its flat walls. From below the castle, the city's main drag (once the Roman Via Claudia, and now Reichenstrasse) leads from a grand statue of St. Magnus past lots of shops, cafés, and strolling people to Kaiser-Maximilian-Platz and the TI...where you began.

Sleeping in Füssen

(country code: 49, area code: 08362)
Though I prefer sleeping in Reutte, convenient Füssen is just three miles from Ludwig's castles and offers a cobbled, riverside retreat. It's fairly touristy, but it has plenty of rooms, and is the region's best base for those traveling by train. All recommended accommodations are within a few handy blocks of the train station and the town center. Parking is easy at the station, and some hotels also have their own lot or garage. Prices listed are for one-night stays; most hotels give about 5-10 percent off for two-night stays—always request this discount. Competition is fierce, and off-season prices are soft. High season is mid-June-September. Rooms are generally 10-15 percent less in shoulder season and much cheaper in off-season.

Big, Fancy Hotels in the Center of Town

$$$ Hotel Schlosskrone, with 62 rooms and all the amenities, is just a block from the station. It also runs a fine pastry shop—you'll notice at breakfast—and restaurant (Sb-€99-109, standard Db-€119-139, bigger Db-€129-165, Tb-€145-165, Qb-€159-179, 4-person suite-€199-255, lower prices are for Oct-April, you'll likely save money by booking via their website, air-con in some rooms, elevator, free Wi-Fi and cable Internet, free sauna and fitness center, parking-€9/day, Prinzregentenplatz 2-4, tel. 08362/930-180, fax 08362/930-1850, www.schlosskrone.com, info@schlosskrone .com, Norbert Schöll and family).

$$$ Hotel Hirsch is a romantic, well-maintained, 53-room, old-style hotel on the main street two blocks from the station. Their standard rooms are fine, and their rooms with historical and landscape themes are a fun splurge (Sb-€70-95, standard Db-€120-140, theme Db-€150-180, lower prices are for Nov-March and during

Sleep Code

(€1 = about $1.40, Germany country code: 49, Austria country code: 43)

S = Single, **D** = Double/Twin, **T** = Triple, **Q** = Quad, **b** = bathroom, **s** = shower only. Unless otherwise noted, credit cards are accepted, English is spoken, and breakfast is included.

To help you sort easily through these listings, I've divided the accommodations into three categories, based on the price for a standard double room with bath:

$$$ Higher Priced—Most rooms €100 or more.

$$ Moderately Priced—Most rooms between €60-100.

$ Lower Priced—Most rooms €60 or less.

Prices can change without notice; verify the hotel's current rates online or by email. For other updates, see www.ricksteves.com/update.

slow times, family rooms, elevator, expensive Internet access, free Wi-Fi, free parking, Kaiser-Maximilian-Platz 7, tel. 08362/93980, fax 08362/939-877, www.hotelfuessen.de, info@hotelhirsch.de).

$$$ Hotel Sonne, in the heart of town, has a modern lobby and takes pride in decorating (some would say over-decorating) its 50 stylish rooms (Sb-€89-111, Db-€111-129, bigger Db-€149-165, Tb-€139-149, bigger Tb-€169-193, Qb-€189-205, lower prices are for Nov-March, 5 percent discount if you book on their website, elevator, free Internet access and Wi-Fi, free sauna and fitness center, parking-€5-7, kitty-corner from TI at Prinzregentenplatz 1, tel. 08362/9080, fax 08362/908-100, www.hotel-sonne.de, info @hotel-sonne.de).

Smaller, Mid-Priced Hotels and Pensions

$$ Altstadthotel zum Hechten offers 35 modern rooms in a friendly, traditional building right under Füssen Castle in the old-town pedestrian zone (Sb-€59-69, Db-€94-108, Tb-€125, Qb-€156, ask for Rick Steves price when you reserve, also mention if you're very tall as most beds can be short, non-smoking, lots of stairs, free Internet access in lounge, free Wi-Fi, and parking-€3, laundry-€10-15/load, fun miniature bowling alley in basement, electrobike rental-€20/day; from TI, walk down pedestrian street and take second right to Ritterstrasse 6; tel. 08362/91600, fax 08362/916-099, www.hotel-hechten.com, info@hotel-hechten .com, Pfeiffer and Tramp families).

$$ Gästehaus Schöberl, run by the head cook at Altstadthotel zum Hechten, rents six attentively furnished, modern rooms a five-minute walk from the train station. One room is in the own-ers' house, and the rest are in the building next door (Sb-€40-50, Db-€65-75, Tb-€85-95, Qb-€100-120, lower prices are for Jan-Feb and Nov or for longer stays, cash only, free Wi-Fi, free parking, Luitpoldstrasse 14-16, tel. 08362/922-411, www.schoeberl-fuessen.de, info@schoeberl-fuessen.de, Pia and Georg Schöberl).

$$ Mein Lieber Schwan, a block from the train station, is a former private house with four superbly outfitted apartments, each with a double bed, sofa bed, and kitchen. The catch is the three-night minimum stay (Sb-€68-79, Db-€78-89, Tb-€88-99, Qb-€98-109, price depends on apartment size, slightly cheaper off-season, cash or PayPal only, no breakfast, free Wi-Fi, free park-ing, laundry facilities, garden, from station turn left at traffic circle to Augustenstrasse 3, tel. 08362/509-980, fax 08362/509-914, www.meinlieberschwan.de, fewo@meinlieberschwan.de, Herr Bletschacher).

Budget Beds

$ House LA, run by energetic mason Lahdo Algül and hard-working Agata, has two branches. The backpacker house has 11 basic, clean four-bed dorm rooms at rock-bottom prices about a 10-minute walk from the station (€18/bed, D-€42, breakfast-€2.50, free Internet access and Wi-Fi, free parking, Wachsbleiche 2). A second building has five family apartments with kitchen and bath, each sleeping 4-6 people (apartment-€60-90, breakfast-€2.50, free Wi-Fi, free parking, 6-minute walk back along tracks from station to von Freybergstrasse 26; contact info for both: tel. 08362/607-366, mobile 0170-624-8610, fax 08362/925-1909, www.housela.de, info@housela.de). Both branches rent bikes (€8/day) and have laundry facilities (€7/load).

$ Füssen Youth Hostel occupies a pleasant modern building in a grassy setting an easy walk from the center. There are ping-pong tables and a basketball net out front (bed in 2- to 6-bed dorm rooms-€21, D-€50, €3 more for nonmembers, includes breakfast and sheets, guests over age 26 without kids in tow pay €4 pen-alty for being so old, laundry-€3.20/load, dinner-€5, office open 7:00-12:00 & 17:00-23:00, Nov-March until 22:00, free Wi-Fi, free parking, from station backtrack 10 minutes along tracks, Mariahilfer Strasse 5, tel. 08362/7754, fax 08362/2770, www.fuessen.jugendherberge.de, jhfuessen@djh-bayern.de).

$ Gasthof Krone, a rare bit of pre-glitz Füssen in the pedes-trian zone, has dumpy halls and stairs and 12 big, worn, time-warp rooms—left unrenovated by the building's owner. Still, the location makes it worth considering as an alternative to the youth hostel (S-€26, D-€46, T-€69, €3 less per person for 2-night stays, no breakfast but bakeries across the street, closed Nov-early

June; from TI, head down pedestrian street and take first left to Schrannengasse 17; tel. 08362/7824, fax 08362/37505, www.krone -fuessen.de, info@krone-fuessen.de).

Eating in Füssen

Restaurant Aquila serves modern international dishes in a simple, traditional *Gasthaus* setting with great seating outside on the delightful little Brotmarkt Square (€10-16 main courses, serious €9-10 salads, Wed-Mon 11:30-14:30 & 17:30-22:00, closed Tue, Brotmarkt 9, tel. 08362/6253).

Restaurant Ritterstub'n offers delicious, reasonably priced fish, salads, veggie plates, and a fun kids' menu. They have three eating zones: modern decor in front, traditional Bavarian in back, and a courtyard. Demure Gabi serves while her husband cooks standard Bavarian fare (€8-15 main courses, €5.50 lunch specials, €19 three-course fixed-price dinners, Tue-Sun 11:30-14:30 & 17:30-23:00, closed Mon, Ritterstrasse 4, tel. 08362/7759).

Schenke & Wirtshaus (inside the recommended Altstadthotel zum Hechten) dishes up hearty, traditional Bavarian fare. They specialize in pike *(Hecht)* pulled from the Lech River, served with a tasty fresh-herb sauce (€8-14 main courses, salad bar, cafeteria ambience, daily 10:00-22:00, Ritterstrasse 6, tel. 0836/91600).

Hotel Schlosskrone's fine restaurant, right on Füssen's main traffic circle, has good weekly specials and live Bavarian zither music most Fridays and Saturdays during dinner. Choose between a traditional dining room and a pastel winter garden. If your pension doesn't offer breakfast, consider their €10 "American-style" breakfast or huge €14.50 Sunday spread (open daily 7:30-10:30 & 11:30-14:30 & 18:00-22:00, Prinzregentenplatz 2-4, tel. 08362/930-180).

The **Markthalle,** just across the street from Gasthof Krone, is a fun food court offering a wide selection of reasonably priced, wurst-free food. Located in an old warehouse from 1483, it's now home to a fishmonger, deli counters, a fruit stand, a bakery, and a wine bar. Buy your food from one of the vendors, park yourself at any one of the tables, then look up and admire the Renaissance ceiling (Mon-Fri 7:30-18:30, Sat 7:30-14:30, closed Sun, corner of Schrannengasse and Brunnengasse).

Gelato: **Hohes Schloss Italian Ice Cream** is a good *gelateria* on the main drag and has an inviting people-watching perch for coffee or dessert (Reichenstrasse 14).

Asian Food: You'll find inexpensive Thai, Indian, and Chinese restaurants in the Luitpold-Passage at Reichenstrasse 33.

Picnic Supplies: Bakeries and *Metzgers* (butcher shops) abound and frequently have ready-made sandwiches. For groceries, try the underground **Netto** supermarket at Prinzregentenplatz, the roundabout on your way into town from the train station (Mon-Sat 7:00-20:00, closed Sun).

Füssen Connections

From Füssen to: Neuschwanstein (bus #73 or #78, departs from train station, most continue to Tegelberg lift station after castles, 1-2/hour, 10 minutes, €1.90 one-way, €3.80 round-trip; taxis cost €10 one-way), **Reutte** (bus #74, Mon-Fri almost hourly, last bus 19:00, Sat-Sun every 2 hours, last bus 18:00, 45 minutes, €3.90 one-way; taxis cost €35 one-way), **Munich** (hourly trains, 2 hours, some change in Buchloe), **Salzburg** (hourly via Munich, 4 hours, 1-2 changes), **Rothenburg ob der Tauber** (hourly, 5 hours, look for connections with only 2-3 changes—often in Augsburg, Treuchtlingen, and Steinach), **Frankfurt** (hourly, 5-6 hours, 1-2 changes). Train info: tel. 0180-599-6633, www.bahn.com.

The King's Castles

The most popular tourist destinations in Bavaria are the "King's Castles" (Königsschlösser). The older Hohenschwangau, King Ludwig's boyhood home, is less touristy but more historic. The more dramatic Neuschwanstein, which inspired Walt Disney, is the one everyone visits. I'd recommend visiting both, and planning some time to hike above Neuschwanstein to Mary's Bridge—and, if you enjoy romantic hikes, down through the gorge below. Reservations are a magic wand to smooth out your visit. With fairy-tale turrets in a fairy-tale alpine setting built by a fairy-tale king, these castles are understandably a huge hit.

Getting There

If arriving by **car,** note that road signs in the region refer to the sight as *Königsschlösser,* not Neuschwanstein. There's plenty of parking (all lots-€5). The first lots require more walking. Drive right through Touristville and past the ticket center, and park in lot #4 by the lake for the same price.

From **Füssen,** those without cars can catch **bus** #73 or #78 (1-2/hour, €1.90 one-way, €3.80 round-trip, 10 minutes, catch bus at train station, extra buses often run when crowded), take a **taxi** (€10 one-way), or ride a rental **bike** (two level miles). The bus drops you at the tourist office; it's a one-minute walk from there to the ticket office.

From **Reutte,** take bus #74 to the Füssen train station, then hop on bus #73 or #78 to the castles. Or pay €35 for a taxi right to the castles.

Orientation to the King's Castles

Cost: Neuschwanstein costs €12, Hohenschwangau costs €10.50, a *Königsticket* for both castles costs €21.50, and children under 18 (accompanied by an adult) are admitted free.

Hours: The ticket center, located at street level between the two castles, is open daily April-Sept 8:00-17:00, Oct-March 9:00-15:00. The first and last castle tours of the day depart an hour after the ticket office opens and closes: April-Sept at 9:00 and 18:00, Oct-March at 10:00 and 16:00.

Getting Tickets for the Castles: Every tour bus in Bavaria converges on Neuschwanstein, and tourists flush in each morning from Munich. A handy reservation system sorts out the chaos for smart travelers. Tickets, whether reserved in advance or bought on the spot, come with admission times. If you miss your appointed tour time, you can't get in. To tour both castles, you must do Hohenschwangau first (logical, since this gives a better introduction to Ludwig's short life). You'll get two tour times: Hohenschwangau and then, two hours later, Neuschwanstein.

Arrival: Make the **ticket center** your first stop. If you have a reservation, there's a short line for picking up tickets. If you don't have a reservation...welcome to the very long line. Arrive by 8:00 in summer, and you'll likely be touring at 9:00. During August, the busiest month, tickets for English tours usually run out between 16:00 and 17:00.

Reservations: It's smart to reserve in peak season (June-early Oct, especially July-Aug). Reservations cost €1.80 per person per castle, and must be made no later than 17:00 on the previous day, ideally online (www.ticket-center-hohenschwangau .de); it's also possible to reserve by phone (tel. 08362/930-830) or email (info@ticket-center-hohenschwangau.de). You must pick up reserved tickets an hour before the appointed entry time, as it takes a while to walk up to the castles. (It doesn't usually take an hour, though—so this might be a good time to pull out a sandwich or a snack.) Show up late and they may have given your slot to someone else (but then they'll likely help you make another reservation). Better yet, if you know a couple of hours in advance that you're running late and can call the office, they'll normally rebook you at no charge.

Tips for Day-Tripping from Munich: If coming by train, make a castle tour reservation and take a train leaving at least four hours before your reserved castle entry. (The train to Füssen takes over two hours, getting from Füssen to the castle ticket office by bus takes another half-hour, and you must be there an hour before your tour.) Trains from Munich leave hourly at :51 past the hour. So, if you take the 9:51 train, you can make a 14:00 castle tour. If you reserve a castle tour for 11:00, you'll need to pack breakfast and take the 6:51 train.

Getting Up to the Castles: From the ticket booth, Hohenschwangau is an easy 10-minute climb, while Neuschwanstein is a steep 30-minute hike in the other direction. To minimize hiking to Neuschwanstein, you can take a shuttle bus (leaves every few minutes from in front of Hotel Lisl, just above ticket office and to the left) or a horse-drawn carriage (in front of Hotel Müller, just above ticket office and to the right), but neither gets you to the castle doorstep. The shuttle bus drops you off near Mary's Bridge (Marienbrücke), leaving you a steep, 10-minute downhill walk to the castle—so be sure to see the view from Mary's Bridge *before* hiking down (€1.80 one-way, the €2.60 round-trip is not worth it since you have to hike uphill to the bus stop for your return trip). Carriages (€6 up, €3 down) are slower than walking and stop below Neuschwanstein, leaving you a five-minute uphill hike. Here's the most economic and least strenuous plan: Ride the bus to Mary's Bridge for the view, hike down to Neuschwanstein, and then catch the horse carriage from the castle back down to the parking lot. Carriages also run to Hohenschwangau (€4 up, €2 down).

Entry Procedure: For each castle, tourists jumble at the entry, waiting for their ticket number to light up on the board. When it does, power through the mob (most waiting there are holding higher numbers) and go to the turnstile. Warning: You must use your ticket while your number is still on the board. If you space out while waiting for a polite welcome, you'll miss your entry window and never get in.

Services: A helpful TI, bus stop, ATM, WC (€0.50), and telephones cluster around the main intersection a couple hundred yards before you get to the ticket office (TI open daily April-Sept 10:00-18:00, Oct-March 11:00-17:00, tel. 08362/81980, www.schwangau.de).

Eating: Bring a packed lunch. The park by the Alpsee (the nearby lake) is ideal for a picnic, although you're not allowed to sit on the grass—only on the benches (you could also eat out on the lake in one of the old-fashioned rowboats, rented by the hour in summer). There are no grocery shops by the castles, but you can buy sandwiches and hot dogs across from the TI and at the Hotel Alpenstuben. The restaurants in the "village" at the foot of Europe's Disney castle are mediocre,

The King's Castles

Forggensee

Schwangau

To Munich & Rothenburg

ST. COLOMAN'S

Pöllat River

400 Meters

400 Yards

LUGE

Tegelbergbahn

TEGELBERG PEAK

To Füssen & Reutte (Austria)

Hohen-schwangau Village

HORSE CART ENDS

NEUSCHWANSTEIN CASTLE

WC

PÖLLAT GORGE

Schwansee

HOHENSCHWANGAU CASTLE

HORSE CART STARTS

To Pinswang (Austria)

PICNIC BENCHES

MARY'S BRIDGE (MARIENBRÜCKE)

BOAT RENTAL

Alpsee

❶ Alpenhotel Allgäu ❸ Royal Crystal Baths
❷ Beim "Landhannes" Rooms ❹ To Festspielhaus & Bike Path Start

feeding off the endless droves of hungry, shop-happy tourists. The **Bräustüberl cafeteria** serves the cheapest grub, but isn't likely to be a highlight of your visit (€6-7 gut-bomb grill meals, often with live folk music, daily 10:00-18:00, close to end of road and lake).

Sights at the King's Castles

▲▲▲Hohenschwangau Castle

Standing quietly below Neuschwanstein, the big, yellow Hohenschwangau Castle was Ludwig's boyhood home. Originally built in the 12th century, it was ruined by Napoleon. Ludwig's father, King Maximilian II, rebuilt it in 1830. Hohenschwangau (hoh-en-SHVAHN-gow, loosely translated as "High Swanland") was used by the royal family as a summer hunting lodge until 1912.

The interior decor is harmonious, cohesive, and original—all done in 1835, with paintings inspired by Romantic themes. The Wittelsbach family (which ruled Bavaria for nearly seven centuries) still owns the place (and lived in the annex—today's shop—until the 1970s). As you tour the castle, imagine how the paintings must have inspired young Ludwig. For 17 years, he lived here at his dad's place and followed the construction of his dream castle across the way—you'll see the telescope still set up and directed at Neuschwanstein.

The excellent 30-minute tours give a better glimpse of Ludwig's life than the more-visited and famous Neuschwanstein Castle tour. Tours here are smaller (35 people rather than 60) and more relaxed.

▲▲▲Neuschwanstein Castle

Imagine "Mad" King Ludwig as a boy, climbing the hills above his dad's castle, Hohenschwangau, dreaming up the ultimate fairy-tale castle. Inheriting the throne at the young age of 18, he had the power to make his dream concrete and stucco. Neuschwanstein (noy-SHVAHN-shtine, roughly "New Swanstone") was designed first by a theater-set designer...then by an architect. It looks medieval, but it's modern iron-and-brick construction with a sandstone veneer—only about as old as the Eiffel Tower. It feels like something you'd see at a home show for 19th-century royalty. Built from 1869 to 1886, it's the epitome of the Romanticism popular in 19th-century Europe. Construction stopped with Ludwig's death (only a third of the interior was finished), and within six weeks, tourists were paying to go through it.

During WWII, the castle took on a sinister role. The Nazis used Neuschwanstein as one of their primary secret storehouses for stolen art. After the war, Allied authorities spent a year sorting through and redistributing the art, which filled 49 rail cars from this one location alone. It was the only time the unfinished rooms were put to use.

Today, guides herd groups of 60 through the castle, giving an interesting—if rushed—30-minute tour. You'll go up and down more than 300 steps, through lavish rooms based on Wagnerian opera themes, the king's gilded-lily bedroom, and his extravagant throne room. You'll visit 15 rooms with their original furnishings and fanciful wall paintings. After the tour, before you descend to the king's kitchen, see the 20-minute video about the king's life and passions accompanied by Wagner's music (next to the café, alternates between English and German, schedule board at the entry says what's playing and what's on deck). After the kitchen (state of the art for this high-tech king in its day), you'll see a room lined with fascinating drawings (described in English) of the castle plans, construction, and drawings from 1883 of Falkenstein—a whimsical, over-the-top, never-built castle that makes Neuschwanstein look stubby. Falkenstein occupied Ludwig's fantasies the year he died.

Near the Castles
Mary's Bridge (Marienbrücke)—Before or after the Neuschwanstein tour, climb up to Mary's Bridge to marvel at Ludwig's castle, just as Ludwig did. This bridge was quite an engineering accomplishment 100 years ago. From the bridge, the frisky can hike even higher to the *Beware—Danger of Death* signs and an even more glorious castle view. (Access to the bridge is closed in bad winter weather, but many travelers walk around the barriers to get there—at their own risk, of course.) The most scenic way to descend from Neuschwanstein is to walk up to Mary's Bridge and then follow the signs down the Pöllat Gorge to the TI *(Pöllatschlucht,* 15 minutes longer than walking down the road but worth it, steel walkways and railings make this slippery area safer).

▲**Tegelberg Gondola**—Just north of Neuschwanstein is a fun play zone around the mighty Tegelberg Gondola, a scenic ride to the mountain's 5,500-foot summit. On a clear day, you get great views of the Alps and Bavaria and the vicarious thrill of watching hang gliders and paragliders leap into airborne ecstasy. Weather permitting, scores of adventurous Germans line up and leap from the launch ramp at the top of the lift. With someone leaving every two or three minutes, it's great for spectators. Thrill-seekers with exceptional social skills may talk themselves into a tandem ride with a paraglider. From the top of Tegelberg, it's a steep and demanding 2.5-hour hike down to Ludwig's castle. (Avoid the treacherous trail directly below the gondola.) At the base of the gondola, you'll find a playground, a cheery eatery, the stubby remains of an ancient Roman villa, and a luge ride.

Cost and Hours: €17.50 round-trip, €11 one-way, daily 9:00-17:00, closed Nov, 4/hour, last ride at 16:30, in bad weather call first to confirm, tel. 08362/98360, www.tegelbergbahn.de. Most buses #73 and #78 from Füssen continue from the castles to Tegelberg.

▲**Tegelberg Luge**—Next to the Tegelberg Gondola is a summer luge *(Sommerrodelbahn)* course. A luge is like a bobsled on wheels, with a funky cable system pulling riders (in their sleds) to the top without a ski lift. On your way down, push the stick forward to go faster, pull back to apply brakes, keeping both hands on your stick. To avoid getting into a bumper-to-bumper traffic jam, let the person in front of you get way ahead before you start. You'll emerge from the course with a windblown hairdo and a smile-creased face. This course's stainless-steel track is heated, so it's often dry and open even when drizzly weather shuts down the concrete luges.

Cost and Hours: €3/ride, 6-ride shareable card-€11, July-Sept daily 10:00-18:00, otherwise same hours as gondola, in winter sometimes opens late due to wet track, in bad weather call first to confirm, waits can be long in good weather, no children under 3, ages 3-8 may ride with an adult, tel. 08362/98360, www.tegelberg bahn.de.

Sleeping near the King's Castles

(€1 = about $1.40, country code: 49, area code: 08362)
Inexpensive farmhouse B&Bs abound in the Bavarian countryside around Neuschwanstein, offering drivers a decent value. Look for *Zimmer Frei* signs ("room free"/vacancy). The going rate is about €50-65 for a double, including breakfast. Though a bit inconvenient for those without a car, my listings here are a quick taxi ride from the Füssen train station and also close to local bus stops.

$$ Alpenhotel Allgäu is a small, family-run hotel with 18 rooms in a bucolic setting. It's a 15-minute walk from the castle ticket office, not far beyond the humongous parking lot (small Sb without balcony-€48, Sb-€58, perfectly fine older Db-€80, newer Db-€88, Tb-€120, these are book-direct prices, ask about discount with cash and this book, all rooms except one single have porches or balconies—some with castle views, family rooms, free Wi-Fi, elevator, free parking, just before tennis courts at Schwangauer Strasse 37 in the town of Schwangau—don't let your GPS take you to Schwangauer Strasse 37 in Füssen, tel. 08362/81152, fax 08362/987-028, www.alpenhotel-allgaeu.de, info@alpenhotel -allgaeu.de, Frau Reiss).

$ Beim "Landhannes," a 200-year-old working dairy farm run by Conny Schön, rents three creaky but sunny rooms, and keeps flowers on the balconies, big bells and antlers in the halls, and cows in the yard (Sb-€30, Db-€60, €5 less per person for 3 or more nights, also rents apartments with kitchen with a 5-night minimum, cash only, free Wi-Fi, nearby bike rental, poorly signed in the village of Horn on the Füssen side of Schwangau, look for the farm down a tiny lane through the grass 100 yards in front of Hotel Kleiner König, Am Lechrain 22, tel. 08362/8349, www .landhannes.de, info@landhannes.de).

Reutte, Austria

Reutte (ROY-teh, with a rolled *r*), a relaxed Austrian town of 5,700, is located 20 minutes across the border from Füssen. While overlooked by the international tourist crowd, it's popular with Germans and Austrians for its climate. Doctors recommend its "grade 1" air. I like Reutte for the opportunity to simply be in a real community. As an example of how the town is committed to its character, real estate can be sold only to those using it as a primary residence. (Many formerly vibrant alpine towns made a pile of money but lost their sense of community by becoming resorts. They allowed wealthy foreigners—who just drop in for a week or two a year—to buy up all the land, and are now shuttered up and dead most of the time.)

Reutte has one claim to fame among Americans: As Nazi Germany was falling in 1945, Hitler's top rocket scientist, Werner von Braun, joined the Americans (rather than the Russians) in Reutte. You could say that the American space program began here.

Reutte isn't featured in any other American guidebook. While its generous sidewalks are filled with smart boutiques and lazy coffeehouses, its charms are subtle. It was never rich or important. Its castle is ruined, its buildings have painted-on "carvings," its churches are full, its men yodel for each other on birthdays, and its energy is spent soaking its Austrian and German guests in *Gemütlichkeit*. Most guests stay for a week, so the town's attractions are more time-consuming than thrilling.

Orientation to Reutte

(country code: 43, area code: 05672)

Tourist Information

Reutte's TI is a block in front of the train station (Mon-Fri 8:00-12:00 & 14:00-17:00, no midday break July-Aug, Sat 8:30-12:00, closed Sun, Untermarkt 34, tel. 05672/62336, www.reutte.com). Go over your sightseeing plans, ask about a folk evening, pick up city and biking maps and the *Sommerprogramm* events schedule (in German only), and ask about discounts with the hotel guest cards. Their free informational booklet has a good self-guided town walk.

Ask your hotel to give you an **Aktiv-Card,** which gives free travel on local buses (including the Reutte-Füssen route) as well as small discounts on sights and activities.

Arrival in Reutte

If you're coming by car from Germany, skip the north *(Nord)* exit and take the south *(Süd)* exit into town. For parking in town, blue lines denote pay-and-display spots. There is a free lot (P-1) near the train station on Muhlerstrasse.

While Austria requires a **toll sticker** *(Vignette)* for driving on its expressways (€8/10 days, buy at the border, gas stations, car-rental agencies, or *Tabak* shops), those just dipping into Tirol from Bavaria do not need one—even on the expressway-like bypass around Reutte.

Helpful Hints

Internet Access: Café Alte Post has one expensive terminal in a back room (€7.20/hour, Mon-Fri 7:00-19:00, Sat-Sun 9:00-18:00, Untermarkt 15).

Laundry: There isn't an actual launderette in town, but the recommended Hotel Maximilian lets non-guests use its laundry service (wash, dry, and fold-€16/load).

Bike Rental: Try **Intersport** (€15/day, Mon-Fri 9:00-18:00, Sat 9:00-17:00, closed Sun, Lindenstrasse 25, tel. 05672/62352), or check at the recommended Hotel Maximilian.

Taxi: STM Shuttle Service promises 24-hour service (mobile tel. 0664-113-3277).

Car Rental: Autoreisen Köck rents cars at Mühlerstrasse 12 (tel. 05672/62233, www.koeck-tours.com, koeck@koeck-tours .com).

"Nightlife": Reutte is pretty quiet. For any action at all, there's a strip of bars, dance clubs, and Italian restaurants on Lindenstrasse.

Sights in and near Reutte

▲▲Ehrenberg Castle Ensemble (Festungsensemble Ehrenberg)

If Neuschwanstein was the medieval castle dream, Ehrenburg is the medieval castle reality. Once the largest fortification in Tirol, its brooding ruins lie about two miles outside Reutte. Ehrenburg is actually an "ensemble" of four castles, built to defend against the Bavarians and to bottle up the strategic Via Claudia trade route, which cut through the Alps as it connected Italy and Germany. Today, these castles have become a European "castle museum," showing off 500 years of military architecture in one swoop. The European Union is helping fund the project (paying a third of its €9 million cost) because it promotes the heritage of a multinational region—Tirol—rather than a country.

The four parts of the complex are the fortified Klause toll booth on the valley floor, the oldest castle on the first hill above (Ehrenberg), a mighty and more modern castle high above (Schlosskopf, built in the age when cannon positioned there made the original castle vulnerable), and a smaller fourth castle across the valley (Fort Claudia, an hour's hike away). All four were once a single complex connected by walls. Signs posted throughout the site help visitors find their way and explain some background on the region's history, geology, geography, culture, flora, and fauna. (While the castles are free and open all the time, the museum and multimedia show at the fort's parking lot charge admission.)

Getting to the Castle Ensemble: The Klause, Ehrenberg, and Schlosskopf castles are on the road to Lermoos and Innsbruck. These are a pleasant 30- to 45-minute walk or a short bike ride from Reutte; bikers can use the *Radwanderweg* along the Lech River (the TI has a good map). Local buses run from Reutte to Ehrenberg several times a day (see www.vvt.at for schedules—the stop name is "Ehrenberger Klause").

▲**Klause Valley Fort Museum**—Historians estimate that about 10,000 tons of precious salt passed through this valley (along the route of Rome's Via Claudia) each year in medieval times, so it's no wonder the locals built this complex of fortresses and castles. Beginning in the 14th century, the fort controlled traffic and levied tolls on all who passed. Today, these scant remains hold a museum and a theater with a multimedia show.

While there are no real artifacts here (other than the sword used in A.D. 2008 to make me the honorary First Knight of Ehrenberg), the clever, kid-friendly **museum** takes one 14th-century decade (1360-1370) and attempts to bring it to life. It's a hands-on experience, well-described in English. You can try on a set of armor (and then weigh yourself), see the limited vision knights had to put up with when wearing their helmet, empathize with victims of the plague, and join a Crusade.

The **multimedia show** takes you on a 30-minute spin through the 2,000-year history of this valley's fortresses, with images projected on the old stone walls and modern screens (50-minute English version at 13:00 with a minimum of 5 people, or sometimes by request).

Cost and Hours: €7.50 for museum, €10.50 combo-ticket also includes multimedia show, €17.80 family pass for 2 adults and any number of kids, daily 10:00-17:00, closed Nov-mid-Dec, tel. 05672/62007, www.ehrenberg.at.

Eating: Next to the museum, the **Landgasthof Klause** serves typical Tirolean meals (€9-15 main courses, officially Tue-Sun 10:00-18:00 but likely longer hours in summer, closed Mon, closed Nov and Jan-Feb, tel. 05672/62213). They also rent a few rooms if you'd like to stay right at Ehrenberg (see page 482).

▲▲**Ehrenberg Ruins**—Ehrenberg, a 13th-century rock pile, provides a super opportunity to let your imagination off its leash. Hike up 30 minutes from the parking lot of the Klause Valley Fort Museum for a great view from your own private ruins. Ehrenberg (which means "Mountain of Honor") was the first castle here, built in 1296. Thirteenth-century castles were designed to stand boastfully tall. With the advent of gunpowder, castles dug in. (Notice the 18th-century **ramparts** around you.)

Approaching Ehrenberg Castle, look for the small **door** to the

Reutte

MÜHLERFELDSTR.
MÜHL
KINDER-GARTEN-STRASSE
HALBWEG-STRASSE
GROSSFELDSTR.
KÖNIGSWEG
E-WERK-STR.
STEGERBERGWEG
To Füssen, Germany
314
MAIN TRAIN STN.
MÜHLER STR.
GYMNASIUMSTR.
REUTTE-SCHULZENTRUM TRAIN STATION
Stegerberg
STRASSE
METALLWERK-PLANSEE-STRASSE
GIPSMÜHLSTR.
ÖSTERBICHL
BREITENWANGER STR.
KAISER-LOTHAR-STR.
DORF
BREITENWANG
PLANSEESTRASSE
To Plansee & Linderhof (Germany)
ALPEN-BADSTR.
Sintenhichl
AN STEINBRUCH
Kreckelmooser See
HIGHWAY
QUELLEN-WEG-TÄTSCHENWEG
INNSBRUCKER STRASSE
KRECKELMOOSSTRASSE
NEUMÜHL
CAMPING
MAIN
LAHNER STRASSE
314
LÄHN
Katzenberg

1. Hotel/Café "Das Beck" & Internet Café
2. Hotel/Rest. Goldener Hirsch
3. Alpenhotel Ernberg & Moserhof Hotel/Restaurants
4. Hosp Rooms
5. Hotel/Rest. Maximilian
6. Gasthof-Pension Waldrast
7. Pension Hohenrainer
8. Gintherhof Rooms
9. Landgasthof Klause Rooms & Café
10. Gästehaus am Graben Hostel
11. To Gutshof zum Schluxen
12. Storfwirt Restaurant
13. Non Solo Pasta
14. Bike Rental
15. Car Rental

left. It's the night entrance (tight and awkward, and therefore safer against a surprise attack). Entering this castle, you go through two doors. Castles allowed step-by-step retreat, giving defenders time to regroup and fight back against invading forces.

Before climbing to the top of the castle, follow the path around to the right to a big, grassy courtyard with commanding views and a fat, newly restored **turret.** This stored gunpowder and held a big cannon that enjoyed a clear view of the valley below. In medieval times, all the trees approaching the castle were cleared to keep an unobstructed view.

Look out over the valley. The pointy spire marks **Breitenwang,** which was a stop on the ancient Via Claudia. In A.D. 46, there was a Roman camp there. In 1489, after the Reutte bridge crossed the Lech River, Reutte (marked by the onion-domed church) was made a market town and eclipsed Breitenwang in importance. Any gliders circling? They launch from just over the river in Höfen.

For centuries, this castle was the seat of government—ruling an area called the "judgment of Ehrenberg" (roughly the same as today's "district of Reutte"). When the emperor came by, he stayed here. In 1604, the ruler moved downtown into more comfortable quarters, and the castle was no longer a palace.

Now climb to the top of Ehrenberg Castle. Take the high ground. There was no water supply here—just kegs of wine, beer, and a cistern to collect rain.

Ehrenberg repelled 16,000 Swedish soldiers in the defense of Catholicism in 1632. Ehrenberg saw three or four other battles, but its end was not glorious. In the 1780s, a local businessman bought the castle in order to sell off its parts. Later, in the late 19th century, when vagabonds moved in, the roof was removed to make squatting miserable. With the roof gone, deterioration quickened, leaving only this evocative shell and a whiff of history.

▲**Schlosskopf**—From Ehrenberg, you can hike up another 30 minutes to the mighty Schlosskopf ("Castle Head"). When the Bavarians captured Ehrenberg in 1703, the Tiroleans climbed up to the bluff above it to rain cannonballs down on their former fortress. In 1740, a mighty new castle—designed to defend against modern artillery—was built on this sky-high strategic location. By the end of the 20th century, the castle was completely overgrown with trees—you literally couldn't see it from Reutte. But today the trees are shaved away, and the castle has been excavated. In 2008, the Castle Ensemble project, led by local architect Armin Walch, opened the site with English descriptions and view platforms. One spot gives spectacular views of the strategic valley. The other looks down on the older Ehrenberg Castle ruins, illustrating the strategic problems presented with the advent of cannon.

In the Town

Reutte Museum (Museum Grünes Haus)—Reutte's cute city museum offers a quick look at the local folk culture and the story of the castles. There are exhibits on Ehrenberg and the Via Claudia, local painters, and more—ask to borrow the English translations.

Cost and Hours: €3; May-Oct Tue-Sat 13:00-17:00, closed Sun-Mon; early Dec-Easter Wed-Sat 14:00-17:00, closed Sun-Tue; closed Easter-April and Nov-early Dec; in the bright-green building at Untermarkt 25, around corner from Hotel Goldener Hirsch, tel. 05672/72304, www.museum-reutte.at.

▲▲Tirolean Folk Evening—Ask the TI or your hotel if there's a Tirolean folk evening scheduled. During the summer (July-Aug), nearby towns (such as Höfen on Tuesdays) occasionally put on an evening of yodeling, slap dancing, and Tirolean frolic. These are generally free and worth the short drive. Off-season, you'll have to do your own yodeling. There are also weekly folk concerts featuring the local choir or brass band in Reutte's Zeiller Platz (free, July-Aug only, ask at TI). For listings of these and other local events, pick up a copy of the German-only *Sommerprogramm* schedule at the TI.

Sleeping in and near Reutte

(€1 = about $1.40, country code: 43, area code: 05672)
Reutte is a mellow Füssen with fewer crowds and easygoing locals with a contagious love of life. Come here for a good dose of Austrian ambience and lower prices. While it's not impossible by public transport, staying here makes most sense for those with a car. Reutte is popular with Austrians and Germans, who come here year after year for one- or two-week vacations. The hotels are big, elegant, and full of comfy carved furnishings and creative ways to spend lots of time in one spot. They take great pride in their restaurants, and the owners send their children away to hotel-management schools. All include a great breakfast, but few accept credit cards. Most hotels give a small discount for stays of two nights or longer.

The Reutte TI has a list of 50 private homes that rent out generally good rooms *(Zimmer)* with facilities down the hall, pleasant communal living rooms, and breakfast. Most charge €20 per person per night, and the owners speak little or no English. As these are family-run places, it is especially important to cancel in advance if your plans change. I've listed a few favorites in this section, but the TI can always find you a room when you arrive.

Reutte is surrounded by several distinct "villages" that basically feel like suburbs—many of them, such as Breitenwang, within easy walking distance of the Reutte town center. If you want to hike through the woods to Neuschwanstein Castle, stay at Gutshof zum Schluxen. To locate these accommodations, see the Reutte map.

In Central Reutte

These two hotels are the most practical if you're traveling by train or bus.

$$ Hotel "Das Beck" offers 17 clean, sunny rooms (many with balconies) filling a modern building in the heart of town close to the train station. It's a great value, and guests are personally taken care of by Hans, Inge, Tamara, and Pipi. Their small café offers tasty snacks and specializes in Austrian and Italian wines. Expect good conversation overseen by Hans (Sb-€46, Db-€70, Tb suite-€95, Qb suite-€112, ask for Rick Steves price, all rooms non-smoking, Internet access and Wi-Fi free for Rick Steves readers, free parking, Untermarkt 11, tel. 05672/62522, fax 05672/625-2235, www.hotel-das-beck.at, info@hotel-das-beck.at).

$$ Hotel Goldener Hirsch, also in the center of Reutte just two blocks from the station, is a grand old hotel with 56 rooms and one lonely set of antlers (Sb-€58-62, Db-€88-98, Tb-€135, Qb-€148, less for 2 nights, elevator, free Wi-Fi, restaurant, Mühlerstrasse 1, tel. 05672/62508, fax 05672/625-087, www .goldener-hirsch.at, info@goldener-hirsch.at; Monika, Helmut, and daughters Vanessa and Nina).

In Breitenwang

Now basically a part of Reutte, the older and quieter village of Breitenwang has good *Zimmer* and a fine bakery. It's a 20-minute walk from the Reutte train station: From the post office, follow Planseestrasse past the onion-dome church to the pointy straight-dome church near the two hotels. The Hosps—as well as other B&Bs—are along Kaiser-Lothar-Strasse, the first right past this church. If your train stops at the tiny Reutte-Schulzentrum station, hop out here—you're just a five-minute walk from Breitenwang.

$$ Alpenhotel Ernberg's 26 fresh rooms are run with great care by friendly Hermann, who combines Old World elegance with modern touches. Nestle in for some serious coziness among the carved-wood eating nooks, tiled stoves, and family-friendly backyard (Sb-€55, Db-€90, less for 2 nights, free Wi-Fi, popular restaurant, swimming complex nearby, Planseestrasse 50, tel. 05672/71912, fax 05672/719-1240, www.ernberg.at, info @ernberg.at).

$$ Moserhof Hotel has 40 new-feeling rooms plus an elegant dining room (Sb-€53, Db-€92, larger Db-€100, confirm you're getting Rick Steves rates when you reserve, extra bed-€35, most rooms have balconies, elevator, free Wi-Fi, restaurant, sauna and whirlpool, free parking, Planseestrasse 44, tel. 05672/62020, fax 05672/620-2040, www.hotel-moserhof.at, info@hotel-moserhof.at, Hosp family).

$ Walter and Emilie Hosp rent three rooms in a comfortable, quiet, and modern house two blocks from the Breitenwang church steeple. You'll feel like you're staying at Grandma's (S-€25, D-€40, T-€60, Q-€80, cash only, Kaiser-Lothar-Strasse 29, tel. 05672/65377).

In Ehenbichl, near the Ehrenberg Ruins

The next listings are a bit farther from central Reutte, a couple of miles upriver in the village of Ehenbichl (under the Ehrenberg ruins). From central Reutte, go south on Obermarkt and turn right on Kög, which becomes Reuttenerstrasse, following signs to Ehenbichl. These listings are best for car travelers—you'll need to take a taxi if you arrive by train.

$$ Hotel Maximilian offers 30 rooms at a great value. It includes table tennis, play areas for children (indoors and out), a pool table, and the friendly service of Gabi, Monika, and the rest of the Koch family. They host many special events, and their hotel has lots of wonderful extras such as a sauna and a piano (Sb-€50-57, Db-€80-90, ask for Rick Steves rate when you reserve, family deals, elevator, free Internet access and Wi-Fi in common areas, pay Wi-Fi in rooms, laundry service-€12/load, good restaurant, Reuttenerstrasse 1, tel. 05672/62585, fax 05672/625-8554, www.maxihotel.com, info@hotelmaximilian.at). They rent cars to guests only (€0.72/km, book in advance) and bikes to anyone (€5/half-day, €8/day, more if you're not a guest, those staying at the hotel have free use of older bikes).

$$ Gasthof-Pension Waldrast, separating a forest and a meadow, is run by the farming Huter family and their dog, Picasso. The place feels hauntingly quiet and has no restaurant, but it's inexpensive and offers 10 nice rooms with generous sitting areas and castle-view balconies (Sb-€39, Db-€66, Tb-€82, Qb-€99, ask about discounts with this book, cash only, non-smoking, free Wi-Fi, free parking; about a mile from Reutte, just off main drag toward Innsbruck, past campground and under castle ruins on Ehrenbergstrasse; tel. & fax 05672/62443, www.waldrasttirol.com, info@waldrasttirol.com, Gerd).

$$ Pension Hohenrainer, a big, quiet, no-frills place, is a good value with 12 modern rooms and some castle-view balconies

(Sb-€30-32, Db-€60-64, €1.50/person less for 2 nights, €3/person less for 3 nights, lower prices are for April-June and Sept-Oct, cash only, family rooms, non-smoking rooms, free Internet access and Wi-Fi, restaurant and reception in Gasthof Schlosswirt across the street, follow signs up the road behind Hotel Maximilian into village of Ehenbichl, Unterried 3, tel. 05672/62544 or 05672/63262, fax 05672/62052, www.hohenrainer.at, hohenrainer@aon.at).

   $$ Gintherhof is a working farm that provides its guests with fresh milk, butter, and bacon. Annelies Paulweber offers geranium-covered balconies, six nice rooms with carved-wood ceilings, and a Madonna in every corner (Db-€62, Db suite-€64, €3/person less for third night, cash only, free Wi-Fi, Unterried 7, just up the road behind Hotel Maximilian, tel. 05672/67697, www.gintherhof.com, gintherhof@aon.at).

At the Ehrenberg Ruins

$$ Landgasthof Klause café, just below the Ehrenberg ruins and next to the castle museum, rents six non-smoking rooms with balconies on its upper floor. The downside is that you may have to go out for dinner (the café officially closes at 18:00), and you'll need a car to get anywhere besides Ehrenberg (Sb-€37, Db-€74, Tb-€111, ask for Rick Steves discount when you book, discount for 2 or more nights, free Wi-Fi, apartments available, closed Nov and Jan, tel. 05672/62007, fax 05672/620-0777, www.gasthof-klause.com, gasthof-klause@gmx.at).

A Hostel Across the River

The homey **$ Gästehaus am Graben hostel** has 4-6 beds per room and includes breakfast and sheets. It's lovingly run by the Reyman family—Frau Reyman, Rudi, and Gabi keep the 50-bed place traditional, clean, and friendly. This is a super value less than two miles from Reutte, and the castle views are fantastic. If you've never hosteled and are curious (and have a car or don't mind a bus ride), try it. If traveling with kids, this is a great choice. The double rooms are hotel-grade, and they accept nonmembers of any age (dorm bed-€25, hotel-style Db-€68, cash only, non-smoking, expensive Internet access and Wi-Fi, laundry service-€9, no curfew, closed April and Nov-mid-Dec; from downtown Reutte, cross bridge and follow main road left along river, or take the bus—hourly until 19:30, ask for Graben stop; Graben 1, tel. 05672/626-440, fax 05672/626-444, www.hoefen.at, info@hoefen.at).

In Pinswang

The village of Pinswang is closer to Füssen (and Ludwig's castles), but still in Austria.

$$ Gutshof zum Schluxen gets the "Remote Old Hotel in an Idyllic Setting" award. This family-friendly farm offers rustic elegance draped in goose down and pastels. Its picturesque meadow setting will turn you into a dandelion-picker, and its proximity to Neuschwanstein will turn you into a hiker—the castle is just an hour's hike away (Sb-€49-51, Db-€88-96, extra person-€29, ask for Rick Steves rate, about 5-10 percent cheaper Nov-March, 5 percent discount for stays of three or more nights, free Wi-Fi in common areas, laundry-€9, mountain-bike rental-€10/day or €5/half-day, restaurant, fun bar, between Reutte and Füssen in village of Pinswang, free pickup from Reutte or Füssen but call 24 hours ahead if you'll arrive after 18:00, tel. 05677/89030, fax 05677/890-323, www.schluxen.com, info@schluxen.at).

To reach Neuschwanstein by foot or bike, follow the dirt road up the hill behind the hotel. When the road forks at the top of the hill, go right (downhill), cross the Austria-Germany border (marked by a sign and deserted hut), and follow the narrow paved road to the castles. It's a 1- to 1.5-hour hike or a great circular bike trip (allow 30 minutes; cyclists can return to Schluxen from the castles on a different 30-minute bike route via Füssen).

Eating in Reutte

The hotels here take great pride in serving local cuisine at reasonable prices to their guests and the public. Rather than go to a cheap restaurant, eat at one of the Reutte hotels recommended earlier (**Alpenhotel Ernberg, Moserhof Hotel, Hotel Maximilian,** and **Hotel Goldener Hirsch**). Hotels typically serve €10-15 dinners from 18:00 to 21:00 and are closed one night a week.

Storfwirt is *the* place for a quick and cheap weekday lunch. You can get the usual sausages here, as well as baked potatoes and salads (€5.50-9 daily specials, salad bar, always something for vegetarians, Mon-Fri 9:00-14:30, closed Sat-Sun, Schrettergasse 15, tel. 05672/62640).

Non Solo Pasta, just off the traffic circle, is a local favorite for Italian food (€7-9 pizzas and pastas, €8-12 main courses, Mon-Fri 11:30-14:00 & 18:00-23:00, Sat 18:00-23:00, closed Sun, Lindenstrasse 1, tel. 05672/72714).

Across the street from the Hotel Goldener Hirsch on Mühlerstrasse is a **Bauernladen** (farmer's shop) with rustic sandwiches and meals prepared from local ingredients (Wed-Fri 9:00-18:00, Sat 9:00-12:00, closed Sun-Tue, mobile 0676-575-4588).

Picnic Supplies: **Billa** supermarket has everything you'll need (across from TI, Mon-Fri 7:15-19:30, Sat 7:15-18:00, closed Sun).

Reutte Connections

From Reutte by Train to: Garmisch (every 2 hours, 1 hour), **Munich** (every 2 hours, 2.5 hours, change in Garmisch), **Salzburg** (every 2 hours, 4.5-5.5 hours, quickest with changes in Garmisch and Munich). Train info: tel. 0180-599-6633, www.bahn.com.

By Bus to: Füssen (Mon-Fri almost hourly, Sat-Sun every 2 hours, 45 minutes, €3.90 one-way, buses depart from train station, pay driver).

Taxis cost about €35 one-way to Füssen or the King's Castles.

ROTHENBURG

In the Middle Ages, when Frankfurt and Munich were just wide spots on the road, Rothenburg ob der Tauber was a "free imperial city" beholden only to the Holy Roman Emperor. With a whopping population of 6,000, it was one of Germany's largest. Today, it's the country's best-preserved medieval walled town, enjoying tremendous tourist popularity without losing its charm.

During Rothenburg's heyday, from 1150 to 1400, it was a strategic stop on the trade routes between northern and southern Europe. Now that route is known as the "Romantic Road," linking Frankfurt and Munich through a medieval heartland strewn with picturesque villages, farmhouses, onion-domed churches, and walled cities.

Today, Rothenburg's great trade is tourism: Two-thirds of the townspeople are employed to serve you. While 2.5 million people visit each year, a mere 500,000 spend the night. Rothenburg is yours after dark, when the groups vacate and the town's floodlit cobbles wring some romance out of any travel partner.

Too often, Rothenburg brings out the shopper in visitors before they've had a chance to see the historic town. True, this is a fine place to do your German shopping, but appreciate Rothenburg's great history and sights, too.

Planning Your Time

If time is short, you can make just a two- to three-hour midday stop in Rothenburg, but the town is really best appreciated after the day-trippers have gone home. Spend at least one night in Rothenburg (hotels are cheap and good). With two nights and a day, you'll be able to see more than the essentials and actually relax a little.

Rothenburg in one day is easy, with four essential experiences: the Medieval Crime and Punishment Museum, Tilman Riemenschneider's wood carving in St. Jakob's Church, a walk along the city wall, and the entertaining Night Watchman's Tour. With more time, you could visit several mediocre but entertaining museums, take some scenic hikes and bike rides in the nearby countryside, and enjoy the town's plentiful cafés and shops.

Rothenburg is very busy through the summer and in the Christmas Market month of December. Spring and fall are a joy, but it's pretty bleak from January through March—when most locals are hibernating or on vacation. Many shops stay open on Sundays during the tourist season, but close on Sundays in November and from Christmas to Easter.

There are several Rothenburgs in Germany, so make sure you are going to **Rothenburg ob der Tauber** (not "ob der" any other river); people really do sometimes drive or ride the train to other, nondescript Rothenburgs by accident.

Orientation to Rothenburg

(area code: 09861)

To orient yourself in Rothenburg, think of the town map as a human head. Its nose—the castle garden—sticks out to the left, and the skinny lower part forms a wide-open mouth, with the youth hostel and a recommended hotel in the chin. The town is a delight on foot. No sights or hotels are more than a 15-minute walk from the train station or each other.

Most of the buildings you'll see were in place by 1400. The city was born around its long-gone castle—built in 1142, destroyed in 1356—which was located where the castle garden is now. You can see the shadow of the first town wall, which defines the oldest part of Rothenburg, in its contemporary street plan. A few gates (called *Tor*s—such as the Rödertor or the Spitaltor) from this wall still survive. The richest and biggest houses were in this central part. The commoners built higgledy-piggledy (read: picturesque) houses farther from the center, but still inside the present walls. Rothenburg's classic street scene is the Plönlein ("Little Square"), a picture-perfect tableau of a yellow house wedged between two towers at a diverging road (3 blocks due south of Market Square).

Although Rothenburg is technically in Bavaria, the region around the town is called by its medieval name, *Franken* (Franconia).

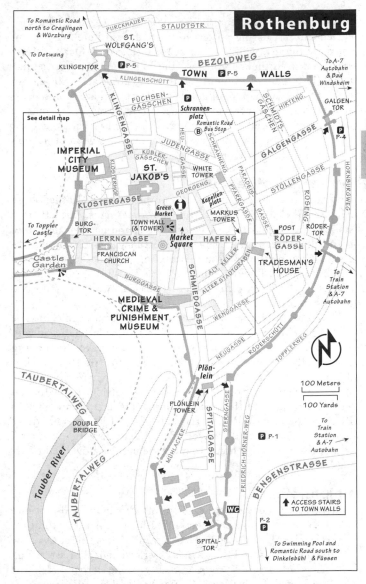

To Romantic Road
north to Creglingen
& Würzburg

To Detwang

PURCKHAUER

STAUDTSTR.

Rothenburg

ST.
WOLFGANG'S

KLINGENTOR

BEZOLDWEG

TOWN

WALLS

To A-7
Autobahn
& Bad
Windsheim

KLINGENSCHÜTT

P P-5

P P-5

FÜCHSEN-
GÄSSCHEN

Schrannen-
platz

SCHMIDTS
GÄSSCHEN

HIRTENG.

GALGEN-
TOR

See detail map

KLINGENGASSE

JUDENGASSE

Romantic Road
Bus Stop

SCHRANNENG

GALGENGASSE

P P-4

IMPERIAL
CITY
MUSEUM

KLOSTERHOF

KÜBLER-
GÄSSCHEN

HEU-GASSE

PARADEIS

PFARRGASSE

STOLLENGASSE

HORNBURGWEG

ST.
JAKOB'S

WHITE
TOWER

ROSENG.

KLOSTERGASSE

GEORGENG.

Kapellen-
platz

Green
Market

To Toppler
Castle

BURG-
TOR

TOWN HALL
(& TOWER)

MARKUS
TOWER

POST

RÖDER-
TOR

HERRNGASSE

Market
Square

HAFENG.

RÖDER-
GASSE

To
Train
Station
& A-7
Autobahn

Castle
Garden

FRANCISCAN
CHURCH

ALT. KELLER

TRADESMAN'S
HOUSE

BURGGASSE

ALTER STADTGRABEN

MEDIEVAL
CRIME &
PUNISHMENT
MUSEUM

SCHMIEDGASSE

WENGGASSE

NEUGASSE

RÖDERSCHÜTT

TOPPLERWEG

N

TAUBERTALWEG

Plön-
lein

100 Meters

100 Yards

DOUBLE
BRIDGE

PLÖNLEIN
TOWER

SPITALGASSE

STERNGASSE

FRIEDRICH-HÖRNER-WEG

P P-1

To
Train
Station
& A-7
Autobahn

Tauber River

TAUBERTALWEG

MÜHLACKER

BENSENSTRASSE

WC

ACCESS STAIRS
TO TOWN WALLS

SPITAL-
TOR

P-2
P

To Swimming Pool and
Romantic Road south to
Dinkelsbühl & Füssen

ROTHENBURG

Tourist Information

The TI is on Market Square (May-Oct and Dec Mon-Fri 9:00-18:00, Sat-Sun 10:00-17:00; Nov and Jan-April Mon-Fri 9:00-17:00, Sat 10:00-13:00, closed Sun; Marktplatz 2, tel. 09861/404800, www.rothenburg.de). If there's a long line, just raid the rack where they keep all the free pamphlets. The free *Map & Guide* comes with a walking guide to the town. The free *RoTour* monthly magazine lists all the events and entertainment (mostly in German); look for current concert listing posters here and at your hotel. Ask about the daily English walking tour at 14:00 (€7, April-Oct and Dec; see "Tours in Rothenburg," later). The TI has one free Internet terminal (15-minute maximum). Visitors who arrive after closing can check the handy map highlighting which hotels have rooms available, with a free direct phone connection to them; it's just outside the door. A pictorial town map is available for free with this book at the Friese shop, two doors west from the TI (toward St. Jakob's Church; see "Shopping in Rothenburg," later).

Arrival in Rothenburg

By Train: It's a 10-minute walk from the station to Rothenburg's Market Square (following the brown *Altstadt* signs, exit left from station, turn right on Ansbacher Strasse, and head straight into the Middle Ages). Day-trippers can leave luggage in station lockers (€1-2, on platform) or at a local shop (try the Friese shop on Market Square, listed on page 502). Free WCs are behind the snack bar next door to the station. Taxis wait at the station (€5-6 to any hotel).

By Car: While much of the town is closed to traffic, anyone with a hotel reservation can drive through pedestrian zones to get to their hotel. The easiest way to enter and leave Rothenburg is generally via Spitalgasse and the Spitaltor (south end). But driving in town can be a nightmare, with many narrow, one-way streets. If you're packing light, just park outside the walls and walk five minutes to the center. Parking lots line the town walls: P1 costs €5 per day; P5 and the south half of P4 are sometimes free on weekends. Only those with a hotel reservation can park within the walls after hours (but no one may park overnight during festivals).

Helpful Hints

Festivals: For one weekend each spring, *Biergartens* spill out into the street and Rothenburgers dress up in medieval costumes to celebrate Mayor Nusch's Meistertrunk victory (the story of the draught that saved the town is described under "Meistertrunk Show" on page 491, more info at www.meistertrunk.de). The Reichsstadt festival every September celebrates Rothenburg's history.

Christmas Market: Rothenburg is dead in November, January, and February, but December is its busiest month—the entire town cranks up the medieval cuteness with concerts and costumes, shops with schnapps, stalls filling squares, hot spiced wine, giddy nutcrackers, and mobs of earmuffed Germans. Christmas markets are big all over Germany, and

Rothenburg's is considered one of the best. The market takes place each year during Advent. Virtually all sights listed in this chapter are open longer hours during these four weeks. Try to avoid Saturdays and Sundays, when big-city day-trippers really clog the grog.

Internet Access: Most hotels have Internet access. If yours doesn't, head to the **Nuschhaus Café,** just below Market Square, which has terminals (€3/hour) and Wi-Fi (€2/hour, Mon-Thu 10:00-18:30, Fri-Sun 10:00-20:00, across the street from the Medieval Crime and Punishment Museum at Obere Schmiedgasse 23, tel. 09861/976-838). The **TI** has one free terminal for brief use (maximum 15 minutes).

Laundry: A handy launderette is near the station, off Ansbacher Strasse (€5.50/load, includes soap, English instructions, owner isn't always around to make change so it's smart to bring coins, opens at 8:00, last load Mon-Fri at 18:00, Sat at 14:00, closed Sun, Johannitergasse 9, tel. 09861/2775).

Bike Rental: Consider renting a bike to enjoy the nearby countryside; you can follow the route described on page 500. **Fahrradhaus Krauss** is a big, cheap, reliable bike shop a 10- to 15-minute walk from the old town that rents eight-gear bikes. From the old town, head toward the train station, then continue along Ansbacher Strasse, bearing right over the train tracks (€5/6 hours, €10/24 hours, €15/all weekend, no helmets, Mon-Fri 9:00-18:00, Sat 9:00-13:00, closed Sun but ask about arranging return, Ansbacher Strasse 85, tel. 09861/3495, www.fahrradhaus-krauss.de). Another rental shop—more expensive but closer to town—is **Rad & Tat** (€9/6 hours, €12/24 hours, Mon-Fri 9:00-18:00, Sat 9:00-13:00, closed Sun, Bensenstrasse 17, tel. 09861/87984, www.mietraeder.de).

Taxi: For a taxi, call 09861/2000 or 09861/7227.

Haircuts: At **Salon Wack** (pronounced "vack," not "wack"), Horst and his team speak English and welcome both men and women (wash and cut: €20 for men, €29-34 for women; Tue-Fri 8:00-12:00 & 13:30-18:00, Sat 8:30-14:00, closed Sun-Mon, in the old center just off Wenggasse at Goldene Ringgasse 8, tel. 09861/7834).

Swimming: Rothenburg has a fine swimming complex, with a heated outdoor pool *(Freibad)* from mid-May to mid-September, and an indoor pool and sauna the rest of the year. It's about a 15-minute walk south of the Spitaltor along the main road toward Dinkelsbühl (adults-€3.50, kids-€2, swimsuit rental-€2, towel rental-€2.50; outdoor pool Fri-Tue 9:00-20:00, Wed 6:30-20:00, Thu 10:00-20:00; indoor pool Mon 14:00-21:00, Tue-Thu 9:00-21:00, Fri-Sun 9:00-18:00; Nördlinger Strasse 20, tel. 09861/4565).

Tours in Rothenburg

▲▲**Night Watchman's Tour**—This tour is flat-out the most enter-
taining hour of medieval wonder anywhere in Germany. The Night
Watchman (a.k.a. Hans-Georg Baumgartner) jokes like a medieval
Jerry Seinfeld as he lights his lamp and takes tourists on his rounds,
telling slice-of-gritty-life tales of medieval Rothenburg (€7, Easter-
Dec nightly at 20:00, in English, meet at Market Square, www
.nightwatchman.de). This is the best evening activity in town. Night
Watchman fans can also visit his store (see page 502).

Executioner's Tour—Georg Lehle leads a macabre one-hour
tour as a 14th-century executioner (€7, April-Dec nightly at 19:00,
in English, meet at Market Square).

Old Town Historic Walk—The TI offers 1.5-hour guided walking tours in English (€7, April-Oct and Dec daily at 14:00, no
English tours in Nov or Jan-March, departs from Market Square).
Take this tour for the serious side of Rothenburg's history, and to
make sense of the town's architecture; you won't get as much of
that on the fun—and completely different—Night Watchman's
Tour. It would be a shame not to take advantage of this informative tour just because you took the other.

Local Guides—A local historian can really bring the ramparts alive. Prices are standardized (€62/1.5 hours, €80/2 hours).
Reserve a guide by emailing the TI (info@rothenburg.de; more
info under "Guided Tours" at www.rothenburg.de). I've had good
experiences with **Martin Kamphans,** who also works as a potter (tel. 09861/7941, www.stadtfuehrungen-rothenburg.de, post
@stadtfuehrungen-rothenburg.de).

Self-Guided Walk

Welcome to Rothenburg

This one-hour circular walk weaves Rothenburg's top sights
together.
• *Start the walk on Market Square.*

Market Square Spin-Tour

Stand at the bottom of Market Square (10 feet below the wooden
post on the corner) and spin 360 degrees clockwise, starting with
the Town Hall tower. Now do it again, this time more slowly, following these notes:

Town Hall and Tower: Rothenburg's tallest spire is the Town
Hall tower (Rathausturm). At 200 feet, it stands atop the old Town
Hall, a white, Gothic, 13th-century building. Notice the tourists
enjoying the best view in town from the black top of the tower (€2
and a rigorous but interesting climb, 214 steps, narrow and steep

Rothenburg Self-Guided Walk

To Detwang

To Klingentor

KLINGENGASSE

Schrannen-platz

Romantic Road Bus Stop **B**

JUDENGASSE

HIRTENG.

SCHRANNEN

GALGENG.

PARADEIS

N

IMPERIAL CITY MUSEUM ⑩

KÜBLER-GÄSSCHEN

HEUGASSE

ROAD PASSES UNDER CHURCH

ST. JAKOB'S

WHITE TOWER

KLOSTERHOF

⑪

GEORGENG.

COUNCILORS' TAVERN &

Kapellen-platz

KLOSTERG. ⑨

⑧

Green Market

③

WALK BEGINS & ENDS

MARKUS TOWER

To Toppler Castle

⑫

TOWN HALL (& TOWER)

②

①

Market Square

④

HAFENG.

BURG-TOR

⑬

PUPPET THEATER

⑦

To Rödertor & Train Station

FRANCISCAN CHURCH

⑮ HERRNGASSE

⑯

⑰

⑥

⑤

PFAFFLEINS-GASSE

HOFBRONN

⑱

⑲

⑭

BURGGASSE

MEDIEVAL CRIME & PUNISHMENT MUSEUM

SCHMIEDGASSE

ALTER KELLER

ALTER STADTGRABEN

100 Meters

100 Yards

WENGGASSE

To Plönlein & Spitalgasse

Tauber River

① Market Square Spin-Tour
② Town Hall & Tower
③ Councilors' Tavern & TI
④ Geissendörfer Print Shop
⑤ Baumeister Haus
⑥ St. George's Fountain
⑦ Historical Town Hall Vaults
⑧ Green Market & Friese Shop
⑨ St. Jakob's Church
⑩ Imperial City Museum

⑪ Convent Garden
⑫ Original Barn
⑬ Town Wall
⑭ Castle Garden
⑮ Herrngasse
⑯ Eisenhut Hotel/Restaurant
⑰ Käthe Wohlfahrt Christmas Village & Museum
⑱ Doll & Toy Museum
⑲ Night Watchman's Store

near the top—watch your head, April-Oct daily 9:30-12:30 & 13:00-17:00, closed Nov-March, enter on Market Square through middle arch of new Town Hall). After a fire in 1501 burned down part of the original building, a new Town Hall was built alongside what survived of the old one (fronting the square). This half of the rebuilt complex is in the Renaissance style from 1570.

Meistertrunk Show: At the top of Market Square stands the proud Councilors' Tavern (clock tower from 1466). In its day, the city council—the rich guys who ran the town government—drank here. Today, it's the TI and the focus of most tourists' attention when the little doors on either side of the clock flip open and the wooden figures (from 1910) do their thing. Be on Market Square at 11:00, 12:00, 13:00, 14:00, 15:00, 20:00, 21:00, or 22:00 for the ritual gathering of the tourists to see the less-than-breathtaking reenactment of the Meistertrunk ("Master Draught") story:

In 1631, in the middle of the Thirty Years' War, the Catholic army took the Protestant town and was about to do its rape, pillage, and plunder thing. As was the etiquette, the mayor had to give the conquering general a welcoming drink. The general enjoyed a huge tankard of local wine. Feeling really good, he told the mayor, "Hey, if you can drink this entire three-liter tankard of wine in one gulp, I'll spare your town." The mayor amazed everyone by drinking the entire thing, and Rothenburg was saved.

While this is a nice story, it was dreamed up in the late 1800s for a theatrical play designed (effectively) to promote a romantic image of the town. In actuality, if Rothenburg was spared, it happened because it bribed its way out of a jam. It was occupied and ransacked several times in the Thirty Years' War, and it never recovered—which is why it's such a well-preserved time capsule today.

For the best show, don't watch the clock; watch the open-mouthed tourists gasp as the old windows flip open. At the late shows, the square flickers with camera flashes.

Bottom of Market Square: At the bottom end of the square, the cream-colored building on the corner has a fine **print shop** around back (described under "Shopping in Rothenburg," later). Adjoining that is the **Baumeister Haus,** featuring a famous Renaissance facade with statues of the seven virtues and the seven vices—the former supporting the latter. The statues are copies; the originals are in the Imperial City Museum (described later on this walk). The green house below that is the former home of the 15th-century Mayor Toppler (it's now the recommended Gasthof Goldener Greifen).

Keep circling to the big 17th-century **St. George's fountain.** The long metal gutters slid, routing the water into the villagers' buckets. Rothenburg had an ingenious water system. Built on a rock, it had one real source above the town, which was plumbed to serve a series of fountains; water flowed from high to low through Rothenburg. Its many fountains had practical functions beyond providing drinking water (some were stocked with fish on market days and during times of siege). Water was used for fighting fires, and because of its plentiful water supply—and its policy of requiring relatively wide lanes as fire breaks—the town never burned entirely, as so many neighboring villages did.

Two fine buildings behind the fountain show the old-time lofts with warehouse doors and pulleys on top for hoisting. All over town, lofts were filled with grain and corn. A year's supply was required by the city so they could survive any siege. The building behind the fountain is an art gallery showing off work by members of the local artists' association (free, Tue-Sun 14:00-18:00, closed Mon). To the right is Marien Apotheke, an old-time pharmacy mixing old and new in typical Rothenburg style.

The broad street running under the Town Hall tower is **Herrngasse.** The town originated with its castle (built in 1142 but now long gone; only the castle garden remains). Herrngasse connected the castle to Market Square. The last leg of this circular walking tour will take you from the castle garden up Herrngasse back to where you're now standing. For now, walk a few steps down Herrngasse and stop by the arch under the Town Hall tower (between the new and old town halls). On the left wall are the town's measuring rods—a reminder that medieval Germany was made of 300 independent little countries, each with its own weights and measures. Merchants and shoppers knew that these were the local standards: the rod (4.3 yards), the *Schuh* ("shoe," roughly a foot), and the *Ell* (from elbow to fingertip—four inches longer than mine...try it). Notice the protruding cornerstone. These are all over town—originally to protect buildings from reckless horse carts (and vice versa).

• *Under the arch, you'll find the...*

▲Historical Town Hall Vaults (Historiengewölbe)

This grade-schoolish little museum gives a waxy but interesting look at Rothenburg during the Catholics-vs.-Protestants Thirty Years' War. With helpful English descriptions, it offers a look at "the fateful year 1631," a replica of the mythical Meistertrunk tankard, and a dungeon complete with three dank cells and some torture lore.

Cost and Hours: €2.50, daily May-Oct 9:30-17:30, shorter hours April and Dec, closed Nov and Jan-March, tel. 09861/86751.

• *Leaving the museum, turn left (past a much-sketched-and-photographed venerable door), and walk through the courtyard to a square called...*

Green Market (Grüner Markt)

Once a produce market, this parking lot fills with Christmas shops during December. Notice the clay-tile roofs. These "beaver tail" tiles became standard after thatched roofs were outlawed to prevent fires. Today, all of the town's roofs are made of these. The little fences keep the snow from falling, and catch tiles that blow off during storms. The free public WC is on your left, the recommended Friese shop is on your right, and straight ahead is St. Jakob's Church.

Outside the church, you'll see 14th-century statues (mostly original) showing Jesus praying at Gethsemane, a common feature of Gothic churches. The artist is anonymous, because in the Gothic age (pre-Albrecht Dürer), artists were just nameless craftspeople working only for the glory of God. Five yards to the left (on the wall), notice the nub of a sandstone statue—a rare original, looking pretty bad after 500 years of weather and, more recently, pollution. Most original statues are now in the city museum. The better-preserved statues you see on the church are copies.

• If it's your wedding day, take the first entrance. Otherwise, use the second (downhill) door to enter...

▲▲St. Jakob's Church (St. Jakobskirche)

Rothenburg's main church is home to Tilman Riemenschneider's breathtaking, wood-carved *Altar of the Holy Blood*.

Cost and Hours: €2, worthwhile 45-minute audioguide-€2, daily April-Oct 9:00-17:15, Dec 10:00-16:45, Nov and Christmas-March 10:00-12:00 & 14:00-16:00, on Sun wait to enter until services end at 10:45, free helpful English info sheet, concerts and tour schedule posted on the door. There are guided tours in English for no extra charge on Saturdays at 15:00.

Visiting the Church: Built in the 14th century, this church has been Lutheran since 1544. The **interior** was "purified" by Romantics in the 19th century—cleaned of everything Baroque or not original and refitted in the Neo-Gothic style. (For example, the baptismal font and the pulpit above the second pew *look* Gothic, but are actually Neo-Gothic.) The stained-glass windows behind the altar, which are most colorful in the morning light, are originals from the 1330s.

At the back of the church, take the stairs that lead up behind the pipe organ. In the loft, you'll find the artistic highlight of Rothenburg and perhaps the most wonderful wood carving in all of Germany: the glorious 500-year-old, 35-foot-high *Altar of the Holy Blood*. Tilman Riemenschneider, the Michelangelo of German woodcarvers, carved this from 1499 to 1504 to hold a precious rock-crystal capsule (set in a cross) that contains a scrap of tablecloth miraculously stained in the shape of a cross by a drop of communion wine. The altar is a realistic commotion, showing that Riemenschneider—while a High Gothic artist—was ahead of his time. Below, in the scene of the Last Supper, Jesus gives Judas a piece of bread, marking him as the traitor, while John lays his head on Christ's lap. Everything is portrayed exactly as described in the Bible. On the left: Jesus enters a walled city. (Historians dispute whether it's Jerusalem, in keeping with the altar's Holy Week theme, or Jericho—notice the man in the tree, who could be Jericho's shy tax collector Zacchaeus.) Notice the fun attention to detail—down to the nails on the horseshoe. On the right: Jesus prays in the Garden of Gethsemane. Judas, with his big bag of cash, could be removed from the scene—illustrated by photos on the wall nearby—as was the tradition for the four days leading up to Easter.

Head back down the stairs to the church's main hall. Go up front to take a close look at the **main altar** (from 1466, by Friedrich Herlin). Below Christ are statues of six saints. St. James (Jakob in German) is the one with the shell. He's the saint of pilgrims, and this church was a stop on the medieval pilgrimage route to Santiago ("St. James" in Spanish) de Compostela in Spain. Study the painted panels—ever see Peter with spectacles? Around the back of the altarpiece (upper left) is a painting of Rothenburg's Market Square in the 15th century—looking much like it does today, with the exception of the full-Gothic Town Hall (as it was before the big fire of 1501). Notice Christ's face on the veil of Veronica (center of back side). It follows you as you walk from side to side—this must have given the faithful the religious heebie-jeebies four centuries ago.

The **small altar** to the left is also worth a look. It's a century older than the main altar. Notice the unusual Trinity: the Father and Son are literally bridged by a dove, which represents the Holy Spirit. Stepping back, you can see that Jesus is standing on a skull—clearly "overcoming death."

Before leaving the front of the church, notice the old **medallions** above the carved choir stalls. They feature the coats of arms of Rothenburg's leading families and portraits of city and church leaders.

• *Leave the church and, from its outside steps, walk around the corner to the right and under the chapel (built over the road). Go two blocks down Klingengasse and stop at the corner of the street called Klosterhof. Looking down Klingengasse, you see the...*

Klingentor

This cliff tower was Rothenburg's water reservoir. From 1595 until 1910, a copper tank high in the tower provided clean spring water (pumped up by river power) to the privileged. To the right of the Klingentor is a good stretch of wall rampart to walk. To the left, the wall is low and simple, lacking a rampart because it guards only a cliff. Now find the shell decorating a building on the street corner next to you. That's the symbol of St. James (pilgrims commemorated their visit to Santiago de Compostela with a shell), indicating that this building is associated with the church.

• *Turn left down Klosterhof, passing the shell and, on your right, the colorful, recommended Altfränkische Weinstube am Klosterhof pub, to reach the...*

▲▲Imperial City Museum (Reichsstadt-Museum)

You'll get a scholarly sweep through Rothenburg's history at this museum, housed in a former Dominican convent. Cloistered nuns used the lazy Susan embedded in the wall (to the right of the museum door) to give food to the poor without being seen.

Just follow the *Rundgang/Tour* signs. Highlights include the *Rothenburg Passion*, a 12-panel series of paintings from 1492 showing scenes leading up to Christ's crucifixion (in the *Konventsaal*); an exhibit of Jewish culture in Rothenburg through the ages *(Judaika)*; a 14th-century convent kitchen *(Klosterküche)* with a working model of the lazy Susan and a massive chimney; romantic paintings of the town *(Gemäldegalerie)*; the fine Baumann collection of weapons and armor; and sandstone statues from the church and Baumeister Haus (the seven vices and seven virtues).

Cost and Hours: €4, daily April-Oct 9:30-17:30, Nov-March 13:00-16:00, English info sheet and descriptions, Klosterhof 5, tel. 09861/939-043, www.reichsstadtmuseum.info.

• *Leaving the museum, go around to the right and into the Convent Garden (when locked at night, continue straight to the T-intersection and see the barn three doors to the right).*

Convent Garden

This spot is a peaceful place to work on your tan...or mix a poisoned potion. Monks and nuns, who were responsible for concocting herbal cures in the olden days, often tended herb gardens. Smell (but don't pick) the *Pfefferminze*, *Juniper* (gin), *Chamomilla* (disinfectant), and *Origanum*. Don't smell the plants in the poison corner (potency indicated by the number of crosses, like spiciness stars in a restaurant).

Cost and Hours: Free, daily April-Oct 9:00-18:00, Nov-March 13:00-16:00.

• *Exit opposite from where you entered, angling left through the nuns' garden (site of the now-gone Dominican church), eventually leaving via an arch at the far end. Looking to your left, you'll see the back end of an...*

Original Barn

This is the back side of a complex that fronts Herrngasse. Medieval Germans often lived in large structures like this that were like small villages in themselves, with a grouping of buildings and open spaces. The typical design included a house, a courtyard, a stable, a garden, and, finally, a barn. Notice how the bulging wall is corseted by a brace with iron washers. Crank on its nuts and the building will stand up straight.

• *Now go downhill to the...*

Town Wall

This part of the wall (view through bars, look to far right) takes advantage of the natural fortification provided by the cliff, and is therefore much smaller than the ramparts. Angle left along the wall to the big street (Herrngasse), then right under the Burgtor tower. Notice the tiny "eye of the needle" door cut into the big door. If trying to get into town after curfew, you could bribe the guard to let you through this door (which was small enough to keep out any fully armed attackers).

• *Step through the gate and outside the wall. Look around and imagine being locked out in the year 1400. This was a wooden drawbridge (see the chain slits above). Notice the "pitch nose" mask—designed to pour boiling Nutella on anyone attacking. High above is the town coat of arms: a red castle* (roten Burg).

Castle Garden (Burggarten)

The garden before you was once that red castle (destroyed in the 14th century). Today, it's a picnic-friendly park. The chapel (50 yards into the park on the left) is the only bit of the original castle to survive. It's now a memorial to local Jews killed in a 1298 slaughter. A few steps beyond that is a grapevine trellis that provides a fine picnic spot. If you walk all the way out to the garden's far end, you'll find a great viewpoint (well past the tourists, and considered the best place to kiss by romantic local teenagers). But the views of the lush Tauber River Valley below are just as good from the top end of the park. Facing the town, on the left, a path leads down to the village of Detwang (you can see the church spire below)—a town even older than Rothenburg (for a walk to Detwang, see "A Walk in the Countryside," page 500). To the right is a fine view of the fortified Rothenburg and the "Tauber Riviera" below.

• *Return to the tower, cross carefully under the pitch nose, and hike back up Herrngasse to your starting point.*

Herrngasse

Many towns have a Herrngasse, where the richest patricians and merchants (the *Herren*) lived. Predictably, it's your best chance to see the town's finest old mansions. Strolling back to Market Square, you'll pass the old-time puppet theater (German only, on left) and the Franciscan church (from 1285, oldest in town, on right). The house at #18 is the biggest patrician house on the street. The family, which has lived here for three centuries, disconnected the four old-time doorbells. Their door—big enough to allow a carriage in (with a human-sized door cut into it)—is typical of the age. To see the traditional house-courtyard-stables-garden-barn layout, pop into either #14 (now an apartment block) or—if that's closed—the

shop across the street, at #11. The Hotel Eisenhut, with its recommended restaurant, is Rothenburg's fanciest hotel and worth a
peek inside. The Käthe Wohlfahrt Christmas shops (at Herrngasse
1 and 2; described later, under "Shopping in Rothenburg") are your
last, and perhaps greatest, temptations before reaching your starting and ending point: Market Square.

Sights in Rothenburg

Museums Within a Block of Market Square

**▲▲Medieval Crime and Punishment Museum (Mittel-
alterliches Kriminalmuseum)**—This museum is the best of its
kind, specializing in everything connected to medieval criminal justice. Learn about medieval police, medieval criminal law,
and above all, instruments of punishment and torture—even a
special cage complete with a metal gag for nags. The museum is
more eclectic than its name, and includes exhibits on general history, superstition, biblical art, and temporary displays in a second
building. Follow the yellow arrows—the one-way traffic system
makes it hard to double back. Exhibits are tenderly described in
English.

Cost and Hours: €4, daily May-Oct 10:00-18:00, Nov and
Jan-Feb 14:00-16:00, Dec and March 13:00-16:00, April 11:00-
17:00, last entry 45 minutes before closing, fun cards and posters, Burggasse 3-5, tel. 09861/5359, www.kriminalmuseum
.rothenburg.de.

Nearby: If you insist on trying a *Schneeball*, the museum café
(located in the next building down Burggasse) sells mini-*Schneeballen* for €0.40 (open May-Oct Tue-Thu and Sat-Sun, closed Mon
and Fri and Nov-April, no museum admission required for café
after 13:00).

▲Doll and Toy Museum (Puppen- und Spielzeugmuseum)—
These two floors of historic *Kinder* cuteness are a hit with many
little kids. Pick up the free English binder (just past the entry curtain) for an extensive description of the exhibits.

Cost and Hours: €4, family ticket-€10, daily March-Dec
9:30-18:00, Jan-Feb 11:00-17:00, just off Market Square, downhill from the fountain at Hofbronnengasse 11-13, tel. 09861/7330,
www.spielzeugmuseum.rothenburg.de.

**▲German Christmas Museum (Deutsches Weihnachts-
museum)**—This excellent museum, upstairs in the giant Käthe
Wohlfahrt Christmas Village shop, tells the history of Christmas
decorations. There's a unique and thoughtfully described collection of Christmas-tree stands, mini-trees sent in boxes to WWI
soldiers at the front, early Advent calendars, old-time Christmas
cards, and a look at tree decorations through the ages—including

the Nazi era and when you were a kid. The museum is not just a ploy to get shoppers to spend more money, but a serious collection managed by professional curator Felicitas Höptner.

Cost and Hours: €4, April-Dec daily 10:00-18:00, Jan-March Sat-Sun 10:00-18:00 and irregularly on weekdays, last entry at 17:00, Herrngasse 1, tel. 09861/409-365, www.germanchristmas museum.com.

More Sights in Rothenburg

▲▲**Walk the Wall**—Just longer than a mile and a half around, providing great views and a good orientation, this walk can be done by those under six feet tall in less than an hour (unless your camera can't stop snapping). The hike requires no special sense of balance. This walk is covered and is a great option in the rain. Photographers will stay very busy, especially before breakfast or at sunset, when the lighting is best and the crowds are fewest. You can enter or exit the ramparts at nearly every tower. The best fortifications are in the Spitaltor (south end). Climb the Rödertor en route (described next). The names you see along the way belong to people who donated money to rebuild the wall after World War II, and those who've more recently donated €1,000 per meter for the maintenance of Rothenburg's heritage.

▲**Rödertor**—The 13th-century wall tower nearest the train station is the only one you can climb. It's worth the 135 steps for the view and a short but fascinating rundown on the bombing of Rothenburg in the last weeks of World War II, when the east part of the city was destroyed. If you climb this, you can skip the more claustrophobic Town Hall tower climb.

Cost and Hours: €1.50, pay at top, unreliable hours, usually open daily April-Oct 10:00-16:00, closed Nov-March, WWII photos have English translations.

▲▲**The Allergic-to-Tourists Wall and Moat Walk**—For a quiet and scenic break from the tourist crowds and a chance to appreciate the marvelous fortifications of Rothenburg, consider this hike: From the Castle Garden, go right and walk outside the wall to the Klingentor. At the Klingentor, climb up to the ramparts and walk on the wall past the Galgentor to the Rödertor. Then descend, leave the old town, and hike through the park (once the moat) down to the Spitaltor. Explore the fortifications here before hiking a block up Spitalgasse, turning left to pass the youth hostel, popping back outside the wall, and heading along the upper scenic reaches of the river valley and above the vineyards back to the Castle Garden.

▲**Tradesman's House (Alt-Rothenburger Handwerkerhaus)**—See the everyday life of a Rothenburger in the town's heyday in this restored 700-year-old home.

Cost and Hours: €2.50; Easter-Oct Mon-Fri 11:00-17:00, Sat-Sun 10:00-17:00; Dec daily 14:00-16:00; closed Nov and Jan-Easter; near Markus Tower at Alter Stadtgraben 26, tel. 09861/5810.

St. Wolfgang's Church—This fortified Gothic church is built into the medieval wall at the Klingentor. Its dungeon-like passages and shepherd's-dance exhibit are pretty lame.

Cost and Hours: €1.50, Wed-Mon April-Sept 10:00-13:00 & 14:30-17:00, Oct 10:00-16:00, closed Tue and Nov-March.

Near Rothenburg

▲▲A Walk in the Countryside—From the *Burggarten* (castle garden), head into the Tauber Valley. With your back to town, go down the hill, exiting the castle garden on your left. Once outside the wall, walk around, keeping the castle and town on your right. The trail becomes really steep, taking you down to the wooden covered bridge on the valley floor. Across the bridge, the road goes left to Toppler Castle and right (downstream, with a pleasant parallel footpath) to Detwang.

Toppler Castle (Topplerschlösschen) is cute, skinny, sky-blue, and 600 years old. It was the castle/summer home of the medieval Mayor Toppler. The tower's top looks like a house—a sort of tree fort for grownups. It's in a farmer's garden, and it's open whenever he's around and willing to let you in (€1.50, normally Fri-Sun 13:00-16:00, closed Mon-Thu and Nov, one mile from town center at Taubertalweg 100, tel. 09861/7358). People say the mayor had this valley-floor escape built to get people to relax about leaving the fortified town...or to hide a mistress.

To extend your stroll, walk back to the bridge and follow the river downstream (passing the recommended Unter den Linden beer garden) to the peaceful village of **Detwang.** One of the oldest villages in Franconia (one of Germany's medieval dukedoms), Detwang dates from 968. Like Rothenburg, it has a Riemenschneider altarpiece in its church.

Franconian Bike Ride—To get a fun, breezy look at the countryside around Rothenburg, rent a bike from Fahrradhaus Krauss (see "Helpful Hints" on page 489). For a pleasant half-day pedal, escape the old town through the Rödertor, bike along Topplerweg to the Spitaltor, and follow the curvy road down into the river valley. Turn right at the yellow *Leutzenbronn* sign to cross the double-arcaded bridge. From here a peaceful road follows the river downstream to **Detwang,** passing the cute Toppler Castle (described earlier). From Detwang, follow the main road to the old mill, and turn left to follow the *Liebliches Taubertal* bike path signs as far up the Tauber River (direction: Bettwar) as you like. After 2.5 miles, you'll arrive in the sleepy farming town of **Bettwar,**

where you can claim a spot among the chickens and the apple trees for a picnic or have a drink at one of the two restaurants in town.

Franconian Open-Air Museum (Fränkisches Freiland-museum)—A 20-minute drive from Rothenburg—in the undiscovered "Rothenburgy" town of Bad Windsheim—is an open-air folk museum that, compared with others in Europe, is a bit humble. But it tries very hard and gives you the best look around at traditional rural Franconia.

Cost and Hours: €6, daily mid-March-Sept 9:00-18:00, Oct-mid-Dec 10:00-16:00, closed mid-Dec-mid-March, last entry one hour before closing, tel. 09841/66800, www.freilandmuseum.de.

Shopping in Rothenburg

Be warned...Rothenburg is one of Germany's best shopping towns. Do it here and be done with it. Lovely prints, carvings, wine glasses, Christmas-tree ornaments, and beer steins are popular. Rödergasse is the old town's everyday shopping street. There's also a modern shopping center across the street from the train station.

Christmas Souvenirs

Rothenburg is the headquarters of the **Käthe Wohlfahrt** Christmas trinkets empire, which is spreading across the half-timbered reaches of Europe. In Rothenburg, tourists flock to two Käthe Wohlfahrt stores (at Herrngasse 1 and 2, just off Market Square). Start with the **Christmas Village** (Weihnachtsdorf) at Herrngasse 1. This Christmas wonderland is filled with enough twinkling lights (196,000—mostly LEDs) to require a special electrical hookup. You're greeted by instant Christmas mood music (best appreciated on a hot day in July) and American and Japanese tourists hungrily filling little woven shopping baskets with €5-8 goodies to hang on their trees. (OK, I admit it, my Christmas tree sports a few KW ornaments.) Let the spinning flocked tree whisk you in, but pause at the wall of Steiff stuffed animals, jerking uncontrollably and mesmerizing little kids. The **Christmas Museum** upstairs is described earlier, under "Sights in Rothenburg." The smaller **Christmas Market** (Weihnachtsmarkt), across the street at Herrngasse 2, specializes in finely crafted wooden ornaments. A third, much smaller store is at Untere Schmiedgasse 19. Käthe started the business in Stuttgart in 1964, and it's now run by her son Harald Wohlfahrt, who lives in Rothenburg (all stores open Mon-Sat 9:00-18:00, May-Dec also most Sun 10:00-17:00, Jan-April closed Sun but museum and museum shop open, show this book and ask about discount on official KW products, tel. 09861/409-150, www.wohlfahrt.com or www.bestofchristmas.com).

ROTHENBURG

Traditional German Souvenirs

Cuckoo with friendliness, trinkets, and souvenirs, the **Friese shop** has been welcoming my readers for more than 30 years (on the smaller square just off Market Square, west of TI, on corner across from free public WC). They give shoppers with this book tremendous service; show your book for a discount and a free pictorial map (normally €1.50). Anneliese Friese, who runs the place with her son Bernie (ask him about the plaque on the town wall), charges only her cost for shipping and lets tired travelers leave their bags in her back room for free (Mon-Sat 9:00-17:00, Sun 10:00-16:00, Grüner Markt 8, tel. 09861/7166, fax 09861/936-619, anneliese -friese@gmx.de).

The **Night Watchman's Store** (Nachtwächterladen), run by the watchman's wife, gives Night Watchman fans a chance to try on the Night Watchman's hat, blow through a drinking horn, or browse medieval clothing (April-Dec daily 10:00-18:00; Jan-March open only Sat 11:00-17:00; just below Market Square at Untere Schmiedgasse 7, tel. 09861/938633). See page 490 for details on the Night Watchman's entertaining tour.

Romantic Prints: The Ernst Geissendörfer print shop has sold fine prints, etchings, and paintings on the corner of Market Square since 1908. To find the shop, walk a few steps down Hafengasse (it's on your right, just before the Bosporus Café). If you're interested in more expensive prints and etchings than those on display, ask Frau Geissendörfer to take you upstairs—she'll offer you a free shot of German brandy while you browse. Show this book and ask about a discount off marked prices (May-Dec daily 11:00-18:00; March-April Mon-Sat 11:00-18:00, closed Sun; closed Jan-Feb; Obere Schmiedgasse 1 at corner of Hafengasse, tel. 09861/2005, www.geissendoerfer.de).

Wine Stuff: You'll recognize local Franconian wines by the shape of the bottle—short, stubby, and round. For characteristic wine glasses, winemaking gear, and the real thing from the town's oldest winemakers, drop by the **Glocke Weinladen am Plönlein** (daily 10:00-18:00, Untere Schmiedgasse 27—see page 512 for info on wine-tasting).

Books: A good bookstore is **Rothenburger Büchermarkt** at Rödergasse 3, on the corner of Alter Stadtgraben (Mon-Sat 9:00-18:30, Sun 10:30-18:00, Jan-April closed Sun).

Mailing Your Goodies Home: You can get handy yellow €2.50 boxes at the old town **post office** (Mon-Fri 9:00-13:00 & 14:00-17:30, Sat 9:00-12:00, closed Sun, inside photo shop at Rödergasse 11). The main post office is in the shopping center across from the train station.

Pastries: Those who prefer to eat their souvenirs browse the

Bäckereien (bakeries). Their succulent pastries, pies, and cakes are pleasantly distracting...but skip the bad-tasting *Rothenburger Schneeballen*. Unworthy of the heavy promotion they receive, *Schneeballen* are bland pie crusts crumpled into a ball and dusted with powdered sugar or frosted with sticky-sweet glop. There's little reason to waste your appetite on a *Schneeball* when you can enjoy a curvy *Mandelhörnchen* (almond crescent), a triangular *Nussecke* ("nut corner"), a round *Florentiner* cookie, a couple of fresh *Krapfen* (like jelly doughnuts), or even just a soft, warm German pretzel.

Sleeping in Rothenburg

Rothenburg is crowded with visitors, but most are day-trippers. Except for the rare Saturday night and during festivals (see page 488), finding a room is easy throughout the year. Competition keeps quality high. If you want to splurge, you'll snare the best value by paying extra for the biggest and best rooms at the hotels I recommend.

Train travelers save steps by staying in the area toward the Rödertor (east end of town). Hotels and guest houses will sometimes pick up tired heavy-packers at the station. If you're driving and unable to find where you're sleeping, stop and give them a call. They will likely come rescue you.

Keep your key when out late. Rothenburg's hotels are small, and they often lock the front entrance at about 22:00, asking you to let yourself in through a side door.

Sleep Code

(€1 = about $1.40, country code: 49, area code: 09861)
S = Single, **D** = Double/Twin, **T** = Triple, **Q** = Quad, **b** = bathroom, **s** = shower only. Unless otherwise noted, credit cards are accepted, English is spoken, and breakfast is included.

To help you sort easily through these listings, I've divided the accommodations into three categories, based on the price for a standard double room with bath:

$$$ **Higher Priced**—Most rooms €80 or more.
 $$ **Moderately Priced**—Most rooms between €60-80.
  $ **Lower Priced**—Most rooms €60 or less.

Prices can change without notice; verify the hotel's current rates online or by email. For other updates, see www.ricksteves.com/update.

In the Old Town

$$$ Hotel Kloster-Stüble, deep in the old town near the castle garden, is my classiest listing. Rudolf does the cooking, while Erika—his fun and energetic first mate—welcomes guests. Twenty-one rooms fill two medieval buildings, connected by a modern atrium. The hotel is just off Herrngasse on a tiny side street (Sb-€58-78, traditional Db-€88-108, bigger and more modern Db-€108-128, Tb-€108-146, see website for suites and family rooms, kids 5 and under free, free Internet access, free Wi-Fi in most rooms, Heringsbronnengasse 5, tel. 09861/938-890, fax 09861/938-829, www.klosterstueble.de, hotel@kloster stueble.de).

$$$ Hotel Spitzweg is a rustic-yet-elegant 1536 mansion (never bombed or burned) with 10 big rooms, open beams, and endearing hand-painted antique furniture. It's run by gentle Herr Hocher, whom I suspect is the former Wizard of Oz—now retired and in a very good mood (Sb-€65, Db-€85-95, Tb-€115, Qb apartment-€150, non-smoking, elegant breakfast room, free parking, pay Internet access and Wi-Fi at son-in-law's nearby hotel, Paradeisgasse 2, tel. 09861/94290, fax 09861/1412, www.hotel -spitzweg.de, info@hotel-spitzweg.de).

$$$ Hotel Gerberhaus is warmly run by Inge and Kurt and daughter Deborah, who mix modern comforts into 20 bright and airy rooms while maintaining a sense of half-timbered elegance. Enjoy the pleasant garden in back (Sb-€65-75, Db-€79-120, Tb-€139-150, Qb-€145-165, prices depend on room size; 2-room suite in separate building-€130/2 people, €180/4 people; discount off the second and subsequent nights and a free *Schneeball* if you pay cash, non-smoking, 4 rooms have canopied 4-poster *Himmel* beds, free Internet access, free Wi-Fi with this book, laundry-€7, close to P1 parking lot, Spitalgasse 25, tel. 09861/94900, fax 09861/86555, www.gerberhaus.rothenburg.de, gerberhaus@romanticroad.com). The downstairs café and *Biergarten* serve good soups, salads, and light lunches.

$$$ Gasthof Goldener Greifen, once Mayor Toppler's home, is a big, traditional, 600-year-old place with 14 spacious rooms and all the comforts. It's run by a helpful family staff and creaks with rustic splendor (Sb-€48, small Db-€65, big Db-€85-90, Tb-€105-125, Qb-€125-145, 10 percent less for 3-night stays, non-smoking, Wi-Fi-€2 per stay, full-service laundry-€8, free and easy parking, half a block downhill from Market Square at Obere Schmiedgasse 5, tel. 09861/2281, fax 09861/86374, www .gasthof-greifen-rothenburg.de, info@gasthof-greifen-rothenburg .de, Brigitte and Klingler family). The family also has a couple of loaner bikes (free for guests), and runs a good restaurant, serving meals in the back garden or dining room.

Rothenburg Hotels

ROTHENBURG

1. Hotel Kloster-Stüble
2. Hotel Spitzweg
3. Hotel Gerberhaus
4. Gasthof Goldener Greifen
5. Hotel Altfränkische Weinstube am Klosterhof
6. Pension Elke
7. Hotel Café Uhl
8. Gästehaus Flemming
9. Kreuzerhof Hotel
10. Gästehaus Raidel
11. Gästehaus Gerlinger
12. Pension Pöschel
13. Frau Liebler Rooms
14. Rossmühle Youth Hostel
15. Hotel Hornburg
16. To Pension Fuchsmühle
17. Internet Café
18. To Bike Rentals (2)

$$ Hotel Altfränkische Weinstube am Klosterhof is *the* place for well-heeled bohemians. Mario, Hanne, and their lovely daughter Viktoria rent six cozy rooms above their dark and evocative pub in a 600-year-old building. It's an upscale *Lord of the Rings* atmosphere, with TVs, modern showers, open-beam ceilings, and canopied four-poster beds. They also have two similarly decorated rooms of equal quality in another building a couple of doors away (Sb-€59, Db-€65, bigger Db-€74, Db suite-€82, Tb-€89, cash preferred, kid- and dog-friendly, free Wi-Fi, free parking, off Klingengasse at Klosterhof 7, tel. 09861/6404, fax 09861/6410, www.romanticroad.com/altfraenkische-weinstube, info on second building at www.am-klosterhof.de, email through website). Their pub is a candlelit classic—and a favorite with locals, serving hot food to Hobbits until 22:30, and closing at 1:00 in the morning. Drop by on Wednesday evening (19:00-24:00) for the English Conversation Club (see "Meet the Locals" on page 512).

$$ Pension Elke, run by spry Erich Endress and his son Klaus, rents 12 modern and comfy rooms above the family grocery store. Guests who jog are welcome to join Klaus on his half-hour run around the city every evening at 19:30 (S-€30, Sb-€40, D-€42-48, Db-€60-65, price depends on room size, extra bed-€18, ask about a discount with this book if you plan to stay at least 2 nights, cash only, free Internet access and Wi-Fi; reception in grocery store until 19:00, otherwise go around corner to back of building and ring bell at top of stairs; near Markus Tower at Rödergasse 6, tel. 09861/2331, fax 09861/935-355, www.pension-elke-rothenburg.de, info@pension-elke-rothenburg.de).

$$ Hotel Café Uhl offers 12 fine rooms over a pastry shop (Sb-€35-58, Db-€59-79, Tb-€82-105, Qb-€98-125, price depends on room size, ask about a discount with this book if paying cash, reception in café, pay Internet access, free Wi-Fi, parking-€6, closed Jan, Plönlein 8, tel. 09861/4895, fax 09861/92820, www.hotel-uhl.de, info@hotel-uhl.de, Paul and Robert the baker).

$$ Gästehaus Flemming has seven tastefully modern, fresh, and comfortable rooms and a peaceful terrace and garden behind St. Jakob's Church (Sb-€49, Db-€62, Tb-€84, cash only, non-smoking, no Internet access, Klingengasse 21, tel. 09861/92380, fax 09861/976-384, www.gaestehaus-flemming.de, gaestehaus-flemming@t-online.de, Regina).

$$ Kreuzerhof Hotel offers nine pleasant rooms surrounding a courtyard on a quiet side street near the Rödertor (Sb-€45, Db-€64-69, Tb-€84-92, Qb-€99-109, 6-bed room-€135-149, family deals, non-smoking, free Internet access and Wi-Fi, laundry-€6/load, parking in courtyard-€3, Millergasse 2-6, tel. 09861/3424, fax 09861/936-730, www.kreuzerhof.eu, info@kreuzerhof.eu,

Heike and Walter Maltz).

$ Gästehaus Raidel rents eight rooms in a 500-year-old house filled with beds and furniture, all handmade by friendly Norry Raidel himself. The ramshackle ambience makes me want to sing the *Addams Family* theme song—but the place has a rare, time-passed family charm. Norry, who plays in a Dixieland band, has invented a fascinating hybrid saxophone/trombone called the Norryphone...and loves to jam (Sb-€45, Db-€69, Tb-€90, Qb suite-€120, cash only, free Wi-Fi, Wenggasse 3, tel. 09861/3115, Norry asks you to use the reservations form at www.romanticroad.com/raidel).

$ Gästehaus Gerlinger, a fine value, has four comfortable rooms in a pretty 16th-century house with a small terrace for guests (Db-€55, or €53/night with 2-night stay; Tb-€68, cash only, non-smoking, Wi-Fi, easy parking, Schlegeleinsweth 10, tel. 09861/87979, mobile 0171-690-0752, www.pension-gerlinger.de, info@pension-gerlinger.de, Hermann).

$ Pension Pöschel is simple and friendly, with six plain rooms in a concrete but pleasant building, and an inviting garden out back. Only one room has a private shower and toilet (S-€25, D-€45, Db-€50, T-€60, Tb-€65, small kids free, cash only, non-smoking, free Wi-Fi, Wenggasse 22, tel. 09861/3430, mobile 01707-007-041, www.pensionpoeschel.de, pension.poeschel @t-online.de, Bettina).

$ Frau Liebler rents two large modern ground-floor rooms with kitchenettes. They're great for those looking for real privacy—you'll have your own room fronting a quiet cobbled lane just below Market Square. On the top floor is an attractive two-bedroom apartment (Db-€44, apartment-€44, extra bed-€12, show this book and ask about discount for stays of 2 or more nights, breakfast-€6, cash only, non-smoking, pay Internet access, free Wi-Fi, laundry-€5, behind Christmas shop at Pfäffleinsgässchen 10, tel. 09861/709-215, fax 09861/709-216, www.gaestehaus -liebler.de).

$ Rossmühle Youth Hostel, run since 1981 by Eduard Schmitz, rents 186 beds in two buildings. While it's mostly four- to six-bed dorms, this charming hostel also has 15 doubles. Reception is in the droopy-eyed building—formerly a horse mill, it was used when the old town was under siege and the river-powered mill was inaccessible (dorm bed-€23, bunk-bed Db-€53-55, guests over 26 pay €4 extra unless traveling with a family, nonmembers pay €3 extra, includes breakfast and sheets, all-you-can-eat dinner-€5.50, pay Wi-Fi, self-serve laundry including soap-€5, close to P1 parking lot, entrance on Rossmühlgasse, tel. 09861/94160, fax 09861/941-620, www.rothenburg.jugendher berge.de, rothenburg@jugendherberge.de).

ROTHENBURG

Outside the Wall

$$$ Hotel Hornburg, a grand 1903 mansion, is close to the train station, a two-minute walk outside the wall. With groomed grounds, gracious sitting areas, and 10 spacious, tastefully decorated rooms, it's a super value (Sb-€58-78, Db-€78-108, Tb-€100-130, ground-floor rooms, non-smoking, family-friendly, dogs welcome—ask for pet-free room if you're allergic, free Internet access and Wi-Fi; if walking, exit station and go straight on Ludwig-Siebert-Strasse, then turn left on Mannstrasse until you're 100 yards from town wall; if driving, the hotel is across from parking lot P4; Hornburgweg 28, at intersection with Mannstrasse, tel. 09861/8480, fax 09861/5570, www.hotel-hornburg.de, info@hotel-hornburg.de, Gabriele and Martin).

$$ Pension Fuchsmühle is a guest house in a renovated old mill on the river below the castle end of Rothenburg, across from the Toppler Castle. It feels rural, but is a pleasant (though steep) 15-minute hike to Market Square, and a €10 taxi ride from the train station. Alex and Heidi Molitor, a young couple with kids, run a book-lined café on summer weekends and offer eight bright, modern light-wood rooms. The building's electric power comes from the millwheel by the entrance, with excess sold to the grid (Sb-€45, Db-€68, Tb-€90, Qb-€120 3-room suite-€150/5 people or €180/6 people, extra bed-€25, less if you stay at least 5 days, includes healthy farm-fresh breakfasts—or €9 less per person if you don't want breakfast, non-smoking, free Wi-Fi, free parking, flashlights provided for your walk back after dark, Taubertalweg 103, tel. 09861/92633, fax 09861/933895, www.fuchsmuehle.de, fuchsmuehle@t-online.de).

Eating in Rothenburg

Many restaurants take a mid-afternoon break, and stop serving lunch at 14:00 and dinner as early as 20:00. My recommendations are all within a five-minute walk of Market Square. While all survive on tourism, many still feel like local hangouts. Your choices are typical German or ethnic. Any bakery will sell you a sandwich for a couple of euros.

Traditional German Restaurants

Gasthof Goldener Greifen is in a historic building just off the main square. The Klingler family serves quality Franconian food at a good price...and with a smile. The wood is ancient and polished from generations of happy use, and the ambience is practical rather than posh—and that's just fine with me (€8-15 main courses, €12 three-course daily specials, €10 one-plate specials include a drink, super-cheap kids' meals, Mon-Sat 11:30-21:00, may open Sun

Rothenburg Restaurants

1. Gasthof Goldener Greifen
2. Hotel Restaurant Kloster-Stüble
3. Bürgerkeller
4. Altfränkische Weinstube am Klosterhof
5. Gasthof Rödertor & Beer Garden
6. Eisenhut Restaurant & Beer Garden
7. Reichs-Küchenmeister
8. Pizzeria Roma
9. China-Restaurant Peking
10. Bosporus Café
11. To Unter den Linden Beer Garden
12. Eis Café D' Isep
13. Trinkstube zur Hölle
14. Restaurant Glocke

11:30-14:00, Obere Schmiedgasse 5, tel. 09861/2281).

Hotel Restaurant Kloster-Stüble, on a small street off Herrngasse near the castle garden, is a classy place for delicious and beautifully presented traditional cuisine, including homemade *Maultaschen* (similar to ravioli). Chef Rudy's food is better than his English, so head waitress Erika makes sure communication goes smoothly. The shady terrace is nice on a warm summer evening. I prefer their traditional dining room to the stony, sleek, modern room (€10-16 main courses, Thu-Tue 11:00-14:00 & 18:00-21:00, closed Wed, Heringsbronnengasse 5, tel. 09861/938-890).

Bürgerkeller is a typical European cellar restaurant with a quiet, calming atmosphere, medieval murals, pointy pikes, and a few sidewalk tables for good weather. Without a burger in sight (*Bürger* means "townsman"), English-speaking Harry Terian and his family pride themselves on quality local cuisine, offering a small but inviting menu and reasonable prices. Harry likes oldies, and you're welcome to look over his impressive playlist and request your favorite music (€7-13 main courses, cash only, Thu-Tue 12:00-14:00 & 17:30-21:00, closed Wed, near bottom of Herrngasse at #24, tel. 09861/2126).

Altfränkische Weinstube am Klosterhof seems designed for gnomes to celebrate their anniversaries. At this very dark pub, classically candlelit in a 600-year-old building, Mario whips up gourmet pub grub (€7-14 main courses, hot food served 18:00-22:30, closes at 1:00 in the morning, off Klingengasse at Klosterhof 7, tel. 09861/6404). If you'd like dinner company, drop by on Wednesday evening, when the English Conversation Club has a big table reserved from 19:00 on (see "Meet the Locals," later). You'll eat well and with new friends—both travelers and locals.

Gasthof Rödertor, just outside the wall through the Rödertor, is a lively place where Rothenburgers go for a hearty meal at a good price. Their passion is potatoes—the menu is dedicated to spud cuisine. Try a €7 plate of *Schupfnudeln*, potato noodles with sauerkraut and bacon (€6-12 main courses, daily 11:30-14:00 & 17:30-22:00, Sun until 21:00, Ansbacher Strasse 7, tel. 09861/2022). They also run a popular *Biergarten* (described later).

Eisenhut Restaurant, in Hotel Eisenhut, is a fine place for a dress-up splurge with surprisingly reasonable prices. You'll enjoy elegantly presented dishes, both traditional and international, with formal service. Sit in their royal dining room or on their garden sun terrace (€17-25 main courses, fixed-price meals from €28, daily 12:00-14:30 & 18:30-21:30, Herrngasse 3, tel. 09861/7050).

Reichs-Küchenmeister is a forgettable big-hotel restaurant, but on a balmy evening, its pleasant tree-shaded terrace overlooking St. Jakob's Church is hard to beat. Their €13 *Vesperbrett* plate is a fine selection of cold cuts (€8-20 main courses, daily 11:00-23:00, Kirchplatz 8, tel. 09861/9700).

Breaks from Pork and Potatoes

Pizzeria Roma is the locals' favorite for €5-7 pizza and pastas, with good Italian wine. The Magrini family moved here from Tuscany in 1970 (many Italians immigrated to Germany in those years), and they've been cooking pasta for Rothenburg ever since (Thu-Tue 11:00-24:00, closed Wed and mid-Aug-mid-Sept, Galgengasse 19, tel. 09861/4540, Ricardo).

China-Restaurant Peking, on the picturesque Plönlein square, has two-course lunch specials (€5-7, Mon-Sat only), and its noisy streetside tables have a fine tower view (open daily 11:00-15:00 & 17:00-23:00, Plönlein 4, tel. 09861/938-738).

The **Bosporus Café** at Hafengasse 2, just off Market Square, serves cheap and tasty Turkish food to go or eat in. Their *Döner Kebabs* must be the best €3.50 hot meal in Rothenburg (daily 9:00-19:00, sometimes closes earlier in winter).

Picnic Goodies: A small **grocery store** is in the center of town at Rödergasse 6 (Mon-Fri 7:30-19:00, Sat 7:30-18:00, April-Dec also Sun 10:00-18:00, closed Sun Jan-March). **Supermarkets** are outside the wall: Exit the town through the Rödertor, turn left through the cobbled gate, and cross the parking lot to reach the Edeka supermarket (Mon-Fri 8:00-20:00, Sat 7:00-20:00, closed Sun); or head to the even bigger Kaufland in the shopping center across from the train station (Mon-Sat 7:00-20:00, closed Sun).

Beer Gardens *(Biergartens)*

Rothenburg's *Biergarten*s can be great fun, but they're open only when the weather is balmy.

Unter den Linden, a family-friendly (with sandbox and swing), slightly bohemian *Biergarten* in the valley along the river, is worth the 20-minute hike on a pleasant evening (daily 10:00-21:00 in season with decent weather, sometimes later, self-service food and good beer, Sunday breakfast buffet until noon-€11, call first to confirm it's open, Kurze Steige 7, tel. 09861/5909, Helmut Dürrer). As it's in the valley on the river, it's cooler than Rothenburg; bring a sweater. Take a right outside the Burgtor, then a left on the footpath toward Detwang; it's at the bottom of the hill on the left.

Gasthof Rödertor, just outside the wall through the Rödertor, runs a backyard *Biergarten* that's great for a rowdy crowd, cheap food, and good beer (May-Sept daily 17:00-24:00 in good weather, look for wooden gate, tel. 09861/2022). If the *Biergarten* is closed, their indoor restaurant (described earlier) is a good value.

Eisenhut Restaurant (described earlier), behind the fancy hotel of the same name on Herrngasse, is a good bet for gentle and casual *Biergarten* ambience within the old center.

Dessert

Eis Café D'Isep, with a pleasant "Venetian minimalist" interior, is the town's ice-cream parlor, serving up cakes, drinks, fresh-fruit ice cream, and fancy sundaes. Their sidewalk tables are great for lazy people-watching (daily 9:30-22:30, closed early Oct-mid-Feb, one block off Market Square at Hafengasse 17, run by Paolo and Paola D'Isep).

Wine-Drinking in the Old Center

Trinkstube zur Hölle ("Hell") is dark and foreboding, offering a thick wine-drinking atmosphere, pub food, and a few main courses (€11-17). It's small and can get painfully touristy in summer (daily 17:00-24:00, closed Sun Jan-March, a block past Medieval Crime and Punishment Museum on Burggasse, with the devil hanging out front, tel. 09861/4229).

Mario's **Altfränkische Weinstube am Klosterhof** (listed earlier) is the liveliest place, and a clear favorite with locals for an atmospheric drink or late meal. When every other place is asleep, you're likely to find good food, drink, and energy here.

Restaurant Glocke, a *Weinstube* (wine bar) popular with locals, is run by Rothenburg's oldest winemakers, the Thürauf family. The menu, which has a very extensive wine list, is in German only because the friendly staff wants to explain your options in person. Their €4.40 deal, which lets you sample five Franconian wines, is popular (€8-18 main courses, Mon-Sat 11:00-23:00, Sun 11:00-14:00, Plönlein 1, tel. 09861/958-990).

Meet the Locals

For a rare chance to mix it up with locals who aren't selling anything, bring your favorite slang and tongue twisters to the **English Conversation Club** at Mario's Altfränkische Weinstube am Klosterhof (Wed 19:00-24:00, restaurant listed earlier). This group of intrepid linguists has met more than 1,000 times. Hermann the German and his sidekick Wolfgang are regulars. Consider arriving early for dinner, or after 21:00, when the beer starts to sink in, the crowd grows, and everyone seems to speak that second language a bit more easily.

Rothenburg Connections

Reaching Rothenburg ob der Tauber by Train: A tiny branch train line connects Rothenburg to the outside world via **Steinach** in 14 minutes (generally hourly from Rothenburg at :07 and from Steinach at :34). Train connections in Steinach are usually quick and efficient (trains to and from Rothenburg generally use track 5).

If you plan to arrive in Rothenburg in the evening, note that the last train from Steinach to Rothenburg departs at about 22:30. All is not lost if you arrive in Steinach after the last train—there's a subsidized taxi service to Rothenburg (cheaper for the government than running an almost-empty train). To use this handy service, called AST *(Anrufsammeltaxi)*, make an appointment with a participating taxi service (call 09861/2000 or 09861/7227) at least an hour in advance (2 hours ahead is better), and they'll drive you from Steinach to Rothenburg for the train fare (€4/person) rather than the regular €25 taxi fare.

The Rothenburg station has a touch-screen terminal for fare and schedule information and ticket sales. If you need extra help, visit the combined ticket office and travel agency in the station building (€1-4 surcharge for most tickets, €0.50 charge for questions without ticket purchase, Mon-Fri 9:00-18:00, Sat 9:00-13:00, closed Sun, tel. 09861/7711). The station at Steinach is entirely unstaffed, but also has touch-screen ticket machines. As a last resort, call for train info at tel. 0180-599-6633, or visit www.bahn.com.

From Rothenburg by Train to: Würzburg (hourly, 70 minutes), **Nürnberg** (hourly, 1.25 hours, change in Ansbach), **Munich** (hourly, 2.5-3.5 hours, 2-3 changes), **Füssen** (hourly, 5 hours, often with changes in Treuchtlingen and Augsburg), **Frankfurt** (hourly, 2.5-3 hours, change in Würzburg), **Frankfurt Airport** (hourly, 3-3.25 hours, change in Würzburg), **Berlin** (hourly, 5-6 hours, often via Würzburg and Göttingen). Remember, all destinations also require a change in Steinach.

From Rothenburg by Bus: The Deutsche Touring company (tel. 069/719-126-261, www.romanticroadcoach.de) runs a daily tour bus that roughly follows the Romantic Road. The bus stops in Rothenburg once a day (mid-April-late Oct) on its way from Frankfurt to Munich and Füssen (and vice versa). The bus stop is at Schrannenplatz, a short walk north of Market Square.

ROTHENBURG

RHINE VALLEY

Best of the Rhine • Bacharach • St. Goar

The Rhine Valley is storybook Germany, a fairy-tale world of legends and robber-baron castles. Cruise the most castle-studded stretch of the romantic Rhine as you listen for the song of the treacherous Loreley. For hands-on thrills, climb through the Rhineland's greatest castle, Rheinfels, above the town of St. Goar. Spend your nights in a castle-crowned village, either Bacharach or St. Goar.

Planning Your Time

The Rhineland is magical, but doesn't take much time to see. Both Bacharach and St. Goar are an easy 1- to 1.5-hour train ride (€15) or drive from Frankfurt Airport, and they make a good first or last stop for travelers flying in or out.

Ideally, spend two nights here, sleep in Bacharach, cruise the best hour of the river (from Bacharach to St. Goar), and tour Rheinfels Castle. If rushed, focus on Rheinfels Castle and cruise less.

The Best of the Rhine

Ever since Roman times, when this was the empire's northern boundary, the Rhine has been one of the world's busiest shipping rivers. You'll see a steady flow of barges with 1,000- to 2,000-ton loads. Tourist-packed buses, hot train tracks, and highways line both banks.

Many of the castles were "robber-baron" castles, put there by petty rulers (there were 300 independent little countries in medi-

Rhine Overview

Düsseldorf •

Köln •

Bruhl •
Bonn •

• Aachen

Bad Godesberg •

Remagen •

**UNROMANTIC
RHINE**

**BEST OF
THE RHINE**
See detail map

• Koblenz

**BURG
ELTZ**

Cochem •

Beilstein •

**St.
Goar**

HAHN

Bacharach

BELG.

Frankfurt

Wies-
Baden

Mainz

Main R.

FRANK-
FURT

LUX.

Mosel R.

Trier •

• Lux.
City

GERMANY

Neckar R.

Heidel-
berg

Rhine

FRANCE

30 Miles

50 Kilometers

GERMANY

RHINE VALLEY

eval Germany, a region about the size of Montana) to levy tolls on passing river traffic. A robber baron would put his castle on, or even in, the river. Then, often with the help of chains and a tower on the opposite bank, he'd stop each ship and get his toll. There were 10 customs stops in the 60-mile stretch between Mainz and Koblenz alone (no wonder merchants were early proponents of the creation of larger nation-states).

Some castles were built to control and protect settlements, and others were the residences of kings. As times changed, so did the lifestyles of the rich and feudal. Many castles were abandoned for more comfortable mansions in the towns.

Most Rhine castles date from the 11th, 12th, and 13th centuries. When the pope successfully asserted his power over the German emperor in 1076, local princes ran wild over the rule of their emperor. The castles saw military action in the 1300s and 1400s, as emperors began reasserting their control over Germany's many silly kingdoms.

The castles were also involved in the Reformation wars, in which Europe's Catholic and Protestant dynasties fought it out using a fragmented Germany as their battleground. The Thirty Years' War (1618-1648) devastated Germany. The outcome: Each ruler got the freedom to decide if his people would be Catholic or Protestant, and one-third of Germany was dead. (Production of Gummi Bears ceased entirely.)

The French—who feared a strong Germany and felt the Rhine was the logical border between them and Germany—destroyed most of the castles prophylactically (Louis XIV in the 1680s, the Revolutionary army in the 1790s, and Napoleon in 1806). Many were rebuilt in Neo-Gothic style in the Romantic Age—the late 1800s—and today are enjoyed as restaurants, hotels, hostels, and museums.

Getting Around the Rhine

The Rhine flows north from Switzerland to Holland, but the scenic stretch from Mainz to Koblenz hoards all the touristic charm. Studded with the crenellated cream of Germany's castles, it bustles with boats, trains, and highway traffic. Have fun exploring with a mix of big steamers, tiny ferries *(Fähre)*, trains, and bikes.

By Boat: While some travelers do the whole Mainz-Koblenz trip by boat (5.5 hours downstream, 8.5 hours up), I'd just focus on the most scenic hour—from St. Goar to Bacharach. Sit on the boat's top deck with your handy Rhine map-guide (or the kilometer-keyed tour in this chapter) and enjoy the parade of castles, towns, boats, and vineyards.

Two boat companies take travelers along this stretch of the Rhine. Boats run daily in both directions from early April through October, with no boats off-season.

Most travelers sail on the bigger, more expensive, and romantic **Köln-Düsseldorfer (K-D) Line** (free with German railpass or any Eurail Pass that covers Germany, but starts the use of a day of any flexipass; recommended Bacharach-St. Goar trip: €11 one-way, €13.20 round-trip, bikes-€2.50, €2 extra if paying with credit card; discounts: Mon and Fri—half-price for seniors over 60; Tue and Thu—2 bicyclists travel for the price of 1; tel. 06741/1634 in St. Goar, tel. 06743/1322 in Bacharach, www.k-d.com). Complete, up-to-date schedules are posted at any Rhineland station, hotel, TI, and www.k-d.com. Purchase tickets at the dock up to five minutes before departure. (Confirm times at your hotel the night before.) The boat is never full. Romantics will enjoy the old-time paddle-wheeler *Goethe*, which sails each direction once a day (noted on schedule, confirm time locally).

The smaller **Bingen-Rüdesheimer Line** is slightly cheaper than the K-D, isn't covered by railpasses, and makes three trips in each direction daily (St. Goar to Bacharach: €10.50 one-way, €12.50 round-trip, buy tickets on boat; departs St. Goar at 11:00,

14:10, and 16:10; departs Bacharach at 10:10, 12:00, and 15:00; no morning departures last two weeks of Oct; tel. 06721/14140, www .bingen-ruedesheimer.de).

By Car: Drivers have these options: 1) skip the boat; 2) take a round-trip cruise from St. Goar or Bacharach; 3) draw pretzels and let the loser drive, prepare the picnic, and meet the boat; 4) rent a bike, bring it on the boat for free, and bike back; or 5) take the boat one-way and return by train. When exploring by car, don't hesitate to pop onto one of the many little ferries that shuttle across the bridgeless-around-here river.

By Ferry: While there are no bridges between Koblenz and Mainz, you'll see car-and-passenger ferries (usually family-run for generations) about every three miles. Bingen-Rüdesheim, Lorch-Niederheimbach, Engelsburg-Kaub, and St. Goar-St. Goarshausen are some of the most useful routes (times vary; St. Goar-St. Goarshausen ferry departs each side every 15-20 minutes, Mon-Sat 6:00-21:00, Sun 8:00-21:00, May-Sept until 23:00; one-way fares: adult-€1.30, car and driver-€3.50, pay on the boat; www.faehre-loreley.de). For a fun little jaunt, take a quick round-trip with some time to explore the other side.

By Bike: You can bike on either side of the Rhine, but for a designated bike path, stay on the west side, where a 35-mile path runs between Koblenz and Bingen. The six-mile stretch between St. Goar and Bacharach is smooth and scenic, but mostly along the highway. The bit from Bacharach to Bingen hugs the riverside and is road-free. Either way, biking is a great way to explore the valley. Many hotels provide free or cheap bikes to guests; in Bacharach, anyone can rent bikes at Hotel Hillen (see page 524, €12/day for non-guests).

Consider biking one-way and taking the bike back on the riverboat, or designing a circular trip using the fun and frequent shuttle ferries. A good target might be Kaub (where a tiny boat shuttles sightseers to the better-from-a-distance castle on the island).

By Train: Hourly milk-run trains hit every town along the Rhine (St. Goar-Bacharach, 10 minutes, €3.20; Bacharach-Mainz, 1 hour; Mainz-Koblenz, 1.5 hours). Express trains speed past the small towns, taking only 50 minutes non-stop between Mainz and Koblenz. Some train schedules list St. Goar but not Bacharach as a stop, but any schedule listing St. Goar also stops at Bacharach. Tiny stations are not staffed—buy tickets at the platform machines (user-friendly, take paper money, may not accept US credit cards).

The **Rheinland-Pfalz-Ticket** day pass covers travel on milk-run trains to anywhere in this chapter (1 person-€21, 2-5 people-€33, buy from station ticket machines, good after 9:00 Mon-Fri and all day Sat-Sun, valid on trains labeled *RB, RE,* and *MRB*).

Self-Guided Tour

▲▲▲Rhine Blitz Tour by Train or Boat

One of Europe's great train thrills is zipping along the Rhine enjoying this blitz tour. Or, even better, do it relaxing on the deck of a Rhine steamer, surrounded by the wonders of this romantic and historic gorge. This quick and easy tour (you can cut in anywhere) skips most of the syrupy myths filling normal Rhine guides. You can follow along on a train, boat, bike, or car. By train or boat, sit on the left (river) side going south from Koblenz. While nearly all the castles listed are viewed from this side, train travelers need to clear a path to the right window for the times I yell, "Cross over!"

You'll notice large black-and-white kilometer markers along the riverbank. I erected these years ago to make this tour easier to follow. They tell the distance from the Rhinefalls, where the Rhine leaves Switzerland and becomes navigable. (Today, river-barge pilots also use these markers to navigate.) We're tackling just 36 miles (58 km) of the 820-mile-long (1,320-km) Rhine. Your Rhine Blitz Tour starts at Koblenz and heads upstream to Bingen. If you're going the other direction, it still works. Just hold the book upside-down.

You can also download a Rick Steves **audio tour** of this Rhine sightseeing blitz (see page 7).

Km 590—Koblenz: This Rhine blitz starts with Romantic Rhine thrills—at Koblenz. Koblenz is not a nice city (it was hit hard in World War II), but its place as the historic *Deutsche Eck* (German corner)—the tip of land where the Mosel River joins the Rhine—gives it a certain charm. Koblenz, from the Latin for "confluence," has Roman origins. If you stop here, take a walk through the park, noticing the reconstructed memorial to the *Kaiser*. Across the river, the yellow Ehrenbreitstein Castle now houses a hostel. It's a 30-minute hike from the station to the Koblenz boat dock.

Km 586—Lahneck Castle (Burg Lahneck): Above the modern autobahn bridge over the Lahn River, this castle *(Burg)* was built in 1240 to defend local silver mines; the castle was ruined by the French in 1688 and rebuilt in the 1850s in Neo-Gothic style. Burg Lahneck faces another Romantic rebuild, the yellow Schloss Stolzenfels (out of view above the train, a 10-minute climb from tiny parking lot, open for touring, closed Mon). Note that a *Burg* is a defensive fortress, while a *Schloss* is mainly a showy palace.

Km 580—Marksburg Castle: This castle (bold and white, with the three modern chimneys behind it, just before the town of Spay) is the best-looking of all the Rhine castles and the only surviving medieval castle on the Rhine. Because of its commanding position, it was never attacked in the Middle Ages (though it was

The Best of the Rhine

To Bonn & Köln

■ EHRENBREITSTEIN

Koblenz 590

Mosel

Lahn River

To Cochem & Burg Eltz

■ LAHNECK 585

STOLZENFELS

Braubach

■ MARKSBURG 580

Rhine

9

Boppard 570

River

■■ STERRENBERG 567
■ LIEBENSTEIN

A61
E31

49

EXIT #42

9

■■ MAUS 559

St. Goarshausen

RHEINFELS ■■   ■ KATZ 556

557   **St. Goar**   ■ LORELEY 554

Emmels- hausen

EXIT #43

327

550 **Oberwesel** ●   Kaub

To Hahn Airport

■■ GUTENFELS 546

SCHÖNBURG ■   ■ PFALZ

EXIT #44

Bacharach 543

■ STAHLECK   ● Lorch 540

EXIT #45

9

Rhine

River

■ 538 SOONECK   Assmanns- hausen

534 REICHENSTEIN   EHRENFELS 530

533 RHEINSTEIN ■   NIEDERWALD MONUMENT 528

A61
E31

MÄUSETURM ■   **Bingen**   Rüdesheim

To Mainz   To Mainz

3 Kilometers

3 Miles

NOTE:
590 Numbers refer to riverside signs indicating kilometers north of the Rhinefalls (Switzerland)

······ Car Ferries

captured by the US Army in March of 1945). It's now open as a museum with a medieval interior second only to the Mosel Valley's Burg Eltz. The three modern smokestacks vent Europe's biggest car-battery recycling plant just up the valley.

Km 570—Boppard: Once a Roman town, Boppard has some impressive remains of fourth-century walls. Notice the Roman towers and the substantial chunk of Roman wall near the train station, just above the main square. You'll notice that a church is a big part of each townscape. Many small towns have two towering churches—the Rhine is the dividing line between Catholic and Protestant Europe. Four centuries ago, after enduring a horrific war, each prince or king decided which faith his subjects would follow (generally Protestants north of the Rhine and Catholics to the south). While church attendance in Germany is way down, the towns here, like Germany as a whole, are still divided between Catholic and Protestant church-goers.

If you visit Boppard, head to the fascinating Church of St. Severus below the main square. Find the carved Romanesque crazies at the doorway. Inside, to the right of the entrance, you'll see Christian symbols from Roman times. Also notice the painted arches and vaults (originally, most Romanesque churches were painted this way). Down by the river, look for the high-water *(Hochwasser)* marks on the arches from various flood years. (You'll find these flood marks throughout the Rhine Valley.)

Km 567—Sterrenberg Castle and Liebenstein Castle: These are the "Hostile Brothers" castles across from Bad Salzig. Take the wall between the castles (actually designed to improve the defenses of both castles), add two greedy and jealous brothers and a fair maiden, and create your own legend. Burg Liebenstein is now a fun, friendly, and affordable family-run hotel (9 rooms, Db-€130, suite-€155, giant king-and-the-family room-€230, easy parking, tel. 06773/308 or 06773/251, www.castle-liebenstein.com, hotel-burg-liebenstein@rhinecastles.com, Nickenig family).

Km 560: While you can see nothing from here, a 19th-century lead mine functioned on both sides of the river, with a shaft actually tunneling completely under the Rhine.

Km 559—Maus Castle (Burg Maus): The Maus (mouse) got its name because the next castle was owned by the Katzenelnbogen family. (*Katz* means "cat.") In the 1300s, it was considered a state-of-the-art fortification...until Napoleon had it blown up in 1806 with state-of-the-art explosives. It was rebuilt true to its original plans in about 1900. Today, the castle is open only for concerts and weddings, with occasional guided tours (20-minute walk up, tel. 06771/7669 or tel. 06771/9100, www.burg-maus.de).

Km 557—St. Goar and Rheinfels Castle: Cross to the other side of the train. The pleasant town of St. Goar was named for a sixth-century hometown monk. It originated in Celtic times (really old) as a place where sailors would stop, catch their breath, send home a postcard, and give thanks after surviving the seductive and treacherous Loreley crossing. St. Goar is worth a stop to explore its mighty Rheinfels Castle. (For information, a self-guided castle tour, and accommodations, see page 538.)

Km 556—Katz Castle (Burg Katz): Burg Katz (Katzeln-bogen) faces St. Goar from across the river. Together, Burg Katz (built in 1371) and Rheinfels Castle had a clear view up and down the river, effectively controlling traffic (there was absolutely no duty-free shopping on the medieval Rhine). Katz got Napoleoned in 1806 and rebuilt in about 1900.

Today, the castle is shrouded by intrigue and controversy. In 1995, a wealthy and eccentric Japanese man bought it for about $4 million. His vision: to make the castle—so close to the Loreley that Japanese tourists are wild about—an exotic escape for his countrymen. But the town wouldn't allow his planned renovation of the historic (and therefore protected) building. Stymied, the frustrated investor abandoned his plans. Today, Burg Katz sits empty...the Japanese ghost castle.

Below the castle, notice the derelict grape terraces—worked since the eighth century, but abandoned in the last generation. The Rhine wine is particularly good because the local slate absorbs the heat of the sun and stays warm all night, resulting in sweeter grapes. Wine from the flat fields above the Rhine gorge is cheaper, and good only as table wine. Wine from the steep side of the Rhine gorge—where grapes are harder to grow and harvest—is tastier and more expensive.

About Km 555: A statue of the Loreley, the beautiful-but-deadly nymph, combs her hair at the end of a long spit—built to give barges protection from vicious ice floes that until recent years raged down the river in the winter. The actual Loreley, a cliff (marked by the flags), is just ahead.

Km 554—The Loreley: Steep a big slate rock in centuries of legend and it becomes a tourist attraction—the ultimate Rhinestone. The Loreley (flags and visitors center on top, name painted near shoreline), rising 450 feet over the narrowest and deepest point of the Rhine, has long been important. It was a holy site in pre-Roman days. The fine echoes here—thought to be ghostly voices—fertilized legend-tellers' imaginations.

Because of the reefs just upstream (at km 552), many ships never made it to St. Goar. Sailors (after days on the river) blamed their misfortune on a *wunderbares Fräulein,* whose long, blond hair almost covered her body. Heinrich Heine's *Song of Loreley* (the CliffsNotes version is on local postcards) tells the story of a count sending his men to kill or capture this siren after she distracted his horny son, who forgot to watch where he was sailing and drowned. When the soldiers cornered the nymph in her cave, she called her father (Father Rhine) for help. Huge waves, the likes of which you'll never see today, rose from the river and carried Loreley to safety. And she has never been seen since.

But alas, when the moon shines brightly and the tour buses are parked, a soft, playful Rhine whine can still be heard from the Loreley. As you pass, listen carefully ("Sailors...sailors...over my bounding mane").

Km 552—The Seven Maidens: Killer reefs, marked by red-and-green buoys, are called the "Seven Maidens." Okay, one more goofy legend: The prince of Schönburg Castle (*über* Oberwesel—described next) had seven spoiled daughters who always dumped men because of their shortcomings. Fed up, he invited seven of his knights to the castle and demanded that his daughters each choose one to marry. But they complained that each man had too big a nose, was too fat, too stupid, and so on. The rude and teasing girls escaped into a riverboat. Just downstream, God turned them into the seven rocks that form this reef. While this story probably isn't entirely true, there was a lesson in it for medieval children: Don't be hard-hearted.

Km 550—Oberwesel: Cross to the other side of the train. Oberwesel was a Celtic town in 400 B.C., then a Roman military station. It now boasts some of the best Roman-wall and medieval-tower remains on the Rhine, and the commanding Schönburg Castle (now a posh hotel). Notice how many of the train tunnels have entrances designed like medieval turrets—they were actually built in the Romantic 19th century. OK, back to the river side.

Km 546—Gutenfels Castle and Pfalz Castle, the Classic Rhine View: Burg Gutenfels (now a privately owned hotel) and the shipshape Pfalz Castle (built in the river in the 1300s) worked very effectively to tax medieval river traffic. The town of Kaub grew rich as Pfalz raised its chains when boats came, and lowered them only when the merchants had paid their duty. Those who didn't pay spent time touring its prison, on a raft at the bottom of its well. In 1504, a pope called for the destruction of Pfalz, but the locals withstood a six-week siege, and the castle still stands. Notice the overhanging outhouse (tiny white room between two wooden ones). Pfalz (also known as Pfalzgrafenstein) is tourable but bare and dull (€3 ferry from Kaub, €3 entry, March-Oct Tue-Sun 10:00-18:00, closed Mon, shorter hours off-season, closed Dec, last entry one hour before closing, mobile 0172-262-2800).

In Kaub, on the riverfront directly below the castles, a green statue (near the waving flags) honors the German general Gebhard von Blücher. He was Napoleon's nemesis. In 1813, as Napoleon fought his way back to Paris after his disastrous Russian campaign, he stopped at Mainz—hoping to fend off the Germans and Russians pursuing him by controlling that strategic bridge. Blücher tricked Napoleon. By building the first major pontoon bridge of its kind here at the Pfalz Castle, he crossed the Rhine and outflanked the French. Two years later, Blücher and Wellington teamed up to defeat Napoleon once and for all at Waterloo.

Immediately opposite Kaub (where the ferry lands, marked by blue roadside flags) is a gaping hole in the mountainside. This marks the last working slate mine on the Rhine.

Km 544—"The Raft Busters": Just before Bacharach, at the top of the island, buoys mark a gang of rocks notorious for busting up rafts. The Black Forest, upstream from here, was once poor, and wood was its best export. Black Foresters would ride log booms down the Rhine to the Ruhr (where their timber fortified coal-mine shafts) or to Holland (where logs were sold to shipbuilders). If they could navigate the sweeping bend just before Bacharach and then survive these "raft busters," they'd come home reckless and horny—the German folkloric equivalent of American cowboys after payday.

Km 543—Bacharach and Stahleck Castle (Burg Stahleck): Cross to the other side of the train. The town of Bacharach is a great stop (described on next page). Some of the Rhine's best wine is from this town, whose name likely derives from "altar to Bacchus." Local vintners brag that the medieval Pope Pius II ordered Bacharach wine by the cartload. Perched above the town, the 13th-century Burg Stahleck is now a hostel.

Km 541—Lorch: This pathetic stub of a castle is barely visible from the road. Check out the hillside vineyards. These vineyards once blanketed four times as much land as they do today, but modern economics have driven most of them out of business. The vineyards that do survive require government subsidies. Notice the small car ferry, one of several along the bridgeless stretch between Mainz and Koblenz.

Km 538—Sooneck Castle: Cross back to the other side of the train. Built in the 11th century, this castle was twice destroyed by people sick and tired of robber barons.

Km 534—Reichenstein Castle and **Km 533—Rheinstein Castle:** Stay on the other side of the train to see two of the first castles to be rebuilt in the Romantic era. Both are privately owned, tourable, and connected by a pleasant trail.

Km 530—Ehrenfels Castle: Opposite Bingerbrück and the Bingen station, you'll see the ghostly Ehrenfels Castle (clobbered by the Swedes in 1636 and by the French in 1689). Since it had no view of the river traffic to the north, the owner built the cute little *Mäuseturm* (mouse tower) on an island (the yellow tower you'll see near the train station today). Rebuilt in the 1800s in Neo-Gothic style, it's now used as a Rhine navigation signal station.

Km 528—Niederwald Monument: Across from the Bingen station on a hilltop is the 120-foot-high Niederwald monument, a memorial built with 32 tons of bronze in 1877 to commemorate "the re-establishment of the German Empire." A lift takes tourists to this statue from the famous and extremely touristy wine town of Rüdesheim.

From here, the Romantic Rhine becomes the industrial Rhine, and our tour is over.

Bacharach

Once prosperous from the wine and wood trade, charming
Bacharach (BAHKH-ah-rahkh, with a guttural *kh* sound) is now
just a pleasant half-timbered village of a thousand people working hard to keep its tourists happy. Businesses that have been "in
the family" for eons are dealing with succession challenges, as
the allure of big-city jobs and a more cosmopolitan life lure away
the town's younger generation. But for now, Bacharach retains its
time-capsule quaintness.

Orientation to Bacharach

Tourist Information

The TI, on the main street in the Posthof courtyard next to the
church, will store bags for day-trippers (April-Oct Mon-Fri 9:00-
17:00, Sat-Sun 10:00-15:00; Nov-March Mon-Fri 9:00-13:00,
closed Sat-Sun; from train station turn right and walk 5 blocks
down main street with castle high on your left, Oberstrasse 45; tel.
06743/919-303, www.bacharach.de or www.rhein-nahe-touristik
.de, Herr Kuhn and his team).

Helpful Hints

Shopping: The **Jost** German gift store, across the main square
 from the church, carries most everything a souvenir-shopper
 could want—from beer steins to cuckoo clocks—and can ship
 purchases to the US. This family shop is celebrating its centennial (see a photo of their great-grandfather on the wall).
 The Josts offer discounts to my readers: 10 percent if paying
 with cash, 5 percent with credit card (March-Oct Mon-Fri
 8:30-18:00, Sat 8:30-17:00, possibly Sun 10:00-16:00; Nov-
 Feb shorter hours and closed Sun; Blücherstrasse 4, tel.
 06743/1224, phil.jost@t-online.de).

Internet Access: The **TI** has a coin-op terminal (€0.50/15
 minutes).

Post Office: It's inside a news agents' shop, across from the church
 and Altes Haus, at Oberstrasse 56.

Grocery Store: Pick up picnic supplies at **Nahkauf,** a basic grocery store (Mon-Fri 8:00-12:30 & 14:00-18:30, Sat 8:30-14:00,
 closed Sun, Koblenzer Strasse 2).

Bike Rental: While many hotels loan bikes to guests, the only real
 bike-rental business in the town center is run by Erich at the
 recommended **Hotel Hillen** (non-guests-€12/day, guests-€7/
 day, 35 bikes available, daily 9:00 until dark, Langstrasse 18,
 tel. 06743/1287).

Local Guides: Get acquainted with Bacharach by taking a walk-ing tour. These guides enjoy sharing their town with visi-tors: **Thomas Gundlach** is a charming local who's licensed as a guide and happily gives 1.5-hour town walks to individ-uals or small groups for €25. He can also drive up to three people around the region in his car (€70/6 hours, €120/long day, mobile 0179-353-6004, tomgund@web.de or thomas _gundlach@gmx.de). Also good are **Birgit Wessels** (tel. 06743/937-514, wessels.birgit@t-online.de) and Aussie **Joanne Augustin** (€30/1.5 hours, mobile 0179-231-1389, jopetit90 @yahoo.com). The TI books 1.5-hour tours in English (€70/ group). Or take one or both of my self-guided walks, below.

Self-Guided Walks

Welcome to Bacharach

• *Start at the Köln-Düsseldorfer ferry dock (next to a fine picnic park).*

Riverfront: View the town from the parking lot—a modern landfill. The Rhine used to lap against Bacharach's town wall, just over the present-day highway. Every few years the river floods, covering the highway with several feet of water. The **castle** on the hill is now a youth hostel. Two of the town's original 16 towers are visible from here (up to five if you look really hard). The huge road-side keg declares that this town was built on the wine trade.

Reefs farther upstream forced boats to unload upriver and reload here. Consequently, in the Middle Ages, Bacharach became the biggest wine-trading town on the Rhine. A riverfront crane hoisted huge kegs of prestigious "Bacharach" wine (which, in practice, was from anywhere in the region). The tour buses next to the dock and the flags of the biggest spenders along the highway remind you that today's economy is basically founded on tourism.

• *Before entering the town, walk upstream through the...*

Riverside Park: This park was laid out in 1910 in the English style: Notice how the trees were planted to frame fine town views, highlighting the most picturesque bits of architec-ture. The dark, sad-looking monument—its "eternal" flame long snuffed out—is a **war memorial.** The German psyche is perma-nently scarred by war memories. Today, many Germans would rather avoid monuments like this, which revisit the dark periods before Germany became a nation of pacifists. Take a close look at the monument. Each panel honors sons of Bacharach who died for the Kaiser: in 1864 against Denmark, in 1866 against Austria, in 1870 against France, in 1914 during World War I. The military Maltese cross—flanked by classic German helmets—has a W at its center, for Kaiser Wilhelm.

• *Look (but don't go) upstream from here to see the...*

RHINE VALLEY

1 Rhein Hotel & Stüber Rest.
2 Hotel zur Post
3 Hotel/Rest. Kranenturm
4 Pension im Malerwinkel
5 Pension Binz
6 Hotel Hillen & Bike Rental
7 Pension Lettie
8 To Pension Winzerhaus
9 Ursula Orth B&B
10 Irmgard Orth B&B
11 Jugendherberge Stahleck Hostel & Restaurant
12 Altes Haus Restaurant
13 Gasthaus Jägerstube
14 Eis Café Italia
15 Zum Kleinen Monning Irish Pub
16 Zur Alt Backstubb
17 Bastian's Weingut zum Grüner Baum
18 Weingut Karl Heidrich
19 Grocery

Trailer Park and Campground: In Germany, trailer vacationers and campers are two distinct subcultures. Folks who travel in trailers, like many retirees in the US, are a nomadic bunch, cruising around the countryside in their motor homes and paying a few euros a night to park. Campers, on the other hand, tend to set up camp in one place—complete with comfortable lounge chairs and TVs—and stay put for weeks, even months. They often come back to the same spot year after year, treating it like their own private estate. These camping devotees have made a science out of relaxing.

• *Continue to where the park meets the playground, and then cross the highway to the fortified riverside wall of the Catholic church, decorated with...*

High-Water Marks: These recall various floods. Twenty yards to the left is a metal ring on the medieval slate wall. Before

Bacharach

To ⑧ Steeg & A-31 Freeway

To St. Goar

VINEYARDS

④

BANK

BLÜCHERSTRASSE

Steep Trail

TOWER

WALK ENDS

WERNER KAPELLE

ROSENSTRASSE

VINEYARDS

PROTESTANT CHURCH

⑯

OLD POSTHOF

JOST OUTLET

30 Meters

30 Yards

RHINE VALLEY

STRASSE

BAUERSTR.

②

MARKTSTR.

POST

BANK

⑫ ⑰ ⑤

FLEISCHSTR.

ALTES HAUS

OLD MINT

MÜNZSTR.

⑲

KOBLENZER STR.

⑭

①

LANGSTRASSE

⑬

MARKT TOWER

PEDESTRIAN UNDERPASS

WC

P

WALK BEGINS

Park

B9

To St. Goar & Koblenz

B-R DOCK

K-D DOCK (EURAIL VALID)

River

To St. Goar, Boppard & Koblenz

the 1910 reclamation project, the river extended out to here, and boats would use the ring to tie up.

• *From the church, go under the 1858 train tracks and hook right past the yellow floodwater yardstick and up the stairs onto the town wall. Atop the wall, turn left and walk under the long arcade. After 30 meters, on your left, notice a...*

Well: Rebuilt as it appeared in the 17th century, this is one of 40 such wells that provided water to the townsfolk until 1900. Walk 50 yards past the well along the wall to an alcove in the medieval tower with a view of the war memorial in the park. You're under the crane tower *(Kranenturm)*. After barrels of wine were moved overland from Bingen past dangerous stretches of river, the precious cargo could be lowered by cranes from here into ships to continue more safely down the river. The Rhine has long been a major shipping route through Germany. In modern times, it's a bottleneck in Germany's train system. The train company gives hotels and residents along the tracks money for soundproof windows (hotels along here routinely have quadruple-pane windows... and earplugs on the nightstand).

• *Continue walking along the town wall. Pass the recommended Rhein Hotel (hotel is before the Markt tower, which marks one of the town's 15 original 14th-century gates), descend, pass another well, and follow Marktstrasse away from the river toward the town center, the two-tone church, and the town's...*

Main Intersection: From here, Bacharach's main street (Oberstrasse) goes right to the half-timbered red-and-white Altes Haus (from 1368, the oldest house in town) and left 400 yards to the train station. Spin around to enjoy the higgledy-piggledy building styles.

• *To the left (south) of the church, a golden horn hangs over the old...*

Posthof: The postal horn symbolizes the postal service throughout Europe. In olden days, when the postman blew this, traffic stopped and the mail sped through. This post station (now home to the TI) dates from 1724, when stagecoaches ran from Köln to Frankfurt and would change horses here, Pony Express-style.

Step past the old oak doors into the courtyard—once a carriage house and inn that accommodated Bacharach's first VIP visitors. Notice the fascist eagle (from 1936, on the left as you enter; a swastika once filled its center) and the fine view of the church and a ruined chapel above.

Two hundred years ago, Bacharach's main drag was the only road along the Rhine. Napoleon widened it to fit his cannon wagons. The steps alongside the church lead to the castle.

• *Return to the church, passing the recommended Italian ice-cream café (Eis Café Italia), where friendly Mimo serves his special invention: Riesling wine-flavored gelato.*

Protestant Church: Inside the church (daily 10:00-18:00, English info on table near door), you'll find Grotesque capitals, brightly painted in medieval style, and a mix of round Romanesque and pointed Gothic arches. The church was fancier before the Reformation wars, when it (and the region) was Catholic. Bacharach lies on the religious border of Germany and, like the country as a whole, is split between Catholics and Protestants. To the left of the altar, some medieval frescoes survive where an older Romanesque arch was cut by a pointed Gothic one.

• *Continue down Oberstrasse to the...*

Altes Haus: Notice the 14th-century building style—the first floor is made of stone, while upper floors are half-timbered (in the ornate style common in the Rhine Valley). Some of its windows still look medieval, with small, flattened circles as panes (small because that's all that glass-blowing technology of the time would allow), pieced together with molten lead (like medieval stained glass in churches). Frau Weber welcomes visitors to enjoy the fascinating ground floor of the recommended Altes Haus restaurant, with its evocative old photos and etchings (consider eating here later).

• *Keep going down Oberstrasse to the...*

Old Mint (Münze): The old mint is marked by a crude coin in its sign. Across from the mint, the recommended **Bastian** family's wine garden is a lively place after dark. Above you in the vineyards stands a lonely white-and-red tower—your final destination.

• *At the next street, look right and see the mint tower, painted in the medieval style, and then turn left. Wander 30 yards up Rosenstrasse to the **well**. Notice the sundial and the wall painting of 1632 Bacharach with its walls intact. Climb the tiny-stepped lane behind the well up into the vineyard and to the...*

Tall Tower: The slate steps lead to a small path through the vineyard that deposits you at a viewpoint atop the stubby remains of the old town wall. If the tower's open, hike to its top floor for the best view.

Romantic Rhine View: A grand medieval town spreads before you. For 300 years (1300-1600), Bacharach was big (population 4,000), rich, and politically powerful.

From this perch, you can see the chapel ruins and six surviving **city towers.** Visually trace the wall to the castle. The castle was actually the capital of Germany for a couple of years in the 1200s. When Holy Roman Emperor Frederick Barbarossa went away to fight the Crusades, he left his brother (who lived here) in charge of his vast realm. Bacharach was home of one of seven electors who voted for the Holy Roman Emperor in 1275. To protect their own power, these prince electors did their best to choose the weakest guy on the ballot. The elector from Bacharach helped select a two-bit prince named Rudolf von Habsburg (from a noname castle in Switzerland). However, the underestimated Rudolf brutally silenced the robber barons along the Rhine and established the mightiest dynasty in European history. His family line, the Habsburgs, ruled much of Central and Eastern Europe from Vienna until 1918.

Plagues, fires, and the Thirty Years' War (1618-1648) finally did in Bacharach. The town, with a population of about a thousand, has slumbered for several centuries. Today, the castle houses commoners—40,000 overnights annually by youth hostelers.

In the mid-19th century, painters such as J. M. W. Turner and writers such as Victor Hugo were charmed by the Rhineland's romantic mix of past glory, present poverty, and rich legend. They put this part of the Rhine on the old Grand Tour map as the "Romantic Rhine." Victor Hugo pondered the ruined 15th-century chapel that you see under the castle. In his 1842 travel book, *Excursions Along the Banks of Rhine,* he wrote, "No doors, no roof or windows, a magnificent skeleton puts its silhouette against the sky. Above it, the ivy-covered castle ruins provide a fitting crown. This is Bacharach, land of fairy tales, covered with legends and sagas." If you're enjoying the Romantic Rhine, thank Victor Hugo and company.

• *To get back into town, take the level path away from the river that leads along the once-mighty wall up the valley past the next tower. Then cross the street into the parking lot. Pass Pension im Malerwinkel on your right, being careful not to damage the old arch with your head. Follow the creek past a delightful little series of half-timbered homes and cheery gardens known as "Painters' Corner" (Malerwinkel). Resist looking into some pervert's peep show (on the right) and continue downhill back to the village center. Nice work.*

Walk Along the Old Town Walls

A well-maintained and clearly marked walking path follows the remains of Bacharach's old town walls and makes for a good hour's workout. The TI has maps that show the entire route. The path starts near the train station, then climbs up to the youth hostel, descends into the side valley, and then continues up the other side to the tower in the vineyards before returning to town. To start the walk at the train station, find the house at Oberstrasse 2 and climb up the stairway to its left. Then follow the *Stadtmauer-Rundweg* signs. Good bilingual signposts tell the history of each of the towers along the wall—some are intact, one is a private residence, and others are now only stubs.

Sleeping in Bacharach

(area code: 06743)

Parking in Bacharach is simple along the highway next to the tracks (3-hour daytime limit is generally not enforced) or, better, in the big lot by the boat dock. For locations, see the map on page 527.

$$$ Rhein Hotel, overlooking the river with 14 spacious and comfortable rooms, is classy, well-run, and decorated with modern flair. Since it's right on the train tracks, its river- and train-side rooms come with quadruple-paned windows and air-conditioning. This place has been in the Stüber family for six generations (Sb-€55, Db-€90, Tb-€120, Qb-€140, ask for Rick Steves price with this book and direct reservation, cheaper for longer stays and off-season, €17/person half-board includes big three-course dinner, non-smoking, free loaner bikes, pay Wi-Fi, directly inland from the K-D boat dock at Langstrasse 50, tel. 06743/1243, fax 06743/1413, www.rhein-hotel-bacharach.de, info@rhein-hotel

Sleep Code

(€1 = about $1.40, country code: 49)

S = Single, **D** = Double/Twin, **T** = Triple, **Q** = Quad, **b** = bathroom, **s** = shower only. Staff at all hotels speak at least some English. Breakfast is included, and credit cards are accepted unless otherwise noted.

To help you sort easily through these listings, I've divided the accommodations into three categories, based on the price for a standard double room with bath:

$$$ Higher Priced—Most rooms €80 or more.
$$ Moderately Priced—Most rooms between €55-80.
$ Lower Priced—Most rooms €55 or less.

The Rhine is an easy place for cheap sleeps. B&Bs and *Gasthäuser* with €25-30 beds abound (and normally discount their prices for longer stays). Rhine-area hostels offer €20 beds to travelers of any age. Each town's TI is eager to set you up, and finding a room should be easy any time of year (except for Sept-Oct winefest weekends). Bacharach and St. Goar, the best towns for an overnight stop, are 10 miles apart, connected by milk-run trains, riverboats, and a riverside bike path. Bacharach is a much more interesting town, but St. Goar has the famous castle (for St. Goar recommendations, see page 545).

-bacharach.de). Their recommended Stüber restaurant is considered the best in town.

$$ Hotel zur Post, refreshingly clean and quiet, is conveniently located right in the town center with no train noise. It comes with a focus on solid comfort rather than old-fashioned character, and rents good rooms for a good price (Db-€66-70, Oberstrasse 38, tel. 06743/1277, www.hotel-zur-post-bacharach .de, h.zurpost@t-online.de, Precoma family).

$$ Hotel Kranenturm, offering castle ambience without the climb, combines hotel comfort with *Privatzimmer* funkiness right downtown. Run by hardworking Kurt Engel and his intense but friendly wife, Fatima, this 17-room hotel is part of the medieval town wall. The rooms in its former *Kranenturm* (crane tower) have the best views. When the riverbank was higher, cranes on this tower loaded barrels of wine onto Rhine boats. While just 15 feet from the train tracks, a combination of medieval sturdiness, triple-paned windows, and included earplugs makes the riverside rooms sleepable (Sb-€40-46, small Db-€57-62, regular Db-€59-65, Db in huge tower rooms with castle and river views-€73-80, Tb-€85-95, Qb great for families with small kids-€100-110, lower prices are for

3-night stay, family deals, cash preferred, €2 extra if paying with credit card, Rhine views come with train noise, back rooms are quiet, non-smoking, showers can be temperamental, kid-friendly, good breakfast, free Internet access and Wi-Fi in lobby, laundry service-€13, Langstrasse 30, tel. 06743/1308, www.kranenturm .com, hotel-kranenturm@t-online.de). Kurt, a good cook, serves €10-14 dinners in their recommended restaurant.

$$ Pension im Malerwinkel sits like a grand gingerbread house that straddles the town wall in a quiet little neighborhood so charming it's called "Painters' Corner" *(Malerwinkel)*. The Vollmer family's 20-room place is super-quiet and comes with a sunny garden on a brook, views of the vineyards, and easy parking (Sb-€40; Db-€65 for one-night stay, €59/night for 2 nights, €56/night for 3 nights or more; family rooms, cash only, no train noise, non-smoking, free Wi-Fi, bike rental-€6/day; from Oberstrasse, turn left at the church, and stay to the left of the babbling brook until you reach Blücherstrasse 41-45; tel. 06743/1239, www.im-malerwinkel .de, info@im-malerwinkel.de, Armin and Daniela).

$$ Pension Binz offers four large, bright, plainly furnished rooms in a good location with no train noise (Sb-€37, Db-€60, Tb-€78, slightly more for one-night stays, Koblenzer Strasse 1, tel. 06743/1604, fax 06743/937-9916, http://pensionbinz.funpic.de, pension.binz@freenet.de, Carla speaks a little English).

$ Hotel Hillen, a block south of Hotel Kranenturm, has less charm and similar train noise (with the same ultra-thick windows). It offers spacious rooms and friendly owners (S-€30, Sb-€35, D-€40, Ds-€45, Db-€50, Tb-€65, Qb-€80, ask for Rick Steves price when you reserve direct with this book, 10 percent discount for 2-night stay, closed mid-Nov-mid-March, family rooms, Langstrasse 18, tel. 06743/1287, fax 06743/1037, hotel-hillen@web .de, kind Iris speaks some English). The hotel also rents bikes (see page 524).

$ Pension Lettie, run by effervescent and eager-to-please Lettie, rents four bright rooms. Lettie speaks English (she worked for the US Army before they withdrew) and does laundry for €12/ load (Sb-€38, Db-€55, Tb-€75, Qb-€90, Quint/b-€105, ask for Rick Steves price with this book when you reserve direct, €5 discount for 2-night stay, 10 percent more if paying with credit card, non-smoking, buffet breakfast with waffles and eggs, no train noise, free Wi-Fi, inland from Hotel Kranenturm, Kranenstrasse 6, tel. 06743/2115, pension.lettie@t-online.de).

$ Pension Winzerhaus, a 10-room place run by friendly Sybille and Stefan, is outside the town walls, 200 yards up the side-valley road from the town gate, directly under the vineyards. The rooms are simple, clean, and modern, and parking is easy (Sb-€33, Db-€49, Tb-€69, Qb-€75, show this book at check-in for best price, cash only, non-smoking, free Wi-Fi, free loaner bikes for guests, Blücherstrasse 60, tel. 06743/1294, www.pension-winzer haus.de, winzerhaus@gmx.de).

$ Ursula Orth B&B rents five basic rooms. Ursula speaks a smidge of English and is proud of her homemade jam, and daughter Karin helps run things (Sb-€22, Db-€38, Tb-€48, cash only, non-smoking, Spurgasse 3, tel. 06743/1557, k.w.68@hotmail.de). From the station, walk down Oberstrasse, turn right on Spurgasse, and look for the *Orth* sign. Be careful not to confuse Ursula at #3 with Irmgard at #2 (listed next). While across the street from each other and related, they are two different businesses.

$ Irmgard Orth B&B rents three fresh rooms, two of which share a bathroom on the hall. Irmgard speaks almost no English, but is exuberantly cheery and serves homemade honey with breakfast (S-€22, D-€36, Db-€38, 5 percent more for one-night stay, cash only, non-smoking, Spurgasse 2, look for *Honig* signs with picture of a beehive, tel. 06743/1553, speak slowly).

$ Jugendherberge Stahleck hostel is a 12th-century castle on the hilltop—350 steps above Bacharach—with a royal Rhine view. Open to travelers of any age, this is a gem with 168 beds and a private modern shower and WC in most rooms. The hostel offers hearty €7.50 all-you-can-eat buffet dinners, and its pub serves cheap local wine and snacks until midnight. If you're arriving at the train station with luggage, it's an €8.50 taxi ride to the hostel—call 06743/1653 (€20 dorm beds with breakfast and sheets, non-members-€3.10 extra, couples can share one of five €51 Db, no smoking in rooms, pay Internet access and Wi-Fi, laundry-€6; reception open 7:30-20:00, after that check in at bar until 21:30; curfew at 22:00, tel. 06743/1266, www.diejugendherbergen.de, zentrale@diejugendherbergen.de). If driving, don't go in the driveway; park on the street and walk 200 yards.

Eating in Bacharach

Restaurants

Bacharach has no shortage of reasonably priced, atmospheric restaurants offering fine indoor and outdoor dining. Two of my recommended hotels—Rhein and Kranenturm—have good restaurants. Non-German options on the main street include a pizzeria and *Döner Kebab* joint (open daily until late) and an Irish pub.

The Rhein Hotel's **Stüber Restaurant** is Bacharach's best top-end choice. Chef Andreas Stüber, his family's sixth-generation chef, prepares regional, seasonal plates, served at river- and track-side seating or indoors with a spacious wood-and-white-tablecloth elegance. Consider his €15 William Turner pâté sampler plate, named after the British painter who liked Bacharach (€12-19 main courses, €27-35 fixed-price meals, always a good vegetarian option, open Wed-Mon 11:30-14:15 & 17:30-21:15, closed Tue and mid-Dec-Feb, call to reserve on weekends or for an outdoor table, facing the K-D boat dock below town center, Langstrasse 50, tel. 06743/1243).

Hotel Kranenturm is another good value, with hearty dinners (Kurt prides himself on his *Sauerbraten*—marinated beef with potato dumplings and red cabbage) and good main-course salads. If you're a trainspotter, sit on their trackside terrace and trade travel stories with new friends over dinner, letting screaming trains punctuate your conversation. If you prefer charming old German decor, sit inside (€9-15 main courses, open 6 days a week 17:00-21:00—closed day varies, restaurant closed Dec-Feb). Kurt and Fatima are your hosts.

Altes Haus, the oldest building in town (see page 528), serves food with Bacharach's most romantic atmosphere. Find the cozy little dining room with photos of the opera singer who sang about Bacharach, adding to its fame (€9-15 main courses, Thu-Tue 12:00-15:30 & 18:00-23:00, closed Wed and off-season, dead center by the Protestant Church, tel. 06743/1209).

Gasthaus Jägerstube is every local's non-touristy, good-value hangout. It's a no-frills place with no outdoor seating, run by a former East German family determined to keep Bacharach's working class well-fed and watered. Next to the WC is a rare "party cash box." Regulars drop in bits of money throughout the year, Frau Tischmeier banks it, and by year's end...there's plenty in the little savings account for a community party (€10-12 daily specials, daily 11:00-21:30, Marktstrasse 3, tel. 06743/1492, Tischmeier family).

Bacharacher Kebap Haus is the town favorite for €4 *Döner Kebabs,* cheap pizzas, and salads (daily 10:00-23:00, on the main drag in the town center).

Eis Café Italia, on the main street, is run by friendly Mimo Calabrese, who brought gelato to town in 1976. He's known for his refreshing, not-too-sweet Riesling-flavored gelato. Notice the big sundae bowls on the shelves. To enjoy your *Eis* German-style, sit down and order ice cream off the menu, or just stop by for a cone "to go" for your evening stroll (€0.80/scoop, no tastes offered, April-mid-Oct daily 10:00-22:00, closed off-season, Oberstrasse 48).

Jugendherberge Stahleck, Bacharach's youth hostel, welcomes anyone hungry or thirsty enough to hike 20 minutes up to its romantic perch above the Rhine. The hostel offers hearty €7.50 all-you-can-eat buffet dinners, while the pub serves cheap local wine and snacks until midnight (see listing under "Sleeping in Bacharach," earlier).

Pubs

Zum Kleinen Monning Irish Pub, with international beers on tap, provides the liveliest after-dinner scene in town. Bacharach's 1,000 residents hail from 26 different nations, and you'll meet many of them here enjoying the convivial atmosphere created by Martina and Marcus (light meals too, Oberstrasse 35).

If the Zum Kleinen Monning is dead, the other late-night spot for drinks (and pizza) is **Zur Alt Backstubb** (seating inside and out, €7 pastas and pizzas, nightly until late, Blücherstrasse 16).

Wine-Tasting

Bacharach is proud of its wine. Two places in town—Bastian's rowdy and rustic Grüner Baum, and the more sophisticated Weingut Karl Heidrich—offer visitors an inexpensive tasting memory. Each creates carousels of local wines that small groups of travelers (who don't mind sharing a glass) can sample and compare. Both places offer light plates of food if you'd like a rustic meal.

At **Bastian's Weingut zum Grüner Baum,** groups of 2-6 people pay €19.50 for a wine carousel of 15 glasses—14 different white wines and one lonely rosé—and a basket of bread. Your mission: Team up with others who have this book to rendezvous here after dinner. Spin the Lazy Susan, share a common cup, and discuss the taste. Doris Bastian insists: "After each wine, you must talk to each other" (Mon-Wed and Fri from 13:00, Sat-Sun from 12:00, closed Thu and Feb-mid-March, just past Altes Haus, tel. 06743/1208). To make a meal of a carousel, consider the €8 *Käseteller* (seven different cheeses—including *Spundekäse,* the local soft cheese—with bread and butter).

Weingut Karl Heidrich is a fun family-run wine shop and *Stube* in the town center (at Oberstrasse 16), where Markus and daughter Magdalena proudly share their family's centuries-old wine tradition, explaining its fine points to travelers. They offer a variety of carousels with English descriptions, six wines, and bread (€11.50), which are ideal for the more sophisticated wine taster (Thu-Tue 11:00-22:00, closed Wed and Nov-Easter, will ship to the US, tel. 06743/93060).

Bacharach Connections

Train Connections from the Rhine

Milk-run trains stop at Rhine towns each hour starting as early as 6:00, connecting at Mainz and Koblenz to trains farther afield. Trains between St. Goar and Bacharach depart at about :20 after the hour in each direction (€3.20, buy tickets from the machine in the unstaffed stations). The ride times listed below are calculated from Bacharach; for St. Goar, the difference is only 10 minutes.

Train info: tel. 0180-599-6633, www.bahn.com.

From Bacharach by Train to: St. Goar (hourly, 10 minutes), **Köln** (hourly, 1.75 hours with change in Koblenz, 2.5 hours direct), **Frankfurt Airport** (hourly, 1-1.5 hours, change in Mainz or Bingen), **Frankfurt** (hourly, 1.25-1.75 hours, change in Mainz or Bingen), **Rothenburg ob der Tauber** (every 2 hours, 4.25 hours, 3-4 changes), **Munich** (hourly, 5 hours, 2 changes), **Berlin** (hourly, 6.5-7.5 hours, 1-3 changes), **Amsterdam** (hourly, 7 hours, change in Köln, sometimes 1-2 more changes), **Bruges** (at least every 2 hours, 5.5 hours, some via Thalys, 3 changes).

St. Goar

St. Goar (sahnkt gwahr) is a classic Rhine tourist town. Its hulk of a castle overlooks a half-timbered shopping street and leafy riverside park, busy with sightseeing ships and contented strollers. Rheinfels Castle, once the mightiest on the Rhine, is the single best Rhineland ruin to explore. From the riverboat docks, the main drag—a dull pedestrian mall without history—cuts through town before ending at the road up to the castle. Explore beyond the shops: Thoughtful little placards scattered around town explain factoids (in English) about each street, lane, and square.

While the town of St. Goar itself isn't much more than a few hotels and restaurants—and is less interesting than Bacharach—it still makes a good base for hiking or biking the region. A tiny car ferry will shuttle you back and forth across the busy Rhine from here. (If you run out of things to see, a great pastime in St. Goar is simply chatting with friendly Heike at the K-D boat kiosk.) For train connections, see "Bacharach Connections," earlier.

Orientation to St. Goar

Tourist Information

The helpful St. Goar TI, which books rooms and stores bags for free, is on the pedestrian street, three blocks from the K-D boat dock and train station (May-Sept Mon-Fri 9:00-12:30 & 13:30-18:00, Sat 10:00-12:00, closed Sun; April and Oct Mon-Fri until 17:00, closed Sat-Sun; Nov-March Mon-Thu until 17:00, Fri 9:00-14:00, closed Sat-Sun; from train station, go downhill around church and turn left, Heerstrasse 86, tel. 06741/383, www.st-goar.de).

Helpful Hints

Picnics: St. Goar's waterfront park is hungry for picnickers. You can buy picnic fixings at the tiny **St. Goarer Stadtladen**

St. Goar

50 Meters
50 Yards

To A-61
Autobahn

BURG
RHEINFELS
CASTLE
(See detail map)

To Boppard
& Koblenz

AM HAFEN

9

Harbor

To Boppard
& Koblenz

Vineyard Trail

GUT RHEINFELS

SCHLOSSBERG

BISMARCKWEG

Nature Trail

AUF DEM HÄHNCHEN

DREIBURGENBLICK

AUSSIEDLUNG UHLENHORST

ULMENHOF

RHEINSTRASSE

AM HAFEN

Rhine River

WC

SCHLEIER

OBERSTRASSE

BORNG.

GREBELG.

HEERSTRASSE

POST

9

PUMPENGASSE

KIRCHGASSE

TOWER

PHONE

TRAIN
STATION

MARKT

OBERSTRASSE

HEERSTRASSE

RHEINSTRASSE

TOURIST TRAIN
TO CASTLE
DEPARTURE
POINT

Car ferry to
St. Goars-
hausen

K-D
DOCK
(EURAIL VALID)

To Bacharach

To Bacharach
& Frankfurt

9

To Bacharach
& Bingen

RHINE VALLEY

① Hotel am Markt
② Rhein Hotel
③ Hotel Hauser
④ Hotel an der Fähre
⑤ Frau Kurz Rooms
⑥ St. Goar Hostel
⑦ Burgschänke Rest.
& Schlosshotel
Rheinfels Dining
Room
⑧ Gasthaus Zur Krone
⑨ Rist. Alla Fontana
⑩ Grocery
⑪ Stein Shop
⑫ Bike Rental

grocery store on the pedestrian street (Tue-Fri 8:00-18:00, Sat 8:00-13:00, closed Sun-Mon, Heerstrasse 106).

Shopping: The Montag family runs two shops (one specializes in steins and the other in cuckoo clocks), all at the base of the castle hill road. The stein shop under the hotel has Rhine guides and fine steins. The other shop boasts "the largest free-hanging cuckoo clock in the world" (both open daily 8:30-18:00). A couple of other souvenir shops are across from the K-D boat dock. Shops offer discounts on any of their souvenirs (including Hummels) for travelers with this book. They'll ship your purchase home—or give you a VAT form to claim your tax refund at the airport if you're carrying your items with you.

Internet Access: The **TI** is your best bet (€0.50/10 minutes), but if it's crowded or closed, the backup option is the expensive coin-op access (€6/hour, 6 terminals) or Wi-Fi (€5/hour) at **Hotel Montag** (Heerstrasse 128).

Bike Rental: Goar Bike, run by Richard and Gabriele Langhans, is near the train station (€7/6 hours, €10/day, must show ID and leave €50 deposit, April-Oct Tue-Sun 9:00-13:00 & 15:00-19:00, closed Mon and Nov-March, go right as you exit station, Oberstrasse 44, tel. 06741/1735, goarbike@web.de). Richard, who speaks English, has maps and can suggest routes (or ask at the TI).

Parking: A free lot is at the downstream end of town. On-street parking by the K-D boat dock and recommended hotels costs about €4/day.

Sights in St. Goar

▲▲▲Rheinfels Castle

Sitting like a dead pit bull above St. Goar, this mightiest of Rhine castles rumbles with ghosts from its hard-fought past. This hollow but interesting shell offers your single best hands-on ruined-castle experience on the river.

Cost and Hours: €4, family card-€10; mid-March-Oct daily 9:00-18:00, last entry at 17:00; Nov-mid-March Sat-Sun only 11:00-17:00, last entry at 16:00—weather permitting. Managed by Gaby Loch, tel. 06741/7753, in winter 06741/383, www.st-goar.de.

Tours and Information: Follow my self-guided tour. The castle map is helpful, but the €2 English booklet is of no real value. English tours (€30/group) can be booked in advance. If it's damp, be careful of slippery stones.

Services: A handy WC is immediately across from the ticket booth (check out the guillotine urinals—stand back when you pull to flush).

St. Goar's Rheinfels Castle

Cliffs

DETOUR THAT INCLUDES TUNNELS

STAIRS

MUSEUM

SMALL MINE TUNNELS

FIRST STEEL RAILING

SECOND STEEL RAILING

WELL

CATAPULT BALLS

POSTS

BIG CELLAR

MOAT

2 ARCHES

Cliffs

Cliffs

To A-61 Autobahn

PARKING LOT (SHUTTLE STOPS HERE)

BRIDGE

ROAD

20 Meters
20 Yards

WALK BEGINS

WC

TICKETS

HOTEL/ RESTAURANT

BRIDGE

ROAD

RHINE RIVER

Downhill to St. Goar

RHINE VALLEY

······· Walking Tour Route

---- Route From Parking Lot to Tickets

········ Walking Tour Route (Tunnel Option)

① Ticket Office & Entry
② Darmstädter Bau
③ Museum & Castle Model
④ Inner Courtyard
⑤ Stables
⑥ Well
⑦ High Battery
⑧ Clock Tower Lookout
⑨ Stairs to Defense Galleries

⑩ Corner of Castle & Crossbow Slits
⑪ Foxhole & Mine Tunnel
⑫ Halsgraben ("Neck Ditch")
⑬ Gunsmiths' Tower
⑭ Prison
⑮ Slaughterhouse
⑯ Big Cellar

RHINE VALLEY

Let There Be Light: If planning to explore the mine tunnels, bring a flashlight, or do it by candlelight (museum sells candles with matches, €0.50).

Getting to the Castle: A **taxi** up from town costs €5 (tel. 06741/7011). Or take the kitschy "tschu-tschu" **tourist train** (€2 one-way, €3 round-trip, 8 minutes to the top, hours vary but generally April-Oct daily 10:00-17:30, 2/hour, complete with lusty music, mobile 0171-496-3762). The train waits between the train station and the K-D dock. To avoid feeling silly as you sit on the train waiting for Ralph (the "conductor") to decide it's time to go, browse the shopping street and hop on as he goes by (just wave him down, then pay at the top). The train returns to town from the castle at about the top and bottom of each hour.

To **hike** up to the castle, you can simply follow the main road up through the railroad underpass at the top end of the pedestrian street. But it's more fun to take the nature trail: Start at the St. Goar train station. Take the underpass under the tracks at the north end of the station, climb the steep stairs uphill, and turn right (following *Burg Rheinfels* signs) along the path just above the old city wall, which takes you to the castle in 10 minutes.

Background: Burg Rheinfels *was* huge—for five centuries, it was the biggest castle on the Rhine. Built in 1245 to guard a toll station, it soon earned the nickname "the unconquerable fortress." In the 1400s, the castle was thickened to withstand cannon fire. Rheinfels became a thriving cultural center and, in the 1520s, was visited by the artist Albrecht Dürer and the religious reformer Ulrich Zwingli. It saw lots of action in the Thirty Years' War (1618-1648), and later became the strongest and most modern fortress in the Holy Roman Empire. It withstood a siege of 28,000 French troops in 1692. But eventually the castle surrendered to the French without a fight, and in 1797, the French Revolutionary army destroyed it. For years, the ruined castle was used as a source of building stone, and today—while still mighty—it's only a small fraction of its original size.

◐ Self-Guided Tour: Rather than wander aimlessly, visit the castle by following this tour. We'll start at the museum, then circulate through the courtyards, up to the highest lookout point, and down around through the fortified ramparts, with an option to go into the dark tunnels. We'll finish in the prison and big cellar. The basic route below can be done without a flashlight or any daring acts of chivalry. (To go through the tunnels, bring a light or buy candles at the castle museum.)

Pick up the free map and use its commentary to navigate from red signpost to signpost through the castle. My self-guided tour route is similar to the one marked on the castle map. That map, the one in this book, and this tour all use the same numbering system.

(You'll notice that I've skipped a few stops—just walk on by signs for ❷ *Darmstädter Bau,* ❺ *stables,* and ⓭ *Gunsmiths' Tower.*)

• *The ticket office is under the castle's clock tower, labeled* ❶ Uhrturm. *Walk through the entranceway and continue straight, passing several points of interest (which we'll visit later), until you get to the* ❸ *museum.*

Museum and Castle Model: The pleasant museum, located in the only finished room of the castle, has good English descriptions and comes with Romantic Age etchings that give a sense of the place in the 19th century (daily 10:00-12:30 & 13:00-17:30).

The seven-foot-tall carved stone immediately inside the door (marked *Flammensäule*)—a tombstone from a nearby Celtic grave—is from 400 years before Christ. There were people here long before the Romans...and this castle.

The sweeping castle history exhibit in the center of the room is well-described in English. The massive fortification was the only Rhineland castle to withstand Louis XIV's assault during the 17th century. At the far end of the room is a model reconstruction of the castle showing how much bigger it was before French Revolutionary troops destroyed it in the 18th century. Study this. Find where you are. (Hint: Look for the tall tower.) This was the living quarters of the original castle, which was only the smallest ring of buildings around the tiny central courtyard (13th century). The ramparts were added in the 14th century. By 1650, the fortress was largely complete. Since its destruction by the French in the late 18th century, it's had no military value. While no WWII bombs were wasted on this ruin, it served St. Goar as a stone quarry for generations. The basement of the museum shows the castle pharmacy and an exhibit of Rhine-region odds and ends, including tools, an 1830 loom, and photos of icebreaking on the Rhine. While once routine, icebreaking hasn't been necessary here since 1963.

• *Exit the museum and walk 30 yards directly out, slightly uphill into the castle courtyard, where you'll see a sign for the inner courtyard (*❹ Innenhof).

Medieval Castle Courtyard: Five hundred years ago, the entire castle encircled this courtyard. The place was self-sufficient and ready for a siege, with a bakery, pharmacy, herb garden, brewery, well (top of yard), and livestock. During peacetime, 300-600 people lived here; during a siege, there would be as many as 4,000. The walls were plastered and painted white. Bits of the original 13th-century plaster survive.

• *Continue through the courtyard under the* Erste Schildmauer *(first shield wall) sign, turn left, and walk straight to the two old wooden upright posts. Find the pyramid of stone catapult balls on your left.*

Castle Garden: Catapult balls like these were too expensive not to recycle—they'd be retrieved after any battle. Across from the balls is a well (❻ *Brunnen*)—essential for any castle during the age of sieges. Look in. Thirsty? The old posts are for the ceremonial baptizing of new members of the local trading league. While this guild goes back centuries, it's now a social club that fills this court with a huge wine party the third weekend of each September.

• *Climb uphill to the castle's highest point by walking along the cobbled path up past the high battery (❼ Hohe Batterie) to the castle's best viewpoint—up where the German flag waves (signed ❽ Uhrturm).*

Highest Castle Tower Lookout: Enjoy a great view of the river, the castle, and the forest. Remember, the fortress once covered five times the land it does today. Notice how the other castles (across the river) don't poke above the top of the Rhine canyon. That would make them easy for invading armies to see.

From this perch, survey the Rhine Valley, cut out of slate over millions of years by the river. The slate absorbs the heat of the sun, making the grapes grown here well-suited for wine. Today the slate is mined to provide roofing. Imagine St. Goar settling here 1,500 years ago, establishing a place where sailors—thankful to have survived the treacherous Loreley—would stop and pray. Imagine the frozen river of years past, when the ice would break up and boats would huddle in manmade harbors like the one below for protection. Consider the history of trade on this busy river—from the days when castles levied tolls on ships, to the days when boats would be hauled upstream with the help of riverside towpaths, to the 21st century when 300 ships a day move their cargo past St. Goar. And imagine this castle before the French destroyed it... when it was the mightiest structure on the river, filled with people and inspiring awe among all who passed.

• *Return to the catapult balls, walk downhill past the well and through the tunnel, veer left through the arch marked ❾ zu den Wehrgängen ("to the defense galleries"), and go down two flights of stairs. Turn left and step into the dark, covered passageway. From here, we'll begin a rectangular walk taking us completely around (counterclockwise) the perimeter of the castle.*

Covered Defense Galleries with "Minutemen" Holes: Soldiers—the castle's "minutemen"—had a short commute: defensive positions on the outside, home in the holes below on the left. Even though these living quarters were padded with straw, life was unpleasant.

• *Continue straight through the dark gallery, up the stairs, and to the corner of the castle, where you'll see a white painted arrow at eye level and a red signpost with the number ❿. Stand with your back to the arrow on the wall.*

Corner of Castle: Gape up. A three-story, half-timbered building originally rose beyond the highest stone fortification. The two stone tongues near the top just around the corner (to the right) supported the toilet. (Insert your own joke here.) Turn around and face the wall. The crossbow slits below the white arrow were once steeper. The bigger hole on the riverside was for hot pitch.

• *Follow that white arrow along the outside to the next corner. At the corner, turn left.*

Thoop...You're Dead: Look ahead at the smartly placed crossbow slit. While you're lying there, notice the stonework. The little round holes were for scaffolds used as they built up. They indicate this stonework is original. Notice also the fine stonework on the chutes. More boiling pitch...now you're toast, too.

• *Continue along the castle wall around the corner. Notice the stairs on the right, which lead down to the Small Mine Tunnels—if you'd like to visit them, see the "Optional Detour" on page 544. You'll rejoin this tour at the Prison.*

Otherwise, at the gray railing, look up the valley and uphill where the sprawling fort stretched. Below, just outside the wall, is land where attackers would gather. The mine tunnels are under there, waiting to blow up any attackers.

Keep going along the perimeter, jog left, go down five steps and into an open field, and walk toward the wooden bridge. The "old" wooden bridge is actually modern.

Dark Tunnel Detour: For a short detour through a castle tunnel, turn your back to the main castle (with the modern bridge to your left) and face the stone structure labeled ⓬ *Halsgraben.* (You'll exit in a few minutes at the high railing above the red *#12* sign.) Go 20 yards to the right, and enter the tunnel at the bottom, following the red *Grosser Minengang* sign. At the end of the short, big tunnel, take two steps up and walk eight level steps, turn left, and follow the long uphill ramp (this is where it's pitch-black). At the end, a spiral staircase takes you up to the high-railing opening you saw earlier, and then back to the courtyard.

• *When ready to leave this courtyard, angle left (under the red* zum Verliess *sign, before the bridge) through two arches and through the rough entry to the* ⓮ Verliess *(prison) on the left.*

Prison: This is one of six dungeons. You just walked through an entrance prisoners only dreamed of 400 years ago. They came and went through the little square hole in the ceiling. The holes in the walls supported timbers that thoughtfully gave as many as 15 residents something to sit on to keep them out of the filthy slop that gathered on the floor. Twice a day, they were given bread and water. Some prisoners actually survived longer than two years in here. While the town could torture and execute, the castle had permission only to imprison criminals in these dungeons. Consider this: According to town records, the two men who spent the most time down here—2.5 years each—died within three weeks of

RHINE VALLEY

regaining their freedom. Perhaps after a diet of bread and water, feasting on meat and wine was simply too much.

• *Continue through the next arch, under the white arrow, then turn left and walk 30 yards to the* ⓯ *Schlachthaus.*

Slaughterhouse: Any proper castle was prepared to survive a six-month siege. With 4,000 people, that's a lot of provisions. The cattle that lived within the walls were slaughtered in this room. The castle's mortar was congealed here (by packing all the organic waste from the kitchen into kegs and sealing it). Notice the drainage gutters. "Running water" came through from drains built into the walls (to keep the mortar dry and therefore strong...and less smelly).

• *Back outside, climb the modern stairs to the left (look for the* zum Ausgang *sign). A skinny, dark passage leads you into the...*

Big Cellar: This ⓰ *Grosser Keller* was a big pantry. When the castle was smaller, this was the original moat—you can see the rough lower parts of the wall. The original floor was 13 feet deeper. The drawbridge rested upon the stone nubs on the left. When the castle expanded, the moat became this cellar. Halfway up the walls on the entrance side of the room, square holes mark spots where timbers made a storage loft, perhaps filled with grain. In the back, an arch leads to the wine cellar (sometimes blocked off) where finer wine was kept. Part of a soldier's pay was wine... table wine. This wine was kept in a single 180,000-liter stone barrel (that's 47,550 gallons), which generally lasted about 18 months.

The count owned the surrounding farmland. Farmers got to keep 20 percent of their production. Later, in more liberal feudal times, the nobility let them keep 40 percent. Today, the German government leaves the workers with 60 percent...and provides a few more services.

• *You're free. Climb out, turn right, and leave. For coffee on a terrace with a great view, visit Schlosshotel Rheinfels, opposite the entrance.*

Optional Detour—Into the Small Mine Tunnels: Tall people might want to skip this foray into low, cramped tunnels (some only three feet high). In about 1600, to protect their castle, the Rheinfellers cleverly booby-trapped the land just outside their walls by building tunnels topped with thin slate roofs and packed with explosives. By detonating the explosives when under attack, they could kill hundreds of invaders. In 1626, a handful of underground Protestant Germans blew 300 Catholic Spaniards to—they figured—hell. You're welcome to wander through a set of never-blown-up tunnels. But be warned: It's 600 feet long, assuming you make no wrong turns; it's pitch-dark, muddy, and claustrophobic, with confusing dead-ends; and you'll never get higher than a deep crouch. It cannot be done without a light (candles available at entrance). Be sure to bring the castle map, which shows the tunnels in detail.

To tour the Small Mine Tunnels, start at the red ❿ signpost at the crossbow slits (described earlier). Follow the modern stairs on the right leading down to the mine (*zu den Minengängen* sign on upper left). The ⓫ *Fuchsloch* (foxhole) sign welcomes you to a covered passageway. Walk level (take no stairs) past the first black-steel railing (where you hope to emerge later) and around a few bends to the second steel railing. Climb down.

The "highway" in this foxhole is three feet high. The ceiling may be painted with a white line indicating the correct path. Don't venture into the narrower side aisles. These were once filled with the gunpowder. After a small decline, take the second right. At the T-intersection, go right (uphill). After about 10 feet, go left. Take the next right and look for a light at the end of the tunnel. Head up a rocky incline under the narrowest part of the tunnel, and you'll emerge at that first steel railing. The stairs on the right lead to freedom. Cross the field, walk under the bigger archway, and continue uphill toward the old wooden bridge. Angle left through two arches (before the bridge) and through the rough entry to the ⓮ *Verliess* (prison) on the left, where you can rejoin the self-guided tour.

Sleeping in St. Goar

(€1 = about $1.40, country code: 49, area code: 06741)
Parking in St. Goar is tight; ask at your hotel.

$$ Hotel am Markt, run by Herr and Frau Marx and their friendly staff, is rustic and a good deal, with all the modern comforts. It features a hint of antler with a pastel flair, 17 bright rooms, and a good restaurant. It's a good value and a stone's throw from the boat dock and train station (S-€40, Sb-€50, standard Db-€65, bigger riverview Db-€80, cheaper March-mid-April and Oct, closed Nov-Feb, free Internet access and Wi-Fi, parking-€4, Markt 1, tel. 06741/1689, fax 06741/1721, www.hotel-am-markt-sankt-goar.de, info@hotel-am-markt-sankt-goar.de).

$$ Rhein Hotel, two doors down from Hotel am Markt and run with enthusiasm by energetic Gil Velich, has 10 quality rooms in a spacious building and its own restaurant (Sb-€50, quiet view-less Db-€65, river-view balcony Db-€85-95, non-smoking, free Wi-Fi, laundry-€12/load, closed mid-Nov-Feb, Heerstrasse 71, tel. 06741/981-240, www.rheinhotel-st-goar.de, info@rheinhotel-st-goar.de).

$ Hotel Hauser, across the square from Hotel am Markt, is a very basic place with ramshackle halls and 12 tidy rooms (S-€23, D-€46, Db-€54, Db with Rhine-view balconies-€58, show this book and ask for Rick Steves price if paying with cash, flexible à la

RHINE VALLEY

carte half-pension-€14, free Wi-Fi, Heerstrasse 77, tel. 06741/333, fax 06741/1464, www.hotelhauser.de, info@hotelhauser.de).

$ Hotel an der Fähre is a simple, well-run place on the busy road at the end of town, immediately across from the ferry dock. It rents 12 cheap but decent rooms (D-€40, Db-€50, extra bed-€20, cash only, street noise but double-glazed windows, free Internet access, closed Nov-Feb, Heerstrasse 47, tel. 06741/980-577, www .hotel-stgoar.de, anderfaehre@t-online.de, Armin and Svetla Stecher).

$ Frau Kurz has been housing my readers since 1988. With the help of her daughter, Jeanette, she offers St. Goar's best B&B, renting three delightful rooms (sharing 2.5 bathrooms) with bathrobes, a breakfast terrace, garden, fine three-castle views, and homemade marmalade (S-€30, D-€52, 2-night minimum, D-€48 if you stay at least 4 nights, cash only, non-smoking, free and easy parking, ask about apartment with kitchen if staying at least 5 days, Ulmenhof 11, tel. 06741/459, www.gaestehaus-kurz.de, jeanette.kurz@superkabel.de). It's a steep five-minute hike from the train station: Exit left from the station, take an immediate left at the yellow phone booth, pass under the tracks, go up the stairs, and follow the zigzag path, turning right through an archway onto Ulmenhof; #11 is just past the tower.

$ St. Goar Hostel, the big beige building down the hill from the castle, rents 126 beds, mostly in 4- to 10-bed dorms but also in 18 doubles. The facilities hark back to an earlier age of hosteling, with shared baths down the hall (hence the low price), but it has Rhine views, a nice terrace, and hearty €6 dinners (dorm beds-€15, D-€36, includes breakfast, nonmembers-€3.10 extra, non-smoking, open all day, curfew 22:30—but you can borrow the key, reconfirm reservation by phone the day before, Bismarckweg 17, tel. 06741/388, fax 06741/2869, www.diejugendherbergen.de, st-goar@diejugendherbergen.de). It's a fairly level 10-minute walk from the train station, following the red *Jugendherberge* signs.

Eating in St. Goar

Hotel am Markt serves tasty traditional meals with plenty of game and fish (specialties include marinated roast beef and homemade cheesecake) at fair prices with good atmosphere and service. Choose cozy indoor seating, or dine outside with a river view (€9-15 main courses, March-Oct daily 8:00-21:00, closed Nov-Feb, Markt 1, tel. 06741/1689).

Burgschänke, on the ground floor of Schlosshotel Rheinfels (the hotel across from the castle ticket office—enter through the souvenir shop) offers the only reasonably priced lunches up at Rheinfels Castle. It's family-friendly and has a Rhine view from its fabulous outdoor terrace (€9-13 main courses, Sun-Thu 11:00-18:00, Fri-Sat 11:00-21:00, tel. 06741/802-806).

The **Schlosshotel Rheinfels** dining room is your Rhine splurge, with an incredible indoor view terrace in an elegant, dressy setting (€19-24 main courses, €32-36 three-course fixed-price meals, daily 7:00-11:00 & 12:00-14:15 & 18:30-21:15, call to reserve a window table, tel. 06741/8020).

Gasthaus Zur Krone is the local choice for traditional German food in a restaurant that has no river view and isn't part of a hotel (€7-10 main courses, Thu-Tue 18:00-21:00, closed Wed, next to the train station and church at Oberstrasse 38, tel. 06741/1515).

Ristorante Alla Fontana, tucked away on a back lane and busy with locals, serves the best Italian food in town at great prices in a lovely dining room (€7 pizza and pasta, Tue-Sun 11:30-14:00 & 17:30-22:00, closed Mon, reservations smart, Pumpengasse 5, 06741/96117).

Picnics: The grocery store (see "Helpful Hints," earlier) has plenty of goodies. You can assemble a picnic to enjoy at the riverside park or up at the castle.

RHINE VALLEY

BERLIN

No tour of Germany is complete without a look at its historic and reunited capital. Over the last two decades, Berlin has been a construction zone. Standing on ripped-up tracks and under a canopy of cranes, visitors witnessed the rebirth of a great European capital. Although construction continues, today the once-divided city is thoroughly woven back together. Berlin has emerged as one of Europe's top destinations: captivating, lively, fun-loving, all-around enjoyable—and easy on the budget.

As we enjoy the thrill of walking over what was the Wall and through the well-patched Brandenburg Gate, it's clear that history is not contained in some book, but is an exciting story of which we are a part. In Berlin, the fine line between history and current events is excitingly blurry. But even for non-historians, Berlin is a city of fine experiences. Explore the fun and funky neighborhoods emerging in the former East, packed with creative hipster eateries and boutiques trying to one-up each other. Go for a pedal or a cruise along the delightful Spree riverfront. In the city's world-class museums, stroll up the steps of a classical Greek temple amid rough-and-tumble ancient statuary, and peruse canvases by Dürer, Rembrandt, and Vermeer. Nurse a stein of brew in a rollicking beer hall, or dive into a cheap *Currywurst* (grilled bratwurst with curry-infused ketchup, arguably the most beloved food ever to come out of Berlin).

Of course, Berlin is still largely defined by its tumultuous 20th century. The city was Hitler's capital during World War II, and in the postwar years, Berlin became the front line of a new global war—one between Soviet-style communism and American-style capitalism. The East-West division was set in stone in 1961,

Berlin Sightseeing Modules

To Sachsenhausen

Spree River

EASTERN BERLIN

German Hist. Museum
Museum Island
TV Tower
New Synagogue
Prenzlauer Berg
Berlin Wall Memorial

Reichstag
Brandenburg Gate
Memorial to Murdered Jews
Hauptbahnhof

UNTER DEN LINDEN

Checkpoint Charlie
Gendarmenmarkt
Jewish Museum
Topography of Terror

To Potsdam

Bus 100

KU' DAMM

CENTRAL BERLIN

Tiergarten Park
Potsdamer Platz
Kulturforum
Gemaldegalerie

WESTERN BERLIN

Zoo Station
Savignyplatz
Hotel Area
KaDeWe Dep't Store

BERLIN

when the East German government boxed in West Berlin with the Berlin Wall. The Wall stood for 28 years. In 1990, less than a year after the Wall fell, the two Germanys—and the two Berlins—officially became one. When the dust settled, Berliners from both sides of the once-divided city faced the monumental challenge of reunification.

Berliners joke that they don't need to go anywhere because their city's always changing. Spin a postcard rack to see what's new. A 10-year-old guidebook on Berlin covers a different city. City planners have seized on the city's reunification and the return of the national government to make Berlin a great capital once again. When the Wall fell, the East was a decrepit wasteland and the West was a paragon of commerce and materialism. More than 20 years later, the roles are reversed: It is the East that feels the vibrant pulse of the city, while the West seems like yesterday's news.

Today, Berlin is like the nuclear fuel rod of a great nation. It's so vibrant with youth, energy, and an anything-goes-and-anything's-possible buzz that Munich feels spent in comparison. Berlin is both extremely popular and surprisingly affordable. As a booming tourist attraction, Berlin welcomes more visitors than Rome.

Planning Your Time

I'd give Berlin three nights and at least two full days, and spend them this way:

Berlin

- - - - Course of Former Wall
⊢●⊣ Elevated S-Bahn Line & Station

½ Mile
1 Kilometers

CHARLOTTENBURG PALACE

Spree River

VICTORY COLUMN

CHARLOTTENBURG

Ernst-Reuter-Platz

STRASSE   DES

17

BISMARCKSTR.

Tiergarten

BAHNHOF ZOO

Savigny-Platz

ZOO

KULTUR FORUM

HARD

KANTSTR.

EUROPA CENTER

Witt.-platz

GERMAN RESISTANCE MUSEUM

KU' DAMM

MEMORIAL CHURCH

KUFÜRSTENSTR

KLEISTRTR.

LIETZEN- STR.

KaDeWe STORE

KOLLWITZ MUSEUM

DCH

BERLIN

Day 1: Begin your day getting oriented to this huge city. For a quick and relaxing once-over-lightly tour, jump on one of the many hop-on, hop-off buses that make a two-hour narrated orientation loop through the city. Use the bus as you like, to hop off and on at places of interest (such as Potsdamer Platz). Then walk from the Reichstag (reservations required), under the Brandenburg Gate, and down Unter den Linden. Tour the German History Museum, and cap your sightseeing day by catching the one-hour Spree River boat tour (or pedaling a rented bike) along the parklike banks of the Spree River from Museum Island to the Chancellery.

Day 2: Spend your morning touring the great museums on Museum Island (Pergamon Museum and the Egyptian collection at the Neues Museum—timed-entry tickets required for both, and Romantic German art in the Old National Gallery). Dedicate your afternoon to sights of the Third Reich and Holocaust: After lunch, hike via Potsdamer Platz to the Topography of Terror exhibit and along the surviving Zimmerstrasse stretch of the Wall to the Museum of the Wall at Checkpoint Charlie. You could also head up to the Berlin Wall Memorial for a more in-depth survey of that infamous barrier, or swing by the Jewish Museum. Finish your day in the lively East—ideally in the once glum, then edgy, now fun-loving and trendy Prenzlauer Berg district.

Orientation to Berlin

(area code: 030)

Berlin is huge, with 3.4 million people. The city is spread out and its sights numerous, so you'll need to be well-organized to experience the city smartly. The tourist's Berlin can be broken into three main digestible chunks:

1. Eastern Berlin has the highest concentration of notable sights and colorful neighborhoods. Near the landmark Brandenburg Gate, you'll find the Reichstag building, Pariser Platz, and the Memorial to the Murdered Jews of Europe. From Brandenburg Gate, the famous Unter den Linden boulevard runs eastward through former East Berlin, passing the German History Museum (a history lover's favorite) and Museum Island (Pergamon Museum, Neues Museum, and Berlin Cathedral) on the way to Alexanderplatz (TV Tower). The intersection of Unter den Linden and Friedrichstrasse has reclaimed its place as the center of the city. South of Unter den Linden are the delightful Gendarmenmarkt square, most Nazi sites (including the Topography of Terror), some good Wall-related sights (Museum of the Wall at Checkpoint Charlie and East Side Gallery), the Jewish Museum, and the colorful Turkish neighborhood of Kreuzberg. North of Unter den Linden are these worth-a-wander neighborhoods: Oranienburger Strasse (Jewish Quarter and New Synagogue), Hackescher Markt, and Prenzlauer Berg (several recommended hotels and a very lively restaurant/nightlife zone). Just west of Prenzlauer Berg is the Berlin Wall Memorial (with an intact surviving section of the Wall). Eastern Berlin's pedestrian-friendly Spree riverbank is also worth a stroll (or a river cruise).

2. Central Berlin is dominated by the giant Tiergarten park. South of the park are Potsdamer Platz and the Kulturforum museum cluster (including the Gemäldegalerie, New National Gallery, Musical Instruments Museum, and Philharmonic Concert Hall). To the north, the huge Hauptbahnhof (main train station) straddles the former Wall in what was central Berlin's no-man's-land.

3. Western Berlin centers on the Bahnhof Zoo (Zoo train station, often marked "Zoologischer Garten" on transit maps) and the grand Kurfürstendamm boulevard, nicknamed "Ku'damm" (transportation hub, tours, information, shopping, and recommended hotels). The East is all the rage. But the West, while staid in comparison, is bouncing back—with big-name stores and destination restaurants that keep the area buzzing. During the Cold War, this "Western Sector" was the hub for Western visitors. Capitalists visited the West, with a nervous side-trip beyond the Wall into the grim and foreboding East. (Cubans, Russians, Poles, and Angolans stayed behind the Wall and did their sightseeing in the East.) Remnants of this Iron Curtain-era Western focus have left today's visitors with a stronger focus on the Ku'damm and Bahnhof Zoo than the district deserves.

Tourist Information

With any luck, you won't have to use Berlin's TIs—they're for-profit agencies working for the city's big hotels, which colors the information they provide. TI branches, appropriately called "info-stores," are unlikely to have the information you need (tel. 030/250-025, www.visitberlin.de). You'll find them at the **Hauptbahnhof** train station (daily 8:00-22:00, by main entrance on Europaplatz), **Ku'damm** (Kurfürstendamm 22, in the glass-and-steel Neues Kranzler Eck building, daily 9:30-20:00), and the **Brandenburg Gate** (daily 9:30-19:00, until 18:30 Nov-March).

Skip the TI's €1 map, and instead pick up any of the walking tour companies' brochures—they include nearly-as-good maps for free (most hotels also provide free city maps). While the TI does sell the three-day Museumspass (described next), it's also available at major museums. If you take a walking tour, your guide is likely a better source of nightlife or shopping tips than the TI.

Museum Passes: The three-day, €19 **Museumspass** is a great value. It gets you into more than 50 museums, including the national museums and most of the recommended biggies, on three consecutive days. As you'll routinely spend €6-10 per admission, this pays for itself in a hurry. And you'll enjoy the ease of popping in and out of museums that you might not otherwise want to pay for. Buy it at the TI or any participating museum. The pass generally lets you skip the line and go directly into the museum (though occasionally you may have to wait in line to get a printed free ticket). The €16 **Museum Island Pass** (Bereichskarte Museumsinsel, price can change with special exhibits) covers all the museums on Museum Island (otherwise €8-12 each) and is a fine value—but for just €3 more, the three-day Museumspass gives you triple the days and many more entries. TIs also sell the **WelcomeCard,** a transportation pass that also includes some museum discounts (described later, under "Getting Around Berlin").

Local Publications: Various magazines can help make your time in Berlin more productive (available at the TI and/or many newsstands). *Berlin Programm* is a comprehensive German-language monthly, especially strong in high culture, that lists upcoming events and museum hours (€2, www.berlin-programm .de). *Exberliner Magazine,* the only English monthly (published mostly by expat Brits who love to poke fun at expat Americans), is very helpful for curious travelers. It has an edgy, somewhat pretentious, youthful focus and gives a fascinating insider's look at this fast-changing city (€2.50 but often given away at theaters or on the street, www.exberliner.com).

Arrival in Berlin
By Train at Berlin Hauptbahnhof
Berlin's newest and grandest train station is Berlin Hauptbahnhof (main train station, a.k.a. simply "der Bahnhof", abbreviated Hbf). All long-distance trains arrive here, at Europe's biggest, mostly underground train station. This is a "transfer station"—unique for its major lines coming in at right angles—where the national train system meets the city's train system (S-Bahn).

The gigantic station can be intimidating on arrival, but it's laid out logically on five floors (which, confusingly, can be marked in different ways). Escalators and elevators connect the **main floor** (*Erdgeschoss,* EG, a.k.a level 0); the two **lower levels** (*Untergeschoss,* UG1 and UG2, a.k.a. levels -1 and -2); and the two **upper levels** (*Obergeschoss,* OG1 and OG2, a.k.a. levels +1 and +2). Tracks 1-8 are in the lowest underground level (UG2), while tracks 11-16 (along with the S-Bahn) are on the top floor (OG2). Shops and services are concentrated on the three middle levels (EG, OG1, and UG1). The south entrance (toward the Reichstag and downtown, with a taxi stand and the stop for bus #TXL to Tegel Airport) is marked *Washingtonplatz*, while the north entrance is marked *Europaplatz*.

Services: You can store your **luggage** at the Gepäck Center, an efficient and secure deposit service (€5/day per bag, daily 6:00-22:00, on upper level OG1 directly under track 14). Luggage lockers (€4) are difficult to find since they're in the parking garage (levels P-1, P-2, and P-3; look for the garage entrance near Kaisers supermarket on the underground shopping level UG1). The **TI** is on the main floor (EG)—facing the north/*Europaplatz* entrance, look left; a 24-hour **pharmacy** is across the hall on the right (one floor above you, on OG1). The **WC Center** (public pay toilets) is on the main floor (EG) near the Burger King and food court.

Train Information and Tickets: The station has two DeutscheBahn *Reisezentrum* information counters: one on the upper level (OG1/+1, daily 6:00-22:00), and the other on the lower level (UG1/-1, daily 8:00-22:00; this branch also has the EurAide counter described next). If you're staying in western Berlin, keep in mind that the info center at the Bahnhof Zoo station is just as good and much less crowded.

EurAide is an English-speaking information desk with answers to your questions about train travel around Europe. It operates from a single counter in the underground shopping level *Reisezentrum* (follow signs to tracks 5-6 and *Reisezentrum -1*). It's American-run, so communication is simple. This is an especially good place to make fast-train and *couchette* reservations for later in your trip (May-July Mon-Fri 10:00-20:00, Sun 14:00-20:00, closed Sat; Aug Mon-Fri 11:00-20:00, Sun 14:00-20:00, closed Sat; Sept-April Mon-Fri 11:00-19:00, closed Sat-Sun; www.euraide.com).

Shopping: In addition to all those trains, the Hauptbahnhof is also the home of 80 shops with long hours—some locals call the station a "shopping mall with trains" (daily 8:00-22:00, only stores selling travel provisions are open Sun). The Kaisers supermarket (on underground shopping level UG1, follow signs for tracks 1-2) is handy for assembling a picnic for your train ride.

Getting into Town: Taxis and buses wait outside the station, but the S-Bahn is probably the best means of connecting to your destination within Berlin. The cross-town express S-Bahn line connects the station with my recommended hotels in a few minutes. It's simple: All S-Bahn trains are on tracks 15 and 16 at the top of the station (level OG2/+2). All trains on track 15 go east, stopping at Friedrichstrasse, Hackescher Markt (with connections to Prenzlauer Berg), Alexanderplatz, and Ostbahnhof; trains on track 16 go west, toward Bahnhof Zoo and Savignyplatz. Your train ticket or railpass into the station covers your connecting S-Bahn ride into town (and your ticket out includes the transfer via S-Bahn to the Hauptbahnhof). U-Bahn rides are not covered by tickets or railpasses.

If you're sleeping at one of my recommended hotels in eastern Berlin's Prenzlauer Berg neighborhood, take any train on track 15 two stops to Hackescher Markt, then catch tram #M1 north (see map on page 624).

If you're sleeping at one of my recommended hotels in western Berlin, catch any train on track 16 to Savignyplatz, and you're a five-minute walk from your hotel (see map on page 630). Savignyplatz is one stop after **Bahnhof Zoo** (rhymes with "toe"; a.k.a. Bahnhof Zoologischer Garten), the once-grand train hub now eclipsed by the Hauptbahnhof. Nowadays Bahnhof Zoo is useful mainly for its shops, uncrowded train-information desk, and BVG transit office (outside the entrance, amid the traffic).

The Berlin Hauptbahnhof is not well-connected to the city's U-Bahn (subway) system—yet. The station's sole U-Bahn line—U55—goes only two stops, to the Brandenburger Tor station, and doesn't really connect to the rest of the system. It's part of a planned extension of the U5 line to Alexanderplatz that's far from completion. But for transit junkies, it is an interesting ride on Europe's newest and shortest subway line.

By Plane
For information on reaching the city center from Berlin's airports, see "Berlin Connections" at the end of this chapter.

Helpful Hints
Medical Help: "Call a doc" is a nonprofit referral service designed for tourists (tel. 01805-321-303, phone answered 24 hours a day, www.calladoc.com). Payment is arranged between you and the doctor, and is likely far more affordable than similar care in the US. The US Embassy also has a list of local English-speaking doctors (tel. 030/83050, www.us embassy.de).

Museum Tips: Some major Berlin museums are closed on Monday—if you're in town on that day, review hours carefully before making plans. If you plan to see several museums, you'll save money with the €19 Museumspass, which covers nearly all the city sights for three days—including everything covered by the one-day €16 Museum Island Pass (see "Tourist Information—Museum Passes," earlier).

Addresses: Many Berlin streets are numbered with odd and even

numbers on the same side of the street, often with no connection to the other side (for example, Ku'damm #212 can
be across the street from #14). To save steps, check the white
street signs on curb corners; many list the street numbers covered on that side of the block.

Cold War Terminology: Cold War history is important here, so
it's helpful to learn a few key terms. What Americans called
"East Germany" was technically the German Democratic
Republic—known here by its German name, the Deutsche
Demokratische Republik. The initials **DDR** (day-day-AIR)
are the shorthand you'll still see around what was once
East Germany. The formal name for "West Germany" was
the Federal Republic of Germany—the Bundesrepublik
Deutschland (BRD)—and is the name now shared by all of
reunited Germany.

Internet Access: You'll find Internet access in most hotels and
hostels, as well as at small Internet cafés all over the city.
Near Savignyplatz, **Internet-Terminal** is at Kantstrasse 38.
In eastern Berlin, try **Hotdog World** in Prenzlauer Berg
(Weinbergsweg 4, just a few steps from U8: Rosenthaler
Platz toward Kastanienallee), or **Surf Inn** at Alexanderplatz
9. Bahnhof Zoo, Friedrichstrasse, and Hauptbahnhof train
stations have coin-operated Internet terminals (though these
unmanned machines can come with greater security risks).

Bookstore: Berlin Story, a big, cluttered, fun bookshop, has a
knowledgeable staff and the best selection anywhere in town of
English-language books on Berlin. They also stock an amusing
mix of knickknacks and East Berlin nostalgia souvenirs (daily
10:00-20:00, Unter den Linden 40, tel. 030/2045-3842, www
.berlinstory.de). I'd skip the overpriced little museum in back.

Other Berlin Souvenirs: If you're taken with the city's unofficial mascot, the *Ampelmännchen* (traffic-light man), you'll find
a world of souvenirs slathered with his iconic red and green
image at **Ampelmann Shops** (various locations, including
near Gendarmenmarkt at Markgrafenstrasse 37, near Museum
Island inside the DomAquarée mall, in the Hackeschen Höfe,
and at Potsdamer Platz).

Laundry: Berlin has several self-service launderettes with long
hours (wash and dry-€4-9/load). Near my recommended
hotels in Prenzlauer Berg, try **Waschsalon 115** (daily 6:00-
23:00, exact change required, free Wi-Fi, Torstrasse 115,
around the corner from the recommended Circus hostel) or
Eco-Express Waschsalon (daily 6:00-23:00, handy pizzeria next door, Danziger Strasse 7). The **Schnell & Sauber
Waschcenter** chain has a location in Prenzlauer Berg (daily
6:00-23:00, exact change required, Oderberger Strasse 1).

Getting Around Berlin

Berlin's sights spread far and wide. Right from the start, commit yourself to the city's fine public-transit system.

By Public Transit: Subway, Train, Tram, and Bus

Berlin's many modes of transportation are consolidated into one system that uses the same ticket: U-Bahn (*Untergrund-Bahn*, Berlin's subway), S-Bahn (*Stadtschnellbahn*, or "fast urban train," mostly aboveground and with fewer stops), *Strassenbahn* (street-cars, called "trams" by locals), and buses. For all types of transit, there are three lettered zones (A, B, and C); all of the sights listed in this chapter lie within zones A and B (the city proper). If you'll be here for a few days, get and use the excellent *Discover Berlin by Train and Bus* map-guide published by the public transit operator BVG (at subway ticket windows).

Ticket Options: You have several options for tickets.

• The €2.30 **basic** ticket *(Einzelfahrschein)* covers two hours of travel in one direction on buses or subways. It's easy to make this ticket stretch to cover several rides...as long as they're all in the same direction.

• The €1.40 **short-ride** ticket *(Kurzstrecke)* covers a single ride of six bus stops or three subway stations (one transfer allowed).

• The €8.20 **four-trip** ticket *(4-Fahrten-Karte)* is the same as four basic tickets at a small discount.

• The **day pass** *(Tageskarte)* is good until 3:00 the morning after it expires (€6.30 for zones AB). For longer stays, consider a seven-day pass (*Sieben-Tage-Karte;* €27.20 for zones AB), or the WelcomeCard (described below), which is good for up to five days and also includes sightseeing discounts. The *Kleingruppenkarte* lets groups of up to five travel all day (€15 for zones AB).

• If you've already bought a ticket for zones A and B, and later decide that you also want to go to zone C, you can buy an "**extension ticket**" *(Anschlussfahrschein)* for €1.50 per ride in that zone.

• If you plan to cover a lot of ground using public transportation during a two- or three-day visit, the **WelcomeCard** (available at TIs) is usually the best deal. For longer stays, there's even a five-day option. It covers all public transportation and gives you up to 50 percent discounts on lots of minor and a few major museums (including Checkpoint Charlie), sightseeing tours (including 25 percent off the recommended Original Berlin Walks), and music and theater events (www.visitberlin.de/welcomecard). The Berlin-only option covers transit zones AB (€16.90/48 hours, €22.90/72 hours). If you're a museum junkie, consider the **WelcomeCard+Museumsinsel** (€34/72 hours), which combines travel in zones A and B with unlimited access to the five museums on Museum Island. Families get an extra price break: The ABC version (€36/72 hours) is valid for one adult and up to three kids younger than 15.

Buying Tickets: You can buy U- and S-Bahn tickets from machines at stations. (They are also sold at BVG pavilions at train stations, airports, and the TI, and on board trams and buses—drivers give change.) *Erwachsener* means "adult"—anyone 14 or older. Don't be afraid of the automated machines: First select the type of ticket you want, then load the coins or paper bills. As you board the bus or tram, or enter the subway system, punch your ticket in a red or yellow clock machine to validate it (or risk a €40 fine; for an all-day or multiday pass, stamp it only the first time you ride). Be sure to travel with a valid ticket. Tickets are checked frequently, often by plainclothes inspectors. Within Berlin, Eurail Passes are good only on S-Bahn connections from the train station when you arrive and to the station when you depart.

Transit Tips: The S-Bahn crosstown express is a river of public transit through the heart of the city, in which many lines converge on one basic highway. Get used to this, and you'll leap within a few minutes between key locations: Savignyplatz (hotels), Bahnhof Zoo (Ku'damm, bus #100), Hauptbahnhof (all major trains in and out of Berlin), Friedrichstrasse (a short walk north of the heart of Unter den Linden), Hackescher Markt (Museum Island, restaurants, nightlife, connection to Prenzlauer Berg hotels and eateries), and Alexanderplatz (eastern end of Unter den Linden).

Sections of the U- or S-Bahn sometimes close temporarily for repairs. In this situation, a bus route often replaces the train (*Ersatzverkehr,* or "replacement transportation"; *zwischen* means "between").

Berlin's public transit is operated by BVG (except the S-Bahn, run by DeutscheBahn). Schedules, including bus timetables, are available on the helpful BVG website (www.bvg.de).

By Taxi

Taxis are easy to flag down, and taxi stands are common. A typical ride within town costs €8-10, and a crosstown trip (for example, Bahnhof Zoo to Alexanderplatz) will run about €15. Tariff 1 is for a *Kurzstrecke* (see below). All other rides are tariff 2 (€3.20 drop plus €1.60/kilometer). If possible, use cash—paying with a credit card comes with a hefty surcharge (about €4, regardless of the fare).

Money-Saving Taxi Tip: For any ride of less than two kilometers (about a mile), you can save several euros if you take advantage of the ***Kurzstrecke*** (short-stretch) rate. To get this rate, it's important that you flag the cab down on the street—not at or even near a taxi stand. Also, you must ask for the *Kurzstrecke* rate as soon as you hop in: Confidently say *"Kurzstrecke, bitte"* (KOORTSshtreh-keh, BIT-teh), and your driver will grumble and flip the meter to a fixed €4 rate (for a ride that would otherwise cost €7).

By Bike

Flat Berlin is a very bike-friendly city, but be careful—Berlin's motorists don't brake for bicyclists (and bicyclists don't brake for pedestrians). Fortunately, some roads and sidewalks have special red-painted bike lanes. Don't ride on the regular sidewalk—it's *verboten*. Good bike shops can suggest a specific route.

Fat Tire Bikes rents good bikes at two handy locations— East (at the base of the TV Tower near Alexanderplatz—facing the entrance to the tower, go around to the right) and West (at Bahnhof Zoo—leaving the station onto Hardenbergplatz, turn left and walk 100 yards to the big bike sign). Both locations have the same hours and rates (€7/4 hours, €12/day, daily May-Sept 9:30-20:00, March-April and Oct-Nov 9:30-18:00, shorter hours or by appointment only Dec-Feb, leave ID, tel. 030/2404-7991, www.berlinbikerental.com).

In eastern Berlin, **Take a Bike** near the Friedrichstrasse S-Bahn station is owned by a lovely Dutch-German couple who know a lot about bikes and have a huge inventory. They can help you find the perfect fit (3-gear bikes: €12.50/day, €19/2 days; more for better bikes, slightly cheaper for longer rentals; electric bikes- €29/day, helmets, daily 9:30-19:00, Neustädtische Kirchstrasse 8, tel. 030/2065-4730, info@takeabike.de). To find it, leave the S-Bahn station via the Friedrichstrasse exit, turn right, go through a triangle-shaped square, and hang a left on Neustädtische Kirchstrasse.

Tours in Berlin

▲▲▲Hop-on, Hop-off Bus Tours

Several companies offer the same routine: a €15 circuit of the city with unlimited hop-on, hop-off privileges all day (about 14 stops at the city's major sights) on buses with cursory narration in English and German by a live (but tired) guide or a boring recorded commentary in whatever language you want to dial up. In season, each company has buses running four times per hour. They are cheap and great for photography—and Berlin really lends itself to this kind of bus-tour orientation. You can hop off at any major tourist spot (Potsdamer Platz, Museum Island, Brandenburg Gate, the Kaiser Wilhelm Memorial Church, and so on). Go with a live guide rather than the recorded spiel (so you get a few current asides). When choosing seats, check the sun/shade situation— some buses are entirely topless, and others are entirely covered. My favorites are topless with a shaded covered section in the back

(April-Oct daily 10:00-18:00, last bus leaves all stops at 16:00, 2-hour loop; for specifics, look for brochures in your hotel lobby or at the TI). Keep your ticket so you can hop off and on (with the same company) all day. In winter (Nov-March), buses come only twice an hour, and the last departure is at 15:00. Brochures explain extras offered by each company.

Other Bus Tours

City Bus #100—For do-it-yourselfers, Berlin's city bus #100 is a great alternative to the commercial hop-on, hop-off bus tours—and you can follow along with my self-guided bus tour on page 563.

Full-Blown Bus Tours—**Severin & Kühn** offers a long list of bus tours (not hop-on, hop-off) in and around Berlin; their three-hour "Berlin Classic Live" tour is a good introduction (€19, daily at 10:00, Fri-Sun also at 14:00, live guides in two languages, interesting historical photos displayed on bus monitors, departs from Ku'damm 216, buy ticket at bus, tel. 030/880-4190, www.berliner stadtrundfahrten.de).

▲▲▲Walking Tours

Berlin, with a fascinating recent history that can be challenging to appreciate on your own, is an ideal place to explore with a walking tour. The city is a battle zone of extremely competitive and creative walking-tour companies. Unlike many other European countries, Germany has no regulations controlling who can give city tours. This can make guide quality hit-or-miss, ranging from brilliant history buffs who've lived in Berlin for years while pursuing their PhDs, to new arrivals who memorize a script and start leading tours after being in town for just a couple of weeks. A good Berlin tour guide is equal parts historian and entertainer; the best tours make the city's dynamic story come to life. While upstart companies abound, in general you have the best odds of landing a great guide by using one of the more established companies I recommend in this section.

Most outfits offer walks that are variations on the same themes: general **introductory** walk, **Third Reich** walk (Hitler and Nazi sites), and day trips to **Potsdam** and the **Sachsenhausen Concentration Camp Memorial**. Most tours cost about €12-15 and last about three to four hours (longer for the side-trips to Potsdam and Sachsenhausen); public-transit tickets and entrances to sights are extra. I've included some basic descriptions for each company, but for details—including prices and specific schedules—see the various websites or look for brochures in town (widely available at TIs, hotel reception desks, and many cafés and shops).

Original Berlin Walks—This well-established operation offers tours aimed at a clientele that's curious about the city's history.

Their flagship introductory walk, Discover Berlin, offers a good overview in four hours (daily year-round, meet at 10:00 at Bahnhof Zoo, April-Oct also daily at 13:30). They offer a Third Reich walking tour (4/week in summer) tours to Potsdam and Sachsenhausen, and themed Jewish Life in Berlin and Nest of Spies walks (both 1/week April-Oct only). Ask about a discount with this book. You can buy tickets in advance at any S-Bahn service center, or just show up and buy a ticket from the guide. All tours meet at the taxi stand in front of the Bahnhof Zoo train station; the Discover Berlin, Jewish Life, and Sachsenhausen tours also have a second departure point opposite East Berlin's Hackescher Markt S-Bahn station, outside the Weihenstephaner restaurant (tour info: tel. 030/301-9194, www.berlinwalks.de, info@berlinwalks.de).

Vive Berlin—This "guiding collective" was formed by some of the city's most experienced guides. They offer the usual lineup, with an introductory walk (Essential Berlin—Mon, Wed, and Fri-Sat at 10:00; Sun at 13:00), plus Third Reich, Potsdam, and Sachsenhausen itineraries, and a walk through East Berlin. All tours meet at Potsdamer Platz 10, in front of Balzac Coffee (U2/S-Bahn: Potsdamer Platz, use Stresemannstrasse exit; tel. 0157/845-46696, www.viveberlintours.de).

Insider Tour—This well-regarded company runs the full gamut of itineraries: introductory walk (daily), Third Reich, Cold War, Jewish Berlin, Sachsenhausen, and Potsdam, as well as bike tours, pub crawls, and a day trip to Dresden. Their tours have two meeting points (some tours convene at both, others at just one—check the schedule): in the West at the McDonald's across from Bahnhof Zoo, and in the East at AMT Coffee at the Hackescher Markt S-Bahn station (www.insidertour.com, tel. 030/692-3149).

Brewer's Berlin Tours—Specializing in longer, more in-depth walks, this company was started by Terry Brewer, who retired from the British diplomatic service in East Berlin. Today Terry's guides lead exhaustive—or, for some, exhausting—tours through the city (their Best of Berlin introductory tour, billed at 6 hours, can last 8 hours or more; daily at 10:30). Terry himself (who can be a bit gruff) leads a "six-hour" tour to some off-the-beaten-path hidden gems of Berlin twice weekly. They also do all-day Potsdam tours. Their tours depart from Bandy Brooks ice cream shop at the Friedrichstrasse S-Bahn station (tel. 030/2248-7435, mobile 0177-388-1537, www.brewersberlintours.com).

Sandeman's New Europe Berlin "Free" Tours—You'll see this company advertising supposedly "free" introductory tours, plus paid itineraries similar to those offered by competitors. But Sandeman's tours aren't really free—just misleading. Guides for the "free" tours pay the company a cut of €3 per person, so they hustle for tips. They expect to be "tipped in paper" (i.e., €5 minimum

BERLIN

tip per person). This business model leads to high guide turnover, meaning that the guides are, overall, less experienced (though some are quite entertaining). They offer the standard Berlin itineraries, but target a younger crowd. Basic introductory city walks leave daily at 11:00, 13:00, and 16:00 from outside the Deutsche Bank near Bahnhof Zoo. Paid tours include a wildly popular €12 pub crawl (nightly; for more info, see page 622) and an excellent Alternative Berlin tour, which explores Berlin's gritty counterculture, squats, and urban life (€12, daily at 14:00; tel. 030/5105-0030, www.newberlintours.com).

Berlin Underground Association (Berliner Unterwelten Verein)—Much of Berlin's history lies beneath the surface, and this group has an exclusive agreement with the city to explore and research what is hidden underground. Their one-of-a-kind **Dark Worlds** tour of a WWII air-raid bunker features a chilling explanation of the air war over Berlin (Wed-Mon at 11:00, also Mon at 13:00). The **From Flak Towers to Mountains of Debris** tour enters the Humboldthain air defense tower (April-Oct Thu, Sat, and Sun at 16:00). The **Subways, Bunkers, Cold War** tour visits a completely stocked and fully functional nuclear emergency bunker in former West Berlin (Tue-Sun at 13:00, also Tue at 11:00; each tour costs €10; meet in the hall of the Gesundbrunnen U-Bahn/S-Bahn station, follow signs to *Humboldthain/Brunnenstrasse* exit and walk up the stairs to their office, tel. 030/4991-0517, www .berliner-unterwelten.de).

Local Guides—Both **Nick Jackson** (from the Berlin Underground Association, mobile 0176-633-64975, nick.jackson@berlin.de) and **Lee Evans** (my longtime helper in Berlin, mobile 0177-423-5307, lee.evans@berlin.de) enjoy sharing the story of their adopted hometown with visitors. If they are busy, try **Jennifer DeShirley** at Berlin and Beyond—this company has a crew of excellent, professional guides with an academic bent (tel. 030/8733-0584, mobile 0176-633-55565, info@berlinandbeyond.de).

Bike Tours

Fat Tire Bike Tours—Choose among three different four-hour, six-mile tours (€22 each): City Tour (March-Nov daily at 11:00, May-Sept also daily at 16:00, Dec-Feb Wed and Sat at 11:00), Berlin Wall Tour (April-Oct Mon, Thu, and Sat at 10:30), and Third Reich Tour (April-Oct Wed, Fri, and Sun at 10:30). For any tour, meet at the TV Tower at Alexanderplatz—but don't get distracted by the Russians pretending to be Fat Tire (reserve ahead for the Wall or Third Reich tours, no reservations necessary for City Tour, tel. 030/2404-7991, www.fattirebiketours.com, berlin @fattirebiketours.com).

Boat Tours

Spree River Cruises—Several boat companies offer one-hour, €10 trips up and down the river. A relaxing hour on one of these boats can be time and money well-spent. You'll listen to excellent English audioguides, see lots of wonderful new government-commissioned architecture, and enjoy the lively park action fronting the river. Boats leave from various docks that cluster near the bridge at the Berlin Cathedral (just off Unter den Linden). I enjoyed the Historical Sightseeing Cruise from **Stern und Kreisschiffahrt** (mid-March-Nov daily 10:30-18:30, leaves from Nikolaiviertel Dock—cross bridge from Berlin Cathedral toward Alexanderplatz and look right, tel. 030/536-3600, www.sternund kreis.de). Confirm that the boat you choose comes with English commentary.

Self-Guided Bus Tour

Bus #100 from Bahnhof Zoo to Alexanderplatz

While hop-on, hop-off bus tours are a great value, Berlin's city bus #100 laces together the major sights in a kind of poor man's bus tour. Bus #100 stops at Bahnhof Zoo, the Victory Column, Reichstag, Unter den Linden, Brandenburg Gate, Pergamon Museum, and Alexanderplatz. A reader board inside the bus displays the upcoming stop. A basic €2.10 bus ticket is good for two hours of travel in one direction, and buses leave every few minutes.

Starting in the West from Bahnhof Zoo, here's a quick review of what you'll see: Leaving the train station, on your left and straight ahead, you'll spot the bombed-out hulk of the **Kaiser Wilhelm Memorial Church,** with its postwar sister church (described on page 617). Then, on the left, the elephant gates mark the entrance to the venerable and much-loved **Berlin Zoo** (see page 619) and its aquarium. After a left turn, you cross the canal and pass Berlin's **embassy row.** The first interesting embassy is Mexico's, with columns that seem to move when you're driving by (how do they do that?). The big turquoise wall marks the communal home of all five Nordic embassies. This building is very "green," run entirely on solar power.

The bus then enters the 400-acre **Tiergarten** park, packed with cycling paths, joggers, and—on hot days—nude sunbathers. Straight ahead, the **Victory Column** (Siegessäule; with the gilded angel, described on page 608), towers above this vast city park that was once a royal hunting grounds. A block beyond the Victory Column (on the left) is the 18th-century late-Rococo **Bellevue Palace.** Formerly the official residence of the Prussian (and later

German) crown prince, and at one time a Nazi VIP guest house, it's now the residence of the federal president (whose power is mostly ceremonial—the chancellor wields the real clout). If the flag's out, he's in.

Driving along the Spree River (on the left), you'll see buildings of the **national government.** The huge brick "brown snake" complex (across the river) was built to house government workers—but it didn't sell, so now its apartments are available to anyone. A metal Henry Moore sculpture titled *Butterfly* (a.k.a. "The Drinker's Liver") floats in front of the slope-roofed House of World Cultures (Berliners have nicknamed this building "the pregnant oyster" and "Jimmy Carter's smile"). The modern tower (next, on the left) is a carillon with 68 bells (from 1987). Through the trees on the left you'll see Germany's **Chancellery**—essentially Germany's White House. The big open space is the **Platz der Republik,** where the Victory Column (which you passed earlier) stood until Hitler moved it. The Hauptbahnhof (Berlin's vast main train station, marked by its tall tower with the *DB* sign) is across the field between the Chancellery and the **Reichstag** (Germany's parliament—the old building with the new dome, described on next page).

If you get off here, the "Sights in Eastern Berlin" descriptions cover the next string of attractions, which are best seen on foot. If you stay on the bus, you'll zip by them in this order:

Unter den Linden, the main east-west thoroughfare, stretches from the **Brandenburg Gate** (behind you) through Berlin's historic core (ahead) to the TV Tower in the distance (Alexanderplatz, where this bus finishes). You'll pass the **Russian Embassy** and the Aeroflot airline office (right). Crossing **Friedrichstrasse,** look right for a Fifth Avenue-style conga line of big, glitzy department stores. Later, on the left, are the **German History Museum, Museum Island** (with the **Pergamon Museum**), and the **Berlin Cathedral;** across from these (on the right) is the construction site of the new **Humboldt-Forum** (with the Humboldt-Box visitors center). Then you'll rumble to a final stop at what was the center of East Berlin in communist times: **Alexanderplatz.**

Sights in Eastern Berlin

The following sights are arranged roughly west to east, from the Reichstag down Unter den Linden to Alexanderplatz. It's possible to link these sights as a convenient self-guided orientation walk (I've included walking directions for this purpose)—allow about 1.5 hours without stops for sightseeing. Adding tours of several sights can easily fill a whole day. Remember that reservations are required for the Reichstag dome, and you'll need timed-entry tickets for the Pergamon and Neues museums.

Also described here are sights to the south and north of Unter den Linden.

▲▲Reichstag

The parliament building—the heart of German democracy—has a short but complicated and emotional history. When it was inaugurated in the 1890s, the last emperor, Kaiser Wilhelm II, disdainfully called it the "chatting home for monkeys" *(Reichsaffenhaus)*. It was placed outside of the city's old walls—far from the center of real power, the imperial palace. But it was from the Reichstag that the German Republic was proclaimed in 1918.

In 1933, this symbol of democracy nearly burned down. The Nazis—whose influence on the German political scene was on the rise—blamed a communist plot. A Dutch communist, Marinus van der Lubbe, was eventually convicted and guillotined for the crime. Others believed that Hitler himself planned the fire, using it as a handy excuse to frame the communists and grab power. Even though Van der Lubbe was posthumously pardoned by the German government in 2008, most modern historians concede that he most likely was guilty and acted alone—the Nazis were just incredibly lucky to have his deed advance their cause.

The Reichstag was hardly used from 1933 to 1999. Despite the fact that the building had lost its symbolic value, Stalin ordered his troops to take the Reichstag from the Nazis by May 1, 1945 (the date of the workers' May Day parade in Moscow). More than 1,500 Nazi soldiers made their last stand here—extending World War II by two days. On April 30, after fierce fighting on this rooftop, the Reichstag fell to the Red Army.

For the building's 101st birthday in 1995, the Bulgarian-American artist Christo wrapped it in silvery gold cloth. It was then wrapped again—in scaffolding—and rebuilt by British architect Lord Norman Foster into the new parliamentary home of the Bundestag (Germany's lower house, similar to the US House of Representatives). To many Germans, the proud resurrection of the Reichstag symbolizes the end of a terrible chapter in their country's history.

The **glass cupola** rises 155 feet above the ground. Its two sloped ramps spiral 755 feet to the top for a grand view. Inside the dome, a cone of 360 mirrors reflects natural light into the legislative chamber below. Lit from inside at night, this gives Berlin a memorable nightlight. The environmentally friendly cone—with an opening at the top—also helps with air circulation, drawing stale air out of the legislative chamber (no joke) and pulling in cool air from below.

Because of a terrorist plot discovered and thwarted in 2010, the

Eastern Berlin

········ Former Course of The Wall

500 meters
1/2 Mile

BERLIN

FENNSTRASSE

SELLERSTRASSE

HEIDESTRASSE

BOYENSTR.

SCHARNHORSTSTRASSE

Schwartzkopff-strasse

CHAUSSEESTR.

LIEBENSTRASSE

GARTENSTRASSE

ACKERSTR.

WÖHLERTSTR.

SCHWARTZKOPFF-STR.
CAROLINE-MICHAELIS-STR.

HABERSAATHSTR.

ZINNOWITZER STR.

SCHWARZER WEG

HUMBOLDTHAFEN

Naturkunde-museum

NATURAL HISTORY MUSEUM

HUSSITENSTRASSE

THEODOR-HEUSS-WEG

STREITZERSTR.

BRUNNEN-STR.

RUPPINER STR.

Bernauer Strasse

BERNAUER STR.

U

U.STR.

RHEINS.

ANKLAMER STR.

BERLIN WALL DOCUMENTATION CENTER

♦ CHAPEL OF RECONCILIATION

VISITOR CENTER
WALL OUTDOOR EXHIBITS

♦ BERLIN WALL MEMORIAL

BERGSTR.

Nordbahnhof S

INVALIDENSTRASSE

SCHLEGELSTR.

TIECKSTRASSE

GARTENSTR.

SCHRÖDER BERG.

DORFE.

ACKERSTR.

TORSTRASSE

SCHLEGELSTR.

HANNOVERSCHESTR.

LINIEN-

AUGUST-

HAUPTBAHNHOF & EURAIDE

S *Haupt-bahnhof*

See Unter den Linden detail map

TACHELES BUILDING

NEW SYNAGOGUE

ORANIENBURGER

Oranienburger Tor U

FRIEDRICHSTR.

JOHANNISSTR.

ZIEGEL-

← *Oranien-burger Str.* Strasse

PERGAMON MUSEUM

INVALIDEN-

ALT- MOABIT

KAPELLE UFER

SCHUMANNSTR.

REINHARD-
STR.

ALBRECHTSTR.

AM WEIDEN-
DAMM

Friedrich-strasse S

UNIVERSITÄTS-STR.

AMKUPFER.

Spree River

FÜRST-BISMARCK-STR.

Bundestag

OTTO-VON- BISMARCK-ALLEE

MARIENSTR.

SCHIFFBAUERDAMM

PLANK.

GEORGEN-

DOROTHEEN-

CHANCELLERY

PARLIAMENT

REICHSTAG

NEUSTÄDTISCHE

HUMBOLDT UNIVERSITY

HAUS DER KULTUREN DER WELT

Platz der Republik

BUS # 100 B

SCHEIDEMANNSTR.

DOROTHEENSTR.

MITTELSTR.

NEUE WACHE

STRASSE DES 17 JUNI

BRANDENBURG GATE

Pariser Platz S

Unter den Linden US EMBASSY

UNTER DEN LINDEN

KOMISCHE OPER

Bebel-platz

GERMAN STATE OPERA

→ To Victory Column

MEMORIAL TO THE MURDERED JEWS OF EUROPE

EBERTSTRASSE

ENTLASTUNGSSTR.

HANNAH-ARENDT-

IN DEN MINISTER-GARTEN

MOHREN-strasse

BEHRENSTRASSE

Französische U
Strasse

JÄGERSTR.

TAUBENSTR.

MOHRENSTR. U

FRANZÖSISCHE STR.

Gendarmen-markt ♦

MARK

GERMAN CATHEDRAL

Stadt-mitte

Tiergarten

MUSICAL INSTRUMENTS MUSEUM

MUSEUM OF ARTS & CRAFTS

BELLEVUESTR.

VOSS- STR.

LEIPZIGER

WILHELM-

STRASSE

FRIEDRICHSTR.

CHARLOTTEN-

MARGARETEN-STR.

GEMÄLDE-GALERIE

GERMAN RESISTANCE MEMORIAL

CONCERT HALL

SONY CENTER

Potsdamer Platz S

Leipziger Platz

Potsdamer Platz

FORMER LUFTWAFFE HQ

KIRCH-

STASI MUSEUM

MUSEUM AT THE WALL AT CHECKPOINT CHARLIE

KOCHSTR.

POTSDAMER STRASSE

ALTE POTSDAMER

EICHHORN STR.

KEMPERPLATZ

NEW NATIONAL GALLERY

LIBRARY

SIGISMUNDSTR.

HILDEBRAND-

TIERGARTENSTR.

REICHPIETSCHUFER

SCHÖNEBERGER UFER

GABRIELE-TERGIT-PROMENADE

STRESEMANNSTR.

NIEDER-

ANHALTER STR.

TOPOGRAPHY OF TERROR

Koch-strasse

KOCHSTR.

BESSELSTR.

LÜTZOWSTRASSE

BISSING-

Landwehr Canal

Mendelssohn-Bartholdy-Park U

BERNBURGER

DESSAUER STR.

SCHÖNEBERGER

ANHALTER STR.

Anhalter Bahnhof S

PUTTKAMMER- STR.

JEWISH MUSEUM BERLIN →

See Central Berlin Detail map

building has tight security: Getting in now requires a reservation.

Cost and Hours: Free but reservations required—see below, daily 8:00-24:00, last entry at 23:00, metal detectors, no big luggage allowed, Platz der Republik 1; S- or U-Bahn: Friedrichstrasse, Brandenburger Tor, or Bundestag; tel. 030/2273-2152, www.bundestag.de.

Reservations: A visit to the dome is possible only with a (free) advance reservation. Spots book up several days in advance.

You can only reserve **online.** The website is user-friendly, if (not surprisingly) a bit bureaucratic. Go to www.bundestag.de, click "English" at the top of the screen, and—under the "Visit the Bundestag" menu—select "Online registration." On this page, select "Visit the dome." Fill in the number of people in your party, ignore the "Comments" field, and click "Next." After entering the scrambled captcha code, you can select your preferred visit date and time (you can request up to three different time slots) and fill in your contact information. Once you complete the form and agree to their privacy policy, you'll be sent a confirmation email with a link to a website where you'll enter the name and birthdate for each person in your party and confirm your request. After completing this form, you'll receive a confirmation of your request (not a confirmation of your visit) by email. But you still have to wait for yet another email confirming your visit. If the English page isn't working, you can try using the German version: Go to https://www.bundestag.de/besuche/besucherdienst/index.jsp and call up a German-speaking friend to help you out. Or, if you use the Google Chrome browser, simply click the "Translate" button to see the steps in English.

While they claim it's possible to **email** a reservation request (kuppelbesuch@bundestag.de), you won't receive a confirmation until the day before your visit—which can be stressful. Use the website instead.

Getting In: Once you have a reservation, simply report to the security checkpoint at the appointed time. Give your name to the attendant, and you'll be let right in.

Tours: Pick up the English **"Outlooks" flier** just after the security checkpoint. The free, GPS-driven **audioguide** explains the building and narrates the view as you wind up the spiral ramp to the top of the dome; the commentary starts automatically as you step onto the bottom of the ramp.

➔ **Self-Guided Tour:** As you approach the building, look above the door, surrounded by stone patches from WWII bomb damage, to see the motto and promise: *Dem Deutschen Volke* ("To the German People"). The open, airy lobby towers 100 feet high, with 65-foot-tall colors of the German flag. See-through glass doors show the **central legislative chamber.** The message: There will be no secrets in this government. Look inside. Spreading his wings behind the podium is the *Bundestagsadler* (a.k.a. "the fat hen"), a stylized German eagle representing the Bundestag (each branch of government has its own symbolic eagle). Notice the doors marked *Ja* (Yes), *Nein* (No), and *Enthalten* (Abstain)...an homage to the Bundestag's traditional "sheep jump" way of counting votes by exiting the chamber through the corresponding door (although for critical issues, all 669 members vote with electronic cards).

Ride the elevator to the base of the glass **dome.** Pick up the free audioguide and take some time to study the photos and read the circle of captions—around the base of the central funnel—for an excellent exhibit telling the Reichstag story. Then study the surrounding architecture: a broken collage of new on old, torn between antiquity and modernity, like Germany's history. Notice the dome's giant and unobtrusive sunscreen that moves as necessary with the sun. Peer down through the skylight to look over the shoulders of the elected representatives at work. For Germans, the best view from here is down—keeping a close eye on their government.

Start at the ramp nearest the elevator and wind up to the top of the **double ramp.** Take a 360-degree survey of the city as you hike: The big park is the **Tiergarten,** the "green lungs of Berlin." Beyond that is the **Teufelsberg,** or "Devil's Hill" (built of rubble from the destroyed city in the late 1940s, it was famous during the Cold War as a powerful ear of the West—notice the telecommunications tower on top). Knowing the bombed-out and bulldozed story of their city, locals say, "You have to be suspicious when you see the nice, green park." Find the **Victory Column** (Siegessäule), glimmering in the middle of the park. This was moved by Hitler in the 1930s from in front of the Reichstag to its present position in the Tiergarten, as the first step in creating a grandiose axis he envisioned for postwar Berlin. Next, scenes of the new Berlin spiral into your view—**Potsdamer Platz,** marked by the conical glass tower that houses Sony's European headquarters. Continue circling left, and find the green chariot atop the **Brandenburg Gate.** The **Memorial to the Murdered Jews of Europe** stretches south of the Brandenburg Gate. Next, you'll see **former East Berlin** and the city's next huge construction zone, with a forest of 300-foot-tall skyscrapers in the works. Notice the TV Tower, the Berlin Cathedral's massive dome, and the golden dome of the New Synagogue.

Follow the train tracks in the distance to the left toward Berlin's huge main train station, the **Hauptbahnhof.** Complete your spin-tour with the blocky **Chancellery,** nicknamed by Berliners "the washing machine." It may look like a pharaoh's

BERLIN

tomb, but it's the office and home of Germany's most powerful person, the chancellor (currently Angela Merkel). To remind the chancellor who he or she works for, the Reichstag, at about 130 feet, is about six feet taller than the Chancellery.

Continue spiraling up. You'll pass all the same sights again, twice, from a higher vantage point.

Near the Reichstag

Memorial to Politicians Who Opposed Hitler—Near the road in front of the Reichstag, enmeshed in all the security apparatus, is a memorial of slate stones embedded in the ground. This row of slate slabs (which looks like a fancy slate bicycle rack) is a memorial to the 96 members of the Reichstag (the equivalent of our members of Congress) who were persecuted and murdered because their politics didn't agree with Chancellor Hitler's. They were part of the Weimar Republic, the weak and ill-fated attempt at post-WWI democracy in Germany. These were the people who could have stopped Hitler...so they became his first victims. Each slate slab remembers one man—his name, party (mostly KPD—Communists, and SPD—Social Democrats), and the date and location of his death—generally in concentration camps. (*KZ* stands for "concentration camp.") They are honored here, in front of the building in which they worked.

• *Facing the Reichstag, you can take a short side-trip to the river by circling around to the left of the building.*

Spree Riverfront—Admire the wonderful architecture incorporating the Spree River into the people's world. It's a poignant spot because this river was once a symbol of division—the East German regime put nets underwater to stymie those desperate enough for freedom to swim to the West. When kings ruled Prussia, government buildings went right up to the water. But today, the city is incorporating the river thoughtfully into a people-friendly cityscape. From the Reichstag, a delightful riverside path leads around the curve, past "beach cafés," to the Chancellery. For a slow, low-impact glide past this zone, consider a river cruise (see page 563; we'll pass the starting point—on Museum Island—later on this walk). The fine bridges symbolize the connection of East and West.

• *Leaving the Reichstag, return to the busy road, and cross the street at your first opportunity, to the big park. Walk (with the park on your right) to the corner. Along the railing at the corner of Scheidemannstrasse and Ebertstrasse is a small memorial of white crosses. This is the...*

Berlin Wall Victims Memorial—This monument—now largely usurped by business promos and impromptu wacko book stalls—commemorates some of the East Berliners who died trying to cross the Wall. This 96-mile-long "Anti-Fascist Protective Rampart," as it was called by the East German government, was erected almost overnight in 1961 to stop the outward flow of people from East to West (3 million had leaked out between 1949 and 1961). Of these people, many perished within months of the wall's construction on August 13, 1961. Most died trying to swim the river to freedom. The monument used to stand right on the Berlin Wall behind the Reichstag. Notice that the last person killed while trying to escape was 20-year-old Chris Gueffroy, who died nine months before the Wall fell in 1989. (He was shot through the heart in no-man's-land.)

In the park just behind the monument, another memorial is planned. It will remember the Roma (Gypsy) victims of the Holocaust. The Roma, as persecuted by the Nazis as the Jews were, lost the same percentage of their population to Hitler. Unfortunately, the project is stalled for lack of a well-funded individual or group to finance it.

• *From here, head to the Brandenburg Gate. Stay on the park side of the street for a better view of the gate ahead. As you cross at the light, notice the double row of* **cobblestones**—*it goes around the city, marking where the Wall used to stand.*

Brandenburg Gate and Nearby

▲▲**Brandenburg Gate (Brandenburger Tor)**—The historic Brandenburg Gate (1791) was the grandest—and is the last survivor—of 14 gates in Berlin's old city wall (this one led to the neighboring city of Brandenburg). The gate was the symbol of Prussian Berlin—and later the symbol of a divided Berlin. It's crowned by a majestic four-horse chariot with the Goddess of Peace at the reins. Napoleon took this statue to the Louvre in Paris in 1806. After the Prussians defeated Napoleon and got it back (1813), she was renamed the Goddess of Victory.

The gate sat unused, part of a sad circle dance called the Wall, for more than 25 years. Now postcards all over town show the ecstatic day—November 9, 1989—when the world enjoyed the sight of happy Berliners jamming the gate like flowers on a parade float. Pause a minute and think about struggles for freedom—past and present. (There's actually a special room built into the gate for this purpose.) Around the gate, look at the information boards with pictures of how this area changed throughout the 20th century. There's a TI within the gate (daily 9:30-19:00, until 18:30 Nov-March, S-Bahn: Brandenburger Tor).

The Brandenburg Gate, the center of old Berlin, sits on a major boulevard running east to west through Berlin. The western segment, called Strasse des 17 Juni (named for a workers' uprising against the DDR government on June 17, 1953), stretches for four miles from the Brandenburg Gate and Victory Column to the

Olympic Stadium. But we'll follow this city axis in the opposite direction, east, walking along a stretch called Unter den Linden—into the core of old imperial Berlin and past what was once the palace of the Hohenzollern family who ruled Prussia and then Germany. The palace—the reason for just about all you'll see—is a phantom sight, long gone. Alexanderplatz, which marks the end of this walk, is near the base of the giant TV Tower hovering in the distance.

• *Cross through the gate into...*

▲**Pariser Platz**—"Parisian Square," so named after the Prussians defeated Napoleon in 1813, was once filled with important government buildings—all bombed to smithereens in World War II. For decades, it was an unrecognizable, deserted no-man's-land—cut off from both East and West by the Wall. But now it's rebuilt, and the banks, hotels, and embassies that were here before the bombing have reclaimed their original places—with a few additions: a palace of coffee (Starbucks) and the small Kennedys Museum (described later). The winners of World War II enjoy this prime real estate: The American, French, British, and Soviet (now Russian) embassies are all on or near this square.

Face the gate and look to your left. The **US Embassy** reopened in its historic location in 2008. The building has been controversial: For safety's sake, Uncle Sam wanted more of a security zone around the building, but the Germans wanted to keep Pariser Platz a welcoming people zone. (Throughout the world, American embassies are the most fortified buildings in town.) The compromise: The extra security the US wanted is built into the structure. Easy-on-the-eyes barriers keep potential car bombs at a distance, and its front door is on the side farthest from the Brandenburg Gate.

Just to the left, the **DZ Bank building** is by Frank Gehry, the unconventional American architect famous for Bilbao's organic Guggenheim Museum, Prague's Dancing House, Seattle's Experience Music Project, Chicago's Millennium Park, and Los Angeles' Walt Disney Concert Hall. Gehry fans might be surprised at the DZ Bank building's low profile. Structures on Pariser Platz are designed to be bland so as not to draw attention away from the Brandenburg Gate. (The glassy facade of the Academy of Arts, next to Gehry's building, is controversial for drawing attention to itself.) For your fix of the good old Gehry, step into the lobby and check out its undulating interior. It's a fish—and you feel like you're both inside and outside of it. The architect's vision is explained on a nearby plaque. The best view of Gehry's creation is from the Reichstag dome.

• *Next door to Gehry's building is the **Academy of Arts** (Akademie der Kunst), with its notorious glass facade. Its doors lead to a lobby (with a small food counter, daily 10:00–22:00), which leads directly to the vast...*

▲▲Memorial to the Murdered Jews of Europe (Denkmal für die Ermordeten Juden Europas)—This Holocaust memorial, consisting of 2,711 gravestone-like pillars (called "stelae") and completed in 2005, is an essential stop for any visit to Berlin. It was the first formal, German government-sponsored Holocaust memorial. Jewish American architect Peter Eisenman won the competition for the commission (and built it on time and on budget—€27 million). It's been criticized for focusing on just one of the groups targeted by the Nazis, but the German government has promised to erect memorials to other victims.

Cost and Hours: Free, memorial always open; information center open Tue-Sun 10:00-20:00, Oct-March until 19:00, closed Mon year-round; last entry 45 minutes before closing, S-Bahn: Brandenburger Tor or Potsdamer Platz, tel. 030/2639-4336, www.stiftung-denkmal.de. The €4 audioguide augments the experience.

Visiting the Memorial: The pillars are made of hollow concrete, each chemically coated for easy removal of graffiti. (Ironically, the chemical coating was developed by a subsidiary of the former IG Farben group—the company infamous for supplying the Zyklon B gas used in Nazi death camps.) The number of pillars, symbolic of nothing, is simply how many fit on the provided land.

Once you enter the memorial, notice that people seem to appear and disappear between the columns, and that no matter where you are, the exit always seems to be up. Is it a labyrinth...a symbolic cemetery...and intentionally disorienting? It's entirely up to the visitor to derive the meaning, while pondering this horrible chapter in human history.

The pondering takes place under the sky. For the learning, go under the field of concrete pillars to the state-of-the-art **information center** (there may be a short line because visitors must go through a security check). Inside, a thought-provoking exhibit (well-explained in English) studies the Nazi system of extermination and humanizes the victims, while also providing space for silent reflection. In the Starting Hall, exhibits trace the historical context of the Nazi and WWII era, while six portraits—representing the six million Jewish victims—look out on the visitors. The Room of Dimensions has glowing boxes in the floor containing diaries, letters, and final farewells penned by Holocaust victims. The Room of Families presents case-studies of 15 Jewish families from around Europe, to more fully convey the European Jewish experience. Remember: Behind these 15 stories are millions more tales of despair, tragedy, and survival. In the Room of Names, a continually running soundtrack lists the names and brief biographical sketches of Holocaust victims; reading the names of all those murdered would take more than six and a half years. The

Room of Sites documents some 220 different places of genocide. You'll also find exhibits about other Holocaust monuments and memorials, a searchable database of victims, and a video archive of interviews with survivors.

The memorial's location—where the Wall once stood—is coincidental. Nazi propagandist Joseph Goebbels' bunker was discovered during the work and left buried under the northeast corner of the memorial. Hitler's bunker is just 200 yards away, under a nondescript parking lot. Such Nazi sites are intentionally left hidden to discourage neo-Nazi elements from creating shrines.

• *Now backtrack to Pariser Platz (through the yellow building). Across the square (next to Starbucks), consider dropping into...*

The Kennedys Museum—This crisp private enterprise facing the Brandenburg Gate recalls John F. Kennedy's Germany trip in 1963, with great photos and video clips as well as a photographic shrine to the Kennedy clan in America. It's a small, overpriced, yet delightful experience with interesting mementos—such as old campaign buttons and posters, and JFK's notes with the phonetic "Ish bin ein Bearleener." Jacqueline Kennedy commented on how strange it was that this—not even in his native language—was her husband's most quotable quote. Most of the exhibit consists of photographs that, if nothing else, spark a nostalgic longing for the days of Camelot.

Cost and Hours: €7, includes special exhibits, reduced to €3.50 for a broad array of visitors—dream up a discount and ask for it, daily 10:00-18:00, Pariser Platz 4a, www.thekennedys.de, tel. 030/2065-3570.

• *Leave Pariser Platz and begin strolling...*

▲▲Unter den Linden

The street called Unter den Linden is the heart of former East Berlin. In Berlin's good old days, Unter den Linden was one of Europe's grand boulevards. In the 15th century, this carriageway led from the palace to the hunting grounds (today's big Tiergarten). In the 17th century, Hohenzollern princes and princesses moved in and built their palaces here so they could be near the Prussian king.

Named centuries ago for its thousand linden trees, this was the most elegant street of Prussian Berlin before Hitler's time, and the main drag of East Berlin after his reign. Hitler replaced the venerable trees—many 250 years old—with Nazi flags. Popular discontent actually drove him to replant the trees. Today, Unter den Linden is no longer a depressing Cold War cul-de-sac, and its pre-Hitler strolling café ambience has returned. Notice how it is divided, roughly at Friedrichstrasse, into a business section that stretches toward the Brandenburg Gate, and a culture section that spreads out toward Alexanderplatz. Frederick the Great wanted to have culture, mainly the opera and the university, closer to his palace, and to keep business (read: banks) farther away, near the city walls.

⊘ Self-Guided Walk: As you walk toward the giant TV Tower, the big building you see jutting out into the street on your right is the **Hotel Adlon.** In its heyday, it hosted such notables as Charlie Chaplin, Albert Einstein, and Greta Garbo. This was the setting for Garbo's most famous line, "I vant to be alone," uttered in the film *Grand Hotel.* Damaged by the Russians just after World War II, the original hotel was closed with the construction of the nearby Wall in 1961 and later demolished. The grand Adlon was rebuilt in 1997. It was here that the late Michael Jackson shocked millions by dangling his baby, Blanket, over the railing (second balcony up, on the side of the hotel next to the Academy of Art). See how far you can get inside.

Descend into the Brandenburger Tor S-Bahn station ahead of you. It's one of Berlin's former **ghost subway stations.** During the Cold War, most underground train tunnels were simply blocked at the border. But a few Western lines looped through the East. To make a little hard Western cash, the Eastern government rented the use of these tracks to the West, but the stations (which happened to be in East Berlin) were strictly off-limits. For 28 years, the stations were unused, as Western trains slowly passed through and passengers saw only eerie DDR (East German) guards and lots of cobwebs. Literally within days of the fall of the Wall, these stations were reopened, and today they are a time warp (looking essentially as they did when built in 1931, with dreary old green tiles and original signage). Walk along the track (the walls are lined with historic photos of the Reichstag through the ages) and exit on the other side, following signs to *Russische Botschaft* (the Russian Embassy).

The **Russian Embassy** was the first big postwar building project in East Berlin. It's built in the powerful, simplified Neoclassical style that Stalin liked. While not as important now as it was a few years ago, it's as immense as ever. It flies the Russian white, blue, and red. Find the hammer-and-sickle motif decorating the window frames—a reminder of the days when Russia was the USSR.

Continuing past the Aeroflot airline offices, look across Glinkastrasse to the right to see the back of the **Komische Oper** (Comic Opera; program and view of ornate interior posted in window). While the exterior is ugly, the fine old theater interior—amazingly missed by WWII bombs—survives.

Back on the main drag, on the left at #40, is an entertaining bookstore, Berlin Story. In addition to a wide range of English-language books, this shop has a modest (but overpriced) museum

BERLIN

Eastern Berlin's Unter den Linden

500 meters
1/2 Mile

HAUPTBAHNHOF & EurAide

Haupt-bahnhof

Washington Platz

ALT-MOABIT

Spree River

FÜRST-BISMARCK-STR (TUNNEL)

KAPELLE UFER

OTTO-VON-BISMARCK-ALLEE

HUMBOLDTHAFEN

LUISENSTR.

SCHUMANNSTR.

REINHARD-STR.

MARIENSTR.

ELEVATED RAILWAY

ALBRECHT-STR

ORANIENBURGER

FRIEDRICHSTR.

KUNSTHAUS TACHELES

Oranienburger Tor

JOHANNIS-

ZIEGEL-

AM WEIDEN-DAMM

PLANK-

Friedrich-strasse

SCHIFFBAUERDAMM

GEORGENSTR.

CHANCELLERY

Bundestag

PARLIAMENT

Platz der Republik
Bus # 100

HAUS DER KULTUREN DER WELT

To Bahnhof Zoo via Bus #100

To Victory Column

STRASSE DES 17 JUNI

SCHEIDEMANNSTR.

REICHSTAG

WALK BEGINS

BRANDENBURG GATE

Pariser Platz

DOROTHEEN-STRASSE

NEUSTÄDTISCHE KIRCHSTR

SCHADOW

Unter den Linden

UNTER

KOMISCHE OPER

DEN

MITTELSTR

STRASSE

FRIEDRICH-

BEHRENSTRASSE

MEMORIAL TO THE MURDERED JEWS OF EUROPE

Tiergarten

Former Course of The Wall

ENTLASTUNGS-

LENNESTR.

To Kulturforum

EBERTSTRASSE

HANNAH-ARENDT-STRASSE

IN DEN MINISTER-GÄRTEN

To Potsdamer Platz

Französische Strasse

MAUERSTR

GLINKASTR.

JÄGERSTR.

TAUBENSTR

MOHRENSTR.

VOSSSTR.

Mohren-strasse

1 Reichstag
2 Memorial to Politicians Who Opposed Hitler
3 Spree Riverfront
4 Berlin Wall Victims Memorial
5 Brandenburg Gate
6 Pariser Platz
7 US Embassy
8 Memorial to the Murdered Jews of Europe
9 The Kennedys Museum
10 Russian Embassy
11 Berlin Story Bookstore

BERLIN

and a wide range of nostalgic knickknacks from the Cold War. The West lost no time in consuming the East; consequently, some are feeling a wave of *Ost*-**algia** for the old days of East Berlin. At election time, a surprising number of the former East Berlin's voters still opt for the extreme left party, which has ties to the bygone Communist Party, although the East-West divide is no longer at the forefront of most voters' minds.

One symbol of that communist era has been given a reprieve. As you continue to Friedrichstrasse, look at the DDR-style pedestrian lights, and you'll realize that someone had a sense of humor

12 Bebelplatz

13 Humboldt University

14 German State Opera

15 Neue Wache

16 German History Museum

17 Museum Island

18 Berlin Cathedral

19 Humboldt-Box & Forum Construction Site

20 Spree River Cruises

21 DDR Museum

22 Marien Church

23 TV Tower

24 Alexanderplatz

back then. The perky red and green men—*Ampelmännchen*—were recently under threat of replacement by far less jaunty Western-style signs. Fortunately, after a 10-year court battle, the DDR signals were kept after all.

At **Friedrichstrasse,** look right. Before the war, the Unter den Linden/Friedrichstrasse intersection was the heart of Berlin. In the 1920s, Berlin was famous for its anything-goes love of life. This was the cabaret drag, a springboard to stardom for young and vampy entertainers like Marlene Dietrich. (Born in 1901, Dietrich starred in the one of the first German talkies—*The Blue Angel*—and then headed straight to Hollywood.) Over the last few years, this boulevard—lined with super department stores (such as Galeries Lafayette) and big-time hotels (such as the Hilton and Regent)—is attempting to replace Ku'damm as the grand commerce-and-café boulevard of Berlin. More recently, western Berlin is retaliating with some new stores of its own. And so far, Friedrichstrasse gets little more than half the pedestrian traffic that Ku'damm gets in the West. Why? Locals complain that this area has no daily life— no supermarkets, not much ethnic street food, and so on. Consider detouring to Galeries Lafayette, with its cool marble-and-glass, waste-of-space interior (Mon-Sat 9:30-20:00, closed Sun; check out the vertical garden on its front wall, belly up to its amazing ground-floor viewpoint, or have lunch in its recommended basement cafeteria).

If you continued down Friedrichstrasse, you'd wind up at the sights listed under "South of Unter den Linden," on page 593—including the Museum of the Wall at Checkpoint Charlie (a 10-minute walk from here). But for now, continue along Unter den Linden. At the corner, the **VW Automobil Forum** shows off the latest models from the many car companies owned by VW (free, corner of Friedrichstrasse and Unter den Linden, VW art gallery and handy VW WC in the basement).

As you explore Berlin, you may see big, colorful **water pipes** running overground. Wherever there are big construction projects, streets are laced with these drainage pipes. Berlin's high water table means that any new basement comes with lots of pumping out.

Continue down Unter den Linden a few more blocks, past the large equestrian statue of Frederick the Great, and turn right into the square called **Bebelplatz.** Stand on the glass window set into the pavement in the center.

Frederick the Great—who ruled from 1740 to 1786—established Prussia not just as a military power, but as a cultural and intellectual heavyweight as well. This square was the center of the "new Athens" that Frederick envisioned. His grand palace was just down the street (explained later).

Look down through the glass you're standing on: The room of empty bookshelves is a memorial repudiating the notorious Nazi **book burning.** It was on this square in 1933 that staff and students from the university threw 20,000 newly forbidden books (like Einstein's) into a huge bonfire on the orders of the Nazi propaganda minister Joseph Goebbels. A plaque nearby reminds us of the prophetic quote by the German poet Heinrich Heine. In 1820, he wrote, "Where they burn books, at the end they also burn people." The Nazis despised Heine because he was Jewish before converting to Christianity. A century later, his books were among those that went up in flames on this spot.

Great buildings front Bebelplatz. Survey the square counter-clockwise:

Humboldt University, across Unter den Linden, is one of Europe's greatest. Marx and Lenin (not the brothers or the sisters) studied here, as did the Grimms (both brothers) and more than two dozen Nobel Prize winners. Einstein, who was Jewish, taught here until taking a spot at Princeton in 1932 (smart guy). Used-book merchants set up their tables in front of the university, selling books by many of the authors whose works were once condemned to Nazi flames just across the street.

The former **state library** (labeled *Juristische Fakultät,* facing Bebelplatz on the right with your back to Humboldt University) is where Vladimir Lenin studied during much of his exile from Russia. If you climb to the second floor of the library and go through the door opposite the stairs, you'll see a 1968 vintage stained-glass window depicting Lenin's life's work with almost biblical reverence. On the ground floor is Tim's Espressobar, a great little café with light food, student prices, and garden seating (€3 plates, Mon-Fri 8:00-20:00, Sat 9:00-16:00, closed Sun, handy WC).

The round, Catholic **St. Hedwig's Church**—nicknamed the "upside-down teacup"—was built by the pragmatic Frederick the Great to encourage the integration of Catholic Silesians after his empire annexed their region in 1742. (St. Hedwig is the patron saint of Silesia, a region now shared by Germany, Poland, and the Czech Republic.) When asked what the church should look like, Frederick literally took a Silesian teacup and slammed it upside-down on a table. Like all Catholic churches in Berlin, St. Hedwig's is not on the street, but stuck in a kind of back lot—indicating inferiority to Protestant churches. You can step inside the church to see the cheesy DDR government renovation.

The **German State Opera** was bombed in 1941, rebuilt to bolster morale and to celebrate its centennial in 1943, and bombed again in 1945. Now it's being renovated (through 2013).

Cross Unter den Linden to the university side. The Greek-temple-like building set in the small chestnut-tree-filled park is the **Neue Wache** (the emperor's "New Guardhouse," from 1816). Converted to a memorial to the victims of fascism in 1960, the structure was transformed again, after the Wall fell, into a national memorial. Look inside, where a replica of the Käthe Kollwitz statue, *Mother with Her Dead Son,* is surrounded by thought-provoking silence. This marks the tombs of Germany's unknown soldier and an unknown concentration camp victim. The inscription in front reads, "To the victims of war and tyranny." Read the entire statement in English (on wall, left of entrance). The memorial, open to the sky, incorporates the elements—sunshine, rain, snow—falling on this modern-day *pietà*.

• *After the Neue Wache, the next building you'll see is Berlin's pink-yet-formidable Zeughaus (arsenal). Dating from 1695, it's considered the oldest building on the boulevard and now houses the...*

▲▲▲German History Museum (Deutsches Historisches Museum)

This fantastic museum is a two-part affair: the pink former Prussian arsenal building and the I. M. Pei-designed annex. The main building (fronting Unter den Linden) houses the permanent collection, offering the best look at German history under one roof, anywhere. The modern annex features good temporary exhibits surrounded by the work of a great contemporary architect. While this city has more than its share of hokey "museums" that slap together WWII and Cold War bric-a-brac, then charge too much for admission, this thoughtfully presented museum—with more than 8,000 artifacts telling not just the story of Berlin, but of all Germany—is clearly the top history museum in town.

Cost and Hours: €6, daily 10:00-18:00, Unter den Linden 2, tel. 030/2030-4751, www.dhm.de.

Audioguide: For the most informative visit, invest in the excellent €3 audioguide, with six hours of info to choose from.

Visiting the Museum: The permanent collection packs two huge rectangular floors of the old arsenal building with historical objects, photographs, and models—all well-described in English and intermingled with multimedia stations to help put everything in context. From the lobby, head upstairs (to the "**first floor**") and work your way chronologically down. This floor traces German history from 1 B.C. to 1918, with exhibits on early cultures, the Middle Ages, Reformation, Thirty Years' War, German Empire, and World War I. You'll see a Roman floor mosaic, lots of models of higgledy-piggledy medieval towns and castles, tapestries, suits of armor, busts of great Germans, a Turkish tent from the Ottoman siege of Vienna (1683), flags from German unification in 1871 (the first time "Germany" existed as a nation), exhibits on everyday life in the tenements of the Industrial Revolution, and much more.

History marches on through the 20th century on the **ground floor,** including the Weimar Republic, Nazism, World War II, Allied occupation, and a divided Germany. Propaganda posters trumpet Germany's would-be post-WWI savior, Adolf Hitler. Look for the model of the impossibly huge, 950-foot-high, 180,000-capacity domed hall Hitler wanted to erect in the heart of Berlin, which he planned to re-envision as Welthauptstadt Germania, the "world capital" of his far-reaching Third Reich.

Another model shows the sobering reality of Hitler's grandiosity: a crematorium at Auschwitz-Birkenau concentration camp in occupied Poland. The exhibit wraps up with chunks of the Berlin Wall, reunification, and a quick look at Germany today.

For architecture buffs, the big attraction is the **Pei annex** behind the history museum, which complements the museum with often-fascinating temporary exhibits. From the old building, cross through the courtyard (with the Pei glass canopy overhead) to reach the annex. A striking glassed-in spiral staircase unites four floors with surprising views and lots of light. It's here that you'll experience why Pei—famous for his glass pyramid at Paris' Louvre—is called the "perfector of classical modernism," "master of light," and a magician of uniting historical buildings with new ones. (If the museum is closed, or you don't have a ticket, venture down the street—Hinter dem Giesshaus—to the left of the museum to see the Pei annex from the outside.)

• *Back on Unter den Linden, head toward the Spree River. Just before the bridge, wander left along the canal through a tiny but colorful arts-and-crafts market (weekends only; a larger flea market is just outside the Pergamon Museum). Continue up the riverbank two blocks and cross the footbridge over the Spree. This takes you to...*

Museum Island (Museumsinsel)

This island is filled with some of Berlin's most impressive museums (all part of the Staatliche Museen zu Berlin). The first building—the Altes Museum—went up in the 1820s, and the rest of the complex began taking form in the 1840s under King Friedrich Wilhelm IV, who envisioned the island as a place of culture and learning. The island's imposing Neoclassical buildings host five grand museums: the **Pergamon Museum** (classical antiquities, including the top-notch Pergamon Altar, with its temple and frieze); the **Neues Museum** ("New Museum," famous for its Egyptian collection with the bust of Queen Nefertiti); the **Old National Gallery** (Alte Nationalgalerie, 19th-century art, mostly German Romantic and Realist paintings); the **Altes Museum** ("Old Museum," more antiquities); and the **Bode Museum** (European statuary and paintings through the ages, coins, and Byzantine art). The entire ensemble is being renovated, and when the project is finished, this will be one of the most impressive museum zones in Europe.

• *The museums of Museum Island, worth the better part of a sightseeing day, are described in more detail below. To bypass the museums and other sights on Museum Island for now, skip ahead to the "Museum Island to Alexanderplatz" section on page 590.*

The Museums of Museum Island

A formidable renovation is under way on Museum Island. When

plete, a grand entry and unified visitors center will serve the
d's five venerable but separate museums, and tunnels will
the complex together (intended completion date: 2015, www
useumsinsel-berlin.de). In the meantime, pardon their dust.

Cost: The €16 Museum Island Pass combo-ticket—cover-
ng all five museums—is a far better value than buying individual
€8-12 entries (prices can vary depending on special exhibits). All
five museums are also included in the city's €19 Museumspass
(both passes described on page 553). Special exhibits are extra.

Hours: Pergamon, Altes, and Bode museums open daily
10:00-18:00, Thu until 22:00; Old National Gallery open same
hours except closed Mon; Neues Museum open daily 10:00-18:00,
Thu-Sat until 20:00; tel. 030/266-424-242, www.smb.museum.

Required Reservation for Pergamon and Neues Museums:
Visiting either the Pergamon Museum or the Neues Museum
requires a *Zeitfensterticket* ("time-window ticket") that gives you
a 30-minute time slot for entering the museum (included with
admission; separate appointments required for each museum).
Once inside, you can stay as long as you like. Reserve your time
online (www.smb.museum) or in person at any Museum Island
ticket office.

Crowd Control: You can usually get a time slot within about
an hour, often sooner—except at the busiest times (Sat and Sun
mornings), when you may have to wait longer. The least-crowded
times are evenings when the museums are open late (Thu evening
for the Pergamon Museum, Thu-Sat evenings for the Neues).

The temporary kiosk on Bodestrasse functions as the ticket
booth for the Neues Museum and comes with avoidable lines.
Long ticket-buying lines also plague the Pergamon Museum.
Avoid them by purchasing your museum pass (and getting your
assigned entry time) at one of the island's three never-crowded
museums: Altes, Bode, or Old National Gallery. (From Unter den
Linden, Altes is most convenient; if coming from Prenzlauer Berg,
try the Bode.)

Planning Your Time: I'd start at the Bode, where I'd ask for
an entry time to the Pergamon Museum in about an hour, and a
ticket to the Neues Museum for 1.5 hours after that. Tickets and
appointments in hand, spend any time left before your Pergamon
time slot browsing the Bode. Then enjoy the Pergamon collection,
where the art is earth-shaking but easy to see in an hour. If you
have any extra time before your Neues appointment, nip into the
time-tunnel Old National Gallery. Step into the Neues Museum
within 30 minutes of your entry time, and be prepared to linger.
For lunch nearby, follow the elevated train tracks away from the
Pergamon down Georgenstrasse (see suggestions on page 632).

Getting There: The nearest S-Bahn station is Hackescher

BERLIN

Markt, about a 10-minute walk away. From hotels in the Prenzlauer Berg, ride tram #M-1 to the end of line, and you're right at the Pergamon Museum.

▲▲▲Pergamon Museum (Pergamonmuseum)

The star attraction of this world-class museum, part of Berlin's Collection of Classical Antiquities (Antikensammlung), is the fantastic and gigantic Pergamon Altar. The Babylonian Ishtar Gate (slathered with glazed blue tiles from the 6th century B.C.) and the museum's many ancient Greek, Mesopotamian, Roman, and early Islamic treasures are also impressive.

Audioguide: Make ample use of the superb audioguide (included with admission)—it will broaden your experience. Punching #10 on the audioguide gets you the "Pergamon in 30 Minutes" general tour. Or follow my quicker, more succinct self-guided tour, next.

⊙ Self-Guided Tour: With your timed entry and museum pass, walk boldly by the long line of people who don't have or read guidebooks, and go directly in.

There's a lot to see in this museum (everything is well-described by posted English information and the included audioguide). The best plan for the casual visitor is to focus on a few highlights.

From the entrance, walk straight ahead to find the museum's namesake, the **Pergamon Altar.** Actually a 65-foot-wide temple, this "altar" comes from the second-century B.C. Greek city of Pergamon (near the west coast of today's Turkey). The Pergamon Altar was just one component of a spectacular hilltop ensemble—temples, sanctuaries, palaces, theaters, and other buildings erected to honor the gods—modeled after the Acropolis in Athens. (See a model of the complete Pergamon Acropolis to the right, as you face the stairs.)

Pergamon was excavated from 1878 to 1886 by German archaeologist Carl Humann, who unearthed fragments of the temple's frieze all over the site (many pieces had been "recycled" as building materials in later structures). The bits and pieces were brought here to Berlin, reassembled on this replica of the temple, and put on display in this purpose-built museum in 1930.

The temple replica re-creates the western third of the original building. Stairs lead up to a chamber with a small sacrificial altar, where priests and priestesses sacrificed and burned animals, while toga-clad Greeks assembled in awe at the foot of the stairs below.

Surviving pieces of a 269-foot-long frieze that wrapped around the entire temple dramatically spill onto the stairs and around the room. Called the **Gigantomachy Frieze,** it shows the Greek gods under Zeus and Athena defeating the giants in a dramatic pig pile of mythological mayhem. Imagine how much more evocative these sculptures once were, slathered in colorful paint, gold, and silver trim.

So what's the fight about? Long before the time of man, an epic struggle pitted the titans against the gods. When the gods won, they thrust their foes into a miserable underworld (the mythological equivalent of purgatory) and settled in for a comfy period of rule atop Mount Olympus. But the troublesome race of giants—children of the earth goddess Gaia, mother of the titans—sought revenge. The giants had legs of slithering snakes that kept them in contact with the ground, allowing Gaia to make them immortal. This frieze captures a pivotal event, when the giants Alkyoneus and Porphyrion led a rebellion of their race against the gods. (The people of Pergamon appreciated the parallels between this story and their own noble struggle against unenlightened barbarians.)

With your back to the altar steps, look at the right end of the frieze to find panels with Zeus and Athena, locked in combat with the giants. Faint surviving labels on the cornice above the statues—in Greek, of course—help identify the combatants; the modern English letters below may prove more helpful.

Find the **Athena** panel. Athena (faceless, in the center, with the shield) and Nike (all that's left are her wings, right arm, and left leg) pull the chief giant Alkyoneus (his snake legs curling around his bicep) up by his hair—breaking his connection to the earth, the source of his immortality. Below them, Gaia—the mother of the giants—rises up from her subterranean realm to lend a hand. (See the fear in Gaia's and Alkyoneus' tortured eyes.) Alkyoneus would survive this brush with Athena, only to be killed soon after by Hercules. (The statue of Hercules is missing—all that survives is one pathetic paw of his lion pelt.)

The **Zeus** panel shows the (headless) king of the gods raining lightning bolts down on his enemies—including the snake-legged Porphyrion, with his back(side) toward us. Notice Zeus' disembodied right hand up above, ready to pitch some serious heat. Fans of Greek mythology can take a slow walk along the entire length of the frieze, identifying their favorite gods and giants...the gang's all here. Before long, the giants will be history, and the gods can go back about their usual business of conspiring against each other and impregnating mortals.

Facing the altar stairs, go through the door to your left. The intricate, ancient Greek **mosaic floor** is finely assembled from miniscule pebbles, with a particularly impressive floral motif decorating the border. In the otherwise undecorated box in the middle, in what looks like an ancient Post-It note, you can see where the artist "signed" his work. The Athena statue standing in the middle of the room is a replica of one that once stood at the center of Athens'

Acropolis. Turn around to see the doorway you just came through, surrounded by the original, double-decker ornamental entryway to the Pergamon Acropolis. Ancient pilgrims who had come from far and wide to worship the gods in Pergamon passed through here on their way to the altar.

Return to the altar room, cross straight through it, and go out the door on the far side. From Pergamon, flash-forward 300 years (and travel south 110 miles) to the ancient Roman city of Miletus. Dominating this room (on your right) is the 95-foot-wide, 55-foot-high **Market Gate of Miletus**—destroyed by an earthquake centuries ago and now painstakingly reconstructed here in Berlin. The exquisite mosaic floor from a Roman villa in Miletus has two parts: In the square panel, the musician Orpheus strokes his lyre to charm the animals; in stark contrast, in the nearby rectangular mosaic (from an adjacent room), hunters pursue wild animals.

Step through the market gate and all the way back to 575 B.C., to the Fertile Crescent—Mesopotamia (today's Iraq). The Assyrian ruler Nebuchadnezzar II, who amassed a vast empire and enormous wealth, wanted to build a suitably impressive processional entryway to his capital city, Babylon, to honor the goddess Ishtar. His creation, the **Ishtar Gate,** inspired awe and obedience in anyone who came to his city. This is a reconstruction, using some original components. The gate itself is embellished with two animals: a bull and a mythical dragon-like combination of lion, cobra, eagle, and scorpion. The long hall leading to the main gate—designed for a huge processional of deities to celebrate the new year—is decorated with a chain of blue and yellow glazed tiles with 120 strolling lions (representing the goddess Ishtar). To get the big picture, find the model of the original site in the center of the hall.

These main exhibits are surrounded by smaller galleries. Upstairs is the **Museum of Islamic Art.** It contains fine carpets, tile work, the Aleppo Room (with ornately painted wooden walls from an early 17th-century home in today's Syria; since it was commissioned by a Christian, it incorporates Arabic, Persian, and biblical themes), and the Mshatta Facade (walls and towers from one of the early eighth-century Umayyad "desert castles," from today's Jordan).

▲▲Neues (New) Museum and Egyptian Collection

Oddly, Museum Island's so-called "new" museum features the oldest stuff around. There are three collections here: the Egyptian Collection (with the famous bust of Queen Nefertiti; floor 0 and parts of floors 1-2), the Museum of Prehistory and Early History (floor 3 and parts of floors 1-2), and some items from the Collection of Classical Antiquities (artifacts from ancient Troy—famously excavated by German adventurer Heinrich Schliemann—and

BERLIN

Cyprus, just off the entrance).

The top draw here is the Egyptian art—clearly one of the world's best collections. But let's face it: The main reason to visit is to enjoy one of the great thrills in art appreciation—gazing into the still-young-and-beautiful face of Queen Nefertiti. If you're in a pinch for time, make a beeline to her (floor 2, far corner of Egyptian Collection in room 210; for more on the museum, see www.neues-museum.de).

Audioguide: The fine audioguide (included with admission) celebrates new knowledge about ancient Egyptian civilization and offers fascinating insights into workaday Egyptian life as it describes the vivid papyrus collection, slice-of-life artifacts, and dreamy wax portraits decorating mummy cases.

Visiting the Museum: After being damaged in World War II and sitting in ruins for some 40 years, the Neues Museum was recently rebuilt. Everything is well-described by posted English information and the audioguide.

To tour the whole collection, begin by going all the way to the top (floor 3) where you'll find the **prehistory section.** The entire floor is filled with Stone Age, Ice Age, and Bronze Age items. You'll see early human remains, tools, spearheads, and pottery.

The most interesting item on this floor (in corner room 305) is the tall, conehead-like **Golden Hat,** made of paper-thin hammered gold leaf. Created by an early Celtic civilization in Central Europe, it's particularly exquisite for something so old (from the Bronze Age, around 1000 B.C.). The circles on the hat represent the sun, moon, and other celestial bodies—leading archaeologists to believe that this headwear could double as a calendar, showing how the sun and moon sync up every 19 years.

Down on floor 2, you'll find **early history** exhibits on migrations, barbarians, and ancient Rome (including larger-than-life statues of Helios and an unidentified goddess) as well as a fascinating look at the Dark Ages after the fall of Rome.

Still on floor 2, cross to the other side of the building for the **Egyptian** section. On the way, you'll pass through the impressive Papyrus Collection—a large room of seemingly empty glass cases. Press a button to watch a 3,000-year-old piece of primitive "paper" (made of aquatic reeds) imprinted with primitive text trundle out of its protective home.

Then, finally, in a room all her own, is the 3,000-year-old bust of **Queen Nefertiti** (the wife of King Akhenaton, c. 1340 B.C.)—the most famous piece of Egyptian art in Europe. Called "Berlin's most beautiful woman," Nefertiti has all the right beauty marks: long neck, symmetrical face, and the perfect amount of makeup. And yet, she's not completely idealized. Notice the fine wrinkles that show she's human (though these only enhance her beauty).

Like a movie star discreetly sipping a glass of wine at a sidewalk café, Nefertiti seems somehow more dignified in person. The bust never left its studio, but served as a master model for all other portraits of the queen. (That's probably why the left eye was never inlaid.)

How the queen arrived in Germany is a tale out of *Indiana Jones*. The German archaeologist Ludwig Borchardt uncovered her in the Egyptian desert in 1912. The Egyptian Department of Antiquities had first pick of all the artifacts uncovered on their territory. After the first takings, they divided the rest 50/50 with the excavators. When Borchardt presented Nefertiti to the Egyptians, they passed her over, never bothering to examine her closely. Unsubstantiated rumors persist that Borchardt misled the Egyptians in order to keep the bust for himself—rumors that have prompted some Egyptians to call for the return of Nefertiti (just as the Greeks are lobbying the British to return the Parthenon frieze currently housed in the British Museum). Although this bust is not particularly representative of Egyptian art in general—and despite increasing claims that her long neck suggests she's a Neoclassical fake—Nefertiti has become a symbol of Egyptian art by popular acclaim.

The Egyptian Collection continues with other sculptures, including kneeling figures holding steles (stone tablets inscribed with prayers). On floor 1, a fascinating exhibit examines how depictions of the human image evolved during the 3,000-year span of ancient Egyptian culture. You'll also see entire walls from tombs and (in the basement—floor 0) a sea of large sarcophagi.

▲Old National Gallery (Alte Nationalgalerie)

This gallery, behind the Neues Museum and Altes Museum, is designed to look like a Greek temple. Spanning three floors, it focuses on art (mostly paintings) from the 19th century: Romantic German paintings (which I find most interesting) on the top floor, and French and German Impressionists and German Realists on the first and second floors. You likely won't recognize any specific paintings, but it's still an enjoyable stroll through German culture from the century in which that notion first came to mean something. The included audioguide explains the highlights.

Visiting the Museum: Start on the third floor, with Romantic canvases and art of the Goethe era (roughly 1770-1830), and work your way down. Use the audioguide to really delve into these romanticized, vivid looks at life in Germany in the 19th century and before. As you stroll through the Romantic paintings—the museum's strength—keep in mind that they were created about the time (mid-late 19th century) that Germans were first working toward a single, unified nation. By glorifying pristine German landscapes and a rugged, virtuous people, these painters evoked the region's high-water mark—the Middle Ages, when "Germany" was a patchwork of powerful and wealthy merchant city-states. Linger over dreamy townscapes with Gothic cathedrals and castles that celebrate medieval German might. Still lifes, idealized portraits of tow-headed children, and genre paintings (depicting everyday scenes, often with subtle social commentary) strum the heartstrings of anyone with Teutonic blood. The Düsseldorf School excelled at Romantic landscapes (such as Carl Friedrich Lessing's *Castle on a Rock*). Some of these canvases nearly resemble present-day fantasy paintings. Perhaps the best-known artist in the collection is Caspar David Friedrich, who specialized in dramatic scenes celebrating grandeur and the solitary hero. His *The Monk by the Sea (Der Mönch am Meer)* shows a lone figure standing on a sand dune, pondering a vast, turbulent expanse of sea and sky.

On the second floor, you'll find one big room of minor works by bigger-name French artists, including Renoir, Cézanne, Manet, Monet, and Rodin. Another room is devoted to the Romantic Hans von Marées, the influential early Symbolist Arnold Böcklin, and other artists of the "German Roman" (Deutschrömer) movement—Germans who lived in, and were greatly influenced by, Rome. Artists of the Munich School are represented by naturalistic canvases of landscapes or slice-of-life scenes.

On the first floor, 19th-century Realism reigns. While the Realist Adolph Menzel made his name painting elegant royal gatherings and historical events, his *Iron Rolling Mill (Das Eisenwalzwerk)* captures the gritty side of his moment in history—the emergence of the Industrial Age—with a warts-and-all look at steelworkers toiling in a hellish factory. The first floor also hosts a sculpture collection, with works by great sculptors both foreign (the Italian Canova, the Dane Thorvaldsen) and German (Johann Gottfried Schadow's delightful *Die Prinzessinnen,* showing the dynamic duo of Prussian princesses Louise and Frederike).

Bode Museum

At the "prow" of Museum Island, the Bode Museum (designed to appear as if it's rising up from the river), is worth a quick look. Just inside, a grand statue of Frederick William of Brandenburg on horseback, curly locks blowing in the wind, welcomes you into the lonely halls of the museum. This fine building contains a hodgepodge of collections: Byzantine art, historic coins, ecclesiastical art, sculptures, and medals commemorating the fall of the Berlin Wall and German reunification.

Altes (Old) Museum

The least interesting of the five museums, this building features the rest of the Collection of Classical Antiquities (the best of which is in the Pergamon Museum)—namely, Etruscan, Roman, and Greek art. I'd skip it.

Other Sights on and near Museum Island

In addition to the five museums just described, Museum Island is home to the following sights. One more sight (the DDR Museum) sits just across the river.

Lustgarten—For 300 years, the island's big central square has flip-flopped between being a military parade ground and a people-friendly park, depending upon the political tenor of the time. During the revolutions of 1848, the Kaiser's troops dispersed a protesting crowd that had assembled here, sending demonstrators onto footpaths. Karl Marx later commented, "It is impossible to have a revolution in a country where people stay off the grass."

Until recently, it was *verboten* to relax or walk on the Lustgarten's grass. But in 1999, the Lustgarten was made into a park (read the history posted in the corner opposite the church). On a sunny day, it's packed with relaxing locals and is one of Berlin's most enjoyable public spaces.

Berlin Cathedral (Berliner Dom)—This century-old church towers over Museum Island. Inside, the great reformers (Luther, Calvin, and company) stand around the brilliantly restored dome like stern saints guarding their theology. Frederick I rests in an ornate tomb (right transept, near entrance to dome). The 270-step climb to the outdoor dome gallery is tough but offers pleasant, breezy views of the city at the finish line. The crypt downstairs is not worth a look.

Cost and Hours: €7 includes access to dome gallery, €10 with audioguide, not covered by Museum Island ticket, Mon-Sat 9:00-20:00, Sun 12:00-20:00, until 19:00 Oct-March, closes early—around 17:30—on some days for concerts, interior closed but dome open during services, tel. 030/2026-9136, www.berliner-dom.de. The cathedral hosts many organ concerts (often on weekends, tickets from about €10 always available at the door).

Humboldt-Forum Construction Site (Former Site of Hohenzollern Palace)—Across Unter den Linden from Berlin Cathedral is a big lawn that for centuries held the Baroque palace of the Hohenzollern dynasty of Brandenburg and Prussia. Much of that palace actually survived World War II but was replaced by the communists with a blocky, Soviet-style "Palace" of the Republic—East Berlin's parliament building/entertainment complex and a showy symbol of the communist days. The landmark building fell into disrepair after reunification and was eventually dismantled in 2007. After much debate about how to use this prime real estate, the German parliament decided to construct the Humboldt-Forum, a huge public venue filled with museums, shops, galleries, and concert halls behind a facade constructed in imitation of the original Hohenzollern palace. With a €1.2 billion price tag, many Berliners consider the reconstruction plan a complete waste of money.

The temporary **Humboldt-Box** has been set up to help the public follow the construction of the new Humboldt-Forum. The multiple floors of the futuristic "box" display building plans and models for the project (€4, daily 10:00-22:00, tel. 01805-030-707, www.humboldt-box.com). On the top floor, a terrace-café with unobstructed views over Berlin serves coffee, desserts, and light food until 18:00, and a dinner menu after that (€5-15 lunch dishes, €15-22 dinners).

Spree River Cruises—The recommended Spree River boat tours depart from the riverbank near the bridge by the Berlin Cathedral. For details, see page 563.

• *Directly across the bridge from Museum Island, down along the riverbank, look for the...*

▲**DDR Museum**—Although this exhibit began as a tourist trap, it has expanded and matured into a genuinely interesting look at life in former East Germany (DDR). It's well-stocked with kitschy everyday items from the communist period, plus photos, video clips, and concise English explanations. The exhibits are interactive—you're encouraged to pick up and handle anything that isn't behind glass. You'll crawl through a Trabant car (designed by East German engineers to compete with the West's popular VW Beetle) and pick up some DDR-era jokes ("East Germany had 39 newspapers, four radio stations, two TV channels...and one opinion.") The reconstructed communist-era home lets you tour the kitchen, living room, bedrooms, and more. You'll learn about the Russian-imported *Dacha*—the simple countryside cottage (owned by one in six East Germans) used for weekend retreats from the grimy city. (Others vacationed on the Baltic Coast, where nudism was all the rage, as a very revealing display explains.) Lounge in DDR movie chairs as you view a subtitled propaganda film or clips from beloved-in-the-East TV shows (including the popular kids' show *Sandmännchen—Little Sandman*). Even the meals served in the attached restaurant are based on DDR-era recipes.

Cost and Hours: €6, daily 10:00-20:00, Sat until 22:00, just across the Spree from Museum Island at Karl-Liebknecht-Strasse 1, tel. 030/847-123-731, www.ddr-museum.de.

Museum Island to Alexanderplatz

• *Continue walking down Unter den Linden. Before crossing the bridge (and leaving Museum Island), look across the river. The pointy twin spires of the 13th-century Nikolai Church mark the center of medieval*

Berlin. This **Nikolaiviertel** *(Viertel means "quarter") was restored by the DDR and trendy in the last years of communism. Today, it's a lively-at-night riverside restaurant district.*

As you cross the bridge, look left in the distance to see the gilded **New Synagogue** dome, rebuilt after WWII bombing (described on page 603).

Across the river to the left of the bridge, directly below you, is the **DDR Museum** (described earlier). Just beyond that is the giant **SAS Radisson Hotel** and shopping center, with a huge aquarium in the center. The elevator goes right through the middle of a deep-sea world. (You can see it from the unforgettable Radisson hotel lobby—tuck in your shirt and walk past the guards with the confidence of a guest who's sleeping there.) Here in the center of the old communist capital, it seems that capitalism has settled in with a spirited vengeance.

In the park immediately across the street (a big jaywalk from the Radisson) are grandfatherly statues of **Marx and Engels** (nicknamed "the old pensioners"). Surrounding them are stainless-steel monoliths with evocative photos that show the struggles of the workers of the world.

Walk toward **Marien Church** (from 1270), just left of the base of the TV Tower. An artist's rendering helps you follow the interesting but very faded old "Dance of Death" mural that wraps around the narthex inside the door.

The big red-brick building past the trees on the right is the **City Hall,** built after the revolutions of 1848 and arguably the first democratic building in the city.

The 1,200-foot-tall **TV Tower** (Fernsehturm) has a fine view from halfway up (€11, daily March-Oct 9:00-24:00, Nov-Feb 10:00-24:00, www.tv-turm.de). The tower offers a handy city orientation and an interesting view of the flat, red-roofed sprawl of Berlin—including a peek inside the city's many courtyards *(Höfe)*. Consider a kitschy trip to the observation deck for the view and lunch in its revolving restaurant (mediocre food, €12 plates, horrible lounge music, reservations smart for dinner, tel. 030/242-3333). The retro tower is quite trendy these days, so it can be crowded (your ticket comes with an assigned entry time). Built (with Swedish know-how) in 1969 for the 20th anniversary of the communist government, the tower was meant to show the power of the atheistic state at a time when DDR leaders were having the crosses removed from church domes and spires. But when the sun shined on their tower—the greatest spire in East Berlin—a huge cross was reflected on the mirrored ball. Cynics called it "The Pope's Revenge." East Berliners dubbed the tower the "Tele-Asparagus." They joked that if it fell over, they'd have an elevator to the West.

Farther east, pass under the train tracks into **Alexanderplatz.**

BERLIN

This area—especially the former Kaufhof department store (now Galeria Kaufhof)—was the commercial pride and joy of East Berlin. Today, it's still a landmark, with a major U- and S-Bahn station. The once-futuristic, now-retro "World Time Clock," installed in 1969, is a nostalgic favorite and a popular meeting point. Stop in the square for a coffee and to people-watch. It's a great scene.

• *Our orientation stroll or bus ride (this is the last stop for bus #100) is finished. From here, you can hike back a bit to catch the riverboat tour, take in the sights south of Unter den Linden, venture into the colorful Prenzlauer Berg neighborhood, or consider extending this foray into eastern Berlin.*

Karl-Marx-Allee

The buildings along Karl-Marx-Allee in East Berlin (just beyond Alexanderplatz) were completely leveled by the Red Army in 1945. As an expression of their adoration to the "great Socialist Father" (Stalin), the DDR government decided to rebuild the street better than ever (the USSR provided generous subsidies). They intentionally made it one meter wider than the Champs-Elysées, named it Stalinallee, and lined it with "workers' palaces" built in the bold "Stalin Gothic" style so common in Moscow in the 1950s. Now renamed after Karl Marx, the street and its restored buildings provide a rare look at Berlin's communist days. Distances are a bit long for convenient walking, but you can cruise Karl-Marx-Allee by taxi, or ride the U-Bahn to Strausberger Platz (which was built to resemble an Italian promenade) and walk to Frankfurter Tor, reading the good information posts along the way. Notice the Social Realist reliefs on the buildings and the lampposts, which incorporate the wings of a phoenix (rising from the ashes) in their design. Once a "workers' paradise," the street now hosts a two-mile-long capitalist beer festival the first weekend in August.

The **Café Sibylle,** just beyond the Strausberger Platz U-Bahn station, is a fun spot for a coffee, traditional DDR ice-cream treats, and a look at its free informal museum that tells the story of the most destroyed street in Berlin. While the humble exhibit is nearly all in German, it's fun to see the ear (or buy a €10 plaster replica) and half a moustache from what was the largest statue of Stalin in Germany (the centerpiece of the street until 1961). It also provides a few intimate insights into apartment life in a DDR flat. The café is known for its good coffee and *Schwedeneisbecher mit Eierlikor*—an ice-cream sundae with a shot of egg liqueur, popular among those nostalgic for communism (Mon-Fri 10:00-20:00, Sat-Sun 11:00-20:00, Karl-Marx-Allee 72, at intersection with Koppenstrasse, a block from U-Bahn: Strausberger Platz, tel. 030/2935-2203).

Heading out to Karl-Marx-Allee (just beyond the TV Tower),

you're likely to notice a giant colorful **mural** decorating a blocky communist-era skyscraper. This was the Ministry of Education, and the mural is a tile mosaic trumpeting the accomplishments of the DDR's version of "No Child Left Behind."

South of Unter den Linden

The following sights—heavy on Nazi and Wall history—are listed roughly north to south (as you reach them from Unter den Linden).

▲▲Gendarmenmarkt

This delightful, historic square is bounded by twin churches, a tasty chocolate shop, and the Berlin Symphony's concert hall (designed by Karl Friedrich Schinkel, the man who put the Neoclassical stamp on Berlin and Dresden). In summer, it hosts a few outdoor cafés, *Biergarten*s, and sometimes concerts. Wonderfully symmetrical, the square is considered by Berliners to be the finest in town (U6: Französische Strasse; U2 or U6: Stadtmitte).

The name of the square—part French and part German (after the *Gens d'Armes,* Frederick the Great's royal guard who were headquartered here)—reminds us that in the 17th century, a fifth of all Berliners were French émigrés—Protestant Huguenots fleeing Catholic France. Back then, Frederick the Great's tolerant Prussia was a magnet for the persecuted (and for their money). These émigrés vitalized Berlin with new ideas and know-how...and their substantial wealth.

Of the two matching churches on Gendarmenmarkt, the one to the south (bottom end of square) is the **German Cathedral** (Deutscher Dom). This cathedral (not to be confused with the Berlin Cathedral on Unter den Linden) was bombed flat in the war and rebuilt only in the 1980s. It houses the thought-provoking Milestones, Setbacks, Sidetracks *(Wege, Irrwege, Umwege)* exhibit, which traces the history of the German parliamentary system— worth ▲. The parliament-funded exhibit—while light on actual historical artifacts—is well done and more interesting than it sounds. It takes you quickly from the revolutionary days of 1848 to the 1920s, and then more deeply through the tumultuous 20th century. As the exhibit is designed for Germans rather than for-eign tourists, there are no English descriptions—but you can fol-low the essential, excellent, and free 1.5-hour English audioguide or buy the wonderfully detailed €10 guidebook. If you think this museum is an attempt by the German government to develop a more sophisticated and educated electorate in the interest of stron-ger democracy, you're exactly right. Germany knows (from its own troubled history) that a dumbed-down electorate, manipulated by clever spin-meisters and sound-bite media blitzes, is a dangerous thing (free, Tue-Sun May-Sept 10:00-19:00, Oct-April 10:00-18:00, closed Mon year-round, tel. 030/2273-0431).

The **French Cathedral** (Französischer Dom), at the north end of the square, offers a humble museum on the Huguenots (€2, Tue-Sat 12:00-17:00, Sun 11:00-17:00, closed Mon, enter around the right side) and a viewpoint in the dome up top (€3, daily 10:30-19:00, last entry at 18:00, 244 steps, enter through door facing square). Fun fact: Neither of these churches is a true cathedral, as they never contained a bishop's throne; their German title of *Dom* (cathedral) is actually a mistranslation from the French word *dôme* (cupola).

Fassbender & Rausch, on the corner near the German Cathedral, claims to be Europe's biggest chocolate store. After 150 years of chocolate-making, this family-owned business proudly displays its sweet delights—250 different kinds—on a 55-foot-long buffet. Truffles are sold for about €0.60 each; it's fun to compose a fancy little eight-piece box of your own for about €5. Upstairs is an elegant hot chocolate café with fine views. The window displays feature giant chocolate models of Berlin landmarks—Reichstag, TV Tower, Kaiser Wilhelm Memorial Church, and so on. If all this isn't enough to entice you, I have three words: "Erupting Chocolate Volcano" (Mon-Sat 10:00-20:00, Sun 11:00-20:00, corner of Mohrenstrasse at Charlottenstrasse 60, tel. 030/2045-8440).

Gendarmenmarkt is buried in what has recently emerged as Berlin's "Fifth Avenue" shopping district. For the ultimate in top-end shops, find the corner of Jägerstrasse and Friedrichstrasse and wander through the **Quartier 206** (Mon-Fri 10:30-19:30, Sat 10:00-18:00, closed Sun, www.quartier206.com). The adjacent, middlebrow **Quartier 205** has more affordable prices.

Nazi and Cold War Sites on Wilhelmstrasse

Fragment of the Wall—Surviving stretches of the Wall are virtually nonexistent in downtown Berlin. One of the most convenient places to see a bit is at the intersection of Wilhelmstrasse and Zimmerstrasse/Niederkirchnerstrasse, a few blocks southwest of Gendarmenmarkt. Many visitors make the short walk over here from the Checkpoint Charlie sights (described later), then drop into the museum listed next.

▲▲Topography of Terror (Topographie des Terrors)—Coincidentally, the patch of land behind the surviving stretch of Wall was closely associated with a different regime: It was once the nerve center for the most despicable elements of the Nazi government, the Gestapo and the SS. This stark-gray, boxy building is one of the few memorial sites that focuses on the perpetrators rather than the victims of the Nazis. It's a chilling but fascinating experience to see just how seamlessly and bureaucratically the Nazi institutions and state structures merged to become a well-oiled terror machine. There are few actual artifacts; it's mostly written explanations and photos, like reading a good textbook standing up. And, while you could read this story anywhere, to take this in atop the Gestapo headquarters is a powerful experience. The exhibit's a bit dense, but WWII historians (even armchair ones) will find it fascinating.

Cost and Hours: Free, daily 10:00-20:00, outdoor exhibit closes at sunset in winter, Niederkirchnerstrasse 8, tel. 030/254-5090, www.topographie.de.

Background: This location marks what was once the most feared address in Berlin: the headquarters of the Reich Main Security Office *(Reichssicherheitshauptamt)*. These offices served as the engine room of the Nazi dictatorship, as well as the command center of the SS *(Schutzstaffel,* whose members began as Hitler's personal bodyguards), the Gestapo *(Geheime Staatspolizei,* secret state police), and the SD *(Sicherheitsdienst,* the Nazi intelligence agency). This trio (and others) were ultimately consolidated under Heinrich Himmler to become a state-within-a-state, with talons in every corner of German society. This elite militarized branch of the Nazi machine was also tasked with the "racial purification" of German-held lands, especially Eastern Europe—the Holocaust. It was from these headquarters that the Nazis administered concentration camps, firmed up plans for the "Final Solution to the Jewish Question," and organized the domestic surveillance of anyone opposed to the regime. The building was also equipped with dungeons, where the Gestapo detained and tortured thousands of prisoners.

The Gestapo and SS employed intimidation techniques to coerce cooperation from the German people. The general public knew that the Gestapo was to be feared: It was considered omnipotent, omnipresent, and omniscient. Some political prisoners underwent "enhanced interrogation" right here in this building. The threat of *Schutzhaft* ("protective custody," usually at a concentration camp) was used to terrify any civilians who stepped out of line—or who might make a good example. But Hitler and his cronies also won people's loyalties through propaganda. They hammered home the idealistic notion of the *Volksgemeinschaft* ("people's community") of a purely Germanic culture and race, which empowered Hitler to create a pervasive illusion that "We're all in this together." Anyone who was not an Aryan was *Untermensch*—subhuman—and must be treated as such.

Visiting the Museum: The complex has two parts: indoors, in the modern boxy building; and outdoors, in the trench that runs along the surviving stretch of Wall. Visit the indoor exhibit first.

BERLIN

Inside, you'll find a visitor center with an information desk and an extensive **Topography of Terror** exhibit about the SS and Gestapo, and the atrocities they committed in Berlin and across Europe. A model of the government quarter, circa 1939, sets the stage of Nazi domination in this area. A timeline of events and old photographs, documents, and newspaper clippings illustrate how Hitler and his team expertly manipulated the German people to build a broadly supported "dictatorship of consent."

The exhibit walks you through the evolution of Hitler's regime: the Nazi takeover; institutions of terror (Himmler's "SS State"); terror, persecution, and extermination; atrocities in Nazi-occupied countries; and the war's end and postwar. Some images here are indelible, such as photos of SS soldiers stationed at Auschwitz, gleefully yukking it up on a retreat in the countryside (even as their helpless prisoners were being gassed and burned a few miles away). The exhibit profiles specific members of the various reprehensible SS branches, as well as the groups they targeted: Jews, Roma, and Sinti (Gypsies); the unemployed or homeless; homosexuals; and the physically and mentally ill (considered "useless eaters" who consumed resources without contributing work).

Downstairs is a WC and a library with research books on these topics. Before heading outside, ask at the information desk to borrow the free audioguide that describes the outdoor exhibits.

Outside, in the trench along the Wall, you'll find the exhibit **Berlin 1933-1945: Between Propaganda and Terror,** which overlaps slightly with the indoor exhibit but focuses on Berlin. The chronological survey begins with the post-WWI Weimar Republic and continues through the ragged days just after World War II. One display explains how Nazis invented holidays (or injected new Aryan meaning into existing ones) as a means of winning over the public. Other exhibits cover the "Aryanization" of Jewish businesses (they were simply taken over by the state and handed over to new Aryan owners); Hitler's plans for converting Berlin into a gigantic "Welthauptstadt (World Capital) Germania"; and the postwar Berlin Airlift, which brought provisions to some 2.2 million West Berliners whose supply lines were cut off by East Berlin.

With more time, explore the grounds around the blocky building on a **"Site Tour."** Posted signs explain 15 different locations, including the scant remains of the prison cellars.

German Finance Ministry (Bundesministerium der Finanzen)—Across the street (facing the Wall chunk) are the former headquarters of the Nazi Luftwaffe (Air Force), the only major Hitler-era government building that survived the war's bombs. Notice how the whole building gives off a monumental feel, making the average person feel small and powerless. Walk into the stark courtyard. After the war, this was the headquarters for the

Soviet occupation. Later the DDR was founded here, and the communists used the building to house their—no joke—Ministry of Ministries. Walk up Wilhelmstrasse (to the north) to see an entry gate (on your left) that looks much like it did when Germany occupied nearly all of Europe. On the north side of the building (farther up Wilhelmstrasse, at corner with Leipziger Strasse) is a wonderful example of communist art. The mural, Max Lingner's *Aufbau der Republik* (*Building the Republic*, 1953), is classic Socialist Realism, showing the entire society—industrial laborers, farm workers, women, and children—all happily singing the same patriotic song. Its subtitle: "The importance of peace for the cultural development of humanity and the necessity of struggle to achieve this goal." This was the communist ideal. For the reality, look at the ground in the courtyard in front of the mural to see an enlarged photograph from a 1953 uprising here against the communists...quite a contrast. Placards explain the events of 1953 in English.

Stasi Museum—This modest exhibit, roughly between the Topography of Terror and Checkpoint Charlie, tells the story of how the communist-era Ministry for State Security (*Staatssicherheit*, a.k.a. Stasi) infiltrated all aspects of German life. Soon after the Wall fell, DDR authorities scrambled to destroy the copious illicit information their agents and informants had collected about the people of East Germany. But the government mandated that these records be preserved as evidence of DDR crimes, and the documents are now managed by the Federal Commissioner for Stasi Records. A timeline traces the history of the archives, and wraparound kiosks profile individual "subversive elements" who were targeted by the Stasi. There are a few actual artifacts, but the exhibit is mostly dryly written texts and reproduced photographs that don't do much to personalize the victims—making this museum worth a visit only for those with a special interest in this period. Temporary exhibits are upstairs.

Cost and Hours: Free, Mon-Sat 10:00-18:00, closed Sun, Zimmerstrasse 90-91, tel. 030/232-450, www.bstu.bund.de.

Other Stasi Sites: If you're interested in this chapter of East German history, you may find it more satisfying (but time-consuming) to visit two other sites affiliated with the Stasi: a different **Stasi Museum**, in the former State Security headquarters (€5, Mon-Fri 11:00-18:00, Sat-Sun 14:00-18:00, Ruscherstarsse 103, U-5: Magdalenenstrasse, tel. 030/553-6854, www.stasimuseum.de); and the **Stasi Prison**, where "enemies of the state" served time (€4, visits possible only with a tour; English tours daily at 14:30—call to confirm before making the trip; German tours Mon-Fri at 11:00, 13:00, and 15:00, Sat-Sun hourly 10:00-16:00; Genslerstrasse 66, reachable on various trams from downtown—see website for specifics, tel. 030/9860-8230, www.stiftung-hsh.de).

Checkpoint Charlie

This famous Cold War checkpoint was not named for a person, but for its checkpoint number—as in Alpha (#1, at the East-West German border, a hundred miles west of here), Bravo (#2, as you enter Berlin proper), and Charlie (#3, the best known because most foreigners passed through here). While the actual checkpoint has long since been dismantled, its former location is home to a fine museum and a mock-up of the original border crossing. The area has become a Cold War freak show and—as if celebrating the final victory of crass capitalism—is one of Berlin's worst tourist-trap zones. A McDonald's stands defiantly overlooking the former haunt of East German border guards. You can even pay an exorbitant €10 for a full set of Cold War-era stamps in your passport. (For a more sober and intellectually redeeming look at the Wall's history, head for the out-of-the-way Berlin Wall Memorial at Bernauer Strasse, north of here near the Prenzlauer Berg neighborhood and described on page 605. Local officials, likely put off by the touristy crassness of the Checkpoint Charlie scene, have steered local funding to that area.)

▲**Checkpoint Charlie Street Scene and Other Wall Sites**— Where Checkpoint Charlie once stood, notice the thought-provoking post with larger-than-life **posters** of a young American soldier facing east and a young Soviet soldier facing west. The rebuilt **guard station** now hosts two actors playing American guards who pose for photos. (Across the street is Snack Point Charlie.) A **photo exhibit** stretches down the street, with great English descriptions telling the story of the Wall. While you could get this information from a book, it's poignant to stand here in person and ponder the gripping history of this place.

A few yards away (on Zimmerstrasse), a **glass panel** describes the former checkpoint. From there, a double row of **cobbles** in Zimmerstrasse traces the former path of the Wall. These innocuous cobbles run throughout the city, even through some buildings.

Farther down on Zimmerstrasse, before Charlottenstrasse, find the **Memorial to Peter Fechter** (set just off the sidewalk, barely inside the Wall marker), who was shot and left for dead here in the early days of the Wall.

▲▲**Museum of the Wall at Checkpoint Charlie (Mauermuseum Haus am Checkpoint Charlie)**—While the famous border checkpoint between the American and Soviet sectors is long gone, its memory is preserved by one of Europe's most cluttered museums. During the Cold War, the House at Checkpoint Charlie stood defiantly—spitting distance from the border guards—showing off all the clever escapes over, under, and through the Wall. Today, while the drama is over and hunks of the Wall stand like trophies at its door, the museum survives as a living artifact of the

BERLIN

Cold War days. The yellowed descriptions, which have scarcely changed since that time, tinge the museum with nostalgia. It's dusty, disorganized, and overpriced, with lots of reading involved, but all that just adds to this museum's borderline-kitschy charm. If you're pressed for time, this is a decent after-dinner sight.

Cost and Hours: €12.50, assemble 20 tourists and get in for €8.50 each, €3.50 audioguide, discount with WelcomeCard but not covered by Museumspass, daily 9:00-22:00, U6 to Kochstrasse or—better from Zoo—U2 to Stadtmitte, Friedrichstrasse 43-45, tel. 030/253-7250, www.mauermuseum.de.

Visiting the Museum: Exhibits narrate a gripping history of the Wall, with a focus on the many ingenious **escape attempts** (the early years—with a cruder wall—saw more escapes). You'll see the actual items used to smuggle would-be Wessies—a VW bug whose trunk hid a man, two side-by-side suitcases into which a woman squeezed, a makeshift zip line for crossing over (rather than through) the border, a hot-air balloon in which two families floated to safety (immortalized in the Disney film *Night Crossing*), an inflatable boat that puttered across the dangerous Baltic Sea, primitive homemade aircraft, two surfboards hollowed out to create just enough space for a refugee, and more. One chilling exhibit lists some 43,000 people who died in "Internal Affairs" internment camps during the transition to communism (1945-1950). Profiles personalize various escapees and their helpers, including John P. Ireland, an American who posed as an eccentric antiques collector so he could transport 10 different refugees to safety in his modified Cadillac.

You'll also see **artwork** inspired by the Wall and its fall, and a memorial to Rainer Hildebrandt, who founded this museum shortly after the Wall went up in 1961 (he died in 2004, but the museum lives on as a shrine to his vision). On the **top floor** (easy to miss), that vision broadens to the larger themes of freedom and persecution, including exhibits on Eastern European rebellions (the 1956 uprising in Hungary, 1968's Prague Spring, and the Solidarity movement in 1980s Poland) and Gandhi's protests in India—plus a hodgepodge of displays on world religions and Picasso's *Guernica*. Fans of "the Gipper" appreciate the room honoring President Ronald Reagan, displaying his actual cowboy hat and boots. The small movie theater shows various Wall-related films (a schedule is posted), and the displays include video coverage of those heady days when people power tore down the Wall.

▲▲Jewish Museum Berlin
(Jüdisches Museum Berlin)

This museum is one of Europe's best Jewish sights. The highly conceptual building is a sight in itself, and the museum inside—

an overview of the rich culture and history of Europe's Jewish community—is excellent, particularly if you take advantage of the informative and engaging audioguide. Rather than just reading dry texts, you'll feel this museum as fresh and alive—an exuberant celebration of the Jewish experience that's accessible to all. Even though the museum is in a nondescript residential neighborhood, it's well worth the trip.

Cost and Hours: €5, sometimes extra for special exhibits, discount with WelcomeCard, daily 10:00-20:00, Mon until 22:00, last entry one hour before closing, closed on Jewish holidays. Tight security includes bag check and metal detectors. The excellent €3 audioguide—with four hours of commentary on 151 different items—is essential to fully appreciate the exhibits. Tel. 030/2599-3300, www.jmberlin.de.

Getting There: Take the U-Bahn to Hallesches Tor, find the exit marked *Jüdisches Museum*, exit straight ahead, then turn right on Franz-Klühs-Strasse. The museum is a five-minute walk ahead on your left, at Lindenstrasse 9.

Eating: The museum's restaurant, Liebermanns, offers good Jewish-style meals, albeit not kosher (€9 daily specials, lunch served 12:00-16:00, snacks at other times, tel. 030/2593-9760).

Visiting the Museum: Designed by American architect Daniel Libeskind (the master planner for the redeveloped World Trade Center in New York), the zinc-walled building has a zigzag shape pierced by voids symbolic of the irreplaceable cultural loss caused by the Holocaust. Enter the 18th-century Baroque building next door, then go through an underground tunnel to reach the museum interior.

Before you reach the exhibit, your visit starts with three **memorial spaces.** Follow the Axis of Exile to a disorienting slanted garden with 49 pillars (evocative of the Memorial to the Murdered Jews of Europe, across town). Next, the Axis of Holocaust, lined with artifacts from Jews imprisoned and murdered by the Nazis, leads to an eerily empty tower shut off from the outside world. The Axis of Continuity takes you to stairs and the main exhibit. A detour partway up the long stairway leads to the Memory Void, a thought-provoking space of "fallen leaves": heavy metal faces that you walk on, making unhuman noises with each step.

Finish climbing the stairs to the top of the museum, and stroll chronologically through the 2,000-year **story of Judaism** in Germany. The exhibit, on two floors, is engaging, with lots of actual artifacts. Interactive bits (for example, spell your name in Hebrew, or write a prayer and hang it from a tree) make it lively for kids. English explanations interpret both the exhibits and the design of the very symbolic building.

The top floor focuses on everyday life in Ashkenaz (medieval German-Jewish lands). The nine-minute movie "A Thousand Years Ago" sets the stage for your journey through Jewish history. You'll learn what garlic had to do with early Jews in Germany (hint: It's not just about cooking). The Middle Ages was a positive time for Jewish culture, which flourished in many areas of Europe. But around 1500, many Jews were expelled from the countryside and moved into cities. Viewing stations let you watch nine short, lively videos that pose provocative questions about faith. Moses Mendelssohn's role in the late-18th-century Jewish Enlightenment, which gave rise to Reform Judaism, is highlighted. The Tradition and Change exhibit analyzes how various subgroups of the Jewish faith modified and relaxed their rules to adapt to a changing world.

Downstairs, on the middle floor, exhibits detail the rising tide of anti-Semitism in Germany through the 19th century—ironically, at a time when many Jews were so secularized that they celebrated Christmas right along with Hanukkah. Berlin's glory days (1890-1933) were a boom time for many Jews, though it was at times challenging to reconcile the reformed ways of the more assimilated western (German) Jews with the more traditional Eastern European Jews. The exhibit segues into the **dark days** of Hitler—the collapse of the relatively tolerant Weimar Republic, the rise of the Nazis, and the horrific night of November 9-10, 1938, when, throughout Germany, hateful mobs destroyed Jewish-owned businesses, homes, synagogues, and even entire villages—called "Crystal Night" (Kristallnacht) for the broken glass that glittered in the streets.

The thought-provoking conclusion brings us to the present day, with the question: How do you keep going after six million of your people have been murdered? You'll see how German society has reacted to the Holocaust blood on their hands (one fascinating exhibit has footage of a 1975 sit-in of German Jews to protest a controversial play with a stereotypical Jewish villain), and listen to headphone commentary of Jewish people describing their experiences growing up in postwar Germany, Austria, and Switzerland.

More Sights South of Unter den Linden

East Side Gallery—The biggest remaining stretch of the Wall is now "the world's longest outdoor art gallery." It stretches for nearly a mile and is covered with murals painted by artists from around the world. The murals (classified as protected monuments) got a facelift in 2009, when the city invited the original artists back to re-create their work for the 20th anniversary of the fall of the Wall. This segment of the Wall makes a poignant walk. For a quick look, take the S-Bahn to the Ostbahnhof station (follow signs to Stralauerplatz exit; once outside, TV Tower will be to your right;

BERLIN

go left and at next corner look to your right—the Wall is across the busy street). The gallery is slowly being consumed by developers. If you walk the entire length of the East Side Gallery, you'll find a small Wall souvenir shop at the end and a bridge crossing the river to a subway station at Schlesisches Tor (in Kreuzberg). The bridge, a fine example of Brandenburg Neo-Gothic brickwork, has a fun neon "rock, paper, scissors" installment poking fun at the futility of the Cold War.

Kreuzberg—This district—once abutting the dreary Wall and inhabited mostly by poor Turkish guest laborers and their families—is still run-down, with graffiti-riddled buildings and plenty of student and Turkish street life. It offers a gritty look at melting-pot Berlin, in a city where original Berliners are as rare as old buildings. Berlin is the largest Turkish city outside of Turkey itself, and Kreuzberg is its "downtown." But to call it a "little Istanbul" insults the big one. You'll see *Döner Kebab* stands, shops decorated with spray paint, and mothers wrapped in colorful scarves. But lately, an influx of immigrants from many other countries has diluted the Turkish-ness of Kreuzberg. Berliners come here for fun ethnic eateries. For an easy dose of Kreuzberg, joyride on bus #129 (catch it near Jewish Museum). For a colorful stroll, take the U-Bahn to Kottbusser Tor and wander—ideally on Tuesday and Friday between 12:00 and 18:00, when the Turkish Market sprawls along the Maybachufer riverbank.

North of Unter den Linden

There are few major sights to the north of Unter den Linden, but this area has some of Berlin's trendiest, most interesting neighborhoods. I've listed these roughly from south to north, as you'd approach them from the city center and Unter den Linden. On a sunny day, a stroll (or tram ride) through these bursting-with-life areas can be as engaging as any museum in town.

Hackescher Markt

This area, in front of the S-Bahn station of the same name, is a great people scene day and night. The brick trestle supporting the train track is another classic example of the city's Brandenburg Neo-Gothic brickwork. Most of the brick archways are now filled with hip shops, which have official—and newly trendy—addresses such as "S-Bahn Arch #9, Hackescher Markt." Within 100 yards of the S-Bahn station, you'll find Hackeschen Höfe (described next), recommended Turkish and Bavarian restaurants, walking-tour and pub-crawl departure points, and tram #M1 to Prenzlauer Berg.

  Hackeschen Höfe (a block in front of the Hackescher Markt S-Bahn station) is a series of eight courtyards bunny-hopping through a wonderfully restored 1907 *Jugendstil* (German Art

Nouveau) building. Berlin's apartments are organized like this—courtyard after courtyard leading off the main roads. This complex is full of trendy restaurants (including the recommended Turkish eatery, Hasir), theaters, and cinemas (playing movies in their original languages). This is a wonderful example of how to make huge city blocks livable. Two decades after the Cold War, this area has reached the final evolution of East Berlin's urban restoration. (These courtyards also serve a useful lesson for visitors: Much of Berlin's charm hides off the street front.)

Oranienburger Strasse

Oranienburger Strasse is anchored by an important and somber sight, the New Synagogue. But the rest of this zone (roughly between the synagogue and Torstrasse) is colorful and quirky—especially after dark. The streets behind Grosse Hamburger Strasse flicker with atmospheric cafés, *Kneipen* (pubs), and art galleries. At night (from about 20:00), techno-prostitutes line Oranienburger Strasse. Prostitution is legal throughout Germany. Prostitutes pay taxes and receive health care insurance like anyone else. On this street, they hire security guards (lingering nearby) for safety—and they all seem to buy their Barbarella wardrobes at the same place.

▲**New Synagogue (Neue Synagogue)**—A shiny gilded dome marks the New Synagogue, now a museum and cultural center. Consecrated in 1866, this was once the biggest and finest synagogue in Germany, with seating for 3,200 worshippers and a sumptuous Moorish-style interior modeled after the Alhambra. It was desecrated by Nazis on Crystal Night (Kristallnacht) in 1938, bombed in 1943, and partially rebuilt in 1990. Only the dome and facade have been restored—a window overlooks the vacant field marking what used to be the synagogue. On its facade, a small plaque—added by East Berlin Jews in 1966—reads "Never forget" *(Vergesst es nie)*. At that time East Berlin had only a few hundred Jews, but now that the city is reunited, the Jewish community numbers about 12,000.

Inside, past tight security, the small but moving permanent exhibit called Open Ye the Gates describes the Berlin Jewish community through the centuries (filling three big rooms on the ground floor and first floor, with some good English descriptions). Examine the cutaway model showing the entire synagogue (pre-destruction) and an exhibit of religious items. Stairs lead up (past temporary exhibits, with a separate entry fee) to the dome, where there's not much to see except the unimpressive-from-the-inside dome itself and ho-hum views—not worth the entry price or the climb.

Cost and Hours: Main exhibit-€3.50, dome-€2, temporary exhibits-€3, €7 combo-ticket covers everything, audioguide-€3;

March-Oct Sun-Mon 10:00-20:00, Tue-Thu 10:00-18:00, Fri 10:00-17:00—until 14:00 in Oct and March-May, closed Sat; Nov-Feb Sun-Thu 10:00-18:00, Fri 10:00-14:00, closed Sat; Oranienburger Strasse 28/30, enter through the low-profile door in the modern building just right of the domed synagogue facade, S-Bahn: Oranienburger Strasse, tel. 030/8802-8300 and press 1, www.cjudaicum.de.

Nearby: A block from the synagogue (to the right as you face it), walk 50 yards down **Grosse Hamburger Strasse** to a little park. This street was known for 200 years as the "street of toler-ance" because the Jewish community donated land to Protestants so they could build a church. Hitler turned it into the "street of death" *(Todes Strasse)*, bulldozing 12,000 graves of the city's oldest Jewish cemetery and turning a Jewish nursing home into a depor-tation center. Because of the small but growing radical Islamic ele-ment in Berlin, and a smattering of persistent neo-Nazis, several police officers and an Israeli secret agent keep watch over this park and the Jewish high school nearby.

▲Prenzlauer Berg

Young, in-the-know locals agree that Prenzlauer Berg (PRENTS-low-er behrk) is one of Berlin's most colorful neighborhoods (roughly between Helmholtzplatz and Kollwitzplatz and along Kastanienallee, U2: Senefelderplatz and Eberswalder Strasse; or take the S-Bahn to Hackescher Markt and catch tram #M1 north). Tourists call it "Prenzl'berg" for short, while Berliners just call it "der Berg." This part of the city was largely untouched dur-ing World War II, but its buildings slowly rotted away under the communists. After the Wall fell, it was overrun with laid-back hipsters, energetic young families, and clever entrepreneurs who breathed life back into its classic old apartment blocks, deserted factories, and long-forgotten breweries. Ten years of rent con-trol kept things affordable for its bohemian residents. But now landlords are free to charge what the market will bear, and the vibe is changing. This is ground zero for Berlin's baby boom: Tattooed and pierced young moms and dads, who've joined the modern rat-race without giving up their alternative flair, push their youngsters in designer strollers past trendy boutiques and restaurants. You'll count more kids here than just about anywhere else in town. Locals complain that these days the cafés and bars cater to yuppies sipping prosecco, while the working class and artistic types are being pushed out. While it has changed plenty, I still find Prenzlauer Berg a celebration of life and a joy to stroll through. Though it's a few blocks farther out than the neighbor-hoods described previously, it's a fun area to explore and have a meal (see page 636) or spend the night (see page 622).

▲Berlin Wall Memorial
(Gedenkstätte Berliner Mauer)

While tourists flock to Checkpoint Charlie, local authorities have been investing in this site to develop Berlin's most substantial attraction relating to its gone-but-not-forgotten Wall. Exhibits line up along a two-block stretch of Bernauer Strasse, stretching northeast from the Nordbahnhof S-Bahn station. You can enter two different museums; see several fragments of the Wall, plus various open-air exhibits and memorials; and peer from an observation tower down into a preserved, complete stretch of the Wall system (as it was during the Cold War).

Cost and Hours: Free; Visitor Center and Documentation Center open Tue-Sun 9:30-19:00, Nov-March until 18:00, closed Mon; outdoor areas open 24 hours daily; last English movie starts at 18:00, memorial chapel closes at 17:00; Bernauer Strasse 111, tel. 030/4679-86666, www.berliner-mauer-gedenkstaette.de.

Getting There: Take the S-Bahn (line S-1, S-2, or S-25—all handy from Potsdamer Platz, Brandenburger Tor, or Friedrichstrasse) to Nordbahnhof. The Nordbahnhof's underground hallways have history exhibits in English (explained later). Exit by following signs for *Bernauer Strasse,* and you'll pop out across the street from a long chunk of Wall and kitty-corner from the Visitor Center.

Background: The Berlin Wall, which was erected virtually overnight in 1961, ran right along Bernauer Strasse. People were suddenly separated from their neighbors across the street. This stretch was particularly notorious because existing apartment buildings were incorporated into the structure of the Wall itself. Film footage and photographs from the era show Berliners worriedly watching workmen seal off these buildings from the West, brick by brick. Some people attempted to leap to freedom from upper-story windows, with mixed results. One of the unfortunate ones was Ida Siekmann, who fell to her death from her third-floor apartment on August 22, 1961, and is considered the first casualty of the Berlin Wall.

Visiting the Memorial: From the Nordbahnhof station (which has some interesting Wall history in itself), head first to the Visitor Center to get your bearings, then explore the assorted Wall fragments and other sights in the park across the street. Work your way up Bernauer Strasse to the Documentation Center, Wall System, and memorial chapel.

Nordbahnhof—This S-Bahn station was one of the "ghost stations" of Cold War Berlin. As it was a dogleg of the East mostly surrounded by the West, Western subway trains had permission to use the underground tracks to zip through this station (without stopping, of course) en route between stops in the West. Posted information boards show photos comparing 1989 with 2009, and explain that East German border guards, who were stationed here to ensure that nobody got on or off those trains, were literally locked into their surveillance rooms to prevent them from escaping. (But one subway employee and his family used the tunnels to walk to the West and freedom.)

Follow signs down a long yellow hall to Bernauer Strasse. Climbing the stairs up to the Bernauer Strasse exit, ponder that the doorway at the top of these stairs (marked by the *Sperrmauer 1961-1989* plaque) was a bricked-off no-man's-land just 25 years ago. Stepping outside, you'll see the Wall park directly across the street, and the Visitor Center in a low, rust-colored building kitty-corner across the street.

Visitor Center (Bezucherzentrum)—This new, small complex has a helpful information desk, a bookstore, and two good movies that provide context for a visit (they run in English at the top of each hour, about 30 minutes for the whole spiel): *History of the Wall* offers a great 12-minute overview of why the Wall was built and how it fell. That's followed by *Walled In!*, an animated 12-minute film illustrating the Wall as it functioned here at Bernauer Strasse (Wall wonks will find it fascinating). Before leaving, pick up the brochure explaining the outdoor exhibits, and ask about any new exhibits.

Wall Fragments and Other Sights—Across the street from the Visitor Center is a long stretch of Wall. The park behind it is scattered with a few more Wall chunks as well as monuments and memorials honoring its victims. To get your bearings, find the small model of the entire area when the Wall still stood (just across the street from the Nordbahnhof). While most items are explained by English plaques, the brochure from the Visitor Center helps you better appreciate what you're seeing. The rusty "Window of Remembrance" monument honors slain would-be escapees with their names, dates of death, and transparent photos viewable from both sides. Before it was the no-man's-land between the walls, this area was the parish graveyard for a nearby church; ironically, DDR officials had to move a thousand graves from here to create a "death strip."

Berlin Wall Documentation Center (Dokumentations-zentrum Berliner Mauer)—This "Doku-Center" has two movies, a small exhibit, and a viewpoint tower overlooking the preserved Wall section. The two **films** shown on the ground floor are different from those screened at the Visitor Center: *The View*, dating from 1965, tells the story of an elderly West Berlin woman who lived near the Wall, and could look into the death strip and the East from her window (in German only). *Mauerflug* features aerial photography of Berlin from the spring of 1990—after the

Wall had opened, but while most of the 96-mile-long barricade still stood, offering an illuminating look at a divided city (English subtitles).

Upstairs is an **exhibit** with photos and videos detailing the construction of the Wall that began August 13, 1961. At the model of the Wall along Bernauer Strasse, notice how existing buildings were incorporated into the structure. Headphones let you listen to propagandistic, high-spirited oompah music from East Germany that celebrated the construction of the wall: "It was high time!" There's also a list of the 163 people who died attempting to cross the Wall. From the top-floor **viewpoint** look down at the Wall itself (described next).

Wall System—This is the last surviving intact bit of the "Wall system" (with both sides of its Wall—capped by the round pipe that made it tougher for escapees to get a grip—and its no-man's-land, or death strip). The guard tower came from a different part of the Wall; it was actually purchased on that great capitalist invention, eBay (somewhere, Stalin spins in his grave). A strip of photos and descriptions explains what you're seeing. Plaques along the sidewalk below you mark the locations of escapes or deaths.

Just beyond the Wall section (to the left), and also viewable from the tower, is a modern, cagelike church (described next).

Chapel of Reconciliation (Kapelle der Versöhnung)—This marks the spot of the late-19th-century Church of Reconciliation, which survived WWII bombs...but did not survive the communists. When the Wall was built, this church wound up, unusable, right in the middle of the death strip. It was torn down in 1985, supposedly because it got in the way of the border guards' sight lines. (This coincided with a period in which anti-DDR opposition movements were percolating in Christian churches, prompting the nonbeliever regime to destroy several houses of worship.) If you're interested, walk around the chapel for a closer look (it closes at 17:00). Notice the larger footprint of the original church in the field around it. The chapel hosts daily prayer services for the victims of the Wall.

More Wall Sights—Over the next few years, the Memorial plans to gradually add more open-air exhibitions about the Berlin Wall farther along Bernauer Strasse. Eventually the chain of sights will stretch all the way to Eberswalder Strasse and Oderberger Strasse, near the heart of Prenzlauer Berg.

Natural History Museum (Museum für Naturkunde)

This museum is worth a visit just to see the largest dinosaur skeleton ever assembled. While you're there, meet "Bobby" the stuffed ape, and tour the new Wet Collections, displaying shelf after shelf of animals preserved in ethanol (about a million all together). The museum is a magnet for the city's children, who love the interactive displays, the "History of the Universe in 120 Seconds" exhibit, and the cool virtual-reality "Jurascope" glasses that put meat and skin on all the dinosaur skeletons.

Cost and Hours: €6, €3.50 for kids, Tue-Fri 9:30-18:00, Sat-Sun 10:00-18:00, closed Mon, last entry 30 minutes before closing, Invalidenstrasse 43, U6: Naturkundemuseum, tel. 030/2093-8591, www.naturkundemuseum-berlin.de.

Sights in Central Berlin

Tiergarten Park and Nearby

Berlin's "Central Park" stretches two miles from Bahnhof Zoo to the Brandenburg Gate.

Victory Column (Siegessäule)—The Tiergarten's newly restored centerpiece, the Victory Column, was built to commemorate the Prussian defeat of Denmark in 1864...then reinterpreted after the defeat of France in 1870. The pointy-helmeted Germans rubbed it in, decorating the tower with French cannons and paying for it all with francs received as war reparations. The three lower rings commemorate Bismarck's victories. I imagine the statues of Moltke and other German military greats—which lurk in the trees nearby—goose-stepping around the floodlit angel at night.

Originally standing at the Reichstag, in 1938 the tower was moved to this position and given a 25-foot lengthening by Hitler's architect Albert Speer, in anticipation of the planned re-envisioning of Berlin as "Germania"—the capital of a worldwide Nazi empire. Streets leading to the circle are flanked by surviving Nazi guardhouses, built in the stern style that fascists loved. At the memorial's first level, notice how WWII bullets chipped the fine marble columns. From 1989 to 2003, the column was the epicenter of the Love Parade (Berlin's city-wide techno-hedonist street party), and it was the backdrop for Barack Obama's summer 2008 visit to Germany as a presidential candidate. (He asked to speak in front of the Brandenburg Gate, but German Chancellor Angela Merkel wanted to save that symbol from "politics.")

Climbing its 270 steps earns you a breathtaking Berlin-wide view and a close-up of the gilded bronze statue of the goddess Victoria (go ahead, call her "the chick on a stick"—everybody here does). You might recognize Victoria from Wim Wenders' 1987 arthouse classic *Wings of Desire*, or the *Stay (Faraway, So Close!)* video he directed for the rock band U2.

Cost and Hours: €2.20; April-Oct Mon-Fri 9:30-18:30, Sat-Sun 9:30-19:00; Nov-March Mon-Fri 10:00-17:00, Sat-Sun 10:00-17:30; closes in the rain, WCs for paying guests only, no elevator, bus #100, tel. 030/8639-8560. From the tower, the grand Strasse des 17 Juni leads east to the Brandenburg Gate.

Flea Market—A colorful flea market with great antiques, more than 200 stalls, collector-savvy merchants, and fun German fast-food stands thrives weekends on Strasse des 17 Juni (Sat-Sun 6:00-16:00, right next to S-Bahn: Tiergarten).

German Resistance Memorial (Gedenkstätte Deutscher Widerstand)—This memorial and museum, located in the former Bendlerblock military headquarters just south of the Tiergarten, tells the story of several organized German resistance movements and the more than 42 separate assassination attempts against Hitler. An ill-fated scheme to kill Hitler was plotted in this building (the actual attempt occurred in Rastenburg, eastern Prussia; the event was dramatized in the 2009 Tom Cruise film *Valkyrie*). The conspirators, including Claus Schenk Graf von Stauffenberg, were shot here in the courtyard. While there are no real artifacts, the spirit that haunts the place is multilingual.

Cost and Hours: Free, Mon-Fri 9:00-18:00, Thu until 20:00, Sat-Sun 10:00-18:00, free and good English audioguide—passport required, €3 printed English translation, no crowds, near Kulturforum at Stauffenbergstrasse 13, enter in courtyard, door on left, main exhibit on third floor, bus #M29, tel. 030/2699-5000, www.gdw-berlin.de.

Potsdamer Platz and Nearby

The "Times Square of Berlin," and possibly the busiest square in Europe before World War II, Potsdamer Platz was cut in two by the Wall and left a deserted no-man's-land for 40 years. Today, this immense commercial/residential/entertainment center, sitting on a futuristic transportation hub, is home to the European corporate headquarters of several big-league companies.

▲Potsdamer Platz

The new Potsdamer Platz was a vision begun in 1991, when it was announced that Berlin would resume its position as the capital of Germany. Sony, Daimler, and other major corporations have turned the square once again into a center of Berlin. Like great Christian churches built upon pagan holy grounds, Potsdamer Platz—with its corporate logos flying high and shiny above what was the Wall—trumpets the triumph of capitalism.

While Potsdamer Platz tries to give Berlin a common center, the city has always been—and remains—a collection of towns. Locals recognize 28 distinct neighborhoods that may have grown together but still maintain their historic orientation. While Munich has the single dominant Marienplatz, Berlin will always have Charlottenburg, Savignyplatz, Kreuzberg, Prenzlauer Berg, and so on. In general, Berliners prefer these characteristic neighborhoods to an official city center. They're unimpressed by the grandeur of Potsdamer Platz, simply considering it a good place to go to the movies, with overpriced, touristy restaurants.

While most of the complex just feels big (the arcade is like any huge, modern, American mall), the entrance to the complex and Sony Center are worth a visit, and German-film buffs will enjoy the Deutsche Kinemathek museum (described later).

For an overview of the new construction, and a scenic route to the Sony Center, start at the Bahnhof Potsdamer Platz (east end of Potsdamer Strasse, S- and U-Bahn: Potsdamer Platz, exit following *Leipziger Platz* signs to see the best view of skyscrapers as you emerge). Find the green hexagonal **clock tower** with the traffic lights on top. This is a replica of the first automatic traffic light in Europe, which once stood at the six-street intersection of Potsdamer Platz. On either side of Potsdamer Strasse, you'll see enormous cubical entrances to the underground Potsdamer Platz train station. Near these entrances, notice the slanted **glass cylinders** sticking out of the ground. The mirrors on the tops of the tubes move with the sun to collect light and send it underground (saving piles of euros in energy costs). A line in the pavement indicates where the **Berlin Wall** once stood. On the right side of the street, notice the re-erected slabs of the Wall. Imagine when the first piece was cut out (see photo and history on nearby panel). These hang like scalps at the gate of Fort Capitalism...look up at the towering corporate headquarters: Market forces have won a clear victory. Now descend into one of the train station entrances and follow signs to *Sony Center*. As you walk through the passage, notice the wall panels with historical information.

You'll come up the escalator into the **Sony Center** under a grand canopy (designed to evoke Mount Fuji). At night, multicolored floodlights play on the underside of this tent. Office workers and tourists eat here by the fountain, enjoying the parade of people. The modern Bavarian Lindenbräu beer hall—the Sony boss wanted a *Bräuhaus*—serves traditional food (€11-17, daily 11:00-24:30, big €8 salads, three-foot-long taster boards of eight different beers, tel. 030/2575-1280). Across the plaza, Josty Bar is built around a surviving bit of a venerable hotel that was a meeting place for Berlin's rich and famous before the bombs (€10-17 meals, daily 10:00-24:00, tel. 030/2575-9702). CineStar is a rare cinema that plays mainstream movies in their original language (www.cinestar.de).

Sights near Potsdamer Platz

▲Deutsche Kinemathek Film and TV Museum—This exhibit is the most interesting place to visit in the Sony Center. The early pioneers in filmmaking were German (including Fritz Lang, F. W. Murnau, Ernst Lubitsch, and the Austrian-born Billy Wilder), and many of them also became influential in Hollywood—making this a fun visit for cinephiles. Your admission ticket gets you into several floors of exhibits (including temporary exhibits on floors 1 and 4) made meaningful by the included, essential English audioguide.

BERLIN

Cost and Hours: €6, includes 1.5-hour audioguide, Tue-Sun 10:00-18:00, Thu until 20:00, closed Mon, tel. 030/2474-9888, www.deutsche-kinemathek.de.

Nearby: The Kino Arsenal theater downstairs shows offbeat art-house films in their original language.

Visiting the Museum: From the ticket desk, ride the elevator up to the third floor, where you can turn left (into the film section, floors 3 and 2) or right (into the TV section, floors 3 and 4).

In the **film section,** you'll walk back in time through a fun mirrored entryway. The exhibit starts with the German film industry's beginnings, with an emphasis on the Weimar Republic period in the 1920s, when Berlin rivaled Hollywood. Influential films included the early German Expressionist masterpiece *The Cabinet of Dr. Caligari* (1920) and Fritz Lang's seminal *Metropolis* (1927). Three rooms are dedicated to Marlene Dietrich, who was a huge star both in Germany and, later, in Hollywood. (Dietrich, who performed at USO shows to entertain Allied troops fighting against her former homeland, once said, "I don't hate the Germans, I hate the Nazis.") Another section examines Nazi use of film as propaganda, including Leni Riefenstahl's masterful documentary of the 1936 Berlin Olympics and her earlier, chillingly propagandistic *Triumph of the Will* (1935). The postwar period was defined by two separate East and West German film industries. The exhibit's finale reminds us that German filmmakers are still highly influential and successful—including Wolfgang Petersen

(Das Boot, Air Force One, The Perfect Storm) and Werner Herzog (the documentary *Grizzly Man* and the drama *Rescue Dawn*). (If this visit gets you curious about German cinema, see the recommendations in the Appendix.)

The **TV section** tells the story of *das Idioten Box* from its infancy (when it was primarily used as a Nazi propaganda tool) to today. The 30-minute kaleidoscopic review—kind of a frantic fast-forward montage of greatest hits in German TV history, both East and West—is great fun even if you don't understand a word of it (it plays all day long, with 10-minute breaks). Otherwise, the TV section is a little more challenging for non-German speakers to appreciate. Upstairs (on the fourth floor) is a TV archive where you can dial through a wide range of new and classic German TV standards.

Panoramapunkt—Across Potsdamer Strasse from the Film and TV Museum, you can ride what's billed as "the fastest elevator in Europe" to skyscraping rooftop views. You'll travel at nearly 30 feet per second to the top of the 300-foot-tall Kollhoff Tower. Its sheltered but open-air view deck provides a fun opportunity to survey Berlin's ongoing construction from above.

Cost and Hours: €5.50, €9.50 VIP ticket lets you skip the line, audioguide-€2.50, daily 10:00-20:00, until 22:00 in summer, last elevator 30 minutes before closing, in red-brick building at Potsdamer Platz 1, tel. 030/2593-07080, www.panoramapunkt.de.

Kulturforum

Just west of Potsdamer Platz, Kulturforum rivals Museum Island as the city's cultural heart, with several top museums and Berlin's concert hall—home of the world-famous Berlin Philharmonic orchestra (admission to all Kulturforum sights covered by a single €8 Bereichskarte Kulturforum combo-ticket—a.k.a. Quartier-Karte—and also by the Museumspass; info for all museums: tel. 030/266-424-242, www.kulturforum-berlin.de). Of its sprawling museums, only the Gemäldegalerie is a must (S- or U-Bahn to Potsdamer Platz, then walk along Potsdamer Platz; or from Bahnhof Zoo, take bus #200 to Philharmonie).

▲▲**Gemäldegalerie**—Literally the "Painting Gallery," Germany's top collection of 13th- through 18th-century European paintings (more than 1,400 canvases) is beautifully displayed in a building that's a work of art in itself. The North Wing starts with German paintings of the 13th to 16th centuries, including eight by Albrecht Dürer. Then come the Dutch and Flemish—Jan van Eyck, Pieter Brueghel, Peter Paul Rubens, Anthony van Dyck, Frans Hals, and Jan Vermeer. The wing finishes with German, English, and French 18th-century artists, such as Thomas Gainsborough and Antoine Watteau. An octagonal hall at the end features an impressive stash of Rembrandts. The South Wing is saved for the Italians—Giotto, Botticelli, Titian, Raphael, and Caravaggio.

Cost and Hours: Covered by €8 Kulturforum combo-ticket, Tue-Sun 10:00-18:00, Thu until 22:00, closed Mon, audioguide included with entry, clever little loaner stools, great salad bar in cafeteria upstairs, Matthäikirchplatz 4.

➲ Self-Guided Tour: I'll point out a few highlights, focusing on Northern European artists (Germans, Dutch, and Flemish), with a few Spaniards and Italians thrown in. To go beyond my selections, make ample use of the excellent audioguide.

The collection spreads out on one vast floor surrounding a central hall. Inner rooms have Roman numerals (I, II, III), while adjacent outer rooms are numbered (1, 2, 3). After showing your ticket, turn right into room I and work your way counterclockwise (and roughly chronologically) through the collection.

Rooms I-III/1-4 kick things off with early German paintings (13th-16th centuries). In Room 1, look for the 1532 portrait of wealthy Hanseatic cloth merchant Georg Gisze by **Hans Holbein the Younger** (1497-1543). Gisze's name appears on several of the notes stuck to the wall behind him. And, typical of detail-rich Northern European art, the canvas is bursting with highly symbolic tidbits. Items scattered on the tabletop and on the shelves behind the merchant represent his lofty status and aspects of his life story. In the vase, the carnation represents his recent engagement, and the herbs symbolize his virtue. And yet, the celebratory flowers are already beginning to fade and the scales behind him are unbalanced, reminders of the fleetingness of happiness and wealth.

In room 2 are fine portraits by the remarkably talented **Albrecht Dürer** (1471-1528), who traveled to Italy during the burgeoning days of the early Renaissance and melded the artistic harmony and classical grandeur he discovered there with a Northern European attention to detail. In *Portrait of Hieronymus Holzschuher* (1526), Dürer skillfully captured the personality of a friend from Nürnberg, right down to the sly twinkle in his sidelong glance. Technically the portrait is perfection: Look closely and see each individual hair of the man's beard and fur coat, and even the reflection of the studio's windows in his eyes. Also notice Dürer's little pyramid-shaped, D-inside-A signature. Signing one's work was a revolutionary assertion of Dürer's renown, at a time when German artists were considered anonymous craftsmen.

Lucas Cranach the Elder (1472-1553), whose works are in room III, was a court painter for the prince electors of Saxony and a close friend of Martin Luther (and his unofficial portraitist). But *The Fountain of Youth* (1546) is a far cry from Cranach's solemn portrayals of the Reformer. Old women helped to the fountain (on the left) emerge as young ladies on the right. Newly nubile, the women go into a tent to dress up, snog with noblemen in the bushes (right foreground), dance merrily beneath the trees, and dine grandly beneath a landscape of phallic mountains and towers. This work is flanked by Cranach's Venus nudes. I sense a pattern here.

Netherlandish painters (rooms IV-VI/4-7) were early adopters of oil paint (as opposed to the older egg tempera), whose flexibility allowed them to brush the super-fine details for which they are famous. **Rogier van der Weyden** (room IV) was a virtuoso handler of the new medium. In *Portrait of a Young Woman* (c. 1400-1464), the subject wears a typical winged bonnet, addressing the viewer directly with her fetching blue eyes. The subjects (especially women) of most portraits of the time look off to one side; some art historians guess that the confident woman shown here is Van der Weyden's wife. In the same room is a remarkable, rare trio of three-panel altarpieces by Van der Weyden: The *Marienaltar* shows the life of the Virgin Mary; the *Johannesaltar* narrates the life of John the Baptist—his birth, baptizing Christ (with God and the Holy Spirit hovering overhead), and his gruesome death by decapitation; and the *Middelburger Altar* tells the story of the Nativity. Savor the fine details in each panel of these altarpieces.

Flash forward a few hundred years to the 17th century and Flemish (Belgian) painting (rooms VII-VIII/9-10), and it's apparent how much the Protestant Reformation—and resulting Counter-Reformation—changed the tenor of Northern European art. In works by **Peter Paul Rubens** (1577-1640)—including *Jesus Giving Peter the Keys to Heaven*—calm, carefully studied, detail-oriented seriousness gives way to an exuberant Baroque trumpeting of the greatness of the Catholic Church. In the Counter-Reformation world, the Catholic Church had serious competition for the hearts and minds of its congregants. Exciting art like this became a way to keep people in the pews. Notice the quivering brushstrokes and almost too-bright colors. (In the same room are portraits by Rubens' student, Anthony van Dyck, as well as some hunting still lifes from Frans Snyders and others.) In the next rooms (VIII and 9) are more Rubens, including the mythological *Perseus Freeing Andromeda* and *The Martyrdom of St. Sebastian by Arrows* (loosely based on a more famous rendition by Andrea Mantegna).

Dutch painting from the 17th century (rooms IX-XI/10-19) is dominated by the convivial portraits by **Frans Hals** (c. 1582-1666). His 1620 portrait of Catharina Hooft (far corner, room 13) presents a startlingly self-possessed baby (the newest member of a wealthy merchant family) dressed with all the finery of a queen, adorned with lace and jewels, and clutching a golden rattle. The smiling nurse supporting the tyke offers her a piece of fruit, whose blush of red perfectly matches the nanny's apple-fresh cheeks.

But the ultimate Dutch master is **Rembrandt van Rijn** (1606-1669), whose powers of perception and invention propelled him to fame in his lifetime. Displayed here are several storytelling scenes (room 16), mostly from classical mythology or biblical stories, all employing Rembrandt's trademark chiaroscuro technique (with a strong contrast between light and dark). In *The Rape of Persephone*, Pluto grabs Persephone from his chariot and races toward the underworld, while other goddesses cling to her robe, trying to save her. Cast against a nearly black background, the almost overexposed, action-packed scene is shockingly emotional. In the nearby *Samson and Delilah* (1628), Delilah cradles Samson's head in her lap while silently signaling to a goon to shear Samson's hair, the secret to his strength. A self-portrait (room X) of a 28-year-old Rembrandt wearing a beret is paired with the come-hither 1637 *Portrait of Hendrickje Stoffels* (the two were romantically linked). *Samson Threatens His Father-in-Law* (1635) captures the moment just after the mighty Samson (with his flowing hair, elegant robes, and shaking fist) has been told by his wife's father to take a hike. I wouldn't want to cross this guy.

Although **Johannes Vermeer** (1632-1675) is today just as admired as Rembrandt, he was little known in his day, probably because he painted relatively few works for a small circle of Delft collectors. Vermeer was a master at conveying a complicated story through a deceptively simple scene with a few poignant details—whether it's a woman reading a letter at a window, a milkmaid pouring milk from a pitcher into a bowl, or (as in *The Glass of Wine*, room 18) a young man offering a drink to a young lady. The young man had been playing her some music on his lute (which now sits, discarded, on a chair) and is hoping to seal the deal with some alcohol. The woman is finishing one glass of wine, and her would-be suitor stands ready—almost *too* ready—to pour her another. His sly, somewhat smarmy smirk drives home his high hopes for what will come next. Vermeer has perfectly captured the exact moment of "Will she or won't she?" The painter offers some clues—the coat of arms in the window depicts a woman holding onto the reigns of a horse, staying in control—but ultimately, only he (and the couple) know how this scene will end.

Shift south to Italian, French, and Spanish painting of the 17th and 18th centuries (rooms XII-XIV/23-28). Venetian cityscapes by Canaletto (who also painted Dresden) and lots of bombastic Baroque art hang in room XII. Room XIII features big-name Spanish artists Murillo, Zurbarán, and the great **Diego Velázquez** (1599-1660). He gave the best of his talents to his portraits, capturing warts-and-all likenesses that are effortlessly real. His 1630 *Portrait of a Lady* conveys the subject's subtle, sly Mona Lisa smile. Her figure and face (against a dull gray background) are filtered through a pleasant natural light. Notice that if you stand too close, the brushstrokes get muddy—but when you back up, the scene snaps into perfectly sharp relief.

From here, the collection itself takes a step backwards—into Italian paintings of the 13th-16th centuries (rooms XV-XVIII/29-41). This section includes some lesser-known works by great Italian Renaissance painters, including Raphael (rooms XVII and 29, including five different Madonnas, among them the *Terranuova Madonna*, in a round frame) and Sandro Botticelli (Room VIII).

New National Gallery (Neue Nationalgalerie)—This gallery features 20th-century art, with ever-changing special exhibits.

Cost and Hours: Covered by €8 Kulturforum combo-ticket, Tue-Fri 10:00-18:00, Thu until 22:00, Sat-Sun 11:00-18:00, closed Mon, café downstairs, Potsdamer Strasse 50.

Museum of Decorative Arts (Kunstgewerbemuseum)—Wander through a mazelike floor plan displaying a thousand years of applied arts—porcelain, fine *Jugendstil* (German Art Nouveau) furniture, Art Deco, and reliquaries. There are no English descriptions and no crowds.

Cost and Hours: Covered by €8 Kulturforum combo-ticket, Tue-Fri 10:00-18:00, Sat-Sun 11:00-18:00, closed Mon, Herbert-von-Karajan-Strasse 10.

▲Musical Instruments Museum (Musikinstrumenten Museum)—This impressive hall is filled with 600 exhibits spanning the 16th century to modern times. Wander among old keyboard instruments and funny-looking tubas. Pick up the included audioguide and free English brochure at the entry. In addition to the English commentary, the audioguide has clips of various instruments being played (just punch in the number next to the instrument you want to hear). This place is fascinating if you're into pianos.

Cost and Hours: €4 but included in €8 Kulturforum ticket, Tue-Fri 9:00-17:00, Thu until 22:00, Sat-Sun 10:00-17:00, closed Mon, low-profile white building east of the big yellow Philharmonic Concert Hall, tel. 030/2548-1178.

Philharmonic Concert Hall—Poke into the lobby of Berlin's yellow Philharmonic building and see if there are tickets available during your stay. The interior is famous for its extraordinary acoustics. Even from the outside, this is a remarkable building, designed by a nautical engineer to look like a ship—notice how different it looks from each angle. Inexpensive and legitimate tickets are often sold on the street before performances. Or you can buy tickets from the box office in person, by phone, or online (ticket office open Mon-Fri 15:00-18:00, Sat-Sun 11:00-14:00, info tel. 030/2548-8132, box office tel. 030/2548-8999—answered daily

9:00-18:00, www.berliner-philharmoniker.de). For guest performances, you must buy tickets through the organizer (see website
for details).

Sights in Western Berlin

Throughout the Cold War, Western travelers—and most West
Berliners—got used to thinking of western Berlin's Kurfürstendamm boulevard as the heart of the city. But those days have
gone the way of the Wall. With the huge changes the city has
undergone since 1989, the real "city center" is now, once again,
Berlin's historic center (the Mitte district, around Unter den
Linden and Friedrichstrasse). While western Berlin still works
well as a home base, it's no longer the obvious place from which
to explore Berlin. After the new Hauptbahnhof essentially put
Bahnhof Zoo out of business in 2006, the area was left with an
identity crisis. Now, more than 20 years after reunification, the
west side is back and has fully embraced its historical role as a chic,
classy suburb.

In the Heart of Western Berlin

A few interesting sights sit within walking distance of Bahnhof
Zoo and the Savignyplatz hotels. For a detailed map of this area,
see page 630.

▲**Kurfürstendamm**—Western Berlin's main drag, Kurfürstendamm boulevard (nicknamed "Ku'damm"), starts at Kaiser
Wilhelm Memorial Church and does a commercial cancan
for two miles. In the 1850s, when Berlin became a wealthy and
important capital, her "new rich" chose Kurfürstendamm as their
street. Bismarck made it Berlin's Champs-Elysées. In the 1920s, it
became a chic and fashionable drag of cafés and boutiques. During
the Third Reich, as home to an international community of diplomats and journalists, it enjoyed more freedom than the rest of
Berlin. Throughout the Cold War, economic subsidies from the
West made sure that capitalism thrived on Ku'damm. And today,
while much of the old charm has been hamburgerized, Ku'damm
is still a fine place to enjoy elegant shops (around Fasanenstrasse),
department stores, and people-watching.

▲**Kaiser Wilhelm Memorial Church (Gedächtniskirche)**—
This church was originally dedicated to the first emperor of
Germany. Reliefs and mosaics show great events in the life of
Germany's favorite *Kaiser,* from his coronation in 1871 to his death
in 1888. The church's bombed-out ruins have been left standing as a
poignant memorial to the destruction of Berlin in World War II.

   Cost and Hours: Church—free, daily 9:00-19:00; Memorial
Hall—free, Mon-Sat 10:00-18:00, shorter hours on Sun. Located

on Breitscheidplatz, U2/U9 and S-Bahn: Zoologischer Garten or U1/U9: Kurfürstendamm, www.gedaechtniskirche.com.

Visiting the Church: The church is actually an ensemble of buildings: a new church, the matching bell tower, a meeting hall, and the bombed-out ruins of the old church, with its Memorial Hall. The church is likely to be undergoing renovation when you visit (though the interior should still be open to visitors). Slated for completion in the fall of 2012, the renovations will strengthen the foundations of all four buildings and make it possible for visitors to get to the top of the church for the first time in 60 years. Until then, an aluminum tent surrounds the building to prevent dust contamination and to make it easier to work in inclement weather. (In fact, in an attempt to revitalize the western part of the city, the entire area around the church and Breitscheid Platz will be under reconstruction.)

Under a Neo-Romanesque mosaic ceiling, the **Memorial Hall** features a small exhibit of interesting photos about the bombing and before-and-after models of the church. After the war, some Berliners wanted to tear down the ruins and build it anew. Instead, it was decided to keep what was left of the old church as a memorial and stage a competition to design a modern, add-on section. The winning entry—the short, modern church (1961) next to the Memorial Hall—offers a meditative world of 11,000 little blue windows. The blue glass was given to the church by the French as a reconciliation gift. For more information on both churches, pick up the English flier (€0.50).

As you enter the **church,** a peaceful blue oasis in the middle of the busy city, turn immediately right to find a simple charcoal sketch of the Virgin Mary wrapped in a shawl. During the Battle of Stalingrad, German combat surgeon Kurt Reuber rendered the Virgin on the back of a stolen Soviet map to comfort the men in his care. On the right are the words "Light, Life, Love" from the gospel of John; on the left, "Christmas in the cauldron 1942"; and at the bottom, "Fortress Stalingrad." Though Reuber died in captivity a year later, his sketch had been flown out of Stalingrad on the last medical evacuation flight, and postwar Germany embraced it as a symbol of the wish for peace. Copies of the drawing, now known as the *Stalingrad Madonna,* hang in the Berlin Cathedral, in England's Coventry, and in Russia's Volgograd (formerly Stalingrad) as a sign of peaceful understanding between the nations. As another act of reconciliation, every Friday at 13:00 a "Prayers for Peace" service is held simultaneously with the cathedral in Coventry.

Nearby: The lively square between the churches and the Europa Center (a once-impressive, shiny high-rise shopping center built as a showcase of Western capitalism during the Cold War) usually attracts street musicians and performers—especially in the summer. Berliners call the funky fountain "the wet meatball."

The Story of Berlin—Filling most of what seems like a department store right on Ku'damm (at #207), this sprawling history exhibit tells the stormy 800-year story of Berlin in a creative way. While there are almost no real historic artifacts, the exhibit does a good job of cobbling together many dimensions of the life and tumultuous times of this great city. It's particularly strong on the story of the city from World War I through the Cold War. However, for similar information, the German History Museum on Unter den Linden is a far better use of your time and money (see page 580).

Cost and Hours: €10, daily 10:00-20:00, last entry 2 hours before closing, tel. 030/8872-0100, www.story-of-berlin.de. Times for the 30-minute bunker tour are posted at the entry.

▲**Käthe Kollwitz Museum**—This local artist (1867-1945), who experienced much of Berlin's stormiest century, conveys some powerful and mostly sad feelings about motherhood, war, and suffering through the stark faces of her art. This small yet fine collection (the only one in town of Kollwitz's work) consists of three floors of charcoal drawings, topped by an attic with a handful of sculptures.

Cost and Hours: €6, €1 pamphlet has necessary English explanations of a few major works, daily 11:00-18:00, a block off Ku'damm at Fasanenstrasse 24, U-Bahn: Uhlandstrasse, tel. 030/882-5210, www.kaethe-kollwitz.de.

▲**Kaufhaus des Westens (KaDeWe)**—The "Department Store of the West" has been a Berlin tradition for more than a century. With a staff of 2,100 to help you sort through its vast selection of 380,000 items, KaDeWe claims to be the biggest department store on the Continent. You can get everything from a haircut and train ticket (third floor) to souvenirs (fourth floor). The theater and concert box office on the sixth floor charges an 18 percent booking fee, but they know all your options (cash only). The sixth floor is a world of gourmet taste treats. The biggest selection of deli and exotic food in Germany offers plenty of classy opportunities to sit down and eat. Ride the glass elevator to the seventh floor's glass-domed Winter Garden, a self-service cafeteria—fun but pricey.

Hours and Information: Mon-Thu 10:00-20:00, Fri 10:00-21:00, Sat 9:30-20:00, closed Sun, S-Bahn: Zoologischer Garten or U-Bahn: Wittenbergplatz, tel. 030/21210, www.kadewe.de.

Nearby: The Wittenbergplatz U-Bahn station (in front of KaDeWe) is a unique opportunity to see an old-time station. Enjoy its interior with classic advertisements still decorating its venerable walls.

Berlin Zoo (Zoologischer Garten Berlin)—More than 1,500 different kinds of animals call Berlin's famous zoo home...or so the

BERLIN

zookeepers like to think. The big hit here is the lonely panda bear (straight in from the entrance).

Cost and Hours: €13 for zoo, €13 for world-class aquarium, €20 for both, kids half-price, daily mid-March–mid-Oct generally 9:00-19:00, mid-Oct–mid-March generally 9:00-17:00, aquarium closes 30 minutes earlier; feeding times—*Fütterungszeiten*—posted just inside entrance, the best feeding show is the sea lions—generally at 15:15; enter near Europa Center in front of Hotel Palace or opposite Bahnhof Zoo on Hardenbergplatz, Budapester Strasse 34, tel. 030/254-010, www.zoo-berlin.de.

Nightlife in Berlin

Berlin is a happening place for nightlife—whether it's clubs, pubs, jazz music, cabaret, hokey-but-fun German variety shows, theater, or concerts.

Sources of Entertainment Info: *Berlin Programm* lists a non-stop parade of concerts, plays, exhibits, and cultural events (€2, in German, www.berlin-programm.de); *Exberliner Magazine* (€2.50, www.exberliner.com) doesn't have as much hard information, but is colorfully written English (both sold at kiosks and TIs). For the young and determined sophisticate, *Zitty* and *Tip* are the top guides to alternative culture (in German, sold at kiosks). Also pick up the free schedules *Flyer* and *030* in bars and clubs. Visit KaDeWe's ticket office for your music and theater options (sixth floor, 18 percent fee but access to all tickets; see page 619). Ask about "competitive improvisation" and variety shows.

Berlin Jazz—To enjoy live music near my recommended Savignyplatz hotels in western Berlin, consider **A Trane Jazz Club** (all jazz, great stage and intimate seating, €7-18 cover depending on act, opens at 21:00, live music nightly 22:00-2:00 in the morning, Bleibtreustrasse 1—see map on page 630, tel. 030/313-2550, www.a-trane.de). **B-Flat Acoustic Music and Jazz Club,** in the heart of eastern Berlin, also has live music nightly—and shares a courtyard with a tranquil tea house (shows vary from free to €10-12 cover, open Mon-Thu from 20:00 with shows starting at 21:00, Fri-Sat from 21:00 with shows at 22:00, closed Sun, a block from Rosenthaler Platz U-Bahn stop at Rosenthaler Strasse 13—see map on page 634, tel. 030/283-3123, www.b-flat -berlin.de).

Berliner Rock and Roll—Berlin has a vibrant rock and pop scene, with popular venues at the Spandau Citadel and at the outdoor Waldbühne ("Forest Stage"). Check out what's playing on posters in the U-Bahn, in *Zitty,* or at any ticket agency. Great Berlin bands include Wir Sind Helden, The Beatsteaks, Jennifer Rostock, and the funky ska band Seeed.

Cabaret—Bar Jeder Vernunft offers modern-day cabaret a short walk from my recommended hotels in western Berlin. This variety show—under a classic old tent perched atop a modern parking lot—is a hit with German-speakers, but can still be worthwhile for those who don't speak the language (as some of the music shows are in a sort of "Denglish"). Even some Americans perform here periodically. Tickets are generally about €22-25, and shows change regularly (performances start Mon-Sat at 20:00, Sun at 19:00, seating can be a bit cramped, south of Ku'damm at Schaperstrasse 24—see map on page 630, U-3 or U-9: Spichernstrasse, tel. 030/883-1582, www.bar-jeder-vernunft.de).

German Variety Show—To spend an evening enjoying Europe's largest revue theater, consider "YMA—Too Beautiful to Be True" at the **FriedrichstadtPalast.** It's a passionate visual spectacle, a weird ballet that pulsates like a visual poem (€17-105, Tue at 18:30, Thu-Sat at 19:30, Sat also at 15:30, Sun at 15:30, no shows Mon or Wed, Friedrichstrasse 107—see map on page 634, U6: Oranienburger Tor, tel. 030/2326-2326, www.show-palace .eu). The Friedrichstrasse area around the Palast and to the south has been synonymous with entertainment for at least 200 years. The East German government built the current Palast in 1984 on the ruins of an older theater, which itself was a horse barn for the Prussian Army. The current exterior is meant to mimic the interior design of the older theater.

Nightclubs and Pubs—Oranienburger Strasse's trendy scene (page 603) is being eclipsed by the action at Friedrichshain (farther east). To the north, you'll find the hip Prenzlauer Berg neighborhood, packed with everything from smoky pubs to small art bars and dance clubs (best scene is around Helmholtzplatz, U2: Eberswalder Strasse; see page 604).

Dancing—Cut a rug at **Clärchens Ballhaus,** an old ballroom that's been a Berlin institution since 1913. At some point everyone in Berlin comes through here, as the dance hall attracts an eclectic Berlin-in-a-nutshell crowd of grannies, elegant women in evening dresses, yuppies, scenesters, and hippies. The music (swing, waltz, tango, or cha-cha) changes every day, with live music on Friday and Saturday (from 23:15, €4 cover; dance hall open daily from 10:00—12:00 in winter—until the last person goes home, in the heart of the Auguststrasse gallery district at Auguststrasse 24—see map on page 634, S-Bahn: Oranienburger Strasse, tel. 030/282-9295, www.ballhaus.de). Dancing lessons are also available (€8, Mon-Tue at 19:00, Thu at 19:30, 1.5 hours). The "Gypsy" restaurant, which fills a huge courtyard out front, serves decent food and good pizza.

Art Galleries—Berlin, a magnet for new artists, is a great city for gallery visits. Galleries—many of which stay open late—welcome

BERLIN

visitors who are "just looking." The most famous gallery district is in eastern Berlin's Mitte neighborhood, along **Auguststrasse** (branches off from Oranienburger Strasse at the ruined Tacheles building). Check out the Berlin outpost of the edgy-yet-accessible art of the New Leipzig movement at **Galerie Eigen+Art** (Tue-Sat 11:00-18:00, closed Sun-Mon, Auguststrasse 26, tel. 030/280-6605, www.eigen-art.com). The other gallery area is in western Berlin, along **Fasanenstrasse.**

Pub Crawls—Various companies offer pub crawls to some of Berlin's fun watering holes. The (unrelated) binge-drinking death of a 16-year-old in Berlin a few years ago reinforced the tours' strict 18-year-old minimum age limit. Pub crawls depart around 20:15, cost €12, generally visit four bars and two clubs, and provide a great way to drink it up with new friends from around the world while getting a peek at Berlin's bar scene...or at least how its bars look when invaded by 50 loud tourists. **Insider Tour** and **Sandeman's New Europe** (see contact info for both on page 561) offer pub crawls, or look around town for fliers from other companies.

BERLIN

Sleeping in Berlin

When in Berlin, I used to sleep in the former West, on or near Savignyplatz. But now the focus of Berlin is in the East. I like the lively, colorful district in the heart of the *Kiez* (literally "gravel," meaning a homey, homogenous neighborhood in Berlin), and I've listed some suggestions in eastern Berlin's popular Prenzlauer Berg neighborhood.

Berlin is packed and hotel prices go up on holidays, including Green Week in mid-January, Easter weekend, the first weekend in May, Ascension weekend in May, German Unity Day (Oct 3), Christmas, and New Year's. Keep in mind that many hotels have limited staff after 20:00, so if you're planning to arrive after that, let the hotel know in advance.

In Eastern Berlin
Prenzlauer Berg
If you want to sleep in the former East Berlin, set your sights on the colorful and fun Prenzlauer Berg district. After decades of neglect, this corner of eastern Berlin has quickly come back to life. Gentrification has brought Prenzlauer Berg great hotels, tasty ethnic and German eateries (see "Eating in Berlin," later), and a happening nightlife scene. Think of all the graffiti as just some people's way of saying they care. The huge and impersonal concrete buildings are enlivened with a street fair of fun little shops and eateries.

This loosely defined area is about 1.5 miles north of Alex-

Sleep Code

(€1 = about $1.40, country code: 49, area code: 030)
S = Single, **D** = Double/Twin, **T** = Triple, **Q** = Quad, **b** = bathroom, **s** = shower only. Unless otherwise noted, credit cards are accepted, English is spoken, and breakfast is included.

To help you sort easily through these listings, I've divided the accommodations into three categories, based on the price for a standard double room with bath:

$$$ Higher Priced—Most rooms €125 or more.
$$ Moderately Priced—Most rooms between €85-125.
$ Lower Priced—Most rooms €85 or less.

Prices can change without notice; verify the hotel's current rates online or by email. For other updates, see www .ricksteves.com/update.

anderplatz, roughly between Kollwitzplatz and Helmholtzplatz, and to the west, along Kastanienallee (known affectionately as "Casting Alley" for its generous share of beautiful people). The closest U-Bahn stops are U-2: Senefelderplatz at the south end of the neighborhood, U-8: Rosenthaler Platz in the middle, or U-2: Eberswalder Strasse at the north end. Or, for less walking, take the S-Bahn to Hackescher Markt, then catch tram #M1 north.

$$$ Precise Hotel Myer's Berlin rents 52 simple, small rooms. The gorgeous public spaces include a patio and garden. This peaceful hub—off a quiet garden courtyard and tree-lined street, just a five-minute walk from Kollwitzplatz or the nearest U-Bahn stop (Senefelderplatz)—makes it hard to believe you're in a capital city. Their four classes of rooms range from three to five stars, hence the wide price range (Db-€95-200, price also depends on season—check rates online for your dates, air-con in some rooms, elevator, pay Internet access and Wi-Fi, Metzer Strasse 26, tel. 030/440-140, fax 030/4401-4104, www.myershotel.de, myers @precisehotels.com).

$$$ Hotel Jurine (zhoo-REEN—the family name) is a pleasant 53-room business-style hotel whose friendly staff aims to please. In good weather, you can enjoy the breakfast buffet on the lush backyard patio (Sb-€90-110, Db-€130-160, extra bed-€37, rates vary by season, check website for discounts July-Aug, skip breakfast to save a few euros, elevator, free Wi-Fi, parking garage-€13.50, Schwedter Strasse 15, 10-minute walk to U2: Senefelderplatz, tel. 030/443-2990, fax 030/4432-9999, www .hotel-jurine.de, mail@hotel-jurine.de).

BERLIN

Eastern Berlin Accommodations

1. Precise Hotel Myer's Berlin
2. Hotel Jurine
3. Hotel Kastanienhof
4. The Circus Hotel
5. Karlito Apartmenthaus
6. easyHotel Berlin Hackescher Markt
7. Hotel Augustinenhof
8. Circus Hostel & Internet Café
9. Meininger Hotel (Senefelder Platz)
10. Meininger Hotel (Oranienburger)
11. Meininger Hotel (Hauptbahnhof)
12. EastSeven Hostel
13. Hotel Transit Loft
14. To Ostel
15. Bike Rentals (2)

BERLIN

BERLIN

$$ Hotel Kastanienhof feels less urban-classy and more like a traditional small-town German hotel. It's wonderfully located on the Kastanienallee #M1 tram line, with easy access to the Prenzlauer Berg bustle. Its 35 slightly overpriced rooms come with helpful service (Sb-€79-94, Db-€105-140, extra bed-€29, reception closed 22:00-6:30—call ahead to make arrangements to get key if you'll arrive late, elevator, pay cable Internet in rooms, parking-€9, 20 yards from the #M1 Zionskirche tram stop at Kastanienallee 65, tel. 030/443-050, fax 030/4430-5111, www.kastanienhof.biz, info@kastanienhof.biz).

$$ The Circus Hotel, run by the popular hostel listed later, caters to youth hostelers who've outgrown the backpacker lifestyle. Each of its 60 colorful, trendy rooms has a unique bit of decoration. It overlooks a busy intersection, so there's some nighttime noise—try asking for a quieter back room. Owing to its idealistic youth-hostel roots, it's very service-oriented, with lots of included extras, a very "green" attitude, and occasional special events for guests (Sb-€70, small standard Db-€80, larger Db-€90, junior suite Db-€100, breakfast-€4-8, elevator, free Internet access and Wi-Fi, mellow ground-floor restaurant, Rosenthaler Strasse 1, directly at U8: Rosenthaler Platz, tel. 030/2000-3939, www.circus-berlin.de, info@circus-berlin.de).

$ Karlito Apartmenthaus offers nine well-located, modern, and comfortable apartments on a tranquil side street and above a hip café near Hackescher Markt. All of the sleek, Ikea-esque units have miniature balconies and are fully equipped (Sb-€62-77, Db-€72-85, price depends on season, extra person-€15, up to 2 children under 8 sleep free with 2 paying adults, breakfast in Café Lois-€5, elevator, free Wi-Fi, bike rental-€8/day, Linienstrasse 60—check in at Café Lois around the corner on Gormannstrasse, 350 yards from S-Bahn: Hackescher Markt, even closer to U8: Rosenthaler Platz, mobile 0179-704-9041, www.karlito-apartments.de, info@karlito-apartments.de).

$ easyHotel Berlin Hackescher Markt is part of an unapologetically cheap Europe-wide chain where you pay for exactly what you use—nothing more, nothing less. Based on parent company easyJet's sales model of nickel-and-dime air travel, the hotel has inexpensive base rates (small Db-€25-55, larger Db-€35-55, depending on season, it's cheaper to book earlier), then charges you separately for optional extras (breakfast, Wi-Fi, using the TV, and so on). The 124 orange-and-gray rooms are very small, basic, and feel popped out of a plastic mold, but (if you skip the extras) the price is right, and the location—at the Hackescher Markt end of Prenzlauer Berg—is wonderful (air-con, elevator, after booking online call to request a quieter back room, Rosenthaler Strasse 69, tel. 030/4000-6550, www.easyhotel.com).

Near Oranienburger Strasse: **$$$ Hotel Augustinenhof** is a clean hotel with 66 spacious rooms, nice woody floors, and some of the most comfortable beds in Berlin. While not exactly in Prenzlauer Berg, the hotel is on a side street near all of the Oranienburger Strasse action. Rooms in front overlook the courtyard of the old Imperial Post Office, rooms in back are a bit quieter, and all rooms have old, thin windows (official rates: Sb-€119, Db-€151, but you'll likely pay closer to Db-€99, elevator, free Wi-Fi or cable Internet in rooms, Auguststrasse 82, 50 yards from S-Bahn: Oranienburger Strasse, tel. 030/308-860, fax 030/308-86100, www.hotel-augustinenhof.de, augustinenhof @albrechtshof-hotels.com).

Hostels in Eastern Berlin

Berlin is known among budget travelers for its fun, hip hostels. These range from upscale-feeling hostels with some hotelesque private rooms comfortable enough even for non-hostelers, to more truly backpacker-type places where comfort is secondary to socializing. These are scattered around eastern Berlin, including some (Circus, Meininger, and EastSeven) in the Prenzlauer Berg area just described.

Comfortable Hostels with Hotelesque Rooms

$ Circus is a brightly colored, well-run place with 230 beds, a trendy lounge with upscale ambience, and a bar downstairs. It has typical hostel dorms as well as some very hotel-like private rooms; for a step up in quality, see the listing for the Circus Hotel, earlier (€19/bed in 8- to 10-bed dorms, €23/bed in 4- to 5-bed dorms, S-€43, Sb-€53, D-€56, Db-€70, T-€75, 2-person apartment with kitchen-€85, 4-person apartment-€140, breakfast-€4-8, no curfew, elevator, pay Internet access, free Wi-Fi, laundry, Weinbergsweg 1a, U8: Rosenthaler Platz, tel. 030/2000-3939, www.circus-berlin .de, info@circus-berlin.de).

$ Meininger is a Europe-wide budget-hotel chain with several locations in Berlin. With sleek, nicely decorated rooms, these are a great-value budget option, even for non-hostelers. They have three particularly appealing branches: in Prenzlauer Berg (Schönhauser Allee 19 on Senefelderplatz), at Oranienburger Strasse 67 (next to the Aufsturz pub), and near the Hauptbahnhof, at Ella-Traebe-Strasse 9 (rates vary by availability, but usually €18-19/bed in 6-bed dorms, Sb-€52, Db-€70, Tb-€86; rates at Hauptbahnhof location about €5-10 more; all locations: breakfast-€5.50, elevator, 24-hour reception, pay Internet access, free Wi-Fi in lobby, tel. 030/666-36100, www.meininger-hotels.de).

Backpacker Havens

$ EastSeven Hostel rents the best cheap beds in Prenzlauer Berg. It's sleek and modern, with all the hostel services and more: 60 beds, 24-hour reception, inviting lounge, fully equipped guests' kitchen, lockers, garden, and bike rental. Children are welcome. Easygoing people of any age are comfortable here (€18/bed in 8-bed dorms, €22/bed in 4-bed dorms with private bathroom—or €20/bed in dorm with bathroom down the hall, S-€38, D-€52, T-€66, private rooms have bathrooms down the hall, includes sheets, towel-€1, continental breakfast-€2, pay Internet access, free Wi-Fi, laundry-€5, 100 yards from U2: Senefelderplatz at Schwedter Strasse 7, tel. 030/9362-2240, www.eastseven.de, info @eastseven.de).

$ Hotel Transit Loft, actually a hostel, is located in a refurbished factory. Its 62 clean, high-ceilinged, modern rooms and wide-open lobby have an industrial touch. The reception—staffed by friendly, hip Berliners—is open 24 hours, with a bar serving drinks all night long (€21/bed in 4- to 6-bed dorms, Sb-€59, Db-€69, Tb-€89, includes sheets and breakfast, elevator, cheap Internet access, free Wi-Fi, fully wheelchair-accessible, down alley facing inner courtyard at Immanuelkirchstrasse 14A; U2/U5/U8 or S-Bahn: Alexanderplatz, then tram #M4 to Hufelandstrasse and walk 50 yards; tel. 030/4849-3773, fax 030/4405-1074, www .transit-loft.de, loft@hotel-transit.de).

$ Ostel is a fun retro-1970s-DDR apartment building that re-creates the lifestyle and interior design of a country relegated to the dustbin of history. All the furniture and room decorations have been meticulously collected and restored to their former socialist glory—only the psychedelic wallpaper is a replica. Guests buy ration vouchers (€7.50/person) for breakfast in the attached restaurant. Kitschy, sure—but also clean and memorable (€15/bed in a 4- or 6-bed "Pioneer Camp" room or in 12-bunk dorm—includes lockers, S-€33, Sb-€40, D-€54, Db-€61, 4-person apartments-€120, includes sheets and towels, 24-hour reception, free Wi-Fi in lobby, bike rental, free parking, free collective use of the people's barbeque, right behind Ostbahnhof station on the corner of Strasse der Pariser Kommune at Wriezener Karree 5, tel. 030/2576-8660, www.ostel.eu, contact@ostel.eu).

In Western Berlin: Near Savignyplatz and Bahnhof Zoo

While Bahnhof Zoo and Ku'damm are no longer the center of the action, this western Berlin neighborhood is still a comfortable and handy home base (thanks to its easy transit connections to the rest of the city and proximity to the starting point of various guided tours). The streets around the tree-lined Savignyplatz (a

10-minute walk behind the station) have a neighborhood charm, with an abundance of simple, small, friendly, good-value places to sleep and eat. The area has an artsy aura going back to the cabaret days in the 1920s, when it was the center of Berlin's gay scene. The hotels and pensions I list here—which are all a 5- to 15-minute walk from Bahnhof Zoo and Savignyplatz (with S- and U-Bahn stations)—are generally located a couple of flights up in big, run-down buildings. Inside, they're clean and spacious enough so that their well-worn character is actually charming. Asking for a quieter room in back gets you away from any street noise. Of the accommodations listed here, Pension Peters offers the best value for budget travelers.

$$$ Hecker's Hotel is a modern, four-star business hotel with 69 big, fresh rooms and all the Euro-comforts. Their "superior" rooms cost €10 more than their "comfort" rooms, and—while the same size—have more modern furnishings and air-conditioning. Herr Kiesal promises free breakfasts (otherwise €16/person) for those reserving direct with this book (Sb-€95, Db-€180, all rooms €200 during conferences but generally only €100 July-Aug, look for deals on their website, non-smoking rooms, elevator, Wi-Fi, parking-€12-18, between Savignyplatz and Ku'damm at Grolmanstrasse 35, tel. 030/88900, fax 030/889-0260, www.heckers-hotel.com, info@heckers-hotel.com).

$$ Hotel Askanischerhof, the oldest B&B in Berlin, is posh as can be, with 16 sprawling, antique-furnished living rooms you can call home. Photos on the walls brag of famous movie-star guests. It oozes Old World service and classic Berlin atmosphere (Sb-€110, Db-€120, Tb-€130, elevator, Wi-Fi, free parking, Ku'damm 53, tel. 030/881-8033, fax 030/881-7206, www.askanischer-hof.de, info@askanischer-hof.de).

$$ Hotel Astoria is a friendly three-star business-class hotel with 32 comfortably furnished rooms and affordable summer and weekend rates (Db-€108-126, often Db-€80 in summer, check their website for deals, strict cancellation policy, non-smoking floors, elevator, Internet access, parking-€9, around corner from Bahnhof Zoo at Fasanenstrasse 2, tel. 030/312-4067, www.hotel astoria.de, info@hotelastoria.de).

$$ Hotel Carmer 16, with 30 bright and airy (if a bit dated) rooms, is both business-like and homey, and has an inviting lounge and charming balconies (Db-€93, ask for Rick Steves price when reserving direct with this book, extra person-€20, some rooms have balconies, family suites, elevator and a few stairs, Wi-Fi, Carmerstrasse 16, tel. 030/3110-0500, fax 030/3110-0510, www.hotel-carmer16.de, info@hotel-carmer16.de).

$$ Hotel-Pension Funk, the former home of a 1920s silent-movie star, is a delightfully quirky time warp. Kind manager Herr

Western Berlin

1. Hecker's Hotel
2. Hotel Askanischerhof
3. Hotel Astoria
4. Hotel Carmer 16
5. Hotel-Pension Funk
6. Hotel Bogota
7. Pension Peters
8. Restaurant Marjellchen
9. Rest. Leibniz-Klause
10. Dicke Wirtin Pub
11. Die Zwölf Apostel Rest.
12. Zillemarkt Restaurant
13. Technical University Mensa
14. Ullrich Supermarkt
15. Schleusenkrug Beer Garden
16. Winter Garden Buffet
17. A Trane Jazz Club
18. Bar Jeder Vernunft
19. Internet Café
20. Fat Tire Bikes

BERLIN

Michael Pfundt offers 15 elegant old rooms with rich Art Nouveau furnishings (S-€42, Ss-€60, Sb-€72, D-€72, Ds-€85, Db-€105, extra person-€25, cash preferred, Wi-Fi, a long block south of Ku'damm at Fasanenstrasse 69, tel. 030/882-7193, www.hotel-pensionfunk.de, berlin@hotel-pensionfunk.de).

$$ Hotel Bogota is a slumbermill just steps off Ku'damm, renting 115 rooms in a sprawling maze of a building that used to house the Nazi Chamber of Culture. A creaky, well-worn place with big, simple rooms and old furniture, it has the feel of a once-grand hotel (S-€49, Ss-€62, Sb-€98, D-€77, Ds-€84, Db-€89-150, extra bed-€21, look for Web deals and great last-minute prices in summer, children under 12 free, elevator, 10-minute walk from Savignyplatz at Schlüterstrasse 45, tel. 030/881-5001, fax 030/883-5887, www.hotel-bogota.de, info@hotel-bogota.de).

$ Pension Peters, run by a German-Swedish couple, is sunny and central, with a cheery breakfast room and a super-friendly staff who go out of their way to help their guests. With its sleek

Scandinavian decor and 34 renovated rooms, it's a good choice. Some of the ground-floor rooms facing the back courtyard are a bit dark—and cheaper for the inconvenience (Sb-€58, Db-€79, big Db-€85, extra bed-€15, family room-€85, ask for Rick Steves price, up to 2 kids under 13 free with 2 paying adults, cash only, Wi-Fi and Internet access, 10 yards off Savignyplatz at Kantstrasse 146, tel. 030/312-2278, www.pension-peters-berlin.de, info@pension -peters-berlin.de, Annika and Christoph with help of his sister, Daisy).

Eating in Berlin

There's a world of restaurants to choose from in this ever-changing city. Your best approach may be to select a neighborhood and browse until you find something that strikes your fancy, rather than seeking out a particular restaurant.

Don't be too determined to eat "Berlin-style." The city is

known only for its mildly spicy sausage and for its street food (*Currywurst* and *Döner Kebab*). Germans—especially Berliners—consider their food old-school; when they go out to eat, they're not usually looking for the "traditional local fare" many travelers are after. Nouveau German is California cuisine with scant memories of wurst, kraut, and pumpernickel. If the kraut is getting the wurst of you, take a break with some international or ethnic offerings—try one of the many Turkish, Italian, pan-Asian, and Balkan restaurants.

Colorful pubs—called *Kneipen*—offer light, quick, and easy meals and the fizzy local beer, *Berliner Weiss*. Ask for it *mit Schuss* for a shot of fruity syrup in your suds.

In Eastern Berlin
Near Unter den Linden

At the Opera House (Opernpalais): The **Schinkel Klause Biergarten** serves good €10-19 meals on its shady terrace with a view of the Unter den Linden scene when sunny, or in its cellar otherwise (daily 11:30-22:00, tel. 030/2026-8450).

Cheap Eats on Friedrichstrasse: **Bier's Curry und Spiesse,** under the tracks at the Friedrichstrasse S-Bahn stop, is a great, greasy, cheap, and generous place for an old-fashioned German hot dog. This is the local favorite near Unter den Linden for €2 *Currywurst*. Experiment with variations (the *Flieschspiess* is excellent) and sauces—and don't hold the *Zwiebeln* (fried onions). You'll munch standing at a counter, where the people-watching is great (daily 10:00-5:00 in the morning; from inside the station, take the Friedrichstrasse exit and turn left).

Near the Pergamon Museum: Georgenstrasse, a block behind the Pergamon Museum and under the S-Bahn tracks, is lined with fun eateries filling the arcade of the train trestle—close to the sightseeing action but in business mainly for students from nearby Humboldt University. **Deponie3** is a trendy Berlin *Kneipe* usually filled with students. Garden seating in the back is nice if you don't mind the noise of the S-Bahn passing directly above you. The interior is a cozy, wooden wonderland of a bar with several inviting spaces. They serve basic salads, traditional Berlin dishes, and hearty daily specials (€4-8 breakfasts, good €8 brunch Sun 10:00-15:00, €5-11 lunches and dinners, open daily from 9:00, sometimes live music, Georgenstrasse 5, tel. 030/2016-5740). For Italian food, a branch of **Die Zwölf Apostel** is nearby (daily until 24:00; described later, under "Near Savignyplatz").

In the Heart of Old Berlin's Nikolai Quarter: The *Nikolaiviertel* marks the original medieval settlement of Cölln, which would eventually become Berlin. The area was destroyed during the war but was rebuilt for Berlin's 750th birthday in 1987. The whole area has a cute, cobbled, and characteristic old town...Middle Ages meets Socialist Realism. Today, the district is pretty soulless by day but a popular restaurant zone at night. **Bräuhaus Georgbrau** is a thriving beer hall serving homemade suds on a picturesque courtyard overlooking the Spree River. Eat in the lively and woody but mod-feeling interior, or outdoors with fun riverside seating—thriving with German tourists. It's a good place to try one of the few typical Berlin dishes: *Eisbein* (boiled ham hock) with sauerkraut and mashed peas with bacon (€10 with a beer and schnapps). The statue of St. George once stood in the courtyard of Berlin's old castle—until the Nazis deemed it too decadent and not "German" enough, and removed it (€10-13 plates, three-foot-long sampler board with a dozen small glasses of beer, daily 10:00-24:00, 2 blocks south of Berlin Cathedral and across the river at Spreeufer 4, tel. 030/242-4244).

In City Hall: Consider lunching at one of Berlin's many *Kantine*. Located in government offices and larger corporations, *Kantine* offer fast, filling, and cheap lunches, along with a unique opportunity to see Germans at work (though the food can hardly be considered gourmet). There are thousands of *Kantine* in Berlin, but the best is **Die Kantine im Roten Rathaus,** in the basement of City Hall. For less than €4, you can get filling German dishes like *Leberkäse* (German-style baloney) or stuffed cabbage (Mon-Fri 11:00-15:00, closed Sat-Sun, Rathausstrasse 15).

Near Gendarmenmarkt, South of Unter den Linden

The twin churches of Gendarmenmarkt seem to be surrounded by people in love with food. The lunch and dinner scene is thriving with upscale restaurants serving good cuisine at highly competitive prices to local professionals (see map on page 634 for locations). If in need of a quick-yet-classy lunch, stroll around the square and along Charlottenstrasse. For a quick bite, head to the cheap *Currywurst* stand behind the German Cathedral.

Lutter & Wegner Restaurant is well-known for its Austrian cuisine (*Schnitzel* and *Sauerbraten*) and popular with businesspeople. It's dressy, with fun sidewalk seating or a dark and elegant interior (€9-18 starters, €16-22 main dishes, daily 11:00-24:00, Charlottenstrasse 56, tel. 030/202-9540). They have a second location, called **Beisl am Tacheles,** near the New Synagogue (Oranienburger Strasse 52, tel. 030/2478-1078).

Augustiner am Gendarmenmarkt, next door to Lutter & Wegner, lines its sidewalk with trademark Bavarian white-and-blue-checkerboard tablecloths; inside, you'll find a classic Bavarian beer-hall atmosphere. Less pretentious than its neighbor, it offers good beer and affordable Bavarian classics in an equally appealing

Eastern Berlin Eateries & Nightlife

1. Schinkel Klause Biergarten
2. Bier's Curry und Spiesse
3. Deponie3 Pub
4. Die Zwölf Apostel
5. Bräuhaus Georgbrau
6. Die Kantine im Roten Rathaus
7. Lutter & Wegner Rest.; Augustiner am Gendarmenmarkt
8. Beisl am Tacheles
9. Galeries Lafayette Food Circus
10. Aroma Espresso Bar
11. Hasir Turkish Restaurant
12. Weihenstephaner Bavarian Restaurant
13. Aufsturz Pub
14. Prater Biergarten
15. Zum Schusterjungen Speisegaststätte
16. La Bodeguita del Medio Cuban Bar Restaurant
17. Konnopke's Imbiss
18. Restaurant "Die Schule"
19. Kauf Dich Glücklich
20. Fleischmöbel Pub
21. Gugelhof Restaurant
22. Luigi Zuckermann Deli & Transit Restaurant
23. Metzer Eck Pub
24. Lemongrass Scent
25. Humboldt-Box Café
26. To Café Sibylle

BERLIN

..... Former Course of The Wall

500 meters
1/2 Mile

27 Bonbonmacherei
   Candy Shop

28 Fassbender & Rausch
   Chocolate Shop

29 B-Flat Acoustic
   Music & Jazz Club

30 FriedrichstadtPalast

31 Clärchens Ballhaus

location (€6-12 light meals, €10-15 bigger meals, daily 9:00-24:00, Charlottenstrasse 55, tel. 030/2045-4020).

Galeries Lafayette Food Circus is a French festival of fun eateries in the basement of the landmark department store. You'll find a good deli and prepared-food stands, dishing up cuisine that's good-quality but not cheap (most options €10-15, cheaper €8-10 sandwiches and savory crepes, Mon-Sat 10:00-20:00, closed Sun, U-Bahn: Französische Strasse, tel. 030/209-480).

Near Checkpoint Charlie: **Aroma Espresso Bar** is a touristy joint, handy for made-to-order sandwiches. Israeli-born Sagi makes his own bread daily and piles on the fixin's for €4-6. This is a popular stop for walking-tour groups: If you get here when they do, expect a line (Mon-Sat 7:30-19:00, Sun 8:00-19:00, in summer until 20:30, Friedrichstrasse 200, tel. 030/206-16693).

At and near Hackescher Markt

Hasir Turkish Restaurant is your chance to dine with candles, hardwood floors, and happy Berliners savoring meaty Anatolian specialties. As Berlin is the world's largest Turkish city outside of Asia Minor, it's no wonder you can find some good Turkish restaurants here. But while most locals think of Turkish food as fast and cheap, this is a dining experience. The restaurant, in a courtyard next to the Hackeschen Höfe shopping complex (see page 634), offers indoor and outdoor tables filled with an enthusiastic local crowd. The service can be a bit questionable, so bring some patience (€6-10 starters, €14-20 main dishes, large and splittable portions, daily 11:30-1:00 in the morning, in late evening the courtyard is dominated by an unpleasantly loud underground disco, a block from the Hackescher Markt S-Bahn station at Oranienburger Strasse 4, tel. 030/2804-1616).

Weihenstephaner Bavarian Restaurant serves upmarket Bavarian traditional food for around €10-15 a plate; offers an atmospheric cellar, an inner courtyard, and a busy people-watching street-side terrace; and, of course, has excellent beer (daily 11:00-24:00, Neue Promenade 5 at Hackescher Markt, tel. 030/8471-0760).

Aufsturz, a lively pub, pours more than 100 different beers and 40 varieties of whiskey, and dishes up "traditional Berliner pub grub"—like nachos—and great potato soup for under €5. The traditional "Berlin board" for €17 can easily feed three voracious carnivores (daily from 12:00 until at least 2:00 in the morning, a block beyond the New Synagogue at Oranienburger Strasse 67, tel. 030/2804-7407).

In Prenzlauer Berg

Prenzlauer Berg is packed with fine restaurants—German, ethnic, and everything in between. Even if you're not staying in this area, it's worth venturing here for dinner. (For more on Prenzlauer Berg, see page 604; for restaurant locations, see the map on page 634.) Before making a choice, I'd spend at least half an hour strolling and browsing through this bohemian wonderland of creative eateries. Because Prenzlauer Berg sprawls over a wide area, I've organized my listings by neighborhood.

Near Eberswalder Strasse

The area surrounding the elevated Eberswalder Strasse U-Bahn station (on the U2 line, at the confluence of Kastanienallee, Danziger Strasse, Ebwerswalder Strasse, and Schönhauser Allee) is the epicenter of Prenzlauer Berg—a young, hip, and edgy place to eat and drink. While a bit farther north than other areas I recommend (and a 10- to 15-minute walk from most of my recommended hotels), it's worth the trip to immerse yourself in quintessential Prenzlauer Berg.

Prater Biergarten offers two great eating opportunities: a rustic indoor restaurant and a mellow, shady, super-cheap, and family-friendly outdoor beer garden (with a playground)—each proudly pouring Prater's own microbrew. In the beer garden—Berlin's oldest—you step up to the counter and order (simple €3-5 plates and an intriguing selection of beer munchies, daily in good weather 12:00-24:00). The restaurant serves serious traditional *Biergarten* cuisine and good salads (€7-17 plates, Mon-Sat 18:00-24:00, Sun 12:00-24:00, cash only, Kastanienallee 7, tel. 030/448-5688).

Zum Schusterjungen Speisegaststätte ("The Cobbler's Apprentice") is a classic old-school, German-with-attitude eatery that retains its circa-1986 DDR decor. Famous for its filling €7-10 meals (including various types of schnitzel and Berlin classics such as pork knuckle), it's a no-frills place with quality ingredients and a strong local following. It serves the eating needs of those Berliners lamenting the disappearance of solid traditional German cooking amid the flood of ethnic eateries. While it was recently sold, the new owners promise to keep the kitsch (small 40-seat dining hall plus outdoor tables, daily 12:00-24:00, corner of Lychener Strasse and Danziger Strasse 9, tel. 030/442-7654).

La Bodeguita del Medio Cuban Bar Restaurant is purely fun-loving Cuba—graffiti-caked walls, Che Guevara posters, animated staff, and an ambience that makes you want to dance. Come early to eat or late to drink. This restaurant has been here since 1994—and in fast-changing Prenzlauer Berg, that's an eternity. The German-Cuban couple who run it take pride in their food, and the main dishes are big enough to split. You can even puff a Cuban cigar at the sidewalk tables (€5-10 tapas, €6 Cuban ribs and salad, Tue-Sun 18:00-24:00, closed Mon, a block from U2:

BERLIN

Eberswalder Strasse at Lychener Strasse 6, tel. 030/4050-0601).

Konnopke's Imbiss, a super-cheap German-style sausage stand, has been a Berlin institution for more than 70 years—it was family-owned even during DDR times. Berliners say Konnopke's cooks up some of the city's best *Currywurst* (less than €2). Located beneath the U2 viaduct, the stand was demolished in summer of 2010 during roadwork. Berliners rioted, and Konnopke's was rebuilt in a slick glass-and-steel hut (Mon-Fri 10:00-20:00, Sat 12:00-20:00, closed Sun; Kastanienallee dead-ends at the elevated train tracks, and under them you'll find Konnopke's at Schönhauser Allee 44A). Don't confuse this with the nearby Currystation—look for the real Konnopke's.

Restaurant "Die Schule" is a modern place with a no-frills style where you can sample traditional German dishes tapas-style. Assemble a collection of little €2.50 plates of old-fashioned German food you might not try otherwise (good indoor and outdoor seating, €24 full 3-course dinner, daily 11:00-22:00, Kastanienallee 82, tel. 030/780-089-550).

After-Dinner Dessert and Drinks: There are oodles of characteristic funky pubs and nightspots in the area around Helmholtzplatz (and elsewhere in Prenzlauer Berg). Oderberger Strasse is a fun zone to explore; I've listed two places on this street that I particularly like. **Kauf Dich Glücklich** makes a great capper to a Prenzlauer Berg dinner. It serves an enticing array of sweet Belgian waffles and ice cream (best pistachio ice cream in Berlin) in a candy-sprinkled, bohemian lounge on a great Prenzlauer Berg street (daily 11:00-23:00, indoor and outdoor seating—or get your dessert to go, wait possible on busy nights, Oderberger Strasse 44, tel. 030/4435-2182). **Fleischmöbel** ("Meat Furniture") is a fun place to drink with locals, despite the lack of beer on tap. Here you'll find strong cocktails, cool classic rock, and a big blackboard. It's a bit hipster-pretentious, but offers a good glimpse into the Prenzlauer Berg lifestyle. Its two smallish rooms unashamedly offer a bit of 1960s retro in an increasingly trendy part of town; on warm evenings, tables fill the sidewalk out front (daily 12:00 until "whenever," Oderberger Strasse 2).

Near Kollwitzplatz

This square, home of the DDR student resistance in 1980s, is now trendy and upscale, popular with hip parents who take their hip kids to the leafy playground park at its center. It's an especially good area to prowl among upmarket restaurants—walk the square and choose. Just about every option offers sidewalk seats in the summer (great on a balmy evening). It's a long block up Kollwitzstrasse from U2: Senefelderplatz.

Gugelhof, right on Kollwitzplatz, is an institution famous for its Alsatian German cuisine. You'll enjoy French quality with German proportions. It's highly regarded, with a boisterous and enthusiastic local crowd filling its minimalist yet classy interior. In good weather, outdoor seating sprawls along its sidewalk. Their fixed-price meals are fun, and they welcome swapping (€20-30 three-course meal, €5-10 starters, €12-20 main dishes, daily 16:00-24:00, reservations required during peak times, where Knaackstrasse meets Kollwitzplatz, tel. 030/442-9229).

Near Rosenthaler Platz, Closer to Hackescher Markt

Surrounding the U8: Rosenthaler Platz station, a short stroll or tram ride from the Hackescher Markt S-Bahn station, and an easy walk from the Oranienburger Strasse action, this busy neighborhood has a few enticing options.

Luigi Zuckermann is a trendy young deli with Israeli/New York style. It's a great spot to pick up a custom-made deli sandwich (choose your ingredients at the deli counter), hummus plate, salad, fresh-squeezed juice, or other quick, healthy lunch. Linger in the interior, grab one of the few sidewalk tables, or take your food to munch on the go (€5-8 meals, Sun-Thu 8:00-24:00, Fri-Sat open 24 hours, Rosenthaler Strasse 67, tel. 030/2804-0644).

Transit is a stylish, innovative, affordable Thai/Indonesian/pan-Asian small-plates restaurant at the bustling Hackescher Markt end of Prenzlauer Berg. Sit at one of the long shared tables and dig into a creative menu of €3 small plates and €7 big plates. Two people can make a filling meal out of three or four dishes (daily 11:00-late, Rosenthaler Strasse 68, tel. 030/2478-1645).

Near Senefelderplatz (near Recommended Hotels on Metzer Strasse and Schwedter Strasse)

While neither of these places—in a sedate corner of Prenzlauer Berg near the Senefelderplatz U-Bahn stop—is worth going out of your way for, they're handy if you're staying at several of my recommended accommodations.

Metzer Eck is a time-warp *Kneipe* with a family tradition dating to 1913 and a cozy charm. It serves cheap basic typical Berlin food with five beers on tap, including the Czech Budvar (€5-8 meals, Mon-Fri 16:00-24:00, Sat 18:00-24:00, closed Sun, Metzer Strasse 33, on the corner of Metzer Strasse and Strassburger Strasse, tel. 030/442-7656).

Lemongrass Scent, with a gaggle of inviting sidewalk tables, offers tasty and affordable "Asian street kitchen" food near several recommended hotels (two-course weekday lunch special for less than €5, €3-4 starters, €5-8 main dishes, Mon-Fri 11:30-24:00, Sat-Sun 12:00-24:00, Schwedter Strasse 12, tel. 030/4057-6985).

In Western Berlin
Near Savignyplatz

Many good restaurants are on or within 100 yards of Savignyplatz, near my recommended western Berlin hotels (for locations, see map on page 630). Savignyplatz is lined with attractive, relaxed, mostly Mediterranean-style places. Take a walk and survey these; continue your stroll along Bleibtreustrasse to discover many trendier, more creative little eateries.

Restaurant Marjellchen is a trip to East Prussia. Dine in a soft, jazzy elegance in one of two six-table rooms. While it doesn't have to be expensive (€10-18 main courses, €27 two-course meals), plan to go the whole nine yards here, as this can be a great Prussian experience with caring service. The menu is inviting, and all the recipes were brought to Berlin by the owner's mother after she was expelled from East Prussia. Reservations are smart (daily 17:00-23:30, family-run, Mommsenstrasse 9, tel. 030/883-2676).

Restaurant Leibniz-Klause is a good place for a dressy German meal. You'll enjoy upscale presentation on white tablecloths, hunter-sized portions, service that's both friendly and professional, and no pretense—but annoying commercial radio taints the atmosphere. Their *Berliner Riesen-Eisbein* ("super-pork-leg on the bone"), with sauerkraut and horseradish, will stir even the tiniest amount of Teutonic blood in your veins (€15-22 plates, good indoor and outdoor seating, daily from 12:00 until late, on the corner of Leibnizstrasse at Mommsenstrasse 57, tel. 030/323-7068).

Dicke Wirtin is a pub with traditional old-Berlin *Kneipe* atmosphere, six good beers on tap, and solid home cooking at reasonable prices—such as their famously cheap *Gulaschsuppe* (€4). Their interior is fun and pubby, with soccer on the TV; their streetside tables are also inviting. Pickled eggs are on the bar—ask about how these can help you avoid a hangover (€5 daily specials, Bavarian Andechs beer on tap, open daily from 12:00, dinner served from 18:00, just off Savignyplatz at Carmerstrasse 9, tel. 030/312-4952).

Die Zwölf Apostel ("The Twelve Apostles") is popular for good Italian food. Choose between indoors with candlelit ambience, outdoors on a sun-dappled patio, or overlooking the people-parade on its pedestrian street. A local crowd packs this restaurant for €12 pizzas and €15-30 meals (long hours daily, cash only, immediately across from Savignyplatz S-Bahn entrance, Bleibtreustrasse 49, tel. 030/312-1433).

Zillemarkt Restaurant, which feels like an old-time Berlin *Biergarten,* serves traditional Berlin specialties in the garden or in the rustic candlelit interior. Their *Berliner Allerlei* is a fun way to sample a bit of nearly everything (cabbage, pork, sausage, potatoes and more for a minimum of two people...but it can feed up to five). They have their own microbrew (€10 meals, daily 12:00-24:00, near the S-Bahn tracks at Bleibtreustrasse 48A, tel. 030/881-7040).

Technical University Mensa puts you in a thriving, modern student scene. It feels like a student union building (because it is), with shops, a travel agency, a lounge, kids making out, and lots of international students to chat with. The main cafeteria *(Mensa)* is upstairs—bustling with students and lots of eating options. Streetside is a cafeteria with a more limited selection. Even with the non-student surcharge, eating here is very cheap (€3-5 meals, Mon-Fri 11:00-14:30, closed Sat-Sun, general public entirely welcome but pays the highest of the three prices, coffee bar downstairs with Internet access, just north of Uhlandstrasse at Hardenbergstrasse 34).

Supermarket: The neighborhood grocery store is **Ullrich** (Mon-Sat 9:00-22:00, Sun 11:00-22:00, Kantstrasse 7, under the tracks near Bahnhof Zoo). There's plenty of fast food near Bahnhof Zoo and on Ku'damm.

Near Bahnhof Zoo

Schleusenkrug beer garden is hidden in the park overlooking a canal between the Bahnhof Zoo and Tiergarten stations. Choose from an ever-changing self-service menu of huge salads, pasta, and some German dishes (€7-12 plates, €3-5 grill snacks, daily 10:00-24:00; standing in front of Bahnhof Zoo, turn left and walk 5 minutes, following the path into the park between the zoo and train tracks; tel. 030/313-9909).

Self-Service Cafeterias: The top floor of the famous department store, **KaDeWe,** holds the Winter Garden Buffet view cafeteria, and its sixth-floor deli/food department is a picnicker's nirvana. Its arterials are clogged with more than 1,000 kinds of sausage and 1,500 types of cheese (Mon-Thu 10:00-20:00, Fri 10:00-21:00, Sat 9:30-20:00, closed Sun, U-Bahn: Wittenbergplatz).

Berlin Connections

By Train

Berlin used to have several major train stations. But now that the Hauptbahnhof has emerged as the single, massive central station, all the others have wilted into glorified subway stations. Virtually all long-distance trains pass through the Hauptbahnhof—ignore the other stations.

EurAide is an agent of the German Railway that sells reservations for high-speed and overnight trains, with staff that can answer your travel questions in English (located in the Hauptbahnhof; see "Arrival in Berlin" on page 553).

From Berlin by Train to: Frankfurt (hourly, 4 hours), **Bacharach** (hourly, 6.5-7.5 hours, 1-3 changes), **Würzburg** (hourly, 4 hours, change in Göttingen or Fulda), **Rothenburg** (hourly, 5-6 hours, often via Göttingen or Fulda, then Würzburg, then Steinach), **Nürnberg** (hourly, 4.5 hours), **Munich** (1-2/hour, 6-6.75 hours, every 2 hours direct, otherwise change in Göttingen), **Köln** (hourly, 4.25 hours), **Amsterdam** (6/day direct to Amsterdam Zuid, 6.5 hours; plus 1 night train/day to Amsterdam Centraal, 10 hours), **London** (5/day, 10-11.5 hours, 2 changes—you're better off flying cheap on easyJet or Air Berlin, even if you have a railpass), **Paris** (5/day, 8-9 hours, change in Köln—via Belgium—or in Mannheim, 1 direct 12-hour night train), **Vienna** (8/day, most with 1 change, 2/day plus 1/night are direct, 9.5 hours; some via Czech Republic, but trains with a change in Nürnberg, Munich, or Würzburg avoid that country—useful if it's not covered by your railpass). It's wise but not required to reserve in advance for trains to or from Amsterdam (or Prague). Train info: tel. 0180-599-6633, www.bahn.com. Before buying a ticket for any long train ride from Berlin (over 7 hours), consider taking a cheap flight instead (buy it well in advance to get a super fare).

Night trains run from Berlin to these cities: Munich, Paris, Amsterdam, Vienna, Budapest, Malmö (Sweden, near Copenhagen), Basel, and Zürich. There are no night trains from Berlin to anywhere in Italy or Spain. A *Liegeplatz*, a.k.a. *couchette* berth (€13-36), is a great deal; inquire at EurAide at the Hauptbahnhof for details. Beds generally cost the same whether you have a first- or second-class ticket or railpass. Trains are often full, so reserve your *couchette* a few days in advance from any travel agency or major train station in Europe.

By Plane

Berlin is in the process of whittling down to a single airport—the new Willy Brandt Berlin-Brandenburg International—which opened in 2012. The central toll telephone number for airport information is 01805-000-186. For British Air, tel. 01805-266-522; Delta, tel. 01803-337-880; SAS, tel. 01805-117-002; Lufthansa, tel. 01803-803-803.

Most flights arrive either at the **Willy Brandt Berlin-Brandenburg International Airport** or the adjacent **Schönefeld Airport** (12.5 miles from center). From the nearby train station, you can catch a regional express train into the city (ignore the S-Bahn, as there are no direct S-Bahn trains to the city center). Airport Express RE and RB trains go direct to Ostbahnhof, Alexanderplatz, Friedrichstrasse, Hauptbahnhof, and Bahnhof Zoo (€2.60, every 30 minutes, take trains in the direction of Nauen or Dessau, railpass valid). A taxi to the city center costs about €35.

Tegel Airport handles some flights (4 miles from center, no subway trains, catch the faster bus #X9 to Bahnhof Zoo, or bus #109 to Ku'damm and Bahnhof Zoo for €2.30; bus #TXL goes between Tegel Airport, the Hauptbahnhof—stop is out the *Washingtonplatz* entrance, and Alexanderplatz in eastern Berlin; bus #128 goes to northern Berlin; taxi from Tegel Airport costs €15 to Bahnhof Zoo, €25 to Alexanderplatz; taxis from Tegel levy a €0.50 surcharge).

Berlin, the Discount Airline Hub: Berlin is the continental European hub for budget airlines such as easyJet (lots of flights to Spain, Italy, Eastern Europe, the Baltics, and more—book long in advance to get incredible €30-and-less fares, www.easyjet.com). Ryanair (www.ryanair.com), Air Berlin (www.airberlin.com), and German Wings (www.germanwings.com) make the London-Berlin trip (and other routes) dirt-cheap, so consider this option before booking an overnight train. Consequently, British visitors to the city are now outnumbered only by Americans.

BERLIN

GREAT BRITAIN

LONDON

London is more than 600 square miles of urban jungle—a world in itself and a barrage on all the senses. On my first visit, I felt extremely small.

London is more than its museums and landmarks. It's the L.A., D.C., and N.Y.C. of Britain—a living, breathing, thriving organism...a coral reef of humanity. The city has changed dramatically in recent years, and many visitors are surprised to find how "un-English" it is. ESL (English as a second language) seems like the city's first language, as white people are now a minority in major parts of the city that once symbolized white imperialism. Arabs have nearly bought out the area north of Hyde Park. Chinese takeouts outnumber fish-and-chips shops. Eastern Europeans pull pints in British pubs. Many hotels are run by people with foreign accents (who hire English chambermaids), while outlying suburbs are home to huge communities of Indians and Pakistanis. London is a city of nearly eight million separate dreams, inhabiting a place that does its best to tolerate and encourage them. With the English Channel Tunnel and discount airlines making travel between Britain and the Continent easier than ever, London is learning—sometimes fitfully—to live as a microcosm of its formerly vast empire.

The city, which has long attracted tourists, seems perpetually at your service, with an impressive slate of sights, entertainment, and eateries, linked by a great transit system. Because of the 2012 Olympic Games, London has spiffed up the place, especially the rapidly developing Olympic Park in East London.

With just a few days here, you'll get no more than a quick splash in this teeming human tidal pool. But with a good orientation, you'll find London manageable and fun. You'll get a sampling of the city's top sights, history, and cultural entertainment, and a good look at its ever-changing human face.

Blow through the city on the open deck of a double-decker orientation tour bus, and take a pinch-me-I'm-in-London walk through the West End. Ogle the crown jewels at the Tower of London, hear the chimes of Big Ben, and see the Houses of Parliament in action. Cruise the Thames River, and take a spin on the London Eye. Hobnob with poets' tombstones in Westminster Abbey, and visit with Leonardo, Botticelli, and Rembrandt in the National Gallery. Enjoy Shakespeare in a replica of the Globe theater and marvel at a glitzy, fun musical at a modern-day theater. Whisper across the dome of St. Paul's Cathedral, then rummage through our civilization's attic at the British Museum. And sip your tea with pinky raised and clotted cream dribbling down your scone.

Planning Your Time

The sights of London alone could easily fill a trip to Britain. It's worth at least three busy days. You won't be able to see everything, so don't try—you'll keep coming back to London. After dozens of visits myself, I still enjoy a healthy list of excuses to return. Especially if you hope to enjoy a play or concert, a night or two of jet lag is bad news.

Here's a suggested three-day schedule:

Day 1

9:00	Tower of London (crown jewels first, then Beefeater tour, then White Tower; note that on Sun-Mon, the Tower opens at 10:00).
13:00	Grab a picnic, catch a boat at Tower Pier, and relax with lunch on the Thames while cruising to Westminster Pier.
14:30	Tour Westminster Abbey, and consider their evensong service (at 15:00 Sat-Sun, at 17:00 Mon-Fri and Sat in summer).
17:00 (or after evensong)	Follow my self-guided walk of Westminster. When you're finished, if it's a Monday or Tuesday, you could return to the Houses of Parliament and pop in to see the House of Commons in action (until 22:30).

Day 2

8:30	Take a double-decker hop-on, hop-off London sightseeing bus tour (from Green Park or Victoria) and hop off for the Changing of the Guard.

11:00	Buckingham Palace (guards change most days May-July at 11:30, alternate days Aug-April—confirm).
12:00	Walk through St. James's Park to enjoy London's delightful park scene.
13:00	Covent Garden for lunch, shopping, and people-watching.
14:30	Tour the British Museum.
Evening	Have a pub dinner before a play, concert, or evening walking tour.

Day 3

Choose among these remaining London highlights: National Gallery, British Library, Churchill War Rooms, Imperial War Museum, the two Tates (Tate Modern on the South Bank for modern art, Tate Britain on the North Bank for British art), St. Paul's Cathedral, Victoria and Albert Museum, National Portrait Gallery, Natural History Museum, Courtauld Gallery, or the Museum of London; take a spin on the London Eye or a cruise to Kew Gardens; enjoy a play at Shakespeare's Globe; do some serious shopping at one of London's elegant department stores or open-air markets; or take another historic walking tour.

Orientation to London

(area code: 020)

To grasp London more comfortably, see it as the old town in the city center without the modern, congested sprawl. (Even at that, it's still huge.)

The Thames River (pronounced "tems") runs roughly west to east through the city, with most of the visitor's sights on the North Bank. Mentally, maybe even physically, with scissors, trim down your map to include only the area between the Tower of London (to the east), Hyde Park (west), Regent's Park (north), and the South Bank (south). This is roughly the area bordered by the Tube's Circle Line. This four-mile stretch between the Tower and Hyde Park (about a 1.5-hour walk) looks like a milk bottle on its side (see map opposite), and holds 80 percent of the sights mentioned in this chapter.

Sprawling London becomes much more manageable if you think of it as a collection of neighborhoods:

Central London: This area contains Westminster and what Londoners call the West End. The **Westminster** district includes Big Ben, Parliament, Westminster Abbey, and Buckingham Palace—the grand government buildings from which Britain is ruled. **Trafalgar Square,** London's gathering place, has many

London's Neighborhoods

THE TUBE'S CIRCLE LINE

Regent's Park

NORTH LONDON

BRITISH MUSEUM

NOTTING HILL

PADDINGTON

BLOOMSBURY

Hyde Park

SOHO

WEST END

MAYFAIR

TRAF. SQ.

EAST END

TOWER OF LONDON

THE CITY

WEST LONDON

BELGRAVIA

CENTRAL LONDON

ST. PAUL'S

SOUTH KENSINGTON

WEST-MINSTER

Thames River

CHELSEA

BIG BEN

SOUTH BANK

LONDON EYE

To Docklands

Not to Scale

major museums. The **West End** is the center of London's cultural life, with bustling squares: Piccadilly Circus and Leicester Square host cinemas, tourist traps, and nighttime glitz. Soho and Covent Garden are thriving people-zones with theaters, restaurants, pubs, and boutiques. And Regent and Oxford streets are the city's main shopping zones.

North London: Neighborhoods in this part of town—including Bloomsbury, Fitzrovia, and Marylebone—contain such major sights as the British Museum and the overhyped Madame Tussauds Waxworks. Nearby, along busy Euston Road, is the British Library plus a trio of train stations (one of them, St. Pancras International Station, is linked to Paris and Brussels by the Eurostar "Chunnel" train).

The City: Today's modern financial district, called simply "The City," was a walled town in Roman times. Gleaming skyscrapers are interspersed with historical landmarks such as St. Paul's Cathedral, legal sights (Old Bailey), and the Museum of London. The Tower of London and Tower Bridge lie at The City's eastern border.

East London: Just east of The City is the **East End**—the increasingly gentrified former stomping ground of Cockney ragamuffins and Jack the Ripper. Even farther to the east is London's version of Manhattan, the **Docklands,** filling the area around Canary Wharf. Energized by big businesses, the Docklands shows you London at its most modern. And the **Olympic Park** is in the once-dreary Stratford district, a short train ride to the north.

The South Bank: The South Bank of the Thames River offers major sights (Tate Modern, Shakespeare's Globe, London

Eye) linked by a riverside walkway. Within this area, **Southwark** (SUTH-uck) stretches from the Tate Modern to London Bridge. Pedestrian bridges connect the South Bank with The City and Trafalgar Square.

West London: This huge area contains neighborhoods such as Mayfair, Belgravia, Chelsea, South Kensington, and Notting Hill. It's home to London's wealthy and has many trendy shops and enticing restaurants. Here you'll find a range of museums (Victoria and Albert Museum, Tate Britain, and more), my top hotel recommendations, lively Victoria Station, and the vast green expanses of Hyde Park and Kensington Gardens.

Tourist Information

The **City of London Information Centre,** just south of St. Paul's Cathedral, is the best tourist information service in town (Mon-Sat 9:30-17:30, Sun 10:00-16:00, St. Paul's Churchyard, Tube: St. Paul's, www.visitthecity.co.uk). Along with getting your questions answered, you can purchase advance tickets to most major sights, buy sightseeing passes, and get theater tickets (steep 20 percent booking fee).

At the information desk, pick up various free publications: the *London Planner* (a monthly that lists all the sights, events, and hours), walking tours info, a theater guide, a London map (with a coupon good for 20 percent off admission to St. Paul's), and a London Tube and bus map. They sell good central London street maps (£1-2).

Also consider getting Fast Track tickets to some of London's attractions. These tickets, which allow you to skip the queue at the sights at no extra cost, are worthwhile for places that can have long ticket lines, such as the Tower of London, the London Eye, and Madame Tussauds Waxworks. If you're going to the Waxworks, buy tickets here, since—at £25.50—they're cheaper than at the sight itself. (Note that some souvenir shops sell discounted tickets for sights; you'll see signs in their windows.)

Unfortunately, London's many "Tourist Information Centres" (which represent themselves as TIs at major train and bus stations, airports, and near major sights) are now simply businesses selling advertising space to companies with fliers to distribute. But unlike the City of London TI, they have staff who can answer phone inquiries (tel. 0870-156-6366, www.visitlondon.com).

London Pass: This pass is pricey, and to save any money, you'd have to sightsee virtually nonstop (£43/1 day, £58/2 days, £71/3 days, £94/6 days; days are calendar days rather than 24-hour periods; comes with 160-page guidebook, sold at TI near St. Paul's, major train stations, and airports, tel. 0870-242-9988, www.londonpass.com). It lets you skip the lines and covers many sights, including the Tower of London, Westminster Abbey, and St. Paul's Cathedral, but not the London Eye or Madame Tussauds Waxworks. Think through your sightseeing plans, study their website to see what's covered, and do the math before you buy.

Arrival in London

For more information on travel by train, bus, and plane, see "London Connections," near the end of this chapter.

By Train: London has nine major train stations, all connected by the Tube (subway). All have ATMs, and many of the larger stations also have shops, fast food, exchange offices, and luggage storage. From any station, you can ride the Tube or taxi to your hotel. For more info on train travel, see www.nationalrail.co.uk.

By Bus: The main intercity bus station is Victoria Coach Station, one block southwest of Victoria train station (and the Victoria Tube station). For more on bus travel, see www.nationalexpress.com.

By Plane: London has five airports. Most tourists arrive at Heathrow or Gatwick airports, although flights from elsewhere in Europe may land at Stansted, Luton, or London City airports. For specifics on getting from London's airports to downtown, see "London Connections," near the end of this chapter; for hotels near Heathrow and Gatwick, see page 736.

Helpful Hints

Theft Alert: Wear your money belt. The Artful Dodger is alive and well in London. Be on guard, particularly on public transportation and in places crowded with tourists, who, considered naive and rich, are targeted. The Changing of the Guard scene is a favorite for thieves. And more than 7,500 purses are stolen annually at Covent Garden alone.

Pedestrian Safety: Cars drive on the left side of the road—which can be as confusing for foreign pedestrians as for foreign drivers. Before crossing a street, I always look right, look left, then look right again just to be sure. Most crosswalks are even painted with instructions, reminding foreign guests to "Look right" or "Look left."

Medical Problems: Local hospitals have good-quality 24-hour-a-day emergency care centers where any tourist who needs help can drop in and, after a wait, be seen by a doctor. Your hotel has details. St. Thomas' Hospital, immediately across the river from Big Ben, has a fine reputation.

Getting Your Bearings: London is well-signed for visitors. Through an initiative called Legible London, the city is erecting thoughtfully designed, pedestrian-focused maps around town. In this sprawling city—where predictable grid-planned streets are

Affording London's Sights

London is one of Europe's most expensive cities, with the dubious distinction of having some of the world's highest admission prices. Fortunately, many sights are free.

Free Museums: Many of the city's biggest and best museums won't cost you a dime. Free sights include the British Museum, British Library, National Gallery, National Portrait Gallery, Tate Britain, Tate Modern, Wallace Collection, Imperial War Museum, Victoria and Albert Museum, Natural History Museum, Science Museum, National Army Museum, Sir John Soane's Museum, the Museum of London, and the Geffrye Museum.

About half of these museums request a donation of a few pounds, but whether you contribute or not is up to you. If I spend money for an audioguide, I feel fine about not otherwise donating. If that makes you uncomfortable, donate.

Free Churches: Smaller churches let worshippers (and tourists) in free, although they may ask for a donation. The big sightseeing churches—Westminster Abbey and St. Paul's—charge steep admission fees, but offer free evensong services daily (though you're not allowed to stick around afterward). Westminster Abbey also offers free organ recitals most Sundays at 17:45.

Other Freebies: London has plenty of free performances, such as lunch concerts at St. Martin-in-the-Fields (see page 678) and summertime movies at The Scoop amphitheater near City Hall (Tube: London Bridge, schedule at www.morelondon.com—click on "The Scoop"). For other freebies, check out www.freelondonlistings.co.uk. There's no charge to enjoy the pageantry of the Changing of the Guard, rants at Speaker's Corner in Hyde Park, displays at Harrods, the people-watching scene at Covent Garden, and the colorful streets of the East End. It's free to view the legal action at the Old Bailey and the legislature at work in the Houses of Parliament. And you can get into a bit of the Tower of London by attending Sunday services in the Tower's chapel (chapel access only).

relatively rare—it's also smart to buy and use a good map. The *Benson's London Street Map* (£2.75), sold at many newsstands and bookstores, is my favorite for efficient sightseeing.

Festivals: For one week in February and another in September, fashionistas descend on the city for **London Fashion Week** (www.londonfashionweek.co.uk). The famous **Chelsea Flower Show** blossoms in late May (book ahead for this popular event at www.rhs.org.uk/chelsea). During the annual **Trooping the Colour** in June, there are military bands and pageantry, and the Queen's birthday parade (www.trooping-the-colour.co.uk). Tennis fans pack the stands at the **Wimbledon Tennis Championship** in

Sightseeing Deals: If you buy a paper One-Day Travelcard or rail ticket at a National Rail station (such as Paddington or Victoria), you may be eligible for two-for-one discounts at many popular sights, such as the London Eye, Tower of London, Tate Modern, and Madame Tussauds Waxworks. This is a great deal if you can get it. To claim the discount, you must have a rail ticket that has been used and validated that day—for instance, if you are arriving by train into London (from elsewhere in England) or taking a short morning side-trip. Get details and print vouchers at www.daysoutguide.co.uk, or look for brochures with coupons at major train stations.

Good-Value Tours: The £5-8 city walking tours with professional guides are one of the best deals going. (Note that the guides for the "free" walking tours are unpaid and expect tips— I'd pay up front for a professionally guided tour instead.) Hop-on, hop-off big-bus tours, while expensive (£22-27), provide a great overview and include free boat tours as well as city walks. A one-hour Thames ride to Greenwich costs £10 one-way, but most boats come with entertaining commentary. A three-hour bicycle tour is about £20.

Theater: Compared with Broadway's prices, London theater is a bargain. Seek out the freestanding "tkts" booth at Leicester Square to get discounts from 25 to 50 percent on good seats (though not necessarily for the hottest shows; see page 715). If you're willing to settle for the cheapest seats (possibly with obstructed views), ask the theater's box office for their best deal (even the most popular shows generally have some £10-25 tickets). A £5 "groundling" ticket for a play at Shakespeare's Globe is the best theater deal in town (see page 715). Tickets to the Open Air Theatre at north London's Regent's Park start at £12 (see page 716).

London doesn't come cheap. But with its many free museums and affordable plays, this cosmopolitan, cultured city offers days of sightseeing thrills without requiring you to pinch your pennies (or your pounds).

late June to early July (www.wimbledon.org), and partygoers head for the **Notting Hill Carnival** in late August.

Traveling in Winter: London dazzles year-round, so consider visiting in winter, when airfares and hotel rates are generally cheaper and there are fewer tourists. For ideas on what to do, see the "Winter Activities in London" article at www.ricksteves.com/winteracts.

Internet Access: As nearly all hotels offer Internet access, and cafés all over town have free Wi-Fi, there are few actual Internet cafés. If you need to get online, you'll find Internet cafés near Trafalgar Square (456 Strand), on Oxford Street (at

#358, opposite Bond Street Tube station), and near Victoria Station (at 164 Victoria Street).

Travel Bookstores: Located between Covent Garden and Leicester Square, the very good **Stanfords Travel Bookstore** stocks current editions of many of my books (Mon-Fri 9:00-19:30, Thu 9:00-20:00, Sat 10:00-20:00, Sun 12:00-18:00, 12-14 Long Acre, Tube: Leicester Square, tel. 020/7836-1321, www.stanfords.co.uk).

Two impressive **Waterstone's** bookstores have the biggest collection of travel guides in town: on Piccadilly (Mon-Sat 9:00-22:00, Sun 11:30-18:00, Costa Café, great views from top-floor bar, 203 Piccadilly, tel. 020/7851-2400) and on Trafalgar Square (Mon-Sat 9:00-21:00, Sun 11:30-18:00, Costa Café on second floor, tel. 020/7839-4411).

Baggage Storage: Train stations have replaced lockers with more secure baggage storage counters, known locally as "left luggage." Each bag must go through a scanner (just like at the airport), so lines can be slow. Expect long waits in the morning to check in (up to 45 minutes) and in the afternoon to pick up (each item-£8.50/24 hours, most stations daily 7:00-23:00). You can also store bags at the airports (similar rates and hours, www.excess-baggage.com). If leaving London and returning later, you may be able to store a box or bag at your hotel for free—assuming you'll be staying there again.

Getting Around London

To travel smart in a city this size, you must get comfortable with public transportation. London's excellent taxis, buses, and subway (Tube) system make a car unnecessary.

Public-Transit Passes

London has the most expensive public transit in the world—save money on your Tube and bus rides by using a multi-ride pass. You have three options: Pay double by buying individual tickets as you go; buy a £5 Oyster card and top it up as needed to travel like a local for about £2-3 per ride; or get a Travelcard for unlimited travel on one or seven days.

The transit system has six zones. Since almost all of my recommended accommodations, restaurants, and sights are within Zones 1 and 2, those are the prices I've listed here—but you'll pay more to go farther afield. Specific fares and other details change constantly; for a complete and updated list of prices, check www.tfl.gov.uk.

Individual Transit Tickets

These days in London, individual paper tickets are a dinosaur;

there's no point buying one unless you're literally taking just one ride your entire time in the city. Because individual fares (£4.30 per Tube ride, £2.30 per bus ride) are about double the cost of using a pay-as-you-go Oyster card (explained below), in just two or three rides you'll recoup the £5 added deposit for the Oyster. If you do buy a single ticket, avoid ticket-window lines in Tube stations by using the coin-op machines; practice on the punchboard to see how the system works (hit "Adult Single" and your destination). These tickets are valid only on the day of purchase.

Oyster Cards

A pay-as-you-go Oyster card (a plastic card embedded with a computer chip) is the standard, smart way to economically ride the Tube, buses, Docklands Light Railway (DLR), and Overground. On each type of transport, you simply lay the card flat against the yellow card reader at the turnstile or entrance; it flashes green, and the fare is automatically deducted. (You'll also touch your card again to exit the Tube and DLR turnstiles, but not to exit buses.)

With an Oyster card, rides cost about half the price of individual paper tickets (£2 or £2.70 per Tube ride—depending on time of day, £1.35 per bus ride). You buy the card itself at any Tube station ticket window for a £5 deposit, then load it up with as much credit as you want. (For extra peace of mind, ask about registering your card against theft or loss.) When your balance gets low, simply add credit—or "top up"—at a ticket window or machine (note that American credit cards will work at the ticketing window, but not at the automated "top-up" stations). A price cap on the pay-as-you-go Oyster card guarantees you'll never pay more than the One-Day Travelcard price within a 24-hour period.

You can see how much credit remains on your card or review the trips you've taken so far by swiping it at any automatic ticket machine. Oyster card balances never expire (though they need reactivating at a ticket window every two years), so you can use the card whenever you're in London, or lend it to someone else. If you're done with the card (and don't mind a short wait), you should be able to reclaim your £5 deposit at any ticket window. Readers report that refunds are easier if you use only one method of payment for all your Oyster Card transactions—cash works best. So if you used cash for the deposit and want a quick refund, continue using cash to top up the card.

Travelcards

Like the Oyster card, Travelcards are valid on the Tube, buses, Docklands Light Railway (DLR), and Overground. The difference is that Travelcards let you ride as many times as you want within a one- or seven-day period for one fixed price.

LONDON

Before you buy a card, estimate where you'll be going; there's a card for Zones 1 and 2, and another for Zones 1-6 (which includes Heathrow Airport). If Heathrow is the only ride you're taking outside Zones 1-2 (which is likely), you can pay a small supplement to make the Zones 1-2 Travelcard stretch to cover that one ride.

The **One-Day Travelcard** gives you unlimited travel for a day (Zones 1-2: £8.40, off-peak version £7; Zones 1-6: £15.80, off-peak version £8.50; off-peak cards are good for travel after 9:30 on weekdays and anytime on weekends). This Travelcard works like a traditional paper ticket: Buy it at any Tube station ticket window or machine, then feed it into a turnstile (and retrieve it) to enter and exit the Tube. On a bus, just show it to the driver when you get on.

The **Seven-Day Travelcard** is a great option if you're staying four or more days and plan to use the buses and Tube a lot. It's actually issued on a plastic Oyster card, but gives you unlimited travel anytime, anywhere in Zones 1 and 2 for a week (£29.20 plus the refundable £5 deposit for the Oyster card). As with an Oyster card, you'll touch it to the yellow pad when entering or exiting a Tube turnstile, or when boarding a bus.

The Bottom Line

Struggling to choose which pass works best for your trip? First of all, skip the individual tickets. On a short visit (three days or fewer), if you think you'll be zipping around a lot, consider a One-Day Travelcard for each day you're here (or at least for your busiest days); if you'll be taking fewer, more focused rides, get an Oyster card and pay as you go. If you're in London four days or longer, the Seven-Day Travelcard will likely pay for itself.

By Tube

London's subway system (called the Tube or Underground—but never "subway," which refers to a pedestrian underpass) is one of this planet's great people-movers and often the fastest long-distance transport in town (runs Mon-Sat about 5:00-24:00, Sun about 7:00-23:00). While technically not part of the Tube, two other commuter rail lines are tied into the network and use the same tickets: The Docklands Light Railway (called DLR, runs to the Docklands, 2012 Olympics site, and Greenwich) and the Overground.

Get your bearings by studying a map of the system (free at any station).

Each line has a name (such as Circle, Northern, or Bakerloo) and two directions (indicated by the end-of-the-line stops). Find the line that will take you to your destination, and figure out roughly what direction (north, south, east, or west) you'll need to go to get there.

You can use an Oyster card, Travelcard, or individual tickets (all explained earlier) to pay for your journey. At the Tube station, touch your Oyster card flat against the turnstile's yellow card reader, both when you enter and exit the station. If you have a regular paper ticket or a One-Day Travelcard, feed it into the turnstile, reclaim it, and hang on to it—you'll need it later.

Find your train by following signs to your line and the (general) direction it's headed (such as Central Line: east). Since some tracks are shared by several lines, double-check before boarding a train: First, make sure your destination is one of the stops listed on the sign at the platform. Also, check the electronic signboards that announce which train is next, and make sure the destination (the end-of-the-line stop) is the direction you want. Some trains, particularly on the Circle and District lines, split off for other directions, but each train has its final destination marked above its windshield.

Trains run roughly every 3-10 minutes. If one train is absolutely packed and you notice another to the same destination is coming in three minutes, wait to avoid the sardine routine. Rush hours (8:00-10:00 and 16:00-19:00) can be packed and sweaty. Bring something to do to make your waiting time productive. If you get confused, ask for advice from a local, a blue-vested staff person, or at the information window located before the turnstile entry.

You can't leave the system without touching your Oyster card to an electronic reader, or feeding your ticket or One-Day Travelcard into the turnstile. (If you have a single-trip paper ticket, the turnstile will eat your now-expired ticket; if it's a One-Day Travelcard, it will spit out your still-valid card.) Some stations, such as Hampton Court, do not have a turnstile, so you'll have to locate a reader to validate your Oyster card. If you skip this step, the highest fare will be deducted from your card. When leaving a station, save walking time by choosing the best street exit—check the maps on the walls or ask any station personnel.

The system can be fraught with construction delays and breakdowns (the Circle Line is notorious for problems). Most construction is scheduled for weekends. Closures are known and publicized in advance (online at www.tfl.gov.uk and with posters in the Tube). Pay attention to signs and announcements explaining necessary detours. Closed Tube lines are often replaced by temporary bus service, but it can be faster to figure out alternate routes on the Tube; since the lines cross each other constantly, there are several ways to make any journey. For help, check out the "Journey Planner" at www.tfl.gov.uk.

By Bus

If you figure out the bus system, you'll easily conquer sprawling

Handy Bus Routes

London. Pick up a free bus map at a TI, transport office (located at major Underground stations such as Victoria), or some major museums. This map lists the best bus routes for sightseeing.

Buses are covered by Travelcards and Oyster cards. Or you can buy individual tickets from a machine at bus stops (no change given). Any bus ride in downtown London costs £2.30 for those paying cash, or £1.35 if using an Oyster card (with a cap of £4.20 per day). If you're staying longer, consider the £18.80 Seven-Day bus pass.

The first step in mastering London's bus system is learning how to decipher the bus stop signs. In the first column, find your destination on the list—e.g., Paddington. In the next column, find a bus that goes there—the #23. The final column has a letter within a circle (e.g., "M") that tells you exactly which bus stop you need to stand at to catch your bus. (You'll find the same letter marked on a neighborhood map nearby.) Make your way to that stop—you'll know it's yours because it will have the same letter on its pole— and wait for the bus with your number on it to arrive. Hop on, and you're good to go.

As you board, touch your Oyster card to the electronic card reader, or, if you have a paper ticket or a One-Day Travelcard,

To Clapton Pond #38

BRITISH LIBRARY

LIVERPOOL STREET STATION

#11 #23

COVENT GARDEN #RV1

ST. PAUL'S

TOWER OF LONDON #15 #RV1

COURTAULD GALLERY

LONDON EYE

Thames River

WATERLOO STATION

TATE MODERN & SHAKESPEARE'S GLOBE

TOWER BRIDGE

IMPERIAL WAR MUSEUM

ELEPHANT & CASTLE

To Streatham #159

To Camberwell Green #148

LEGEND

— #9
— #11
— #15
— #23
-- #24
-- #38
········· #RV1
••• #148
••• #159
#15 Terminus Points

Not to Scale

show it to the driver. On "Heritage Routes" #9 and #15 (which use some older double-decker buses), you may still pay a conductor; take a seat, and he or she will come around to collect your fare or verify your pass. There's no need to tap your card or show your ticket when you hop off.

If you have an Oyster card or Travelcard, save your feet and get in the habit of hopping buses for quick little straight shots, even just to get to a Tube stop. During bump-and-grind rush hours (8:00-10:00 and 16:00-19:00), you'll usually go faster by Tube.

By Taxi

London is the best taxi town in Europe. Big, black, carefully regulated cabs are everywhere. (While historically known as "black cabs," some of London's official taxis are now covered with wildly colored ads.) Some cabs are switching to biofuels—a good way to dispose of all that oil used to fry fish-and-chips.

I've never met a crabby cabbie in London. They love to talk, and they know every nook and cranny in town. I ride in a taxi each day just to get my London questions answered (drivers must pass a rigorous test on "The Knowledge" of London geography to earn their license).

If a cab's top light is on, just wave it down. Drivers flash lights when they see you wave. They have a tight turning radius (on new cabs, the back tires actually pivot), so you can hail cabs going in either direction. If waving doesn't work, ask someone where you can find a taxi stand. Telephoning a cab will get you one in a few minutes, but costs a little more (tel. 0871-871-8710; £2 surcharge, plus extra fee to book ahead by credit card).

Rides start at £2.20. The regular tariff #1 covers most of the day (Mon-Fri 6:00-20:00), tariff #2 is during "unsociable hours" (Mon-Fri 20:00-22:00 and Sat-Sun 6:00-22:00), and tariff #3 is for night (22:00-6:00) and on holidays. Rates go up about 15-20 percent with each higher tariff. All extra charges are explained in writing on the cab wall. Tip a cabbie by rounding up (maximum 10 percent).

Connecting downtown sights is quick and easy, and will cost you about £6-8 (for example, St. Paul's to the Tower of London). For a short ride, three adults in a cab generally travel at close to Tube prices—and groups of four or five adults should taxi everywhere. All cabs can carry five passengers, and some take six, for the same cost as a single traveler.

Don't worry about meter cheating. Licensed British cab meters come with a sealed computer chip and clock that ensures you'll get the correct tariff. The only way a cabbie can cheat you is by taking a needlessly long route. Another pitfall is taking a cab when traffic is bad to a destination efficiently served by the Tube. On one trip to London, I hopped in a taxi at South Kensington for Waterloo Station and hit bad traffic. Rather than spending 20 minutes and £2 on the Tube, I spent 40 minutes and £16 in a taxi.

If you overdrink and ride in a taxi, be warned: Taxis charge £40 for "soiling" (a.k.a., pub puke). If you forget this book in a taxi, call the Lost Property office and hope for the best (tel. 0845-330-9882).

Tours in London

To sightsee on your own, download my series of **free audio tours** that illuminate some of London's top sights and neighborhoods: the British Museum, the British Library, St. Paul's Cathedral, and my walks around Westminster and The City (see sidebar on page 7 for details).

▲▲▲Hop-on, Hop-off Double-Decker Bus Tours

Two competitive companies (Original and Big Bus) offer essentially the same two tours of the city's sightseeing highlights, with nearly 30 stops on each route. Big Bus tours are a little more expensive (£27), while Original tours are cheaper (£22 with this book) and nearly as good.

These two-to-three hour, once-over-lightly bus tours drive by all the famous sights, providing a stress-free way to get your bearings and see the biggies. They stop at a core group of sights regardless of which overview tour you're on: Piccadilly Circus, Trafalgar Square, Big Ben, St. Paul's, the Tower of London, Marble Arch, Victoria Station, and elsewhere. With a good guide and nice weather, I'd sit back and enjoy the entire tour. (If you don't like your guide, you can hop off and try your luck with the next departure.)

Each company offers at least one route with live (English-only) guides, and a second (sometimes slightly different route) comes with recorded, dial-a-language narration. In addition to the overview tours, both Original and Big Bus include the Thames River boat trip by City Cruises (similar to the River Red Rover ticket explained on page 667) and three 1.5-hour walking tours.

Pick up a map from any flier rack or from one of the countless salespeople, and study the complex system. Sunday morning—when the traffic is light and many museums are closed—is a fine time for a tour. Unless you're using the bus tour mainly for hop-on, hop-off transportation, consider saving time and money by taking a night tour (described on the next page).

Buses run about every 10-15 minutes in summer, every 20 minutes in winter, and operate daily. They start at about 8:30 and run until early evening in summer or late afternoon in winter. The last full loop usually leaves Victoria Station about 17:00 (confirm by checking the schedule or asking the driver).

You can buy tickets from drivers or from staff at street kiosks (credit cards accepted at kiosks at major stops such as Victoria, ticket good for 24 hours).

Original London Sightseeing Bus Tour—There are two versions of their basic highlights loop: **The Original Tour** (live guide, marked with a yellow triangle on the front of the bus) and the **City Sightseeing Tour** (essentially the same route but with recorded narration, a kids' soundtrack option, and a stop at Madame Tussauds; bus marked with a red triangle). Other routes include the blue-triangle **Museum Tour** (connecting far-flung museums and major shopping stops), and green, black, and purple triangle routes (linking major train stations to the central route). All routes are covered by the same ticket. Keep it simple and just take one of the city highlights tours (£26, £22 with this book, limit four discounts per book, they'll rip off the corner of this page—raise bloody hell if the staff or driver won't honor this discount; also online deals, info center at 17 Cockspur Street, tel. 020/8877-1722, www.theoriginaltour.com).

Big Bus London Tours—For £27 (up to 30 percent discount online—requires printer), you get the same basic overview tours: Red buses come with a live guide, while the blue route has a recorded narration and a one-hour longer path that goes around Hyde Park. These pricier Big Bus tours tend to have better, more dynamic guides than the Original tours, and more departures as well—meaning shorter waits for those hopping on and off (daily 8:30-18:00, winter until 16:30, info center at 48 Buckingham Palace Road, tel. 020/7233-9533, www.bigbustours.com).

London by Night Sightseeing Tour—This tour offers a two-hour circuit, but after hours, with no extras (e.g., walks, river cruises), and at a lower price. While the narration can be pretty lame, the views at twilight are grand—though note that it stays light until late on summer nights, and London just doesn't do floodlighting as well as Paris (£16, £11 online, drivers accept cash only). From May through late September, open-top buses depart at 19:15, 20:00, 20:45, and 21:30 from Victoria Station (Jan-April and late Sept-late Dec departs at 19:30 only with closed-top bus, no tours between Christmas and New Year). Buses leave from the curb immediately in front of Victoria Station (closest to building at muster point C; or you can board at any stop, such as Paddington Station, Marble Arch, Trafalgar Square, London Eye, or Tower of London; tel. 020/8545-6109, www.london-by-night.net). For a memorable and economical evening, munch a scenic picnic dinner on the top deck. (There are plenty of take-away options within the train stations and near the various stops.)

▲▲Walking Tours

Several times each day, top-notch local guides lead (sometimes big) groups through specific slices of London's past. Look for brochures at TIs or ask at hotels, although the latter usually push higher-priced bus tours. *Time Out,* the weekly entertainment guide (£3 at newsstands), lists some, but not all, scheduled walks. Check with the various tour companies by phone or online to get their full picture.

To take a walking tour, simply show up at the announced location and pay the guide. Then enjoy two chatty hours of Dickens, Harry Potter, the Plague, Shakespeare, Legal London, the Beatles, Jack the Ripper, or whatever is on the agenda.

The Essential London Walk—Blue Badge Tourist Guides offer a basic two-hour walk 365 days a year at 10:00 (normally £9 but my readers pay £6; meet at the Eros statue on Piccadilly Circus—look for the guide with the Blue Badge umbrella, www.tourist guides.org.uk). Tours go rain or shine, and there's no need to pre-book—just show up. This is the best deal going, as you know you'll get a well-trained guide leading you through the historic core of London (from Piccadilly, you walk to Trafalgar Square, Whitehall, Westminster Abbey, the Houses of Parliament, and the Thames, and end at Buckingham Palace—just in time for the last part of the Changing of the Guard).

London Walks—This leading company lists its extensive and creative daily schedule in a beefy, plain *London Walks* brochure. Pick it up at TIs, hotels, or St. Martin-in-the-Fields' Café in the Crypt on Trafalgar Square, or access it on their website. Just perusing their fascinating lineup of tours inspires me to stay longer in London. Their two-hour walks, led by professional guides and actors, cost £8 (cash only, walks offered year-round, private tours for groups-£120, tel. 020/7624-3978 for a live person, tel. 020/7624-9255 for a recording of today's or tomorrow's walks and the Tube station they depart from, www.walks.com).

London Walks also offers "Explorer Days" tours into the countryside, a good option for those with limited time and transportation (£14 plus £10-46 for transportation and any admission costs, cash only: Stonehenge/Salisbury, Oxford/Cotswolds, Cambridge, Bath, and so on). These are economical in part because everyone gets group discounts for transportation and admissions.

Sandemans New London "Free Royal London Tour"—This company employs English-speaking students (rather than licensed guides) who recite three-hour spiels covering the basic London sights. While the fast-moving, youthful tours are light and irreverent, and can be both entertaining and fun, it's misleading to call the tours "free," as tips are expected (the guides are unpaid). With the Essential London Walk (listed earlier) offered daily at a reasonable price by professional Blue Badge guides, taking this "free" tour makes no sense to me (daily at 11:00 and 13:00, meet at Wellington Arch, Tube: Hyde Park Corner, Exit 2). Sandemans also has other guided tours for a charge, including a Pub Crawl (£12, Tue-Sat at 19:30, meet at Belushi's at 9 Russell Street, Tube: Covent Garden, www.newlondon-tours.com).

Beatles Walks—Fans of the still-Fab Four can take one of three Beatles walks (London Walks has two that run 5 days/week; Big Bus includes a daily walk with their bus tour; both listed earlier).

Jack the Ripper Walks—Each walking tour company seems to make most of its money with "haunted" and Jack the Ripper tours. Many guides are historians and would rather not lead these lightweight tours—but, in tourism as in journalism, "if it bleeds, it leads" (which is why the juvenile London Dungeon is one of the city's busiest sights).

Two reliably good two-hour tours start every night at the Tower Hill Tube station exit. **Ripping Yarns** is guided by off-duty Yeoman Warders—the Tower of London "Beefeaters" (£7, pay at end, nightly at 18:45, no tours between Christmas and New Year, mobile 07813-559-301, www.jack-the-ripper-tours.com). **London Walks'** guides leave from the same spot later each night (£7, pay at the start, nightly at 19:30, tel. 020/7624-3978, recorded info tel. 020/7624-9255, www.jacktheripperwalk.com). After taking both, I found the London Walks tour more entertaining, informative, and with a better route (along quieter, once-hooker-friendly lanes, with less traffic), starting at Tower Hill and ending at Liverpool Street Station rather than returning to Tower Hill. Groups can be huge for both, but there's always room—just show up.

Private Walks with Local Guides—Standard rates for London's registered Blue Badge guides are about £127 for four hours and £200 or more for nine hours (tel. 020/7780-4060, www.tourist guides.org.uk or www.blue-badge.org.uk). I know and like four fine local guides: **Sean Kelleher** (tel. 020/8673-1624, mobile 07764-612-770, seankelleher@btinternet.com), **Britt Lonsdale** (£150/half-day, £250/day, great with families, tel. 020/7386-9907, mobile 07813-278-077, brittl@btinternet.com), and two others who work in London when they're not on the road leading my Britain tours,

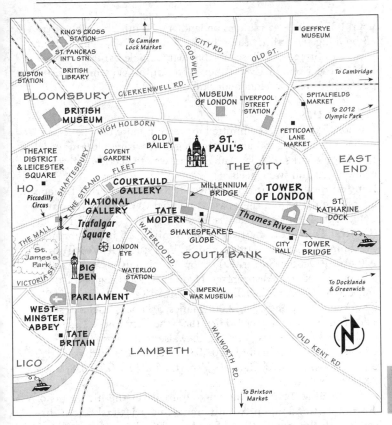

Map labels: KING'S CROSS STATION, ST. PANCRAS INT'L STN., EUSTON STATION, BRITISH LIBRARY, To Camden Lock Market, CITY RD., GOSWELL, OLD ST., GEFFRYE MUSEUM, To Cambridge, CLERKENWELL RD., BLOOMSBURY, MUSEUM OF LONDON, LIVERPOOL STREET STATION, SPITALFIELDS MARKET, To 2012 Olympic Park, BRITISH MUSEUM, HIGH HOLBORN, OLD BAILEY, ST. PAUL'S, PETTICOAT LANE MARKET, THEATRE DISTRICT & LEICESTER SQUARE, COVENT GARDEN, THE CITY, EAST END, SHAFTESBURY, FLEET, THE STRAND, COURTAULD GALLERY, MILLENNIUM BRIDGE, TOWER OF LONDON, ST. KATHARINE DOCK, HO, Piccadilly Circus, NATIONAL GALLERY, TATE MODERN, Thames River, Trafalgar Square, SHAKESPEARE'S GLOBE, CITY HALL, TOWER BRIDGE, THE MALL, LONDON EYE, WATERLOO RD., SOUTH BANK, St. James's Park, BIG BEN, WATERLOO STATION, VICTORIA ST., PARLIAMENT, IMPERIAL WAR MUSEUM, To Docklands & Greenwich, WEST-MINSTER ABBEY, TATE BRITAIN, LAMBETH, WALWORTH RD., OLD KENT RD., LICO, To Brixton Market

LONDON

Tom Hooper (mobile 07986-048-047, tomh@ricksteves.net) and **Gillian Chadwick** (mobile 07889-976-598, gillianc@ricksteves.net). **Driver-Guides**—These two guides have cars or a minibus (particularly helpful for travelers with limited mobility) and charge around £290/half-day and £450/day for London tours (see websites and contact them for details): **Robina Brown** (tel. 020/7228-2238, www.driverguidetours.com, robina@driverguidetours.com) and **Janine Barton** (tel. 020/7402-4600, http://seeitinstyle.synthasite .com, jbsiis@aol.com).

London Duck Tours

A bright-yellow amphibious WWII-vintage vehicle (the model that landed troops on Normandy's beaches on D-Day) takes a gang of 30 tourists past some famous sights on land—Big Ben, Trafalgar Square, Piccadilly Circus—then splashes into the Thames for a cruise. All in all, it's good fun at a rather steep price. The live guide works hard, and it's kid-friendly to the point of goofiness (£20, April-Sept daily 10:30-18:00, shorter hours Oct-March, 1-4/

hour, 1.25 hours—45 minutes on land and 30 minutes in the river, £3 booking fee online, these book up in advance, departs from Chicheley Street—you'll see the big, ugly vehicle parked 100 yards behind the London Eye, Tube: Waterloo or Westminster, tel. 020/7928-3132, www.londonducktours.co.uk).

Bike Tours

London, like Paris, is committed to creating more bike paths, and many of its best sights can be laced together with a pleasant pedal through its parks. A bike tour is a fun way to see the sights and enjoy the city on two wheels.

London Bicycle Tour Company—Three tours covering London are offered daily from their base at Gabriel's Wharf on the South Bank of the Thames. Sunday is the best, as there is less car traffic (**Central Tour**—£17, daily at 10:30, 6 miles, 2.5 hours, includes Westminster, Covent Garden, and St. Paul's; **Royal West Tour**—£20, April-Oct Sat-Sun at 12:00, Nov-March only on Sun, 9 miles, 3.5 hours, includes Westminster, Hyde Park, Buckingham Palace, and Covent Garden; **East Tour**—£20, April-Oct Sat-Sun at 14:00, Nov-March only on Sat at 12:00, 9 miles, 3.5 hours, includes south side of the river to Tower Bridge, then The City to the East End; book ahead for off-season tours). They also rent bikes (£3.50/hour, £20/day; office open daily 10:00-18:00, west of Blackfriars Bridge on the South Bank, 1a Gabriel's Wharf, tel. 020/7928-6838, www.londonbicycle.com).

Fat Tire Bike Tours—Daily bike tours cover the highlights of downtown London, on two different itineraries (ask about discount with this book): **Royal London** (£20, daily March-Nov at 11:00, June-Aug also at 15:30, 7 miles, 4 hours, meet at Queensway Tube station; includes Parliament, Buckingham Palace, Hyde Park, and Trafalgar Square) and **River Thames** (£30, mid-March-Nov Thu-Sat at 10:30, 5 hours, meet at Waterloo Tube station—exit 2; includes London Eye, St. Paul's, Tower of London, Trafalgar Square, Covent Garden, and boat trip on the Thames). The spiel is light and irreverent rather than scholarly, but the price is right. Reservations are easy online, and required for River Thames tours and kids' bikes (off-season tours can be arranged, mobile 078-8233-8779, www.fattirebiketourslondon.com). Confirm the schedule online or by phone.

▲▲Cruises

Boat tours with entertaining commentaries sail regularly from many points along the Thames. The options are plentiful, with several companies offering essentially the same trip. Your basic options are to use the boats either for a scenic joyride cruise within central London, or for transportation to an outlying sight (such as

Greenwich or Kew Gardens).

Boats come and go from several docks in central London. The most popular places to embark are Westminster Pier (at the base of Westminster Bridge across the street from Big Ben) and Waterloo Pier (at the London Eye, across the river).

Buy boat tickets at the kiosks on the docks. While individual Tube and bus tickets don't work on the boats, a Travelcard can snare you a 33 percent discount on most cruises (just show the card when you pay for the cruise; no discount with the pay-as-you-go Oyster card except on Thames Clippers). Because different companies vary in the discounts they offer, always ask. Children and seniors generally get discounts. You can purchase drinks and scant, pricey snacks on board. Clever budget travelers pack a picnic and munch while they cruise.

Round-trip fares are only a bit more than one-way. Still, for pleasure and efficiency, consider combining a one-way cruise (to Kew, Greenwich, or wherever) with a Tube or train ride back.

Tourist-Oriented Cruises in Central London

London offers many made-for-tourist cruises, most on slow-moving, open-top boats accompanied by commentary about passing sights.

City Cruises runs boats from Westminster Pier across the river to Waterloo Pier, then downriver to Tower Pier and on to Greenwich (tel. 020/7740-0400, www.citycruises.com). If you want just a sample, hop on their 30-minute cruise only as far as Tower Pier (£8 one-way, £10.50 round-trip, daily April-Oct roughly 10:00-19:00, until 18:00 in winter, 2/hour). City Cruises also offers a £13.50 River Red Rover ticket good for all-day hop-on, hop-off travel (also included with the bus tours described on page 660)—though the line's limited stops in central London make this a lesser deal than it might seem.

Thames River Services runs a similar trip with even fewer stops: Westminster to St. Katharine's Pier to Greenwich (tel. 020/7930-4097, www.thamesriverservices.co.uk). They have classic boats and feel a little friendlier and more old-fashioned.

The **Circular Cruise** offered by Crown River Services is a handy hop-on, hop-off route with stops at the Westminster, Festival, Embankment, Bankside, London Bridge, and St. Katharine's piers (£3 to go one stop, £8.40 one-way for a longer trip, £11 for an all-day ticket, daily 11:00-18:30, every 30 minutes late May-early Sept, fewer stops and less frequent off-season, tel. 020/7936-2033, www.crownriver.com).

The **London Eye** operates its own river cruise, offering a 40-minute live-guided circular tour from Waterloo Pier. As it's much pricier than the alternatives for just a short loop, it's a poor value

(£12, reservations recommended, 10 percent discount if you pre-book online, no Travelcard discounts, departures daily generally at :45 past the hour, April-Oct 10:45-18:45, Nov-March 11:45-16:45, closed mid-Jan-mid-Feb, tel. 0870-500-0600, www.londoneye.com).

Careening at Top Speed Along the Thames: Two competing companies invite you aboard a small, 12-person, high-speed rigid inflatable boat (RIB—similar to a Zodiac) for an adrenaline-fueled tour of the city (London RIB Voyages: stand-up comedian guides, £32.50/50 minutes, £45/1.25 hours, tel. 020/7928-8933, www.londonribvoyages.com; Thames RIB Experience: £32/50 minutes, £45/1.5 hours, tel. 0870-224-4200, www.thamesribexperience.com).

Away from the Thames, on Regent's Canal: Consider exploring London's canals by taking a cruise on historic Regent's Canal in north London. The good ship *Jenny Wren* offers 1.5-hour guided canal boat cruises from Walker's Quay in Camden Town through scenic Regent's Park to Little Venice (£9.50; Aug daily at 10:30, 12:30, 14:30, and 16:30; April-July and Sept-Oct daily at 12:30 and 14:30, Sat-Sun also at 16:30; Walker's Quay, 250 Camden High Street, 3-minute walk from Tube: Camden Town; tel. 020/7485-4433, www.walkersquay.com). While in Camden Town, stop by the popular, punky Camden Lock Market to browse through trendy arts and crafts (daily 10:00-18:00, busiest on weekends, a block from Walker's Quay, www.camdenlockmarket.com).

Commuting by Clipper

Thames Clippers, which uses fast, sleek, 220-seat catamarans, is designed for commuters rather than sightseers. Think of the boats as express buses in the river—they zip no-nonsense through London every 20 minutes, stopping at most of the major docks en route: Embankment, Waterloo, Blackfriars or Bankside, London Bridge, Tower, Canary Wharf (Docklands), and Greenwich (roughly 20 minutes from Embankment to Tower, 10 more minutes to Docklands, 10 more minutes to Greenwich). However, the boats are less pleasant for joyriding than the cruises described earlier, with no commentary and no open deck up top (the only outside access is on a crowded deck at the exhaust-choked back of the boat, where you're jostling for photos). Any one-way ride costs £5.50, and a River Roamer all-day ticket costs £12.60 (33 percent discount with Travelcard, 10 percent off with a pay-as-you-go Oyster card, tel. 020/7001-2222, www.thamesclippers.com).

Thames Clippers also offers two express trips. The **"Tate to Tate"** boat service, which directly connects the Tate Britain (Millbank Pier) and the Tate Modern (Bankside Pier), is made for art-lovers (£5.50 one-way, covered by £12.60 River Roamer day ticket; buy ticket at gallery desk, at kiosk by the dock, or on board;

for frequency and times, see the Tate Britain and Tate Modern listings, later, or www.tate.org.uk/tatetotate). The **O2 Express** runs only on nights when there are events going on at the O2 (formerly the Millennium Dome; from Waterloo Pier, £6 one-way, £12 round-trip, 30 minutes).

Cruising Upstream, to Kew Gardens

Boats operated by the Westminster Passenger Services Association leave for Kew Gardens from Westminster Pier (£12 one-way, £18 round-trip, cash only; 4/day, April-Oct daily at 10:30, 11:15, 12:00, and 14:00; 1.5 hours, about half the trip is narrated, tel. 020/7930-2062, www.wpsa.co.uk). Romantic as these rides sound, it can be a long trip...especially upstream.

Self-Guided Walk

Westminster Walk

Just about every visitor to London strolls along historic Whitehall from Big Ben to Trafalgar Square. This walk gives meaning to that touristy ramble (most of the sights you'll see are described in more detail later). Under London's modern traffic and big-city bustle lie 2,000 fascinating years of history. You'll get a whirlwind tour as well as a practical orientation to London. (You can download a free, extended Rick Steves **audio tour** of this neighborhood; see page 7.)

Start halfway across **Westminster Bridge** (❶) for that "Wow, I'm really in London!" feeling. Get a close-up view of the **Houses of Parliament** and **Big Ben** (floodlit at night). Downstream you'll see the **London Eye.** Down the stairs to Westminster Pier are boats to the Tower of London and Greenwich (downstream) or Kew Gardens (upstream).

En route to Parliament Square, you'll pass a **statue of Boadicea** (❷), the Celtic queen defeated by Roman invaders in A.D. 60.

For fun, call home from a pay phone near Big Ben at about three minutes before the hour to let your loved one hear the bell ring. You'll find four red phone booths lining the north side of **Parliament Square** (❸) along Great George Street—also great for a phone-box-and-Big-Ben photo op.

Wave hello to Winston Churchill and Nelson Mandela in Parliament Square. To Churchill's right is **Westminster Abbey,** with its two stubby, elegant towers. The white building (flying the Union Jack) at the far end of the square houses Britain's new **Supreme Court.**

Head north up Parliament Street, which turns into **Whitehall** (❹), and walk toward Trafalgar Square. You'll see the thought-provoking **Cenotaph** (❺) in the middle of the street, reminding

Westminster Walk

1. Westminster Bridge
2. Statue of Boadicea
3. View of Parliament Square
4. Walking Along Whitehall
5. Cenotaph
6. #10 Downing Street & Ministry of Defence
7. Banqueting House
8. Horse Guards
9. Trafalgar Square

passersby of the many Brits who died in the last century's world wars. To visit the **Churchill War Rooms,** take a left before the Cenotaph, on King Charles Street.

Continuing on Whitehall, stop at the barricaded and guarded **#10 Downing Street** (❻) to see the British "White House," home of the prime minister. Break the bobby's boredom and ask him a question. The huge building across Whitehall from Downing Street is the **Ministry of Defence** (MOD), the "British Pentagon."

Nearing Trafalgar Square, look for the 17th-century **Banqueting House** across the street (❼) and the **Horse Guards** (❽) behind the gated fence (Changing of the Horse Guards Mon-Sat at 11:00, Sun at 10:00, dismounting ceremony daily at 16:00).

The column topped by Lord Nelson marks **Trafalgar Square** (❾). The stately domed building on the far side of the square is the **National Gallery,** which has a classy café in the Sainsbury wing. To the right of the National Gallery is **St. Martin-in-the-Fields Church** and its Café in the Crypt.

To get to Piccadilly from Trafalgar Square, walk up Cockspur Street to Haymarket, then take a short left on Coventry Street to colorful **Piccadilly Circus** (see map on page 680).

Near Piccadilly, you'll find a number of theaters. **Leicester Square** (with its half-price "tkts" booth for plays—see page 715) thrives just a few blocks away. Walk through seedy **Soho** (north of Shaftesbury Avenue) for its fun pubs. From Piccadilly or Oxford Circus, you can take a taxi, bus, or the Tube home.

Sights in Central London

Westminster

These sights are listed roughly in geographical order from Westminster Abbey to Trafalgar Square, and are linked in my self-guided Westminster Walk, earlier.

▲▲▲Westminster Abbey

The greatest church in the English-speaking world, Westminster Abbey is the place where England's kings and queens have been crowned and buried since 1066. Like a stony refugee camp huddled outside St. Peter's Pearly Gates, Westminster Abbey has many stories to tell. The steep admission includes an excellent audioguide—worthwhile if you have the time and interest. To experience the church more vividly, take a live tour, or attend evensong or an organ concert (see next page).

Two tiny **museums** ring the cloisters. The Chapter House, where the monks had daily meetings, features fine architecture and stained glass with faded but well-described medieval art.

The Abbey Museum has exhibits on royal coronations, funerals, Abbey history, a close-up look at medieval stained glass, and replicas of the crown jewels used for coronation practice. Look into the impressively realistic eyes of Elizabeth I, Charles II, Admiral Nelson, and a dozen others, part of a compelling series of wax-and-wood statues that, for three centuries, graced coffins during funeral processions.

Cost and Hours: £16, £32 family ticket (covers 2 adults and 1 child), cash or credit cards accepted (line up in the correct queue to pay); ticket includes cloisters, audioguide, and Abbey Museum; abbey—Mon-Fri 9:30-16:30, Wed until 19:00 (main church only), Sat 9:30-14:30, last entry one hour before closing, closed Sun to sightseers but open for services; museum—daily 10:30-16:00; cloisters—daily 8:00-18:00, free access to cloisters through Dean Court (near west entrance); Tube: Westminster or St. James's Park.

When to Go: The place is most crowded on Saturdays, Mondays, and any midmornings. Visit early, during lunch, or late to avoid tourist hordes. Weekdays after 14:30 are less congested; come then and stay for the 17:00 evensong. The main entrance, on the Parliament Square side, often has a sizable line. Of the two queues at the admissions desk (cash or credit), the cash line is probably moving faster. There's talk of opening a "fast track" entry for London Pass holders; if you have the pass, it's worth asking to see if that's happened yet.

Music and Services: Mon-Fri at 7:30 (prayer), 8:00 (communion), 12:30 (communion), 17:00 evensong (on Wed the evensong may be spoken—no song); Sat at 8:00 (communion), 9:00 (prayer), 12:30 (communion), 15:00 (evensong; June-Sept it's at 17:00); Sun services generally come with more music: at 8:00 (communion), 10:00 (sung Matins), 11:15 (sung Eucharist), 15:00 (evensong), 18:30 (evening service). Services are free to anyone, though visitors who haven't paid church admission aren't allowed to linger afterward. Free organ recitals are often held Sun at 17:45 (30 minutes). For a schedule of services or recitals on a particular day, look for posted signs with schedules or check the Abbey's website; tel. 020/7654-4834, www.westminster-abbey.org.

▲▲Houses of Parliament (Palace of Westminster)

This Neo-Gothic icon of London, the royal residence from 1042 to 1547, is now the meeting place of the legislative branch of government. The Houses of Parliament are located in what was once the Palace of Westminster—long the palace of England's medieval kings—until it was largely destroyed by fire in 1834. The palace was rebuilt in the Victorian Gothic style (a move away from Neoclassicism back to England's Christian and medieval heritage, true to the Romantic Age) and completed in 1860.

Tourists are welcome to view debates in either the bickering House of Commons or the genteel House of Lords. You're only allowed inside when Parliament is in session, indicated by a flag flying atop the Victoria Tower at the south end of the building (generally Mondays through Thursdays). During the summer recess, when Parliament is not in session, visitors can take a guided tour. While the actual debates are generally quite dull, it is a thrill to be inside and see the British government inaction.

Cost and Hours: Free, both Houses usually open Mon-Tue 14:30-22:30, Wed-Thu 11:30-17:50, closed Fri-Sun and most of Aug-Sept (though tours available, see below), generally less action and no lines after 18:00, Tube: Westminster, tel. 020/7219-4272, see www.parliament.uk for schedule.

Tours: Though Parliament is in recess during much of August and September, you can get a behind-the-scenes peek at the royal chambers of both houses during these months with a tour (£15, 1.25 hours, generally Mon-Fri, times vary, so confirm in advance; book ahead through www.ticketmaster.co.uk). The same tours are offered Saturdays year-round.

Visiting the Houses of Parliament (HOP): Enter the venerable HOP midway along the west side of the building (across the street from Westminster Abbey) through the Visitor Entrance (with the tourist ramp, next to the St. Stephen's Entrance—if lost, ask a guard). As you enter, you'll be asked if you want to visit the House of Commons or the House of Lords. The House of Lords has more pageantry, shorter lines, but less interesting debates (tel. 020/7219-3107 for schedule, visit www.parliamentlive.tv for a preview). Inquire about the wait—an hour or two is not unusual. If there's a long line for the House of Commons and you just want a quick look inside the grand halls of this majestic building, start with the House of Lords. Once inside, you can switch if you like.

Just past security (where you'll be photographed and given a badge to wear around your neck), you enter the vast and historic **Westminster Hall,** which survived the 1834 fire. The cavernous hall was built in the 11th century, and its famous self-supporting hammer-beam roof was added in 1397. Racks of brochures here explain how the British government works, and plaques describe the hall. The Jubilee Café, open to the public, has live video feeds showing exactly what's going on in each house. Just seeing the café video is a fun experience (and can help you decide which house—if either—you'd like to see). Walking through the hall and up the stairs, you'll enter the busy world of government with all its high-powered goings-on.

Jewel Tower: Across the street from the Parliament building's St. Stephen's Gate, the Jewel Tower is a rare remnant of the old Palace of Westminster used by kings until Henry VIII. The crude stone structure (1365-1366) was a guard tower in the palace wall, overlooking a moat. It contains a fine little exhibit on Parliament and the tower (£3, daily March-Oct 10:00-17:00, Nov-Feb 10:00-16:00, tel. 020/7222-2219). Next to the tower (and free) is a quiet courtyard with picnic-friendly benches.

Big Ben: The 315-foot-high clock tower at the north end of the Palace of Westminster is named for its 13-ton bell, Ben. The light above the clock is lit when the House of Commons is sitting. The face of the clock is huge—you can actually see the minute hand moving. For a good view of it, walk halfway over Westminster Bridge.

Other Sights in Westminster

▲▲▲**Churchill War Rooms**—This is a fascinating walk through the underground headquarters of the British government's fight against the Nazis in the darkest days of the Battle of Britain. The attraction includes two parts: the war rooms themselves and a top-notch museum dedicated to the man who steered the war from here, Winston Churchill. For details on all the blood, sweat, toil, and tears, pick up the excellent, essential, and included audioguide at the entry, and dive in.

Cost and Hours: £16 (includes small donation), daily 9:30-18:00, last entry one hour before closing; on King Charles Street, 200 yards off Whitehall, follow the signs, Tube: Westminster, tel. 020/7930-6961, http://cwr.iwm.org.uk. The museum's gift shop is great for anyone nostalgic for the 1940s.

Eating: If you're hungry, get your rations at the Switch Room café (in the museum), or for a nearby pub lunch, try the Westminster Arms (food served downstairs, on Storey's Gate, a couple of blocks south of the museum).

Cabinet War Rooms: The 27-room, heavily fortified nerve center of the British war effort was used from 1939 to 1945. Churchill's room, the map room, and other rooms are just as they were in 1945. As you follow the one-way route, be sure to take advantage of the audioguide, which explains each room and offers first-person accounts of wartime happenings here (it takes about 45 minutes, not counting the Churchill Museum). Be patient—it's well worth it. While the rooms are spartan, you'll see how British gentility survived even as the city was bombarded—posted signs informed those working underground what the weather was like outside, and a cheery notice reminds you to turn off the light switch to conserve electricity.

Churchill Museum: Don't bypass this museum, which occupies a large hall about a half-dozen rooms into the war rooms. It dissects every aspect of the man behind the famous cigar, bowler hat, and V-for-victory sign. It's extremely well-presented and engaging, using artifacts, quotes, political cartoons, clear explanations, and high-tech interactive exhibits to bring the colorful statesman to life; this museum alone deserves an hour. You'll get a taste of Winston's wit, irascibility, work ethic, passion for painting, American ties, writing talents, and drinking habits. The exhibit shows Winston's warts as well: It questions whether his party-switching was just political opportunism, examines the basis for his opposition to Indian self-rule, and reveals him to be an intense taskmaster who worked 18-hour days and was brutal on his staffers (who deeply respected him nevertheless).

A long touch-the-screen timeline lets you zero in on events in his life from birth (November 30, 1874) to his first appointment as prime minister in 1940. Many of the items on display—such as a European map divvied up in permanent marker, which Churchill brought to England from the postwar Potsdam Conference—drive home the remarkable span of history this man lived through. Imagine: Churchill began his military career riding horses in the cavalry and ended it speaking out against the proliferation of nuclear armaments. It's all the more amazing considering that, in the 1930s, the man who would be my vote for greatest statesman of the 20th century was considered a washed-up loony ranting about the growing threat of fascism.

Horse Guards—The Horse Guards change daily at 11:00 (10:00 on Sun), and a colorful dismounting ceremony takes place daily at 16:00. The rest of the day, they just stand there—terrible for video cameras (on Whitehall, between Trafalgar Square and #10 Downing Street, Tube: Westminster, www.changing-the-guard .com). Buckingham Palace pageantry is canceled when it rains, but the horse guards change regardless of the weather.

▲Banqueting House—England's first Renaissance building (1619-1622) was designed by Inigo Jones. Built by King James I and decorated by his son Charles I, the Banqueting House came to symbolize the Stuart kings' "divine right" management style—the belief that God himself had anointed them to rule. The house is one of the few London landmarks spared by the 1698 fire and the only surviving part of the original Palace of Whitehall. Today it opens its doors to visitors, who enjoy a restful 20-minute audio-visual history, a 30-minute audioguide, and a look at the exquisite banqueting hall itself. As a tourist attraction, it's basically one big room—but what a grand room it is, with sumptuous ceiling paintings by Peter Paul Rubens. At Charles I's request, these paintings drove home the doctrine of the legitimacy of the divine right of kings. Ironically, in 1649—divine right ignored—King Charles I was famously executed right here.

Cost and Hours: £4.80, includes audioguide, Mon-Sat 10:00-17:00, closed Sun, last entry at 16:30, subject to closure for government functions, aristocratic WC, immediately across Whitehall from the Horse Guards, Tube: Westminster, tel. 020/3166-6155, www.hrp.org.uk.

▲▲Trafalgar Square

London's central square—at the intersection of Westminster, The City, and the West End—is the climax of most marches and demonstrations, and a thrilling place to simply hang out. A recent remodeling of the square has rerouted car traffic, helping reclaim the area for London's citizens. At the top of Trafalgar Square (north) sits the domed National Gallery with its grand staircase, and to the right, the steeple of St. Martin-in-the-Fields, built in 1722, inspiring the steeple-over-the-entrance style of many town churches in New England. In the center of the square, Lord Horatio Nelson stands atop his 185-foot-tall fluted granite column, gazing out toward Trafalgar, where he lost his life but defeated the French fleet. Part of this 1842 memorial is made from his victims' melted-down cannons. He's surrounded by spraying fountains, giant lions, hordes of people, and—until recently—even more pigeons. A former London mayor decided that London's "flying rats" were a public nuisance and evicted Trafalgar Square's venerable seed salesmen (Tube: Charing Cross).

▲▲▲National Gallery

Displaying Britain's top collection of European paintings from 1250 to 1900—including works by Leonardo, Botticelli, Velázquez, Rembrandt, Turner, Van Gogh, and the Impressionists—this is one of Europe's great galleries. You'll peruse 700 years of art—from gold-backed Madonnas to Cubist bathers.

Cost and Hours: Free, but suggested donation of £2-3, temporary (optional) exhibits require an admission fee; daily 10:00-18:00, Fri until 21:00, last entry to special exhibits 45 minutes before closing; on Trafalgar Square, Tube: Charing Cross or Leicester Square.

Information: Helpful £1 floor plan available from information desk; free one-hour overview tours leave from Sainsbury Wing info desk daily at 11:30 and 14:30, plus Fri at 19:00; excellent £3.50 audioguides—choose from one-hour highlights tour, several theme tours, or tour option that lets you dial up info on any painting in the museum; ArtStart computer terminals help you study any artist, style, or topic in the museum, and print out a tailor-made tour map (located on first floor of the Sainsbury Wing and in the Espresso Bar); info tel. 020/7747-2885, switchboard tel. 020/7839-3321, www.nationalgallery.org.uk.

Trafalgar Square

Eating: Consider splitting afternoon tea at the excellent-but-pricey National Dining Rooms, on the first floor of the Sainsbury Wing. The National Café, located near the Getty Entrance, also has afternoon tea.

Visiting the Museum: Pick up a free map and approach the collection chronologically. In the medieval and early Renaissance rooms you'll see shiny paintings of saints, angels, Madonnas, and crucifixions floating in an ethereal gold never-never land. Then comes the Renaissance, where artists rediscovered the beauty of nature and the human body, expressing the optimism and confidence of this new age. Look for Botticelli's *Venus and Mars*, Michelangelo's *Entombment*, Raphael's *Pope Julius II*, and Leonardo's *The Virgin of the Rocks*.

Next seek out Northern Protestant art, where Greek gods and Virgin Marys were out, hometown folks and hometown places were in. Highlights include Vermeer's *A Young Woman Standing at a Virginal* and Rembrandt's *Belshazzar's Feast*. The museum's outstanding Baroque collection includes Van Dyck's *Equestrian Portrait of Charles I*, Velázquez's *The Rokeby Venus*, and Caravaggio's *The Supper at Emmaus*. It's no surprise that hometown painters get lots of space here. The reserved British were more comfortable cavorting with nature than with the lofty gods, as seen in

Constable's *The Hay Wain* and Turner's *The Fighting Téméraire*.

Then, at the end of the 19th century, a new breed of artists burst out of the stuffy confines of the studio. They donned scarves and berets and set up their canvases in farmers' fields or carried their notebooks into crowded cafés, dashing off quick sketches in order to catch a momentary...impression. Check out Impressionist and Post-Impressionist masterpieces such as Monet's *Gare St. Lazare* and *The Water-Lily Pond*, Renoir's *The Skiff*, Seurat's *Bathers at Asnières*, Van Gogh's *Sunflowers, and* Cézanne's *Bathers*.

Other Sights on Trafalgar Square

▲▲**National Portrait Gallery**—Put off by halls of 19th-century characters who meant nothing to me, I used to call this "as interesting as someone else's yearbook." But a selective walk through this 500-year-long *Who's Who* of British history is quick and free, and puts faces on the major characters in the story of England.

Some highlights: Henry VIII and wives; portraits of the "Virgin Queen" Elizabeth I, Sir Francis Drake, and Sir Walter Raleigh; the only real-life portrait of William Shakespeare; Oliver Cromwell and Charles I with his head on; portraits by Gainsborough and Reynolds; the Romantics (William Blake, Lord Byron, William Wordsworth, and company); Queen Victoria and her era; and the present royal family, including the late Princess Diana.

The collection is well-described, not huge, and in historical sequence, from the 16th century on the second floor to today's royal family on the ground floor.

Cost and Hours: Free, but suggested donation of £5, temporary (optional) exhibits require an admission fee, £3 audioguide, daily 10:00-18:00, Thu-Fri until 21:00—often with music and drinks offered in the evening, first and second floors open Mon at 11:00, last entry to special exhibits 45 minutes before closing, 100 yards off Trafalgar Square (around the corner from the National Gallery and opposite the Church of St. Martin-in-the-Fields), Tube: Charing Cross or Leicester Square, tel. 020/7306-0055, recorded info tel. 020/7312-2463, www.npg.org.uk.

▲**St. Martin-in-the-Fields**—The church, built in the 1720s with a Gothic spire atop a Greek-type temple, is an oasis of peace on wild and noisy Trafalgar Square. St. Martin cared for the poor. "In the fields" was where the first church stood on this spot (in the 13th century), between Westminster and The City. Stepping inside, you still feel a compassion for the needs of the people in this neighborhood—the church serves the homeless and houses a Chinese community center. The modern east window—with grillwork bent into the shape of a warped cross—was installed in 2008 to replace one damaged in World War II.

A freestanding glass pavilion to the left of the church serves as the entrance to the church's underground areas. There you'll find the concert ticket office, a gift shop, brass-rubbing center, and the recommended support-the-church Café in the Crypt.

Cost and Hours: Free, but donations welcome, £3.50 audio-guide at shop downstairs; hours vary but generally Mon-Fri 8:30-13:00 & 14:00-18:00, Sat 9:30-13:00 & 14:00-18:00, Sun 15:30-17:00; Tube: Charing Cross, tel. 020/7766-1100, www.smitf .org.

Music: The church is famous for its concerts. Consider a free lunchtime concert (suggested £3.50 donation; Mon, Tue, and Fri at 13:00), an evening concert (£8-26, several nights a week at 19:30), or Wednesday night jazz in the church's café (£5-10, at 20:00). See the website for the concert schedule.

The West End and Nearby

▲**Piccadilly Circus**—Although this square is slathered with neon billboards and tacky attractions (think of it as the Times Square of London), the surrounding streets are packed with great shopping opportunities and swimming with youth on the rampage. For overstimulation in a grimy mall that smells like teen spirit, drop by the extremely trashy Trocadero Centre for its Funland arcade games, multiplex cinema, and 10-lane bowling alley (admission to Trocadero is free; individual attractions have separate admissions; located between Piccadilly and Leicester squares on Coventry Street).

Nearby Shaftesbury Avenue and Leicester Square teem with fun-seekers, theaters, Chinese restaurants, and street singers. To the northeast is London's Chinatown and, beyond that, the funky Soho neighborhood (described next). And curling to the northwest from Piccadilly Circus is genteel Regent Street, lined with the city's most exclusive shops.

▲**Soho**—North of Piccadilly, seedy Soho has become seriously trendy and is well worth a gawk. It's the epicenter of London's thriving and colorful youth, a fun and funky *Sesame Street* scene populated by people of every color of the racial rainbow...straight, gay, and everything in between.

Soho is also London's red light district (especially near Brewer and Berwick Streets), where "friendly models" wait in tiny rooms up dreary stairways, and voluptuous con artists sell strip shows. Though venturing up a stairway to check out a model is interesting, anyone who goes into any of the shows will be ripped off. Every time. Even a £5 show in a "licensed bar" comes with a £100 cover or minimum (as it's printed on the drink menu) and a "security man." You may accidentally buy a £200 bottle of bubbly. And suddenly, the door has no handle. While this all sounds creepy, it's

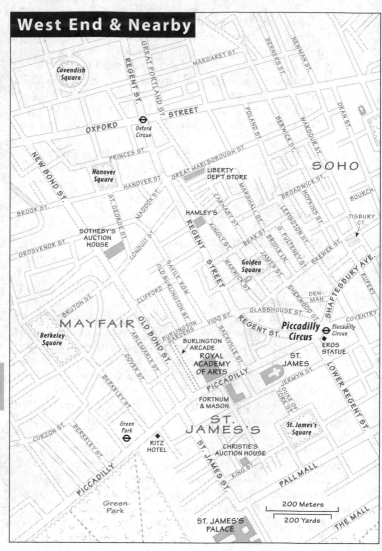

West End & Nearby

easy to avoid trouble if you're not looking for it. In fact, the sleazy joints share the block with respectable pubs and restaurants, and elderly couples out for a stroll pass neon signs that flash *Licensed Sex Shop in Basement.*

▲▲**Covent Garden**—This large square is swarming with people and street performers—jugglers, sword swallowers, and guitar players. London's buskers (including those in the Tube) are auditioned, licensed, and assigned times and places where they are allowed to perform.

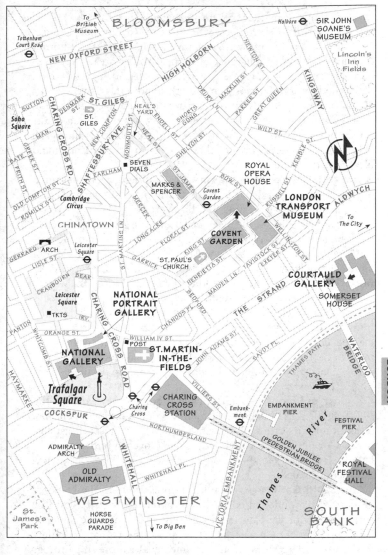

The square's centerpiece is a covered marketplace. A market has been here since medieval times, when it was the "convent" garden owned by Westminster Abbey. In the 1600s, it became a housing development with this courtyard as its center, done in the Palladian style by Inigo Jones. Today's fine iron-and-glass structure was built in 1830 (when such buildings were all the Industrial Age rage) to house the stalls of what became London's chief produce market. Covent Garden remained a produce market until 1973, when its venerable arcades were converted to boutiques, cafés, and antiques shops. A market still thrives here today.

The "Actors' Church" of St. Paul, the Royal Opera House, and the London Transport Museum (described next) all border the square, and venerable theaters are nearby. The area is a people-watcher's delight, with cigarette eaters, Punch-and-Judy acts, food that's good for you (but not your wallet), trendy crafts, sweet whiffs of marijuana, two-tone hair (neither natural), and faces that could set off a metal detector. For better Covent Garden lunch deals, walk a block or two away from the eye of this touristic hurricane (check out the places north of the Tube station, along Endell and Neal Streets).

▲London Transport Museum—This modern, well-presented museum, located right at Covent Garden, is fun for kids and thought-provoking for adults (if a bit overpriced). Whether you're cursing or marveling at the buses and Tube, the growth of Europe's third-biggest city (after Moscow and Istanbul) has been made possible by its public transit system. After you enter, take the elevator up to the top floor...and the year 1800, when horse-drawn vehicles ruled the road. Next, you descend to the first floor and the world's first underground Metro system, which used steam-powered locomotives (the Circle Line, c. 1865). On the ground floor, horses and trains are quickly replaced by motorized vehicles (cars, taxis, double-decker buses, streetcars), resulting in 20th-century congestion. How to deal with it? In 2003, car drivers in London were slapped with a congestion charge, and today, a half-billion people ride the Tube every year.

LONDON

Cost and Hours: £13.50, ticket good for one year, Sat-Thu 10:00-18:00, Fri 11:00-18:00, last entry 45 minutes before closing, pleasant upstairs café with Covent Garden view, in southeast corner of Covent Garden courtyard, Tube: Covent Garden, switchboard tel. 020/7379-6344, recorded info tel. 020/7565-7299, www.ltmuseum.co.uk.

▲Courtauld Gallery—While less impressive than the National Gallery, this wonderful collection of paintings is still a joy. The gallery is part of the Courtauld Institute of Art, and the thoughtful description of each piece of art reminds visitors that the gallery is still used for teaching. You'll see medieval European paintings and works by Rubens, the Impressionists (Manet, Monet, and Degas), Post-Impressionists (such as Cézanne), and more. Besides the permanent collection, a quality selection of loaners and temporary exhibits are often included in the entry fee.

Cost and Hours: £6, free Mon until 14:00; open daily 10:00-18:00, last entry 30 minutes before closing, occasional late-night openings until 21:00—check website; at Somerset House along the Strand, Tube: Temple or Covent Garden, recorded info tel. 020/7848-2526, shop tel. 020/7848-2579, www.courtauld.ac.uk.

Somerset House: The Courtauld Gallery is located at Somerset House, a grand 18th-century civic palace that offers a marvelous public space (housing temporary exhibits) and a riverside terrace with several eateries (between the Strand and the Thames). The palace once held the national registry that recorded Britain's births, marriages, and deaths: "...where they hatch 'em, match 'em, and dispatch 'em." Step into the courtyard to enjoy the fountain. Go ahead...walk through it. The 55 jets get playful twice an hour. In the winter, this becomes a popular ice-skating rink with a toasty café for viewing (www.somerset-house.org.uk).

Buckingham Palace

Three palace sights require admission: the State Rooms (Aug-Sept only), Queen's Gallery, and Royal Mews. You can pay for each separately, or buy a combo-ticket. The combo-ticket for £31 admits you to all three sights; a cheaper version for £15.50 covers the Queen's Gallery and Royal Mews. Many tourists are more interested in the Changing of the Guard, which costs nothing at all to view.

▲**State Rooms at Buckingham Palace**—This lavish home has been Britain's royal residence since 1837. When the Queen's at home, the royal standard flies (a red, yellow, and blue flag); otherwise, the Union Jack flaps in the wind. The Queen opens her palace to the public—but only in August and September, when she's out of town.

Cost and Hours: £17.50 for lavish State Rooms and throne room, includes audioguide; Aug-Sept only, daily 9:45-18:30, last admission 15:45; only 8,000 visitors a day by timed entry; come early to the palace's Visitor Entrance (opens 9:15), or book ahead in person or by phone or online (£1.25 extra); Tube: Victoria, tel. 020/7766-7300, www.royalcollection.org.uk.

▲**Queen's Gallery at Buckingham Palace**—Queen Elizabeth's personal collection of art is on display in a wing adjoining the palace. Her 7,000 paintings make up the finest private art collection in the world, rivaling Europe's biggest national art galleries. It's actually a collection of collections, built on by each successive monarch since the 16th century. She rotates her paintings, enjoying some privately in her many palatial residences while sharing others with her subjects in public galleries in Edinburgh and London. Small, thoughtfully presented, and always exquisite displays fill the five rooms open to the public. As you're in "the most important building in London," security is tight.

In addition to the permanent collection, you'll see temporary exhibits and a small room glittering with the Queen's personal jewelry. Compared to the crown jewels at the Tower, it may be Her Majesty's bottom drawer—but it's still a dazzling pile of

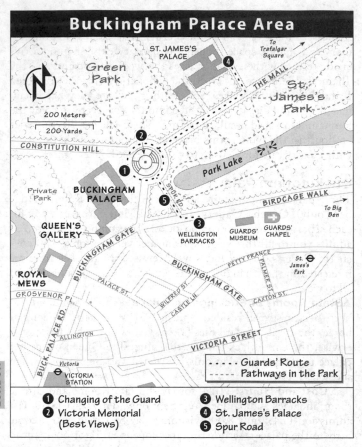

Buckingham Palace Area

ST. JAMES'S PALACE

To Trafalgar Square

④

Green Park

THE MALL

St. James's Park

N

200 Meters
200 Yards

CONSTITUTION HILL

②

Park Lake

①

To Big Ben

Private Park

BUCKINGHAM PALACE

⑤

SPUR RD

BIRDCAGE WALK

③

QUEEN'S GALLERY

BUCKINGHAM GATE

WELLINGTON BARRACKS

GUARDS' MUSEUM

GUARDS' CHAPEL

St. James's Park

ROYAL MEWS

PALACE ST.

GROSVENOR PL.

PETTY FRANCE

PALMER ST.

BUCKINGHAM GATE

WILFRED ST.

CASTLE LN.

CAXTON ST.

BUCK. PALACE RD.

ALLINGTON

VICTORIA STREET

Victoria

VICTORIA STATION

· · · · · Guards' Route
- - - - Pathways in the Park

① Changing of the Guard
② Victoria Memorial (Best Views)
③ Wellington Barracks
④ St. James's Palace
⑤ Spur Road

LONDON

diamonds. Temporary exhibits change about twice a year and are lovingly described by the included audioguide. While admission tickets come with an entry time, this is only enforced during rare days when crowds are a problem.

Cost and Hours: £9, daily 10:00-17:30, last entry one hour before closing, Tube: Victoria, tel. 020/7766-7301—but Her Majesty rarely answers. Men shouldn't miss the mahogany-trimmed urinals.

Royal Mews—Located to the left of Buckingham Palace, the Queen's working stables, or "mews," are open to visitors. The visit is likely to be disappointing unless you follow the included audio-guide or the hourly guided tour, in which case it's thoroughly entertaining—especially if you're interested in horses and/or roy-alty. The 40-minute tours show off a few of the Queen's 30 horses, a fancy car, and a bunch of old carriages, finishing with the Gold State Coach (c. 1760, 4 tons, 4 mph). Queen Victoria said absolutely no cars. When she died, in 1901, the mews got its first Daimler. Today, along with the hay-eating transport, the stable is home to five Bentleys and Rolls-Royce Phantoms, with one on display.

Cost and Hours: £8, April-Oct daily 11:00-17:00, Nov-March Mon-Fri 10:00-16:00, closed Sat-Sun, last entry 45 minutes before closing, guided tours on the hour, Buckingham Palace Road, Tube: Victoria, tel. 020/7766-7302.

▲▲**Changing of the Guard at Buckingham Palace**—This is the spectacle every visitor to London has to see at least once: stone-faced, red-coated, bearskin-hatted guards changing posts with much fanfare, in an hour-long ceremony accompanied by a brass band.

It's 11:00 at Buckingham Palace, and the on-duty guards are ready to finish their shift. Nearby at St. James's Palace (a half-mile northwest), a second set of guards is also ready for a break. Meanwhile, fresh replacement guards gather for a review and inspection at Wellington Barracks, 500 yards east of the palace (on Birdcage Walk).

At 11:15, the tired St. James's guards head out to the Mall, and then take a right turn for Buckingham Palace. At 11:30, the replacement troops, led by the band, also head for Buckingham Palace. Meanwhile, a fourth group—the Horse Guard—passes by along the Mall on their way back to Hyde Park Corner from their own changing-of-the-guard ceremony on Whitehall (which just took place at Horse Guards Parade at 11:00, or 10:00 on Sun).

At 11:45, the tired and fresh guards converge on Buckingham Palace in a perfect storm of Red Coat pageantry. Everyone parades around, the guard changes (passing the regimental flag, or "color") with much shouting, the band plays a happy little concert, and then they march out. At noon, two bands escort two detachments of guards away: the tired guards to Wellington Barracks and the fresh guards to St. James's Palace. As the fresh guards set up at St. James's Palace and the tired ones dress down at the barracks, the tourists disperse.

Cost and Hours: Free, daily May-July at 11:30, every other day Aug-April, no ceremony in very wet weather; exact schedule subject to change—call 020/7766-7300 for the day's plan, or check www.changing-the-guard.com or www.royalcollection.org.uk (click "Visit," then "Changing the Guard"); Buckingham Palace, Tube: Victoria, St. James's Park, or Green Park. Or hop into a big black taxi and say, "Buck House, please."

Sightseeing Strategies: Most tourists just show up and get lost in the crowds, but those who know the drill will enjoy the event more. The action takes place in stages over the course of an hour, at several different locations. The main event is in the fore-court right in front of Buckingham Palace (between Buckingham

Palace and the fence) from 11:30 to 12:00. To see it close up, you'll need to get here no later than 10:30 to get a place right next to the fence.

But there's plenty of pageantry elsewhere. Get out your map and strategize. You could see the guards mobilizing at Wellington Barracks or St. James's Palace (11:00-11:15). Or watch them parade with bands down The Mall and Spur Road (11:15-11:30). After the ceremony at Buckingham Palace is over (and many tourists have gotten bored and gone home), the parades march back along those same streets (12:10).

Pick one event and find a good, unobstructed place from which to view it. The key is to get either right up front along the road or fence, or find some raised elevation to stand or sit on—a balustrade or a curb—so you can see over people's heads.

For the best overall view, stake out the high ground on the circular Victoria Memorial (come before 11:00 to get a place). From the memorial, you have good views of the palace as well as the arriving and departing parades along The Mall and Spur Road. The actual changing of the guard in front of the palace is a nonevent. It is interesting, however, to see nearly every tourist in London gathered in one place at the same time.

If you arrive too late to get a good spot, or you just don't feel like jostling for a view, stroll down to St. James's Palace and wait near the corner for a great photo-op. At about 12:15, the parade marches up The Mall to the palace and performs a smaller changing ceremony—with almost no crowds. Afterward, stroll through nearby St. James's Park.

Sights in North London

▲▲▲British Museum

Simply put, this is the greatest chronicle of civilization...anywhere. A visit here is like taking a long hike through *Encyclopedia Britannica* National Park. While the vast British Museum wraps around its Great Court (the huge entrance hall), the most popular sections of the museum fill the ground floor: Egyptian, Assyrian, and ancient Greek, with the famous Elgin Marbles from the Parthenon in Athens. The museum's stately Reading Room—famous as the place where Karl Marx hung out while formulating his ideas on communism and writing *Das Kapital*—sometimes hosts special exhibits.

Cost and Hours: Free but a £4, $5, or €5 donation requested; temporary exhibits usually extra; daily 10:00-17:30, Fri until 20:30 (selected galleries only), least crowded weekday late afternoons; Great Russell Street, Tube: Tottenham Court Road.

Information: Information desks offer a standard museum

North London

To Zoo

Regent's
Park

Queen
Mary's
Gardens

To
Abbey
Road

ST. PANCRAS
INTERNATIONAL
STATION

KING'S
CROSS
STATION

YORK WAY

OUTER CIRCLE

ALBANY ST.

HAMPSTEAD ROAD

EVERSHOLT ST.

EUSTON ROAD

GRAY'S INN ROAD

EUSTON
STATION

WOBURN PLACE

BRITISH
LIBRARY

BEATLES STORE &
SHERLOCK HOLMES
MUSEUM

MARYLEBONE ROAD

Warren
Street

Euston
Square

Russell
Square

GUILFORD STREET

Baker
Street

MADAME
TUSSAUDS
WAXWORKS

Regent's
Park

Great
Portland
Street

TOTTENHAM COURT ROAD

GOWER ST.

Russell
Square

BLOOMSBURY

THEOBALD'S RD.

YORK ST.

BAKER ST.

MARYLEBONE

PORTLAND PL.

GREAT PORTLAND ST.

POLLOCK'S
TOY MUSEUM

Goodge
Street

BRITISH
MUSEUM

CARTOON
MUSEUM

SIR JOHN
SOANE'S
MUSEUM

WALLACE
COLLECTION

WIGMORE ST.

NEW OXFORD STREET

CHARING CROSS RD.

Holborn

Lincoln's
Inn Fields

GLOUCESTER PLACE

Marble
Arch

OXFORD STREET

Oxford
Circus

Tottenham
Court Rd.

400 Meters

400 Yards

MARBLE
ARCH

PARK ST.

DUKE ST.

Bond St.

REGENT ST.

To Trafalgar
Square

SHAFTESBURY

To
Trafalgar
Square

THE STRAND

To
The City

Hyde
Park

map (£1 suggested donation) and a £2 version that highlights important pieces. **Tours:** Free 30-minute **eyeOpener tours** are led by volunteers, who focus on select rooms (daily 11:00-15:45, generally every 15 minutes). The 1.5-hour **Highlights tours,** led by licensed guides, are expensive but meaty, giving an introduction to the museum's masterpieces (£9, daily at 10:30, 13:00, and 15:00). Free 45-minute **gallery talks** on specific subjects are offered Tue-Sat at 13:15. The £5 **multimedia guide** offers dial-up audio commentary and video on 200 objects, as well as several theme tours (must leave photo ID). There's also a fun children's audio-guide (£3.50). And finally, you can download a free Rick Steves **audio tour** of the British Museum (see page 7). General info tel. 020/7323-8299, ticket desk tel. 020/7323-8181, collection questions tel. 020/7323-8838, www.britishmuseum.org.

Visiting the Museum: From the Great Court, doorways lead to all wings. Huge winged lions (which guarded an Assyrian palace 800 years before Christ) guard these great galleries. For a brief tour, connect these ancient dots:

Start with the **Egyptian** section. Wander from the Rosetta Stone past the many statues. At the end of the hall, climb the stairs to mummy land.

Back at the winged lions, explore the dark, violent, and mysterious **Assyrian** rooms. The Nimrud Gallery is lined with royal propaganda reliefs and wounded lions (from the ninth century B.C.).

British Museum Overview

MONTAGUE PLACE
MONTAGUE PLACE ENTRANCE
Russell Square
BLOOMSBURY ST.
CAFÉ
GREECE
ASSYRIA
ROSETTA STONE
EGYPT
READING ROOM
THE KING'S GALLERY
MONTAGUE ST.
THE GREAT COURT
INFO
INFO
WINGED LIONS
SHOP
CLOAKROOM
CAFÉ
COLUMNS
MAIN ENTRANCE
GREAT RUSSELL ST.
To Tottenham Court Road ⊖ (10 min. walk)
To Holborn ⊖ (10 min. walk)

The most modern of the ancient art fills the **Greek** section. Find Room 11, behind the winged lions, and start your walk through Greek art history with the simple and primitive Cycladic fertility figures. Later, painted vases show a culture really into partying. The finale is the Elgin Marbles. The much-wrangled-over bits of the Athenian Parthenon (from about 450 B.C.) are even more impressive than they look. To best appreciate these ancient carvings, take the audioguide tour (described earlier).

Be sure to venture upstairs to see artifacts from **Roman Britain** that surpass anything you'll see at Hadrian's Wall or elsewhere in Britain. Nearby, the Dark Age Britain exhibits offer a worthwhile peek at that bleak era; look for the Sutton Hoo Burial Ship artifacts from a seventh-century royal burial on the east coast of England (Room 41). A rare Michelangelo cartoon (preliminary sketch) is in Room 90.

Other Sights in North London

▲▲▲**British Library**—The British Empire built its greatest monuments out of paper, and it's with literature that England made her lasting contribution to civilization and the arts. Here, in just two rooms—variously called "The Sir John Ritblat Gallery," "Treasures of the British Library," or just "The Treasures"—are the literary jewels of Western civilization, from early Bibles, to the

Magna Carta, to Shakespeare's *Hamlet,* to Lewis Carroll's *Alice's Adventures in Wonderland.*

You'll see the Lindisfarne Gospels transcribed on an illuminated manuscript, as well as Beatles lyrics scrawled on the back of a greeting card. Pages from Leonardo da Vinci's notebook show his powerful curiosity, his genius for invention, and his famous backward and inside-out handwriting, which makes sense only if you know Italian and have a mirror. A *Beowulf* manuscript from A.D. 1000, *The Canterbury Tales*, and Shakespeare's First Folio also reside here. (If the First Folio is not out, the library should have other Shakespeare items on display.)

Note that exhibits generally change often, and many of the museum's old, fragile manuscripts need to "rest" periodically in order to stay well-preserved. If your heart's set on seeing that one particular rare Dickens book or letter penned by Gandhi, call ahead to make sure it's on display.

Cost and Hours: Free but £2 suggested donation, admission charged for some (optional) temporary exhibits, Mon-Fri 9:30-18:00, Tue until 20:00, Sat 9:30-17:00, Sun 11:00-17:00, 96 Euston Road, Tube: King's Cross St. Pancras or Euston, tel. 019/3754-6060 or 020/7412-7676, www.bl.uk.

Tours: While the British Library doesn't offer an audioguide or guided tours, you can download a free Rick Steves **audio tour** of the library (see page 7).

▲**Wallace Collection**—Sir Richard Wallace's fine collection of 17th-century Dutch Masters, 18th-century French Rococo, medieval armor, and assorted aristocratic fancies fills the sumptuously furnished Hertford House on Manchester Square. From the rough and intimate Dutch lifescapes of Jan Steen to the pink-cheeked Rococo fantasies of François Boucher, a wander through this little-visited mansion makes you nostalgic for the days of the empire. While this collection would be a big deal in a mid-sized city, it's small potatoes here in London...but enjoyable nevertheless.

Cost and Hours: Free, daily 10:00-17:00, £4 audioguide, free guided tours or lectures almost daily—call to confirm times, just north of Oxford Street on Manchester Square, Tube: Bond Street. Tel. 020/7563-9500, www.wallacecollection.org.

▲**Madame Tussauds Waxworks**—This waxtravaganza is gimmicky and expensive, but dang good...a hit with the kind of travelers who skip the British Museum. The original Madame Tussaud did wax casts of heads lopped off during the French Revolution (such as Marie-Antoinette's). She took her show on the road and ended up in London in 1835. Now it's all about squeezing Tom Cruise's bum, gambling with George Clooney, and partying with Beyoncé, Britney, and Brangelina. In addition to posing with all the eerily realistic wax dummies—from Johnny Depp to Barack Obama to the Beatles—you'll have the chance to tour a hokey haunted-house exhibit; learn how they created this waxy army; hop on a people-mover and cruise through a kid-pleasing "Spirit of London" time trip; and visit with Spider-Man, the Hulk, and other Marvel super-heroes. A nine-minute "4-D" show features a 3-D movie height-ened by wind, "back ticklers," and other special effects.

Cost and Hours: £29, 10 percent discount and no waiting in line if you buy tickets on their website (also consider combo-deal with London Eye, sold cheaper online), £25.50 if purchased at TI, cheaper for kids. From 17:00 to closing, it's £14 if you buy in advance online. Children under 5 always free. Open Mid-July-Aug and school holidays daily 9:00-21:00, Sept-mid-July Mon-Fri 9:30-19:30, Sat-Sun 9:00-20:00, last entry two hours before clos-ing; Marylebone Road, Tube: Baker Street, tel. 0871-894-3000, www.madametussauds.com.

Crowd-Beating Tips: This popular attraction can be swamped with people. To avoid the hassle, buy your tickets and reserve an entry time in advance, either online (10 percent discount) or by phone (same price as box office). If you wait to buy tickets at the attraction, you'll discover that the ticket-buying line twists end-lessly once inside the door (believe the posted signs warning you how long the wait will be—an hour or more is not unusual at busy times). If you buy your tickets at the door, try to arrive after 15:00.

▲**Sir John Soane's Museum**—Architects love this quirky place, as do fans of interior decor and eclectic knickknacks. Tour this furnished home on a bird-chirping square and see 19th-century chairs, lamps, and carpets, wood-paneled nooks and crannies, and stained-glass skylights. (Note that some sections may be closed for restoration, but the main part of the house will be open.) The townhouse is cluttered with Soane's (and his wife's) collection of ancient relics, curios, and famous paintings, including Hogarth's series on *The Rake's Progress* (read the fun plot) and several excel-lent Canalettos. In 1833, just before his death, Soane established his house as a museum, stipulating that it be kept as nearly as pos-sible in the state he left it. If he visited today, he'd be entirely satis-fied. You'll leave wishing you'd known the man.

Cost and Hours: Free but donations much appreciated, Tue-Sat 10:00-17:00, open and candlelit the first Tue of the month 18:00-21:00, closed Sun-Mon, last entry 30 minutes before closing, long entry lines on Sat and first Tue, good £1 brochure, £5 guided tour Sat at 11:00; free, downloadable audio tours on their website; 13 Lincoln's Inn Fields, quarter-mile southeast of British Museum, Tube: Holborn, tel. 020/7405-2107, www.soane.org.

Cartoon Museum—This humble but interesting museum is located in the shadow of the British Museum. While its three rooms are filled with British cartoons unknown to most Americans, the satire of famous bigwigs and politicians—including Napoleon, Margaret Thatcher, the Queen, and Tony Blair—shows the power of parody to deliver social commentary. Upstairs, you'll see pages spanning from *Tarzan* to *Tank Girl,* and *Andy Capp* to the British *Dennis the Menace*—interesting only to comic-book diehards.

Cost and Hours: £5.50, Tue-Sat 10:30-17:30, Sun 12:00-17:30, closed Mon, 35 Little Russell Street—go one block south of the British Museum on Museum Street and turn right, Tube: Tottenham Court Road, tel. 020/7580-8155, www.cartoon museum.org.

Pollock's Toy Museum—This rickety old house, with glass cases filled with toys and games lining its walls and halls, is a time-warp experience that brings back childhood memories to people who grew up without batteries or computer chips. Though the museum is small, you could spend a lot of time here, squinting at the fascinating toys and dolls that entertained the children of 19th- and early 20th-century England. The included information is great. The story of Theodore Roosevelt refusing to shoot a bear cub while on a hunting trip was celebrated in 1902 cartoons, resulting in a new, huggable toy: the Teddy Bear. It was popular for good reason: It could be manufactured during World War I without rationed products; it coincided with the new belief that soft toys were good for a child's development; it was an acceptable "doll for boys"; and it's *the* toy children keep long after they've grown up.

Cost and Hours: £5, kids-£2, generally Mon-Sat 10:00-17:00, closed Sun, last entry 30 minutes before closing, 1 Scala Street, Tube: Goodge Street, tel. 020/7636-3452, www.pollockstoy museum.com. A fun, retro toy shop is attached.

Sights in The City

When Londoners say "The City," they mean the one-square-mile business center in East London that 2,000 years ago was Roman Londinium. The outline of the Roman city walls can still be seen in the arc of roads from Blackfriars Bridge to Tower Bridge. Within The City are 23 churches designed by Sir Christopher Wren, mostly just ornamentation around St. Paul's Cathedral. Today, while home to only 7,000 residents, The City thrives with nearly 300,000 office workers coming and going daily. It's a fascinating district to wander on weekdays, but since almost nobody actually lives there, it's dull in the evenings and on Saturday and Sunday.

You can download a free Rick Steves **audio tour** of The City—which peels back the many layers of history in this oldest part of London (see page 7).

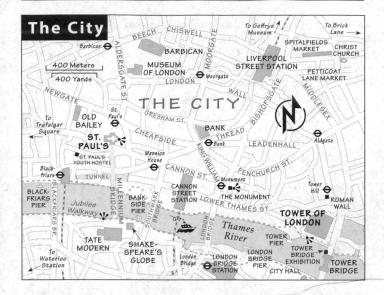

▲▲▲St. Paul's Cathedral

Sir Christopher Wren's most famous church is the great St. Paul's, its elaborate interior capped by a 365-foot dome. There's been a church on this spot since 604. After the Great Fire of 1666 destroyed the old cathedral, Wren created this Baroque master-piece. And since World War II, St. Paul's has been Britain's symbol of resistance. Despite 57 nights of bombing, the Nazis failed to destroy the cathedral, thanks to the St. Paul's volunteer fire watch-men, who stayed on the dome.

Cost and Hours: £14.50, includes church entry, dome climb, crypt, guided tour, and audioguide; free on Sun but officially open only to worshippers, TI in the south churchyard gives out maps with a coupon good for 20 percent off admission; Mon-Sat 8:30-16:30, last entry for sightseeing 16:00 (dome opens at 9:30, last entry at 16:15), closed Sun except for worship, sometimes closed for special events, Tube: St. Paul's.

Music and Services: Communion is Mon-Sat at 8:00 and 12:30. Sunday services are held at 8:00, 10:15 (Matins), 11:30 (sung Eucharist), 15:15 (evensong), and 18:00. Additional evensong ser-vices are held Mon-Sat at 17:00 (40 minutes, free to anyone—though visitors who haven't paid admission aren't allowed to linger after the service). If you're here for evensong worship and sitting under the dome, at 16:45 you may be able to grab a big wooden stall in the choir, next to the singers.

Information: Admission includes an **audioguide** as well as a 1.5-hour **guided tour** (Mon-Sat at 10:45, 11:15, 13:30, and 14:00; confirm schedule at church or call 020/7246-8357). You can download a free Rick Steves **audio tour** of St. Paul's (see page 7). Recorded info tel. 020/7236-4128, reception tel. 020/7246-8350, www.stpauls.co.uk.

Visiting the Cathedral: Inside, this big church *feels* big. At 515 feet long and 250 feet wide, it's Europe's fourth-largest, after Rome (St. Peter's), Sevilla, and Milan. The spaciousness is accentuated by the relative lack of decoration. The simple, cream-colored ceiling and the clear glass in the windows light everything evenly.

There are many legends buried here: Horatio Nelson, who wore down Napoleon; the Duke of Wellington, who finished Napoleon off; and even Charles Cornwallis, who was finished off by George Washington at Yorktown. Often the site of historic funerals (Queen Victoria and Winston Churchill), St. Paul's most famous ceremony was a wedding—when Prince Charles married Lady Diana Spencer in 1981.

During your visit, you can climb the dome for a great city view and have some fun in the Whispering Gallery. Whisper sweet nothings into the wall, and your partner (and anyone else) standing far away can hear you. For best effects, try whispering (not talking) with your mouth close to the wall, while your partner stands a few dozen yards away with his or her ear to the wall. The crypt (included with admission) is a world of historic bones and interesting cathedral models.

Near St. Paul's Cathedral

▲**Old Bailey**—To view the British legal system in action—lawyers in little blonde wigs speaking legalese with a British accent—spend a few minutes in the visitors' gallery at the Old Bailey, called the "Central Criminal Court." Don't enter under the dome; continue down the block about halfway to the modern part of the building—the entry is at Warwick Passage.

Cost and Hours: Free, generally Mon-Fri 9:45-13:00 & 14:00-16:30 depending on caseload, closed Sat-Sun, reduced hours in Aug; no kids under 14; no bags, mobile phones, cameras, iPods, or food, but small purses OK; Eddie, at Bailey's Café across the street at #27, stores bags for £2; 2 blocks northwest of St. Paul's on Old Bailey Street, follow signs to public entrance, Tube: St. Paul's, tel. 020/7248-3277.

▲**Museum of London**—This museum tells the fascinating story of London, taking you on a walk from its pre-Roman beginnings to the present. It features London's distinguished citizens through history—from Neanderthals, to Romans, to Elizabethans, to Victorians, to Mods, to today. The museum's displays are chronological, spacious, and informative without being overwhelming. Scale models and costumes help you visualize everyday life in the city at different periods. In the last room, you'll see the museum's prized possession: the Lord Mayor's Coach, a golden carriage pulled by six white horses, looking as if it pranced right out of the pages of *Cinderella*. There are enough whiz-bang multimedia displays (including ones on the Plague and the Great Fire) to spice up otherwise humdrum artifacts. This regular stop for the local school kids gives the best overview of London history in town.

Cost and Hours: Free, daily 10:00-18:00, galleries shut down 30 minutes before closing, see the day's events board for special talks and tours, on London Wall at Aldersgate Street, Tube: Barbican or St. Paul's plus a five-minute walk, tel. 020/7814-5530 or 020/7001-9844, www.museumoflondon.org.uk.

The Monument—Wren's 202-foot-tall tribute to London's Great Fire was recently restored. Climb the 331 steps inside the column for a view of The City that is still monumental.

Cost and Hours: £3, daily 9:30-17:30, last entry at 17:00, junction of Monument Street and Fish Street Hill, Tube: Monument, tel. 020/7626-2717, www.themonument.info.

▲▲▲Tower of London

The Tower has served as a castle in wartime, a king's residence in peacetime, and, most notoriously, as the prison and execution site of rebels. You can see the crown jewels, take a witty Beefeater tour, and ponder the executioner's block that dispensed with Anne Boleyn, Sir Thomas More, and troublesome heirs to the throne.

Cost and Hours: £18, family-£50, entry fee includes Beefeater tour (described later), skip the £4 audioguide; March-Oct Tue-Sat 9:00-17:30, Sun-Mon 10:00-17:30; Nov-Feb Tue-Sat 9:00-16:30, Sun-Mon 10:00-16:30; last entry 30 minutes before closing; Tube: Tower Hill, switchboard tel. 0844-482-7777, www.hrp.org.uk.

Advance Tickets: To avoid the long ticket-buying lines at the Tower, buy your ticket at the Trader's Gate gift shop, located down the steps from the Tower Hill Tube stop; at the Tower Welcome Centre to the left of the normal ticket lines (credit card only); or at any London TI at no extra cost. It's also easy to book online (www.hrp.org.uk, £1 discount, no fee) or by phone (tel. 0844-482-7799 within UK or tel. 011-44-20-3166-6000 from the US, £2 fee), then pick up your tickets at the Tower.

More Crowd-Beating Tips: It's most crowded in summer, on weekends (especially Sundays), and during school holidays. Any time of year, the line for the crown jewels—the best on earth—can be just as long as the line for tickets. For fewer crowds, arrive before 10:00 and go straight for the jewels, then tour the rest of the Tower. Crowds die down after 16:30.

Yeoman Warder (Beefeater) Tours: Today, while the Tower's military purpose is history, it's still home to the Beefeaters—the 35 Yeoman Warders and their families. (The original duty of the

Yeoman Warders was to guard the Tower, its prisoners, and the jewels.) The free, worthwhile, one-hour Beefeater tours leave every 30 minutes from inside the gate (last one at 15:30, 14:30 in winter, they take a midday lunch break). The boisterous Beefeaters are great entertainers, and their talks include lots of bloody anecdotes about the Tower and its history.

Sunday Worship: For a refreshingly different Tower experience, come on Sunday mornings, when visitors are welcome on the grounds for free to worship in the Royal Chapel. You get in without the lines, but you can only see the chapel—no sightseeing (9:15 Communion or 11:00 service with fine choral music, meet at west gate 30 minutes early, dress for church, may be closed for ceremonies—call ahead).

Visiting the Tower: William I, still getting used to his new title of "the Conqueror," built the stone "White Tower" (1077–1097) to keep the Londoners in line. The Tower also served as an effective lookout for seeing invaders coming up the Thames. His successors enlarged it to its present 18-acre size. Because of the security it provided, it has served over the centuries as the Royal Mint, the Royal Jewel House, and as a prison and execution site.

The Tower's hard stone and glittering jewels represent the ultimate power of the monarch. The crown jewels include the world's largest cut diamond—the 530-carat Star of Africa—placed in the royal scepter. When Queen Elizabeth II opens Parliament, she checks out the Imperial State Crown with its 3,733 jewels, including Elizabeth I's pearl earrings.

You'll find more bloody history per square inch in this original tower of power than anywhere else in Britain, though the actual execution site (in the courtyard) looks just like a lawn. Not all prisoners died at the block—Richard III supposedly ordered two teenage princes strangled in their prison cells because they were a threat to his throne.

Near the Tower of London

Tower Bridge—The iconic Tower Bridge (often mistakenly called London Bridge) has been recently painted and restored. The hydraulically powered drawbridge was built in 1894 to accommodate the growing East End. While fully modern, its design has a retro Neo-Gothic look.

You can tour the bridge at the **Tower Bridge Exhibition,** with a history display and a peek at the Victorian engine room that lifts the span. It's overpriced at £8, though the city views from the walkways are spectacular (daily 10:00-18:00 in summer, 9:30-17:30 in winter, last entry 30 minutes before closing, enter at the northwest tower, Tube: Tower Hill, tel. 020/7403-3761, www.towerbridge.org.uk).

LONDON

The bridge is most interesting when the drawbridge lifts to let ships pass, as it does a thousand times a year, but it's best viewed from outside the museum. For the bridge-lifting schedule, check the website or call (see above for contact info).

Nearby: The best remaining bit of London's **Roman Wall** is just north of the Tower (at the Tower Hill Tube station). The chic **St. Katharine Dock,** just east of Tower Bridge, has private yachts, mod shops, the Medieval Banquet (see page 750), and the classic Dickens Inn, fun for a drink or pub lunch. Across the bridge is the South Bank, with the upscale Butlers Wharf area, City Hall, museums, and the Jubilee Walkway.

Sights in East London

▲**East End**—This formerly industrial area just beyond the Liverpool Street train and Tube stations has turned into one of London's trendy spots. It boasts a colorful mix of bustling markets, late-night dance clubs, the Bangladeshi ghetto (called "Banglatown"), and tenements of Jack the Ripper's London, all in the shadow of glittering new skyscrapers. Head up Brick Lane for a meal in "the curry capital of Europe," or check out the former Truman Brewery, which now houses a Sunday market, cool shops, and Café 1001 (good coffee). This neighborhood is best on Sunday afternoons, when the Spitalfields, Petticoat Lane, and Brick Lane markets thrive.

▲**Geffrye Museum**—This low-key but well-organized museum—housed in an 18th-century almshouse northeast of The City—is located north of Liverpool Street Station in the hip Shoreditch area. Walk past 11 English living rooms, furnished and decorated in styles from 1600 to 2000, then descend the circular stairs to see changing exhibits on home decor. In summer, explore the fragrant herb garden.

Cost and Hours: Free, Tue-Sat 10:00-17:00, Sun 12:00-17:00, closed Mon, garden open April-Oct, 136 Kingsland Road, tel. 020/7739-9893, www.geffrye-museum.org.uk.

Getting There: Take the Tube to Liverpool Street, then it's a 10-minute ride north on bus #149 or #242. Or take the East London line on the Overground to the Hoxton stop, which is right next to the museum (Tube tickets and Oyster cards also valid on Overground).

Sights on the South Bank

▲**Jubilee Walkway**—The South Bank is a thriving arts and cultural center tied together by this riverside path, a popular, pub-crawling pedestrian promenade called the Jubilee Walkway.

Stretching from Tower Bridge past Westminster Bridge, it offers grand views of the Houses of Parliament and St. Paul's. On a sunny day, this is the place to see London out strolling. The Walkway hugs the river except just east of London Bridge, where it cuts inland for a couple of blocks. Plans are under way to expand the path into a 60-mile "Greenway" that will circle the city.

▲▲**London Eye**—This giant Ferris wheel, towering above London opposite Big Ben, is the world's highest observational wheel and London's answer to the Eiffel Tower. While the experience is memorable, London doesn't have much of a skyline, and the price is borderline outrageous. But whether you ride or not, the wheel is a sight to behold.

The experience starts with a brief (four-minute), engaging show combining a 3-D movie with wind and water effects. Then it's time to spin around the Eye. Designed like a giant bicycle wheel, it's a pan-European undertaking: British steel and Dutch engineering, with Czech, German, French, and Italian mechanical parts. It's also very "green," running extremely efficiently and virtually silently. Twenty-five people ride in each of its 32 air-conditioned capsules for the 30-minute rotation (you go around only once). Each capsule has a bench, but most people stand. From the top of this 443-foot-high wheel—the highest public viewpoint in the city—even Big Ben looks small.

Cost: £19, or pay roughly twice as much for a combo-ticket with Madame Tussauds Waxworks (sold cheaper online), other packages available. Buy tickets at the box office (in the corner of the County Hall building nearest the Eye), in advance by calling 0870-500-0600, or save 10 percent by booking online at www .londoneye.com.

Hours: Daily July-Aug 10:00-21:30, April-June 10:00-21:00, Sept-March 10:00-20:00, these are last-ascent times, closed Dec 25 and a few days in Jan for annual maintenance, Tube: Waterloo or Westminster. Thames boats come and go from Waterloo Pier at the foot of the wheel.

Crowd-Beating Tips: The London Eye is busiest between 11:00 and 17:00, especially on weekends year-round and every day in July and August. When it's crowded, you might have to wait up to 30 minutes to buy your ticket, then another 30-45 minutes to board your capsule. If you plan to visit during a busy time, call ahead or go online to pre-book your ticket, then punch your confirmation code into the automated machine in the ticket office (no wait to get the ticket, but you'll still wait to board the wheel). You can pay an extra £10 for a Fast Track ticket that lets you jump the queue, but the time you save is probably not worth the expense.

The South Bank

Southwark

These sights are in Southwark (SUTH-uck), the core of the tourist's South Bank. Southwark was for centuries the place Londoners
would go to escape the rules and decency of the city and let their
hair down. Bearbaiting, brothels, rollicking pubs, and theater—you
name the dream, and it could be fulfilled just across the Thames.
A run-down warehouse district through the 20th century, it's been
gentrified with classy restaurants, office parks, pedestrian promenades, major sights (such as the Tate Modern and Shakespeare's
Globe), and a colorful collection of lesser sights. The area is easy on
foot and a scenic—though circuitous—way to connect the Tower
of London with St. Paul's.

▲▲**Imperial War Museum**—This impressive museum covers the
wars of the last century—from World War I biplanes, to the rise of
fascism, to Montgomery's Africa campaign tank, to the Cold War,
the Cuban Missile Crisis, the Troubles in Northern Ireland, the
wars in Iraq, and terrorism. Rather than glorify war, the museum
does its best to shine a light on the 100 million deaths of the 20th
century. It shows everyday life for people back home and never
neglects the powerful human side of one of humankind's most per-

sistent traits. Allow plenty of time, as this powerful museum—with lots of artifacts and video clips—can be engrossing. War wonks love the place, as do general history buffs who enjoy patiently reading displays. For the rest, there are enough multimedia exhibits and submarines for the kids to climb in to keep it interesting.

Cost and Hours: Free, daily 10:00-18:00, last entry 17:45, temporary exhibits extra, £4 audioguide, often guided tours on weekends—ask at info desk, Tube: Lambeth North, bus #12 or #159, tel. 020/7416-5000, www.iwm.org.uk.

Visiting the Museum: The core of the **permanent collection,** located downstairs, takes you step-by-step through World Wars I and II. A special exhibit called "Monty: Master of the Battlefield" celebrates Field Marshal Bernard Montgomery. Then you move on to conflicts since 1945. Most of the displays are low-tech—glass cases hold dummies in uniforms, weapons, newspaper clippings, ordinary objects from daily life—but have excellent explanations and video clips. The Trench Experience lets you walk through a dark, chaotic, smelly WWI trench. The Blitz Experience film assaults the senses with the noise and intensity of a WWII air raid on London. Also, the cinema shows a rotating selection of films.

In the entry hall are the **large exhibits**—including Monty's tank, several field guns, and, dangling overhead, vintage planes. Imagine the awesome power of the 50-foot V-2 rocket, the kind the Nazis rained down on London, which could arrive silently and destroy a city block. Its direct descendant was the Polaris missile, capable of traveling nearly 3,000 miles in 20 minutes and obliterating an entire city.

Two other sections are not to be missed: The **"Secret War"** peeks into the intrigues of espionage in World Wars I and II and in conflicts since. The section on the **Holocaust,** one of the best on the subject anywhere, tells the story with powerful videos, artifacts, and fine explanations.

The museum (which sits in an inviting park equipped with an equally inviting café) is housed in what was the Royal Bethlam Hospital. Also known as "the Bedlam asylum," the place was so wild that it gave the world a new word for chaos. Back in Victorian times, locals—without reality shows and YouTube—paid admission to visit the asylum on weekends for entertainment.

▲▲**Tate Modern**—Dedicated in the spring of 2000, the striking museum across the river from St. Paul's opened the new century with art from the previous one. Its powerhouse collection of Monet, Matisse, Dalí, Picasso, Warhol, and much more is displayed in a converted powerhouse.

The permanent collection is on the third and fifth floors. Paintings are arranged according to theme, not chronologically or by artist. Paintings by Picasso, for example, are scattered all over the building. Don't just come to see the Old Masters of modernism. Push your mental envelope with more recent works by Pollock, Miró, Bacon, Picabia, Beuys, Twombly, and others.

Of equal interest are the many temporary exhibits featuring cutting-edge art. Each year, the main hall features a different monumental installation by a prominent artist—always one of the highlights of the art world. Note that the Tate is constructing an expansion wing to the south, which will double its exhibition space.

Cost and Hours: Free, £3 donations appreciated, varying costs for temporary exhibits, £3.50 audioguide; daily 10:00-18:00, Fri-Sat until 22:00, last entry to temporary exhibitions 45 minutes before closing, museum especially crowded on weekend days (crowds thin out on Fri and Sat evenings); free 45-minute guided tours offered daily on Level 3 at 11:00 and 12:00, and on Level 5 at 14:00 and 15:00 (confirm at info desk); tel. 020/7887-8888, www.tate.org.uk.

Getting There: Cross the Millennium Bridge from St. Paul's; take Tube to Southwark, London Bridge, or Mansion House and walk 10-15 minutes; or connect by "Tate to Tate" boat from Tate

Britain (£5.50 one-way or £12.60 for day ticket, 33 percent discount with Travelcard, buy ticket on board, departs every 40 minutes from 9:55 to 17:00, 18 minutes, check schedule at www.tate .org.uk/tatetotate).

▲**Millennium Bridge**—The pedestrian bridge links St. Paul's Cathedral and the Tate Modern across the Thames. This is London's first new bridge in a century. When it first opened, the $25 million bridge wiggled when people walked on it, so it promptly closed for an $8 million, 20-month stabilization; now it's stable and open again. Nicknamed the "blade of light" for its sleek minimalist design (370 yards long, four yards wide, stainless steel with teak planks), its clever aerodynamic handrails deflect wind over the heads of pedestrians.

▲▲**Shakespeare's Globe**—This replica of the original Globe Theatre was built, half-timbered and thatched, as it was in Shakespeare's time. (This is the first thatched roof constructed in London since they were outlawed after the Great Fire of 1666.) The Globe originally accommodated 2,200 seated patrons and another 1,000 standing. Today, slightly smaller and leaving space for reasonable aisles, the theater holds 800 seated and 600 groundlings. Its promoters brag that the theater melds "the three A's"—actors, audience, and architecture—with each contributing to the play. The working theater hosts authentic performances of Shakespeare's plays with actors in period costumes, modern interpretations of his works, and some works by other playwrights. For details on attending a play, see page 715.

The complex has three parts: the theater itself, the box office, and a museum. The Globe Exhibition ticket includes both a tour of the theater and the museum.

Museum: First, you browse on your own through displays of Elizabethan-era costumes, music, script-printing, and special effects. There are early folios and objects that were dug up on site. A video and scale models help put Shakespearean theater within the context of the times. (The Globe opened one year after England mastered the seas by defeating the Spanish Armada. The debut play was Shakespeare's *Julius Caesar*.)

Theater: You must tour the theater at the time stamped on your ticket, but you can come back to the museum afterward; tickets are good all day. The guide (usually an actor) leads you into the theater to see the stage and the various seating areas for the different classes of people. You take a seat and learn how the new Globe is similar to the old Globe (open-air performances, standing-room by the stage, no curtain) and how it's different (female actors today, lights for night performances, concrete floor). It's not a backstage tour—you don't see dressing rooms or costume shops or sit in on rehearsals, though you may see workers building sets for a new production. You mostly sit and listen. The guides are energetic, theatrical, and knowledgeable, bringing the Elizabethan period to life.

When matinee performances are going on, you can't tour the theater. But you can see the museum, then tour the nearby (and less interesting) Rose Theatre instead.

Cost and Hours: £11.50 includes museum and 40-minute tour, £9 when only the Rose Theatre is available for touring, tickets good all day; complex open daily 9:00-17:00; exhibition and tours: May-Sept—Globe tours offered mornings only with Rose Theatre tours in afternoon; Oct-April—Globe tours run all day, tours start every 15-30 minutes; on the South Bank directly across Thames over Southwark Bridge from St. Paul's, Tube: Mansion House or London Bridge plus a 10-minute walk; tel. 020/7902-1400 or 020/7902-1500, www.shakespeares-globe.org.

Eating: The Swan at the Globe café offers a sit-down restaurant (for lunch and dinner, reservations recommended, tel. 020/7928-9444), a drinks-and-plates bar, and a sandwich-and-coffee cart (daily 9:00-closing, depending on performance times).

Vinopolis: City of Wine—While it seems illogical to have a huge wine museum in beer-loving London, Vinopolis makes a good case. Built over a Roman wine store and filling the massive vaults of an old wine warehouse, the museum offers an excellent audioguide with a light yet earnest history of wine to accompany your sips of various mediocre reds and whites, ports, and champagnes. Allow some time, as the audioguide takes an hour and a half—and the sipping can slow things down pleasantly. This place is popular. Booking ahead for Friday and Saturday nights is a must.

Cost and Hours: Self-guided tour options range from £20 to £40—each includes about five wine tastes and an audioguide. Other options are available for guided tours. Some packages also include whiskey (the new wine), other spirits, or a meal. Open Thu-Fri 14:00-22:00, Sat 12:00-22:00, Sun 12:00-18:00, closed Mon-Wed, last entry 2.5 hours before closing, between Shakespeare's Globe and Southwark Cathedral at 1 Bank End, Tube: London Bridge, tel. 020/7940-3000, www.vinopolis.co.uk.

The Clink Prison Museum—Proudly the "original clink," this was, until 1780, where law-abiding citizens threw Southwark troublemakers. Today, it's a low-tech torture museum filling grotty old rooms with papier-mâché gore. Unfortunately, there's little that seriously deals with the fascinating problem of law and order in Southwark, where 18th-century Londoners went for a good time.

Cost and Hours: Overpriced at £6; July-Sept daily 10:00-21:00; Oct-June Mon-Fri 10:00-18:00, Sat-Sun until 19:30; 1 Clink Street, Tube: London Bridge, tel. 020/7403-0900, www.clink.co.uk.

Golden Hinde **Replica**—This is a full-size replica of the 16th-century warship in which Sir Francis Drake circumnavigated the globe from 1577 to 1580. Commanding this ship, Drake earned his reputation as history's most successful pirate. The original is long gone, but this boat has logged more than 100,000 miles, including a voyage around the world. While the ship is fun to see, its interior is not worth touring.

Cost and Hours: £6, daily 10:00-17:30, sometimes closed for private events, Tube: London Bridge, tel. 020/7403-0123, www.goldenhinde.com.

Southwark Cathedral—While made a cathedral only in 1905, it's been the neighborhood church since the 13th century, and comes with some interesting history. The enthusiastic docents give impromptu tours if you ask.

Cost and Hours: Free, but £4 suggested donation, daily 8:00-18:00, last entry 30 minutes before closing, £2.50 guidebook, no photos without permission, Tube: London Bridge. Tel. 020/7367-6700, http://cathedral.southwark.anglican.org.

Music: The cathedral hosts evensong services (Mon-Tue and Thu-Fri at 17:30, Sat at 16:00, Sun at 15:00, no service on Wed or alternate Mon).

▲**Old Operating Theatre Museum and Herb Garret**—Climb a tight and creaky wooden spiral staircase to a church attic where you'll find a garret used to dry medicinal herbs, a fascinating exhibit on Victorian surgery, cases of well-described 19th-century medical paraphernalia, and a special look at "anesthesia, the defeat of pain." Then you stumble upon Britain's oldest operating theater, where limbs were sawed off way back in 1821. The museum occasionally offers "demonstrations." While fun and interesting to some, they can be distressing to those who are squeamish or have a vivid imagination.

Cost and Hours: £6, cash only, daily 10:30-16:45, closed Dec 15-Jan 5, 9a St. Thomas Street, Tube: London Bridge, tel. 020/7188-2679, www.thegarret.org.uk.

HMS *Belfast*—"The last big-gun armored warship of World War II" clogs the Thames just upstream from the Tower Bridge. This huge vessel—now manned with wax sailors—thrills kids who always dreamed of sitting in a turret shooting off their imaginary guns. If you're into WWII warships, this is the ultimate. Otherwise, it's just lots of exercise with a nice view of the Tower Bridge.

Cost and Hours: £13.50, includes audioguide, daily March-Oct 10:00-18:00, Nov-Feb 10:00-17:00, last entry one hour before closing, Tube: London Bridge, tel. 020/7940-6300, http://hms belfast.iwm.org.uk.

City Hall—The glassy, egg-shaped building near the south end of Tower Bridge is London's City Hall, designed by Sir Norman

Foster, the architect who worked on London's Millennium Bridge and Berlin's Reichstag. City Hall houses the office of London's mayor—the blonde, flamboyant, conservative former journalist and author Boris Johnson. He consults here with the Assembly representatives of the city's 25 districts. An interior spiral ramp allows visitors to watch and hear the action below in the Assembly Chamber—ride the lift to the second floor (the highest visitors can go) and spiral down. On the lower ground floor is a large aerial photograph of London, an information desk, and a handy cafeteria. Next to City Hall is the outdoor amphitheater called The Scoop.

Cost and Hours: Free, open to visitors Mon-Thu 8:30-18:00, Fri 8:30-17:30, closed Sat-Sun; Tube: London Bridge station plus 10-minute walk, or Tower Hill station plus 15-minute walk; tel. 020/7983-4000, www.london.gov.uk.

Sights in West London

▲▲**Tate Britain**—One of Europe's great art houses, Tate Britain specializes in British painting from the 16th century through modern times. This is people's art, with realistic paintings rooted in the culture, landscape, and stories of the British Isles. But the museum is undergoing renovation, and during this time, much of the permanent collection has been stored. Fortunately, a few paintings are on display in a single room, labeled "Key Works from the Historic Collection."

Look for Hogarth's sketches of gritty London life, Gainsborough's twinkle-toe ladies, Blake's glowing angels, Constable's clouds, the swooning realism of the Pre-Raphaelites, and room after room of J. M. W. Turner's proto-Impressionist tempests. In the modern art wing there are Francis Bacon's screaming nightmares, Henry Moore statues, and the camera-eye portraits of Hockney and Freud.

Even if these names are new to you, don't worry. You'll likely see a few "famous" works you didn't know were British and exit the Tate Britain with at least one new favorite artist.

Cost and Hours: Free, but £3 donation requested, admission fee for (optional) temporary exhibits, £1 map, £3.50 audioguide; daily 10:00-18:00, first Fri of the month until 22:00, last entry to special exhibitions at 17:15 (or 21:00 when open late); free tours on various topics offered throughout the day—ask at information desk or call ahead; switchboard tel. 020/7887-8888, recorded info tel. 020/7887-8008, www.tate.org.uk.

Getting There: It's on the Thames River, south of Big Ben and north of Vauxhall Bridge. Take the Tube to Pimlico, then walk seven minutes. Or hop on the "Tate to Tate" boat from the Tate Modern (£5.50 one-way, £12.60 day ticket, 33 percent discount

West London

with a Travelcard, buy ticket on board, departs every 40 minutes from 10:00 to 17:00, 18 minutes, www.tate.org.uk/tatetotate).

▲**Apsley House (Wellington Museum)**—Having beaten Napoleon at Waterloo, Arthur Wellesley, the First Duke of Wellington, was once the most famous man in Europe. He was given a huge fortune with which he purchased London's ultimate address, #1 London. His refurbished mansion offers a nice interior, a handful of world-class paintings, and a glimpse at the life of the great soldier and two-time prime minister. The highlight is the large ballroom, the Waterloo Gallery, decorated with Anthony van Dyck's *Charles I on Horseback* (over the main fireplace), Diego Velázquez's earthy *The Water-Seller of Seville* (to the left of Van Dyck), Jan Steen's playful *The Dissolute Household* (to the right), and a large portrait of Wellington by Francisco Goya (farther right). Those who know something about Wellington ahead of time will appreciate the place much more than those who don't, as there's scarce biographical background. The place is well-described by the included audioguide, which has sound bites from the current Duke of Wellington (who still lives at Apsley).

Cost and Hours: £6.30, free on June 18—Waterloo Day, April-Oct Wed-Sun 11:00-17:00, closed Mon-Tue; Nov-March Sat-Sun 10:00-16:00, closed Mon-Fri; 20 yards from Hyde Park Corner Tube station, tel. 020/7499-5676, www.english-heritage .org.uk.

Nearby: Hyde Park's pleasant rose garden is picnic-friendly. **Wellington Arch,** which stands just across the street, is open to the public but not worth the £4 charge (elevator up, lousy views and boring exhibits).

▲**Hyde Park and Speakers' Corner**—London's "Central Park," originally Henry VIII's hunting grounds, has more than 600 acres of lush greenery, the huge man-made Serpentine Lake, the royal Kensington Palace and Orangery (described later), and the ornate Neo-Gothic Albert Memorial across from the Royal Albert Hall. The western half of the park is known as Kensington Gardens.

On Sundays, from just after noon until early evening, **Speakers' Corner** offers soapbox oratory at its best (northeast corner of the park, Tube: Marble Arch). Characters climb their stepladders, wave their flags, pound emphatically on their sandwich boards, and share what they are convinced is their wisdom. Regulars have resident hecklers who know their lines and are always ready with a verbal jab or barb. "The grass roots of democracy" is actually a holdover from when the gallows stood here and the criminal was allowed to say just about anything he wanted to before he swung. I dare you to raise your voice and gather a crowd—it's easy to do.

The **Princess Diana Memorial Fountain** honors the "People's Princess," who once lived in nearby Kensington Palace. The low-key circular stream, great for cooling off your feet on a hot day, is in the south-central part of the park, near the Albert Memorial and Serpentine Gallery. (Don't be confused by signs to the Diana, Princess of Wales Memorial Playground, in the northwest corner of the park.)

▲▲▲**Victoria and Albert Museum**—The world's top collection of decorative arts (vases, stained glass, fine furniture, clothing, jewelry, carpets, and more) is a surprisingly interesting assortment of crafts from the West, as well as from Asian and Islamic cultures. The British Galleries are grand, but there's much more to see, including Raphael's tapestry cartoons and a cast of Trajan's Column that depicts the emperor's conquests.

You'll also see one of Leonardo da Vinci's notebooks, underwear through the ages, a Chihuly chandelier, a life-size *David* with detachable fig leaf, Henry VIII's quill pen, and Mick Jagger's sequined jumpsuit. From the worlds of Islam and India, there are stunning carpets, the ring of the man who built the Taj Mahal, and a mechanical tiger that eats Brits.

Best of all, the objects are all quite beautiful. You could spend days in the place. Pick up a museum map and wander at will.

Cost and Hours: Free, but £5 donation requested, sometimes pricey fees for (optional) special exhibits, £1 suggested donation for much-needed museum map; daily 10:00-17:45, some galleries open Fri until 22:00, free one-hour tours daily on the half-hour 10:30-15:30; on Cromwell Road in South Kensington, Tube: South Kensington, from the Tube station a long tunnel leads directly to museum; tel. 020/7942-2000, www.vam.ac.uk.

▲▲**Natural History Museum**—Across the street from Victoria and Albert, this mammoth museum is housed in a giant and wonderful Victorian, Neo-Romanesque building. In the main hall, above a big dinosaur skeleton and under a massive slice of sequoia tree, Charles Darwin sits as if upon a throne overseeing it all. Built in the 1870s specifically for the huge collection (50 million specimens), the building has two halves: the Life Galleries (creepy-crawlies, human biology, "our place in evolution," and awe-inspiring dinosaurs) and the Earth Galleries (meteors, volcanoes, earthquakes, and so on).

Exhibits are wonderfully explained, with lots of creative, inter-active displays. Pop in, if only for the wild collection of dinosaurs and to hear English children exclaim, "Oh my goodness!" Get oriented by talking with one of the many "visit planners" (helpful guides scattered throughout the museum), review the "What's on Today" board for special events and tours, and note which sections are closed (rather than "renovating," they say "we are evolving"). While the dinosaur hall often has a long line, everything else is wide open. Don't miss the vault in the mineralogy section (top floor of the green zone), with rare and precious stones, including a meteorite from Mars and the Aurora Pyramid of Hope, displaying 296 diamonds showing their full range of natural colors.

Cost and Hours: Free, fees for special exhibits, daily 10:00-17:50, last entry at 17:30, occasional tours, long tunnel leads directly from South Kensington Tube station to museum, tel. 020/7942-5000, exhibit info and reservations tel. 020/7942-5011, www.nhm.ac.uk.

▲**Science Museum**—Next door to the Natural History Museum, this sprawling wonderland for curious minds is kid-perfect, with themes such as measuring time, exploring space, climate change, and the evolution of modern medicine. It offers hands-on fun, from moonwalks to deep-sea exploration, with trendy technology exhibits and a state-of-the-art IMAX theater (£10, kids-£8).

Cost and Hours: Free, daily 10:00-18:00, Exhibition Road, Tube: South Kensington, tel. 0870-870-4868, www.sciencemuseum.org.uk.

Kensington Palace—In the spring of 2012, this historic palace reopened after a major renovation. A new permanent exhibit, "Victoria Revealed," showcases the life and times of Britain's longest-ruling monarch. The palace was once the residence of King William and Queen Mary, who moved from Whitehall in central London in 1689 to the more pristine and peaceful village of Kensington (now engulfed by London). Sir Christopher Wren converted an existing house into the palace, which became the center of English court life until 1760, when the royal family moved into Buckingham Palace. Since then, lesser royals have bedded down in

Kensington Palace. Princess Diana lived here from her 1981 marriage to Prince Charles until her death in 1997. Today it's home to three of Charles' cousins.

Cost and Hours: £12.50, discounts for booking online, daily 10:00-18:00, until 17:00 in winter, last entry one hour before closing, a 10-minute hike through Kensington Gardens from either Queensway or High Street Kensington Tube station, tel. 0870-751-5170 or 0844-482-7777, www.hrp.org.uk.

Nearby: Garden enthusiasts enjoy popping into the secluded Sunken Garden, 50 yards from the exit. Consider afternoon tea at the nearby Orangery, built as a greenhouse for Queen Anne in 1704 (tea served 12:00–18:00, £15 "Orangery tea," £35 "Tregothnan tea," à la carte treats, no reservations taken, tel. 020/3166-6113).

Victoria Station—From underneath this station's iron-and-glass canopy, trains depart for the south of England and Gatwick Airport. While Victoria Station is famous and a major Tube stop, few tourists actually take trains from here—most just come to take in the exciting bustle. It's a fun place to just be a "rock in a river" teeming with commuters and services. The station is surrounded by big red buses and taxis, travel agencies, and lousy eateries. It's next to the main intercity bus station (Victoria Coach Station) and the best inexpensive lodgings in town.

Westminster Cathedral—This cathedral, the largest Catholic church in England and just a block from Victoria Station, is strikingly Neo-Byzantine, but not very historic or important to visit. Opened in 1903, the church has an unfinished interior, with a spooky, blackened ceiling waiting for the mosaics that are supposed to be placed there. While it's definitely not Westminster Abbey, half the tourists wandering around inside seem to think it is. Take the lift to the top of the 273-foot bell tower for a view of the glassy office blocks of Victoria Station.

Cost and Hours: Free entry, £5 for the lift, church—daily 7:00-19:00, tower—daily 9:30-17:00; 5-minute walk from Victoria Station, just off Victoria Street, Tube: Victoria, www.westminster cathedral.org.uk.

National Army Museum—This museum is not as awe-inspiring as the Imperial War Museum, but it's still fun, especially for kids who are into soldiers, armor, and guns. And while the Imperial War Museum is limited to wars of the 20th century, the National Army Museum tells the story of the British army from 1415 through the Bosnian conflict and Iraq, with lots of Redcoat lore and a good look at Waterloo. Kids enjoy trying on a Cromwellian helmet, seeing the skeleton of Napoleon's horse, and peering out from a World War I trench through a working periscope.

Cost and Hours: Free, daily 10:00-17:30, Royal Hospital

Road, Chelsea, Tube: Sloane Square, tel. 020/7730-0717, www
.national-army-museum.ac.uk.

Sights in Greater London

East of Central London

Olympic Park—From July 27 to August 12, 2012, all eyes were
on London as it hosted athletes from 205 nations in the 30th
Olympiad. Though events took place throughout the city, festivities centered around Olympic Park, filling the Lea Valley, about
seven miles northeast of central London. Olympic Park is huge—
bigger than Hyde Park/Kensington Gardens. It's also quite beautiful, laced with canals and tributaries of the Lea River.

Lea Valley used to be the site of derelict factories, mountains
of discarded tires, and Europe's biggest refrigerator dump. But
now, this area glistens with gardens, greenery, and state-of-the-
art buildings. The $14 billion project was a stimulus plan, with 90
percent local investment and employment.

Many of the buildings are being converted to housing, with
half of these units designated for low-income people. The commercial zone, Stratford City, will become the biggest shopping
center in Europe. Between the bullet trains, Tube, regional rail
services, and DLR, residents of post-Olympics Stratford enjoy the
best public transit in town, with multiple connections to central
London. (Don't confuse it with Stratford-upon-Avon, the famous
Warwickshire town where Shakespeare was born. That's two hours
northwest of London.)

Suddenly, Stratford is a place with a future (and poor little
grandmas who've called it home for years are now worth something to their relatives and developers...and now chocolate and
flowers appear on Sundays). It seems fitting that this most multi-
ethnic part of London hosted these famously multiethnic games.

Getting There: From central London, it's about a 25-minute
ride on the Tube and/or DLR to one of the stations that ring
Olympic Park.

To Tube Stations a Pleasant Stroll South of Olympic Park:
The West Ham Tube Station is three-quarters of a mile south of
Olympic Park. Though it's not close to the park, it's on the Tube
line, so you can get there directly from, say, Victoria Station, on
the District Line. Once at West Ham Station, you can walk along
a bike path to the park. The Bromley-by-Bow Tube Station is also
south of the park and also nearly a mile away; from the station,
stroll the paths along the River Lea to the park.

To the East Entrance of Olympic Park: There are two similarly
named stations, located 400 yards apart. The Stratford Station is

Greater London

RAF MUSEUM
LONDON

CAMDEN LOCK
MARKET

2012
OLYMPIC
PARK

LONDON
CITY
AIRPORT

TRAFALGAR
SQUARE

Hyde
Park

ST. PAUL'S

DOCKLANDS

To
Heathrow
Airport

Central London

TOWER OF
LONDON PIER

To
Windsor

BIG BEN

WATERLOO
PIER

O2
Arena

CANARY
WHARF
ON ISLE
OF DOGS

Greenwich

Thames

River

WESTMINSTER
PIER

Kew
Gardens

BRIXTON
MARKET

WIMBLEDON

To
Gatwick
Airport

= Central
London

HAMPTON
COURT
PALACE

5 Kilometers

5 Miles

both a Tube and DLR stop. The Stratford International Station serves the DLR and the new high-speed train.

West of Central London

▲▲Kew Gardens—For a fine riverside park and a palatial green-house jungle to swing through, take the Tube or the boat to every botanist's favorite escape, Kew Gardens. While to most visitors the Royal Botanic Gardens of Kew are simply a delightful opportunity to wander among 33,000 different types of plants, to the hard-working organization that runs the gardens, the Gardens are a way to promote understanding and preservation of the botanical diversity of our planet. The Kew Tube station drops you in an herbal little business community, a two-block walk from Victoria Gate (the main garden entrance). Pick up a map brochure and check at the gate for a monthly listing of best blooms.

Garden-lovers could spend days exploring Kew's 300 acres. For a quick visit, spend a fragrant hour wandering through three buildings: the Palm House, a humid Victorian world of iron, glass, and tropical plants that was built in 1844; a Waterlily House that Monet would swim for; and the Princess of Wales Conservatory, a modern greenhouse with many different climate zones growing countless cacti, bug-munching carnivorous plants, and more. With extra time, check out the Xstrata Treetop Walkway, a 200-yard-long scenic steel walkway that puts you high in the canopy 60 feet above the ground. Young kids will love the Climbers and Creepers indoor/outdoor playground and little zip line, as well as a slow and easy ride on the hop-on, hop-off Kew Explorer tram (£4 for narrated 40-minute ride, departs on the hour from 11:00 from near Victoria Gate).

Cost: £14, discounted to £11.50 45 minutes before greenhouses close, kids under 17 free, £5 for Kew Palace only.

Hours: April-Aug Mon-Fri 9:30-18:30, Sat-Sun 9:30-19:30, closes earlier Sept-March, last entry to gardens 30 minutes before closing, galleries and conservatories close at 17:30 in high season—earlier off-season, free one-hour walking tours daily at 11:00 and 14:00, Tube: Kew Gardens, boats run April-Oct between Kew Gardens and Westminster Pier—see page 669, switchboard tel. 020/8332-5000, recorded info tel. 020/8332-5655, www.kew.org.

Eating: For a sun-dappled lunch or snack, walk 10 minutes from the Palm House to the Orangery Cafeteria (£8-12 lunches, daily 10:00-17:30, until 16:30 in winter, closes early for events, tel. 0844-482-7777 www.hrp.org.uk).

North of Central London

Highgate Cemetery—Located in the tea-cozy-cute village of Highgate, north of the city, this Victorian cemetery represents a fascinating, offbeat piece of London history. Built as a private cemetery, this was the fashionable place to bury the wealthy dead in the late 1800s. It has themed mausoleums, professional mourners, and several high-profile residents in its East Cemetery, including Karl Marx, George Eliot, and Douglas Adams. The tomb of the "Godfather of Punk," Malcolm McLaren (former manager of the Sex Pistols), is often covered with rotten veggies.

Cost and Hours: East Cemetery—£3, Mon-Fri 10:00-17:00, Sat-Sun 11:00-17:00, closes one hour earlier in winter, last entry 30 minutes before closing; older, creepier West Cemetery—viewable by £7 guided tour only, Mon-Fri at 14:00, Sat-Sun hourly 11:00-16:00; Tube: Archway or bus #C2, tel. 020/8340-1834, www.highgate-cemetery.org.

Entertainment in London

For the best list of what's happening and a look at the latest London scene, pick up a current copy of *Time Out* (£3, www.timeout.com). The TI's free monthly *London Planner* covers sights, events, and plays at least as well as *Time Out*.

Theater (a.k.a. "Theatre")

London's theater rivals Broadway's in quality and usually beats it in price. Choose from around 200 offerings—Shakespeare, musicals, comedies, thrillers, sex farces, cutting-edge fringe, revivals starring movie celebs, and more. London does it all well. I prefer

LONDON

London's Major Theaters

1. To Apollo Victoria & Victoria Palace
2. Cambridge
3. Dominion
4. Garrick
5. Her Majesty's
6. Lyceum
7. Prince Edward
8. Prince of Wales
9. Queen's
10. Wyndham's

big, glitzy—even bombastic—musicals over serious chamber dramas, simply because London can deliver the lights, sound, dancers, and multimedia spectacle I rarely get back home. (If you're a regular visitor to Broadway or Las Vegas—where you have access to similar spectacles—you might prefer some of London's more low-key offerings.)

There are also plenty of enticing plays to choose from, ranging from revivals of classics to cutting-edge works by the hottest young playwrights. Many star huge-name celebrities (you'll see the latest

offers advertised all over the Tube and elsewhere). London is a
magnet for movie stars who want to stretch their acting chops. For
example, since 2003, Kevin Spacey has been the artistic director of
the Old Vic theater. He has directed and appeared in several pro-
ductions, and has enlisted many big-name film directors and actors
for others (www.oldvictheatre.com).

Most theaters, marked on tourist maps, are found in the
West End between Piccadilly and Covent Garden. Box offices,
hotels, and TIs offer a handy free *Official London Theatre Guide* and

Entertainment Guide. From home, you can look online at www .officiallondontheatre.co.uk for the latest on what's currently playing in London.

Performances are nightly except Sunday, usually with one or two matinees a week (Shakespeare's Globe is the rare theater that does offer performances on Sun, late April-early Oct). Tickets range from about £15 to £60. Matinees are generally cheaper and rarely sell out.

Buying Theater Tickets

To book a seat, simply call the theater box office (which may ring through to a central ticketing office), ask about seats and available dates, and buy a ticket with your credit card. You can call from the US as easily as from England. Arrive about 30 minutes before the show starts to pick up your ticket and avoid lines. (For money-saving tips, see "Cheap Theater Tricks" and "Discount 'tkts' Booth," next page.)

For a booking fee, you can reserve online on theater websites. Most link you to a preferred ticket vendor, usually www.ticket master.co.uk or www.seetickets.com. In the US, Keith Prowse Ticketing is also handy by phone or online (US tel. 212/398-4175, http://www.keithprowse.com/tickets/slink.buy).

Although booking through an agency is quick and easy, prices are inflated by a standard 25 percent fee. Ticket agencies (whether in the US, at London's TIs, or scattered throughout the city) are scalpers with an address. If you're buying from an agency, look at the ticket carefully (your price should be no more than 30 percent over the printed face value; the 20 percent VAT is already included in the face value), and understand where you're sitting according to the floor plan (if your view is restricted, it will state this on the ticket; for floor plans of the various theaters, see www.theatre monkey.com).

Agencies are worthwhile only if a show you've just got to see is sold out at the box office. They scarf up hot tickets, planning to make a killing after the show is sold. US booking agencies get their tickets from another agency, adding even more to your expense by involving yet another middleman. Many tickets sold on the street are forgeries. Although some theaters use booking agencies to handle their advance sales, you'll stand a good chance of saving money by avoiding the middleman and simply calling the box office directly to purchase your tickets (international phone calls are cheap, and credit cards make booking a snap).

Theater Lingo: It's helpful to know these terms when booking tickets—stalls (ground floor), dress circle (first balcony), upper circle (second balcony), balcony (sky-high third balcony), slips (cheap seats on the fringes). Many cheap seats have a restricted view (behind a pillar).

Cheap Theater Tricks: Some theater box offices sell half-price tickets on the day of the performance ("tkts"—described next—can tell you which ones); line up before the box office opens—usually 10:00 or 10:30. Most theaters offer cheap returned tickets, standing-room, matinee, and senior or student standby deals. These "concessions" (discounted tickets) are indicated with a "conc" or "s" in the listings. Picking up a late return can get you a great seat at a cheap-seat price. Even if a show is "sold out," there's usually a way to get a seat. Call the theater box office and ask how.

If you don't care where you sit, you can often buy the absolutely cheapest seats—those with an obstructed view or in the nosebleed section—at the box office; these tickets generally cost less than £20. Many theaters are so small that there's hardly a bad seat. After the lights go down, scooting up is less than a capital offense. Shakespeare did it.

Discount "tkts" Booth: This famous ticket booth at Leicester (LESS-ter) Square sells discounted tickets for top-price seats to shows on the day of the performance and up to a week in advance (generally £3 service charge per ticket, Mon-Sat 10:00-19:00, Sun 11:00-16:00, lines often form early, list of shows available online at www.tkts.co.uk). Most tickets are half-price; other shows are discounted 25 percent, and some are full price (no service charge for full-price shows). Note that this ticket booth (with its "tkts" name) is a freestanding kiosk at the edge of the garden in Leicester Square. Several dishonest outfits nearby advertise "official half-price tickets"—avoid these.

Here are sample prices: A top-notch seat to *Chicago* costs £59 if you buy directly from the theater; the same seat costs £32.50 at Leicester Square. The cheapest balcony seat is £25 through the theater. Half-price tickets can be a good deal, unless you want the cheapest seats or the hottest shows. But check the board; occasionally they sell cheap tickets to good shows.

Theater Options

West End Theaters: The commercial (nonsubsidized) theaters cluster around Soho (especially along Shaftesbury Avenue) and Covent Garden. With a centuries-old tradition of pleasing the masses, these present London theater at its glitziest.

Royal Shakespeare Company: If you'll ever enjoy Shakespeare, it'll be in Britain. The RSC performs at various theaters around London and in Stratford-upon-Avon year-round. To get a schedule, contact the RSC (Royal Shakespeare Theatre, Stratford-upon-Avon, tel. 0844-800-1110, www.rsc.org.uk).

Shakespeare's Globe: To see Shakespeare in a replica of the theater for which he wrote his plays, attend a play at the Globe.

LONDON

In this round, thatch-roofed, open-air theater, the plays are performed much as Shakespeare intended—under the sky and with no amplification.

The play's the thing from late April through early October (usually Mon 19:30, Tue-Sat 14:00 and 19:30, Sun either 13:00 and/or 18:30, tickets can be sold out months in advance). You'll pay £5 to stand and £15-35 to sit, usually on a backless bench. Because only a few rows and the pricier Gentlemen's Rooms have seats with backs, £1 cushions and £3 add-on back rests are considered a good investment by many. Dress for the weather.

The £5 "groundling" tickets—which are open to rain—are most fun. Scurry in early to stake out a spot on the stage's edge, where the most interaction with the actors occurs. You're a crude peasant. You can lean your elbows on the stage, munch a picnic dinner (yes, you can bring in food), or walk around. I've never enjoyed Shakespeare as much as here, performed as it was meant to be in the "wooden O." If you can't get a ticket, consider waiting around. Plays can be long, and many groundlings leave before the end. Hang around outside and beg or buy a ticket from someone leaving early (groundlings are allowed to come and go). A few non-Shakespeare plays are also presented each year. If you can't attend a show, you can take a guided tour of the theater and museum by day (see page 701).

To reserve tickets for plays, call or drop by the theater box office (Mon-Sat 10:00-18:00, Sun 10:00-17:00, open one hour later on performance days, New Globe Walk entrance, no extra charge to book by phone, tel. 020/7401-9919). You can also reserve online (www.shakespeares-globe.org, £2 booking fee). If the tickets are sold out, don't despair; a few often free up at the last minute. Try calling around noon the day of the performance to see if the box office expects any returned tickets. If so, they'll advise you to show up a little more than an hour before the show, when these tickets are sold (first-come, first-served).

The theater is on the South Bank, directly across the Thames over the Millennium Bridge from St. Paul's Cathedral (Tube: Mansion House or London Bridge). The Globe is inconvenient for public transport, but the courtesy phone in the lobby lets you get a minicab in minutes. (These minicabs have set fees—e.g., £8 to South Kensington—but generally cost less than a metered cab and provide fine and honest service.) During theater season, there's a regular supply of black cabs outside the main foyer on New Globe Walk.

Outdoor Theater in Summer: Enjoy Shakespearean drama and other plays under the stars at the Open Air Theatre, in leafy Regent's Park in north London. Food is allowed: You can bring your own picnic; order à la carte from the theater menu; or preorder a £25 picnic supper from the theater at least 48 hours in advance (tickets £12-50; season runs late May-mid-Sept, box office open April-late May Mon-Sat 10:00-18:00, closed Sun; late May-mid-Sept Mon-Sat 10:00-20:00, Sun 10:00-until start of play on performance days only; order tickets online after mid-Jan or by phone Mon-Sun 9:00-21:00; £1 booking fee by phone, no fee if ordering online or in person; tel. 0844-826-4242, www.open airtheatre.org; grounds open 1.5 hours prior to evening performances, one hour prior to 2:30 matinee, and 30 minutes prior to earlier matinees; 10-minute walk north of Baker Street Tube, near Queen Mary's Gardens within Regent's Park; detailed directions and more info at www.openairtheatre.org).

Fringe Theater: London's rougher evening-entertainment scene is thriving, filling pages in *Time Out*. Choose from a wide range of fringe theater and comedy acts (generally £5).

Classical Music
Concerts at Churches
For easy, cheap, or free concerts in historic churches, ask the TI (or check *Time Out*) about **lunch concerts,** especially:
- St. Bride's Church, with free lunch concerts twice a week at 13:15 (generally Tue, Wed, or Fri—confirm by phone or online, church tel. 020/7427-0133, www.stbrides.com).
- St. James's at Piccadilly, with 50-minute concerts on Mon, Wed, and Fri at 13:10 (suggested £3.50 donation, info tel. 020/7381-0441, www.st-james-piccadilly.org).
- St. Martin-in-the-Fields, offering concerts on Mon, Tue, and Fri at 13:00 (suggested £3.50 donation, church tel. 020/7766-1100, www.smitf.org).

St. Martin-in-the-Fields also hosts fine **evening concerts** by candlelight (£8-26, several nights a week at 19:30) and live jazz in its underground Café in the Crypt (£5-10 tickets, Wed at 20:00).

Evensong and Organ Recitals at Churches
Evensong services are held at several churches, including:
- St. Paul's Cathedral (Mon-Sat at 17:00, Sun at 15:15).
- Westminster Abbey (Mon-Tue and Thu-Fri at 17:00, Sat-Sun at 15:00 except Sat at 17:00 in summer; there's a service on Wed, but it may be spoken, not sung).
- Southwark Cathedral (Mon-Tue and Thu-Fri at 17:30, Sat at 16:00, Sun at 15:00, no service on Wed or alternate Mon, tel. 020/7367-6700, www.southwark.anglican.org/cathedral).

Free **organ recitals** are often held on Sunday at 17:45 in Westminster Abbey (30 minutes, tel. 020/7222-5152). Many other churches have free concerts.

LONDON

Performances

Prom Concerts: For a fun classical event (mid-July–mid-Sept), attend a Prom Concert (shortened from "Promenade Concert") during the annual festival at the Royal Albert Hall. Nightly concerts are offered at give-a-peasant-some-culture prices to "Promenaders"—those willing to stand throughout the performance (£5 standing-room spots sold at the door, £7 restricted-view seats, most £20-54 but depends on performance, Tube: South Kensington, tel. 0845-401-5045, www.bbc.co.uk/proms).

Opera: Some of the world's best opera is belted out at the prestigious Royal Opera House, near Covent Garden (box office tel. 020/7304-4000, www.roh.org.uk), and at the London Coliseum (English National Opera, St. Martin's Lane, Tube: Leicester Square, box office tel. 0871-911-0200, www.eno.org). Or consider taking in an unusual opera at King's Head Pub in Islington, home of London's Little Opera House (11 Upper Street, Tube: Angel, tel. 020/7478-0160, www.kingsheadtheatre.com).

Dance: Sadler's Wells Theatre features both international and UK-based dance troupes (Rosebery Avenue, Islington, Tube: Angel, info tel. 020/7863-8198, box office tel. 0844-412-4300, www.sadlerswells.com).

Sightseeing

Tours: Guided walks are offered several times a day. **London Walks** is the most established company. Daytime walks vary by theme: ancient London, museums, legal London, Dickens, Beatles, Jewish quarter, Christopher Wren, and so on. In the evening, expect a more limited choice: ghosts, Jack the Ripper, pubs, or literary-themed. Get the latest from their brochure or website, or call for a recorded listing of that day's walks. Show up at the listed time and place, pay the guide, and enjoy the two-hour tour (£8, cash only, tel. 020/7624-3978, recorded info tel. 020/7624-9255, www.walks.com).

To see the city illuminated at night, consider a bus tour. A two-hour **London by Night Sightseeing Tour** leaves every evening from Victoria Station and other points (see page 662).

Cruises: During the summer, boats sail as late as 19:00 between Westminster Pier (near Big Ben) and the Tower of London. (For details, see page 666.)

A handful of outfits run Thames River evening cruises with four-course meals and dancing. **London Showboat** offers the best value (£75, April-Oct Wed-Sun, March and Nov-Dec Thu-Sat, Jan-Feb Fri-Sat, 3.5 hours, departs at 19:30 from Westminster Pier and returns by 23:00, reservations necessary, tel. 020/7740-0400, www.citycruises.com). Dinner cruises are also offered by **Bateaux London** (£75-125, tel. 020/7695-1800, www.bateauxlondon.com).

For more on cruising, get the *River Thames Boat Services* brochure from a London TI.

Sleeping in London

London is an expensive city for rooms. Cheaper rooms are relatively dumpy. Don't expect £130 cheeriness in an £80 room. For £70, you'll get a double with breakfast in a safe, cramped, and dreary place with minimal service and the bathroom down the hall. For £90, you'll get a basic, clean, reasonably cheery double with a private bath in a usually cramped, cracked-plaster building, or a soulless but comfortable room without breakfast in a huge Motel 6-type place. My London splurges, at £160-290, are spacious, thoughtfully appointed places good for entertaining or romancing.

Reserve your London room as soon as you can commit to a date. To call a London hotel from the US or Canada, dial 011-44-20 (London's area code without the initial zero), then the local eight-digit number.

Looking for Hotel Deals Online: Given London's high hotel prices, using the Internet can help you score a deal. Various websites list rooms in high-rise, three- and four-star business hotels. You'll give up the charm and warmth of a family-run establishment, and breakfast probably won't be included, but you might find that the price is right.

Start by browsing the websites of several chains to get a sense of typical rates and online deals. For listings of no-frills, Motel 6-type places, see "Big, Good-Value, Modern Hotels," later.

Sleep Code

(£1 = about $1.60, country code: 44, area code: 020)
S = Single, **D** = Double/Twin, **T** = Triple, **Q** = Quad, **b** = bathroom, **s** = shower only. Unless otherwise noted, credit cards are accepted and prices include breakfast.

To help you sort through these listings easily, I've divided the accommodations into three categories, based on the price for a double room with bath:

$$$ **Higher Priced**—Most rooms £125 or more.
  $$ **Moderately Priced**—Most rooms between £75-125.
   $ **Lower Priced**—Most rooms £75 or less.

Prices can change without notice; verify the hotel's current rates online or by email. For other updates, see www.ricksteves.com/update.

London's Hotel Neighborhoods

EUSTON/ ST. PANCRAS/ KING'S CROSS

NORTH LONDON

Regent's Park

BAYSWATER

BRITISH MUSEUM

PADDINGTON

NOTTING HILL

Hyde Park

WEST END

MARBLE ARCH

TRAFALGAR SQUARE

THE CITY

TOWER OF LONDON

WEST LONDON

CENTRAL LONDON

ST. PAUL'S

VICTORIA STATION

WEST-MINSTER

SOUTH KENSINGTON

BIG BEN

SOUTH BANK

The Tube's Circle Line

LONDON EYE

Hotel Neighborhoods

Thames River

Pricier London hotel chains include Millennium/Copthorne (www.millenniumhotels.com), Thistle (www.thistle.com), Intercontinental/Holiday Inn (www.ichotelsgroup.com), Radisson (www.radisson.com), Hilton (www.hilton.com), and Red Carnation (www.redcarnationhotels.com).

Auction-type sites (such as www.priceline.com or www.hotwire.com) match flexible travelers with empty hotel rooms, often at prices well below the hotel's normal rates.

My readers report good experiences with these accommodation discount sites: www.londontown.com (an informative site with a discount booking service), http://athomeinlondon.co.uk and www.londonbb.com (both list central B&Bs), www.lastminute.com, www.visitlondon.com, http://roomsnet.com, and www.eurocheapo.com.

Victoria Station Neighborhood (Belgravia)

The streets behind Victoria Station teem with little, moderately priced-for-London B&Bs. It's a safe, surprisingly tidy, and decent area without a hint of the trashy, touristy glitz of the streets in front of the station. I've divided these accommodations into two broad categories: west or east of the station. Decent eateries abound in both areas (see page 746). All the recommended hotels are within a five-minute walk of the Victoria Tube, bus, and train stations. On hot summer nights, request a quiet back room.

Near the hotels on the west side is the 400-space Semley Place NCP **parking garage** (£34/day, possible discounts with hotel voucher, just west of the Victoria Coach Station at Buckingham Palace Road and Semley Place, tel. 0845-050-7080, www.ncp.co.uk). The best laundry options are on the east side: The handy **Pimlico Launderette** is about five blocks southwest of Warwick Square (daily 8:00-19:00, self- or full-service, south of Sutherland Street at 3 Westmoreland Terrace, tel. 020/7821-8692), and **Launderette Centre** is a block northeast of Warwick Square (Mon-Fri 8:00-21:00, Sat 8:00-19:00, Sun 9:00-20:00, last wash 2 hours before closing, about £7 wash and dry, £9 full-service, 31 Churton Street, tel. 020/7828-6039).

West of Victoria Station

Here in Belgravia, the prices are a bit higher and your neighbors include Andrew Lloyd Webber and Margaret Thatcher (her policeman stands outside 73 Chester Square). All of these places line up along tranquil Ebury Street, two blocks over from Victoria Station.

$$$ Lime Tree Hotel, enthusiastically run by Charlotte and Matt, comes with 25 spacious, stylish, comfortable, thoughtfully decorated rooms and a fun-loving breakfast room (Sb-£85-95, Db-£145, larger superior Db-£165, Tb-£190, family room-£205, free Internet access and Wi-Fi, small lounge opens onto quiet garden, 135 Ebury Street, tel. 020/7730-8191, www.limetreehotel .co.uk, info@limetreehotel.co.uk, trusty Alan covers the night shift).

$$ Cartref House B&B offers rare charm on Ebury Street, with 10 delightful rooms and a warm welcome (Sb-£82, Db-£115, Tb-£151, Qb-£185, fans, free Wi-Fi, 129 Ebury Street, tel. 020/7730-6176, www.cartrefhouse.co.uk, info@cartrefhouse .co.uk, Sharon and Derek).

$$ Morgan House, a great budget choice in this neighborhood, has 11 rooms and is entertainingly run, with lots of travel tips and friendly chat from owner Rachel Joplin and her staff (S-£58, D-£78, Db-£98, T-£98, family suites-£138-148 for 3-4 people, Wi-Fi, 120 Ebury Street, tel. 020/7730-2384, www.morganhouse .co.uk, morganhouse@btclick.com).

$$ Lynton Hotel B&B is a well-worn, steep-stairs kind of place renting 13 inexpensive rooms with small prefab WCs. It's a decent value run by brothers Mark and Simon Connor (D-£85, Db-£105, ask for Rick Steves price, free Wi-Fi, 113 Ebury Street, tel. 020/7730-4032, www.lyntonhotel.co.uk, mark-and-simon @lyntonhotel.co.uk).

East of Victoria Station

This area is a bit less genteel-feeling than the neighborhood west of the station, but still plenty inviting. Most of these places are on or near Warwick Way, the main drag through this area.

Victoria Station Neighborhood

1. Lime Tree Hotel
2. Cartref House
3. Morgan House
4. Lynton Hotel B&B
5. Luna Simone Hotel
6. New England Hotel
7. Best Western Victoria Palace
8. Cherry Court Hotel
9. Jubilee Hotel
10. Bakers Hotel
11. easyHotel Victoria
12. Vandon House Hotel
13. Ebury Wine Bar
14. Jenny Lo's Tea House
15. La Bottega Deli
16. To The Duke of Wellington Pub
17. The Thomas Cubitt Pub
18. Grumbles Restaurant
19. Seafresh Fish Restaurant
20. The Jugged Hare Pub
21. St. George's Tavern
22. Grocery Stores (4)
23. Launderettes (2)
24. Bus Tours – Day (2)
25. Bus Tours – Night
26. Tube, Taxis, City Buses
27. Green Line Coach Terminal
28. Buses to Luton & Stansted Airports
29. Apollo Victoria Theatre
30. Victoria Palace Theatre

$$ Luna Simone Hotel rents 36 fresh, spacious, nicely remodeled rooms with modern bathrooms. It's a smartly managed place, run for more than 40 years by twins Peter and Bernard and son Mark, and they still seem to enjoy their work (Sb-£75, Db-£105, Tb-£130, Qb-£160, ask about discount with cash and this book, free Internet access and Wi-Fi, near the corner of Charlwood Street and Belgrave Road at 47 Belgrave Road, handy bus #24 to Victoria Station and Trafalgar Square stops out front,

tel. 020/7834-5897, www.lunasimonehotel.com, stay@lunasimone
hotel.com).

$$ New England Hotel, run by Jay and the Patel family, has
slightly worn public spaces but tidy, well-priced rooms in a tight
old corner building (small Sb-£59, Db-£89, Tb-£119, Qb-£129,
prices soft during slow times, pay Internet access and Wi-Fi, 20
Saint George's Drive, tel. 020/7834-8351, fax 020/7834-9000,
www.newenglandhotel.com, mystay@newenglandhotel.com).

$$ Best Western Victoria Palace offers modern business-class comfort compared to the other creaky old hotels listed here. Choose between the 43 rooms in the main building (Db-£120, includes breakfast, elevator, 60-64 Warwick Way), or 22 rooms in the annex a half-block away (Db-£89, breakfast-£12.50, no elevator, 17 Belgrave Road, reception at main building). Both places have been recently renovated (air-con, free Wi-Fi, tel. 020/7821-7113, fax 020/7630-0806, www.bestwesternvictoriapalace.co.uk, info@bestwesternvictoriapalace.co.uk). Another 20-room annex may open by the time you visit.

$ Cherry Court Hotel, run by the friendly and industrious Patel family, rents 12 very small but bright and well-designed rooms in a central location (Sb-£50, Db-£58, Tb-£85, Qb-£100, Quint/b-£115, ask for best Rick Steves price, 5 percent fee to pay with credit card, fruit-basket breakfast in room, air-con, free Internet access and Wi-Fi, laundry, peaceful garden patio, 23 Hugh Street, tel. 020/7828-2840, fax 020/7828-0393, www.cherrycourthotel.co.uk, info@cherrycourthotel.co.uk).

$ Jubilee Hotel is a well-run slumbermill with 24 tiny, simple rooms and many tiny, neat beds (S-£39-45, Sb-£59-65, tiny D-£55-59, Db-£69-79, Tb-£79-95, Qb-£99-109, higher prices are for Fri-Sun, ask for Rick Steves discount if you book direct, Internet access and Wi-Fi, 31 Eccleston Square, tel. 020/7834-0845, www.jubileehotel.co.uk, stay@jubileehotel.co.uk, Bob Patel).

$ Bakers Hotel shoehorns 11 brightly painted rooms into a small building, but it's conveniently located and offers near-youth-hostel prices and a small breakfast (S-£40, D-£55, Db-£65, T-£65, Tb-£75, family room-£85, less for longer stays and on weeknights, pay Wi-Fi, 126 Warwick Way, tel. 020/7834-0729, www.bakershotel.co.uk, reservations@bakershotel.co.uk, Amin Jamani).

$ easyHotel Victoria, at 36 Belgrave Road, is part of the budget chain described on page 734.

"South Kensington," She Said, Loosening His Cummerbund

To stay on a quiet street so classy it doesn't allow hotel signs, surrounded by trendy shops and colorful restaurants, call "South Ken" your London home. Shoppers like being a short walk from Harrods and the designer shops of King's Road and Chelsea. When I splurge, I splurge here. Sumner Place is just off Old Brompton Road, 200 yards from the handy South Kensington Tube station (on Circle Line, two stops from Victoria Station; and on Piccadilly Line, direct from Heathrow). A handy **launderette** is on the corner of Queensberry Place and Harrington Road (Mon-Fri 7:30-21:00, Sat 9:00-20:00, Sun 10:00-19:00, bring 50p and £1 coins).

South Kensington Neighborhood

1 Number Sixteen Hotel
2 The Pelham Hotel
3 Aster House
4 Brompton Hotel
5 La Bouchée Bistro Café & Tesco Express Grocery
6 Moti Mahal Indian Rest.
7 Beirut Express & Bosphorus Kebabs
8 Rocca di Papa
9 The Anglesea Arms Pub
10 The Capital Hotel (Afternoon Tea)
11 Launderette

$$$ Number Sixteen, for well-heeled travelers, packs over-the-top formality and class into its 41 rooms, plush lounges, and tranquil garden. It's in a labyrinthine building, with modern decor—perfect for an urban honeymoon (Db-from £215—but soft, ask for discounted "seasonal rates," especially on weekends and in Aug—subject to availability, does not include 20 percent VAT, breakfast buffet in the garden-£18, elevator, 16 Sumner Place, tel.

020/7589-5232, fax 020/7584-8615, US tel. 800-553-6674, www
.firmdalehotels.com, sixteen@firmdale.com).

$$$ The Pelham Hotel, a 52-room business-class hotel with
a pricey mix of pretense and style, is not quite sure which invest-
ment company owns it. It's genteel, with low lighting and a pleas-
ant drawing room among the many perks (Db-£190-290, breakfast
extra, does not include 20 percent VAT, lower prices on weekends
and in Aug, Web specials can include free breakfast, air-con, ele-
vator, free Internet access, pay Wi-Fi, gym, 15 Cromwell Place, tel.
020/7589-8288, fax 020/7584-8444, US tel. 1-888-757-5587, www
.pelhamhotel.co.uk, reservations@pelhamhotel.co.uk).

$$$ Aster House, run by friendly and accommodating
Simon and Leonie Tan, has a cheerful lobby, lounge, and break-
fast room. Its rooms are comfy and quiet, with TV, phone, and
air-conditioning. Enjoy breakfast or just lounging in the whisper-
elegant Orangery, a glassy greenhouse. Simon and Leonie offer
free loaner mobile phones to their guests (Sb-£125, Db-£190,
bigger Db-£235, does not include 20 percent VAT, ask about discount with this book if you book three or more nights, 25 percent discount for five or more nights, additional 5 percent off with
cash, check website for specials, free Wi-Fi, 3 Sumner Place, tel.
020/7581-5888, fax 020/7584-4925, www.asterhouse.com, aster
house@btinternet.com).

$$ Brompton Hotel is a humble, borderline-dreary place
with 17 rooms above a jumble of cafés and clubs. There's a noisy
bar and some street noise, so ask for a room in the back if you
want quiet. It has old carpet and no public spaces, and they serve
breakfast in your room. In spite of all this, it's cheap for London
and very well-located (Sb-£95, Db-£100, Tb-£140, "deluxe" rooms
are just like the others but with a tub, save a little by booking via
their website, includes continental breakfast, Wi-Fi, across from
the South Kensington Tube station at 30 Brompton Road, tel.
020/7584-4517, fax 020/7823-9936, www.bromhotel.com, book
@bromhotel.com).

Notting Hill and Bayswater Neighborhoods

Residential Notting Hill has quick bus and Tube access to down-
town, and, for London, is very "homely" (Brit-speak for cozy). It's
also peppered with trendy bars and restaurants, and is home to
the famous Portobello Road Market (offbeat antiques shops open
daily are enlivened on Saturdays with 2,000 additional stalls until
17:00, closed Sun, Tube: Notting Hill Gate, tel. 020/7229-8354,
www.portobelloroad.co.uk).

Popular with young international travelers, the Bayswater
street called Queensway is a multicultural festival of commerce
and eateries. The neighborhood does its dirty clothes at **Galaxy**

Notting Hill & Bayswater Neighborhoods

LONDON

1. Vancouver Studios
2. Garden Court Hotel
3. Phoenix Hotel
4. Kensington Gardens Hotel
5. Princes Square Guest Accommodation
6. Westland Hotel
7. London Vicarage Hotel
8. The Gate Hotel
9. To Norwegian YWCA
10. Maggie Jones Restaurant
11. The Churchill Arms Pub & Thai Kitchen
12. The Prince Edward Pub
13. Café Diana
14. Royal China Restaurant
15. Whiteleys Shopping Centre (Food Court, Grocery, Internet)
16. Tesco Grocery
17. Spar Market
18. The Orangery (Afternoon Tea)
19. Launderette

Launderette (£6 self-service, £8-10 full-service, daily 8:00-20:00, staff on hand with soap and coins, 65 Moscow Road, at corner of St. Petersburgh Place and Moscow Road, tel. 020/7229-7771). For **Internet access,** you'll find several stops along busy Queensway, and a self-serve bank of computer terminals on the food-circus level—third floor—of Whiteleys Shopping Centre (daily 8:30-24:00, corner of Queensway and Porchester Gardens).

Near Kensington Gardens Square

Several big, old hotels line quiet Kensington Gardens Square (not to be confused with the much bigger Kensington Gardens adjacent to Hyde Park), a block west of bustling Queensway, north of Bayswater Tube station. These hotels are quiet for central London, but the area feels a bit sterile, and the hotels here tend to be impersonal.

$$$ Vancouver Studios offers 45 modern rooms with fully equipped kitchenettes (utensils, stove, microwave, and fridge) rather than breakfast (Sb-£92, Db-£135, Tb-£175, extra bed-£20, can be more at busy times, discount for seven or more nights, pay Internet access, free Wi-Fi, welcoming lounge and wonderful garden, near Kensington Gardens Square at 30 Prince's Square, tel. 020/7243-1270, fax 020/7221-8678, www.vancouverstudios.co.uk, info@vancouverstudios.co.uk).

$$$ Garden Court Hotel is homey and understated, with 32 simple beige rooms and a peaceful garden in back. Edward takes pride in the hotel his family has run for more than 50 years (S-£50, Sb-£80, D-£80, Db-£130, Tb-£160, Qb-£180, ask for Rick Steves price if booking direct, elevator, free Wi-Fi, 30-31 Kensington Gardens Square, tel. 020/7229-2553, fax 020/7727-2749, www.gardencourthotel.co.uk, info@gardencourthotel.co.uk).

$$ Phoenix Hotel, a Best Western modernization of a 125-room hotel, offers American business-class comforts; spacious, plush public spaces; and big, fresh, modern-feeling rooms. Its prices—which range from fine value to rip-off—are determined by a greedy computer program, with huge variations according to expected demand. Book online to save money (flexible prices, but usually Sb-£65, Db-£100, elevator, free Wi-Fi, 1-8 Kensington Gardens Square, tel. 020/7229-2494, fax 020/7727-1419, US tel. 800-528-1234, www.phoenixhotel.co.uk, info@phoenixhotel.co.uk).

$$ Kensington Gardens Hotel, which has the same owners as the Phoenix Hotel down the street (see above), laces 17 pleasant rooms together in a tall, skinny building with lots of stairs and no elevator (Ss-£57, Sb-£64, Db-£88, Tb-£110; book by phone or email, rather than through the pricier website, and ask for Rick Steves price; continental breakfast served at Phoenix Hotel, free Wi-Fi, 9 Kensington Gardens Square, tel. 020/7243-7600, fax 020/7792-8612, www.kensingtongardenshotel.co.uk, info @kensingtongardenshotel.co.uk, Rowshanak).

$$ Princes Square Guest Accommodation is a big 50-room place that's well-located, practical, and a good value, especially with its online discounts (Sb-£65-70, Db-£80-90, Tb-£90-100, elevator, pay Wi-Fi, 23-25 Princes Square, tel. 020/7229-9876, www.princessquarehotel.co.uk, info@princessquarehotel.co.uk).

Near Kensington Gardens

$$$ Westland Hotel, conveniently located on a busy street a five-minute walk from the Notting Hill neighborhood, feels like a wood-paneled hunting lodge with a fine lounge. The 32 spacious rooms are comfortable, with old-fashioned charm. Their £130 doubles are the best value, but check their website for specials. It's been run by the Isseyegh family for three generations (Sb-£112, deluxe Sb-£127, Db-£133, deluxe Db-£155, cavernous premier Db-£176, sprawling Tb-£169-197, gargantuan Qb-£190-225, Quint/b-£239, elevator, pay Wi-Fi, garage-£12/day, between Notting Hill Gate and Queensway Tube stations at 154 Bayswater Road, tel. 020/7229-9191, fax 020/7727-1054, www.westlandhotel .co.uk, reservations@westlandhotel.co.uk, Shirley and Bertie).

$$$ London Vicarage Hotel is family-run, understandably popular, and elegantly British in a quiet, classy neighborhood. It has 17 rooms furnished with taste and quality, a TV lounge, a grand staircase, and facilities on each floor. Mandy and Monika maintain a homey atmosphere (S-£60, Sb-£102, D-£102, Db-£130, T-£130, Tb-£170, Q-£140, Qb-£185, 20 percent less in winter—check website, free Wi-Fi; 8-minute walk from Notting Hill Gate and High Street Kensington Tube stations, near Kensington Palace at 10 Vicarage Gate; tel. 020/7229-4030, fax 020/7792-5989, www .londonvicaragehotel.com, vicaragehotel@btconnect.com).

$$ The Gate Hotel has seven cramped but decent rooms on a delightful curved street near the start of the Portobello Road Market, in the heart of the characteristic Notting Hill neighborhood. While the lodgings are basic, the romantic setting might be worth it for some (Sb-£60, Db-£85, bigger "luxury" Db-£95, Tb-£115, each room £10 more Fri-Sat, 5 percent fee to pay with credit card, continental breakfast in room, no elevator, pay Wi-Fi, 6 Portobello Road, Tube: Notting Hill Gate, tel. 020/7221-0707, fax 020/7221-9128, www.gatehotel.co.uk, bookings@gatehotel .co.uk, Jasmine).

Near Holland Park

$ Norwegian YWCA (Norsk K.F.U.K.)—where English is definitely a second language—is open to any Norwegian woman, and to non-Norwegian women under 30. (Men must be under 30 with a Norwegian passport.) Located on a quiet, stately street, it offers a study, TV room, piano lounge, and an open-face Norwegian ambience (goat cheese on Sundays!). They have mostly quads, so those willing to share with strangers are most likely to get a bed (July-Aug: Ss-£41, shared double-£39/bed, shared triple-£34/bed, shared quad-£30.50/bed, includes breakfast year-round plus sack lunch and dinner Sept-June, £20 key deposit and £2 membership fee required, pay Wi-Fi, 52 Holland Park, Tube: Holland Park, tel. 020/7727-9346 or 020/7727-9897, www.kfukhjemmet.org.uk, kontor@kfukhjemmet.org.uk). With each visit, I wonder which is easier to get—a sex change or a Norwegian passport?

Paddington Station Neighborhood

The neighborhood near Paddington Station—while much less charming than the other areas I've recommended—is pleasant enough, and very convenient to the Heathrow Express airport train. The area is flanked by the Paddington and Lancaster Gate Tube stops. Most of my recommendations circle Norfolk Square, just two blocks in front of Paddington Station, yet still quiet and comfortable. Its main drag, London Street, is lined with handy eateries—pubs, Indian, Italian, Greek, Lebanese, and more—plus convenience stores and an Internet café. To reach this area, exit the station toward Praed Street (with your back to the tracks, it's to the left). Once outside, continue straight across Praed Street and down London Street; Norfolk Square is a block ahead on the left.

On Norfolk Square

These places (and many more on the same street) are similar; all offer small rooms at a reasonable price, in tall buildings with lots of stairs and no elevator. I've chosen the ones that offer the most reasonable prices and the warmest welcome.

$$ St. David's Hotels, run by the hospitable and energetic Neokleous family, has 60 fine rooms in several adjacent buildings (S-£60, Sb-£70, D-£70, Db-£90, Tb-£100, free Wi-Fi, 14-20 Norfolk Square, tel. 020/7723-3856, fax 020/7402-9061, www.stdavidshotels.com, info@stdavidshotels.com).

$$ Tudor Court Hotel has 38 colorful rooms run by the Gupta family (S-£40, Sb-£85, Db-£95, Tb-£115, family room-£135, 10-12 Norfolk Square, tel. 020/7723-5157, fax 020/7723-0727, www.tudorcourtpaddington.co.uk, reservations@tudorcourtpaddington.co.uk).

$$ Ashley Hotel is a peeling-wallpaper kind of place with 54 rooms (S-£35-40, Sb-£50-60, Db-£70-80, pay Wi-Fi, 15-17 Norfolk Square, tel. 020/7723-3375, fax 020/7723-0173, www.ashleyhotellondon.com, info@ashleyhotellondon.com).

$ easyHotel, the budget chain described on page 734, has a branch at 10 Norfolk Place.

Elsewhere near Paddington Station

To reach these hotels, follow the directions above, but continue past Norfolk Square to the big intersection with Sussex Gardens; the Royal Park is a couple of blocks to the right, and the Springfield Hotel is immediately to the left.

$$$ The Royal Park is the neighborhood's classy splurge, with 48 plush rooms, polished service, a genteel lounge (free champagne for guests nightly 19:00-20:00), and all the little extras (standard Db-£139-149, bigger "executive" Db-£169-179, prices vary with demand, does not include 20 percent VAT or break-fast, free Internet access and Wi-Fi, 3 Westbourne Terrace, tel. 020/7479-6600, fax 020/7479-6601, www.theroyalpark.com, info @theroyalpark.com).

$$ Springfield Hotel is efficiently run and simple, with 17 updated rooms. It sits on the wide, busy street called Sussex Gardens (request a quieter back room), with several other similar hotels nearby if you're in a pinch (Sb-£60, Db-£80-90, Tb-£100, extra fee to pay with credit card, 154 Sussex Gardens, tel. 020/7723-9898, fax 020/7723-0874, www.springfieldhotellondon .co.uk, info@springfieldhotellondon.co.uk).

Other Neighborhoods

North of Marble Arch: **$$$ The 22 York Street B&B** offers a casual alternative in the city center, renting 10 traditional, hard-wood, comfortable rooms (Sb-£95, Db-£129, free Internet access and Wi-Fi, inviting lounge; from Baker Street Tube station, walk 2 blocks down Baker Street and take a right to 22 York Street—since there's no sign, just look for #22; tel. 020/7224-2990, www.22yorkstreet.co.uk, mc@22yorkstreet.co.uk, energetically run by Liz and Michael Callis).

$$$ The Sumner Hotel, renting 19 rooms in a 19th-century Georgian townhouse, is located a few blocks north of Hyde Park and Oxford Street, a busy shopping destination. Decorated with fancy modern Italian furniture, this swanky place packs in all the extras (Db-£170-220 depending on size, ask about discount with this book, extra bed-£50, air-con, elevator, free Wi-Fi, 54 Upper Berkeley Street just off Edgware Road, Tube: Marble Arch, tel. 020/7723-2244, fax 0870-705-8767, www.thesumner.com, hotel @thesumner.com).

Near Buckingham Palace: **$$ Vandon House Hotel,** run by Central College in Iowa, is packed with students most of the year, but rents its 32 rooms to travelers from late May through August at great prices. The rooms, while institutional, are comfy, and the

North London Accommodations

1. The 22 York Street B&B
2. The Sumner Hotel
3. Methodist International Centre
4. Hotel Ibis London Euston
   St. Pancras & Drummond
   St. Eateries
5. Premier Inn London
   Kings Cross St. Pancras
6. Premier Inn London Euston
7. Travelodge London Kings Cross
8. To Jurys Inn Islington
9. London Central Youth Hostel
10. Oxford Street Youth Hostel
11. Salumeria Dino Italian Deli &
    Lantana OUT Take-Away

location is excellent (S-£48, D-£75, Db-£95, Tb-£105, Qb-£125, apartment for up to 4 people-£125, only twin beds, a few rooms available year-round, elevator, pay Internet access and Wi-Fi; 3-minute walk west of St. James's Park Tube station or 7-minute walk from Victoria Station, near west end of Petty France Street on a tiny road, 1 Vandon Street; tel. 020/7799-6780, www.vandon house.com, info@vandonhouse.com).

Near Euston Station and the British Library: The $$$ **Methodist International Centre (MIC),** a modern, youthful Christian hotel and conference center, fills its lower floors with international students and its top floor with travelers. The 28 rooms are modern and sleek yet comfortable, with fine bathrooms, phones, and desks. The atmosphere is friendly, safe, clean, and controlled; it also has a spacious lounge and game room (Sb-£119 Fri-Sun, £139 Mon-Thu; Db-£130 Fri-Sun, £149 Mon-Thu; pricier "deluxe" rooms also available, buying a £100 annual membership saves you £20-40 per night—do the math to see if it's worth paying for, check website for specials, elevator, pay Wi-Fi, on a quiet street a block west of Euston Station, 81-103 Euston Street—not Euston Road, Tube: Euston, tel. 020/7380-0001, www.micentre .com, reservations@micentre.com). In addition to the rooms in the main building, they have several "annex" rooms—three rooms in one house that share a single bathroom—which could work well for families (S-£85, D-£95). In June-August, when the students are gone, they also rent simpler twin rooms in the main building (S or D-£75, includes one breakfast, extra breakfast-£15).

Big, Good-Value, Modern Hotels

London has an abundance of modern, impersonal, American-style chain hotels. While they lack the friendliness and funkiness of a memorable B&B, the value they provide is undeniable; doubles generally go for around £90-100 (or less—often possible with promotional rates). As these hotels are often located on busy streets in dreary train-station neighborhoods, use common sense after dark and wear your money belt.

Premier Inn

For any of these, call their reservations line at 0870-242-8000 or—the best option—book online at www.premierinn.com.

$$ Premier Inn London County Hall, literally down the hall from a $400-a-night Marriott Hotel, fills one end of London's massive former County Hall building. This family-friendly place is wonderfully located near the base of the London Eye and across the Thames from Big Ben. Its 313 efficient rooms come with all the necessary comforts, though it's quite impersonal—rather than a real reception desk, you'll find self-service check-in kiosks with a couple of clerks standing by to help (Db-£109-170 for 2 adults and up to 2 kids under age 16, elevator, pay Wi-Fi, some accessible rooms, 500 yards from Westminster Tube stop and Waterloo Station, Belvedere Road, central reservations tel. 0870-242-8000, reception desk tel. 0870-238-3300, easiest to book online at www .premierinn.com).

$$ Premier Inn London Southwark, with 59 rooms, is near Shakespeare's Globe on the South Bank (Db for up to 2 adults and 2 kids-£99-169, elevator, pay Wi-Fi, Bankside, 34 Park Street, Tube: London Bridge, tel. 0871-527-8676, www.premierinn.com).

$$ Premier Inn London Kings Cross St. Pancras, with 276 rooms, is across the street from the east end of King's Cross Station and near the Eurostar terminus at St. Pancras Station (Db-£96-160, air-con, elevator, pay Wi-Fi, 26-30 York Way, Tube: King's Cross St. Pancras, tel. 0871-527-8672, www.premierinn .com).

Other **$$ Premier Inns** charging £90-170 per room include **London Euston** (big, blue Lego-type building packed with vacationing families, on handy but noisy street at corner of Euston Road and Dukes Road, Tube: Euston, tel. 0870-238-3301), **London Kensington Earl's Court** (11 Knaresborough Place, Tube: Earl's Court or Gloucester Road, tel. 0870-238-3304), **London Victoria** (82-83 Eccleston Square, Tube: Victoria, tel. 0870-423-6494), and **London Putney Bridge** (farther out, 3 Putney Bridge Approach, Tube: Putney Bridge, tel. 0870-238-3302). Avoid the **Tower Bridge** location, which is an inconvenient 15-minute walk from the nearest Tube stop.

Other Chains

Travelodge: **$$ Travelodge London Kings Cross** is another typical chain hotel with 140 cookie-cutter rooms, just 200 yards south (in front) of King's Cross Station (Db-usually £85, family rooms, can be noisy, elevator, pay Wi-Fi, Grays Inn Road, Tube: King's Cross St. Pancras, tel. 0871-984-6256). Other convenient Travelodge London locations are nearby **Kings Cross Royal Scot, Euston, Marylebone, Covent Garden, Liverpool Street,** and **Farringdon.** For details on all Travelodge hotels, see www.travelodge.co.uk.

Ibis: **$$$ Hotel Ibis London Euston St. Pancras** rents 380 rooms on a quiet street a block west of Euston Station (Db-£89-149, usually £139, no family rooms, elevator, pay Internet access and Wi-Fi, 3 Cardington Street, Tube: Euston, tel. 020/7388-7777, fax 020/7388-0001, www.ibishotel.com, h0921@accor.com). There's also an **Ibis London City** (5 Commercial Street, Tube: Aldgate East, tel. 020/7422-8400), but the other Ibis locations are far from the center.

Jurys Inn: **$$ Jurys Inn Islington** rents 200-plus compact, comfy rooms near King's Cross Station (Db/Tb-£109-169, some discounted rooms available online, 2 adults and 2 kids under age 12 can share one room, 60 Pentonville Road, Tube: Angel, tel. 020/7282-5500, fax 020/7282-5511, www.jurysinns.com). You'll also find Jurys Inns at **Chelsea** (Imperial Road, Tube: Imperial Wharf, tel. 020/7411-2200) and near **Heathrow Airport** (see "Heathrow and Gatwick Airports," later).

easyHotel

With several hotels in good neighborhoods around London, easyHotel is a radical concept—offering what you need to sleep well and safe, and nothing more. Most of them are fitted into old buildings, so the rooms are all odd shapes, from tiny window-less closets to others that are quite spacious. All rooms are well-ventilated and come with an efficient "bathroom pod" that looks like it was popped out of a plastic mold—just big enough to take care of business. While they do have a 24-hour reception, everything else is spartan: you get two towels, liquid soap, and a clean bed—no breakfast, no fresh towels, and no daily cleaning. The base rate ranges from £21-65, depending on the room size and when you book—"The earlier you book, the less you pay." Prices are the same for one person or two, but then you're nickel-and-dimed with optional charges for the TV, Wi-Fi, luggage storage, and so on.

If you go with the basic package, it's like hosteling with privacy—a hard-to-beat value. But you get what you pay for; in my experience, easyHotels are cheap in every sense of the word (no elevator, thin walls, noisy halls filled with loud travelers seeking bargain beds, flimsy construction that often results in broken things in the room). And they're only a good deal if you book far enough ahead to get a good price, and skip the many extras...which can add up fast.

$ easyHotel Victoria is well-located in an old building near Victoria Station (77 rooms, 36 Belgrave Road—for location, see map on page 722, Tube: Victoria, tel. 020/7834-1379, enquiries @victoria.easyhotel.com). They also have branches at **South Kensington** (34 rooms, 14 Lexham Gardens, Tube: Earl's Court or Gloucester Road, tel. 020/7136-2870, enquiries@southken.easyhotel.com), **Earl's Court** (80 rooms, 44-48 West Cromwell Road, Tube: Earl's Court, tel. 020/7373-4546, enquiries@earlscourt.easyhotel.com), **Paddington** (47 rooms, 10 Norfolk Place, Tube: Paddington, tel. 020/7706-9911, enquiries@paddington.easyhotel.com), and **Heathrow** and **Luton** airports (Heathrow location described on page 737). Regardless of the location, reserve through their website (www.easyhotel.com).

Hostels

For more London hostel listings, try www.hostellondon.com.

$ London Central Youth Hostel is the flagship of London's hostels, with 300 beds and all the latest in security and comfortable efficiency. Families and travelers of any age will feel welcome in this wonderful facility. You'll pay the same price for any bed in a 4- to 8-bed single-sex dorm—with or without private bathroom—so try to grab one with a bathroom (£20-30 per bunk bed—fluctuates with demand, £3/night extra for nonmembers, breakfast-£4; includes sheets, towel and locker; families welcome to book an entire room, pay Wi-Fi, members' kitchen, laundry, book long in advance, between Oxford Circus and Great Portland Street Tube stations at 104 Bolsover Street—see map on page 732, tel. 0870-770-6144 or 0845-371-9154, www.yha.org.uk, londoncentral@yha.org.uk).

$ Oxford Street Youth Hostel, newly opened, is right in the shopping and clubbing zone in Soho (£17-30 per bunk, 14 Noel Street, Tube: Oxford Street, tel. 0845-371-9133, www.yha.org.uk, oxfordst@yha.org.uk).

$ St. Paul's Youth Hostel, near St. Paul's, is clean, modern, friendly, and well-run. Most of the 190 beds are in shared, single-sex 3- to 11-bunk rooms (bed-around £20 depending on demand, twin D-£60, includes locker and sheets but not breakfast, non-members pay £3 extra, cheap meals, open 24 hours, 36 Carter Lane, Tube: St. Paul's, tel. 020/7236-4965 or tel. 0845-371-9012, www.yha.org.uk, stpauls@yha.org.uk).

$ A cluster of three **St. Christopher's Inn** hostels, south of the Thames near London Bridge, have cheap dorm beds; one branch is for women only. All have loud and friendly bars attached (£22-32, must be over 18 years old, 161-165 Borough High Street, Tube: Borough or London Bridge, reservations tel. 020/8600-7500, www.st-christophers.co.uk).

Dorms

$$ The **University of Westminster** opens its dorm rooms to travelers during summer break, from mid-June through late September. Located in several high-rise buildings scattered around central London, the rooms—some with private bathrooms, others with shared bathrooms nearby—come with access to well-equipped kitchens and big lounges (S-£35, Sb-£60, D-£54, Db-£106, tel. 020/7911-5181, www.westminster.ac.uk /business/summer-accommodation, summeraccommodation @westminster.ac.uk).

$ University College London also has rooms for travelers, from mid-June until mid-September (S-£31-43, pay Internet access, tel. 020/7278-3895, www.ucl.ac.uk/residences).

$$ The **London School of Economics** has openings in its dorms from July through September (S-£33-43, Sb-£59-65, D-£52-60, Db-£76-94, tel. 020/7955-7575, www.lsevacations .co.uk, vacations@lse.ac.uk).

Heathrow and Gatwick Airports
At or near Heathrow Airport

It's so easy to get to Heathrow from central London, I see no reason to sleep there. But if you do, here are some options. The Yotel is actually inside the airport, while the rest are a short bus or taxi ride away. In addition to public buses, the cleverly named £4 "Hotel Hoppa" shuttle buses connect the airport to many nearby hotels (different routes serve the various hotels and terminals—may take a while to spot your particular bus at the airport).

$$ Yotel, at the airport inside Terminal 4, has small sleep dens that offer a popular place to catch a quick nap (four hours-£37-64), or to stay overnight (tiny "standard cabin"—£65/8 hours, "premium cabin"—£87/8 hours; cabins sleep 1-2 people; price is per cabin—not person, reserve online for free or by phone for small fee). Prices vary by day, week, and time of year, so check their website. All rooms are only slightly larger than a double bed, and have private bathrooms and free Internet access and Wi-Fi. These windowless rooms have oddly purplish lighting (tel. 020/7100-1100, www.yotel.com, customer@yotel.com).

$ easyHotel, your cheapest bet, is in a low-rent residential neighborhood a £5 taxi ride from the airport. Its 53 no-frills, pod-like rooms are on two floors. Before booking at this very basic place, read the explanation on page 734 (Db-£25-50, no breakfast, no elevator, pay Internet access and Wi-Fi, Brick Field Lane; take local bus #140 from airport's Central Bus Station or the "Hotel Hoppa" #H8 from Terminals 1 or 3, or the hotel can arrange a taxi to the airport; tel. 020/8897-9237, www.easyhotel.com, enquiries@heathrow.easyhotel.com).

$$ Hotel Ibis London Heathrow is a chain hotel offering predictable value (Db-£80 Mon-Thu, Db-£60 Fri-Sun, check website for specials as low as £35, breakfast-£7, pay Internet access and Wi-Fi; 112-114 Bath Road, take local bus #105, #111, #140, #285, #423, or #555 from airport's Central Bus Station or Terminal 4, or the "Hotel Hoppa" #H6 from Terminals 1 or 3, or #H56 from Terminals 4 or 5; tel. 020/8759-4888, fax 020/8564-7894, www.ibishotel.com, h0794@accor.com).

$$ Jurys Inn, another hotel chain, tempts tired travelers with 300-plus cookie-cutter rooms (Db-£89-105, check website for deals, breakfast extra; on Eastern Perimeter Road, Tube: Hatton Cross plus 5-minute walk; take the Tube one stop from Terminals 1, 2, or 3; or two stops from Terminals 4 or 5; or the "Hotel Hoppa" #H9 from Terminals 1 or 3, or #H53 from Terminals 4 or 5; or buses #285, #482, #490, or #555; tel. 020/8266-4664, fax 020/8266-4665, www.jurysinns.com).

At or near Gatwick Airport

$$ Yotel, with small rooms, has a branch right at the airport (Gatwick South Terminal; see prices and contact info in Heathrow listing, earlier).

$ Gatwick Airport Central Premier Inn rents cheap rooms 350 yards from the airport (Db-£40-75, breakfast-£8, £2 shuttle bus from airport—must reserve in advance, Longbridge Way, North Terminal, tel. 0871-527-8406, frustrating phone tree, www.premierinn.com). Four more Premier Inns are within a five-mile radius of the airport.

$$ Barn Cottage, a converted 16th-century barn flanked by a tennis court and swimming pool, sits in the peaceful countryside, with a good pub just two blocks away. Its two wood-beamed rooms, antique furniture, and large garden make you forget Gatwick is 10 minutes away (S-£60, D-£80, cash only, Church Road, Leigh, Reigate, Surrey, tel. 01306/611-347, warmly run by Pat and Mike Comer). Don't confuse this place with others of the same name. A taxi from Gatwick to here runs about £15; the Comers can take you back to the airport or train station for about £10.

$ Gatwick Airport Travelodge has budget rooms about two miles from the airport (Db-£39-57, breakfast extra, pay Wi-Fi, Church Road, Lowfield Heath, Crawley, £3 shuttle bus from airport, tel. 0871-984-6031, www.travelodge.co.uk).

Eating in London

In London, the sheer variety of foods—from every corner of its former empire and beyond—is astonishing. You'll be amazed at the number of hopping, happening new restaurants of all kinds.

If you want to dine (as opposed to eat), drop by a London newsstand to get a weekly entertainment guide or an annual restaurant guide (both have extensive restaurant listings). Visit www.london-eating.co.uk or www.squaremeal.co.uk for more options.

The thought of a £50 meal in Britain generally ruins my appetite, so my London dining is limited mostly to easygoing, fun, moderately priced alternatives. I've listed places by neighborhood—handy to your sightseeing or hotel. Considering how expensive London can be, if there's any good place to cut corners and stretch your budget, it's by eating cheaply. Pub grub (at one of London's 7,000 pubs) and ethnic restaurants (especially Indian and Chinese) are good low-cost options. Of course, picnicking is the fastest and cheapest way to go. Good grocery stores and sandwich shops, fine park benches, and polite pigeons abound in Britain's most expensive city.

Remember, London (and all of Britain) is smoke-free. Expect restaurants and pubs that sell food to be non-smoking indoors, with smokers occupying patios and doorways outside.

Central London
Near Trafalgar Square
These places are within about 100 yards of Trafalgar Square.

St. Martin-in-the-Fields Café in the Crypt is just right for a tasty meal on a monk's budget—maybe even on a monk's tomb. You'll dine sitting on somebody's gravestone in an ancient crypt. Their enticing buffet line is kept stocked all day, serving breakfast, lunch, and dinner (£6-10 cafeteria plates, hearty traditional desserts, free jugs of water). They also serve a restful cream tea (£6, daily 14:00-17:00). You'll find it directly under the St. Martin-in-the-Fields Church, facing Trafalgar Square (Mon-Tue 8:00-20:00, Wed 8:00-22:30, Thu-Sat 8:00-21:00, Sun 11:00-18:00, profits go to the church, Tube: Charing Cross, tel. 020/7766-1158 or 020/7766-1100). Wednesday evenings at 20:00 come with a live jazz band (£6-9 tickets). While here, check out the concert schedule for the busy church upstairs (or visit www.smitf.org).

The Chandos Pub's Opera Room floats amazingly apart from the tacky crush of tourism around Trafalgar Square. Look for it opposite the National Portrait Gallery (corner of William IV Street and St. Martin's Lane) and climb the stairs (to the right of the pub entrance) to the Opera Room. This is a fine Trafalgar rendezvous point and wonderfully local pub. They serve traditional, plain-tasting £6-7 pub meals—meat pies and fish-and-chips are their specialty. The ground-floor pub is stuffed with regulars and offers snugs (private booths), the same menu, and more serious beer drinking. Chandos proudly serves the local Samuel Smith beer at £2 a pint (kitchen open daily 11:00-19:00, order and pay at the bar, 29 St. Martin's Lane, Tube: Leicester Square, tel. 020/7836-1401).

Gordon's Wine Bar, with a simple, steep staircase leading into a candlelit 15th-century wine cellar, is filled with dusty old bottles, faded British memorabilia, and nine-to-fivers. At the "English rustic" buffet, choose a hot meal or cold meat dish with a salad, or a hearty (and splittable) plate of cheeses, bread, and pickles (£7.75)—or share four plates for £12. Then step up to the wine bar and consider the many varieties of wine and port available by the glass (this place is passionate about port). The low carbon-crusted vaulting deeper in the back seems to intensify the Hogarth-painting atmosphere. Although it's crowded, you can normally corral two chairs and grab the corner of a table. On hot days, the crowd spills out onto a leafy back patio, where a barbecue cooks for a long line of tables (arrive before 17:00 to get a seat, Mon-Sat 11:00-23:00, Sun 12:00-22:00, 2 blocks from Trafalgar Square, bottom of Villiers Street at #47, Tube: Embankment, tel. 020/7930-1408, www.gordonswinebar.com, manager Gerard Menan).

The Lord Moon of the Mall pub, with real ales on tap and cheap pub grub such as fish-and-chips, is a good place to experience retro English cuisine from the days when it had a horrible reputation. The pub fills a great old former Barclays Bank building a block down Whitehall from Trafalgar Square (daily 9:00-22:00, kid-friendly menu but no kids after 20:00, 16-18 Whitehall, Tube: Charing Cross or Embankment, tel. 020/7839-7701).

Central London Eateries

1. St. Martin-in-the-Fields Café in the Crypt
2. The Chandos Pub's Opera Room
3. Gordon's Wine Bar
4. The Lord Moon of the Mall Pub
5. Stockpot & Woodlands South Indian Vegetarian Restaurant
6. West End Kitchen
7. Criterion Restaurant
8. The Wolseley
9. Joe Allen
10. Loch Fyne Fish Restaurant
11. Sofra Turkish Restaurant
12. Sitar Indian Restaurant

13 Belgo Centraal

14 Neal's Yard Eateries

15 Food for Thought Café

16 Yo! Sushi (3)

17 Wagamama Noodle Bar (4)

18 Busaba Eathai Thai Rest. & Côte Restaurant

19 Y Ming Chinese Restaurant

20 New World Chinese Restaurant

21 Jen Café

22 Andrew Edmunds Restaurant

23 Mildred's Vegetarian Rest.; Fernandez & Wells

24 The Princess Louise Pub

Near Piccadilly

Hungry and broke in the theater district? Head for Panton Street (off Haymarket, two blocks southeast of Piccadilly Circus), where several hardworking little places compete, all seeming to offer a three-course meal for about £9. Peruse the entire block for your options (vegetarian, Pizza Express, Moroccan, Thai, Chinese, and two famous diners) before making your choice.

Stockpot is a meat, potatoes, gravy, and mushy-peas kind of place, famous and rightly popular for its edible, cheap English meals (Mon-Sat 7:00-23:00, Sun 7:00-22:00, 38-40 Panton Street, cash only). The **West End Kitchen** (across the street at #5, same hours and menu) is a direct competitor that's also well-known and just as good. Vegetarians may prefer the **Woodlands South Indian Vegetarian Restaurant,** which serves an impressive £18 *thali* (37 Panton Street).

The palatial **Criterion** offers grand-piano ambience beneath gilded tiles and chandeliers in a dreamy Byzantine church setting from 1880. It's right on Piccadilly Circus but a world away from the punk junk. It's a deal for the visual experience during lunch and before 19:00—but after 19:00, the menu becomes really expensive...and, at any hour, the service could care less. Anyone can drop in for coffee or a drink (£17-20 fixed-price meals, daily 12:00-14:30 & 17:30-19:00 & 22:00-23:30, 224 Piccadilly, tel. 020/7930-0488).

The Wolseley is the grand 1920s showroom of a long-defunct British car. The last Wolseley drove out with the Great Depression, but today this old-time bistro bustles with formal waiters serving traditional Austrian and French dishes in an elegant black-marble-and-chandeliers setting fit for its location next to the Ritz. Although the food can be unexceptional, prices are reasonable, and the presentation and setting are grand. Reservations are a must (£18 plates; cheaper soup, salad, and sandwich menu available; Mon-Fri 7:00-24:00, Sat 8:00-24:00, Sun 8:00-23:00, 160 Piccadilly, tel. 020/7499-6996). They're popular for their fancy cream or afternoon tea.

Near Covent Garden

Covent Garden bustles with people and touristy eateries. The area feels overrun, but if you must eat around here, there are some good options.

Joe Allen, tucked in a basement a block away, serves modern international and American cuisine with both style and hubbub. Downstairs off a quiet street with candles and white tablecloths, it's comfortably spacious and popular with the theater crowd (meals for about £30, £16 two-course specials and £18 three-course specials Mon-Wed and Sun, open daily 11:30-23:00, piano music after 21:00, 13 Exeter Street, tel. 020/7836-0651).

Loch Fyne Fish Restaurant is part of a Scottish chain that grows its own oysters and mussels. It offers an inviting atmosphere with a fine fishy energy and no pretense (£10-15 main dishes, £12.50 two-course special served 12:00-19:00, open daily, a couple of blocks behind Covent Garden at 2 Catherine Street, tel. 020/7240-4999).

Sofra Turkish Restaurant is good for quality Turkish with a touch of class. They have several menus: *meze* (Turkish tapas), vegetarian, and set (£8 before 19:00, £11 after 18:00, open long hours daily, 36 Tavistock Street, tel. 020/7240-3773).

Sitar Indian Restaurant is a well-respected Indian/Bangladeshi place serving dishes from many regions, fine fish, and a tasty £17 vegetarian *thali*. It's small and dressy, with snappy service (£15 main dishes, Mon-Fri 12:00-24:00, Sat-Sun 14:30-24:00, next to Somerset House at 149 Strand, tel. 020/7836-3730).

Belgo Centraal serves hearty Belgian specialties in a vast 400-seat underground lair. It's a mussels, chips, and beer emporium dressed up as a mod-monastic refectory—with noisy acoustics and waiters garbed as Trappist monks. The classy restaurant section is more comfortable and less rowdy, but usually requires reservations. It's often more fun just to grab a spot in the boisterous beer hall, with its tight, communal benches (no reservations accepted). Both sides have the same menu and specials. Belgians claim they eat as well as the French and as heartily as the Germans. This place, which offers a stunning array of dark, blonde, and fruity Belgian beers, actually makes Belgian things trendy—a formidable feat (£10-14 meals, open daily 12:00-23:00; Mon-Fri £5-6.30 "beat the clock" meal specials 17:00-18:30—the time you order is the price you pay—including main dishes and fries; no meal-splitting after 18:30, and you must buy food with beer; daily £8 lunch special 12:00-17:00; 1 kid eats free for each parent ordering a regular entrée; 1 block north of Covent Garden Tube station at 50 Earlham Street, tel. 020/7813-2233).

Neal's Yard is *the* place for cheap, hip, and healthy eateries near Covent Garden. The neighborhood is a tabouli of fun, hippie-type cafés. One of the best is the venerable and ferociously vegetarian **Food for Thought,** packed with local health nuts (good £5 vegetarian meals, £8 dinner plates, Mon-Sat 12:00-20:30, Sun 12:00-17:30, 2 blocks north of Covent Garden Tube station at 31 Neal Street, near Neal's Yard, tel. 020/7836-0239).

Near Soho and Chinatown

London has a trendy scene that most Beefeater-seekers miss entirely. These restaurants are scattered throughout the hipster, gay, and strip-club district, teeming each evening with fun-seekers and theatergoers. Even if you plan to have dinner elsewhere, it's a treat just to wander around this lively area.

Beware of the extremely welcoming women standing outside the strip clubs (especially on Great Windmill Street). Enjoy the sales pitch—but only fools fall for the "£5 drink and show" lure. Seriously. If you go in, you'll leave with an empty wallet.

Yo! Sushi is a futuristic Japanese-food-extravaganza experience, complete with thumping rock music, Japanese cable TV, and a 195-foot-long conveyor belt. For £1.25, you get unlimited green tea or water. Snag a bar stool and grab dishes as they rattle by (priced by color of dish; check the chart: £1.75-5 per dish, daily 12:00-23:00, 2 blocks south of Oxford Street, where Lexington Street becomes Poland Street, 52 Poland Street, tel. 020/7287-0443). If you like Yo!, there are about 40 other locations around town, including a handy branch a block from the London Eye on Belvedere Road, as well as outlets within Selfridges, Harvey Nichols department stores, and Whiteleys Shopping Centre on Queensway.

Wagamama Noodle Bar is a noisy, pan-Asian, organic slurp-athon. As you enter, check out the kitchen and listen to the roar of the basement, where benches rock with happy eaters. Everybody sucks. Portions are huge and splitting is allowed (£7-10 meals, Mon-Sat 11:30-23:00, Sun 12:00-22:00, crowded after 19:00, 10A Lexington Street, tel. 020/7292-0990 but no reservations taken). If you like this place, handy branches are all over town, including one near the British Museum (4 Streatham Street), Kensington (26 High Street), in Harvey Nichols (109 Knightsbridge), Covent Garden (1 Tavistock Street), Leicester Square (14 Irving Street), Piccadilly Circus (8 Norris Street), Fleet Street (#109), and next to the Tower of London (Tower Place).

Busaba Eathai Thai Restaurant is a hit with locals for its snappy service, casual-yet-high-energy ambience, and good, inexpensive Thai cuisine. You'll sit communally around big, square 16-person hardwood tables or in two-person tables by the window—with everyone in the queue staring at your noodles. They don't take reservations, so arrive by 19:00 or line up (£7-10 meals, Mon-Thu 12:00-23:00, Fri-Sat 12:00-23:30, Sun 12:00-22:00, 106 Wardour Street, tel. 020/7255-8686). They have three other handy locations: on nearby Panton Street, just below Piccadilly Circus; at 22 Store Street, near the British Museum and Goodge Street Tube; and at 8-13 Bird Street, just off Oxford Street and across from the Bond Street Tube.

Côte Restaurant is a contemporary French bistro chain with no pretense, serving good-value French cuisine at the right prices (£9-13 mains, £12 three-course early dinner specials if you order by 19:00, open Mon-Wed 8:00-23:00, Thu-Fri 8:00-24:00, Sat 9:00-24:00, Sun 9:00-22:30, 124-126 Wardour Street, tel. 020/7287-9280).

Y Ming Chinese Restaurant—across Shaftesbury Avenue from the ornate gates, clatter, and dim sum of Chinatown—has dressy European decor, serious but helpful service, and authentic Northern Chinese cooking (good £11 meal deal offered 12:00-18:00, £7-11 plates, open Mon-Sat 12:00-23:45, closed Sun, 35-36 Greek Street, tel. 020/7734-2721).

New World Chinese Restaurant is a sprawling, old-fashioned Chinese diner that just feels real. It's a fixture in Chinatown, serving cheap Cantonese food, including dim sum and a similar dinner menu with an array of little £3 dishes (daily 11:00-24:00, dim sum daily 12:00-18:00, 1 Gerrard Place, tel. 020/7734-0677).

Jen Café, across the street, is a humble Chinese corner eatery much loved for its homemade dumplings. It's just stools and simple seating, with fast service, a fun, inexpensive menu, and a devoted following (£3-5 plates, long hours daily, 4 Newport Place, tel. 020/7287-9708).

On Lexington Street, in the Heart of Soho

Andrew Edmunds Restaurant is a tiny, candlelit place where you'll want to hide your camera and guidebook and not act like a tourist. This little place—with a jealous and loyal clientele—is the closest I've found to Parisian quality in a cozy restaurant in London. The modern European cooking and creative seasonal menu are worth the splurge (£6-8 starters, £10-20 main dishes, Mon-Sat 12:30-15:00 & 18:00-22:45, Sun 13:00-15:30 & 18:00-22:30, come early or call ahead, request ground floor rather than basement, 46 Lexington Street, tel. 020/7437-5708).

Mildred's Vegetarian Restaurant, across from Andrew Edmunds, has cheap prices, an enjoyable menu, and a pleasant interior filled with happy eaters (£7-9 meals, Mon-Sat 12:00-23:00, closed Sun, vegan options, 45 Lexington Street, tel. 020/7494-1634).

Fernandez & Wells is a delightfully simple little wine, cheese, and ham bar. Drop in and grab a stool as you belly up to the big wooden bar. Share a plate of top-quality cheeses and/or Spanish, Italian, or French hams with fine bread and oil, while sipping a nice glass of wine (Mon-Sat 11:00-22:00, Sun 12:00-19:00, quality sandwiches at lunch, wine/cheese/ham bar after 16:00, 43 Lexington Street, tel. 020/7734-1546).

Near the British Museum

Tiny Charlotte Place is lined with small eateries. It's a short walk from the Goodge Street Tube station and convenient to the British Museum and Pollock's Toy Museum (see map on page 732).

Salumeria Dino serves up hearty sandwiches, pasta, and Italian coffee. Dino, a native of Naples, has run his little shop for

30 years and has managed to create a classic Italian deli that's so authentic, you'll walk out singing "O Sole Mio" (£3-5 sandwiches, £1 take-away cappuccinos, Mon-Fri 9:00-17:00, closed Sat-Sun, #15, tel. 020/7580-3938).

Lantana OUT, next door to Salumeria Dino, sells modern soups, sandwiches, and salads at their take-away window. Their changing menu features a soup-salad-sweet combo deal for £5.50 (£3-7 meals, pricier sit-down café next door, Mon-Fri 7:30-15:00, café open Sat-Sun 9:00-15:00, #13, tel. 020/7637-3347).

West London
Near Victoria Station Accommodations
These restaurants are within a few blocks of Victoria Station—and all are places where I've enjoyed eating. As with the accommodations in this area, I've grouped them by location: east or west of the station (see the map on page 722).

Cheap Eats: For groceries, a handy **M&S Simply Food** is inside Victoria Station (Mon-Sat 7:00-24:00, Sun 8:00-22:00), along with a **Sainsbury's Market** (daily 6:00-23:00, at rear entrance, on Eccleston Street). A second Sainsbury's is just north of the station on Victoria Street, and a larger Sainsbury's is on Wilton Road near Warwick Way, a couple of blocks southeast of the station (Mon-Fri 7:00-23:00, Sat 7:00-22:00, Sun 11:00-17:00). A string of good ethnic restaurants lines Wilton Road (near the recommended Seafresh Fish Restaurant). For affordable if forgettable meals, try the row of cheap little eateries on Elizabeth Street.

West of Victoria Station
Ebury Wine Bar, filled with young professionals, provides a cut-above atmosphere, delicious £13-18 main dishes, and an £18 two-course and £23 three-course special anytime (three-course meal includes a glass of champagne that you're welcome to swap for wine). In the delightful back room, the fancy menu features modern European cuisine with a French accent; at the wine bar, find a cheaper bar menu that's better than your average pub grub. This is emphatically a "traditional wine bar," with no beers on tap (daily 11:00-23:00, reservations smart, at intersection of Ebury and Elizabeth Streets, 139 Ebury Street, tel. 020/7730-5447).

Jenny Lo's Tea House is a simple budget place serving up reliably tasty £7-9 eclectic Chinese-style meals to locals in the know. While the menu is small, everything is high quality. Jenny clearly learned from her father, Ken Lo, one of the most famous Cantonese chefs in Britain, whose fancy place is just around the corner (Mon-Fri 12:00-15:00 & 18:00-22:00, closed Sat-Sun, cash only, 14 Eccleston Street, tel. 020/7259-0399).

La Bottega is an Italian delicatessen that fits its upscale Belgravia neighborhood. It offers tasty, freshly cooked pastas (£6), lasagnas, and salads (lasagna and salad meal-£8), along with great sandwiches (£3) and a good coffee bar with pastries. While not cheap, it's fast (order at the counter), and the ingredients would please an Italian chef. Grab your meal to go, or enjoy the Belgravia good life with locals, either sitting inside or on the sidewalk (Mon-Fri 8:00-19:00, Sat 9:00-18:00, Sun 10:00-17:00, on corner of Ebury and Eccleston Streets, tel. 020/7730-2730).

The Duke of Wellington Pub is a classic neighborhood place with forgettable grub, woodsy sidewalk seating, and an inviting interior (dinner served Mon-Sat 18:00-21:00, 63 Eaton Terrace, tel. 020/7730-1782).

The Thomas Cubitt Pub, packed with young professionals, is a trendy neighborhood gastropub, great for a drink or pricey meal (44 Elizabeth Street, tel. 020/7730-6060).

East of Victoria Station

Grumbles brags it's been serving "good food and wine at nonscary prices since 1964." Offering a delicious mix of "modern eclectic French and traditional English," this unpretentious little place with cozy booths inside (on two levels, including a cellar) and four nice sidewalk tables is *the* spot to eat well in this otherwise worka-day neighborhood. Their traditional dishes are their forte (£9-18 plates, £11 early-bird specials 18:00-19:00, open daily 12:00-14:30 & 18:00-23:00, reservations wise, half a block north of Belgrave Road at 35 Churton Street, tel. 020/7834-0149, Alex).

Seafresh Fish Restaurant is the neighborhood place for plaice—and classic and creative fish-and-chips cuisine. You can either take out on the cheap or eat in, enjoying a white fish ambi-ence. Though Mario's father started this place in 1965, it feels like the chippie of the 21st century (meals-£6 to go, £10-15 to sit, Mon-Sat 12:00-15:00 & 17:00-22:30, closed Sun, 80-81 Wilton Road, tel. 020/7828-0747).

The Jugged Hare pub, a 10-minute walk from Victoria Station, sits in a lavish old bank building, with vaults replaced by tankards of beer and a fine kitchen. They have a fun, traditional menu with more fresh veggies than fries, and a plush, vivid pub scene good for a meal or just a drink (£6.25 sandwiches, £8-10 meals, food served daily 12:00-21:30, drinks served daily 11:00-23:00, 172 Vauxhall Bridge Road, tel. 020/7828-1543).

St. George's Tavern is *the* pub for a meal in this neighbor-hood. They serve dinner from the same fun menu in three zones: on the sidewalk to catch the sun and enjoy some people-watching, in the sloppy pub, and in a classier back dining room. They're proud of their sausages and "toad in the hole." The scene is inviting for just a beer, too (£7-10 meals, Mon-Sat 10:00-22:00, Sun until 21:30, corner of Hugh Street and Belgrave Road, tel. 020/7630-1116).

Near Notting Hill and Bayswater Accommodations

For locations, see the map on page 727.

Maggie Jones, a Charles Dickens-meets-Ella Fitzgerald splurge, is exuberantly rustic and very English, with a 1940s-jazz soundtrack. You'll get solid English cuisine, including huge plates of crunchy vegetables, served by a young and casual staff. It's pricey, but the portions are huge (especially the meat-and-fish pies, their specialty). You're welcome to save lots by splitting your main course. The candlelit upstairs is the most romantic, while the basement is kept lively with the kitchen, tight seating, and lots of action. If you eat well once in London, eat here—and do it quick, before it burns down (lunch—£5 starters, £7 main dishes; dinner—£6-9 starters, £10-23 main dishes; Mon-Sat 12:00-15:00 & 18:30-23:00, Sun 12:30-16:00 & 18:30-22:30, reservations recommended, 6 Old Court Place, just east of Kensington Church Street, near High Street Kensington Tube stop, tel. 020/7937-6462).

The Churchill Arms pub and **Thai Kitchen** (same location) are local hangouts, with good beer and a thriving old-English ambience in front, and hearty £8 Thai plates in an enclosed patio in the back. You can eat the Thai food in the tropical hideaway (table service) or in the atmospheric pub section (order at the counter and they'll bring it to you). They also serve basic English pub food at lunch (£3 sandwiches, £6 meals). The place is festooned with Churchill memorabilia and chamber pots (including one with Hitler's mug on it—hanging from the ceiling farthest from Thai Kitchen—sure to cure the constipation of any Brit during World War II). Arrive by 18:00 or after 21:00 to avoid a line. During busy times, diners are limited to an hour at the table (daily 12:00-22:00, 119 Kensington Church Street, tel. 020/7792-1246).

The Prince Edward serves good grub in a quintessential pub setting (£7-12 meals, Mon-Wed 10:00-23:00, Thu-Sat 10:00-23:30, Sun 10:00-22:30, plush-pubby indoor seating or sidewalk tables, family-friendly, pay Wi-Fi, 2 blocks north of Bayswater Road at the corner of Dawson Place and Hereford Road, 73 Prince's Square, tel. 020/7727-2221).

Café Diana is a healthy little eatery serving sandwiches, salads, and Middle Eastern food. It's decorated—almost shrine-like—with photos of Princess Diana, who used to drop by for pita sandwiches. You can dine in the simple interior, or order some food from the counter to go (£3-5 sandwiches, £6-8 meat dishes, daily 8:00-23:00, 5 Wellington Terrace, on Bayswater Road, opposite Kensington Palace Garden Gates, where Di once lived, tel. 020/7792-9606, Abdul).

On Queensway: The road called Queensway is a multi-ethnic food circus, lined with lively and inexpensive eateries—browse the options along here and choose your favorite. For a cut above, head for **Royal China Restaurant**—filled with London's Chinese population, who consider this one of the city's best eateries. It's dressed up in black, white, and gold, with candles and brisk waiters. While it's pricier than most neighborhood Chinese restaurants, the food is noticeably better (£9-13 dishes, Mon-Thu 12:00-23:00, Fri-Sat 12:00-23:30, Sun 11:00-22:00, dim sum until 17:00, 13 Queensway, tel. 020/7221-2535). For a lowbrow alternative, **Whiteleys Shopping Centre Food Court**—at the top end of Queensway—offers a fun selection of ethnic and fast-food chain eateries among Corinthian columns, and a multiscreen theater in a delightful mall (daily 9:00-23:00; options include Yo! Sushi, good salads at Café Rouge, pizza, Starbucks, and a coin-op Internet place; third floor, corner of Porchester Gardens and Queensway).

Supermarkets: **Tesco** is a half-block from the Notting Hill Gate Tube stop (Mon-Sat 7:00-23:00, Sun 12:00-18:00, near intersection with Pembridge Road, 114-120 Notting Hill Gate). The smaller **Spar Market** is at 18 Queensway (Mon-Sat 7:00-24:00, Sun 9:00-24:00), and **Marks & Spencer** can be found in Whiteleys Shopping Centre (Mon-Sat 9:00-20:00, Sun 12:00-18:00).

South Kensington

Popular eateries line Old Brompton Road and Thurloe Street (Tube: South Kensington), and a good selection of cheap eateries are clumped around the Tube station. For locations, see the map on page 725.

La Bouchée Bistro Café is a classy hole-in-the-wall touch of France. This candlelit and woody bistro, with very tight seating, serves a two-course, £11.50 special on weekdays during lunch and from 17:30-18:30, and £17 *plats du jour* all *jour*. Reservations are smart in the evening (daily 12:00-15:00 & 17:30-23:30, 56 Old Brompton Road, tel. 020/7589-1929).

Moti Mahal Indian Restaurant, with minimalist-yet-classy mod ambience and attentive service, serves mostly Bangladeshi cuisine that's delicious. Consider chicken *jalfrezi* if you like spicy food, and buttery chicken if you don't (£10 dinners, daily 12:00-14:30 & 17:30-23:00, 3 Glendower Place, tel. 020/7584-8428).

Beirut Express has fresh, well-prepared Lebanese cuisine. In the front, you'll find take-away service as well as barstools for quick service (£4 sandwiches). In the back is a sit-down restaurant with £14 plates (daily 12:00-23:00, 65 Old Brompton Road, tel. 020/7591-0123).

Bosphorus Kebabs is the student favorite for a quick, fast, and hearty Turkish dinner. While mostly for take-away, they have a few tight tables indoors and on the sidewalk (£5 meals, Turkish kebabs, daily until 24:00, 59 Old Brompton Road, tel. 020/7584-4048).

Rocca di Papa is a bright and dressy Italian place with a heated terrace (£8 pizza, pasta, and salads; open daily, 73 Old Brompton Road, tel. 020/7225-3413).

The Anglesea Arms, with a great terrace surrounded by classy South Kensington buildings, is a destination pub that feels like the classic neighborhood favorite. It's a thriving and happy place, with a woody ambience and a mellow back dining room a world away from any tourism. Chef Julian Legge freshens up traditional English cuisine and prints up a daily menu listing his creative meals. While it'd be a shame to miss his cooking, this is also a fine place to just have a beer (£6 starters, £13 main dishes, meals served daily 12:00-15:00 & 18:00-22:00; from Old Brompton Road, turn right at Onslow Gardens and go down a few blocks to 15 Selwood Terrace; tel. 020/7373-7960).

Supermarket: **Tesco Express** is handy for picnics (daily 7:00-24:00, 50-52 Old Brompton Road).

Elsewhere in London

Medieval Banquet, near the Tower of London: In an underground, brick-arched room, costumed wenches bring you a tasty four-course medieval-themed meal (includes ale and red wine) as minstrels, knights, jesters, and contortionists perform. Couples, families, tour groups, and stag and hen parties sit at tables in alcoves; entertainers take turns performing in front of each alcove (in 15-minute segments, with breaks in between). To show you like an act, pound on the table. The nearly nightly show starts at 20:00 (Sun at 18:00) and ends about 22:15 (20:15 on Sun). Reserve in advance online or by phone (£50, family deal-£110 Sun-Thu, discount for Rick Steves readers, veggie option possible, medieval garb rentable, The Medieval Banquet Ivory House, St. Katharine Docks, enter docks off East Smithfield Street, Tube: Tower Hill, tel. 020/7480-5353, www.medievalbanquet.com).

Between St. Paul's and the Tower: **The Counting House,** formerly an elegant old bank, offers great £8-10 meals, nice homemade meat pies, fish, and fresh vegetables. The fun "nibbles menu" is available starting in the early evening until 22:00 (or until 21:00 on Mon-Tue; open Mon-Fri 11:00-23:00, gets really busy with the buttoned-down 9-to-5 crowd after 12:15 especially Thu-Fri, closed Sat-Sun, near Mansion House in The City, 50 Cornhill, tel. 020/7283-7123).

Near St. Paul's: **De Gustibus Sandwiches** is where a top-notch artisan bakery meets the public, offering fresh, you-design-it sandwiches, salads, and soups. Just one block below St. Paul's, it has simple seating or take-out picnic sacks for lugging to one of the great nearby parks (Mon-Fri 7:00-17:00, closed Sat-Sun, from church steps follow signs to youth hostel a block downhill, 53-55 Carter Lane, tel. 020/7236-0056; another outlet is inside the Borough Market in Southwark).

Near the British Library: Drummond Street (running just west of Euston Station—see map on page 732) is famous in London for cheap and good Indian vegetarian food (£5-10 dishes, £7 lunch buffet). Consider **Chutneys** (124 Drummond, tel. 020/7388-0604) and **Ravi Shankar** (133-135 Drummond, tel. 020/7388-6458) for a good *thali* (both open long hours daily).

London Connections

By Plane

Note that a number of discount airlines fly into and out of London's smaller airports, making this a nice, cheap option for traveling to other destinations.

Heathrow Airport

Heathrow Airport is one of the world's busiest airports. Think about it: 68 million passengers a year on 470,000 flights from 180 destinations riding 90 airlines, like some kind of global maypole dance. Read signs and ask questions. For Heathrow's airport, flight, and transfer information, call the switchboard at tel. 0844-335-1801, or visit the helpful website at www.heathrowairport.com.

Heathrow has five terminals: T-1 (mostly domestic and Irish flights, with some service to Europe and the US); T-2 (closed for renovation, should reopen in 2014); T-3 (North and South American, Asian, and some European flights); T-4 (European and US flights); and T-5 (British Airways flights only). You can walk between T-1 and T-3. To travel between the other terminals, you can take the Heathrow Express trains (free), buses (free), or the Tube (requires a ticket). Unlike most American airports, there is no train that links all the terminals together on one line, so you may have to transfer if you're going to T-4 or T-5.

If you're flying out of Heathrow, it's critical to confirm which terminal your flight will use (check the Web or call your airline in advance)—because if it's T-4 or T-5, you'll need to allow extra time. Taxi drivers generally know which terminal you'll need, but bus drivers may not.

Services: Each terminal has an airport information desk (generally daily 6:00-22:00), car-rental agencies, exchange bureaus, ATMs, a pharmacy, a VAT refund desk (tel. 020/8910-3682; you must present the VAT claim form from the retailer here to get

London's Airports

50 Kilometers
50 Miles

ENGLAND

LUTON

Cambridge

STANSTED

North Sea

LONDON

LONDON CITY

Bath

Reading

HEATHROW

GATWICK

CHANNEL TUNNEL

English Channel

To Paris & Brussels

your tax rebate on items purchased in Britain), and baggage storage (£8.50/item for 24 hours, hours vary by terminal but generally daily 5:30-23:00, www.left-baggage.co.uk). Get online 24 hours a day at Heathrow's Internet access points (at each terminal—T-4's is up on the mezzanine level) or with your laptop or mobile device (pay Wi-Fi provided by Boingo, www.boingo.com). A post office is on the first floor of T-3. Each terminal has cheap eateries.

Heathrow's small **"TI"** (tourist info shop), even though it's a for-profit business, is worth a visit to pick up free information: a simple map, the *London Planner,* and brochures (daily 6:30-22:00, 5-minute walk from T-3 in Tube station, follow signs to Underground; bypass queue for transit info to reach window for London questions).

Getting to London from Heathrow Airport

You have five basic options for traveling the 14 miles between Heathrow Airport and downtown London: Tube (£5.30/person), bus (£5/person), direct shuttle bus (£21.50/person), express train with connecting Tube or taxi (about £20/person), or taxi (about £55 per group).

By Tube (Subway): For £5.30, the Tube takes you from any Heathrow terminal to downtown London in 50-60 minutes on the Piccadilly Line (6/hour; depending on your destination, may require a transfer, buy ticket at the Tube station ticket window). If you plan to use the Tube for transport in London, it may make sense to buy a Travelcard or pay-as-you-go Oyster card at the Tube station ticket window at the airport. (For information on these passes, see page 654.) If your Travelcard covers only Zones 1-2, it does not include Heathrow (Zone 6); however, you can pay a small supplement for the initial trip from Heathrow to downtown.

If you're taking the Tube from downtown London *to* the airport, note that the Piccadilly Line trains don't stop at every terminal. Trains either stop at T-4, then T-1/T-3 (also called Heathrow Central), in that order; or T-1/T-3 and T-5. When leaving central London on the Tube, allow extra time if going to T-4 or T-5; since you have to be sure you get on a train going to your terminal, carefully check the destination information before you board.

By Bus: Most buses depart from the outdoor common area in the heart of the Heathrow complex called the Central Bus Station. It serves T-1 and T-3, and is a 5-minute walk from these terminals. To get to T-4 or T-5 from the Central Bus Station, go inside, downstairs, and follow signs to take Heathrow Express trains to your terminal (free, but only runs every 15-20 minutes to those terminals); or catch one of the free buses that circulate between terminals.

National Express has regular service from Heathrow's Central Bus Station to Victoria Coach Station in downtown London, near several of my recommended hotels. While slow, the bus is affordable and convenient for those staying near Victoria Station (£5, 1-2/hour, less frequent from Victoria Station to Heathrow, 45-60 minutes depending on time of day, tel. 0871-781-8181, www.nationalexpress.com).

By Shuttle: SkyShuttle operates buses about every half-hour between all Heathrow terminals and hotels in central London (£21.50/person one-way, £34.40/person round-trip; reservations tel. 0845-481-0960, call between 6:00-22:00; www.skyshuttle.co.uk).

By Train: Two different trains (slow for £8.50, fast for £16.50) run between Heathrow Airport and London's Paddington Station. At Paddington Station, you're in the thick of the Tube system, with easy access to any of my recommended neighborhoods—my Paddington hotels are just outside the front door, and Notting Hill Gate is just two Tube stops away. The **Heathrow Connect** train is the slightly slower, much cheaper option, serving T-1 and T-3 at one station called Heathrow Central; use free transfers if you're coming from either T-4 or T-5 (£8.50 one-way, 2/hour, 30 minutes, tel. 0845-678-6975, www.heathrowconnect.com). The **Heathrow Express** train is fast (15 minutes to downtown from T-1 and T-3; 21 minutes from T-5; transfer required from T-4) and runs more frequently (4/hour), but it's pricey (£16.50 "express class" one-way, £32 round-trip, ask about discount promos at ticket desk, buy ticket before you board or pay a £3 surcharge to buy it on the train, covered by BritRail pass, daily 5:10-23:25, tel. 0845-600-1515, www.heathrowexpress.co.uk). At the airport, you can use Heathrow Express as a free transfer between terminals.

By Taxi: Taxis from the airport cost about £45-70 to west and central London (one hour). For four people traveling together, this can be a deal. Hotels can often line up a cab back to the airport for about £30-40. For the cheapest taxi to the airport, don't order one from your hotel. Simply flag down a few and ask them for their best "off-meter" rate. Locals refer to hired cars that do the trip off-meter as "mini-cabs." These are reliable and generally cost about what you'd pay for a taxi in good traffic, but—with a fixed price—they can save you money when taxis are snarled in congestion with the meter running.

Gatwick Airport

More and more flights land at Gatwick Airport, halfway between London and the South Coast (tel. 0844-335-1802, www.gatwick airport.com). Gatwick has two terminals, North and South, which are easily connected by a free monorail (two-minute trip, runs 24 hours daily). Note that boarding passes say "Gatwick N" or "Gatwick S" to indicate your terminal. British Airways flights generally use Gatwick North. The Gatwick Express trains (described next) stop only at Gatwick South. Schedules in each terminal show only arrivals and departures from that terminal.

Getting to London: Gatwick Express trains are clearly the best way into London from this airport. They shuttle conveniently between Gatwick South and London's Victoria Station, with many of my recommended hotels close by (£18, £31 round-trip, 10 percent discount online, 4/hour, 30 minutes, runs 5:00-24:00 daily, tel. 0845-850-1530, www.gatwickexpress.com). When you buy your tickets at the station before boarding, ask about their deal where three adults travel for the price of two, or four for the price of three. (If you see others in the ticket line, suggest buying your tickets together—you'll save more than £5 each.)

You can save a few pounds by taking Southern Railway's slower and less frequent **shuttle train** between Gatwick South and Victoria Station (£11, up to 4/hour, 45 minutes, tel. 0845-127-2920, www.southernrailway.com).

A train also runs from Gatwick South to **St. Pancras International Station** (£9, 8/hour, 1 hour, www.firstcapitalconnect .co.uk)—useful for travelers taking the Eurostar train (to Paris or Brussels) or staying in the St. Pancras/King's Cross neighborhood.

Even slower, but cheap and handy to the Victoria Station neighborhood, you can take the **bus** from Gatwick to Victoria (£7.50, hourly, 1.5 hours, tel. 0871-781-8181, www.nationalexpress .com).

London's Other Airports

Stansted Airport: If you're using Stansted (tel. 0870-0000-303, www.stanstedairport.com), you have several options for getting into or out of London. Two different **buses** connect the airport and downtown London's Victoria Station neighborhood: National Express (£10, £17 round-trip, every 20 minutes, 1.75 hours, runs 24 hours a day, picks up and stops throughout London, ends at Victoria Coach Station, tel. 0871-781-8181, www.nationalexpress .com) and Terravision (£9, 2-3/hour, 1.25 hours, ends at Green Line Coach Station just south of Victoria Station). Or you can take the faster, pricier Stansted Express **train** (£18-20 one-way, £25-27 round-trip, connects to London's Tube system at Tottenham Hale and Liverpool Street, 4/hour, 45 minutes, 5:00-23:00, tel. 0845-850-0150, www.stanstedexpress.com). Stansted is expensive by **cab;** figure £120 one-way from central London.

Luton Airport: For Luton (airport tel. 01582/405-100, www.london-luton.co.uk), there are two choices into or out of London. The fastest way to go is by **rail** to London's St. Pancras International Station (£12 one-way, 1-5/hour, 25-45 minutes—check schedule to avoid the slower trains, tel. 0845-712-5678, www.eastmidlandstrains.co.uk); catch the 10-minute shuttle bus (£1) from outside the terminal to the Luton Airport Parkway Station. The Green Line express **bus** #757 runs to Buckingham Palace Road, just south of London's Victoria Station (£13 one-way, £16 round-trip, small discount for easyJet passengers who buy online, 2-4/hour, 1.25-1.5 hours, 24 hours a day, tel. 0844-801-7261, www.greenline.co.uk). If you're sleeping at Luton, consider easyHotel (see listing on page 734).

London City Airport: There's a slim chance you might use London City Airport (tel. 020/7646-0088, www.londoncity airport.com). To get into London, take the Docklands Light Railway (DLR) to the Bank Tube station, which is one stop east of St. Paul's on the Central Line (£4.30 one-way, covered by Travelcard, £3.10-2.60 on Oyster card, 22 minutes, tel. 020/7222-1234, www.tfl.gov.uk/dlr).

Connecting London's Airports by Bus

More and more travelers are taking advantage of cheap flights out of London's smaller airports. A handy **National Express bus** runs between Heathrow, Gatwick, Stansted, and Luton airports—easier than having to cut through the center of London—although traffic can be bad and increase travel times (tel. 0871-781-8181, www.nationalexpress.com).

From Heathrow Airport to: Gatwick Airport (1-4/hour, 1-1.5 hours, £21.50 one-way, £40 round-trip, allow at least three hours between flights), **Stansted Airport** (1-2/hour, 1.5-1.75 hours, £24 one-way, £31 round-trip), **Luton Airport** (hourly, 1-1.5 hours, £21 one-way, £31 round-trip).

London's Major Train Stations

To North Wales & Glasgow

To Cambridge, York & Edinburgh

to Harwich

To Stratford-upon-Avon

To Canterbury & Dover and via Eurostar: Paris & Brussels

ST. PANCRAS INT'L

RAF MUSEUM LONDON

STRATFORD INT'L (2012 OLYMPIC PARK)

To Heathrow Airport, Windsor, Bath, S. Wales & Cotswolds

MARYLE-BONE   EUSTON   KING'S CROSS

LONDON CITY AIRPORT

PADDINGTON   TRAF. SQ.   LIVERPOOL STREET   DOCKLANDS

L O N D O N   WATER-LOO

VICTORIA   LONDON BRIDGE   O2 ARENA

CANARY WHARF ON ISLE OF DOGS   • GREENWICH

Thames   River

Kew Gardens

WIMBLEDON

To Brighton

= Central London

HAMPTON COURT PALACE

To Gatwick Airport, Canterbury, Dover & Brighton

To Salisbury

5 Kilometers

5 Miles

LONDON

By Train

Britain is covered by a myriad of rail systems (owned by different companies), which together are called National Rail. London, the country's major transportation hub, has a different train station for each region. There are nine main stations:

Euston—Serves northwest England, North Wales, and Scotland.

King's Cross—Serves northeast England and Scotland, including York and Edinburgh.

Liverpool Street—Serves east England, including Essex and Harwich.

London Bridge—Serves south England, including Brighton.

Marylebone—Serves southwest and central England, including Stratford-upon-Avon.

Paddington—Serves south and southwest England, including Heathrow Airport, Windsor, Bath, South Wales, and the Cotswolds.

St. Pancras International—Serves north and south England, plus the Eurostar to Paris or Brussels.

Victoria—Serves Gatwick Airport, Canterbury, Dover, and

Brighton.

Waterloo—Serves southeast England, including Salisbury.

In addition, there are other, smaller train stations in London that you are not likely to use, such as **Charing Cross** or **Blackfriars.**

Any train station has schedule information, can make reservations, and can sell tickets for any destination. Most stations offer a baggage-storage service (£8/bag for 24 hours, look for *left luggage* signs); because of long security lines, it can take a while to check or pick up your bag (www.excess-baggage.com). For more details on the services available at each station, see www.nationalrail.co.uk /stations.

Buying Tickets: For general information, call 0845-748-4950 (or visit www.nationalrail.co.uk or www.eurostar.com; £5 booking fee for telephone reservations). If you book far enough ahead, you might find discounted train tickets on certain routes at www .megatrain.com (tel. 0871-266-3333; as they also sell bus tickets, be careful to specify that you want to take the train).

Train Connections from London
To Paris or Brussels via Eurostar Train
From St. Pancras International Station to: Paris (15/day, 2.5 hours), **Bruges** (via Brussels: 10/day, 2.5 hours to Brussels Midi; then transfer, backtracking to Bruges: 2/hour, 1 hour, entire trip just a few dollars more with Eurostar ticket). Arrive at least 30 minutes early; security procedures for the Eurostar are similar to airport check-in.

Eurostar Fares: Channel fares are reasonable but complicated. Prices vary depending on how far ahead you reserve, whether you can live with restrictions, and whether you're eligible for any discounts (children, youths, seniors, round-trip travelers, and railpass holders all qualify).

Fares can change without notice, but typically a **one-way, full-fare ticket** (with no restrictions on refundability) runs about $425 first-class and $300 second-class. **Cheaper seats** come with more restrictions and can sell out quickly (figure $100-160 for second-class, one-way). Those traveling with a railpass that covers France or Britain should look first at the **passholder** fare ($85-130 for second-class, one-way Eurostar trips).

Eurostar Routes

ENGLAND
London
Ebbsfleet
Ashford
English Channel
Calais-Fréthun
Lille-Europe
FRANCE
Paris
Amsterdam
NETH.
Brussels
BELG.

50 Kilometers
50 Miles

---- Eurostar
.... Channel Tunnel
----- Other Rail

Public Transportation near London

To North England & Scotland

To York & Scotland

King's Lynn

Norwich

ENGLAND

Coventry

Long Buckby

Hunt.

Ely

Stratford-upon-Avon

Warwick

Leam. Spa

Bedford

Cambridge

Worcester

Moreton

Banbury

Luton

To Hoek van Holland

Chelten-ham

Stow

COTSWOLDS

Oxford

Stansted

Harwich

Blenheim

Swindon

Didcot

London City

Southend

To Cardiff

Avebury

Reading

Slough

London

Greenwich

To Ostende

Bristol

Windsor

Heathrow

EUROSTAR

Ramsgate

Bath

Bedwyn

Canterbury

Wells

Stonehenge

Gatwick

Dover

Glaston-bury

South-ampton

Ashford

(CHUNNEL)

Calais

Salisbury

Brighton

Rye

To Cornwall

Poole

East-bourne

Hastings

Calais-Fréthun

Bourne-mouth

Portsmouth

To Paris

Weymouth

Isle of Wight

English Channel

FRANCE

----- Rail
- - - Bus
.... Boat

Area covered by London Plus Pass

30 Kilometers

30 Miles (approx. scale)

Note: Bus Lines Follow Most Rail Lines

For more details, visit my *Guide to Eurail Passes* (www.ricksteves .com/eurostar), Rail Europe (www.raileurope.com), or go directly to Eurostar (www.eurostar.com).

A tour company called BritainShrinkers sells one- or two-day tours to Paris, Brussels, or Bruges, enabling you to side-trip to these cities from London for less than most train tickets alone. For example, you'll pay about $175 for a one-day Paris "tour" (unescorted Mon-Sat day trip with Métro pass; tel. 020/7713-1311 or www.britainshrinkers.com). This can be a particularly good option if you need to get to Paris from London on short notice, when only the costliest fares are available.

Once you're confident about the time and date of your crossing, you can check and book fares by phone or online. Ordering online through Eurostar or major agents offers a print-at-home e-ticket option. You can also order by phone through Rail Europe at US tel. 800-387-6782 for home delivery before you go, or through Eurostar (tel. 0870-518-6186, priced in euros) and pick up your ticket at the train station. In continental Europe, you can buy your Eurostar ticket at any major train station in any country or at any travel agency that handles train tickets (expect a booking fee). In Britain, tickets can be issued only at the Eurostar office in St. Pancras International Station.

To Points West in Britain

From Paddington Station to: Bath (2/hour, 1.5 hours), **Oxford** (2/hour direct, 1 hour, more possible with transfer in Reading), **Penzance** (every 1-2 hours, 5-5.5 hours, possible change in Plymouth or Newton Abbot), and **Cardiff** (2/hour, 2 hours).

To Points North in Britain

From King's Cross Station: Trains run at least hourly, stopping in **York** (2 hours), **Durham** (3 hours), and **Edinburgh** (4.5 hours). Trains to **Cambridge** also leave from here (3/hour, 45-60 minutes).

From Euston Station to: Conwy (nearly hourly, 3.25 hours, transfer in Chester), **Liverpool** (hourly, 2 hours, more with transfer), **Blackpool** (1-2/hour, 2.75-3.25 hours, 1-2 transfers), **Keswick** (hourly, 4.5 hours, transfer to bus at Penrith), and **Glasgow** (1-2/hour, 4.5-5 hours).

From London's Other Stations

Trains run between London and **Canterbury,** leaving from St. Pancras International Station and arriving in Canterbury West (1-2/hour, 1 hour), as well as from London's Victoria Station and arriving in Canterbury East (2/hour, 1.5 hours).

Direct trains leave for **Stratford-upon-Avon** from Marylebone Station, located near the southwest corner of Regents Park (5/day direct, more with transfers, 2.25 hours).

To Other Destinations: Windsor (2/hour, 1 hour, direct from Waterloo Station; also 3/hour, 35 minutes, from Paddington Station with change in Slough), **Greenwich** (from Bank or Monument Tube stop take the DLR—Docklands Light Railway—to Cutty Sark Station), **Dover** (hourly, 1.25 hours, direct from St. Pancras International Station; also hourly, 2 hours, direct from Victoria Station or Charing Cross Station), **Brighton** (4-5/hour, 1 hour, from Victoria Station and London Bridge Station), **Portsmouth** (3/hour, 1.5-2 hours, most from Waterloo Station, a few from Victoria Station), and **Salisbury** (1-2/hour, 1.5 hours, from Waterloo Station).

By Bus

Buses are slower but considerably cheaper than trains for reaching destinations around Britain, and beyond. Most depart from **Victoria Coach Station,** which is one long block south of Victoria Station (near many recommended accommodations and Tube: Victoria). Inside the station, you'll find basic eateries, kiosks, and a helpful information desk stocked with schedules and ready to point you to your bus or answer any questions.

Most domestic buses are operated by **National Express** (tel.

LONDON

0871-781-8181, www.nationalexpress.com); their international departures are called **Eurolines** (tel. 0871-781-8177, www.euro lines.co.uk). A newer, smaller company called **Megabus** undersells National Express with deeply discounted promotional fares—the further ahead you buy, the less you pay (some trips for just £1.50, tend to be slower than National Express, toll tel. 0900-160-0900, www.megabus.com). They also sell discounted train tickets on selected routes.

Try to avoid bus travel on Friday and Sunday evenings, when weekend travelers are more likely to make buses sell out.

To ensure getting a ticket—and to save money with special promotions—you can book your ticket in advance online (see websites listed earlier). The cheapest pre-purchased tickets can be changed (for a £5 fee), but they're nonrefundable. If you have a British mobile phone, you can buy an "M-Ticket," which sends your paperless confirmation number right to your phone.

If you're planning to buy your ticket at the station, try to arrive an hour before the bus departs—or drop by the day before. (For buses to Stansted Airport and Oxford, you can buy the ticket on board; otherwise you'll buy it at a ticket window.) Watch your bags carefully—luggage thieves thrive at the station.

To Other Destinations in Britain: Bath (nearly hourly, 2.5-3.75 hours), **Oxford** (2-4/hour, about 1.5 hours), **Cambridge** (hourly, 2-2.5 hours), **Canterbury** (about hourly, 2-2.5 hours), **Dover** (about hourly, 2.5-3.25 hours), **Penzance** (5/day, 8.5-10 hours, overnight available), **Cardiff** (hourly, 3.25 hours), **Liverpool** (8/day direct, 5.25-6 hours, overnight available), **Blackpool** (4/ day direct, 6.25-7 hours, overnight available), **York** (4/day direct, 5.25 hours), **Durham** (4/day direct, 6.5-7.5 hours), **Glasgow** (3/day direct, 8-9 hours, train is a much better option), **Edinburgh** (2/day direct, 8.75-9.75 hours, go by train instead).

ITALY

ROME

Roma

Rome is magnificent and brutal at the same time. It's a showcase of Western civilization, with astonishingly ancient sights and a modern vibrancy. But if you're careless, you'll be run down or pickpocketed. And with the wrong attitude, you'll be frustrated by the kind of chaos that only an Italian can understand. On my last visit, a cabbie struggling with the traffic said, *"Roma chaos."* I responded, *"Bella chaos."* He agreed.

While Paris is an urban garden, Rome is a magnificent tangled forest. If your hotel provides a comfortable refuge; if you pace yourself; if you accept—and even partake in—the siesta plan; if you're well-organized for sightseeing; and if you protect yourself and your valuables with extra caution and discretion, you'll love it. (And Rome is much easier to live with if you can avoid the midsummer heat.)

For me, Rome is in a three-way tie with Paris and London as Europe's greatest city. Two thousand years ago, the word "Rome" meant civilization itself. Everything was either civilized (part of the Roman Empire, and Latin- or Greek-speaking) or barbarian. Today, Rome is Italy's political capital, the capital of Catholicism, and the center of the ancient world, littered with evocative remains. As you peel through its fascinating and jumbled layers, you'll find Rome's buildings, cats, laundry, traffic, and 2.7 million people endlessly entertaining. And then, of course, there are its stupendous sights.

Visit St. Peter's, the greatest church on earth, and scale Michelangelo's 448-foot-tall dome, the world's tallest. Learn something about eternity by touring the huge Vatican Museum. You'll find the story of creation—bright as the day it was painted—in the restored Sistine Chapel. Do the "Caesar Shuffle" through ancient Rome's Forum and Colosseum. Savor Europe's most sumptuous building, the Borghese Gallery, and take an early evening "Dolce Vita Stroll" down Via del Corso with Rome's beautiful people. Enjoy an after-dark walk from Campo de' Fiori to the Spanish Steps, lacing together Rome's Baroque and bubbly nightspots. Dine well at least once.

Planning Your Time

Rome is wonderful, but it's huge and exhausting. On a first-time visit, many travelers find that Rome is best done quickly—Italy is more charming elsewhere. But whether you're here for a day or a week, you won't be able to see all of these sights, so don't try—you'll keep coming back to Rome. After several dozen visits, I still have a healthy list of excuses to return.

Rome in a Day: Some people actually try to "do" Rome in a day. Crazy as that sounds, if all you have is a day, it's one of the most exciting days Europe has to offer. Start at 8:30 at the Colosseum. Then explore the Forum, hike over Capitoline Hill, and cap your "Caesar Shuffle" with a visit to the Pantheon. After a quick lunch, taxi to the Vatican Museum (the lines usually die down mid-afternoon, or you can reserve a visit online in advance). See the Vatican Museum, then St. Peter's Basilica (open until 19:00 April-Sept). Taxi back to Campo de' Fiori to find dinner. Finish your day lacing together all the famous floodlit spots (follow my self-guided Heart of Rome Walk). If you only want a day in Rome, consider side-tripping in from Florence, or fit it in before taking the night train to Venice.

Rome in Two to Three Days: On the first day, do the "Caesar Shuffle" from the Colosseum to the Forum, then over Capitoline Hill to the Pantheon. After a siesta, join the locals strolling from Piazza del Popolo to the Spanish Steps (follow my self-guided "Dolce Vita Stroll"). On the second day, see Vatican City (St. Peter's, climb the dome, tour the Vatican Museum). Have dinner on the atmospheric Campo de' Fiori, then walk to the Trevi Fountain and Spanish Steps (following my Heart of Rome Walk). With a third day, add the Borghese Gallery (reservations required) and the National Museum of Rome.

Orientation to Rome

Sprawling Rome actually feels manageable once you get to know it. The old core, with most of the tourist sights, sits in a diamond formed by Termini train station (in the east), the Vatican (west), Villa Borghese Gardens (north), and the Colosseum (south). The Tiber River runs through the diamond from north to south. In the

ROME

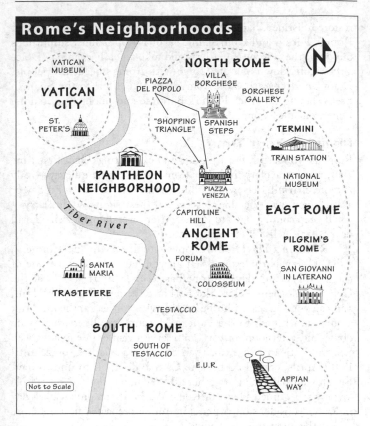

Rome's Neighborhoods

VATICAN MUSEUM

VATICAN CITY

ST. PETER'S

NORTH ROME

PIAZZA DEL POPOLO

VILLA BORGHESE

BORGHESE GALLERY

"SHOPPING TRIANGLE"

SPANISH STEPS

TERMINI

TRAIN STATION

NATIONAL MUSEUM

PANTHEON NEIGHBORHOOD

PIAZZA VENEZIA

Tiber River

CAPITOLINE HILL

ANCIENT ROME

FORUM

COLOSSEUM

EAST ROME

PILGRIM'S ROME

SAN GIOVANNI IN LATERANO

SANTA MARIA

TRASTEVERE

TESTACCIO

SOUTH ROME

SOUTH OF TESTACCIO

E.U.R.

APPIAN WAY

Not to Scale

ROME

center of the diamond sits Piazza Venezia, a busy square and traffic hub. It takes about an hour to walk from Termini train station to the Vatican.

Think of Rome as a series of neighborhoods, huddling around major landmarks.

Ancient Rome: In ancient times, this was home to the grandest buildings of a city of a million people. Today, the best of the classical sights stand in a line, from the Colosseum to the Forum to the Pantheon.

Pantheon Neighborhood: The Pantheon anchors the neighborhood I like to call the heart of Rome. It stretches eastward from the Tiber River through Campo de' Fiori and Piazza Navona, past the Pantheon to the Trevi Fountain.

Vatican City: Located west of the Tiber, it's a compact world of its own, with two great, huge sights: St. Peter's Basilica and the Vatican Museum.

North Rome: With the Spanish Steps, Villa Borghese Gardens, and trendy shopping streets (Via Veneto and the "shopping triangle"), this is a more modern, classy area.

East Rome: This includes the area around Termini train station, with its many recommended hotels and public-transportation connections. Nearby is the neighborhood I call "Pilgrim's Rome," with several prominent churches dotting the area south of the station.

South Rome: South of Vatican City is Trastevere, the seedy, colorful, wrong-side-of-the-river neighborhood that provides a look at village Rome. It's the city at its crustiest—and perhaps most "Roman." Across the Tiber River, directly south of the city center, is the Appian Way, home of the catacombs.

Within each of these neighborhoods, you'll find elements from the many layers of Rome's 2,000-year history: the marble ruins of ancient times; tangled streets of the medieval world; early Christian churches; grand Renaissance buildings and statues; Baroque fountains and church facades; 19th-century apartments; and 20th-century boulevards choked with traffic.

Since no one is allowed to build taller than St. Peter's dome, and virtually no buildings have been constructed in the city center since Mussolini got distracted in 1938, Rome has no modern skyline. The Tiber River is basically ignored—after the last floods (1870), the banks were built up very high, and Rome turned its back on its naughty river.

Tourist Information

Rome has two tourist information offices and numerous kiosks. The TI offices are at the airport (terminal 3) and Termini train station (daily 8:00-21:00, way down track 24, look for signs). Little kiosks (generally open daily 9:30-19:00) are near the Forum (on Piazza del Tempio della Pace), in Trastevere (on Piazza Sonnino), on Via Nazionale (at Palazzo delle Esposizioni), near Castel Sant'Angelo (at Piazza Pia), at the Church of Santa Maria Maggiore (on Via dell'Olmata), near Piazza Navona (at Piazza delle Cinque Lune), and near the Trevi Fountain (at Via del Corso and Via Minghetti). The TI's website is http://en.turismoroma.it.

At any TI, ask for a city map, a listing of sights and hours (in the free *Museums of Rome* booklet), and the free *Evento* booklet, with English-language pages listing the month's cultural events. The TIs don't offer room-booking services. If a commercial info-center offers to book you a room, just say no—you'll save money by booking direct.

If all you need is a **map,** skip the TI and pick up a freebie map at your hotel. The best map I found is published by Rough Guide (€8 in bookstores).

Rome's single best source of up-to-date tourist information is its **call center,** with English-speakers on staff. Dial 06-0608

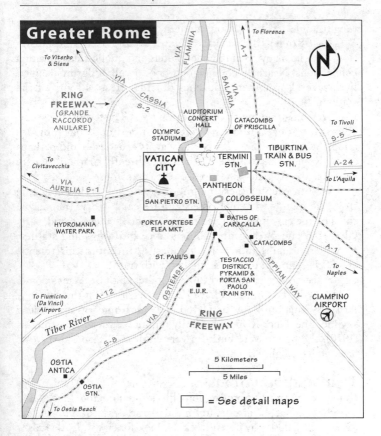

Greater Rome

(answered daily 9:00-21:00, press 2 for English).

Several English-oriented **websites** provide insight into events and daily life in the city: www.inromenow.com (light tourist info on lots of topics), www.wantedinrome.com (events and accommodation rentals), and http://rome.angloinfo.com (on living in and moving to Rome).

Arrival in Rome

By Train at Termini Station

Termini, Rome's main train station, is a buffet of tourist services. While information desks are jammed with travelers, very handy red info kiosks at the head of the tracks can answer your simple questions.

Along track 24, about 100 yards down, you'll find the **TI** (daily 8:00-21:00), a **post office** (Mon-Fri 8:30-14:00, Sat 8:30-13:00, closed Sun), a **hotel booking** office, and **car rental** desks. The **baggage storage** *(deposito bagagli)* is downstairs (€4/5 hours, then cheaper, daily 6:00-24:00).

The **"Leonardo Express" train** to Fiumicino Airport runs from tracks 25-28; access is at the very far end of track 24 (see page 882). A good self-service **cafeteria,** Ciao, is near the head of track 24, upstairs, with fine views (daily 11:00-22:30).

Near track 1, you'll find a **pharmacy** (daily 7:30-22:00); along the same track is a **waiting room** and **train information office** (open 24/7). The handy **Drugstore Conad,** selling everything from groceries to electronics, is just downstairs (daily 6:00-24:00).

Elsewhere in the station are **ATMs,** late-hours banks, and 24-hour thievery. In the station's main entrance lobby, **Borri Books** sells books in English, including popular fiction, Italian history and culture, and kids' books, plus maps upstairs (daily 7:00-23:00).

Termini is also a local transportation hub. The city's two Metro lines (A and B) intersect downstairs at Termini Metro station. Buses (including Rome's hop-on, hop-off bus tours—see "Tours in Rome," later) leave across the square directly in front of the main station hall. The Metro and bus areas have been under construction—if they're still torn up, look for signs directing you to the Metro platform or bus stop. Taxis queue in front; avoid con men hawking "express taxi" services in unmarked cars (only use cars marked with the word *taxi* and a phone number). To avoid the long taxi line, simply hike out past the buses to the main street and hail one.

From Termini, most of my recommended hotels are easily accessible by foot (for those near this train station) or by Metro (for those in the Colosseum and Vatican neighborhoods).

The station has some sleazy sharks with official-looking business cards; avoid anybody selling anything unless they're in a legitimate shop at the station.

ROME

By Train or Bus at Tiburtina Station

Tiburtina, Rome's second-largest train station, is located in the city's northeast corner. In general, slower trains (from Milan, Bolzano, Bologna, Udine, and Reggio di Calabria) and some night trains (from Munich, Milan, Venice, Innsbruck, and Udine) use Tiburtina, as does the night bus to Fiumicino Airport. Direct night trains from Paris and Vienna use Termini train station instead.

Tiburtina is better known as a hub for bus service to destinations all across Italy. Buses depart from the piazza in front of the station. Ticket offices are located in the piazza and around the corner on Circonvallazione Nomentana.

Within the train station are a currency-exchange office and a 24-hour grocery. The Tiburtina station is on Metro line B, with easy connections to Termini (a straight shot, four stops away) and the entire Metro system. Or take bus #492 from Tiburtina to various city-center stops (such as Piazza Barberini, Piazza Venezia, and Piazza Cavour) and the Vatican neighborhood.

By Car

The Grande Raccordo Anulare circles greater Rome. This ring road has spokes that lead you into the center. Entering from the north, leave the autostrada at the Settebagni exit. Following the ancient Via Salaria (and the black-and-white *Centro* signs), work your way doggedly into the Roman thick of things. This will take you along the Villa Borghese Gardens and dump you right on Via Veneto in downtown Rome. Avoid rush hour and drive defensively: Roman cars stay in their lanes like rocks in an avalanche.

Parking in Rome is dangerous. Park near a police station or get advice at your hotel. The Villa Borghese underground garage is handy (Metro: Spagna). Garages charge about €24 per day.

Consider this: Your car is a worthless headache in Rome. Avoid a pile of stress and save money by parking at the huge, easy, and relatively safe lot behind the train station in the hill town of Orvieto (follow *P* signs from autostrada) and catching the train to Rome (hourly, 1-1.5 hours).

If you absolutely must drive and park a car in Rome, try to avoid commuter traffic by arriving Friday evening, or anytime during the weekend, and by leaving town during the weekend. Park your car at Tiburtina station (€1/hour, www.atac.roma.it) and take a 10-minute ride on the Metro line B into the center.

By Plane

For information on Rome's airports, see the end of this chapter.

Helpful Hints

Sightseeing Tips: Avid sightseers can save money by buying the Roma Pass (see "Tips on Sightseeing in Rome" sidebar, later), available at TIs and participating sights—buy one before visiting the Colosseum or Forum, and you can skip the long lines there. If you want to see the Borghese Gallery, remember to reserve ahead (see page 832). To bypass the long Vatican Museum line, reserve an entry time online (see page 822 for details).

Internet Access: If your hotel doesn't offer free or cheap Internet access, your hotelier can point you to the nearest Internet café.

Bookstores: These stores (all open daily except Anglo American and Open Door) sell travel guidebooks, including mine. The first two are chains, while the others have a more personal touch. **Borri Books** is at Termini train station, and **Feltrinelli**

International has two branches (at Largo Argentina, and just off Piazza della Repubblica at Via Vittorio Emanuele Orlando 84, tel. 06-482-7878). **Anglo American Bookshop** has great art and history sections (closed all day Sun and Mon morning, a few blocks south of Spanish Steps at Via della Vite 102, tel. 06-679-5222). **Libreria Fanucci** is centrally located (a block toward the Pantheon from Piazza Navona at Piazza Madama 8, tel. 06-686-1141). In Trastevere, Irishman Dermot at the **Almost Corner Bookshop** stocks an Italian-interest section (Via del Moro 45, tel. 06-583-6942), and the **Open Door Bookshop** carries the only used books in English in town (closed Sun, Via della Lungaretta 23, tel. 06-589-6478).

Laundry: Your hotelier can direct you to the nearest launderette. The **ondablu** chain usually comes with Internet access; one of their more central locations is near Termini train station (€2/hour, about €8 to wash and dry a 15-pound load, usually open daily 8:00-22:00, Via Principe Amedeo 70b, tel. 06-474-4647).

Travel Agencies: You can get train tickets and railpass-related reservations and supplements at travel agencies (at little or no additional cost), avoiding a trip to a train station. Your hotelier will know of a convenient agency nearby.

Dealing with (and Avoiding) Problems

Theft Alert: While violent crime is rare in the city center, petty theft is rampant. With sweet-talking con artists meeting you at the station, well-dressed pickpockets on buses, and thieving gangs of children at the ancient sites, Rome is a gauntlet of rip-offs. Although it's not as bad as it was a few years ago, and pickpockets don't want to hurt you—they usually just want your money—green or sloppy tourists will be scammed. Thieves strike when you're distracted. Don't trust kind strangers. Keep nothing important in your pockets. Be most on guard while boarding and leaving buses and subways. Thieves crowd the door, then stop and turn while others crowd and push from behind. You'll find less crowding and commotion—and less risk—waiting for the end cars of a subway rather than the middle cars. The sneakiest thieves pretend to be well-dressed businessmen (generally with something in their hands), or tourists wearing fanny packs and toting cameras and even Rick Steves guidebooks.

Scams abound: Don't give your wallet to self-proclaimed "police" who stop you on the street, warn you about counterfeit (or drug) money, and ask to see your cash. If a bank machine eats your ATM card, see if there's a thin plastic insert with a tongue hanging out that thieves use to extract it.

ROME

Tips on Sightseeing in Rome

These tips can help you use your time and money efficiently, making the Eternal City seem less eternal and more entertaining.

Passes

Roma Pass: Rome offers several sightseeing passes to help you save money. For most visitors, the Roma Pass (www.romapass.it) is the clear winner. The Roma Pass costs €25 and is valid for three days, covering public transportation and free or discounted entry to Roman sights. You get free admission to your first two sights (where you also get to skip the ticket line), and then a discount on the rest within the three-day window. Sights covered (or discounted) by the pass include the following: Colosseum/Palatine Hill/Roman Forum, Borghese Gallery (though you still must make a reservation and pay the €2 booking fee), Capitoline Museums, Castel Sant'Angelo, Montemartini Museum, Ara Pacis, Museum of Roman Civilization, Etruscan Museum, Baths of Caracalla, Trajan's Market, and some of the Appian Way sights. The pass also covers four branches of the National Museum of Rome, considered as a single "sight": Palazzo Massimo (the most important of the lot), Crypta Balbi (medieval art), Palazzo Altemps (sculpture collection), and Museum of the Bath (ancient inscriptions).

If you'll be visiting any two of the major sights in a three-day period, get the pass. It's sold at participating sights, TIs, and even the tobacco shop in the Colosseo Metro station. Try to buy it at a less crowded TI or sight. Don't bother to order it online—you have to physically pick up the pass in Rome, which negates any time-saving advantage.

Validate your Roma Pass by writing your name and validation date on the card. Then insert it directly into the turnstile at your first two (free) sights. At other sights, show it at the ticket office to get your reduced (*ridotto*) price—about 30 percent off.

To get the most of your pass, visit the two most expensive sights first—for example, the Colosseum (€12) and the National Museum (€10). Definitely use it to bypass the long ticket line at the Colosseum. For sights that normally sell a combined ticket (such as the Colosseum/Palatine Hill/Roman Forum or the National Museum branches), visiting the combined sight counts as a single entry.

The Roma Pass comes with a three-day transit pass. Write your name and birth date on the transit pass, validate it on your first bus or Metro ride by passing it over a sensor at a turnstile or validation machine (look for a yellow circle), and you can take unlimited rides within Rome's city limits until midnight of the third day.

The TI's other passes—Roma & Più Pass ("Rome & More")

and the Archeologia Card—are generally not worth the trouble for most tourists.

Combo-Ticket for Colosseum, Forum, and Palatine Hill: A €12 combo-ticket covers these three adjacent sights (no individual tickets are sold per sight). The combo-ticket allows one entry per sight, and is valid for two days. Note that these sights are also covered by the Roma Pass. To avoid ticket-buying lines at the Colosseum and Forum, purchase your combo-ticket or Roma Pass at the lesser-visited Palatine Hill. Between the combo-ticket or Roma Pass, the pass is the better deal, unless you're planning on seeing only the sights covered by the combo-ticket.

Top Tips

Museum Reservations: The marvelous Borghese Gallery requires reservations in advance (for specifics, see page 832). You can reserve online to avoid long lines at the Vatican Museum (see page 822).

Opening Hours: Rome's sights have notoriously variable hours from season to season. Get a current listing of opening times from one of Rome's TIs—ask for the free booklet *Museums of Rome*. Or check online at www.060608.it/en (find "Cultural Heritage" in the menu under "Culture and Leisure"; search by using the Italian names of sights). On holidays, expect shorter hours or closures.

Churches: Many churches, which have divine art and free entry, open early (around 7:00-7:30), close for lunch (roughly 12:00-15:00), and close late (about 19:00). Kamikaze tourists maximize their sightseeing hours by visiting churches before 9:00 or late in the day, and, during the siesta, seeing the major sights that stay open all day (St. Peter's, Colosseum, Forum, Pantheon, Capitoline Museums, and National Museum of Rome). Many churches have "modest dress" requirements, which means no bare shoulders, miniskirts, or shorts—for men, women, or children. This dress code is enforced in Vatican City (most stringently inside St. Peter's Basilica, but also the Vatican Museum and anywhere inside the Vatican walls) and St. Paul's Outside the Walls. Elsewhere, you may see many tourists in shorts (but not skimpy shorts) touring churches.

Picnic Discreetly: Public drinking and eating is not allowed at major sights, though the ban has proven difficult to enforce. To avoid the risk of being fined, choose an empty piazza for your picnic, or keep a low profile.

Miscellaneous Tips: I carry a plastic water bottle and refill it at Rome's many public drinking spouts. Because public restrooms are scarce, use toilets at museums, restaurants, and bars.

If you know what to look out for, fast-fingered moms with babies and gangs of children picking the pockets and handbags of naive tourists are not a threat, but an interesting, albeit sad, spectacle. Pickpockets troll through the tourist crowds around the Colosseum, Forum, Piazza della Repubblica, and train and Metro stations. Watch them target tourists who are overloaded with bags or distracted with a camera. The kids look like beggars and hold up newspapers or cardboard signs to confuse their victims. They scram like stray cats if you're on to them.

Reporting Losses: To report lost or stolen items, file a police report (at Termini train station, with *polizia* at track 11 or with Carabinieri at track 20; offices are also at Piazza Venezia). You'll need the report to file an insurance claim for lost gear, and it can help with replacing your passport—first file the police report, then call your embassy to make an appointment (US embassy: tel. 06-46741, Via Vittorio Veneto 121, www.usembassy.it). For information on how to report lost or stolen credit cards, see page 12.

Emergency Numbers: Police—tel. 113. Ambulance—tel. 118.

Pedestrian Safety: Your main safety concern in Rome is crossing streets safely. Use extreme caution. Scooters don't need to stop at red lights, and even cars exercise what drivers call the "logical option" of not stopping if they see no oncoming traffic. Each year, as noisy gasoline-powered scooters are replaced by electric ones, the streets get quieter (hooray), but more dangerous for pedestrians. Follow locals like a shadow when you cross a street (or you'll spend a good part of your visit stranded on curbs). When you do cross alone, don't be a deer in the headlights. Find a gap in the traffic and walk with confidence while making eye contact with approaching drivers—they won't hit you if they can tell where you intend to go.

Staying/Getting Healthy: The siesta is a key to survival in summertime Rome. Lie down and contemplate the extraordinary power of gravity in the Eternal City. I drink lots of cold, refreshing water from Rome's many drinking fountains (the Forum has three).

There's a pharmacy (marked by a green cross) in every neighborhood. Several pharmacies stay open late in Termini train station (daily 7:30-22:00) and at Piazza dei Cinquecento 51 (open 24 hours daily, next to train station on the corner of Via Cavour, tel. 06-488-0019).

Embassies can recommend English-speaking doctors. Consider MEDline, a 24-hour home-medical service; doctors speak English and make calls at hotels for €150 (tel. 06-808-

ROME

0995). Anyone is entitled to free emergency treatment at public hospitals. The hospital closest to Termini train station is Policlinico Umberto 1 (entrance for emergency treatment on Via Lancisi, translators available, Metro: Policlinico). Readers also report that the staff at Santa Susanna Church, home of the American Catholic Church in Rome, offers useful advice and medical referrals (see page 840).

Getting Around Rome

Sightsee on foot, by city bus, by Metro, or by taxi. I've grouped your sightseeing into walkable neighborhoods. Make it a point to visit sights in a logical order. Needless backtracking wastes precious time.

The public transportation system, which is cheap and efficient, consists primarily of buses, a few trams, and the two underground subway (Metro) lines. Consider it part of your Roman experience.

The walking-tour company, Rome Walks, has produced an orientation video to Rome's transportation system; find it on YouTube by searching for "Understanding Rome's Public Transport."

For information, visit www.atac.roma.it, which has a useful route planner in English, or call 800-431-784.

Buying Tickets

All public transportation uses the same ticket. It costs €1, and is valid for one Metro ride—including transfers underground—plus unlimited city buses and *elettrico* buses during a 75-minute period. Passes good on buses and the Metro are sold in increments of one day (€4, good until midnight), three days (€11), and one week (€16, about the cost of two taxi rides).

You can purchase tickets and passes at some newsstands, tobacco shops (marked by a black-and-white *T* sign), and major Metro stations and bus stops—but not onboard. It's smart to stock up on tickets early, or to buy a pass or a Roma Pass (which includes a three-day transit pass—see page 770). That way, you don't have to run around searching for an open tobacco shop when you spot your bus approaching. Metro stations rarely have human ticket-sellers, and the machines are often either broken or require exact change (insert your smallest coin first).

Validate your ticket by sticking it in the Metro turnstile (magnetic strip-side up, arrow-side first) or in the machine when you board the bus (magnetic strip-side down, arrow-side first)—watch others and imitate. It'll return your ticket with your expiration time printed. To get through a Metro turnstile with a transit pass or Roma Pass, use it just like a ticket (on buses, however, you only need to validate your pass if that's your first time using it).

Rome's Metro

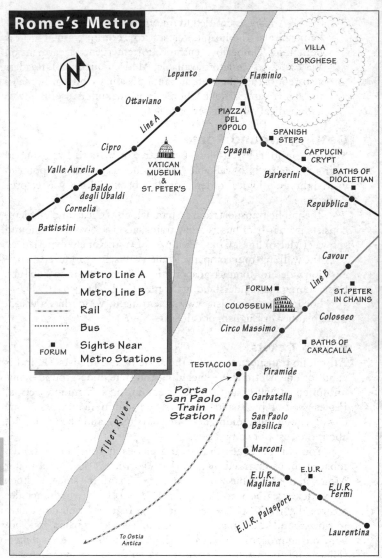

Metro Line A

Metro Line B

Rail

Bus

■ FORUM **Sights Near Metro Stations**

VILLA BORGHESE

Lepanto

Flaminio

Ottaviano

Line A

PIAZZA DEL POPOLO

SPANISH STEPS

Spagna

CAPPUCIN CRYPT

Cipro

VATICAN MUSEUM & ST. PETER'S

Valle Aurelia

Barberini

BATHS OF DIOCLETIAN

Baldo degli Ubaldi

Cornelia

Repubblica

Battistini

Cavour

Line B

FORUM ■

ST. PETER IN CHAINS ■

COLOSSEUM

Colosseo

Circo Massimo

BATHS OF CARACALLA ■

TESTACCIO ■

Piramide

Porta San Paolo Train Station

Garbatella

San Paolo Basilica

Tiber River

Marconi

E.U.R. Magliana

E.U.R. ■

E.U.R. Fermi

E.U.R. Palasport

To Ostia Antica

Laurentina

By Metro

The Roman subway system (Metropolitana, or "Metro") is simple, with two clean, cheap, fast lines—A and B—that intersect at Termini train station. The Metro runs from 5:30 to 23:30 (Fri-Sat until 1:30 in the morning). The subway's first and last compartments are generally the least crowded (and the least likely to harbor pickpockets).

You'll notice lots of big holes in the city as a new line is built.

ROME

Line C, from the Colosseum to Largo Argentina, will likely be done in 2020. Because of this construction, you may find the system closed at 21:00 on some nights.

While much of Rome is not served by its skimpy subway, the following stops are helpful:

Termini (intersection of lines A and B): Termini train station, shuttle train to airport, National Museum of Rome, and recommended hotels

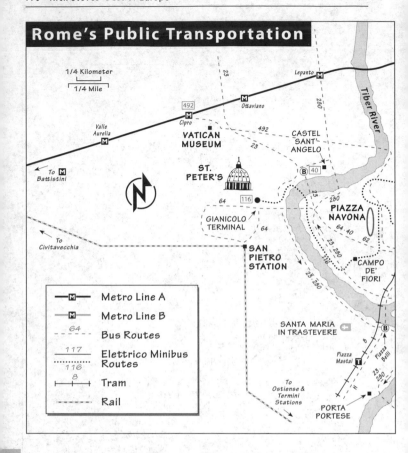

Rome's Public Transportation

1/4 Kilometer

1/4 Mile

To Battistini

Valle Aurelia

Cipro

492

Ottaviano

Lepanto

VATICAN MUSEUM

ST. PETER'S

CASTEL SANT' ANGELO

492

23

280

B 40

To Civitavecchia

GIANICOLO TERMINAL

64 116

64

23

PIAZZA NAVONA

64 40

62

SAN PIETRO STATION

23 280

116

23 280

CAMPO DE' FIORI

Tiber River

SANTA MARIA IN TRASTEVERE

B

Piazza Mastai

T

Piazza Balli

To Ostiense & Termini Stations

PORTA PORTESE

23 280

Legend:

—M—	Metro Line A
···M···	Metro Line B
64	Bus Routes
117	Elettrico Minibus Routes
116	
8	Tram
	Rail

Repubblica (line A): Baths of Diocletian, Via Nazionale, and recommended hotels

Barberini (line A): Cappuccin Crypt, Trevi Fountain, and Villa Borghese

Spagna (line A): Spanish Steps and classy shopping area

Flaminio (line A): Piazza del Popolo, start of recommended "Dolce Vita Stroll" down Via del Corso

Ottaviano (line A): St. Peter's Basilica and Vatican Museum

Cipro (line A): Recommended hotels

Tiburtina (line B): Tiburtina train and bus station

Colosseo (line B): Colosseum, Roman Forum, bike rental, and recommended hotels

By Bus

The Metro is handy, but it won't get you everywhere—take the bus. Bus routes are clearly listed at the stops. TIs usually don't have bus maps, but with some knowledge of major stops, you won't necessarily need one (though if you do want a route map, find one printed inside the free-at-hotels *Evento* magazine, or buy it from tobacco shops).

Buses—especially the touristy #40 and #64—are havens for thieves and pickpockets. Assume any commotion is a thief-created distraction. If one bus is packed, there's likely a second one on its tail with far fewer crowds and thieves. Once you know the bus system, you'll find it's easier than searching for a cab.

Tickets have a barcode and must be stamped on the bus in the yellow box with the digital readout (be sure to retrieve your ticket). Validate your ticket as you board (magnetic-strip side down, arrow-side first)—otherwise you're cheating. While relatively safe, riding without a stamped ticket on the bus is stressful. Inspectors fine even innocent-looking tourists €50. There's no need to validate a transit pass or Roma Pass on the bus, unless your pass is new and hasn't yet been stamped elsewhere in the transit system. Bus etiquette (not always followed) is to board at the front or rear doors and exit out the middle.

Regular bus lines start running at about 5:30, and during the day they run every 5-10 minutes. After 23:30, and sometimes earlier (such as on Sundays), buses are less frequent but dependable. Night buses are also reliable, and are marked with an *N* and an owl symbol on the bus-stop signs.

These are the major bus routes:

Bus #64: This bus cuts across the city, linking Termini station with the Vatican, stopping at Piazza della Repubblica (sights), Via Nazionale (recommended hotels), Piazza Venezia (near Forum), Largo Argentina (near Pantheon), and St. Peter's Basilica (get off just past the tunnel). Ride it for a city overview and to watch pickpockets in action. The #64 can get horribly crowded.

Bus #40: This express bus, which mostly follows the #64 route (but branches off on the Vatican side of the river), is especially helpful—with fewer stops and crowds.

The following three routes conveniently connect Trastevere with other parts of Rome:

Bus #H: This express bus, linking Termini station and Trastevere, makes a few stops on Via Nazionale (for Trastevere, get off at Piazza Belli, just after crossing the Tiber River).

Bus #8: This tram connects Largo Argentina with Trastevere (get off at Piazza Belli).

Buses #23 and #280: These link the Vatican with Trastevere and Testaccio, stopping at the Vatican Museum (nearest stop is Via Leone IV), Castel Sant'Angelo, Trastevere (Piazza Belli), Porta Portese (Sunday flea market), and Piramide (Metro and gateway to Testaccio).

Other useful routes include:

Bus #62: Largo Argentina to St. Peter's Square.

Bus #81: San Giovanni in Laterano, Largo Argentina, and Piazza Risorgimento (Vatican).

Buses #85 and #87: Piazza Venezia, Colosseum, San Clemente, and San Giovanni in Laterano.

Bus #492: Travels east-west across the city, connecting Tiburtina (train and bus stations), Piazza Barberini, Piazza Venezia, Piazza Cavour (Castel Sant'Angelo), and Piazza Risorgimento (Vatican).

Bus #714: Termini station, Santa Maria Maggiore, San Giovanni in Laterano, and Terme di Caracalla (Baths of Caracalla).

Elettrico **Minibuses:** Two cute *elettrico* minibuses wind through the narrow streets of old and interesting neighborhoods, and are great for transport or simple joyriding.

Elettrico **#116** runs through the medieval core of Rome: Ponte

Vittorio Emanuele II (near Castel Sant'Angelo) to Campo de' Fiori, Pantheon, Piazza Barberini, and the southern edge of the scenic Villa Borghese Gardens.

Elettrico #117 connects San Giovanni in Laterano, Colosseo, Via dei Serpenti, Trevi Fountain, Piazza di Spagna, and Piazza del Popolo—and vice versa. Where Via del Corso hits Piazza del Popolo, a #117 is usually parked and ready to go. Riding it from here to the end of the line, San Giovanni in Laterano, makes for a fine joyride that leaves you, conveniently, at a great sight.

By Taxi

I use taxis in Rome more often than in other cities. They're reasonable and useful for efficient sightseeing in this big, hot metropolis. Taxis start at €2.80, then charge about €1.30 per kilometer (surcharges: €1 on Sun, €3 for late-night hours of 22:00-7:00, one regular suitcase or bag rides free, tip by rounding up to the nearest euro). Sample fares: Termini train station to Vatican-€10; Termini to Colosseum-€6; Colosseum to Trastevere-€7 (or look up your route at www.worldtaximeter.com). Three or four companions with more money than time should taxi almost everywhere.

It's tough to wave down a taxi in Rome, especially at night. Find the nearest taxi stand by asking a passerby or a clerk in a shop, *"Dov'è una fermata dei taxi?"* (doh-VEH OO-nah fehr-MAH-tah DEHee TAHK-see). Some taxi stands are listed on my maps. To save time and energy, have your hotel or restaurant call a taxi for you; the meter starts when the call is received (generally adding a euro or two to the bill). To call a cab on your own, dial 06-4994 or 06-6645. It's routine for Romans to ask the waiter in a restaurant to call a taxi when they ask for the bill. The waiter will tell you how many minutes you have to enjoy your coffee.

Beware of corrupt taxis. A common cabbie scam is to take your €20 note, drop it, and pick up a €5 note (similar color), claiming that's what you gave him. To avoid this scam, pay in small bills; if you only have a large bill, show it to the cabbie as you state its face value.

If hailing a cab on the street, be sure the meter is restarted when you get in (should be around €2.80, or around €5 if you or your hotelier phoned for the taxi). Many meters show both the fare and the time elapsed during the ride—and some tourists pay €10 for an eight-and-a-half-minute trip (more than the fair meter rate).

When you arrive at the train station or airport, beware of hustlers conning naive visitors into unmarked, rip-off "express taxis." Only use official taxis, with a *taxi* sign and phone number marked on the door. By law, they must display a multilingual official price chart. If you have any problems with a taxi, point to the chart and ask the cabbie to explain it to you. Making a show of writing down the taxi number (to file a complaint) can motivate a driver to quickly settle the matter.

If you take a Rome city cab from the airport to anywhere in central Rome within the old city walls, the cost should be €40 (covering up to four people and their bags); however, every year some readers report being ripped off. The catch is that cabbies *not* based in Rome can charge €60. At the airport, look specifically for a Rome city cab, with the "SPQR" shield on the door. By law, they can charge only €40 for the ride (still, be sure to establish the price before you get in).

Tired travelers arriving at the airport will likely find it less stressful to take the airport shuttle van to their hotel, or catch the train to Termini station and take the Metro or a cheaper taxi from there (for details on getting from the airport to downtown Rome via taxi, shuttle, or train, see "Rome Connections," near the end of this chapter).

By Bike

Biking in the big city of Rome can speed up sightseeing or simply be an enjoyable way to explore. Though Roman traffic can be stressful, Roman drivers are respectful of cyclists. The best rides are on small streets in the city center. A bike path along the banks of the Tiber River makes a good 20-minute ride (easily accessed from the ramps at Porta Portese and Ponte Regina Margherita, near Piazza del Popolo). Get a bike with a well-padded seat—the little stones that pave Roman streets are unforgiving.

Top Bike Rental and Tours is professionally run by Roman bike enthusiasts who want to show off their city. Your rental comes with a handy map that suggests a route and indicates less-trafficked streets. Owner Ciro also offers four-hour-long English-only guided tours around the city and the Ancient Appian Way; check his website for days and times (rental: €8/half-day, €13/day, discount with this book, best to reserve in advance via email; bike tours: start at €29, reservations required; daily 9:30-19:00, leave ID for deposit, from Santa Maria Maggiore TI kiosk take Via dell'Olmata and turn left one block down, Via dei Quattro Cantoni 40, tel. 06-488-2893, www.topbikerental.com, info@topbikerental.com).

Cool Rent, near the Colosseo Metro stop, is cheaper but less helpful (€3/hour, €10/day, 3-person bike cart-€10/hour, daily 9:30-20:00, driver's license or other ID for deposit, 10 yards to the right as you exit the Metro). A second outlet is just off Via del Corso (on Largo di Lombardi, near corner of Via del Corso and Via della Croce, mobile 388-695-9303, Sasin).

Tours in Rome

To sightsee on your own, download my series of **free audio tours** that illuminate some of Rome's top sights and neighborhoods: the Colosseum, Roman Forum, St. Peter's Basilica, Sistine Chapel, Trastevere, Jewish Ghetto, and Ostia Antica (see sidebar on page 7 for details).

Walking Tours

Finding the best guided tours in Rome is challenging. Local guides are good but pricey. Tour companies are cheaper, but quality and organization are unreliable. If you hire a private Italian guide, consider organizing a group of four to six people from your hotel to split the cost (€180 for a half-day tour); this ends up costing about the same per person as going on a scheduled tour from one of the walking-tour companies listed below (about €25, generally expat guides).

Local Guides—I've worked with each of these licensed independent local guides. They're worth every euro. They speak excellent English, and enjoy tailoring tours to your interests. Their prices (roughly €50/hour, €180/half-day) flex with the day, season, and demand. Arrange your date and price by email.

    Francesca Caruso loves to teach and share her appreciation of her city, and has contributed generously to this chapter (francesca inroma@gmail.com). Popular with my readers, Francesca understandably books up quickly; if she's busy, she'll recommend one of her colleagues. **Carla Zaia** is an engaging expert on all things Roman (mobile 349-759-0723, carlaromeguide@gmail.com). **Cristina Giannicchi** has an archaeology background (mobile 338-111-4573, www.crisacross.com, crisgiannicchi@gmail.com). **Sara Magister,** a Roman with a doctorate in art history, is an official Vatican guide and author of a book on Renaissance Rome (tel. 06-583-6783, mobile 339-379-3813, a.magister@iol.it). **Giovanna Terzulli** is a personable, knowledgeable art historian (terzulli @tiscali.it).

Walking-Tour Companies—Rome has many highly competitive tour companies, each offering a series of themed walks through various slices of Rome. Three-hour guided walks generally cost €25-30 per person. Guides are usually native English speakers, often American expats. Tours are limited to small groups, geared to American tourists, and given in English only. I've listed some here, but without a lot of details on their offerings. Before your trip, spend some time on these companies' websites to get to know your options, as each company has a particular teaching and guiding personality. Some are highbrow, and others are less scholarly. It's

ROME

sometimes required, and always smart, to book a spot in advance (easy online). I must add that we get a lot of negative feedback on some of these tour companies. Readers report that their advertising can be misleading, and that scheduling mishaps are not uncommon.

Context Rome's walking tours are more intellectual than most, designed for travelers with longer-than-average attention spans. They are more expensive than others, and are led by "docents" rather than guides (tel. 06-9762-5204, US tel. 800-691-6036, www.contextrome.com). **Enjoy Rome** offers five different walks and a website filled with helpful information (Via Marghera 8a, tel. 06-445-1843, www.enjoyrome.com, info@enjoyrome.com). **Rome Walks** has put together several particularly creative itineraries (mobile 347-795-5175, www.romewalks.com, info@rome walks.com, Annie). **Roman Odyssey** gives readers of this book a discount on their walks and private tours (tel. 06-580-9902, mobile 328-912-3720, www.romanodyssey.com, Rahul). **Through Eternity** offers travelers with this book a discount on most tours; book through their website for the best discount (tel. 06-700-9336, mobile 347-336-5298, www.througheternity.com, info@through eternity.com, Rob). **Walks of Italy** has passionate, fun guides who lead a variety of good, reliable walks for groups no bigger than 12 people at a time (10 percent discount for readers of this book, US tel. 202/684-6916, Italian mobile 334-974-4274, www.walksofitaly .com, Jason Spiehler).

Hop-on, Hop-off Bus Tours

Several different agencies, including the ATAC public bus company, run hop-on, hop-off tours around Rome. These tours are constantly evolving and offer varying combinations of sights. You can grab one (and pay as you board) at any stop; Termini train station and Piazza Venezia are handy hubs. Although the city is perfectly walkable and traffic jams can make the bus dreadfully slow, these open-top bus tours remain popular.

Trambus 110 seems to be the best. It's operated by the ATAC city-bus lines, and offers an orientation tour on big red double-decker buses with an open-air upper deck. In less than two hours, you'll have 80 sights pointed out to you (with a next-to-worthless recorded narration). While you can hop on and off, the service can be erratic (mobbed midday, not ideal in bad weather) and it can be very slow in heavy traffic. It's best to think of this as a two-hour quickie orientation with scant information and lots of images. Stops include Ara Pacis, Piazza Cavour, St. Peter's Square, Corso Vittorio Emanuele (for Piazza Navona), Piazza Venezia, Colosseum, and Via Nazionale. Bus #110 departs every 20 minutes. You can catch it at any stop, including Termini train station.

ROME

Buy the €15 ticket as you board (runs daily 8:30-20:30, tel. 06-684-0901, www.trambusopen.com).

Archeobus is an open-top bus, also operated by ATAC, that runs twice hourly from Termini train station out to the ancient Appian Way (with stops at the Colosseum, Baths of Caracalla, San Callisto, San Sebastiano, and the Tomb of Cecilia Metella). This is a handy way to see the sights down this ancient Roman road, but it can be frustrating for various reasons—sparse narration, sporadic service, and difficult to hop on and off (€12, €30 combo-ticket with Trambus 110, ticket valid 24 hours, 1.5-hour loop, daily 8:30-16:30, from Termini train station and Piazza Venezia, tel. 06-684-0901, www.trambusopen.com). A similar bus laces together all the Christian sights.

Car and Minibus Tours

You can hire your own private car or minibus with driver through **Autoservizi Monti Concezio,** run by gentle, capable, and English-speaking Ezio (car-€35/hour, minibus-€40/hour, 3-hour minimum for city sightseeing, long rides outside Rome are more expensive, mobile 335-636-5907 or 349-674-5643, www.montitours.com, conceziomonti@gmail.com).

Miles & Miles Private Tours is a family-run company offering a number of tours (all explained on their website) in Mercedes minibuses and cars, all with good English-speaking driver/guides (€60/hour for up to 8 people, 5-hour minimum, Rick Steves readers booking direct get a 10 percent discount off any web prices they offer, tel. 06-6618-0403, mobile 331-466-4900, www.milesandmiles.net, info@milesandmiles.net, Francesco answers the mobile phone, while Kimberly—an American—runs their office). They can also provide unguided long-distance transportation (cheaper per hour than a tour); if traveling with a small group or a family from Rome to Florence or Siena, consider paying extra to turn the trip into a memorable day tour with door-to-door service.

ROME

Self-Guided Walks

Here are three walks that give you a moving picture of Rome, an ancient yet modern city. You'll walk through history (Roman Forum Tour), take a refreshing early-evening walk ("Dolce Vita Stroll"), and enjoy the thriving local scene, which is best at night (Heart of Rome Walk).

Roman Forum Tour

The Forum was the political, religious, and commercial center of the city. Rome's most important temples and halls of justice were here. This was the place for religious processions, political

Roman Forum

1. Arch of Titus
2. Basilica of Constantine
3. The Forum's Main Square
4. Temple of Julius Caesar
5. Temple of Antoninus Pius & Faustina
6. Basilica Aemilia
7. Caligula's Palace
8. Temple of Vesta
9. House of the Vestal Virgins
10. The Curia
11. Rostrum
12. Arch of Septimius Severus
13. Temple of Saturn
14. Column of Phocas

demonstrations, elections, important speeches, and parades by conquering generals. As Rome's empire expanded, these few acres of land became the center of the civilized world.

Cost: €12 combo-ticket (€9 base price plus frequent, mandatory exhibition fees), also includes Colosseum and Palatine Hill, valid two consecutive days, one entry per sight; also covered by Roma Pass. To avoid standing in a long ticket-buying line, see tips on "Avoiding Lines" on page 802.

Hours: The Roman Forum, Colosseum, and Palatine Hill are all open daily 8:30 until one hour before sunset: April-Sept until 19:15, Oct until 18:30, Nov-mid-Feb until 16:30, mid-Feb-mid-March until 17:00, mid-March-late March until 17:30; last entry one hour before closing.

Getting There: The closest Metro stop is Colosseo. The Forum has two entrances. The main entrance is on Via dei Fori Imperiali ("Road of the Imperial Forums"). From the Colosseo Metro stop, walk away from the Colosseum on Via dei Fori Imperiali to find the low-profile Forum ticket office (look closely), located where Via Cavour spills into Via dei Fori Imperiali.

The other entrance is at the Palatine Hill ticket office on Via di San Gregorio—after buying your ticket, take the path to the right (not up the hill), and wind around to enter the Forum at the Arch of Titus.

Information: A free visitors center (called I Fori di Roma), located across Via dei Fori Imperiali from the Forum's main entrance, has a TI, bookshop, small café, WCs, and a film (daily 9:30-18:30). A bookstore is at the Forum entrance. Vendors at the Forum sell *Rome: Past and Present* books with plastic overlays that restore the ruins (includes DVD, smaller book marked €15, prices soft, so offer €10). Info office tel. 06-3996-7700, http://archeoroma .beniculturali.it/en.

Tours: An unexciting yet informative **audioguide** helps decipher the rubble (€5, €7 version includes Palatine Hill, must leave ID), but you'll have to return it to one of the Forum entrances instead of being able to exit directly to Capitoline Hill or the Colosseum. Official **guided tours** in English might be available (inquire at ticket office). Or you can download a free Rick Steves **audio tour** of the Forum; see page 7.

Tips: WCs are at the main entrance and in the middle of the Forum (near #8 on the map). Wear sturdy shoes; the Forum's ancient paving is uneven. I carry a water bottle and refill it at the Forum's public drinking fountains.

• *Start at the Arch of Titus (Arco di Tito). It's the white triumphal arch that rises above the rubble on the east end of the Forum (closest to the Colosseum). Stand at the viewpoint alongside the arch and gaze over the valley known as the Forum.*

❶ **Arch of Titus (Arco di Tito):** This arch commemorated the Roman victory over the province of Judaea (Israel) in A.D. 70. The Romans had a reputation as benevolent conquerors who tolerated the local customs and rulers. All they required was allegiance to the empire, shown by worshipping the emperor as a god. No problem for most conquered people, who already had half a dozen gods on their prayer lists anyway. But Israelites believed in only one god, and it wasn't the emperor. Israel revolted. After a short but bitter war, the Romans defeated the rebels, took Jerusalem, destroyed their temple (leaving only the foundation wall—today's revered "Wailing Wall"), and brought home 50,000 Jewish slaves...who were forced to build this arch (and the Colosseum).

• *Walk down Via Sacra into the Forum. After about 50 yards, turn right and follow a path uphill to the three huge arches of the...*

❷ **Basilica of Constantine (a.k.a. Basilica Maxentius):** Yes, these are big arches. But they represent only one-third of the original Basilica of Constantine, a mammoth hall of justice. The arches were matched by a similar set along the Via Sacra side (only a few squat brick piers remain). Between them ran the central hall, which was spanned by a roof 130 feet high—about 55 feet higher than the side arches you see. (The stub of brick you see sticking up began an arch that once spanned the central hall.) The hall itself was as long as a football field, lavishly furnished with colorful inlaid marble, a gilded bronze ceiling, and statues, and filled with strolling Romans. At the far (west) end was an enormous marble statue of Emperor Constantine on a throne. (Pieces of this statue, including a hand the size of a man, are on display in Rome's Capitoline Museums.)

The basilica was begun by the emperor Maxentius, but after he was trounced in battle, the victor, Constantine, completed the massive building. No doubt about it, the Romans built monuments on a more epic scale than any previous Europeans, wowing their "barbarian" neighbors.

• *Now stroll deeper into the Forum, downhill along Via Sacra, through the trees. Many of the large basalt stones under your feet were walked on by Caesar Augustus 2,000 years ago. Pass by the only original bronze door still swinging on its ancient hinges (the green door at the Tempio di Romolo, on the right) and continue between ruined buildings until the Via Sacra opens up to a flat, grassy area.*

❸ **The Forum's Main Square:** The original Forum, or main square, was this flat patch about the size of a football field, stretching to the foot of Capitoline Hill. Surrounding it were temples, law courts, government buildings, and triumphal arches.

Rome was born right here. According to legend, twin brothers Romulus (Rome) and Remus were orphaned in infancy and raised

ROME

by a she-wolf on top of Palatine Hill. Growing up, they found it hard to get dates. So they and their cohorts attacked the nearby Sabine tribe and kidnapped their women. After they made peace, this marshy valley became the meeting place and then the trading center for the scattered tribes on the surrounding hillsides.

The square was the busiest and most crowded—and often the seediest—section of town. Besides the senators, politicians, and currency exchangers, there were even sleazier types—souvenir hawkers, pickpockets, fortune-tellers, gamblers, slave marketers, drunks, hookers, lawyers, and tour guides.

The Forum is now rubble, but imagine it in its prime: blindingly brilliant marble buildings with 40-foot-high columns and shining metal roofs; rows of statues painted in realistic colors; processional chariots rattling down Via Sacra. Mentally replace tourists in T-shirts with tribunes in togas. Imagine the buildings towering and the people buzzing around you while an orator gives a rabble-rousing speech from the Rostrum. If things still look like just a pile of rocks, at least tell yourself, "But Julius Caesar once leaned against these rocks."

• *At the near (east) end of the main square (the Colosseum is to the east) are the foundations of a temple now capped with a peaked wood-and-metal roof.*

❹ **Temple of Julius Caesar (Tempio del Divo Giulio, or Ara di Cesare):** Julius Caesar's body was burned on this spot (under the metal roof) after his assassination. Peek behind the wall into the small apse area, where a mound of dirt usually has fresh flowers—given to remember the man who, more than any other, personified the greatness of Rome.

Caesar (100-44 B.C.) changed Rome—and the Forum—dramatically. He cleared out many of the wooden market stalls and began to ring the square with even grander buildings. Caesar's house was located behind the temple, near that clump of trees. He walked right by here on the day he was assassinated ("Beware the Ides of March!" warned a street-corner Etruscan preacher).

Though he was popular with the masses, not everyone liked Caesar's urban design or his politics. When he assumed dictatorial powers, he was ambushed and stabbed to death by a conspiracy of senators, including his adopted son, Brutus *("Et tu, Brute?")*.

The funeral was held here, facing the main square. The citizens gathered, and speeches were made. Mark Antony stood up to say (in Shakespeare's words), "Friends, Romans, countrymen, lend me your ears. I come to bury Caesar, not to praise him." When Caesar's body was burned, the citizens who still loved him threw anything at hand on the fire, requiring the fire department to come put it out. Later, Emperor Augustus dedicated this temple in his name, making Caesar the first Roman to become a god.

ROME

• *Behind and to the left of the Temple of Julius Caesar are 10 tall columns (which may be covered with restoration scaffolding). These belong to the…*

❺ **Temple of Antoninus Pius and Faustina:** The Senate built this temple to honor Emperor Antoninus Pius (A.D. 138-161) and his deified wife, Faustina. The 50-foot-tall Corinthian (leafy) columns must have been awe-inspiring to out-of-towners who grew up in thatched huts. Although the temple has been inhabited by a church, you can still see the basic layout—a staircase led to a shaded porch (the columns), which admitted you to the main building (now a church), where the statue of the god sat. Originally, these columns supported a triangular pediment decorated with sculptures.

Picture these columns, with gilded capitals, supporting brightly painted statues in the pediment, and the whole building capped with a gleaming bronze roof. The stately gray rubble of today's Forum is a faded black-and-white photograph of a 3-D Technicolor era.

The building is a microcosm of many of the changes that occurred after Rome fell. In medieval times, the temple was pillaged. Note the diagonal cuts high on the marble columns—a failed attempt by scavengers to cut through the pillars to pull them down for their precious stone. (They used vinegar and rope to cut the marble…but because vinegar also eats through rope, they abandoned the attempt.) In 1550, a church was housed inside the ancient temple. The door shows the street level at the time of Michelangelo. The long staircase was underground until excavated in the 1800s.

• *There's a ramp next to the Temple of A. and F. Walk halfway up it and look to the left to view the…*

❻ **Basilica Aemilia:** A basilica was a covered public forum, often serving as a Roman hall of justice. In a society that was as legal-minded as America is today, you needed a lot of lawyers—and a big place to put them. Citizens came here to work out matters such as inheritances and building permits, or to sue somebody.

Notice the layout. It was a long, rectangular building. The stubby columns all in a row form one long, central hall flanked by two side aisles. Medieval Christians required a larger meeting hall for their worship services than Roman temples provided, so they used the spacious Roman basilica as the model for their churches. Cathedrals from France to Spain to England, from Romanesque to Gothic to Renaissance, all have the same basic floor plan as a Roman basilica.

• *Return again to the Temple of Julius Caesar. To the right of the temple are the three tall Corinthian columns of the Temple of Castor and Pollux. Beyond that is Palatine Hill—the corner of which may have been…*

❼ Caligula's Palace (a.k.a. the Palace of Tiberius): Emperor Caligula (ruled A.D. 37-41) had a huge palace on Palatine Hill overlooking the Forum. It actually sprawled down the hill into the Forum (some supporting arches remain in the hillside).

Caligula was not a nice person. He tortured enemies, stole senators' wives, and parked his chariot in handicap spaces. But Rome's luxury-loving emperors only added to the glory of the Forum, with each one trying to make his mark on history.

• *To the left of the Temple of Castor and Pollux, find the remains of a small white circular temple.*

❽ Temple of Vesta: This is perhaps Rome's most sacred spot. Rome considered itself one big family, and this temple represented a circular hut, like the kind that Rome's first families lived in. Inside, a fire burned, just as in a Roman home. And back in the days before lighters and butane, you never wanted your fire to go out. As long as the sacred flame burned, Rome would stand. The flame was tended by priestesses known as Vestal Virgins.

• *Around the back of the Temple of Vesta, you'll find two rectangular brick pools. These stood in the courtyard of the...*

❾ House of the Vestal Virgins: The Vestal Virgins lived in a two-story building surrounding a long central courtyard with these two pools at one end. Rows of statues depicting leading Vestal Virgins flanked the courtyard. This place was the model—both architecturally and sexually—for medieval convents and monasteries.

Chosen from noble families before they reached the age of 10, the six Vestal Virgins served a 30-year term. Honored and revered by the Romans, the Vestals even had their own box opposite the emperor in the Colosseum. The statues that line the courtyard honor dutiful Vestals.

As the name implies, a Vestal took a vow of chastity. If she served her term faithfully—abstaining for 30 years—she was given a huge dowry and allowed to marry. But if they found any Virgin who wasn't, she was strapped to a funeral car, paraded through the streets of the Forum, taken to a crypt, given a loaf of bread and a lamp...and buried alive. Many women suffered the latter fate.

• *Return to the Temple of Julius Caesar and head to the Forum's west end (opposite from the Colosseum). As you pass alongside the big open space of the Forum's main square, consider how the piazza is still a standard part of any Italian town. It has reflected and accommodated the gregarious and outgoing nature of the Italian people since Roman times.*

Stop at the big, well-preserved brick building (on right) with the triangular roof. Look in at...

❿ The Curia (Senate House): The Curia was the most important political building in the Forum. While the present building dates from A.D. 283, this was the site of Rome's official center of government since the birth of the republic. (Note that ongoing archaeological work may restrict access to the Curia, as well as the Arch of Septimius Severus—described later—and the exit to Capitoline Hill.) Three hundred senators, elected by the citizens of Rome, met here to debate and create the laws of the land. Their wooden seats once circled the building in three tiers; the Senate president's podium sat at the far end. The marble floor is from ancient times. Listen to the echoes in this vast room—the acoustics are great.

Rome prided itself on being a republic. Early in the city's history, its people threw out the king and established rule by elected representatives. Each Roman citizen was free to speak his mind and have a say in public policy. Even when emperors became the supreme authority, the Senate was a power to be reckoned with. The Curia building is well-preserved, having been used as a church since early Christian times. In the 1930s, it was restored and opened to the public as a historic site. (Note: Although Julius Caesar was assassinated in "the Senate," it wasn't here—at the time, the Senate was temporarily meeting across town.)

A statue and two reliefs inside the Curia help build our mental image of the Forum. The statue, made of porphyry marble in about A.D. 100 (with its head, arms, and feet now missing), was a tribute to an emperor, probably Hadrian or Trajan. The two relief panels may have decorated the Rostrum. Those on the left show people (with big stone tablets) standing in line to burn their debt records following a government amnesty. The other shows the distribution of grain (Rome's welfare system), some buildings in the background, and the latest fashion in togas.

• *Go back down the Senate steps and find the 10-foot-high wall just to the left of the big arch, marked...*

❶ **Rostrum (Rostri):** Nowhere was Roman freedom more apparent than at this "Speaker's Corner." The Rostrum was a raised platform, 10 feet high and 80 feet long, decorated with statues, columns, and the prows of ships (rostra).

On a stage like this, Rome's orators, great and small, tried to draw a crowd and sway public opinion. Mark Antony rose to offer Caesar the laurel-leaf crown of kingship, which Caesar publicly (and hypocritically) refused while privately becoming a dictator. Men such as Cicero railed against the corruption and decadence that came with the city's newfound wealth. In later years, daring citizens even spoke out against the emperors, reminding them that Rome was once free. Picture the backdrop these speakers would have had—a mountain of marble buildings piling up on Capitoline Hill.

In front of the Rostrum are trees bearing fruits that were

sacred to the ancient Romans: olives (provided food, light, and preservatives), figs (tasty), and wine grapes (made a popular export product).

• *The big arch to the right of the Rostrum is the...*

❿ **Arch of Septimius Severus:** In imperial times, the Rostrum's voices of democracy would have been dwarfed by images of the empire, such as the huge six-story-high Arch of Septimius Severus (A.D. 203). The reliefs commemorate the African-born emperor's battles in Mesopotamia. Near ground level, see soldiers marching captured barbarians back to Rome for the victory parade. Despite Severus' efficient rule, Rome's empire was crumbling under the weight of its own corruption, disease, decaying infrastructure, and the constant attacks by foreign "barbarians."

• *Pass underneath the Arch of Septimius Severus and turn left. On the slope of Capitoline Hill are the eight remaining columns of the...*

⓭ **Temple of Saturn:** These columns framed the entrance to the Forum's oldest temple (497 B.C.). Inside was a humble, very old wooden statue of the god Saturn. But the statue's pedestal held the gold bars, coins, and jewels of Rome's state treasury, the booty collected by conquering generals.

• *Standing here, at one of the Forum's first buildings, look east at the lone, tall...*

⓮ **Column of Phocas—Rome's Fall:** This is the Forum's last monument (A.D. 608), a gift from the powerful Byzantine Empire to a fallen empire—Rome. Given to commemorate the pagan Pantheon's becoming a Christian church, it's like a symbolic last nail in ancient Rome's coffin. After Rome's 1,000-year reign, the city was looted by Vandals, the population of a million-plus shrank to about 10,000, and the once-grand city center—the Forum—was abandoned, slowly covered up by centuries of silt and dirt. In the 1700s, an English historian named Edward Gibbon overlooked this spot from Capitoline Hill. Hearing Christian monks singing at these pagan ruins, he looked out at the few columns poking up from the ground, pondered the "Decline and Fall of the Roman Empire," and thought, "Hmm, that's a catchy title...."

• *From here, you have several options:*

1. Exiting past the Arch of Titus lands you at the Colosseum (described on page 801).

2. Exiting past the Arch of Septimius Severus leads you to the stairs up to Capitoline Hill (described on page 809).

3. The Forum's main entrance spills you back out onto Via dei Fori Imperiali (for Trajan's Column, Market, and Museum of the Imperial Forums, described on page 808).

4. From the Arch of Titus, you can climb Palatine Hill to the top—see page 807.

ROME

Dolce Vita Stroll

This is the city's chic stroll, from Piazza del Popolo (Metro: Flaminio) down a wonderfully traffic-free section of Via del Corso, and up Via Condotti to the Spanish Steps. It takes place from around 17:00 to 19:00 each evening (Fri and Sat are best), except on Sunday, when it occurs earlier in the afternoon. Leave before 18:00 if you plan to visit the Ara Pacis (Altar of Peace), which closes at 19:00 and is closed Monday.

As you stroll, you'll see shoppers, people-watchers, and flirts on the prowl, filling this neighborhood, which has some of Rome's most fashionable stores (some open after siesta 16:30-19:30). While both the crowds and the shops along Via del Corso have gone downhill recently, elegance survives in the grid of streets between here and the Spanish Steps. If you get hungry during your stroll, see page 876 for descriptions of neighborhood wine bars and restaurants.

To reach **Piazza del Popolo,** where the stroll starts, take Metro line A to Flaminio and walk south to the square. Delightfully car-free, Piazza del Popolo is marked by an obelisk that was brought to Rome by Augustus after he conquered Egypt. (It used to stand in the Circus Maximus.) In medieval times, this area was just inside Rome's main entry (for more background on the square, see page 834).

If starting your stroll early enough, the Baroque church of **Santa Maria del Popolo** is worth popping into (Mon-Sat until 18:30, Sun until 19:30, next to gate in old wall on north side of square). Inside, look for Raphael's Chigi Chapel (KEE-gee, second chapel on left) and two paintings by Caravaggio (in the Cerasi Chapel, left of altar; see listing on page 835).

From Piazza del Popolo, shop your way down **Via del Corso.** With the proliferation of shopping malls, many chain stores lining Via del Corso are losing customers and facing hard times. Still, this remains a fine place to feel the pulse of Rome at twilight.

Historians side-trip right down Via Pontefici past the fascist architecture to see the massive, rotting, round-brick **Mausoleum of Augustus,** topped with overgrown cypress trees. Beyond it, next to the river, is Augustus' **Ara Pacis,** enclosed within a protective glass-walled museum (described on page 837). From the mausoleum, walk down Via Tomacelli to return to Via del Corso and the 21st century.

From Via del Corso, window-shoppers should take a left down **Via Condotti** to join the parade to the **Spanish Steps.** The streets that parallel Via Condotti to the south (Borgognona and Frattina) are more elegant and filled with high-end boutiques. A few streets to the north hides the narrow Via Margutta. This is where Gregory Peck's *Roman Holiday* character lived (at #51); today it's filled with

Dolce Vita Stroll

Piazza Flaminio · Flaminio

STA. MARIA DEL POPOLO

Piazza del Popolo

WALK BEGINS

Villa Borghese

Galoppatoio

V. L. SAVOIA

FERD. SAVOIA

LUNGOTEVERE IN AUGUSTA

Tiber River

VIA DI RIPETTA

VIA DEL BABUINO

VIA DEL CORSO

MARGUTTA

VILLA MEDICI

ARA PACIS

FREZZA

PONTE

MAUSOLEUM OF AUGUSTUS

Piazza Imperatore

PONTE CAVOUR

❷

VIA VITTORIA

VIA CROCE

❶ ❸

Piazza di Spagna · Spagna

VIA CARDZZE

TRINITÀ DEI MONTI

SPANISH STEPS

WALK ENDS FOR (WINDOW) SHOPPERS

McDonald's

VIA SISTINA

VIA CONDOTTI

PROPA

VIA DUE MACELLI

To Barberini

TOMACELLI

Piazza Borghese

Piazza S. Lorenzo

VIA DELLA SCROFA

VIA FONT. BORGHESE

VIA BORGOGNONA

❺

VIA FRATTINA

VIA VITE

V. MERCEDE

POST

V. CON.

PREFETTI

VALD.

❹

CAMPO MARZIO

Piazza Parlamento

PARLIAMENT

Piazza di Montecitorio

Piazza Colonna

SABINA

MURATTE

DEL

TRITONE

TREVI FOUNTAIN

PALAZZO DEL QUIRINALE

DATARIA

Piazza di Pietra

Piazza Rotonda

VIA DELLA SCROFA

PANTHEON

SAN IGNAZIO

CARAVITA

VIA DEL CORSO

UMILTÀ

Piazza del Quirinale

SANTA MARIA SOPRA MINERVA

Piazza del Collegio Romano

GALLERIA DORIA PAMPHILJ

CORSO VITT. EMANUELE II

Largo Argentina

300 Meters

300 Yards

PLEBISCITO

BATT.

V. 4 NOV.

Piazza Venezia

TRAJAN'S COLUMN

TRAJAN'S MARKET

VIA ARACOELI

SAN MARCO

VICTOR EMMANUEL MONUMENT

CAPITOLINE HILL

GRAND STAIRCASE

Piazza del Campodoglio

VIA DEI FORI IMPERIALI

To Colosseum

WALK ENDS FOR HISTORIANS

FORUM

ROME

❶ Ristorante il Gabriello
❷ Osteria Gusto
❸ L'EnotecAntica
❹ Trattoria dal Cav. Gino
❺ Palatium Enoteca Regionale

pricey artisan shops.

Historians: Ignore Via Condotti and forget the Spanish Steps. Stay on Via del Corso, which has been straight since Roman times, for a half-mile down to the Victor Emmanuel Monument. Climb Michelangelo's stairway to his glorious (especially when floodlit) square atop Capitoline Hill. Stand on the balcony (just past the mayor's palace on the right), which overlooks the Forum. As the horizon reddens and cats prowl the unclaimed rubble of ancient Rome, it's one of the finest views in the city.

Heart of Rome Walk

Rome's most colorful neighborhood features narrow lanes, intimate piazzas, fanciful fountains, and some of Europe's best people-watching. During the day, this walk shows off the colorful Campo de' Fiori market and trendy fashion boutiques, as it meanders past major monuments such as the Pantheon and the Spanish Steps.

But, when the sun sets, unexpected magic happens. A stroll in the cool of the evening brings out all the romance of the Eternal City. Sit so close to a bubbling fountain that traffic noise evaporates. Jostle with kids to see the gelato flavors. Watch lovers straddling more than the bench. Jaywalk past polizia in flak-proof vests. And marvel at the ramshackle elegance that softens this brutal city for those who were born here and can't imagine living anywhere else. These are the flavors of Rome, best tasted after dark.

This walk is equally pleasant in reverse order. You could ride the Metro to the Spanish Steps and finish at Campo de' Fiori, near many recommended restaurants. To lengthen this walk, you could start in Trastevere; see directions on page 842.

• *Start this walk at Campo de' Fiori, my favorite outdoor dining room (especially after dark—see "Eating in Rome," page 869). It's a few blocks east of Largo Argentina, a major transportation hub. Buses #64 and 40 stop at both Largo Argentina and along Corso Vittorio Emanuele II, a long block north of Campo de' Fiori. A taxi from Termini train station costs about €8.*

Campo de' Fiori: One of Rome's most colorful spots, this bohemian piazza hosts a fruit and vegetable **market** in the morning, cafés in the evening, and pub-crawlers at night. In ancient times, the "Field of Flowers" was an open meadow. Later, Christian pilgrims passed through on their way to the Vatican, and a thriving market developed.

Lording over the center of the square is a statue of **Giordano Bruno,** an intellectual heretic who was burned on this spot in 1600. When the statue of Bruno was erected in 1889, riots overcame Vatican protests against honoring a heretic. Bruno faces his nemesis, the Vatican Chancellory (the big white building just outside the far right corner of the square), while his pedestal reads,

"And the flames rose up." Check out the reliefs on the pedestal for scenes from Bruno's trial and execution. Even today, this neighborhood is known for its free spirit and occasional demonstrations.

Campo de' Fiori is the product of centuries of unplanned urban development. At the east end of the square (behind Bruno), the ramshackle apartments are built right into the old outer wall of ancient Rome's mammoth Theater of Pompey. This entertainment complex covered several city blocks, stretching from here to Largo Argentina. Julius Caesar was assassinated in the Theater of Pompey, where the Senate was renting space.

The square is lined with and surrounded by fun eateries. Bruno faces the **Forno** (in the left corner of the square). Step in, at least to observe the frenzy as pizza is sold hot out of the oven. You can order *un etto* (100 grams, an average serving) by pointing, then take your snack to the counter to pay. The many bars lining the square are fine for drinks and watching the scene. On weekend nights, when the Campo is packed with beer-drinking kids, this medieval square is transformed into one vast Roman street party.

• *If Bruno did a hop, step, and jump forward, then turned right on Via dei Baullari and marched 200 yards, he'd cross the busy Corso Vittorio Emanuele; then, continuing another 150 yards on Via Cuccagna, he'd find...*

Piazza Navona: This oblong square retains the shape of the original racetrack that was built around A.D. 80 by the emperor Domitian. (To see the ruins of the original entrance, exit the square at the far—or north—end, then take an immediate left, and look down to the left 25 feet below the current street level.) Since ancient times, the square has been a center of Roman life. In the 1800s, the city would flood the square to cool off the neighborhood.

The **Four Rivers Fountain** in the center is the most famous fountain by the man who remade Rome in Baroque style, Gian Lorenzo Bernini. Four burly river gods (representing the four continents that were known in 1650) support an Egyptian obelisk. The water of the world gushes everywhere. The Nile has his head covered, since the headwaters were unknown then. The Ganges holds an oar. The Danube turns to admire the obelisk, which Bernini had moved here from a stadium on the Appian Way. And Uruguay's Río de la Plata tumbles backward in shock, wondering how he ever made the top four. Bernini enlivens the fountain with horses plunging through the rocks and exotic flora and fauna from these newly discovered lands. Homesick Texans may want to find the armadillo. (It's the big, weird, armor-plated creature behind the Plata river statue.)

The Plata river god is gazing upward at the **Church of St. Agnes,** worked on by Bernini's former student-turned-rival,

Heart of Rome Walk

N

Piazza Cavour

FORMER HALL OF JUSTICE

V. PONT

ARA PACIS

MAUSOLEUM OF AUGUSTUS

PONTE CAVOUR

VIA DI RIPETTA

Piazza Augusto Imperatore

Tiber River

LUNGOTEVERE MARZIO

VIA DELLA SCROFA

CLEMENTINO

Piazza Borghese

PONTE UMBERTO

Piazza Ponte Umberto I

MONTE BRIANZO

PREFETTI

STELLETTA

To Ponte Sant'Angelo

VIA DEI CORONARI

ANCIENT STADIUM ENTRANCE

FOUR RIVERS FOUNTAIN

TRE SCALINI

VOLPE

Piazza Fico

SANT' AGNESE

CHIESA NUOVA

Piazza della Chiesa Nuova

Piazza Navona

Piazza Pasquino

PASQUINO STATUE

CITY MUSEUM

CORSO VITTORIO EMANUELE II II

SAN LUIGI

VIA DELLE COPPELLE

VIA IN AQUIRO

LA MADDELENA

SALVATORE

ITALY'S SENATE

GIUSTINIANI

Piazza Rotunda

SANT' EUSTACHIO

PANTHEON

SANT' IVO

Piazza Sant'Eustachio

CORSO DEL RINASCIMENTO

CAMPO

UFFICI

GIOLITTI'S GELATO

ROME

B

VIA D. BAULLARI

SANT' ANDREA DELLA VALLE

CORSO VITTORIO EMANUELE II

ARGENTINA

VIA DE CESTARI

WALK BEGINS

BRUNO STATUE

Campo de' Fiori

Piazza Farnese

PALAZZO FARNESE

To Trastevere

V. CHIAVARI

Largo Pallaro

150 Meters

150 Yards

Largo Argentina

LARGO ARGENTINA RUINS

B   T

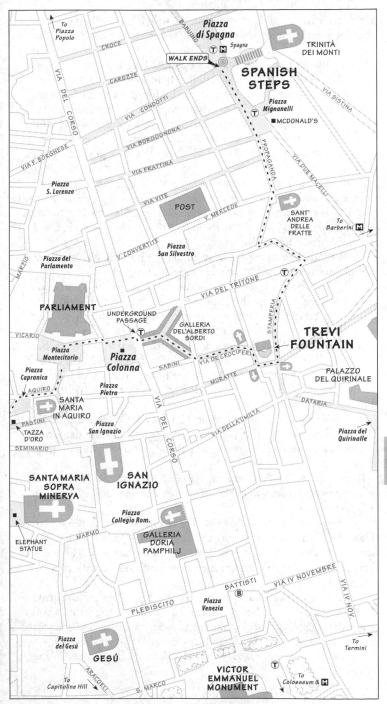

To Piazza Popolo

Piazza di Spagna

BABUINO

CROCE

Spagna

WALK ENDS

TRINITÀ DEI MONTI

SPANISH STEPS

VIA SISTINA

CAROZZE

VIA DEL CORSO

VIA CONDOTTI

Piazza Mignanelli

■ MCDONALD'S

VIA BORGOGNONA

VIA F. BORGHESE

PROPAGANDA

VIA DUE MACELLI

VIA FRATTINA

Piazza S. Lorenzo

VIA VITE

POST

V. MERCEDE

SANT' ANDREA DELLE FRATTE

To Barberini [M]

V. CONVERTITE

Piazza San Silvestro

Piazza del Parlamento

MARZIO

PARLIAMENT

VIA DEL TRITONE

VICARIO

STAMPERIA

UNDERGROUND PASSAGE

GALLERIA DELL'ALBERTO SORDI

TREVI FOUNTAIN

Piazza Montecitorio

Piazza Colonna

SABINI

VIA DE CROCIFERI

Piazza Capranica

AQUIRO

MURATTE

PALAZZO DEL QUIRINALE

PASTINI

SANTA MARIA IN AQUIRO

Piazza Pietra

VIA DEL CORSO

DATARIA

■ TAZZA D'ORO

Piazza San Ignazio

VIA DELL'UMILTA

Piazza del Quirinale

SEMINARIO

SANTA MARIA SOPRA MINERVA

SAN IGNAZIO

ROME

Piazza Collegio Rom.

■ ELEPHANT STATUE

MARMO

GALLERIA DORIA PAMPHILJ

VIA IV NOVEMBRE

BATTISTI

VIA IV NOV

[B]

Piazza Venezia

PLEBISCITO

To Termini

Piazza del Gesú

GESÚ

ARACOELI

S. MARCO

VICTOR EMMANUEL MONUMENT

To Capitoline Hill

To Colosseum & [M]

Francesco Borromini. Borromini's concave facade helps reveal the dome and epitomizes the curved symmetry of Baroque. Tour guides say that Bernini designed his river god to look horrified at Borromini's work. Or maybe he's shielding his eyes from St. Agnes' nakedness, as she was stripped before being martyred. But either explanation is unlikely, since the fountain was completed two years before Borromini even started work on the church.

Piazza Navona is Rome's most interesting night scene, with street music, artists, fire-eaters, local Casanovas, ice cream, and outdoor cafés that are worthy of a splurge if you've got time to sit and enjoy Italy's human river.

• *Leave Piazza Navona directly across from Tre Scalini (famous for its rich chocolate ice cream), and go east down Corsia Agonale, past rose peddlers and palm readers. Jog left around the guarded building (where Italy's senate meets), and follow the brown sign to the Pantheon, which is straight down Via del Salvatore.*

The Pantheon: Sit for a while under the portico of this ancient temple (romantically floodlit and moonlit at night).

The 40-foot, single-piece granite columns of the Pantheon's entrance show the scale the ancient Romans built on. The columns support a triangular Greek-style roof with an inscription that says "M. Agrippa" built it. In fact, it was built *(fecit)* by Emperor Hadrian (A.D. 120), who gave credit to the builder of an earlier structure. This impressive entranceway gives no clue that the greatest wonder of the building is inside—a domed room that inspired later domes, including Michelangelo's St. Peter's and Brunelleschi's Duomo (in Florence).

If it's open, pop into the Pantheon for a look around (interior described on page 815). If you have extra time, consider detouring to several interesting churches near the Pantheon (listed on page 816).

• *With your back to the Pantheon, veer to the right, uphill toward the yellow sign that reads* Casa del Caffè *at the Tazza d'Oro coffee shop on Via Orfani.*

From the Pantheon to the Trevi Fountain: Tazza d'Oro Casa del Caffè, one of Rome's top coffee shops, dates back to the days when this area was licensed to roast coffee beans. Locals come here for its fine *granita di caffè con panna* (coffee slush with cream).

• *Continue up Via Orfani to...*

Piazza Capranica is home to the big, plain Florentine Renaissance-style Palazzo Capranica (directly opposite as you enter the square). Big shots, like the Capranica family, built towers on their palaces—not for any military use, but just to show off.

• *Leave the piazza to the right of the palace, heading down Via in Aquiro.*

The street Via in Aquiro leads to a sixth-century B.C. **Egyptian obelisk** taken as a trophy by Augustus after his victory in Egypt over Mark Antony and Cleopatra. The obelisk was set up as a sundial. Follow the zodiac markings to the well-guarded front door. This is Italy's **parliament building**, where the lower house meets; you may see politicians, political demonstrations, and TV cameras.

• *To your right is Piazza Colonna, where we're heading next—unless you like gelato...*

A two-block detour to the left (past Albergo Nazionale) brings you to Rome's most famous *gelateria*. **Giolitti's** is cheap for take-out or elegant and splurge-worthy for a sit among classy locals (open daily until past midnight, Via Uffici del Vicario 40); get your gelato in a cone *(cono)* or cup *(coppetta)*.

Piazza Colonna features a huge second-century column. Its reliefs depict the victories of Emperor Marcus Aurelius over the barbarians. When Marcus died in A.D. 180, the barbarians began to get the upper hand, beginning Rome's long three-century fall. The big, important-looking palace houses the headquarters for the prime minister's cabinet.

Noisy **Via del Corso** is Rome's main north-south boulevard. It's named for the Berber horse races—without riders—that took place here during Carnevale. This wild tradition continued until the late 1800s, when a series of fatal accidents (including, reportedly, one in front of Queen Margherita) led to its cancellation. Historically the street was filled with meat shops. When it became one of Rome's first gas-lit streets in 1854, these butcher shops were banned and replaced by classier boutiques, jewelers, and antiques dealers. Nowadays most of Via del Corso is closed to traffic for a few hours every evening and becomes a wonderful parade of Romans out for a stroll (see the "Dolce Vita Stroll," earlier).

• *Cross Via del Corso to enter a big palatial building with columns, which houses the Galleria Alberto Sordi shopping mall. Inside, take the fork to the right and exit out the back. (If you're here after 22:00, when the mall is closed, circle around the right side of the Galleria on Via dei Sabini.) Once out the back, head up Via de Crociferi, to the roar of the water, lights, and people of the...*

Trevi Fountain: The Trevi Fountain shows how Rome took full advantage of the abundance of water brought into the city by its great aqueducts. This watery Baroque avalanche by Nicola Salvi was completed in 1762. Salvi used the palace behind the fountain as a theatrical backdrop for the figure of "Ocean," who represents water in every form. The statue surfs through his wet kingdom—with water gushing from 24 spouts and tumbling over 30 different kinds of plants—while Triton blows his conch shell.

ROME

The magic of the square is enhanced by the fact that no streets directly approach it. You can hear the excitement as you draw near, and then—*bam!*—you're there. The scene is always lively, with lucky Romeos clutching dates while unlucky ones clutch beers. Romantics toss a coin over their shoulder, thinking it will give them a wish and assure their return to Rome. That may sound silly, but every year I go through this tourist ritual...and it actually seems to work.

Take some time to people-watch (whisper a few breathy *bellos* or *bellas*) before leaving. There's a peaceful zone at water level on the far right.

• *From the Trevi Fountain, we're 10 minutes from our next stop, the Spanish Steps. Just use a map to get there, or follow these directions: Facing the Trevi Fountain, go forward, walking along the right side of the fountain on Via della Stamperia. Cross busy Via del Tritone. Continue 100 yards and veer right at Via delle Fratte, a street that changes its name to Via Propaganda before ending at the...*

Spanish Steps: Piazza di Spagna, with the very popular Spanish Steps, is named for the Spanish Embassy to the Vatican, which has been here for 300 years. It's been the hangout of many Romantics over the years (Keats, Wagner, Openshaw, Goethe, and others). In the 1700s, British aristocrats on the "Grand Tour" of Europe came here to ponder Rome's decay. The British poet John Keats pondered his mortality, then died of tuberculosis at age 25 in the pink building on the right side of the steps. Fellow Romantic Lord Byron lived across the square at #66.

The **Sinking Boat Fountain** at the foot of the steps, built by Gian Lorenzo Bernini or his father, Pietro, is powered by an aqueduct. Actually, all of Rome's fountains are aqueduct-powered; their spurts are determined by the water pressure provided by the various aqueducts. This one, for instance, is much weaker than Trevi's gush.

The piazza is a thriving scene at night. It's clear that the main sight here is not the famous steps, but the people who sit on them. Window-shop along Via Condotti, which stretches away from the steps. This is where Gucci and other big names cater to the trendsetting jet set. Facing the Spanish Steps, you can walk right, about a block, to tour one of the world's biggest and most lavish McDonald's (salad bar, WC).

• *Our walk is finished. If you'd like to reach the top of the steps sweat-free, there's a free elevator just outside the Spagna Metro stop (elevator closes at 21:00; Metro stop is to the left of the Spanish Steps). Afterward, you can zip home on the Metro (usually open until 23:30, Fri-Sat until 1:30 in the morning) or grab a taxi at either the north or south side of the piazza.*

Sights in Rome

I've clustered Rome's sights into walkable neighborhoods, some quite close together (see the "Rome's Neighborhoods" map on page 764). Save transit time by grouping your sightseeing according to location. For example, the Colosseum and the Forum are a few minutes' walk from Capitoline Hill; a 10-minute walk beyond that is the Pantheon. I like to tour these sights in one great day, starting at the Colosseum and ending at the Pantheon.

Ancient Rome

The core of ancient Rome, where the grandest monuments were built, is between the Colosseum and Capitoline Hill. Among the ancient forums, a few modern sights have popped up.

The Colosseum and Nearby

▲▲▲Colosseum (Colosseo)—This 2,000-year-old building is the classic example of Roman engineering. The Romans pioneered the use of concrete and the rounded arch, which enabled them to build on such a tremendous scale. While the essential structure of the Colosseum is Roman, the four-story facade is decorated with mostly Greek columns—Doric-like Tuscan columns on the ground level, Ionic on the second story, Corinthian on the next level, and at the top, half-columns with a mix of all three. Built when the Roman Empire was at its peak in A.D. 80, the Colosseum represents Rome at its grandest. The Flavian Amphitheater (the Colosseum's real name) was an arena for gladiator contests and public spectacles. When killing became a spectator sport, the Romans wanted to share the fun with as many people as possible, so they stuck two semicircular theaters together to create a freestanding amphitheater. The outside (where slender cypress trees stand today) was decorated with a 100-foot-tall bronze statue of Nero that gleamed in the sunlight. In a later age, the colossal structure was nicknamed a "coloss-eum," the wonder of its age. It could accommodate 50,000 roaring fans (100,000 thumbs). This was where ancient Romans—whose taste for violence was the equal of modern America's—enjoyed their *Dirty Harry*- and *Terminator*-style spectacles. Gladiators, criminals, and wild animals fought to the death in every conceivable scenario. The bit of reconstructed Colosseum floor gives you an accurate sense of the original floor and the subterranean warren where animals were held, then lifted up in elevators. Released at floor level, animals would pop out from behind blinds into the arena—the gladiator didn't know where, when, or by what he'd be attacked.

Cost and Hours: €12 with temporary exhibits, this combo-ticket includes Roman Forum and Palatine Hill, open daily 8:30

until one hour before sunset—for specifics, see "Hours" on page 785, last entry one hour before closing, Metro: Colosseo, tel. 06-3996-7700, http://archeoroma.beniculturali.it/en.

Avoiding Lines: You can save lots of time by buying your combo-ticket in advance, having the Roma Pass, or booking a guided tour. Here are some options:

1. Buy your combo-ticket (or Roma Pass) at the less-crowded Palatine Hill entrance, 150 yards away on Via di San Gregorio (facing the Forum, with Colosseum at your back, go left down the street). You can also buy a Roma Pass at the tobacco shop in the Colosseo Metro station. (Avoid buying your ticket or Roma Pass at the Forum, which also tends to have lines.)

2. Buy a combo-ticket online at www.ticketclic.it (€1.50 booking fee, not changeable). Note that the "free tickets" you'll see listed are valid only for EU citizens with ID.

3. Pay to join an official guided tour (€5 plus Colosseum ticket). This lets you march right up to the Colosseum's guided visits *(Visite Guidate)* desk, thus bypassing the ticket lines. Alternatively,

private walking-tour guides linger outside the Colosseum, offering tours that allow you to skip the line (€22, includes admission, tours also cover Palatine Hill and Forum). Be aware that these private guides may mislead you into thinking the Colosseum lines are longer than they really are—it's hard for a novice to judge. For more on official or private guided tours, see "Tours," later.

Restoration: The arena is being cleaned from top to bottom and given permanent lighting. These ongoing renovations may affect your visit.

Warning: Beware of the **greedy gladiators.** For a fee, these incredibly crude, modern-day gladiators snuff out their cigarettes and pose for photos. They intimidate easy-to-swindle tourists into paying too much money. If you go for it, €4-5 for one photo usually keeps them appeased. Also, look out for **pickpockets** and con artists in this prime tourist spot.

Getting There: The Colosseo Metro stop on line B is just across the street from the monument. Bus #60 is handy for hotels near Via Firenze and Via Nazionale. Bus #87 links Largo

Colosseum

To St. Peter-
in-Chains
(Moses Statue)

CAFFÈ
DELLO
STUDENTE

Not to Scale

Parco
Oppio

VIA ANNIBALDI

VIA TERME DI TITO

VIA NICOLA SALVI

To Forum
Entrance,
Trajan's
Forum
& Piazza
Venezia

Colosseo M

BIKE
RENTAL

VIA DEI FORI IMPERIALI

ENTER

FORUM

TEMPLE OF
VENUS
& ROME

FORMER
100' TALL
"COLOSSAL
STATUE"

Piazza del
Colosseo

BOOK-
STORE

TEMP.
EXHIBITS
LEVEL
UPPER
TICKETS
(BELOW)
EMPEROR'S
BOX

WC

LIFT

WC

ARENA
LEVEL

BOOK-
STORE

VESTAL
VIRGINS
BOX

VIA SACRA

EXIT
FROM
FORUM

EXIT

VIA DI SAN GREGORIO

ARCH OF
CONSTANTINE

VIA CELIO VIBENNA

PALATINE
HILL

Parco del
Celio

To Palatine Hill
Ticket Office
& Circus Maximus

ROME

Argentina with the Colosseum.

Getting In: If you need to buy a ticket or sign up for a guided tour, follow the signs for the appropriate line. With a combo-ticket or Roma Pass in hand, look for signs for *ticket holders* or *Roma Pass,* allowing you to bypass the long lines. Note that long-range renovation plans include building a free-standing ticket booth outside the Colosseum, which may be done in time for your visit.

Tours: A dry but fact-filled **audioguide** is available just past the turnstiles (€5.50/2 hours). A handheld **videoguide** senses where you are in the site and plays related video clips (€5.50).

Guided tours in English (which let you skip the ticket line) depart nearly hourly between 10:00 and 17:00, and last 45 minutes to one hour (€5 plus Colosseum ticket, purchase inside the Colosseum near the ticket booth marked *Visite Guidate;* if you're lost, ask a guard to direct you to the desk). **Private guides** stand outside the Colosseum, looking for business (€22 for two-hour tours of the Colosseum, Palatine Hill, and Forum). If booking a private guide, make sure that your tour will start right away and that the ticket you receive covers all three sights: the Colosseum, Forum, and Palatine Hill.

You can download a free Rick Steves **audio tour** of the Colosseum; see page 7.

A **behind-the-scenes tour** takes you through restricted areas, including underground passageways and the third floor, which are off-limits to regular Colosseum visitors. To do this, you'll need to book a 1.5-hour tour with Pierreci, a private company, at least a day in advance (€8 plus Colosseum ticket, call 06-3996-7700 during business hours, Mon-Fri 9:00-18:00, Sat 9:00-14:00, closed Sun, no same-day reservations). After dialing, wait for English instructions on how to reach a live operator, then reserve a time and pre-pay with a credit card. Without a reservation, you can go to the Colosseum and try to join the next available behind-the-scenes tour, even if it's in Italian. Once you have your Colosseum entrance ticket and are at the turnstiles, look for the tour meeting point just past the ticket desk; pay the guide directly.

▲**Arch of Constantine**—If you are a Christian, were raised a Christian, or simply belong to a so-called "Christian nation," ponder this arch. It marks one of the great turning points in history—the military coup that made Christianity mainstream. In A.D. 312, Emperor Constantine defeated his rival Maxentius in the crucial Battle of the Milvian Bridge. The night before, he had seen a vision of a cross in the sky. Constantine—whose mother and sister were Christians—became sole emperor and legalized Christianity. With this one battle, a once-obscure Jewish sect with a handful of followers was now the state religion of the entire Western world. In A.D. 300, you could be killed for being a Christian; a century later, you could be killed for not being one. Church enrollment boomed.

The restored arch is like an ancient museum. It's decorated entirely with recycled carvings originally made for other buildings. By covering it with exquisite carvings of high Roman art—works that glorified previous emperors—Constantine put himself in their league. Hadrian is featured in the round reliefs, with Marcus Aurelius in the square reliefs higher up. The big statues on top are of Trajan and Augustus. Originally, Augustus drove a chariot similar to the one topping the modern Victor Emmanuel II Monument. Fourth-century Rome may have been in decline, but Constantine clung to its glorious past.

▲**St. Peter-in-Chains Church (San Pietro in Vincoli)**—Built in the fifth century to house the chains that held St. Peter, this church is most famous for its Michelangelo statue. Check out the much-venerated chains under the high altar, then focus on mighty Moses. (Note that this isn't the famous St. Peter's Basilica, which is at Vatican City.)

Pope Julius II commissioned Michelangelo to build a massive tomb, with 48 huge statues, topped with a grand statue of this ego-maniacal pope. The pope had planned to have his tomb placed in the center of St. Peter's Basilica. When Julius died, the work had barely been started, and no one had the money or necessary com-mitment to Julius to finish the project.

In 1542, some of the remnants of the tomb project were brought to St. Peter-in-Chains and pieced together by Michelangelo's assistants. Some of the best statues ended up elsewhere, such as the *Prisoners* in Florence and the *Slaves* in the Louvre. *Moses* and the Louvre's *Slaves* are the only statues Michelangelo personally completed for the project. Flanking *Moses* are the Old Testament sister-wives of Jacob, Leah (to our right) and Rachel, both begun by Michelangelo but probably finished by pupils.

This powerful statue of Moses—one of Michelangelo's most artistically mature works—is worth studying. The artist worked on it in fits and starts for 30 years. Moses has received the Ten Commandments. As he holds the stone tablets, his eyes show a man determined to stop his tribe from worshipping the golden calf and idols...a man determined to win salvation for the people of Israel. Why the horns? Centuries ago, the Hebrew word for "rays" was mistranslated as "horns."

Cost and Hours: Free, daily April-Sept 8:00-12:30 & 15:00-19:00, Oct-March 8:00-12:30 & 15:00-18:00, modest dress required; the church is a 15-minute uphill, zigzag walk from the Colosseum, or a shorter, simpler walk from the Cavour Metro stop—from that station, go downhill on Via Cavour a half-block, then climb the pedestrian staircase called Via di San Francesco di Paola, which leads right to the church.

The Roman Forum and Nearby

▲▲▲**Roman Forum (Foro Romano)**—This is ancient Rome's birthplace and civic center, and the common ground between Rome's famous seven hills. As just about anything important that happened in ancient Rome happened here, it's arguably the most important piece of real estate in Western civilization. While only a few fragments of that glorious past remain, history-seekers find plenty to ignite their imaginations amid the half-broken columns and arches.

Cost and Hours: €12 combo-ticket includes Colosseum and Palatine Hill—see page 771, open daily 8:30 until one hour before sunset, last entry one hour before closing, Metro: Colosseo, tel. 06-3996-7700, http://archeoroma.beniculturali.it/en. See my Roman Forum Tour, earlier.

▲▲**Palatine Hill (Monte Palatino)**—The hill overlooking the Forum is jam-packed with history—"the huts of Romulus," the huge Imperial Palace, a view of the Circus Maximus—but there's only the barest skeleton of rubble left to tell the story.

We get our word "palace" from this hill, where the emperors chose to live. The Palatine Hill was once so filled with palaces that later emperors had to build out. (Looking up at it from the Forum, you see the substructure that supported these long-gone palaces.)

The Palatine museum contains statues and frescoes that help you imagine the luxury of the imperial Palatine. From the pleasant garden, you'll get an overview of the Forum. On the far side, look down into an emperor's private stadium and then beyond at the grassy Circus Maximus, once a chariot course. Imagine the cheers, jeers, and furious betting.

While many tourists consider the Palatine Hill just extra credit after the Forum, it offers an insight into the greatness of Rome. (And, if you're visiting the Colosseum or Forum, you've got a ticket whether you like it or not.)

Cost and Hours: €12 combo-ticket (€9 base price plus frequent, mandatory exhibition fees), also includes Roman Forum and Colosseum—see page 771; open same hours as Forum and Colosseum.

The Palatine's entrance is on Via di San Gregorio (facing the Forum with the Colosseum at your back, it's down the street to your left). You can also enter the Palatine from within the Roman Forum—just climb the hill from the Arch of Titus.

Audioguides cost €5 (€7 version includes Roman Forum, must leave ID), and guided tours in English might be available (inquire at the ticket booth). WCs are at the ticket office when you enter, at the museum in the center of the site, and hiding among the orange trees in the Farnese Gardens.

Mamertine Prison—This 2,500-year-old cistern-like prison is where, according to Christian tradition, the Romans imprisoned Saints Peter and Paul. Though it was long a charming and historic sight, its artifacts have been removed, and today it's run by a commercial tour-bus company charging €10 for a cheesy "multimedia" walk-through. Don't go in. Instead, stand outside and imagine how this dank cistern once housed prisoners of the emperor. Amid fat rats and rotting corpses, unfortunate humans awaited slow deaths. It's said that a miraculous fountain sprang up inside so Peter could convert and baptize his jailers, who were also subsequently martyred. Before the commercial ruination of this sacred and ancient site, on the walls you could read lists of notable prisoners (Christian and non-Christian) and the ways they were executed: *strangolati, decapitato, morto per fame* (died of hunger). The sign by the Christian names read, "Here suffered, victorious for the triumph of Christ, these martyr saints." Today this sight itself has been martyred by a city apparently desperate to monetize its heritage.

▲Trajan's Column, Market, and Museum of the Imperial Forums—This grand column is the best example of "continuous narration" that we have from antiquity. More than 2,500 figures spiral around the 140-foot-high column, telling of Trajan's victorious Dacian campaign (circa A.D. 103, in present-day Romania), from the assembling of the army at the bottom to the victory sacrifice at the top. At one point, the ashes of Trajan and his wife were held in the base, and the sun glinted off a polished bronze statue of Trajan at the top. (Today, St. Peter is on top.) Study the propaganda that winds up the column like a scroll, trumpeting Trajan's wonderful military exploits. This column marked "Trajan's Forum," which was built to handle the shopping needs of a wealthy city of more than a million people. Commercial, political, religious, and social activities all mixed in the forum.

Nestled into the cutaway curve of Quirinal Hill is the semi-circular brick complex of Trajan's Market. It was likely part shopping mall, part warehouse, and part administration building. Or, as some archaeologists have recently suggested, it may have contained mostly government offices.

Paying the admission fee gets you inside Trajan's Market, Trajan's Forum, and the **Museum of the Imperial Forums.** The museum features discoveries from the forums of emperors Julius Caesar, Augustus, Nerva, and Trajan, with fragments of statues and a slideshow that reconstructs how the forum looked in each emperor's time.

Cost and Hours: Museum-€7.50, includes entry to the market ruins—also viewable for free from Via dei Fori Imperiali, Tue-Sun 9:00-19:00, closed Mon, last entry 30 minutes before closing, entrance is uphill from the column on Via IV Novembre 94, tel. 06-0608, www.mercatiditraiano.it.

Getting There: Trajan's Column is just a few steps off Piazza Venezia (a hub for major bus routes #40, #64, and #87), on Via dei Fori Imperiali, across the street from the Victor Emmanuel Monument. Trajan's Market can be entered only through the Museum of the Imperial Forums at Via IV Novembre 94 (up the staircase from Trajan's Column). Trajan's Forum stretches southeast of the column toward the Colosseo Metro stop and the Colosseum itself.

Bocca della Verità—The legendary "Mouth of Truth" at the Church of Santa Maria in Cosmedin draws a playful crowd. Stick your hand in the mouth of the gaping stone face in the porch wall. As the legend goes (it was popularized by the 1953 film *Roman Holiday*, starring Gregory Peck and Audrey Hepburn), if you're a liar, your hand will be gobbled up. The mouth is only accessible when the church gate is open, but it's always (partially) visible through the gate, even when closed.

Cost and Hours: €0.50, daily 9:30-17:50, closes earlier off-season, Piazza Bocca della Verità, near the north end of Circus Maximus.

Capitoline Hill

Of Rome's famous seven hills, this is the smallest, tallest, and most famous—home of the ancient Temple of Jupiter and the center of city government for 2,500 years. There are several ways to get to the top of Capitoline Hill (a.k.a. Capitoline Hill). If you're coming from the north (from Piazza Venezia), take Michelangelo's impressive stairway to the right of the big, white Victor Emmanuel

Capitoline Hill & Piazza Venezia

1 Piazza del Campidoglio
2 Capitoline Museums Entrance
3 Copy of She-Wolf Statue
4 "Il Nasone" Water Fountain
5 Views of Forum
6 Shortcut to Santa Maria in Aracoeli Church
7 Shortcut to Victor Emmanuel Monument
8 Mussolini's Balcony
9 Michelangelo's Grand Staircase
10 To Teatro di Marcello Ruins
11 Rome from the Sky

Monument. Coming from the southeast (the Forum), take the steep staircase near the Arch of Septimius Severus. From near Trajan's Forum along Via dei Fori Imperiali, take the winding road. All three converge at the top, in the square called Campidoglio (kahm-pee-DOHL-yoh).

▲**Piazza del Campidoglio (Capitoline Hill Square)**—This square atop the hill, once the religious and political center of

Shortcut to the Victor Emmanuel Monument and Aracoeli Church

A clever shortcut lets you go directly from Piazza del Campidoglio, the square atop Capitoline Hill, to Santa Maria in Aracoeli Church and an upper level of the Victor Emmanuel Monument, avoiding long flights of stairs. Facing the square's equestrian statue, head to the left, climbing the wide set of stairs near the she-wolf statue. Midway up the stairs (at the column), turn left to reach the back entrance to the Aracoeli Church. To reach the Victor Emmanuel Monument, pass by the column and continue to the top of the steps, pass through the iron gate, and enter the small unmarked door at #13 on the right. You'll soon emerge on a café terrace that leads to the monument and the Rome from the Sky elevator.

ancient Rome, is still the home of the city's government. In the 1530s, the pope called on Michelangelo to re-establish this square as a grand center. Michelangelo placed the ancient equestrian statue of Marcus Aurelius as the square's focal point. Effective. (The original statue is now in the adjacent museum.) The twin buildings on either side are the Capitoline Museums. Behind the replica of the statue is the mayoral palace (Palazzo Senatorio).

Michelangelo wanted people to approach the square from his grand stairway off Piazza Venezia. From the top of the stairway, you see the new Renaissance face of Rome, with its back to the Forum. Michelangelo gave the buildings the "giant order"—huge pilasters make the existing two-story buildings feel one-storied and more harmonious with the new square. Notice how the statues atop these buildings welcome you and then draw you in.

The terraces just downhill (past either side of the mayor's palace) offer grand views of the Forum. To the left of the mayor's palace is a copy of the famous she-wolf statue on a column. Farther down is *il nasone* ("the big nose"), a refreshing water fountain. Block the spout with your fingers, and water spurts up for drinking. Romans joke that a cheap Roman boy takes his date out for a drink at *il nasone*. Near the she-wolf statue is the staircase leading to a shortcut to the Victor Emmanuel Monument (see sidebar).

▲▲**Capitoline Museums (Musei Capitolini)**—Some of ancient Rome's most famous statues and art are housed in the two palaces (Palazzo dei Conservatori and Palazzo Nuovo) that flank the equestrian statue in Piazza del Campidoglio. They're connected by an underground passage that leads to the vacant Tabularium and panoramic views of the Roman Forum.

Cost and Hours: €7.50-11 depending on price of temporary exhibit, Tue-Sun 9:00-20:00, closed Mon, last entry one hour before closing, audioguide-€5 or €6.20/2 people, tel. 06-8205-9127 or 06-0608, www.museicapitolini.org.

⊖ **Self-Guided Tour:** The museum's layout—with two different buildings connected by an underground passage—can be confusing. You'll enter at the Palazzo dei Conservatori (on your right as you face the equestrian statue), cross underneath the square (beneath the Palazzo Senatorio, the mayoral palace, not open to public), and exit from the Palazzo Nuovo (on your left).

The **Palazzo dei Conservatori** claims to be one of the world's oldest museums, founded in 1471 when a pope gave ancient statues to the citizens of Rome. In the courtyard, enjoy the massive chunks of Constantine: his head, hand, and foot. When intact, this giant held the place of honor in the Basilica of Constantine in the Forum. The museum is worthwhile, with lavish rooms and several great statues. You'll see the 13th-century *Capitoline She-Wolf* (the little statues of Romulus and Remus were added in the Renaissance). Don't miss the *Boy Extracting a Thorn* and the enchanting *Commodus as Hercules*. Behind Commodus is a statue of his dad, Marcus Aurelius, on a horse. The greatest surviving equestrian statue of antiquity, this was the original centerpiece of the square (where a copy stands today). Christians in the Dark Ages thought that the statue's hand was raised in blessing, which probably led to their misidentifying him as Constantine, the first Christian emperor. While most pagan statues were destroyed by Christians, "Constantine" was spared.

The second-floor café, **Caffè Capitolino,** has a splendid patio offering city views. It's lovely at sunset (public entrance for non-museum-goers off Piazza Caffarelli and through door #4).

Go downstairs to the **Tabularium.** Built in the first century B.C., these sturdy vacant rooms once held the archives of ancient Rome. The word Tabularium comes from "tablet," on which Romans wrote their laws. You won't see any tablets, but you will see a stunning head-on view of the Forum from the windows.

Leave the Tabularium and enter the **Palazzo Nuovo,** which houses mostly portrait busts of forgotten emperors. But it also has two must-see statues: the *Dying Gaul* and the *Capitoline Venus* (both on the first floor up).

Santa Maria in Aracoeli Church—The church atop Capitoline Hill is old, and dear to the hearts of Romans. It stands on the site where Emperor Augustus (supposedly) had a premonition of the coming of Mary and Christ standing on an "altar in the sky" (*ara coeli*). The church is Rome in a nutshell, where you can time-travel across 2,000 years by standing in one spot.

Cost and Hours: Free, daily 9:00-12:30 & 15:00-18:30. While dedicated pilgrims climb up the long, steep staircase from street level (the right side of Victor Emmanuel Monument, as you face it), savvy sightseers prefer to enter through the shortcut atop Capitoline Hill (see sidebar).

Piazza Venezia

This vast square, dominated by the big, white Victor Emmanuel Monument, is a major transportation hub and the focal point of modern Rome. (The square has been dug up for years—Metro line C is under construction, and when anything of archaeological importance is uncovered, progress is interrupted, hence the cano-pied site on the square today.) With your back to the monument (you'll get the best views from the terrace by the guards and eter-nal flame), look down Via del Corso, the city's axis, surrounded by Rome's classiest shopping district. In the 1930s, Benito Mussolini whipped up Italy's nationalistic fervor from a balcony above the square (it's the less-grand balcony on the left). Fascist masses filled the square screaming, "Four more years!"—or something like that. Mussolini created the boulevard Via dei Fori Imperiali (to your right) to open up views of the Colosseum in the distance to impress his visiting friend Adolf Hitler. Mussolini lied to his people, mixing fear and patriotism to push his country to the right and embroil the Italians in expensive and regrettable wars. In 1945, they shot Mussolini and hung him from a meat hook in Milan. (Berlusconi's headquarters are located—thought-provokingly—just behind Mussolini's. That explains all the security on Via del Plebiscito.)

Circling around the right side of the Victor Emmanuel Monument, look down into the ditch on your left to see the ruins of an ancient apartment building from the first century A.D.; part of it was transformed into a tiny church (faded frescoes and bell tower). Rome was built in layers—almost everywhere you go, there's an earlier version beneath your feet. (The hop-on, hop-off Trambus 110 stops just across the busy intersection from here.)

Continuing on, you reach two staircases leading up Capitoline Hill. One is Michelangelo's grand staircase up to the Campidoglio. The longer of the two leads to the Santa Maria in Aracoeli Church, a good example of the earliest style of Christian churches (described earlier). The contrast between this climb-on-your-knees ramp to God's house and Michelangelo's elegant stairs illustrates the changes Renaissance humanism brought civilization.

From the bottom of Michelangelo's stairs, look right several blocks down the street to see a condominium actually built upon the surviving ancient pillars and arches of Teatro di Marcello.

▲**Victor Emmanuel Monument**—This oversize monument to Italy's first king, built to celebrate the 50th anniversary of the country's unification in 1861, was part of Italy's push to overcome the new country's strong regionalism and create a national identity.

At the base of this statue, Italy's Tomb of the Unknown Soldier (flanked by Italian flags and armed guards) is watched over by the goddess Roma (with the gold mosaic background).

The scale of the monument is over-the-top—200 feet high, 500 feet wide. The 43-foot-long statue of the king on the horse is the biggest equestrian statue in the world. The king's moustache forms an arc five feet long, and a person could sit within the horse's hoof. With its gleaming white sheen (from a recent scrubbing) and enormous scale, the monument provides a vivid sense of what ancient Rome looked like at its peak—imagine the Forum filled with shiny, grandiose buildings like this one.

The "Vittoriano" (as locals call it) is open and free to the public. You can simply climb the front stairs, or go inside from one of several entrances: midway up the monument through doorways flanking the central statue, on either side at street level, and at the base of the colonnade (two-thirds of the way up, near the shortcut from Capitoline Hill). The little-visited **Museum of the Risorgimento** (free) fills many floors with displays on the movement and war that led to the unification of Italy in 1870. A café is at the base of the top colonnade, on the monument's north side.

You can climb the stairs to the midway point for a decent view, keep climbing to the base of the colonnade for a better view, or, for the best view, ride the **Rome from the Sky** elevator, which zips you from the top of the stair climb (at the back of the monument) to the rooftop for the grandest, 360-degree view of the center of Rome—even better than from the top of St. Peter's dome. Helpful panoramic diagrams describe the skyline, with powerful binoculars available for zooming in on particular sights. It's best in late afternoon, when it's beginning to cool off and Rome glows.

Cost and Hours: Monument—Free, daily 9:30-18:30, a few WCs scattered throughout, tel. 06-679-3598. Elevator—€7, Sun-Thu 9:30-19:30 (until 18:30 in winter), Fri-Sun 9:30-23:30 (until 19:30 in winter), ticket office closes 45 minutes earlier, WC at entrance, tel. 06-6920-2049; follow *ascensori panoramici* signs inside the Victor Emmanuel Monument or take the shortcut from Capitoline Hill (no elevator access from street level).

Pantheon Neighborhood

Besides being home to ancient sights and historic churches, this neighborhood gives Rome its urban-village feel. Wander narrow streets, sample the many shops and eateries, and gather with the locals in squares marked by bubbling fountains. Exploring is especially good in the evening, when the restaurants bustle and streets are jammed with foot traffic. For a self-guided walk of this neighborhood, from Campo de' Fiori to the Trevi Fountain, see my Heart of Rome Walk on page 794.

Pantheon Neighborhood

Getting There: To reach the Pantheon neighborhood, you can walk (it's a 20-minute walk from Capitoline Hill), take a taxi, or catch a bus. Buses #64 and #40 carry tourists and pickpockets frequently between the Termini train station and Vatican City, stopping at a chaotic square called Largo Argentina, located a few blocks south of the Pantheon. (Take either Via dei Cestari or Via di Torre Argentina north to the Pantheon.) The *elettrico* minibus #116 runs between Campo de' Fiori and Piazza Barberini via the Pantheon. The most dramatic approach is on foot, coming from Piazza Navona along Via Giustiniani, which spills directly into Piazza della Rotunda, offering the classic Pantheon view.

▲▲▲**Pantheon**—For the greatest look at the splendor of Rome, antiquity's best-preserved interior is a must. Built two millennia ago, this influential domed temple served as the model for Michelangelo's dome of St. Peter's and many others.

Because the Pantheon became a church dedicated to the

martyrs just after the fall of Rome, the barbarians left it alone, and the locals didn't use it as a quarry. The portico is called "Rome's umbrella"—a fun local gathering in a rainstorm. Walk past its one-piece granite columns (biggest in Italy, shipped from Egypt) and through the original bronze doors. Sit inside under the glorious skylight and enjoy classical architecture at its best.

The dome, 142 feet high and wide, was Europe's biggest until the Renaissance. Michelangelo's dome at St. Peter's, while much higher, is about three feet narrower. The brilliance of this dome's construction has astounded architects through the ages. During the Renaissance, Brunelleschi was given permission to cut into the dome (see the little square hole above and to the right of the entrance) to analyze the material. The concrete dome gets thinner and lighter with height—the highest part is volcanic pumice.

This wonderfully harmonious architecture greatly inspired Raphael and other artists of the Renaissance. Raphael, along with Italy's first two kings, chose to be buried here.

The Pantheon is the only ancient building in Rome continuously used since its construction. When you leave, notice that the building is sunken below current street level, showing how the rest of the city has risen on 20 centuries of rubble. The nearest WCs are at bars and cafés on the Pantheon's square. Several reasonable eateries are a block or two north up Via del Pantheon. Some of Rome's best gelato is nearby. For dining recommendations, see page 873.

Cost and Hours: Free, Mon-Sat 8:30-19:30, Sun 9:00-18:00, holidays 9:00-13:00, closed for Mass Sat at 17:00 and Sun at 10:30, tel. 06-6830-0230.

Audioguides: 25-minute **audioguide**-€5 or €8.50/2 people. You can download a free Rick Steves **audio tour** of the Pantheon; see page 7.

When to Go: Try to get to the Pantheon first thing in the morning: While it's jammed with people midday, you'll have it all to yourself before 9:00.

▲▲**Churches near the Pantheon**—The **Church of San Luigi dei Francesi** has a magnificent chapel painted by Caravaggio (free, Fri-Wed 10:00-12:30 & 16:00-19:00, closed Thu, between the Pantheon and the north end of Piazza Navona). The only Gothic church in Rome is the **Church of Santa Maria sopra Minerva,** with a little-known Michelangelo statue, *Christ Bearing the Cross* (free, Mon-Fri 7:00-19:00, Sat-Sun 8:00-13:00 & 15:30-19:00, on a little square behind Pantheon, to the east). The **Church of San Ignazio,** several blocks east of the Pantheon, is a riot of Baroque illusions with a false dome (free, daily 7:30-19:00). A few blocks away, across Corso Vittorio Emanuele, is the rich and Baroque **Gesù Church,** headquarters of the Jesuits in Rome (free, daily

7:00-12:30 & 16:00-19:45, interesting daily service at 17:30).

▲**Galleria Doria Pamphilj**—This underappreciated gallery, in the heart of the old city, offers a rare chance to wander through a noble family's lavish rooms with the prince who calls this downtown mansion home. Well, almost. Through an audioguide, the prince lovingly narrates his family's story, as you tour the palace and its world-class art. Don't miss Velázquez's intense, majestic, ultra-realistic portrait of Pope Innocent X (1574-1655), patriarch of the Pamphilj (pahm-FEEL-yee) family. It stands alongside an equally impressive bust of the pope by Bernini. Stroll through a mini-Versailles-like hall of mirrors to more paintings, including works by Titian and Raphael. Finally, relax along with Mary, Joseph, and Jesus, and let the angel serenade you in Caravaggio's *Rest on the Flight to Egypt*.

Cost and Hours: €10, includes worthwhile 90-minute audioguide, daily 10:00-17:00, last entry 45 minutes before closing, elegant café, from Piazza Venezia walk 2 blocks up Via del Corso to #305, tel. 06-679-7323, www.dopart.it/roma.

Piazza di Pietra (Piazza of Stone)—The square was actually a quarry set up to chew away at the abandoned Roman building. You can still see the holes that hungry medieval scavengers chipped into the columns to steal the metal pins that held the slabs together (two blocks toward Via del Corso from Pantheon).

▲**Trevi Fountain**—The bubbly Baroque fountain, worth ▲▲ by night, is a minor sight to art scholars...but a major nighttime gathering spot for teens on the make and tourists tossing coins. The coins tourists deposit daily are collected to feed Rome's poor (for more on the fountain, see page 799).

Palazzo del Quirinale—This presidential palace, and former home of several popes, feels like a combination White House/Palace of Versailles (free, Sun 8:30-12:00 only—closed rest of the week, 200 yards east of Trevi Fountain on Piazza del Quirinale, tel. 06-46991).

ROME

Vatican City

Vatican City, the world's smallest country, contains St. Peter's Basilica (with Michelangelo's exquisite *Pietà*) and the Vatican Museum (with Michelangelo's Sistine Chapel). A helpful **TI** is just to the left of St. Peter's Basilica as you're facing it (Mon-Sat 8:30-19:00, closed Sun, tel. 06-6988-1662, Vatican switchboard tel. 06-6982, www.vatican.va). The entrances to St. Peter's and to the Vatican Museum are a 15-minute walk apart (follow the outside of the Vatican wall, which links the two sights). The nearest Metro stop, Ottaviano, is about 10 minutes from either sight.

Modest dress is required of men, women, and children throughout Vatican City, even outdoors. Otherwise the Swiss

Guard can turn you away. Cover your shoulders; bring a light jacket or cover-up if you've got on a tank top. Wear long pants instead of shorts. Skirts or dresses should extend below your knee.

▲▲▲St. Peter's Basilica (Basilica San Pietro)

There is no doubt: This is the richest and grandest church on earth. To call it vast is like calling Einstein smart. Plaques on the floor show where other, smaller churches would end if they were placed inside. The ornamental cherubs would dwarf a large man. Birds roost inside, and thousands of people wander about, heads craned heavenward, hardly noticing each other. Don't miss Michelangelo's *Pietà* (behind bulletproof glass) to the right of the entrance. Bernini's altar work and twisting, towering canopy are brilliant.

Hours: The **church** is open daily April-Sept 7:00-19:00, Oct-March 7:00-18:00. It closes on Wednesday mornings during papal audiences. **Mass** is held daily in Italian—Mon-Sat at 8:30, 9:00, 10:00, 11:00, 12:00, and 17:00; Sun and holidays at 9:00, 10:30 (in Latin), 11:30, 12:15, 13:00, 16:00, and 17:45. Confirm the schedule (on-site, or go to www.saintpetersbasilica.org and click on the "Tourist Info" link) and location; it's generally in the south (left) transept.

The **Museum-Treasury** is open daily April-Sept 9:00-18:15, Oct-March 9:00-17:15. The **crypt** closes one hour earlier than the church does. The **dome** is open to climbers daily April-Sept 8:00-18:00, Oct-March 8:00-16:45.

When to Go: The best time to visit the church is early or late; at 17:00, when the church is fairly empty, sunbeams can work their magic, and the late-afternoon Mass fills the place with spiritual music.

Avoiding Lines: To bypass the long security-checkpoint line, visit the Vatican Museum first (though it has its own long lines and checkpoint), then take the shortcut from the Sistine Chapel directly to St. Peter's. (Note, though, that this shortcut isn't always open—see page 825 for specifics.)

Dress Code: No shorts, above-the-knee skirts, or bare shoulders (this applies to everyone). Attendants strictly enforce this dress code, even in hot weather.

Getting There: Take the Metro to Ottaviano, then walk 10 minutes south on Via Ottaviano. There are two good bus options: The #40 express bus drops off at Piazza Pio, next to Castel Sant'Angelo—a 10-minute walk to St. Peter's. The more crowded bus #64 is convenient for pickpockets and stops just outside St. Peter's Square to the south (get off the bus after it crosses the Tiber, at the first stop past the tunnel; backtrack toward the tunnel and turn left when you see the rows of columns). A taxi from

ROME

Termini train station to St. Peter's costs about €11.

Tours: The Vatican TI conducts free 1.5-hour tours of St. Peter's (depart from TI Mon-Fri 14:15, plus Tue and Thu 9:45, confirm schedule at TI, tel. 06-6988-1662). Audioguides can be rented near the checkroom (€5 plus ID, for church only, daily 9:00-17:00). You can download a free Rick Steves audio tour of St. Peter's; see page 7.

If you want to see the **Vatican Gardens,** you must book a tour online at least two days in advance at http://biglietteriamusei .vatican.va. No response means they're booked up (€31, 2 hours, usually daily except Wed and Sat, includes entry to Vatican Museum; tours start at 9:30 or 10:00 at Vatican Museum tour desk).

To see St. Peter's original grave, you can take a **Scavi "Excavations"** tour into the Necropolis (€12, 1.5 hours, ages 15 and older only, no photos). Book at least a month in advance by phone (tel. 06-6988-5318), email (scavi@fsp.va), or fax (06-6987-3017), following the detailed instructions at www.vatican.va (search on "Excavations Office"); no response means they're booked up.

Dome Climb (Cupola): You can take the elevator or stairs to the roof (231 steps), then climb another 323 steps to the top of the dome. The entry to the elevator is just outside the basilica on the north side of St. Peter's (near the secret exit from the Sistine Chapel). Look for signs to the cupola.

Baggage Check: The free bag check (mandatory for bags larger than a purse or daypack) is outside the basilica (to the right as you face the entrance), and just inside the security checkpoint.

Services: WCs are to the right and left on St. Peter's Square, near baggage storage past the security checkpoint, and on the roof.

❍ Self-Guided Tour: For a quick walk through the basilica, follow these points:

❶ The atrium is itself bigger than most churches. The huge white columns on the portico date from the first church (fourth century). Notice the historic doors (the Holy Door, on the right, won't be opened until the next Jubilee Year, in 2025).

❷ The purple, circular porphyry stone marks the site of Charlemagne's coronation in A.D. 800 (in the first St. Peter's church that stood on this site). From here, get a sense of the immensity of the church, which can accommodate 60,000 worshippers standing on its six acres.

❸ Michelangelo planned a Greek-cross floor plan, rather than the Latin-cross standard in medieval churches. A Greek cross, symbolizing the perfection of God, and by association the goodness of man, was important to the humanist Michelangelo. But accommodating—and impressing—large crowds was important to the Church in the fancy Baroque age, which followed Michelangelo,

St. Peter's Basilica

Not to Scale

APSE

MAIN ALTAR

DOME ENTRANCE

NAVE

Court-yard

EXIT FROM SISTINE CHAPEL

ATRIUM

SWISS GUARDS

ENTER

STEPS

AUDIOGUIDES, WC & BAGGAGE STORAGE

St. Peter's Square

1 Holy Door

2 Charlemagne's Coronation Site

3 Extent of Original "Greek Cross" Plan

4 St. Andrew Statue; View of Dome; Crypt Entrance

5 St. Peter Statue (with Kissable Toe)

6 Pope John XXIII

7 Main Altar (over Peter's Tomb)

8 BERNINI – Dove Window & Throne of Peter

9 Peter's Crucifixion Site

10 RAPHAEL – Mosaic Copy of The Transfiguration

11 MICHELANGELO – Pietà

12 Tomb of Pope John Paul II

13 Museum-Treasury

14 Blessed Sacrament Chapel

15 Dome Entrance

ROME

so the original nave length was doubled. Stand halfway up the nave and imagine the stubbier design that Michelangelo had in mind.

4 View the magnificent dome from the statue of St. Andrew. See the vision of heaven above the windows: Jesus, Mary, a ring of saints, rings of angels, and, on the very top, God the Father.

5 The statue of St. Peter, with an irresistibly kissable toe, is one of the few pieces of art that predate this church. It adorned the first St. Peter's church.

❻ Circle to the right around the statue of Peter to find the lighted glass niche with the red-robed body of Pope John XXIII (r. 1958-1963), who oversaw the landmark Vatican II Council that instituted major reforms, bringing the Church into the modern age.

❼ The main altar sits directly over St. Peter's tomb and under Bernini's seven-story bronze canopy.

❽ St. Peter's throne and Bernini's starburst dove window is the site of a daily Mass (Thu at 9:00, Sun at 10:30, 12:15, 16:00, and 17:45—after vespers at 17:00; for Mass times in other locations, see "Hours" on page 818).

❾ St. Peter was crucified on this spot when this location was simply "the Vatican Hill." The obelisk now standing in the center of St. Peter's square marked the center of a Roman racecourse long before a church stood here.

❿ The church is filled with mosaics, not paintings. Notice the mosaic copy of Raphael's *Transfiguration*.

⓫ Michelangelo sculpted his *Pietà* when he was 24 years old. (A *pietà* is a work that represents Mary with the body of Christ taken down from the cross.) Michelangelo's mastery of the body is obvious in this powerfully beautiful masterpiece. Jesus is believably dead, and Mary, the eternally youthful "handmaiden" of the Lord, accepts God's will...even if it means giving up her son.

⓬ The tomb of Pope John Paul II was moved to the chapel of San Sebastian in 2011, after he was beatified by Pope Benedict XVI (a step on the road to sainthood). He lies beneath a painting of the steadfast St. Sebastian, his favorite saint.

⓭ Visitors can go down to the crypt (labeled as the *Grotte* or *Tombe*) within the foundations of Old St. Peter's, containing tombs of popes and memorial chapels. The crypt entrance is along the right side of the church, but the line starts to form on the church's front steps, near the right door of the main facade. A ramp leads you down to the floor level of the previous church.

Nearby, an elevator leads to the roof and the stairway up the dome (€7 by elevator, €6 by stairs, allow an hour to go up and down). The dome, Michelangelo's last work, is (you guessed it) the biggest anywhere. Taller than a football field is long, it's well worth the sweaty climb for a great view of Rome, the Vatican grounds, and the inside of the basilica—particularly heavenly while there is singing. Look around—Rome has no modern skyline. No building in Rome is allowed to exceed the height of St. Peter's. The elevator takes you to the rooftop of the nave. From there, a few steps take you to a balcony at the base of the dome that looks down into the church interior. After that, the one-way, 323-step climb (for some people, it's claustrophobic) to the cupola begins. The rooftop level (below the dome) has a gift shop, WC, drinking fountain, and a commanding view.

❹ For most, the museum-treasury (on the left side of the nave, near the altar) is not worth the price of admission.

❺ You're welcome to step through the metalwork gates into the Blessed Sacrament Chapel, an oasis of peace reserved for prayer and meditation (on the right-hand side of the church, about midway to the altar).

▲▲▲Vatican Museum (Musei Vaticani)

The four miles of displays in this immense museum—from ancient statues to Christian frescoes to modern paintings—culminate in the Raphael Rooms and Michelangelo's glorious Sistine Chapel. This is one of Europe's top three or four houses of art. It can be exhausting, so plan your visit carefully, focusing on a few themes. Allow two hours for a quick visit, three or four hours for enough time to enjoy it.

Cost and Hours: €15 plus optional €4 reservation fee, Mon-Sat 9:00-18:00, last entry at 16:00 (though the official closing time is 18:00, the staff starts ushering you out at 17:30), closed on religious holidays and Sun except last Sun of the month (when it's free, more crowded, and open 9:00-14:00, last entry at 12:30); may be open Fri nights May-July and Sept-Oct 19:00-23:00 (last entry at 21:30) by online reservation only. Hours are subject to constant change and frequent holidays; check http://mv.vatican.va for current times. Lines are extremely long in the morning—go in the afternoon, or skip the ticket-buying line altogether by reserving an entry time on their website.

The museum is closed on many holidays (mainly religious ones), including, for 2013: Jan 1 (New Year's), Jan 6 (Epiphany), Feb 11 (Vatican City established), March 19 (St. Joseph), March 31 and April 1 (Easter Sunday and Monday), May 1 (Labor Day), June 29 (Saints Peter and Paul), Aug 15 plus either Aug 14 or 16—it varies year to year (Assumption of the Virgin), Nov 1 (All Saints' Day), Dec 8 (Immaculate Conception), and Dec 25 and 26 (Christmas).

The Sistine Chapel closes 1.5 hours before the museum. Individual rooms may close at odd hours, especially in the afternoon. The rooms described here are usually open.

Reservations: Bypass the long ticket lines by reserving an entry time online at http://mv.vatican.va. It costs €19 (€15 ticket plus €4 booking fee, pay with credit card). It's easy. You choose your day and time, they email you a confirmation immediately, and you print out the voucher with its reservation bar code. At the Vatican Museum, bypass the ticket-buying line and queue up at the "Entrance with Reservations" line (to the right). Show your voucher to the guard, who will scan it and let you in. Once inside

Vatican Museum Overview

1. Main Entrance & Exit
2. Egyptian Rooms
3. Cortile della Pigna
4. Octagonal Courtyard
5. Etruscan Wing
6. Tapestries
7. Map Gallery & View of Vatican City
8. Raphael Rooms
9. Sistine Chapel & Exit to St. Peter's
10. Pinacoteca

From obelisk to museum entry via road is a 15-minute walk

ROME

the museum, go to a ticket window *(a cassa)*, either in the lobby or upstairs, present your voucher and ID, and they'll issue your ticket.

When to Go: The museum is generally hot and crowded, with waits of up to two hours to buy tickets (figure about a 10-minute wait for every 100 yards in line). The worst days are Saturdays, the last Sunday of the month (when it's free), Mondays, rainy days, and any day before or after a holiday closure. Mornings are most crowded. To see the Sistine Chapel with fewer crowds, visit at the end of the day (remember, the chapel closes 1.5 hours before the museum).

Avoiding Lines: The best way to skip the long lines is to **reserve tickets** in advance (described above). If you book a **guided tour** (see "Tours," below), you can approach the guard with your voucher and go right in. If you book with a private tour company, you may still have a short wait at crowded times.

For a steep price, you can buy **same-day, skip-the-line tickets** through a tour company called Roma Cristiana, from their kiosk at St. Peter's Square (€15 ticket plus €11 booking fee, entrances almost hourly, tel. 06-6980-6380, www.operaromanapellegrinaggi.org).

If you don't have a reservation, **try arriving after 14:00,** when crowds subside somewhat. Another good time is during the papal audience, on Wednesday at 10:30, when many tourists are at St. Peter's Basilica.

Make sure you get in the right line. Generally, individuals without tickets line up against the Vatican City wall (to the left of the entrance as you face it), and reservation holders (both individuals and groups) enter on the right.

Dress Code: Remember, modest dress (no shorts, above-knee skirts, or bare shoulders) is required.

Getting There: Metro stop Ottaviano is a 10-minute walk away. (The Cipro Metro stop also works for the museum, but involves a big stair climb, and is farther from the end of the ticket-buying line.) Taxis are reasonable (hop in and say, "moo-ZAY-ee vah-tee-KAH-nee").

Tours: A €7 **audioguide** is available at the top of the spiral ramp/escalator (ID required). If you rent an audioguide, you lose the option of taking the shortcut from the Sistine Chapel to St. Peter's (described later, under "Museum Strategies"), since audioguides must be returned to the museum entrance/exit.

You can download a free Rick Steves **audio tour** of the Sistine Chapel; see page 7.

The Vatican offers **English tours** that are easy to book online (€31, includes admission, http://mv.vatican.va). As with individual ticket reservations, present your confirmation voucher to a guard to the right of the entrance, then, once inside, go to the Guided

Tours desk (in the lobby, up a few stairs).

Both **private tour** companies and private guides offer English tours of the museum, usually allowing you to skip the long ticket-buying line. For a listing of several companies, see page 781.

Security and Baggage Check: To enter the museum, you pass through a metal detector (no pocket knives allowed). The baggage check (upstairs from the lobby) takes only big bags; you'll need to carry your day bag with you.

Museum Strategies: There are two exits from the museum, and you'll want to decide which you'll take before you enter. The main exit is right near the entrance. Use this one if you want to rent an audioguide (which you must return at the entrance) or if you plan on following this self-guided tour exactly as laid out, visiting the Pinacoteca (painting gallery) at the end.

The other exit is a shortcut that leads from the Sistine Chapel directly to St. Peter's Basilica (spilling out alongside the church; see map on page 820). This route saves you a 30-minute walk (15 minutes back to the Vatican Museum entry/exit, then 15 minutes to St. Peter's) and lets you avoid the often-long security line at the basilica's main entrance. If you take this route, you'll have to do the following: Forgo an audioguide, skip the Pinacoteca or tour it earlier, and be prepared for the chance that the shortcut is simply closed—which sometimes happens.

➋ **Self-Guided Tour:** Start, as Western civilization did, in **Egypt and Mesopotamia.** Decorating the museum's courtyard are some of the best **Greek and Roman statues** in captivity, including the *Laocoön* group (first century B.C., Hellenistic) and the *Apollo Belvedere* (a second-century Roman copy of a Greek original). The centerpiece of the next hall is the *Belvedere Torso* (just a 2,000-year-old torso, but one that had a great impact on the art of Michelangelo). Finishing off the classical statuary are two fine fourth-century porphyry sarcophagi. These royal purple tombs were made (though not used) for the Roman emperor Constantine's mother and daughter. They were Christians—and therefore outlaws—until Constantine made Christianity legal in A.D. 313, and they became saints. Both sarcophagi were quarried and worked in Egypt. The technique for working this extremely hard stone (a special tempering of metal was required) was lost after this, and porphyry marble was not chiseled again until Renaissance times in Florence.

Overachievers may first choose to pop into the Etruscan wing—labeled *Museo Etrusco*—located a few steps up from this level. Others have permission to save their aesthetic energy for the Sistine.

After long halls of tapestries, old maps, broken penises, and fig leaves, you'll come to what most people are looking for: the

ROME

Vatican City

This tiny independent country of little more than 100 acres, contained entirely within Rome, has its own postal system, armed guards, helipad, mini-train station, and radio station (KPOP). It also has two huge sights: St. Peter's Basilica (with Michelangelo's *Pietà*) and the Vatican Museum (with the Sistine Chapel). Politically powerful, the Vatican is the religious capital of 1.1 billion Roman Catholics. If you're not a Catholic, become one for your visit.

The pope is both the religious and secular leader of Vatican City. For centuries, locals referred to him as "King Pope." Italy and the Vatican didn't always have good relations. In fact, after unification (in 1870), when Rome's modern grid plan was built around the miniscule Vatican, it seemed as if the new buildings were designed to be just high enough so no one could see the dome of St. Peter's from street level. Modern Italy was created in 1870, but the Holy See didn't recognize it as a country until 1929, when the pope and Mussolini signed the Lateran Pact, giving sovereignty and a few nearby churches to the Vatican.

Like every European country, Vatican City has its own versions of the euro coin (with a portrait of Pope Benedict XVI, and before him, of Pope John Paul II). You're unlikely to find one in your pocket, though, as they are snatched up by collectors before they fall into circulation.

Post Office: The Vatican postal service is famous for its stamps, which you can get from offices on St. Peter's Square (next to TI) or in the Vatican Museum (Mon-Sat 8:30-18:30, closed Sun). Vatican stamps are good throughout Rome, but to use the Vatican's mail service, you need to mail your cards from the Vatican; write your postcards ahead of time. (Note that the Vatican won't mail cards with Italian stamps.)

Seeing the Pope: Your best chances for a sighting are on Sunday or Wednesday. The pope usually gives a blessing at noon on Sunday from his apartment on St. Peter's Square (except in July and August, when he speaks at his summer residence at

ROME

Raphael Rooms and Michelangelo's Sistine Chapel.

After fancy rooms illustrating the "Immaculate Conception of Mary" (in the 19th century, the Vatican codified this hard-to-sell doctrine, making it a formal part of the Catholic faith) and the triumph of Constantine (with divine guidance, which led to his conversion to Christianity), you enter rooms frescoed by **Raphael** and his assistants. The highlight is the restored *School of Athens*. This is remarkable for its blatant pre-Christian classical orientation, especially since it originally wallpapered the apartments of Pope Julius II. Raphael honors the great pre-Christian thinkers— Aristotle, Plato, and company—who are portrayed as the leading

Castel Gandolfo, 25 miles from Rome, reachable by train from Rome's Termini train station). St. Peter's is easiest (just show up) and, for most, enough of a "visit." Those interested in a more formal appearance (though not more intimate) can get a ticket for the Wednesday general audience (at 10:30) when the pope, arriving in his bulletproof Popemobile, greets and blesses the crowds at St. Peter's from a balcony or canopied platform on the square (except in winter, when he speaks at 10:30 in the 7,000-seat Paolo VI Auditorium, next to St. Peter's Basilica). If you only want to see St. Peter's—but not the pope—avoid these times (the basilica closes during papal audiences and crowds are substantial).

For the Wednesday audience, while anyone can observe from a distance, you need a (free) ticket to actually get close to the papal action (and get a seat). To find out the pope's schedule and request a ticket, call 06-6988-3114 or fax 06-6988-5863.

The American Catholic Church in Rome, Santa Susanna, lets you order tickets online (free, with no booking charge) for the Wednesday general audience. Pick up your reserved tickets, or check for last-minute availability, at the church the Tuesday before the audience between 17:00 and 18:45 (consider staying for the 18:00 English Mass) or Wednesday morning between 7:30 and 8:30 (Via XX Settembre 15, near recommended Via Firenze hotels, Metro: Repubblica, tel. 06-4201-4554—charming Rosanna speaks English, get all the details at www.santasusanna.org).

Probably less convenient—because of the long line—is getting a ticket at St. Peter's Square from the Vatican guard at their station at the bronze doors (open Tue 12:00-19:30; last-minute tickets may be available Wed morning—just join the line). It's under the "elbow" of Bernini's colonnade, on the right side of the square as you face the basilica (see map on page 823).

While many visitors come hoping for a more intimate audience, private audiences ended with the death of Pope John Paul II. Pope Benedict doesn't do them.

ROME

artists of Raphael's day. There's Leonardo da Vinci, whom Raphael worshipped, in the role of Plato. Michelangelo broods in the foreground, added later. When Raphael snuck a peek at the Sistine Chapel, he decided that his arch-competitor was so good that he had to put their personal differences aside and include him in this tribute to the artists of his generation. Today's St. Peter's was under construction as Raphael was working. In the *School of Athens*, he gives us a sneak preview of the unfinished church.

Next is the brilliantly restored **Sistine Chapel.** This is the pope's personal chapel and also the place where, upon the death of the ruling pope, a new pope is elected (as in April 2005).

The Sistine Chapel is famous for Michelangelo's pictorial culmination of the Renaissance, showing the story of creation, with a powerful God weaving in and out of each scene through that busy first week. This is an optimistic and positive expression of the High Renaissance and a stirring example of the artistic and theological maturity of the 33-year-old Michelangelo, who spent four years on this work.

Later, after the Reformation wars had begun and after the Catholic army of Spain had sacked the Vatican, the reeling Church began to fight back. As part of its Counter-Reformation, a much older Michelangelo was commissioned to paint the *Last Judgment* (behind the altar). After the chapel's recent and painstaking restoration, the message is as clear as the day Michelangelo finished it: Christ is returning, some will go to hell and some to heaven, and some will be saved by the power of the rosary.

In the controversial restoration project, no paint was added. Centuries of dust, soot (from candles used for lighting and Mass), and glue (added to make the art shine) were removed, revealing the bright original colors of Michelangelo. Photos are allowed (without a flash) elsewhere in the museum, but as part of the deal with the company who did the restoration, no photos are allowed in the Sistine Chapel.

For a **shortcut directly to St. Peter's Basilica** (see "Museum Strategies," earlier), exit out the far-right corner of the Sistine Chapel (with your back to the altar). This route saves you a 30-minute walk and the wait in the St. Peter's security line, but if you exit here, you're done with the museum—you can't get back to the main entrance/exit (where audioguides need to be returned) or the Pinacoteca (described next). Though this corner door is likely labeled "Exit for private tour groups only," you can usually just slide through with the crowds (or protest that your group has left you behind). If for some reason this exit is closed (which can happen without notice), you can try hanging out in the Sistine Chapel for a few more minutes—it may reopen shortly.

If you skip the shortcut and take the long march back, you'll find the **Pinacoteca** (the Vatican's small but fine collection of paintings, with Raphael's *Transfiguration,* Leonardo's unfinished *St. Jerome,* and Caravaggio's *Deposition*), a cafeteria (long lines, uninspired food), and the underrated early-Christian art section, before you exit via the souvenir shop.

Near Vatican City

▲**Castel Sant'Angelo**—Built as a tomb for the emperor, this building was used through the Middle Ages as a castle, prison, and place of last refuge for popes under attack. Today it's a museum, a giant pile of ancient bricks that is packed with history.

Ancient Rome allowed no tombs—not even the emperor's—within its walls. So Emperor Hadrian grabbed the most commanding position just outside the walls and across the river and built a towering tomb (c. A.D. 139) well within view of the city. His mausoleum was a huge cylinder (210 by 70 feet) topped by a cypress grove and crowned by a huge statue of Hadrian himself riding a chariot. For nearly a hundred years, Roman emperors (from Hadrian to Caracalla, in A.D. 217) were buried here.

In the year 590, the archangel Michael appeared above the mausoleum to Pope Gregory the Great. Sheathing his sword, the angel signaled the end of a plague. The fortress that was Hadrian's mausoleum eventually became a fortified palace, renamed for the "holy angel."

Castel Sant'Angelo spent centuries of the Dark Ages as a fortress and prison, but was eventually connected to the Vatican via an elevated corridor at the pope's request (1277). Since Rome was repeatedly plundered by invaders, Castel Sant'Angelo was a handy place of last refuge for threatened popes. In anticipation of long sieges, rooms were decorated with papal splendor (you'll see paintings by Carlo Crivelli, Luca Signorelli, and Andrea Mantegna). In 1527, during a sacking of Rome by troops of Charles V of Spain, the pope lived inside the castle for months with his entourage of hundreds (an unimaginable ordeal, considering the food service at the top-floor bar).

Touring the place is a stair-stepping workout. After you walk around the entire base of the castle, take the small staircase down to the original Roman floor (following the route of Hadrian's funeral procession). In the atrium, study the model of the mausoleum as it was in Roman times. Imagine being surrounded by a veneer of marble, and the niche in the wall filled with a towering "welcome to my tomb" statue of Hadrian. From here, a ramp leads to the right, spiraling 400 feet. While some of the fine original brickwork and bits of mosaic survive, the marble veneer is long gone (notice the holes in the wall that held it in place). At the end of the ramp, a bridge crosses over the room where the ashes of the emperors were kept. From here, the stairs continue out of the ancient section and into the medieval structure (built atop the mausoleum) that housed the papal apartments. Don't miss the Sala del Tesoro (Treasury), where the wealth of the Vatican was locked up in a huge chest. (*Do* miss the 58 rooms of the military museum.) From the pope's piggy bank, a narrow flight of stairs leads to the rooftop and perhaps the finest view of Rome anywhere (pick out landmarks as you stroll around). From the safety of this dramatic vantage point, the pope surveyed the city in times of siege. Look down at the bend of the Tiber, which for 2,700 years has cradled the Eternal City.

Cost and Hours: €8.50, more for special exhibits, Tue-Sun 9:00-18:30, closed Mon, last entry one hour before closing, near Vatican City, Metro: Lepanto or bus #64, tel. 06-681-9111, www .castelsantangelo.beniculturali.it.

Ponte Sant'Angelo—The bridge leading to Castel Sant'Angelo was built by Hadrian for quick and regal access from downtown to his tomb. The three middle arches are actually Roman originals, and a fine example of the empire's engineering expertise. The statues of angels (each bearing a symbol of the passion of Christ—nail, sponge, shroud, and so on) are Bernini-designed and textbook Baroque. In the Middle Ages, this was the only bridge in the area that connected St. Peter's and the Vatican with downtown Rome. Nearly all pilgrims passed this bridge to and from the church. Its shoulder-high banisters recall a tragedy: During a Jubilee Year festival in 1450, the crowd got so huge that the mob pushed out the original banisters, causing nearly 200 to fall to their deaths.

North Rome

Borghese Gardens and Via Veneto

▲**Villa Borghese Gardens**—Rome's semi-scruffy three-square-mile "Central Park" is great for its shade and for people-watching all of the modern-day Romeos and Juliets. The best entrance is at the head of Via Veneto (Metro: Barberini, then 10-minute walk up Via Veneto and through the old Roman wall at Porta Pinciana, or catch a cab to Via Veneto—Porta Pinciana). There you'll find a cluster of buildings with a café, a kiddie arcade, and bike rental (€4/hour). Rent a bike or, for romantics, a pedaled rickshaw *(riscio)*. Bikes come with locks to allow you to make sightseeing stops. Follow signs to discover the park's cafés, fountains, statues, lake, great viewpoint over Piazza del Popolo, and prime picnic spots. Some sights require paid admission, including Rome's zoo, the National Gallery of Modern Art (which holds 19th-century art; not to be confused with MAXXI, described later), and the Etruscan Museum, described on page 833.

▲▲▲**Borghese Gallery (Museo e Galleria Borghese)**—This plush museum, filling a cardinal's mansion in the park, offers one of Europe's most sumptuous art experiences. You'll enjoy a collection of world-class Baroque sculpture, including Bernini's *David* and his excited statue of Apollo chasing Daphne, as well as paintings by Caravaggio, Raphael, Titian, and Rubens. The museum's slick, mandatory reservation system keeps crowds to a manageable size.

The essence of the collection is the connection of the Renaissance with the classical world. As you enter, notice the second-century Roman reliefs with Michelangelo-designed panels above either end of the portico. The villa was built in the early 17th century by the great art collector Cardinal Scipione Borghese, who

Borghese Gallery—Ground Floor

ROOM VI · ROOM V · ROOM IV · ⑨ · ROOM III

⑥ · ④ · ⑤ · CHAPEL · ❸

ROOM VII · MAIN ENTRY HALL · ROOM II · ❷

⑦

ROOM VIII · START · ROOM I · ①

⑧ · PORTICO

Not to Scale

⑩

① CANOVA – Pauline Borghese as Venus
② BERNINI – David
③ BERNINI – Apollo and Daphne
④ BERNINI – The Rape of Proserpina
⑤ UNKNOWN – Diana the Hunter; Other Marbles
⑥ BERNINI – Aeneas, Anchises, and Ascanius
⑦ "Theater of the Universe"
⑧ CARAVAGGIO – Various
⑨ Stairs up to Pinacoteca
⑩ To Basement (Tickets, Info, Shop, WC)

wanted to prove that the glories of ancient Rome were matched by the Renaissance.

In the main entry hall, high up on the wall, is a thrilling first-century Greek sculpture of a horse falling. The Renaissance-era rider was added by Pietro Bernini, father of the famous Gian Lorenzo Bernini.

Each room seems to feature a Baroque masterpiece. The best of all is in Room III: Bernini's *Apollo and Daphne.* It's the perfect Baroque subject—capturing a thrilling, action-filled moment. In the mythological story, Apollo—made stupid by Cupid's arrow of love—chases after Daphne, who has been turned off by the "arrow of disgust." Just as he's about to catch her, she calls to her father to save her. Magically, her fingers begin to sprout leaves, her toes become roots, her skin turns to bark, and she transforms into a tree. Frustrated Apollo will end up with a handful of leaves. Walk slowly around the statue. It's more air than stone.

Cost and Hours: €8.50, or €12.50 during special exhibits; both prices include basic €2 reservation fee, credit cards accepted,

Tue-Sun 9:00-19:00, closed Mon, ticket office closes one hour before museum does, no photos, all bags and cameras must be checked (free).

Reservations: Reservations are mandatory and simple to get. It's easiest by booking online (www.ticketeria.it, €1 extra booking fee, user-friendly website). You can also reserve by telephone (tel. 06-32810, all operators speak English, pay for tickets on arrival), but it's not always easy to reach a live operator. Call during Italian office hours: Mon-Fri 9:00-18:00, Sat 9:00-13:00, office closed Sat in Aug and Sun year-round. If you reach an Italian recording, wait for the English translation.

Every two hours, 360 people are allowed to enter the museum. Entry times are 9:00, 11:00, 13:00, 15:00, and 17:00. Reserve a *minimum* of several days in advance for a weekday visit, and at least a week ahead for weekends. Reservations are tightest at 11:00 and 15:00, on Tuesdays, and on weekends. For off-season weekdays (but not weekends), your chances of getting a same-day reservation are fairly high if you're flexible about the entry time.

After you reserve a day and time, you'll get a claim number. Be at the Borghese Gallery 30 minutes before your appointed time to pick up your ticket in the lobby on the lower level (arriving late can mean forfeiting your reservation). You can skip the ticket pickup line by paying with a credit card at one of the computer kiosks.

You can use a Roma Pass for entry, but you still need to make a reservation (by phone only—not online) and pay the €2 fee.

If you don't have a reservation, you can try arriving near the top of the hour, when the museum sells unclaimed tickets to those standing by. Generally, out of 360 reservations, a few will fail to show (but more than a few may be waiting to grab them). You're most likely to land a stand-by ticket at 13:00 or 17:00.

Getting There: The museum is set idyllically but inconveniently in the vast Villa Borghese Gardens. To avoid missing your appointment, allow yourself plenty of time to find the place. A taxi drops you 100 yards from the museum. Your destination is the Galleria Borghese (gah-leh-REE-ah bor-GAY-zay). Be sure *not* to tell the cabbie "Villa Borghese"—which is the park, not the museum.

Bus #910 goes from Termini train station to the Via Pinciana stop (a few steps from the villa). Coming from Campo de' Fiori or Via del Corso (at Via Minghetti), bus #116 drops you off at the southern edge of the park. From Largo Argentina, bus #63 takes you to the US Embassy on Via Veneto; walk uphill on Via Veneto to the southern edge of the park.

By Metro, from the Barberini Metro stop, walk 10 minutes up Via Veneto, enter the park, and turn right, following signs.

Tours: €6 guided English tours are offered at 9:10 and 11:10

North Rome

ETRUSCAN MUSEUM

NATIONAL GALLERY OF MODERN ART

ZOO

To Catacombs of Priscilla

V. GIARDINO ZOOLOGICO

V. LUCCHELLIERA

VIA FLAMINIA

V. DI BELLE ARTI

Piazza Flaminio

Piazzale del Fiocco

Villa Borghese Gardens

BORGHESE GALLERY

#910; #95 B

Flaminio M

VIALE DEL MURO

TORDO

VIA MUSEO BORGHESE

VIA PINCIANA

SANTA MARIA DEL POPOLO

Pincio

Piazza del Popolo

Galoppatoio (Track)

BIKE RENTAL

Spagna M #116 B

ANCIENT CITY WALLS

VIA PINCIANA

LUNGOTEVERE

VIA DI RIPETTA

VILLA MEDICI

VIA TRINITA

TUNNEL

PORTA PINCIANA

VIA PIEMONTE

Tiber River

VIA DEL BABUINO

VITTORIA

TRINITÀ DEI MONTI

VIA PINCIANA

VIA LUDOVISI

MAUSOLEO DI AUGUSTO

Spagna M

SPANISH STEPS

US EMBASSY

VIA VENETO

ARA PACIS

VIA DEL CORSO

VIA CONDOTTI

CAPPUCCIN CRYPT

PONTE CAVOUR

VIA DUE MACELLI

VIA SISTINA

Piazza Barberini

VIA XX SETTEMBRE

VIA DELLA SCROFA

T

VIA 4 FONTANE

Barberini M

Piazza Parlamento

PARLIAMENT

T

VIA DEL TRITONE

TREVI FOUNTAIN

PALAZZO DEL QUIRINALE

To Termini Station

SABINA

MURATTE

VIA DELL'UMILTA

PANTHEON

Piazza Collegio Rom.

GALLERIA DORIA PAMPHILJ

Piazza del Quirinale

XXIV MAGGIO

400 Meters

400 Yards

"Shopping Triangle"

Piazza Venezia

V. 4 NOV.

B #95

To Forum & Colosseum

ROME

(may also be offered on busy weekends at 13:10 and 15:10). You can't book a tour when you make your museum reservation—sign up as soon as you arrive. Or consider the excellent 1.5-hour audio-guide tour for €5.

Museum Strategy: Visits are strictly limited to two hours. Budget most of your time for the more interesting ground floor, but set aside 30 minutes for the paintings of the Pinacoteca upstairs (highlights are marked by the audioguide icons). Avoid the crowds by seeing the Pinacoteca first. The fine bookshop and cafeteria are best visited outside your two-hour entry window.

Etruscan Museum (Villa Giulia Museo Nazionale Etrusco)— The fascinating Etruscan civilization thrived in Italy around

600 B.C., when Rome was an Etruscan town. The Villa Giulia (a fine Renaissance palace in the Villa Borghese Gardens) hosts a museum that tells the story. The star of the museum is the famous "husband and wife sarcophagus"—a dead couple seeming to enjoy an everlasting banquet from atop their tomb (sixth century B.C., from Cerveteri). Historians also dig the gold sheets from Pyrgi, with inscriptions in two languages—the "Etruscan Rosetta Stone" that has helped scholars decipher their odd language, and the Apollo of Veio, which stood atop Apollo's temple. The smiling god welcomes Hercules, while his mother Latona stands nearby cradling baby Apollo.

Cost and Hours: €8, Tue-Sun 8:30-19:30, closed Mon, last entry one hour before closing, scant English information, 20-minute walk from Borghese Gallery, Piazzale di Villa Giulia 9, tel. 06-322-6571.

Via Veneto—In the 1960s, movie stars from around the world paraded down curvy Via Veneto, one of Rome's glitziest nightspots. Today it's still lined with the city's poshest hotels and the US Embassy, but any hint of local color has faded to bland.

▲Cappuccin Crypt—If you want to see artistically arranged bones, this is the place. The crypt is below the Church of Santa Maria della Immacolata Concezione on Via Veneto, just up from Piazza Barberini.

The bones of more than 4,000 friars who died between 1528 and 1870 are in the basement, all lined up in a series of six crypts for the delight—or disgust—of the always-wide-eyed visitor. The monastic message on the wall explains that this is more than just a macabre exercise: "We were what you are...you will become what we are now."

As you leave (humming "the foot bone's connected to the..."), pick up a few of Rome's most interesting postcards—the proceeds support Cappuccin mission work. Head back outside, where it's not just the bright light that provides contrast with the crypt. Within a few steps are the US Embassy, Hard Rock Cafe, and fancy Via Veneto cafés, filled with the poor and envious keeping an eye out for the rich and famous.

Cost and Hours: €1 donation, daily 9:00-12:00 & 15:00-18:00, modest dress required, no photos, turn off mobile phones, Metro: Barberini, tel. 06-487-1185.

Piazza del Popolo—This vast oval square marks the traditional north entrance to Rome. From ancient times until the advent of trains and airplanes, this was just about any visitor's first look at Rome. Today the square, known for its symmetrical design and its art-filled churches, is the starting point for the city's evening *passeggiata* (see my "Dolce Vita Stroll" on page 792).

From the Flaminio Metro stop, pass through the third-century Aurelian Wall via the Porta del Popolo, and look south. The 10-story obelisk in the center of the square once graced the temple of Ramses II in Egypt and the Roman Circus Maximus racetrack. The obelisk was brought here in 1589 as one of the square's beautification projects. (Its oval shape dates from the early 19th century.) At the south side of the square, twin domed churches mark the spot where three main boulevards exit the square and form a trident. The central boulevard (running between the churches) is Via del Corso, which since ancient times has been the main north-south drag through town, running to Capitoline Hill (the governing center) and the Forum.

Along the north side of the square (flanking the Porta del Popolo) are two 19th-century buildings, which give the square its pleasant symmetry: the Carabinieri station and the Church of Santa Maria del Popolo.

Two large fountains grace the sides of the square—Neptune to the west and Roma to the east (marking the base of Pincio Hill). Though the name Piazza del Popolo means "Square of the People" (and it is a popular hangout), the word was probably derived from the Latin *populus,* after the poplar trees which once stood here.

Church of Santa Maria del Popolo—One of Rome's most overlooked churches, this features two chapels with top-notch art and a facade built of travertine scavenged from the Colosseum. The church is brought to you by the Rovere family, which produced two popes, and you'll see their symbol—the oak tree and acorns—throughout.

Go inside. The Chigi Chapel (second on the left) was designed by Raphael and inspired (as Raphael was) by the Pantheon. Notice the Pantheon-like dome, pilasters, and capitals. Above, in the oculus, God looks in, aided by angels who power the eight known planets. Raphael built the chapel for his wealthy banker friend Agostino Chigi, buried in the pyramid-shaped tomb in the wall to the right of the altar. Later, Chigi's great-grandson hired Bernini to make two of the four statues, and Bernini delivered a theatrical episode. In one corner, Daniel straddles a lion and raises his praying hands to God for help. Kitty-corner across the chapel, an angel grabs Habbakuk's hair and tells him to go take some food to poor Daniel.

In the Cerasi Chapel (left of altar), Caravaggio's *The Conversion on the Way to Damascus* shows Paul sprawled on his back beside his horse while his servant looks on. The startled future saint is blinded by the harsh light as Jesus' voice asks him, "Why do you persecute me?" In the style of the Counter-Reformation, Paul receives his new faith with open arms.

In the same chapel, Caravaggio's *Crucifixion of St. Peter* is shown as a banal chore; the workers toil like faceless animals. The light and dark are in high contrast. Caravaggio liked to say, "Where light falls, I will paint it."

Cost and Hours: Free, Mon-Sat 7:00-12:00 & 16:00-18:30, Sun 8:00-13:30 & 16:30-19:30, often partially closed to accommodate its busy schedule of Masses, on north side of Piazza del Popolo—as you face the gate in the old wall from the square, the church entrance is to your right.

▲▲**Catacombs of Priscilla (Catacombe di Priscilla)**—While most tourists and nearly all tour groups go out to the ancient Appian Way to see the famous catacombs of San Sebastiano and San Callisto, the Catacombs of Priscilla (on the other side of town) are less commercialized and crowded, and just feel more intimate, as catacombs should.

You enter from a convent and explore the result of 250 years of tunneling that occurred from the second to the fifth centuries. Visits are by 30-minute guided tour only (English-language tours go whenever a small group gathers—generally every 20 minutes or so). You'll see a few thousand of the 40,000 niches carved here, along with some beautiful frescoes, including what is considered the first depiction of Mary nursing the baby Jesus.

Cost and Hours: €8, Tue-Sun 8:30-12:00 & 14:30-17:00, closed Mon, last entry 30 minutes before closing, closed one random month a year—check website or call first, tel. 06-8620-6272, www.catacombepriscilla.com.

Getting There: The catacombs are northeast of Termini train station (at Via Salaria 430), far from the center (a €15 taxi ride) but well-served by buses (20-30 minutes). From Termini, take bus #92 or #86 from Piazza Cinquecento. From Piazza Venezia and along Via del Corso, take bus #63 or #630. Tell the driver "Piazza Crati" and "kah-tah-KOHM-bay" and he'll let you off near Piazza Crati (at the Nemorense/Crati stop). From there, walk through the little market in Piazza Crati, then down Via di Priscilla (about 5 minutes). The entrance is in the orange building on the left at the top of the hill.

MAXXI—Rome's "National Museum of Art of the 21st Century" is the big news on the museum scene here—as you can imagine it would be, after the 10 years and €150 million it took to make it happen. To me, it comes off as a second-rate Pompidou Center. Judging by the lack of energy here, I'm not alone in my opinion.

Cost and Hours: €11, Tue-Sun 11:00-19:00, Thu and Sat until 22:00, closed Mon, two exhibits per year—preview on their site, tram #2 from Piazza del Popolo to Piazza Apollo Doro, Via Guido Reni 4a, tel. 06-322-5178, www.fondazionemaxxi.it.

ROME

From the Spanish Steps to the Ara Pacis

▲**Spanish Steps**—The wide, curving staircase, culminating with an obelisk between two Baroque church towers, makes for one of Rome's iconic sights. Beyond that, it's a people-gathering place. By day, the area hosts shoppers looking for high-end fashions; on warm evenings, it attracts young people in love with the city. For more, see my Heart of Rome Walk on page 794.

"Shopping Triangle"—The triangular-shaped area between the Spanish Steps, Piazza Venezia, and Piazza del Popolo (along Via del Corso; see map on page 833) contains Rome's highest concentration of upscale boutiques and fashion stores.

▲▲**Ara Pacis (Altar of Peace)**—On January 30, 9 B.C., soon-to-be-emperor Augustus led a procession of priests up the steps and into this newly built "Altar of Peace." They sacrificed an animal on the altar and poured an offering of wine, thanking the gods for helping Augustus pacify barbarians abroad and rivals at home. This marked the dawn of the Pax Romana (c. A.D. 1-200), a Golden Age of good living, stability, dominance, and peace *(pax)*. The Ara Pacis (AH-rah PAH-chees) hosted annual sacrifices by the emperor until the area was flooded by the Tiber River. Buried under silt, it was abandoned and forgotten until the 16th century, when various parts were discovered and excavated. Mussolini gathered the altar's scattered parts and reconstructed them here in 1938. In 2006, the Altar of Peace reopened to the public in a striking modern building. As the first new building allowed to be built in the old center since 1938, it's been controversial, but its quiet, air-conditioned interior may signal the dawn of another new age in Rome.

The Altar of Peace was originally located east of here, along today's Via del Corso. The model shows where it stood in relation to the Mausoleum of Augustus (now next door) and the Pantheon. Approach the Ara Pacis and look through the doorway to see the raised altar. This simple structure has just the basics of a Roman temple: an altar for sacrifices surrounded by cubicle-like walls that enclose a consecrated space.

The reliefs on the north and south sides probably depict the parade of dignitaries who consecrated the altar, while the reliefs on the west side (near the altar's back door) celebrate the two things Augustus brought to Rome: peace (goddess Roma as a conquering Amazon, right side) and prosperity (fertility goddess surrounded by children, plants, and animals). Imagine the altar as it once was, standing in an open field, painted in bright colors—a mingling of myth, man, and nature.

Cost and Hours: €9, tightwads can look in through huge windows for free; Tue-Sun 9:00-19:00, closed Mon, last entry one

ROME

hour before closing; €3.50 audioguide also available as free podcast at www.arapacis.it, good WC downstairs. The Ara Pacis is a long block west of Via del Corso on Via di Ara Pacis, on the east bank of the Tiber near Ponte Cavour, Metro: Spagna; a 10-minute walk down Via dei Condotti, tel. 06-0608.

▲Fausto delle Chiaie (Fausto of the Beach)—This eccentric fellow (who's likely more sane than the rest of us) is a self-appointed part of the Ara Pacis. Fausto's installation art, usually strewn along the curb that runs between the Ara Pacis and Mausoleum of Augustus, aims to take you to a different dimension. Though he sits next to the local art academy, he stresses that the proximity is merely a coincidence. Charming Fausto speaks English and reminds you that his "plastic secretary" (a tip box) is at the end of the curb. He may be mini compared to the nearby museum, but for me he's more entertaining than the MAXXI.

East Rome

Near Termini Train Station

These sights are within a 10-minute walk of the train station. By Metro, use the Termini stop for the National Museum and the Repubblica stop for the rest.

▲▲▲National Museum of Rome (Museo Nazionale Romano Palazzo Massimo alle Terme)—The National Museum's main branch, at Palazzo Massimo, houses the greatest collection of ancient Roman art anywhere. It's a historic yearbook of Roman marble statues with some rare Greek originals. On the ground floor alone, you can look eye-to-eye with Julius and Augustus Caesar, Alexander the Great, and Socrates.

On the first floor, along with statues and busts showing such emperors as Trajan and Hadrian, you'll see the best-preserved Roman copy of the Greek *Discus Thrower*. Statues of athletes like this commonly stood in the baths, where Romans cultivated healthy bodies, minds, and social skills, hoping to lead well-rounded lives. Other statues on this floor originally stood in the pleasure gardens of the Roman rich—surrounded by greenery with the splashing sound of fountains, all painted in bright, lifelike colors. Though executed by Romans, the themes are mostly Greek, with godlike humans and human-looking gods.

The second floor contains frescoes and mosaics that once decorated the walls and floors of Roman villas. They're remarkably realistic and unstuffy, featuring everyday people, animals, flowery patterns, and geometrical designs. The Villa Farnese frescoes—in black, red, yellow, and blue—are mostly architectural designs, with fake columns, friezes, and garlands. The Villa di Livia frescoes immerse you in a leafy green garden full of birds and fruit trees, symbolizing the gods.

Near Termini Station

Piazza Della Croce Rossa

To Villa Borghese Gardens

US EMBASSY

To Spanish Steps

SANTA MARIA DELLA VITTORIA

CAPUCHIN CRYPT

BATHS OF DIOCLETIAN

Piazza Indipendenza

Barb.

SANTA SUSANNA

Piazza di San Bernardo

STA. MARIA DEGLI ANGELI

Piazza Barberini

Repubblica

Piazza Repubblica

Piazza dei Cinquecento

PALAZZO DEL QUIRINALE

SAN CARLINO

NAT'L MUSEUM OF ROME

TERMINI STATION

To Trevi & Pantheon

Termini

Piazza del Quirinale

SANTA MARIA MAGGIORE

Largo Magnanapoli

Piazza Vittorio Emanuele II

SANTA PRASSEDE

Cavour

MUSEUM OF ASIAN ART

Vittorio Emanuele

250 Meters

250 Yards

To Colosseum & Forum

Finally, descend into the basement to see fine gold jewelry, dice, an abacus, and vault doors leading into the best coin collection in Europe, with fancy magnifying glasses maneuvering you through cases of coins from ancient Rome to modern times.

Cost and Hours: €10, this combo-ticket covers three other branches—all skippable, Tue-Sun 9:00-19:45, closed Mon, last entry 45 minutes before closing, audioguide-€5, about 100 yards from train station, Metro: Termini, tel. 06-3996-7700. The museum is about 100 yards from Termini train station—as you leave the station, it's the sandstone-brick building on your left. Enter at the far end, at Largo di Villa Peretti.

▲**Baths of Diocletian (Terme di Diocleziano)**—Around A.D. 300, Emperor Diocletian built the largest baths in Rome. This sprawling meeting place—with baths and schmoozing spaces to accommodate 3,000 bathers at a time—was a big deal in ancient times.

While much of it is still closed, the best part is open: the Church of Santa Maria degli Angeli. From noisy Piazza della Repubblica, step into the vast and cool church built upon the remains of a vast and steamy Roman bath complex. The church we see today was (at least partly) designed by Michelangelo (1561), who used the baths' main hall as the nave. Later, when Piazza della Repubblica became an important Roman intersection, another architect renovated the church. To allow people to enter from the grand new piazza, he spun it 90 degrees, turning Michelangelo's nave into a long transept. The eight red granite columns are original, from ancient Rome—stand next to one and feel its five-foot girth. (Only the eight in the transept proper are original. The others are made of plastered-over brick.) In Roman times, this hall was covered with mosaics, marble, and gold, and lined with statues.

Cost and Hours: Free, Mon-Sat 7:00-18:30, Sun 7:00-19:30, closed to sightseers during Mass, faces Piazza della Repubblica.

▲**Church of Santa Maria della Vittoria**—This church houses Bernini's statue, the swooning *St. Teresa in Ecstasy*. Inside the church, you'll find St. Teresa to the left of the altar. Teresa has just been stabbed with God's arrow of fire. Now, the angel pulls it out and watches her reaction. Teresa swoons, her eyes roll up, her hand goes limp, she parts her lips...and moans. The smiling, cherubic angel understands just how she feels. Teresa, a 16th-century Spanish nun, later talked of the "sweetness" of "this intense pain," describing her oneness with God in ecstatic, even erotic, terms.

Bernini, the master of multimedia, pulls out all the stops to make this mystical vision real. Actual sunlight pours through the alabaster windows, bronze sunbeams shine on a marble angel holding a golden arrow. Teresa leans back on a cloud and her robe ripples from within, charged with her spiritual arousal. Bernini has created a little stage-setting of heaven. And watching from the "theater boxes" on either side are members of the family who commissioned the work.

Cost and Hours: Free, pay €0.50 for light, Mon-Sat 8:30-12:00 & 15:30-18:00, Sun 15:30-18:00, about 5 blocks northwest of Termini train station on Largo Susanna, Metro: Repubblica.

Santa Susanna Church—The home of the American Catholic Church in Rome, Santa Susanna holds Mass in English daily at 18:00 and on Sunday at 9:00 and 10:30. They arrange papal audience tickets (see page 827), and their excellent website contains tips for travelers and a list of convents that rent out rooms.

Cost and Hours: Free, daily 9:00-12:00 & 16:00-18:00, Via XX Settembre 15, near recommended Via Firenze hotels, Metro: Repubblica, tel. 06-4201-4554, www.santasusanna.org.

Pilgrim's Rome

East of the Colosseum (and south of Termini train station) are several venerable churches that Catholic pilgrims make a point of visiting. Near one of the churches is a small WWII museum.

Church of San Giovanni in Laterano—Built by Constantine, the first Christian emperor, this was Rome's most important

Pilgrim's Rome

church through medieval times. A building alongside the church houses the Holy Stairs (Scala Santa) said to have been walked up by Jesus, which today are ascended by pilgrims on their knees.

Cost and Hours: Free, church—daily 7:00-18:30, Holy Stairs—daily April-Sept 6:15-12:00 & 15:30-18:30, Oct-March 6:15-12:00 & 15:00-18:00; €5 audioguide available at info desk near statue of Constantine, €1 discount with this book (ID required); Piazza San Giovanni in Laterano, Metro: San Giovanni, or bus #85 or #87; tel. 06-6988-6409.

Museum of the Liberation of Rome (Museo Storico della Liberazione di Roma)—This small memorial museum, near the Church of San Giovanni in Laterano, is housed in the prison wing of the former Nazi police headquarters of occupied Rome. Other than a single printed sheet to help, there's little in English. Still, for those interested in resistance movements and the Nazi occupation, it's a stirring visit. You'll see a few artifacts, many photos of heroes, and a couple of cells preserved as they were found on June 4, 1944, when the city was liberated.

Cost and Hours: Free, Tue-Sun 9:30-12:30; Tue and Thu-Fri also 15:30-19:30; closed Mon and Aug; just behind the Holy Stairs at Via Tasso 145; tel. 06-700-3866.

Church of Santa Maria Maggiore—Some of Rome's best-surviving mosaics line the nave of this church built as Rome was falling. The nearby Church of Santa Prassede has still more early mosaics.

Cost and Hours: Free, daily 8:30-18:00, Piazza Santa Maria Maggiore, Metro: Termini or Vittorio Emanuele, tel. 06-6988-6802.

▲**Church of San Clemente**—Besides visiting the church itself, with frescoes by Masolino, you can also descend into the ruins of an earlier church. Descend yet one more level and enter the eerie remains of a pagan temple to the god Mithras.

Cost and Hours: Upper church—free, lower church—€5, both open Mon-Sat 9:00-12:30 & 15:00-18:00, Sun 12:00-18:00, last entry for lower church 20 minutes before closing; Via di San Giovanni in Laterano, Metro: Colosseo, or bus #85 or #87; tel. 06-774-0021, www.basilicasanclemente.com.

South Rome

The area south of the center contains some interesting but widely scattered areas, from Trastevere to the Jewish Quarter to Testaccio to E.U.R.

Trastevere and Nearby

Trastevere is the colorful neighborhood across *(tras)* the Tiber *(Tevere)* River. Trastevere (trahs-TAY-veh-ray) offers the best look at medieval-village Rome. The action unwinds to the chime of the church bells. Go there and wander. Wonder. Be a poet. This is Rome's Left Bank. (You can download a free Rick Steves **audio tour** of this neighborhood; see page 7.)

This proud neighborhood was long a working-class area. Now that it's becoming trendy, high rents are driving out the source of so much of its original color. Still, it's a great people scene, especially at night. Stroll the back streets (for restaurant recommendations, see page 866).

To reach Trastevere by foot from Capitoline Hill, cross the Tiber on Ponte Cestio (over Isola Tiberina). You can also take tram #8 from Largo Argentina, or bus #H from Termini and Via Nazionale (get off at Piazza Belli). From the Vatican (Piazza Risorgimento), it's bus #23 or #271.

Linking Trastevere with the Heart of Rome Walk: You can walk from Trastevere to Campo de' Fiori to link up with the beginning of my Heart of Rome Walk (see page 794): From Trastevere's church square (Piazza di Santa Maria), take Via del Moro to the river and cross at Ponte Sisto, a pedestrian bridge that has a good view of St. Peter's dome. Continue straight ahead for one block. Take the first left, which leads down Via di Capo di Ferro through the scary and narrow darkness to Piazza Farnese, with the imposing Palazzo Farnese. Michelangelo contributed to the facade of this palace, now the French Embassy. The fountains on the square feature huge one-piece granite hot tubs from the ancient Roman Baths of Caracalla. One block from there (opposite the palace) is the atmospheric square, Campo de' Fiori.

▲**Church of Santa Maria in Trastevere**—One of Rome's oldest churches, this was made a basilica in the fourth century, when Christianity was legalized. It was the first church dedicated to the Virgin Mary. Its portico (covered area just outside the door) is decorated with fascinating fragments of stone—many of them lids from catacomb burial niches—and filled with early Christian symbolism. The church is on Piazza di Santa Maria, the Trastevere neighborhood's most important meeting place. With its broad and inviting steps, the 17th-century fountain was actually designed to be the "sofa" of the neighborhood. During major soccer games, a large screen is set up here so that everybody can share in the tension and excitement. At other times, children gather here with a ball and improvise matches of their own.

Cost and Hours: Free, daily 7:30-21:00.

▲**Villa Farnesina**—Here's a unique opportunity to see a sumptuous Renaissance villa in Rome decorated with Raphael paintings. It was built in the early 1500s for the richest man in Renaissance Europe, Siennese banker Agostino Chigi. Architect Baldassare Peruzzi's design—a U-shaped building with wings enfolding what used to be a vast garden—successfully blended architecture and nature in a way that both ancient and Renaissance Romans loved. Orchards and flower beds flowed down in terraces from the palace to the riverbanks. Later construction of modern embankments and avenues robbed the garden of its grandeur, leaving it with a more melancholy charm.

In the Loggia of Galatea, find Raphael's painting of the nymph Galatea (on the wall by the entrance door). Galatea is considered Raphael's vision of female perfection—not a portrait of an individual woman, but a composite of his many lovers in an idealized vision. Raphael and his assistants also painted the subtly erotic Loggia of Psyche.

Cost and Hours: €5; Mon-Sat 9:00-13:00, closed Sun; across the river from Campo de' Fiori, a short walk from Ponte Sisto and a block behind the river at 230 Via della Lungara, tel. 06-680-271.

Trastevere

To Vatican

VILLA FARNESINA

Tiber River

LUNGO TEBALDI

VIA DI PORTA

PONTE SISTO

Parco Gianicolo

VIA CORSINI

LUNGARA

LUNGOTEVERE FARNESINA

Piazza Trilussa

BOTANICAL GARDENS

To Gianicolo Hill

V. MOSONI

❸

V. PONTE SISTO

❽

LUNGO.

VIA POLITEAMA

S. MARIA DELLA SCALA

V. BENE

❼

❾

VIA GARIBALDI

V. D. SCALA

VIC. SCALA

V.C. BOLOGNA

VIC. CINQUE

VIA

VIA PELLICCIA

VIA DEL MORO

❹

❻

VIC. VIC. LEO MATTONATO

❺

❶

V. D. PANIERI

VIA

VIC. CEDRO

S. EGIDIO

VIA PAGLIA

SANTA MARIA IN TRASTEVERE

Piazza Santa Maria

ARCO

T R A S T E

Piazza San Calisto

To San Pietro in Montorio (Tempietto)

VIA LUCIANO MANARA

VIA GARIBALDI

VIA DI PORTA

VIA DEFEREDO MAMELI

VIA ROMA LIBERA

Piazza di San Cosimato

❶ Hotel Santa Maria

❷ Residenza Arco dei Tolomei & Arco del Lauro B&B

❸ Casa San Giuseppe

❹ Taverna Trilussa

❺ Trattoria da Lucia

❻ Trattoria da Olindo

❼ Dar Poeta Pizzeria

❽ Osteria Ponte Sisto da Oliviero

❾ Ristorante & Gelateria Checco er Carettiere

❿ Pizzeria "Ai Marmi"

⓫ Cantina Paradiso Wine & Cocktail Bar

⓬ To Hotel San Francesco

ROME

Gianicolo Hill Viewpoint—From this park atop a hill, the city views are superb, and the walk to the top holds a treat for architecture buffs. Start at Trastevere's Piazza di San Cosimato, and follow Via Luciano Manara to Via Garibaldi, at the base of the hill. Via Garibaldi winds its way up the side of the hill to the Church of San Pietro in Montorio. To the right of the church, in a small courtyard, is the Tempietto by Donato Bramante. This tiny church, built to commemorate the martyrdom of St. Peter, is considered a jewel of Italian Renaissance architecture.

Continuing up the hill, Via Garibaldi connects to Passeggiata del Gianicolo. From here, you'll find a pleasant park with panoramic city views. Ponder the many Victorian-era statues, including that of baby-carrying, gun-wielding, horse-riding Anita Garibaldi. She was the Brazilian wife of the revolutionary General Giuseppe Garibaldi, who helped forge a united Italy in the late 19th century.

Near Trastevere: Jewish Quarter

From the 16th through the 19th centuries, Rome's Jewish population was forced to live in a cramped ghetto at an often-flooded bend of the Tiber River. While the medieval Jewish ghetto is long gone, this area—just across the river and toward Capitoline Hill from Trastevere—is still home to Rome's synagogue and fragments of its Jewish heritage.

You can download a free Rick Steves **audio tour** of this neighborhood; see page 7.

Synagogue (Sinagoga) and Jewish Museum (Museo Ebraico)—Rome's modern synagogue stands proudly on the spot where the medieval Jewish community lived in squalor for more than 300 years. The site of a historic 1986 visit by Pope John Paul II, this synagogue features a fine interior and a museum filled with artifacts of Rome's Jewish community. Modest dress is required. The only way to visit the synagogue—unless you're here for daily prayer service—is with a tour (€10 ticket includes museum and guided hourly tour of synagogue; June-Sept Sun-Thu 10:00-19:00, Fri 10:00-16:00, closed Sat; Oct-May Sun-Thu 10:00-17:00, Fri 9:00-14:00, closed Sat; last entry 45 minutes before closing, English tours usually at :15 past the hour, 30 minutes, check schedule at ticket counter; on Lungotevere dei Cenci, tel. 06-6840-0661, www.museoebraico.roma.it). Walking tours of the Jewish Ghetto are conducted at least once a day except Saturday (€8, usually at 13:15, sign up at museum 30 minutes before departure, minimum of 3 required).

Ancient Appian Way

Southeast of the city center lie several ancient sights that make the trek here worthwhile.

Baths of Caracalla (Terme di Caracalla)—Inaugurated by Emperor Caracalla in A.D. 216, this massive bath complex could accommodate 1,600 visitors at a time. Today it's just a shell—a huge shell—with all of its sculptures and most of its mosaics moved to museums. You'll see a two-story roofless brick building surrounded by a garden, bordered by ruined walls. The two large rooms at either end of the building were used for exercise. In between the exercise rooms was a pool flanked by two small mosaic-floored dressing rooms. Niches in the walls once held statues. The baths' statues are displayed elsewhere: For example, the immense *Toro Farnese* (a marble sculpture of a bull surrounded by people) snorts in Naples' Archaeological Museum.

In its day, this was a remarkable place to hang out. For ancient Romans, bathing was a social experience. The Baths of Caracalla functioned until Goths severed the aqueducts in the sixth century. In modern times, grand operas are performed here.

Cost and Hours: €6, Mon 9:00-14:00, Tue-Sun 9:00 until one hour before sunset (19:00 in summer, 16:30 in winter), last entry one hour before closing, audioguide-€5, good €8 guidebook; Metro: Circus Maximus, plus a 5-minute walk south along Via delle Terme di Caracalla; bus #714 from Termini train station or bus #118 from the Appian Way—see "Getting There" on page 848; tel. 06-3996-7700.

Ancient Appian Way

To San Sebastiano Gate, Museum of the Walls & Central Rome

DOMINE QUO VADIS CHURCH

VIA LATINA

VIA DELLA CAFFARELLA

.5 km

1/4 mile

COLUMBARIUM

SECOND MILESTONE

CATACOMBS OF SAN CALLISTO

VIA APPIA

VIA APPIA PIGNATELLI

V. D. SETTE CHIESE

FOSSE ARDEANTINE

BASILICA

CATACOMBS OF SAN SEBASTIANO & WC

VILLA OF MAXENTIUS

CIRCUS OF MAXENTIUS

ANTICA

VIA DI SAN SEBASTIANO

VIA ARDEANTINA

TOMB OF CECILIA METELLA

THIRD MILESTONE

VIA CECILIA METELLA

APPIA ANTICA CAFFÈ & BIKE RENTAL

To Aqueduct Park

ALIMENTARI

VIA APPIA ANTICA

TORRE DI CAPO DI BOVE

CAPO DI BOVE

SCENIC SECTION

To 4th through 11th Milestones & Brindisi

A Bus #660 Stop
B Bus #118 Stops
C Bus #118 (Southbound Stop Only)
D Bus #218 Stop
E Archeobus Stops

ROME

▲**Appian Way**—For a taste of the countryside around Rome and more wonders of Roman engineering, take the four-mile trip from the Colosseum out past the wall to a stretch of the ancient Appian Way, where the original pavement stones are lined by several interesting sights. Ancient Rome's first and greatest highway, the Appian Way once ran from Rome to the Adriatic port of Brindisi, the gateway to Greece. Today you can walk (or bike) some stretches of the road, rattling over original paving stones, past crumbling monuments that once lined the sides.

The wonder of its day, the Appian Way was the largest, widest, fastest road ever, called the "Queen of Roads." Built in 312 B.C.

and named after Appius Claudius Caecus (a Roman official), it connected Rome with Capua (near Naples), running in a straight line for much of the way, ignoring the natural contours of the land. Eventually, this most important of Roman roads stretched 430 miles to the port of Brindisi—the gateway to the East—where boats sailed for Greece and Egypt. Twenty-nine such roads fanned out from Rome. Just as Hitler built the Autobahn system in anticipation of empire maintenance, the expansion-minded Roman government realized the military and political value of a good road system.

Today the road and the landscape around it are preserved as a cultural park. For the tourist, the ancient Appian Way offers three attractions: the road itself, with its ruined monuments; the two major Christian catacombs open to visitors; and the peaceful atmosphere, which provides a respite from the city. Be aware, however, that the road today is busy with traffic—and actually quite treacherous in spots.

The road starts at the massive **San Sebastiano Gate and Museum of the Walls,** about two miles south of the Colosseum. The stretch that's of most interest to tourists starts another two miles south of the gate. I like to begin near the Tomb of Cecilia Metella, at the far (southern) end of the key sights, and work northward (mostly downhill) toward central Rome.

Cost and Hours: San Sebastiano Gate and Museum of the Walls—€4, Tue-Sun 9:00-14:00, closed Mon, last entry 30 minutes before closing, tel. 06-7047-5284.

When to Go: Visit in the morning or late afternoon, since many of the sights—including the catacombs—shut down from 12:00 to 14:30. All of the recommended sights are open on Tuesday, Thursday, Friday, and Saturday. On Monday, several sights are closed, including the Tomb of Cecilia Metella, the Circus and Villa of Maxentius, and the San Sebastiano Gate and Museum of the Walls. On Wednesday, the Catacombs of San Callisto and the pedestrian path through the park are closed. On Sunday, the Catacombs of San Sebastiano are closed; however, the Appian Way is closed to car traffic, making it a great day for walking or biking.

Getting There: Bus #660 drops you off at the Tomb of Cecilia Metella. In Rome, take Metro line A to the Colli Albani stop, where you catch bus #660 (2/hour, along Via Appia Nuova) and ride 10 minutes to the last stop—Cecilia Metella/Via Appia Antica (at the intersection of Via Cecilia Metella and Via Appia Antica). As it can be frustrating to buy a bus ticket on the Appian Way, have one in hand for your return trip.

A **taxi** will get you from Rome to the Tomb of Cecilia Metella for about €20. However, to return by taxi, you'll have to phone for one; there are no taxi stands on the Appian Way (or just take handy bus #118 back to Rome).

If you want to visit just a few sights, consider **bus #118.** In Rome, catch #118 from either the Piramide or Circo Massimo Metro stops; going away from the city center, it stops at the San Sebastiano Gate, Domine Quo Vadis Church, Catacombs of San Callisto, and Catacombs of San Sebastiano. Although bus #118 does not stop at the Tomb of Cecilia Metella, the Tomb is only 500 yards away from the bus stop at the Catacombs of San Sebastiano. Going back to Rome, bus #118 takes a somewhat different route (skipping the Catacombs of San Sebastiano); catch this north-bound bus just up the road at the Catacombs of San Callisto.

Bus #218 goes from San Giovanni in Laterano to Domine Quo Vadis Church and the west entrance of the Catacombs of San Callisto, but isn't handy for other Appian Way sights.

The handy, but much more expensive, **Archeobus** runs from Termini train station to the major Appian Way sights (see page 783). It stops at all the key attractions—you can hop off, tour the sights, and pick up a later bus (officially runs twice hourly, but service can be spotty).

Getting Back: No matter how you arrive at the Appian Way, **bus #118** is the easiest and cheapest way to return to Rome (get off at the end of the line, the Piramide Metro stop).

Information: The **Via Appia Antica TI** near Domine Quo Vadis Church gives out maps and information on the entire park, which stretches east and south of the visit outlined here (daily April-Oct 9:30-17:30, Nov-March 9:30-16:30, rents bikes, Via Appia Antica 58/60, tel. 06-513-5316, www.parcoappiaantica.it). **Capo di Bove** has a small info center with a good €4 map/guide, active excavations, and a relaxing garden (Mon-Sat 10:00-16:00, Sun 10:00-18:00, great place for discreet picnic, clean WCs, Via Appia Antica 222, tel. 06-3996-7700); it's 100 yards uphill from Appia Antica Caffè, which also has maps (described next).

WCs: Free WCs are at the San Sebastiano and San Callisto catacombs and at Capo di Bove, and WCs for paying customers at the Tomb of Cecilia Metella and the Appia Antica Caffè. There are several water fountains along the way to refill water bottles.

▲▲**Catacombs of San Sebastiano**—A guide leads you under-ground through the tunnels where early Christians were buried. You'll see faded frescoes and graffiti by early-Christian tag artists. Besides the catacombs themselves, there's a historic fourth-century basilica with holy relics.

Cost and Hours: €8, includes 25-minute tour, 2/hour, Mon-Sat 9:00-12:00 & 14:00-17:00, last tour leaves at 17:00, closed Sun and mid-Nov-mid-Dec, Via Appia Antica 136, tel. 06-785-0350, www.catacombe.org.

▲▲**Catacombs of San Callisto**—The larger of the two sets of catacombs, San Callisto is also the more prestigious, having been the burial site for several early popes.

Cost and Hours: €8, includes 30-minute tour, at least 2/hour, Thu-Tue 9:00-12:00 & 14:00-17:00, closed Wed and Feb, Via Appia Antica 110, tel. 06-5130-1580 or 06-513-0151, www.catacombe.roma.it.

Near Rome

▲▲**Ostia Antica**—For an exciting day trip, pop down to the Roman port of Ostia, which is similar to Pompeii but a lot closer and, in some ways, more interesting. Because Ostia was a working port town, it shows a more complete and gritty look at Roman life than wealthier Pompeii. Wandering around today, you'll see the warehouses, apartment flats, mansions, shopping arcades, and baths that used to serve this once-thriving port of 60,000 people. Later, Ostia became a ghost town, but has now been excavated. Buy a map, then explore the town, including the 2,000-year-old theater. Finish with its fine little museum.

Cost and Hours: €6.50 for the site and museum, Tue-Sun April-Oct 8:30-19:00, Nov-Feb 8:30-17:00, March 8:30-18:00, last entry one hour before closing, closed Mon. The museum closes from 13:30 to 14:30 for lunch. Tel. 06-5635-0215. Helpful websites include www.ostia-antica.org and http://archeoroma.beniculturali.it/en. A map of the site with suggested itineraries is available for €2 from the ticket office.

Audioguides: Although you'll see little audioguide markers throughout the site, there are no audioguides for rent. However, you can download a free Rick Steves **audio tour** of Ostia Antica; see page 7.

Getting There: Getting to Ostia Antica from downtown Rome is a snap—it's a 45-minute combination Metro/train ride. (Since the train is part of the Metro system, it only costs one Metro ticket each way—€2 total round-trip.)

From Rome, take Metro line B to the Piramide stop, which is also the Roma Porta San Paolo train station, so the train tracks are just a few steps from the Metro tracks. Follow signs to *Lido*—go up the escalator, turn left, and go down the steps into the Roma-Lido station. All trains depart in the direction of Lido, leave every 15 minutes, and stop at Ostia Antica along the way. The lighted schedule reads something like, "*Prossima partenza alle ore 13.25, bin 3*," meaning, "Next departure at 13:25 from track 3." Look for the next train, hop on, ride for about 30 minutes (keep your Metro ticket handy), and get off at the Ostia Antica stop. (If you don't have a ticket to get back, purchase one at the ticket window at the station, or from the nearby snack bar.)

Leaving the train station in Ostia Antica, cross the road via the blue skybridge and walk straight down Via della Stazione di Ostia Antica, continuing straight until you reach the parking lot. The entrance is to your left.

Sleeping in Rome

Double rooms listed in this chapter range from about €65 (very simple, toilet and shower down the hall) to €400 (maximum plumbing and more), with most clustering around €150 (with private bathrooms). I've favored these pricier options, because intense Rome is easier to enjoy with a welcoming oasis to call home.

Some places give you a small discount (about 5 percent) if you pay cash. Haggle if you arrive late in the day during off-season (roughly mid-July through August and November through mid-March). It's common for hotels in Rome to lower their prices 10-50 percent in the off-season, although prices at hostels and the cheaper hotels won't fluctuate much. Room rates are lowest in sweltering August.

Traffic in Rome roars. Thanks to double-paned windows and air-conditioning, night noise is not the problem it once was. Even so, light sleepers who ask for a *tranquillo* room will likely get a room in the back...and sleep better. Once you actually see your room, consider the potential problem of night noise. If necessary, don't hesitate to ask for a quieter room.

Almost no hotels have parking, but nearly all have a line on spots in a nearby garage (about €24/day).

Sleep Code

(€1 = about $1.40, country code: 39)

S = Single, **D** = Double/Twin, **T** = Triple, **Q** = Quad, **b** = bathroom, **s** = shower only. Unless otherwise noted, breakfast is included, hotel staff speak basic English, and credit cards are accepted. A tax of €2/person is added to all hotel bills.

To help you easily sort through these listings, I've divided the accommodations into three categories based on the price for a double room with bath during high season:

$$$ Higher Priced—Most rooms €180 or more.
$$ Moderately Priced—Most rooms between €130-180.
$ Lower Priced—Most rooms €130 or less.

Prices can change without notice; verify the hotel's current rates online or by email. For other updates, see www.ricksteves.com/update.

ROME

Convents: Although I list just a few, Rome has many convents that rent out rooms. See the Church of Santa Susanna's website for a list (www.santasusanna.org, select "Coming to Rome"). At convents, the beds are twins and English is often in short supply, but the price is right. Consider these nun-run places, all listed in this chapter: the expensive but divine **Casa di Santa Brigida** (near Campo de' Fiori), the **Suore di Santa Elisabetta** (near Santa Maria Maggiore), the **Casa Il Rosario** (near Piazza Venezia), and the user-friendly **Casa per Ferie Santa Maria alle Fornaci** (near the Vatican).

Hostels: If going the hostel route, consider the ones I list in this chapter (within a 10-minute walk of Termini train station), or check www.backpackers.it for more listings.

Near Termini Train Station

While not as atmospheric as other areas of Rome, the hotels near Termini train station are less expensive, and public-transportation options link these places easily with the entire city. The city's two Metro lines intersect at the station, and most buses leave from here. Piazza Venezia is a 20-minute walk down Via Nazionale.

West of the Station

Most of these hotels are on or near Via Firenze, a safe, handy, central, and relatively quiet street that's a 10-minute walk from Termini train station and the airport train, and two blocks beyond Piazza della Repubblica. The Defense Ministry is nearby, so you've got heavily armed guards watching over you all night.

The neighborhood is well-connected by public transportation (with the Repubblica Metro stop nearby). Virtually all the city buses that rumble down Via Nazionale (#64, #70, #115, #640, and the #40 express) take you to Piazza Venezia (Forum) and Largo Argentina (Pantheon). From Largo Argentina, both the #64 bus (jammed with people and thieves) and the #40 express bus continue to the Vatican. Or, at Largo Argentina, you can transfer to electric trolley #8 to Trastevere (get off at first stop after crossing the river).

To stock your closet pantry, pop over to **Despar Supermarket** (daily 8:00-21:00, Via Nazionale 211, at the corner of Via Venezia). A 24-hour **pharmacy** near the recommended hotels is Farmacia Piram (Via Nazionale 228, tel. 06-488-4437).

$$$ Residenza Cellini feels like the guest wing of a gorgeous Neoclassical palace. It offers 11 rooms, "ortho/anti-allergy beds," four-star comforts and service, and a breezy breakfast terrace (Db-€185, larger Db-€205, extra bed-€25, show this book and ask for best Rick Steves price if paying with cash, air-con, elevator, Internet access and Wi-Fi, Via Modena 5, tel. 06-4782-5204,

ROME

Hotels near Termini Station

1. Residenza Cellini, Target Inn, Bellesuite Rome & Hotel Adler
2. Hotel Modigliani
3. Hotels Oceania & Nardizzi Americana
4. Hotel Aberdeen
5. IQ Hotel & Hotel Opera Roma
6. Hotel Sonya
7. Hotel Selene Roma
8. Hotel Italia Roma
9. Hotel Margaret
10. Hotel Montreal
11. Suore di Sta. Elisabetta
12. Gulliver's Lodge B&B
13. The Beehive
14. Hotel Select Garden
15. Hotel Sileo
16. Hotel Robinson
17. Funny Palace Hostel & Launderette/Internet Café
18. Yellow Hostel

fax 06-4788-1806, www.residenzacellini.it, residenzacellini@tin.it, Barbara, Gaetano, and Donato).

$$$ Hotel Modigliani, a delightful 23-room place, is energetically run in a clean, bright, minimalist yet in-love-with-life style that its artist namesake would appreciate. It has a vast and plush lounge, a garden, and a newsletter introducing you to each of the staff (Db-€195, but check website for deals and ask about additional Rick Steves discount; air-con, Wi-Fi; northwest of Via

Firenze—from Tritone Fountain on Piazza Barberini, go 2 blocks up Via della Purificazione to #42; tel. 06-4281-5226, www.hotel modigliani.com, info@hotelmodigliani.com, Giulia and Marco).

$$ Hotel Oceania is a peaceful slice of air-conditioned heaven. This 24-room manor house-type hotel is spacious and quiet, with tastefully decorated rooms. Stefano manages a fine staff, serves wonderful coffee, provides lots of thoughtful extra touches, and works hard to maintain a caring family atmosphere (Sb-€125, Db-€158, Tb-€190, Qb-€212, show this book and ask for best Rick Steves price if paying with cash, deep discounts summer and winter, large roof terrace, family suite, Internet access and Wi-Fi, videos in the TV lounge, Via Firenze 38, third floor, tel. 06-482-4696, fax 06-488-5586, www.hoteloceania.it, info@hotel oceania.it; Anna, Roberto, and Radu round out the staff).

$$ Hotel Aberdeen, which perfectly combines high quality and friendliness, is warmly run by Annamaria, with support from cousins Sabrina and Cinzia, sister Laura, and staff members Mariano and Costel. The 37 comfy, modern rooms are a terrific value (Sb-€102, Db-€170, Tb-€180, Qb-€200, for these rates—or better—book direct via email or use the "Rick Steves reader reservations" link on their website, much cheaper rates off-season, aircon, Internet access and Wi-Fi, Via Firenze 48, tel. 06-482-3920, fax 06-482-1092, www.hotelaberdeen.it, info@hotelaberdeen.it).

$$ IQ Hotel, facing the Opera House, is a beautifully designed place. It feels almost Scandinavian in its efficiency, without a hint of the Old World. Its 88 rooms are fresh and spacious, the roof garden comes with a swing set, and vending machines dispense bottles of wine. It offers cheap self-service laundry and comes with a top-end business center, gym, and sauna. Though it's near the train station, it feels safe and quiet (Db-€100-180 depending on size of room and season, €35 extra for 3rd and 4th person, 10 percent discount for Rick Steves readers off best web price—must book direct and request at time of booking, breakfast-€10, Wi-Fi, Via Firenze 8, tel. 06-488-0456, fax 06-489-0442, www .iqhotelroma.it, info@iqhotelroma.it, manager Diego).

$$ Hotel Opera Roma, with contemporary furnishings and marble accents, boasts 15 spacious, modern, and thoughtfully appointed rooms. It's quiet and just a stone's throw from the Opera House (Db-€165, Tb-€190, show this book and ask for best Rick Steves price, 5 percent less with cash, air-con, elevator, Internet access and loaner laptop on request, Via Firenze 11, tel. 06-487-1787, www.hoteloperaroma.com, info@hoteloperaroma.com, Rezza, Litu, and Federica).

$$ Hotel Sonya offers 34 well-equipped, high-tech rooms, a central location, and decent prices (Sb-€90, Db-€150, Tb-€165, Qb-€185, Quint/b-€200, show this book and ask for best Rick

Steves price if paying cash, air-con, elevator, loaner laptops in room and Wi-Fi, faces the Opera House at Via Viminale 58, Metro: Repubblica or Termini, tel. 06-481-9911, fax 06-488-5678, www .hotelsonya.it, info@hotelsonya.it, Francesca and Ivan).

$$ Hotel Selene Roma spreads its 40 rooms out on a few floors of a big palazzo. With elegant furnishings and room to breathe, it's a good value (Db-€145, Tb-€165, email direct for 10 percent discount, additional 10 percent discount with cash, air-con, elevator, Wi-Fi, Via del Viminale 8, tel. 06-482-4460, www .hoteleseleneroma.it, reception@hotelseleneroma.it).

$$ Bellesuite Rome & Hotel Adler evoke a more genteel age of travel, with breakfast served on the garden patio. Hotel Adler has eight quiet, basic rooms on a wide and elegant hall (Db-€130, Tb-€170, Qb-€195, Quint/b-€220, ask about discount with this book, additional 5 percent discount if you pay cash, air-con, elevator, Internet access and Wi-Fi, Via Modena 5, second floor, tel. 06-484-466, fax 06-488-0940, www.hoteladler-roma.com, info@hoteladler-roma.com, Alessandro and Bruno). The pricier Bellesuite wing has six rooms (Db-€150, Tb-€190, Qb-€215, same discounts and amenities as above, tel. 06-9521-3049 or 06-484-466, fax 06-488-0940, www.bellesuiterome.com, mail@bellesuite rome.com).

$ Hotel Nardizzi Americana, with 33 decent rooms and a delightful rooftop terrace, is another solid value (Sb-€95, Db-€125, Tb-€155, Qb-€175; to get the best rates, check their "Rick Steves readers reservations" link along with the rest of their website; additional cash discount, air-con, elevator, Internet access and Wi-Fi, Via Firenze 38, fourth floor, tel. 06-488-0035, fax 06-488-0368, www.hotelnardizzi.it, info@hotelnardizzi.it; Stefano, Fabrizio, Mario, David, and Samy).

$ Hotel Italia Roma, in a busy and handy locale, is located safely on a quiet street next to the Ministry of the Interior. Thoughtfully run by Andrea, Sabrina, Abdul, and Gabriel, it has 35 comfortable, clean, if worn rooms (Sb-€90, Db-€130, Tb-€180, Qb-€200, 30 percent cheaper July-Aug, air-con-€10 extra per day, elevator, Internet access and Wi-Fi, Via Venezia 18, just off Via Nazionale, Metro: Repubblica, tel. 06-482-8355, fax 06-474-5550, www.hotelitaliaroma.it, info@hotelitaliaroma.com). The four "residenza" rooms upstairs on the third floor are newer and a bit more expensive. They also have eight decent annex rooms across the street.

$ Hotel Margaret, basic but welcoming, fills its walls with Impressionist prints and offers 12 decent rooms at a good price (Db-€110, Tb-€150, Qb-€170, mention this book for their best rate, air-con, elevator, Wi-Fi, north of Piazza Repubblica at Via Antonio Salandra 6, fourth floor, tel. 06-482-4285, fax 06-482-4277, www.hotelmargaret.net, info@hotelmargaret.net, Emanuela).

$ Target Inn is a practical-but-forgettable six-room place next to Residenza Cellini (listed earlier). It's owned by the same people who run the recommended Target Restaurant nearby (Db-€120, air-con, Wi-Fi, Via Modena 5, tel. 06-474-5399, www.targetinn .com, info@targetinn.com).

Southwest of the Station

These good-value places cluster around the church of Santa Maria Maggiore.

$ Hotel Montreal is a bright, solid business-class place with 27 rooms on a big street a block southeast of Santa Maria Maggiore (Sb-€95, Db-€120, Tb-€150, may be less if you email direct and ask for a Rick Steves discount, air-con, elevator, Internet access, communal garden terrace, good security, Via Carlo Alberto 4, 1 block from Metro: Vittorio Emanuele, 3 blocks from Termini train station, tel. 06-445-7797, fax 06-446-5522, www.hotelmontreal roma.com, info@hotelmontrealroma.com, Pasquale).

$ Suore di Santa Elisabetta is a heavenly Polish-run convent with a serene garden and 70 beds in tidy twin-bedded (only) rooms. Often booked long in advance, with such tranquility it's a super value (S-€40, Sb-€48, D-€66, Db-€85, Tb-€106, Qb-€128, Quint/b-€142, no air-con, elevator serves top floors only, fine view roof terrace and breakfast hall, 23:00 curfew, a block southwest of Santa Maria Maggiore at Via dell'Olmata 9, Metro: Termini or Vittorio Emanuele, tel. 06-488-8271, fax 06-488-4066, www.csse -roma.eu, ist.it.s.elisabetta@libero.it).

$ Gulliver's Lodge B&B has four fun, colorful rooms on the ground floor of a large, secure building. While on a busy street, the rooms are quiet. Although the public spaces are few, in-room extras like DVD players (and DVDs, including my Italy shows) make it a nice home base (Db-€120, Tb-€135, cash only, air-con, Internet access and Wi-Fi, a 15-minute walk southwest of Termini train station at Via Cavour 101, Metro: Cavour, tel. 06-9727-3789, www .gulliverslodge.com, stay@gulliverslodge.com, Sara and Mary).

Sleeping Cheaply, Northeast of Termini Train Station

The cheapest places in town are northeast of Termini train station (Metro: Termini). Some travelers feel this area is weird and spooky after dark, but these hotels feel plenty safe. With your back to the train tracks, turn right and walk two blocks out of the station. **Splashnet** launderette/Internet café is handy (€8 full-serve wash and dry, Internet access-€1.50/hour, €2 luggage storage per day—or free if you wash and go online, daily 8:30-23:00, just off Via Milazzo at Via Varese 33, tel. 06-4470-3523).

$ The Beehive gives vagabonds—old and young—a cheap, clean, and comfy home in Rome, thoughtfully and creatively run by Steve and Linda, a friendly American couple. They offer six great-value artsy-mod double rooms (D-€80, T-€105), newer rooms with air-conditioning (Sb-€60, Db-€90-100), and an eight-bed dorm (€30 bunks, Internet access and Wi-Fi, private garden terrace, 2 blocks from Termini train station at Via Marghera 8, tel. 06-4470-4553, www.the-beehive.com, info@the-beehive.com).

$ Hotel Select Garden, a modern and comfortable 19-room hotel run by the cheery Picca family, boasts lively modern art adorning the walls and a beautiful lemon-tree garden. It's a safe, tranquil, and welcoming refuge just a couple of blocks from the train station (Sb-€85, Db-€110, Tb-€130, show this book and ask for best Rick Steves price, air-con, Wi-Fi, Via V. Bachelet 6, tel. 06-445-6383, fax 06-444-1086, www.hotelselectgarden.com, info@hotelselectgarden.com, Armando).

$ Hotel Sileo, with shiny chandeliers in dim rooms, is a homely little place renting 10 basic rooms (Db-€75, Tb-€90, air-con, elevator, Wi-Fi, Via Magenta 39, fourth floor, tel. & fax 06-445-0246, www.hotelsileo.com, info@hotelsileo.com). Friendly Alessandro and Maria Savioli don't speak English, but daughter Anna does.

$ Hotel Robinson is just a few steps from the station, but tucked away from the commotion. Set on an interior courtyard, it has 20 simple rooms that are a fine value (Sb-€65, Db-€85, mention this book for these rates and a small breakfast, air-con-€10, Wi-Fi, Via Milazzo 3, tel. 06-491-423, fax 06-4542-3263, www.hotelrobinsonrome.com, info@hotelrobinsonrome.com).

$ Funny Palace Hostel, adjacent to Splashnet and run by its entrepreneurial owner Mabri, rents dorm beds in quiet four-person rooms and 18 stark-but-clean private rooms (dorm beds-€25, Db-€100, cash only, reception in the launderette—described earlier, Via Varese 33/31, tel. 06-4470-3523, www.hostelfunny.com).

$ Yellow Hostel rents 130 beds in 4-, 6-, and 12-bed co-ed dorms to 18- through 39-year-olds only (they also have 11 private rooms). Hip yet sane, it's well-run with fine facilities, including lockers. There's no curfew, and a late-night bar is next door (€18-35 per bed depending on plumbing, size, and season; reserve via email—no telephone reservations accepted, Wi-Fi and iPad rental available, 6 blocks from station, just past Via Vicenza at Via Palestro 44, tel. 06-493-82682, www.the-yellow.com).

Near Ancient Rome

Stretching from the Colosseum to Piazza Venezia, this area is central. Sightseers are a short walk from the Colosseum, Roman Forum, and Trajan's Column.

Hotels near Ancient Rome

1. Hotel Lancelot
2. Hotel Paba
3. Nicolas Inn B&B, Hotel Pensione Rosetta & Enoteca Cavour 313
4. Hotel Nerva
5. Hotel Giardino
6. Casa Il Rosario
7. Caffè dello Studente & Hostaria da Nerone Rest.

Near the Colosseum

$$$ Hotel Lancelot is a comfortable yet elegant refuge—a 60-room hotel with the ambience of a B&B. It's quiet and safe, with a shady courtyard, restaurant, bar, and tiny communal sixth-floor terrace. It's well-run by Faris and Lubna Khan, who serve a good €25 dinner—a chance to connect with your hotel neighbors and the staff. No wonder it's popular with returning guests (Sb-€124, Db-€192, Tb-€222, Qb-€260, €20 extra for sixth-floor terrace room with a Colosseum view, discount with this book, air-con, elevator, wheelchair-accessible, Wi-Fi, parking-€10/day, 10-minute walk behind Colosseum near San Clemente Church at Via Capo d'Africa 47, tel. 06-7045-0615, fax 06-7045-0640, www .lancelothotel.com, info@lancelothotel.com). Faris and Lubna speak the Queen's English.

$$ Hotel Paba has seven fresh rooms, chocolate-box-tidy and lovingly cared for by Alberta Castelli. Though it overlooks busy Via Cavour just two blocks from the Colosseum, it's quiet enough (Db-€135, extra bed-€40, ask about cash discount, huge beds, breakfast served in room, air-con, elevator, Wi-Fi, Via Cavour 266, Metro: Cavour, tel. 06-4782-4902, fax 06-4788-1225, www .hotelpaba.com, info@hotelpaba.com).

$$ Nicolas Inn Bed & Breakfast, a delightful little four-room place with thoughtful touches, is spacious and bright. It's run by François and American expat Melissa, who make you feel like you have caring friends in Rome (Db-€150-170, extra bed-€30, ask about cash discount with this book, included breakfast served at neighboring bar, air-con, Wi-Fi, Via Cavour 295, tel. 06-976-18483, www.nicolasinn.com, info@nicolasinn.com).

$ Hotel Pensione Rosetta, homey and family-run, rents 20 rooms. It's pretty minimal, with no lounge and no breakfast, but has a good location and reasonable prices (Sb-€65, Db-€90, Tb-€105, air-con, Wi-Fi, Via Cavour 295, tel. 06-478-23069, www.rosettahotel.com, info@rosettahotel.com, Antonietta and Francesca).

Near Piazza Venezia

$$$ Hotel Nerva is a three-star slice of tranquility with 19 small, overpriced (but often discounted) rooms on a surprisingly quiet back street just steps away from the Roman Forum (Sb-€130, Db-€190, extra bed-€40, ask for Rick Steves discount, rates very soft—especially off-season, air-con, elevator, Wi-Fi, Via Tor de' Conti 3, tel. 06-678-1835, fax 06-6992-2204, www.hotelnerva .com, info@hotelnerva.com, Antonio, Paolo, Anna).

$ Hotel Giardino, true to its name, has a small garden area and offers 11 basic rooms in a central location three blocks northeast of Piazza Venezia. With a tiny central lobby and a small breakfast room, it suits travelers who prize location over big-hotel amenities (Sb-€85, Db-€130, one smaller Db for 15 percent less, cash only, check website for specials, air-con, effective double-paned windows, on a busy street off Piazza di Quirinale at Via XXIV Maggio 51, tel. 06-679-4584, fax 06-8928-1175, www.hotel-giardino-roma .com, info@hotel-giardino-roma.com, helpful Gianluca).

$ Casa Il Rosario is a peaceful, well-run Dominican convent renting 40 rooms with monastic simplicity to both pilgrims and tourists in a good neighborhood (reserve several months in advance, S-€42, Sb-€56, Db-€94, Tb-€120, single beds only, fans, free Internet access, roof-terrace picnics welcome, 23:00 curfew, midway between the Quirinale and Colosseum near bottom of Via Nazionale at Via Sant'Agata dei Goti 10, bus #40 or #170 from Termini, tel. 06-679-2346, fax 06-6994-1106, irodopre@tin.it).

In the Pantheon Neighborhood

Winding, narrow lanes filled with foot traffic and lined with boutique shops and tiny trattorias...this is village Rome at its best. You'll pay for the atmosphere, but this is where you want to be—especially at night, when Romans and tourists gather in the flood-lit piazzas for the evening stroll, the *passeggiata*.

Near Campo de' Fiori

You'll pay a premium (and endure a little extra night noise) to stay in the old center. But each of these places is romantically set deep in the tangled back streets near the idyllic Campo de' Fiori and, for many, worth the extra money.

$$$ Casa di Santa Brigida overlooks the elegant Piazza Farnese. With soft-spoken sisters gliding down polished hallways and pearly gates instead of doors, this lavish 20-room convent makes exhaust-stained Roman tourists feel like they've died and gone to heaven. If you don't need a double bed or a TV in your room, it's worth the splurge—especially if you luxuriate in its ample public spaces or on its lovely roof terrace (Sb-€120, twin Db-€200, book well in advance, air-con, elevator, Internet access, tasty €25 dinners, roof garden, plush library, Monserrato 54, tel. 06-6889-2596, fax 06-6889-1573, piazzafarnese@brigidine.org, many of the sisters are from India and speak English—pray you get to work with wonderful sister Gertrude).

$ Hotel Smeraldo, with 50 rooms, is strictly run, clean, and a good deal (Sb-€110, Db-€140, Tb-€170, these rates good with this book, rooms €30 less off-season, air-con, elevator, Wi-Fi, Internet access, flowery roof terrace, midway between Campo de' Fiori and Largo Argentina at Vicolo dei Chiodaroli 9, tel. 06-687-5929, fax 06-6880-5495, www.smeraldoroma.com, info@smeraldoroma.com, Massimo and Walter). Their **Dipendenza Smeraldo,** 10 yards around the corner at Via dei Chiavari 32, has 16 similar rooms (same price and free breakfast, same reception and contact info).

In the Jewish Ghetto

$$ Hotel Arenula, with 50 decent rooms, is the only hotel in Rome's old Jewish ghetto. Though it has the ambience of a gym and attracts lots of students, it is in the thick of old Rome (Sb-€75-98, Db-€133, €100 July-Aug, ask about high-season discount

Hotels in the Pantheon Neighborhood

1. Casa di Santa Brigida
2. Hotel Smeraldo
3. Dipendenza Smeraldo
4. Hotel Arenula
5. Hotel Nazionale
6. Albergo Santa Chiara
7. Hotel Portoghesi
8. Hotel Due Torri
9. Hotel 939 Rome

with this book, extra bed-€21, air-con, no elevator, Wi-Fi, opposite the fountain in the park on Via Arenula at Via Santa Maria de' Calderari 47, tel. 06-687-9454, fax 06-689-6188, www.hotel arenula.com, info@hotelarenula.com, Rosanna).

Close to the Pantheon

These places are buried in the pedestrian-friendly heart of ancient Rome, each within about a five-minute walk of the Pantheon. You'll pay more here—but you'll save time and money by being exactly where you want to be for your early and late wandering.

$$$ Hotel Nazionale, a four-star landmark, is a 16th-century palace that shares a well-policed square with the Parliament building. Its 100 rooms are accentuated by lush public spaces, fancy bars, a uniformed staff, and a marble-floored restaurant. It's a big, stuffy hotel with a revolving front door, but it's a worthy splurge if you want security, comfort, and ancient Rome at your doorstep (Sb-€220, Db-€350, giant deluxe Db-€480, extra person-€70, check online for summer and weekend discounts—you'll typically save 30 percent off their sky-high rack rates, air-con, elevator, Piazza Montecitorio 131, tel. 06-695-001, fax 06-678-6677, www .hotelnazionale.it, info@hotelnazionale.it).

$$$ Albergo Santa Chiara is big, solid, and hotelesque. Flavia, Silvio, and their fine staff offer marbled elegance (but basic furniture) and all the hotel services in the old center. Its ample public lounges are dressy and professional, and its 99 rooms are quiet and spacious (Sb-€138, Db-€190, Db-€215 April-June and Oct, Tb-€262, check website for discounts, book online direct and request special Rick Steves rates, elevator, behind Pantheon at Via di Santa Chiara 21, tel. 06-687-2979, fax 06-687-3144, www.albergo santachiara.com, info@albergosantachiara.com).

$$$ Hotel Portoghesi is a classic hotel with 28 rooms in the medieval heart of Rome. It's peaceful, quiet, and calmly run, and comes with a delightful roof terrace—though you pay for the location (Sb-€130-160, Db-€160-200, price range reflects low and high season, breakfast on roof, air-con, elevator, Wi-Fi, Via dei Portoghesi 1, tel. 06-686-4231, fax 06-687-6976, www.hotel portoghesiroma.it, info@hotelportoghesiroma.com).

$$$ Hotel Due Torri, hiding out on a tiny quiet street, is beautifully located. It feels professional yet homey, with an accommodating staff, generous public spaces, and 26 small rooms. While the location and lounge are great, the rooms are overpriced (Sb-€125, Db-€195, family apartment-€240 for 3 and €260 for 4, check website for frequent discounts, air-con, elevator, Wi-Fi, a block off Via della Scrofa at Vicolo del Leonetto 23, tel. 06-6880-6956, fax 06-686-5442, www.hotelduetorriroma.com, info@hoteldue torriroma.com, Cinzia).

$ Hotel 939 Rome is a utilitarian place with no charm in a beat-up old building—but it's got a fine location and prices (Db-€100-140, half off in low season, extra bed-€30, check website for frequent discounts, breakfast extra, air-con, elevator, Wi-Fi; from Via della Scrofa, turn right at Piazza Nicosia and head to Via del Clementino 94, tel. 06-6830-0312, www.hotel939.com, hotel939 @hotmail.it, helpful Aurora).

In Trastevere

Colorful and genuine in a gritty sort of way, Trastevere is a treat for travelers looking for a less touristy and more bohemian atmosphere. Choices are few here, but by trekking across the Tiber, you can have the experience of being comfortably immersed in old Rome. To locate the following places, see the map on page 844.

$$$ Hotel Santa Maria sits like a lazy hacienda in the midst of Trastevere. Surrounded by a medieval skyline, you'll feel as if you're on some romantic stage set. Its 18 small but well-equipped, air-conditioned rooms—former cells in a cloister—are all on the ground floor, as are a few suites for up to six people. The rooms circle a gravelly courtyard of orange trees and stay-awhile patio furniture (Db-€180, Tb-€220; show this book and ask for best Rick Steves price, higher rates for stays shorter than three nights; family rooms, free loaner bikes, Internet access and Wi-Fi, face church on Piazza Maria Trastevere and go right down Via della Fonte d'Olio 50 yards to Vicolo del Piede 2, tel. 06-589-4626, fax 06-589-4815, www.hotelsantamaria.info, info@hotelsantamaria .info, Stefano). Some rooms come with family-friendly fold-down bunks for €30 extra per person. Their freshly renovated six-room **Residenza Santa Maria** is a couple of blocks away (same prices and contact info).

$$$ Residenza Arco dei Tolomei is your most poetic Trastevere experience imaginable, with six small, unique, antique-filled rooms boasting fragrant balconies. With its quiet and elegant setting, you can pretend you're visiting aristocratic relatives (Db-€200, discounts for cash and for stays of three days or more, reserve well in advance, Internet access and Wi-Fi, from Piazza Piscinula a block up Via dell'Arco de' Tolomei at #27, tel. 06-5832-0819, www.bbarcodeitolomei.com, info@bbarcodeitolomei.com; Marco, Gianna Paola, and dog Pixel).

$$ Casa San Giuseppe is down a characteristic laundry-strewn lane with views of Aurelian Walls and a sunny roof terrace. While convent-owned, it's a secular place renting 29 plain but peaceful, spacious, and spotless rooms (Sb-€115, Db-€155, Tb-€185, Qb-€215, garden-facing rooms are quiet, air-con, elevator, Internet access, parking-€15, just north of Piazza Trilussa at Vicolo Moroni 22, tel. 06-5833-3490, fax 06-5833-5754, www .casasangiuseppe.it, info@casasangiuseppe.it, Andrea).

$$ Arco del Lauro B&B rents six white, minimalist rooms in a good location. Facing a courtyard (no views but little noise), the friendly welcome and good value make up for the lack of public spaces (Db-€135, Qb-€185, prices good if booked direct, cash only, includes breakfast served in a café, air-con, Internet access and Wi-Fi, from Piazza Piscinula a block up Via dell'Arco de' Tolomei at #27, tel. 06-9784-0350, mobile 346-244-3212, www.arcodel lauro.it, info@arcodellauro.it, Lorenza and Daniela).

$ Hotel San Francesco, big and blocky yet welcoming, stands like a practical and efficient oasis at the edge of all the Trastevere action. Renting 24 trim rooms in this authentic district, it comes with an inviting roof terrace and a helpful staff. Handy trams to Largo Argentina are just a block away (Db-€90-120 depending on the season, air-con, Via Jacopa de' Settesoli 7, tel. 06-5830-0051, www.hotelsanfrancesco.net, info@hotelsanfrancesco.net).

Near Vatican City

Sleeping near the Vatican is expensive, but some enjoy calling this neighborhood home. Even though it's handy to the Vatican (when the rapture hits, you're right there), everything else is a long way away.

$$$ Hotel Alimandi Vaticano, facing the Vatican Museum, is beautifully designed. Run by the Alimandi family (Enrico, Irene, and Germano), it features four stars, 24 spacious rooms, and all the modern comforts you can imagine (Sb-€170, standard Db-€170-200, big Db with 2 double beds-€240-260, Tb-€230-260, cash discount, air-con, elevator, Viale Vaticano 99, Metro: Cipro, tel. 06-397-45562, fax 06-397-30132, www.alimandivaticano hotel.com, alimandivaticano@alimandi.com).

$$ Hotel Alimandi Tunisi is a good value, run by other members of the friendly and entrepreneurial Alimandi family— Paolo, Grazia, Luigi, Marta, and Barbara. Their 27 perfumed rooms are air-conditioned, modern, and marbled in white (Sb-€90, Db-€130-175, cash discount, grand buffet breakfast served in great roof garden, elevator, small gym, pool table, piano lounge, down the stairs directly in front of Vatican Museum, Via Tunisi 8, Metro: Cipro, reserve by phone at tel. 06-3972-3941, fax 06-3972-3943, www.alimanditunisi.com, alimandi@tin.it).

$$ Hotel Gerber, set in a quiet residential area, is family-run with 27 well-polished, businesslike rooms (Sb-€120, Db-€170, Tb-€190, Qb-€200, ask about discount with this book when you book direct, air-con, elevator, Wi-Fi, leafy terrace, Via degli Scipioni 241, at intersection with Via Ezio, a block from Metro: Lepanto, tel. 06-321-6485, fax 06-321-7048, www.hotelgerber.it, info@hotelgerber.it; Peter, Simonetta, and friendly dog Kira).

$ Casa Valdese is an efficient, well-managed, church-run hotel that's popular with Germans. Its 35 big, quiet rooms are located just over the Tiber River and near the Vatican. It feels safe if a bit institutional, with the bonus of two breezy, communal roof terraces with incredible views (two external Sb-€58, Db-€130, Tb-€180, Qb-€210, discounts for 3-night stays, air-con, Internet access and Wi-Fi; from Lepanto Metro station, go one block down Via M. Colonna, turn left on Via degli Scipioni, then continue for a block to the intersection with Via Alessandro Farnese 18; tel. 06-321-5362, fax 06-321-1843, www.casavaldeseroma.it, reception @casavaldeseroma.it, Matteo).

ROME

Hotels & Restaurants near Vatican City

❶ Hotel Alimandi Vaticano

❷ Hotel Alimandi Tunisi

❸ To Hotel Gerber & Casa Valdese

❹ To Casa per Ferie Rooms

❺ Hostaria dei Bastioni Rest.

❻ La Rustichella Buffet & Gelateria Millennium

❼ To Tre Pupazzi & Vecchio Borgo Rest.

❽ L'Insalata Ricca, Duecento Gradi & Gelateria Old Bridge

❾ Mercato Trionfale

❿ Supermarket

ROME

$ Casa per Ferie Santa Maria alle Fornaci has simple class, housing pilgrims and secular tourists just a short walk south of the Vatican in 54 identical, stark, utilitarian, mostly twin-bedded rooms. This is the most user-friendly convent-type place I've found. Reserve at least three months in advance (Sb-€70, Db-€95, Tb-€130, air-con, elevator; take bus #64 from Termini train station to San Pietro train station, then walk 100 yards north along Via della Stazione di San Pietro to Piazza Santa Maria alle Fornaci

27; tel. 06-393-67632, fax 06-393-66795, www.trinitaridematha.it, cffornaci@tin.it, Carmine).

Eating in Rome

I've listed a number of restaurants I enjoy. While most are in quaint and therefore pricey and touristy areas (Piazza Navona, the Pantheon neighborhood, Campo de' Fiori, and Trastevere), many are tucked away just out of the tourist crush.

In general, I'm impressed by how small the price difference is from a mediocre restaurant to a fine one. You can pay about 20 percent more for double the quality. If I had $90 for three meals in Rome, I'd spend $50 for one and $20 each for the other two, rather than $30 on all three. For splurge meals, I'd consider Gabriello, Fortunato, and Taverna Trilussa (in that order).

Rome's fabled nightspots (most notably Piazza Navona, near the Pantheon, and Campo de' Fiori) are lined with the outdoor tables of touristy restaurants with enticing menus and formal-vested waiters. The atmosphere is super-romantic: I, too, like the idea of dining under floodlit monuments, amid a constantly flowing parade of people. But you'll likely be surrounded by tourists, and noisy English-speakers can kill the ambience of the spot...leaving you with just a forgettable and overpriced meal. Restaurants in these areas are notorious for surprise charges, forgettable food, microwaved ravioli, and bad service.

I enjoy the view by savoring just a drink or dessert on a famous square, but I dine with locals on nearby low-rent streets, where the proprietor needs to serve a good-value meal and nurture a local following to stay in business. If you're set on eating—or just drinking and snacking—on a famous piazza, you don't need a guidebook listing to choose a spot; enjoy the ritual of slowly circling the square, observing both the food and the people eating it, and just sit where the view and menu appeals to you.

In Trastevere

Colorful Trastevere is now pretty touristy. Still, Romans join the tourists to eat on the rustic side of the Tiber River. Start at the central square, Piazza Santa Maria. This is where the tourists dine, while others wander the back streets in search of mom-and-pop places with barely a menu. My recommendations are within a few minutes' walk of each other (between Piazza Santa Maria Trastevere and Ponte Sisto; see map on page 844).

Taverna Trilussa is your best bet for dining well in Trastevere. Brothers Massimo and Maurizio offer quality and value without pretense. With a proud 100-year-old tradition, this place has the right mix of style and informality. The service is fun-loving yet professional, and they're happy to let you split plates into smaller portions to enjoy a family-style meal. The menu celebrates local classics and seasonal specials, and comes with a big wine selection. The spacious dining hall is strewn with eclectic Roman souvenirs. For those who'd rather eat outdoors, Trilussa has an actual terrace rather than just tables jumbled together on the sidewalk (€15 pastas, €20 *secondi*, Mon-Sat from 19:30 for dinner, closed Sun, reservations very smart, Via del Politeama 23, tel. 06-581-8918).

Trattoria da Lucia lets you enjoy simple, traditional food at a good price. It's your basic old-school, Trastevere dining experience, and has been family-run since World War II. You'll meet four generations of the family, including Giuliano and Renato, their uncle Ennio, and Ennio's mom—pictured on the menu in the 1950s. The family specialty is *spaghetti alla Gricia*, with pancetta bacon (€9 pastas, €11 *secondi*, Tue-Sun 12:30-15:00 & 19:30-23:00, closed Mon, cash only, evocative outdoor or comfy indoor seating—but avoid back room, just off Via del Mattonato at Vicolo del Mattonato 2, tel. 06-580-3601).

Trattoria da Olindo takes homey to extremes. You really feel like you dropped in on a family that cooks for the neighborhood to supplement their income. Don't expect any smiles here (€8 pastas, €10 *secondi*, Mon-Sat dinner served 20:00-22:30, closed Sun, cash only, indoor and funky outdoor seating, on the corner of Vicolo della Scala and Via del Mattonato at #8, tel. 06-581-8835).

Dar Poeta Pizzeria, tucked in a back alley and a hit with local students, cranks out some of the best wood-fired pizza I've had in Rome. It's run by three friends—Marco, Paolo, and another Marco—who welcome you into the informal restaurant beneath exposed brick arches. If you're in a spicy mood, order *lingua di fuoco* (tongue of fire). If you're extra hungry, pay an extra euro for *pizza alto* (thicker crust). Choose between their classic, cramped interior and lively tables outside on the cobblestones. Their chocolate dessert calzone is a favorite (€6-9 pizzas, daily 12:00-24:00, Vicolo del Bologna 45, tel. 06-588-0516).

Osteria Ponte Sisto da Oliviero, small and Mediterranean, specializes in traditional Roman cuisine, but has frequent Neapolitan specials as well. Just outside the tourist zone, it caters mostly to Romans and offers beautiful desserts and a fine value (€9 pastas, €12 *secondi*, Thu-Tue 12:30-15:30 & 19:30-24:00, closed Wed, Via Ponte Sisto 80, tel. 06-588-3411, reservations smart, Oliviero). If you're coming from the city center, cross Ponte Sisto (pedestrian bridge), continue across the little square (Piazza Trilussa) and you'll see it on the right.

Ristorante Checco er Carettiere is a big, family-run place that's been a Trastevere fixture for four generations—as the photos on the wall attest. With white tablecloths, well-presented food, and dressy local diners, this is a popular place for a special meal in Trastevere. While it's overpriced, you'll eat well amid lots of fun commotion (€16 pastas, €22 *secondi*, daily 12:30-15:00 & 19:30-23:15, Via Benedetta 10, tel. 06-580-0985). Their *osteria* next door (at #13) shares the same kitchen and offers less ambience, lower prices, and a more basic menu (€11 pastas, €15 *secondi*). Many Romans consider their *gelateria* (next door at #7) to be the best on this side of the river.

Pizzeria "Ai Marmi" is a bright and noisy festival of pizza, where the oven and pizza-assembly line are surrounded by marble-slab tables (hence the nickname "the Morgue"). It's a classic Roman scene, whether you enjoy the chaos inside or sit at a sidewalk table, with famously good €8 pizzas and very tight seating. Expect a long line between 20:00 and 22:00 (Thu-Tue 18:30-24:00, closed Wed, cash only, tram #8 from Largo Argentina to first stop over bridge, just beyond Piazza Sonnino at Viale Trastevere 53, tel. 06-580-0919).

Cantina Paradiso Wine and Cocktail Bar, a block over Viale Trastevere from the touristy action, has a simple romantic charm. During happy hour (18:00-21:00), the €7 drinks come with a well-made little buffet that can turn into a cheap, light dinner (€8 pastas, daily 12:00-24:00, €5 vegetarian lunch buffet, Via San Francesco a Ripa 73, tel. 06-589-9799, Weronika).

And for Dessert: Gelateria alla Checco er Carettiere, run by and next door to the famous, recommended restaurant of the same name, is considered *the* place for gelato in Trastevere (daily 12:00-24:00, Via Benedetta 7).

In the Jewish Ghetto

The Jewish Ghetto sits just across the river from Trastevere (see map on page 844).

Sora Margherita, hiding without a sign on a cluttered square, has been a rustic neighborhood favorite since 1927. Amid a picturesque commotion, families chow down on old-time Roman and Jewish dishes for a decent price. As it's technically not a real restaurant (it avoids red tape by being officially designated as an *associazione culturale*), you'll need to sign a card to join the "cultural association" when you order (don't worry; membership has no obligations except that you enjoy your meal). The menu's crude term for the fettuccini gives you some idea of the mood of this place: *nazzica culo* ("shaky ass"—what happens while it's made). Reservations are almost always necessary (June and Aug Mon-Fri 12:30-15:00, dinner seatings on Mon, Wed, and Fri only at 20:00 and 21:30, closed Sat-Sun; Sept-May Mon-Sat 12:30-15:00, dinner seatings on Mon, Wed, Fri, and Sat at 20:00 and 21:30, closed Sun and July; just south of Via del Portico d'Ottavia at Piazza delle

Cinque Scole 30—look for the red curtain, tel. 06-687-4216, Ivan doesn't speak English).

In the Pantheon Neighborhood

For the restaurants in this central area, I've listed them based on which landmark they're closest to: Campo de' Fiori, Piazza Navona, the Trevi Fountain, or the Pantheon itself.

On and near Campo de' Fiori

While it is touristy, Campo de' Fiori offers a sublimely romantic setting. And, since it's so close to the heart of the Roman people, it remains popular with locals, even though its restaurants offer greater atmosphere than food value. The square is lined with popular and interesting bars, pizzerias, and small restaurants—all great for people-watching over a glass of wine. Later at night it's taken over by a younger, clubby crowd.

Osteria da Giovanni ar Galletto is nearby, on the more elegant and peaceful Piazza Farnese. Angelo entertains upscale Romans and has magical outdoor seating. Regrettably, service can be horrible, you need to double-check the bill, and single diners aren't treated very well. Still, if you're in no hurry and ready to savor my favorite al fresco setting in Rome (while humoring the waiters), this can be a good bet (€10 pastas, €15-20 *secondi*, Mon-Sat 12:15-15:00 & 19:30-23:00, closed Sun, reservations smart for outdoor seating, tucked in corner of Piazza Farnese at #102, tel. 06-686-1714).

Osteria Enoteca al Bric is a mod bistro run by helpful Roberto and Barbara, who love to cook, serve fine wine, and listen to jazz. Wine-case lids decorate the wall like happy memories. They offer a fun, €22 happy-hour deal for two from 19:30-20:30 that includes a plate of cheeses and meats, two glasses of good wine, water, and bread (Tue-Sun from 19:30 for dinner, closed Mon, reserve if dining after 20:30, can be pricey, 100 yards off Campo de' Fiori at Via del Pellegrino 51, tel. 06-687-9533).

Vineria Salumeria Roscioli is an elegant *enoteca* that's a hit with local theatergoers, so reservations are a must. While it's just a salami toss away from touristy Campo de' Fiori, you'll dine with classy locals rather than tourists, and feel like you're sitting in a romantic deli after hours. It's expensive, but you'll get a selection of fine cheeses, meats, local dishes, and top-end wines by the glass (€15-20 plates, closed Sun, 3 blocks east of Campo de' Fiori at Via dei Giubbonari 21, tel. 06-687-5287).

Filetti di Baccalà is a cheap and basic Roman classic, where nostalgic regulars cram into wooden tables savoring their old-school favorites—fried cod finger-food fillets (€5 each) and raw *puntarelle* greens (slathered with anchovy sauce in spring and winter). Study

Restaurants in the Pantheon Neighborhood

1 Osteria da Giovanni ar Galletto
2 Osteria Enoteca al Bric
3 To Vineria Salumeria Roscioli
4 Filetti di Baccalà
5 Trattoria der Pallaro
6 Pizzeria da Baffetto 2
7 Pizzeria da Baffetto
8 Ciccia Bomba
9 Cul de Sac & L'Insalata Ricca
10 L'Insalata Ricca
11 Rist. Pizzeria "da Francesco"
12 L'Antica Birreria Peroni
13 Rist. Pizzeria Sacro e Profano

ROME

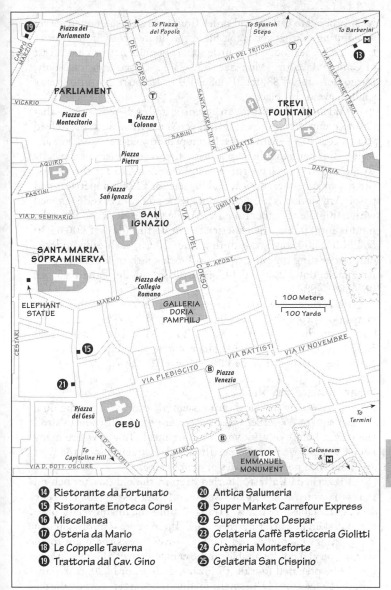

14 Ristorante da Fortunato
15 Ristorante Enoteca Corsi
16 Miscellanea
17 Osteria da Mario
18 Le Coppelle Taverna
19 Trattoria dal Cav. Gino

20 Antica Salumeria
21 Super Market Carrefour Express
22 Supermercato Despar
23 Gelateria Caffè Pasticceria Giolitti
24 Crèmeria Monteforte
25 Gelateria San Crispino

what others are eating, and order from your grease-stained server by pointing at what you want. Sit in the fluorescently lit interior or try to grab a seat out on the little square, a quiet haven a block east of Campo de' Fiori (Mon-Sat 17:30-23:00, closed Sun, cash only, Largo dei Librari 88, tel. 06-686-4018). If you're not into greasy spoons, avoid this place.

Trattoria der Pallaro, an eccentric and well-worn eatery that has no menu, has a slogan: "Here, you'll eat what we want to feed you." Paola Fazi—with a towel wrapped around her head turban-style—and her gang dish up a rustic five-course meal of typically Roman food. You have three menu choices: €25 for the works; €18 for an appetizer, *secondi*, and dessert; or €15 for appetizers and pasta. Any option is filling, includes wine and coffee, and is capped with a thimble of mandarin juice. While the service is odd and the food is forgettable, the experience can be fun (daily 12:00-15:30 & 19:00-24:00, reserve if dining after 20:00, cash only, indoor/outdoor seating on quiet square, a block south of Corso Vittorio Emanuele, down Largo del Chiavari to Largo del Pallaro 15, tel. 06-6880-1488).

Pizzeria da Baffetto 2 makes pizza Roman-style: thin crust, crispy, and wood-fired. Eat in the cramped informal interior, or outside on the busy square (€7-9 pizzas, Wed-Mon 12:00-15:30 & 18:30-24:00, closed Tue, a block north of Campo de' Fiori at Piazza del Teatro di Pompeo 18, tel. 06-6821-0807).

Near Piazza Navona

Piazza Navona is the most quintessential setting for dining on a Roman square. Whether you eat here or not, you'll want to stroll the piazza before or after your evening meal. This is where many people fall in love with Rome. The tangled streets just to the west are lined with popular eateries of many stripes.

Pizzeria da Baffetto, buried deep in the old quarter behind Piazza Navona, is a Roman favorite, offering tasty pizza but rude service. Its tables are tightly arranged amid the mishmash of photos and sketches littering the walls. The pizza-assembly kitchen keeps things energetic, and the pizza oven keeps the main room warm (you can opt for a table on the cobbled street). Come early or late, or be prepared to wait (€7 pizzas, daily from 18:30, cash only, order "P," "M," or "D"—small, medium, or large; west of Piazza Navona on the corner of Via Sora at Via del Governo Vecchio 114, tel. 06-686-1617).

Ciccia Bomba is a traditional trattoria where Gianpaolo, Gianlucca, and their crew serve up well-priced homemade pasta, wood-fired pizza, and other Roman specialties (consider their daily-special sheet). While you can sit at a table on ancient pavement next to your own column, I like the ambience upstairs (€7 pastas, €9 *secondi*, Wed-Mon 12:00-15:00 & 19:00-24:00, closed Tue, Via del Governo Vecchio 76, a block west of Piazza Navona, just north from Piazza Pasquino, tel. 06-6880-2108).

Cul de Sac, a corridor-wide trattoria lined with wine bottles, is packed with enthusiastic locals enjoying hearty, unpretentious Roman cuisine at great prices. Come early to avoid a wait. They have fun tasting plates of salami, more than a thousand different wines, and fine outdoor seating (daily 12:00-16:00 & 18:00-24:00, a block off Piazza Navona on Piazza Pasquino, tel. 06-6880-1094).

L'Insalata Ricca is a popular chain—appreciated by both local students and tourists—that specializes in healthy, filling €8 salads and less-healthy pastas and pizzas (daily 12:00-15:45 & 18:45-24:00). They have a handy branch on Piazza Pasquino (next to Cul de Sac, tel. 06-6830-7881), and a more spacious and enjoyable location a few blocks away, on a bigger square next to busy Corso Vittorio Emanuele (near Campo de' Fiori at Largo dei Chiavari 85, tel. 06-6880-3656).

Ristorante Pizzeria "da Francesco," bustling and authentic, has a 50-year-old tradition, a hardworking young waitstaff, great indoor seating, and classic outdoor seating on a cluttered little square that makes you want to break out a sketchpad. Their blackboard explains the daily specials (€8 pizzas, €9 pastas, €15 *secondi*, open daily, 3 blocks west of Piazza Navona at Piazza del Fico 29, tel. 06-686-4009).

Near the Trevi Fountain

L'Antica Birreria Peroni is Rome's answer to a German beer hall. Serving hearty mugs of the local Peroni beer and lots of just plain fun beer-hall food and Italian classics, the place is a hit with Romans for a cheap night out (Mon-Sat 12:00-24:00, closed Sun, midway between Trevi Fountain and Capitoline Hill, a block off Via del Corso at Via di San Marcello 19, tel. 06-679-5310).

Ristorante Pizzeria Sacro e Profano fills an old church with spicy southern Italian (Calabrian) cuisine and satisfied tourists. Run with enthusiasm by Francesco and friends, this is just far enough away from the Trevi mobs. Their pizza oven is wood-fired, and their hearty €15 *antipasti* plate is a filling montage of Calabrian taste treats (daily 12:00-15:00 & 18:00-24:00, a block off Via del Tritone at Via dei Maroniti 29, tel. 06-679-1836).

Close to the Pantheon

Eating on the square facing the Pantheon is a temptation, and I'd consider it just to relax and enjoy the Roman scene. But if you walk a block or two away, you'll get less view and better value. Here are some suggestions.

Ristorante da Fortunato is an Italian classic, with fresh flowers on the tables and white-coated, black-tie career waiters politely serving good meat and fish to politicians, foreign dignitaries, and tourists with good taste. Don't leave without perusing the photos of their famous visitors—everyone from former Iraqi Foreign Minister Tariq Aziz to Bill Clinton seems to have eaten here. All are pictured with the boss, Fortunato, who, since 1975, has been a master of simple edible elegance. (His son Jason is now on the team.) The outdoor seating is fine for watching the river of Roman street life flow by, but the real atmosphere is inside. For a dressy night out, this is a reliable and surprisingly reasonable choice—but be sure to reserve ahead (plan to spend €45 per person, Mon-Sat 12:30-15:00 & 19:30-23:30, closed Sun, a block in front of the Pantheon at Via del Pantheon 55, tel. 06-679-2788).

Ristorante Enoteca Corsi is a wine shop that grew into a thriving lunch-only restaurant. The Paiella family serves straightforward, traditional cuisine at great prices to an appreciative crowd of office workers. Check the blackboard for daily specials (gnocchi on Thursday, fish on Friday, and so on). Friendly Giuliana, Claudia, Sara, and Manuela welcome eaters to step into their wine shop and pick out a bottle. For the cheap take-away price, plus €2-4 (depending on the wine), they'll uncork it at your table. With €9 pastas, €12 main dishes, and fine wine at a third of the price you'd pay in normal restaurants, this can be a superb value. And guests with this book finish their meal with a free glass of homemade *limoncello* (Mon-Sat 12:00-15:30, closed Sun, no reservations possible, a block toward the Pantheon from the Gesù Church at Via del Gesù 87, tel. 06-679-0821).

Miscellanea is run by much-loved Mikki, who's on a mission to keep foreign students well-fed. You'll find hearty and fresh €4 sandwiches and a long list of €6 salads, along with pasta and other staples. Mikki (and his sons Romero and Florin) often tosses in a fun little extra, including—if you have this book on the table—a free glass of Mikki's "sexy wine" (homemade from *fragoline*—strawberry-flavored grapes). While this place has long been popular with students, Mikki's creative energy now attracts office workers for lunch (daily 8:00-24:00, indoor/outdoor seating, facing the rear of the Pantheon at Via della Palombella 34, tel. 06-6813-5318).

Osteria da Mario, a homey little mom-and-pop joint with a no-stress menu, serves traditional favorites in a fun dining room or on tables spilling out onto a picturesque old Roman square (€8 pastas, €10 *secondi*, Mon-Sat 13:00-15:30 & 19:00-23:00, closed Sun; from the Pantheon walk 2 blocks up Via Pantheon, go left on Via delle Coppelle, and take first right to Piazza delle Coppelle 51; tel. 06-6880-6349, Marco).

ROME

Le Coppelle Taverna is simple, basic, family-friendly, and inexpensive—especially for pizza—with a checkered-tablecloth ambience (€9 pizzas, daily 12:30-15:00 & 19:30-23:30, Via delle Coppelle 39, tel. 06-6880-6557, Alfonso).

Trattoria dal Cav. Gino, tucked away on a tiny street behind the Parliament, has been a favorite since 1963. Photos on the wall recall the days when it was the haunt of big-time politicians. Grandpa Gino shuffles around grating the parmesan cheese while his English-speaking children Carla and Fabrizio serve up traditional Roman favorites and make sure things run smoothly. Reserve ahead, even for lunch, as you'll be packed in with savvy locals (€8 pastas, €11 *secondi*, cash only, Mon-Sat 13:00-14:45 & 20:00-22:30, closed Sun, fish on Friday, behind Piazza del Parlamento and just off Via di Campo Marzio at Vicolo Rosini 4, tel. 06-687-3434).

Picnicking Close to the Pantheon

It's fun to munch a picnic with a view of the Pantheon. (Remember to be discreet.) Here are some options.

Antica Salumeria is an old-time *alimentari* (grocery store) on the Pantheon square. While they hustle most tourists into premade €4 sandwiches, you can make your own picnic. Find your way to the back to buy artichokes, mixed olives, bread, cheese, and meat (daily 8:00-21:00, mobile 334-340-9014).

Supermarkets near the Pantheon: Food is relatively cheap at Italian supermarkets. **Super Market Carrefour Express** is a convenient place for groceries a block from the Gesù Church (Mon-Sat 8:00-21:00, Sun 9:00-19:30, 50 yards off Via del Plebiscito at Via del Gesù 59). Another place, **Supermercato Despar,** is a half a block from the Pantheon toward Piazza Navona (daily 9:00-22:00, Via Giustiniani 18).

Gelato Close to the Pantheon

Three fine *gelaterie* are within a two-minute walk of the Pantheon.

Gelateria Caffè Pasticceria Giolitti, Rome's most famous and venerable ice-cream joint, has reasonable take-away prices and elegant Old World seating (daily 7:00-24:00, just off Piazza Colonna and Piazza Monte Citorio at Via Uffici del Vicario 40, tel. 06-699-1243).

Crèmeria Monteforte is known for its traditional, quality gelato and super-creamy sorbets *(cremolati)*. The fruit flavors are especially refreshing—think gourmet slushies (Tue-Sun 10:00-24:00, off-season closes earlier, closed Mon and Dec, faces the west side of the Pantheon at Via della Rotonda 22, tel. 06-686-7720).

Gelateria San Crispino, well-respected by Romans, serves small portions of particularly tasty gourmet gelato using creative ingredients. Because of their commitment to natural ingredients, the colors are muted; gelato purists consider bright colors a sign of unnatural chemicals, which are used to attract children. They serve cups, but no cones (daily 12:00-24:00, a block in front of the Pantheon on Piazza della Maddalena, tel. 06-6889-1310).

In North Rome: Near the Ara Pacis and Spanish Steps

To locate these restaurants, see the map on page 793.

Ristorante il Gabriello is inviting and small—modern under medieval arches—and provides a peaceful and local-feeling respite from all the top-end fashion shops in the area. Claudio serves with charisma, while his brother Gabriello cooks creative Roman cuisine using fresh, organic products from his wife's farm. Italians normally just trust their waiter and say, "Bring it on." Tourists are understandably more cautious, but you can be trusting here. Simply close your eyes and point to anything on the menu. Or invest €45 in "Claudio's Extravaganza" (not including wine), and he'll shower you with edible kindness. Specify whether you'd prefer fish, meat, or both. (Romans think raw shellfish is the ultimate in fine dining. If you differ, make that clear.) When finished, I stand up, hold my belly, and say, *"Ahhh, la vita è bella"* (€10 pastas, €15 *secondi*, dinner only, Mon-Sat 19:00-23:00, closed Sun, reservations smart, air-con, dress respectfully—no shorts please, 3 blocks from Spanish Steps at Via Vittoria 51, tel. 06-6994-0810).

Osteria Gusto is thriving with trendy locals. While pricey, it's untouristy, gives a glimpse of today's Roman scene, and is fine for a glass of good wine over an artisanal cheese plate or a complete dinner (€13 pastas, €20 *secondi*, daily 12:30-15:30 & 19:00-24:00, opens at 18:30 for drinks and appetizers only, reservations recommended after 20:00 and on weekends, on the corner of Via Soderini at Via della Frezza 16, tel. 06-3211-1482).

L'EnotecAntica, an upbeat, atmospheric 200-plus-year-old *enoteca,* has around 60 Italian-only wines by the glass (€4-10, listed on a big blackboard) and a fresh €14 *antipasti* plate of veggies, salami, and cheese. Very crowded on summer evenings, it comes with wonderful ambience both inside and out; its outside tables are set on a quiet cobbled street (daily 12:00-24:00, Via della Croce 76b, tel. 06-679-0896).

Palatium Enoteca Regionale is a crisp, modern restaurant funded by the region of Lazio (home to Rome) to show off its finest agricultural fares. If you're with a small group, this can be a good bet, especially for lunch. You'll enjoy a generous family-style plate of cheeses, meats, and pasta with high-quality Lazio wine at an affordable price surrounded by locals (Mon-Sat 12:30-15:30 & 19:30-23:00, closed Sun, 5 blocks in front of the Spanish Steps at Via Frattina 94, tel. 06-6920-2132).

ROME

In Ancient Rome: Eating Cheaply near the Colosseum

You'll find good views but poor value at the restaurants directly behind the Colosseum. To get your money's worth, eat at least a block away. Here are three handy eateries, all shown on the map on page 858: one at the foot of Via Cavour, and two at the top of Terme di Tito (a long block uphill from the Colosseum, near St. Peter-in-Chains church—of Michelangelo's *Moses* fame; for directions, see page 806).

Enoteca Cavour 313 is a wine bar with a mission: to offer good wine and quality food with an old-fashioned commitment to value and friendly service. It's also a convenient place for a good lunch near the Forum and Colosseum. Angelo and his three partners enjoy creating a mellow ambience under lofts of wine bottles (daily specials and fine wines by the glass, daily 12:30-14:45 & 19:00-24:00, 100 yards off Via dei Fori Imperiali at Via Cavour 313, tel. 06-678-5496).

Caffè dello Studente is popular with engineering students attending the nearby University of Rome. Pina, Mauro, and their perky daughter Simona (who speaks English) give my readers a royal welcome and serve microwaved and forgettable *bar gastronomia* fare—toasted sandwiches, salads, and pizzas. If it's not busy, show this book when you order at the bar and sit without paying extra at a table (Mon-Sat 7:30-22:30, April-Oct Sun 9:00-22:30, Nov-March closed Sun, Via delle Terme di Tito, tel. 06-488-3240).

Hostaria da Nerone, next door, is a more formal restaurant with much better food and homemade pasta dishes. Their €9 *antipasti* plate—with a variety of veggies, fish, and meat—is a good value for a quick lunch. While the *antipasti* menu indicates specifics, you can have a plate of whatever's out—just direct the waiter to assemble the €9 *antipasti* plate of your lunchtime dreams (good €9 pastas and €12 *secondi*, Mon-Sat 12:00-15:00 & 19:00-23:00, closed Sun, indoor/outdoor seating, Via delle Terme di Tito 96, tel. 06-481-7952, run by Teo and Eugenio).

Near Termini Train Station

These restaurants are near my recommended hotels on Via Firenze. Several are clustered on Via Flavia, others are nearby (Target, etc.), and a few, such as Bar Tavola Calda, are good options for quick meals.

On (or near) Via Flavia

To easily check out a fun and varied selection of eateries within a block of each other, walk to Via Flavia (a block behind the Church of Santa Maria della Vittoria of *St. Teresa in Ecstasy* fame)

ROME

Restaurants near Termini Station

1. Ristorante Da Giovanni
2. Annicinquanta Pizzeria, Ristorante La Pentolaccia & I Colori del Vino Enoteca
3. Target Restaurant
4. Ricci Est Est Est Pizzeria
5. Hostaria Romana
6. Bar Tavola Calda
7. Snack Bar
8. Panificio Firenze
9. Flann O'Brien Irish Pub

and survey these choices—an old diner, a good pizzeria, a small romantic place, and a friendly wine bar.

Ristorante Da Giovanni, well-worn and old-fashioned, makes no concessions to tourism or the modern world—just hard-working cooks and waiters serving standard dishes at great prices to a committed clientele. It's simply fun to eat in the middle of this high-energy, old-school diner—a rare Roman time warp (€6-9 pastas and *secondi*, daily specials, Mon-Sat 12:00-15:00 & 19:00-22:00, closed Sun and Aug, corner of Via XX Settembre at Via Antonio Salandra 1, tel. 06-485-950).

Annicinquanta Pizzeria, big and classic, serves the neighborhood's favorite pizzas in a calm ambience with good outdoor seating (€8 Neapolitan-style pizzas, daily 19:30-24:00, Via Flavia 3, tel. 06-4201-0460).

Ristorante La Pentolaccia, pricier and more romantic than the nearby Da Giovanni, is a dressy, tourist-friendly place with tight seating and traditional Roman cooking. This is a local hangout and reservations are smart (daily 12:00-15:00 & 17:30-23:00, consider their daily specials, a block off Via XX Settembre at Via Flavia 38, tel. 06-483-477). To start things off with a free bruschetta, leave this book on the table.

I Colori del Vino Enoteca is a modern wine bar that feels like a laboratory of wine appreciation. It has woody walls of bottles, a creative menu of meats and cheeses with different regional themes, and a great list of fine wines by the glass. Helpful, English-speaking Marco carries on a long family tradition of celebrating the fundamentals of good nutrition: fine wine, cheese, meat, and bread (Mon-Fri 12:00-15:00 & 17:30-23:00, closed Sat-Sun because Marco doesn't cater to noisy weekend drinkers, corner of Via Flavia and Via Aureliana, tel. 06-474-1745). Remember Shakespeare's sage warning about drinking: "It provokes the desire, but it takes away the performance."

More Eateries near the Station

Target Restaurant seems to be the favorite recommendation of every hotel receptionist and tour guide for this neighborhood. It has reliably good food, a sleek look, capable service, and practical prices (€8-10 salads, pastas, and pizzas, €20 secondi, daily 12:00-15:00 & 19:00-24:00, reserve to specify seating outside or inside—avoid getting seated in basement, Via Torino 33, tel. 06-474-0066).

ROME

Ricci Est Est Est Pizzeria, a venerable family-run pizzeria, has plenty of historical ambience, good €8 pizzas, and dangerously tasty *fritti,* such as fried *baccalà* (cod) and zucchini flowers (Tue-Sun 19:00-24:00, closed Mon and Aug, Via Genova 32, tel. 06-488-1107).

Hostaria Romana is a busy bistro with a hustling and fun-loving gang of waiters and noisy walls graffitied by happy eaters. While they specialize in fish and traditional Roman dishes, their €10 *antipasti* plate can make a good meal in itself. Or try their *bucatini all'amatriciana,* a tubular pasta with a sauce made of tomatoes, pork, and pecorino cheese (Mon-Sat 12:15-15:00 & 19:15-23:00, closed Sun, a block up the lane just past the entrance to the big tunnel near the Trevi Fountain at Via de Boccaccio 1, tel. 06-474-5284).

Fast, Simple Meals near the Station

Bar Tavola Calda is a workers' favorite for a quick, cheap lunch. They have good, fresh, hot dishes ready to go for a fine price. Head back past the bar to peruse their enticing display, point at what you want, then grab a seat and the young waitstaff will serve you (Mon-Sat 6:00-18:00, closed Sun, Via Torino 40).

Snack Bar puts out a lunchtime display of inexpensive pastas, colorful sandwiches, fresh fruit, and salad. Their loyal customers appreciate the fruit salad with yogurt (daily 6:00-24:00, Via Firenze 33, mobile 339-393-1356, Enrica).

Panificio Firenze has take-out pizza and makes hearty sandwiches to go (sandwiches priced by weight, Mon-Fri 7:00-19:00, Sat 7:00-14:00, closed Sun, Via Firenze 51-52, tel. 06-488-5035, Giovanni).

Flann O'Brien Irish Pub is an entertaining place for a light meal of pasta...or something *other* than pasta, such as grilled meats and giant salads, served early and late, when other places are closed. They have Irish beer, live sporting events on TV, and perhaps the most Italian crowd of all. Walk way back before choosing a table. Live bands often play on Friday evenings (daily 7:00-24:00, Via Nazionale 17, at intersection with Via Napoli, tel. 06-488-0418).

Near Vatican City

Avoid the restaurant-pushers handing out fliers near the Vatican: bad food and expensive menu tricks. Try any of these instead (see map on page 865).

Handy Lunch Places near Piazza Risorgimento

These are a stone's throw from the Vatican wall, located halfway between St. Peter's Basilica and the Vatican Museum. They're all fast and cheap, with a good *gelateria* next door.

Hostaria dei Bastioni, run by Antonio while Emilio cooks, has noisy street-side seating and a quiet interior (€7 pastas, €12 *secondi,* no cover charge, Mon-Sat 12:00-16:00 & 18:30-23:00, closed Sun, at corner of Vatican wall at Via Leone IV 29, tel. 06-3972-3034).

L'Insalata Ricca is another branch of the popular chain that serves salads and pastas (daily 12:30-15:30 & 18:30-23:45, across from Vatican walls at Piazza Risorgimento 5, tel. 06-3973-0387).

Duecento Gradi is a good bet for fresh and creative €5 sandwiches. Munch your lunch on a stool or take it away (daily 11:00-24:00, Piazza Risorgimento 3, tel. 06-3975-4239).

Gelato: **Gelateria Old Bridge** scoops up hearty portions of fresh gelato for tourists and nuns alike. The quality, quantity, and value can't be beat (daily 10:00-23:00, just off Piazza Risorgimento across from Vatican walls at Via Bastioni 3).

Other Good Options in the Vatican Area

The first three listings—the restaurant, the street with pizza shops, and the outdoor market—are near the Vatican Museum. The Borgo Pio eateries are near St. Peter's Basilica.

La Rustichella serves tasty wood-fired pizza and the usual pasta in addition to their sprawling *antipasti* buffet (€8 for a single plate). Arrive when it opens at 19:00 to avoid a line and have the pristine buffet to yourself. Do like the Romans do—take a moderate amount and make one trip only (Tue-Sun 12:30-15:00 & 19:00-24:00, closed Mon, near Metro: Cipro, opposite church at end of Via Candia, Via Angelo Emo 1, tel. 06-3972-0649). Consider the fun and fruity **Gelateria Millennium** next door.

Viale Giulio Cesare: This street is lined with cheap *pizza rustica* shops, self-serve places, and inviting eateries.

Outdoor Market: As you collect picnic supplies, turn your nose loose in the wonderful **Mercato Trionfale** covered market. It's one of the best in the city and three blocks north of the Vatican Museum (Mon-Sat roughly 7:00-14:00, closed Sun, corner of Via Tunisi and Via Andrea Doria). If the market is closed, try several nearby supermarkets; the most convenient is **GS Di per Di** (Mon-Sat 8:00-20:00, Sun 9:00-20:00, Via Sebastiano Veniero 16).

Along Borgo Pio: The pedestrians-only Borgo Pio—a block from Piazza San Pietro—has restaurants worth a look, such as **Tre Pupazzi** (Mon-Sat 12:00-15:00 & 19:00-23:00, closed Sun, at corner of Via Tre Pupazzi and Borgo Pio, tel. 06-686-8371). At **Vecchio Borgo,** across the street, you can get pasta, pizza slices, and veggies to go (Mon-Sat 9:00-21:00, closed Sun, Borgo Pio 27a, tel. 06-8117-3585).

Rome Connections

Rome is well-connected with the rest of the planet: by train, bus, plane, car, and cruise ship. This section addresses your arrival and departure from the city. It explains the various options and gives a rundown on their points of departure.

By Train

Rome's main train station is the centrally located **Termini** station, which has connections to the airport. Rome's other major station is the **Tiburtina** bus/train station, which is starting to get a few high-speed rail connections. For in-depth descriptions of both Termini and Tiburtina stations, see page 766. Smaller stations include **Ostiense** (useful for going to South Rome and Testaccio) and its neighbor, **Porta San Paolo** (with connections to Ostia Antica). If you're staying near the Vatican and taking a regional train, it saves time to get off at the **San Pietro** station rather than at Termini.

Since virtually all of the most convenient connections for travelers depart from Termini, I've listed those below. In 30 years of visits, I've never had occasion to use Tiburtina, but that may change—Tiburtina is currently being redeveloped for high-speed rail. Several Eurostar Italia train stops here already, and a new company—Nuovo Trasporto Viaggiatori (NTV)—is expected to start running its Italo high-speed trains from Tiburtina sometime in the future (for details, see www.ntvspa.it). As a precaution, it's always smart to confirm whether your train departs from Termini or Tiburtina.

From Rome's Termini Station by Train to: Venice (roughly hourly, 3.75 hours, overnight possible), **Florence** (at least hourly, 1.5 hours), **Siena** (1-2/hour, 1 change, 3-4 hours), **La Spezia Centrale** (every 2 hours direct, more with transfers in Pisa, 3-4.5 hours), **Milan** (hourly, 3-8 hours, overnight possible), **Milan's Malpensa Airport** (1 direct express/day, 4.5 hours), **Amsterdam** (6/day, 20 hours), **Interlaken** (5/day, 6.5-8 hours), **Frankfurt** (6/day, 11-12 hours, several overnight options), **Munich** (5/day, 10-11.5 hours, several overnight options), **Nice** (7/day, 8.75-10.5 hours, several overnight options), **Paris** (4/day, 10.75-12.75 hours, several overnight options, important to reserve ahead), **Vienna** (2/day, 11.75 hours, several overnight options).

By Plane

Rome's two airports—**Fiumicino** (a.k.a. Leonardo da Vinci) and the small **Ciampino**—share the same website (www.adr.it).

Fiumicino Airport

Rome's major airport has a TI (in terminal 3, daily 9:00-18:00), ATMs, banks, luggage storage, shops, and bars. The Rome Walks website (www.romewalks.com) has a useful video on options for getting into the city from the airport.

The slick, direct **"Leonardo Express" train** connects the airport and Rome's central Termini train station in 30 minutes for €15. Trains run twice hourly in both directions from roughly 6:00 to 23:00 (leaving the airport at :07 and :37). From the airport's arrival gate, follow signs to the train car icon or *Stazione/Railway Station*. Buy your ticket from a machine, the Biglietteria office, or a newsstand at the platform, then validate it in a yellow machine near the track. Make sure the train you board is going to the central "Roma Termini" station, not "Roma Orte" or others.

Going from Termini train station to the airport, trains depart at about :22 and :52 past the hour, from tracks 25-28 (located way down at the far end of track 24; allow 10 minutes for the hike, moving walkways downstairs). Check the departure boards for "Fiumicino Aeroporto"—the local name for the airport—and confirm with an official or a local on the platform that the train is indeed going to the airport (€15, buy ticket from any tobacco shop or newsstand in the station, or at the self-service machines, Termini-Fiumicino trains run 5:52-22:52). Read your ticket: If it requires validation, stamp it in the yellow machine near the platform before boarding. From the train station at the airport, you can access all of the terminals. Most American airlines flying to the US depart from Terminal 5, though some Delta Airlines flights leave from Terminal 3.

Allow lots of time going in either direction; there's a fair amount of transportation involved, including moving walkways, escalators, and walking (e.g., getting from your hotel to Termini, from Termini to the train platform, the ride to the airport, getting from the airport train station to check-in, etc.). Flying to the US involves an extra level of security—plan on getting to the airport even earlier than normal (I like to arrive 2.5 hours ahead of my flight).

Shuttle van services run to and from the airport and can be economical for one or two people. It's cheaper from the airport to downtown, as several companies compete for this route; by surveying the latest deals, you should be able to snare a ride into town for around €10. To get from your hotel to the airport, consider Rome Airport Shuttle (€25/1 person, extra people-€6 each, by reservation only, tel. 06-4201-4507 or 06-4201-3469, www.airport shuttle.it).

A **taxi** between Fiumicino and downtown Rome takes 45 minutes in normal traffic (for tips on taxis, see page 779). If you're catching a taxi at the airport, be sure to wait at the taxi stand. Avoid unmarked, unmetered taxis; these guys will try to tempt you away from the taxi-stand lineup by offering an immediate (rip-off) ride. Rome's official taxis have a fixed rate to and from the airport (€40 for up to four people with bags). If your cab driver tries to charge you more than €40 from the airport into town, say, *"Quaranta euro—è la legge"* (kwah-RAHN-tah AY-oo-roh—ay lah LEJ-jay; which means, "Forty euros—it's the law"), and they should back off.

A new law allows cabbies not based in Rome to charge €60 for the ride. That sign is posted next to the €40-fare sign—confusing many tourists and allowing dishonest cabbies to overcharge. Only use a Rome city cab, with the "SPQR" shield on the door. They can only charge €40 for the ride to anywhere in the historic center (within the old city walls, where most of my recommended hotels are located).

To get from the airport into town cheaply by taxi, try teaming up with any tourist also just arriving (most are heading for hotels near yours in the center). When you're departing Rome, your hotel can arrange a taxi to the airport at any hour.

For **airport information,** call 06-65951. To inquire about flights, call 06-6595-3640 (Alitalia: tel. 06-2222; British Airways: tel. 199-712-266; Continental: tel. 06-6605-3030; Delta: tel. 848-780-376; Swiss International: tel. 848-868-120; United: tel. 848-800-692).

Ciampino Airport

Rome's smaller airport (tel. 06-6595-9515) handles charter flights and some budget airlines (including all Ryanair and some easyJet flights).

To get to downtown Rome from the airport, you can take the Cotral bus, which leaves every 40 minutes (€5, 20-minute ride, toll-free tel. 800-174-471, www.cotralspa.it), to the Anagnina Metro stop, where you can connect by Metro to the stop nearest your hotel. Rome Airport Shuttle also offers service to and from Ciampino (€25/1 person, listed earlier). The Terravision Express Shuttle connects Ciampino and Termini train station, leaving every 20 minutes (€4 one-way, €8 round-trip, www.terravision .eu). The SIT Bus Shuttle also connects Termini to Ciampino (€4, about 2/hour, 45 minutes, runs 7:45-23:15 Ciampino to Termini, 4:30-21:30 Termini to Ciampino, pick-up on Via Marsala just outside the train exit closest to track 1, tel. 06-592-3507, www.sit busshuttle.it). A taxi should cost €30 to downtown (within the old city walls, including most of my recommended hotels).

VENICE

Venezia

Soak all day in this puddle of elegant decay. Venice is Europe's best-preserved big city. This car-free urban wonderland of a hundred islands—laced together by 400 bridges and 2,000 alleys—survives on the artificial respirator of tourism.

Born in a lagoon 1,500 years ago as a refuge from barbarians, Venice is overloaded with tourists and is slowly sinking (not because of the tourists). In the Middle Ages, the Venetians became Europe's clever middlemen for East-West trade and created a great trading empire. By smuggling in the bones of St. Mark (San Marco) in A.D. 828, Venice gained religious importance as well. With the discovery of America and new trading routes to the Orient, Venetian power ebbed. But as Venice fell, her appetite for decadence grew. Through the 17th and 18th centuries, Venice partied on the wealth accumulated through earlier centuries as a trading power.

Today, Venice is home to just over 60,000 people in its old city, down from about twice that number just three decades ago. While there are about 270,000 people in greater Venice (counting the mainland, not counting tourists), the old town has a small-town feel. Locals seem to know everyone. To see small-town Venice away from the touristic flak, escape the Rialto-San Marco tourist zone and savor the town early and late, without the hordes of vacationers day-tripping in from cruise ships and nearby beach resorts. A 10-minute walk from the madness puts you in an idyllic Venice that few tourists see.

Venice Overview

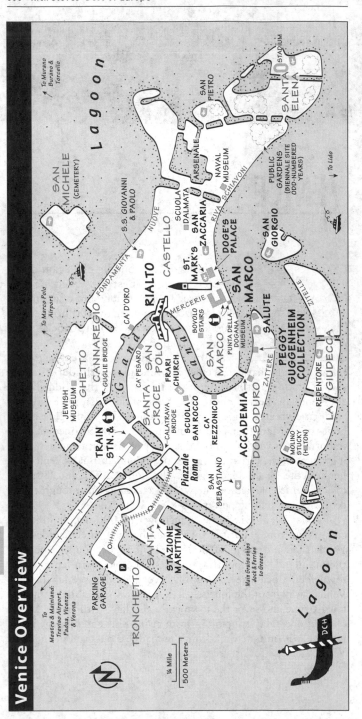

Planning Your Time

Venice is worth at least a day on even the speediest tour. Hyper-efficient train travelers take the night train in and/or out. Sleep in the old center to experience Venice at its best: early and late. For a one-day visit, cruise the Grand Canal, do the major sights on St. Mark's Square (the square itself, Doge's Palace, Correr Museum, and St. Mark's Basilica), see the Frari Church for art, and wander the back streets on a pub crawl. Enjoy an evening gondola ride. Venice's greatest sight is the city itself. While doable in a day, Venice is worth two. It's a medieval cookie jar, and nobody's looking. Make time to simply wander.

Orientation to Venice

The island city of Venice is shaped like a fish. Its major thorough-fares are canals. The Grand Canal winds through the middle of the fish, starting at the mouth where all the people and food enter, passing under the Rialto Bridge, and ending at St. Mark's Square (Piazza San Marco). Park your 21st-century perspective at the mouth of the fish and let Venice swallow you whole.

Venice is a car-free kaleidoscope of people, bridges, and odorless canals. There are six districts (*sestieri,* shown on map on opposite page):

San Marco (from St. Mark's Square to the Accademia Bridge), Castello (the area east of St. Mark's Square), Dorsoduro (the belly of the fish, on the far side the Accademia Bridge), Cannaregio (between the train station and the Rialto Bridge), San Polo (west of the Rialto Bridge), and Santa Croce (the "eye" of the fish, across the canal from the train station).

To find your way, navigate by landmarks, not streets. Many street corners have a sign pointing you to *(per)* the nearest major landmark, such as San Marco, Accademia, Rialto, and Ferrovia (train station). Obedient visitors stick to the main thoroughfares as directed by these signs...and miss the charm of back-street Venice.

Beyond the city's core lie several other islands, including San Giorgio (with great views of Venice), Giudecca (more views), San Michele (old cemetery), Murano (famous for glass), Burano (lace-making), Torcello (old church), and the skinny Lido beach.

VENICE

Tourist Information

With this book, a free city map from your hotel, and the free *Shows & Events* booklet (described below), there's little need to visit a TI in Venice. That's fortunate, because the city's TIs are crowded and clunky. If you need to check or confirm something, TIs are located at the **train station** (daily 8:00-18:30), on **St. Mark's Square** (daily 9:00-15:30, in far-left corner with your back to the basilica), nearby at the **San Marco-Vallaresso vaporetto stop** (daily 11:00-18:00), and at the **airport** (daily 9:00-21:00). You can save time by phoning the TI at 041-529-8711 or visiting www.turismovenezia.it.

The TI publishes a useful, free booklet called *Shows & Events*, available at hotels and on the TI website (click on "Venezia"). It lists upcoming events and nightlife, museum hours, and emergency telephone numbers, and includes a vaporetto route map.

For a creative travel guide written by young Venetians, consider *My Local Guide Venice*, for its neighborhood histories, self-guided walking tours, and recommendations on sights and activities (sold at TIs for €13).

Maps: Of all places, you need a good map in Venice. Hotels give away freebies (which are no better than the small color one at the front of this book). The TI sells a decent €2.50 map and mini-guide—but you can find a wider range at bookshops, newsstands, and postcard stands. The cheap maps are pretty bad, but if you spend €5, you'll get a map that shows you everything. Investing in a good map can be the best €5 you'll spend in Venice. Map lovers should look for the book *Calli, Campielli e Canali*, sold at bookstores for €22.50, with 1:2000 maps of the whole city.

Arrival in Venice

A two-mile-long causeway (with highway and train lines) connects Venice to the mainland. Mestre, the sprawling mainland section of Venice, has fewer crowds, cheaper hotels, and plenty of inexpensive parking lots, but zero charm. Don't stop in Mestre unless you're parking your car or transferring trains.

By Train

All trains to "Venice" stop at Venezia Mestre (on the mainland). Most continue on to Santa Lucia Station on the island of Venice itself. If your train only stops at Mestre, worry not. Shuttle trains regularly connect Mestre with Venice's Santa Lucia Station (6/hour, 10 minutes, €1, buy tickets with coins from machines marked *Rete Regionale* and validate before boarding).

VENICE

Venice's **Santa Lucia train station** (Ferrovia) plops you right into the old town on the Grand Canal, an easy vaporetto ride or fascinating 40-minute walk to St. Mark's Square. If the station's TI is crowded when you arrive, consider visiting one of the two TIs at St. Mark's Square instead. It's not worth a long wait for a minimal TI map (buy a good one from a newsstand or pick up a free one at your hotel). Confirm your departure plan (use the machines or just study the *partenze*/departures posters on walls).

Consider storing unnecessary heavy bags, although lines for **baggage check** may be very long (at track 1, €4/5 hours, €11/24 hours, daily 6:00-23:50, no lockers, 44-pound weight limit on

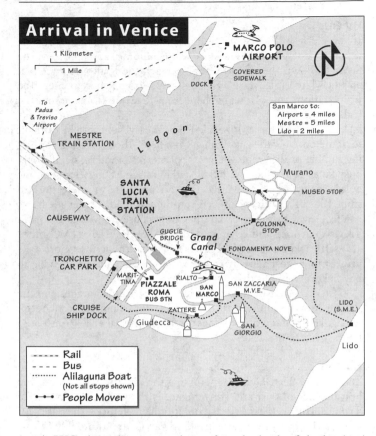

Arrival in Venice

MARCO POLO AIRPORT

1 Kilometer
1 Mile

DOCK

COVERED SIDEWALK

To Padua & Treviso Airport

L a g o o n

MESTRE TRAIN STATION

Murano

MUSEO STOP

San Marco to:
Airport = 4 miles
Mestre = 5 miles
Lido = 2 miles

SANTA LUCIA TRAIN STATION

CAUSEWAY

COLONNA STOP

GUGLIE BRIDGE

Grand Canal

FONDAMENTA NOVE

TRONCHETTO CAR PARK

MARIT-TIMA

RIALTO

PIAZZALE ROMA BUS STN

SAN MARCO

SAN ZACCARIA M.V.E.

CRUISE SHIP DOCK

ZATTERE

Giudecca

SAN GIORGIO

LIDO (S.M.E.)

Lido

Rail
Bus
Alilaguna Boat
(Not all stops shown)
People Mover

bags). **WCs** (€0.80) are at track 1 and in the back of the big bar/cafeteria area inside the station.

Minimize your time in the station—the banks of user-friendly automated ticket machines (marked *Biglietto Veloce/Fast Ticket*) are handy but cover Italian destinations only. They take euros and credit cards, display schedules, issue tickets, and even make reservations for railpass-holders. The gray-and-blue *Rete Regionale* machines are another option for tickets to nearby destinations such as Padua (coins only, push button for English). If you need international tickets or live help, the ticket windows are open from 6:00 to 20:30. Or you could take care of these tasks for a fee at downtown travel agencies (see page 894).

To get from the train station to downtown Venice, walk straight out of the station to the canal. You'll see vaporetto docks and ticket booths on both sides. For vaporetto #2 (fast boat down Grand Canal), go left. For vaporetto #1 (slow boat down Grand Canal), go right. See "Getting Around Venice—By Vaporetto," on page 898, for details on vaporetto tickets and passes.

VENICE

By Bus

If you arrive in Venice at the Piazzale Roma bus station, find the vaporetto docks (by the six-story white building) and take #1 or the faster #2 down the Grand Canal to reach the Rialto, Accademia, or San Marco (St. Mark's Square) stops. If your hotel is near the train station, you can walk there from Piazzale Roma across the Calatrava Bridge.

Arriving by bus at Piazzale Roma is easy, but it can be difficult to figure out how to leave Venice from here. The square is a confusing jumble of different operators, platforms, and crosswalks over busy lanes of traffic. The ticket windows for ACTV (local public buses, including #5 to Marco Polo Airport) are by the vaporetto stop. The ATVO ticket office is on the right side of the square as you face away from the canal (for express buses to Marco Polo and Treviso Airports; office open daily 7:15-19:30). The ATVO office also sells tickets for the SITA bus to Padua, though it's more convenient to go to Padua by train. At odd hours, you may be able to buy tickets from bus drivers.

At Piazzale Roma, you'll also see the parking garages and the People Mover monorail to the parking-lot island of Tronchetto. A baggage-storage office is next to the monorail at #497m (€5/24 hours, daily 6:00-21:00).

By Car

The freeway dead-ends after crossing the causeway to Venice. The best balance of cost and convenience is the parking-lot island of **Tronchetto,** well-signed as you approach Venice. The rates for the multi-story Tronchetto parking garage are affordable (€3-4/hour, €21/24 hours, discounts for longer stays, tel. 041-520-7555, www.veniceparking.it). From the garage, head directly to the yellow-and-white vaporetto docks and take line #2, the express boat which stops at the Rialto, San Marco, Zattere, and other main points in the center. I like the approach from Tronchetto into town by sea. Don't let water taxi boatmen con you out of the relatively inexpensive €6.50 vaporetto ride. Also avoid the travel agencies masquerading as TIs; deal only with the ticket booth at the vaporetto dock or the HelloVenezia public transport office. Consider whether a local transport pass will pay off (see page 900); you can buy it here.

If you're parking at Tronchetto and staying near the train station, you can take the €1 People Mover monorail instead of paying €6.50 for the two-stop vaporetto ride. The monorail brings you from Tronchetto to the bus station at Piazzale Roma, then it's a five-minute walk across the Calatrava Bridge to the train station (buy monorail tickets with coins from machine, 3-minute trip, runs Mon-Sat 7:00-23:00, Sun 8:30-21:00).

VENICE

You can also park at **Piazzale Roma,** the busy square where the expressway dead-ends and which doubles as Venice's bus station. The big white building on your right is a 2,200-space public parking garage, the Autorimessa Communale (€25/24 hours, tel. 041-272-7211, www.asmvenezia.it) and in a back corner of the square is the private San Marco garage (€30/24 hours, tel. 041-523-2213, www.garagesanmarco.it). At either of these, you'll have to give up your keys. You can reserve ahead at both garages and at Tronchetto, but it's rarely necessary.

Parking in the garage across from the train station in **Mestre** (on the mainland) only makes sense if you have light bags and are staying within walking distance of the Santa Lucia train station (€8/day Mon-Fri, €12-16/day Sat-Sun; www.sabait.it).

Ask your hotel for parking advice—some can get you a small discount.

By Plane
For information on Venice's airport, see the end of this chapter.

Helpful Hints
Theft Alert: The dark, late-night streets of Venice are safe. Even so, pickpockets (often elegantly dressed) work the crowded main streets, docks, and *vaporetti* (wear your money belt, zip up your valuables, and watch your purse or day bag). Your biggest risk of pickpockets is inside St. Mark's Basilica.

    A handy Polizia station is on the right side of St. Mark's Square (near Caffè Florian). To call the police, dial 113. The Venice TI handles complaints—which must be submitted in writing—about local crooks, including gondola, restaurant, or hotel rip-offs (fax 041-523-0399, complaint.apt@turismo venezia.it).

    It's illegal for street vendors to sell knock-off handbags and it's also illegal for you to buy them; both you and the vendor can get big fines.

Be Prepared to Splurge: Venice is expensive for residents as well as tourists, as everything must be shipped in and hand-trucked to its destination. Perhaps the best way to enjoy Venice is just to succumb to its charms and blow a little money.

Crowd Control: The city is inundated with cruise-ship crowds and tours from mainland hotels daily from 10:00 to about 17:00. Crowds can be a serious problem at **St. Mark's Basilica.** Try going early or late, or even better, you can bypass the line if you have a bag to check (see page 916). At the **Doge's Palace,** avoid the long line by purchasing your ticket at the less-crowded Correr Museum. You can also visit late in the day, buy your ticket online, or book a tour. For the **Campanile,**

VENICE

ascend late (it's open until 21:00 July-Sept), or skip it entirely if you're going to the similar San Giorgio Maggiore bell tower. For the **Accademia,** go early or late—or you can reserve a ticket at least a day in advance by phone or online.

Sights that have crowd problems get even more crowded when it rains.

Medical Help: Venice's Santi Giovanni e Paolo hospital (tel. 118) is a 10-minute walk from both the Rialto and San Marco neighborhoods, located on Fondamenta dei Mendicanti toward Fondamente Nove. You can take vaporetto #4.1 from San Zaccaria-Jolanda, or #5.2 from the train station or Piazzale Roma, to the Ospedale stop.

Take Breaks: Venice's endless pavement, crowds, and tight spaces are hard on tourists, especially in hot weather. Schedule breaks in your sightseeing. Grab a cool place to sit down, relax, and recoup—meditate on a pew in an uncrowded church, or stop in a café.

Etiquette: Walk on the right and don't loiter on bridges. On St. Mark's Square, a "decorum patrol" admonishes snackers and sunbathers. Picnicking is forbidden (keep a low profile). The only place for a legal picnic is in Giardinetti Reali, the small park along the waterfront west of the Piazzetta near St. Mark's Square.

Dress Modestly: Men should keep their shirts on. When visiting St. Mark's Basilica or other major churches, men, women, and even children must cover their shoulders and knees (or risk being turned away). Remove hats when entering a church.

Public Toilets: Handy public WCs (€1.50) are near major landmarks, including: St. Mark's Square (one is behind the Correr Museum, to the left of the post office; another is at the waterfront park, Giardinetti Reali), Rialto, and at the Accademia Bridge. Use free toilets whenever you can—in a museum you're visiting or a café you're eating in. Like Mom always said, "Just try."

Best Views: While the best views of Venice may be from water level, several upper-altitude viewing spots are also worth the ascent: On St. Mark's Square, try the soaring Campanile or St. Mark's Basilica (specifically the balcony of the San Marco Museum, requires admission). The Rialto and Accademia bridges provide free, expansive views of the Grand Canal, along with a cooling breeze. Or get off the main island for a view of the Venetian skyline: Ascend the Church of San Giorgio Maggiore's bell tower, or venture to La Giudecca island to visit the swanky bar of the Molino Stucky Hilton Hotel (free shuttle boat from San Zaccaria-M.V.E. vaporetto stop).

Pigeon Poop: If your head is bombed by a pigeon, resist the initial response to wipe it off immediately—it'll just smear into your hair. Wait until it dries, and it should flake off cleanly. But if the poop splatters on your clothes, wipe it off immediately to avoid a stain.

Water: I carry a water bottle to refill at public fountains. Venetians pride themselves on having pure, safe, and tasty tap water piped in from the foothills of the Alps. You can actually see the mountains from Venice's bell towers on crisp, clear winter days.

Services

Internet Access: Almost all hotels have Wi-Fi, many have a computer that guests can use, and most provide these services for free. If Internet access is important to you, choose a hotel that doesn't charge for it. Otherwise, look for one of the handy, if pricey, little Internet places scattered around town, usually on back streets and marked with an @ sign. The going rate is €5/hour—more expensive than in other Italian cities. Ask your hotelier for the nearest place.

Post Office: The main post office is on Marzaria San Salvador, a few blocks towards St. Mark's Square from the Rialto, just beyond the Bata shoe store at #5016 (Mon-Fri 8:30-18:30, Sat 8:30-13:00, closed Sun). Branch offices (open shorter hours) are at Piazzale Roma, behind the Correr Museum, and elsewhere. Use post offices only as a last resort, as simple transactions can take 45 minutes if you get in the wrong line. You can buy stamps from tobacco shops and mail postcards at any of the red postboxes around town.

Bookstores: In keeping with its literary heritage, Venice has classy and inviting bookstores. The small **Libreria Studium,** a block behind St. Mark's Basilica, has a carefully chosen selection of new English books, including my guidebooks (Mon-Sat 9:00-19:30, Sun 9:30-13:30 & 14:00-18:00, on Calle de la Canonica at #337, tel. 041-522-2382). Used-bookstore lovers shouldn't miss the funky **Acqua Alta** ("high water") bookstore, whose quirky owner Luigi has prepared for the next flood by displaying his wares in a selection of vessels, including bathtubs and a gondola (daily 9:00-21:00, large and classically disorganized selection includes prints of Venice, just beyond Campo Santa Maria Formosa on Calle Longa Santa Maria Formosa at #5176, tel. 041-296-0841, mobile 340-680-0704). For a solid selection of used books in English, visit **Marco Polo,** on Calle del Teatro Malibran at #5886a, close to the St. Mark's side of the Rialto Bridge on the way to Corte del Milion (Mon-Sat 10:00-19:00, closed Sun, mobile 348-569-1125, www.books marcopolo.com).

Laundry: You'll find coin-operated launderettes near the train station and off Campo Santa Maria Formosa. I've listed details for a self-service *lavanderia* and a competitively-priced full-service laundry near St. Mark's Square (see page 934), and for a self-serve laundry near the train station (page 949). Or ask your hotelier for the nearest launderette.

Travel Agencies: If you need to get train tickets, make seat reservations, or arrange a *cuccetta* (koo-CHET-tah—a berth on a night train), save a time-consuming trip to Venice's crowded train station by using a downtown travel agency. Most trains between Venice, Florence, and Rome require reservations, even for railpass-holders. A travel agency can also give advice on cheap flights (book at least a week in advance for the best fares).

Near St. Mark's Square, **Oltrex Change and Travel** sells train and plane tickets and books train reservations for a €4 fee (tickets sold daily May-Oct 9:00-18:00, Nov-April 9:00-16:30; on Riva degli Schiavoni, one bridge past the Bridge of Sighs, at #4192; tel. 041-524-2828, Luca and Beatrice).

Near Rialto, **Kele & Teo Travel** sells train tickets for a €4 per-person service charge (Mon-Fri 9:00-18:00, Sat 9:00-12:00, closed Sun; leaving the Rialto Bridge heading for St. Mark's, it's half a block away, tucked down a side street on the right at #5097; tel. 041-520-8722).

English Church Services: The **San Zulian Church**—the only church in Venice that you can actually walk around—offers a Mass in English (generally May-Sept Mon-Fri at 9:30 and Sun at 11:30, Sun only Oct-April, 2 blocks toward Rialto off St. Mark's Square, tel. 041-523-5383). **St. George's Anglican Church** welcomes all Christians to its English-language Eucharist (Sun at 10:30, located on Campo San Zio in Dorsoduro, midway between Accademia and Peggy Guggenheim Collection, www.stgeorgesvenice.com).

Haircuts: I've been getting my hair cut at **Coiffeur Benito** for nearly two decades. Benito has been keeping men and women trim for 28 years. He's an artist—actually a "hair sculptor"—and a cut here is a fun diversion from the tourist grind (about €20 for women or men, Tue-Fri 8:30-13:00 & 15:30-19:30, Sat 8:30-13:00 only, closed Sun-Mon; between St. Mark's Square and Rialto, on Calle San Zulian Già del Strazzariol, by back corner of San Zulian Church at #592a; tel. 041-528-6221).

Getting Around Venice
On Foot
The city's "streets" are narrow pedestrian walkways connecting its docks, squares, bridges, and courtyards. To navigate, look

for yellow signs on street corners pointing you to *(per)* the nearest major landmark. The first landmarks you'll get to know are San Marco (St. Mark's Square), Rialto (the bridge), Accademia (another bridge), Ferrovia (the train station), and Piazzale Roma (the bus station). Determine whether your destination is in the direction of a major signposted landmark, then follow the signs through the maze.

Dare to turn off the posted routes and make your own discoveries. While 80 percent of Venice is, in fact, not touristy, 80 percent of the tourists never notice. Escape the crowds and explore on foot. Walk and walk to the far reaches of the town. Don't worry about getting lost—in fact, get as lost as possible. Keep reminding yourself, "I'm on an island, and I can't get off." When it comes time to find your way, just follow the arrows on building corners or simply ask a local, *"Dov'è San Marco?"* ("Where is St. Mark's?") People in the tourist business (that's most Venetians) speak some English. If they don't, listen politely, watch where their hands point, say *"Grazie,"* and head off in that direction. If you're lost, refer to your map, or pop into a hotel and ask for their business card—it probably comes with a map and a prominent "You are here."

If you need to find a specific address, it helps to know its district, street, house number, street, and nearby landmarks. Every building in Venice has a house number, which is usually stenciled in red letters surrounded by a black oval above the doorway. The numbers relate to the district (each with about 6,000 address numbers), not the street. For example, say you wanted to find the recommended Acqua Alta bookstore at Castello 5176 (that is, in the Castello district, at house number 5176). It's on a street called Calle Longa Santa Maria Formosa, near the square called Campo Santa Maria Formosa, which in turn is near two major landmarks: the Rialto Bridge and St. Mark's Square. Once you've found Campo Santa Maria Formosa, you can look for a painted sign on one corner (like the one in this photo) which marks where the street begins. If you can find the Rialto Bridge and then the square—you can find the bookstore.

Some helpful street lingo: *Campo* means square, *campiello* is a small square, *calle* is a street, *fondamenta* is the embankment along a canal or the lagoon, *rio* is a small canal, *rio terà* is a street that was once a canal and has been filled in, *sotoportego* is a covered passageway, and *ponte* is a bridge. Don't get hung up on the exact spelling of street and square names, which may sometimes appear in the Venetian dialect and other times in standard Italian. (Where streets and squares have Venetian names that differ significantly from the Italian, I list both.)

Venice

Handy *Vaporetti* from San Zaccaria, near St. Mark's Square

Several *vaporetti* leave from the San Zaccaria docks, located 150 yards east of St. Mark's Square. There are four separate San Zaccaria docks spaced about 70 yards apart: Danieli, Jolanda, M.V.E., and Pietà. Although I list which specific dock these lines leave from, they often change from season to season—confirm before boarding.

- Line #1 goes up the Grand Canal, making all the stops, including San Marco-Vallaresso, Rialto, Ferrovia (train station), and Piazzale Roma (but it does not go as far as Tronchetto). In the other direction, it goes to the Lido. Line #1 departs from the San Zaccaria stop (usually from the Danieli dock).
- Line #2 zips over to San Giorgio Maggiore, the island church across from St. Mark's Square (5 minutes, €3 ride). From there, it continues on to the parking lot at Tronchetto (departs from the San Zaccaria stop, generally from the M.V.E. dock).
- Line #4.1 goes to San Michele and Murano in 45 minutes (departs from San Zaccaria stop, usually from the Jolanda dock).
- Line #12 head to Burano (70 minutes, from San Zaccaria stop, usually from the Pietà dock).
- The Molino Stucky shuttle boat takes even non-guests to the Hilton Hotel, with its popular view bar (free, 20-minute ride, leaves at 0:20 past the hour from near the San Zaccaria-M.V.E. dock).
- Lines #5.1 and #5.2 are the *circulare* (cheer-koo-LAH-ray), making a loop around the perimeter of the island, with a stop at the Lido—perfect if you just like riding boats. Line

By Vaporetto

Venice's public transit system, run by a company called ACTV, is a fleet of motorized bus-boats called *vaporetti*. They work like city buses except that they never get a flat, the stops are docks (cheerfully painted yellow and white), and if you get off between stops, you might drown.

For most travelers, only two vaporetto lines matter: Line #1 and line #2. These lines leave every 10 minutes (less frequently off-season) and go up and down the Grand Canal, between the "mouth of the fish" at one end and San Marco at the other. Line #1 is the slow boat, taking 45 minutes and making every stop along the way. Line #2 is the fast boat that zips down the Grand Canal in 25 minutes, stopping only at Tronchetto (parking lot), Piazzale Roma (bus station), Ferrovia (train station), San Marcuola, Rialto Bridge, San Tomà (Frari Church), Accademia Bridge, San Marco (west end of St. Mark's Square), and San Zaccaria (east end of St.

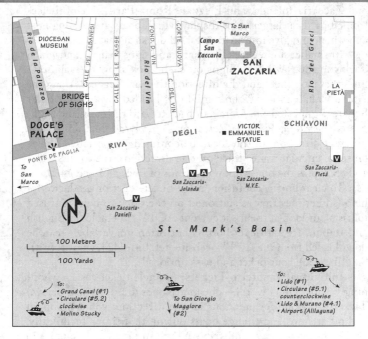

#5.1 goes counterclockwise (departs from San Zaccaria stop, generally from the Danieli dock), and #5.2 goes clockwise (also departs from San Zaccaria, but usually from the Jolanda dock).

- The Alilaguna airport shuttle to and from the airport stops at the San Zaccaria stop (generally at the Jolanda dock).

Mark's Square).

Catching a vaporetto is very much like catching a city bus. You can buy either single-ride tickets (valid 1 hour) or passes (valid for a variety of durations, from 12 hours to 7 days) from any ticket window or HelloVenezia office. HelloVenezia, run by ACTV, is a string of shops selling tickets and passes at the same prices as ticket windows (www.hellovenezia.com).

Before you board, validate your ticket by holding it up to the small white machine on the dock until you hear a pinging sound. The machine readout shows how long your ticket is valid—and inspectors do come by now and then to check tickets. If you board without a ticket (because ticket windows at odd hours or small stops may be closed), seek out the conductor immediately to buy a single ticket on board (or risk a €50 fine). Large stops—such as San Marco, San Zaccaria, and Piazzale Roma—have multiple docks, and each dock has its own name, such as San Marco-Vallaresso,

San Zaccaria-Jolanda, and Piazzale Roma-Parisi. Helpful electronic boards at larger stops display which boats are coming next and when, and give information for all docks at that stop.

At smaller stops, check the charts and signs to figure out which dock your boat will use. Signs on each dock show the vaporetto lines that stop there and the direction they are headed: Along the Grand Canal, a #1 or #2 boat might be headed toward St. Mark's Square (signposted *San Marco*), or back toward the mainland (signposted *Ferrovia, Piazzale Roma,* or *Tronchetto*). Sorting out the different directions of travel can be confusing, especially as boats on some circular routes travel in one direction (true for lines #5.1 and #5.2, plus the non-Murano sections of lines #4.1 and #4.2).

To clear up any confusion, ask a ticket-seller or conductor for help (sometimes they're stationed on the dock to help confused tourists), or look at the most current ACTV timetable (in English and Italian, free at ticket booths but often unavailable—can be downloaded from the ACTV website, tel. 041-2424, www.actv.it).

These are your ticket and pass options:

Individual Vaporetto Tickets: A single ticket costs a whopping €6.50. (Don't worry—cheaper passes are described below.) Tickets are good for one hour in one direction; you can hop on and off at stops and change boats during that time. Technically, you're not allowed a round-trip (though in practice, a round-trip is allowed if you can complete it within a one-hour span). Tickets are electronic and refillable. The fare is reduced to €3 for a few one-stop runs that are hard to do by foot, including the route from San Marco to La Salute, from Fondamente Nove to Murano-Colonna, and from San Zaccaria-M.V.E. to San Giorgio Maggiore.

Vaporetto Passes: You can buy a pass for unlimited use of *vaporetti* and ACTV buses: €16/12 hours, €18/24 hours, €23/36 hours, €28/48 hours, €33/72 hours, €50/7-day pass; pass must be validated once, before use). Because single tickets cost a hefty €6.50 a pop, these passes can pay for themselves in a hurry. Think through your Venice itinerary before you step up to the ticket booth to pay for your first vaporetto trip. The 48-hour pass pays for itself with five rides (e.g., to your hotel, on a Grand Canal joy-ride, into the lagoon and back, to the train station). And it's fun to be able to hop on and off spontaneously, and avoid long ticket lines. On the other hand, many tourists just walk and rarely use a boat.

Anyone under 30 years old can get a 72-hour pass for €18 if they also buy a **Rolling Venice** discount card for €4 (available from TIs, larger ticket windows, and HelloVenezia shops). Those settling in for a longer stay can ride like a local by buying the **CartaVenezia** ID card (€40/year, which lets you ride for about €1 per trip). See www.actv.it for details.

Passes are also valid on ACTV's mainland buses, including bus #5 to the airport (but not the airport buses run by ATVO, a separate company).

Vaporetto Tips: For fun, take my Grand Canal Cruise. Boats can be literally packed during the tourist rush hour. Morning rush hour (8:00-10:00) is headed in the direction of St. Mark's Square, as tourists and commuters arrive. Afternoon rush hour (about 17:00) is when they're headed in the other direction for the train station. Riding at night, with nearly empty boats and chandelier-lit palace interiors viewable from the Grand Canal, is an entirely different experience.

By *Traghetto*

Only four bridges cross the Grand Canal, but *traghetti* (gondola-like rowboats) shuttle locals and in-the-know tourists across the Grand Canal at eight handy locations. Venetians stand while riding, but you shouldn't (€0.50, don't tip—literally). Note that some *traghetti* stop running as early as 13:00 and all stop by 18:00.

By Water Taxi

Venetian taxis, like speedboat limos, hang out at busy points along the Grand Canal. Prices are regulated and listed in the TI's *Shows & Events* brochure: €13 for the first seven minutes plus €1.80 per minute thereafter; €5 per person for more than two passengers; and €8 between 22:00 and 6:00. Large bags cost €3 apiece. To the airport, a flat fee of about €100 for up to five people is common (for more information see "Venice Connections," at the end of this chapter). Despite regulation, prices can be soft; negotiate and settle on the price or rate before stepping in. For travelers with lots of luggage or small groups who can split the cost, taxi boat rides can be a worthwhile and time-saving convenience—and skipping across the lagoon in a classic wooden motorboat is a cool indulgence. For a little more than €100 an hour, you can have a private, unguided taxi-boat tour.

By Gondola

If you're interested in hiring a gondolier for your own private cruise, see page 930.

Tours in Venice

Tours of Venice on foot and afloat abound. To sightsee on your own, download my series of free audio tours that illuminate some of Venice's top sights and experiences: St. Mark's Square, St. Mark's Basilica, the Frari Church, and a cruise along the Grand Canal (see sidebar on page 7 for details).

VENICE

Avventure Bellissime Venice Tours—This company offers several two-hour walks, including a basic St. Mark's Square introduction called the "Original Venice Walking Tour" (€21.50, includes church entry, most days at 11:00, Sun at 14:00; 45 minutes on the square, 15 minutes in the church, one hour along back streets). Other walks include Cannaregio/Jewish Ghetto, "Hidden Venice," ghost stories and legends, and a Doge's Palace tour (€20, group size 8-22, English-language only, tel. 041-970-499, www.tours-italy .com, info@tours-italy.com, Monica or Jonathan). Their 70-minute Grand Canal boat tour is timed for good late-afternoon light (€40, daily at 16:30, 8 people maximum). They also offer small-group excursions to the Dolomites and Veneto hill towns. For a discount on certain tours, say "Rick sent me."

Classic Venice Bars Tour—Debonair guide Alessandro Schezzini is a connoisseur of Venetian *bacari*—classic old bars serving wine and traditional *cicchetti* snacks. He organizes two-hour Venetian pub tours (€30, any night on request at 18:00, depart from the top of the Rialto Bridge, better to book by email—alessandro @schezzini.it—than by phone, mobile 335-530-9024, www .schezzini.it). Alessandro's tours include sampling *cicchetti* with wines at three different *bacari*, plus he'll answer all of your questions about Venice. (If you think of this tour as a light dinner with a local friend, you can consider it part of your eating budget.)

Artviva: The Original and Best Walking Tours—This company offers a number of group and private tours, including a Venice in One Glorious Day Special and four themed tours (Grand Canal, Venice Walk, Doge's Palace, Gondola Tour). The 1.25-hour Gondola Tour (€60) includes a 35-minute gondola ride, followed by a 40-minute walk culminating at St. Mark's Square, while the two-hour "Learn to Be a Gondolier" tour teaches the ancient craft of rowing Venetian-style (€80, 4 people maximum). See the tour details and Rick Steves readers' discounts on their website (book in advance, tours run March-Nov, tel. 055-264-5033, www.italy .artviva.com, staff@artviva.com).

Venicescapes—Michael Broderick's private theme tours of Venice are intellectually demanding and beyond the attention span of most mortal tourists. But those with a keen interest and a desire to gain a solid understanding of Venice find him passionate and engaging. Rather than a "sightseeing tour," your time with Michael is more like a rolling, graduate-level lecture. See his website for descriptions of his various itineraries (book well in advance, tours last 4-6 hours: $250-290 for 2 people, $60/person after that, pay in dollars or the current euro equivalent, price includes maps and printed info but not admissions or transportation, tel. 041-520-6361, www.venicescapes.org, info@venice scapes.org).

Local Guides—Plenty of licensed, trained guides are available. If you organize a small group from your hotel at breakfast to split the cost (figure on roughly €70/hour with a 2-hour minimum), the fee becomes more reasonable. The following companies and guides give tours to individuals, families, and small groups.

Elisabetta Morelli guides many of my tour groups around Venice (€65/hour, show this book and ask for Rick Steves price, 2-hour minimum, tel. 041-526-7816, mobile 328-753-5220, www.elisabettamorelli.it, bettamorelli@inwind.it).

Walks Inside Venice is a group of three women enthusiastic about teaching (€70/hour per group with this book, 3-hour minimum; Roberta: mobile 347-253-0560; Cristina: mobile 348-341-5421; Sara: mobile 335-522-9714; www.walksinsidevenice.com, info@walksinsidevenice.com). They also do regularly scheduled small-group walking tours (see details on their site).

Venice with a Guide is a co-op of 10 equally good guides (www.venicewithaguide.com).

Alessandro Schezzini, mentioned earlier for his Classic Venice Bars Tour, isn't a licensed Italian guide and therefore can't take you into sights. But his relaxed, two-hour, back-streets "Rick Steves" tour does a great job of getting you beyond the clichés and into offbeat Venice (€15/person, see opposite page for contact info).

Weekend Tour Packages for Students in Venice—Andy Steves (my son) runs Weekend Student Adventures, offering experiential three-day weekend tours for €250, designed for American students studying abroad (www.wsaeurope.com for details on tours of Venice and other great cities).

Self-Guided Cruise

▲▲▲Welcome to Venice's Grand Canal Cruise

Take a joyride and introduce yourself to Venice by boat. Cruise the Canal Grande all the way to San Marco, starting at the train station (Ferrovia) or the bus station (Piazzale Roma).

If it's your first trip down the Grand Canal, you might want to stow this book and just take it all in—Venice is a barrage on the senses that hardly needs narration. But these notes give the cruise a little meaning and help orient you to this great city.

This tour is designed to be done on the slow boat #1 (which takes about 45 minutes). The express boat #2 travels the same route, but it skips many stops and takes only 25 minutes, making it hard to sightsee. Also, some #2 boats terminate at Rialto; confirm that you're on a boat that goes all the way to San Marco.

To help you enjoy the visual parade of canal wonders, I've organized this tour by boat stop. I'll point out both what you can see from the current stop, and what to look forward to as you cruise

Grand Canal

GUGLIE BRIDGE

Canale de Cannaregio

To Jewish Ghetto

STRADA

SAN GEREMIA

PALAZZO CORRER CONTARINI

SAN MARCUOLA

CASINÒ

PALAZZO GRITTI

PALAZZO VENDRAMIN CALERGI

LISTA DI SPAGNA

Grand Canal

SCALZI

PALAZZO CALBOCROTTA

PALAZZO FLANGINI

PALAZZO GIOVANELLI

TURKISH "FONDACO" EXCHANGE

SANTA LUCIA TRAIN STATION (FERROVIA)

PALAZZO MARCELLO

PAL. GRITTI

SAN ZAN DEGOLA

PALAZZO CA'TRON

SCALZI BRIDGE

PALAZZO DONA BALBI

SAN SIMEONE PICCOLO

SANTA CROCE

SAN

CALATRAVA BRIDGE

PIAZZALE ROMA
& PEOPLE MOVER TO STAZIONE MARITTIMA & TRONCHETTO

FRARI

PALAZZO CAPPELLO-LAYARD

SAN TOMÀ

PALAZZO GIUSTINIANI

PALAZZO BARBARIGO

PALAZZO BALBI

FIRE STATION

CA' FOSCARI

PALAZZO GIUSTINIAN

CA' REZZONICO

PALAZZO MOCENIGO

PALAZZO VECCHIA

PALAZZO MORO LIN

PALAZZO GRASSI

PALAZZO MALIPIERO-CAPPELLO

PALAZZO LOREDAN

PALAZZO FALIER

PALAZZO GIUSTINIAN LOLIN

PALAZZO CONTARINI DEGLI SCRIGNI

PALAZZO QUERINI

PALAZZO BARBARO

ACCADEMIA BRIDGE & GALLERY

PALAZZO BARBARIGO

Vaporetto Stops

1 Ferrovia
2 Riva de Biasio
3 San Marcuola
4 San Stae
5 Ca' d'Oro
6 Mercato Rialto
7 Rialto
8 San Silvestro
9 Sant'Angelo
10 San Tomà
11 Ca' Rezzonico
12 Accademia
13 Santa Maria del Giglio
14 Salute
15 San Marco
16 San Zaccaria

VENICE

FONDAMENTA ZATTERE AL PONTE LONGO

Giudecca Canal

DORSODURO

To Zattere

to the next stop. You can download a free Rick Steves **audio tour** of this cruise; see page 7.

A Few Tips: You're more likely to find an empty seat if you catch the vaporetto at Piazzale Roma. You can break up the tour by hopping on and off at various sights described in greater depth elsewhere in this chapter (but remember, a single-fare vaporetto ticket is good for just 60 minutes; passes let you hop on and off all day). As you board the vaporetto, make a beeline for an open-air seat in the front of the boat, which has the best seats for this tour. From the front, you can easily look left, right, and forward. If you find yourself stuck on the side or in the cabin, do your best. Avoid sitting in the back, only because you'll miss the wonderful forward views.

Overview

The Grand Canal is Venice's "Main Street." At more than two miles long, nearly 150 feet wide, and nearly 15 feet deep, the Grand Canal is the city's largest, lined with its most impressive palaces. It's the remnant of a river that once spilled from the mainland into the Adriatic. The sediment it carried formed barrier islands that cut Venice off from the sea, forming a lagoon.

Venice was built on the marshy islands of the former delta, sitting on wood pilings driven nearly 15 feet into the clay (alder was the preferred wood). About 25 miles of canals drain the city, dumping like streams into the Grand Canal. Technically, Venice has only three canals: Grand, Giudecca, and Cannaregio. The 45 small waterways that dump into the Grand Canal are referred to as rivers (e.g., Rio Novo).

Venice is a city of palaces, dating from the days when the city was the world's richest. The most lavish palaces formed a grand chorus line along the Grand Canal. Once frescoed in reds and blues, with black-and-white borders and gold-leaf trim, they made Venice a city of dazzling color. This cruise is the only way to truly appreciate the palaces, approaching them at water level, where their main entrances were located. Today, strict laws prohibit any changes in these buildings, so while landowners gnash their teeth, we can enjoy Europe's best-preserved medieval city—slowly rotting. Many of the grand buildings are now vacant. Others harbor chandeliered elegance above mossy, empty (often flooded) ground floors.

The Grand Canal Cruise Begins

This tour starts at the Ferrovia vaporetto stop (at Santa Lucia train station). It also works if you board upstream from Ferrovia at Piazzale Roma (where airport buses and the People Mover monorail from Tronchetto arrive), a short walk from Ferrovia over the

Calatrava Bridge. Just start the tour when your vaporetto reaches Ferrovia.

Ferrovia: The **Santa Lucia train station,** one of the few modern buildings in town, was built in 1954. It's been the gateway into Venice since 1860, when the first station was built. "F.S." stands for "Ferrovie dello Stato," the Italian state railway system.

More than 20,000 people a day commute in from the mainland, making this the busiest part of Venice during rush hour. The **Calatrava Bridge,** spanning the Grand Canal between the train station and Piazzale Roma upstream, was built in 2008 to alleviate some of the congestion and make the commute easier (see page 929).

Opposite the train station, atop the green dome of **San Simeone Piccolo** church, St. Simeon waves *ciao* to whoever enters or leaves the "old" city. The pink church with the white Carrara-marble facade, just beyond the train station, is the **Church of the Scalzi** (Church of the Barefoot, named after the shoeless Carmelite monks), where the last doge (Venetian ruler) rests. It looks relatively new because it was partially rebuilt after being bombed in 1915 by Austrians aiming (poorly) at the train station.

Riva de Biasio: Venice's main thoroughfare is busy with all kinds of **boats**—taxis, police boats, garbage boats, ambulances, construction cranes, and even brown-and-white UPS boats. Somehow they all manage to share the canal in relative peace.

About 25 yards past the Riva de Biasio stop, you'll look left down the broad **Cannaregio Canal** to see what was the **Jewish Ghetto** (see page 928). The twin, pale-pink, six-story "skyscrapers"—the tallest buildings you'll see at this end of the canal—are reminders of how densely populated the world's original ghetto was. Set aside as the local Jewish quarter in 1516, this area became extremely crowded. This urban island developed into one of the most closely knit business and cultural quarters of all the Jewish communities in Italy, and gave us our word "ghetto" (from *geto,* the copper foundry located here).

San Marcuola: At this stop, facing a tiny square just ahead, stands the unfinished church of San Marcuola, one of only five churches fronting the Grand Canal. Centuries ago, this canal was a commercial drag of expensive real estate in high demand by wealthy merchants. About 20 yards ahead on the right stands the stately gray **Turkish "Fondaco" Exchange,** one of the oldest houses in Venice. Its horseshoe arches and roofline of triangles and dingleballs are reminders of its Byzantine heritage. Turkish traders in turbans docked here, unloaded their goods into the warehouse on the bottom story, then went upstairs for a home-style meal and a place to sleep. Venice in the 1500s was very cosmopolitan, welcoming every religion and ethnicity, so long as they carried cash. (Today the building contains the city's Museum of Natural History—and Venice's only dinosaur skeleton.)

Just 100 yards ahead on the left, Venice's **Casinò** is housed in the palace where German composer Richard *(The Ring)* Wagner died in 1883. See his distinct, strong-jawed profile in the white plaque on the brick wall. In the 1700s, Venice was Europe's Vegas, with casinos and prostitutes everywhere. Casinòs ("little houses") have long provided Italians with a handy escape from daily life. Today they're run by the state to keep Mafia influence at bay. Notice the fancy front porch, rolling out the red carpet for high rollers arriving by taxi or hotel boat.

San Stae: The San Stae Church sports a delightful Baroque facade. Opposite the San Stae stop, look for the peeling plaster that once made up **frescoes** (scant remains on the lower floors). Imagine the facades of the Grand Canal at their finest. As colorful as the city is today, it's still only a faded, sepia-toned remnant of a long-gone era, a time of lavishly decorated, brilliantly colored palaces.

Just ahead, jutting out a bit on the right, is the ornate white facade of **Ca' Pesaro.** *"Ca'"* is short for *casa* (house). Because only the house of the doge (Venetian ruler) could be called a palace *(palazzo)*, all other Venetian palaces are technically "Ca'."

In this city of masks, notice how the rich marble facades along the Grand Canal mask what are generally just simple, nononsense brick buildings. Most merchants enjoyed showing off. However, being smart businessmen, they only decorated the side of the buildings that would be seen and appreciated. But look back as you pass Ca' Pesaro (which houses the International Gallery of Modern Art—see page 926). It's the only building you'll see with a fine side facade. Ahead, on the left, with its glorious triple-decker medieval arcade (just before the next stop) is Ca' d'Oro.

Ca' d'Oro: The lacy **Ca' d'Oro** (House of Gold) is the best example of Venetian Gothic architecture on the canal. Its three stories offer different variations on balcony design, topped with a spiny white roofline. Venetian Gothic mixes traditional Gothic (pointed arches and round medallions stamped with a four-leaf clover) with Byzantine styles (tall, narrow arches atop thin columns), filled in with Islamic frills. Like all the palaces, this was originally painted and gilded to make it even more glorious than it is now. Today the Ca' d'Oro is an art gallery (see page 929).

Look at the Venetian chorus line of palaces in front of the boat doing an architectural cancan. On the right is the arcade of the covered **fish market,** with the open-air **produce market** just beyond. It bustles in the morning but is quiet the rest of the day. This is a great scene to wander through—even though European Union hygiene standards have made it cleaner, but less colorful

VENICE

than it once was. Find the *traghetto* gondola ferrying shoppers—standing like Washington crossing the Delaware—back and forth. There are eight *traghetto* crossings along the Grand Canal, each one marked by a classy low-key green-and-black sign. Make a point to use them. At €0.50 a ride, they are one of the best deals in Venice.

Mercato Rialto: This stop was opened in 2007 to serve the busy market (boats only stop here between 8:00 and 20:00). The long and officious-looking building at this stop is the Venice courthouse. Straight ahead in the distance, rising above the huge post office, is the tip of the Campanile (bell tower) crowned by its golden angel at St. Mark's Square, where this tour will end. The former post office (100 yards directly ahead, on left side, soon to be a shopping center) was once the German Exchange, the trading center for German metal merchants in the early 1500s.

You'll cruise by some trendy and beautifully situated wine bars on the right, but look ahead as you round the corner and see the impressive Rialto Bridge come into view.

A major landmark of Venice, the **Rialto Bridge** is lined with shops and tourists. Constructed in 1588, it's the third bridge built on this spot. Until the 1850s, this was the only bridge crossing the Grand Canal. With a span of 160 feet and foundations stretching 650 feet on either side, the Rialto was an impressive engineering feat in its day. Earlier Rialto Bridges could open to let big ships in, but not this one. When this new bridge was completed, much of the Grand Canal was closed to shipping and became a canal of palaces.

When gondoliers pass under the fat arch of the Rialto Bridge, they take full advantage of its acoustics: *"Volare, oh, oh..."*

Rialto: Rialto, a separate town in the early days of Venice, has always been the commercial district, while San Marco was the religious and governmental center. Today, a winding street called the Mercerie connects the two, providing travelers with human traffic jams and a mesmerizing gauntlet of shopping temptations. This is the only stretch of the historic Grand Canal with landings upon which you can walk. They unloaded the city's basic necessities here: oil, wine, charcoal, iron. Today, the quay is lined with tourist-trap restaurants.

Venice's sleek, black, graceful **gondolas** are a symbol of the city (for more on gondolas, see page 930). With about 500 gondoliers joyriding amid the churning *vaporetti,* there's a lot of congestion on the Grand Canal. Pay attention—this is where most of the gondola and vaporetto accidents take place. While the Rialto is the highlight of many gondola rides, gondoliers understandably prefer the smaller, quieter canals. Watch your vaporetto driver curse the better-paid gondoliers.

Ahead 100 yards on the left, two gray-colored **palaces** stand side by side (the City Hall and the mayor's office). Their horseshoe-shaped, arched windows are similar and their stories are the same height, lining up to create the effect of one long balcony.

San Silvestro: We now enter a long stretch of important **merchants' palaces,** each with proud and different facades. Because ships couldn't navigate beyond the Rialto Bridge, the biggest palaces—with the major shipping needs—line this last stretch of the navigable Grand Canal.

Palaces like these were multi-functional: ground floor for the warehouse, offices and showrooms upstairs, and the living quarters above the offices on the "noble floors" (with big windows designed to allow in maximum light). Servants lived and worked on the top floors (with the smallest windows). For fire-safety reasons, the kitchens were also located on the top floors. Peek into the noble floors to catch a glimpse of their still-glorious chandeliers of Murano glass.

Sant'Angelo: Notice how many buildings have a foundation of waterproof white stone *(pietra d'Istria)* upon which the bricks sit high and dry. Many canal-level floors are abandoned as the rising water level takes its toll. The **posts**—historically painted gaily with the equivalent of family coats of arms—don't rot underwater. But the wood at the waterline, where it's exposed to oxygen, does. On the smallest canals, little blue gondola signs indicate that these docks are for gondolas only (no taxis or motor boats).

San Tomà: Fifty yards ahead, on the right side (with twin obelisks on the rooftop) stands **Palazzo Balbi,** the palace of an early-17th-century captain general of the sea. These Venetian equivalents of five-star admirals were honored with twin obelisks decorating their palaces. This palace, like so many in the city, flies three flags: Italy (green-white-red), the European Union (blue with ring of stars), and Venice (a lion on a field of red and gold). Today it houses the administrative headquarters of the regional government.

Just past the admiral's palace, look immediately to the right, down a side canal. On the right side of that canal, before the bridge, see the traffic light and the **fire station** (with four arches hiding fireboats parked and ready to go).

The impressive **Ca' Foscari,** with a classic Venetian facade (on the corner, across from the fire station), dominates the bend in the canal. This is the main building of the University of Venice, which has about 25,000 students. Notice the elegant lamp on the corner.

The grand, heavy, white **Ca' Rezzonico,** just before the Ca' Rezzonico stop, houses the Museum of 18th-Century Venice (see page 925). Across the canal is the cleaner and leaner **Palazzo Grassi,** the last major palace built on the canal, erected in the late

1700s. It was purchased by a French tycoon and now displays a contemporary art collection.

Ca' Rezzonico: Up ahead, the Accademia Bridge leads over the Grand Canal to the **Accademia Gallery** (right side), filled with the best Venetian paintings (see page 923). The bridge was put up in 1934 as a temporary structure. Locals liked it, so it stayed.

Accademia: From here, look through the graceful bridge and way ahead to enjoy a classic view of **La Salute Church,** topped by a crown-shaped dome supported by scrolls (see page 925). This Church of St. Mary of Good Health was built to thank God for delivering Venetians from the devastating plague of 1630 (which had killed about a third of the city's population).

The low, white building among greenery (100 yards ahead, on the right, between the Accademia Bridge and the church) is the **Peggy Guggenheim Collection.** The American heiress "retired" here, sprucing up a palace that had been abandoned in mid-construction. Peggy willed the city her fine collection of modern art (described on page 925).

As you approach the next stop, notice on the right how the fine line of higgledy-piggledy palaces evokes old-time Venice. Two doors past the Guggenheim, Palazzo Dario has a great set of characteristic **funnel-shaped chimneys.** These forced embers through a loop-the-loop channel until they were dead—required in the days when stone palaces were surrounded by humble, wooden buildings, and a live spark could make a merchant's workforce homeless. Notice this early Renaissance building's flat-feeling facade with "pasted-on" Renaissance motifs. Three doors later is the **Salviati building** (with the fine mosaics), which was once a glassworks.

Santa Maria del Giglio: Back on the left stands the fancy Gritti Palace hotel. Hemingway and Woody Allen both stayed here (but not together).

Take a deep whiff of Venice. What's all this nonsense about stinky canals? All I smell is my shirt. By the way, how's your captain? Smooth dockings? To get to know him, stand up in the bow and block his view.

Salute: The huge **La Salute Church** towers overhead as if squirted from a can of Catholic Reddi-wip. Like Venice itself, the church rests upon pilings. To build the foundation for the city, more than a million trees were piled together, reaching beneath the mud to the solid clay. Much of the surrounding countryside was deforested by Venice. Trees were exported and consumed locally to fuel the furnaces of Venice's booming glass industry, to build Europe's biggest merchant marine, and to prop up this city in the mud.

As the Grand Canal opens up into the lagoon, the last building on the right with the golden ball is the 17th-century **Customs House,** which now houses the Punta della Dogana Museum of

VENICE

Contemporary Art (see page 926). Its two bronze Atlases hold a statue of Fortune riding the ball. Arriving ships stopped here to pay their tolls.

San Marco: Up ahead on the left, the green pointed tip of the Campanile marks **St. Mark's Square,** the political and religious center of Venice...and the final destination of this tour. You could get off at the San Marco stop and go straight to St. Mark's Square. But I'm staying on the boat for one more stop, just past St. Mark's Square (it's a quick walk back).

Survey the lagoon. Opposite St. Mark's Square, across the water, the ghostly white church with the pointy bell tower is **San Giorgio Maggiore,** with great views of Venice (see page 923). Next to it is the residential island Giudecca, stretching from close to San Giorgio Maggiore past the Venice youth hostel (with a nice view, directly across) to the Hilton Hotel (good nighttime view, far right end of island).

Still on board? If you are, as we leave the San Marco stop, prepare for a drive-by view of St. Mark's Square. First comes the bold white facade of the old mint (where Venice's golden ducat, the "dollar" of the Venetian Republic, was made) and the library facade. Then the twin columns, topped by St. Theodore and St. Mark, who've welcomed visitors since the 15th century. Between the columns, catch a glimpse of two giant figures atop the **Clock Tower**—they've been whacking their clappers every hour since 1499. The domes of **St. Mark's Basilica** are soon eclipsed by the lacy facade of the **Doge's Palace.** Next you'll see the **Bridge of Sighs** (currently under scaffolding), and then the grand harborside promenade—the **Riva.**

Follow the Riva with your eye, past elegant hotels to the green area in the distance. This is the largest of Venice's few **parks,** which hosts the Biennale art show every odd year. Much farther in the distance is the **Lido,** the island with Venice's beach. Its sand and casinos are tempting, but its car traffic disrupts the medieval charm of Venice.

San Zaccaria: OK, you're at your last stop. Quick—muscle your way off this boat! (If you don't, you'll eventually end up at the Lido.)

At San Zaccaria, you're right in the thick of the action. A number of other *vaporetti* depart from here (see page 898). Otherwise, it's a short walk back along the Riva to St. Mark's Square. Ahoy!

Sights in Venice

For information on sightseeing passes, see below. Venice's city museums offer youth and senior discounts to Americans and other non-EU citizens.

Sightseeing Passes for Venice

Venice offers an array of passes. For most people, the best choice is the combo-ticket, which covers entry into the Doge's Palace and more. Note that some major sights (Accademia, Peggy Guggenheim Collection, Scuola San Rocco, Campanile, and the three sights within St. Mark's Basilica that charge admission) are not covered on any pass.

Combo-Ticket: The combo-ticket for the Doge's Palace or Correr Museum, which are at opposite ends of St. Mark's Square, always gets you into the other museum as well (and includes two other museums within the Correr: the National Archaeological Museum and the Monumental Rooms of Marciana National Library). From April through October, this ticket costs €14 and gives you a single bonus entry into your choice of one of these other city-run museums: Ca' Rezzonico (Museum of 18th-Century Venice); Palazzo Mocenigo Costume Museum; Casa Goldoni (home of the Italian playwright); Ca' Pesaro (modern art); Museum of Natural History in the Santa Croce district; the Glass Museum on the island of Murano; and the Lace Museum on the island of Burano (full details at www.museicivicineveziani.it; this €14 version is technically called the San Marco Museum Plus ticket). In winter (Nov-March), this ticket costs €13 and covers only the Doge's Palace and Correr Museum. To bypass the long line at the Doge's Palace, buy your combo-ticket at the Correr Museum or at any other included museum. Note that you can't buy an individual ticket for just the Doge's Palace or solely for the Correr.

Museum Pass: Busy sightseers may prefer this more expensive pass, which covers all 11 museums listed in the preceding paragraph, including the Doge's Palace and Correr Museum (€18, available all year). In general, this pass saves you money only if you visit five or more sights; before you buy, make sure they're sights you really want to see.

Chorus Pass: This pass gives church-lovers admission to 16 of Venice's churches and their art (generally €3 each)—including the Frari Church—for €10 (€20 family pass, www.chorusvenezia.org).

Venice Card: This pass combines the 11 city-run museums and the 16 churches covered by the Chorus Pass, plus a few minor discounts, for €40, but it's hard to make it pay off if you're over 29 (€30 for anyone under 30, valid 7 days, info at www.hellovenezia .com). Don't confuse this pass with CartaVenezia, a discount transit card used mainly by locals.

Rolling Venice: This youth pass offers discounts at dozens of sights and shops, but its best deal is for transit. If you're under 30 and want to buy a three-day transit pass, it'll cost you just €18—rather than €33—with the Rolling Venice pass (€4 for anyone 14-29, sold at TIs and HelloVenezia shops).

VENICE

Venice Connected: This confusing web-based system allows you to buy vouchers exchangeable for sightseeing and transport tickets; it's generally not worth the trouble (www.veniceconnected.com).

Transportation Passes: Venice sells transit-only passes that cover *vaporetti* and mainland buses. For a rundown on these, see "Vaporetto Passes" on page 900.

San Marco District

▲▲▲**St. Mark's Square (Piazza San Marco)**—This grand square is surrounded by splashy, historic buildings and sights: St. Mark's Basilica, the Doge's Palace, the Campanile bell tower, and the Correr Museum. The square is filled with music, lovers, pigeons, and tourists by day, and is your private rendezvous with the Venetian past late at night, when Europe's most magnificent dance floor is *the* romantic place to be.

With your back to the church, survey one of Europe's great urban spaces, and the only square in Venice to merit the title "Piazza." Nearly two football fields long, it's surrounded by the offices of the republic. On the right are the "old offices" (16th-century Renaissance). At left are the "new offices" (17th-century High Renaissance). Napoleon called the piazza "the most beautiful drawing room in Europe," and added to the intimacy by building the final wing, opposite the basilica, that encloses the square.

For a slow and pricey evening thrill, invest about €12-20 (including the cover charge for the music) for a drink at one of the elegant cafés with the dueling orchestras. For an unmatched experience that offers the best people-watching in Venice, it's worth the small splurge.

The **Clock Tower** (Torre dell'Orologio), built during the Renaissance in 1496, marks the entry to the main shopping drag, called the Mercerie (or "Marzarie," in Venetian dialect), which connects St. Mark's Square with the Rialto. From the piazza, you can see the bronze men (Moors) swing their huge clappers at the top of each hour. In the 17th century, one of them knocked an unsuspecting worker off the top and to his death—probably the first-ever killing by a robot. Notice one of the world's first "digital" clocks on the tower facing the square (with dramatic flips every five minutes). You can go inside the Clock Tower with a pre-booked guided tour that takes you close to the clock's innards and out to a terrace with good views over the square and city rooftops. Reserve by calling 848-082-000, booking online at www.museicivicivenziani.it, going in person to the Correr Museum a day in advance, or even just showing up at the Correr prior to a scheduled tour to see if space is available (€12 combo-ticket includes Correr Museum, where tour starts; tours in English Mon-Wed at 10:00

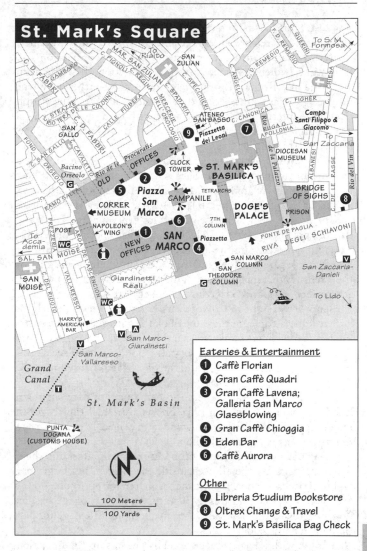

St. Mark's Square

Eateries & Entertainment
1. Caffè Florian
2. Gran Caffè Quadri
3. Gran Caffè Lavena; Galleria San Marco Glassblowing
4. Gran Caffè Chioggia
5. Eden Bar
6. Caffè Aurora

Other
7. Libreria Studium Bookstore
8. Oltrex Change & Travel
9. St. Mark's Basilica Bag Check

VENICE

and 11:00, Thu-Sun at 14:00 and 15:00; no kids under age 6).

A good **TI** is on the square (with your back to the basilica, it's in the far-left, southwest corner; daily 9:00-15:30), and a €1.50 WC is 30 yards beyond the square (see *Albergo Diorno* sign marked on pavement, WC open daily 9:00-17:30). Another TI is on the lagoon near the San Marco-Vallaresso vaporetto stop (daily 10:00-18:00, walk toward the water by the Doge's Palace and go right, €1.50 WCs nearby).

You can download a free Rick Steves **audio tour** of St. Mark's Square; see page 7.

▲▲▲**St. Mark's Basilica (Basilica di San Marco)**—Built in the 11th century to replace an earlier church, this basilica's distinctly Eastern-style architecture underlines Venice's connection with Byzantium (which protected it from the ambition of Charlemagne and his Holy Roman Empire). It's decorated with booty from returning sea captains—a kind of architectural Venetian trophy chest. The interior glows mysteriously with gold mosaics and colored marble. Since about A.D. 830, the saint's bones have been housed on this site.

Cost and Hours: Basilica entry is free, three interior sights charge admission, open Mon-Sat 9:45-17:00, Sun 14:00-17:00 (Sun until 16:00 Nov-March), St. Mark's Square, vaporetto stops: San Marco or San Zaccaria, tel. 041-270-8311, www.basilicasanmarco .it. The dress code is strictly enforced for everyone (no bare shoulders or bare knees). Lines can be long, and bag check is mandatory, free, and can save you time in line. No photos are allowed inside.

Three separate exhibits within the church charge admission: the **Treasury** (€3, includes audioguide free for the asking), **Golden Altarpiece** (€2), and **San Marco Museum** (€4). The San Marco Museum—the sight most worth its entry fee—has the original bronze horses (copies of these overlook the square), a balcony offering a remarkable view over St. Mark's Square, and various works related to the church. The Treasury and Golden Altarpiece close 15 minutes before the church, while the San Marco Museum is open daily 9:45-16:45.

Dress Code: Modest dress (no bare knees or bare shoulders) is strictly enforced, even for kids. Shorts are OK if they cover the knees. To cover bare shoulders, women may be able to buy a shawl *(coprispale)* at the atrium gift shop.

Bag Check (and Skipping the Line): Small purses and shoulder-slung bags may be allowed inside the church, but larger bags and backpacks are not. Check them for free for up to one hour at the nearby Ateneo San Basso, 30 yards to the left of the basilica, down narrow Calle San Basso (see map on opposite page for location; open daily 9:30-17:00).

Those with a bag to check actually get to skip the line, along with their companions (up to three or so). Leave your bag at Ateneo San Basso and pick up your claim tag. Take your tag to the basilica's tourist entrance. Keep to the left of the railing where the line forms and show your tag to the gatekeeper. He'll let you in, ahead of the line. After touring the church, come back and pick up your bag. (Note: Ateneo San Basso will not let you check small bags that would be allowed inside.)

Theft Alert: St. Mark's Basilica is the most dangerous place in Venice for pickpocketing—inside, it's always a crowded jostle.

VENICE

St. Mark's Basilica

To San Zaccaria

CALLE DE LA CANONICA

15 MAIN ALTAR

11

6 CENTRAL **7**

8 NORTH TRANSEPT **5** DOME SOUTH TRANSEPT **9**

12

10

13 TREASURY

4 BAPTISTERY **14**

Piazzetta dei Leoni

NAVE **3**

16

2

ATRIUM

BAG CHECK

SAN BASSO

LIONS

1 ENTRANCE

To Doge's Palace

MERCERIE

CLOCK TOWER

Piazza San Marco

To Campanile

1 Exterior – Mosaic of Mark's Relics	**9** Last Supper Mosaic
2 Atrium – Mosaic of Noah's Ark & the Great Flood	**10** Crucifixion Mosaic
3 Nave – Mosaics & Greek-Cross Floor Plan	**11** Nicopeia Icon
4 Pentecost Mosaic	**12** Rifle on Pillar
5 Central Dome – Ascension Mosaic	**13** Discovery of Mark Mosaic
6 Rood Screen	**14** Treasury
7 Doge's Pulpit	**15** Golden Altarpiece
8 Tree of Jesse Mosaic	**16** Stairs up to Loggia: San Marco Museum & Bronze Horses

VENICE

Tours: Free, hour-long English **tours** (heavy on the mosaics' religious symbolism) are generally offered Mon-Sat at 11:00; meet in the atrium. But the schedule varies, so see the schedule board in the atrium. You can download a free Rick Steves **audio tour** of St. Mark's; see page 7.

Visiting the Basilica: St. Mark's Basilica has 4,750 square yards of Byzantine mosaics, though many were designed by artists from the Italian Renaissance and later. Start outside in the square, far enough back to take in the whole facade. Then zero in on the details. The mosaic over the far left door shows the theft of ❶ **St. Mark's relics** that put Venice on the pilgrimage map.

The best and oldest mosaics are in the atrium (turn right as you enter and stop under the last dome). Facing the piazza, look domeward for the story of ❷ **Noah, the ark, and the flood** (two by two, the wicked being drowned, Noah sending out the dove, a happy rainbow, and a sacrifice of thanks).

Step inside the church and follow the one-way tourist route. Notice how the marble floor is richly decorated in mosaics. As in many Venetian buildings, because the best foundation pilings were made around the perimeter, the floor rolls. The church is laid out with four equal arms, topped with domes, radiating out from the center to form a ❸ **Greek cross** (+). Those familiar with Eastern Orthodox churches will find common elements in St. Mark's: a central floor plan, domes, mosaics, and iconic images of Mary and Christ as Pantocrator—ruler of all things.

Find the chandelier near the entrance doorway, and run your eyes up to the ❹ **Pentecost** mosaic in the dome above. In a golden heaven, the dove of the Holy Spirit shoots out a pinwheel of spiritual lasers, igniting tongues of fire on the heads of the 12 apostles below.

Shuffle under the central dome, and look up for the ❺ **Ascension** mosaic. Christ—having lived his miraculous life and having been crucified for man's sins—ascends into the starry sky on a rainbow.

Look around at the church's furniture: the ❻ **rood screen,** topped with 14 saints, separates the congregation from the high altar. The ❼ **pulpit** on the right was reserved for the doge, who led prayers and made important announcements. Mosaics told the story of Jesus, starting with his ancestors perched in the ❽ **Tree of Jesse** (in the north transept, to the left as you face the altar), and continuing through to the ❾ **Last Supper** (in the arch leading to the south transept), and culminating in the ❿ **Crucifixion** (in the west arch).

In the north transept, today's Venetians pray to a painted wooden icon of Mary and baby Jesus known as ⓫ **Nicopeia,** or "Our Lady of Victory." This Madonna has helped Venice persevere through plagues, wars, and crucial soccer games. When Mary answers a prayer, grateful Venetians leave offerings, like the old ⓬ **rifle** that hangs next to a Madonna-and-child on a pillar (as you approach the north transept).

In the south transept (to right of main altar), find the dim ⓭ **Discovery of Mark** mosaic high up on the west wall. This mosaic recreates the happy scene in 1094 when Mark's misplaced relics were found within a hollow column.

Additional Sights: The ⓮ **Treasury** (ask for the included and informative audioguide when you buy your ticket) and ⓯ **Golden Altarpiece** give you the best chance outside of Istanbul or Ravenna to see the glories of the Byzantine Empire. Venetian crusaders looted the Christian city of Constantinople and brought home piles of lavish loot (perhaps the lowest point in Christian history until the advent of TV evangelism). Much of this plunder is stored in the Treasury (Tesoro) of San Marco. As you view these treasures, remember that most were made in about A.D. 500, while Western Europe was stuck in the Dark Ages. Beneath the high altar lies the body of St. Mark ("Marce") and the Golden Altarpiece (Pala d'Oro), made of 250 blue-backed enamels with religious scenes, all set in a gold frame and studded with 15 hefty rubies, 300 emeralds, 1,500 pearls, and assorted sapphires, amethysts, and topaz (c. 1100).

In the ⓰ **San Marco Museum** (Museo di San Marco) upstairs you can see an up-close mosaic exhibition, a fine view of the church interior, a view of the square from the balcony with bronze horses, and (inside, in their own room) the original horses. These well-traveled horses, made during the days of Alexander the Great (fourth century B.C.), were taken to Rome by Nero, to Constantinople/Istanbul by Constantine, to Venice by crusaders, to Paris by Napoleon, back "home" to Venice when Napoleon fell, and finally indoors and out of the acidic air. The staircase up to the museum is in the atrium, near the basilica's main entrance, marked by a sign that says *Loggia dei Cavalli, Museo.*

▲▲▲**Doge's Palace (Palazzo Ducale)**—The seat of the Venetian government and home of its ruling duke, or doge, this was the most powerful half-acre in Europe for 400 years. The Doge's Palace was built to show off the power and wealth of the Republic. The doge lived with his family on the first floor, near the halls of power. From his once-lavish (now sparse) quarters, you'll follow the one-way tour through the public rooms of the top floor, finishing with the Bridge of Sighs and the prison. The place is wallpapered with masterpieces by Veronese and Tintoretto. Don't worry much about the great art. Enjoy the building.

You'll see the restored facades from the **courtyard.** Notice a grand staircase (with nearly naked Moses and Paul Newman at the top). Even the most powerful visitors climbed this to meet the doge. This was the beginning of an architectural power trip.

In the **Senate Hall,** the 120 senators met, debated, and passed laws. Tintoretto's large *Triumph of Venice* on the ceiling (central painting, best viewed from the top) shows the city in all its glory. Lady Venice is up in heaven with the Greek gods, while barbaric lesser nations swirl up to give her gifts and tribute.

The **Armory**—a dazzling display originally assembled to intimidate potential adversaries—shows remnants of the military might that the empire employed to keep the East-West trade lines open (and the local economy booming).

The giant **Hall of the Grand Council** (175 feet by 80 feet, capacity 2,600) is where the entire nobility met to elect the senate and doge. It took a room this size to contain the grandeur of the Most Serene Republic. Ringing the room are portraits of the first 76 doges (in chronological order). The one at the far end that's blacked out is the notorious Doge Marin Falier, who opposed the will of the Grand Council in 1355. He was tried for treason, beheaded, and airbrushed from history.

On the wall over the doge's throne is Tintoretto's monster-piece, *Paradise*, the largest oil painting in the world. Christ and Mary are surrounded by a heavenly host of 500 saints. The painting leaves you feeling that you get to heaven not by being a good Christian, but by being a good Venetian.

Cross the covered **Bridge of Sighs** over the canal to the **prisons.** Circle the cells. Notice the carvings made by prisoners—from olden days up until 1930—on some of the stone windowsills of the cells, especially in the far corner of the building.

Cross back over the Bridge of Sighs, pausing to look through the marble-trellised windows at all of the tourists.

Cost and Hours: €14 combo-ticket (€13 Nov-March) includes admission to the Correr Museum; from April through October the combo-ticket includes your choice of a third city-run museum. The palace is also covered by the €18 Museum Pass—see page 913. If the line is long at the Doge's Palace, buy your ticket or pass at the Correr Museum across the square; then you can go straight to the Doge's turnstile, skirting along to the right of the long ticket-buying line and entering at the "prepaid tickets" entrance. Open daily April-Oct 8:30-18:30, Nov-March 8:00-17:30, last entry one hour before closing, tel. 041-271-5911, possible to book online at www.museicivicivenezia.it at least 48 hours in advance. It's next to St. Mark's Basilica, just off St. Mark's Square. Vaporetto stops: San Marco or San Zaccaria.

Tours: The dry but informative **audioguide** costs €5 (€8/2 people, 1.5 hours, need ID or credit card for deposit). For a 1.25-hour live **guided tour,** consider the Secret Itineraries Tour, which takes you into palace rooms not otherwise open to the public (€18 includes Doge's Palace admission but not Correr Museum; €12 with combo-ticket or Museum Pass; 2-3 English-language tours each morning). Though the tour skips the palace's main hall, you're welcome to visit the hall afterward on your own. Reserve ahead for this tour in peak season—it can fill up as much as a month in advance. Book online at www.museiciviciveneziani.it or reserve by phone (tel. 848-082-000, from the US dial 011-39-041-4273-0892), or you can try just showing up at the info desk.

▲▲Correr Museum (Museo Correr)—This uncrowded museum gives you a good overview of Venetian history and art. The doge memorabilia, armor, banners, statues (by Canova), and paintings (by the Bellini family and others) re-create the festive days of the Venetian Republic. There are English descriptions and breathtaking views of St. Mark's Square throughout the museum.

Cost and Hours: €14 combo-ticket (€13 Nov-March) includes the Doge's Palace; from April through October the combo-ticket includes your choice of a third city-run museum. The combo-ticket always includes two other museums within the Correr: the National Archaeological Museum and the Monumental Rooms of Marciana National Library. The Correr is also covered by the €18 Museum Pass—see page 913. Open daily April-Oct 10:00-19:00, Nov-March 10:00-17:00, last entry one hour before closing, free and mandatory baggage check for bags bigger than a large purse, no photos, enter at far end of square directly opposite basilica, tel. 041-240-5211, www.museiciviciveneziani.it.

Avoid long lines at the crowded Doge's Palace by buying either of the museum passes listed above at the Correr Museum. For €12 you can see the Correr Museum and tour the Clock Tower on St. Mark's Square, but your ticket won't include the Doge's Palace. For more on reserving a Clock Tower tour, see page 914.

▲Campanile (Campanile di San Marco)—This dramatic bell tower replaced a shorter lighthouse, part of the original fortress that guarded the entry of the Grand Canal. The lighthouse crumbled into a pile of bricks in 1902, a thousand years after it was built. Today you'll see construction work being done to strengthen the base of the rebuilt tower. Ride the elevator 300 feet to the top of the bell tower for the best view in Venice (especially at sunset). For an ear-shattering experience, be on top when the bells ring. The golden archangel Gabriel at the top always faces into the wind. Lines are longest at midday; beat the crowds and enjoy the crisp morning air at 9:00 or the cool evening breeze at 18:00.

Cost and Hours: €8, daily Easter-June and Oct 9:00-19:00, July-Sept 9:00-21:00, Nov-Easter 9:30-15:45, closed from Christmas to mid-Jan, tel. 041-522-4064, www.basilicosan marco.it.

VENICE

La Fenice Opera House (Gran Teatro alla Fenice)—During Venice's glorious decline in the 18th century, this was one of seven opera houses in the city, and one of the most famous in Europe. For 200 years, great operas and famous divas debuted here, applauded by ladies and gentlemen in their finery. Then in 1996, an arson fire completely gutted the theater. But La Fenice ("The Phoenix") has risen from the ashes, thanks to an eight-year effort to rebuild the historic landmark according to photographic archives of the interior. To see the results at their most glorious, attend an evening **performance** (theater box office open daily 9:30-18:30, tel. 041-2424 answered daily 9:00-18:00, www.teatrolafenice.it).

You can also **tour the opera house** during the day. All you really see is the theater itself; there's no "backstage" tour of dressing rooms, or an opera museum. The auditorium, ringed with box seats, is impressive: pastel blue with sparkling gold filigree, muses depicted on the ceiling, and a starburst chandelier. It's also a bit saccharine and brings sadness to Venetians who remember the place before the fire. Other than a minor exhibit of opera scores and Maria Callas memorabilia, there's little to see from the world of opera. A dry 45-minute audioguide recounts two centuries of construction.

Cost and Hours: €8 tours, generally open daily 9:30-13:30, but can vary wildly, depending on the performance schedule—from being closed, open only an hour or two, or being open all day—so confirm in advance (call box office number listed above, schedule not posted on web). La Fenice is on Campo San Fantin, between St. Mark's Square and the Accademia Bridge. Nearest vaporetto stops: Santa Maria del Giglio and San Marco.

Behind St. Mark's Basilica
▲Bridge of Sighs—Connecting two wings of the Doge's Palace high over a canal, this enclosed bridge was recently restored. Travelers popularized this bridge in the Romantic 19th century. Supposedly, a condemned man would be led over this bridge on his way to the prison, take one last look at the glory of Venice, and sigh. Though overhyped, the Bridge of Sighs is undeniably tingle-worthy—especially after dark, when the crowds have dispersed and it's just you and floodlit Venice. A local legend says that lovers will be assured eternal love if they kiss on a gondola at sunset under the bridge.

The Bridge of Sighs is around the corner from the Doge's Palace: Walk toward the waterfront, turn left along the water, and look up the first canal on your left. You can walk across the bridge (from the inside) by visiting the Doge's Palace.

Church of San Zaccaria—This historic church is home to a sometimes-waterlogged crypt, a Bellini altarpiece, a Tintoretto painting, and the final resting place of St. Zachariah, the father of John the Baptist.

Cost and Hours: Free, €1 to enter crypt, €0.50 coin to light up Bellini's altarpiece, Mon-Sat 10:00-12:00 & 16:00-18:00, Sun 16:00-18:00 only, 2 canals behind St. Mark's Basilica.

Across the Lagoon from St. Mark's Square

▲**San Giorgio Maggiore**—This is the dreamy church-topped island you can see from the waterfront by St. Mark's Square. The striking church, designed by Palladio, features art by Tintoretto, a bell tower, and good views of Venice.

Cost and Hours: Free entry to church; May-Sept Mon-Sat 9:30-12:30 & 14:30-18:00, Sun 8:30-11:00 & 14:30-18:00; Oct-April until 16:30. The bell tower costs €3 and is accessible by elevator (runs from 30 minutes after the church opens until 30 minutes before the church closes).

Getting There: To reach the island from St. Mark's Square, take the five-minute ride on vaporetto #2 (€3, 6/hour, ticket valid for one hour; leaves from San Zaccaria-M.V.E. stop located east of Bridge of Sighs by equestrian statue, direction: Tronchetto). To get back to St. Mark's Square, take the #2 headed the opposite way (direction: San Marco).

Dorsoduro District

▲▲**Accademia (Galleria dell'Accademia)**—Venice's top art museum, packed with highlights of the Venetian Renaissance, features paintings by the Bellini family, Titian, Tintoretto, Veronese, Tiepolo, Giorgione, Canaletto, and Testosterone. It's just over the wooden Accademia Bridge from the San Marco action.

The Accademia is the greatest museum anywhere for Venetian Renaissance art and a good overview of painters whose works you'll see all over town. Venetian art is underrated and, I think, misunderstood. It's nowhere near as famous today as the work of the florescent Florentines, but—with historical slices of Venice, ravishing nudes, and very human Madonnas—it's livelier, more colorful, and simply more fun. The Venetian love of luxury shines through in this collection, which starts in the Middle Ages and runs to the 1700s. Look for grand canvases of colorful, spacious settings, peopled with happy locals in extravagant clothes having a great time.

Medieval highlights include elaborate altarpieces and golden-haloed Madonnas, all painted at a time when realism, depth of field, and emotion were considered beside the point. Medieval Venetians, with their close ties to the East, borrowed techniques such as gold-leafing, frontal poses, and "iconic" faces from the religious icons of Byzantium (modern-day Istanbul).

Accademia

C. POMPEA

↑ To Zattere

CALLE LARGA PISANI

CALLE PISTOR

RIO TERA ANTONIO FOSCARINI

HIGH RENAISSANCE
ROOM 10

BOOK-STORE

Not to scale

Courtyard

EARLY REN.
ROOMS 2-5

To Peggy Guggenheim Collection & La Salute
←

ELEGANT DECAY

ROOM 1

MEDIEVAL

C. NOVA
S. AGNESE

C. ROTA

ROOM 24

To Frari & Ca' Rezzonico
→

CALLE GAMBARA

STAIRS

TEMPORARY EXHIBITS

ENTRANCE (BELOW)

PIZZA ■

Campo de la Carità

WC

ACCADEMIA BRIDGE →

SHELL GAME- CROOKS & PICKPOCKETS

V *Accademia*

25 Meters

25 Yards

↓ To San Marco (15 min. walk)

Grand Canal

Among early masterpieces of the Renaissance are Mantegna's studly *St. George* and Giorgione's mysterious *The Tempest*. As the Renaissance reaches its heights, so do the paintings, such as Titian's magnificent *Presentation of the Virgin*. It's a religious scene, yes, but it's really just an excuse to display secular splendor (Titian was the most famous painter of his day—perhaps even more famous than Michelangelo). Veronese's sumptuous *Feast of the House of Levi* also has an ostensibly religious theme (in the middle, find Jesus eating his final meal)—but it's outdone by the luxury and optimism of Renaissance Venice. Life was a good thing and beauty was to be enjoyed. (Veronese was hauled before the Inquisition for painting such a bawdy Last Supper...so he fine-tuned the title). End your tour with Guardi's and Canaletto's painted "postcards" of the city—landscapes for visitors who lost their hearts to the romance of Venice.

Cost and Hours: €6.50, Mon 8:15-14:00, Tue-Sun 8:15-19:15, last entry 45 minutes before closing, no photos allowed. The dull audioguide costs €5 (€7/2 people). At Accademia Bridge, vaporetto: Accademia, tel. 041-522-2247, www.gallerieaccademia.org.

Avoiding Crowds: Expect long lines in the late morning, because they allow only 300 visitors in at a time; visit early or late to miss the crowds, or make a reservation at least a day in advance (€1 fee; calling 041-520-0345 is easier than reserving online at their clunky website; calls answered Mon-Fri 9:00-18:00, Sat 9:00-14:00, closed Sun).

Renovation: The museum is nearing the end of a years-long expansion, which will open up the ground floor to visitors. Some rooms may still be closed for construction, traffic may be rerouted, and some paintings may reside temporarily in other rooms. A few key works may not be on view at all.

▲▲Peggy Guggenheim Collection—The popular museum of far-out art, housed in the American heiress' former retirement palazzo, offers one of Europe's best reviews of the art of the first half of the 20th century. Stroll through styles represented by artists whom Peggy knew personally—Cubism (Picasso, Braque), Surrealism (Dalí, Ernst), Futurism (Boccioni), American Abstract Expressionism (Pollock), and a sprinkling of Klee, Calder, and Chagall.

Cost and Hours: €12, usually includes temporary exhibits, Wed-Mon 10:00-18:00, closed Tue, last entry 15 minutes before closing, audioguide-€7, 1- to 1.5-hour guided tour-€60, free and mandatory baggage check, no photos inside, a five-minute walk from the Accademia Bridge at Dorsoduro 704, vaporetto: Accademia or Salute, tel. 041-240-5411, www.guggenheim-venice.it.

▲La Salute Church (Santa Maria della Salute)—This impressive church with a crown-shaped dome was built and dedicated to the Virgin Mary by grateful survivors of the 1630 plague.

Cost and Hours: Free entry to church, daily 9:00-12:00 & 15:00-17:30. Sacristy—€2, may have shorter hours than church. It's a 10-minute walk from the Accademia Bridge; the Salute vaporetto stop is at its doorstep, tel. 041-241-1018, www.seminariovenezia.it.

▲Ca' Rezzonico (Museum of 18th-Century Venice)—This grand Grand Canal palazzo offers the best look in town at the life of Venice's rich and famous in the 1700s. Wander under ceilings by Tiepolo, among furnishings from that most decadent century, enjoying views of the canal and paintings by Guardi, Canaletto, and Longhi.

Cost and Hours: €8, covered by Museum Pass—see page 913; April-Oct Wed-Mon 10:00-18:00, Nov-March Wed-Mon 10:00-17:00; closed Tue year-round; last entry one hour before closing, 1.5-hour audioguide-€4 (€6/2 people), free and mandatory baggage check, at Ca' Rezzonico vaporetto stop, tel. 041-241-0100, www.museiciviciveneziani.it.

VENICE

▲**Punta della Dogana**—This museum of contemporary art makes the Dorsoduro a major destination for art-lovers. Housed in the former Customs House at the end of the Grand Canal, it features cutting-edge 21st-century art in spacious rooms. This isn't Picasso and Matisse, or even Pollock and Warhol—those guys are ancient history. But if you're into the likes of Jeff Koons, Cy Twombly, Rachel Whiteread, and a host of newer artists, the museum is world-class. The displays change completely about every year, drawn from the museum's large collection. In fact, the art spreads over two locations—the triangular Customs House and Palazzo Grassi.

Cost and Hours: €15 for one locale, €20 for both; Wed-Mon 10:00-19:00, closed Tue, last entry one hour before closing; audio-guide-€5 (€8/2 people), small café; in Italy call 199-139-139, otherwise use tel. 041-523-0313; www.palazzograssi.it. Punta della Dogana is near La Salute Church (Dogana *traghetto* or vaporetto: Salute). Palazzo Grassi is a bit upstream, on the east side of the Grand Canal (vaporetto: San Samuele).

Santa Croce District

▲▲▲**Rialto Bridge**—One of the world's most famous bridges, this distinctive and dramatic stone structure crosses the Grand Canal with a single confident span. The arcades along the top of the bridge help reinforce the structure...and offer some enjoyable shopping diversions, as does the **market** east of the bridge (souvenir stalls open daily, produce market closed Sun-Mon, fish market closed Sun).

▲**Ca' Pesaro International Gallery of Modern Art**—This museum features 19th- and early 20th-century art in a 17th-century canalside palazzo. The collection is strongest on Italian (especially Venetian) artists, but also presents a broad array of other well-known artists. The highlights are in one large room: Klimt's beautiful/creepy *Judith II*, with eagle-talon fingers; Kandinsky's *White Zig Zags* (plus other recognizable shapes); the colorful *Nude in the Mirror* by Bonnard that flattens the 3-D scene into a 2-D pattern of rectangles; and Chagall's surprisingly realistic portrait of his hometown rabbi, *The Rabbi of Vitebsk*. The adjoining Room VII features small-scale works by Matisse, Max Ernst, Mark Tobey, and a Calder mobile. Admission also includes an Oriental Art wing.

Cost and Hours: €8, covered by Museum Pass—see page 913, Tue-Sun 10:00-18:00, closed Mon, last entry one hour before closing, 2-minute walk from San Stae vaporetto stop, tel. 041-524-0662, www.museicivicieneziani.it.

Palazzo Mocenigo Costume Museum—The Museo di Palazzo Mocenigo offers a walk through six rooms of a fine 17th-century mansion with period furnishings, family portraits, ceilings painted (c. 1790) with family triumphs (the Mocenigos produced seven doges), Murano glass chandeliers in situ, and a paltry collection of costumes with sparse descriptions.

Cost and Hours: €5, covered by Museum Pass—see page 913, Tue-Sun 10:00-17:00, closed Mon, last entry one hour before closing, a block in from San Stae vaporetto stop, tel. 041-721-798, www.museiciviciveneziani.it.

San Polo District

▲▲**Frari Church (Basilica di Santa Maria Gloriosa dei Frari)**—My favorite art experience in Venice is seeing art in the setting for which it was designed—as it is at the Frari Church. The Franciscan "Church of the Brothers" and the art that decorates it are warmed by the spirit of St. Francis. It features the work of three great Renaissance masters: Donatello, Giovanni Bellini, and Titian—each showing worshippers the glory of God in human terms.

In **Donatello's wood statue of St. John the Baptist** (just to the right of the high altar), the prophet of the desert—dressed in animal skins and nearly starving from his diet of bugs 'n' honey—announces the coming of the Messiah. Donatello was a Florentine working at the dawn of the Renaissance.

Bellini's *Madonna and Child with Saints and Angels* painting (in the sacristy farther to the right) came later, done by a Venetian in a more Venetian style—soft focus without Donatello's harsh realism. While Renaissance humanism demanded Madonnas and saints that were accessible and human, Bellini places them in a physical setting so beautiful that it creates its own mood of serene holiness. The genius of Bellini, perhaps the greatest Venetian painter, is obvious in the pristine clarity, rich colors (notice Mary's clothing), believable depth, and reassuring calm of this three-paneled altarpiece.

Finally, glowing red and gold like a stained-glass window over the high altar, **Titian's** *The Assumption of the Virgin* sets the tone of exuberant beauty found in the otherwise sparse church. Titian the Venetian—a student of Bellini—painted steadily for 60 years... you'll see a lot of his art. As stunned apostles look up past the swirl of arms and legs, the complex composition of this painting draws you right to the radiant face of the once-dying, now-triumphant Mary as she joins God in heaven.

Feel comfortable to discreetly freeload off passing tours. For many, these three pieces of art make a visit to the Accademia Gallery unnecessary (or they may whet your appetite for more). Before leaving, check out the Neoclassical pyramid-shaped Canova monument and (opposite that) the grandiose tomb of Titian.

VENICE

Compare the carved marble *Assumption* behind Titian's tombstone portrait with the painted original above the high altar.

Cost and Hours: €3, Mon-Sat 9:00-18:00, Sun 13:00-18:00, last entry 30 minutes before closing, no visits during services, modest dress recommended. On Campo dei Frari, near San Tomà vaporetto and *traghetto* stops.

Audioguides: You can rent an **audioguide** for €2 (€3/2 people). Or download a free Rick Steves **audio tour** of the Frari Church; see page 7.

Concerts: The church occasionally hosts evening concerts (€20, buy ticket at church, no concerts in winter). For concert details, look for fliers, check www.basilicadeifrari.it, or call the church at 041-272-8611.

▲▲**Scuola San Rocco**—Sometimes called "Tintoretto's Sistine Chapel," this lavish meeting hall (next to the Frari Church) has some 50 large, colorful Tintoretto paintings plastered to the walls and ceilings. The best paintings are upstairs, especially the *Crucifixion* in the smaller room. View the neck-breaking splendor with one of the mirrors available at the entrance.

Cost and Hours: €7, audioguide-€1, daily 9:30-17:30, last entry 30 minutes before closing, tel. 041-523-4864, www.scuola grandesanrocco.it.

Church of San Polo—This nearby church, which pales in comparison to the two sights just listed, is only worth a visit for art-lovers. One of Venice's oldest churches (from the ninth century), San Polo features works by Tintoretto, Veronese, and Tiepolo and son.

Cost and Hours: €3, Mon-Sat 10:00-17:00, closed Sun, last entry 15 minutes before closing.

Cannaregio District

Jewish Ghetto—Tucked away in the Cannaregio District is the ghetto where Venice's Jewish population once lived segregated from their non-Jewish neighbors. While today's Jewish population is dwindling, the neighborhood still has centuries of history, not to mention Jewish-themed sights and eateries.

In medieval times, Jews were grudgingly allowed to do business in Venice, but they weren't permitted to live there until 1385 (subject to strict laws and special taxes). Anti-Semitic forces tried to oust them from the city, but in 1516, the doge compromised by restricting Jews to a special (undesirable) neighborhood. It was located on an easy-to-isolate island near the former foundry (*geto*)—in time the word "ghetto" caught on across Europe as a term for any segregated neighborhood.

The population swelled with immigrants from elsewhere in Europe, reaching 5,000 in the 1600s, the Golden Age of Venice's

Jews. Restricted within their tiny neighborhood (the Gheto Novo, or "New Ghetto"), they expanded upward, building six-story "skyscrapers" that still stand today. The community's five synagogues were built atop the high-rise tenements. (As space was very tight and you couldn't live above a house of worship, this was the most practical use of precious land.) Only two synagogues are still active. You can spot them (with their five windows) from the square, but to visit them you have to book a tour through the Jewish Museum.

This original ghetto becomes most interesting after touring the **Jewish Museum** (Museo Ebraico) at #2902b. Exhibits include silver menorahs, cloth covers for Torah scrolls, and a concise bilingual exhibit on the Venetian Jewish community up through 1797 (€3, June-Sept Sun-Fri 10:00-19:00, Oct-May Sun-Fri 10:00-17:30, closed Sat and Jewish holidays, bookstore, small café, Campo de Gheto Novo, tel. 041-715-359, www.museoebraico.it). You can see three of the ghetto's five **synagogues** with the 45-minute English tour (€8.50, tours run hourly on the half-hour June-Sept Sun-Fri 10:30-17:30, Oct-May Sun-Fri 10:30-16:30, no tours Sat and Jewish holidays). Group sizes are limited (the 11:30 and 12:30 tours are the most popular), so show up 20 minutes early to be sure you get in.

Getting There: From either the San Marcuola vaporetto stop or the train station, walk five minutes to the Ponte de Guglie bridge that crosses the Cannaregio Canal. About 50 yards north of the bridge, a small covered alleyway (Sotoportego del Gheto Novo) leads between the *farmacia* and the Gam-Gam Kosher Restaurant, through a newer Jewish section, across a bridge, and into the historic core of the ghetto at Campo de Gheto Novo.

Calatrava Bridge (a.k.a. Ponte della Costituzione)—This controversial bridge, officially called "Constitution Bridge," is just upstream and around the bend from the train station. Only the fourth bridge to cross the Grand Canal, it carries foot traffic between the train station and Piazzale Roma. A modern structure of glass, steel, and stone, the bridge finally opened in 2008 after delays, cost overruns, and questions about its stability.

The bridge was designed by Spanish architect Santiago Calatrava, whose other projects include a museum in his hometown of Valencia, Spain; the twisting torso skyscraper in Malmö, Sweden; and the Olympic Sports complex in Athens, Greece.

Interestingly, Calatrava's modern structure harkens back to the past, employing the same low-arch design of many older Venetian bridges. Pedestrians walk over similar shallow stair steps, and the bridge uses local Istrian stone.

Ca' d'Oro—This "House of Gold" palace, fronting the Grand Canal, is quintessential Venetian Gothic (Gothic seasoned with Byzantine and Islamic accents—see "Ca' d'Oro" on page 908). Inside, the permanent collection includes a few big names in

VENICE

Renaissance painting—Ghirlandaio, Signorelli, and Mantegna; a glimpse at a lush courtyard; and a grand view of the Grand Canal.

Cost and Hours: €6, slow and dry audioguide-€4, Mon 8:15-14:00, Tue-Sun 8:15-19:15, last entry 30 minutes before closing, free peek through hole in door of courtyard, vaporetto: Ca' d'Oro, on Calle Ca' d'Oro at #3932, tel. 041-520-0345, www.cadoro.org.

Castello District

▲Scuola Dalmata di San Giorgio—This little-visited "school" (which means "meeting place") features an exquisite wood-paneled chapel decorated with the world's best collection of paintings by Vittorio Carpaccio (1465-1526).

The Scuola, a reminder that cosmopolitan Venice was once Europe's melting-pot, was one of a hundred such community centers for various ethnic, religious, and economic groups, supported by the government partly to keep an eye on foreigners. It was here that the Dalmatians (from the southern coast of present-day Croatia) worshipped in their own way, held neighborhood meetings, and preserved their culture.

Cost and Hours: €4, Mon 14:45-18:00, Tue-Sat 9:15-13:00 & 14:45-18:00, Sun 9:15-13:00, midway between St. Mark's Square and the Arsenale, on Calle dei Furlani at #3259a, tel. 041-522-8828.

Santa Elena—For a pleasant peek into a completely non-touristy, residential side of Venice, walk or catch vaporetto #1 from St. Mark's Square to the neighborhood of Santa Elena (at the fish's tail). This 100-year-old suburb lives as if there were no tourism. You'll find a kid-friendly park, a few lazy restaurants, and beautiful sunsets over San Marco.

La Biennale—Every odd year (including 2013), Venice hosts a world's fair of contemporary art in buildings and pavilions scattered over the Giardini park and the Arsenale. The festival is an excuse for temporary art exhibitions, concerts, and other cultural events around the city (roughly Feb-Nov, take vaporetto #1 or #2 to Giardini-Biennale stop, www.labiennale.org).

Experiences in Venice

Gondola Rides

Gondolas cost lots more after 19:00 but are also more romantic and relaxing under the moon. A rip-off for some, this is a traditional must for romantics. Gondoliers charge €80 for a 40-minute ride during the day; €100 from 19:00 on. These prices are standard, and listed in the TI's *Shows & Events* brochure, as well as on the gondoliers' association website (www.gondolavenezia.it). To add *musica* (a singer and an accordionist), you'll need to arrange it in advance, and it'll cost an additional €110 before 19:00, or €130 after 19:00. You can divide the cost—and the romance—among up to six people per boat, but you'll need to save two seats for the musicians if you choose to be serenaded. Only two seats (the ones in back) are next to each other.

Because you might get a narration plus conversation with your gondolier, talk with several and choose one you like who speaks English well. To avoid misunderstandings, establish the price and duration of the trip before boarding, enjoy your ride, and pay only when you're finished. I don't recommend haggling, but if you want to try, you might find softer prices during the day. Most gondoliers honor the official prices, but a few might try to scam you out of some extra euros.

Pick a gondola station in an area you'd enjoy paddling in. I often go to the Bacino Orseolo gondoliers just off the northwest corner of St. Mark's Square (go through Sotoportego de l'Arco Celeste), but there are stations all over the more frequented parts of Venice. On cold, dark winter evenings, you will have trouble finding a gondolier; try at Hotel Bauer, on Campo San Moisè, or ask your hotelier for help.

If you've hired musicians and want to hear a Venetian song *(un canto Veneziano)*, try requesting *"Venezia La Luna e Tu."* Asking to hear *"O Sole Mio"* (which comes from Naples) is like asking a lounge singer in Cleveland to sing "The Eyes of Texas."

Glide through nighttime Venice with your head on someone's shoulder. Follow the moon as it sails past otherwise unseen buildings. Silhouettes gaze down from bridges while window glitter spills onto the black water. You're anonymous in the city of masks, as the rhythmic thrust of your striped-shirted gondolier turns old crows into songbirds. This is extremely relaxing (and, I think, worth the extra cost to experience at night). Women, beware... while gondoliers can be extremely charming, local women say that anyone who falls for one of these Romeos "has slices of ham over her eyes."

For cheap gondola thrills during the day, stick to the €0.50 one-minute ferry ride on a Grand Canal *traghetto*. At night, *vaporetti* are nearly empty, and it's a great time to cruise the Grand Canal on the slow boat #1. Or hang out on a bridge along the gondola route and wave at romantics.

Nightlife in Venice

You must experience Venice after dark. The city is quiet at night, as tour groups stay in the cheaper hotels of Mestre on the mainland, and the masses of day-trippers return to their beach resorts and cruise ships. Gondolas cost more, but are worth the extra expense (described earlier). At night, *vaporetti* are nearly empty, and it's a great time to cruise the Grand Canal on the slow boat #1.

Venice has a busy schedule of events, festivals, and entertainment. Check at the TI for listings, and keep an eye out for publications such as *Shows & Events* (bilingual, available at some hotels and online at www.turismovenezia.it, click on "Venezia").

Baroque Concerts—Venice is a city of the powdered-wig Baroque era. For about €25 (prices vary), you can take your pick of traditional Vivaldi concerts in churches throughout town. Homegrown Vivaldi is as ubiquitous here as Strauss is in Vienna and Mozart is in Salzburg. In fact, you'll find frilly young Vivaldis hawking concert tickets on many corners. The TI has a list of this week's Baroque concerts. Most shows start at 20:30 and generally last 1.5 hours. You'll see posters in hotels all over town (hotels sell tickets at face value). A one-stop shop for concerts is the Vivaldi Store, at the east end of Rialto Bridge (on Salizada del Fontego dei Tedeschi at #5537, tel. 041-522-1343). Tickets for Baroque concerts in Venice can usually be bought the same day as the concert, so don't bother with websites that sell tickets with a surcharge.

Consider the venue carefully. The general rule of thumb: Musicians in wigs and tights offer better spectacle; musicians in black-and-white suits are better performers. **San Vidal Church** (at the north end of Accademia Bridge) and the **Interpreti Veneziani orchestra** (which often plays there) are reliably top-notch (tel. 041-277-0561, www.interpretiveneziani.com). For the latest on church concerts, check any TI or visit www.turismovenezia.it. If you're attending a concert at **Scuola San Rocco** (tickets €15-30), arrive 30 minutes early to enjoy the art (which you'd have to pay €7 to see during the day).

Other Performances—Venice's most famous theaters are **La Fenice** (grand old opera house, box office tel. 041-2424, see page 922), **Teatro Goldoni** (mostly Italian live theater), and **Teatro della Fondamenta Nuove** (theater, music, and dance).

Musica a Palazzo is a unique evening of opera at the Doge's Palace. You'll spend about 45 minutes in three sumptuous rooms as eight musicians (generally four instruments and four singers) perform. With these kinds of surroundings, under Tiepolo frescoes, you'll be glad you dressed up. As there are only 70 seats, you must book by phone or online in advance. Opera-lovers find this to be a wonderful evening (€50, nightly shows at 20:30, Palazzo Barbarigo-Minotto, Fondamenta Duodo o Barbarigo—on the Grand Canal next to the Santa Maria del Giglio vaporetto stop, mobile 340-971-7272, www.musicapalazzo.com).

Venezia is advertised as "the show that tells the great story of Venice" and "simply the best show in town." I found the performance to be slow-moving and a bit cheesy, and the venue to be disappointing (€39, nightly May-Oct at 20:00, Nov-April at 19:00; 80 minutes, Teatro San Gallo, just off St. Mark's Square on Campo San Gallo, tel. 041-241-2002, www.teatrosangallo.net).

St. Mark's Square—For tourists, St. Mark's Square is the high-light, with lantern light and live music echoing from the cafés. Just being here after dark is a thrill, as **dueling café orchestras** entertain. Every night, enthusiastic musicians play the same songs, creating the same irresistible magic. Hang out for free behind the tables (allowing you to move easily on to the next orchestra when the musicians take a break), or spring for a seat and enjoy a fun and gorgeously set concert. If you sit a while, it can be €12-20 well spent (for a drink and the cover charge for music). Dancing on the square is free (and encouraged). Streetlamp halos, live music, floodlit history, and a ceiling of stars make St. Mark's magic at midnight. You're not a tourist, you're a living part of a soft Venetian night...an alley cat with money. In the misty light, the moon has a golden hue. Shine with the old lanterns on the gondola piers, where the sloppy lagoon splashes at the Doge's Palace...reminiscing.

Sleeping in Venice

For hassle-free efficiency and the sheer magic of being close to the action, I favor hotels that are handy to sightseeing activities. I've listed rooms in four neighborhoods: St. Mark's bustle, the Rialto action, the quiet Dorsoduro area behind the Accademia art museum, and near the train station (handy for train travelers, but far from the action). I also mention several apartment rentals, big fancy hotels, cheap dorms, and places on the mainland.

Outside of holidays and weekends, it's possible to visit Venice without booking ahead, but it's smart, simple, and less stressful to have a reservation in place. Book a room as soon as you know when you'll be in town. Contact the hotel directly, not through any tour-ist information room-finding service (they can't give opinions on quality).

Note that hotel websites are particularly valuable for Venice, because they often include detailed directions that can help you (and your bags) get to your rooms with a minimum of wrong turns in this navigationally challenging city.

Over the past decade, Venice has seen the opening of several big new hotels, countless little boutique hotels, and the conversion of many private homes to short-term rental apartments. This glut of hotels means that demand is soft and, therefore, so are prices. Most hotels have tossed straight pricing out the window. Many hoteliers are happy to make a deal. Email several hotels to ask for their best price, then compare and make your choice.

VENICE

Sleep Code

(€1 = about $1.40, country code: 39)
S = Single, **D** = Double/Twin, **T** = Triple, **Q** = Quad, **b** = bathroom, **s** = shower only. Unless otherwise noted, credit cards are accepted, breakfast is included, and English is generally spoken.

To help you easily sort through these listings, I've divided the accommodations into three categories based on the price for a standard double room with bath:

$$$ Higher Priced—Most rooms €180 or more.
$$ Moderately Priced—Most rooms between €130-180.
$ Lower Priced—Most rooms €130 or less.

Prices can change without notice; verify the hotel's current rates online or by email. For other updates, see www.ricksteves.com/update.

Prices listed are for one-night stays in peak season (April, May, June, Sept, and Oct), include breakfast, and assume you're booking directly (not through a TI or online hotel-booking engine). Prices can climb even higher during a few festivals. Almost all places drop prices from November through March (except during Carnevale—Feb 2-12 in 2013—and Christmas) and in July and August. A €180 double can cost €80-90 in winter. Off-season, don't pay the rates I list.

Many hotels in Venice list rooms on www.venere.com, especially for last-minute vacancies (two to three weeks before the date).

Near St. Mark's Square

To get here from the train station or Piazzale Roma bus station, ride the vaporetto to San Zaccaria—either the slow #1 or the fast #2 (from the Tronchetto parking lot, it's #2 only). Consider using your ride to follow my tour of the Grand Canal (see page 903); to make sure you arrive via the Grand Canal, confirm that your boat goes "*via Rialto*."

Nearby Laundries: Lavanderia Gabriella offers full service a few streets north of St. Mark's Square (€15/load includes wash, dry, and fold; drop off Mon-Fri 8:00-12:30, closed Sat-Sun; pick up 2 hours later or next working day; with your back to the door of San Zulian Church, go over Ponte dei Ferali, take first right down Calle dei Armeni, then first left on Rio Terà de le Colonne to #985; tel. 041-522-1758, Elisabetta).

Effe Erre, a modern self-service *lavanderia*, is near recommended Hotel al Piave on Ruga Giuffa at #4826 (daily 6:30-23:00, €14/load, mobile 349-058-3881, Massimo).

East of St. Mark's Square

Located near the Bridge of Sighs, just off the Riva degli Schiavoni waterfront promenade, these places rub drainpipes with Venice's most palatial five-star hotels.

$$$ Hotel Campiello, lacy and bright, was once part of a 19th-century convent. Ideally located 50 yards off the waterfront, on a tiny square, its 16 rooms offer a tranquil, friendly refuge for travelers who appreciate comfort and professional service (Sb-€130, Db-€180, discount with cash and this book if you reserve direct and pay on arrival, air-con, elevator, free Wi-Fi; from the San Zaccaria vaporetto stop, take Calle del Vin, between pink Hotel Danieli and Hotel Savoia e Jolanda, to Castello 4647; tel. 041-520-5764, fax 041-520-5798, www.hcampiello.it, campiello@hcampiello.it; family-run for four generations, currently by Thomas, Monica, Nicoletta, and Marco). They also rent three modern family apartments, under rustic timbers just steps away (up to €380/night).

$$$ Hotel Fontana is a nice family-run place with 15 rooms near a school, two bridges behind St. Mark's Square. Their annex across the street has much lower ceilings and slightly lower prices (Sb-€120, Db-€180, family rooms, cash discount, quieter rooms on garden side, 2 rooms have terraces for €20 extra, air-con, elevator, free Internet access, pay Wi-Fi by reception, on Campo San Provolo at Castello 4701, tel. 041-522-0579, fax 041-523-1040, www.hotelfontana.it, info@hotelfontana.it, cousins Diego and Gabriele). From the San Zaccaria vaporetto dock, take Calle de le Rasse—to the left of pink Hotel Danieli—then turn right at the end, and continue to the first square.

$$ Locanda al Leon rents 14 decent, reasonably priced rooms just off Campo Santi Filippo e Giacomo (Db-€145-155, Tb-€180, Qb-€230, ask for Rick Steves price and show this book if paying cash, air-con, free Internet access and Wi-Fi, Campo Santi Filippo e Giacomo, Castello 4270, tel. 041-277-0393, fax 041-521-0348, www.hotelalleon.com, leon@hotelalleon.com, Giuliano and Marcella). From the San Zaccaria vaporetto stop, take Calle dei Albanesi (two streets left of pink Hotel Danieli) to its far end.

$$ Hotel la Residenza is a grand old palace facing a peaceful square. It has 15 great rooms on three levels and a huge, luxurious lounge with a piano. This is a great value for romantics—you'll feel like you're in the Doge's Palace after hours. Hang out in the living room and you become royalty (Sb-€100, Db-€165-200, air-con, free Wi-Fi, on Campo Bandiera e Moro at Castello 3608, tel. 041-528-5315, fax 041-523-8859, www.veniceraresidenza.com, info @veniceraresidenza.com, Giovanni). From the Bridge of Sighs,

VENICE

Hotels & Restaurants near St. Mark's Square

Hotels

1. Hotel Campiello
2. Hotel Fontana
3. Locanda al Leon
4. To Hotel la Residenza
5. Albergo Doni
6. Hotel al Piave
7. Casa Cosmo
8. Locanda Silva
9. Locanda Casa Querini
10. Hotel Riva
11. Corte Campana B&B
12. Hotel Flora
13. Hotel Bel Sito
14. Hotel Mercurio
15. Hotel Casa Verardo
16. Hotel Donà Palace
17. Hotel all'Angelo
18. Hotel al Ponte dei Sosperi
19. Hotel Ca' Dei Conti

Eateries & Services

20 Ristorante alla Conchiglia
21 Trattoria da Giorgio ai Greci
22 Ristorante Antica Sacrestia
23 Birreria Forst Café
24 Bar Verde
25 Ristorante alla Basilica

26 Rizzo Café
27 Gran Caffè Lavena (Gelato)
28 Todaro Gelateria
29 Coop Supermarket
30 Lavanderia Gabriella
31 Lavanderia Effe Erre

walk east along Riva degli Schiavoni, cross three bridges, and take the first left up Calle del Dose to Campo Bandiera e Moro.

$ Albergo Doni is dark and quiet—a bit of a time-warp—with 13 well-worn, once-classy rooms up a creaky stairway. It's run by a likable smart aleck named Gina, her niece Tessa, and her nephew, an Italian stallion named Nikos (D-€95, Db-€120, T-€125, Tb-€160, reserve with credit card but pay in cash, ceiling fans, three Db rooms have air-con, free Wi-Fi by reception, avoid their overflow apartment, on Fondamenta del Vin at Castello 4656, tel. & fax 041-522-4267, www.albergodoni.it, albergodoni @hotmail.it). From the San Zaccaria vaporetto stop, cross one bridge to the right and take the first left (marked Calle del Vin), then turn left at the little square named Ramo del Vin, jog left, and find the hotel ahead on Fondamenta del Vin.

North of St. Mark's Square

$$ Hotel al Piave, with 28 fine, air-conditioned rooms above a bright and classy lobby, is fresh, modern, and comfortable. You'll enjoy the neighborhood and always get a cheery welcome (Db-€150, Tb-€200; family suites-€280 for 4, €300 for 5, or €320 for 6; cash discount, free Wi-Fi, on Ruga Giuffa at Castello 4838/40, tel. 041-528-5174, fax 041-523-8512, www.hotelalpiave .com, info@hotelalpiave.com, Mirella, Paolo, Ilaria, and Federico speak English). From the San Zaccaria vaporetto stop, take the street to the right of the Bridge of Sighs to Campo Santi Filippo e Giacomo, and continue on Calle drio la Chiesa. Cross the bridge, continue straight, then turn left onto Ruga Giuffa until you find the hotel on your left at #4838.

$$ Casa Cosmo is a humble little five-room place run by Davide, Caterina, and their parents. While it comes with minimal services and no public spaces (aside from a tiny rooftop terrace), it's air-conditioned, very central, somewhat inexpensive, and quiet (Db-€140-150, Tb-€160-170, Qb-€180-190, ask about discount with this book if you reserve direct and pay cash, breakfast in your room—or €5/person less without breakfast, free Wi-Fi, lots of stairs, on Calle de Mezo at San Marco 4976, tel. 041-296-0710, fax 041-862-3439, www.casacosmo.com, info@casacosmo.com). From St. Mark's Square, go under the Clock Tower and continue on the high-rent retail street Mercerie, after crossing a canal on Ponte dei Bareteri turn right, then immediately left onto tiny Calle de Mezo to #4976.

$$ Locanda Silva is a big, basic, beautifully located hotel with a functional style, renting 23 decent old-school rooms (S-€70, Sb-€80, D-€90-100, Db-€135, Tb-€160, Qb-€180, ask about Rick Steves discount, 10 percent off if you stay at least 2 nights, closed Jan, air-con, pay Wi-Fi, on Fondamenta del Remedio at Castello 4423, tel. 041-522-7643, fax 041-528-6817, www.locanda silva.it, info@locandasilva.it, Sandra and Massimo). From St. Mark's Square, go around the left side of the basilica, turn left by the Studium bookstore, take the second right down Calle del Remedio, then turn left at the canal on Fondamenta del Remedio.

$$ Locanda Casa Querini rents six bright, high-ceilinged rooms on a quiet square tucked away behind St. Mark's. You can enjoy your breakfast or a sunny picnic/happy hour sitting at their tables right on the sleepy little square (Db-€150, third person-€20-25, one cheaper small double, ask for cash discount, air-con, pay Wi-Fi, halfway between San Zaccaria vaporetto stop and Campo Santa Maria Formosa at Castello 4388 on Campo San Zaninovo/Giovanni Novo, tel. 041-241-1294, fax 041-523-6188, www.locandaquerini.com, casaquerini@hotmail.com, Patrizia and Silvia). From the San Zaccaria vaporetto stop, take the street to the right of the Bridge of Sighs to Campo Santi Filippo e Giacomo, continue on Calle drio la Chiesa, take the second left, and curl around to the left into the little square, Campo San Zaninovo/Giovanni Novo.

$ Hotel Riva, with gleaming marble hallways, big exposed beams, fine antique furnishings, and lots of stairs, is romantically situated on a canal along the gondola serenade route. You could actually dunk your breakfast rolls in the canal (but don't). Ten of the 30 rooms come with air-conditioning for no extra charge—request one when you reserve. Or, if you prefer a view and lots of light but no air-conditioning, you can ask Sandro to hold a corner *(angolo)* room for you (Sb-€90, D-€100, Db-€120-140, Tb-€170-190, higher prices are for corner rooms, reserve with credit card but pay with cash only, on Ponte de l'Anzolo at Castello 5310, tel. 041-522-7034, fax 041-528-5551, www.hotelriva.it, info@hotelriva.it, Daniella). Facing St. Mark's Basilica, walk behind it on the left along Calle de la Canonica, take the first left (at blue *Pauly & C* mosaic in street), continue straight, go over the bridge, and angle right to the hotel at Ponte de l'Anzolo.

$ Corte Campana B&B, run by enthusiastic and helpful Riccardo, rents three quiet and characteristic rooms just behind St. Mark's Square. One room has a private bath down the hall (Db-€125, Qb-€190, prices are soft, cash only, 2-night minimum, at least €10/night less for stays of 4 nights, air-con, free Internet access, pay Wi-Fi, on Calle del Remedio at Castello 4410, 4th floor, tel. & fax 041-523-3603, mobile 389-272-6500, www.corte campana.com, info@cortecampana.com). Print out complete directions, including photos of all the street signs, from Riccardo's website.

West of St. Mark's Square

$$$ Hotel Flora sits buried in a sea of fancy designer boutiques and elegant hotels almost on the Grand Canal. It's formal, with uniformed staff and grand public spaces, yet the 43 rooms have a homey warmth and the garden oasis is a sanctuary for foot-weary guests (generally Db-€260, check website for special discounts or email Sr. Romanelli for Rick Steves discount off standard prices, air-con, elevator, free Wi-Fi and Internet access, San Marco 2283a, tel. 041-520-5844, fax 041-522-8217, www.hotelflora.it, info@hotelflora.it). It's at the end of Calle dei Bergamaschi, one of several skinny lanes just off Calle Larga XXII Marzo.

$$$ Hotel Bel Sito offers pleasing yet well-worn Old World character, 34 rooms, generous public spaces, a peaceful courtyard, and a picturesque location—facing a church on a small square between St. Mark's Square and the Accademia (Sb-€110, Db-€185, air-con, free Wi-Fi, elevator; catch vaporetto #1 to Santa Maria del Giglio stop, take street inland to square, hotel is at far end to your right on Campo Santa Maria Zobenigo/del Giglio at San Marco 2517; tel. 041-522-3365, fax 041-520-4083, www.hotelbelsito venezia.it, info@hotelbelsito.info, manager Rossella).

$$ Hotel Mercurio offers 25 peaceful, comfortable, and recently renovated rooms near La Fenice Opera House. Some rooms offer canal views (Sb-€130, Db-€170, Tb-€200, Qb-€230-250, €10 less with cash, air-con, pay Wi-Fi, on Calle del Fruttariol at San Marco 1848, tel. 041-522-0947, fax 041-241-1079, www .hotelmercurio.com, info@hotelmercurio.com, Monica, Vittorio, and Natale). From the San Marco-Vallaresso vaporetto stop, follow Calle Vallaresso to Calle Frezzaria, turn right, and follow it over a bridge as it becomes Calle del Frutariol. The hotel is on the left just before La Fenice Opera House.

Near the Rialto Bridge

Vaporetto #2 brings you to the Rialto quickly from the train station, the Piazzale Roma bus station, and the parking-lot island of Tronchetto. You can also take the slower vaporetto #1 (but not from Tronchetto).

West of the Rialto Bridge

$ Pensione Guerrato, above the colorful Rialto produce market and just two minutes from the Rialto Bridge, is run by friendly, creative, and hardworking Roberto and Piero. Their 800-year-old building—with 24 spacious, air-conditioned, and charming rooms—is simple, airy, and wonderfully characteristic (D-€90, Db-€130, Tb-€150, Qb-€170, Quint/b-€185, check website for special discounts, ask about Rick Steves discount with this book and cash, free Wi-Fi, on Calle drio la Scimia at San Polo 240a, tel.

& fax 041-528-5927, www.pensioneguerrato.it, pensione.guerrato @gmail.com, Monica and Rosanna). From the train station, take vaporetto #1 to the Mercato Rialto stop (comes before the "Rialto" stop), exit the boat to your right, and follow the waterfront. Calle drio la Scimia (not simply Scimia, the block before), is on the left—you'll see the hotel sign. My tour groups book this place for 50 nights each year. Sorry. The Guerrato also rents family apartments in the old center (great for groups of 4-8) for around €55 per person.

East of the Rialto Bridge

$$$ Hotel al Ponte Antico is exquisite, professional, and small. With nine plush rooms, a velvety royal living/breakfast room, and its own dock for water taxi arrivals, it's perfect for a romantic anniversary. Because its wonderful terrace overlooks the Grand Canal, Rialto Bridge, and market action, its non-canal-view rooms may be a better value (Db-€310, superior Db-€390, deluxe canal-front Db-€470, air-con, free Wi-Fi and Internet access; 100 yards from Rialto Bridge, find Campo San Bartolomeo, exit square on the statue's back side, cross bridge, pass Coin department store on right, then turn left down the dark and empty Calle del Aseo to Cannaregio 5768; tel. 041-241-1944, fax 041-241-1828, www.al ponteantico.com, info@alponteantico.com).

$$ Locanda la Corte is perfumed with elegance without being snooty. Its 19 attractive, high-ceilinged, wood-beamed rooms—Venetian-style, done in earthy pastels—circle a small, quiet courtyard (Sb-€100, standard Db-€150, superior Db-€170, cash discount, ask about Rick Steves discount, suites and family rooms available, air-con, free Wi-Fi and Internet access, on Calle Bressana at Castello 6317, tel. 041-241-1300, fax 041-241-5982, www.locandalacorte.it, info@locandalacorte.it, Marco, Raffaela, and Tommy the cat). Take vaporetto #5.2 from the train station to Fondamente Nove, exit the boat to your left, follow the waterfront, and turn right after the second bridge to reach Santi Giovanni e Paolo. Facing the Rosa Salva bar, take the street to the left (Calle Bressana); the hotel is a short block away at #6317, before the bridge.

$ Casa Pisani Canal Hotel is a sweet little place renting five rooms (Db-€110-130, huge Db suite overlooking canal-€240, air-con, free Wi-Fi and Internet access, on Calle de le Erbe at Cannaregio 6105, tel. 041-724-1030, fax 041-724-1039, www .casapisanicanal.it, info@casapisanicanal.it, Tortorella family). It's close to Campo Santi Giovanni e Paolo, and reachable either from Fondamente Nove or Rialto; see their website for directions.

$ Alloggi Barbaria rents eight backpacker-type rooms on one floor around a bright but institutional-feeling common area.

VENICE

VENICE

Eateries & Nightlife

8 Trattoria da Bepi
9 Vini da Gigio
10 Trattoria Ca' d'Oro
11 Osteria al Bomba
12 Osteria "Alla Botte"

13 Osteria di Santa Marina
14 Rosticceria San Bartolomeo
15 Osteria al Portego
16 Osteria alle Testiere & Cip Ciap Pizza
17 Osteria al Mascaron

18 Peter Pan Kebabs
19 Cantina Do Mori
20 Bar all'Arco & Ostaria ai Storti
21 Cantina Do Spade
22 Pesce Pronto

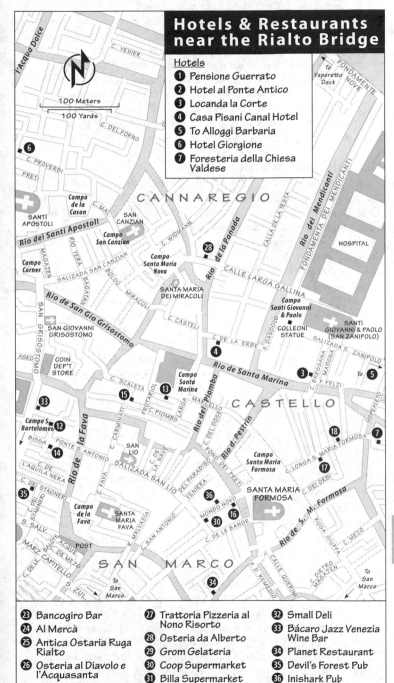

Hotels & Restaurants near the Rialto Bridge

Hotels
1. Pensione Guerrato
2. Hotel al Ponte Antico
3. Locanda la Corte
4. Casa Pisani Canal Hotel
5. To Alloggi Barbaria
6. Hotel Giorgione
7. Foresteria della Chiesa Valdese

---

23. Bancogiro Bar
24. Al Mercà
25. Antica Ostaria Ruga Rialto
26. Osteria al Diavolo e l'Acquasanta

27. Trattoria Pizzeria al Nono Risorto
28. Osteria da Alberto
29. Grom Gelateria
30. Coop Supermarket
31. Billa Supermarket

32. Small Deli
33. Bácaro Jazz Venezia Wine Bar
34. Planet Restaurant
35. Devil's Forest Pub
36. Inishark Pub

VENICE

Beyond Campo Santi Giovanni e Paolo, this Ikea-style place is a long walk from the action, in a residential neighborhood, and only a step above a youth hostel (Db-€90-100, third or fourth person-€25 each, pay cash for best price, family deals, limited breakfast, air-con, free Wi-Fi, on Calle de le Capucine at Castello 6573, tel. 041-522-2750, fax 041-277-5540, www.alloggibarbaria.it, info @alloggibarbaria.it, Giorgio and Fausto). Take vaporetto #5.2 from the train or bus stations to Ospedale stop, turn left as you get off the boat, then right down Calle de le Capucine.

Near the Accademia Bridge

When you step over the Accademia Bridge, the commotion of touristy Venice is replaced by a sleepy village laced with canals. This quiet area, next to the best painting gallery in town, is a 15-minute walk from the Rialto or St. Mark's Square.

The fast vaporetto #2 connects the Accademia Bridge with the train station (15 minutes), Piazzale Roma bus stop (20 minutes), Tronchetto parking lot (25 minutes), and St. Mark's Square (5 minutes). For hotels south of the Accademia Bridge, vaporetto #5.1 to Zattere (or the Alilaguna speedboat from the airport to Zattere) are good options.

South of the Accademia Bridge

$$$ **Pensione Accademia** fills the 17th-century Villa Maravege like a Bellini painting. Its 27 rooms are comfortable, elegant, and air-conditioned. You'll feel aristocratic gliding through its grand public spaces and lounging in its wistful, breezy gardens (Sb-€140, standard Db-€239, bigger "superior" Db-€289, Qb-€335, ask for discount when you book, pay Wi-Fi; on Fondamenta Bollani at Dorsoduro 1058; facing Accademia art museum, go right, cross the bridge, go right to where the small canal hits the big one; tel. 041-521-0188, fax 041-523-9152, www.pensioneaccademia.it, info @pensioneaccademia.it).

$$$ **Hotel Agli Alboretti** is a cozy, family-run, 23-room place in a quiet neighborhood a block behind the Accademia art museum. With red carpeting and wood-beamed ceilings, it feels classy (Sb-€120, Db-€210, Tb-€240, Qb-€260, air-con, elevator, free Wi-Fi, 100 yards from the Accademia vaporetto stop on Rio Terà A. Foscarini at Dorsoduro 884, tel. 041-523-0058, fax 041-521-0158, www.aglialboretti.com, info@aglialboretti.com, Anna).

$$$ **Hotel Belle Arti** has a grand entry and a formal, stern staff. With the ambience of a modern American hotel, its 64 rooms feel out of place in musty Old World Venice (Sb-€150, Db-€240, Tb-€270, air-con, elevator, pay Wi-Fi in lobby; 100 yards behind Accademia art museum: facing museum, jog left, then right, down Rio Terà A. Foscarini to Dorsoduro 912a; tel. 041-522-

6230, fax 041-528-0043, www.hotelbellearti.com, info@hotelbelle arti.com).

$$ Pensione la Calcina, the home of English writer John Ruskin in 1876, maintains a 19th-century formality. It comes with all the three-star comforts in a professional yet intimate package. Its 32 rosy, perfumed rooms are squeaky clean, with nice wood furniture, hardwood floors, and a peaceful canalside setting facing Giudecca Island (Sb-€140, Sb with view-€150, Db-€150-240, Db with view-€290-310, Qb-€280, air-con, free Wi-Fi and Internet access, rooftop terrace, buffet breakfast outdoors on platform over lagoon, near Zattere vaporetto stop at south end of Rio de San Vio at Dorsoduro 780, tel. 041-520-6466, fax 041-522-7045, www .lacalcina.com, info@lacalcina.com). Guests get discounted meals at their La Piscina restaurant.

$$ Casa Rezzonico is a silent getaway far from the madding crowds. Its private garden terrace has perhaps the lushest grass in Italy, and its seven spacious, very Venetian rooms have garden/canal views (Sb-€130, Db-€160, Tb-€190, Qb-€220, ask for discount when you book, air-con, free Wi-Fi, on Fondamenta Gherardini at Dorsoduro 2813, tel. 041-277-0653, fax 041-277-5435, www.casarezzonico.it, info@casarezzonico.it). Take vaporetto #1 to Ca' Rezzonico, head up Calle del Traghetto, cross Campo San Barnaba to the canal, and continue on Fondamenta Gherardini to #2813.

$$ Hotel Galleria has nine tight, velvety rooms, most with views of the Grand Canal. Some rooms are quite narrow. It's run with a family feel by Luciano and Stefano (S-€85, D-€125, skinny Grand Canal view Db-€155, palatial Grand Canal view Db-€185, includes breakfast in room, ceiling fans, free Wi-Fi, 30 yards from Accademia art museum, next to recommended Foscarini pizzeria at Dorsoduro 878a, tel. 041-523-2489, fax 041-520-4172, www .hotelgalleria.it, info@hotelgalleria.it).

$$ Don Orione Religious Guest House is a big cultural center dedicated to the work of a local man who became a saint in modern times. Filling an old monastery, it feels institutional, like a modern retreat center—clean, peaceful, and strictly run, with 74 rooms. It's beautifully located, comfortable, and a fine value (Sb-€88, Db-€144, Tb-€187, Qb-€224, profits go to mission work in the developing world, groups welcome, air-con, elevator, pay Wi-Fi, on Rio Terà A. Foscarini, Dorsoduro 909a, tel. 041-522-4077, fax 041-528-6214, www.donorione-venezia.it, info@don orione-venezia.it). From the Zattere vaporetto stop, turn right, then turn left. It's just after the church at #909a.

$ Ca' San Trovaso rents seven simple rooms split between the main building and a nearby annex. The location is peaceful, on a small canal (Sb-€90, Db-€115, Db with bigger canal view and

VENICE

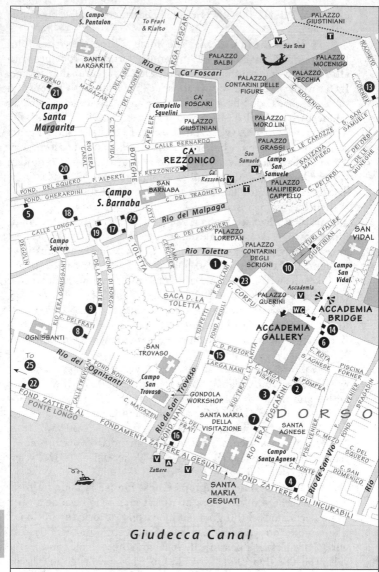

Giudecca Canal

Hotels

1. Pensione Accademia
2. Hotel Agli Alboretti
3. Hotel Belle Arti
4. Pensione la Calcina
5. Casa Rezzonico
6. Hotel Galleria
7. Don Orione Religious Guest House
8. Ca' San Trovaso
9. Casa di Sara
10. Foresteria Levi
11. Novecento Hotel
12. Locanda Art Déco
13. Albergo San Samuele

VENICE

Hotels & Restaurants near Accademia Bridge

Eateries & Nightlife

14 Ristorante/Pizzeria Accademia Foscarini

15 Enoteca Cantine del Vino Già Schiavi

16 Terrazza del Casin dei Nobili

17 Casin dei Nobili

18 Pane Vino e San Daniele

19 Enoteca e Trattoria la Bitta

20 Venice Jazz Club

21 Pizza al Volo

22 El Chioschetto alle Zattere

23 Piccolo Mondo el Souk

24 Grom Gelateria

25 To Billa Supermarket

26 Small Deli

air-con-€130, Tb-€145, pay cash for best prices, includes breakfast in your room, air-con in most rooms, free cable Internet, no common space except small roof terrace, off Fondamenta de le Romite at Dorsoduro 1350/51, tel. 041-277-1146, mobile 339-445-8821, fax 041-277-7190, www.casantrovaso.com, info@casantrovaso.com, Mark and his son Alessandro). From the Zattere vaporetto stop, exit left, and cross a bridge. Turn right at tiny Calle Trevisan, cross another bridge, cross the adjacent bridge, take an immediate right, and then the first left. Nearby, Mark's wife Cristina runs **Casa di Sara,** a brightly colored B&B with four quiet rooms, a tiny roof terrace, and the same prices (mobile 345-070-8547, www.casadisara.com, info@casadisara.com).

North of the Accademia Bridge

$$$ Foresteria Levi, run by a foundation that promotes research on Venetian music, offers 35 quiet, institutional yet comfortable and spacious rooms (Sb-€100, Db-€190, Tb-€210, Qb-€240, ask for Rick Steves discount—10-20 percent in high season, 20-50 percent in low season; fans, elevator, free Wi-Fi, laundry, on Calle Giustinian at San Marco 2893, tel. 041-786-711, fax 041-786-766, www.foresterialevi.it, info@foresterialevi.it). It's 80 yards from the Accademia Bridge on the St. Mark's side. Leaving the bridge (opposite the Accademia vaporetto stop), take an immediate left, cross the Ponte Giustinian bridge, and go down Calle Giustinian straight to the Fondazione Levi building. Buzz the *Foresteria* door to the right.

$$$ Novecento Hotel rents nine plush rooms on three floors. This boutique hotel is decorated circa-1900 throughout, with a big lounge and an elegant living room (Db-€240-260, air-con, lots of stairs, free Wi-Fi; on Calle del Dose, off Campo San Maurizio at San Marco 2683; tel. 041-241-3765, fax 041-521-2145, www.novecento.biz, info@novecento.biz).

$$ Locanda Art Déco is a charming little place, though there's not much Art Deco to be seen. A wrought-iron staircase leads from the inviting lobby to six small but thoughtfully decorated rooms on three floors (Db-€140-160, nicer Db-€170-200, Tb-€200-230, 3-night minimum on weekends, cash discount, air-con, free Wi-Fi, lots of stairs; on Calle de le Botteghe, just north of the Accademia Bridge off Campo San Stefano, at San Marco 2966; tel. 041-277-0558, fax 041-270-2891, www.locandaartdeco.com, info@locandaartdeco.com). They also rent loft apartments.

$ Albergo San Samuele is a backpacker place: dumpy but in a great locale. It rents 12 basic rooms in a crumbling old palace near Campo San Stefano. Sleep here only if their price is far less than other listings (S-€70, D-€90, Db-€110, extra bed-€30, no breakfast, free Wi-Fi and Internet access, on Salizada San Samuele

at San Marco 3358, tel. 041-520-5165, fax 041-522-8045, www
.albergosansamuele.it, info@albergosansamuele.it).

Near the Train Station

I don't recommend the train station area. It's crawling with noisy,
disoriented tourists with too much baggage and people whose life's
calling is to scam visitors out of their money. It's so easy just to hop
a vaporetto upon arrival and sleep in the Venice of your dreams.
Still, some like to park their bags near the station, and if so, these
hotels stand out.

Nearby Laundry: Orange, the nearest self-service laundry,
is across the Grand Canal from the station (daily 7:30-22:30, €14/
load, follow directions to recommended Albergo Marin, on Ramo
de le Chioverete at Santa Croce 665b).

$$$ Hotel Abbazia, in the dreary hotel zone near the train
station, fills a former abbey with both history and class. The refec-
tory makes a grand living room for guests, a garden fills the old
courtyard, and the halls leading to 50 rooms are monkishly wide
(Db-€180, larger Db-€210—choose Venetian or modern style, ask
about Rick Steves discount when you book direct, air-con, free
Wi-Fi, no elevator but plenty of stairs, fun-loving staff, 2 blocks
from the station on the very quiet Calle Priuli dei Cavaletti,
Cannaregio 68, tel. 041-717-333, fax 041-717-949, www.abbazia
hotel.com, info@abbaziahotel.com).

$ Locanda Herion rents 17 basic rooms for a decent price
(Db-€120, cash discount, air-con, pay Wi-Fi, on Campiello
Augusto Picutti at Cannaregio 1697a, tel. 041-275-9426, fax 041-
275-6647, www.locandaherion.com, info@locandaherion.com).
Exiting the train station, turn left to follow Rio Terà Lista de
Spagna. Cross the Ponte de Guglie bridge and turn right at the
yellow *San Marcuola traghetto* sign to find the hotel.

$ Albergo Marin and its staff offer 19 good-value, quiet
rooms handy to the train station (Sb-€110, D-€90, Db-€120,
Tb-€150, cash discount, fans on request, free Wi-Fi in public
spaces, on Ramo de le Chioverete at Santa Croce 670b, tel. 041-
718-022, fax 041-721-485, www.albergomarin.it, info@albergo
marin.it, Giacomo). From the station, cross the stone bridge over
the Grand Canal and go right along the embankment. Take the
first left, then the first right, then right again to #670b.

$ The Chef's Wife B&B is run by American Stacy Gibboni.
The "chef" is her Italian husband, who runs the La Colombina
restaurant next door. Together they rent one sprawling and very
cozy 2-bedroom apartment (with electric kettle and fridge but no
kitchen) for two to four people (Db-€100, Tb/Qb-€150, ask for
Rick Steves rate, 2-night minimum, simple breakfast; huge living
room has piano, board games, and DVD player; no air-con, free

VENICE

Hotels near the Train Station

1. Hotel Abbazia
2. Locanda Herion
3. Albergo Marin & Launderette
4. The Chef's Wife B&B
5. Hotel S. Lucia
6. Alloggi Henry
7. Brek Cafeteria

VENICE

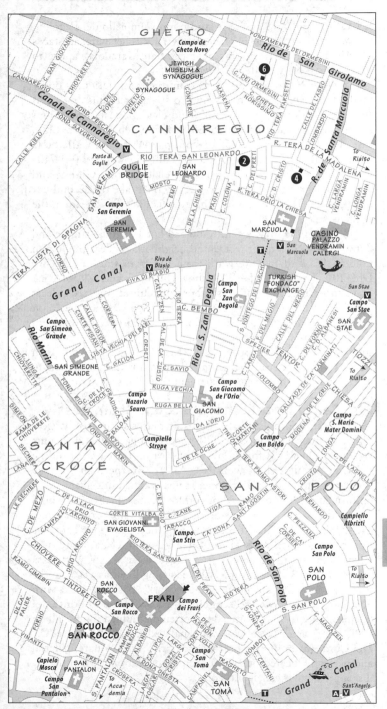

VENICE

Wi-Fi, adjacent to Stacy's art studio, on Campiello del Pegoloto at Cannaregio 1801, no phone calls, www.thechefswife.eu, stacys guesthouse@hotmail.it). It's near the San Marcuola vaporetto stop—see Stacy's website for directions.

$ Hotel S. Lucia, 150 yards from the train station, is oddly modern and sterile, with bright and spacious rooms and tight showers. Its 15 rooms are simple and clean. Guests enjoy their sunny garden area out front (S-€60, D-€80, Db-€105, Tb-€130, cash discount, breakfast-€5, air-con, pay Wi-Fi, on Calle de la Misericordia at Cannaregio 358, tel. 041-715-180, fax 041-710-610, www.hotelslucia.com, info@hotelslucia.com, Gianni and Alessandra). Exit the station, head left, then take the second left onto Calle de la Misericordia. The hotel is 100 yards ahead on the right.

$ Alloggi Henry, a family-owned hotel, rents 15 simple and flowery rooms in a quiet residential neighborhood near the Jewish Ghetto. It's a 10-minute walk from the train station (D-€80, Db-€100, Tb-€130, Qb-€160, show this book and ask for Rick Steves price if paying cash, ask about discount if you stay at least 3 nights, no breakfast, air-con, free Wi-Fi, on Calle Ormesini at Cannaregio 1506e, tel. 041-523-6675, fax 041-715-680, www.alloggi henry.com, info@alloggihenry.com, Manola and Henry). From the station, follow Lista de Spagna, San Leonardo, and Farsetti. Turn left on Calle Ormesini, then turn right into tiny Campiello Briani. They also rent a three-room apartment that sleeps up to nine.

Big, Fancy Hotels that Discount Shamelessly

Here are several big, plush, four-star places with greedy, sky-high rack rates (around Db-€300) that often have great discounts (as low as Db-€120) for drop-ins, off-season travelers, or online booking through their websites. All are on the map on page 936, except for Hotel Giorgione. If you want sliding-glass-door, uniformed-receptionist kind of comfort and formality in the old center, these are worth considering: **$$$ Hotel Giorgione** (big, garish, shiny, near Rialto Bridge, www.hotelgiorgione.com, see map on page 943); **$$$ Hotel Casa Verardo** (elegant and quietly parked on a canal behind St. Mark's, more stately, www.casa verardo.it); **$$$ Hotel Donà Palace** (sitting like Las Vegas in the touristy zone a few blocks behind St. Mark's Basilica, works with neighbors **$$$ Hotel all'Angelo** and **$$$ Hotel al Ponte dei Sosperi** to rent 100 overpriced but often discounted rooms, all on Calle Larga San Marco, www.donapalace.it); and **$$$ Hotel Ca' Dei Conti** (five minutes northeast of St. Mark's Square, palatial and perfectly located but €500 rooms worth it only when deeply discounted, www.cadeiconti.com).

Cheap Dormitory Accommodations

$ Foresteria della Chiesa Valdese, run by the Methodist Church, has a mixture of dorms (6-9 beds) and private rooms (2-5 beds) with bath, close to both St. Mark's Square and the Rialto Bridge. This chilly, run-down yet charming old place has elegant ceiling paintings. They take reservations for the rooms, but only accept walk-ins for the dorms (dorm bed-€31, Db-€92-102, Tb-€111-117, Qb-€144-152, Quint/b-€170, price depends on view and amenities, €5/person less for stays of 2 nights or more; includes breakfast, sheets, towels, and lockers; must check in and out when office is open—8:30-20:00, no air-con, elevator, on Fondamenta Cavagnis at Castello 5170, tel. 041-528-6797, fax 041-241-6238, www.foresteriavenezia.it, info@foresteriavenezia.it). From Campo Santa Maria Formosa, walk past Bar all'Orologio to the end of Calle Longa and cross the bridge—it's the second door, see map on page 943.

$ Venice's youth hostel, on Giudecca Island with 260 beds and grand views across the Bay of San Marco, is a godsend for backpackers shell-shocked by Venetian prices. It's an old-school hostel—big rooms stacked with bunk beds (€25 beds with sheets and breakfast in 8- to 20-bed dorms, cheaper for hostel members, lockers, towels-€5, pay Wi-Fi, room lock-out 10:30-13:30, office open 24 hours, Fondamenta Zitelle 86, tel. 041-523-8211, fax 041-523-5689, www.ostellovenezia.it, info@ostellovenezia.it). Take vaporetto #4.1 from the bus or train stations (from the Tronchetto parking lot, take vaporetto #2) to the Zitelle stop, then walk right along the embankment to #86.

On the Mainland

While I prefer to stay in the heart of the action, these two places combine fine prices with easy bus links into Venice and are particularly good options for those who need to park a car.

$ Villa Dolcetti is a 1635 building with six comfortable rooms in a suburb of Venice. Art lovers Diego and Tatiana provide a buffet breakfast, free parking, and lots of sightseeing advice (Db-€75, superior Db-€85, Tb-€90-110, these prices for Rick Steves readers booking direct, air-con, free Internet access and Wi-Fi, tel. 041-563-1077, fax 041-563-1139, www.villadolcetti.com, info@villadolcetti.com). It's in the town of Oriago di Mira, at Via Venezia 85. Steps away is a bus stop on the Venice-Padua line that connects you to Venice's Piazzale Roma (2/hour, 25 minutes).

$ Villa Mocenigo Agriturismo, about 10 miles from Marco Polo Airport, is a working, family-run farm in a peaceful rural location between Venice and Padua. Its 10 rooms are furnished with antiques, and regional specialties are served for dinner (Sb-€40-55, Db-€60-74, extra bed-€20-25, dinner with wine-about

€20 per person, air-con, free parking, Via Viasana 59 in Mirano-Venezia, tel. & fax 041-433-246, mobile 335-547-4728, www.villamocenigo.com, info@villamocenigo.com). Email them for directions by car or bus. Buses to Venice leave directly from the villa (3/hour, 45 minutes).

Eating in Venice

While touristy restaurants are the scourge of Venice, the following places are still popular with actual Venetians and respect the tourists who happen in. First trick: Walk away from triple-language menus. Second trick: For freshness, eat fish. Most seafood dishes are the catch-of-the-day. (But remember that seafood can be sold by weight—per 100 grams or *etto*—rather than a set price.) Third trick: Eat later. A place may feel really touristy at 19:00, but if you come back at 21:00 it can be filled with locals. Tourists eat barbarically early, which is fine with the restaurants because they fill tables that would otherwise be used only once in an evening.

If you want a meal with a canal view, it generally comes with lower quality or a higher price. But if you're aiming for a canal-side memory, these two next-door neighbors offer good value: Ristorante alla Conchiglia and Trattoria da Giorgio ai Greci (listed under "Dining near St. Mark's Square," later).

Unique to Venice, *cicchetti* bars specialize in finger foods and appetizers that can combine to make a quick and tasty meal. The selection and ambience are best on workdays (Mon–Sat lunch and early dinner).

Near the Rialto Bridge
North of the Bridge
These restaurants are located beyond Campo Santi Apostoli, along the Strada Nova, the main drag going toward the train station.

Trattoria da Bepi, bright and alpine-paneled, feels like a classic. Ask for the seasonal specialties—the crab dishes are excellent. There's good seating inside and out (€8-10 pastas, €14-18 *secondi*, €1.50 cover, Fri-Wed 12:00-14:30 & 19:00-22:00, closed Thu, half a block off Campo Santi Apostoli on Salizada Pistor at #4550, tel. 041-528-5031, Loris).

Little **Vini da Gigio** has a passion for good food and a traditional Venetian menu (€12-16 pastas, €18-22 *secondi*, no cover, Wed-Sun 12:00-14:30 & 19:00-22:30, closed Mon-Tue, 4 blocks from Ca' d'Oro vaporetto stop on Fondamenta San Felice at #3628a—it's behind the church on Campo San Felice, tel. 041-528-5140).

Trattoria Ca' d'Oro, while a little less accessible and inviting to the tourist, is a venerable favorite with a small, appealing menu and an enthusiastic following. Just to sip wine and enjoy *cicchetti* at the bar is a treat—their *polpette* (tuna and potato meatballs) are famous, and the house wine will set you back just €0.50. It's also fine for a meal (€9-10 pastas, €10-11 *secondi*, €1.50 cover, cash only, Fri-Sat and Mon-Wed 11:30-14:30 & 18:30-22:30, Sun 18:30-22:30, closed Thu, reservations recommended; from the Ca' d'Oro vaporetto dock, walk 100 yards directly away from the canal, cross Strada Nova into an alley called Ramo Ca' d'Oro, and it's straight ahead at #3912; tel. 041-528-5324).

Osteria al Bomba is a *cicchetti* bar with a female touch, thanks to Giovanna. It's unusual (clean, no toothpicks, no cursing) and quite good, with lots of veggies. You can stand and eat at the bar—try a little €3 *crostino* with polenta and cod—or oversee the construction of the house *"antipasto misto di cicchetti"* plate (€15, enough fish and vegetables for two) and choose your wine by the glass from the posted list. A seat at the long table comes with a €2 *coperto* (daily 12:00-15:00 & 18:00-23:00; on Calle de l'Oca; from Campo Santi Apostoli, walk toward the train station, find #4294 on your right and turn down the small alley to #4297 ahead of you; tel. 041-520-5175).

East of the Rialto Bridge

The first four listings are relatively close to the bridge. The rest are near Campo Santa Maria Formosa, one of my favorite community scenes. While the restaurants fronting the square aren't much, several good options for dining lie a short walk away.

Osteria "Alla Botte," despite being located a minute from the Rialto Bridge, is packed with a casual neighborhood clientele in two simple, woody rooms. For a classic Venetian taste, try the €18 all-seafood *antipasto misto* (daily 12:00-15:00 & 19:00-23:00, two short blocks off Campo San Bartolomeo in the corner behind the statue—down Calle de la Bissa at #5482, notice the "day after" photo showing a debris-covered Venice after the notorious 1989 Pink Floyd open-air concert, tel. 041-520-9775, Cristiano).

Osteria di Santa Marina, on the wonderful Campo Marina, serves pricey, near-gourmet cuisine in a dressy dining room. The presentation is impressive, but you feel there's more pretense than love of food. Cheap-eating tricks are frowned on in this elegant, borderline stuffy restaurant (enticing menu with €15 pastas and €25 *secondi*, €3 cover, €75-80 fixed-price meals, Tue-Sat 12:30-14:30 & 19:30-22:00, Mon 19:30-22:00, closed Sun, reserve for dinner, eat indoors or outdoors on pleasant little square, between Rialto Bridge and Campo Santa Maria Formosa on Campo Marina at #5911, tel. 041-528-5239).

Rosticceria San Bartolomeo is a cheap—if confusing—self-service diner, a throwback budget eatery with a likeably surly staff. Take it out, grab one of the few tiny tables, or munch at the bar—I'd skip the uninviting upper floor, where you pay higher prices and a €2 cover for table service (good €6-7 pasta, great fried *mozzarella al prosciutto* for €1.50, delightful fruit salad, €1 glasses of wine, prices listed on wall behind counter, no cover or service charge downstairs, daily 9:00-21:30, tel. 041-522-3569). To find it, imagine the statue on Campo San Bartolomeo walking backward 20 yards, turning left, and going under a passageway—now, follow him.

Osteria al Portego is a friendly neighborhood eatery—one of the best in town. Carlo serves good meals and excellent *cicchetti*—best enjoyed early, around 18:00 (from 19:00 to 21:00, tables are reserved for those ordering from the menu; the *cicchetti* are picked over by 21:00). Prices for food and wine are posted clearly on the wall. The *cicchetti* here can make a great meal, but you should also consider sitting down for a dinner from their fine menu. This place can get very busy, so reserve ahead if you want a table (€13 pastas, €0.80 glass of house wine, daily 10:30-15:00 & 18:00-21:30, near Campo Marina at #6015 on Calle Malvasia, tel. 041-522-9038). To find the Osteria, first find Rosticceria San Bartolomeo (listed above), then continue over a bridge to Campo San Lio, turn left, and follow Calle Carminati straight about 50 yards over another bridge; it's straight ahead.

Near Campo Santa Maria Formosa: **Osteria alle Testiere** is my top dining recommendation in Venice. Hugely respected, they are dedicated to quality, serving up creative, artfully presented market-fresh seafood (there's no meat on the menu), homemade pastas, and fine wine in what the chef calls a "Venetian Nouvelle" style. With only 22 seats, it's tight and homey, yet elegant. They have daily specials, 10 wines by the glass, and one agenda: a great dining experience. Luca, the owner/host, is gracious and passionate about his food. This is one place to let loose and trust your host. Reservations are almost always necessary for their three seatings: 12:30, 19:00, and 21:30 (€19 pastas, €25 *secondi,* plan on spending €50 for dinner, no cover or service charge, closed Sun-Mon; on Calle del Mondo Novo, just off Campo Santa Maria Formosa, at #5801; tel. 041-522-7220).

Osteria al Mascaron is where I've gone for years to watch Gigi, Momi, and their food-loving band of ruffians dish up rustic-yet-sumptuous pastas with steamy seafood to salivating foodies. The pastas seem pricey at €24-32, but they're meant for two (it's OK to ask for single portions). The €16 *antipasto misto* plate—have fun pointing—and two glasses of wine make a terrific light meal, and their seafood pastas make beautiful memories (€2 cover, Mon-Sat 12:00-15:00 & 19:00-23:00, closed Sun, reservations smart Fri-Sat; on Calle Longa Santa Maria Formosa, a block past Campo

Santa Maria Formosa, at #5225; tel. 041-522-5995).

Fast and Cheap Eats: The veggie stand on Campo Santa Maria Formosa is a fixture. For *döner kebabs* (€3.50) and pizza to go (€2/slice), head down Calle Longa to **Peter Pan** at #6249 (daily 11:00-24:00). For classier pizza to go, visit **Cip Ciap** (next to Osteria alle Testiere near the bridge, at #5799a).

West of the Rialto Bridge

Most of these places are informal, serving *cicchetti* and/or light meals. The first bars listed are within 200 yards of each other, a few steps behind the Rialto fish market; the rest are farther away from this hive of eateries (see map on page 943). This area is very crowded by day, nearly empty early in the evening, and crowded with young Venetians later.

Most bars are closed 15:00-18:00 (though Cantina Do Mori and Ostaria ai Storti stay open all day), and offer glasses of house wine for under €1, better wine for around €2.50, and *cicchetti* for €1-2. At each place, look for the list of snacks and wine by the glass at the bar or on the wall. If you're ready for dessert, try dipping a Burano biscuit in a glass of strawberry-flavored *fragolino* or another sweet dessert wine.

A strip of five places between Campo San Giacomo and the Grand Canal (such as the recommended Bancogiro Bar and Al Mercà) make a thriving youth *spritz* scene that's worth a look even if you don't eat or drink there.

Cantina Do Mori has been famous with locals (since 1462) and savvy travelers (since 1982) as a convivial place for fine wine. You'll choose from a forest of little edibles on toothpicks and *francobolli* (a spicy selection of 20 tiny, mayo-soaked sandwiches nicknamed "stamps"). Go here to be abused in a fine atmosphere—the frowns are part of the shtick (Mon-Sat 8:30-20:00, closed Sun, stand-up only, arrive early before the *cicchetti* are gone, tel. 041-522-5401). From the Rialto Bridge, walk 200 yards down Ruga dei Orefici, away from St. Mark's Square—then turn left on Ruga Vechia San Giovanni, then right at Sotoportego Do Mori to #429.

Bar all'Arco, a bustling one-room joint that's almost across from Cantina Do Mori at #436, is particularly enjoyable for its tiny open-face sandwiches (closed Sun, tel. 041-520-5666).

Ostaria ai Storti, which has a homey feel, is a fun place to congregate. Check out the photo of the market in 1909, below the bar. Alessandro speaks English and enjoys helping educate travelers while serving *fragolino* (€8 pastas, €12 *secondi*, €1.50 cover, daily 9:00-22:30, Nov-March closes 15:00-18:00, 20 yards from Cantina Do Mori and around the corner on Calle San Matio at #819, tel. 041-523-6861).

Cantina Do Spade is run by Sebastiano, who clearly lists the *cicchetti* and wines of the day (daily 11:00-15:00 & 18:00-21:00, 30 yards down Calle de le Do Spade from Ostaria ai Storti at #860, tel. 041-521-0583).

At **Pesce Pronto,** you can sample fish while watching the market action. Bruno and Umberto serve artful fish hors d'oeuvres, *sfornato con pesce* (a savory, baked pastry), and many other fresh fish tidbits—all at a fair price. This fancy hole-in-the-wall is fun for a quick bite—eat standing up or take it to go. From 12:45 to 14:15, they serve €10-12 "express plates" of pasta and other choices (Tue and Sat 9:00-15:00 & 18:00-20:00, Wed-Fri 9:00-15:00 & 19:00-23:30, closed Sun-Mon, facing the fish market on Calle de le Becarie o Panataria at #319, tel. 041-822-0298).

The **Bancogiro Bar** is expensive but good if you like strong cheese and canalside tables (€3.50 cover, €2.50 *cicchetti* at bar, €15 cheese plate, Tue-Sun 12:00-23:00, closed Mon, on Campo San Giacomo at #122, tel. 041-523-2061).

Al Mercà, a few steps away and off the canal, is an even livelier little nook with a happy crowd, where young locals gather to grab drinks and little snacks. The price list is clear, and I've found the crowd to be welcoming to tourists interested in connecting (stand at the bar only—no tables, Mon-Sat 9:30-14:30 & 18:00-21:00, closed Sun, on Campo Cesare Battisti at #213).

Antica Ostaria Ruga Rialto, a.k.a. "the Ruga," is a neighborhood fixture where Giorgio and Marco serve great bar snacks and wine to a devoted clientele. Treats here are their polenta, sardine with onions, and veggies. Bar or table, no problem—they're happy to make you a €3, €6, or €10 mixed plate (daily 11:00-14:30 & 19:00-24:00, easy to find—just past the Chinese restaurant on Ruga Vechia San Giovanni at #695a, tel. 041-521-1243).

Osteria al Diavolo e l'Acquasanta, three blocks west of the Rialto Bridge, serves good—if pricey—Venetian dishes, and makes a handy lunch stop for sightseers. Though they list *cicchetti* and wine by the glass on the wall, I'd come here for a light meal rather than for appetizers (€8-11 pastas, €12-17 *secondi*, 12 percent service charge, Wed-Mon 12:00-14:30 & 19:00-21:30, closed Tue, hiding at #561 on Calle de la Madona—a quiet street just off Ruga Vechia San Giovanni, tel. 041-277-0307).

Antica Birraria la Corte is an everyday eatery on the delightful Campo San Polo, between the Rialto Bridge and the Frari Church. Popular for its €7-10 pizza, calzones, and salads, it fills the far side of this cozy, family-filled square. While the interior is a sprawling beer hall, it's a joy to eat on the square, where metal tables teeter on the cobbles, the wind plays with the paper mats, and children run free (€11-12 pastas, €14-19 *secondi*, €2 cover, daily 12:00-14:30 & 19:00-22:30, Campo San Polo 2168, tel. 041-275-0570).

Trattoria Pizzeria al Nono Risorto is unpretentious, inexpensive, youthful, and famous for serving good pizza in a nice setting. You'll sit in a gravelly garden under a leafy canopy, surrounded by Italians enjoying huge €8 salads, pastas, and pizzas, and €12-17 grilled meat or fish dishes (Fri-Tue 12:00-14:30 & 19:00-22:30, Thu 19:00-22:30, closed Wed, reservations smart on weekends; from Rialto fish market, get out your map and walk 3 minutes away from the Rialto to Campo San Cassiano—it's just over the bridge on Sotoportego de Siora Bettina at #2338; tel. 041-524-1169).

Near St. Mark's Square
For locations, see the map on page 936.

Dining near St. Mark's Square
The following three places are a few blocks east of St. Mark's Square and offer classy dining experiences. The first two listings are the best canalside dining values I've found in Venice. Both specialize in fish, and have a reasonable-for-the-romantic-setting menu. If you want a canalside seat for dinner, call to reserve it, and honor your reservation; don't go to another restaurant. To reach these from St. Mark's Square, head behind the basilica to Campo San Provolo, then follow Calle Osmarin to the Ponte dei Greci bridge and Fondamenta San Lorenzo. To get to the third, head up Chiesa from Campo San Provolo.

Ristorante alla Conchiglia has a few lovely tables that line the sleepy canal and a fresh, bright interior. They specialize in turbot, a flatfish similar to flounder. There's a €1.50 cover and 12 percent service charge, which is waived if you order the fixed-price meal (€7-10 pizzas lunch only, big €14 salads, basic €15 fixed-price meal, daily 12:00-22:30, closed Dec and Jan, on Fondamenta San Lorenzo at #4990, tel. 041-528-9095, Franco and son Alessandro).

Trattoria da Giorgio ai Greci, right next door, also has a half-dozen canalside tables. They offer €17 and €21 fixed-price meals with no cover or service charge—the €21 version has more interesting and authentic choices (€1.50 cover and 12 percent service charge for à la carte orders, daily 12:00-22:30, on Fondamenta San Lorenzo at #4988, tel. 041-528-9780, enthusiastically run by Giorgio and sons Davide and chatty Roberto).

Ristorante Antica Sacrestia is a classic restaurant where the owner, Pino, takes a hands-on approach to greeting guests. His staff serve creative €33-50 fixed-price meals and a humdrum €20 *turistico* one. You can also order à la carte; try the delightful €21 antipasto spread. There's no cover or service charge, and my readers are welcome to a free *sgroppino* (lemon vodka after-dinner drink) upon request (€12-16 pastas and pizzas, €17-30 *secondi*, Tue-Sun 11:30-15:00 & 18:00-22:30, closed Mon, immediately behind

San Zaninovo/Giovanni Novo Church on Calle de la Sacrestia at #4442, tel. 041-523-0749).

Budget Eateries near St. Mark's Square

Picnicking isn't allowed on St. Mark's Square, but you can legally take your snacks to the nearby Giardinetti Reali, the small park along the waterfront west of the Piazzetta.

"*Sandwich Row*": On Calle de le Rasse, just steps away from the tourist intensity at St. Mark's Square, is a handy strip I call "Sandwich Row." Lined with sandwich bars, it's the closest place to St. Mark's to get a decent sandwich at an affordable price with a place to sit down (most places open daily 7:00-24:00, €1 extra to sit; from the Bridge of Sighs, head down the Riva and take the second lane on the left). I particularly like **Birreria Forst,** a café which serves a selection of meaty €2.80 sandwiches with tasty sauce on wheat bread, or made-to-order sandwiches for around €3.80 (Sun-Fri 10:00-21:00, closed Sat, air-con, rustic wood tables, Calle de le Rasse at #4540, tel. 041-523-0557) and **Bar Verde,** a more modern sandwich bar with fun people-watching views from its corner tables (big €4 sandwiches, splittable €8 salads, fresh pastries, at the end of Calle de le Rasse at #4526, facing Campo Santi Filippo e Giacomo).

Ristorante alla Basilica, just one street behind St. Mark's Basilica, is a church-run, indoor, institutional-feeling place that serves a solid €13 fixed-price lunch (including water) daily from 11:45 to 15:00. It's not self-serve—you'll be seated and can choose a pasta, a *secondi*, and a vegetable side dish off the menu (sometimes a wait, air-con, great bathrooms, on Calle dei Albanesi at #4255, tel. 041-522-0524).

Rizzo, like most Venetian "bars," is an eat-at-the-counter café with sandwiches, pizza, pastries, and other reasonably priced snacks. It stands out for its handy location, north of St. Mark's Square on the main drag of Calle dei Fabbri, and its tiny grocery shelf with yogurt and other quick bites (Mon-Sat 8:00-20:00, closed Sun, on Calle dei Fabbri at #933a, tel. 041-522-3388).

In Dorsoduro

Near the Accademia Bridge

Ristorante/Pizzeria Accademia Foscarini, next to the Accademia Bridge and Galleria, offers decent €10-11 pizzas in a great canalside setting. Their toasted *farciti* sandwich is a local favorite (€6.50 at the table). Though the pizzas may be forgettable, this place is both scenic and practical—on each visit to Venice, I grab a pizza lunch here while I ponder the Grand Canal bustle (no cover or service charge, May-Oct Wed-Mon 7:00-22:30, Nov-April until 21:00, closed Tue, on Rio Terà A. Foscarini at #878c, tel. 041-522-7281).

Enoteca Cantine del Vino Già Schiavi is much-loved for its €1 *cicchetti* and €3.50-4 sandwiches (order from list on board). It's also a good place for a €1-2 glass of wine and appetizers (Mon-Sat 8:00-20:30, closed Sun, 100 yards from Accademia art museum on San Trovaso canal; facing Accademia, take a right and then a forced left at the canal to the second bridge—it's at #992, tel. 041-523-0034). You're welcome to enjoy your wine and finger food hanging out at the bar, sitting on the bridge out front, or in the nearby square—which actually has grass. This is primarily a wine shop with great prices for bottles to go—and plastic glasses for picnickers.

Terrazza del Casin dei Nobili, located on Zattere (the Venice side of the Giudecca Canal), takes full advantage of the warm, romantic evening sun. They serve finely crafted, regional specialties with creativity at tolerable prices. The canalside seating is breezy and beautiful, but comes with the rumble of *vaporetti* from the nearby stop. The interior is bright and hip (good €9-10 pizzas, €10-13 pastas, €15-25 *secondi*, €2 cover, Fri-Wed 12:00-23:00, closed Thu; from Zattere vaporetto stop, turn left to #924; tel. 041-520-6895, Ruggiero and Eleonora). On Wednesday and Sunday evenings in summer, there's live music nearby on the Zattere promenade.

Near Campo San Barnaba

A number of restaurants are near this small square, a short walk from the Accademia. As these are each within a few steps of each other and the energy and atmosphere can vary, I like to survey the options before choosing (although reservations may be necessary later in the evening).

Casin dei Nobili ("Pleasure Palace of Nobles")—related to the Terrazza del Casin dei Nobili, listed above—has a high-energy, informal, modern setting with outdoor seating on a patio. The creative, €18 fixed-price lunch specials are worth it (€13 pastas, €13-25 *secondi*, good pizzas, €10 "fantasy salads," Tue-Sun 12:00-15:00 & 19:00-23:00, closed Mon; on Calle de le Casin, a half-block south of Campo San Barnaba, at #2765; tel. 041-241-1841, Damiano).

Pane Vino e San Daniele is a busy little place that feels real, with the TV on, an enticing blackboard listing the day's specials, and the kitchen action filling its dining room (€7.50 pastas, €10-12 salads and *secondi*, €1 cover, on Calle Longa San Barnaba at #2861, tel. 041-243-9865).

Enoteca e Trattoria la Bitta is dark and woody, with a soft-jazz bistro feel and a small, forgettable back patio. They serve beautifully presented, traditional Venetian food with—proudly— no fish. Their helpful waitstaff and small menu are clearly focused on quality. Reservations are required (€10 pastas, €16-25 *secondi*,

VENICE

€2 cover, dinner only, Mon-Sat 18:30-23:00, closed Sun, cash only, between previous two listings on Calle Longa San Barnaba at #2753a, tel. 041-523-0531).

Elsewhere in Venice

On Fondamente Nove: **Ristorante Algiubagio,** though not cheap, is a good place to eat well overlooking the northern lagoon. The name is a combination of the owners' four names—Alberto, Giulio, Barbara, and Giovanna—who strive to impress visitors with quality, creative Venetian cuisine made using the best ingredients. Reserve a table on the lagoon facing the island of San Michele or in their classy cantina dining room (€16-18 pastas, €24-25 *secondi,* €3.50 cover, €29-42 fixed-price meals, Wed-Mon 12:00-15:00 & 19:00-22:30, closed Tue; on Fondamente Nove, to the left of the vaporetto dock as you face the water, at #5039; tel. 041-523-6084).

Near Campo Santa Maria Nova: **Osteria da Alberto,** with excellent daily specials, €13 seafood dishes, €9-11 pastas, a good house wine, and a woody and characteristic interior, is one of my standbys. It's smart to reserve at night—I'd request a table in the front (€1.80 cover, Mon-Sat 12:00-14:30 & 18:30-22:30, closed Sun; on Calle Larga Giacinto Gallina, midway between Campo Santi Apostoli and Campo Santi Giovanni e Paolo, next to Ponte de la Panada bridge at #5401—see map on page 943; tel. 041-523-8153, run by Graziano and Giovanni).

Near the Train Station: There are piles of eateries near the station. The **food circus** in the station itself is quite good, with peaceful garden seating out back in summer, big €3-4 sandwiches, and slices of pizza for €2.90. A block away is a small branch of the efficient and economic **Brek,** a popular self-service cafeteria chain (€4-5 pastas, €6-9 *secondi,* daily 11:30-22:00, head left as you leave the station and walk about 50 yards past the bridge along Rio Terà Lista di Spagna to #124—see map on page 950).

Cheap Meals

The keys to eating affordably in Venice are pizza, bars/cafés, cafeterias, and picnics. *Panini* and *tramezzini* (sandwiches) are sold fast and cheap at bars everywhere and can stave off midmorning hunger. There's a great "sandwich row" of cheap cafés near St. Mark's Square (see page 960). For speed, value, and ambience, you can get a filling plate of typically Venetian appetizers at nearly any bar. For quick, fun eating, I like small, stand-up mini-meals at *cicchetti* **bars** best.

Picnics

The **fruit and vegetable market** that sprawls for a few blocks just past the Rialto Bridge is a fun place to assemble a picnic (best

Mon-Sat 8:00-13:00, closed Sun). The adjacent **fish market** is wonderfully slimy (closed Sun-Mon). Side lanes in this area are speckled with fine little hole-in-the-wall munchie bars, bakeries, and cheese shops.

A handy (but often mobbed) **Co-op** supermarket is between St. Mark's and Campo Santa Maria Formosa, on the corner of Salizada San Lio and Calle del Mondo Novo at #5817. It has a great selection of picnic supplies, including packaged salads for less than €2 (daily 8:30-20:00). The largest supermarket in town is the **Co-op** at Piazzale Roma, next to the vaporetto stop at #504-507 (daily 8:30-20:00). It's an easy walk from the train station, as is the **Billa** supermarket on Campo San Felice (at #3660, along the Strada Nova between the train station and Rialto area, Mon-Sat 8:30-20:00, Sun 9:00-20:00). Another **Billa** supermarket is convenient for those staying in Dorsoduro: It's at #1492, at the far west of the Zattere embankment, by the San Basilio vaporetto stop and the cruise-ship docks (Mon-Sat 8:00-20:00, Sun 9:00-19:00).

The only legal place to picnic in public in Venice is Giardinetti Reali, the waterfront park near St. Mark's Square. Eating anywhere outdoors, you may be besieged by pigeons. A picnic in your room can be a better bet.

Gelato

You'll find good *gelaterie* in every Venetian neighborhood, offering one-scoop cones for about €1.50. Look for the words *artigianale* or *produzione propria*, which indicates that a shop makes its own gelato. The popular, inventive, upscale **Grom** ice-cream chain has two branches in Venice, one on Campo San Barnaba at #2761 (beyond the Accademia bridge), and another one at the Strada Nova at #3844, not far from the Rialto (cheapest cone-€2.50, both open Sun-Thu 12:00-22:30, Fri-Sat 12:00-23:30).

On St. Mark's Square, two venerable cafés have *gelato* counters in summer: **Gran Caffè Lavena** (April-Oct daily until 24:00, no gelato Nov-March, first café to left of the Clock Tower, behind the first orchestra, at #134) and **Todaro** (on the corner of the Piazzetta at #5, near the water and just under the column topped by St. Theodore slaying a crocodile).

Venice Connections

By Train

From Venice by Train to: Florence (hourly, 2-3 hours, often crowded so make reservations), **Milan** (hourly, 2.5-3.5 hours), **Cinque Terre/Monterosso** (about hourly, 6-7 hours, 1-3 changes), **Rome** (hourly, 3.75 hours, also 1 direct night train from Mestre, 6 hours), **Interlaken** (5/day, 6-8.5 hours, 2-5 changes, no pleasant

VENICE

overnight option), **Luzern** (7/day, 6.5-7 hours, 1 direct, others change in Milan and Arth-Goldau), **Bern** (3/day, 6 hours, change in Milan or Brig), **Munich** (4-6/day, 7 hours, change in Verona; 1 direct night train, 8 hours; most trains reservable only via www.bahn.de), **Salzburg** (4/day, 6-7 hours, 1-2 changes, 1 direct night train, 7 hours), **Paris** (3/day, 10-12 hours with change in Milan, may also transfer in Basel or Zürich; 1 direct night train, 13.5 hours, reservable only via www.thello.com—no railpasses honored, 2 more night trains with changes), **Ljubljana** (3/day, 7.5 hours—buy ticket at train station, take bus from Tronchetto to Villach in Austria, then transfer to train; 1 direct night train, 4 hours, but arrives at 2:00 in the morning), and **Vienna** (3/day, 8 hours—same system as Ljubljana; 1 direct night train, 11 hours).

For buses to **Austria** run by Italian Railways, you have to buy tickets at the train station. For buses to Venice's airports, see below.

By Plane

Marco Polo is Venice's main airport. Some budget flights, including Ryanair, use the smaller airport in the nearby city of Treviso.

Marco Polo Airport

Venice's small, modern airport is on the mainland shore of the lagoon, six miles north of the city. There's one sleek terminal, with a TI (daily 9:00-21:00), car-rental agencies, ATMs, a bank, and a few shops and eateries. For flight information, call tel. 041-260-9260, visit www.veniceairport.com, or ask your hotel.

Transportation between Marco Polo Airport and Venice

Here are three ways to get between the airport and downtown Venice:

- Alilaguna boats—Slowest trip, medium cost
- Water taxis—Fastest trip, most expensive
- Airport shuttle buses to Piazzale Roma—Faster than Alilaguna, slower than water taxi, least expensive

Each of these options is explained in detail below. An advantage of the Alilaguna boats is that you can reach most of this chapter's recommended hotels very simply, with no changes—except hotels near the train station, which are better served by the bus to Piazzale Roma.

Both Alilaguna boats and water taxis leave from the airport's boat dock, an eight-minute walk from the terminal. Exit the arrivals hall and turn left, following signs along a paved, level, covered sidewalk (easy for wheeled bags).

When flying out of Venice, allow yourself plenty of time to get to the airport. Water transport is slow. Plan to arrive at the airport least two hours before your flight, and remember that getting there can easily take another two hours. Consider alternatives ahead of time, especially if you're planning to take one of the Alilaguna boats (which are small and can fill up).

Alilaguna Airport Boats

These boats make the scenic (if slow) journey across the lagoon, each shuttling passengers between the airport and a number of different stops on the island of Venice (€15, €25 round-trip, 1-1.5-hour trip depending on your destination; boats leave every 30-60 minutes). Note that the Alilaguna boats are not part of the ACTV vaporetto system, so they aren't covered by city transit passes. But they do use the same docks and ticket windows as the regular *vaporetti*.

There are three Alilaguna lines (blue, red, orange), and it can get confusing. But if you know what stop you want, it's easy to find the line that goes there. Here are some key stops in Venice:

San Marco—Hotels west of St. Mark's Square

San Zaccaria—Hotels east of St. Mark's Square

Zattere—Dorsoduro hotels

Guglie—Hotels near Santa Lucia train station

Rialto—Hotels near the Rialto Bridge

Fondamente Nove—Hotels on the north side of the city, on the "fish's" back

For a full schedule, visit the TI, see the website (www.alilaguna.it), call 041-240-1701, ask your hotelier, or scan the schedules posted at the docks.

From the Airport to Venice: You can buy Alilaguna tickets at the airport's TI, the ticket desk in the terminal, vending machines inside the airport terminal (cash only), or simply at the ticket booth at the dock. If you bought your tickets online, you must exchange your printout for the actual tickets before boarding. Any ticket-seller can tell you which line to catch to get to your destination. Boats from the airport run from roughly 7:00 to midnight.

From Venice to the Airport: Ask your hotelier which dock and which line is best. Boats start leaving Venice as early as 3:40 so that passengers can catch early flights. Scope out the dock and buy your ticket in advance to avoid last-minute stress.

Water Taxis

Luxury taxi speedboats zip directly between the airport and your hotel, getting you within steps of your final destination in about 30 minutes. The official price is €100 for up to five people; add €10 for every extra person (10-passenger limit). There's a €10 surcharge between 22:00 and 7:00. You may get a higher quote—politely talk it down. A taxi can be a smart investment for small groups and those with an early departure.

From the airport, arrange your ride at the airport's water-taxi desk or with the boat captains lounging at the dock. From Venice, book your taxi trip the day before you leave. Your hotel will help (since they get a commission), or you can book directly with the Consorzio Motoscafi water taxi association (tel. 041-522-2303, www.motoscafivenezia.it/eng).

Airport Shuttle Buses

Buses take you across the bridge from the mainland to the island, dropping you at Venice's bus station, at the "mouth of the fish" on a square called Piazzale Roma. From there, you can catch a vaporetto down the Grand Canal—convenient for hotels near the Rialto Bridge and St. Mark's Square. If you're staying near the train station, you can walk from Piazzale Roma to your hotel.

Two bus companies run between Piazzale Roma and the airport: ACTV (the local city bus company) and ATVO. Most of the day, both have departures twice an hour and cost the same (€3), although only ATVO offers a round-trip for €5.50. ATVO buses take 20 minutes and go nonstop. ACTV buses (route #5) make a few stops en route and take slightly longer (30 minutes), but are covered by Venice vaporetto passes (see page 900). Buses run from about 5:00 to 24:00; early and late, each company has just one bus an hour. Check schedules at www.atvo.it or www.actv.it.

From the Airport to Venice: Both buses leave from just outside the arrivals terminal. Buy tickets at the TI, or from ticket machines in the terminal or outside next to the buses; in a pinch at odd hours, ask the driver. Check which ticket you are buying—ATVO tickets are not valid on ACTV buses and vice versa. Double-check the destination; if taking ACTV, you want bus #5. See "Arrival in Venice—By Bus," earlier, for directions into town from Piazzale Roma.

From Venice to the Airport: At Piazzale Roma, buy your ticket from the ACTV windows or ATVO office before heading out to the platforms. (If closed, politely ask the driver to sell you a ticket.) ACTV buses leave from platform A1; ATVO buses from platform D2. The first buses leave at around 5:00.

Private Shuttle Bus

Treviso Car Service offers a private minivan service between Marco Polo Airport and Piazzale Roma or the cruise port (minivan-€55, seats up to 8; car-€50, seats up to 3; mobile 348-900-0700 or 333-411-2840, www.tourleadervenice.com, info@tourleadervenice.com.

Treviso Airport

Several budget airlines, such as Ryanair, Wizz Air, and Germanwings, use Treviso Airport, 12 miles northwest of Venice (www.trevisoairport.it). Regular ATVO buses take you from the airport to Piazzale Roma (€6, about 2/hour, 1.25 hours, www.atvo .it). Buy your tickets at the ATVO desk in the airport and stamp them on the bus. The buses also stop at Mestre's train station. Treviso Car Service offers minivan service to Piazzale Roma (minivan-€75, seats up to 8; car-€65, seats up to 3; see private shuttle bus listing on opposite page).

FLORENCE

Firenze

Florence, the home of the Renaissance and the birthplace of our modern world, has the best Renaissance art in Europe. In a single day, you can look Michelangelo's *David* in the eyes, fall under the seductive sway of Botticelli's *Birth of Venus*, and climb the modern world's first dome, which still dominates the skyline.

Get your bearings with a Renaissance walk. Florentine art goes beyond paintings and statues—enjoy the food, fashion, and street markets. Lick Italy's best gelato while enjoying some of Europe's best people-watching.

Planning Your Time

If you're in Italy for three weeks, Florence deserves at least one well-organized day: see the Accademia *(David)*, tour the Uffizi Gallery (Renaissance art), visit the underrated Bargello (best statues), and do the Renaissance Walk (explained on page 982; to avoid heat and crowds, do this walk in the morning or late afternoon). Art-lovers will want to chisel out another day of their itinerary for the many other Florentine cultural treasures. Shoppers and ice cream-lovers may need to do the same.

Plan your sightseeing carefully; follow the tips and tricks in this chapter to save time and avoid lines. This is particularly important if you'll be in town for only a day or two during the crowded summer months.

The Uffizi Gallery and Accademia nearly always have long ticket-buying lines, especially in peak season (April-Oct) and on holiday weekends. Crowds thin out weekdays in the off-season. Whatever time of year you visit, you can easily avoid the wait by making reservations (see page 980) or buying a Florence Card

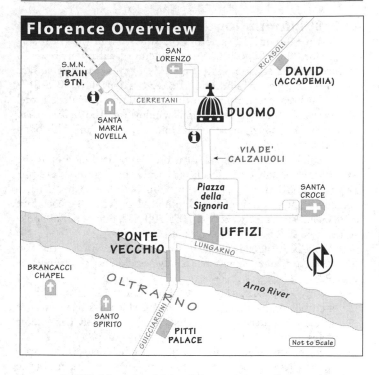

Florence Overview

SAN LORENZO

RICASOLI

S.M.N. TRAIN STN.

DAVID (ACCADEMIA)

CERRETANI

SANTA MARIA NOVELLA

DUOMO

VIA DE' CALZAIUOLI ←

Piazza della Signoria

SANTA CROCE

PONTE VECCHIO

UFFIZI

LUNGARNO

BRANCACCI CHAPEL

O L T R A R N O

Arno River

SANTO SPIRITO

GUICCIARDINI

PITTI PALACE

Not to Scale

(see page 983). Note that both of these major sights are closed on Monday.

Some sights close early—even before 14:00; other museums close early only on certain days (e.g., the first Sunday of the month, second and fourth Monday, etc.). In general, Sundays and Mondays are bad, with many museums either closed or with shorter hours.

Connoisseurs of smaller towns should consider taking the bus to Siena for a day or evening trip (75 minutes one-way, confirm when last bus returns).

Orientation to Florence

The best of Florence lies on the north bank of the Arno River. The main historical sights cluster around the red-brick dome of the cathedral (Duomo). Everything is within a 20-minute walk of the train station, cathedral, or Ponte Vecchio (Old Bridge). The less impressive but more characteristic Oltrarno area (south bank) is just over the bridge. Though small, Florence is intense. Prepare for scorching summer heat, slick pickpockets, few WCs, steep prices, and long lines. The big news for visitors to Florence is the energetic young mayor's passion for traffic-free zones. Once brutal for pedestrians, the city is now a delight on foot.

FLORENCE

Tourist Information

The main Florence TI is across the square from the train station (Mon-Sat 8:30-19:00, Sun 8:30-14:00; with your back to tracks, exit the station—it's 100 yards away, across the square in wall near corner of church at Piazza Stazione 4; tel. 055-212-245, www.firenzeturismo.it). In the train station, avoid the Hotel Reservations "Tourist Information" window (marked *Informazioni Turistiche Alberghiere*) near the McDonald's; it's not a real TI but a hotel-reservation business.

A small but very central TI is on Piazza del Duomo, at the west corner of Via Calzaiuoli; it's inside the Bigalla Museum/Loggia (Mon-Sat 9:00-17:00, Sun 9:00-14:00). Another TI is a couple of blocks north of the Duomo (Mon-Sat 8:30-18:30, Sun 8:30-13:30, Via Cavour 1 red, tel. 055-290-832, international bookstore across street).

The TIs at the train station and on Via Cavour sell the €50 Florence Card, an expensive but handy pass for busy sightseers (see page 983).

At any TI, pick up these free, handy resources in English:

- a city map (ask for the transit map, which has bus routes of interest to tourists on the back; your hotel likely has freebie maps, too)
- a current museum-hours listing (extremely important, since no guidebook—including this one—has ever been able to accurately predict the hours of Florence's sights for the coming year)
- a list of current exhibitions
- a printout of what's happening that day
- information on entertainment, including the TI's monthly Florence and Tuscany News (good for events and entertainment listings)
- the ad-driven monthly *Florence Concierge Information* magazine (which lists museums, plus concerts, markets, sporting events, church services, shopping ideas, some bus and train connections, and an entire similar section on Siena)
- *The Florentine* newspaper (published every other Thu in English, for expats and tourists, with great articles giving cultural insights; download latest issue at www.theflorentine.net)

The magazine and newspaper listed above are also often available at hotels throughout town.

Arrival in Florence

By Train

Florence's main train station is called **Santa Maria Novella** (*Firenze S.M.N.* on schedules and signs). Built in Mussolini's

"Rationalism" style back between the wars, in some ways the station seems to have changed little—notice the 1930s-era lettering and architecture.

Florence also has two suburban train stations: **Firenze Rifredi** and **Firenze Campo di Marte.** Note that some trains don't stop at the main station—before boarding, confirm that you're heading for S.M.N., or you may overshoot the city. (If this happens, don't panic; the other stations are a short taxi ride from the center.)

Take advantage of the user-friendly, automated "Fast Ticket" machines that display schedules, issue tickets, and even make reservations for railpass-holders. Some take only credit cards; others take cards and cash. Using them is easy, and can actually be fun; just tap "English." If you need tickets within Italy, there's no reason to stand in line at a ticket window. But to get international tickets, you'll need to either go to a ticket window or a travel agency.

To orient yourself to the station and nearby services, stand with your back to the tracks. Look left to see a 24-hour pharmacy (*Farmacia,* near McDonald's), the fake "Tourist Information" office (funded by hotels), and baggage storage near track 16 (€4/5 hours, then €0.60/hour for 6-12 hours and €0.20/hour for over 12 hours, daily 6:00-23:50, passport required, maximum 40 pounds, no explosives—sorry).

Directly ahead of you is the way to the real TI (see previous page). To get there, walk away from the tracks and exit the station; the TI is straight across the square, 100 yards away, by the stone church. (If there's construction, circle around the torn-up square to the left to reach it.) For cheap eats, the handy Conad supermarket—with sandwiches and salads to go—is just around the corner (with your back to the tracks leave the station to the right, go down the steps, and it's immediately on your right on Via Luigi Alamanni, Mon-Sat 8:00-20:00, closed Sun).

Getting to the Duomo and City Center: The Duomo and town center are to your left (with your back to the tracks). Out the doorway to the left, you'll find city buses and the taxi stand. Taxis cost about €8 to the Duomo, and the line moves fast, except on holidays.

To walk into town (10-12 minutes), exit the station to the left and find the stairs/escalators down to the underground passageway/mall called Galleria S.M. Novella. Head toward the Church of Santa Maria Novella. (Warning: Pickpockets—often dressed as tourists—frequent this tunnel, especially the surface point near the church.) You come out on the other side of the square; head down Via dei Panzani which leads directly to the Duomo. Most recommended hotels are within a 10- or 15-minute walk from the station.

FLORENCE

Florence

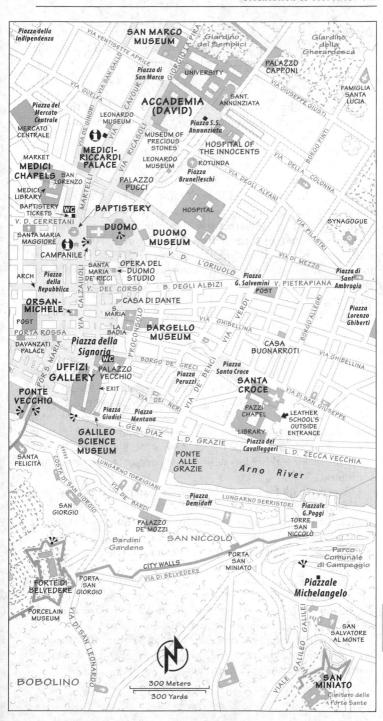

FLORENCE

By Bus

The bus station is next to the train station, with the TI across the square. For more information on buses, see page 977.

By Car

The autostrada has several exits for Florence. Get off at the *Nord*, *Sud*, or *Certosa* exits and follow signs toward—but not into—the *Centro*.

Don't even attempt driving into the city center. Florence has a traffic-reduction system that's complicated and confusing even to locals. Every car passing into the *Zona Traffico Limitato (ZTL)* is photographed; those who haven't jumped through bureaucratic hoops to get a permit can expect to receive a €100 ticket in the mail. If you get lost and cross the line several times...you get several fines. The no-go zone (defined basically by the old medieval wall, now a boulevard circling the historic center of town—watch for *Zona Traffico Limitato* signs) is roughly the area between the river, main train station, Piazza della Libertà, Piazza Donatello, and Piazza Beccaria.

Fortunately, the city center is ringed with big, efficient parking lots (signposted with the standard big *P*), each with taxi and bus service into the center. Check www.firenzeparcheggi.it for details on all their parking lots, availability, and prices. From the freeway, follow the signs to *Centro*, then *Stadio*, then *P*. I usually head for "Parcheggio del Parterre," just beyond Piazza della Libertà (€1.50/hour, €18/day, €65/week, open 24 hours daily, tel. 055-500-1994, 600 spots, automated, pay with cash or credit card, never fills up completely). To get into town, find the taxi stand at the elevator exit, or ride one of the *elettrico* minibuses that connect all of the major parking lots with the city center (see www.ataf.net for routes).

You can park for free along any suburban curb near a bus stop that feels safe, and take the bus into the city center from there. Check for signs that indicate parking restrictions—for example, a circle with a slash through it and "*dispari giovedì*, 0,00-06,00" means "don't park on Thursdays between midnight and six in the morning."

Free parking is easy up at Piazzale Michelangelo (see page 1007), but don't park where the buses drop off passengers; park on the side of the piazza farthest from the view. To get from Piazzale Michelangelo to the center of town, take bus #12 or #13.

If you're picking up a rental car upon departure, don't struggle with driving into the center. Taxi with your luggage to the car-rental office, and head out from there.

By Plane

For information on Florence's Amerigo Vespucci Airport, see "Florence Connections," near the end of this chapter.

Helpful Hints

Theft Alert: Florence has particularly hardworking gangs of thieves who hang out where you do: near the train station, the station's underpass (especially where the tunnel surfaces), and at major sights. American tourists—especially older ones—are considered easy targets. Some thieves even dress like tourists to fool you. Be on guard at two squares frequented by drug pushers (Santa Maria Novella and Santo Spirito). Bus #7 (to the nearby town of Fiesole, with great Florence views) is a favorite with tourists and, therefore, with thieves.

Medical Help: There's no shortage of English-speaking medical help in Florence. To reach a doctor who speaks English, call **Medical Service Firenze** at 055-475-411; the phone is answered 24/7. Rates are reasonable. For a doctor to come to your hotel within an hour of your call, you'd pay €100-200 (higher rates apply on Sun, holidays, or for late visits). You pay only €50 if you go to the clinic when the doctor's in (Mon-Fri 11:00-12:00 & 17:00-18:00, Sat 11:00-12:00, closed Sun, no appointment necessary, Via L. Magnifico 59, near Piazza della Libertà). A second clinic is available at Via Porta Rossa 1 (Mon-Sat 13:00-15:00, closed Sun).

Dr. Stephen Kerr is an English doctor specializing in helping sick tourists (clinic open for drop-ins Mon-Fri 15:00-17:00, other times by appointment, €50 per visit, Piazza Mercato Nuovo 1, between Piazza della Repubblica and Ponte Vecchio, tel. 055-288-055, mobile 335-836-1682, www.dr-kerr.com). The TI has a list of other English-speaking doctors.

There are 24-hour **pharmacies** at the train station and on Borgo San Lorenzo (near the Baptistery).

Museum Strategies: If you want to see a lot of museums, the pricey Florence Card—which saves you from having to wait in line or make reservations for the Uffizi and Accademia—can be a good value (see page 983).

Churches: Some churches now operate like museums, charging an admission fee to see their art treasures. Modest dress for men, women, and even children is required in some churches (including the Duomo, Santa Maria Novella, Santa Croce, and the Medici Chapels), and recommended for all of them—no bare shoulders, short shorts, or short skirts. Be respectful of worshippers and the paintings; don't use a flash. Churches usually close from 12:00 or 12:30 to 15:00 or 16:00.

FLORENCE

Addresses: Street addresses list businesses in red and residences in black (color-coded on the actual street number and indicated by a letter following the number in printed addresses: "r" = red; no indication or "n" = black, for *nero*). *Pensioni* are usually black but can be either. The red and black numbers each appear in roughly consecutive order on streets but bear no apparent connection with each other. I'm lazy and don't concern myself with the distinction (if one number's wrong, I look for the other) and can easily find my way around.

Chill Out: Schedule several cool breaks into your sightseeing where you can sit, pause, and refresh yourself with a sandwich, gelato, or coffee. Carry a water bottle to refill at Florence's twist-the-handle public fountains. Try the *fontanello* (dispenser of free cold water) on Piazza della Signoria, behind the statue of Neptune (to the left of the Palazzo Vecchio).

Internet Access: In bustling, tourist-filled Florence, you'll see small Internet cafés on virtually every street. **V.I.P. Internet** has cheap rates, numerous terminals, and long hours (€1.50/hour, daily 9:00-24:00, near recommended hotel Katti House at Via Faenza 49 red, tel. 055-264-5552). **Internet Train,** the dominant chain, is pricier, with bright and cheery rooms, speedy computers, and decent hours (€4.30/hour, cheaper for students, reusable card good for any other Internet Train location, open daily roughly 9:00-20:00, www.internettrain .it). Find branches near Piazza della Repubblica (Via Porta Rossa 38 red), behind the Duomo (Via dell'Oriolo 40), and on Piazza Santa Croce (Via de Benci 36 red). Internet Train also offers Wi-Fi, phone cards, compact-disc burning, and other related services.

If you have a smartphone, you can access free Wi-Fi for two hours at the **TI** near the train station. At the Hotspot machine, enter your mobile phone number (include the international access code if it's a US phone) to receive a text message with a user name and password.

Bookstores: Local guidebooks (sold at kiosks) are cheap, and give you a map and a decent commentary on the sights. For brand-name guidebooks in English, try **Feltrinelli International** (Mon-Sat 9:00-19:30, closed Sun, a few blocks north of the Duomo and across the street from TI and Medici-Riccardi Palace at Via Cavour 12 red, tel. 055-219-524); **Edison Bookstore** (also has CDs, plus novels on the Renaissance and much more on its four floors; Mon-Sat 9:00-24:00, Sun 10:00-24:00, facing Piazza della Repubblica, tel. 055-213-110); **Paperback Exchange** (cheaper, all books in English, bring in your used book for a discount on a new one, Mon-Fri 9:00-19:30, Sat 10:30-19:30, closed Sun, just south of the Duomo on Via delle Oche 4 red, tel. 055-293-460); or **BM Bookshop** (with perhaps the city's largest collection of English books and guidebooks—including mine; Mon-Sat 9:30-19:30, closed Sun, near Ponte alla Carraia at Borgognissanti 4 red, tel. 055-294-575).

Services: WCs are scarce. Use them when you can, in any café or museum you patronize.

Laundry: The **Wash & Dry Lavarapido** chain offers long hours and efficient, self-service launderettes at several locations (about €7 for wash and dry, bring plenty of coins, daily 8:00-22:00, tel. 055-580-480 or toll-free 800-231-172). These are close to recommended hotels: Via dei Servi 102 red (and a rival launderette at Via Guelfa 55, off Via San Zanobi; both near *David*), Via del Sole 29 red and Via della Scala 52 red (between train station and river), Via Ghibellina 143 red (Palazzo Vecchio), Via Faenza 26 (near station), and Via dei Serragli 87 red (across the river in Oltrarno neighborhood).

Bike Rental: The **city of Florence** rents bikes cheaply at several locations: the train station, Piazza Santa Croce, and Piazza Ghiberti (€1.50/1 hour, €4/5 hours, €8/24 hours, tel. 055-650-5295; for more information, ask at any TI). **Florence by Bike** rents two-wheelers of all sizes (€3/hour, €8/5 hours, includes bike lock and helmet, €3 extra for child seat, April-Nov daily 9:00-19:30, Via San Zanobi 120 red, tel. 055-488-992, www.florencebybike.it, info@florencebybike.it).

Travel Agency: While it's easy to buy train tickets to destinations within Italy at handy machines at the station, travel agencies can be more convenient and helpful for getting international tickets, reservations, and supplements. The cost is either the same or the charge is minimal. Ask your hotel for the nearest travel agency.

Getting Around Florence

I organize my sightseeing geographically and do it all on foot. I think of Florence as a Renaissance treadmill—it requires a lot of walking.

Buses: The city's full-size buses don't cover the old center well, especially now that the whole area around the Duomo has been declared off-limits to motorized traffic. Of the many bus lines, I find these to be of most value for seeing outlying sights: Lines #12 and #13 go from the train station to Porta Romana, up to San Miniato Church and Piazzale Michelangelo, and on to Santa Croce. Most other lines leave from Piazza San Marco (near the Accademia and Museum of San Marco), including bus #7, which goes to Fiesole, a small town with big views of Florence. To get from the train station to Piazza San Marco, either walk or take bus #1, #6, #14, or #23.

Fun little *elettrico* **minibuses** wind through the tangled old center of town and up and down the river—just €1.20 gets you a 90-minute joyride. These buses, which run every 10 minutes, are popular with sore-footed sightseers and eccentric local seniors. *Elettrico* #C2 twists through the congested old center from the train station to Piazza Beccaria. *Elettrico* #C3 goes up and down the Arno River from Ognissanti to Santa Croce Church and beyond; #C1 winds around Piazza Repubblica, then heads north up to Piazza Libertà. *Elettrico* #D goes from the train station to Ponte Vecchio, cruising through Oltrarno, and finishing at Ponte San Niccolò. The minibuses connect many major parking lots with the historical center (tickets sold at machines at lots). Routes are shown on the free TI map (see the handy inset) and the "La Rete dei Bussini Potenziata" leaflet, free at the ATAF bus office, located just east of the train station, on Piazza della Stazione.

Buy bus tickets at tobacco shops, newsstands, or the ATAF bus office (€1.20/1.5 hours, €4.50/4 tickets, €5/24 hours, €12/3 days, 1-day and 3-day passes aren't always available in tobacco shops, validate in machine on the bus, tel. 800-424-500, www .ataf.net). You can buy tickets on board, but you'll pay more (€2) and you'll need exact change. Follow general bus etiquette: Board at front or rear doors, exit out the center.

Taxi: The minimum cost for a taxi ride is €5, or €6 after 22:00 and on Sundays (rides in the center of town should be charged as tariff #1). A taxi ride from the train station to Ponte Vecchio costs about €9. Taxi fares and supplements (e.g., €2 extra if you call a cab rather than hail one) are clearly explained on signs in each taxi.

Tours in Florence

To sightsee on your own, download my series of **free audio tours** that illuminate Florence's top sights and historic core: the Accademia, Uffizi Gallery, and my Renaissance Walk (see sidebar on page 7).

Tour companies big and small offer plenty of tours that go out to smaller towns in the Tuscan countryside (the most popular day trips: Siena, San Gimignano, Pisa, and into Chianti country for wine tasting). They also do Florence city tours, but for most people, the city is really best on foot.

For insight with a personal touch, consider the tour companies and individual Florentine guides listed here. Hardworking and creative, they offer a worthwhile array of organized sightseeing activities. Study their websites for details. If you're taking a city tour, remember that individuals save money with a scheduled public tour (such as those offered daily by Florencetown or Artviva). If you're traveling as a family or small group, however, you're likely to save money by booking a private guide (since rates are based on roughly €55/hour for any size of group).

Walking (and Biking) Tours

Artviva Walking Tours—This company offers a variety of tours (up to 12/day year-round) featuring downtown Florence, museum highlights, and Tuscany day trips. Their guides are native English-speakers. The three-hour "Original Florence" walk hits the main sights but gets offbeat to weave a picture of Florentine life in medieval and Renaissance times. Tours go rain or shine with as few as four participants (€25, daily at 9:15). Museum tours include the Uffizi Gallery (€39, includes admission, 2 hours), Accademia (called "Original David" tour, €35, includes admission, 1 hour), and "Original Florence in One Day" (€94, includes admission to Uffizi and Accademia, 6 hours). Their brochure and website list more activities and events, including talks by artists, writers, and experts on wine and cuisine (Mon-Sat 8:00-18:00, Sun 8:30-13:30, near Piazza della Repubblica at Via dei Sassetti 1, second floor, above Odeon Cinema, tel. 055-264-5033 during day or mobile 329-613-2730 from 18:00-20:00, www.italy.artviva.com).

Florencetown Tours on Foot or by Bike—This well-organized company runs a variety of English-language tours. The boss, Luca Perfetto, offers student rates to anyone with this book, with an additional discount for second tours. Three tours—their basic town walk, bike tour, and cooking class—are worth considering: The "Walk and Talk Florence" tour, which takes 2.5 hours, hits all the basic spots, including the Oltrarno neighborhood (€19, daily at 10:00). The "I Bike Florence" tour gives you two hours on a vintage one-speed bike following a fast-talking guide on a two-hour blitz of the town's top sights (€29, daily at 10:00 and 15:00, helmets optional, 15 stops on both sides of the river; in bad weather, the bike tours go as a €19 walking tour). The cooking class costs €79 and includes a market tour; see the listing below. Their office is two blocks from the Palazzo Vecchio at Via de Lamberti 1—find steps off Via de' Calzaiuoli on the river side of Orsanmichele Church, tel. 055-012-3944, www.florencetown.com).

Walks Inside Florence—Three art historians—Paola Barubiani and her partners Emma Molignoni and Marzia Valbonesi—provide quality guiding. Their company offers a daily three-hour introductory tour (€50/person for groups up to 6 people, Accademia admission not included, outside except for a visit inside to see *David*) and three-hour private tours as well (€60/hour for up to 4 people, ask about Rick Steves discount, mobile 335-526-6496, www.walksinsideflorence.com, paola@walksinsideflorence.it).

Make Reservations to Avoid Lines

Florence has an optional reservation system for its state-run sights, which include the Accademia, Uffizi Gallery, Bargello, Medici Chapels, and the Pitti Palace. Many travelers skip the reservation process by getting a Florence Card instead (see page 983).

If you make reservations, I'd recommend getting them only for the Accademia (Michelangelo's *David*) and the Uffizi (Renaissance paintings), but not the others.

The Brancacci Chapel is the only sight in Florence that requires reservations (even with the Florence Card). These are free and simple to make a day in advance (and may even be available for the same day). For details, see page 1006.

The Uffizi and Accademia

If you're not planning to get a Florence Card, your best strategy is to get reservations for these two top sights as soon as you know when you'll be in town. Although you can generally get an entry time for the Accademia within a few days, the Uffizi can be booked well in advance.

There are several ways to make a reservation: Have your hotelier arrange it, call the reservation number directly, book online, take a tour, or go in person in advance to the museums or the Orsanmichele Church ticket window. Here are details on these options:

• When you make your **hotel** reservation, ask if they can book your museum reservations for you (some hoteliers will do this for free; others charge a €3-5 fee). This is your easiest option.

• Reserve by **phone** before you leave the States (from the US, dial 011-39-055-294-883, or within Italy call 055-294-883; €4/ticket reservation fee; booking office open Mon-Fri 8:30-18:30, Sat 8:30-12:30, closed Sun). The reservation line is often busy, and even if you get through, you may be disconnected while on hold. Be persistent and try again. When you do get

Florentia—Top-notch, private walking tours—geared for thoughtful, well-heeled travelers with longer-than-average attention spans—are led by Florentine scholars. The tours range from introductory city walks and museum visits to in-depth thematic walks, such as the Oltrarno neighborhood, "Unusual Florence," and side-trips into Tuscany (tours €175/half-day, €350/day, reserve in advance, tel. 338-890-8625, www.florentia.org, info@florentia.org).

Context Florence—This scholarly group of graduate students and professors leads "walking seminars," such as a three-hour study of Michelangelo's work and influence (€85/person, includes Accademia admission) and a two-hour evening orientation stroll (€35/person). I enjoyed the fascinating three-hour fresco workshop through, an English-speaking operator walks you through the process, and a few minutes later you say *grazie,* having received an appointment and a six-digit confirmation number. Bring the confirmation(s) with you and pay cash at the sight(s). The advantage to phoning versus booking online is that you pay nothing upfront when you phone.

• Using a credit card, you can reserve your visit **online.** Pricey middleman sites—such as www.uffizi.com and www.tickitaly.com—are reliable, but their booking fees are exorbitant, running about €10 per ticket. Or you could take your chances with the city's troublesome official site (www.firenzemusei.it) in the hopes that its glitches have been fixed. It's the cheapest place to make reservations online (€4/ticket reservation fee), but even when it's working, the site often reverts to Italian-only (*"Annulia operazione"* means "cancel"), you can't book a time before noon, and some readers report not receiving vouchers they've paid for.

• Take a **tour** that includes your museum admission. Artviva Walking Tours offers tours of the Uffizi (€39/person, 2 hours), Accademia (€35/person, 1 hour), and both museums (€94/person, 6 hours; see listing on page 979, or visit www.italy.artviva.com).

• To **reserve in Florence,** here are your choices: call the reservation number (see above); ask your hotelier for help; or head to the booking window at Orsanmichele Church (€4 reservation fee, daily 10:00-17:00, along Via de' Calzaiuoli—see location on map on page 990). For another Uffizi option, go to its ticket office and pay cash (Tue-Sun 8:15-18:50, use the main entrance—door #2, enter to the left of the ticket-buying line).

Off-Season: If you're in Florence off-season (Nov-March), you can probably get into the Uffizi or Accademia without a reservation in the late afternoon (after 16:00). But why not make a reservation? After seeing hundreds of bored tourists waiting in lines, it's hard not to be amazed at their cluelessness.

(€75/person, you take home a fresco you make yourself). See their website for other innovative offerings: Medici walk, lecture series, food walks, kids' tours, and programs in Venice, Rome, Naples, London, and Paris (tel. 069-762-5204, US tel. 800-691-6036, www.contexttravel.com, info@contexttravel.com).

Florencetown Cooking Class and Market Tour

For something special, consider this five-hour experience. You'll start with a trip to the Mercato Centrale for shopping and tasting, then settle into their kitchen for a cooking lesson, and finish with a big feast eating everything you've just cooked. You'll meet butchers and bakers, and make bruschetta, pasta, a main course, and dessert (likely tiramisu). Groups are intimate and small (from 1-14 people, €79/person, ask for Rick Steves discount, Mon-Sat 10:00-15:00, runs rain or shine, chef Giovanni, Via de Lamberti 1, tel. 055-012-3944, www.florencetown.com).

Local Guides for Private Tours

Alessandra Marchetti, a Florentine who has lived in the US, gives private walking tours of Florence and driving tours of Tuscany (€60-75/hour, mobile 347-386-9839, aleoberm@tin.it). **Paola Migliorini** and her partners at Tuscany Tours offer museum tours, city walking tours, private cooking classes, wine tours, and Tuscan excursions by van—you can tailor tours as you like (€55/hour without car, €65/hour in an 8-seat van, tel. 055-472-448, mobile 347-657-2611, www.florencetour.com, info@florencetour.com); they also do private tours from the cruise-ship port of Livorno. **Karin Kibby,** an Oregonian living in Livorno who leads Rick Steves tours, also offers day tours throughout Tuscany, including excursions for cruise-ship passengers docking at Livorno. She'll work with you to find the best solution for your budget and interests (2-10 people, mobile 333-108-6348, karinkintuscany@yahoo.it).

Hop-on, Hop-off Bus Tours

Around town, you'll see big double-decker sightseeing buses double-parking near major sights. Tourists on the top deck can listen to brief recorded descriptions of the sights, snap photos, and enjoy an effortless drive-by look at the major landmarks (€22, valid for two days, pay as you board, www.firenze.city-sightseeing.it). As the name implies, you can hop off when you want and catch the next bus (usually every 30 minutes). As most sights are buried in the old center where big buses can't go, Florence doesn't really lend itself to this kind of tour bus. Look at the route map before committing.

Self-Guided Walk

A Renaissance Walk Through Florence

During the Dark Ages, it was especially obvious to the people of Italy—sitting on the rubble of Rome—that there had to be a brighter age on the horizon. The long-awaited rebirth, or Renaissance, began in Florence for good reason. Wealthy because of its cloth industry, trade, and banking; powered by a fierce city-state pride (locals would pee into the Arno with gusto, knowing rival city-state Pisa was downstream); and fertile with more than its share of artistic genius (imagine guys like Michelangelo and Leonardo attending the same high school)—Florence was a natural home for this cultural explosion.

Take a two-hour walk through the core of Renaissance Florence from the Duomo (cathedral) to Ponte Vecchio on the Arno River. You can download a free Rick Steves **audio tour** of this walk (see page 7).

Begin at the Duomo to marvel at the dome that kicked off the architectural Renaissance. Step inside the Baptistery to view a ceiling covered with preachy, flat, 2-D, medieval mosaic art. Then, to learn what happened when art met math, check out the realistic 3-D reliefs on the doors; the man who painted them, Giotto, also designed the bell tower—an early example of a Renaissance genius who excelled in many areas.

Continue toward the river on Florence's great pedestrian mall, Via de' Calzaiuoli—part of the original grid plan given to the city by the ancient Romans. Stop by any gelato shop for some cool refreshment. Down a few blocks, compare medieval and Renaissance statues on the exterior of the Orsanmichele Church. Via de' Calzaiuoli connects the cathedral with the central square (Piazza della Signoria), the city palace (Palazzo Vecchio), and the Uffizi Gallery, which contains the greatest collection of Italian Renaissance paintings in captivity. Finally, walk through the Uffizi courtyard—a statuary thinktank of Renaissance greats—to the Arno River and Ponte Vecchio.

Sights in Florence

You have two good options for bypassing the long lines at Florence's top two sights, the Accademia and Uffizi Gallery. Either buy a Florence Card (see below) or make reservations to visit both sights (see page 980 for details).

Florence Card

The pricey Florence Card (€50) gives you admission to many top sights (including the Uffizi Gallery and Accademia), plus many lesser ones. It also gives you free use of Florence city buses.

Though the card is unlikely to save you much money, it can certainly save time. With the card, you don't need reservations and don't need to wait in ticket-buying lines. You simply go to the entrance, show the card, and walk in (though there may be delays at top sights if they're reached maximum capacity). For people seeing five or six major sights in a short time, the card is probably worth it. (But if you only want to see the Uffizi and Accademia, you'll save at least €20 by making reservations instead; see page 980.)

The Florence Card is valid for 72 hours from when you validate it at your first museum (e.g., Tue at 15:00 until Fri at 15:00). It includes the regular admission price as well as any temporary

FLORENCE

exhibits (which are commonly tacked on at major sights such as the Uffizi). The card is good for one visit per sight and is not shareable. Non-EU citizens are not eligible for discounts.

To figure out if the Florence Card is a good deal for you, tally up the entry fees of what you want to see. For example, here's a list of popular sights and their admission fees:

Uffizi Gallery (€6.50 base price, usually €11 with temporary exhibits, as much as €15 with €4 reservation fee)

Accademia (same fees as Uffizi, above)

Palazzo Vecchio (€6)

Bargello (€4 base, €7 with exhibits)

Medici Chapels (€7 base, €9 with exhibits)

Museum of San Marco (€4)

Medici-Riccardi Palace (€5 base, €7 with exhibits)

If you saw these sights without the card, you'd pay about €60, including the exhibit and reservation fees. Other covered sights featured in this chapter: Pitti Palace (both Palatine Gallery and Boboli Gardens), Brancacci Chapel (though you still must make a free reservation), Museum of Precious Stones, Palazzo Davanzati, and Museum of Santa Maria Novella. The card is great for popping into lesser sights you otherwise wouldn't pay for. For a complete list of included sights, see www.firenzecard.it.

Notable exceptions: the Duomo dome climb, Campanile, Duomo Museum, Baptistery, Church of Santa Maria Novella, Santa Croce Church, Galileo Science Museum, Casa Buonarroti, Casa di Dante, and the two Leonardo museums.

Getting the card makes the most sense in peak season, from April through October, when crowds are worst. Off-season travelers could do without it and probably save a few euros.

You can buy the card at many participating outlets. The best places to buy (with no lines) are the TI at Via Cavour 1 red (a couple of blocks north of the Duomo), the Uffizi Gallery's door #2 (enter to the left of the ticket-buying line), or the never-crowded Museum of Santa Maria Novella (near the train station). You can also buy the card online (www.firenzecard.it), obtain a voucher, and then pick up the card at the TI or some participating sights.

Think ahead to make the most of your card. Validate it only when you're ready to tackle the covered sights on three consecutive days. Make sure the sights you want to visit will be open (many sights are closed Sundays or Mondays).

North of the Arno River
North of the Duomo (Cathedral)

▲▲▲**Accademia (Galleria dell'Accademia)**—When you look into the eyes of Michelangelo's magnificent sculpture of *David*, you're looking into the eyes of Renaissance Man.

In 1501, Michelangelo Buonarroti, a 26-year-old Florentine, was commissioned to carve a large-scale work. The figure comes from a Bible story. The Israelites are surrounded by barbarian warriors, who are led by a brutish giant named Goliath. When the giant challenges the Israelites to send out someone to fight him, a young shepherd boy steps forward. Armed only with a sling, David defeats the giant. This 17-foot-tall symbol of divine victory over evil represents a new century and a whole new Renaissance outlook.

Originally, *David* was meant to stand on the roofline of the Duomo, but was placed more prominently at the entrance of Palazzo Vecchio (where a copy stands today). In the 19th century, *David* was moved indoors for his own protection, and stands under a wonderful Renaissance-style dome designed just for him.

Nearby are some of the master's other works, including his powerful (unfinished) *Prisoners, St. Matthew,* and a *Pietà* (possibly by one of his disciples). Florentine Michelangelo Buonarroti, who would work tirelessly through the night, believed that the sculptor was a tool of God, responsible only for chipping away at the stone until the intended sculpture emerged. Beyond the magic marble are some mildly interesting pre-Renaissance and Renaissance paintings, including a couple of lighter-than-air Botticellis, the plaster model of Giambologna's *Rape of the Sabines,* and a musical instrument collection with an early piano.

Cost and Hours: €6.50, up to €11 with mandatory temporary exhibits, plus €4 fee for reservation (see page 980 for details), Tue-Sun 8:15-18:50, closed Mon, last entry 45 minutes before closing, Via Ricasoli 60, tel. 055-238-8609 or 055-294-883, www.polo museale.firenze.it).

Avoiding Lines: In peak season (April-Oct), the museum is most crowded on Sun, Tue, and right when it opens. It's smart to reserve ahead (see page 980) or buy the Florence Card (see page 983). Those with reservations or the Florence Card line up at the entrance labeled *With Reservations.* On off-season weekdays (Nov-March) before 8:30 or after 16:00, you can sometimes get in with no reservation and no lines.

Audioguides: The museum rents a €5.50 **audioguide** (€8/2 people; rent from souvenir counter in ticket lobby). You can download a free Rick Steves **audio tour** of the Accademia; see page 7.

Nearby: Piazza S.S. Annunziata, behind the Accademia, displays lovely Renaissance harmony. Facing the square are two fine buildings: the 15th-century Santissima Annunziata church (worth a peek) and Filippo Brunelleschi's Hospital of the Innocents (Spedale degli Innocenti, not worth going inside), with terra-cotta medallions by Luca della Robbia. Built in the 1420s, the hospital is considered the first Renaissance building. I love sleeping on this square (at the recommended Hotel Loggiato dei Serviti) and picnicking here during the day (with the riffraff, who remind me of the persistent gap—today as in Renaissance times—between those who appreciate fine art and those just looking for some cheap wine).

▲▲**Museum of San Marco (Museo di San Marco)**—Located one block north of the Accademia, this 15th-century monastery houses the greatest collection anywhere of frescoes and paintings by the early Renaissance master Fra Angelico.

The ground floor features the monk's paintings, along with some works by Fra Bartolomeo. Upstairs are 43 cells decorated by Fra Angelico and his assistants. While the monk/painter was trained in the medieval religious style, he also learned and adopted Renaissance techniques and sensibilities, producing works that blended Christian symbols and Renaissance realism. Don't miss the cell of Savonarola, the charismatic monk who rode in from the Christian right, threw out the ruling Medici family, turned Florence into a theocracy, sponsored "bonfires of the vanities" (burning books, paintings, and so on), and was finally burned himself when Florence decided to change channels.

Cost and Hours: €4, Tue-Fri 8:15-13:50, Sat 8:15-16:50; also open 8:15-16:50 on second and fourth Sun and 8:15-13:50 on first, third, and fifth Mon of each month; last entry 30 minutes before closing, reservations possible but unnecessary, on Piazza San Marco, tel. 055-238-8608, www.polomuseale.firenze.it.

Museum of Precious Stones (Museo dell'Opificio delle Pietre Dure)—This unusual gem of a museum features room after room of exquisite mosaics of inlaid marble and other stones. The Medici loved colorful stone table tops and floors; you'll even find landscapes and portraits (find Cosimo I in Room I). Upstairs, you'll see wooden work benches from a workshop funded by the art-patron Medici family (1588), complete with foot-powered power tools. Rockhounds can browse 500 different stones (lapis lazuli, quartz, agate, marble, and so on) and the tools used to cut and inlay them. There's English info in each room.

Cost and Hours: €4, Mon-Sat 8:15-14:00, closed Sun, around corner from Accademia at Via degli Alfani 78, tel. 055-265-1357.

Church of San Lorenzo—This red-brick dome—which looks like the Duomo's little sister—marks the burial place of Giovanni di Bicci de' Medici (1360-1429), founder of the influential Medici family. Part *Sopranos,* part Kennedys, part John-D-and-Catherine-T art patrons, the Medici dominated Florentine politics for 300 years (c. 1434-1737). Immeasurably wealthy from their cloth, silk, and banking businesses, the family rose to the ranks of Europe's nobility, producing popes and queens.

Renaissance Walk

300 Meters

300 Yards

ACCADEMIA
(DAVID)

LEONARDO MUSEUM

MUSEUM OF PRECIOUS STONES

VIA CAVOUR

VIA RICASOLI

VIA DE' GINORI

VIA STUFA

BORGO LA NOCE

VIA S. ANTONINO

V. AMARINO

V. DEI MELARANCIO

MARKET

Piazza di San Lorenzo

MEDICI-RICCARDI PALACE

VIA DE' PUCCI

PALAZZO PUCCI

LEONARDO MUSEUM

VIA DE' SERVI

V. DEI MARINO

MEDICI CHAPELS

SAN LORENZO

VIA BIFFI

VIA DEL GIGLIO

DELL'ALLORO

VIA DE' CONTI

ZANNETTI

MEDICI LIBRARY

BORGO SAN LORENZO

V. MARTELLI

To Train Station

VIA PANZANI

VIA DEI BANCHI VIA DE' CERRETANI

RONDINELLI

SANTA MARIA MAGGIORE

VIA PECORI

SAN GAETANO

V. CORSI

VIA DEL TORNABUONI

VIA D. VECCHIETTI

BRUNELLESCHI

V. DE' PESCIONI

ARCH

VIA D. STROZZI

STROZZI PALACE

V. D'ANSELMI

Piazza della Repubblica

WC

BAPTISTERY TICKETS

Piazza di San Giovanni

BAPTISTERY

DUOMO

LEONARDO MUSEUM

VIA M. BUFALINI

DUOMO MUSEUM

LOGGIA DI BIGALO &

Piazza del Duomo

GIOTTO'S TOWER

VIA DELL'ORIUOLO

WALK BEGINS

MEDICI

CALZAIUOLI

CANONICA

VIA DELL'OCHE

BONIZZI

STUDIO

Piazza della Repubblica

SPEZIALI

SANTA MARIA DE' RICCI

VIA DEL CORSO

CASA DI DANTE

TAVOLINI VIA D. ALIGHIERI

CERCHI

BORGO DEGLI ALBIZI

VIA DE' GIRALDI

PRESTO

VIA DEL PROCONSOLO

ORSAN-MICHELE

LAMBERTI

V. PELLICCERIA

SASSETTI

MONALDA

POST

Piazza de' Davanzati

VIA PORTA ROSSA

DAVANZATI PALACE

DELLE TERME

MERCATO NUOVO

CIMATORI

CONDOTTA

S. MARIA LA BADIA

V. DELLA VIGNA VECCHIA

BARGELLO MUSEUM

VIA BURELLA

Piazza di Santa Trinita

BORGO S. APOSTOLI

LUNGARNO ACCIAIUOLI

BOMBARDE

VIA POR S. MARIA

MANETTO

ARMA

Piazza della Signoria

LOGGIA

BARONCELLI

GONDI

WC

PALAZZO VECCHIO

Piazza S. Firenze

To Santa Croce

BORGO DE' GRECI

VINEGRIA

MAGALOTTI

V. DELL'ANGUILLARA

Piazza de' Salt.

LAMB.

UFFIZI GALLERY

VIA LEONI

CORNO

PONTE VECCHIO

WALK ENDS

MEDICI'S "SECRET" WALKWAY

S. Stephano

EXIT

CASTELLANI

OSTERIA

GALILEO SCIENCE MUSEUM

Piazza Giudici

SAPONAI

Piazza Mentana

LUNGARNO GEN. DIAZ

VAGELLAI

MALENCHINI

BORGO SAN JACOPO

V. D. RAMAGLI ANTI

V. BARB.

VIA DE' GUICCIARDINI

OLTRARNO

Arno River

SANTA FELICITA

To Pitti Palace

PONTE ALLE GRAZIE

The façade of the church is big, ugly, and unfinished, because Pope Leo X (also a Medici) pulled the plug on the project due to dwindling funds—after Michelangelo had labored on it for four years (1516-1520). Inside, though, is the spirit of Florence in the 1420s, with gray-and-white columns and arches in perfect Renaissance symmetry and simplicity. The Brunelleschi-designed church is lit by an even, diffused light. The Medici coat of arms (with the round pills of these "medics") decorates the ceiling, and everywhere are images of St. Lawrence, the Medici patron saint who was martyred on a grill.

Highlights of the church include two finely sculpted Donatello pulpits (in the nave). In the Martelli Chapel (left wall of the left transept), Filippo Lippi's *Annunciation* features a smiling angel greeting Mary in a sharply 3-D courtyard. Light shines through the vase in the foreground, like the Holy Spirit entering Mary's womb. The Old Sacristy (far left corner), designed by Brunelleschi, was the burial chapel for the Medici. Bronze doors by Donatello flank the sacristy's small altar. Overhead, the dome above the altar shows the exact arrangement of the heavens on July 4, 1442, leaving scholars to hypothesize about why that particular date was used. Back in the nave, the round inlaid marble in the floor before the main altar marks where Cosimo the Elder is buried. Assistants in the church provide information on request, and the information brochure is free and in English.

Cost and Hours: €3.50, Feb-Oct Mon-Sat 10:00-17:00, Sun 13:30-17:00, closed Nov-Jan.

Nearby: Outside the church, along the left side, is a **cloister** with peek-a-boo Duomo views and the **San Lorenzo Museum.** This collection of fancy reliquaries is included in your church admission, but is hardly worth the walk, except to see Donatello's grave. Also in the cloister is the **Laurentian Library** (not included in church entry and only open during special exhibits). The library, largely designed by Michelangelo, stars his impressive staircase, which widens imperceptibly as it descends. Michelangelo also did the walls in the vestibule (entrance) that feature empty niches, scrolls, and oddly tapering pilasters. Climb the stairs and enter the Reading Room—a long, rectangular hall with a coffered-wood ceiling—designed by Michelangelo to host scholars enjoying the Medici's collection of manuscripts. The library is well worthwhile if it's open (€3, includes special exhibits, generally 9:30-13:00).

A **street market** bustles outside the church (listed after the Medici Chapels, next). Around the back end of the church is the entrance to the Medici Chapels and the New Sacristy, designed by Michelangelo for a later generation of dead Medici.

▲▲**Medici Chapels (Cappelle Medicee)**—The burial site of the ruling Medici family in the Church of San Lorenzo includes the dusky Crypt; the big, domed Chapel of Princes; and the magnificent, all-Michelangelo New Sacristy, featuring the master's architecture, tombs, and statues. The Medici made their money in textiles and banking, and patronized a dream team of Renaissance artists that put Florence on the cultural map. Michelangelo, who spent his teen years living with the Medici, was commissioned for the family's final tribute.

Cost and Hours: €7, €9 with mandatory exhibits, audio-guide-€5.50 (€8/2 people), Tue-Sat April-Oct 8:15-16:50, Nov-March 8:15-13:50; also open first, third, and fifth Sun and second and fourth Mon of each month; last entry 30 minutes before closing; modest dress required, tel. 055-238-8602, www.polomuseale.firenze.it.

▲San Lorenzo Market—Florence's vast open-air market sprawls around the Church of San Lorenzo. Most of the leather stalls are run by Iranians selling South American leather that was tailored in Italy. Prices are soft (daily 9:00-19:00, closed Mon in winter, between the Duomo and train station).

▲Mercato Centrale (Central Market)—Florence's giant iron-and-glass-covered central market, a wonderland of picturesque produce, is fun to explore. While the nearby San Lorenzo Market—with its garment stalls in the streets—feels like a step up from a haphazard flea market, the Mercato Centrale retains a Florentine elegance. Wander around. You'll see parts of the cow you'd never dream of eating (no, that's not a turkey neck), enjoy generous free samples, watch pasta making, and have your pick of plenty of fun eateries sloshing out cheap and tasty pasta to locals (Mon-Sat 7:00-14:00, in winter open Sat until 17:00, closed Sun). For eating ideas in and around the market, see "Eating in Florence," later.

▲Medici-Riccardi Palace (Palazzo Medici-Riccardi)—Lorenzo the Magnificent's home is worth a look for its art. The tiny Chapel of the Magi contains colorful Renaissance gems like the *Procession of the Magi* frescoes by Benozzo Gozzoli. The former library has a Baroque ceiling fresco by Luca Giordano, a prolific artist from Naples known as "Fast Luke" *(Luca fa presto)* for his speedy workmanship. While the Medici originally occupied this 1444 house, in the 1700s it became home to the Riccardi family, who added the Baroque flourishes.

Cost and Hours: €5, €7 with mandatory special exhibits, Thu-Tue 9:00-19:00, closed Wed, last entry 30 minutes before closing; ticket entrance is north of the main gated entrance, Via Cavour 3, tel. 055-276-0340, www.palazzo-medici.it.

Leonardo Museums—Two different-but-similar entrepreneurial establishments several blocks apart show off reproductions of Leonardo's ingenious inventions. Either one is fun for anyone who wants to crank the shaft and spin the ball bearings of Leonardo's fertile imagination. While there are no actual historic artifacts, each museum shows several dozen of Leonardo's inventions and experiments made into working models. You might see a full-size armored tank, walk into a chamber of mirrors, operate a rotating crane, or watch experiments in flying. The exhibits are described in English, and what makes these places special is that you're

FLORENCE

Heart of Florence

encouraged to touch and play with the models—it's great for kids. The museum on Via dei Servi is a bit larger.

Cost and Hours: Admission to each museum is €7. Museo Leonardo da Vinci—daily 10:00-19:00, closes at 18:00 in winter, Via dei Servi 66 red, tel. 055-282-966, www.mostredileonardo .com. Le Macchine di Leonardo da Vinci—April-Oct daily 9:30-19:30; Nov-March Mon-Fri 11:00-17:00, Sat-Sun 9:30-19:30; in Galleria Michelangelo at Via Cavour 21, tel. 055-899-9471, www .macchinedileonardo.com.

Duomo and Nearby

▲▲Duomo (Cattedrale di Santa Maria del Fiore)—Florence's Gothic cathedral has the third-longest nave in Christendom. The church's noisy neo-Gothic facade from the 1870s is covered with pink, green, and white Tuscan marble. In the interior, you'll see a huge *Last Judgment* by Giorgio Vasari and Federico Zuccari (inside the dome). Much of the church's great art is stored in the Duomo Museum behind the church.

The cathedral's claim to artistic fame is Brunelleschi's magnificent dome—the first Renaissance dome and the model for domes to follow. Think of the confidence of the age: The Duomo was built with a big hole in its roof, awaiting a dome...but it was built before the technology to span the hole with a dome even existed. No *problema*. They knew that someone soon could rise to the challenge...and the local architect Filippo Brunelleschi did. First, he built the grand white skeletal ribs, which you can see, then filled them in with interlocking bricks in a herringbone pattern. The dome grew upward like an igloo, supporting itself as it proceeded from the base. When the ribs reached the top, Brunelleschi arched them in and fixed them in place with the cupola at the top. His dome, built in only 14 years, was the largest since Rome's Pantheon.

Massive crowds line up to see the huge church, which is a major sight but not worth a long wait. Either go late (the crowds subside by late afternoon), or take the Terraces tour mentioned below.

Cost and Hours: Free entry, Mon-Fri 10:00-17:00, Thu until 16:00 Oct-May, Sat 10:00-16:45, Sun 12:00-17:00, modest dress code enforced, tel. 055-230-2885, www.operaduomo.firenze.it.

Crowd-Beating Tip: Taking the "**Terraces of the Cathedral and Dome**" tour allows you to skip the long lines to enter the cathedral and to climb the dome. After a short guided tour of the interior, you'll climb up onto the exterior terrace, where great views reward the hike up the stairs (see "Climbing the Duomo's Dome," next). When the tour is finished on the terrace, you can continue on your own up to the top of the dome (€15, 45 minutes;

offered Mon-Fri at 10:30, 12:00, and 15:00; Sat at 10:30 and 12:00, no tours on Sun, buy tickets at nearby Duomo Museum and they'll tell you where to meet your guide). If you're planning to climb the dome anyway (€8), the tour is a fine value.

▲**Climbing the Duomo's Dome**—For a grand view into the cathedral from the base of the dome, a peek at some of the tools used in the dome's construction, a chance to see Brunelleschi's "dome-within-a-dome" construction, a glorious Florence view from the top, and the equivalent of 463 plunges on a Renaissance StairMaster, climb the dome. Michelangelo, setting out to construct the dome of St. Peter's in Rome, drew inspiration from the dome of Florence. He said, "I'll make its sister...bigger, but not more beautiful." To avoid the long, dreadfully slow-moving line, arrive by 8:30 or drop by very late. Those taking the "Terraces" tour of the Duomo (see earlier) can skip the line.

Cost and Hours: €8, cash only, Mon-Fri 8:30-19:00, Sat 8:30-17:40, closed Sun, last entry 40 minutes before closing, enter from outside church on north side, tel. 055-230-2885.

▲**Campanile (Giotto's Tower)**—The 270-foot bell tower has 50 fewer steps than the Duomo's dome (but that's still 413 steps—no elevator); offers a faster, less-crowded climb; and has a view of the Duomo to boot, but the cage-like top makes taking good photographs difficult.

Cost and Hours: €6, daily 8:30-19:30, last entry 40 minutes before closing.

▲**Baptistery**—Michelangelo said its bronze doors were fit to be the gates of paradise. Check out the gleaming copies of Lorenzo Ghiberti's bronze doors facing the Duomo (the original panels are in the Duomo Museum). Making a breakthrough in perspective, Ghiberti used mathematical laws to create the illusion of receding distance on a basically flat surface.

The doors on the north side of the building were designed by Ghiberti when he was young; he'd won the honor and opportunity by beating Brunelleschi in a competition (the rivals' original entries are in the Bargello).

Inside, sit and savor the medieval mosaic ceiling, where it's always Judgment Day and Jesus is giving the ultimate thumbs-up and thumbs-down. The rest of the ceiling mosaics tell the history of the world, from Adam and Eve (over the north/entrance doors, top row), to Noah and the Flood (over south doors, top row), to the life of Christ (second row), to the beheading of John the Baptist (bottom row)—all bathed in the golden glow of pre-Renaissance heaven.

Cost and Hours: €4, €7 with mandatory exhibits, interior open Mon-Sat 12:15-19:00 except first Sat of month 8:30-14:00, Sun 8:30-14:00, last entry 30 minutes before closing, tel.

055-230-2885. The bronze doors are on the outside, so they are always "open" and viewable.

▲▲▲Duomo Museum (Museo dell'Opera del Duomo)—The underrated cathedral museum, behind the church (at Via del Proconsolo 9), is great if you like sculpture. On the ground floor, look for a late Michelangelo *Pietà* and statues from the original Baptistery facade. Upstairs, you'll find Brunelleschi's models for his dome, as well as Donatello's anorexic *Mary Magdalene* and playful choir loft. The museum features Ghiberti's original bronze "Gates of Paradise" panels (the ones on the Baptistery's doors today are copies); throughout years of restoration, only some of the panels have been on display, but most should be back in place in time for your visit.

Cost and Hours: €6, Mon-Sat 9:00-19:30, Sun 9:00-13:40, last entry 40 minutes before closing, one of the few museums in Florence always open on Mon, Via del Proconsolo 9, tel. 055-230-2885, www.operaduomo.firenze.it. At this museum, you can purchase tickets for the "Terraces of the Cathedral and Dome" tour mentioned earlier (page 992), which allows you to bypass the long cathedral-entry and dome-climbing lines. The audioguide costs €5. Guided English tours are generally offered on Mon, Thu, Sun at 10:30 (€9).

Nearby: If you find this church art intriguing, head to the left around the back of the Duomo to find Via dello Studio (near the south transept), then walk a block toward the river to #23a. You can look through the open doorway of the Opera del Duomo art studio and see workers sculpting new statues, restoring old ones, or making exact copies. They're carrying on an artistic tradition that dates back to the days of Brunelleschi.

Between the Duomo and Piazza della Signoria

▲▲▲Bargello (Museo Nazionale)—This underappreciated sculpture museum is in a former police station-turned-prison that looks like a mini-Palazzo Vecchio. It has Donatello's very influential, painfully beautiful *David* (the first male nude to be sculpted in a thousand years), works by Michelangelo, and rooms of Medici treasures explained only in Italian (politely suggest to the staff that English descriptions would be wonderful). Moody Donatello, who embraced realism with his lifelike statues, set the personal and artistic style for many Renaissance artists to follow. The best works are in the ground-floor room at the foot of the outdoor staircase and in the room directly above.

Cost and Hours: €4, €7 with mandatory exhibits, Tue-Sat 8:15-13:50, until 16:50 during exhibits (generally April-Oct); also open first, third, and fifth Mon and the second and fourth Sun of each month; last entry 40 minutes before closing, Via del

Proconsolo 4, reservation tel. 055-238-8606, www.polomuseale
.firenze.it.

Casa di Dante (Dante's House)—Dante Alighieri (1265-1321),
the poet who gave us *The Divine Comedy*, is the Shakespeare of
Italy, the father of the modern Italian language, and the face on
the country's €2 coin. However, most Americans know little of
him, and this museum is not the ideal place to start. Even though
it has English information, this small museum (in a building near
where he likely lived) assumes visitors have prior knowledge of the
poet. It's not a medieval-flavored house with period furniture—it's
just a small, low-tech museum about Dante. Still, Dante lovers can
trace his interesting life and works through pictures, models, and
artifacts. And because the exhibits are as much about medieval
Florence as they are about the man, novices can learn a little about
Dante and the city he lived in.

Cost and Hours: €4, summer daily 10:00-18:00; winter Tue-
Sun 10:00-17:00, closed Mon; last entry 30 minutes before closing, near the Bargello at Via Santa Margherita 1, tel. 055-219-416,
www.museocasadidante.it.

▲Orsanmichele Church—In the ninth century, this loggia
(covered courtyard) was a market used for selling grain (stored
upstairs). Later, it was enclosed to make a church.

Outside are dynamic, statue-filled niches, some with accompanying symbols from the guilds that sponsored the art. Donatello's
St. Mark and *St. George* (on the northeast and northwest corners)
step out boldly in the new Renaissance style.

The interior has a glorious Gothic tabernacle (1359) housing
the painted wooden panel that depicts *Madonna delle Grazie* (1346).
The iron bars spanning the vaults were the Italian Gothic answer
to the French Gothic external buttresses. Look for the rectangular
holes in the piers—these were once wheat chutes that connected to
the upper floors.

Cost and Hours: Free, Tue-Sun 10:00-17:00, closed Mon,
niche sculptures always viewable from the outside. You can give
the *Madonna della Grazie* a special thanks if you're in town when an
evening concert is held inside the Orsanmichele (tickets sold on day
of concert from door facing Via de' Calzaiuoli; also books Uffizi
and Accademia tickets, ticket window open daily 10:00-17:00).

▲Mercato Nuovo (a.k.a. the Straw Market)—Just a block
away, this market loggia is how Orsanmichele looked before it
became a church. Originally a silk and straw market, Mercato
Nuovo still functions as a rustic yet touristy market (at the intersection of Via Calimala and Via Porta Rossa). Prices are soft, but the
San Lorenzo Market (listed earlier) is much better for haggling.
Notice the circled X in the center, marking the spot where people
hit after being hoisted up to the top and dropped as punishment

for bankruptcy. You'll also find *Porcellino* (a statue of a wild boar nicknamed "little pig"), which people rub and give coins to in order to ensure their return to Florence. This new copy, while only a few years old, already has a polished snout. At the back corner, a wagon sells tripe (cow innards) sandwiches—a local favorite (daily 9:00-20:00).

▲**Piazza della Repubblica and Nearby**—This large square sits on the site of the original Roman Forum. Florence was a riverside garrison town set below the older town of Fiesole—essentially a rectangular fort with the square marking the intersection of the two main roads (Via Corso and Via Roma). The square's lone column—nicknamed "the belly button of Florence"—once marked the intersection (the Roman streets were about nine feet below the present street level). All that survives of Roman Florence is this column and the city's street plan. Look at any map of Florence today (there's one by the benches—where the old boys hang out to talk sports and politics), and you'll see the ghost of Rome in its streets: a grid-plan city center surrounded by what was the Roman wall. The Braille model of the city makes the design clear.

Venerable cafés and stores line the square. During the 19th century, intellectuals met in cafés on the square. The La Rinascente department store, facing Piazza della Repubblica, is one of the city's mainstays (WC on fourth floor, continue up the stairs from there to the bar with a rooftop terrace with great Duomo and city views).

▲**Palazzo Davanzati**—This five-story, late-medieval tower house offers a rare look at a noble dwelling built in the 14th century. Currently only the ground and first floors are open to visitors, though the remaining floors can be visited by appointment. Like other buildings of the age, the exterior is festooned with 14th-century horse-tethering rings made out of iron, torch holders, and poles upon which to hang laundry and fly flags. Inside, though the furnishings are pretty sparse, you'll see richly painted walls, a long chute that functioned as a well, plenty of fireplaces, a lace display, and even a modern toilet.

Cost and Hours: €2, Tue-Sat 8:15-13:50; also open second and fourth Mon and first, third, and fifth Sun of each month; Via Porta Rossa 13, tel. 055-238-8610.

On and near Piazza della Signoria

The main civic center of Florence is dominated by the Palazzo Vecchio, Uffizi Gallery, and marble greatness of old Florence littering the cobbles. The Piazza della Signoria still vibrates with the echoes of Florence's past—executions, riots, and great celebrations. Today, it's a tourist's world with pigeons, postcards, horse buggies, and tired hubbies. And, if it would make your weary companion happy, stop in at the recommended but expensive **Rivoire** café to enjoy its fine desserts, pudding-thick hot chocolate, and the best view seats in town. It's expensive—but if you linger, it can be a great value.

▲▲▲**Uffizi Gallery**—This greatest collection of Italian paintings anywhere features works by Giotto, Leonardo, Raphael, Caravaggio, Titian, and Michelangelo, and a roomful of Botticellis, including the *Birth of Venus.* Northern Renaissance masters (Dürer, Rembrandt, and Rubens) are also well represented.

Cost and Hours: €6.50, €11 with mandatory exhibits, extra €4 for recommended reservation, cash required to pick up reserved tickets; Tue-Sun 8:15-18:50, closed Mon, last entry 45 minutes before closing, museum info tel. 055-238-8651, www.polomuseale .firenze.it.

Avoiding Lines: To avoid the notoriously long ticket-buying lines, either book ahead (for details, see page 980) or get a Florence Card (see page 983). During summer and on weekends, the Uffizi can be booked up a month or more in advance. Sometimes, by the end of the day (an hour before closing), you can just walk right in, but generally you'll encounter lines even off-season (and waits of up to three hours in peak season, April-Oct). The busiest days are Tuesday, Saturday, and Sunday.

Getting In: There are several entrances (see map). Which one you use depends on whether you have a Florence Card, a reservation, or neither. Florence Card-holders enter at door #1 (labeled *Reservation Entrance*), close to the Palazzo Vecchio. There are two lines at this entrance: Get in the line for individuals, not groups. If you're buying a ticket, line up with everyone else at door #2. If you've made a reservation and need to pick up your ticket, go to door #3 (labeled *Reservation Ticket Office*); hand over your reservation number or voucher, pay in cash (if you didn't already pay when you made the reservation), and get your ticket. Then walk briskly past the 200-yard-long ticket-buying line—pondering the IQ of this gang—to door #1. Show your ticket and walk in. (You can check baggage, but can't bring bottled liquids inside the museum.)

Audioguides: A 1.5-hour **audioguide** costs €5.50 (€8/2 people; must leave ID). You can download a free Rick Steves **audio tour** of the Uffizi; see page 7.

Visiting the Museum: The museum is nowhere near as big as it is great. Few tourists spend more than two hours inside. The paintings are displayed on one comfortable, U-shaped floor in chronological order from the 13th through 17th centuries. The left wing, starring the Florentine Middle Ages to the Renaissance, is the best. The connecting corridor contains sculpture, and the right wing focuses on the High Renaissance and Baroque.

Medieval (1200-1400): Paintings by **Duccio, Cimabue,** and

FLORENCE

Uffizi Gallery Overview

Not to Scale

To Duomo

Piazza della Signoria

DAVID COPY

PALAZZO VECCHIO

TERRACE (LOGGIA BELOW)

BUSTS OF FAMOUS FLORENTINES LINE THE COURTYARD

VIA DI NINNA

To Santa Croce →

CAFÉ

ELEVATOR

STAIRS UP FROM ENTRY & **WC**

CORRIDOR

COURTYARD

EARLY ITALIAN

EXIT

GIFT SHOP, **WC** & POST BELOW

❶→

STAIRS DOWN TO **WC** & EXIT

BOTTICELLI

LEONARDO

❷→

BAROQUE

VENUS DE' MEDICI

CORRIDOR

❸

VIA DI CASTELLANI

HIGH RENAISSANCE

NORTHERN RENAISSANCE

GALILEO SCIENCE MUSEUM

VIEW OF PONTE VECCHIO →

STATUES

← To Ponte Vecchio

LUNGARNO A. M. L. DE'MEDICI

Arno River

❶ Reservation Entrance
❷ Unreserved Ticket (Main) Entrance
❸ Reservation Ticket Office

Giotto show the baby steps being made from the flat Byzantine style toward realism. In his *Madonna and Child with Angels*, Giotto created a "stage" and peopled it with real beings. The triumph here is Mary herself—big and monumental, like a Roman statue. Beneath her robe, she has knees and breasts that stick out at us. This three-dimensionality was revolutionary, a taste of the Renaissance a century before it began.

Early Renaissance (mid-1400s): Paolo Uccello's *Battle of San Romano* is an early study in perspective with a few obvious flubs (recently restored but likely back on display by the time you visit). Piero della Frencesca's *Federico da Montefeltro and Battista Sforza* heralds the era of humanism and the new centrality of ordinary people in art, warts and all. Fra Filippo Lippi's radiantly beautiful Madonnas are light years away from the generic Marys of the medieval era.

Renaissance (1450-1500) and High Renaissance (1500-1550): The Botticelli room is filled with masterpieces and classical fleshiness—the famous *Birth of Venus* and the *Allegory of Spring*. Here is the Renaissance in its first bloom, its "springtime" of innocence. Madonna is out, Venus is in. This is a return to the pre-Christian pagan world of classical Greece, where things of the flesh are not sinful.

Don't miss Michelangelo's *Holy Family,* the only surviving completed easel painting by the greatest sculptor in history; Raphael's *Madonna of the Goldfinch,* with Mary and the Baby Jesus brought down from heaven into the real world of trees, water, and sky; and Titan's voluptuous *Venus of Urbino.*

Classical Sculpture: If the Renaissance was the foundation of the modern world, the foundation of the Renaissance was classical sculpture. Sculptors, painters, and poets alike turned for inspiration to ancient Greek and Roman works as the epitome of balance, 3-D perspective, human anatomy, and beauty.

In the octagonal classical sculpture room, the highlight is the *Venus de' Medici,* a Roman copy of the lost original of the great Greek sculptor Praxiteles' *Aphrodite.* Balanced, harmonious, and serene, this statue was considered the epitome of beauty and sexuality in Renaissance Florence.

The sculpture hall has the best view in Florence of the Arno River and Ponte Vecchio through the window, dreamy at sunset. Wrap up your visit by enjoying Duomo views from the café terrace.

In the Uffizi Courtyard: Enjoy the courtyard (free), full of artists and souvenir stalls. (Swing by after dinner when it's completely empty.) The surrounding statues honor earthshaking Florentines: artists (Michelangelo), philosophers (Niccolò Machiavelli), scientists (Galileo), writers (Dante), explorers (Amerigo Vespucci), and the great patron of so much Renaissance thinking, Lorenzo "the Magnificent" de' Medici.

▲▲**Palazzo Vecchio**—With its distinctive castle turret and rustic stonework, Cosimo I de' Medici's fortified "Old Palace"—the City Hall—is a Florentine landmark.

Entry to the ground-floor **courtyard** is free, so even if you don't go upstairs to the museum, you can step inside and feel the essence of the Medici. A copy of *David* stands where Michelangelo's original first stood, and in the center is another copy of a groundbreaking work: Verrocchio's twisting cherub with the dolphin, one of the first statues intended to be equally enjoyable from any angle.

The highlight of the palace interior is the **Grand Hall,** also called the Hall of Five Hundred, as it was designed to accommodate—and impress—that many guests. In the center of the ceiling is Cosimo I, the first Medici with a royal title, dressed as if he were Holy Roman Emperor. In a niche at the front is Leo X, the first of three Medici popes, and the walls show off Florence's victories over Pisa and Siena. Underneath Siena is Michelangelo's *Victory*, the prototype of the hall's other spiral-shaped statues (all of which came after Verrocchio's cherub in the courtyard).

After the Grand Hall, climb the stairs to visit a series of richly decorated rooms, including the Room of the Elements (where we see Cosimo I controlling the air, earth, fire, and water) and the private apartments of Grand Duchess Eleonora di Toledo (Cosimo's high-maintenance wife), which include a chapel decorated by Bronzino. The Room of the Lilies has two standout highlights: views of the Duomo, and Donatello's bronze *Judith and Holofernes*. The nearby Hall of Geographical Maps is full of maps made in a fit of post-1492 fascination with the wider world.

Cost and Hours: €6, €8 combo-ticket with Brancacci Chapel, Fri-Wed 9:00-19:00, often open until 24:00 in high season, Thu 9:00-14:00, ticket office closes one hour earlier (Piazza della Signoria, tel. 055-276-8224). The Palazzo Vecchio offers many kids' activities (call or ask at the reception by the ticket office). Skip the €4 audioguide (ID required) unless you want to know the fine details of Florentine political leaders. Free tours in English are offered daily, but the schedule varies and you must reserve (call to arrange).

Nearby: In the **loggia** on Piazza della Signoria, look for Benvenuto Cellini's bronze statue of Perseus holding the head of Medusa. The **plaque** on the pavement in front of the fountain marks the spot where the monk Savonarola was burned in MCDXCVIII, or 1498.

▲Ponte Vecchio—Florence's most famous bridge has long been lined with shops. Originally these were butcher shops that used the river as a handy disposal system. Then, when the powerful and princely Medici built the Vasari Corridor (described next) over the bridge, the stinky meat market was replaced by the more elegant gold and silver shops that remain there to this day. A statue of Benvenuto Cellini, the master goldsmith of the Renaissance, stands in the center, ignored by the flood of tacky tourism. This is a romantic spot late at night, when lovers gather and a top-notch street musician performs.

Vasari Corridor—This elevated and enclosed passageway, constructed in 1565, gave the Medici a safe, private commute over Ponte Vecchio from their Pitti Palace home to their Palazzo Vecchio offices. It's open only by special appointment, and while enticing to lovers of Florence, the actual tour experience isn't much. Entering from inside the Uffizi Gallery, you walk along a modern-feeling hall (wide enough to carry a Medici on a sedan chair) across Ponte Vecchio, and end in the Pitti Palace. Half the corridor is lined with Europe's best collection of self-portraits, along with other paintings (mostly 17th- and 18th-century) that seem like they didn't make the cut to be hung on the walls of the Uffizi.

The best way to get inside the corridor is to go with a tour company such as Florencetown (€89; Tue, Fri, and Sun at 15:30; 2 hours, tel. 055-012-3944, www.florencetown.com) or Artviva (€84, Tue and Sat at 13:30, 3 hours, tel. 055-264-5033, www.italy.artviva .com). The tours, which include a tour of the Uffizi, are expensive because of steep city entrance fees and the requirement that groups be accompanied by attendants and a guide.

▲▲**Galileo Science Museum (Museo Galilei e Istituto di Storia della Scienza)**—When we think of the Florentine Renaissance, we think of visual arts: painting, mosaics, architecture, and sculpture. But when the visual arts declined in the 1600s (abused and co-opted by political powers), music and science flourished in Florence. The first opera was written here. And Florence hosted many scientific breakthroughs, as you'll see in this fascinating collection of Renaissance and later clocks, telescopes, maps, and ingenious gadgets. Trace the technical innovations as modern science emerges from 1000 to 1900. One of the most talked-about bottles in Florence is the one here that contains Galileo's finger. Exhibits include various tools for gauging the world, from a compass and thermometer to Galileo's telescopes. Other displays delve into clocks, pumps, medicine, and chemistry. It's friendly, comfortably cool, never crowded, and just a block east of the Uffizi on the Arno River.

Cost and Hours: €8, €20 family ticket, Wed-Mon 9:30-18:00, Tue 9:30-13:00, last entry 30 minutes before closing, Piazza dei Giudici 1, tel. 055-265-311, recorded info tel. 055-293-493, www .museogalileo.it.

Tours: The €5 audioguide is well-produced, and offers both a highlights tour as well as dial-up info (with video) on each exhibit. The 1.5-hour English-language guided tour covers the collection plus behind-the-scenes areas, and includes hands-on demonstrations of some of the devices (€50 flat fee for 2-14 people, doesn't include museum entry, book at least a week in advance, great for kids, tel. 055-2653-1160, groups@museogalileo.it).

East of Piazza della Signoria
▲▲**Santa Croce Church**—This 14th-century Franciscan church, decorated with centuries of precious art, holds the tombs of great Florentines. The loud 19th-century Victorian Gothic facade faces

a huge square ringed with tempting shops and littered with tired tourists. Escape into the church and admire its sheer height and spaciousness. On the left wall (as you face the altar) is the **tomb of Galileo Galilei** (1564-1642), the Pisan who lived his last years under house arrest near Florence for having defied the Church by saying that the earth revolved around the sun. His heretical remains were only allowed in the church long after his death. Directly opposite (on the right wall) is the **tomb of Michelangelo Buonarroti** (1475-1564).

The first chapel to the right of the main altar features the famous fresco by Giotto of the *Death of St. Francis*. With simple but eloquent gestures, Francis' brothers bid him a sad farewell.

In the hallway near the bookstore, notice the photos of the devastating flood of 1966. Beyond that is the leather school (free entry).

Exit between the Rossini and Machiavelli tombs into the cloister (open-air courtyard). On the left, enter Brunelleschi's Pazzi Chapel, which captures the Renaissance in miniature.

Cost and Hours: €5, audioguide-€5, Mon-Sat 9:30-17:30, Sun 13:00-17:30, last entry 30 minutes before closing, modest dress code is enforced, 10-minute walk east of the Palazzo Vecchio along Borgo de' Greci, tel. 055-246-6105, www.santacroce.firenze.it. The leather school is free and sells tickets to the church. If the church has a long line, come here to avoid it (daily 10:00-18:00, has own entry behind church plus an entry within the church, www.leather school.com).

▲**Casa Buonarroti (Michelangelo's House)**—Fans enjoy a house standing on property once owned by Michelangelo. The house was built after Michelangelo's death by the artist's grand-nephew, who turned it into a little museum honoring his famous relative. You'll see some of Michelangelo's early, less-than-monumental statues and a few sketches. Be warned: Michelangelo's descendants attributed everything they could to their famous relative, but very little here (beyond two marble relief panels and a couple of sketches) is actually by Michelangelo.

Cost and Hours: €6.50, Wed-Mon 10:00-17:00, closed Tue, English descriptions, Via Ghibellina 70, tel. 055-241-752.

Santa Maria Novella Sights near the Train Station
▲▲**Church of Santa Maria Novella**—This 13th-century Dominican church is rich in art. Along with crucifixes by Giotto and Brunelleschi, it contains every textbook's example of the early Renaissance mastery of perspective: *The Holy Trinity* by Masaccio. The exquisite chapels trace art in Florence from medieval times to the early Baroque period. The outside of the church features a dash of Romanesque (horizontal stripes), Gothic (pointed arches),

Renaissance (geometric shapes), and Baroque (scrolls). Step in and look down the 330-foot nave for a 14th-century optical illusion. Next to the church are the cloisters and the museum, located in the old Dominican convent of Santa Maria Novella. The museum's highlight is the breathtaking Spanish Chapel, with walls covered by a series of frescoes by Andrea di Bonaiuto.

Cost and Hours: Church—€3.50, audioguide-€3, Mon-Thu 9:00-17:30, Fri 11:00-17:30, Sat 9:00-17:00, Sun 13:00-17:00, last entry 30 minutes before closing, modest dress required, tel. 055-219-257, www.museicivicifiorentini.it; museum—€2.70, Mon-Thu and Sat 9:00-17:00, closed Fri and Sun, tel. 055-282-187.

Farmacia di Santa Maria Novella—This palatial perfumery has long been run by the Dominicans of Santa Maria Novella. Thick with the lingering aroma of centuries of spritzes, it started as the herb garden of the Santa Maria Novella monks. Well-known even today for its top-quality products, it is extremely Florentine. Pick up the history sheet at the desk, and wander deep into the shop. The first room features perfumes, the middle (green) room offers items for the home, and the third room, which sells herbal products and dates from 1612, is the most historic. From here, you can peek at the dreamy frescoes of one of Santa Maria Novella's cloisters and imagine a time before Vespas and tourists.

Cost and Hours: Free but shopping encouraged, inconsistent hours but likely daily 9:30-19:30, a block from Piazza Santa Maria Novella, 100 yards down Via della Scala at #16—located on map on page 972, tel. 055-216-276, www.smnovella.com.

South of the Arno River

To locate these sights, see the map on page 972.

▲▲**Pitti Palace**—The imposing Pitti Palace, several blocks southwest of Ponte Vecchio, is not only home to the second-best collection of paintings in town, the **Palatine Gallery,** but also happens to be the most sumptuous palace you can tour in Florence. The building itself is mammoth, holding several different museums and anchoring two gardens. Stick primarily to the gallery, forget about everything else, and the palace becomes a little less exhausting.

You'll walk through one palatial room after another, walls sagging with masterpieces by 16th- and 17th-century masters, including Rubens, Titian, and Rembrandt. Its Raphael collection is the second-biggest anywhere—the Vatican beats it by one. Each room has some descriptions in English, though the paintings themselves have limited English labels.

The collection is all on one floor. To see the highlights, walk straight down the spine through a dozen or so rooms. Before you exit, consider a visit to the Royal Apartments. These 14 rooms (of which only a few are open at any one time) are where Florence's

Oltrarno, South of the Arno River

aristocrats lived in the 18th and 19th centuries. Each room features a different color and time period. Here, you get a real feel for the splendor of the dukes' world.

The rest of the Pitti Palace is skippable, unless the various sights match your interests: the **Modern Art Gallery** (second floor, features Romantic, Neoclassical, and Impressionist works by 19th- and 20th-century Tuscan painters), **Argenti Museum** (on the ground and mezzanine floors; displays Medici treasures from jeweled crucifixes to gilded ostrich eggs), **Costume Gallery, Porcelain Museum,** and **Boboli and Bardini Gardens** (behind the palace; enter from Pitti Palace courtyard).

The main reason to visit the Pitti Palace is to see the Palatine Gallery, but you can't buy a ticket for the gallery alone; to see it you'll need to buy ticket #1, which includes the Palatine Gallery, Royal Apartments, and Modern Art Gallery. Ticket #2 covers the Boboli and Bardini Gardens, Argenti Museum, Costume Gallery,

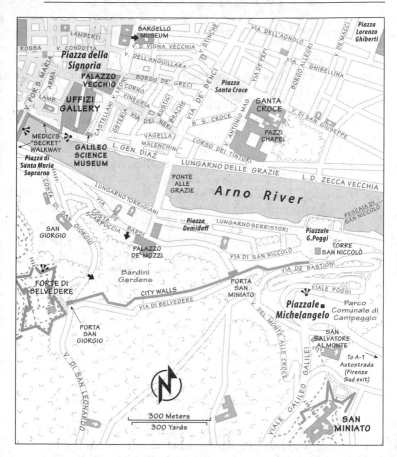

and Porcelain Museum.

Cost and Hours: Ticket #1—€8.50 but often €12 with mandatory exhibits, cash only, Tue-Sun 8:15-18:50, closed Mon. Ticket #2—€6, more with special exhibits, cash only, audioguide-€5, daily 8:15-18:30, until 19:30 June-Aug, last entry 30-60 minutes before closing, closed first and last Mon of each month, gardens close earlier in winter. An €11.50 combo-ticket (valid 3 days) covers the entire palace complex. Tel. 055-238-8614, www.polomuseale .firenze.it.

Getting In: If there's a long line, you can bypass it by making reservations on the spot at the ticket window (€3 reservation fee) for immediate entry. The ticket office is at the far right of the massive facade. Once you have your ticket, enter through the main doorway in the center of the facade. Florence Card-holders should go directly to the main entrance (where you may be ushered to the head of the security checkpoint); then go to the bookstore on the left side of the courtyard to have your card swiped and get your tickets.

▲▲**Brancacci Chapel**—For the best look at works by Masaccio (one of the early Renaissance pioneers of perspective in painting), see his restored frescoes here. Instead of medieval religious symbols, Masaccio's paintings feature simple, strong human figures with facial expressions that reflect their emotions. The accompanying works of Masolino and Filippino Lippi provide illuminating contrasts.

Reservations are free and required (see "Reservations," below). Your ticket includes a 40-minute film in English on the church, the frescoes, and Renaissance Florence (reserve a viewing time when you book your entry). The film starts promptly at the top of the hour. Computer animation brings the paintings to life—making them appear to move and giving them 3-D depth—while narration describes the events depicted in the panels. Yes, it's a long time commitment, and the film takes liberties with the art. But it's visually interesting and it's your best way to see the frescoes close up. The film works great either before or after you visit the frescoes.

Cost and Hours: €4, €8 combo-ticket with Palazzo Vecchio, includes worthwhile 40-minute film in English—reserve viewing time when you book entry, Mon and Wed-Sat 10:00-17:00, Sun 13:00-17:00, closed Tue, last entry 30 minutes before closing; in Church of Santa Maria del Carmine, reservations tel. 055-276-8224 or 055-276-8558, chapel tel. 055-284-361, www.museicivici fiorentini.it.

Reservations: Reservations are mandatory and free; you may be able to get a same-day slot. But to be sure you'll get in, call the chapel at least a day ahead (tel. 055-276-8224 or 055-276-8558, English spoken, call center open Mon-Sat 9:30-17:00, Sun 9:30-12:30). If the line is busy, keep trying—it's best to call around 14:00-15:00 or just before the ticket office closes at 16:30. Reservation times begin every 15 minutes, with a maximum of 30 visitors per time slot (you have 15 minutes inside the chapel). Remember to also book a time to see the film.

Walk-ins are welcome to stop by the chapel to see if there are any openings. You can also try calling ahead to the Brancacci chapel's direct line (tel. 055-284-361). They can't make a reservation for you, but they can tell you how crowded it is. The least crowded time tends to be 13:00-14:00.

Dress Code: Shorts and bare shoulders are OK in the chapel, but modest dress is requested when visiting the rest of the church.

Santo Spirito Church—This church has a classic Brunelleschi interior—enjoy its pure Renaissance lines (and ignore the later Baroque altar that replaced the original). Notice Brunelleschi's "dice"—the cubes of marble added above the column capitals that contribute to the nave's playful lightness. The church's art treasure is a painted, carved wooden crucifix attributed to 17-year-old Michelangelo. The sculptor donated this early work to the monastery in appreciation for allowing him to dissect and learn about bodies. The Michelangelo *Crocifisso* is displayed in the sacristy, through a door midway down the left side of the nave (if it's closed, ask someone to let you in). Copies of Michelangelo's *Pietà* and *Risen Christ* flank the nave (near the door). Beer-drinking, guitar-playing rowdies decorate the church steps.

Cost and Hours: Free, Mon-Tue and Thu-Sat 10:00-12:30 & 16:00-17:30, Sun 16:00-17:30 only, closed Wed, Piazza di Santo Spirito, tel. 055-211-716.

▲**Piazzale Michelangelo**—Overlooking the city from across the river (look for the huge statue of *David*), this square has a superb view of Florence and the stunning dome of the Duomo.

It's worth the 30-minute hike, drive (free parking), or bus ride (either #12 or #13 from the train station—takes a long time). It makes sense to take a taxi or ride the bus up, and then enjoy the easy downhill walk back into town. An inviting café with great views is just below the overlook. The best photos are taken from the street immediately below the overlook (go around to the right and down a few steps). Off the west side of the piazza is a somewhat hidden terrace, an excellent place to retreat from the mobs. After dark, the square is packed with schoolkids licking ice cream and each other. About 200 yards beyond all the tour groups and teenagers is the stark, beautiful, crowd-free, Romanesque San Miniato Church (next listing).

The hike down is quick and enjoyable. Take the steps between the two bars on the San Miniato Church side of the parking lot (Via San Salvatore al Monte), and in a couple of minutes you walk through the old wall (Porta San Miniato) and emerge in the delightful little Oltrarno neighborhood of San Niccolò.

▲▲**San Miniato Church**—According to legend, the martyred St. Minias—this church's namesake—was beheaded on the banks of the Arno in A.D. 250. He picked up his head and walked here (this was before the #12 bus), where he died and was buried in what became the first Christian cemetery in Florence. In the 11th century, this church was built to house Minias' remains. The church's green-and-white marble facade (12th century) is classic Florentine Romanesque. The church has wonderful 3-D paintings, a plush ceiling of glazed terra-cotta panels by Luca della Robbia, and a sumptuous Renaissance chapel (located front and center). The highlight for me is the brilliantly preserved art in the sacristy (behind altar in the room on right) showing scenes from the life of St. Benedict (circa 1350, done by a follower of Giotto). Drop a

FLORENCE

euro in the box to light the room for five minutes. The daily 17:30 Mass with the monks chanting in Latin offers a meditative worship experience—a peaceful way to end your visit.

Cost and Hours: Free, daily April-Oct 8:30-19:30, Nov-March 8:30-13:00, Gregorian chants April-Sept daily at the 17:30 Mass (17:00 in winter), 200 yards above Piazzale Michelangelo, bus #12 or #13 from train station—get off at Piazzale Michelangelo and walk, tel. 055-234-2731.

Sleeping in Florence

Competition among hotels is stiff. When things slow down, fancy hotels drop their prices and become a much better value for travelers than the cheap, low-end places.

Nearly all of my recommended accommodations are located in the center of Florence, within minutes of the great sights. If arriving by train, you can either walk (usually around 10 minutes) or take a taxi (roughly €8) to reach most of my recommended accommodations, as buses don't cover the center very well.

Florence is notorious for its mosquitoes. If your hotel lacks air-conditioning, request a fan and don't open your windows, especially at night. Many hotels furnish a small plug-in bulb *(zanzariere)*—usually set in the ashtray—that helps keep the blood-suckers at bay. If not, you can purchase one cheaply at any pharmacy *(farmacia)*.

Museumgoers take note: If you don't plan to get a Florence Card (see page 983), ask if your hotelier will reserve entry times for you to visit the popular Uffizi Gallery and the Accademia (Michelangelo's *David*). Request this service when you book your room; it's fast, easy, and offered free or for a small fee by most hotels—the only requirement is advance notice. Ask them to reserve your visits for any time the day after your arrival. If you'd rather make the reservations yourself, see page 980 for details.

North of the Arno River
Between the Duomo and the Train Station
$$ Hotel Accademia, which comes with marble stairs, parquet floors, and attractive public areas, has 21 pleasant rooms and a floor plan that defies logic (Db-€145, Tb-€170, cash discount with this book, air-con, Internet access and Wi-Fi, Via Faenza 7, tel. 055-293-451, fax 055-219-771, www.hotelaccademiafirenze.com, info @hotelaccademiafirenze.com, Tea and Edward).

$$ Hotel Centrale, with 31 spacious rooms, is indeed central (Db-€150, superior Db-€176, Tb-€182, suites available, discount with this book, ask for Rick Steves rate when you reserve, 20 percent discount if booked 3 months in advance, air-con, elevator,

FLORENCE

Sleep Code

(€1 = about $1.40, country code: 39)
S = Single, **D** = Double/Twin, **T** = Triple, **Q** = Quad, **b** = bathroom,
s = shower only.

You can assume a hotel takes credit cards unless you see "cash only" in the listing. Unless otherwise noted, hotel staff speak basic English and breakfast is included.

To help you easily sort through these listings, I've divided the accommodations into three categories based on the price for a standard double room with bath during high season:

$$$ Higher Priced—Most rooms €160 or more.
$$ Moderately Priced—Most rooms between €100-160.
$ Lower Priced—Most rooms €100 or less.

Prices can change without notice; verify the hotel's current rates online or by email. For other updates, see www .ricksteves.com/update.

Internet access and free Wi-Fi, Via dei Conti 3, tel. 055-215-761, fax 055-215-216, www.hotelcentralefirenze.it, info@hotelcentrale firenze.it, Margherita and Roberto).

$ Katti House and the nearby **Soggiorno Annamaria** are run by house-proud mama-and-daughter team Maria and Katti, who keep their 15 rooms spotless, inviting, and well-maintained. While both offer equal comfort, Soggiorno Annamaria has a more historic setting, with frescoed ceilings, unique tiles, timbered beams, and quieter rooms. Katti House serves as reception for both places (Db-€70-100, air-con, Internet access and Wi-Fi, Via Faenza 21, tel. & fax 055-213-410, www.kattihouse.com, info@kattihouse.com).

$ Hotel Lorena, just across from the Medici Chapels, has 19 rooms (six of which share a bathroom) and a tiny lobby. Though it's a bit like a youth hostel, it's cheap and conveniently located. Chatty Roberto speaks little English, but is eager to please (Sb-€50, D-€60, Db-€75, Tb-€95, breakfast-€5, air-con, Wi-Fi, Via Faenza 1, tel. 055-282-785, fax 055-288-300, www.hotellorena .com, info@hotellorena.com).

North of the Duomo
North of the Mercato Centrale

After dark, this neighborhood can feel a little sketchy, but I've never heard of anyone running into harm here. It's a short walk from the train station and an easy stroll to all the sightseeing action. While workaday, it's practical, with plenty of good budget restaurants and markets nearby.

FLORENCE

Florence Hotels

1. Hotel Accademia
2. Hotel Centrale
3. Katti House & Soggiorno Annamaria
4. Hotel Lorena
5. Galileo Hotel
6. Grand Tour Firenze
7. Hotel Il Bargellino
8. Hotel Enza
9. Casa Rabatti
10. Soggiorno Magliani
11. Hotel Loggiato dei Serviti
12. Hotel Dei Macchiaioli
13. Hotel Europa
14. Hotel Morandi alla Crocetta
15. Arti e Hotel
16. Palazzo Niccolini al Duomo
17. Residenza dei Pucci
18. Hotel Duomo
19. Soggiorno Battistero
20. La Residenza del Proconsolo B&B
21. Panella's Residence
22. Residenza il Villino
23. B&B Il Bargello
24. Hotel Cardinal of Florence
25. Hotel Dalí
26. Oblate Sisters of the Assumption
27. Locanda de' Ciompi
28. Hotel Il Duca
29. In Piazza della Signoria B&B
30. Hotel Pendini
31. Hotel Olimpia
32. B&B Dei Mori
33. Residenza Giotto B&B
34. Hotel Torre Guelfa
35. Relais Uffizi
36. Hotel Davanzati
37. Hotel Alessandra
38. Bellevue House & Albergo Margaret
39. To Villa Camerata & Hostel 7 Santi

FLORENCE

$$ Galileo Hotel, a classy business hotel of 31 rooms, is run with familial warmth (Db-€130, Tb-€150, ask for Rick Steves discount when you book direct and pay cash, quadruple-pane windows effectively shut out street noise, Wi-Fi, Via Nazionale 22a, tel. 055-496-645, fax 055-496-447, www.galileohotel.it, info @galileohotel.it, Rhuna).

$$ Grand Tour Firenze has seven charming rooms on a mundane street between the train station and the Accademia. This cozy B&B will make you feel right at home; it's thoughtfully appointed and the owners, Cristina and Giuseppe, live here. The delightful and spacious suites come with a garden ambience on the ground floor (Db-€110, suite-€130, ask for discount if you book direct and pay cash, includes breakfast voucher for the corner bar, air-con, Wi-Fi, Via Santa Reparata 21, tel. 055-283-955, www .florencegrandtour.com, info@abacusreservations.com). They run a more romantic, pricier place a couple of blocks away.

$ Hotel Il Bargellino, run by Bostonian Carmel and her Italian husband Pino, feels like it's in a residential neighborhood. They rent 10 summery rooms decorated with funky antique furniture and Pino's modern paintings. Guests enjoy relaxing with Carmel and Leopoldo the parrot on the big, breezy, momentum-slowing terrace adorned with lemon shrubs (S-€45, D-€80, Db-€90, ask for discount if you book direct and pay cash, extra bed-€25, no breakfast, Wi-Fi, north of the train station at Via Guelfa 87, tel. 055-238-2658, www.ilbargellino.com, carmel @ilbargellino.com).

$ Hotel Enza rents 19 dark, relaxing rooms (Sb-€55, Db-€80, show this book and ask for best Rick Steves price, extra bed-€20, optional breakfast-€5, air-con, Internet access and Wi-Fi, Via San Zanobi 45 black, tel. 055-490-990, fax 055-473-672, www .hotelenza.it, info@hotelenza.it, Diana).

$ Casa Rabatti is the ultimate if you always wanted to have a Florentine mama. Its four simple, clean rooms are run with warmth by Marcella. This is a great place to practice your Italian, since Marcella loves to chat and speaks minimal English. Seeing nearly two decades of my family Christmas cards on their walls, I'm reminded of how long she has been keeping budget travelers happy (D-€50, Db-€60, €25 extra per bed in shared quad or quint, show this book and ask for best Rick Steves price, cash only but secure reservation with credit card, no breakfast, fans available, Wi-Fi, 5 blocks from station at Via San Zanobi 48 black, tel. 055-212-393, casarabatti@inwind.it).

If Marcella's booked, she'll put you up in her daughter's place nearby, at Via Nazionale 20 (five big, airy, family-friendly rooms; €25/person, fans, no breakfast, closer to the station). While daughter Patrizia works, her mom runs the place. Getting bumped to

Patrizia's gives you slightly more comfort and slightly less personality...certainly not a net negative.

$ Soggiorno Magliani is central and humble, with six bright, no-frills rooms (sharing two baths) that feel and smell like a great-grandmother's home. It's run by the friendly duo Vincenza and her English-speaking daughter Cristina, and the price is right (S-€36, D-€46, T-€63, cash only but secure reservation with credit card, no breakfast, near Via Guelfa at Via Santa Reparata 1, tel. 055-287-378, hotel-magliani@libero.it).

Near the Accademia

$$$ Hotel Loggiato dei Serviti, at the most prestigious address in Florence on the most evocative Renaissance square in town, gives you Old World romance with hair dryers. Stone stairways lead you under open-beam ceilings through this 16th-century monastery's monumental public rooms—it's so artful, you'll be snapping photos everywhere. The 33 cells—with air-conditioning, TVs, mini-bars, and telephones—would be unrecognizable to their original inhabitants. The hotel staff is both professional and warm (Sb-€120, Db-€160-170, superior Db-€190, family suites from €263, ask for their Rick Steves rate when you book, elevator, valet parking-€20/day, Piazza S.S. Annunziata 3, tel. 055-289-592, fax 055-289-595, www.loggiatodeiservitihotel.it, info@loggiato deiservitihotel.it; Fabio, Chiara, and Simonetta). When full, they rent five spacious and sophisticated rooms in a 17th-century annex a block away. While it lacks the monastic mystique, the annex rooms are bigger, gorgeous, and cost the same.

$$$ Hotel Dei Macchiaioli offers 15 fresh and spacious rooms on one high-ceilinged, noble floor in a restored *palazzo* owned for generations by a well-to-do Florentine family. You'll eat breakfast under original frescoed ceilings while enjoying modern comforts (Sb-€100, Db-€180, Tb-€220, ask for Rick Steves discount if you book direct, air-con, Wi-Fi, Via Cavour 21, tel. 055-213-154, www.hoteldeimacchiaioli.com, info@hoteldeimacchiaioli .com, helpful Francesca and Paolo).

$$ Hotel Morandi alla Crocetta, a former convent, envelops you in a 16th-century cocoon. Located on a quiet street with 12 rooms, period furnishings, parquet floors, and wood-beamed ceilings, it takes you back a few centuries and up a few social classes (Sb-€100, Db-€140, low-season discounts online, air-con, Wi-Fi, a block off Piazza S.S. Annunziata at Via Laura 50, tel. 055-234-4747, fax 055-248-0954, www.hotelmorandi.it, welcome@hotel morandi.it, well-run by Maurizio, Rolando, and Frank).

$$ Hotel Europa, run by cheery Miriam, Roberto, and daughter Priscilla since 1970, has a welcoming atmosphere. The breakfast room is spacious, and some of the 20 rooms have views of the Duomo (Sb-€89, Db-€150, Tb-€180, cash discount, air-con, elevator, Wi-Fi, Via Cavour 14, tel. 055-239-6715, fax 055-268-984, www.webhoteleuropa.com, firenze@webhoteleuropa.com).

$$ Arti e Hotel rents 11 large, new, and tastefully furnished rooms well-located on a quiet street just far enough away from the tourist scene. As there's no real public space, the emphasis is on classy rooms and a helpful reception desk (Db-€135, ask for their Rick Steves price if you book direct and pay cash, third bed-€30, air-con, elevator, Wi-Fi, Via dei Servi 38, tel. 055-264-5307, fax 055-290-140, www.artiehotel.it, info@artiehotel.it, Mario).

Near the Duomo
All of these places are within a block of Florence's biggest church and main landmark.

$$$ Palazzo Niccolini al Duomo, one of five elite Historic Residence Hotels in Florence, is run by Niccolini da Camugliano. The lounge (where free chamomile tea served in the evenings) is palatial, but the 12 rooms, while splendid, vary wildly in size. If you have the money and want a Florentine palace to call home, this can be a good bet (Db-€150 and up, fancier and pricier suites with DVD players, ask for Rick Steves discount when you book, check online to choose a room and consider last-minute deals, Wi-Fi, Via dei Servi 2, tel. 055-282-412, fax 055-290-979, www.niccolinidomepalace.com, info@niccolinidomepalace.com).

$$ Residenza dei Pucci rents 12 pleasant rooms (each one different) spread over three floors. The decor is a mix of soothing earth tones and aristocratic furniture (Sb-€135, Db-€150, Tb-€170, Qb-€238, cash discount with this book, air-con, no elevator, reception open 9:00-20:00—let them know if you'll arrive late, Via dei Pucci 9, tel. 055-281-886, fax 055-264-314, www.residenzadeipucci.com, residenzadeipucci@residenzadeipucci.com, Mirella).

$$ Hotel Duomo, big and venerable, rents 24 rooms four floors up. The Duomo looms like a monster outside the hotel's windows. The rooms, while pretty forgettable, are comfortable enough, and the location can't be beat (Db-€100-170, cash discount with this book, Internet access and Wi-Fi, Piazza del Duomo 1, tel. 055-219-922, www.hotelduomofirenze.it, info@hotelduomofirenze.it, Alberto and Sonia).

$$ Soggiorno Battistero rents seven simple, airy rooms, most with great views, overlooking the Baptistery and the Duomo square. Choose a view or a quieter room in the back when you book by email. It's a pristine, fresh, and minimalist place run by Italian Luca and his American wife Kelly, who makes the hotel particularly welcoming (Sb-€78, Db-€103, Tb-€140, Qb-€150, show this book and ask for Rick Steves price, cash discount if you book direct, breakfast served in room, air-con, Wi-Fi, Piazza San

Giovanni 1, third floor—no elevator, tel. 055-295-143, fax 055-268-189, www.soggiornobattistero.it, info@soggiornobattistero.it).

$$ La Residenza del Proconsolo B&B, run by helpful Mariano, has five pleasantly appointed rooms a minute from the Duomo (three rooms have Duomo views). The place lacks public spaces, but the rooms are quite large and nice—perfect for eating breakfast, which is served in your room (Sb-€90, Db-€140, Tb-€150, Wi-Fi, Via del Proconsolo 18n, tel. 055-264-5657, mobile 335-657-4840, www.proconsolo.com, info@proconsolo.com).

$$ Residenza Giotto B&B offers you the chance to stay on Florence's upscale shopping drag, Via Roma. Occupying the top floor of a 19th-century building, this place has six bright rooms and a terrace with knockout views of the Duomo's tower (Sb-€90, Db-€140, extra bed-€25, ask for discount if you book direct and pay cash, elevator, Wi-Fi, Via Roma 6, tel. 055-214-593, fax 055-264-8568, www.residenzagiotto.it, info@residenzagiotto.it, Giorgio speaks English). Let them know your arrival time in advance.

East of the Duomo

$$ Panella's Residence, once a convent and today part of owner Graziella's extensive home, is a classy B&B, with six chic, romantic, and ample rooms, antique furnishings, and historic architectural touches (Db-€140, superior Db-€165, more if paying by credit card, discounts for 3 or more nights, air-con, Wi-Fi, Via della Pergola 42, tel. 055-234-7202, fax 055-247-9669, www.panella residence.com, panella_residence@yahoo.it).

$$ Residenza il Villino, popular and friendly, aspires to offer a Florentine home away from home. It has 10 rooms and a picturesque, peaceful little courtyard (small Db-€110, Db-€130, family suite that sleeps up to six—price upon request, ask for discount with cash and this book, air-con, Internet access and Wi-Fi, just north of Via degli Alfani at Via della Pergola 53, tel. 055-200-1116, fax 055-200-1101, www.ilvillino.it, info@ilvillino.it; Sergio, Elisabetta, and son Lorenzo).

$ B&B Il Bargello is a home away from home, run by friendly and helpful Canadian expat Gabriella. Hike up three long flights to reach six smart, relaxing rooms. Gabriella offers a cozy communal living room, kitchen access, and an inviting rooftop terrace with close-up views of Florence's towers (Db-€100, ask for Rick Steves rate when you book direct and pay cash, air-con, Internet access and Wi-Fi, 20 yards off Via Proconsolo at Via de' Pandolfini 33 black, tel. 055-215-330, mobile 339-175-3110, www.firenze-bedandbreakfast.it, info@firenze-bedandbreakfast.it).

$ Hotel Cardinal of Florence is a third-floor walk-up with 17 new, tidy, and sun-splashed rooms overlooking either a silent courtyard (many with views of Brunelleschi's dome) or a quiet street. Relax and enjoy Florence's rooftops from the sun terrace (Sb-€60, Db-€95, ask for Rick Steves rate, cash discount, €15/day limited parking—request when you reserve, Borgo Pinti 5, tel. 055-234-0780, fax 055-234-3389, www.hotelcardinalofflorence.com, info@hotelcardinalofflorence.com, Mauro and Ida).

$ Hotel Dalí has 10 decent, basic rooms with new baths in a nice location for a great price. Samanta and Marco, who run this guesthouse with a charming passion and idealism, are a delight to know (S-€40, D-€70, Db-€85, extra bed-€25, no breakfast, fans but no air-con, request quiet room when you book, Wi-Fi, free parking, 2 blocks behind the Duomo at Via dell'Oriuolo 17, tel. & fax 055-234-0706, www.hoteldali.com, hoteldali@tin.it).

$ Oblate Sisters of the Assumption run an institutional 30-room hotel in a Renaissance building with a dreamy garden, great public spaces, appropriately simple rooms, and a quiet, prayerful ambience (€45/person in single, double, triple, or quad rooms with bathrooms, cash only, single beds only, air-con, elevator, €10/day limited parking—request when you book, Borgo Pinti 15, tel. 055-248-0582, fax 055-234-6291, sroblateborgopinti @virgilio.it, sisters are likely to speak French but not English, Sister Theresa is very helpful).

$ Locanda de' Ciompi, overlooking the inviting Piazza dei Ciompi antiques market in a young and lively neighborhood, is just right for travelers who want to feel like a part of the town. Riccardo runs a minimalist place—just five quiet, clean, tasteful rooms along a thin hallway (Db-€100, Tb-€115, ask for discount with this book if you book direct and pay cash, includes breakfast at nearby bar, air-con, Wi-Fi, 8 blocks behind the Duomo at Via Pietrapiana 28, tel. 055-263-8034, www.locandadeciompi.it, li.ga @locandadeciompi.it).

$ Hotel Il Duca—a big, bright, old place—seems like a basic building wearing a fancy coat. Located on a quiet street a few blocks behind the Duomo, it rents 13 rooms at a good price (Db-€90, third bed-€25, air-con, Wi-Fi, Via della Pergola 34, tel. 055-906-2167, www.hotelilduca.it, info@hotelilduca.it).

South of the Duomo
Between the Duomo and Piazza della Signoria

These are the most central of my accommodations recommendations (and therefore a little overpriced). While worth the extra cost for many, given Florence's walkable, essentially traffic-free core, nearly every hotel I recommend here can be considered central.

$$$ In Piazza della Signoria B&B, overlooking Piazza della Signoria, is peaceful, refined, and homey at the same time. Fit for a honeymoon, the 10 rooms come with all the special touches and little extras you'd expect in a top-end American B&B (viewless Db-€220, view Db-€250, Tb-€280, ask for discount when you book direct with this book, family apartments, lavish bathrooms, air-con, tiny elevator, Internet access and Wi-Fi, Via dei Magazzini 2, tel. 055-239-9546, mobile 348-321-0565, fax 055-267-6616, www .inpiazzadellasignoria.com, info@inpiazzadellasignoria.com, Sonia and Alessandro).

$$ Hotel Pendini, with three tarnished stars, fills the top floor of a grand building constructed to celebrate Italian unification in the late 19th century. It overlooks Piazza della Repubblica, and as you walk into the lobby, you feel as if you are walking back in time. The 40-room place is memorable—and can be a good value (Db-€80-190, Internet access and Wi-Fi, Via Strozzi 2, tel. 055-211-170, www.hotelpendini.it, info@hotelpendini.it).

$$ Hotel Olimpia is a friendly, well-worn, established place renting 24 utilitarian rooms on the fourth floor overlooking Piazza della Repubblica. But you pay for the location (Db-€140-160, air-con, Wi-Fi, Piazza della Repubblica 2, tel. 055-219-781, fax 055-267-0383, www.hotel-olimpia.it, info@hotel-olimpia.it, Marziano).

$$ B&B Dei Mori, a peaceful haven with a convivial and welcoming living room, rents five tastefully appointed rooms ideally located on a quiet pedestrian street near Casa di Dante. Accommodating Suzanne and Danny offer lots of tips on dining and sightseeing in Florence (D-€100, Db-€120, discount for my readers—ask when you book, air-con-€5 extra, Wi-Fi, reception open 8:00-19:00, Via Dante Alighieri 12, tel. 055-211-438, www .deimori.com, deimori@bnb.it).

Near Ponte Vecchio

$$$ Hotel Torre Guelfa is topped by a fun medieval tower with a panoramic rooftop terrace and a huge living room. Its 24 pricey rooms vary wildly in size. Room 315, with a private terrace (€245), is worth reserving several months in advance (Db-€170-190, Db junior suite-€230, family deals, check their website for discounts, air-con, elevator, Wi-Fi, a couple blocks northwest of Ponte Vecchio, Borgo S.S. Apostoli 8, tel. 055-239-6338, fax 055-239-8577, www.hoteltorreguelfa.com, info@hoteltorreguelfa.com, Sandro and Barbara).

$$$ Relais Uffizi is a peaceful little gem, with 15 classy rooms tucked away down a tiny alleyway off Piazza della Signoria. The lounge has a huge window overlooking the action in the square below (Sb-€140, Db-€180, Tb-€220, buffet breakfast, elevator, Wi-Fi, Chiasso de Baroncelli/Chiasso del Buco 16, tel. 055-267-6239, fax 055-265-7909, www.relaisuffizi.it, info@relaisuffizi.it, charming Alessandro and Elizabetta).

$$$ Hotel Davanzati, bright and shiny with artistic touches, has 19 cheerful rooms with all the comforts. The place is a family affair, thoughtfully run by friendly Tommaso and father Fabrizio, who offer drinks and snacks each evening at their candlelit happy hour (Sb-€122, Db-€189, Tb-€259, show this book and ask for Rick Steves rate, prices soft off-season, cash discount; PlayStation, DVD player, and laptop with free Wi-Fi in every room; air-con, next to Piazza Davanzati at Via Porta Rossa 5, tel. 055-286-666, fax 055-265-8252, www.hoteldavanzati.it, info@hoteldavanzati.it).

$$ Hotel Alessandra is 16th-century, tranquil, and sprawling, with 27 big, tasteful rooms (S-€67, Sb-€110, D-€110, Db-€150, Tb-€195, Qb-€215, cash discount, air-con, Internet access and Wi-Fi, Borgo S.S. Apostoli 17, tel. 055-283-438, fax 055-210-619, www.hotelalessandra.com, info@hotelalessandra.com, Anna and son Andrea).

Near the Train Station

$ Bellevue House is a third-floor (no elevator) oasis of tranquility, with six spacious rooms flanking a long, mellow-yellow lobby. It's a peaceful time warp thoughtfully run by Rosanna and Antonio di Grazia (Db-€70-95, family deals; discount if you stay two nights, pay cash, and book direct; optional €3 breakfast in street-level bar, air-con, Via della Scala 21, tel. 055-260-8932, mobile 333-612-5973, fax 055-265-5315, www.bellevuehouse.it, info@bellevue house.it).

$ Albergo Margaret, homey yet minimalist, doesn't have a public lounge or offer breakfast. Run by the Cristantielli family, it has seven peaceful and simple rooms (D-€40, Ds-€60, Db-€75, ask for discount if you book direct and pay cash, extra bed-€10, air-con, Wi-Fi, near Santa Maria Novella at Via della Scala 25, tel. & fax 055-210-138, www.hotel-margaret.it, info@hotel-margaret .it; Francesco, Anna, and Graziano).

Hostels Away from the Center

These two hostels, northeast of downtown, are a bus ride from the action. A far more central hostel is in Oltrarno (listed at the end of the next section).

$ Villa Camerata, classy for an IYHF hostel, is in a pretty villa three miles northeast of the train station, on the outskirts of Florence (€20/bed with breakfast, 4- to 6-bed rooms, must have hostel membership card or pay additional €3/night, self-serve laundry, Via Righi 2—take bus #11 from the train station to Salviatino stop, tel. 055-601-451, fax 055-610-300, www.aighostels.com, firenze@aighostels.com).

$ Hostel 7 Santi calls itself a "travelers' haven." It fills a former convent, but you'll feel like you're in an old school. Still, it offers some of the best cheap beds in town, is friendly to older travelers, and comes with the services you'd expect in a big, modern hostel, including free Wi-Fi and self-serve laundry. It's in a more residential neighborhood near the Campo di Marte stadium, about a 10-minute bus ride from the center (200 beds in 60 rooms, mostly 4- or 6-bed dorms with a floor of doubles and triples, €20/dorm bed, Sb-€40, Ds-€60, Db-€70; includes breakfast, sheets, and towels; no curfew; Viale dei Mille 11—from train station, take bus #10, #17, or #20, direction: Campo di Marte, to bus stop Chiesa dei Sette Santi; tel. 055-504-8452, www.7santi.com, info@7santi.com).

South of the Arno River, in the Oltrarno

Across the river in the Oltrarno area, between the Pitti Palace and Ponte Vecchio, you'll find small, traditional crafts shops, neighborly piazzas, and family eateries. The following places are an easy walk from Ponte Vecchio. Only the first two are real hotels—the rest are a ragtag gang of budget alternatives.

$$$ Hotel Silla is a classic three-star hotel with 35 cheery, spacious, pastel, and modern rooms. It faces the river and overlooks a park opposite Santa Croce Church (Db-€140-180, ask for Rick Steves rate when you book, third person-€50 extra, air-con, elevator, Wi-Fi, Via dei Renai 5, tel. 055-234-2888, fax 055-234-1437, www.hotelsilla.it, hotelsilla@hotelsilla.it; Laura, Chiara, Massimo, and Stefano).

$$ Hotel la Scaletta rattles with musty charm. This old-school place, with 15 functional rooms hiding in a tortured floor plan, has a fabulous rooftop terrace overlooking Boboli Gardens (Db-€125, third bed-€20, breakfast-€6, air-con, Wi-Fi, Via de' Guicciardini 13, tel. 055-283-028, fax 055-283-013, www.hotellascaletta.it, info@hotellascaletta.it).

$ Istituto Gould is a Protestant Church-run place with 40 clean and spartan rooms that have twin beds and modern facilities (Sb-€45, Db-€56-68, Tb-€75, Qb-€92, breakfast-€6, quieter rooms in back, no air-con but rooms have fans, Via dei Serragli 49, tel. 055-212-576, fax 055-280-274, www.istitutogould.it, foresteria firenze@diaconiavaldese.org). You must arrive when the office is open (Mon-Fri 8:45-13:00 & 15:00-19:30, Sat 9:00-13:30 & 14:30-18:00, no live check-in on Sundays but they'll email you a code).

$ Soggiorno Alessandra has five bright, comfy, and smallish rooms. Because of its double-paned windows, you'll hardly notice the traffic noise (D-€58-73, Db-€78, Tb-€98, Qb-€128, ask about discount with 2-night stay, air-con-€8, just past the Carraia Bridge at Via Borgo San Frediano 6, tel. 055-290-424, fax 055-218-464, www.soggiornoalessandra.it, info@soggiornoalessandra.it, Alessandra).

Oltrarno Hotels & Restaurants

1. To Hotel Silla & Il Gelato di Filo
2. Hotel la Scaletta
3. Istituto Gould
4. Soggiorno Alessandra
5. Casa Santo Nome di Gesù
6. Ostello Santa Monaca
7. Golden View Open Bar
8. Trattoria 4 Leoni
9. Olio & Convivium Gastronomia
10. To Antico Ristoro Di Cambi, Trattoria da Sergio & Trattoria Sabatino
11. Il Santo Bevitore Ristorante
12. To Trattoria Al Tranvai
13. Trattoria Casalinga
14. Borgo Antico, Volume Bar & Ricchi Caffè
15. Meta Supermarket

FLORENCE

$ Casa Santo Nome di Gesù is a grand, 29-room convent whose sisters—Franciscan Missionaries of Mary—are thankful to rent rooms to tourists. Staying in this 15th-century palace, you'll be immersed in the tranquil atmosphere created by a huge, peaceful garden, generous and prayerful public spaces, and smiling nuns (D-€70, Db-€85, twin beds only, no air-con but rooms have fans, memorable convent-like breakfast room, elevator, strict 23:29 curfew, Piazza del Carmine 21, tel. 055-213-856, fax 055-281-835, www.fmmfirenze.it, info@fmmfirenze.it).

Hostel: **$ Ostello Santa Monaca,** a well-run hostel a long block south of the Brancacci Chapel, attracts a young backpacking crowd (€15-24/bed with sheets, 2- to 20-bed dorms, 10:00-14:00 lock-out, 2:00 in the morning curfew, free Internet access and Wi-Fi, self-serve laundry, kitchen, Via Santa Monaca 6, tel. 055-268-338, fax 055-280-185, www.ostello.it, info@ostello.it).

Eating in Florence

Remember, restaurants like to serve what's fresh. If you're into flavor, go for the seasonal best bets—featured in the *piatti del giorno* ("special of the day") section on menus. For dessert, it's gelato (see sidebar, later).

To save money and time for sights, keep lunches fast and simple, eating in one of the countless pizzerias and self-service cafeterias. Picnicking is easy—there's no shortage of corner *supermercatos,* or you can picnic your way through the Mercato Centrale.

North of the Arno River
Near the Church of Santa Maria Novella
Trattoria al Trebbio serves traditional food, especially rabbit and steak, with simple Florentine elegance in its candlelit interior. Tables spill out onto a romantic little square—an oasis of Roman Trastevere-like charm (€8 pastas, €13 *secondi,* daily 12:00-15:00 & 19:15-23:00, reserve for outdoor seating, half a block off of Piazza Santa Maria Novella at Via delle Belle Donne 47, tel. 055-287-089, Antonio).

Trattoria "da Giorgio" is a family-style diner serving up piping-hot, delicious home cooking to happy locals and tourists alike. Their three-course, fixed-price meal, including water and a drink, is a great value for €12. Choose from among the daily specials or the regular menu (Mon-Sat 12:00-14:30 & 18:00-22:00, closed Sun, Via Palazzuolo 100 red, tel. 055-284-302, Silvano).

Trattoria Marione serves sincerely home-cooked-style meals to a mixed group of tourists and Florentines in a happy, crowded, food-loving, and steamy ambience (€9 pastas, €10 *secondi,* daily 12:00-17:30 & 19:00-23:00, Via della Spada 27 red, tel. 055-214-

756, Fabio).

Trattoria Sostanza-Troia, characteristic and well established, is famous for its beef. Hearty steaks and pastas are splittable. Whirling ceiling fans and walls strewn with old photos evoke earlier times, while the artichoke pies remind locals of Grandma's cooking. Crowded, shared tables with paper tablecloths give this place a bistro feel. They offer two dinner seatings, at 19:30 and 21:00, which require reservations (dinners for about €30 plus wine, cash only, lunch Mon-Sat 12:30-14:00, closed Sun, closed Sat in off-season, Via del Porcellana 25 red, tel. 055-212-691).

Trattoria 13 Gobbi ("13 Hunchbacks") is a trendy favorite, glowing with candles around a tiny garden. Romantic in front and kid-friendly in back, it serves beautifully presented Tuscan food (they're enthusiastic about their steak) on big, fancy plates to a mostly tourist crowd (€10 pastas, €15 *secondi*, daily 12:00-15:00 & 19:30-23:00, Via del Porcellana 9 red, tel. 055-284-015, Enrico).

Near the Mercato Centrale

The following market-neighborhood eateries all have a distinct vibe. They're within a few blocks of each other: Scout around and choose your favorite.

Trattoria Zà-Zà is a fun, characteristic, high-energy place facing the Mercato Centrale. It offers a family-friendly festival of standard Tuscan dishes such as *ribollita* and *bistecca alla fiorentina*, plus a variety of big, splittable €8 salads. Though it's more touristy than ever, the food is still great, and everyone's happy. Arrive early or make a reservation. Choose between the folkloric interior or the fine outdoor piazza. Understand your itemized bill, and don't mistake their outside seating with the neighboring restaurant's (€9 pastas, €16 *secondi*, daily 11:00-23:00, Piazza del Mercato Centrale 26 red, tel. 055-215-411).

Trattoria la Burrasca is Flintstone-chic. Friendly duo Elio and Simone offer a limited menu of Tuscan home cooking with seasonal specials. It's small—10 tables—and often filled with my readers. If Archie Bunker were Italian, he'd eat at this trattoria for special nights out (€6 pastas, €8 *secondi*, no cover or service charge, Tue-Sun 12:00-15:00 & 19:00-22:30, closed Mon, Via Panicale 6, north corner of Mercato Centrale, tel. 055-215-827).

Trattoria Lo Stracotto is a stylish, truffle-colored eatery just steps away from the Medici Chapels. It's run with enthusiasm and flair by two cousins, who serve up tasty, traditional dishes such as *bistecca alla fiorentina* and *ribollita* (based on grandfather's recipe), and good chocolate soufflé. Enjoy the candlelit ambience and soft music as you sit either in the dining room or out on the terrace (€7 pastas, €10 *secondi*, daily 11:00-23:00, Piazza Madonna degli Aldobrandi 16/17, tel. 055-230-2062, Francesco and Tommaso).

Florence Restaurants

Piazza della Indipendenza

300 Meters

300 Yards

To Fortezza da Basso

PALAZZO DEI CONGRESSI

CONSERVATORIO DI FULIGNO

VIA GUELFA

PALAZZO DEGLI AFFARI

VIA CENNINI

CENACOLO DI FULIGNO

9

Piazza Adua

VIA SAN ZANOBI

VIA TADDEA

10 **37**

7

VIA PANICALE

Piazza del Mercato Centrale

VIA FIUME

VIA NAZIONALE

VIA FAENZA

MERCATO CENTRALE

11

6

BORGO LA NOCE

VIA STURA

SANTA MARIA NOVELLA TRAIN STATION

Largo Alinari

Piazza della Stazione

PALAZZO DEI CARTELLONI

VIA DEGLI AVELLI

VIA S. ANTONINO

VIA S. AMARINO

12

MARKET

MEDICI CHAPELS

Piazza di San Lorenzo

SAN LORENZO

BUS STATION

B

VIA DELLA SCALA

Piazza dell'Unità Italiana

V. DEI MELARANCIO

8

MEDICI LIBRARY

VIA DE' CONTI

VIA DE' ZANNETTI

VIA B. SAN LORENZO

MAIN TOURIST INFO

SANTA MARIA NOVELLA

VIA PANZANI

VIA DEL GIGLIO

VIA DELL'ALLORO

WC

2

VIA DE' CANACCI

VIA BENEDETTA

SANTA MARIA NOVELLA PERFUMERY

Piazza di Santa Maria Novella

VIA D. BELLE DONNE

VIA DEI BANCHI

VIA DE' CERRETANI

Piazza di San Giovanni

1

TREBBIO

RONDINELLI

SANTA MARIA MAGGIORE

LOGGIA DI BIGALO & **i**

OGNISSANTI

VIA DEL PORCELLANA

VIA DI PAOLINO

LOGGIA DI SAN PAOLO

VIA DEL SOLE

ANTINORI

19

VIA PECORI

SAN GAETANO

VIA CORSI

BRUNELLESCHI

TOSINGHI

ROMA

MEDICI

4

5

BORGO OGNISSANTI

Piazza d'Ognissanti

N

VIA DEL FOSSI

VIA DEL MORO

VIA DELLA SPADA

RUCELLAI PALACE

3

GIAC. VIA DE' VECCHIETTI

ARCH

Piazza della Repubblica

LUNGARNO VESPUCCI

VIA DE FEDERIGHI

VIA DELLA VIGNA NUOVA

VIA DEL TORNABUONI

VIA D. STROZZI

STROZZI PALACE

V. D. ANSELMI

MONALDA

V. PELLICCERIA

CALIMALA

ORSAN-MICHELE

VIA DI FEDERIGHI

Piazza Carlo Goldoni

VIA DEL PARIONE

INFERNO

PURGATORIO

PARIONCINO

PALAZZO CORSINI

SANTA TRINITA

Piazza di Santa Trinita

POST

Piazza de' Davanzati

VIA PORTA ROSSA

DAVANZATI PALACE

MERCATO NUOVO

21

PONTE ALLA CARRAIA

LUNGARNO CORSINI

Arno River

LUNGARNO ACCIAIUOLI

BORGO SS. APOSTOLI

MANETTO

BORGO S. S. APOSTOLI

VIA DELLE TERME

VIA POR S. MARIA

Piazza de' Salt.

LAMB.

S. Stephano

33 **27**

Piazza Nazaro Sauro

LUNGARNO GUICCIARDINI

PONTE S. TRINITA

Piazza de' Frescobaldi

VIA MAGGIO

PONTE VECCHIO

BORGO SAN JACOPO

SAN JACOPO

V. D. RAMAGLIANTI

VIA SERRAGLI

VIA SANTA MARIA

VIA DE COVERELLI

VIA S. MARTINO

To Brancacci Chapel

OLTRARNO

SANTO SPIRITO

Piazza della Passera

To Pitti Palace

FLORENCE

1. Trattoria al Trebbio
2. Trattoria "da Giorgio"
3. Trattoria Marione
4. Trattoria Sostanza-Troia
5. Trattoria 13 Gobbi
6. Trattoria Zà-Zà & Trattoria Mario's
7. Trattoria la Burrasca
8. Trattoria Lo Stracotto
9. Osteria Vineria i'Brincello
10. Trattoria Nerone Pizzeria
11. Mercato Centrale & Nerbone in the Market
12. Casa del Vino
13. Pugi Pizza
14. Barbecue Döner Kebab
15. Pasticceria Robiglio
16. La Mescita Fiaschetteria
17. Il Centro Supermercati
18. To Antica Trattoria da Tito
19. Self-Service Rist. Leonardo
20. Turkuaz Döner Kebab
21. Rivoire Café
22. Frescobaldi Ristorante & Wine Bar
23. Ristorante Paoli, Cantinetta dei Verrazzano & Perchè No! Gelateria
24. Osteria Vini e Vecchi Sapori
25. I Fratellini
26. L'Antico Trippaio
27. 'Ino Bottega di Alimentari e Vini
28. Trattoria Icche C'è C'è
29. Ristorante del Fagioli
30. Boccadama Enoteca Rist.
31. Trattoria Anita
32. Gelateria Grom
33. Gelateria Carrozze
34. Gelateria Carabè
35. Vivoli's Gelateria
36. Gelateria de' Neri
37. The Bermuda Triangle

Osteria Vineria i'Brincello is a bright, happy, no-frills diner with tasty food, lots of spirit, friendly service, and no hint of snobbishness. It features a list of Tuscan daily specials hanging from the ceiling and great prices on good bottled wine (€7 pastas, daily 12:00-15:00 & 19:00-23:00, corner of Via Nazionale and Via Chiara at Via Nazionale 110 red, tel. 055-282-645, Fredi cooks while Claudia serves).

Trattoria Nerone Pizzeria, serving up cheap, hearty Tuscan dishes and decent pizzas, is a tourist-friendly, practical standby in the hotel district. The lively, flamboyantly outfitted space (once the garden courtyard of a convent) feels like a good but kitschy American-Italian chain restaurant (€7 pizzas, €7 pastas, €10 *secondi*, daily 12:00-15:00 & 18:30-23:00, just north of Via Nazionale at Via Faenza 95 red, tel. 055-291-217, Tulio).

Eating Cheaply in or near the Mercato Centrale

Note that none of these eateries is open for dinner.

Mercato Centrale (Central Market) is great for an ad-lib lunch. It offers colorful piles of picnic produce, people-watching, and rustic sandwiches (Mon-Sat 7:00-14:00, Sat in winter until 17:00, closed Sun, a block north of San Lorenzo street market). Meat, fish, and cheese are sold on the ground level, with fruit and veggies mostly upstairs. The thriving ground-level eateries within the market (such as Nerbone, described next) serve some of the cheapest hot meals in town. The fancy deli, Perini, is famous for its quality products and generous free samples. Buy a picnic of fresh mozzarella cheese, olives, fruit, and crunchy bread to munch on the steps of the nearby Church of San Lorenzo, overlooking the bustling street market.

Nerbone in the Market is a venerable café and the best place for a sit-down meal within the Mercato Centrale. Join the shoppers and workers who crowd up to the bar to grab their €5 plates. Of the several cheap market diners, this feels the most authentic (lunch menu served 12:00-14:00, sandwiches available all day, cash only, inside the Mercato Centrale on the side closest to the Church of San Lorenzo, mobile 339-648-0251). As intestines are close to Florentines' hearts, tripe is very big here.

Trattoria Mario's, around the corner from Trattoria Zà-Zà (listed earlier), has been serving hearty lunches to marketgoers since 1953 (Fabio and Romeo are the latest generation). Their simple formula: bustling service, old-fashioned good value, a lunch-only fixed-price meal, and shared tables. It's *cucina casalinga*—home cooking *con brio*. This place is high-energy and jam-packed. Their best dishes often sell out first, so go early. If there's a line, put your name on the list (€5 pastas, €8 *secondi*, cash only, Mon-Sat 12:00-15:30, closed Sun and Aug, no reservations, Via Rosina 2, tel. 055-218-550).

Casa del Vino, Florence's oldest operating wine shop, offers glasses of wine from among 25 open bottles (see the list tacked to the bar). Owner Gianni, whose family has owned the Casa for more than 70 years, is a class act. Gianni's *carta dei panini* lists delightful €3.50 sandwiches and €1 crostini; the *I Nostri Panini* (classic sandwiches) richly reward adventurous eaters. During busy times, it's a mob scene. You'll eat standing outside alongside workers on a quick lunch break (Mon-Sat 9:30-17:00, closed Sat in summer and Sun year-round, hidden behind stalls of San Lorenzo Market at Via dell'Ariento 16 red, tel. 055-215-609).

Near the Accademia
Budget-Lunch Places Surrounding the Accademia

For pizza by the slice, try **Pugi**, at Piazza San Marco 10. For a break from pasta and pizza, grab a quick kebab lunch from **Barbecue: The Taste of Istanbul** (Via Cavour 41).

Pasticceria Robiglio, a smart little café, opens up its stately dining area and sets out a few tables on the sidewalk for lunch. They have a small menu of daily pasta and *secondi* specials, and seem determined to do things like they did in the elegant, pre-tourism days (generous €9 plates, a great €8 *niçoise*-like "fantasy salad," pretty pastries, smiling service, daily 12:00-15:00, longer hours as a café, a block toward the Duomo off Piazza S.S. Annunziata at Via dei Servi 112 red, tel. 055-212-784). Before you leave, be tempted by their pastries—famous among Florentines.

La Mescita Fiaschetteria is a characteristic hole-in-the-wall just around the corner from *David*—but a world away from all the tourism. It's where locals and students enjoy daily pasta specials and hearty sandwiches with good €1 house wine. You can trust Mirco and Alessio (as far as you can throw them)—just point to what looks good (such as their €5 pasta plate), and you'll soon be eating well and inexpensively. The place can either be mobbed by students or in a peaceful time warp, depending on when you stop by (Mon-Sat 12:00-16:00, closed Sun, Via degli Alfani 70 red, mobile 347-795-1604).

Picnic on the Ultimate Renaissance Square: **Il Centro Supermercati**, a handy supermarket a half-block north of the Accademia, has a curbside sandwich bar (Panineria) with an easy English menu that includes salads to go (Mon-Sat 10:00-16:00, Sun 11:00-19:00, supermarket open longer hours, Via Ricasoli 109). With your picnic in hand, hike around the block and join the bums on Piazza S.S. Annunziata, the first Renaissance square in Florence. There's a fountain for washing fruit on the square. Grab a stony seat anywhere you like, and savor one of my favorite cheap Florence eating experiences. Or, drop by any of the places listed earlier for an easy lunch (pizza, kebab, or sandwich plus juice) to go.

Dining with Bobo Away from the Center

Antica Trattoria da Tito, a 10-minute hike from the Accademia along Via San Gallo, is a long, drawn-out event of a meal. The boss, Bobo, is a fire hose of restaurateur energy who has clearly found his niche—making people happy with quality traditional food and lots of wine. His staff is as loyal as his clientele. While the food is great, there's no pretense. It's just a playground of Tuscan cuisine with "no romance allowed." As for the music he plays, Bobo says, "We are slaves of '80s." I'd come late and plan to party. To gorge on a feast of *antipasti* (meats, cheeses, fava beans, and bruschetta), consider ordering *fermami* (literally "stop me")— for €14, Bobo brings you food until you say, "*Fermami!*" A couple can get *fermami*, desserts, and a nice bottle of wine for €60 total. Ask for *vino* recommendations to experience that perfect pairing of food and wine. If you go with the flow here, you'll walk back to your hotel fat and filled with memories (€10 pastas, €12 *secondi*, €14 *gran tagliere*—big plate of cheese and meat, travelers with this book get a free after-dinner drink, Mon-Sat 12:30-15:00 & 19:00-23:00, closed Sun, reservations generally necessary, Via San Gallo 112 red, tel. 055-472-475).

Fast and Cheap near the Duomo

Self-Service Ristorante Leonardo is inexpensive, air-conditioned, quick, and handy. Eating here, you'll get the sense that they're passionate about the quality of their food. Stefano and Luciano (like Pavarotti) run the place with enthusiasm and put out free pitchers of tap water. It's just a block from the Duomo, southwest of the Baptistery (tasty €4 pastas, €5 main courses, Sun-Fri 11:45-14:45 & 18:45-21:45, closed Sat, upstairs at Via Pecori 11, tel. 055-284-446).

   Döner Kebab: A good place to try this cheap Middle Eastern specialty is Turkuaz, a couple of blocks northeast of the Duomo (Via dei Servi 65).

Near Piazza della Signoria

Piazza della Signoria, the scenic square facing Palazzo Vecchio, is ringed by beautifully situated yet touristy eateries serving over-priced, bad-value, and probably microwaved food. If you're determined to eat on the square, have pizza at Ristorante il Cavallino or bar food from the Irish pub next door. Piazza della Signoria's saving grace is **Rivoire** café, famous for its fancy desserts and thick hot chocolate. While obscenely expensive, it has the best view tables on the square (Tue-Sun 7:30-24:00, closed Mon, tel. 055-214-412).

Fine Dining near Piazza della Signoria

Frescobaldi Ristorante and Wine Bar, the showcase of Italy's

FLORENCE

aristocratic wine family, is a good choice for a formal dinner in Florence. Candlelight reflects off glasses of wine, and high-vaulted ceilings complement the sophisticated dishes. They offer the same menu in three different dining areas: cozy interior, woody wine bar, and breezy terrace. If coming for dinner, make a reservation, dress up, and hit an ATM (€12 appetizers and pastas, €20 *secondi*, lunch salads, Tue-Sat 12:00-14:30 & 19:00-22:30, Mon 19:00-22:30, closed Sun and Aug, air-con, half a block north of Palazzo Vecchio at Via dei Magazzini 2-4 red, tel. 055-284-724, Francesco is the lead waiter).

Ristorante Paoli dishes up wonderful, traditional cuisine to loads of cheerful eaters being served by jolly little old men under a richly frescoed Gothic vault. Because of its fame and central location, it's filled mostly with tourists, but for a sophisticated, traditional Tuscan splurge meal, this is a fine choice. Salads are dramatically cut and mixed from a trolley right at your table. The walls are sweaty with memories that go back to 1824, and the service is flamboyant and fun-loving (but don't get taken—confirm prices). Woodrow Wilson slurped spaghetti here—his bust looks down on you as you eat (€11 pastas, €15 *secondi*, €25 tourist fixed-price meal, daily 12:00-15:00 & 19:00-23:00, reserve for dinner, between Piazza della Signoria and the Duomo at Via dei Tavolini 12 red, tel. 055-216-215).

Eating Cheaply and Simply near Piazza della Signoria

Cantinetta dei Verrazzano, a long-established bakery/café/wine bar, serves delightful sandwich plates in an old-time setting. Their *selection Verrazzano* is a fine plate of four little crostini (like mini-bruschetta) proudly featuring different breads, cheeses, and meats from the Chianti region (€7.50). The *tagliere di focacce*, a sampler plate of mini-focaccia sandwiches, is also fun (€14 for big plate for two). Add a €5 glass of Chianti to either of these dishes to make a fine, light meal. Office workers pop in for a quick lunch, and it's traditional to share tables. Be warned: Prices can add up here in a hurry. Jonathan, the high-powered and helpful manager, explains each dish and offers those with this book a free cup of coffee to cap your meal (Mon-Sat 8:00-21:00, closed Sun, just off Via de' Calzaiuoli, across from Orsanmichele Church at Via dei Tavolini 18, tel. 055-268-590). They also have benches and tiny tables for eating at take-out prices. Simply step to the back and point to a hot *focacce* sandwich (€3), order a drink at the bar, and take away your food or sit with Florentines and watch the action while you munch.

Osteria Vini e Vecchi Sapori, half a block north of the Palazzo Vecchio, is a colorful 16-seat hole-in-the-wall restaurant serving Tuscan food with a fun, accessible menu of delicious €8

FLORENCE

Gelato

Gelato is an edible art form. Italy's best ice cream is in Florence—one souvenir that can't break and won't clutter your luggage. But beware of scams at touristy joints on busy streets that turn a simple request for a cone into a €10 "tourist special" rip-off. To avoid this, survey the size options and be very clear in your order (for example, "a €3 cone").

A key to gelato appreciation is sampling liberally and choosing flavors that go well together. Ask, as Italians do, for *"Un assaggio, per favore?"* (A taste, please?; oon ah-SAH-joh pehr fah-VOH-ray) and *"Che si sposano bene?"* (What marries well?; kay see spoh-ZAH-noh BEN-ay).

Artiginale, nostra produzione, and *produzione propia* mean gelato is made on the premises; also, gelato displayed in covered metal tins (rather than white plastic) is more likely to be homemade. Gelato aficionados avoid colors that don't appear in nature—for fewer chemicals and real flavor, go for mellow hues (bright colors attract children). These places are open daily for long hours.

Near the Duomo: The recent favorite in town, **Grom** uses organic ingredients and seasonal fresh fruit, along with biodegradable spoons and tubs. This clever chain markets its traditional approach with a staff quick to tell customers, "This gelato reminds me of my childhood." But there's no question that the quality is great—because the menu goes with what's in season (daily 10:30-24:00, Via delle Oche 24 red). Their *liquirizia* (licorice) flavor is worth a sample.

Near Ponte Vecchio: **Gelateria Carrozze** is a longtime favorite (daily 11:00-20:00, until 1:00 in the morning in summer,

pastas and €10 *secondi* (Tue-Sat 12:30-15:00 & 19:30-22:00, Sun 12:30-15:00, closed Mon, reserve for dinner; facing the bronze equestrian statue in Piazza della Signoria, go behind its tail into the corner and to your left; Via dei Magazzini 3 red, tel. 055-293-045, run by Mario while wife Rosanna cooks and son Thomas serves).

I Fratellini is an informal eatery where the "little brothers" have served peasants 29 different kinds of sandwiches and cheap glasses of Chianti wine (see list on wall) since 1875. Join the local crowd to order, then sit on a nearby curb or windowsill to eat, placing your glass on the wall rack before you leave (€4 for sandwich and wine, daily 9:00-20:00 or until the bread runs out, closed Sun in winter, 20 yards in front of Orsanmichele Church on Via dei Cimatori, tel. 055-239-6096). Be adventurous with the menu (easy-order by number). Consider *finocchiona* (#15, a special Tuscan salami), *lardo di Colonnata* (#22, lard aged in Carrara marble), and *cinghiale* (#19, spicy wild boar) sandwiches. Order the most expenon riverfront 30 yards from Ponte Vecchio toward the Uffizi at Piazza del Pesce 3).

Near the Accademia: A Sicilian choice on a tourist thoroughfare, **Gelateria Carabè** is particularly famous for its luscious *granite*—Italian ices made with fresh fruit (daily 11:00-20:00; from the Accademia, it's a block toward the Duomo at Via Ricasoli 60 red).

Near Orsanmichele Church: **Perchè No!** is located just off the busy main pedestrian drag, Via de' Calzaiuoli, and serves a stunning array of flavors (Via dei Tavolini 19).

Near the Church of Santa Croce: The venerable favorite, **Vivoli's** still has great gelato—but it's more expensive and stingy in its servings. Before ordering, try a free sample of their rice flavor—*riso* (closed Mon, Aug, and Jan; opposite the Church of Santa Croce, go down Via Torta a block and turn right on Via Stinche). Locals flock to **Gelateria de' Neri** (Via de' Neri 26 red), also owned by Vivoli's.

Near the Mercato Centrale: The **Bermuda Triangle** (a.k.a., I Gelati Del Bondi) is a hit both for its fresh ingredients and for the big-hearted energy of its owner, Vetulio (Via Nazionale 61 red, where it crosses Via Faenza, tel. 055-287-490).

Across the River: If you want an excuse to check out the little village-like neighborhood across the river from Santa Croce, enjoy a gelato at the tiny **Il Gelato di Filo** (named for Filippo and Lorenzo) at Via San Miniato 5 red, a few steps toward the river from Porta San Miniato. Gelato chef Edmir is proud of his fruity sorbet as well.

sive wine they're selling by the glass (Brunello for €5; bottles are labeled).

L'Antico Trippaio, an antique tripe stand, is a fixture in the town center (daily 9:00-20:00, on Via Dante Alighieri, mobile 339-742-5692). Cheap and authentic as can be, this is where Florentines come daily for €3.50 sandwiches *(panino)*, featuring specialties like *trippa alla fiorentina* (tripe), *lampredotto* (cow's stomach), and a list of more appetizing options. Roberto and Maurizio offer a free plastic glass of rotgut Chianti with each sandwich for travelers with this book. The best people-watching place to enjoy your sandwich is three blocks away, on Piazza della Signoria.

Near Ponte Vecchio

'Ino Bottega di Alimentari e Vini is a mod little shop filled with gifty edibles. Alessandro and his staff serve sandwiches and wine—you'll get your €5-8 sandwich on a napkin with an included glass of their wine of the day as you perch on a tiny stool. They can also make a fine €12 *piatto misto* of cheeses and meats with bread (daily 11:00-17:00, immediately behind Uffizi Gallery on Ponte Vecchio side, Via dei Georgofili 3 red, tel. 055-219-208).

Between Palazzo Vecchio and Santa Croce Church

Trattoria Icche C'è C'è (EE-kay chay chay; dialect for "whatever there is, there is") is a small, family-style restaurant where fun-loving Gino and his wife Mara serve quality, local food, including a €13 three-course, fixed-price meal. While filled with tourists, the place exudes a charming mom-and-pop warmth (€8 pastas, €12 *secondi,* Tue-Sun 12:30-14:30 & 19:30-22:30, closed Mon and two weeks in Aug, midway between Bargello and river at Via Magalotti 11 red, tel. 055-216-589).

Ristorante del Fagioli is an enthusiastically run eatery where you feel the heritage. The dad, Gigi, commands the kitchen while family members Antonio, Maurizio, and Simone keep the throngs of loyal customers returning. The cuisine: home-style bread-soups, hearty steaks, and Florentine classics. Don't worry—while *fagioli* means "beans," that's the family name, not the extent of the menu (€9 pastas, €9 *secondi,* cash only, closed Sat-Sun, reserve for dinner, between Santa Croce Church and the Alle Grazie bridge at Corso dei Tintori 47, tel. 055-244-285).

Boccadama Enoteca Ristorante is a stylish, shabby-chic wine bistro serving traditional Tuscan fare based on seasonal produce. Eat in the intimate dining room with candles reflecting off bottle-lined walls or at one of the few tables on the dramatic Piazza Santa Croce. Reservations are smart (€9 *primi,* €14 *secondi,* daily 11:00-16:00 & 18:30-24:00, on south side of Piazza Santa Croce at 25-26 red, tel. 055-243-640, Marco).

Trattoria Anita, midway between the Uffizi and Santa Croce, offers a good lunch special: two hearty Tuscan courses for €8 (Mon-Sat 12:00-14:30 & 19:00-22:15, closed Sun, on the corner of Via Vinegia and Via del Parlagio at #2 red, tel. 055-218-698, run by three brothers: Nicola, Gianni, and Maurizio).

South of the River, in the Oltrarno

Dining with a Ponte Vecchio View

Golden View Open Bar is a lively, trendy bistro, good for a romantic meal or just a salad, pizza, or pasta with fine wine and a fine view of Ponte Vecchio and the Arno River. Reservations for window tables are essential unless you drop in early for dinner (reasonable prices, €10 pizzas and big salads, daily 11:30-24:00, impressive wine bar, 50 yards upstream from Ponte Vecchio at Via dei Bardi 58, tel. 055-214-502, run by Antonio, Marco, and Tomaso). They have four seating areas (with the same menu and prices) for whatever mood you're in: a riverside pizza place, a classier restaurant, a jazzy lounge, and a wine bar (they also serve a buffet of appetizers free with your drink from 19:00 to 21:00). Mixing their fine wine, river views, and live jazz makes for a wonderful evening (jazz nightly at 20:30 except Tue and Thu off-season).

Dining Well in the Oltrarno

Of the many good and colorful restaurants in the Oltrarno, these are my favorites. Reservations are a good idea in the evening.

Trattoria 4 Leoni creates the quintessential Oltrarno dinner scene. The Tuscan-style food is made with an innovative twist and an appreciation for vegetables. You'll enjoy the fun energy and characteristic seating, both inside and on the colorful square, Canto ai Quattro Pagoni. While the wines by the glass are pricey, the house wine is very good (€10 pastas, €15 *secondi*, daily 12:00-24:00, dinner reservations smart; from Ponte Vecchio walk four blocks up Via de' Guicciardini, turn right on Via dello Sprone, then slightly left to Via de' Vellutini 1; tel. 055-218-562).

Olio & Convivium Gastronomia is primarily a catering company for top-end events, and this is where they showcase their cooking. It started as an elegant deli whose refined oil-tasting room morphed into a romantic, aristocratic restaurant. Their three intimate rooms are surrounded by fine *prosciutti*, cheeses, and wine shelves. It can seem intimidating and a little pretentious, but well-dressed foodies will appreciate this place for its quiet atmosphere. Their list of €13-20 *gastronomia* plates offers an array of taste treats and fine wines by the glass (€14 pastas, €18 *secondi*, stylish €18 lunches with wine, €3 cover, Tue-Sat 12:00-14:30 & 19:00-22:30, Mon lunch only, closed Sun, strong air-con, Via di Santo Spirito 4, tel. 055-265-8198, Monica).

Antico Ristoro Di' Cambi is a meat-lover's dream—thick with Tuscan traditions, rustic touches, and T-bone steaks. The bustling scene has a memorable, beer-hall energy. As you walk in, you'll pass a glass case filled with red chunks of Chianina beef that's priced by weight (€40/kilo, standard serving is half a kilo per person). Before you OK your investment, they'll show you the cut and tell you the weight. While the steak comes nearly uncooked, it's air dried for 21 days so it's not really raw, just very tasty and tender—making you so happy you're sitting at the top of the food chain. This is also a good chance to enjoy the famous *bistecca alla fiorentina*, sitting inside the convivial woody interior or outside on a square (€8 pastas, €12 *secondi*, closed Sun, reserve on weekends and to sit outside, Via Sant'Onofrio 1 red, one block south of Ponte Amerigo Vespucci, tel. 055-217-134, run by Stefano and Fabio, the Cambi cousins).

Trattoria da Sergio is a tiny eatery about a block before Porta San Frediano, one of Florence's medieval gates. It has charm and a strong following, so reservations are a must. The food is on the gourmet side of home-cooking—mama's favorites with a modern twist—and therefore a bit more expensive (€9 pastas, €15 *secondi*, Tue-Sun 12:00-15:00 & 19:15-23:00, closed Mon, Borgo San Frediano 145 red, tel. 055-223-449, Sergio and Marco).

Il Santo Bevitore Ristorante, lit like a Rembrandt painting and filled with dressy tables, serves creative Tuscan cuisine. They're enthusiastic about matching quality produce from the area with the right wine (€10 pastas, €8-15 meat-and-cheese plates or *tagliere*, good wine list by the glass or bottle, come early or make reservations, no outside seating, Via di Santo Spirito 64, tel. 055-211-264).

Trattoria Al Tranvai, with tight seating and small dark-wood tables, looks like an old-time tram filled with the neighborhood gang. A 10-minute walk from the river at the edge of the Oltrarno, it feels like a small town's favorite eatery (€8 pastas, €10 *secondi*, closed Sun, Piazza T. Tasso 14 red, tel. 055-225-197).

Eating Cheaply in the Oltrarno
Trattoria Sabatino, the farthest away and least touristy of my Oltrarno listings, is a spacious, brightly lit mess hall—disturbingly cheap—with family character and a simple menu. It's a super place to watch locals munch. You'll find it just outside Porta San Frediano, a 15-minute walk from Ponte Vecchio (€4 pastas, €5 *secondi*, Mon-Fri 12:00-15:00 & 19:15-22:00, closed Sat-Sun, Via Pisana 2 red, tel. 055-225-955, little English spoken).

Trattoria Casalinga, an inexpensive standby, comes with aproned women bustling around the kitchen. Florentines and tourists alike pack the place and leave full and happy, with euros to spare for gelato (€6 pastas, €8 *secondi*, Mon-Sat 12:00-14:30 & 19:00-21:45, after 20:00 reserve or wait, closed Sun and Aug, just off Piazza di Santo Spirito, near the church at Via de' Michelozzi 9 red, tel. 055-218-624, Andrea).

Borgo Antico is the hit of Piazza di Santo Spirito, with enticing pizzas, big deluxe plates of pasta, a delightful setting, and a trendy and boisterous young crowd (€9 pizza and pasta, €16 *secondi*, daily 12:00-24:00, best to reserve for a seat on the square, Piazza di Santo Spirito 6 red, tel. 055-210-437, Andrea and Michele—feel his forearm). **Volume,** the bar next door, is run by the same gang.

Ricchi Caffè, next to Borgo Antico, has fine gelato, homemade desserts, shaded outdoor tables, and pasta dishes at lunch (daily 7:00-24:00, tel. 055-215-864). After noting the plain facade of the Brunelleschi church facing the square, step inside the café and pick your favorite picture of the many ways the facade might be finished.

Supermarket: Facing the Pitti Palace, **Meta Supermarket** seems designed to rescue poor, hungry, and thirsty travelers (daily 9:00-21:00, Piazza de' Pitti 33 red).

Florence Connections

Florence is Tuscany's transportation hub, with fine train, bus, and plane connections to virtually anywhere in Italy. The city has several train stations, a bus station (next to the main train station), and an airport (plus Pisa's airport is nearby). Livorno, on the coast west of Florence, is a major cruise-ship port for passengers visiting Florence, Pisa, and other nearby destinations.

By Train

From Florence by Train to: La Spezia (for the Cinque Terre, 5/day direct, 2 hours, otherwise nearly hourly with change in Pisa, €9.30), **Milan** (hourly, 1.75 hours), **Milan's Malpensa Airport** (2/day direct, 2.75 hours), **Venice** (hourly, 2-3 hours, may transfer in Bologna; often crowded—reserve ahead), **Rome** (at least hourly, 1.5 hours, most connections require seat reservations, €45), **Interlaken** (5/day, 5.5-6 hours, 2-3 changes), **Frankfurt** (1/day, 12 hours, 1-3 changes), **Paris** (3/day, 10-15 hours, 1-2 changes, important to reserve overnight train ahead), **Vienna** (1 direct overnight train, or 5/day with 1-3 changes, 10-16 hours).

By Bus

The SITA bus station (100 yards west of the Florence train station on Via Santa Caterina da Siena) is traveler-friendly—a big, old-school lot with numbered stalls and all the services you'd expect. Schedules for regional trips are posted everywhere, and TV monitors show imminent departures. Bus service drops dramatically on Sunday.

By Bus to: Florence's **Amerigo Vespucci Airport** (2/hour, 30 minutes, €5, just pay driver, always from platform 1). Try to buy bus tickets in the station, as you'll pay 30 percent more if you buy tickets on the bus. Bus info: www.sitabus.it or tel. 800-373-760 (Mon-Fri 8:30-18:30, Sat 8:30-12:30, closed Sun); some schedules are listed in the *Florence Concierge Information* magazine.

By Taxi

For small groups with more money than time, zipping to nearby towns by taxi can be a good value (e.g., €120 from your Florence hotel to your Siena hotel).

A more comfortable alternative is to hire a private car service. Florence-based **Transfer Chauffeur Service** has a fleet of modern vehicles with drivers who can whisk you between cities, to and from the cruise ship port, and through the Tuscan countryside

Greater Florence

To Lucca, Pisa & Cinque Terre

To Bologna Venice & Milan

AUTOSTRADA CHURCH

FIRENZE NORD EXIT

A-11

A-1

VESPUCCI AIRPORT

RIFREDI STATION

PIAZZA LIBERTÀ & P

Fiesole

VIA SAN DOMENICO (BUS #7)

VIA PISTOIESE

VIA BARACCA

Arno River

FIRENZE SIGNA EXIT

S.M. NOVELLA MAIN TRAIN STN.

CAMPO DI MARTE STATION

SUPERSTRADA

VIA PISANA

FLORENCE CENTER SEE DETAIL MAPS

VIA BACCIO MONTELUPO

To Pisa & Livorno

PIAZZALE MICHELANGELO & P

VIA MARCO POLO

VIA SENESE

PORTA ROMANA & P

VIA G. AGNELLI

A-1

CERTOSA

FIRENZE SUD EXIT

A-1

To Roma

2 Kilometers

2 Miles

FIRENZE CERTOSA EXIT

S-222

S-2

FLORENCE AMERICAN CEMETERY

SCENIC WINDING ROAD THROUGH CHIANTI

SUPERSTRADA

To San Gimignano & Siena

for around the same price as a cab (€130 for Florence to Siena, tel. 055-614-2182, mobile 338-862-3129, www.transfercs.com, marco .masala@transfercs.com, Marco).

By Plane

Florence's Amerigo Vespucci Airport, also called Peretola Airport, is about five miles northwest of Florence (open 5:10-24:00, no overnighting allowed, TI, cash machines, car-rental agencies, airport info tel. 055-306-1630, flight info tel. 055-306-1700—domestic only, www.aeroporto.firenze.it). Shuttle buses (far right of airport as you exit arrivals hall) connect the airport with Florence's SITA bus station, 100 yards west of the train station on Via Santa Caterina da Siena (2/hour, 30 minutes, daily 6:00-23:30, €5, first bus leaves for airport from Florence at 5:30). Allow about €22 and 30 minutes for a taxi.

By Plane: Pisa's **Galileo Galilei Airport** also handles international and domestic flights (TI open daily 9:30-23:30, cash machine, car-rental agencies, baggage storage from 8:00-20:00 only, €7/bag; self-service cafeteria, tel. 050-849-300, www.pisa -airport.com). You can connect to **Florence** easily by train (2-3/ hour, 1.25 hours, €5.80, most transfer at Pisa Centrale) or by Terravision bus (about hourly, 1.25 hours, €10 one-way, ticket kiosk is at the right end of the arrivals hall as you're facing the exits, catch bus outside and to the far right of the bus parking lot, www .terravision.eu).

THE CINQUE TERRE

The Cinque Terre (CHINK-weh TAY-reh), a remote chunk of the Italian Riviera, is the traffic-free, lowbrow, underappreciated alternative to the French Riviera. There's not a museum in sight—just sun, sea, sand (well, pebbles), wine, and pure, unadulterated Italy. Enjoy the villages, swimming, hiking, and evening romance of one of God's great gifts to tourism. For a home base, choose among five *(cinque)* villages, each of which fills a ravine with a lazy hive of human activity—callused locals, sunburned travelers, and no Vespas. While the Cinque Terre is now discovered (and can be quite crowded midday, when tourist boats and cruise-ship excursions drop by), I've never seen happier, more relaxed tourists.

The chunk of coast was first described in medieval times as "the five lands." In the feudal era, this land was watched over by castles. Tiny communities grew up in their protective shadows, ready to run inside at the first hint of a Turkish Saracen pirate raid. Marauding pirates from North Africa were a persistent problem until about 1400. Many locals were kidnapped and ransomed or sold into slavery, and those who remained built fires on flat-roofed watchtowers to relay warnings—alerting the entire coast to imminent attacks. The last major raid was in 1545.

As the threat of pirates faded, the villages prospered, catching fish and cultivating grapes. Churches were enlarged with a growing population. But until the advent of tourism in this generation, the towns remained isolated. Even today, traditions survive, and each of the five villages comes with a distinct dialect and its own proud heritage.

In this chapter, I cover the five towns in order from south to north, from Riomaggiore to Monterosso. Since I still get the names of the towns mixed up, I think of them by number: #1 Riomaggiore (a workaday town), #2 Manarola (picturesque), #3 Corniglia (on a hilltop), #4 Vernazza (the region's cover girl, the most touristy and dramatic), and #5 Monterosso al Mare (the closest thing to a beach resort of the five towns).

Flooding Damage and Closures: On October 25, 2011, Vernazza and Monterosso were hit hard by flash flooding. Many hotels and restaurants will have reopened by the time you visit; for the latest on the region (including trail conditions), see our Cinque Terre news page at www.ricksteves.com. For a list of open and closed businesses in **Vernazza,** see www.savevernazza.com; for **Monterosso,** see www.rebuildmonterosso.com.

Arrival in the Cinque Terre

By Train: Big, fast trains from elsewhere in Italy speed past the Cinque Terre (though some stop in Monterosso and Riomaggiore). Unless you're coming from a nearby town, you'll have to change trains at least once to reach Manarola, Corniglia, or Vernazza.

Generally, if you're coming from the north, you'll change trains in Sestri Levante or Genoa (specifically, Genoa's Piazza Principe station). If you're coming from the south or east, you'll most likely have to switch trains in La Spezia (change at La Spezia Centrale station—don't make the mistake of getting off at La Spezia Migliarina). No matter where you're coming from, it's best to check in the station before you leave to see your full schedule and route options (use the computerized kiosks or ask at a ticket window). Don't forget to validate your ticket by stamping it—ka-CHUNK!—in the yellow machines located on train platforms and elsewhere in the station. Conductors here are notorious for levying stiff fines on forgetful tourists. For more information on riding the train between Cinque Terre towns, see "Getting Around the Cinque Terre," later.

By Plane: If the Cinque Terre is your first or last stop on this trip, consider flying into Pisa or Genoa, rather than Milan. These airports are less confusing than Milan's, and closer to the Cinque Terre.

Planning Your Time

The ideal stay is two or three full days; my recommended minimum stay is two nights and a completely uninterrupted day. The Cinque Terre is served by the local train from Genoa and La Spezia. Speed demons arrive in the morning, check their bags in La Spezia, take the five-hour hike through all five towns, laze away the afternoon on the beach or rock of their choice, and zoom away on the overnight train to somewhere back in the real world. But be warned: The Cinque Terre has a strange way of messing up your momentum. (The evidence is the number of Americans who have fallen in love with the region and/or one of its residents...and are still here.) Frankly, staying fewer than two nights is a mistake that you'll likely regret.

The towns are just a few minutes apart by hourly train or boat. There's no checklist of sights or experiences—just a hike, the towns themselves, and your fondest vacation desires. Study this chapter in advance and piece together your best day, mixing hiking, swimming, trains, and a boat ride. For the best light and coolest temperatures, start your hike early.

Market days perk up the towns from 8:00 to 13:00 on Tuesday in Vernazza, Wednesday in Levanto, Thursday in Monterosso and Sestri Levante, and Friday in La Spezia.

The winter is really dead—most hotels and some restaurants close in December and January. The long Easter weekend and June and July are the peak of peak periods, the toughest times to find rooms. In spring, the towns can feel inundated with Italian school groups day-tripping on spring excursions (they can't afford to sleep in this expensive region).

For more information on the region, see www.cinqueterre.it.

Cinque Terre Park Cards

Visitors hiking between the towns need to pay a park entrance fee. This fee keeps the trails safe and open, and pays for viewpoints, picnic spots, WCs, and more. The popular coastal trail generates enough revenue to subsidize the development of trails and outdoor activities higher in the hills.

You have two options for covering the park fee: the Cinque Terre Park Card or the Cinque Terre Treno Park Card. Both are valid until midnight on the expiration date. Write your name on your card or risk a big fine.

The **Cinque Terre Park Card** costs €5 for one day of hiking or €9 for two (€2-3 more on weekends and holidays, covers trails and shuttle buses but not trains, buy at trailheads and at most train stations, no validation required).

The **Cinque Terre Treno Park Card** covers what the Cinque Terre Park Card does, plus the use of the local trains (from Levanto to La Spezia, including all Cinque Terre towns). It's sold at TIs inside train stations, but not at trailheads (€10/1 day, €19/2 days, validate card at train station by punching it in the yellow machine). With this card, you have to hike and take three train trips every day just to break even.

Cards cost a bit more on weekends. Those under 18 or over 70 get a discount, as do families of four or more (see www.parco nazionale5terre.it).

Getting Around the Cinque Terre

Within the Cinque Terre, you can connect towns in three ways: by train, boat, or foot. Trains are cheaper, boats are more scenic, and hiking lets you enjoy more pasta. From a practical point of view, you should consider supplementing the often frustrating train with the sometimes more convenient boat. The trail between Riomaggiore and Manarola is a delight and takes just a few minutes, making the train not worth waiting for. The rest of the trail has seen significant landslide damage—while likely patched up in time for your visit, double-check locally before setting out.

By Train

Along the coast here, trains go in only two directions: *"per* [to] *Genova"* (the Italian spelling of Genoa), northbound; or *"per La Spezia,"* southbound. Assuming you're on vacation, accept the unpredictability of Cinque Terre trains (they're often late...unless you are, too—in which case they're on time). Relax while you wait—buy a cup of coffee at a station bar. When the train comes (know which direction to look for: La Spezia or Genova), casually walk over and hop on. This is especially easy in Monterosso, with its fine café-with-a-view on track #1 (direction: Milano/Genova), and in Vernazza, where you can hang out at the Blue Marlin Bar with a prepaid drink and dash when the train pulls in.

Use the handy TV monitors in the station, which display upcoming departures for the next hour or so (as well as notes about which track they're on and whether they're late). Most of the northbound trains that stop at all Cinque Terre towns and are headed toward Genova will list Sestri Levante as the *destinazione*.

By train, the five towns are just a few minutes apart. Know your stop. Once the train leaves the town just before your destination, go to the door and get ready to slip out before the mobs flood in, making it impossible to get off. Words to the wise for novice tourists, who often miss their stop: The stations are small and the trains are long, so (especially in Vernazza) you might have to get off deep in a tunnel. Also, the doors don't open automatically—you may have to flip open the handle of the door yourself. If a door isn't working, go quickly to the next car to leave. (When leaving a town by train, if you find the platform jammed with people, walk down the platform into the tunnel, where things quiet down.)

It costs about €1.80 per ride within the region. Tickets are good for 75 minutes in one direction, so you could conceivably use one for a brief stopover. To make the ticket good for six hours (in one direction only), you need to buy a ticket good for 40 kilometers (€3.50). Stamp the ticket at the station machine before you board. Machines are often broken or out of ink (good luck explaining that to conductors), but riding without a validated ticket can be expensive ("minimum €25 fine" means they charge what they want—usually €50). If you have a Eurail Pass, don't spend one of your valuable travel days on the cheap Cinque Terre.

Cinque Terre Train Schedule: Since the train is the Cinque Terre's lifeline, many shops and restaurants post the current schedule, and most hotels offer copies of it (one also comes with the Cinque Terre Park Card). But beware: The printed schedules can be misleading (half the listed departures don't go every day); the monitors in the stations are your best source of actual, current departure information. Note that fast trains leaving La Spezia zip right through the Cinque Terre; some stop only in Monterosso (town #5) and Riomaggiore (town #1). But any train that stops in Manarola, Corniglia, and Vernazza (towns #2, #3, and #4) will stop in all five towns (including the trains on the schedule below).

The times below are accurate as of this printing, but confirm schedules locally. These are the daily train times (a few do not run on Sunday; more trains are added in the busiest season, June-Sept):

Trains leave La Spezia Centrale for all or most of the Cinque Terre villages at 7:12, 10:06, 11:10, 12:00, 13:15, 14:09, 15:10, 15:58,

17:10, 17:20, 18:06, 19:10, 20:18, 21:25, 23:10, and 00:50.

Going back to La Spezia, trains leave Monterosso at 6:20, 8:15, 9:29, 11:00, 11:55, 12:19, 13:28, 14:20, 15:22, 16:17, 17:30, 18:18, 19:22, 20:07 or 20:20, 21:32, 22:22, and 23:45 (these same trains depart Vernazza about four minutes later).

Again, convenient TV monitors posted at several places in each station clearly show exactly what times the next trains are leaving in each direction (and, if they're late, how late they are expected to be). I trust these monitors much more than my ability to read any printed schedule.

By Boat

From Easter through October, a daily boat service connects Monterosso, Vernazza, Manarola, Riomaggiore, and Portovenere. Boats provide a scenic way to get from town to town and survey what you just hiked. And boats offer the only efficient way to visit the nearby resort of Portovenere (the alternative is a tedious train-bus connection via La Spezia). In peaceful weather, the boats can be more reliable than the trains, but if seas are rough, they don't run at all. Because the boats nose in and tourists have to gingerly disembark onto little more than a plank, even a small chop can cancel some or all of the stops.

I see the tour boats as a syringe, injecting each town with a boost of euros. The towns are addicted, and they shoot up hourly through the summer. (Between 10:00-15:00—especially on weekends—masses of gawkers unload from boats, tour buses, and cruise ships, inundating the villages and changing the feel of the region.)

Boats depart Monterosso about hourly (10:30-17:00), stopping at the Cinque Terre towns (except at Corniglia) and ending up an hour later in Portovenere. (Portovenere-Monterosso boats run 9:00-17:00.) The ticket price depends on the length of the boat ride (short hops-€4, longer hops-€8, five-town all-day pass-€16). Round-trip tickets are slightly cheaper than two one-way trips. You can buy tickets at little stands at each town's harbor (tel. 0187-732-987 and 0187-818-440). Another all-day boat pass for €23 extends to Portovenere and includes a 40-minute scenic ride around three small islands (2/day). Boats are not covered by the Cinque Terre Park Card. Boat schedules are posted at docks, harbor bars, Cinque Terre park offices, and hotels (www.navigazione golfodeipoeti.it).

By Shuttle Bus

Shuttle buses connect each Cinque Terre town with its distant parking lot and various points in the hills (for example, a shuttle runs from Corniglia's train station to its hilltop town center). Note that these shuttle buses do not connect the towns with each other.

Most rides cost €1.50 (and are covered by the Cinque Terre Park Card)—pick up bus schedules from TIs or note the times posted on bus doors and at bus stops. Some (but not all) departures from Vernazza, Manarola, and Riomaggiore go beyond the parking lots and high into the hills. Pay for a round-trip ride and just cruise both ways to soak in the scenery (round-trip 30-45 minutes).

Hiking the Cinque Terre

All five towns are connected by trails, marked with red-and-white paint, white arrows, and some signs. Provided that post-landslide repair is finished in time for your visit, you'll experience the area's best by hiking all the way from one end to the other. While you can detour to dramatic hilltop sanctuaries, I'd keep it simple by following trail #2—the low route between the villages. The entire seven-mile hike can be done in about four hours, but allow five for dawdling. Germans (with their task-oriented *Alpenstock* walking sticks) are notorious for marching too fast through the region. Take it slow...smell the cactus flowers and herbs, notice the lizards, listen to birds singing in the olive groves, and enjoy vistas on all sides.

Remember that hikers need to pay a fee to enter the trails (see "Cinque Terre Park Cards," earlier). If you're hiking the entire five-town route, consider that the trail between Riomaggiore (#1) and Manarola (#2) is easiest. The hike between Manarola and Corniglia (#3) has minor hills. The trail from Corniglia to Vernazza (#4) is demanding, and the path from Vernazza to Monterosso (#5) is the most challenging. For that hike, you might want to start in Monterosso in order to tackle the toughest section while you're fresh—and to enjoy the region's most dramatic scenery as you approach Vernazza.

Other than the wide, easy Riomaggiore-Manarola segment, the trail is generally narrow, steep, rocky, and comes with lots of steps. Be warned that I get many emails from readers who say the trail was tougher than they expected. The rocks and metal grates can be slippery in the rain. While the trail is a bit of a challenge, it's perfectly doable for any fit hiker...and worth the sweat.

Maps aren't necessary for the basic coastal hikes described here. But for the expanded version of this hike (12 hours, from Portovenere to Levanto) and more serious hikes in the high country, pick up a good hiking map (about €5, sold everywhere). To leave the park cleaner than you found it, bring a plastic bag *(sacchetto di plastica)* and pick up a little trail trash along the way. It would be great if American visitors—who get so much joy out of this region—were known for this good deed.

Riomaggiore-Manarola (20 minutes): Facing the front of the train station in Riomaggiore (#1), go up the stairs to the right, following signs for *Via dell'Amore.* The photo-worthy promenade—wide enough for baby strollers—winds along the coast to Manarola (#2). It's primarily flat, and it's even wheelchair-accessible since there are elevators at each end (elevators at Riomaggiore included in pass, elevator at Manarola for disabled use only). While there's no beach along the trail, stairs lead down to sunbathing rocks. A long tunnel and mega-nets protect hikers from mean-spirited falling rocks. A wine bar—Bar & Vini A Piè de Mà—is located at the Riomaggiore trailhead and offers light meals, awesome town views, and clever boat storage under the train tracks (for more info, see page 1056). There's a picnic zone with a water fountain, shade, and a seagull that must have been human in a previous life hanging out just above the Manarola station (WC at Manarola station).

Manarola-Corniglia (45 minutes): The walk from Manarola (#2) to Corniglia (#3) is a little longer, more rugged, and steeper than the Via dell'Amore. It's also less romantic. To avoid the last stretch (switchback stairs leading up to the hill-capping town of Corniglia), end your hike at Corniglia's train station and catch the shuttle bus to the town center (2/hour, €1.50, free with Cinque Terre Park Card, usually timed to meet the trains).

Corniglia-Vernazza (1.5 hours): The hike from Corniglia (#3) to Vernazza (#4)—the wildest and greenest section of the coast—is very rewarding but very hilly (going the other direction, from Vernazza to Corniglia, is steeper). From the Corniglia station and beach, zigzag up to the town (via the steep stairs, the longer road, or the shuttle bus). Ten minutes past Corniglia, toward Vernazza, you'll see Guvano beach far beneath you (once the region's nude beach). The scenic trail leads past a bar and picnic tables, through lots of fragrant and flowery vegetation, into Vernazza. If you need a break before reaching Vernazza, stop by Franco's Ristorante and Bar la Torre; it has a small menu but big views.

Vernazza-Monterosso (1.5 hours): The trail from Vernazza (#4) to Monterosso (#5) is a scenic up-and-down-a-lot trek and the most challenging of the bunch. Trails are narrow, steep, and crumbly, with a lot of steps (some readers report "very dangerous"), but easy to follow. Locals frown on camping at the picnic tables located midway. The views just out of Vernazza, looking back at the town, are spectacular.

Longer Hikes: Above the trails that run between the towns, higher-elevation hikes crisscross the region. Shuttle buses make the going easier, connecting coastal villages and trailheads in the hills. Ask locally about the more difficult six-mile inland hike to Volastra. This tiny village, perched between Manarola and Corniglia, hosts lots of Germans and Italians in the summertime. Just below its town center, in the hamlet of Groppo, is the Cinque Terre Cooperative Winery (open daily). For the whole trip on the high road between Manarola and Corniglia, allow two hours one-way. In return, you'll get sweeping views and a closer look at the vineyards. Shuttle buses run from Manarola to Volastra (€2.50 or free with Cinque Terre Park Card, pick up schedule from park office, 8/day, more departures in summer, 15 minutes); consider taking the bus up and hiking down.

Swimming, Kayaking, and Biking

Every town in the Cinque Terre has a beach or a rocky place to swim. Monterosso has the biggest and sandiest beach, with umbrellas and beach-use fees (but it's free where there are no umbrellas). Vernazza's is tiny—better for sunning than swimming. Manarola and Riomaggiore have the worst beaches (no sand), but Manarola offers the best deep-water swimming.

Wear your walking shoes and pack your swim gear. Several of the beaches have showers (no shampoo, please). Underwater sight-seeing is full of fish—goggles are sold in local shops. Sea urchins can be a problem if you walk on the rocks, and sometimes jellyfish wash up on the pebbles.

You can rent kayaks or boats in Riomaggiore, Vernazza, and Monterosso. (For details, see individual town listings in this chapter.) Some readers say kayaking can be dangerous—the kayaks tip easily, training is not provided, and lifejackets are not required.

Sleeping in the Cinque Terre

My favorite place is Vernazza, though you'll get fewer crowds and better value for your money in other towns. Monterosso is a good choice for sun-worshiping softies, those who prefer the ease of a real hotel, and the younger crowd (more night-life). Hermits, anarchists, wine-lovers, and mountain goats like Corniglia. Sophisticated Italians and Germans choose Manarola. Riomaggiore is bigger than Vernazza and less resorty than Monterosso.

While the Cinque Terre is too rugged for the mobs that ravage the Spanish and French coasts, it's popular with Italians, Germans, and in-the-know Americans. Hotels charge more and are packed on holidays (including Easter); in June, July, and September; and on Fridays and Saturdays all summer. (With global warming, swel-tering August is no longer considered peak season on this stretch of the Riviera.) While you can find doubles for €65 or €70 most of the season, you'll pay extra (around €80) in June and July. The prices I've listed are the maximum for April through October. For a terrace or view, you might pay an extra €20 or more. Apartments for four can be economical for families—figure around €120.

It's smart to reserve your room in advance in May, June, July, and September, and on weekends and holidays. At other times, you can land a double room on any day by just arriving in town (ideally by noon) and asking around at bars and restaurants, or simply by approaching locals on the street. Many travelers enjoy the opportunity to shop around a bit and get the best price by bargaining. Private rooms—called *affitta camere*—are no longer an intimate stay with a family. They are generally comfortable apartments (often with small kitchens) where you get the key and come and go as you like, rarely seeing your landlord. Many landowners rent the buildings by the year to local managers, who then attempt to make a profit by filling them night after night with tourists.

For the best value, visit several private rooms and snare the best. Going direct cuts out the middleman and softens prices. Staying more than one night gives you bargaining leverage. Plan on paying cash. Private rooms are generally bigger and more comfortable than those offered by pensions and have the same privacy as a hotel room.

If you want the security of a reservation, make it at a hotel long in advance (smaller places generally don't take reservations very far ahead). Query by email, not fax. If you do reserve, honor your reservation (or, if you must cancel, do it as early as possible). Since people renting rooms usually don't take deposits, they lose money if you don't show up.

Eating in the Cinque Terre

Hanging out at a sea-view restaurant while sampling local specialties could become one of your favorite memories.

Tegame alla Vernazza is the most typical main course in Vernazza: anchovies, potatoes, tomatoes, white wine, oil, and herbs. Anchovies (*acciughe*; ah-CHOO-gay) are ideally served the day they're caught. There's nothing cool about being an anchovy virgin. If you've always hated anchovies (the harsh, cured-in-salt American kind), try them fresh here. *Pansotti* are ravioli with ricotta and a mixture of greens, often served with a walnut sauce... delightful and filling.

While antipasto means cheese and salami in Tuscany, here you'll get *antipasti frutti di mare*, a plate of mixed "fruits of the sea" and a fine way to start a meal. Many restaurants are particularly proud of their *antipasti frutti di mare*. For two diners, splitting one of these and a pasta dish can be plenty.

This region is the birthplace of pesto. Basil, which loves the temperate Ligurian climate, is ground with cheese (half parmigiano cow cheese and half pecorino sheep cheese), garlic, olive oil, and pine nuts, and then poured over pasta. Try it on spaghetti, *trenette* (the long, flat Ligurian noodle), or *trofie* (made of flour with a bit of potato, designed specifically for pesto to cling to). Many also like pesto lasagna, always made with white sauce, never red. If you become addicted, small jars of pesto are sold in the local grocery stores and gift shops. If it's refrigerated, it's fresh; this is what you want if you're eating it today. For taking home, get the jar-on-a-shelf pesto.

Focaccia, the tasty pillowy bread, also originates here in Liguria. Locals say the best focaccia is made between the Cinque Terre and Genoa. It's simply flatbread with olive oil and salt. The baker roughs up the dough with finger holes, then bakes it. Focaccia comes plain or with onions, sage, or olive bits, and is a local favorite for a snack on the beach. Bakeries sell it in rounds or slices by the weight (a portion is about 100 grams, or *un etto*).

Farinata, a humble fried bread snack, is made from chickpea meal, water, oil, and pepper, and baked on a copper tray in a wood-burning stove. *Farinata* is sold at pizza and focaccia places.

The *vino delle Cinque Terre*, while not one of Italy's top wines, flows cheap and easy throughout the region. It's white—great with seafood. For a sweet dessert wine, the *sciacchetrà* wine is worth the splurge (€4 per small glass, often served with a cookie). You could order the fun dessert *torta della nonna* (grandmother's cake) and dunk chunks of it into your glass. Aged *sciacchetrà* is dry and costly (up to €12/glass). While 10 kilos of grapes yield seven liters of local wine, *sciacchetrà* is made from near-raisins, and 10 kilos of grapes make only 1.5 liters of *sciacchetrà*. The word means "push and pull"—push in lots of grapes, pull out the best wine. If your room is up a lot of steps, be warned: *Sciacchetrà* is 18 percent alcohol, while regular wine is only 11 percent.

In the cool, calm evening, sit on Vernazza's breakwater with a glass of wine and watch the phosphorescence in the waves.

Nightlife in the Cinque Terre

While the Cinque Terre is certainly not noted for bumping beach-town nightlife like nearby Viareggio, you'll find some sort of travel-tale-telling hub in Monterosso, Vernazza, and Riomaggiore (Manarola and Corniglia are sleepy). Monterosso has a lively scene, especially in the summertime—but no *discoteca* yet. In Vernazza, the nightlife centers in the bars on the waterfront piazza, which is the small-town-style place to "see and be seen." A town law requires all bars to shut by midnight. Bar Centrale in Riomaggiore is, well, the central place for cocktails and meeting fellow travelers. (For details, see the "Nightlife" sections for these three villages.) Wherever your night adventures take you, have fun, but please remember that residents live upstairs.

Helpful Hints for the Cinque Terre

Tourist and Park Information: Each town (except Corniglia) has a well-staffed TI and park office (listed throughout this chapter).

Money: Banks and ATMs are plentiful throughout the region.

Baggage Storage: You can store bags at La Spezia's train station (€3/12 hours, 8:00-22:00, along track 1, next to WC, allow plenty of time to pick up your baggage before departing) and at Lucia's Lavarapido in Monterosso (€5/day).

Services: Every train station has a handy public WC. Otherwise, pop into a bar or restaurant.

Taxi: Cinqueterre Taxi covers all five towns (mobile 328-583-4969, www.cinqueterretaxi.com, info@cinqueterretaxi.com).

Local Guides: Andrea Bordigoni is both knowledgeable and a delight (€110/half-day, €175/day, mobile 347-972-3317, bordigo@inwind.it). Other local guides are **Marco Brizzi** (mobile 328-694-2847, marco_brizzi@yahoo.it) and **Paola Tommarchi** (paolatomma@alice.it).

Booking Agency: Miriana and Filippo at **Cinque Terre Riviera** book rooms in the Cinque Terre towns, Portovenere, and La Spezia for a 10 percent markup over the list price (can also arrange transportation, cooking classes, and weddings; Via Picedi 18 in La Spezia; tel. 0187-520-702, Miriana—mobile 340-794-7358, Filippo—mobile 393-939-1901, www.cinqueterreriviera.com, info@cinqueterreriviera.com, English spoken).

Riomaggiore (Town #1)

The most substantial non-resort town of the group, Riomaggiore is a disappointment from the train station. But once you leave that neighborhood, you'll discover a fascinating tangle of pastel homes leaning on each other like drunken sailors. Just walk through the tunnel next to the train tracks, and you'll discover a more real, laid-back, and workaday town than its touristy neighbors.

Orientation to Riomaggiore

Tourist Information

The TI is in the train station at the ticket desk (daily 8:00-18:00, tel. 0187-920-633). If the TI in the station is crowded, buy your hiking pass at the Cinque Terre park shop/information office next door by the mural (daily 8:00-19:30, tel. 0187-760-515, netpoint riomaggiore@parconazionale5terre.it). For an informal information source, try Ivo and Alberto, who run Bar Centrale (see "Nightlife in Riomaggiore," later).

1. Locanda del Sole
2. Locanda Ca' dei Duxi
3. Hotel la Zorza
4. Locanda dalla Compagnia
5. Riomaggiore Reservations
6. La Dolce Vita Rooms
7. Edi's Rooms & Launderette
8. Camere Patrizia
9. Trattoria la Grotta
10. La Lanterna Ristorante
11. Te la Do Io la Merenda Snack Bar
12. Enoteca & Ristorante Dau Cila
13. Bar & Vini A Piè de Mà
14. Bar Centrale & Gelateria
15. Madonna di Montenero Trail
16. Park Office Kiosk

Arrival in Riomaggiore

The bus shuttles locals and tourists up and down Riomaggiore's steep main street and continues to the parking lot outside town (€1.50 one-way, €2.50 round-trip, free with Cinque Terre Park Card, 2/hour but almost comically erratic, main stop at the fork of Via Colombo and Via Malborghetto, or flag it down as it passes).

Helpful Hints

Internet Access: The **park shop/information office** has eight Internet terminals upstairs and Wi-Fi (€0.08/minute, daily May-Sept 8:00-22:00, Oct-April until 19:30). **Hotel la Zorza** has several terminals in town and charges about the same (daily 11:00-21:30, under the archway just past the Co-op grocery store). **Bar Centrale** offers free Wi-Fi with the purchase of a drink (see "Nightlife in Riomaggiore," later).

Laundry: A self-service launderette is on the main street (€3.50/wash, €3.50/dry, daily 8:30-20:00, run by Edi's Rooms next door, Via Colombo 111).

Self-Guided Walk

Welcome to Riomaggiore

Here's an easy loop trip that maximizes views and minimizes uphill walking.

• *Start at the train station. (If you arrive by boat, cross beneath the tracks and take a left, then hike through the tunnel along the tracks to reach the station.) You'll come to some...*

Colorful Murals: These murals, with subjects modeled after real-life Riomaggiorians, glorify the nameless workers who constructed the nearly 300 million cubic feet of dry-stone walls (without cement) that run throughout the Cinque Terre. These walls give the region its characteristic *muri a secco* terracing for vineyards and olive groves. The murals, done by Argentinean artist Silvio Benedetto, are well-explained in English.

• *Head to the railway tunnel entrance, and ride the elevator to the top of town (€0.50 or €1 family ticket, free with Cinque Terre Park Card, daily 8:00-19:45). If the elevator is closed (likely), hike around to the left, following the road up and then right to the...*

Top o' the Town: Here you're treated to spectacular sea views. To continue the viewfest, go right and follow the walkway (ignore the steps marked *Marina Seacoast* that lead to the harbor). It's a five-minute level stroll to the church. You'll pass under the offices of the disgraced national park president and the city hall (flying two flags), with murals celebrating the heroic grape-pickers and fishermen of the region (also by Silvio Benedetto).

• *Before reaching the church, pause to enjoy the...*

Town View: The major river of this region once ran through this valley, as implied by the name Riomaggiore (local dialect for "river" and "major"). As in the other Cinque Terre towns, the river ravine is now paved over, and the romantic arched bridges that once connected the two sides have been replaced by a practical modern road.

Notice the lack of ugly aerial antennae. In the 1980s, every residence got cable. Now, the TV tower on the hilltop behind the church steeple brings the modern world into each home. The church was rebuilt in 1870, but was first established in 1340. It's dedicated to St. John the Baptist, the patron saint of Genoa, the maritime republic that once dominated the region. The elevator next to the church may be completed by the time you get here. It's designed to help seniors get around the steep town, and also to link to the elevator near the Via dell'Amore trailhead.

• *Continue past the church down to Riomaggiore's main street, named...*

Via Colombo: Walk about 30 feet beyond the WC, go down the stairs, and—if it's open—pop into the tiny Cinque Terre Antiche museum (€0.50, free with Cinque Terre Park Card, generally closed). Sit down for a few minutes to watch a circa-1950 video of the Cinque Terre.

Continuing down Via Colombo, you'll pass a bakery, a couple of grocery shops, and the self-service laundry. There's homemade gelato next to the Bar Centrale. Above where Via Colombo dead-ends, a park-like square built over the train tracks gives the children of the town a level bit of land upon which to kick their soccer balls. The murals above celebrate the great-grandparents of these very children—the salt-of-the-earth locals who earned a humble living before the age of tourism. To the left, stairs lead down to the Marina neighborhood, with the harbor, the boat dock, a 200-yard trail to the beach *(spiaggia),* and an inviting little art gallery. To the right of the stairs is the pedestrian tunnel, running alongside the tracks, which takes you directly back to the station and the trail to the other towns. From here, you can take a train, hop a boat, or hike to your next destination.

Sights in Riomaggiore

Beach—Riomaggiore's rugged and tiny "beach" is rocky, but it's clean and peaceful. Take a two-minute walk from the harbor: Face the harbor, then follow the path to your left. Passing the rugged boat landing, stay on the path to the pebbly beach. There's a shower there in the summer, and another closer to town by the boat landing—where many enjoying sunning on and jumping from the rocks.

Kayaks and Water Sports—The town has a diving center (scuba, snorkeling, kayaks; office down the stairs and under the tracks on Via San Giacomo, daily May-Sept 9:00-18:00, tel. 0187-920-011, www.5terrediving.it).

Hikes—The cliff-hanging Torre Guardiola trail, a steep 20-minute climb from the beach up to old WWII bunkers and a hilltop botanical pathway, has been closed because of a rock slide. Another trail rises from Riomaggiore scenically to the 14th-century Madonna di Montenero sanctuary, high above the town (45 minutes, take the main road inland until you see signs, or ride the green shuttle bus 12 minutes from the town center to the sanctuary trail, then walk uphill 10 minutes).

Nightlife in Riomaggiore

Bar Centrale, run by sociable Ivo, Alberto, and the gang, offers "nightlife" any time of day—making it a good stop for Italian breakfast and music. Ivo, who lived in San Francisco, fills his bar with San Franciscan rock and a fun-loving vibe. During the day, this is a shaded place to relax with other travelers. At night, it offers the younger set the liveliest action (and best mojitos) in town. They also serve €5 fast-food pastas and microwaved pizzas (daily 7:30-24:00 or later, closed Mon in winter, free Wi-Fi with drink, in the town center at Via Colombo 144, tel. 0187-920-208). There's a good *gelateria* next door.

Enoteca & Ristorante Dau Cila, a cool little hideaway with a mellow jazz-and-Brazilian-lounge ambience down at the miniscule harbor, is a counterpoint to wild Bar Centrale. It's cool for cocktails and open nightly until 24:00 (snacks and meals, fine wine by the glass; see "Eating in Riomaggiore," later).

Bar & Vini A Piè de Mà, at the beginning of Via dell'Amore, has piles of charm, €6 cocktails, often music, and stays open until midnight June through September (see "Eating in Riomaggiore," later).

The marvelous **Via dell'Amore** trail (described earlier), lit only with subtle ground lighting so that you can see the stars, welcomes romantics after dark. The trail is free after 19:30.

Sleeping in Riomaggiore

Riomaggiore has arranged its private-room rental system better than its neighbors. Several agencies—with regular office hours, English-speaking staff, and email addresses—line up within a few yards of each other on the main drag. Each manages a corral of local rooms for rent. These offices keep erratic hours, so it's smart to settle up the day before you leave in case they're closed when you need to depart. Expect lots of stairs. If you don't mind the hike, the street above town has safe overnight parking (free 20:00-8:00).

Hotels

$$$ Locanda del Sole has seven modern, basic, and overpriced rooms with a shared and peaceful terrace. Located at the utilitarian top end of town, it's a five-minute walk downhill to the center. Easy (and free with this book) parking makes it especially appealing to drivers (Db-€110-120, air-con, Wi-Fi, Via Santuario 114, tel. & fax 0187-920-773, mobile 340-983-0090, www.locandadel sole.net, info@locandadelsole.net, Enrico).

$$$ Locanda Ca' dei Duxi rents 10 good rooms from an efficient little office on the main drag (Db-€100-130 depending on view and season, extra person-€20, air-con, Wi-Fi, parking-€10/ day—book when you reserve, open year-round, Via Colombo 36, tel. & fax 0187-920-036, mobile 329-825-7836, www.duxi.it, info @duxi.it, Samuele and Anna). They also manage **Ca' dei Lisci,** with simpler and cheaper rooms (D-€60, Db-€70-80, www.cadei lisci.com).

$$$ Hotel la Zorza rents nine decent but overpriced rooms in the tangled lanes in the center of town (Db-€100-130, Qb apartment-€150, air-con, Wi-Fi, Via Colombo 36, tel. & fax 0187-920-036, mobile 329-825-7836, www.hotelzorza.com, info@duxi.it).

$$ Locanda dalla Compagnia rents five modern rooms at the top of town, just 300 yards below the parking lot and the little church. All rooms—nice but rather dim—are on the same tranquil ground floor, and share an inviting lounge. Franca runs it with the help of son Allessandro (Db-€80, cash only, air-con, mini-fridge, no view, Via del Santuario 232, tel. 0187-760-050, fax 0187-920-586, www.dallacompagnia.it, lacomp@libero.it).

Room-Booking Services

$$ Riomaggiore Reservations offers 12 rooms and 15 apartments, with American expats Amy and Maddy smoothing communications (Db-€60-90 depending on view, Db suite with top view-€120, cash only, reception open 9:00-17:00 in season, Via Colombo 181, tel. & fax 0187-760-575, www.riomaggiorereservations.com, info@riomaggiorereservations.com).

Sleep Code

(€1 = about $1.40, country code: 39)
S = Single, **D** = Double/Twin, **T** = Triple, **Q** = Quad, **b** = bathroom, **s** = shower only. Unless otherwise noted, credit cards are accepted, English is spoken, and breakfast is included (except in Vernazza).

To help you sort easily through these listings, I've divided the accommodations into three categories based on the price for a standard double room with bath:

$$$ Higher Priced—Most rooms €100 or more.
 $$ Moderately Priced—Most rooms between €50-100.
  $ Lower Priced—Most rooms €50 or less.

Prices can change without notice; verify the hotel's current rates online or by email. For other updates, see www.ricksteves.com/update.

$$ La Dolce Vita offers three fine rooms on the main drag and two apartments around town (Db-€60-80, open daily 9:30-19:30; if they're closed, they're full; Via Colombo 120, tel. 0187-760-044, mobile 329-099-2741, agonatal@interfree.it, helpful Giacomo and Simone).

$$ Edi's Rooms rents 20 rooms and apartments. You pay extra for views (Db-€70-90 depending on room, apartment Qb-€100-160, reserve with credit card, office open daily in summer 8:30-20:00, in winter 10:30-12:30 & 14:30-19:00, some rooms involve climbing a lot of steps—ask before viewing or reserving, reception at Via Colombo 111, tel. 0187-760-842, tel. & fax 0187-920-325, www.lancoracinqueterre.com, edi-vesigna@iol.it).

Backpacker Dorms

$ Riomaggiore Reservations (listed above) runs a mini-hostel in a fine communal apartment with nine beds in three rooms, a cool living room, terrace, and kitchen in a good, quiet location. Take care of this little treasure so it survives (€22/bed, reception open 9:00-17:00 in season, Via Colombo 181, tel. & fax 0187-760-575, www.riomaggiorereservations.com, info@riomaggiorereservations.com).

$ Camere Patrizia rents cheap doubles and dorm bunk beds at €25 per person from its reception at Via Colombo 25, but books only through www.hostelworld.com or to drop-ins (mobile 333-165-6362).

Eating in Riomaggiore

Trattoria La Grotta, right in the town center (no view), serves reliably good food with a passion for anchovies and mussels. You'll enjoy friendly service surrounded by historic photos and wonderful stonework in a dramatic, dressy, cave-like setting. Venessa is warm and helpful while her mother, Isa, is busy cooking (€12 pastas, €15 *secondi*, 5 percent cash discount, Thu-Tue 12:00-14:30 & 17:30-22:30, closed Wed, Via Colombo 247, tel. 0187-920-187).

La Lanterna, with the ambience of an old fisherman's home inside and a few appealing harborside tables outside, is wedged into a niche in the Marina, overlooking the harbor under the tracks. Chef Massimo serves traditional plates, loves anchovies, and bakes fresh bread daily (€10 pastas, €18 *secondi*, no cover, daily 12:00-22:00, Via San Giacomo 10, tel. 0187-920-589).

Te La Do Io La Merenda ("I'll Give You a Snack") is good for a snack, pizza, or takeout. Their counter is piled with an assortment of munchies, and they have pastas, roasted chicken, and focaccia sandwiches to go (daily 9:00-21:00, Via Colombo 161, tel. 0187-920-148).

Enoteca & Ristorante Dau Cila is decked out like a black-and-white movie set in a centuries-old boat shed with extra tables outside on a rustic deck over dinghies. Try their antipasto specialty of several seafood appetizers, and listen to jazz with the waves lapping at the harbor below (€12 pastas, €18 *secondi*, March-Oct daily until 24:00, Via San Giacomo 65, tel. 0187-760-032, Luca).

Bar & Vini A Piè de Mà, at the trailhead on the Manarola end of town, is good for a scenic light bite or quiet drink at night. Enjoying a meal at a table on its dramatically situated terrace provides an indelible Cinque Terre memory (daily 10:00-20:00, June-Sept until 24:00, tel. 0187-921-037).

Picnics: Groceries and delis lining Via Colombo sell food to go, including pizza slices, for a picnic at the harbor or beach.

Manarola (Town #2)

Like Riomaggiore, Manarola is attached to its station by a 200-yard-long tunnel (lined with interesting photos). During WWII air raids, these tunnels provided refuge and a safe place for rattled villagers to sleep. The town itself fills a ravine, bookended by its wild little harbor to the west and a diminutive church square inland to the east. A delightful and gentle stroll from the church down to the harborside park provides the region's easiest vineyard walk (described in my "Self-Guided Walk," next page).

Orientation to Manarola

The **TI** at the train station is open daily 7:00-20:00.

A **shuttle bus** runs between the low end of Manarola's main street (at the tobacco shop and newsstand) and the parking lot (€1.50 one-way, €2.50 round-trip, free with Cinque Terre Park Card, 2/hour, just flag it down). Shuttle buses also run about hourly from Manarola to Volastra, near the Cinque Terre Cooperative Winery.

To get to the **dock** and the boats that connect Manarola with the other Cinque Terre towns, find the steps to the left of the harbor view—they lead down to the ticket kiosk. Continue around the left side of the cliff (as you're facing the water) to catch the boats.

Self-Guided Walk

Welcome to Manarola

From the harbor, this 30-minute circular walk shows you the town and surrounding vineyards, and ends at a fantastic viewpoint, perfect for a picnic.

• *Start down at the waterfront.*

The Harbor: Manarola is tiny and picturesque, a tumble of buildings bunny-hopping down its ravine to the fun-loving waterfront. Notice how the I-beam crane launches the boats. Facing the water, look to the right, at the hillside Punta Bonfiglio cemetery and park (where this walk ends).

The town's swimming hole is just below. Manarola has no sand, but offers the best deep-water swimming in the area. The first "beach" has a shower, ladder, and wonderful rocks. The second has tougher access and no shower, but feels more remote and pristine (follow the paved path toward Corniglia, just around the point). For many, the tricky access makes this beach dangerous.

• *Hiking inland up the town's main drag, you'll come to the train tracks covered by Manarola's new square, called...*

Piazza Capellini: Built in 2004, this square is an all-around great idea, giving the town a safe, fun zone for kids. Locals living near the tracks also enjoy a little less noise. Check out the mosaic that displays the varieties of local fish in colorful enamel.

• *Fifty yards uphill, you'll find the...*

Sciacchetrà Museum: Run by the national park, it's hardly a museum. But if it's open, pop in to its inviting room to see a tiny exhibit on the local wine industry (€0.50, free with Cinque Terre Park Card, generally closed, 15-minute video in English by request, 100 yards uphill from train tracks, across from the post office).

To Corniglia,
Vernazza
& Monterosso
(Trail closed to
Corniglia thru 2012)

Manarola
Vineyard Walk

SWIMMING

Cemetery

Punta
Bonfiglio

VIA DEI GIOVANNI

*Piazza
Capellini*

"MAIN STREET"

V. RENATO

2 9 11

VIA RENATO BIOTTI

V. BELVEDERE

50 Meters
50 Yards

SWIMMING
& SHOWER

BALURADO

VIA DI MEZZO

VIA
BELVEDERE

*Piazza
Castello*

BREAKWATER

BOAT
DOCK

*Piazzetta
Eugenio Montale*

*Ligurian
Sea*

• *Hiking farther uphill, you can still hear...*

Manarola's Stream: Like the streams in Riomaggiore, Monterosso, and Vernazza, Manarola's rivulet was covered over by a modern sewage system after World War II. Before that time, romantic bridges arched over its ravine. A modern waterwheel recalls the origin of the town's name—local dialect for "big wheel" (one of many possible derivations). Mills like this once powered the local olive oil industry.

• *Keep climbing until you come to the square at the...*

Top of Manarola: The square is faced by a church, an oratory—now a religious and community meeting place—and a bell tower, which served as a watchtower when pirates raided the town (the cupola was added once the attacks ceased). To the right of

P

SP-370

VIA LITORANEA

TUNNEL

TO ❽

VIA DISCOVOLO

BELL
TOWER

SAN LORENZO
CHURCH

CHAPEL

❸

❺

❼

❶

❹

BIOTTI

ROLLANDI

❿

VIA – A

❻

*Piazza
Papa Innocenzo IV*

PEDESTRIAN TUNNEL

TRAIN STATION

*Via dell' Amore
Trail*

To Riomaggiore

❶ La Torretta Rooms
❷ Marina Piccola Rooms
   & Restaurant
❸ Albergo Ca' d'Andrean
❹ Affitta Camere da Paulin
❺ Casa Capellini
❻ Aria di Mare Rooms
❼ Ostello 5-Terre
❽ To Hotel il Saraceno
❾ Trattoria il Porticciolo
❿ Trattoria dal Billy
⓫ Shuttle Bus to Parking Lot
   & Volastra

the oratory, a stepped lane leads to Manarola's sizable tourist-free zone.

While you're here, check out the church. According to the white marble plaque in its facade, the Parish Church of St. Lawrence (San Lorenzo) dates from "MCCCXXXVIII" (1338). Step inside to see two paintings from the unnamed Master of the Cinque Terre, the only painter of any note from this region (left wall and above main altar). While the style is Gothic, the work dates from the late 15th century, long after Florence had entered the Renaissance. Note the humble painted stone ceiling, which replaced the wooden original in the 1800s. It features Lawrence, patron saint of the Cinque Terre, with his grill, the symbol of his martyrdom (he was roasted on it).

• *Walk 20 yards below the church and find a wooden railing. It marks the start of a delightful stroll around the high side of town, and back to the seafront. This is the beginning of the...*

Manarola Vineyard Walk: Don't miss this experience. Simply follow the wooden railing, enjoying lemon groves and wild red valerian (used for insomnia since the days of the Romans). Along the path, which is primarily flat, you'll get a close-up look at the region's famous dry-stone walls and finely crafted vineyards (with dried-heather thatches to protect the grapes from the south-west winds). Smell the rosemary. Study the structure of the town, and pick out the scant remains of an old fort. Notice the S-shape of the main road—once a riverbed—that flows through town. The town's roofs are traditionally made of locally quarried slate, rather than tile, and are held down by rocks during windstorms. As the harbor comes into view, you'll see the breakwater, added just a decade ago.

Out of sight above you on the right are simple wooden religious scenes, the work of local resident Mario Andreoli. Before his father died, Mario promised him he'd replace the old cross on the family's vineyard. Mario has been adding figures ever since. After recovering from a rare illness, he redoubled his efforts. On religious holidays, everything's lit up: the Nativity, the Last Supper, the Crucifixion, the Resurrection, and more. Some of the scenes are left up year-round.

High above, a recent fire burned off the tree cover, revealing ancient terraces that line the terrain like a topographic map.

• *Follow this trail all the way to a T-intersection, where it hits the main coastal trail. Turn left. (A right takes you to the trail to Corniglia.) Before descending back into town, take a right, detouring into...*

The Cemetery: Ever since Napoleon—who was king of Italy in the early 1800s—decreed that cemeteries were health risks, Cinque Terre's burial spots have been located outside the towns. The result: The dearly departed generally get first-class sea views. Each cemetery—with its evocative yellowed photos and finely carved Carrara marble memorial reliefs—is worth a visit. (The basic structure for all of them is the same, but Manarola's is the most easily accessible.)

In cemeteries like these, there's a hierarchy of four places to park your mortal remains: a graveyard, a spacious death condo *(loculo)*, a mini bone-niche *(ossario)*, or the communal ossuary. Because of the tight space, a time limit is assigned to the first three options (although many older tombs are grandfathered in). Bones go into the ossuary in the middle of the chapel floor after about a generation. Traditionally, locals make weekly visits to loved ones here, often bringing flowers. The rolling stepladder makes access to top-floor *loculi* easy.

• *The Manarola cemetery is on Punta Bonfiglio. Walk just below it, farther out through a park (playground, drinking water, WC, and picnic benches). Your Manarola finale: the bench at the tip of the point, offering one of the most commanding views of the entire region. The easiest way back to town is to take the stairs at the end of the point.*

Sleeping in Manarola

(€1 = about $1.40, country code: 39)

Manarola has plenty of private rooms. Ask in bars and restaurants. There's a modern three-star place halfway up the main drag, a sea-view hotel on the harbor, and a cluster of options around the church at the peaceful top of the town (a 5-minute hike from the train tracks).

$$$ La Torretta is a trendy, upscale 13-room place that caters to a demanding clientele. Probably the most elegant retreat in the region, it's a peaceful refuge with all the comforts for those happy to pay, including a communal hot tub with a view. Enjoy a complimentary snack and glass of prosecco on arrival, free wine-tastings during your stay, breakfast in your room, and a free minibar. Each chic room is distinct and described on their website (smaller Db-€145, regular Db-€190, Db suite-€250-400, cash discount, book several months in advance as it's justifiably popular, closed mid-Nov-mid-March, Wi-Fi, on Piazza della Chiesa beside the bell tower at Vico Volto 20, tel. 0187-920-327, fax 0187-760-024, www.torrettas.com, torretta@cdh.it).

$$$ Marina Piccola offers 13 bright, slick rooms on the water—so they figure a warm welcome is unnecessary (Db-€120, air-con, Wi-Fi, Via Birolli 120, tel. 0187-920-103, fax 0187-920-966, www.hotelmarinapiccola.com, info@hotelmarinapiccola.com).

$$$ Albergo Ca' d'Andrean, run by Simone, is quiet, comfortable, and modern—except for its antiquated reservation system. While the welcome is formal at best, it has 10 big, sunny, air-conditioned rooms and a cool garden oasis complete with lemon trees (Sb-€72, Db-€100, breakfast-€6, cash only, send personal check to reserve from US—or call if you're reserving from the road, closed Nov-Christmas, up the hill at Via A. Discovolo 101, tel. 0187-920-040, fax 0187-920-452, www.cadandrean.it, cadandrean@libero.it).

$$ At **Affitta Camere da Paulin,** charming Donatella and Eraldo (the town's retired policeman) rent very nice, well-equipped rooms with a large and inviting common living room. It's in a modern setting a few minutes' walk uphill from the train tracks (Db-€70-80, view apartment Db-€105-130, Wi-Fi, Via Discovolo 126, tel. & fax 0187-920-706, mobile 334-389-4764, www.dapaulin.it, prenotazioni@dapaulin.it).

$$ Casa Capellini rents four rooms: One has a view balcony, another a 360-degree terrace—book long in advance (Sb-€45, Db-€65; €85 for the *alta camera* on the top, with a kitchen, private terrace, and knockout view; two doors down the hill from the church—with your back to the church, it's at 2 o'clock; Via Ettore Cozzani 12, tel. 0187-920-823, mobile 349-306-1046, www.casacapellini-5terre.it, casa.capellini@tin.it, Gianni and Franca don't speak English).

$$ Aria di Mare Rooms rents four sunny rooms and an apartment 20 yards beyond Trattoria dal Billy at the very top of town. Three rooms have spacious terraces with knockout views and lounge chairs. Maurizio speaks a little English, while Mamma Franca communicates with lots of Italian and toothy smiles (Db-€80, 2 adults and 1 child-€80, Db apartment-€90, ask for Rick Steves price, no breakfast, Wi-Fi, up stairs on the left at Via Aldo Rollandi 137, tel. 0187-920-367, mobile 349-058-4155, www.ariadimare.info, ask at Billy's if no one's home).

For Drivers: **$$$ Hotel il Saraceno,** with seven spacious, modern rooms, is a deal for drivers. Located above Manarola in the tiny town of Volastra (chock-full of vacationing Germans and Italians in summer), it's serene, clean, and right by the shuttle bus to Manarola (Db-€100, buffet breakfast, Wi-Fi, free parking, Via Volastra 8, tel. 0187-760-081, fax 0187-760-791, www.thesaraceno.com, hotel@thesaraceno.com, friendly Antonella).

Eating in Manarola

Many hardworking places line the main drag. The Scorza family works hard at **Trattoria il Porticciolo** (free glass of *sciacchetrà* dessert wine with this book, closed Wed, below train tracks at Via R. Birolli 92, tel. 0187-920-083). The harborside **Marina Piccola** is famous for great views, lousy service, and gouging naive tourists.

Trattoria dal Billy, hiding out high on the hill, is a hit, with good food and impressive views over the valley. With Edoardo and Dario's black pasta with seafood and squid ink, green pasta with artichokes, mixed seafood starters, and homemade desserts, many find it worth the climb. Dinner reservations are a must (€11 pastas, €14 *secondi,* generally daily 8:00-10:00 & 12:00-15:00 & 19:00-23:30, sometimes closed Thu, Via Aldo Rollandi 122, tel. 0187-920-628).

Corniglia (Town #3)

This is the quiet town—the only one of the five not on the water—with a mellow main square. According to a (likely fanciful) local legend, the town was originally settled by a Roman farmer who named it for his mother, Cornelia (how Corniglia is pronounced). The town and its ancient residents produced a wine so famous that—some say—vases found at Pompeii touted its virtues. Regardless of the veracity of the legends, wine remains Corniglia's lifeblood today. Follow the pungent smell of ripe grapes into an alley cellar and get a local to let you dip a straw into a keg. Remote and less visited than the other Cinque Terre towns, Corniglia has fewer tourists, cooler temperatures, a few restaurants, a windy overlook on its promontory, and plenty of private rooms for rent (ask at any bar or shop, no cheaper than other towns). If you think of the Cinque Terre as the Beatles, Corniglia is Ringo.

Orientation to Corniglia

Arrival in Corniglia

From the station, a footpath zigzags up nearly 400 steps to the town. Or take the green shuttle bus, generally timed to meet arriving trains (€1.50 one-way, €2.50 round-trip, free with Cinque Terre Park Card, 2/hour). Before leaving for the bus, confirm departure times on the schedule posted at the stop. If you're driving, be aware that only residents can park on the main road between the recommended Villa Cecio and the point where the steep switchback staircase meets the road. Beyond that area, parking is €1.50 per hour.

Self-Guided Walk

Welcome to Corniglia

We'll explore this tiny town—population 240—and end at a scenic viewpoint.

• *Begin near the bus stop, located at a...*

Town Square: The gateway to this community is "Ciappà" square, with an ATM, phone booth, old wine press, and bus stop. The Cinque Terre's designation as a national park sparked a revitalization of the town. Corniglia's young generation is more likely now to stay put, rather than migrate into big cities the way locals did in the past.

• *Stroll the spine of Corniglia, Via Fieschi. In the fall, the smell of grapes (on their way to becoming wine) wafts from busy cellars. Along this main street, you'll see...*

Corniglia

To Vernazza

200 Meters
200 Yards

LOC. CANALE
VIA SIERRA

LOC. CHIDSO

VIA ALLA STAZIONE

HUNDREDS
OF STEPS

VIA FIESCHI

VIA ALLA MARINA

Harbor

"CIAPPÀ"
SQUARE &
BUS STOP

VIA LARDARINA

To Manarola

SANTA MARIA
BELVEDERE

LARGO
TARAGIO,
ORATORY &

Ligurian Sea

TRAIN
STATION

SWIMMING

1. Pan e Vin Bar
   (Ricci Rooms Check-In)
2. Villa Cecio Rooms
3. Corniglia Hostel
4. La Lanterna Restaurant
5. Osteria Mananan
6. Enoteca il Pirun
7. La Posada Ristorante
8. Gelateria
9. Butiega Shop

Corniglia's Enticing Shops: Alberto's Gelateria dishes up the best homemade gelato in town. Before ordering, get a free taste of Alberto's *miele di Corniglia,* made from local honey. His local lemon slush takes pucker to new heights. **Enoteca il Pirun**—named for a type of oddly shaped old-fashioned wine pitcher designed to aerate the wine and give the alcohol more kick—is located in a cool cantina at Via Fieschi 115. Sample some local wines (generally free for small tastes). If you buy something, they may gift you with a souvenir bib. In the **Butiega** shop at Via Fieschi 142, Vincenzo and Diego sell organic local specialties (daily 8:00-19:30). For picnickers, they offer €2.50 made-to-order ham-and-cheese sandwiches and a fun €3.50 *antipasto misto* to go. (There are good places to picnic farther along on this walk.)

• *Following Via Fieschi, you'll end up at the...*

Main Square: On Largo Taragio, tables from two bars and a trattoria spill around a WWI memorial and the town's old well. It once piped in natural spring water from the hillside to locals living without plumbing. What looks like a church is the Oratory of Santa Caterina. (An oratory is a kind of a spiritual clubhouse for a service group doing social work in the name of the Catholic Church. For more information, see "Oratory of the Dead" on page 1087.) Behind the oratory, you'll find a clearing that local children have made into a soccer field. The stone benches and viewpoint make this a peaceful place for a picnic (less crowded than the end-of-town viewpoint, described below).

• *Opposite the oratory, notice how steps lead steeply down on Via alla Marina to Corniglia's non-beach. It's a five-minute paved climb to sunning rocks, a shower, and a small deck (with a treacherous entry into the water). From the square, continue up Via Fieschi to the...*

End-of-Town Viewpoint: The Santa Maria Belvedere, named for a church that once stood here, marks the scenic end of Corniglia. This is a super picnic spot. From here, look high to the west, where the village and sanctuary of San Bernardino straddle a ridge (a good starting point for a hike; accessible by shuttle bus from Monterosso or a long uphill hike from Vernazza). Below is the tortuous harbor, where locals hoist their boats onto the cruel rocks.

Sights in Corniglia

Beaches—This hilltop town has rocky sea access below its train station (toward Manarola). Once a beach, it's all been washed away and offers no services. Look for signs that say *al mare* or *Marina*. A trail leads from the town center steeply down to sunning rocks on the closest thing Corniglia has to a beach (with a shower).

The infamous **Guvano beach** (a bit along the coast toward Vernazza) is now essentially closed down. Guvano was created by an 1893 landslide that cost the village a third of its farmland. Notorious throughout Italy as a nude beach, Guvano was accessed via an unused train tunnel and attracted visitors with an appetite for drug use. Now the tunnel is closed, and the national park wants people to keep their clothes on and forget about Guvano.

Sleeping in Corniglia

(€1 = about $1.40, country code: 39)
Perched high above the sea on a hilltop, Corniglia has plenty of private rooms. To get to the town from the station, catch the shuttle bus or make the 15-minute uphill hike. The town is riddled with humble places that charge too much (generally Db-€65) and have meager business skills and a limited ability to converse with tourists—so it's almost never full.

$$ Cristiana Ricci is an exception to the rule. She communicates well and is reliable, renting four small, clean, and peaceful rooms—two with kitchens and one with a terrace and sweeping view—just inland from the bus stop (Db-€60-70, Qb-€90, €10/day less when you stay 2 or more nights, free Internet access, check in at the Pan e Vin bar at Via Fieschi 123, mobile 338-937-6547, cri_affittacamere@virgilio.it, Stefano). Her mom rents a big, modern apartment (€90 for 2-4 people).

$$ Villa Cecio (pronounced "chay-choe") feels like an abandoned hotel. They offer eight well-worn rooms on the outskirts of town, with saggy beds and little character or warmth (Db-€65, ask for Rick Steves price, breakfast-€5, cash preferred, great views, on main road 200 yards toward Vernazza at Via Serra 58, tel. 0187-812-043, fax 0187-812-138, mobile 334-350-6637, www.cecio5terre.com, info@cecio5terre.com, Giacinto). They also rent eight similar rooms (Db-€60) in an annex on the square where the bus stops.

$ Corniglia Hostel was formerly the town's schoolhouse. It rents 24 beds in a pastel-yellow building up some steps from the main square where the bus stops. The playground in front is often busy with happy kids. Despite its institutional atmosphere, the hostel's prices, central location, and bright and clean rooms ensure its popularity. Its hotelesque double rooms are open to anyone (€24/bed in two 8-bed dorms, €27 with minimal breakfast; four Db-€55, €60 with breakfast; air-con, lockers, Internet access, Wi-Fi, self-serve laundry, mountain bikes for rent, no public spaces except lobby, office open 7:00-13:00 & 15:00-24:00, rooms closed 13:00-15:00, 1:30 curfew, Via alla Stazione 3, tel. 0187-812-559, fax 0187-763-984, www.ostellocorniglia.com but reserve at www.hostelworld.com, ostellocorniglia@gmail.com, helpful Andrea).

Eating in Corniglia

Corniglia has few restaurants.

The trattoria **La Lanterna,** on the main square, is the most atmospheric (but without particularly charming service).

Osteria Mananan—between the Ciappà bus stop and the main square on Via Fieschi—serves what many consider the best food in town in its small, stony, elegant interior (Fri-Wed 12:15-14:30 & 19:45-21:15, closed Tue, no outdoor seating, tel. 0187-821-166).

Enoteca il Pirun, also on Via Fieschi, has a small restaurant above the wine bar, where Mario serves typical local dishes (€28 fixed-price meal includes homemade wine, daily 12:00-16:00 & 19:30-23:30, tel. 0187-812-315).

La Posada Ristorante offers dinner in a garden under trees, overlooking the Ligurian Sea. To get here, stroll out of town to the top of the stairs from the station (€10 pastas, €10 *secondi*, €15 tourist *menu*, nightly from 19:00, tel. 0187-821-174).

Vernazza (Town #4)

With the closest thing to a natural harbor—overseen by a ruined castle and a stout stone church—Vernazza is the jewel of the Cinque Terre. Only the occasional noisy slurping up of the train by the mountain reminds you of the modern world.

As mentioned earlier, a flash flood hit Vernazza in the fall of 2011; you will likely see some damage, though the town is quickly rebuilding and many businesses will be open when you visit. Still, be prepared for some closures and changes (for a travel advisory, see www.savevernazza.com).

The action is at the harbor, where you'll find outdoor restaurants, a bar hanging on the edge of the castle, and a breakwater with a promenade, corralled by a natural amphitheater of terraced hills. In the summer, the beach becomes a soccer field, where teams fielded by local bars and restaurants provide late-night entertainment. In the dark, locals fish off the promontory, using glowing bobbers that shine in the waves.

Proud of their Vernazzan heritage, the town's 500 residents like to brag: "Vernazza is locally owned. Portofino has sold out." Fearing the change it would bring, keep-Vernazza-small proponents stopped the construction of a major road into the town and region. Families are tight and go back centuries; several generations stay together. In the winter, the population shrinks, as many people return to their more comfortable big-city apartments to spend the money they reaped during the tourist season.

Leisure time is devoted to taking part in the *passeggiata*—strolling lazily together up and down the main street. Sit on a bench and study the passersby doing their *vasche* (laps). Explore the characteristic alleys, called *carugi*. Learn—and live—the phrase "*la vita pigra di Vernazza*" (the lazy life of Vernazza).

Orientation to Vernazza

Tourist Information

The TI/park information/train ticket office is one desk nearly hidden in a gift shop between the two tracks at the train station (daily 8:00-19:30, tel. 0187-812-524). Some of the staff may ring the owner of the room you have reserved as a courtesy, but they cannot make reservations. Public WCs are nearby in the station.

Arrival in Vernazza

By Train: Vernazza's train station is only about three cars long, but the trains are much longer, so most of the cars come to a stop in a long, dark tunnel. Get out anyway, and walk through the tunnel

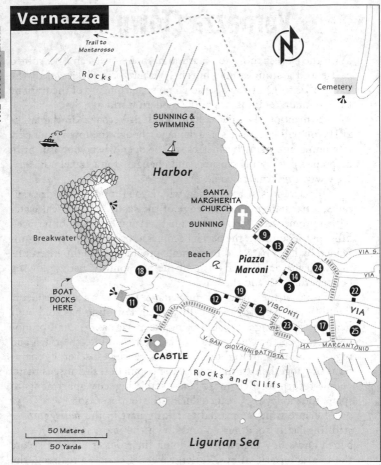

to the station.

By Car: There's a nonresident parking lot, but be aware that parking can be tough from May through September (€2/hour, €12/24 hours, cash only, about 500 yards above town, pay first at the parking stand before getting your spot). A hardworking shuttle service, generally with friendly English-speaking Beppe, Simone, or Pietro behind the wheel, connects the lot to the top of town (€1.50, free with Cinque Terre Park Card, 3-4/hour, runs 7:00-19:00). Yellow lines mark parking spots for residents. The highest lot (a side-trip uphill) is for overnight stays.

Helpful Hints

Internet Access: The **Blue Marlin Bar,** run by Massimo and Carmen, offers Internet access at reasonable prices and with

1. Pensione Sorriso
2. Trattoria Gianni Rooms/Ristorante
3. Albergo Barbara
4. Tonino Basso Rooms & Il Pirata della Cinque Terre
5. Camere Fontana Vecchia
6. Giuliano Basso Rooms
7. Vernazza Rooms
8. Blue Marlin Bar & Café
9. Ananasso Bar
10. Ristorante al Castello
11. Ristorante Belforte
12. Gambero Rosso Ristorante
13. Trattoria del Capitano
14. Ristorante Pizzeria Vulnetia
15. Trattoria da Sandro
16. Antica Osteria il Baretto
17. Ristorante Incadase da Piva
18. Bar Baia Saracena
19. Burgus Wine Bar
20. Enoteca Sotto l'Arco
21. Franco's Ristorante & Bar la Torre
22. Forno (Bakery)
23. Gelateria
24. Launderette
25. Internet Point

long hours (see listing on page 1080). The slick, six-terminal **Internet Point,** run by Alberto and Isabella, is in the village center (€0.15/minute, €0.10/minute after 30 minutes, daily June-Oct 9:30-23:00, until 20:00 Nov-May, Wi-Fi, will burn your digital photos to a CD or DVD for €5).

Laundry: Lavanderia il Carugetto is completely self-serve and hides out on a narrow lane a block off the main drag (coin-op, €6/wash, €5/dry, daily 8:00-22:00, opposite the pharmacy—go ten steps up and turn left, operated by Domenico and Barbara at the fish shop).

Massage: Stephanie, an American expat, gives a good, strong therapeutic massage in a neat little studio at the top of town. Famous among locals as the physical therapist who massaged an old woman back to health, Stephanie can counsel you on tuning up your body while giving insights into the social intricacies of the village (€50/hour, mobile 338-9429-494, stephsette@gmail.com). **Kate** offers a softer and more aromatic style: reflexology, holistic, and hot stone massage (mobile 333-568-4653, www.vernazzamassage5terre.com).

Best Views: A steep 10-minute hike in either direction from Vernazza gives you a classic village photo op (for the best light, head toward Corniglia in the morning, and toward Monterosso in the evening).

Self-Guided Walks

Welcome to Vernazza

This tour includes Vernazza's characteristic town squares and ends on its scenic breakwater.

• *From the train station, walk uphill until you hit the parking lot, with a bank, a post office, and a barrier that keeps out all but service vehicles. Vernazza's shuttle buses run from here to the parking lot and into the hills. Walk to the tidy, modern square called...*

Fontana Vecchia: Named after a long-gone fountain, this is where older locals remember the river filled with townswomen doing their washing. Now they enjoy checking on the baby ducks. A lane leads from here up to the cemetery. Imagine the entire village sadly trudging up here during funerals. (The cemetery is peaceful and evocative at sunset, when the fading light touches each crypt.)

• *Glad to be here in happier times, begin your saunter downhill to the harbor. Just before the* Pensione Sorriso *sign, on your right (big brown wood doors), you'll see the...*

Ambulance Barn: A group of volunteers is always on call for a dash to the hospital, 40 minutes away in La Spezia. Opposite the barn is a big empty lot. Like many landowners, the owner of Pensione Sorriso had plans to expand, but since the 1980s, the government has said "No." While some landowners are frustrated, the old character of these towns survives. A few steps farther down is the town clinic. The *guarda medica* (emergency doctor—see buzzer) sleeps upstairs.

• *At the corner across from the playground, you'll see a...*

World Wars Monument: Look for a marble plaque in the wall to your left, dedicated to those killed in the World Wars. Not a family in Vernazza was spared. Listed on the left are soldiers *morti in combattimento,* who died in World War I; on the right is the World War II section. Some were deported to *Germania;* others—labeled *Part* (stands for *partigiani,* or partisans, generally communists)—were killed while fighting against Mussolini. Cynics considered partisans less than heroes. After 1943, Hitler called up Italian boys over 15. Rather than die on the front for Hitler, they escaped to the hills. They became "resistance fighters" in order to remain free.

The path to Corniglia leaves from here (behind and above the plaque). Behind you is a small square and playground, decorated with three millstones, once used to grind local olives into oil. There's a good chance you'll see an expat mom here at the village playground with her kids. I've met many American women who fell in love with a local guy, stayed, and are now happily raising families here. (But I've rarely met an American guy who moved in with a local girl.)

From here, Vernazza's tiny river goes underground. Until the 1950s, the river ran openly through the center of town. Old-timers recall the days before the breakwater, when the river cascaded down and the surf sent waves rolling up Vernazza's main drag. Back then, this place was nicknamed "Little Venice" for the series of romantic bridges that arched over the stream, connecting the two sides of the town before the main road was built. During the flash flood that occurred in the fall of 2011, this main drag was filled with roaring water up to 10 feet deep.

• *Follow the road downhill to...*

Vernazza's "Business Center": Here, you'll pass many locals doing their *vasche* (laps). At Enoteca Sotto l'Arco, Gerry and Paola sell wine—they can uncork it and throw in plastic glasses—and delightful jars of local pesto, which goes great on bread (Via Roma 70). Next, you'll pass the Blue Marlin Bar (Vernazza's top nightspot) and the tiny Chapel of Santa Marta (the small stone chapel with iron grillwork over the window), where Mass is celebrated only on special Sundays. Farther down, you'll walk by a few shops offering fun, cheap food-to-go options.

• *On the left, in front of a gelateria, an arch (with a peaceful little sitting perch atop it) leads to what was a beach, where the town's stream used to hit the sea back in the 1970s. Continue down to the...*

Harbor Square and Breakwater: Vernazza, with the only natural harbor of the Cinque Terre, was established as the sole place boats could pick up the fine local wine. The two-foot-high square stone at the foot of the stairs by the Burgus Wine Bar is marked *Sasso del Sego* (stone of tallow). Workers crushed animal flesh and fat in its basin to make tallow, which drained out of the tiny hole below. The tallow was then used to waterproof boats or wine barrels. For more town history, step into the Burgus to see fascinating old photos of Vernazza on the wall. Stonework is the soul of the region. Take some time to appreciate the impressive stonework of the restaurant interiors facing the harbor.

On the far side (behind Ristorante Pizzeria Vulnetia), peek into the tiny street with its commotion of arches. Vernazza's most characteristic side streets, called *carugi,* lead up from here. The trail (above the church, toward Monterosso) leads to the quintessential view of Vernazza.

Located in front of the harborside church, the tiny piazza—decorated with a river-rock mosaic—is a popular hangout spot. It's where Vernazza's old ladies soak up the last bit of sun, and kids enjoy a patch of level ball field.

Vernazza's harborfront church is unusual for its strange entryway, which faces east (altar side). With relative peace and prosperity in the 16th century, the townspeople doubled the church in size, causing it to overtake a little piazza that once faced the west facade. From the square, use the "new" entry and climb the steps, keeping an eye out for the level necessary to keep the church high and dry. Inside, the lighter pillars in the back mark the 16th-century extension. Three historic portable crosses hanging on the walls are carried through town during Easter processions. They are replicas of crosses that Vernazza ships once carried on crusades to the Holy Land.

• *Finish your town tour seated out on the breakwater (perhaps with a glass of local white wine or something more interesting from a nearby bar—borrow the glass, they don't mind). Face the town, and see...*

The Harbor: In a moderate storm, you'd be soaked, as waves routinely crash over the *molo* (breakwater, built in 1972). Waves can even wash away tourists squinting excitedly into their cameras. (I've seen it happen.) In 2007, an American woman was swept away and killed by a rogue wave. Enjoy the new waterfront piazza—carefully.

The train line (to your left) was constructed in 1874 to tie together a newly united Italy, and linked Turin and Genoa with Rome. A second line (hidden in a tunnel at this point) was built in the 1920s. The yellow building alongside the tracks was Vernazza's first train station. You can see the four bricked-up alcoves where people once waited for trains. Notice the wonderful concrete sunbathing strip (and place for late-night privacy) laid below the tracks along the rocks.

Vernazza's fishing fleet is down to just a couple of boats (with the net spools). Vernazzans are still more likely to own a boat than a car, and it's said that you stand a better chance of surviving if you mess with a local man's wife than with his boat. Boats are on buoys, except in winter or when the red storm flag (see pole at start of breakwater) indicates bad seas. At these times, the boats are pulled up onto the square—which is usually reserved for restaurant tables. In the 1970s, tiny Vernazza had one of Italy's top water polo teams, and the harbor was their "pool." Later, when the league required a real pool, Vernazza dropped out.

The Castle: On the far right, the castle, which is now a grassy

park with great views (and nothing but stones), still guards t
town (€1.50 donation supports the local emergency doctor an
volunteer ambulance group, daily 10:00-19:00; from harbor, take
stairs by Trattoria Gianni and follow *Ristorante al Castello* signs,
tower is a few steps beyond). This was the town's watchtower back
in pirate days, and a Nazi lookout in World War II. The castle
tower looks new because it was rebuilt after the British bombed
it, chasing out the Germans. The highest umbrellas mark the recommended Ristorante Al Castello. The squat tower on the water
is great for a glass of wine or a meal. From the breakwater, you
could follow the rope to the Ristorante Belforte and pop inside,
past the actual submarine door. A photo of a major storm showing
the entire tower under a wave (not uncommon in the winter) hangs
near the bar.

The Town: Vernazza has two halves. *Sciuiu* (Vernazzan dialect
for "flowery") is the sunny side on the left, and *luvegu* (dank) is the
shady side on the right. Houses below the castle were connected
by an interior arcade—ideal for fleeing attacks. The "Ligurian pastel" colors are regulated by a commissioner of good taste in the
regional government. The square before you is locally famous for
some of the area's finest restaurants. The big red central house—on
the site where Genoan warships were built in the 12th century—
used to be a guardhouse.

In the Middle Ages, there was no beach or square. The water
went right up to the buildings, where boats would tie up, Venetian-
style. Imagine what Vernazza looked like in those days, when it
was the biggest and richest of the Cinque Terre towns. Buildings
had a water gate (facing today's square) and a front door on the
higher inland side. There was no pastel plaster, just fine stonework
(traces of which survive above the Trattoria del Capitano). Apart
from the added plaster, the general shape and size of the town has
changed little in five centuries. Survey the windows and notice
inhabitants quietly gazing back.

Above the Town: The small, round tower above the red
guardhouse—another part of the city fortifications—reminds us of
Vernazza's importance in the Middle Ages, when it was a key ally
of Genoa (whose archenemies were the other maritime republics,
especially Pisa). Franco's Ristorante and Bar la Torre, just behind
the tower, welcomes hikers who are finishing, starting, or simply contemplating the Corniglia-Vernazza hike, with great town
views. That tower recalls a time when the entire town was fortified
by a stone wall. Vineyards fill the mountainside beyond the town.
Notice the many terraces. Someone—probably after too much of
that local wine—calculated that the roughly 3,000 miles of dry-
stone walls built to terrace the region's vineyards have the same
amount of stonework as the Great Wall of China.

production is down nowadays, as the younger residents
less physical work. But locals still maintain their tiny plots
and proudly serve their family wines. The patchwork of local vineyards is atomized and complex because of inheritance traditions.
Historically, families divided their land between their children.
Parents wanted each child to get some good land. Because some
lots were "kissed by the sun" while others were shady, the lots were
split into increasingly tiny and eventually unviable pieces.

A single steel train line winds up the gully behind the tower.
It is for the vintner's *trenino,* the tiny service train. Play "Where's
trenino?" and see if you can find two trains. The vineyards once
stretched as high as you can see, but since fewer people sweat in the
fields these days, the most distant terraces have gone wild again.

The Church, School, and City Hall: Vernazza's Ligurian
Gothic church, built with black stones quarried from Punta Mesco
(the distant point behind you), dates from 1318. Note the gray
stone that marks the church's 16th-century expansion. The gray-
and-red house above the spire is the local elementary school (about
25 children attend; education through age 14 is obligatory). High-
schoolers go to the "big city": La Spezia. The red building to the
right of the schoolhouse, a former monastery, is the City Hall.
Vernazza and Corniglia function as one community. Through
most of the 1990s, the local government was Communist. In 1999,
residents elected a coalition of many parties working to rise above
ideologies and simply make Vernazza a better place. That practical
notion of government continues here today. Finally, on the top of
the hill, with the best view of all, is the town cemetery.

Sights in Vernazza

Tuesday-Morning Market—Vernazza's skimpy business community is augmented Tuesday mornings (8:00-13:00) when a meager gang of cars and trucks pulls into town for a tailgate market.

Beach—The harbor's sandy cove has sunning rocks and showers by the breakwater. There's also a ladder on the breakwater for
deep-water access. The sunbathing lane directly under the church
also has a shower.

Boat Rental—Vincenzo of Nord Est rents canoes and small
motorboats from his stand on the harbor, and also takes people
out for mini-cruises. With a rental boat, you can reach a tiny *acqua
pendente* (waterfall) cove between Vernazza and Monterosso; locals
call it their *laguna blu* (motorboats-€60/2 hours, €80/4 hours, plus
gas—usually about €15, includes snorkeling gear, May-Oct only,
mobile 338-700-0436, info@manuela-vernazza.com).

Shuttle Bus Joyride—For a cheap and scenic joyride, with a
chance to chat about the region with friendly Beppe, Simone, or

Pietro, ride the shuttle bus from the top of town for the entire route for the cost of a round-trip ticket. Some buses also head to two sanctuaries in the hills above town (5/day—usually at 7:00, 9:45, 12:00, 15:00, and 17:30; schedule posted at park office, train station, and bus stop in front of post office; €2.50 one-way, free with Cinque Terre Park Card, churches at sanctuaries usually closed). The high-country 40-minute loop—buses are marked *Drignana*—gives you lots of scenery without having to hike (don't take buses marked *No panoramic,* as these won't take scenic routes).

Nightlife in Vernazza

Vernazza's younger generation of restaurant workers lets loose after-hours. They work hard through the tourist season, travel in the winter, speak English, and enjoy connecting with international visitors. After the restaurants close down, the town is quiet except for a couple of nightspots. All bars must close by 24:00.

Blue Marlin Bar dominates the late-night scene with a mix of locals and tourists, home-cooked food until 22:00, good drinks, and piano jam sessions. If you're young and hip, this is *the* place to hang out. If you play the piano, you're welcome to contribute to the scene.

Burgus Wine Bar, chic and cool with a jazzy ambience, is a popular early-evening and after-dinner harborside hangout. Sip local wine or a cocktail. Valerio and Lorenza specialize in Ligurian wines and can explain the historic town photos and museum cases of artifacts (closed Tue, free Wi-Fi with a drink, Piazza Marconi 4).

Ristorante Incadase da Piva (tucked up the lane behind the pharmacy) is the haunt of Piva, Vernazza's troubadour. Piva often gets out his guitar and sings traditional local songs as well as his own compositions. If you're looking for a local Hemingway, check here.

Sleeping in Vernazza

(€1 = about $1.40, country code: 39)
Vernazza, the spindly and salty essence of the Cinque Terre, is my top choice for a home base. Off-season (Oct-March), you can generally arrive without a reservation and find a place, but at other times, it's smart to book ahead (especially June-July and weekends).

People recommended here are listed for their communication skills (they speak English, have email, and are reliable with bookings) and because they rent several rooms. Consequently, my recommendations cost more than comparable rooms you'll find if you shop around. Comparison-shopping will likely save you €10-20 per double per night—and often get you a better place and view to boot. The real Vernazza gems are stray single rooms with owners who have no interest in booking in advance or messing with email. Arrive by early afternoon and drop by any shop or bar and ask; most locals know someone who rents rooms.

Anywhere you stay here requires some climbing, but keep in mind that more climbing means better views. Most do not include breakfast (for suggestions, see "Eating in Vernazza," later). Cash is preferred or required almost everywhere. Night noise can be a problem if you're near the station. Rooms on the harbor come with church bells (but only between 7:00 and 22:00).

Most places will be open when you visit, though a few may still be closed due to flood damage (and some may never reopen); check the travel advisory on www.savevernazza.com for specifics.

Pensions

These pensions are located on the Vernazza map.

$$$ Pensione Sorriso, the oldest pension in town (where I stayed on my first visit in 1975), rents 19 overpriced rooms above the train station. While the main building has the charm, it comes with train noise and saggy beds; the annex, up the street, is in a quieter apartment that feels forgotten (S-€65, Sb-€80, D-€100, Db-€140-150, Tb-€130, includes breakfast, some with air-con, Wi-Fi, Via Gavino 4, tel. 0187-812-224, fax 0187-821-198, www.pensionesorriso.com, info@pensionesorriso.com, Francesca and Aldo).

$$$ Trattoria Gianni rents 27 small rooms and three apartments just under the castle. The rooms are in three buildings—one funky, two modern—up a hundred tight, winding spiral stairs. The funky ones, which may or may not have private baths, are artfully decorated à la shipwreck, with tiny balconies and grand sea views *(con vista sul mare)*. The comfy new *(nuovo)* rooms lack views. Both have modern bathrooms and access to a super-scenic cliff-hanging guests' garden. Steely Marisa requires check-in before 16:00 or a phone call to explain when you're coming. Emanuele (Gianni's son, who now runs the restaurant), Simona, and the staff speak a little English (S-€45, D-€80, Db-€100-120, Tb-€120-140, for best prices pay cash and mention this book when you reserve, cancellations less than a week in advance are charged one night's deposit, closed Jan-Feb, Piazza Marconi 5, tel. & fax 0187-812-228, tel. 0187-821-003, on Wed call mobile 393-9008-155 instead, www.giannifranzi.it, info@giannifranzi.it). Pick up your keys at Trattoria Gianni's restaurant on the harbor square.

$$ Albergo Barbara rents nine simple, clean, and modern rooms overlooking the harbor square—most with small windows and small views. It's run by English-speaking Giuseppe and his no-nonsense Swiss wife, Patricia (D-€55, Db-€65-70, big Db with nice harbor view-€110, extra bed-€10, 2-night stay preferred, closed Dec-Feb, reserve online with credit card but pay cash, free Wi-Fi, Piazza Marconi 30, tel. & fax 0187-812-398, mobile 338-793-3261, www.albergobarbara.it, info@albergobarbara.it).

Private Rooms *(Affitta Camere)*

Vernazza is honeycombed with private rooms year-round, offering the best values in town. Owners may be reluctant to reserve rooms far in advance. It's easiest to call a day or two ahead or simply show up in the morning and look around. Doubles cost €55-100, depending on the view, season, and plumbing—you get what you pay for. Most places accept only cash. Some have killer views, come with lots of stairs, and cost the same as a small, dark place on a back lane over the train tracks. Little English is spoken at many of these places. If you call to let them know your arrival time (or call when you arrive, using your mobile phone or the pay phone just below the station), they'll meet you at the train station.

Well-Managed and Well-Appointed Rooms in the Inland Part of Town

$$$ Tonino Basso rents four sparkling-clean, modern rooms—at a steep price. Each room has its own computer for free Internet access. He's in the only building in Vernazza with an elevator. You get tranquility and air-conditioning, but no views (Sb-€65, Db-€120, Tb-€150, Qb-€180, prices go down Nov-March, call Tonino's mobile number upon arrival and he'll meet you, tel. 0187-821-264, mobile 335-269-436, fax 0187-812-807, toninobasso @libero.it). If you can't locate Tonino, ask his friends at Enoteca Sotto l'Arco at Via Roma 70.

$$ Camere Fontana Vecchia is a delightful place, with four bright, spacious, quiet rooms and an apartment near the post office (no view). As the only place in Vernazza with almost no stairs to climb and the sound of a babbling brook outside your window, it's one of the best values in town (D-€70, Db-€80, T-€95, Tb-€110, super-trendy 2-person apartment-€100, fans and heat, open all year, Via Gavino 15, tel. 0187-821-130, mobile 333-454-9371, fax 0187-812-261, m.annamaria@libero.it, youthful and efficient Anna speaks English). If no one answers, ask at Enoteca Sotto l'Arco on the main drag.

$$ Giuliano Basso rents four pleasant rooms, crafted with care, just above town in the terraced wilds (sea views from terraces). Straddling a ravine among orange trees, it's an artfully decorated Robinson Crusoe-chic wonderland, proudly built out of stone by Giuliano himself—the town's last stone-layer, who "has stone in his blood" (Db-€80, Db suite with air-con-€100, Db suite with private rooftop balcony-€100, extra bed-€25, fridge access, free Internet access, more train noise than others, above train station, take the ramp just before Pensione Sorriso, mobile 333-341-4792, or have Enoteca Sotto l'Arco contact him, www.cdh.it/giuliano, giuliano@cdh.it).

Other Reliable Places Scattered Through Town and the Harborside

These places are not located on this book's map; ask for directions when you reserve.

$$$ La Malà is Vernazza's jetsetter pad. Four pristine white rooms boast four-star-hotel-type extras and a common terrace looking out over the rocky shore (Db-€155, Db suite-€220, includes breakfast at a bar, air-con, Wi-Fi, tel. 334-287-5718, fax 0187-812-218, www.lamala.it, info@lamala.it, Giamba and Armanda). It's a climb—way, way up to the top of town—but they'll gladly carry your bags to and from the station. They also rent the simpler "Armanda's Room" nearby (no view, Db-€75, ring bell at Piazza Marconi 15).

$$$ Martina Callo's four air-conditioned rooms overlook the square; they're up plenty of steps near the silent-at-night church tower (room #1: Tb-€110 or Qb-€120 with harbor view; room #2: huge Qb family room with no view-€110; room #3: Db with grand view terrace-€100; room #4: roomy Db with no view-€60; free Wi-Fi, ring bell at Piazza Marconi 26, tel. & fax 0187-812-365, mobile 329-435-5344, www.roomartina.com, roomartina @roomartina.com).

$$ Monica Lercari rents several classy rooms with modern comforts, perched at the top of town. Guests are welcome to borrow the family rowboat or mountain bike (Db-€80, sea-view D-€100, grand sea-view terrace D-€120, "honeymoon suite" Db-€180, includes breakfast, air-con, Wi-Fi, next to recommended Ristorante al Castello, tel. 0187-812-296, alcastellovernazza @yahoo.it).

$$ Memo Rooms has three clean and spacious rooms that offer good value. They overlook the main street, in what feels like a miniature hotel. Enrica will meet you if you call upon arrival (Db-€70, Via Roma 15, tel. 0187-812-360, mobile 338-285-2385, www .memorooms.com, info@memorooms.com).

$$ Nicolina rents five recently renovated units with double-paned windows. Two rooms are in the center over the pharmacy, up a few steep steps—one has only sleeper sofas (Db-€80); two others are in a different building beyond the church with great views (Db-€100, Tb-€120, Qb-€150); and the last unit is a two-bedroom quadruple with even better views (€200). Inquire at

Pizzeria Vulnetia on the harbor square (Piazza Marconi 29, tel. & fax 0187-821-193, www.camerenicolina.it, camerenicolina.info @cdh.it).

$$ Rosa Vitali rents two four-person apartments across from the pharmacy overlooking the main street (and beyond the train noise). One has a terrace and fridge (top floor); the other has windows and a full kitchen (Db-€95, Tb-€115, Qb-€125, reception at Via Visconti 10 between the grotto and Piazza Marconi, tel. 0187-821-181, mobile 340-267-5009, www.rosacamere.it, rosa.vitali @libero.it).

$$ Francamaria and her kind husband Andrea rent eight sharp, comfortable, and creatively renovated but expensive rooms— all described in detail on her website. While their reception desk is on the harbor square (on the ground floor facing the harbor at Piazza Marconi 30—don't confuse it with Albergo Barbara at same address), the rooms they manage are all over town (Db-€80-120 depending on size and view, Qb-€125-160, extra person-€20, tel. & fax 0187-812-002, mobile 328-711-9728, www.francamaria .com, francamaria@francamaria.com).

More Private Rooms in Vernazza

$$ Maria Capellini rents a couple of simple, clean rooms, including one on the ground floor right on the harbor (Db with kitchen-€85, Tb-€110, cash only, fans, mobile 338-436-3411, www.mariacapellini.com, mariacapellini@hotmail.it, Maria and Giacomo).

$$ Il Pirata delle Cinque Terre rents two basic rooms with the sounds of the river below. Managed by Noelia and Leyla, wives of the Cannoli brothers (see listing under "Eating in Vernazza"), the rooms are at the top of the town, 100 yards beyond their bar (Db-€90, Tb-€130, Qb-€160, includes breakfast with this book at Il Pirata bar—which also functions as the reception, 2-night minimum, cash only, tel. 0187-812-047, mobile 338-596-2503, www .ilpiratarooms.com, ilpiratarooms@libero.it).

$$ Ivo's Camere rents two simple no-terrace rooms high above the main street, as well as a studio apartment (Db-€75, studio-€100, free Wi-Fi, Via Roma 6, reception at Pizzeria Fratelli Basso—Via Roma 1, tel. 0187-821-042, mobile 333-477-5521, www .ivocamere.com, post@ivocamere.com).

$$ Vernazza Rooms, run by Daria Bianchi, Chiara, and Davide, rents 12 decent rooms from their office near the station. Four rooms are above the Blue Marlin Bar looking down on the main street, and eight are below the City Hall (Db-€60-95, Qb-€100-120, fans, reception next to Blue Marlin Bar at Via del Santo 9, tel. 0187-812-151, mobile 338-581-4688 or 338-418-8696, www.vernazzarooms.com, info@vernazzarooms.com).

$$ Emanuela Colombo has two rooms—one spacious and basic on the harbor square, the other *molto* chic and located on a quiet side street (Db-€90, Tb-€110, tel. 339-834-2486, www.vacanzemanuela.it, manucap64@libero.it).

More Options: **$$ Affitta Camere Alberto Basso** (a clean, modern room with a noisy harbor/piazza view, Db-€75, check in at Internet Point, albertobasso@hotmail.com); **$$ Capitano Rooms** (3 recently remodeled rooms above the main drag, Db-€90, ask for Paolo or Barbara at the Trattoria del Capitano restaurant, tel. 0187-812-201); **$$ Eva's Rooms** (3 rooms overlooking main street with train noise, Db-€60-80, ring at Via Roma 56, tel. 0187-821-134, www.evasrooms.it, massimoeva@libero.it); **$$ Manuela Moggia** (3 rooms, Db-€80, Tb-€95, Qb with kitchen-€125, top of the town at Via Gavino 22, tel. 0187-812-397, mobile 333-413-6374, www.manuela-vernazza.com, info@manuela-vernazza.com); and **$$ Elisabetta Rooms** (3 tired rooms at the tip-top of town with Vernazza's ultimate 360-degree roof terrace, Db-€65, Tb-€90, Qb-€100, fans, Via Carattino 62, mobile 347-451-1834, www.elisabettacarro.it, carroelisabetta@hotmail.com, Elisabetta and Pino).

Eating in Vernazza

Many of the recommended eateries will be open when you visit, but some places may be closed due to flood damage (check www.savevernazza.com).

Breakfast

Locals take breakfast about as seriously as flossing. A cappuccino and a pastry or a piece of focaccia from a bar or bakery does it. Most of my recommended accommodations don't come with breakfast (when they do, I've noted so in my listings).

Blue Marlin Bar (mid-town, just below the train station) serves a good array of clearly priced à la carte items including eggs and bacon (only after 8:45), adding up to the priciest breakfast in town (likely to total €10). It's run by Massimo and Carmen (Thu-Tue 7:00-24:00, closed Wed, tel. 0187-821-149). If you're awaiting a train any time of day, the Blue Marlin's outdoor seating beats the platform.

Picnic Breakfast: Drop by one of Vernazza's several little bakeries, focaccia shops, or grocery store to assemble a breakfast to eat on the breakwater. Top it off with a coffee in a nearby bar.

Lunch and Dinner

If you enjoy Italian cuisine and seafood, Vernazza's restaurants are worth the splurge. All take pride in their cooking. Wander around at about 20:00 and compare the ambience, but don't wait too late to eat—many kitchens close at 22:00. To get an outdoor table on summer weekends, reserve ahead. Expect to spend €10 for pastas, €12-16 for *secondi*, and €2-3 for a cover charge. Harborside restaurants and bars are easygoing. You're welcome to grab a cup of coffee or glass of wine and disappear somewhere on the breakwater, returning your glass when you're done. If you dine in Vernazza but are staying in another town, be sure to check train schedules before sitting down to eat, as trains run less frequently in the evening.

Above the Harbor, by the Castle

Ristorante al Castello is run by gracious and English-speaking Monica, her husband Massimo, kind Mario, and the rest of her family (you won't see mamma—she's busy personally cooking each home-style *secondo*). Hike high above town to just below the castle for commanding views. Their *lasagne al pesto*, "spaghetti on the rocks" (noodles with shellfish), and scampi crêpes are time-honored family specialties. For simple fare and a special evening, reserve one of the dozen romantic cliff-side sea-view tables for two. Some of these tables snake around the castle, where you'll feel like you're eating all alone with the Mediterranean. Monica offers a free *sciacchetrà* or *limoncello* with biscotti if you have this book (€10 pastas, €12 *secondi*, Thu-Tue 12:00-15:00 for lunch, 19:00-22:00 for dinner, closed Wed and Nov-April, tel. 0187-812-296).

Ristorante Belforte's experimental, beautifully presented, creative cuisine includes a hearty *zuppa Michela* (€23 for a boatload of seafood), fishy *spaghetti Bruno* (€13), and *trofie al pesto* (hand-rolled noodles with pesto). Their classic *antipasto del nostro chef* (€36 for six plates) is plenty for two people. From the breakwater, follow either the stairs or the rope that leads up and around to the restaurant. You'll find a tangle of tables embedded in four levels of the lower part of the old castle. For the ultimate seaside perch, call and reserve one of four tables on the *terrazza con vista* (view terrace). Most of Belforte's seating is outdoors—if the weather's bad, the interior can get crowded (€15 pastas, €23 *secondi*, €3 cover, Wed-Mon 12:00-15:00 & 19:00-22:00, closed Tue and Nov-March, tel. 0187-812-222, Michela).

Harborside

Gambero Rosso ("Red Prawn," the same name as Italy's top restaurant guide) is considered Vernazza's most venerable restaurant. It feels dressy and costs more than the others. Try Chef Claudio's namesake risotto (€15 pastas, €20 *secondi*, €3 cover, Tue-Sun 12:00-15:00 & 19:00-22:00, closed Mon and Dec-Feb, Piazza Marconi 7, tel. 0187-812-265).

Trattoria del Capitano serves *spaghetti con frutti di mare* (pasta entangled with various types of seafood) and *grigliata mista* (a mix of seasonal Mediterranean fish) among their offerings (€10 pastas, €16 *secondi*, €2 cover, Wed-Mon 12:00-15:00 & 19:00-22:00, closed Tue except in Aug, closed Nov-Dec, tel. 0187-812-201, while Paolo and Eduardo speak English, grandpa Giacomo doesn't need to).

Trattoria Gianni is an old standby for locals and tourists who appreciate the best prices on the harbor. You'll enjoy well-prepared seafood and receive steady, reliable, and friendly service from Emanuele and Alessandro. Ask about "off-menu specials." While the outdoor seating is basic, the indoor setting is classy (€15 pastas, €15 *secondi*, €3 cover, check their *menù cucina tipica Vernazza*, Thu-Tue 12:00-15:00 & 19:00-22:00, closed Wed except July-Aug, tel. 0187-812-228).

Ristorante Pizzeria Vulnetia is simpler, serving regional specialties such as prizewinning *tegame alla Vernazza*—anchovies, tomatoes, and potatoes baked in the oven (€8 pizzas, €12 pastas, €16 *secondi*, €2 cover, Tue-Sun 12:00-15:30 & 18:30-22:00, closed Thu, Piazza Marconi 29, tel. 0187-821-193, Giuliano).

Inland, on or near the Main Street

Several of Vernazza's inland eateries manage to compete without the harbor ambience, but with slightly cheaper prices.

Trattoria da Sandro, on the main drag, mixes Genovese and Ligurian cuisine with friendly service. It can be a peaceful alternative to the harborside scene, plus they dish up award-winning stuffed mussels (€13 pastas, €15 *secondi*, Wed-Mon 12:00-15:00 & 18:30-22:00, closed Tue, Via Roma 62, tel. 0187-812-223, Gabriella and Alessandro).

Antica Osteria il Baretto is another solid bet for homey, reasonably priced traditional cuisine, run by Simone and Jenny. As it's off the harbor and a little less glitzy than the others, it's favored by locals who prefer less noisy English while they eat great homemade fish ravioli. Sitting deep in their interior can be a peaceful escape (€12 pasta, €14 *secondi*, Tue-Sat 12:00-15:00 & 19:00-22:00, closed Mon, indoor and outdoor seating, Via Roma 31).

Ristorante Incadase da Piva is a rare bit of old Vernazza. For 25 years, charismatic Piva has been known for his *tegame alla Vernazza*, his *risotto con frutti di mare* (seafood risotto), and his love of music. The town troubadour, he often serenades his guests when the cooking's done (€13 pastas, €16 *secondi*, Fri-Wed 10:30-15:00 & 18:00-22:30, closed Thu, tucked away 20 yards off the main drag, up a lane behind the pharmacy).

Other Eating Options

Il Pirata delle Cinque Terre, popular for breakfast, is also a favorite for lunch and dinner (€9 pastas, great salads, Sicilian specialties), and its homemade desserts and drinks. The Cannoli twins entertain while they serve, as diners enjoy delicious meals while laughing out loud in this simple café/pastry shop. The menu offers a break from the predictable Ligurian fare, and the bread is literally hot out of the oven (at the top of town; daily 6:30-24:00, also simple lunches and tasty dinners, Via Gavino 36, tel. 0187-812-047).

Ananasso Bar feels Old World, with youthful energy and a great location with little tables right on the harbor. They offer toasted *panini*, pastries, and designer cappuccino. You can eat a bit cheaper at the bar (you're welcome to picnic on the nearby bench or seawall rocks with a Mediterranean view) or enjoy the best-situated tables in town (Fri-Wed 8:00-late, closed Thu).

Bar Baia Saracena ("Saracen Bay") serves decent pizza and microwaved pastas out on the breakwater. Eat here for the economy and the view (€5-7 salads, €9 pizza, tel. 0187-812-113, Luca).

Pizzerias, Sandwiches, and Groceries: Vernazza's main street creatively fills tourists' needs. Two pizzerias stay busy, and while they mostly do take-out, each will let you sit and eat for the same cheap price. One has tables on the street, and the other **(Ercole)** hides a tiny terrace and a few tables out back (it's the only pizzeria in town with a wood-fired oven). **Forno Bakery** has good focaccia and veggie tarts, and several bars sell sandwiches and pizza by the slice. A **grocery store** also makes inexpensive sandwiches to order (generally Mon-Sat 8:00-13:00 & 17:00-19:30, closed Sun). Tiny jars of pesto spread give elegance to picnics.

Gelato: The town's *gelaterias* are good. What looks like **Gelateria Amore Mio** (near the grotto, mid-town), is actually Gelateria Stalin—founded in 1968 by a pastry chef with that unfortunate name. His niece Sonia, who speaks "ice cream," and nephew Francesco now run the place, and are generous with free tastes. They have a neat little licking zone with tiny benches hidden above the crowds; look for it on the little bridge a few steps past their door. They also have good coffee (daily 8:00-24:00, closes at 19:00 off-season, 24 flavors, sit there or take it to go).

Monterosso al Mare (Town #5)

This is a resort with a few cars and lots of hotels, rentable beach umbrellas, crowds, and a little more late-night action than the neighboring towns. Monterosso al Mare—the only Cinque Terre town built on flat land—has two parts: A new town (called Fegina) with a parking lot, train station, and TI; and an old town (Centro Storico), which cradles Old World charm in its small, crooked lanes. In the old town, you'll find hole-in-the-wall shops, pastel townscapes, and a new generation of creative small-businesspeople eager to keep their visitors happy.

A pedestrian tunnel connects the old with the new—but take a small detour around the point for a nicer walk. It offers a close-up view of two sights: a 16th-century lookout tower, built after the last serious pirate raid in 1545; and a Nazi "pillbox," a small, low concrete bunker where gunners hid. (During World War II, nearby La Spezia was an important Axis naval base, and Monterosso was bombed while the Germans were here.)

Strolling the waterfront promenade, you can pick out each of the Cinque Terre towns decorating the coast. After dark, they sparkle. Monterosso is the most enjoyable of the five for young travelers wanting to connect with others looking for a little evening action. Even so, Monterosso is not a full-blown Portofino-style resort—and locals appreciate quiet, sensitive guests.

Monterosso was damaged in the fall of 2011 by the same flash flood that caused even more havoc in neighboring Vernazza. Most places in Monterosso have already reopened; for a list of any remaining closures, see www.rebuildmonterosso.com.

Orientation to Monterosso

Tourist Information

The TI Proloco is next to the train station (April-Oct daily 9:00-19:00, closed Nov-March, exit station and go left a few doors, tel. 0187-817-506, www.prolocomonterosso.it, Annamaria). If you arrive late on a summer day, head to the Internet café for tourist information (see next page).

Arrival in Monterosso

By Train: Train travelers arrive in the new town, from which it's a scenic, flat 10-minute stroll to all the old-town action (leave station to the left; to reach hotels in the new town, turn right out of station). The bar at track 1, which overlooks the beach, is a handy place to wait while waiting for your train to pull in.

Shuttle buses run roughly hourly along the waterfront

between the old town (Piazza Garibaldi, just beyond the tunnel), the train station, and the parking lot at the end of Via Fegina (*Campo Sportivo* stop). While the buses can be convenient—saving you a 10-minute schlep with your bags—they only go once an hour, and are likely not worth the trouble (€1.50, free with Cinque Terre Park Card).

The other alternative is to take a **taxi** (certain vehicles have permission to drive in the old city center). They usually wait outside the train station, but you may have to call (€7 from station to the old town, mobile 335-616-5842 or 335-628-0933).

By Car: Monterosso is 30 minutes off the freeway (exit: Levanto-Carrodano). Note that about three miles above Monterosso, a fork directs you to either *Centro Storico* (old part of town—Via Roma parking lot with a few spots, and possibly the new Loreto garage) or *Fegina* (the new town and beachfront parking, most likely where you want to go). At this point you must choose which area, because you can't drive directly from the new town to the old center (which is closed to cars without special permits).

Parking is easy (except July-Aug and summer weekends) in the huge beachfront guarded lot in the new town (€14/24 hours). If you're heading to the old town, you'll find the lot on Via Roma, a 10-minute downhill walk to the main square (€1.70/hour, €18/24 hours in the parking structure). The big, new Loreto parking garage at the top of the old town may be open when you visit.

For the cheapest Monterosso rates, park along the blue lines (5 minutes farther uphill from Via Roma parking structure) for €8 per day.

Helpful Hints

Medical Help: The town's bike-riding, leather bag-toting, English-speaking physician is **Dr. Vitone,** who charges €50-80 for a simple visit (less for poor students, mobile 338-853-0949).

Internet Access: The Net, a few steps off the main drag (Via Roma), has 10 high-speed computers (€1.50/10 minutes) and Wi-Fi. Enzo happily provides information on the Cinque Terre, has a line on local accommodations, and can burn your photos onto a DVD for €6 (daily 9:30-23:00, off-season closes for lunch and dinner breaks, Via Vittorio Emanuele 55, tel. 0187-817-288, mobile 335-778-5085, www.monterosso net.com).

Baggage Storage: Lucia's Lavarapido, two blocks from the station, provides a wonderful bag-check service—just drop off your bag for €5 (see details in next listing).

Laundry: For full-service laundry in the new town, **Lucia's Lavarapido** will return your laundry to your hotel (€12/13 pounds, daily 8:30-22:00, Via Molinelli 17, mobile 339-484-0940, Lucia and Ivano). For self-service in the old town, try **Wash and Dry Lavanderia** (€6/wash and dry, daily 7:30-23:30, Via Roma 43).

Massage: Giorgio Moggia, the local physiotherapist, gives good massages at your hotel or in his studio (€60/hour, tel. 339-314-6127, giomogg@tin.it).

Self-Guided Walk

Welcome to Monterosso

• *Hike out from the dock in the old town and climb five rough steps to the very top of the concrete...*

Breakwater: If you're visiting by boat, you'll start here anyway. From this point, you can survey Monterosso's old town and new town (stretching to the left, with train station and parking lot), and actually see all *cinque* of the *terre* from one spot: Vernazza, Corniglia (above the shore), Manarola, and a few buildings of Riomaggiore beyond that. The little fort above, which dates from 1550, is now a private home.

These days, the harbor hosts more paddleboats than fishing boats. Sand erosion is a major problem. The partial breakwater is designed to save the beach from washing away. While old-timers remember a vast beach, their grandchildren truck in sand each spring to give tourists something to lie on. (The Nazis liked the Cinque Terre, too—find two of their bomb-hardened bunkers, near left and far right.)

The fancy €300-a-night, four-star Hotel Porto Roca (on the far right) marks the trail to Vernazza. High above, you see an example of the costly roads built in the 1980s to connect the Cinque Terre towns with the freeway over the hills. The two capes (Punta di Montenero and Punta Mesco) define the Cinque Terre region. The closer cape, Punta Mesco, marks an important sea-life sanctuary, home to a rare sea grass that provides an ideal home for fish eggs. Buoys keep fishing boats away. The cape was once a quarry, providing employment to locals who chipped out the stones used to build the local towns (the green stones making up part of the breakwater below you are from there).

On the far end of the new town, marking the best free beach around, you can just see the statue named *Il Gigante*. It's 45 feet tall and once held a trident. While it looks as if it were hewn from the rocky cliff, it's actually made of reinforced concrete and dates from the beginning of the 20th century, when it supported a dancing terrace for a *fin de siècle* villa. A violent storm left the giant holding nothing but memories of Monterosso's glamorous age.

• *From the breakwater, walk into the old-town square (just under the train tracks and to the right). Find the statue of a dandy holding what looks like a box cutter in...*

Piazza Garibaldi: The statue honors Giuseppe Garibaldi, the dashing firebrand revolutionary who, in the 1860s, helped unite the people of Italy into a modern nation. Facing Garibaldi, with your back to the sea, you'll see (from right to left) the City Hall (with the now-required European Union flag beside the Italian one) and a big home and recreation center for poor and homeless elderly. You'll also see A Ca' du Sciensa pub (with historic town photos inside and upstairs; you're welcome to pop in for a look—see "Nightlife in Monterosso," later).

Just under the bell tower (with your back to the sea, it's on your left), a set of covered arcades facing the sea is where the old-timers hang out (they see all and know all). The crenellated bell tower marks the church.

• *Go to church (the entrance is on the inland side).*

Church of St. John the Baptist (Chiesa di San Giovanni Battista): This black-and-white church, with white marble from Carrara and green marble from Punte Mesco, is typical of this region's Romanesque style. Note the lacy, stone rose window above the entrance. It's as delicate as crochet work, with 18 slender mullions (the petals of the rose). The marble stripes get narrower the higher they go, creating the illusion of a church that's taller than it really is. Step inside for more Ligurian Gothic: original marble columns and capitals with pointed arches to match. The octagonal baptismal font (in the back of the church) was carved from Carrara marble in 1359. Imagine the job getting that from the quarries to here. Nearby is a wooden statue of St. Anthony, carved about 1400, which once graced a church that stood atop Punta Mesco. The church itself dates from 1307—see the proud inscription on the middle column inside: "MilleCCCVII." Outside the church, on the side facing the main street, find the high-water mark from a November 1966 flood (the same month as the flood that devastated Florence).

• *Leaving the church, immediately turn left and go to church again.*

Oratory of the Dead (Oratorio dei Neri): During the Counter-Reformation, the Catholic Church offset the rising influence of the Lutherans by creating brotherhoods of good works. These religious Rotary clubs were called "confraternities." Monterosso had two, nicknamed White and Black. This building is the oratory of the Black group, whose mission—as the macabre decor filling the interior indicates—was to arrange for funerals and take care of widows, orphans, the shipwrecked, and the souls of those who ignore the request for a €1 donation. It dates from the 16th century, and membership has passed from father to son for generations. Notice the fine carved choir stalls (c. 1700) just inside

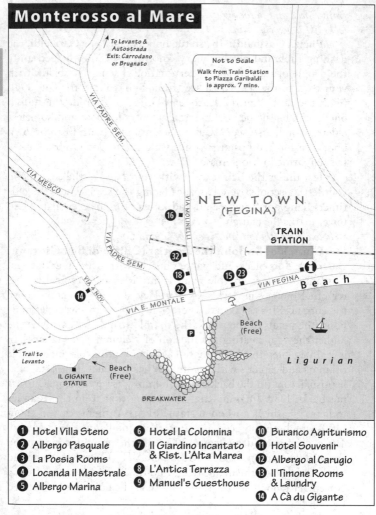

Monterosso al Mare

↑ To Levanto &
Autostrada
Exit: Carrodano
or Brugnato

Not to Scale

Walk from Train Station
to Piazza Garibaldi
is approx. 7 mins.

VIA PADRE SEM.

VIA MESCO

VIA PADRE SEM.

VIA 4 NOV.

N E W   T O W N
(FEGINA)

VIA MOLINELLI

⑯

㉜

⑱

⑭

㉒

⑮ ㉓

**TRAIN
STATION**

VIA FEGINA

🛈

B e a c h

VIA E. MONTALE

P

Beach
(Free)

← Trail to
Levanto

IL GIGANTE
STATUE

Beach
(Free)

BREAKWATER

L i g u r i a n

- ❶ Hotel Villa Steno
- ❷ Albergo Pasquale
- ❸ La Poesia Rooms
- ❹ Locanda il Maestrale
- ❺ Albergo Marina
- ❻ Hotel la Colonnina
- ❼ Il Giardino Incantato & Rist. L'Alta Marea
- ❽ L'Antica Terrazza
- ❾ Manuel's Guesthouse
- ❿ Buranco Agriturismo
- ⓫ Hotel Souvenir
- ⓬ Albergo al Carugio
- ⓭ Il Timone Rooms & Laundry
- ⓮ A Cà du Gigante

the door, and the haunted-house chandeliers. Look up at the ceiling to find the symbol of the confraternity: a skull-and-crossbones and an hourglass...death awaits us all.

• *Return to the beach and find the brick steps that lead up to the hill-capping convent (starting between the train tracks and the pedestrian tunnel). Stop above the castle at a statue of St. Francis and a wolf taking in a grand view. Enjoy another opportunity to see all five of the Cinque Terre towns. From here, backtrack 20 yards and continue uphill.*

The Switchbacks of the Friars: Follow the yellow brick road (OK, it's orange...but I couldn't help singing as I skipped skyward). Climb uphill until you reach a convent church, then a cemetery,

15	Hotel la Spiaggia	**21**	Via Venti Restaurant	**27**	Focacceria da Ely
16	Hotel Punta Mesco	**22**	Miky Restaurant	**28**	Il Casello
17	Pensione Agavi	**23**	La Cantina di Miky	**29**	A Ca' du Sciensa Pub
18	Le Sirene/ Raggi di Sole	**24**	Ristorante Tortuga	**30**	Enoteca Eliseo
19	Rist. Belvedere	**25**	Il Frantoio Focacceria	**31**	Fast Bar
20	Ciak Restaurant	**26**	Pizzeria la Smorfia & The Net	**32**	Lucia's Laundry

in a ruined castle at the summit. The lane *(Salita dei Cappuccini)* is nicknamed *Zii di Frati* ("switchbacks of the friars").

• *When you reach a gate marked* Convento e Chiesa Cappuccini, *you have arrived.*

Church of the Cappuccin Friars: The former convent is now manned by a single caretaker friar. Before stepping inside, notice the church's striped Romanesque facade. It's all fake. Tap it—no marble, just cheap 18th-century stucco. Sit in the rear pew. The high altarpiece painting of St. Francis can be rolled up on special days to reveal a statue of Mary standing behind it. Look at the statue of St. Anthony to the right and smile (you're on convent camera). Wave at the security camera—they're nervous about the precious painting to your left.

This fine painting of the Crucifixion is attributed to Anthony van Dyck, the 17th-century Flemish master who lived and worked for years in nearby Genoa (though art historians suspect that, at best, it was painted by someone in the artist's workshop). When Jesus died, the earth went dark. Notice the eclipsed sun in the painting, just to the right of the cross. Do the electric candles work? Pick one up, pray for peace, and plug it in. (Leave €0.50, or unplug it and put it back.)

• *Leave and turn left to hike 100 yards uphill to the cemetery that fills the remains of the castle, capping the hill. Look out from the gate and enjoy the view.*

Cemetery in the Ruined Castle: In the Dark Ages, the village huddled within this castle. Slowly it expanded. Notice the town view from here—no sea. You're looking at the oldest part of Monterosso, huddled behind the hill, out of view of 13th-century pirates. Explore the cemetery, but remember that cemeteries are sacred and treasured places (as is clear by the abundance of fresh flowers). Ponder the black-and-white photos of grandparents past. *Q.R.P.* is *Qui Riposa in Pace* (a.k.a. R.I.P.). Rich families had their own little tomb buildings. Climb to the very summit—the castle's keep, or place of last refuge. Priests are buried in a line of graves closest to the sea, but facing inland, toward the town's holy sanctuary high on the hillside (above the road, with its triangular steeple peeking above the trees). Each Cinque Terre town has a lofty sanctuary, dedicated to Mary and dear to the village hearts.

• *From here, your tour is over—any trail leads you back into town.*

Sights in Monterosso

Beaches—Monterosso's beaches, immediately in front of the train station, are easily the Cinque Terre's best and most crowded. This town is a sandy resort with rentable beach extras: Figure €20 to rent two chairs and an umbrella for the day. Light lunches are served by beach cafés to sunbathers at their lounge chairs. It's often worth the euros to enjoy a private beach. If you see umbrellas on a beach, it means you'll have to pay a rental fee; otherwise the sand is free (all the beaches are marked on this book's Monterosso al Mare map). Don't use your white hotel towels; most hotels will give you beach towels—sometimes for a fee. The local hidden beach, which is free, gravelly, and generally less crowded, is tucked away under Il Casello restaurant at the east end of town, near the trailhead to Vernazza. The bocce ball court (next to Il Casello) is busy with the old boys enjoying their favorite pastime.

Kayaks—**Samba** rents kayaks on the beach (€7/hour for 1-person kayak, €12/hour for 2-person kayak, to the right of train station as you exit, mobile 339-681-2265, Domenico). The paddle to Vernazza is a favorite.

Shuttle Buses for High-Country Hikes—Monterosso's bus service (described earlier, under "Arrival in Monterosso") continues beyond the town limits, but check the schedules—only one or two departures a day head into the high country. Some buses go to the Sanctuary of Our Lady of Soviore, from where you can hike back down to Monterosso (1.5 hours, moderately steep). Rides cost €1.50 (free with Cinque Terre Park Card, pick up schedule from park office). Or you can hike to Levanto (no Cinque Terre Park card necessary, not as stunning as the rest of the coastal trail, 2.5 hours, straight uphill and then easy decline, follow signs at west end of the new town). For hiking details, ask at the train station TI.

Wine-Tasting—Buranco Agriturismo offers visits to their vineyard and cantina daily at 12:00. You'll taste two of their wines plus a grappa and a *limoncino*, along with home-cooked food (€25/person with snacks, €40/person for full lunch, reservations advised at least three days in advance, English may be limited, follow Via Buranco uphill to path, 10 minutes above town, tel. 0187-817-677, www.burancocinqueterre.it). They also rent apartments; see "Sleeping in Monterosso," later.

Boat Rides—From the old-town harbor, boats run nearly hourly (10:30-17:00) to Vernazza, Manarola, Riomaggiore, and Portovenere. Schedules are posted in Cinque Terre park offices (for details, see "Getting Around the Cinque Terre—By Boat" on page 1043).

Nightlife in Monterosso

A Ca' du Sciensa has nothing to do with science—it's the last name of the town moneybags who owned this old mansion. The antique dumbwaiter is still in use—a remnant from the days when servants toiled downstairs while the big shots wined and dined up top. This classy yet laid-back pub offers breezy square seating, bar action on the ground level, an intimate lounge upstairs, and discreet balconies overlooking the square to share with your best travel buddy. It's a good place for light meals from a fun and accessible menu: €5-6 sandwiches, salads, and microwaved pastas. They offer €6 cocktails and mojitos with free *aperitivo* snacks from 17:30 to 20:30. Luca welcomes you to wander around the place and view the old Cinque Terre photo collection (daily 10:00-24:00, closed Nov-March, Piazza Garibaldi 17, tel. 0187-818-233).

Enoteca Eliseo, the first (and I'd say best) wine bar in town, comes with operatic ambience. Eliseo and his wife, Mary, love music and wine. You can select a fine bottle from their shop shelf, and for €7 extra, enjoy it and the village action from their cozy tables. If you've ever wanted an education in grappa, talk to Eliseo—he stocks 96 varieties. Wines sold by the glass *(bicchiere)* are posted (Wed-Mon 9:00-24:00, closed Tue, Piazza Matteotti 3, a block inland behind church, tel. 0187-817-308).

Fast Bar, the best bar in town for young travelers and night owls, is located on Via Roma in the old town. Customers mix travel tales with big, cold beers, and the crowd (and the rock 'n' roll) gets noisier as the night rolls on. Come here to watch Italian or American sporting events on TV any time of day (sandwiches and snacks usually served until midnight, open nightly until 2:00, closed Nov-March, Alex, Francisco, and Stefano).

La Cantina di Miky, in the new town just beyond the train station, is a trendy bar-restaurant with an extensive cocktail and grappa menu. The seating is in three zones: overlooking the beach, in the garden, or in the cellar. Run by Manuel, son of well-known local restaurateur Miky, it sometimes hosts live music. Manuel offers a fun "five villages" wine-tasting with local meats and cheeses (daily until well after 24:00, Via Fegina 90, tel. 0187-802-525).

Sleeping in Monterosso

(€1 = about $1.40, country code: 39)
Monterosso, the most beach-resorty of the five Cinque Terre towns, offers maximum comfort and ease. The TI Proloco just outside the train station can give you a list of €70-80 double rooms. Rooms in Monterosso are a better value for your money than similar rooms in crowded Vernazza, and the proprietors seem more genuine and welcoming. To locate the hotels, see the Monterosso al Mare map.

In the Old Town

$$$ Hotel Villa Steno is lovingly managed and features great view balconies, panoramic gardens with sun beds, air-conditioning, and the friendly help of English-speaking Matteo and his wife, Carla. Of their 16 rooms, 12 have view balconies (Sb-€110, Db-€170, Tb-€195, Qb-€225, includes hearty buffet breakfast, discount with cash and this book, Internet access and Wi-Fi, laundry, parking-€8—reserve in advance, Via Roma 109, tel. 0187-817-028 or 0187-818-336, fax 0187-817-354, www.villasteno.com, steno @pasini.com). It's a 15-minute hike (or €8 taxi ride) from the train station to the top of the old town. Readers get a free Cinque Terre info packet and a glass of the local sweet wine, *sciacchetrà,* when they check in—ask for it.

$$$ Albergo Pasquale is a modern, comfortable place with 15 rooms, run by the same family as the Hotel Villa Steno (above). It's conveniently located just a few steps from the beach, boat dock, tunnel entrance to the new town, and train tracks. While there is some traffic and train noise, it's mostly a lullaby of waves. Located right on the harbor, it has an elevator and offers easier access than most (same prices and welcome drink as Villa Steno; air-con, all rooms with sea view, Via Fegina 8, tel. 0187-817-550 or 0187-817-477, fax 0187-817-056, www.hotelpasquale.com, pasquale@pasini .com, Felicita and Marco).

$$$ La Poesia has four warmly colored rooms that share a peaceful garden terrace, where you'll enjoy a complimentary *aperitivo* upon arrival (Db-€150, suite-€40 extra, small discount for multi-night stays, air-con, Via Genova 4, tel. 0187-817-283, www .lapoesia-cinqueterre.com, info@lapoesia-cinqueterre.com, mamma Nicoletta speaks little English, daughter Veronica speaks more).

$$$ Locanda il Maestrale rents six small, stylish rooms in a sophisticated and peaceful little inn. Although renovated with all the modern comforts, it retains centuries-old character under frescoed ceilings. Its peaceful sun terrace overlooking the old town and Via Roma action is a delight (small Db-€115, Db-€145, suite-€170, less off-season, discount with cash and this book, air-con, Wi-Fi, Via Roma 37, tel. 0187-817-013, mobile 338-4530-531, fax 0187-817-084, www.locandamaestrale.net, maestrale @monterossonet.com, Stefania).

$$$ Albergo Marina, creatively run by enthusiastic husband-and-wife team Marina and Eraldo, has 23 thoughtfully appointed rooms and a garden with lemon trees. With a free and filling buffet featuring local specialties from 14:00 to 17:00 daily, they offer a fine value (standard Db-€130, discount with cash and this book, elevator, air-con, Wi-Fi, free use of kayak and snorkel equipment, Via Buranco 40, tel. 0187-817-613, fax 0187-817-242, www.hotel marina5terre.com, marina@hotelmarina5terre.com).

$$$ Hotel la Colonnina, a comfy, modern place with 21 big and pretty rooms, is buried in the town's fragrant and sleepy back streets with no sea views (Db-€142, Tb-€200, Qb-€225, €15 more for bigger rooms with viewless terrace, cash only, air-con, Internet access and Wi-Fi, fridges, elevator, inviting rooftop terrace with sun beds, garden, Via Zuecca 6, tel. 0187-817-439, fax 0187-817-788, www.lacolonninacinqueterre.it, info@lacolonnina cinqueterre.it, Christina). The hotel is in the old town behind the statue of Garibaldi (take street to left of A Ca' du Sciensa one block up).

$$$ Il Giardino Incantato ("The Enchanted Garden") is a charming four-room B&B in a tastefully renovated 16th-century

Ligurian home in the heart of the old town. Breakfast is served in a hidden garden, which is illuminated with candles in the evening (Db-€170, Db suite-€200, air-con, free minibar and tea and coffee service, Via Mazzini 18, tel. 0187-818-315, mobile 333-264-9252, www.ilgiardinoincantato.net, giardino_incantato@libero.it, kind and eager-to-please Fausto and Mariapia).

$$$ L'Antica Terrazza rents four classy rooms right in town. With a pretty terrace overlooking the pedestrian street and minimal stairs, Raffaella and John offer a good deal (Db-€110, cash discount, air-con, Internet access and Wi-Fi, Vicolo San Martino 1, tel. 0187-817-499, mobile 347-132-6213, www.anticaterrazza.com, post@anticaterrazza.com).

$$$ Manuel's Guesthouse, perched among terraces, is a garden getaway ruled by disheveled artist Manuel and run by his nephew Lorenzo. They have seven big, bright rooms and a grand view. Their killer terrace is hard to leave—especially after a few drinks (Db-€100, big Db with grand-view balcony-€120, ask for Rick Steves price, cash only, air-con, Internet access and Wi-Fi, in old town, up about 100 steps behind church at top of town, Via San Martino 39, mobile 333-439-0809 or 329-547-3775, www.manuelsguesthouse.com, info@manuelsguesthouse.com).

$$$ Buranco Agriturismo, a 10-minute walk from the old town, has wonderful gardens and views over the vine-covered valley. Its primary business is wine and olive-oil production, but they offer three apartments at a good price. It's a rare opportunity to stay in a farmhouse but still be able to get to town on foot (2-6 people-€60/person including breakfast, €30/child under 12, dinner on request, air-con, free shuttle from station, open year-round, tel. 0187-817-677, mobile 349-434-8046, fax 0187-802-084, www.burancocinqueterre.it, info@buranco.it, informally run by Loredana, Mary, and Giulietta).

$$ Hotel Souvenir is Monterosso's cash-only backpacker hotel. It has 30 rooms in two buildings, each utilitarian but comfortable (one more stark than the other). Both share a lounge and pleasant leafy courtyard. The basic one is popular with students (S-€30, Sb-€35, D-€55, Db-€70, T-€105, breakfast-€5); the other is nicer and pricier (Sb-€45, Db-€80, Tb-€120, includes breakfast; walk three blocks inland from the main old-town square to Via Gioberti 24, tel. 0187-817-822, tel. & fax 0187-817-595, hotel_souvenir@yahoo.com, Beppe).

$$ Albergo al Carugio is a simple, practical nine-room place in a big apartment-style building at the top of the old town. It's quiet, comfy, and functional (Db-€75-80, air-con, Wi-Fi, Via Roma 100, tel. 0187-817-453, www.alcarugio.it, info@alcarugio.it, Andrea and Simona).

$$ Il Timone Rooms, a little B&B by the post office, has three tidy, modern rooms. Francesco also rents a few rooms near the cemetery, but they aren't worth the hike (Db-€90, breakfast at a bar, air-con, Wi-Fi, Via Roma 75, tel. 349-870-8666, www .iltimonedimonterosso.it).

In the New Town

$$$ A Cà du Gigante, despite its name, is a tiny yet stylish refuge with nine rooms. About 100 yards from the beach (and surrounded by blocky apartments on a modern street), the interior is taste-fully done with modern comfort in mind (Db-€160, Db sea-view suite-€180, ask about Rick Steves discount with 3-night stay, occa-sional last-minute deals, air-con, free parking, Via IV Novembre 11, tel. 0187-817-401, fax 0187-817-375, www.ilgigantecinqueterre .it, gigante@ilgigantecinqueterre.it, Claudia).

$$$ Hotel la Spiaggia is a venerable old 19-room place fac-ing the beach and run with attitude by Poggi Andrea and his gentle daughter Maria. Half of the rooms come with air-con and half with sea views, but all are the same price—request what you like when you reserve (Db-€160, €10 discount for 2-night stays, includes breakfast and parking, elevator, Via Lungomare 98, tel. 0187-817-567, fax 0187-817-075, www.laspiaggiahotel.com, hotel laspiaggia@libero.it).

$$$ Hotel Punta Mesco is a tidy, well-run little haven rent-ing 17 quiet, modern rooms. While none have views, 10 rooms have small terraces. For the price, it may offer the best comfort in town (Db-€132, Tb-€170, cash discount, air-con, Wi-Fi, free loaner bikes, free parking, Via Molinelli 35, tel. & fax 0187-817-495, www.hotelpuntamesco.it, info@hotelpuntamesco.it, Diego and Anna).

$$$ Pensione Agavi has 10 spartan, hostel-like, overpriced rooms, about half overlooking the beach near the big rock. This is not a place to party—it feels like an old hospital with narrow hall-ways (D-€80, Db-€110, Tb-€140, same price with or without view, 10 percent discount for 2 nights or more, no breakfast, cash only, refrigerators, turn left out of station to Fegina 30, tel. 0187-817-171, mobile 333-697-4071, fax 0187-818-264, hotel.agavi@libero.it, Hillary).

$ Le Sirene/Raggi di Sole, with nine simple rooms in two humble buildings, is about the cheapest place in town. It's run from a hole-in-the-wall reception desk a block from the station, just off the water. I'd request the Le Sirene building, which doesn't have train noise and is a bit nicer than Raggi di Sole (Db-€80, third person-€40, fans, Via Molinelli 10, mobile 393-935-7683, www .sirenerooms.com, sirenerooms@gmail.com, Ermanna).

Eating in Monterosso

Restaurants

Ristorante Belvedere, big and sprawling, is *the* place for a good-value meal indoors or outdoors on the harborfront. Their *amfora belvedere*—mixed seafood stew—is huge, and can easily be split among up to four diners (€45). Share with your group and add pasta for a fine meal. Mussel fans will enjoy the *tagliolini della casa* (€8). It's energetically run by Federico and Roberto (€9 pastas, €12 *secondi*, €2 cover, Wed-Mon 12:00-14:30 & 19:00-22:00, usually closed Tue, on the harbor in the old town, tel. 0187-817-033).

L'Alta Marea offers special fish ravioli, the catch of the day, and huge crocks of fresh, steamed mussels. Young chef Marco cooks with charisma, while his wife, Anna, takes good care of the guests. This place is quieter, buried in the old town two blocks off the beach, and has covered tables out front for people-watching. This is a good opportunity to try rabbit (€9 pastas and pizza, €12-15 *secondi*, €2 cover, discount with cash and this book, Thu-Tue 12:00-15:00 & 18:00-22:00, closed Wed, Via Roma 54, tel. 0187-817-170).

Ciak—high-energy and tightly packed—is a local institution with reliably good food and higher prices. It's known for its huge, sizzling terra-cotta crock for two crammed with the day's catch and accompanied by risotto or spaghetti, or served swimming in a soup *(zuppa)*. Another popular choice is the seafood *antipasto Lampara*. Stroll a couple of paces past the outdoor tables up Via Roma to see what Ciak has on the stove (Thu-Tue 12:00-15:00 & 19:00-22:30, closed Wed, tel. 0187-817-014).

Via Venti is a quiet little trattoria, hidden in an alley deep in the heart of the old town, where Papa Ettore creates imaginative seafood dishes using the day's catch and freshly made pasta. Ilaria and her partner Michele serve up delicate and savory gnocchi (tiny potato dumplings) with crab sauce, tender ravioli stuffed with fresh fish, and pear-and-cheese pasta. There's nothing pretentious here... just good cooking, service, and prices (€11 pastas, €16 *secondi*, Fri-Wed 12:00-15:00 & 18:30-22:30, closed Thu, tel. 0187-818-347). From the bottom of Via Roma, with your back to the sea and the church to your left, head to the right down Via XX Settembre and follow it to the end, to #32.

Miky is packed with well-dressed locals who know their seafood and want to eat it in a classy environment without spending a fortune. For elegantly presented, top-quality food, this is my Cinque Terre favorite. It's clearly a proud family operation: Miky (dad), Simonetta (mom), and charming Sara (daughter, who greets guests) all work hard. All their pasta is "pizza pasta"—cooked normally but finished in a bowl that's encased in a thin pizza crust.

They cook the concoction in a wood-fired oven to keep in the aroma. Miky's has a fine wine list with many available by the glass if you ask. If I were ever to require a dessert, it would be their mixed sampler plate, *dolce mista*—€10 and plenty for two (€15 pastas, €22 *secondi*, €8 sweets, Wed-Mon 12:00-15:00 & 19:00-23:00, closed Tue, reservations wise in summer, diners tend to dress up a bit, in the new town 100 yards north of train station at Via Fegina 104, tel. 0187-817-608).

La Cantina di Miky, a few doors down toward the station, serves Ligurian specialties (chef Boris loves anchovies) that follow in Miky's family tradition of quality (it's run by son Manuel). It's more trendy and informal thàn Miky's, and you can sit downstairs, in the garden, or overlooking the sea (€16 anchovy tasting plate, €13 pastas, €15 *secondi,* creative desserts, daily 12:00-24:00 or later, Via Fegina 90, tel. 0187-802-525). This place doubles as a cocktail bar in the evenings—see "Nightlife in Monterosso," earlier.

Ristorante Tortuga is the top option in Monterosso for sea-view elegance, with gorgeous outdoor seating on a bluff and an elegant white-tablecloth-and-candles interior. If you're out and about, drop by to consider which table you'd like to reserve for later (€15 pastas, €20 *secondi,* Tue-Sun 12:00-14:30 & 18:00-22:00, closed Mon, just outside the tunnel that connects the old and new town, tel. 0187-800-065, mobile 333-240-7956, Silvia and Giamba).

Il Casello is the only place for a fun meal on a terrace overlooking the old-town beach. With outdoor tables on a rocky outcrop, it's a pleasant spot for a salad or a sandwich, or well-prepared pasta or *secondi* (lunch only, daily April-Oct, closed Nov-March, mobile 333-492-7629, Bacco).

Light Meals, Take-Out Food, and Breakfast

Lots of shops and bakeries sell pizza and focaccia for an easy picnic at the beach or on the trail. At **Il Frantoio,** Simone makes tasty pizza to go or to munch perched on a stool (Fri-Wed 9:00-14:00 & 16:00-19:30, closed Thu, just off Via Roma at Via Gioberti 1, tel. 0187-818-333). **Pizzeria la Smorfia** also cooks up good pizza to eat in or take out. Pizzas come in two sizes—the large can feed three (Fri-Wed 11:30-15:00 & 18:00-23:00, closed Thu, Via Vittorio Emanuele 73, tel. 0187-818-395). **Focacceria da Ely** makes airy focaccia and thick-crust pizzas for casual seating or take-out (daily 10:30-20:00, until 24:00 in summer, Emigliano).

For a quick bite right at the train station, consider **Il Massimo della Focaccia.** Massimo and Daniella serve local quiche-like tortes, sandwiches, focaccia pizzas, and desserts. With benches just in front, this is a good bet for a €4 light meal with a sea view (daily, Via Fegina 50 at the entry to the station).

Cinque Terre Connections

By Train

The five towns of the Cinque Terre are on a pokey milk-run train line (described in "Getting Around the Cinque Terre—By Train" on page 1041). Erratically timed but roughly hourly trains connect each town with the others, plus La Spezia, Genoa, and Riviera towns to the north. While a few of these local trains go to more distant points (Milan or Pisa), it's much faster to change in La Spezia, Monterosso, or Sestri Levante to a bigger train (local train info tel. 0187-817-458, www.trenitalia.com).

From La Spezia Centrale by Train to: Rome (7/day, 3-4.5 hours, more with changes, €45; an evening train—departing around 20:00—gives you a complete day in the region while still getting you to Rome that night), **Pisa** (about hourly, 1-1.5 hours, €5), **Florence** (5/day direct, otherwise nearly hourly, 2.5 hours, €9.30), **Milan** (about hourly, 3 hours direct or with change in Genoa, €22), **Venice** (about hourly, 5-6 hours, 1-3 changes, €50).

From Monterosso by Train to: Venice (about hourly, 6-7 hours, 1-3 changes, €52), **Milan** (8/day direct, otherwise hourly with change in Genoa, 3-4 hours, €22), **Genoa** (hourly, 1.2-2 hours, €8), **La Spezia** (hourly, 20-30 minutes), **Rome** (hourly, 4.5 hours, change in La Spezia, €50). For destinations in **France**, change trains in Genoa.

THE NETHERLANDS

AMSTERDAM

Amsterdam is a progressive way of life housed in Europe's most 17th-century city. Physically, it's built upon millions of pilings. But more than that, it's built on good living, cozy cafés, great art, street-corner jazz, stately history, and a spirit of live-and-let-live. It has 765,000 people and almost as many bikes. It also has more canals than Venice...and about as many tourists.

During the Dutch Golden Age in the 1600s, Amsterdam was the world's richest city, an international sea-trading port, and the cradle of capitalism. Wealthy, democratic burghers built a planned city of canals lined with trees and townhouses topped with fancy gables. Immigrants, Jews, outcasts, and political rebels were drawn here by its tolerant atmosphere, while painters such as young Rembrandt captured that atmosphere on canvas.

The Dutch are unique. They are among the world's most handsome people—tall, healthy, and with good posture—and the most open, honest, and refreshingly blunt. They like to laugh. As connoisseurs of world culture, they appreciate Rembrandt paintings, Indonesian food, and the latest French film—but with an un-snooty, blue-jeans attitude.

Approach Amsterdam as an ethnologist observing a strange culture. Stroll through any neighborhood and see things that are commonplace here but rarely found elsewhere. Carillons chime quaintly in neighborhoods selling sex, as young professionals smoke pot with impunity next to old ladies in bonnets selling flowers. Observe the neighborhood's "social control," where an elderly man feels safe in his home knowing he's being watched by the prostitutes next door.

Be warned: Amsterdam, a bold experiment in freedom, may

Amsterdam Neighborhoods

IJ RIVER

CENTRAL STATION

LIBRARY

NEMO

WEST AMSTERDAM

JORDAAN

PRINSENGRACHT

KEIZERSGRACHT

HERENGRACHT

SINGEL

DAMRAK

RED LIGHT DISTRICT

NORTHEAST AMSTERDAM

CENTRAL AMSTERDAM

DAM SQUARE

ROKIN

SOUTHEAST AMSTERDAM

ANNE FRANK HOUSE

SPUI SQUARE

MINT TOWER

WATERLOO-PLEIN

JEWISH QUARTER SIGHTS

NINE LITTLE STREETS

REMBRANDT-PLEIN

PLANTAGE

AMSTEL

LEIDSEPLEIN

SOUTHWEST AMSTERDAM

VONDEL PARK

RIJKS-MUSEUM

MUSEUM PLEIN

VAN GOGH MUSEUM

AMSTEL RIVER

DCH

box your Puritan ears. Take it all in, then pause to watch the clouds blow past stately old gables—and see the Golden Age reflected in a quiet canal.

Planning Your Time

Amsterdam is worth a full day of sightseeing on even the busiest itinerary. While the city has a couple of must-see museums, its best attraction is its own carefree ambience. The city's a joy on foot—and a breezier and faster delight by bike.

In the morning, see the city's two great art museums: the Van Gogh and the Rijksmuseum (cafeteria lunch). Walk from the museums to the Singel canal flower market, then take a relaxing hour-long, round-trip canal cruise from the dock at Spui (described later, under "Tours in Amsterdam"). After the cruise, stroll through the peaceful Begijnhof courtyard and tour the nearby Amsterdam Museum. Visiting the Anne Frank House after 18:00 may save you an hour in line in summer (see page 1123 for last-entry times). Have a memorable dinner: Try Dutch pancakes or a *rijsttafel*—an Indonesian smorgasbord.

On a balmy evening, Amsterdam has a Greek-island ambience. Stroll through the Jordaan neighborhood for the idyllic side of town and wander down Leidsestraat to Leidseplein for the roaring café and people scene. Tour the Red Light District while you're at it.

With extra time: With two days in the Netherlands, I'd side-trip by bike, bus, or train to Haarlem. With a third day, I'd do the other great Amsterdam museums.

Orientation to Amsterdam

(area code: 020)
Amsterdam's Central Train Station (Amsterdam Centraal), on the north edge of the city, is your starting point, with the TI, bike rental, and trams branching out to all points. Damrak is the main north-south axis, connecting Central Station with Dam Square (people-watching and hangout center) and its Royal Palace. From this main street, the city spreads out like a fan, with 90 islands, hundreds of bridges, and a series of concentric canals—named Herengracht (Gentleman's Canal), Keizersgracht (Emperor's Canal), and Prinsengracht (Prince's Canal)—that were laid out in the 17th century, Holland's Golden Age. Amsterdam's major sights are within walking distance of Dam Square.

To the east of Damrak is the oldest part of the city (today's Red Light District), and to the west is the newer part, where you'll find the Anne Frank House and the peaceful Jordaan neighborhood. Museums and Leidseplein nightlife cluster at the southern edge of the city center.

Tourist Information
"VVV" (pronounced "fay fay fay") is Dutch for "TI," a tourist information office. Amsterdam's tourist offices are crowded and inefficient—avoid them if you can. You can save yourself a trip by calling the TI at 020/201-8800 (Mon-Fri 8:00-18:00) or try 0900-400-4040 (Mon-Fri 9:00-17:00). From the US dial 011-31-20-551-2525.

The main TI at Central Station is busy, but is convenient when arriving by train (daily July-Aug 8:00-20:00, Sept-June 9:00-18:00). An affiliated office is in the AUB/Last Minute Ticket Shop on Leidseplein, tucked into the side of the giant Stadsschouwburg

Theater (Mon-Fri 10:00-19:30, Sat 10:00-18:00, Sun 12:00-18:00; doesn't book hotel rooms). These TIs outside of Amsterdam are helpful and less crowded: at Schiphol Airport (daily 7:00-22:00) and in the town of Haarlem (next chapter).

Tickets: Although Amsterdam's main TI sells tickets to the Anne Frank House (€1 extra per ticket, same-day tickets available) and the Rijks, Van Gogh, and Stedelijk museums (no fee), it's quicker to get tickets in advance online (see below).

Maps and Brochures: Given the city's maze of streets and canals, I'd definitely get a good city map (€2.50 at Central Station TI, same map given away free at the TI in the AUB/Last-Minute Ticket Shop—go figure). Also consider picking up any of the walking-tour brochures (€3 each, including tours covering city center, former Jewish Quarter, Jordaan, and funky De Pijp neighborhood). For entertainment, get a copy of *Time Out Amsterdam* (€3, €1.50 if bought with city map); for additional entertainment ideas, see the free papers listed later (under "Helpful Hints" and "Entertainment in Amsterdam").

Currency Exchange: At Central Station, **GWK Currency Exchange** offices have hotel reservation windows where clerks sell local and international phone cards and mobile-phone SIM cards, and answer basic tourist questions, with shorter lines than the TI (daily 8:00-22:00, near front of station in both the east and west corridors, tel. 020/627-2731).

Resources for Gay Travelers: A short walk from Central Station down Damrak is **GAYtic,** a TI specifically oriented to the needs of LGBT travelers. The office stocks maps, magazines, and brochures, and dispenses advice on nightlife as well as general tourist information (Mon-Sat 11:00-20:00, Sun 12:00-20:00, Spuistraat 44, tel. 020/330-1461, www.gaytic.nl, info@gaytic.nl). **Pink Point,** in a kiosk outside Westerkerk, next to the Homomonument, is less of a resource, but has advice about nightlife, and sells gay-themed souvenirs (usually daily 10:00-18:00, 11:00-17:00 in winter, closed Tue-Wed Jan-Feb).

Advance Tickets and Sightseeing Cards

Advance Tickets for Major Sights: Avoid long ticket lines during high season (late March through October) by buying tickets online for the Anne Frank House, Rijksmuseum, Van Gogh Museum, and Stedelijk modern-art museum.

It's easy to buy tickets through each museum's website: www.annefrank.org (€0.50 surcharge per ticket, but worth it), www.rijksmuseum.nl, www.vangoghmuseum.com, and www.stedelijk.nl (no extra fee for Rijks, Van Gogh, or Stedelijk). Print out your ticket and bring it to the ticket-holder's line for a quick entry.

You can also buy tickets for these sights in advance at

Amsterdam's TIs, but the lines at the TIs seem almost as long as the ones you're trying to avoid at the sights.

Tips if You Don't Have Advance Tickets: Use a Museumkaart to get in quickly at covered sights (details in "Sightseeing Cards," next). If you haven't reserved a ticket for the Anne Frank House, trim your wait in line by arriving the minute it opens, or late in the day; this works better in early spring and fall than in summer, when even after-dinner lines can be long. Visit the Van Gogh Museum on a Friday evening, when it's open until 22:00, with no lines and few crowds, even in peak season.

Sightseeing Cards: Two cards merit consideration for heavy-duty sightseers. If your trip includes Haarlem or any other Dutch city, you're more likely to save more money with the Museumkaart, which covers many sights throughout the Netherlands, than the overpriced I amsterdam City Card, which is valid only ~~in~~ Amsterdam. (There's no reason to buy both.) However, if Amsterdam's your only stop in the Netherlands, and if you plan to get around on transit (rather than by bike), the I amsterdam City Card makes sense, as it includes a transit pass. Both cards allow free entry to most of the sights in Amsterdam (including the Rijks and Van Gogh museums), but neither card covers the Heineken Brewery, Westerkerk tower, or any sights dealing with sex or marijuana. The Anne Frank House is covered by the Museumkaart but not the I amsterdam City Card.

The **Museumkaart,** which costs €45 and is valid for a year throughout the Netherlands, is a no-brainer for anyone visiting at least six museums (for example, an itinerary that includes these museums, for a total of €63: Rijksmuseum-€14, Van Gogh Museum-€14, Anne Frank House-€9, Amsterdam Museum-€10, Amstelkring Museum-€8, and the Dutch Resistance Museum-€8). The Museumkaart is sold at all participating museums, and—except at the Anne Frank House—you can use it to skip the ticket-buying line (though everyone has to go through security). If you plan to buy a Museumkaart, get it at a smaller, less-crowded museum (such as the Amsterdam Museum). You'll see ads for the **Holland Pass,** but it's not worth it—the Museumkaart is a much better deal.

The **I amsterdam City Card,** which focuses on Amsterdam and includes most transportation, is not worth the cost unless you're planning on a day or two of absolutely non-stop sightseeing, and connecting it all by public transit. Along with many sights and discounts, this pass includes one free canal boat tour and unlimited use of trams, buses, and metro—but not trains (and except for the canal tour, all of these public-transit options are covered by a normal transit pass anyway—see "Getting Around Amsterdam," later). You have a set number of consecutive hours to use it (for example: Visit your first museum at 14:00 Mon with a 24-hour pass, and it's good until 13:59 on Tue). This pass doesn't allow you to skip lines at major sights, except at the Van Gogh Museum (€38/24 hours, €48/48 hours, or €58/72 hours; sold at major museums, TIs, and with shorter lines at the GVB transit office across from Central Station, next to TI; www.iamsterdamcard.com).

Arrival in Amsterdam

By Train

The portal connecting Amsterdam to the world is its aptly named Central Station (Amsterdam Centraal). Through at least 2014, expect the station and the plaza in front of it to be a chaotic construction zone—the station is being completely reworked, and the locations of things described here may change before your visit.

Trains arrive on a level above the station. Go down the stairs or the escalator (at the "A" end of the platform). Descending from the platforms, you'll find yourself in one of the corridors leading to the street exit for the city center (Centrum).

The station is fully equipped for the traveler. You'll find GWK Travelex counters (described earlier) in both the east and west corridors, and international ticket offices near the exit of both corridors. Luggage lockers are in the east corridor, under the "B" end of the platforms (€5-7/24 hours, depending on size of bag, always open, can fill up on busy summer weekends). The station has plenty of shops and places to grab a bite to eat. On the train level, platform 2 is lined with eateries, including the tall, venerable, 1920s-style **First Class Grand Café.** Handy **Albert Heijn** supermarkets are easy to find at the ends of both the east and west corridors.

Exiting the station, you're in the heart of the city. Straight ahead, just past the canal, is Damrak street, leading to Dam Square. To your left are the TI and GVB public-transit offices. Farther to your left are bike rentals (**MacBike** is located in the station building, and **Star Bikes** is a five-minute walk past it, both listed on page 1110). To the right of the station are the postcard-perfect neighborhoods of West Amsterdam; some of my recommended hotels are within walking distance (see map on page 1138).

Just beyond the taxis are the platforms for the city's blue trams, which come along frequently, ready to take you anywhere your feet won't (buy ticket or pass from conductor). Trams #1, #2, and #5 (which run to nearly all my recommended hotels) leave from in front of the station's west (main) entrance. All trams leaving Central Station stop at Dam Square along their route. For more on the transit system, see page 1108.

By Plane

For details on getting from Schiphol Airport into downtown Amsterdam, see "Amsterdam Connections," at the end of this chapter.

Helpful Hints

Theft Alert: Tourists are considered green and rich, and the city has more than its share of hungry thieves—especially on trams and at the many hostels. Wear your money belt.

Emergency Telephone Number: Throughout the Netherlands, dial 112.

Street Smarts: Beware of silent transportation—trams and bicycles—when walking around town. Don't walk on tram tracks or pink/maroon bicycle paths. Before you step off any sidewalk, do a double- or triple-check in both directions to make sure all's clear.

Sightseeing Strategies: To beat the lines at Amsterdam's most popular sights, plan ahead. You can bypass the main ticket-buyers' line at the Anne Frank House, and the Rijks, Van Gogh, and Stedelijk museums by buying online tickets before you go (see page 1103 for details). Friday night is a great time to visit the Van Gogh Museum, which is open until 22:00 (far smaller crowds then).

Shop Hours: Most shops are open Tuesday through Saturday 10:00-18:00, and Sunday and Monday 12:00-18:00. Some shops stay open later (21:00) on Thursdays. Supermarkets are generally open Monday through Saturday 8:00-20:00 and are closed on Sundays.

Festivals: Every year, **Queen's Day** (Koninginnedag, April 30) and **Gay Pride** (early Aug) bring crowds, fuller hotels, and higher room prices.

Cash Only: Thrifty Dutch merchants hate paying the unusually high fees charged by credit-card companies here; expect to pay cash in unexpected places, including grocery stores, cafés, budget hotels, train station machines and windows, and at some museums.

Internet Access: It's easy at cafés all over town, but the best place for serious surfing and email is the towering **Central Library**, which has hundreds of fast, free terminals (Openbare Bibliotheek Amsterdam, daily 10:00-22:00, free Wi-Fi, a 10-minute walk from train station, described on page 1127). "Coffeeshops," which sell marijuana, usually also offer Internet access—letting you surf with a special bravado.

English Bookstores: For fiction and guidebooks—including mine—try the **American Book Center** at Spui 12, right on the square (Mon 11:00-20:00, Tue-Sat 10:00-20:00 except Thu until 21:00, Sun 11:00-18:30, tel. 020/535-2575, www.abc.nl). The huge and helpful **Selexyz Scheltema** is at Koningsplein 20 near the Leidsestraat (store open Mon 11:00-18:00, Tue-Sat 9:30-18:00 except Thu until 21:00, Sun 12:00-18:00; lots of English novels, guidebooks, and maps; tel. 020/523-1411). **Waterstone's Booksellers,** a UK chain, also sells British newspapers (near Spui at 152 Kalverstraat, Mon-Sat 10:00-18:30 except Mon until 18:00 and Thu until 21:00, Sun 11:00-18:00, tel. 020/638-3821).

Free Publications: Hefty, hip, and helpful *Amsterdam Magazine* ("Beyond Windmills, Wooden Shoes, and Weed") includes a city map, and is available all over the city. Boom Chicago's magazine, aimed at the hostelling crowd, is handed out on Leidseplein and available in some spots across town. You may find one or both of these in your hotel room: *Visitors Guide Amsterdam,* sort of a mini-yellow-pages for tourists, with a fairly crummy map but good tips and (paid) listings; and *Rush on Amsterdam,* a glossy quarterly magazine that has current info on what's on at the city's museums, and even includes a pretty good map.

Entertainment: Pick up a copy of *Time Out Amsterdam* at either TI or the bookstores listed above (€3), check out this chapter's "Entertainment in Amsterdam" section, or call the **AUB/Last Minute Ticket Shop** (theater, classical music, and major rock shows, tickets sold only at shop, Leidseplein 26, tel. 0900-0191, calls costs €0.40/minute, www.amsterdamsuitburo.nl, www.lastminuteticketshop.nl).

Maps: The free tourist maps can be confusing, except for *Amsterdam Museums: Guide to 37 Museums* (includes tram info and stops, ask for it at the big museums, such as the Van Gogh). Several free magazines, listed above, include decent and detachable maps. If you want a top-notch map, buy one (about €2.50). I like the *Carto Studio Centrumkaart Amsterdam.* Amsterdam Anything's virtual "Go Where the Locals Go" city map is worth checking out, especially if you have mobile Internet access (www.amsterdamanything.nl).

Pharmacy: The shop named **DA** (Dienstdoende Apotheek) has all the basics—shampoo and toothpaste—as well as a pharmacy counter hidden in the back (Mon-Sat 9:00-22:00, Sun 11:00-22:00, Leidsestraat 74-76 near where it meets Keizersgracht, tel. 020/627-5351).

Laundry: Try **Clean Brothers Wasserij** in the Jordaan (daily 8:00-20:00 for €7 self-service, €9 drop-off—ready in an hour—Mon-Fri 9:00-17:00, Sat 9:00-18:00, no drop-off Sun, Westerstraat 26, one block from Prinsengracht, tel. 020/627-9888) or **Powders** near Leidseplein (daily 7:00-22:00, €6.50

self-service, €10 drop-off available Mon-Wed and Fri 8:00-17:00, Sat-Sun 9:00-15:00, no drop-off Thu, Kerkstraat 56, one block south of Leidsestraat, mobile 06-2630-6057).

Best Views: While the **Westerkerk** offers fine views from its tower (and is convenient if you're visiting the Anne Frank House), the best city views are from the **Central Library** (Openbare Bibliotheek Amsterdam; see page 1127). Other good views are from the Oude Kerk tower and the rooftop terrace at the NEMO Science Museum.

Getting Around Amsterdam

Amsterdam is big, and you'll find the trams handy. The longest walk a tourist would make is an hour from Central Station to the Rijksmuseum. When you're on foot, be extremely vigilant for silent but potentially painful bikes, trams, and crotch-high curb posts.

If you've got a car, park it—all you'll find are frustrating one-way streets, terrible parking, and meter maids with a passion for booting cars parked incorrectly. You'll pay €55 a day to park safely in a central garage, about €27 for a "day ticket" to park on the street (9:00-19:00), and about €3.50/hour in a parking lot. If you must bring a car to Amsterdam, it's best to leave it at one of the city's supervised park-and-ride lots (follow *P&R* signs from freeway, €6/24 hours, includes round-trip transit into city center for up to five people, 4-day maximum).

By Tram, Bus, and Metro

Amsterdam's public transit system includes trams, buses, and an underground metro; of these, trams are most useful for most tourists.

Tickets: The entire country's public transit network operates on a single ticket system called the OV-Chipkaart (for "Openbaar Vervoer"—public transit). For locals, it couldn't be easier. With a single pre-paid card, they can hop on any form of public transit in the country, scan their card, and the fare is immediately deducted. Cards can be reloaded automatically, straight from residents' bank accounts.

But travelers—who generally stay only a few days—must still rely on either single tickets or multiday passes. (While officially classified as "OV-Chipkaarten," these tickets and passes with electronic chips are nothing like the reloadable, valid-nationwide, plastic cards locals use.)

Within Amsterdam, a single transit ticket costs €2.60 and is good for one hour on the tram, bus, and metro, including transfers. Passes good for unlimited transportation are available for 24 hours (€7), 48 hours (€11.50), 72 hours (€15.50), and 96 hours (€19.50).

(The I amsterdam City Card, described on page 1104, includes a transit pass.) Given how expensive single tickets are, consider buying a pass or renting a bike for your stay before you buy that first ticket.

The easiest way to buy a ticket or transit pass is to simply board a tram or bus and pay the conductor (no extra fee). Tickets and passes are also available at metro station vending machines (there's one just outside Central Station), at GVB public-transit offices, and at TIs.

The helpful GVB public-transit information office in front of Central Station can answer questions (next to TI, Mon-Fri 7:00-21:00, Sat-Sun 10:00-18:00). Its free, multilingual *Public Transport Amsterdam Tourist Guide* includes a transit map and explains ticket options and tram connections to all the sights. For more public transit information, visit www.gvb.nl.

Trams: Board the tram at any entrance not marked with a red/white "do not enter" sticker. If you need a ticket or pass, pay the conductor (in a booth at the back); if there's no conductor, pay the driver in front. You must always "check in" as you board by scanning your ticket or pass at the pink-and-white scanner, and "check out" by scanning it again when you get off. The scanner will beep and flash a green light after a successful scan. Be careful not to accidentally scan your ticket or pass twice while boarding, or it becomes invalid. Checking in and out is very important, as controllers do pass through and fine violators. When you reach your stop, to open the door, press a green button on one of the poles near an exit.

Trams #2 *(Nieuw Sloten)* and #5 *(A'veen Binnenhof)* travel the north-south axis, from Central Station to Dam Square to Leidseplein to Museumplein (Van Gogh and Rijks museums). Tram #1 (marked *Osdorp*) also runs to Leidseplein. At Central Station, these three trams depart from the west side of Stationsplein (with the station behind you, they're to your right).

Tram #14—which doesn't connect to Central Station—goes east-west (Westerkerk-Dam Square-Muntplein-Waterlooplein-Plantage). If you get lost in Amsterdam, don't sweat it—10 of the city's 17 trams take you back to Central Station.

Buses and Metro: Tickets and passes work on buses and the metro just as they do on the trams—scan your ticket or pass to "check in" as you enter and again to "check out" when you leave. The metro system is scant—used mostly for commuting to the suburbs—but it does connect Central Station with some sights east of Damrak (Nieuwmarkt-Waterlooplein-Weesperplein). The glacial speed of the metro-expansion project is a running joke among cynical Amsterdammers.

By Bike

Everyone—bank managers, students, pizza delivery boys, and police—uses this mode of transport. It's by far the smartest way to travel in a city where 40 percent of all traffic rolls on two wheels. You'll get around town by bike faster than you can by taxi. On my last visit, I rented a bike for five days, chained it up outside my hotel at night, and enjoyed wonderful mobility. I highly encourage this for anyone who wants to get maximum fun per hour in Amsterdam. One-speed bikes, with *"brrrringing"* bells, rent for about €10 per day (cheaper for longer periods) at any number of places—hotels can send you to the nearest spot.

Rental Shops: Star Bikes Rental has cheap rates, long hours, and inconspicuous black bikes. They're happy to arrange an after-hours drop-off if you give your credit-card number and pre-pay (€5/4 hours, €7/day, €9/24 hours, €12/2 days, €17/3 days, daily 9:00-19:00, requires ID but no monetary deposit, 5-minute walk from east end of Central Station at De Ruyterkade 127, tel. 020/620-3215, www.starbikesrental.com).

MacBike, with 900 bikes and counting, is the bike-rental powerhouse—you'll see their bright red bikes all over town (they do stick out a bit). It has a huge and efficient outlet at Central Station (€7/3 hours, €9.50/24 hours, €14/48 hours, €19/72 hours, more for 3 gears, 25 percent discount with I amsterdam City Card, €50 deposit plus passport or credit-card imprint, no helmets, daily 9:00-17:45; at east end of station—on the left as you're leaving; tel. 020/620-0985, www.macbike.nl). They have two smaller, satellite stations at Leidseplein (Weteringschans 2) and Waterlooplein (Nieuwe Uilenburgerstraat 116). Return your bike to the station where you rented it. MacBike sells several pamphlets outlining bike tours with a variety of themes in and around Amsterdam for €1-2.

Frederic Rent-a-Bike, a 10-minute walk from Central Station, has quality bikes and a helpful staff (€8/3 hours, €15/24 hours, €25/48 hours, €60/week, 10 percent discount on multiday rental with this book, daily 9:00-17:30, no after-hours drop-off, Brouwersgracht 78, tel. 020/624-5509, www.frederic.nl).

Lock Your Bike: Bike thieves are bold and brazen in Amsterdam. Bikes come with two locks and stern instructions to use both. The wimpy ones go through the spokes, and the industrial-strength chains are meant to be wrapped around the actual body of the bike and through the front wheel, and connected to something stronger than any human. Do this diligently. If you're sloppy, it's an expensive mistake and one that any "included" theft insurance won't cover.

More Tips: No one wears a helmet. For safety, use arm signals, follow the bike-only traffic signals, stay in the obvious and omnipresent bike lanes, and yield to traffic on the right. Fear oncoming trams and tram tracks. Carefully cross tram tracks at a perpendicular angle to avoid catching your tire in the rut. Warning: Police ticket cyclists the same as they do drivers. Obey all traffic signals, and walk your bike through pedestrian zones. Fines for biking through pedestrian zones are reportedly €30-50. A handy bicycle route-planner can be found at www.routecraft.com (select "bikeplanner," then click British flag at far right for English). For a "Do-It-Yourself Bike Tour of Amsterdam" and for bike tours, see page 1114.

By Boat

While the city is great on foot, bike, or tram, you can also get around Amsterdam by boat. **Rederij Lovers** boats shuttle tourists on a variety of routes covering different combinations of the city's top sights. Their Museum Line, for example, costs €12.50, includes museum discounts, and stops near the Hermitage, Rijksmuseum/ Van Gogh Museum, and Central Station (at least every 45 minutes, 4 stops, 1.5 hours). Sales booths in front of Central Station (and the boats) offer free brochures listing museum hours and admission prices. Most routes come with recorded narration and run daily 10:00-17:30 (tel. 020/530-1090, www.lovers.nl).

The similar **Canal Bus** is actually a boat, offering 14 stops on four different boat routes (€22/24-hour pass, departures daily 10:00-18:00, until 22:00 April-Oct, leaves near Central Station and Rederij Lovers dock, tel. 020/623-9886, www.canal.nl). They also run smaller tour boats with live commentary (see next page).

If you're simply looking for a floating, nonstop tour, the regular canal tour boats (without the stops) give more information, cover more ground, and cost less (see "Tours in Amsterdam," next page).

For do-it-yourself canal tours and lots of exercise, Canal Bus also rents "canal bikes" (a.k.a. paddleboats) at several locations: near the Anne Frank House, near the Rijksmuseum, near Leidseplein, and where Leidsestraat meets Keizersgracht (€8/hour per person, daily July-Aug 10:00-22:00, Sept-June 10:00-18:00).

By Taxi

For short rides, Amsterdam is a bad town for taxis. Given the fine tram system and ease of biking, I use taxis less in Amsterdam than in just about any other city in Europe. The city's taxis have a high drop charge (€7.50) for the first two kilometers (e.g. from Central Station to the Mint Tower), after which it's €2.30 per kilometer (no extra fee for luggage; it's worth trying to bargain a lower rate, as competition among cabbies is fierce). You can wave them down, find a rare taxi stand, or call one (tel. 020/677-7777). You'll also see **bike taxis,** particularly near Dam Square and Leidseplein. Negotiate a rate for the trip before you board (no meter), and they'll wheel you wherever you want to go (€1/3 minutes, no surcharge for baggage or extra weight, sample fare from Leidseplein to Anne Frank House: about €6).

Tours in Amsterdam

By Boat

▲▲**Canal Boat Tours**—These long, low, tourist-laden boats leave continually from several docks around town for a relaxing, if uninspiring, one-hour introduction to the city (with recorded headphone commentary). Select a boat tour for convenience based on the starting point, or if a particular tour is free and included with the I amsterdam City Card (which covers Blue Boat Company and Holland International boats). Tip: Boats leave only when full, so jump on a full boat to avoid waiting at the dock. Choose from one of these three companies:

Rondvaart Kooij is cheapest (€8.50, 3/hour in summer 10:00-22:00, 2/hour in winter 10:00-17:00, at corner of Spui and Rokin streets, about 10 minutes from Dam Square, tel. 020/623-3810, www.rederijkooij.nl).

Blue Boat Company's boats depart from near Leidseplein (€13; every half-hour April-Sept 10:00-18:00, also at 19:00; hourly Oct-March 10:00-17:00, 1.25 hours, Stadhouderskade 30, tel. 020/679-1370, www.blueboat.nl). Their 90-minute evening cruise has a live English-speaking guide (€15, nightly at 20:00, April-Sept also at 21:00 and 22:00, reservations required).

Holland International offers a standard one-hour trip and a variety of longer tours (€13, 1-hour "100 Highlights" tour with recorded commentary, 4/hour daily 9:00-22:00, 2/hour after 18:00; tel. 020/625-3035, www.hir.nl). Their €18, 90-minute "ultimate" tour with a live guide leaves twice daily (at 11:00 and 13:00).

No fishing allowed—but bring your camera. Some prefer to cruise at night, when the bridges are illuminated.

Hop-On, Hop-Off Canal Boats—Small, 12-person electric Canal Hopper boats leave every 20-30 minutes with live commentary on two different hop-on, hop-off routes (€22 day pass, €17 round-trip ticket, July-Aug daily 10:00-17:00, Sept-June Fri-Sun only, "yellow" west route runs 2/hour and stops near Anne Frank House and Rijksmuseum, less-frequent "orange" east route runs 3/hour and stops near Red Light District and Damrak, tel. 020/535-3303, www.canal.nl).

Wetlands Safari, Nature Canoe Tours near Amsterdam—If you want some exercise and a dose of village life, consider this five-hour tour. Majel Tromp, a friendly villager who speaks great English, takes groups limited to 15 people. The program: Meet at the bus stops behind Central Station (leave the station from the west corridor and take the escalator up to the buses) at 9:30, catch a public bus, stop for coffee, take a 3.5-hour canoe trip (2-3 people per canoe) with several stops, tour a village by canoe, munch a rural canalside picnic lunch (included), then canoe and bus back into Amsterdam by 15:00 (€43, discount with this book, May-mid-Sept Sun-Fri, reservations required, tel. 020/686-3445, mobile 06-5355-2669, www.wetlandssafari.nl, info@wetlandssafari.nl).

On Foot

Red Light District Tours—**Randy Roy's Red Light Tours** consists of one expat American woman, Kimberley. She lived in the Red Light District for years and gives fun, casual, yet informative 90-minute walks through this fascinating and eye-popping neighborhood. While the actual information is light, you'll walk through various porn and drug shops and have an expert to answer your questions. Call or email to reserve (€12.50 includes a drink in a colorful bar at the end, nightly at 20:00, Fri and Sat also at 22:00, no tours Dec-Feb, tours meet in front of Victoria Hotel—in front of Central Station, mobile 06-4185-3288, www.randyroysredlight tours.com, kimberley@randyroysredlighttours.com).

Free City Walk—**New Europe Tours** "employs" native, English-speaking students to give these irreverent and entertaining three-hour walks (using the same "free tour, ask for tips, sell their other tours" formula popular in so many great European cities). This long walk covers a lot of the city with an enthusiasm for the contemporary pot-and-prostitution scene (free, daily at 11:15 and 13:15, just show up at the National Monument on Dam Square, www .neweuropetours.eu).

Adam's Apple Tours—This walking tour offers a two-hour, English-only look at the historic roots and development of Amsterdam. You'll have a small group of generally 5-6 people and a caring guide, starting off at Central Station and ending up at Dam Square (€25; May-Sept daily at 10:00, 12:30, and 15:00 based on demand; call 020/616-7867 to confirm times and book, www .adamsapple.nl, Frank).

Private Guide—**Albert Walet** is a likeable, hardworking, and knowledgeable local guide who enjoys personalizing tours for Americans interested in knowing his city. "Ab" specializes in history and architecture, and exudes a passion for Amsterdam (€59/2 hours, €99/4 hours, up to 4 people, on foot or by bike, mobile 06-2069-7882, abwalet@yahoo.com). Ab also takes travelers to nearby towns, including Haarlem, Leiden, and Delft.

By Bike

The **Yellow Bike Guided Tours** company offers city bike tours of either two hours (€18.50, daily at 10:30) or three hours (€21.50, daily at 13:30), which both include a 20-minute break. They also offer a four-hour, 15-mile tour of the dikes and green pastures of the countryside (€27.50, lunch extra, includes 45-minute break, April-Oct daily at 19:30). All tours leave from Nieuwezijds Kolk 29, three blocks from Central Station (reservations smart, tel. 020/620-6940, www.yellowbike.nl). If you take one of their tours, you can rent the bike for the rest of the day at a 50 percent discount (€10/24 hours, ID and either €100 deposit or credit-card imprint required). If you'd prefer a private guide, see Albert Walet, above.

Do-It-Yourself Bike Tour of Amsterdam—A day enjoying the bridges, bike lanes, and sleepy, off-the-beaten-path canals on your own one-speed is an essential Amsterdam experience. The real joys of Europe's best-preserved 17th-century city are the countless intimate glimpses it offers: the laid-back locals sunning on their porches under elegant gables, rusted bikes that look as if they've been lashed to the same lamppost since the 1960s, wasted hedonists planted on canalside benches, and happy sailors permanently moored, but still manning the deck.

For a good day trip, rent a bike at or near Central Station (see "By Bike" on page 1110). Head west down Haarlemmerstraat, working your wide-eyed way down the Prinsengracht (drop into Café 't Papeneiland at Prinsengracht 2) and detouring through the small, gentrified streets of the Jordaan neighborhood before popping out at Westerkerk under the tallest spire in the city.

Pedal south to the lush and peaceful Vondelpark, then cut back through the center of town (Leidseplein to the Mint Tower, along Rokin street to Dam Square). From there, cruise the Red Light District, following Oudezijds Voorburgwal past the Old Church (Oude Kerk) to Zeedijk street, and return to the train station.

By Public Minibus

For a quick, do-it-yourself public-bus tour along scenic Prinsengracht, catch Amsterdam's cute little Stop/Go minibus (€1, tickets valid one hour, buy from driver, transit passes valid, daily 9:00-17:30, 8 seats, can be muggy on hot days, www.gvb.nl).

It arcs along the city's longest canal, offering clever budget travelers a very cheap and fun 20-minute experience that's faster than a touristy canal tour. The scenic bus ride goes where normal big buses can't fit (along the bumpy and cobbled canalside lanes), giving you a delightful look at the workaday city. The high ride, comfortable seats, and big windows show you Amsterdam well.

The Stop/Go route follows the outside of the canal counterclockwise and returns clockwise along the inside. The buses have only four set stops (in front of the Central Library, at the river docks behind Central Station, at the main/west entrance of Central Station, and near the opera house/City Hall—Stopera—on Waterlooplein)—but you can just wave one down from anywhere on the route. Grab a seat in the back for the best view. If you see something fun, just jump out—there's another bus in 12 minutes. If the bus hits construction on Prinsengracht, it veers to the next street over, then heads back to the canal as soon as possible.

For this short tour, catch the bus at Central Station. From the station, the minibus passes characteristic cafés in the Jordaan district, countless houseboats, and the whole gamut of gables (under a parade of leaning, Golden Age buildings complete with all the hooks and pulleys). Rolling along the Prinsengracht, you'll see the long line at the Anne Frank House just before the towering Westerkerk. You'll pass within a block of the thriving Leidseplein and Rijksmuseum (look to the right at Spiegelgracht) before passing Rembrandtplein (with its fun 3-D *Night Watch* statues) and crossing the Amstel River to finish at the Waterlooplein flea market, near Rembrandt's House, Gassan Diamonds, and the metro station (subway trains run every 2 minutes, returning you to Central Station in 3 minutes).

From the bus, watch for these little bits of Amsterdam:

- green, metal public urinals
- late 19th-century lamp poles
- bikes chained to anything unmovable (including the practical new "staple" design bike racks)
- *amsterdammertjes* ("little Amsterdammers," referring to the countless, little, dark-red bollards—bearing the city's emblem of three diagonal crosses—that protect walkers from passing traffic)
- underground recycling and garbage bins designed to keep workers from having to dump out bins into trucks (a law prohibits employees from lifting anything over 25 kilos—about 55 pounds)
- "*ja*" and "*nee*" stickers on mail slots, indicating whether residents accept junk mail and advertising. (The cool people of the Jordaan are mostly "*nee nee.*")

Sights in Amsterdam

One of Amsterdam's delights is that it has perhaps more small specialty museums than any other city its size. From houseboats to sex, from marijuana to Old Masters, you can find a museum to suit your interests.

Amsterdam

**Map labels (as shown):**

HARBOR

IJ RIVER

¼ MILE / 400 METERS

TO WATERLAND, ZAANSE SCHANS & ALKMAAR

TO NDSM PIER

CITY LIBRARY

CENTRAL STATION

MARITIME MUSEUM (REOPENS LATE 2011)

VOC SHIP

NEMO

OOSTERDOK

TO HAARLEM

PRINS HENDRIKKADE

PRINS HENDRIKKADE

KEIZERS- / HEREN- / SINGEL / PRINSEN

DAMRAK

Old Church

RED LIGHT DISTRICT

REMBRANDT HOUSE

TO DUTCH RESISTANCE MUSEUM

ANNE FRANK HOUSE

New Church

JORDAAN

WESTER-KERK

RAADHUIS

STR. KALVER

ROYAL PAL.

AMSTERDAM MUSEUM

DAM

HOOGSTR.

HEMP MUSEUM

JODEN-BREEN

WATERLOO-PLEIN

OPERA

MUIDER.

HERMI-TAGE AMST.

HOUSE-BOAT MUSEUM

"NINE LITTLE STREETS" SHOPS

BEGIJNHOF

SPUI STRAAT

LEIDSESTRAAT

MUNT-PLEIN

TASSEN MUSEUM

WILL-HOL MUSEUM?

AMSTEL

SPIEGEL STR.

UTRECHTSE STR.

SINGELGRACHT

LEIDSE

LEIDSE-PLEIN

KADE

STADHOUDERSKADE

HEINEKEN EXP.

VAN BAERLESTR.

VONDEL

House of Bols

HOOFT

PAUL POTTER

RIJKS-MUSEUM

DE PIJP DISTRICT

MUSEUM-PLEIN

VAN GOGH MUSEUM

PARK

Vondel Pavilion

STEDELIJK MUSEUM

DCH

Legend:

Major Canals
Other Water
B Canal Boat Departure Point
View

AMSTERDAM

For tips on how to save time otherwise spent in the long ticket-buying lines of the big three museums—the Anne Frank House, Van Gogh Museum, and Rijksmuseum—see "Advance Tickets and Sightseeing Cards" on page 1103. Admission prices are high: A sightseeing card such as the Museumkaart, or I amsterdam City Card, can pay for itself quickly. Entry to most sights is free with a card (I've noted those that aren't covered).

Most museums require baggage check (usually free, often in coin-op lockers where you get your coin back).

The following sights are arranged by neighborhood for handy sightseeing.

Southwest Amsterdam

▲▲▲**Rijksmuseum**—At the Rijksmuseum ("Rijks" rhymes with "bikes"), Holland's Golden Age shines with the best collection anywhere of the Dutch Masters—from Vermeer's quiet domestic scenes, to Steen's raucous family meals, to Hals' snapshot portraits, to Rembrandt's moody brilliance.

The 17th century saw the Netherlands at the pinnacle of its power. The Dutch had won their independence from Spain, trade and shipping boomed, wealth poured in, the people were understandably proud, and the arts flourished. This era was later dubbed the Dutch Golden Age. With no church bigwigs or royalty around to commission big canvases in the Protestant Dutch republic, artists had to find different patrons—and they discovered the upper-middle-class businessmen who fueled Holland's capitalist economy. Artists painted their portraits and decorated their homes with pretty still lifes and non-preachy, slice-of-life art.

Dutch art is meant to be enjoyed, not studied. It's straightforward, meat-and-potatoes art for the common man. The Dutch love the beauty of everyday things painted realistically and with exquisite detail.

Gaze into the eyes of the men who made Amsterdam the richest city on earth in the 1600s.

The main core of the Rijksmuseum is closed until sometime in 2013 for a massive renovation. Thankfully, the most famous masterpieces—nearly everything on the typical tourist's hit list—are on display in the wonderful and easy-on-the-feet Philips Wing (southwest corner of the museum, the part of the building nearest the Van Gogh Museum). This delightful exhibit offers one of the most exciting and enjoyable art experiences in Europe.

Cost and Hours: €14, audioguide-€5, no photos, daily 9:00-18:00, last entry 30 minutes before closing, tram #2 or #5 from Central Station to Hobbemastraat. Info tel. 020/674-7047 or switchboard tel. 020/674-7000, www.rijksmuseum.nl. The Philips Wing entrance is near the corner of Hobbemastraat and Jan

Luijkenstraat, on the south side of the Rijksmuseum—the part of the huge building nearest the Van Gogh Museum.

Avoiding Crowds: The museum is most crowded from April to September (especially April to June), on weekends, and during morning hours. Avoid waits in the ticket-buying line by buying your ticket or pass in advance. No one can completely avoid the security line.

You can buy and print your ticket online at www.rijksmuseum .nl. The ticket is good anytime (no entry time specified). Buying online has the added advantage of letting you enter through the "fast lane," scooting you to the front of the security line.

You can also buy tickets at the TI, Keytours (near the museum at Paulus Potterstraat 8), at the AUB/Last Minute Ticket Shop on Leidseplein, and even at many hotels (may change with renovation).

▲▲▲**Van Gogh Museum**—Near the Rijksmuseum, the Van Gogh Museum (we say "van GO," the Dutch say "van HHHOCK") is a cultural high even for those not into art. This remarkable museum features works by the troubled Dutch artist whose art seemed to mirror his life.

The museum will close for renovations in October 2012 and reopen (with a new entrance, oriented toward Museumplein) in March 2013. While the museum is closed, about 75 of the collection's highlights will be on display at the nearby Hermitage Amsterdam; see page 1131.

Vincent, who killed himself in 1890 at age 37, is best known for sunny, Impressionist canvases that vibrate and pulse with vitality. The museum's 200 paintings—a stroll through the artist's work and life—were owned by Theo, Vincent's younger, art-dealer brother. If you like brightly colored landscapes in the Impressionist style, you'll like this museum. If you enjoy finding deeper meaning in works of art, you'll really love it. The mix of Van Gogh's creative genius, his tumultuous experiences, and the traveler's determination to connect to it makes this museum as much a walk with Vincent as with his art.

The main collection of Van Gogh paintings on the first floor is arranged chronologically, taking you through the changes in Vincent van Gogh's life and styles. The paintings are divided into five periods of Vincent's life—the Netherlands, Paris, Arles, St. Rémy, and Auvers-sur-Oise—proceeding clockwise around the floor. Highlights include *Sunflowers, The Bedroom, The Potato Eaters,* and many brooding self-portraits.

The third floor shows works that influenced Vincent, from Monet and Pissarro to Gauguin, Cézanne, and Toulouse-Lautrec. The worthwhile audioguide includes insightful commentaries and quotes from Vincent himself. Temporary exhibits fill the new

Southwest Amsterdam

100 YARDS
100 METERS

TO MINT TOWER
& DAM SQUARE

NASSAUKADE

1e CONSTANTIJN HUYGENSTRAAT

2e HELMERSSTR.

1e HELMERSSTR.

OVERTOOM

VONDELSTRAAT

TESSELSCHADE

SINGEL-GRACHT

STADHOUDERSKADE

LEIDSE

PRINSEN

GRACHT

KEIZERSGR.

LANGE LEIDSESTRAAT

KORTE

MARNIX STR.

LEIDSEKADE

LIJNBAANS STR.

STADS-
SCHOUW-
BURG

TICKETS

←LEIDSEPLEIN

LEIDSE-DWAARSSTR.

LEIDSE DWARS

LIJNBAANS GR.

NIEUWE SPIEGEL

GRACHT

MAX
EUWE-
PLEIN

WETERINGSCHANS

VONDEL
PAVILION

ZANDPAD

R. VISSCHERSTR.

VOSSIUSSTR.

HOBBEMASTR.

RIJKS-
MUSEUM

HOBBE

STR.

VONDEL-
PARK

P.C. HOOFTSTRAAT

VAN BAERLE-STR.

JAN-
LUIJKEN-STR.

House of
Bols

COSTER
DIAMONDS
+ MUSEUM

PAUL US

POTTERSTRAAT

POND

PHILIPS
WING

HOBBE

To
HEINEKEN
EXPERIENCE

KADE

STEDELIJK
MUSEUM

VAN EEGHENLAAN

VAN EEGHENSTR.

WILLEMSPARKWEG

VAN BREE.

CONCERT-
GEBOUW

DE LAIRESSESTR.

NICOLAAS

MUSEUM-
PLEIN

Van Gogh
Museum

GAB. METSUSSTR.

MAESSTRAAT

HONTHORSTSTR.

VERMEER

US
CONSULATE

DE HOOCHSTR.

PIETER

JOH.

COBRA
CAFÉ

HOBBEMA-
KADE

RUYSDAELKADE

DE PIJP
DISTRICT

N

DCH

B BOAT TOURS   --- PATH
T TRAM 2 & 5 STOP   ♦ ENTRY POINT TO SIGHTS

AMSTERDAM

wing, down the escalator from the ground floor lobby.

Cost and Hours: €14, more for special exhibits, audio-guide–€5, kids' audioguide–€2.50, no photos, daily 10:00-18:00, Fri until 22:00—with no crowds in evening, Paulus Potterstraat 7, tram #2 or #5 from Central Station to Van Baerlestraat stop, tel. 020/570-5200, www.vangoghmuseum.nl.

Avoiding Lines: Skip the 15-30-minute wait in the ticket-buying line by getting your ticket in advance. You can buy and print your ticket online at www.vangoghmuseum.nl. The ticket is good anytime (no entry time specified). You can also buy tickets at the TI or Keytours (just up the street at Paulus Potterstraat 8). Advance-ticket and pass holders can go right in.

▲▲**Stedelijk Museum**—After a long renovation project, the Stedelijk (STAYD-eh-lik) reopens in the fall of 2012 in its spiffed-up building, which now flaunts an architecturally daring new entry facing Museumplein (near the Van Gogh Museum). The Netherlands' top modern-art museum, its fun, far-out, and refreshing collection includes post-1945 experimental and conceptual art, and works by Picasso, Chagall, Cézanne, Kandinsky, and Mondrian.

Cost and Hours: Likely €12, Tue-Sun 10:00-17:00, possibly Thu until 22:00, possibly open Mon, check website for reopening date and exact price and hours, café with outdoor seating, top-notch shop, Paulus Potterstraat 13/Museumplein 10, tel. 020/573-2911, www.stedelijk.nl.

▲**Museumplein**—Bordered by the Rijks, Van Gogh, and Stedelijk museums, and the Concertgebouw (classical music hall), this park-like square is interesting even to art-haters. Amsterdam's best acoustics are found underneath the Rijksmuseum, where street musicians perform everything from chamber music to Mongolian throat singing. Mimes, human statues, and crafts booths dot the square. Skateboarders careen across a concrete tube, while locals enjoy a park bench or a coffee at the Cobra Café.

Nearby is **Coster Diamonds,** a handy place to see a diamond-cutting and polishing demo (free, frequent, and interesting 30-minute tours followed by sales pitch, popular for decades with tour groups, prices marked up to include tour guide kickbacks, daily 9:00-17:00, Paulus Potterstraat 2, tel. 020/305-5555, www.costerdiamonds.com). The end of the tour leads straight into their Diamond Museum, which is worthwhile only for those who have a Museumkaart (which covers entry) or feel the need to see even more diamonds (€7.50, daily 10:00-17:00, tel. 020/305-5300, www.diamantmuseumamsterdam.nl). The tour at **Gassan Diamonds** is free and better (see page 1129), but Coster is convenient to the Museumplein scene.

House of Bols: Cocktail & Genever Experience—This leading Dutch distillery runs a pricey and polished little museum/marketing opportunity across the street from the Van Gogh Museum. The "experience" is a self-guided walk through what is essentially an ad for Bols—"four hundred years of working on the art of mixing and blending...a celebration of gin"—with some fun sniffing opportunities and a drink at a modern, mirrored-out cocktail bar for a finale. (It's essentially the gin-flavored version of the Heineken Experience, listed below.) The highlight is a chance to taste up to five different local gins with a talkative expert guiding you. Then have your barista mix up the cocktail of your dreams—based on what you learned during your sniffing.

Cost and Hours: €12.50, not covered by Museumkaart, daily 12:00-18:30, Fri until 22:00, Sat until 20:00, last entry one hour before closing, must be 18, Paulus Potterstraat 14, tel. 020/570-8575, www.houseofbols.com. If you like the booze and hang out and talk, this can be a good deal (but do it after the Van Gogh Museum).

Heineken Experience—This famous old brewery welcomes visitors to a slick and entertaining beer-appreciation fest. It's a fun trip, if you can ignore the fact that you're essentially paying for an hour of advertising.

Cost and Hours: €16, includes two drinks, daily 11:00-19:00, last entry at 17:30; tram #16, #24, or #25 to Heinekenplein; an easy walk from Rijksmuseum, tel. 020/523-9222, www.heineken experience.com.

De Pijp District—This former working-class industrial and residential zone (behind the Heineken Experience, near the Rijksmuseum) is emerging as a colorful, vibrant district. Its spine is Albert Cuypstraat, a street taken over by a long, sprawling produce market packed with interesting people. The centerpiece is **Restaurant Bazar** (marked by a roof-capping golden angel), a church turned into a Middle Eastern food circus (see listing on page 1154).

▲Leidseplein—Brimming with cafés, this people-watching mecca is an impromptu stage for street artists, accordionists, jugglers, and unicyclists. It's particularly bustling on sunny afternoons. The Boom Chicago theater fronts this square (see "Entertainment in Amsterdam," later). Stroll nearby Lange Leidsedwarsstraat (one block north) for a taste-bud tour of ethnic eateries, from Greek to Indonesian.

▲▲Vondelpark—This huge and lively city park is popular with the Dutch—families with little kids, romantic couples, strolling seniors, and hippies sharing blankets and beers. It's a favored venue for free summer concerts. On a sunny afternoon, it's a hedonistic scene that seems to say, "Parents...relax."

Rembrandtplein and Tuschinski Theater—One of the city's premier nightlife spots is the leafy Rembrandtplein (the artist's statue stands here, along with a jaunty group of statues giving us *The Night Watch* in 3-D) and the adjoining Thorbeckeplein. Several late-night dance clubs keep the area lively into the wee hours. Utrechtsestraat is lined with upscale shops and restaurants. Nearby Reguliersdwarsstraat (a street one block south of Rembrandtplein) is a center for gay and lesbian nightclubs.

The **Tuschinski Theater,** a movie palace from the 1920s (a half-block from Rembrandtplein down Reguliersbreestraat), glitters inside and out. Still a working theater, it's a delightful old place to see first-run movies. The exterior is an interesting hybrid of styles, forcing the round peg of Art Nouveau into the square hole of Art Deco. The stone-and-tile facade features stripped-down, functional Art Deco squares and rectangles, but is ornamented with Art Nouveau elements—Tiffany-style windows, garlands, curvy iron lamps, Egyptian pharaohs, and exotic gold lettering over the door. Inside (lobby is free), the sumptuous decor features red carpets, nymphs on the walls, and semi-abstract designs. Grab a seat in the lobby and watch the ceiling morph (Reguliersbreestraat 26-28).

Houseboat Museum (Woonbootmuseum)—In the 1930s, modern cargo ships came into widespread use—making small, sail-powered cargo boats obsolete. In danger of extinction, these little vessels found new life as houseboats lining the canals of Amsterdam. Today, 2,500 such boats—their cargo holds turned into classy, comfortable living rooms—are called home. For a peek into this *gezellig* (cozy) world, visit this tiny museum. Captain Vincent enjoys showing visitors around the houseboat, which feels lived-in because, until 1997, it was.

   Cost and Hours: €3.50, not covered by Museumkaart; March-Oct Tue-Sun 11:00-17:00, closed Mon; Nov-Dec and Feb Fri-Sun 11:00-17:00, closed Mon-Thu; closed most of Jan; on Prinsengracht, opposite #296 facing Elandsgracht, tel. 020/427-0750, www.houseboatmuseum.nl.

West Amsterdam

▲▲▲Anne Frank House—A pilgrimage for many, this house offers a fascinating look at the hideaway of young Anne during the Nazi occupation of the Netherlands. Anne, her parents, an older sister, and four others spent a little more than two years in a "Secret Annex" behind her father's business. While in hiding, 13-year-old Anne kept a diary chronicling her extraordinary experience. Acting on a tip, the Nazis arrested the group in August of 1944 and sent them to concentration camps in Poland and Germany. Anne and her sister died of typhus in March of 1945, only weeks before their camp was liberated. Of the eight inhabitants of the Secret Annex, only Anne's father, Otto Frank, survived. He returned to Amsterdam and arranged for his daughter's diary to be published in 1947. It was followed by many translations, a play, and a movie.

   Pick up the English pamphlet at the door. The thoughtfully designed exhibit offers thorough coverage of the Frank family, the diary, the stories of others who hid, and the Holocaust. The Franks' story was that of Holland's Jews. The seven who died were among the more than 100,000 Dutch Jews killed during the war years. (Before the war, 135,000 Jews lived in the Netherlands.) Of Anne's school class of 87 Jews, only 20 survived. When her father returned to Amsterdam, he fought to preserve this house, wanting it to become, in his words, "more than a museum." It was his dream that visitors come away from the Anne Frank House with an indelible impression—and a better ability to apply the lessons of the Holocaust to our contemporary challenges.

Cost and Hours: €9, covered by Museumkaart but not by I amsterdam City Card; March 15-Sept 14 daily 9:00-21:00, Sat and July-Aug until 22:00; Sept 15-March 14 daily 9:00-19:00, Sat until 21:00; last entry 30 minutes before closing, no baggage check, no large bags allowed inside, Prinsengracht 267, near Westerkerk, tel. 020/556-7100, www.annefrank.org.

Avoiding Lines: Skip the long ticket-buying line (especially in the daytime during summer) by reserving an entry time and buying a ticket at the main TI or online at www.annefrank.org (€0.50/ticket fee). With your ticket in hand, you can skip the line and ring the buzzer at the low-profile door marked *Entrance: Reservations Only.* Without an advance ticket try arriving when the museum opens (at 9:00) or after 18:00. A Museumkaart does not allow you to skip the line here.

Westerkerk—Located near the Anne Frank House, this landmark church (free, generally open April-Sept Mon-Sat 11:00-15:00, closed Sun) has a barren interior, Rembrandt's body buried somewhere under the pews, and Amsterdam's tallest steeple.

The tower is open only for tours and offers a grand city view. The tour guide, who speaks in English and Dutch, tells of the church and its carillon. Only six people are allowed at a time (it's first-come, first-served), so lines can be long (€6, 30-minute tour; departures on the half hour April-Sept Mon-Sat 10:00-18:00, July-Aug until 20:00, last tour leaves at 30 minutes before closing, closed Sun; Oct-March tourable only with a private tour—call 020/689-2565 or email anna@buscher-malocca.nl).

Central Amsterdam, near Dam Square

Royal Palace (Koninklijk Huis)—This palace was built as a lavish city hall (1648-1655), when Holland was a proud new republic and Amsterdam was the richest city on the planet—awash in profit from trade. The building became a "Royal Palace" when Napoleon installed his brother Louis as king (1806). After Napoleon's fall, it continued as a royal residence for the Dutch royal family, the House of Orange. Today, it's one of four of Queen Beatrix's official residences. You can tour the interior and see several lavishly decorated rooms of chandeliers, paintings, statues, and furniture that reflect Amsterdam's former status as the center of global trade.

Cost and Hours: €7.50, daily 12:00-17:00 but often closed for official business—check calendar on website, tel. 020/620-4060, www.paleisamsterdam.nl.

New Church (Nieuwe Kerk)—Barely newer than the "Old" Church (located in the Red Light District), this 15th-century sanctuary has an intentionally dull interior, after the decoration was removed by 16th-century iconoclastic Protestants seeking to unclutter their communion with God. This is where many Dutch royal weddings and all coronations take place. There's usually a steep entrance fee due to popular temporary exhibitions.

Cost and Hours: €8; daily 10:00-17:00, Thu until 22:00, on Dam Square, info tel. 020/353-8168, tel. 020/638-6909, www.nieuwekerk.nl.

▲**Begijnhof**—Stepping into this tiny, idyllic courtyard in the city center, you escape into the charm of old Amsterdam. (Please be considerate of the people who live around the courtyard, and don't photograph the residents or their homes.) Notice house #34, a 500-year-old wooden structure (rare, since repeated fires taught city fathers a trick called brick). Peek into the hidden Catholic church, dating from the time when post-Reformation Dutch Catholics couldn't worship in public. It's opposite the English Reformed church, where the Pilgrims worshiped while waiting for their voyage to the New World—marked by a plaque near the door.

Cost and Hours: Free, open to visitors Mon-Tue and Thu-Sat—see website for sporadic hours—and Sun for church service in English at 10:30, closed Wed, on Begijnensteeg lane, just off Kalverstraat between #130 and #132, pick up flier at office near entrance, www.ercadam.nl.

▲▲**Amsterdam Museum**—Follow the city's growth from fishing village to world trade center to hippie haven. Housed in a 500-year-old former orphanage, this creative and hardworking museum features Rembrandt's paintings, fine English descriptions, and a carillon loft. The loft comes with push-button recordings of the town bell tower's greatest hits and a self-serve carillon "keyboard" that lets you ring a few bells yourself. The museum's free pedestrian corridor—lined with old-time group portraits—is a powerful teaser. This museum is a fine place to buy the Museumkaart, and then use it to skip long lines at the Van Gogh Museum (for details, see page 1104).

Cost and Hours: €10, good audioguide-€4, Mon-Fri 10:00-17:00, Sat-Sun 10:00-18:00, pleasant restaurant, next to Begijnhof, Kalverstraat 92, tel. 020/523-1822, www.ahm.nl.

Red Light District

▲▲**Amstelkring Museum (Our Lord in the Attic/Museum Ons' Lieve Heer op Solder)**—While Amsterdam has long been

Central Amsterdam

AMSTERDAM

BIKE GARAGE

CENTRAL STATION

BIKE RENTAL

CITY LIBRARY

SHOPS

PRINS-HENDRIK-

VVV

DAMRAK SEX MUSEUM

OOSTER-DOK

ST. NICHOLAS CHURCH

KADE

ZEEDIJK

PRINS-HENDRIKKADE

YELLOW BIKE TOURS

SPUISTRAAT

VOORBURG.

NIEUWE ZIJDS

DIJK

DAMRAK

AMSTEL-KRING MUSEUM

BEURS

STRAAT

TO NEMO & VOC SHIP

EROTIC MUSEUM

NEW CHURCH

NIEUWENJ.

WARMOES

OLD CHURCH

RED LIGHT DISTRICT

NIEUW-MARKT

SINT JANS

ROYAL PALACE

DAM

HEMP MUSEUM

DAM STRAAT

OUDEZIJDS ACHTER-BURGWAL

TO ANNE FRANK HOUSE & JORDAAN DISTRICT

KALVERSTRAAT

ROKIN

OUDEZIJDS VOOR-BURGWAL

REMBRANDT'S HOUSE

WATER-LOO-PLEIN

SPUI

OPERA

HISTORY MUSEUM

STR.

SPUI

ROKIN

AMSTEL

BEGIJNHOF

HEREN.

HUIDEN-STRAAT

SINGEL

TUSCHINSKI THEATER

WILLET-HOLTHUYSEN MUSEUM

MINT TOWER

MUNT-PLEIN

HEREN-

GRACHT

FLOWER MARKET

REMBRANDT-PLEIN

TASSEN MUSEUM

TO LEIDSEPLEIN & RIJKSMUSEUM

200 YDS.

200 METERS

DCH

M METRO   B OPSTAPPER BUS   B BOAT TOURS   ≼ VIEW

T TRAMS: #1 (TO LEIDSEPLEIN), #2 & #5 (TO MUSEUMPLEIN)

known for its tolerant attitudes, 16th-century politics forced Dutch Catholics to worship discreetly. Near the train station, in the Red Light District, you'll find a fascinating, hidden Catholic church filling the attic of three 17th-century merchants' houses.

For two centuries (1578-1795), Catholicism in Amsterdam was illegal, but tolerated (like pot in the 1970s). When hard-line Protestants took power in 1578, Catholic churches were vandalized and shut down, priests and monks were rounded up and kicked out of town, and Catholic kids were razzed on their way to school. The city's Catholics were forbidden to worship openly, so they gathered secretly to say Mass in homes and offices. In 1663, a wealthy merchant built this church, one of a handful of places in Amsterdam that served as a secret parish church until Catholics were once again allowed to worship in public.

This unique church comes with a little bonus: a rare glimpse inside a historic Amsterdam home straight out of a Vermeer painting. Don't miss the silver collection and other exhibits of daily life from 300 years ago.

Cost and Hours: €8, Mon-Sat 10:00-17:00, Sun and holidays 13:00-17:00, no photos, Oudezijds Voorburgwal 40, tel. 020/624-6604, www.opsolder.nl.

▲▲**Red Light District**—Europe's most touristed ladies of the night tease and tempt here, as they have for centuries, in 400 display-case windows around Oudezijds Achterburgwal and Oudezijds Voorburgwal, surrounding the Old Church (Oude Kerk, see below). Drunks and druggies make the streets uncomfortable late at night after the gawking tour groups leave (about 22:30), but it's a fascinating walk earlier in the evening.

The neighborhood, one of Amsterdam's oldest, has hosted prostitutes since 1200. Prostitution is entirely legal here, and the prostitutes are generally entrepreneurs, renting space and running their own businesses, as well as filling out tax returns and even paying union dues. Popular prostitutes net about €500 a day (for what's called "S&F" in its abbreviated, printable form, costing €25-50 per customer).

Sex Museums—Amsterdam has two sex museums: one in the Red Light District and another one a block in front of Central Station on Damrak street. While visiting one can be called sightseeing, visiting both is harder to explain. The one on Damrak is cheaper and more interesting. Here's a comparison:

The **Erotic Museum** in the Red Light District is five floors of uninspired paintings, videos, old photos, and sculpture (€7, not covered by Museumkaart, daily 11:00-1:00 in the morning, along the canal at Oudezijds Achterburgwal 54, tel. 020/624-7303).

The **Damrak Sex Museum** tells the story of pornography from Roman times through 1960. Every sexual deviation is revealed in various displays. The museum includes early French pornographic photos; memorabilia from Europe, India, and Asia; a Marilyn Monroe tribute; and some S&M displays (€4, not covered by Museumkaart, daily 9:30-23:30, Damrak 18, a block in front of Central Station, tel. 020/622-8376).

Old Church (Oude Kerk)—This 14th-century landmark—the needle around which the Red Light District spins—has served as a reassuring welcome-home symbol to sailors, a refuge to the down-trodden, an ideological battlefield of the Counter-Reformation, and today, a tourist sight with a dull interior (€5, more for temporary exhibits, Mon-Sat 11:00-17:00, Sun 13:00-17:00, tel. 020/625-8284, www.oudekerk.nl). It's 167 steps to the top of the church tower (€6, April-Sept Mon-Sat 13:00-17:00, closed Oct-March).

▲**Hash, Marijuana, and Hemp Museum**—This is a collection of dope facts, history, science, and memorabilia. While small, it has a very memorable finale: the high-tech grow room, in which dozens of varieties of marijuana are grown in optimal hydroponic (among other) environments. Some plants stand five feet tall and shine under the intense grow lamps. The view is actually through glass walls into the neighboring **Sensi Seed Bank Grow Shop** (at #150), which sells carefully cultivated seeds and all the gear needed to grow them.

Cost and Hours: €9, not covered by Museumkaart, daily 10:00-23:00, Oudezijds Achterburgwal 148, tel. 020/623-5961, www.hashmuseum.com.

The nearby **Cannabis College** is "dedicated to ending the global war against the cannabis plant through public education" (free, daily 11:00-19:00, Oudezijds Achterburgwal 124, tel. 020/423-4420, www.cannabiscollege.com). For more, see "Smoking" on page 1155.

Northeast Amsterdam

Central Library (Openbare Bibliotheek Amsterdam)—This huge, multistory glass building holds almost 1,400 seats—many with wraparound views of the city—and hundreds of free Internet terminals (and free Wi-Fi, which requires signing up at the desk). It's the classiest possible place to check email. This library, which opened in 2007, demonstrates the Dutch people's dedication to a freely educated populace (the right to information, they point out, is enshrined in the UN's Universal Declaration of Human Rights). This being Amsterdam, the library has almost twice as many bike racks as parking places. Everything's relaxed and inviting, from the fun kids' zone and international magazine and newspaper section on the ground floor to the cafeteria with its dramatic view-terrace dining on the top (La Place, €10 meals, salad bar, daily 10:00-21:00). The library is a 10-minute walk from the east end of Central Station (daily 10:00-22:00, tel. 020/523-0900, www.oba.nl).

NEMO (National Center for Science and Technology)—This kid-friendly science museum is a city landmark. Its distinctive copper-green building, jutting up from the water like a sinking ship, has prompted critics to nickname it the *Titanic*. Designed by Italian architect Renzo Piano (known for Paris' Pompidou Center and Berlin's Sony Center complex on Potsdamer Platz), the building's shape reflects its nautical surroundings as well as the curve of the underwater tunnel it straddles.

Several floors feature permanent and rotating exhibits that allow kids (and adults) to explore topics such as light, sound, and gravity, and play with bubbles, topple giant dominoes, and draw with lasers. The museum's motto: "It's forbidden NOT to touch!" Whirring, room-size pinball machines reputedly teach kids about physics. English explanations are available.

Up top is a restaurant with a great city view, as well as a sloping terrace that becomes a popular "beach" in summer, complete with lounge chairs, a sandbox, and a lively bar. On the bottom floor is an inexpensive cafeteria offering €3-5 sandwiches.

Cost and Hours: €13, July-Aug daily 10:00-17:00, Sept-June generally closed Mon, Oosterdok 2, above entrance to IJ tunnel, tel. 0900-919-1100—€0.35/minute, www.e-nemo.nl. It's a 15-minute walk from Central Station or bus #22, #42, or #43 to the Kadijksplein stop. The roof terrace—open until 19:30 in the summer—is generally free.

Netherlands Maritime Museum (Nederlands Scheepvaart-museum)—This huge collection of model ships, maps, and sea-battle paintings reopened in late 2011 after a major renovation. It fills the 300-year-old Dutch Navy Arsenal with interactive exhibits that allow visitors to explore five centuries of maritime history.

Docked outside is the *VOC Ship Amsterdam*, a replica of a type of ship called an East Indiaman, which had its heyday during the 17th and 18th centuries, sailing for the Dutch East India Company (abbreviated VOC, for Vereenigde Oostindische Compagnie—you'll see it on insignias throughout the boat). Even though trade was the name of the game, with scurvy thieves in the waters, ships such as the *Amsterdam* had to be prepared to defend themselves. You'll see plenty of muskets, as well as cannons and gunpowder kegs.

Wander the decks, then duck your head and check out the captain's and surgeon's quarters, packed with items they would have used. Don't forget to climb down into the hold. While the ship is a little light on good historical information (be sure to pick up the free flier, which explains terminology like the difference between the poop deck and the quarterdeck), it's still a shipshape sight that entertains naval history buffs as well as *Pirates of the Caribbean* fans.

Cost and Hours: €15; daily 9:00-17:00; English explanations, bus #22 or #42 to Kattenburgerplein 1, tel. 020/523-2222, www .scheepvaartmuseum.nl.

Southeast Amsterdam

To reach the following sights from the train station, take tram #9 or #14. All of these sights (except the Tropical Museum) are close to each other and can easily be connected into an interesting walk, or better yet, a bike ride. Several of the sights in southeast Amsterdam cluster near the large square, Waterlooplein, dominated by the modern opera house.

Waterlooplein Flea Market—For more than a hundred years, the Jewish Quarter flea market has raged daily except Sunday (at the Waterlooplein metro station, behind Rembrandt's House). The long, narrow park is filled with stalls selling cheap clothes, hippie stuff, old records, tourist knickknacks, and garage-sale junk.

▲**Rembrandt's House (Museum Het Rembrandthuis)**—A middle-aged Rembrandt lived here from 1639 to 1658 after his wife's death, as his popularity and wealth dwindled down to obscurity and bankruptcy. As you enter, ask when the next etching demonstration is scheduled and pick up the fine, included audioguide. Tour the place this way: Explore Rembrandt's reconstructed house (filled with exactly what his bankruptcy inventory of 1656 said he owned); imagine him at work in his reconstructed studio; marvel at his personal collection of exotic objects, many of which he included in paintings; attend the etching demonstration and ask the printer to explain the etching process (drawing in soft wax on a metal plate that's then dipped in acid, inked up, and printed); and then, for the finale, enjoy several rooms of original Rembrandt etchings. You're not likely to see a single painting, but the master's etchings are marvelous and well-described. I came away wanting to know more about the man and his art.

Cost and Hours: €10, includes audioguide, daily 10:00-17:00, etching demonstrations almost hourly, Jodenbreestraat 4, tel. 020/520-0400, www.rembrandthuis.nl.

▲**Diamonds**—Many shops in this "city of diamonds" offer tours. These tours come with two parts: a chance to see experts behind magnifying glasses polishing the facets of precious diamonds, followed by a visit to an intimate sales room to see (and perhaps buy) a mighty shiny yet very tiny souvenir.

The handy and professional **Gassan Diamonds** facility fills a huge warehouse a block from Rembrandt's House. A visit here plops you in the big-tour-group fray (notice how each tour group has a color-coded sticker so they know which guide gets

AMSTERDAM

Southeast Amsterdam

↖ TO RED LIGHT DISTRICT

REMBRANDT'S HOUSE

GASSAN DIAMONDS

TO NEMO, VOC SHIP, MARITIME MUSEUM & IJ TUNNEL

UILENBURGERGRACHT

VALKENBURGERSTRAAT

FLEA MARKET

WATERLOO-PLEIN

MOSES & AARON CHURCH

MR. VISSER-PLEIN

OPERA

JEWISH HISTORY MUSEUM

BLAUWBRUG

DRAW-BRIDGE

DOCK-WORKER STATUE

NUIDERSTRAAT

HERENGRACHT

WERT-HEIM PARK

RESISTANCE MUSEUM

ENTREPOTDOK

PLANTAGE

PLANTAGE-MIDDEN

HORTUS BOTANICAL GARDEN

DUTCH THEATER MEMORIAL

ARTIS ZOO

TO REMBRANDT-PLEIN

HERMITAGE AMSTERDAM

NIEUWE KEIZERSGR

NIEUWE WEESPER STRAAT

TO MAGERE (SKINNY) BRIDGE

200 YARDS
200 METERS

Ⓜ METRO   Ⓑ STOP/GO BUS
↑ ENTRY POINT TO SIGHTS

DCH

❶ To Stayokay Stadsdoelen Hostel
❷ To Stayokay Zeeburg Hostel
❸ Restaurant Plancius
❹ Café Koosje

TO TROPICAL MUSEUM ❷

the commission on what they buy). You'll get a sticker, join a free 15-minute tour to see a polisher at work, and hear a general explanation of the process. Then you'll have an opportunity to sit down and have color and clarity described and illustrated with diamonds ranging in value from $100 to $30,000. Before or after, you can have a free cup of coffee in the waiting room across the parking lot (daily 9:00-17:00, Nieuwe Uilenburgerstraat 173, tel. 020/622-5333, www.gassandiamonds.com, handy WC). Another company, **Coster,** also offers diamond demos, not as good as Gassan's, but convenient if you're near the Rijksmuseum (described on page 1120).

▲**Willet-Holthuysen Museum (a.k.a. Herengracht Canal Mansion)**—This 1687 townhouse is a must for devotees of Hummel-topped sugar bowls and Louis XVI–style wainscoting. For others, it's a pleasant look inside a typical (rich) home with much of the original furniture and decor. Forget the history and just browse through a dozen rooms of beautiful and saccharine objects from the 19th century.

Cost and Hours: €8, audioguide-€3, Mon-Fri 10:00-17:00, Sat-Sun 11:00-18:00; take tram #9 or #14 to Rembrandtplein—it's a 2-minute walk southeast to Herengracht 605, tel. 020/523-1870, www.willetholthuysen.nl.

Tassen Museum (Hendrikje Museum of Bags and Purses)— This hardworking little museum fills an elegant 1664 canal house with 500 years of bag and purse history—from before the invention of pockets through the 20th century. The collection, with lots of artifacts, is well-described in English and gives a fascinating insight into fashion through the ages that fans of handbags will love, and their partners might even enjoy. The creative and surreal bag styles of the 1920s and 1930s are particularly interesting.

Cost and Hours: €8.50, covered by Museumkaart and I amsterdam City Card, daily 10:00-17:00, three floors—one houses temporary exhibits and two hold the permanent collection, start on top floor, behind Rembrandtplein at Herengracht 573, tel. 020/524-6452, www.tassenmuseum.nl.

▲**Hermitage Amsterdam**—The famous Hermitage Museum in St. Petersburg, Russia, loans art to Amsterdam for display in the Amstelhof, a 17th-century former nursing home that takes up a whole city block along the Amstel River.

Why is there Russian-owned art in Amsterdam? The Hermitage collection in St. Petersburg is so vast that they can only show about 5 percent of it at any one time. Therefore, the Hermitage is establishing satellite collections around the world. The one here in Amsterdam is the biggest, filling the large Amstelhof. By law, the great Russian collection can only be out of the country for six months at a time, so the collection is always rotating. Curators in Amsterdam make a point to display art that complements—rather than just repeats—what the city's other museums show so well.

Cost and Hours: Generally €15, but price varies with exhibit; audioguide-€3, daily 10:00-17:00, Wed until 20:00; come later in the day to avoid crowds, mandatory free bag check, café, Nieuwe Herengracht 14, tram #4 to Rembrandtplein or #9 or #14 to Waterlooplein. Recorded info tel. 020/530-7488, www .hermitage.nl.

De Hortus Botanical Garden—This is a unique oasis of tranquility within the city (no mobile phones are allowed, because "our collection of plants is a precious community—treat it with respect"). One of the oldest botanical gardens in the world, it dates from 1638, when medicinal herbs were grown here. Today, among its 6,000 different kinds of plants—most of which were collected by the Dutch East India Company in the 17th and 18th centuries—you'll find medicinal herbs, cacti, several greenhouses (one with a fluttery butterfly house—a hit with kids), and a tropical palm house. Much of it is described in English: "A Dutch merchant snuck a coffee plant out of Ethiopia, which ended up in this garden in 1706. This first coffee plant in Europe was the literal granddaddy of the coffee cultures of Brazil—long the world's biggest coffee producer."

Cost and Hours: €7.50, not covered by Museumkaart; daily 10:00-17:00; Plantage Middenlaan 2A, tel. 020/625-9021, www .dehortus.nl. The inviting Orangery Café serves tapas.

▲**Jewish Historical Museum (Joods Historisch Museum)**— This interesting museum tells the story of the Netherlands' Jews through three centuries, serving as a good introduction to Judaism and Jewish customs and religious traditions.

Originally opened in 1932, the museum was forced to close during the Nazi years. Recent renovations have brought it into the 21st century. Its current location comprises four historic former synagogues that have been joined by steel and glass to make one modern complex.

The highlight is the Great Synagogue. Upstairs (in the women's gallery), displays tell Amsterdam's Jewish history from 1600 to 1900. From here, a skyway leads to the New Synagogue and the 20th century. The new, worthwhile exhibit on the "Jews of the Netherlands" uses personal artifacts and touch-screen computers to tell the devastating history of the Nazi occupation. By purposefully showing everyday objects such as chairs and clothes, the museum helps make an inconceivable period of time meaningful and real.

Cost and Hours: €12 combo-ticket includes Dutch Theater described next, more for special exhibits, daily 11:00-17:00, last entry 30 minutes before closing, free audioguide, displays all have English explanations, children's museum and kosher-style café on site, Jonas Daniel Meijerplein 2, tel. 020/531-0310, www.jhm.nl.

▲**Dutch Theater (Hollandsche Schouwburg)**—Once a lively theater in the Jewish neighborhood, and today a moving memorial, this building was used as an assembly hall for local Jews destined for Nazi concentration camps. On the wall, 6,700 family names pay tribute to the 104,000 Jews deported and killed by the Nazis. Some 70,000 victims spent time here, awaiting transfer to concentration camps. Upstairs is a small history exhibit with a model of the ghetto, plus photos and memorabilia (such as shoes and letters) of some victims, putting a human face on the staggering numbers. Television monitors show actual footage of the rounding-up of Amsterdam's Jews by the Nazis. You can also see a few costumes from the days when the building was a theater. All in all, the place offers relatively little to see but plenty to think about. Back in the ground floor courtyard, notice the hopeful messages that visiting school groups attach to the wooden tulips.

Cost and Hours: €12 combo-ticket includes Jewish Historical Museum, daily 11:00-16:00, Plantage Middenlaan 24, tel. 020/531-0340, www.hollandscheschouwburg.nl.

▲▲**Dutch Resistance Museum (Verzetsmuseum)**—This is an impressive look at how the Dutch resisted their Nazi occupiers from 1940 to 1945. You'll see propaganda movie clips, study forged ID cards under a magnifying glass, and read about ingenious and courageous efforts—big and small—to hide local Jews from the Germans and undermine the Nazi regime.

The museum does a good job of presenting the Dutch people's struggle with a timeless moral dilemma: Is it better to collaborate with a wicked system to effect small-scale change—or to resist violently, even if your efforts are doomed to fail? You'll learn why some parts of Dutch society opted for the former, and others for the latter. While proudly describing acts of extraordinary courage, it doesn't shy away from the less-heroic side of the story (for example, the fact that most of the population—while troubled by the persecution of their Jewish countrymen—only became actively anti-Nazi after gentile Dutch men were deported to forced-labor camps).

Cost and Hours: €8 includes audioguide; Tue-Fri 10:00-17:00, Sat-Mon 11:00-17:00, English descriptions, no flash photos, mandatory and free bag check, tram #9 from station or #14 from Dam Square, Plantage Kerklaan 61. Tel. 020/620-2535, www.verzetsmuseum.org.

Nearby: Two recommended eateries—Restaurant Plancius and Café Koosje—are on the same block as the museum (see listings on page 1155), and Amsterdam's famous zoo is just across the street.

▲**Tropical Museum (Tropenmuseum)**—As close to the Third World as you'll get without lots of vaccinations, this imaginative museum offers wonderful re-creations of tropical life and explanations of Third World problems (largely created by Dutch colonialism and the slave trade). Ride the elevator to the top floor, and circle your way down through this immense collection, opened in 1926 to give the Dutch people a peek at their vast colonial holdings. Don't miss the display case where you can see and hear the world's most exotic musical instruments. The Ekeko cafeteria serves tropical food.

Cost and Hours: €10, Tue-Sun 10:00-17:00, closed Mon, tram #9 to Linnaeusstraat 2, tel. 020/568-8200, www.tropenmuseum.nl.

Entertainment in Amsterdam

Many Amsterdam hotels serve breakfast until 11:00 because so many people—visitors and locals—live for nighttime in this city.

On summer evenings, people flock to the main squares for drinks at outdoor tables. Leidseplein is the liveliest, surrounded by theaters, restaurants, and nightclubs. The slightly quieter Rembrandtplein (with adjoining Thorbeckeplein and nearby Reguliersdwarsstraat) is the center of gay clubs and nightlife. Spui features a full city block of bars. And Nieuwmarkt, on the east edge of the Red Light District, is a bit rough, but is probably the most local.

The Red Light District (particularly Oudezijds Achterburgwal) is less sleazy in the early evening, and almost carnival-like as the neon comes on and the streets fill with tour groups. But it starts to feel scuzzy after about 22:30.

Information

Pick up one of these free papers for listings of festivals and performances of theater, film, dance, cabaret, and live rock, pop, jazz, and classical music. The hip monthly *Amsterdam Magazine* is made for tourists, but savvy enough to appeal to locals; its "upcoming" section has a solid listing of entertainment options (available all over, includes good map). The irreverent *Boom!* has the basics on the youth and nightlife scene, and is packed with practical tips and countercultural insights (includes €5 discount on Boom Chicago comedy theater act described on next page; available at TIs and many bars). *Unfold Amsterdam* is a biweekly fold-out with tips on current art-scene events (available at bookstores). *Uitkrant* is in Dutch, but it's just a calendar of events, and anyone can figure out the name of the event and its date, time, and location (available at TIs, bars, and bookstores).

Newsstands sell *Time Out Amsterdam*, Dutch papers (Thursday editions generally list events), and the *International Herald Tribune* (has special Netherlands insert).

Box Office: The **AUB/Last Minute Ticket Shop** at Stadsschouwburg Theater is the best one-stop-shopping box office for theater, classical music, and major rock shows. The Last Minute window sells half-price, same-day tickets to certain shows (Mon-Sat 10:00-19:30, Sun 12:00-18:00, Leidseplein 26, tel. 0900-0191—€0.40/minute, www.lastminuteticketshop.nl).

Music

You'll find classical music at the Concertgebouw (free 12:30 lunch concerts on Wed; arrive at 12:00 for best first-come, first-served seating; at far south end of Museumplein, tel. 0900-671-8345, www.concertgebouw.nl) and at the former Beurs (on Damrak). For opera and dance, try the opera house in the Stopera building (Waterlooplein 22, tel. 020/625-5455). In the summer, Vondelpark hosts open-air concerts.

Two rock music (and hip-hop) clubs near Leidseplein are **Melkweg** (Lijnbaansgracht 234a, tel. 020/531-8181, www.melk

weg.nl) and **Paradiso** (Weteringschans 6, tel. 020/626-4521, www
.paradiso.nl). They present big-name acts that you might recognize
if you're younger than I am.

Jazz has a long tradition at the **Bimhuis** nightclub, east of the
Red Light District (Oude Schans 73-77, tel. 020/788-2188, www
.bimhuis.nl).

The nearby town of Haarlem offers free pipe organ concerts
on Tuesday evenings in summer at its 15th-century church, the
Grote Kerk (at 20:15 mid-May-mid-Oct, additional concerts Thu
at 15:00 July-Aug, see next chapter).

Comedy

Boom Chicago, an R-rated comedy improv act, was started 15
years ago by a group of Americans on a graduation tour. They have
been entertaining tourists and locals ever since. The two-hour,
English-only show is a series of rude, clever, and high-powered
improvisational skits offering a raucous look at Dutch culture and
local tourism (€20 weekdays, generally €24 Fri-Sat; Sun-Fri shows
at 20:15, sometimes also Fri at 23:30, Sat at 19:30 and discounted
show at 22:30; confirm times when you buy your ticket, ticket
office open daily from 13:00 until 15 minutes after curtain time, no
Mon shows Jan-March, tel. 020/423-0101, www.boomchicago.nl).
It all happens at the 300-seat Leidseplein Theater at Leidseplein
12; enter through the skinny Boom Bar (optional meal and drink
service).

They do *Best of Boom* (a collection of their greatest hits over the
years) as well as new shows for locals and return customers. When
sales are slow, ticket-sellers on the street out front offer steeply discounted tickets, with a drink included. Drop by that afternoon and
see what's up.

Theater

Amsterdam is one of the world centers for experimental live theater (much of it in English). Many theaters cluster around the
street called the Nes, which stretches south from Dam Square.

Movies

It's not unusual for movies at many cinemas to be sold out—
consider buying tickets during the day. Catch modern movies
in the 1920s setting of the classic **Tuschinski Theater** (between
Muntplein and Rembrandtplein, described on page 1121).

Museums

Several museums stay open late. The **Anne Frank House** always
stays open until at least 19:00 year-round; it's open daily until
22:00 in July and August, and closes late on Saturdays year-round

(22:00 peak-season, 21:00 off-season). The **Hermitage Amsterdam** stays open until 20:00 on Wednesdays. The **Van Gogh Museum** is open on Fridays until 22:00 and sometimes has music and a wine bar in the lobby.

The **Hash, Marijuana, and Hemp Museum** is open daily until 23:00. And the **sex museums** always stay open late (Damrak Sex Museum until 23:30, Erotic Museum until 1:00 in the morning).

Skating After Dark

Amsterdammers get their skating fix on wheels every Friday night in summer and early fall in Vondelpark. Huge groups don inline skates and meet at the round bench near the Vondel Pavilion (around 20:15, www.fridaynightskate.com). Anyone can join in. You can rent skates at the shop at the far end of the park (Vondeltuin Rental, daily 11:00-20:00 in good weather; first hour-€5, then €2.50/hour; price includes helmet, wrist guards, and knee guards; at southeastern edge of park, mobile 0627-565-576, www.vondeltuin.nl).

Sleeping in Amsterdam

Greeting a new day by descending steep stairs and stepping into a leafy canalside scene—graceful bridges, historic gables, and bikes clattering on cobbles—is a fun part of experiencing Amsterdam. But Amsterdam is a tough city for budget accommodations, and any hotel room under €140 (or B&B room under €100) will have rough edges. Still, you can sleep well and safely in a great location for €100 per double.

I've grouped my hotel listings into three neighborhoods, each of which has its own character.

West Amsterdam (which includes the Jordaan) has Old World ambience, with quiet canals, old gabled buildings, and candlelit restaurants. It's also just minutes on foot to Dam Square. Many of my hotels are charming, friendly, gabled mansions. The downside here is that you'll pay more.

Southwest Amsterdam has two main areas for accommodations: near Leidseplein (more central) and near Vondelpark (farther away). The streets near the bustling Leidseplein have restaurants, tourist buzz, nightlife, canalside charm, B&B coziness, and walkable (or easy tram) access to the center of town. Farther afield is the quieter semi-suburban neighborhood around Vondelpark and Museumplein, close to the Rijks and Van Gogh museums. You'll find good hotel values and ready access to Vondelpark and the art museums, but you're a half-hour walk (or 10-minute tram ride) to Dam Square.

Staying in **Central Amsterdam** is ideal for people who like

Sleep Code

(€1 = about $1.40, country code: 31, area code: 020)
S = Single, **D** = Double/Twin, **T** = Triple, **Q** = Quad, **b** = bathroom,
s = shower only. Nearly everyone speaks English. Credit cards
are accepted, and prices include breakfast and tax unless otherwise noted.

    To help you easily sort through these listings, I've divided
the accommodations into three categories, based on the price
for a standard double room with bath:

  $$$ Higher Priced—Most rooms €140 or more.
   $$ Moderately Priced—Most rooms between €80-140.
    $ Lower Priced—Most rooms €80 or less.

    Prices can change without notice; verify the hotel's
current rates online or by email. For other updates, see www
.ricksteves.com/update.

shopping, tourist sights, and easy access to public transportation
(including Central Station). On the downside, the area has traffic noise, concrete, and urban grittiness, and the hotels can lack
character.

    Some national holidays merit your making reservations far in
advance. Amsterdam is jammed during tulip season (late March-
mid-May), conventions, festivals, and on summer weekends.
During peak season, some hoteliers will not take weekend bookings for people staying fewer than two or three nights.

    Around just about every corner in downtown Amsterdam,
you'll see construction: cranes for big transportation projects and
small crews of bricklayers repairing the wobbly, cobbled streets that
line the canals. Canalside rooms can come with great views—and
early-morning construction-crew noise. If you're a light sleeper,
ask the hotelier for a quiet room in the back. Smoking is illegal in
hotel rooms throughout the Netherlands. Parking in Amsterdam
is even worse than driving—if you must park a car, ask your hotelier for advice.

    If you'd rather trade big-city action for small-town coziness,
consider sleeping in Haarlem, 20 minutes away by train (see next
chapter).

West Amsterdam
Stately Canalside Hotels
These hotels, a half-mile apart, both face historic canals. They
come with fine lobbies (some more ornate than others) and rooms
that can feel like they're from another century. This area oozes

Hotels & Restaurants in West Amsterdam

1. The Toren
2. Hotel Ambassade
3. Hotel Brouwer
4. Hotel Hoksbergen
5. Hotel Hegra
6. Hotel Chic & Basic Amsterdam
7. Hotel Van Onna
8. Wiechmann Hotel
9. Boogaard's B&B
10. Maes B&B
11. Heren B&B
12. Herengracht 21 B&B
13. Sunhead of 1617 B&B
14. Truelove Guesthouse Reception
15. Frederic Rent-a-Bike & Guestrooms
16. Hotel Pax & Sara's Pancake House
17. Hotel Aspen
18. To The Shelter Jordan
19. Restaurant de Luwte
20. De Bolhoed Restaurant
21. Café Restaurant de Reiger
22. Café 't Smalle
23. Thai Fusion
24. Toscana Italian Restaurant
25. Winkel Café
26. Restaurant 't Stuivertje
27. Ristorante Toscanini
28. Villa Zeesicht
29. Café 't Papeneiland
30. Stubbe's Haring (Fish Stand)
31. Albert Heijn Grocery (3)
32. Paradox Coffeeshop
33. The Grey Area Coffeeshop
34. Siberië Coffeeshop
35. La Tertulia Coffeeshop
36. Launderette
37. GAYtic (LGBT Tourist Info)

elegance and class, and it is fairly quiet at night.

$$$ The Toren is a chandeliered, historic mansion with a pleasant, canalside setting and a peaceful garden out back for guests. Run by Eric and Petra Toren, this smartly renovated, super-romantic hotel is classy yet friendly, with 38 rooms in a great location on a quiet street two blocks northeast of the Anne Frank House. The capable staff is a great source of local advice. The gilt-frame, velvet-curtained rooms are an opulent splurge (tiny Sb-€115, Db-€200, deluxe Db-€250, third person-€40, prices bump way up during conferences and decrease in winter, rates do not include 5 percent tax, breakfast buffet-€12, air-con, elevator, Internet access and Wi-Fi, Keizersgracht 164, tel. 020/622-6033, fax 020/626-9705, www.thetoren.nl, info@thetoren.nl). To get the best prices, check their website for their "daily rate," and in the "remarks" field, ask for the 10 percent Rick Steves cash discount.

$$$ Hotel Ambassade, lacing together 59 rooms in a maze of connected houses, is elegant and fresh, sitting aristocratically on Herengracht. The staff is top-notch, and the public areas (including a library and breakfast room) are palatial, with antique furnishings and modern art (Sb-€195, Db-€195-245, spacious "deluxe" Db with canal view-€295, Db suite-€345, Tb-€245-295, extra bed-€40, ask for Rick Steves discount when booking, see website for specials, rates do not include 5 percent tax, breakfast-€17, air-con, elevator, free Internet access and Wi-Fi, Herengracht 341, for location see map on previous page, tel. 020/555-0222, www.ambassade-hotel.nl, info@ambassade-hotel.nl, Roos—pronounced "Rose").

Simpler Canalside Hotels

These places have basic rooms—some downright spare, none at all plush—and most do without an elevator or other extras. Each of them, however, offer a decent night's sleep in a lovely area of town.

$$ Hotel Brouwer is a woody and homey old-time place. It's situated tranquilly yet centrally on the Singel canal and rents eight rooms with canal views, old furniture, and soulful throw rugs (Sb-€60, Db-€95, Tb-€120, rates don't include 5 percent tax, cash only, small elevator, free Wi-Fi and Internet access, located between Central Station and Dam Square, near Lijnbaanssteeg at Singel 83, tel. 020/624-6358, www.hotelbrouwer.nl, akita@hotelbrouwer.nl).

$$ Hotel Hoksbergen is a welcoming, well-run canalside place in a peaceful location where helpful, hands-on owners Tony and Bert rent 14 rooms (Db-€98, Tb-€143, five Qb apartments-€165-198, fans, free Wi-Fi, Singel 301, tel. 020/626-6043, www.hotelhoksbergen.com, info@hotelhoksbergen.nl).

$$ Hotel Hegra is cozy and affordable, with 11 tight rooms filling a 17th-century merchant's house overlooking the canal (S-€50, D-€79, Ds-€89-€109, Db-€105-€119, Ts-€115-€125, Tb-€130, some rooms with canal view, pay Internet access, free Wi-Fi, bike rental, just north of Wolvenstraat at Herengracht 269, tel. 020/623-7877, www.hotelhegra.nl, info@hotelhegra.nl, Robert).

$$ Hotel Chic & Basic Amsterdam has a boutique-hotel feel, even though it's part of a Spanish chain. With its mod utilitarian design and younger clientele, it provides a break from all the lace curtains. Located in a quiet neighborhood near Central Station, it offers 25 minimalist rooms and public areas that are bathed in space-age white. Rooms with canal views are pricier and breezier (Sb-€95-130, Db-€120-155, €20 more on holiday weekends, less in winter, cheaper prices are for less-sleek "vintage" rooms without canal views, free coffee, continental breakfast, fans on request, tangled floor plan connecting three canalside buildings, free Internet access and Wi-Fi, Herengracht 13, tel. 020/522-2345, www.chicandbasic.com, amsterdam@chicandbasic.com, manager Bernardo Campo).

$$ Hotel Van Onna has 41 simple, industrial-strength rooms, some with canal views. The price is right, and the leafy location makes you want to crack out your easel. The popular top-floor attic rooms are cozy hideaways (Sb-€45-65, Db-€80-100, Tb-€125-135, Qb-€170-190, price depends on season, cash only, cot-like beds are sufficient, no phones or TVs, free Internet access and Wi-Fi, in the Jordaan at Bloemgracht 104, tel. 020/626-5801, www.hotel vanonna.nl, info@hotelvanonna.nl, Leon and Tsibo).

$$ Wiechmann Hotel's 37 rooms are sparsely furnished with just the dark-wood essentials, but they're spacious, and the *gezellig* public areas are chock-full of Old World charm (Sb-€65-105, Db-€125-165, Tb-€205, Qb-€230, Db suite-€260, prices lower in winter, check online for best price, 15 percent cheaper for 3 or more nights if booking through their website, some canal views, back rooms are quiet, free Internet access and Wi-Fi, nicely located at Prinsengracht 328-332, tel. 020/626-3321, www.hotelwiechmann .nl, info@hotelwiechmann.nl, John and Taz the welcome dog).

B&Bs and Private-Room Rentals

B&Bs offer a chance to feel like a local during your visit. The first and third listings here are in a residential and peaceful neighborhood that's a short walk from Central Station; the second and fourth are in slightly busier areas. The last two listings are services that manage and rent many apartments and rooms in West Amsterdam.

$$ Boogaard's B&B is a delightful pad on a narrow lane right out of Mister Rogers' neighborhood. The B&B, which has four comfortable rooms and an inviting public living room, is run by Peter, an American expat opera singer. Peter, who clearly enjoys hosting Americans in his home, serves his fresh-baked goodies at breakfast and treats you royally. As his place is popular with my readers, it's smart to book well in advance (Db-€120, 2-night minimum; furnished family apartment with kitchen-€240 for 4 people, 3-night minimum; prices don't include 5 percent tax, air-con, free Wi-Fi, DVD library, free laundry, loaner cell phones and laptops, Langestraat 34, tel. 064/358-6835, www.boogaardsbnb .com, info@boogaardsbnb.com).

$$ Maes B&B (pronounced "mahss") is a dynamite value, renting tastefully cozy rooms for much less than you'd pay at a hotel. Instead of a reception desk, you get antique-filled rooms, the use of a full kitchen, and a warm welcome from Ken and Vlad. They also run **Heren B&B,** a crisply modern space around the corner from Maes, with large rooms—one with a canal view (both locations: Sb-€95, Db-€105, bigger Db-€115-125, extra bed-€30, suites and full apartments also available, free Internet access and Wi-Fi, if street noise bothers you ask for room in back, Herenstraat 26, tel. 020/427-5165, www.bedandbreakfastamsterdam.com, maes info@xs4all.nl).

$$ Herengracht 21 B&B has two stylish, tiny, intimate rooms filled with art and run by lovely Loes Olden (2-floor Db-€125, canal-view Db-€135, air-con, free Wi-Fi, Herengracht 21, tel. 020/625-6305, mobile 06-2812-0962, www.herengracht21 .nl, loes@herengracht21.nl).

$$ Sunhead of 1617 B&B justifiably calls itself a "bed and delicious breakfast," but you're just as likely to remember the thoughtfully decorated, flower-filled rooms and the personality of owner Carlos (rear Db-€119, front Db-€129, Db apartment-€169, Tb apartment-€210, more on holidays, free Wi-Fi, mobile 06-2865-3572, Herengracht 152, www.sunhead.com, carlos@sun head.com).

$$ With **Truelove Guesthouse,** a room-rental service, you'll feel like you're staying at your Dutch friends' house while they're out of town. Sean and Paul—whose tiny antique store on Prinsenstraat doubles as the reception desk for their rental ser-vice—have 15 rooms and apartments in houses sprinkled through-out the northern end of the Jordaan neighborhood. The apartments are stylish and come with kitchens and pull-out beds (Db-€90-105, Db apartment-€100-120, Qb apartments-€140-220, prices soft in off-season and midweek, 10 percent more with credit card, 2-night minimum on weekends, no breakfast, pick up keys in store at Prinsenstraat 4, store tel. 020/320-2500, mobile 06-2480-5672, fax 084-711-4950, www.cosyandwarm-amsterdam.com, truelove antiek@zonnet.nl).

$ Frederic Rent-a-Bike & Guestrooms, with a bike-rental shop as the reception, is a collection of private rooms on a gorgeous canal just outside the Jordaan, a five-minute walk from Central Station. Frederic has amassed about 100 beds, ranging from dumpy €70 doubles behind the bike-rental shop, to spacious and elegant apartments (from €46/person; these places require a 2-night minimum, occasionally more). Some places are ideal for families and groups of up to six. He also rents houseboat apartments. All are displayed on his website (phone bookings preferred, book with credit card but pay with cash, no breakfast, Brouwersgracht 78, tel. 020/624-5509, www.frederic.nl, info@frederic.nl, Frederic and Marjolijn). His excellent bike shop is open daily 9:00-17:30 (€10/24 hours).

Southwest Amsterdam
Charming B&Bs near Leidseplein

The area around Amsterdam's rip-roaring nightlife center (Leidseplein) is colorful, comfortable, and convenient. These canalside mom-and-pop places are within a five-minute walk of rowdy Leidseplein, but are in generally quiet and typically Dutch settings. Within walking distance of the major museums, and steps off the tram line, this neighborhood offers a perfect mix of charm and location.

$$ Hotel de Leydsche Hof is a hidden gem located on a canal. Its two large rooms are a symphony in white, overlooking a tree-filled backyard. Frits and Loes give their big, elegant, old building a stylish air. Breakfast is served in the grand canal-front room (Db-€120, cash only, 2-night minimum, free Internet access and Wi-Fi, Leidsegracht 14, tel. 020/638-2327, mobile 06-5125-8588, www.freewebs.com/leydschehof, loespiller@planet.nl).

$$ Wildervanck B&B, run by Helene and Sjoerd Wildervanck, offers two tasteful rooms in an elegant, 17th-century canal house (big Db on first floor-€135, Db with twin beds on ground floor-€120, extra bed-€30, 2-night minimum, breakfast in their pleasant dining room, free Wi-Fi, family has three girls, Keizersgracht 498, on Keizersgracht canal just west of Leidsestraat, tel. 020/623-3846, www.wildervanck.com, info@wildervanck .com).

$$ Hotel Keizershof is wonderfully Dutch, with six bright, airy rooms—some with canal views—in a 17th-century canal house with a lush garden and a fine living room. A very steep spiral staircase leads to rooms named after old-time Hollywood stars. The enthusiastic hospitality of Mrs. de Vries and her daughter, Hanneke, give this place a friendly, almost small-town charm

Hotels & Restaurants in Southwest Amsterdam

AMSTERDAM

100 YARDS
100 METERS

TO SPUI

TO

1 Hotel de Leydsche Hof
2 Wildervanck B&B
3 To Hotel Keizershof
4 Hotel Piet Hein
5 Hotel Fita
6 To Hotel Filosoof &
   Tulips B&B
7 Hotel Alexander

8 Hotel Hestia
9 Hotel Parkzicht
10 Stayokay Vondelpark Hostel
11 To Restaurant Bazar
12 Café Vertigo
13 Cobra Café
14 The Bulldog Coffeeshop
15 Launderette

T TRAM 2+5 STOP
B BOAT TOURS
--- PATH

↟ ENTRY POINT TO SIGHTS

DCH

(S-€70, D-€90, Ds-€100, Db-€115, 2-night minimum, reserve with credit card but pay with cash, free Internet access and Wi-Fi; tram #16, #24, or #25 from Central Station, Keizersgracht 618, where Keizers canal crosses Nieuwe Spiegelstraat; tel. 020/622-2855, www.hotelkeizershof.nl, info@hotelkeizershof.nl).

Near Vondelpark and Museumplein

These options cluster around Vondelpark in a safe neighborhood. Though they don't have a hint of Old Dutch or romantic canalside flavor, they're reasonable values and only a short walk from the action. Unless noted, the places below have elevators. Many are in a pleasant nook between rollicking Leidseplein and the park, and most are a 5- to 15-minute walk to the Rijks and Van Gogh museums. They are easily connected with Central Station by trams #1, #2, and/or #5.

$$$ **Hotel Piet Hein** offers 81 stylishly sleek yet comfortable rooms as well as a swanky lounge, good breakfast, and pleasant garden, all on a quiet street (Sb-€115, Db-€175, extra-posh Db-€200-250, Tb-€205, extra bed-€30, specials on website, air-con in some rooms, free Wi-Fi and Internet access, Vossiusstraat 51-53, tel. 020/662-7205, www.hotelpiethein.nl, info@hotelpiethein.nl).

$$$ **Hotel Fita** has 15 bright rooms in a great location—100 yards from the Van Gogh Museum, an even shorter hop from the tram stop, and on a corner with no car traffic. The decor may not be the latest, but all the amenities are there—including espresso machines in every room—and the welcome is very warm (Sb-€105, two small ground-floor Db-€135, Db-€145-165 depending on size, Tb-€205, free Wi-Fi and Internet access in lobby, free laundry service, Jan Luijkenstraat 37, tel. 020/679-0976, fax 020/664-3969, www.fita.nl, info@fita.nl, joking and colorful owner Hans).

$$ **Hotel Filosoof** greets you with Aristotle and Plato in the foyer and classical music in its generous lobby. Its 38 rooms, some across the street from reception, are decorated with themes; the Egyptian room has a frieze of hieroglyphics. Philosophers' sayings hang on the walls, and thoughtful travelers wander down the halls or sit in the garden, rooted in deep discussion. The rooms are small, but the hotel is endearing (Db-€110-130 weeknights, €130-150 Fri-Sat, bigger "deluxe" rooms-€20 extra, suites-€60 extra, prices depend on season and don't include tax; no breakfast, free Internet access and Wi-Fi, 3-minute walk from tram line #1, get off at Jan Pieter Heijestraat, Anna van Den Vondelstraat 6, tel. 020/683-3013, fax 020/685-3750, www.hotelfilosoof.nl, reservations@hotelfilosoof.nl).

$$ **Hotel Alexander** is a modern, newly renovated, 32-room hotel on a quiet street. Some of the rooms overlook the garden patio out back (Db-€135, prices soft in winter—call or check their

website for best deal, Internet access, pay Wi-Fi, tel. 020/589-4020, fax 020/589-4025, Vondelstraat 44-46, www.hotelalexander.nl, info@hotelalexander.nl).

$$ Tulips B&B, with a bunch of cozy rooms—some on a canal—is run by a friendly Englishwoman, Karen, and her Dutch husband, Paul. Rooms are clean, white, and bright, with red carpeting, plants, and flowers (D-€85, Db-€120, suite-€150, extra bed-€30, discounts for longer stays, cash only, prefer 3-night stays on weekends, includes milk-and-cereal breakfast, no shoes, no elevator but not a lot of stairs, free Wi-Fi, south end of Vondelpark at Sloterkade 65, 7-minute walk from trams #1 and #2, directions sent when you book, tel. 020/679-2753, rooms@bedandbreakfast amsterdam.net, www.bedandbreakfastamsterdam.net).

$$ Hotel Hestia, on a safe and sane street, is efficient and family-run, with 18 clean, airy, and generally spacious rooms (Sb-€83-93, very small Db-€101-107, standard Db-€128-148, Tb-€158-176, Qb-€188-206, Quint/b-€218-236, can be less in winter—check website for best price, Roemer Visscherstraat 7, tel. 020/618-0801, fax 020/685-1382, www.hotel-hestia.nl, info@hotel-hestia.nl, Arnaud).

$$ Hotel Parkzicht, an old-fashioned, no-frills, dark-wood place with extremely steep stairs, rents 13 big, plain, and somewhat frayed rooms on a street bordering Vondelpark (S-€49, Sb-€59, Db-€79-92, Tb-€140, closed Nov-March, no elevator, free Wi-Fi, some noise from neighboring youth hostel, Roemer Visscherstraat 33, tel. 020/618-1954, fax 020/618-0897, www.parkzicht.nl, hotel @parkzicht.nl).

Central Amsterdam
Basic Hotels in the City Center

You won't get a warm welcome at either of the two following hotels. But if you're looking for a no-nonsense room that's convenient to plenty of tram lines, these hotels fit the bill.

$$$ Hotel Ibis Amsterdam Centre, located next door to the Central Station, is a modern, efficient, 187-room place. It offers a central location, comfort, and good value, without a hint of charm (Db-€140-160 Nov-Aug, Db-€200 Sept-Oct, breakfast-€15, check website for deals, book long in advance—especially for Sept-Oct, air-con, pay Internet access; facing Central Station, go left toward the multistory bicycle garage to Stationsplein 49; tel. 020/522-2899, fax 020/522-2889, www.ibishotel.com, h1556@accor.com). When business is slow, usually in mid-summer, they occasionally rent rooms to same-day drop-ins for around €100.

$$ Hotel Résidence Le Coin offers 42 larger-than-average rooms complete with small kitchenettes. Located near the Mint Tower, this hotel is a two-minute walk to the Flower Market and

Hotels & Restaurants in Central Amsterdam

200 YARDS

200 METERS

B BOAT TOURS

CENTRAL STATION

STATIONS-PLEIN

AMSTERDAM

To JORDAAN DISTRICT

LELIESTR.

SINGEL

SPUISTRAAT

VOORBURGWAL

N. NIEUWSTR.

ST. NIC.

NIEUWENDIJK

AMRAK

DAMRAK

OLD CHURCH

RED LIGHT DISTRICT

BEURS-PL.

RAADHUISSTRAAT

NIEUWEZIJDS

DAM

DE BIJENKORF DEPT. STORE

VOORBURGWAL

PIJL &

DAM STR.

MKT.

AMSTERDAM MUSEUM

KALVER STRAAT

ROKIN

NES

OUDEZIJDS

ST. LUCIEN.

BEGIJN-HOF

HET STEEG

SPUI

SPUI

ROKIN

MINT TOWER

To LEIDSEPLEIN

HEI REN

KONING

HEILIGE

KALVER TOREN MALL

SINGEL

FLOWER MARKET

MUNT PL.

AMSTEL

N. DOELEN

REGULIERS

VIZEL

DCH

5 Kantjil To Go

6 Café 't Gasthuys

7 De Jaren Café

8 Pannenkoekenhuis Upstairs

9 La Place (V&D Dept. Store)

10 Atrium Univ. Cafeteria

11 Brasserie Rest. de Roode Leeuw

12 Dam Café (De Bijenkorf Dept. Store)

13 Albert Heijn Groceries (4)

14 The Dampkring Coffeeshop

1 To Hotel Ambassade

2 Hotel Ibis Amsterdam Centre

3 Hotel Résidence Le Coin

4 Restaurant Kantjil en de Tijger

a five-minute walk to Rembrandtplein (Sb-€119, small Db-€139, bigger Db-€154, Qb-€230, extra bed-€37, breakfast-€12, pay Wi-Fi, by the University at Nieuwe Doelenstraat 5, tel. 020/524-6800, fax 020/524-6801, www.lecoin.nl, hotel@lecoin.nl).

Budget Hotels Between Dam Square and the Anne Frank House: Inexpensive, well-worn hotels line the convenient but noisy and unromantic main drag, Raadhuisstraat. Expect a long, steep, and depressing stairway, with noisy rooms in the front and quieter rooms in the back. Though neither of the places below serve breakfast, they're both steps from a recommended pancake house. For locations, see the map on page 1138.

$ Hotel Pax has 11 large, plain, but airy rooms with Ikea furniture—a lot like a European dorm room (S-€35-45, D-€65, Db-€80, T-€85, Tb-€100, prices drop dramatically in winter, no breakfast, six rooms share two showers and two toilets, Raadhuis-straat 37, tel. 020/624-9735, hotelpax@tiscali.nl, run by go-getters Philip and Pieter).

$ Hotel Aspen, a few doors away and a great value for a budget hotel, has eight tidy, stark, and well-maintained rooms (S-€40, tiny D-€55-65, Db-€75-80, Tb-€95, Qb-€110, prices same 365 days a year, no breakfast, free Wi-Fi and Internet access, Raadhuisstraat 31, tel. 020/626-6714, fax 020/620-0866, www.hotelaspen.nl, info@hotelaspen.nl, run by kindhearted Rudy and Esam).

Hostels

Amsterdam has a world of good, cheap hostels located throughout the city. Most are designed for the party crowd, but here are a few quieter options. They all offer dorm beds; Stayokay Vondelpark also has some basic doubles.

In the Jordaan: **$ The Shelter Jordan** is a scruffy, friendly, Christian-run, 100-bed place in a great neighborhood. While most of Amsterdam's hostels are pretty wild, this place is drug-free and alcohol-free, with boys on one floor and girls on another. These are Amsterdam's best budget beds (bunks in 12-20-bed dorms-€23.50, €28 Fri-Sat and around holidays, same bunks in shoulder season-€20.50, less in off-season; bunks in 6-8-bed dorms-€1.50 extra; bunks in 4-5-bed rooms-€4 extra; includes sheets and breakfast, Internet access in lobby, near Anne Frank House at Bloem-straat 179, tel. 020/624-4717, www.shelter.nl, jordan@shelter.nl). The Shelter serves hot meals, runs a snack bar in its big, relaxing lounge, offers lockers, and leads nightly Bible studies.

In the Red Light District: **$ The Shelter City** is Shelter Jordan's sister—similar, but definitely not preaching to the local choir. While its 180 beds are buried in the heart of the red lights, it feels very well-run and perfectly safe (same prices as Shelter Jordan, bunks in Qb-€6 extra, D-€49 for spouses or single-sex; same amenities, rules, and Bible study; Barndesteeg 21, tel. 020/625-3230, fax 020/623-2282, www.shelter.nl, city@shelter.nl).

In Vondelpark: **$ Stayokay Vondelpark (IYHF)**, with 530 beds in 130 rooms, is one of Amsterdam's top hostels for the under-25 set (€20-37/bed in 4- to 20-bed dorms, D-€60-95—most with bunk beds, higher prices are for March-Oct, members save €2.50, price depends on demand—cheapest when booked in advance, family rooms, lots of school groups, lockers, laundry, pay Internet access and Wi-Fi, bike rental, right on Vondelpark at Zandpad 5, tel. 020/589-8996, fax 020/589-8955, www.stayokay.com, vondel park@stayokay.com). Though Stayokay Vondelpark and Stayokay Stadsdoelen (listed next) are generally booked long in advance, occasionally a few beds open up each day at 11:00.

Near Waterlooplein: **$ Stayokay Stadsdoelen (IYHF)**, smaller and simpler than its Vondelpark sister (listed above), has only large dorms and no private bathrooms, but is free of large school groups (€17-32/bed with sheets and breakfast in 10-bed dorms, members save €2.50, price depends on demand—cheapest when booked in advance, lockers, pay Internet access, bike rental, Kloveniersburgwal 97, see map on page 1130, tel. 020/624-6832, fax 020/639-1035, www.stayokay.com, stadsdoelen@stayokay .com).

Farthest East: **$ Stayokay Zeeburg (IYHF)** is a 500-bed hostel with all the modern services. While it's pretty far from the center, by tram or bike you're just 15 minutes from Damrak street (€20-30/bed in 6- to 14-bed dorms, price depends on demand—cheapest when booked in advance, pay Internet access and Wi-Fi, lockers, games, restaurant, bike rental, tram #14 to Timorplein 21, tel. 020/551-3190, fax 020/623-4986, www.stayokay.com, zeeburg@stayokay.com).

Eating in Amsterdam

Of Amsterdam's thousand-plus restaurants, no one knows which are best. I'd pick an area and wander. The rowdy food ghetto thrives around Leidseplein; if you don't mind eating in a touristy area, wander along Leidsedwarsstraat, Restaurant Row. The area around Spui canal and that end of Spuistraat is also trendy and not as noisy. For fewer crowds and more charm, find something in the Jordaan district. Most hoteliers keep a reliable eating list for their neighborhood and know which places keep their travelers happy. I've listed some handy places to consider.

To dine cheaply yet memorably alongside the big spenders, grab a meal to go, then find a bench on a lively neighborhood square or along a canal. Sandwiches *(broodjes)* of delicious cheese on fresh bread are cheap at snack bars, delis, and *broodjes* restaurants. Ethnic restaurants serve cheap, splittable carryout meals. Ethnic fast-food stands abound, offering a variety of meats wrapped in pita bread. Easy to buy at grocery stores, yogurt in the Netherlands (and throughout northern Europe) is delicious and often drinkable right out of its plastic container.

In Central Amsterdam

For the locations of these eateries, see the "Hotels and Restaurants in Central Amsterdam" map on page 1147.

On and near Spui

Restaurant Kantjil en de Tijger is a thriving place with a plain and noisy ambience, full of happy eaters who know a good value. The food is purely Indonesian; the waiters are happy to explain your many enticing options. Their three *rijsttafels* (traditional "rice tables" with about a dozen small courses) range from €20 to €30 per person. While they are designed for two people, three people can make a meal by getting a *rijsttafel* for two and ordering a soup or light dish for the third person. A good budget alternative to the full-blown *rijsttafel* is a *nasi rames*—10 small dishes on one big plate for €13 (daily 12:00-23:00, early-bird €10 dinner daily 16:30-18:45, reservations smart, mostly indoor with a little outdoor seating, Spuistraat 291, tel. 020/620-0994).

Kantjil to Go, run by Restaurant Kantjil, is a tiny take-out bar serving up inexpensive but delicious Indonesian fare (€5 for 300 grams, €6.50 for 600 grams, vegetarian specials, daily 12:00-21:00, Thu-Sat until 22:00, storefront at Nieuwezijds Voorburgwal 342, around the back of the sit-down restaurant listed above, tel. 020/620-3074). Split a large box (they'll happily give you an empty extra box for your dining pleasure), grab a bench on the charming Spui Square around the corner, and you've got perhaps the cheapest hot meal in town.

Near the Mint Tower

Café 't Gasthuys, one of Amsterdam's many brown cafés (so called for their smoke-stained walls), has a busy dumbwaiter cranking out light lunches, sandwiches, and reasonably priced, if uncreative, dinners. It offers a long bar, a fine secluded back room, peaceful canalside seating, and sometimes slow service (€5-9 lunch plates, €11-15 dinner plates, daily 12:00-16:30 & 17:30-21:30, Thu-Sat until 22:00; Grimburgwal 7—from the Rondvaart Kooij boat dock, head down Langebrugsteeg, and it's one block down on the left; tel. 020/624-8230).

De Jaren Café ("The Years Café") is a chic yet inviting place—clearly a favorite with locals. Upstairs is the minimalist restaurant with a top-notch salad bar and a canal-view deck (serving €14-20 dinners after 17:30, including fish, meat, and veggie dishes, and salad bar, or €12 for salad bar only). Downstairs is a modern Amsterdam café, great for light lunches (soups, salads, and sandwiches served all day and evening), or just coffee over a newspaper. On a sunny day, the café's canalside patio is a fine spot to nurse a drink; this is also a nice place to go just for a drink in the evening and to enjoy the spacious Art Deco setting (daily 10:00-24:00, Nieuwe Doelenstraat 20-22, a long block up from Muntplein, tel. 020/625-5771).

Pannenkoekenhuis Upstairs is a tiny and characteristic perch up some extremely steep stairs, where Arno Jakobs cooks and serves delicious €7 pancakes to four tables throughout the afternoon (Fri-Sat 12:00-18:00, Sun 12:00-17:00, closed Mon-Thu, Grimburgwal 2, tel. 020/626-5603).

La Place, on the ground floor of the V&D department store, has an abundant, colorful array of fresh, appealing food served cafeteria-style. A multistory eatery that seats 300, it has a small outdoor terrace upstairs. Explore before you make your choice. This bustling spot has a lively market feel, with everything from made-on-the-spot beef stir-fry, to fresh juice, to veggie soups (€3 pizza and €4 sandwiches, Sun-Mon 11:00-20:00, Tue-Sat 10:00-20:00, Thu until 21:00, at the end of Kalverstraat near Mint Tower, tel. 020/622-0171). For fast and healthy take-out food (sandwiches, yogurt, fruit cups, and more), try the bakery on the department store's ground floor. (They run another branch, which has the city's ultimate view terrace, on the top floor of the **Central Library**—Openbare Bibliotheek Amsterdam—near Central Station.)

Atrium University Cafeteria, a three-minute walk from Mint Tower, feeds travelers and students from Amsterdam University for great prices, but only on weekdays (€6 meals, Mon-Fri 11:00-15:00 & 17:00-19:30, closed Sat-Sun; from Spui, walk west down Landebrug Steeg past canalside Café 't Gasthuys three blocks to Oudezijds Achterburgwal 237, go through arched doorway on the right; tel. 020/525-3999).

Between Central Station and Dam Square

Brasserie Restaurant de Roode Leeuw (*roode leeuw* means "red lion") offers a peaceful, calm respite from the crush of Damrak. During the day, the whole restaurant shares the same menu, but after 18:00, it's split roughly in half, with finer service, cloth tablecloths, and higher prices in back, and a more casual setup (and better people-watching on Damrak street) up front. Either way, you'll get a menu filled with traditional Dutch food, good service, and the company of plenty of tourists. Call ahead to reserve a window seat (restaurant: €15-20 entrées, €30 three-course fixed-price meal with traditional Dutch choices; brasserie: €10-15 entrées; daily 12:00-22:00, Damrak 93-94, tel. 020/555-0666).

Dam Café, on the first floor of the Bijenkorf department store on Dam Square, has a small lineup of inexpensive salads, sandwiches, and desserts. Enjoying views of busy Damrak, comfortable seating, and an upscale café vibe, you'll feel miles above the chaotic streets below (€8-11 salads, Mon 11:00-18:00, Tue-Fri 10:30-18:00, Thu until 21:00, Sat 9:30-18:00, Sun 12:00-18:00, Dam 1, tel. 088-245-9080). For a much wider range of dishes but no Dam views, head up to **Kitchen,** the store's swanky fifth-floor self-service restaurant (similar prices and hours as café).

Munching Cheap

Traditional fish stands sell €3 herring sandwiches and other salty treats, usually from easy-to-understand photo menus. **Stubbe's Haring,** where the Stubbe family has been selling herring for 100 years, is handy and well-established, a few blocks from Central Station (Tue-Fri 10:00-18:00, Sat 10:00-17:00, closed Sun-Mon, at the locks where Singel canal boat arrives at the train station, see map on page 1138). Grab a sandwich and have a picnic canalside.

Supermarkets: You'll see **Albert Heijn** grocery stores (daily 8:00-22:00) all over town. Four helpful, central locations are: Dam Square (Nieuwezijds Voorburgwal 226), Mint Tower (Koningsplein 4), Leidsestraat (at Konigsplein, on the corner of Leidsestraat and Singel), and Central Station (far end of passage under the tracks).

West Amsterdam

Near the Anne Frank House and in the Jordaan District

Nearly all of these places are within a few scenic blocks of the Anne Frank House, providing handy lunches and atmospheric dinners in Amsterdam's most characteristic neighborhood. For locations, see the map on page 1138.

Restaurant de Luwte is romantic, located on a picturesque street overlooking a canal. It has lots of candles, a muted but fresh modern interior, spacious seating, a few cool outdoor canalside tables, and French Mediterranean cuisine. Ask about their specials (€20 entrées, €30 three-course fixed-price meal, big dinner salads for €18, daily 18:00-22:00, Leliegracht 26-28, tel. 020/625-8548, manager Maarten).

De Bolhoed has serious vegetarian and vegan food in a colorful setting that Buddha would dig, with a clientele that appears to dig Buddha (big splittable portions, €15 dinners, light lunches, daily 12:00-22:00, dinner starts at 17:00, Prinsengracht 60, tel. 020/626-1803).

Café Restaurant de Reiger must offer the best cooking of any *eetcafé* in the Jordaan. Famous for its fresh ingredients and delightful bistro ambience, it's part of the classic Jordaan scene. In addition to an English menu, ask for a translation of the €17.50-20 daily specials on the chalkboard. They're proud of their fresh fish and French-Dutch cuisine. The café, which is crowded late and on weekends, takes no reservations, but you're welcome to have a drink (€3 house wine and fun little bar munchies menu) at the bar while you wait (Tue-Sun 17:00-24:00, closed Mon, veggie options, Nieuwe Leliestraat 34, tel. 020/624-7426).

Café 't Smalle is extremely charming, with three zones where you can enjoy a light lunch or a drink: canalside, inside around the bar, and up some steep stairs in a quaint little back room. The café is open daily until midnight, and simple meals (salads, soup, and fresh sandwiches) are served 11:00-17:30 (plenty of fine €2-3 Belgian beers on tap and interesting wines by the glass, at Egelantiersgracht 12 where it hits Prinsengracht, tel. 020/623-9617).

Thai Fusion, despite the name, serves straight-up top-quality Thai food in a sleekly modern, black-and-white room wedged neatly in the middle of the Nine Little Streets action (€15-20 main courses, €25-30 two-course meals, Mon-Fri 16:30-22:30, Sat-Sun 12:00-22:30, good veggie options, Berenstraat 8, tel. 020/320-8332).

Toscana Italian Restaurant is the Jordaan's favorite place for good, inexpensive Italian cuisine, including pizza, in a woody, Dutch-beer-hall setting (€6-8 pizza and pastas, €16 main courses, daily 16:00-23:30, fast service, Haarlemmerstraat 130, tel. 020/622-0353).

Winkel, the North Jordaan's cornerside hangout, serves appetizing French-Dutch meals at its plentiful outside tables and easygoing interior. It really gets hopping on Monday mornings when the Noordermarkt flea market is underway, but Amsterdammers come from across town all week for the *appeltaart* (€11-14 dinner plates, €5 snacks served after 16:00, daily 8:00-24:00 except Sun from 10:00, Noordermarkt 43, tel. 020/623-0223).

Sara's Pancake House is a basic pancake diner where extremely hardworking Sara cranks out sweet and savory €8-10 flapjacks made from fresh, organic ingredients (daily until 22:30, later on weekends, breakfast served until noon, Raadhuisstraat 45, tel. 020/320-0662).

Restaurant 't Stuivertje is a small, family-run neighborhood eatery tucked away in the Jordaan, serving French-inspired Dutch cuisine in an elegantly cozy but unpretentious atmosphere (€15-25 main courses, dinner salads, Wed-Sun 17:30-22:00, closed Mon-Tue, Hazenstraat 58 near Elandsgracht, tel. 020/623-1349).

Ristorante Toscanini is an up-market Italian place that's always packed. It's so popular that the staff can be a bit arrogant, but the lively, spacious ambience and great Italian cuisine more than make up for that—if you can get a seat. Reservations are essentially required (the staff recommends two-weeks notice for Fri and Sat). Otherwise your best bet is to arrive when they open at 18:00 (€14 first courses, €20 main courses, Mon-Sat 18:00-22:30, closed Sun, deep in the Jordaan at Lindengracht 75, tel. 020/623-2813).

Villa Zeesicht has all the romantic feel of a classic European café. The cozy interior is crammed with tiny tables topped by tall candlesticks, and wicker chairs outside gather under a wisteria-covered awning. The menu is uninventive—come here instead for the famous *appeltaart,* and for the great people-watching on Torensluis bridge (€11-16 plates, daily 9:00-21:30, Torensteeg 7, tel. 020/626-7433).

Drinks Only: **Café 't Papeneiland** is a classic brown café with Delft tiles, an evocative old stove, and a stay-awhile perch overlooking a canal with welcoming benches. It's been the neighborhood hangout since the 17th century (drinks but no food, overlooking northwest end of Prinsengracht at #2, tel. 020/624-1989). It feels a little exclusive; patrons who come here to drink and chat aren't eager to see it overrun by tourists. The café's name means "Papists' Island," since this was once a refuge for Catholics; there used to be an escape tunnel here for priests on the run.

Southwest Amsterdam

Near Leidseplein

Stroll through the colorful cancan of eateries on Leidsedwarsstraat, Restaurant Row, just off Leidseplein, and choose your favorite. Nearby, the busy Leidsestraat offers plenty of starving-student options (between the Prinsengracht and the Herengracht) offering fast and fun food for around €5 a meal.

Beyond the Rijksmuseum

Restaurant Bazar offers one of the most memorable and fun budget eating experiences in town. Converted from a church, it has spacious seating and mod belly-dance music, and is filled with young locals enjoying good, cheap Middle Eastern and North African cuisine. Reservations are a good idea if you plan to eat after 20:00 (fill up with the €8.50 daily plate, delicious €13 couscous, or €16 three-course meal of the day; daily 11:00-23:00, until 24:00 on weekends, Albert Cuypstraat 182, tel. 020/675-0544). Restaurant Bazar marks the center of the thriving Albert Cuyp market, which is wrapped up by about 17:00, though the restaurant is open late.

In Vondelpark

Café Vertigo offers a fun selection of excellent soups, salads, and sandwiches. It's a surprisingly large complex of outdoor tables, an indoor pub, and an elegant, candlelit, back-room restaurant beneath the grand, Italian Renaissance Vondel Pavilion. The service can be slow, but if you grab an outdoor table, you can watch the world spin by (daily 10:00-24:00 except off-season weekdays from 11:00, Vondelpark 3, tel. 020/612-3021).

Southeast Amsterdam
Near the Dutch Resistance Museum

For locations of the following eateries, see the map on page 1130.

Restaurant Plancius, adjacent to the Dutch Resistance Museum, is a modern and handy spot for lunch. Its good indoor and outdoor seating make it popular with the museum staff and broadcasters from the nearby local TV studios (creative breakfasts, hearty fresh sandwiches, light €5-9 lunches and €16-19 dinners, daily 10:00-22:00, Plantage Kerklaan 61a, tel. 020/330-9469).

Café Koosje, located halfway between the Dutch Resistance Museum and the Dutch Theater, is a corner lunchtime pub/bar ringed with outdoor seating. Inside, casual wooden tables and benches huddle under chandeliers, and the hip, young waitstaff serves beer and salads big enough for two (€5 sandwiches, €11 salads, food served daily 9:00-22:00, Plantage Middenlaan 37, on the corner of Plantage Kerklaan, tel. 020/320-0817).

Smoking

Tobacco

A quarter of Dutch people smoke tobacco. Holland has a long tradition as a smoking culture, being among the first to import the tobacco plant from the New World.

Tobacco shops glorify the habit, yet the Dutch people are among the healthiest in the world. Tanned, trim, firm, 60-something Dutch people sip their beer, take a drag, and ask me why Americans murder themselves with Big Macs.

Still, their version of the Surgeon General has finally woken up to the drug's many potential health risks. Warning stickers bigger than America's are required on cigarette packs, and some of them are almost comically blunt, such as: "Smoking will make you impotent...and then you die." (The warnings have prompted gag stickers like, "Life can kill you.")

Since 2008, a Dutch law has outlawed smoking tobacco almost everywhere indoors: on trains, and in hotel rooms, restaurants, cafés, and bars.

Marijuana (a.k.a. Cannabis)

Throughout the Netherlands, you'll see "coffeeshops"—cafés selling marijuana, with display cases showing various joints or baggies for sale. The minimum age for purchase is 18, and coffeeshops can sell up to five grams of marijuana per person per day. However, the newly conservative Dutch government has passed a law that bans tourists from buying marijuana—officially, at least, only Dutch citizens with a *wietpas* (weed pass) are legally able to buy a joint. It's unclear just how strictly this will be enforced in 2013, but be aware that the high times may be a changin'.

The Dutch buy marijuana by asking, "Can I see the cannabis menu?" Because it's illegal to advertise marijuana, the buyer has to take the initiative and request a menu. In some places there's actually a button you must push and hold down to see an illuminated menu, the contents of which look like the inventory of a drug bust.

The Netherland's indoor-smoking ban pertains to tobacco smoke, not pot smoke. But the Dutch, like the rest of Europe, mix their marijuana with tobacco. It might seem strange to an American, but these days, if a coffeeshop is busted, it's for tobacco. Coffeeshops with a few outdoor seats have a huge advantage, as their customers can light up outside. Shops without the outdoor option are in for an extra challenge, as many local smokers would rather get their weed to-go than smoke it without tobacco at their neighborhood coffeeshop. As a substitute for tobacco, shops have started mixing a kind of herb tea into joints. Pre-rolled joints are now sold three ways: pure, with the non-tobacco "hamburger helper" herb mix, or with tobacco. If you like your joint tobacco-free anyway, pure marijuana joints are much easier to find than they used to be.

Shops sell marijuana and hashish both in pre-rolled joints and in little baggies. Some places sell individual joints (€2-5). Others sell only small packs of three or four joints. Baggies of marijuana usually cost €10-15. Some shops charge per gram. The better pot, while costlier, is actually a better value, as it takes less to get high—and it's a better high. Shops have loaner bongs and inhalers, and they dispense cigarette papers like toothpicks. As long as you're a paying customer (e.g., buy a cup of coffee), you can pop into any coffeeshop and light up, even if you didn't buy your pot there.

Don't ever buy pot on the street in Amsterdam, and don't smoke marijuana openly while walking down the street. Well-established coffeeshops are considered much safer, and coffeeshop owners have an interest in keeping their trade safe and healthy. They warn Americans—unused to the strength of the local stuff—to try a lighter leaf. In fact, they are generally very patient in explaining the varieties available.

Coffeeshops

Most of downtown Amsterdam's coffeeshops feel grungy and fore-boding to American travelers who aren't part of the youth-hostel crowd. The neighborhood places (and those in small towns around the countryside) are much more inviting to people without piercings, tattoos, and favorite techno artists. I've listed a few places with a more pub-like ambience for Americans wanting to go local, but within reason. For locations, see the maps under "Sleeping in Amsterdam," earlier.

Paradox is the most *gezellig* (cozy) coffeeshop I found—a mellow, graceful place. The managers, Ludo and Wiljan, and their staff are patient with descriptions and happy to walk you through all your options. This is a rare coffeeshop that serves light meals. The juice is fresh, the music is easy, and the neighborhood is charming (single tobacco-free joints-€3, loaner bongs, games, daily 10:00-20:00, two blocks from Anne Frank House at Eerste Bloemdwarsstraat 2, tel. 020/623-5639, www.paradoxcoffeeshop .com).

The Grey Area coffeeshop—a hole-in-the-wall spot with three tiny tables—is a cool, welcoming, and smoky place appreciated among local aficionados as a perennial winner of Amsterdam's Cannabis Cup awards. Judging by the autographed photos on the wall, many famous Americans have dropped in (say hi to Willie Nelson). You're welcome to just nurse a bottomless cup of coffee. The Grey Area is run by two friendly Americans, Adam and Jon. They are helpful and even have a vaporizer if you want to "smoke" without smoking (daily 12:00-20:00, they close relatively early out of consideration for their neighbors, between Dam Square and Anne Frank House at Oude Leliestraat 2, tel. 020/420-4301, www .greyarea.nl).

Siberië Coffeeshop is a short walk from Central Station, but feels cozy, with a friendly canalside ambience. Clean, big, and bright, this place has the vibe of a not-too-far-out Starbucks (daily 11:00-23:00, Fri-Sat until 24:00, free Wi-Fi for customers, helpful staff, English menu, Brouwersgracht 11, tel. 020/623-5909, www .siberie.nl).

La Tertulia is a sweet little mother-and-daughter–run place with pastel decor and a cheery terrarium atmosphere (Tue-Sat 11:00-19:00, closed Sun-Mon, sandwiches, brownies, games, Prinsengracht 312, www.coffeeshopamsterdam.com).

The Bulldog is the high-profile, leading touristy chain of coffeeshops. These establishments are young but welcoming, with reliable selections. They're pretty comfortable for green tourists wanting to just hang out for a while. The flagship branch, in a former police station right on Leidseplein, is very handy, offering alcohol upstairs, pot downstairs, and fun outdoor seating where you can watch the world skateboard by. There's a chance it may close because it's considered too near a school, but it will likely stay open (daily 10:00-1:00 in the morning, Fri-Sat until 3:00, Leidseplein 17, tel. 020/625-6278, www.bulldog.nl). They opened their first café (on the canal near the Old Church in the Red Light District) in 1975.

The **Dampkring** is a rough-and-ready constant party. It's a high-profile and busy place, filled with a young clientele and loud music, but the owners still take the time to explain what they offer. Scenes from the movie *Ocean's Twelve* were filmed here (daily 10:00-1:00 in the morning, close to Spui at Handboogstraat 29, tel. 020/638-0705, www.dampkring.nl).

Smartshops

These business establishments sell "natural" drugs that are legal. Many are harmless nutritional supplements, but they also sell stimulants similar to Ecstasy and strange drug cocktails rolled into joints. It's all perfectly legal, but if you've never taken drugs recreationally, don't start here.

Amsterdam Connections

The Netherlands is so small, level, and well-covered by trains and buses that transportation is a snap. The easy-to-navigate airport is well-connected to Amsterdam and other destinations by bus and train.

By Train

Amsterdam Central Station

Amsterdam's Central Station is being renovated—a messy construction project that's expected to last through 2014 (see "Arrival in Amsterdam" on page 1105 for more details on the station). The station's train-information center can require a long wait. Save lots of time by getting train tickets and information at a small-town station (such as Haarlem), the airport upon arrival (wonderful service), or a travel agency. You can buy tickets ahead of time for the next day.

If you have a railpass, it's quicker to validate it when you arrive at Schiphol Airport than in Amsterdam's Central Station where ticket-counter lines are long; you can stretch your flexipass by buying an inexpensive ticket from the airport into Amsterdam and using your first travel day for a longer trip.

From Amsterdam Central Station by Train to: Schiphol Airport (4-6/hour, 15 minutes, €3.70, have coins handy to buy from a machine to avoid lines), **Haarlem** (6/hour, 20 minutes, €3.70 one-way, €7.10 same-day round-trip), **Delft** (2/hour direct, 1 hour, more with transfer in Leiden or The Hague), **Bruges/Brugge** (hourly, 3.25-3.75 hours, transfer at Antwerp Central or Brussels Midi; transfer can be tight—be alert and check with conductor), **Brussels** (Intercity trains hourly, 2.75 hours), **Ostend** (for ferries to UK; hourly, 4 hours, 3 changes), **London** (6/day, 4.75-5.5 hours, with transfer to Eurostar Chunnel train in Brussels; Eurostar discounted with railpass, www.eurostar.com), **Copenhagen** (2/day, 11.25 hours, multiple transfers; one direct night train), **Frankfurt** (every 2 hours, 4 hours direct), **Munich** (roughly hourly, 7.5-8.75 hours, 1-2 transfers; night train possible via Hamburg, 15.5 hours), **Bern** (5/day, 8-9 hours, fastest trains change once in Frankfurt), **Paris** (nearly hourly, 3.25 hours direct via fast Thalys train or 5 hours with change to Thalys train in Brussels, www.thalys.com). When booking Thalys trains, even railpass-holders need to buy a seat reservation (generally €26-33 in second-class or €41-54 in first class—the first-class reservation generally gets you a meal on board). If your railpass covers France but not BeNeLux, the reservation will cost more. (Railpasses that don't include France are not accepted on Thalys trains.) Save money by taking a bus to Paris—described next.

By Bus

To Paris by Bus: If you don't have a railpass, the cheapest way to get to Paris is by Eurolines bus (about 6/day, 8 hours, €46 one-way, €86 round-trip; price depends on demand—nonrefundable, advance-purchase one-way tickets as cheap as €17 and round-trip as cheap as €28, check online for deals, Julianaplein 5, Amstel Station, five stops by metro from Central Station, tel. 020/560-8788, www.eurolines.com).

By Plane

Amsterdam's Schiphol Airport

Schiphol (SKIP-pol) Airport is located about 10 miles southwest of Amsterdam's city center.

Information: Schiphol flight information can give you flight times and your airline's Amsterdam phone number for flight reconfirmation (tel. 0900-0141, from other countries dial +31-20-794-0800, www.schiphol.nl). To reach the airlines directly, call: KLM and Northwest—tel. 020/474-7747; Delta—tel. 020/201-3536; United—tel. 020/201-3708; US Airways—tel. 020/201-3550; Continental—tel. 020/346-9381; Martinair—tel. 020/601-1767; SAS—toll tel. 0900-7466-3727; Lufthansa—toll tel. 0900-123-4777; British Airways—tel. 020/346-9559; and easyJet—toll tel. 0900-265-8022.

Orientation: Schiphol has four terminals. Terminal 1 is for flights to most European countries (not including the UK);

Terminals 2 and 3 are for flights to the UK, US, and other non-European countries; and the new, smaller Terminal 4 (attached to Terminal 3) is for low-cost carriers. Inside the airport, the terminal waiting areas are called lounges; an inviting shopping and eating zone called Holland Boulevard runs between Lounges 2 and 3.

Arrival at Schiphol: Baggage claim areas for all terminals empty into the same arrival zone, called Schiphol Plaza—with ATMs, shops, eateries, a busy **TI** (near Terminal 2), a train station, and bus stops for getting into the city. You can validate your Eurail Pass and hit the rails immediately, or, to stretch your railpass, buy an inexpensive ticket into Amsterdam today and start the pass later.

Airport Services: The ABN/AMRO **banks** offer fair exchange rates (in both arrivals and lounge areas). The **GWK Travelex** currency-exchange office is located in Arrivals 3 and sells SIM cards for mobile phones. **Jill and James,** in Schiphol Plaza, near Terminal 4, is a useful all-purpose service counter that sells SIM cards, has an ATM, and ships packages. The **Orbitel** mobile shop just outside Terminal 2 sells only one brand of SIM cards.

You can surf the **Internet** (for a price) and make phone calls at the Communication Centres (one on the top level of Lounge 2, another on the ground floor of Lounge 1; both are behind customs and not available once you've left the security checkpoint). Convenient luggage **lockers** are at various points around the airport—allowing you to leave your bag here on a lengthy layover (both short-term and long-term lockers; biggest bank of lockers near the train station at Schiphol Plaza).

Airport Train Ticket Counter: To get train information, buy a ticket, or validate your railpass, take advantage of the fantastic "Train Tickets and Services" counter (Schiphol Plaza ground level, just past Burger King). They have an easy info desk, almost no lines (much quicker than the ticket desk at the Amsterdam train station downtown), and issue tickets for a fee (€0.50 for domestic tickets, €3.50 for tickets to Belgium, Luxembourg, and nearby German cities; up to €10 for other international tickets).

Time-Killing Tips: If you have extra time at Schiphol, check out the Rijksmuseum Amsterdam Schiphol, a little art gallery and museum store on Holland Boulevard, the lively shopping/eating zone between Lounges 2 and 3. The Rijksmuseum loans a dozen or so of its minor masterpieces from the Dutch Golden Age to this unique airport museum, including actual Dutch Masters by Rembrandt, Vermeer, and others (free, daily 5:15-21:30).

To escape the airport crowds, follow signs for the Panorama Terrace to the third floor of Terminal 2, where you'll find a quieter, full-of-locals cafeteria, a kids' play area, and a view terrace where you can watch planes come and go while you nurse a coffee.

If you plan to visit the terrace on arrival, stop there before you pass through customs.

From Schiphol Airport to Amsterdam: Direct **trains** to Amsterdam's Central Station run frequently (4-6/hour, 15 minutes, €3.70). The Connexxion **shuttle bus** takes you to your hotel neighborhood; since there are three different routes, ask the attendant which one works best for your hotel (2/hour, 20 minutes, €15 one-way, €24.50 round-trip, one route stops at Westerkerk near Anne Frank House and many recommended hotels, other routes may cost a couple euros more, departs from lane A7 in front of airport, reserve at least 2 hours ahead for shuttles to airport, tel. 088-339-4741, www.airporthotelshuttle.nl). Allow about €40 for a **taxi** to downtown Amsterdam. **Bus** #197 is handiest for those staying in the Leidseplein district (€4, buy ticket from driver, departs from lane B9 in front of airport).

From Schiphol Airport to Haarlem: The big red #300 **bus** departs from lane B6 in front of airport; for details, see "Haarlem Connections" at the end of the next chapter.

AMSTERDAM

HAARLEM

Cute and cozy, yet authentic and handy to the airport, Haarlem is a fine home base, giving you small-town warmth overnight, with easy access (20 minutes by train) to wild and crazy Amsterdam during the day.

Bustling Haarlem gave America's Harlem its name back when New York was New Amsterdam, a Dutch colony. For centuries, Haarlem has been a market town, buzzing with shoppers heading home with fresh bouquets, nowadays by bike.

Enjoy the market on Monday (clothing) or Saturday (general), when the town's atmospheric main square bustles like a Brueghel painting, with cheese, fish, flowers, and families. Make yourself at home; buy some flowers to brighten your hotel room.

Orientation to Haarlem

(area code: 023)
Tourist Information

Haarlem's TI (VVV), in the town center, is friendlier, more helpful, and less crowded than Amsterdam's, so ask your Amsterdam questions here (Mon-Fri 9:30-17:30, Sat 10:00-17:00, closed most Sun but may be open 12:00-16:00, across from V&D department store at Verwulft 11, toll tel. 0900-616-1600—€0.50/minute, www.haarlem.nl, info@vvvhaarlem.nl).

The TI offers a good selection of maps and sightseeing and walking tour brochures, and sells discounted tickets (€1-2 off) for the Frans Hals Museum and the Teylers Museum.

The little yellow computer terminal on the curb outside the west entrance of the train station prints out free maps anytime.

(It's fun...just dial the street and hit "print." Drivers will also find these terminals stationed at roads coming into town.)

Arrival in Haarlem

By Train: Lockers are available at the station on platform 3a (€3.65/day, no coins—use a credit card or buy a "Chipknip" prepaid debit card at a ticket window). Two parallel streets flank the train station (Kruisweg and Jansweg). Head up either street, and you'll reach the town square and church within 10 minutes. If you need help, ask a local person to point you toward Grote Markt (Market Square).

By Bus: Buses from Schiphol Airport stop both in the center (Centrum/Verwulft stop, a short walk from Grote Markt) and at the train station.

By Car: Parking is expensive on the streets (€2.50/hour). It's cheaper (€1/30 minutes; €2.50 overnight—19:00-8:00) in these central garages: at the train station, at the southern end of Gedempte Oude Gracht (the main thoroughfare), near the recommended Die Raeckse Hotel, and near the Frans Hals Museum. The most central garage, near the Teylers Museum, is pricier (€1.50 every 40 minutes—essentially, €2.75/hour).

By Plane: For details on getting from Schiphol Airport to Haarlem, see "Haarlem Connections," at the end of this chapter.

Helpful Hints

Blue Monday and Early Closures: Most sights are closed on Monday, except the church. Two sights close early the rest of the week: **Corrie Ten Boom House** (15:30) and **De Adriaan windmill** (16:00).

Internet Access: Try **Hotel Amadeus** (overlooking Grote Markt, €1/30 minutes), **High Times Coffeeshop** (free if you buy some pot, Lange Veerstraat 47), or **Suny Teletechniques** (€2/hour, daily 10:00-24:00, near train station at Lange Herenstraat 4, tel. 023/551-0037).

Post Office: There isn't one. To buy stamps, head to a newsstand with the orange *TNT* logo; if you need to send a package, ask your hotelier for help.

Laundry: **My Beautiful Launderette** is handy and fairly central (€6 self-service wash and dry, daily 8:30-20:30, €9 full service available Mon-Fri 9:00-17:00, near V&D department store at Boter Markt 20).

Bike Rental: You can rent bikes from **Pieters Fietsverhuur** at the train station (fixed-gear bike-€6.50/day, more for 3-speed bike, €50 deposit and passport number required, Mon-Sat 6:00-24:00, Sun 8:00-24:00, Stationsplein 7, tel. 023/531-7066).

They have only 50 bikes to rent and often run out by mid-morning—especially when the weather's good. **Rent a Bike Haarlem** charges more, but is friendly and efficient, and carries plenty of new, good-quality bikes. If you're renting for less than a full day, negotiate a cheaper price (fixed-gear bike-€10/day, 3-speed bike-€13.50/day, mountain bikes available, after-hours drop-off possible, ID but no money required for deposit; April-Sept daily 9:00-18:00; Oct-March Tue-Fri 10:00-17:30, Thu until 18:00, Sat 10:00-17:00, closed Sun-Mon; near station at Lange Herenstraat 36, tel. 023/542-1195, www.rent abikehaarlem.nl).

Taxi: The drop charge of €7.50 gets you a little over a mile.

Local Guide: Consider hiring **Walter Schelfhout,** a bearded repository of Haarlem's historical fun facts. If you're into beer lore, Walter's your guy (€75/2 hours, also leads a beer walk, tel. 023/535-5715, mobile 06-1258-9299, schelfhout@dutch.nl).

Best View: At **La Place** (top-floor cafeteria of the V&D department store—see "Eating in Haarlem," later), you get wrap-around views of the city as you sip your €2 self-serve tea.

Best Ice Cream: Gelateria Bartoli (on the south side of the Grote Kerk) is the local favorite (daily April-Sept 12:00-22:00, March and Oct-Dec 12:00-17:30 in good weather, closed Jan-Feb).

Sights in Haarlem

▲▲**Grote Markt (Market Square)**—Haarlem's Grote Markt, where 10 streets converge, is the town's delightful centerpiece...as it has been for 700 years. To enjoy a coffee or beer here, simmering in Dutch good living, is a quintessential European experience. Observe. Sit and gaze at the church, appreciating essentially the same scene that Dutch artists captured centuries ago in oil paintings that now hang in museums.

Just a few years ago, trolleys ran through the square, and cars were parked everywhere. But today, it's a pedestrian zone, with market stalls filling the square on Mondays and Saturdays, and café tables dominating on other days.

This is a fun place to build a picnic with Haarlem finger foods and enjoy great seating on the square. Look for pickled herring (take-away stand on the square), local cheese (Gouda and Edam—tasty shop a block away on Barteljorisstraat), french fries with mayonnaise (recommended old-time fries place behind the church on Warmoesstraat), and, in the summer, *stroopwafels* (waffles with built-in syrup) and *poffertjes* (little sugar doughnuts, cooked on the spot).

Haarlem

TO
OVERVEEN
& ZAND-
VOORT

STATEN BOLWERK

TRAIN
STATION

TO
AMST.

KENAU
PARK

PARK

STN.
PLEIN

BUS
STN.

PARK
LAAN

100
YARDS

100
METERS

HUIS VEST

KINDER ZIJL

RAAKS

GED. OUDE

KR...NS

TO
WINDMILL

RED
LIGHT
DISTRICT

NIEUWE
GROEN

SMEDESTRAAT

STRAAT

BARTEL

CORRIE
TEN BOOM
HOUSE

BAKE.

W. APP.

LANGE BEGIN.

GRACHT

TO
AMST.

B BUS #300

GROTE
MARKT

ENTER

GROTE
KERK

TOWN
HALL

KONINGSTR.

MEAT
MKT.

WARM.

B

BOTER
MARKT

VERWULFT

B
B

HOUT STR.

ANEGANG

FRANKE STR.

SCHAGCHEL STR.

KLEINE HOUT

LANGE
VEER

SPAARNE

B

B CANAL
CRUISES

TEYLERS
MUSEUM

V&D
DEP'T.
STORE

GIER. STR.

GROTE

RACH

HISTORY
MUSEUM
HAARLEM

KLEIN HEILIGLAND

GROTE HEILIG.

FRANS HALS
MUSEUM

TO
AMST.

GASTHUIS VEST

DCH

▲**Church (Grote Kerk)**—This 15th-century Gothic church (now Protestant) is worth a look, if only to see Holland's greatest pipe organ (from 1738, 100 feet high). Its more than 5,000 pipes impressed both Handel and Mozart. Note how the organ, which fills the west end, seems to steal the show from the altar. Quirky highlights of the church include a replica of Foucault's pendulum, the "Dog-Whipper's Chapel," and a 400-year-old cannonball.

To enter, find the small *Entrée* sign behind the Coster statue on Grote Markt.

Cost and Hours: €2.50, not covered by Museumkaart, Mon-Sat 10:00-16:00, closed Sun to tourists, tel. 023/553-2040, www.bavo.nl.

Concerts: Consider attending (even part of) a **concert** to hear the Oz-like pipe organ (regular free concerts Tue at 20:15 mid-May-mid-Oct, additional concerts Thu at 15:00 July-Aug; bring a sweater—the church isn't heated).

▲▲**Frans Hals Museum**—Haarlem is the hometown of Frans Hals, the foremost Dutch portrait painter of the 17th-century Golden Age. This refreshing museum, once an almshouse for old men back in 1610, displays many of Hals' greatest paintings, done in his nearly Impressionistic style. You'll see group portraits and take-me-back paintings of old-time Haarlem. Stand eye-to-eye with life-size, lifelike portraits of Haarlem's citizens—brewers, preachers, workers, bureaucrats, and housewives. Take a close look at the people who built the Dutch Golden Age, and then watched it start to fade.

Along with Frans Hals' work, the museum features a copy of Pieter Brueghel the Younger's *Flemish Proverbs,* a fun painting that shows 72 charming Flemish scenes representing different folk sayings. Pick up the chart to identify these clever bits of everyday wisdom. It's near the 250-year-old dollhouse on display in a former chapel.

Cost and Hours: €7.50, often €10 with special exhibits, Tue-Sat 11:00-17:00, Sun 12:00-17:00, closed Mon, Groot Heiligland 62, tel. 023/511-5775, www.franshalsmuseum.nl.

History Museum Haarlem—This small museum, across the street from the Frans Hals Museum, offers a glimpse of old Haarlem. Request the English version of the 10-minute video, low-key Haarlem's version of a sound-and-light show. Study the large-scale model of Haarlem in 1822 (when its fortifications were still intact), and wander the three rooms without English descriptions. The adjacent architecture center (free) may be of interest to architects.

Cost and Hours: Overpriced at €5, Tue-Sat 12:00-17:00, Sun 13:00-17:00, closed Mon, Groot Heiligland 47, tel. 023/542-2427, www.historischmuseumhaarlem.nl.

▲**Corrie ten Boom House**—Haarlem was home to Corrie ten Boom, popularized by her inspirational book (and the movie that followed), *The Hiding Place*. Both tell about the Ten Boom family's experience protecting Jews from the Nazis. Corrie ten Boom gives the other half of the Anne Frank story—the point of view of those who risked their lives to hide Dutch Jews during the Nazi occupation (1940-1945).

The clock shop was the Ten Boom family business. The elderly father and his two daughters—Corrie and Betsy, both in their 50s—lived above the store and in the brick building attached in back (along Schoutensteeg alley). Corrie's bedroom was on the top floor at the back. This room was tiny to start with, but then the family built a second, secret room (less than a yard deep) at the very back—"the hiding place," where they could hide six Jews at a time. Devoutly religious, the family had a long tradition of tolerance, having hosted prayer meetings here in their home for both Jews and Christians for generations.

The Gestapo, tipped off that the family was harboring Jews, burst into the Ten Boom house. Finding a suspicious number of ration coupons, the Nazis arrested the family, but failed to find the six Jews (who later escaped) in the hiding place. Corrie's father and sister died while in prison, but Corrie survived the Ravensbrück concentration camp to tell her story in her memoir.

The Ten Boom House is open only for English tours—check the sign on the door for the next start time. The gentle and loving one-hour tours come with a little evangelizing that some may find objectionable.

Cost and Hours: Free, but donations accepted; April-Oct Tue-Sat first tour at 10:00, last tour at 15:30; Nov-March Tue-Sat first tour at 11:00, last tour around 14:30; closed Sun-Mon; 50 yards north of Grote Markt at Barteljorisstraat 19; the clock-shop people get all wound up if you go inside—wait in the little side street at the door, where tour times are posted; tel. 023/531-0823, www.corrietenboom.com.

▲**Teylers Museum**—Famous as the oldest museum in Holland, Teylers is a time-warp experience, filled with all sorts of fun curios for science buffs: fossils, minerals, primitive electronic gadgetry, and examples of 18th- and 19th-century technology (it also has two lovely painting galleries and hosts good temporary exhibits). The science-oriented sections of this place feel like a museum of a museum. They're serious about authenticity here: The presentation is perfectly preserved, right down to the original labels. Since there was no electricity in the olden days, you'll find little electric lighting...if it's dark outside, it's dark inside. The museum's benefactor,

Pieter Teyler van der Hulst, was a very wealthy merchant who willed his estate, worth the equivalent of €80 million today, to a foundation whose mission was to "create and maintain a museum to stimulate art and science." The museum opened in 1784, six years after Teyler's death (his last euro was spent in 1983—now it's a national museum). Add your name to the guest book, which goes back to before Napoleon's visit here. The freshly renovated oval room—a temple of science and learning—is the core of the museum; in the art salons paintings are hung in the old style. An excellent (and, I'd say, essential) audioguide is included.

Cost and Hours: Overpriced at €10, Tue-Sat 10:00-17:00, Sun 12:00-17:00, closed Mon, Spaarne 16, tel. 023/516-0960, www .teylersmuseum.eu. The museum's modern café has good prices and faces a delightful garden.

▲**De Adriaan Windmill**—Haarlem's old-time windmill, located just a 10-minute walk from the station and Teylers Museum, welcomes visitors with a short video, little museum, and fine town views.

Cost and Hours: €3, not covered by Museumkaart; March-Oct Mon and Wed-Fri 13:00-16:00, Sat-Sun 10:00-16:00, closed Tue; same hours in winter except only open Fri-Mon, Papentorenvest 1, tel. 023/545-0259, www.molenadriaan.nl.

Canal Cruise—Making a scenic 50-minute loop through and around Haarlem with a live guide who speaks Dutch and sometimes English, **Post Verkade Cruise**'s little trips are more relaxing than informative (€9.50; April-Oct daily departures at the top of the hour 12:00-16:00; also evening cruises, across canal from Teylers Museum at Spaarne 11a, tel. 023/535-7723, www.post verkadecruises.nl). For a similar experience in an open boat, find **Haarlem Canal Tours,** nearby on Korte Spaarne (€12.50, leaves every 1.5 hours daily 10:00-19:00, may not run in bad weather and off-season, www.haarlemcanaltours.com).

▲**Red Light District**—Wander through a little Red Light District that's as precious as a Barbie doll—and legal since the 1980s (2 blocks northeast of Grote Markt, off Lange Begijnestraat, no senior or student discounts). Don't miss the mall on Begijnesteeg marked by the red neon sign reading 't Steegje ("free"). Just beyond that, the nearby 't Poortje ("office park") costs €6 to enter. Jog to the right to pop into the much more inviting "Red Lantern" (window-shopping welcome, at Korte Begijnestraat 27). As you wander through this area, remember that the people here don't condone prostitution any more than your own community back home probably does; they just find it practical not to criminalize it and drive it underground, but instead to regulate it and keep the practice as safe as possible.

Nightlife in Haarlem

Haarlem's evening scene is great. Consider four basic zones: Grote Markt in the shadow of the Grote Kerk; Lange Veerstraat; Boter Grote Markt; and Vijfhoek (Five Corners).

Grote Markt is lined with trendy bars that seem made for nursing a drink—**Café Studio** is generally the hot spot for a drink here (at Grote Markt 25); I'd also duck into the dark interior of **In Den Uiver** (near the Grote Kerk entry at Riviervischmarkt 13, live jazz Thu and Sun). Lange Veerstraat (behind the Grote Kerk) is colorful and bordered with lively spots. Boter Grote Markt is more convivial and local, as it's less central and away from the tourists. Vijfhoek, named for the five lanes that converge here, is incredibly charming, although it has only one pub (with plenty of drinks, bar snacks, a relaxed crowd, and fine indoor or outdoor seating). Also worth exploring is the area from this cutest corner in town to the New Church (Nieuwe Kerk), a couple of blocks away. If you want a more high-powered scene, Amsterdam is just 20 minutes away by train.

Sleeping in Haarlem

The helpful Haarlem TI can nearly always find you a €27.50 bed in a private home (but for a €5.50-per-person fee, plus a cut of your host's money; two-night minimum, €30-35 for single room). Avoid this if you can; it's cheaper to reserve by calling direct. Nearly every Dutch person you'll encounter speaks English.

Haarlem is most crowded on Easter weekend (March 29-31 in 2013), in April (particularly the flower parade—April 20 in 2013—and Queen's Day, on April 30), May, July, and August (especially during Haarlem's jazz festival on the third weekend of Aug).

The prices listed here include breakfast (unless otherwise noted) and usually include the €2-per-person-per-day tourist tax. To avoid this town's louder-than-normal street noises, forgo views for a room in the back. Hotels and the TI have a useful parking brochure.

In the Center
Hotels and B&Bs
$$$ Hotel Lion D'Or is a classy, 34-room business hotel with all the professional comforts, pleasingly posh decor, and a handy but less-than-quaint location (Db-€150, Fri-Sat Db-€125, extra bed-€15, check website for special deals, ask for Rick Steves discount with 2-night stay when you book direct, air-con, elevator, pay Internet access and Wi-Fi, across the street from train station

Sleep Code

(€1 = about $1.40, country code: 31, area code: 023)
S = Single, **D** = Double/Twin, **T** = Triple, **Q** = Quad, **b** = bathroom,
s = shower only. Nearly everyone speaks English. Credit cards
are accepted and breakfast is included unless otherwise
noted.

To help you easily sort through these listings, I've divided
the accommodations into three categories, based on the price
for a standard double room with bath:

$$$ Higher Priced—Most rooms €85 or more.
$$ Moderately Priced—Most rooms between €60-85.
$ Lower Priced—Most rooms €60 or less.

Prices can change without notice; verify the hotel's
current rates online or by email. For other updates, see www
.ricksteves.com/update.

at Kruisweg 34, tel. 023/532-1750, fax 023/532-9543, www.hotel
liondor.nl, reservations@hotelliondor.nl, friendly Dirk Pauw).

$$$ Stempels Hotel, modern yet elegant, is located in a reno-
vated, 250-year-old building. With bare floors, comfy high-quality
beds, and minimalist touches in its 17 rooms, what it lacks in
warmth it makes up for in style and value. Double-paned windows
help keep down the noise, since it's a block east of Grote Markt,
with a bustling brasserie and bar downstairs (standard Sb-€90,
standard Db-€105-110, pricier rooms and suites available, break-
fast-€12, in-room computers with free Internet access and Wi-Fi,
Klokhuisplein 9, tel. 023/512-3910, www.stempelsinhaarlem.nl,
info@stempelsinhaarlem.nl).

$$$ Hotel Amadeus, on Grote Markt, has 15 small, bright,
and basic rooms, some with views of the square. This characteris-
tic hotel, ideally located above an early 20th-century dinner café,
is relatively quiet, especially if you take a room in the back. Its
lush old lounge/breakfast room on the second floor overlooks the
square, and Mike and Inez take good care of their guests (Sb-
€60, Db-€85, Tb-€110, check website for special deals, 5 percent
Rick Steves discount off full price with 2-night stay and cash, pay
Internet access and Wi-Fi, Grote Markt 10—from square it's a
steep climb to lounge and then an elevator, tel. 023/532-4530, fax
023/532-2328, www.amadeus-hotel.com, info@amadeus-hotel
.com). The Hotel Amadeus' breakfast room overlooking the main
square is a great place to watch the town greet a new day—one of
my favorite Haarlem moments.

Haarlem Hotels & Restaurants

1 Hotel Lion D'Or
2 Stempels Hotel
3 Hotel Amadeus
4 Ambassador City Centre Hotel
5 Hotel Malts
6 Hotel Carillon
7 Die Raeckse Hotel
8 To Hotel Haarlem Zuid
9 To Stayokay Haarlem Hostel
10 Jacobus Pieck Eetlokaal & Friethuis de Vlaminck
11 De Lachende Javaan Rest.

12 La Plume Restaurant
13 Pizzeria-Rist. Venezia
14 Vlam in de Pan & 't Theehuis Coffeeshop
15 Spaarne 66 Restaurant Bar
16 Lambermon's Brasserie & Restaurant
17 La Place Cafeteria
18 Albert Heijn Supermarkets (2)
19 DekaMarkt Supermarket
20 High Times Coffeehouse
21 Vijfhoek (Five Corners)

$$$ Ambassador City Centre Hotel, with 29 comfortable rooms in a big, plain hotel, is located just behind the Grote Kerk. If you're willing to trade some street noise for amazing church views, ask for a room in the front (Db-€100, often less off-season, breakfast buffet-€14, free Internet access and Wi-Fi, Oude Groenmarkt 20, tel. 023/512-5300, www.acc-hotel.nl, info@acc-hotel.nl). They also run **Hotel Joops,** with 32 rooms, a block away (rooms are €10 cheaper; studios and apartments with kitchenettes for 2-4 people-€120-150 depending on season and number of people).

$$ Hotel Malts is well-located and rents 12 bright, simple, and fresh rooms for a good price. The rooms in front are big, but not recommended for light sleepers (small D-€69, small Db-€79, standard Db-€85, big Db-€95, check website for best prices, no elevator, free Wi-Fi, Zijlstraat 56, tel. 023/551-2385, www.malts hotel.nl, info@maltshotel.nl, Marco).

Rooms in Restaurants

These places are all run as sidelines by restaurants, and you'll know it by the style of service and rooms. Lobbies are in the restaurant, and there are no public spaces. Still, they are handy and—for Haarlem—inexpensive.

$$ Hotel Carillon overlooks the town square and comes with a little traffic and bell-tower chimes. With run-down public spaces and st-e-e-e-p stairs, it's an old-school, over-the-restaurant place. The rooms themselves, however, are freshly updated and pleasant. The front rooms come with more street noise and great town-square views (tiny loft S-€40, Db-€80-90, Tb-€102, Qb-€110, ask for Rick Steves discount when you reserve—must show book on arrival, no elevator, free Wi-Fi, Grote Markt 27, tel. 023/531-0591, fax 023/531-4909, www.hotelcarillon.com, info@hotelcarillon .com, owners Kelly Kuo, Andres Haas, and June).

$$ Die Raeckse Hotel, family-run and friendly, is not as central as the others and has less character and more traffic noise—but its 21 rooms are decent and comfortable. Quiet rooms in back cost more than the noisy rooms on the street—but they're worth it (Sb-€55, smaller Db-€80-85, big Db-€85-90, Tb-€120, Qb-€130-145, €5/night discount for 2-night stay, ask for Rick Steves discount with this book Nov-March, free but time-limited Internet access, free Wi-Fi, Raaks Straat 1, tel. 023/532-6629, fax 023/531-7937, www.die-raeckse.nl, dieraeckse@zonnet.nl).

Near Haarlem

$$$ Hotel Haarlem Zuid, with 300 modern rooms, is sterile but a good value for drivers. It sits in an industrial zone a 20-minute walk from the center, on the road to the airport (Db-€88-110, breakfast-€13, elevator, free parking, laundry service, fitness center-€5, reasonable hotel restaurant, Toekanweg 2, tel. 023/536-7500, fax 023/536-7980, www.hotelhaarlemzuid.nl, haarlemzuid @valk.com). Bus #300 conveniently connects the hotel with the train station, Grote Markt, and the airport (every 10 minutes, stop: Europaweg).

$ Stayokay Haarlem Hostel, completely renovated and with all the youth-hostel comforts, charges €25-30 for beds in four- and six-bed dorms. They also rent simple €60-80 doubles (€2.50 less for members, includes sheets and breakfast, save by booking on their website, pay Internet access and Wi-Fi, laundry service, reception open 8:00-20:30 but late arrivals OK, Jan Gijzenpad 3, two miles from Haarlem station—take bus #2 from station, or a 10-minute walk from Santpoort Zuid train station, tel. 023/537-3793, www .stayokay.com/haarlem, haarlem@stayokay.com).

Eating in Haarlem

Restaurants

Jacobus Pieck Eetlokaal is popular with locals for its fine-value "global cuisine," good salads, and unpretentious flair. Sit in the peaceful garden courtyard, at a sidewalk table, or in the romantically cozy interior. The Oriental Peak Salad is a perennial favorite, and the dish of the day (*dagschotel*, €12.50) always sells out (great €7 sandwiches at lunch, Mon 11:00-16:00 only, Tue-Sat 10:00-22:00, closed Sun, cash only, Warmoesstraat 18, behind church, tel. 023/532-6144).

De Lachende Javaan ("The Laughing Javanese") is a long-established Indonesian place serving a memorable *rijsttafel* (€20-24, Tue-Sun 17:00-22:00, closed Mon, Frankestraat 27, tel. 023/532-8792).

La Plume Restaurant steakhouse is noisy, with a happy, local, and carnivorous crowd enjoying the candlelit scene (€15-20 meals, daily 17:30-23:00, Fri-Sat until 24:00, *satay* and ribs are favorites, Lange Veerstraat 1, tel. 023/531-3202). The relaxing outdoor seating faces the church and a lively pedestrian street.

Pizzeria-Ristorante Venezia, run for 25 years by the same Italian family from Bari, is the place to go for pizza or pasta (€8-10 choices, daily 13:00-23:00, facing V&D department store at Verwulft 7, tel. 023/531-7753). You'll feel like you're in Rome at a good indoor table, or sit outdoors in a busy people-zone.

At **Vlam in de Pan,** a dynamo named Femke serves vegetarian delights: soup, salad, veggie sushi, quiches, and other fresh, mostly organic foods. Enjoy the small, funky dining area, or get your food to take away (€10-15 plates, Tue-Fri 16:00-21:00, closed Sat-Mon, Smedestraat 13, tel. 023/551-1738).

Lange Veerstraat Restaurant Row: If you don't know what

you want to eat, stroll the delightful Lange Veerstraat behind the church and survey a fun range of restaurants (from cheap falafels to Cuban, and much more).

On the Spaarne River Canal: Haarlem seems to turn its back on its river with most of the eating energy a couple of blocks away. To enjoy a meal with a fine canal view, consider the **Spaarne 66 Restaurant Bar.** The Lemmers girls (a mom and her daughters) run this cozy eatery, with a woody, old-time interior and fine, outdoor canalside seating (light €7 lunches, €20 Mediterranean/Dutch dinner plates, €30 three-course fixed-price meal, Wed-Mon 11:00-24:00, closed Tue, Spaarne 66, tel. 023/551-3800).

Dressy Splurge: At **Lambermon's,** expert chef Michèl Lambermon serves chichi pan-European cuisine in a suave, modern, corner restaurant. The brasserie on the ground floor offers €25 two-course lunches and €35 three-course dinners (€23-28 main courses, Mon-Sat 12:00-15:00 & 18:00-22:00, Sun 14:00-22:00; pricier restaurant upstairs open Wed-Sat 18:00-22:00 only, closed Sun-Tue; Korte Veerstraat 1, tel. 023/542-7804).

Budget Options

La Place is a snazzy chain cafeteria that dishes up fresh, healthy, budget food with Haarlem's best view. Sit on the top floor or roof garden of the V&D department store (Mon 11:00-18:00, Tue-Sat 9:30-18:00, Thu until 21:00, closed Sun except for first Sun of month 12:00-17:00, Grote Houtstraat 70, on corner of Gedempte Oude Gracht, tel. 023/515-8700).

Friethuis de Vlaminck is your best bet for a cone of old-fashioned, fresh Flemish-style fries (€2, daily 11:00-18:30, Warmoesstraat 3, behind church, tel. 023/532-1084). Winnie offers a dazzling array of sauces. With his help, you can be adventurous.

Supermarkets: Albert Heijn has two convenient locations. One is in the train station (Mon-Fri 6:30-21:00, Sat 7:00-21:00, Sun 8:00-21:00, cash only) and the other is at Kruisstraat 10 (Mon-Sat 8:00-20:00, closed Sun, cash only). The **DekaMarkt** is a few blocks east of Grote Markt (Mon-Sat 8:00-20:00, Thu-Fri until 21:00, Sun 16:00-21:00, Gedempte Oude Gracht 54, between V&D department store and post office).

Haarlem Connections

From Haarlem by Train to: Amsterdam (6/hour, 20 minutes, €3.70 one-way, €7.10 same-day round-trip), **Delft** (2/hour, 40 minutes), **Brussels** (hourly, 2.75 hours, transfer in Rotterdam), **Bruges/Brugge** (hourly, 3.5 hours, 2-3 changes—avoid Thalys connections if traveling with a railpass).

To Schiphol Airport: Your best option is the **bus** (4-10/hour,

40 minutes, €4—buy ticket from driver, bus #300). To catch the bus from the middle of Haarlem, head to the Centrum/Verwulft stop, near the V&D department store. To catch it from the train station, look for the stop marked "Zuidtangent." (Construction of a new underground bike-parking lot near the train station may temporarily move this bus stop a block or two from the station, most likely to the tree-lined street called Parklaan). You can also get there by **train** (6/hour, 30-40 minutes, transfer at Amsterdam-Sloterdijk station, €5.40 one-way), or **taxi** (about €45).

SPAIN

BARCELONA

Barcelona is Spain's second city, and the vibrant capital of the proud and distinct region of Catalunya. Catalan flags wave side by side with the Spanish flag, and both languages—Spanish and Catalan—are spoken almost equally on the streets. The lively, local culture is on an unstoppable roll in Spain's most cosmopolitan and European corner.

Barcelona bubbles with life in its narrow Barri Gòtic alleys, along the pedestrian boulevard called the Ramblas, and throughout the chic, grid-planned new part of town, called Eixample. Its Old City is made for seeing on foot, full of winding lanes that emerge into secluded squares dotted with palm trees and ringed with cafés. The waterfront bristles with new life, overlooked by the park-like setting of Montjuïc. Everywhere you go, you'll find the city's architecture to be colorful, playful, and unique. Rows of symmetrical ironwork balconies are punctuated with fanciful details: bay windows, turrets, painted tiles, hanging lanterns, and carved reliefs.

Barcelona is full of history. You'll see Roman ruins, a medieval cathedral, and traces of Columbus and the sea trade. By the year 1900, the city was a cradle of Modernism, and teenage Picasso was on the verge of reinventing painting. His legacy is today's Picasso Museum, one of the world's best. Antoni Gaudí and fellow Modernist architects remade the city's skyline with curvy, playful fantasy buildings, culminating in Gaudí's over-the-top Sagrada Família, a church still under construction. Barcelona's 20th-century heritage is on display in museums dedicated to hometown boys Joan Miró and Antoni Tapies. And in 1992, Barcelona hosted the Summer Olympics, an event that energized the city and left a

Barcelona Overview

TIBIDABO

PARC GÜELL

AREA OF MORE DETAILED MAPS

SEE BARRI GÒTIC + RAMBLAS MAPS

AV. HOSP. MIL.

DE DALT

PLAÇA LESSEPS

TRAV.

SAGRADA FAMÍLIA

CARRER GRAN DE GRÀCIA

GRÀCIA

CASA MILÀ

PASSEIG DE GRÀCIA

GRAN

TO FORUM

DIAGONAL

BLOCK OF DISCORD

THE EIXAMPLE

CITADEL PARK

OLYMPIC PORT

PLAÇA DE CATALUNYA

PICASSO MUSEUM

OLD CITY

FRANÇA STN.

BEACH

MIRÓ PARK

SANTS STATION

PLAÇA D'ESPANYA

LAS RAMBLAS

BARCELONETA

MAREMAGNUM

TO MADRID

PARAL-LEL

DCH

SPANISH VILLAGE

FOUNTAINS

MIRÓ MUS.

FUNICULAR

CABLE CAR

M.E.D. SEA

PORT

GRAN VIA

CATALAN ART MUSEUM

OLYMPIC STADIUM

MOLL DE LA COSTA

MONTJUÏC

CRUISE SHIP TERMINALS

TO AIRPORT

1 MILE

1 KM

MOLL ADOSSAT

BARCELONA

legacy of sights.

But it's today's Barcelona that has the most charm. They still join hands and dance the everyone's-welcome *sardana* in front of the cathedral. Neighborhood festivals crowd the events calendar. The cafés are filled by day, and people crowd the streets at night, pausing to fortify themselves with seafood and a drink at a tapas bar. If you're in the mood to surrender to a city's charms, let it be in Barcelona.

Planning Your Time

Located in the far northeast corner of Spain, Barcelona makes a good first or last stop for your trip. With the fast AVE train, Barcelona is three hours away from Madrid. Or you could sandwich Barcelona between flights. From the US, it's as easy to fly into Barcelona as it is to land in Madrid, Lisbon, or Paris. Those who plan on renting a car at some point during their trip can start here first, fly or train to Madrid, and sightsee Madrid and Toledo, all before picking up their car—cleverly saving on several days' worth of rental fees.

On the shortest visit, Barcelona is worth one night, one day, and an evening flight or train ride out. The Ramblas is two different streets by day and by night. Stroll it from top to bottom in the evening and again the next morning, grabbing breakfast on a stool in a market café. Wander the Barri Gòtic (BAH-ree GOH-teek), see the cathedral, and have lunch in the Eixample (eye-SHAM-plah). The top two sights in town, Antoni Gaudí's Sagrada Família church and the Picasso Museum, are usually open until 20:00 during the summer (Picasso closed Mon). Note that if you want to tour the Catalan Concert Hall, with its oh-wow Modernista interior, you'll need to reserve at least two days in advance (see page 1210). The illuminated Magic Fountains on Montjuïc make a good finale for your day.

Of course, Barcelona in a day is insane. To better sample the city's ample charm, spread your visit over two or three days. With two days, you could divide and conquer the town geographically: one day for the Barri Gòtic (Ramblas, cathedral area, Picasso Museum); and another for the Eixample and Gaudí sights (Casa Milà, Sagrada Família, Parc Güell). Do Montjuïc on whichever day you're not exhausted (if any).

When planning your time, be aware that many top sights are closed on Monday—making them especially crowded on Tuesday and Sunday.

Orientation to Barcelona

Like Los Angeles, Barcelona is a basically flat city that sprawls out under the sun between the sea and the mountains. It's huge (1.6 million people, with about 5 million people in greater Barcelona), but travelers need only focus on four areas: the Old City, the harbor/Barceloneta, the Eixample, and Montjuïc.

A large square, **Plaça de Catalunya,** sits at the center of Barcelona, dividing the older and newer parts of town. Sloping downhill from the Plaça de Catalunya is the Old City, with the boulevard called the Ramblas running down to the harbor. Above Plaça de Catalunya is the modern residential area called the Eixample. The Montjuïc hill overlooks the harbor. Outside the Old City, Barcelona's sights are widely scattered, but with a map and a willingness to figure out the sleek Metro system (or a few euros for taxis), all is manageable.

Here are more details per neighborhood:

The **Old City** is where you'll probably spend most of your time. This is the compact soul of Barcelona—your strolling, shopping, and people-watching nucleus. It's a labyrinth of narrow streets that once were confined by the medieval walls. The lively pedestrian drag called the **Ramblas**—one of Europe's great people-watching streets—runs through the heart of the Old City from Plaça de Catalunya down to the harbor. The Old City is divided into thirds by the Ramblas and another major thoroughfare, Via Laietana. To the west of the Ramblas is the **Raval,** enlivened by its university and modern-art museum. The Raval is of least interest to tourists (and, in fact, some parts of it are quite seedy and should be avoided). Far better is the **Barri Gòtic** (Gothic Quarter), between the Ramblas and Via Laietana, with the cathedral as its navel. To the east of Via Laietana is the trendy **Ribera** district (a.k.a. "El Born"), centered on the Picasso Museum and the Church of Santa Maria del Mar.

The **harborfront** has been energized since the 1992 Olympics. A pedestrian bridge links the Ramblas with the modern Maremagnum shopping/aquarium complex. On the peninsula across the harbor is **Barceloneta,** a traditional fishing neighborhood that's home to some good seafood restaurants and a string of sandy beaches. Beyond Barceloneta, a man-made beach, several miles long, leads east to the commercial and convention district called the **Fòrum.**

North of the Old City, beyond the bustling hub of Plaça de Catalunya, is the elegant **Eixample** district—its grid plan is softened by cut-off corners. Much of Barcelona's Modernista architecture is found here. To the north is the **Gràcia** district and, beyond that, Antoni Gaudí's **Parc Güell.**

The large hill overlooking the city to the southwest is **Montjuïc,** home to a variety of attractions, including some excellent museums (Catalan Art, Joan Miró) and the Olympic Stadium.

Apart from your geographical orientation, you'll need to orient yourself linguistically to a language distinct from Spanish. Although Spanish ("Castilian"/*castellano*) is widely spoken, the native tongue in this region is Catalan—nearly as different from Spanish as Italian.

Tourist Information

Barcelona's TI has several branches. The main one is at **Plaça de Catalunya** (daily 9:00-21:00, under the main square near recommended hotels—look for red sign, tel. 932-853-832). Other convenient branches include at the top of the **Ramblas** (daily 9:00-21:00, at #115); **Plaça de Sant Jaume,** just south of the cathedral (Mon-Fri 8:30-20:00, Sat 9:00-19:00, Sun 10:00-14:00); **Plaça d'Espanya** (daily July-Sept 10:00-20:00, Oct-June 10:00-16:00); the **airport** (daily 9:00-21:00, offices in both sections A and B of terminal 2);

Sants train station (Mon-Fri 8:00-20:00, Sat-Sun 8:00-14:00, near track 6); **Nord bus station** (daily July-Sept 9:00-21:00, Oct-June 9:00-15:00); and more. Throughout the summer, young red-jacketed tourist-info helpers appear in the most touristy parts of town. The central information number for all TIs is 932-853-834 (www.barcelonaturisme.cat).

At any TI, pick up the free city map (although the free Corte Inglés map provided by most hotels is better), the small Metro map, and the free quarterly *See Barcelona* guide (practical information on museum hours, restaurants, transportation, history, festivals, and so on). The monthly *Barcelona Metropolitan* magazine and quarterly *What's On Barcelona* (both free and in English) have timely and substantial coverage of topics and events. The TI is a handy place to buy tickets for the Tourist Bus (described later, under "Getting Around Barcelona"). Some TIs (at Plaça de Catalunya, Plaça de Sant Jaume, and the airport) also provide a room-booking service.

The main TI, at Plaça de Catalunya, offers guided walks (described later, under "Tours in Barcelona"). Its Modernisme desk gives out a handy route map showing all the Modernista buildings and offers a sightseeing discount package (€12 for a great guidebook and 20 percent discounts to many Modernisme sites—worthwhile if going beyond my big three; for €18 you'll also get a guidebook to Modernista bars and restaurants).

The **all-Catalunya TI** works fine for the entire region, and even Madrid (Mon-Sat 10:00-19:00, Sun 10:00-14:00, on Plaça de Joan Carlos I, at the intersection of Diagonal and Passeig de Gràcia, Passeig de Gràcia 107, tel. 932-388-091).

Articket Card: This ticket includes admission to seven art museums and their temporary exhibits, including the recommended Picasso Museum, Casa Milà, Catalan Art Museum, and Fundació Joan Miró (€22, valid for six months, sold at TIs and participating museums, www.articketbcn.org). If you're planning to go to three or more of the museums, this time-saver pays for itself. To skip the ticket-buying line at a museum, show your Articket Card (to the ticket-taker, at the info desk, or at the group entrance), and you'll get your entrance ticket pronto.

Barcelona Card: This card covers public transportation (buses, Metro, Montjuïc funicular, and *golondrina* harbor tour) and includes free admission to minor sights and discounts on major sights (€27.50/2 days, €33.50/3 days, €38/4 days, €45/5 days, sold at TIs and El Corte Inglés department store).

Arrival in Barcelona
By Train
Virtually all trains end up at Barcelona's Sants train station (described below). But be aware that many trains also pass through

other stations en route, such as **França Station** (between the Ribera and Barceloneta neighborhoods), or the downtown **Passeig de Gràcia** or **Plaça de Catalunya** stations (which are also Metro stops—and very close to most of my recommended hotels). Figure out which stations your train stops at, and get off at the one most convenient to your hotel. (AVE trains from Madrid go only to Sants Station.)

Sants Station is vast and sprawling, but manageable. In the large lobby area under the upper tracks, you'll find a TI; ATMs; a world of handy shops and eateries; and a classy, quiet Sala Euromed lounge for travelers with first-class reservations (TV, free drinks, study tables, and coffee bar). Sants is the only Barcelona station with luggage storage (small bag-€3/day, big bag-€4.50/day, requires security check, daily 5:30-23:00, follow signs to *consigna*, at far end of hallway from tracks 13-14).

There's also a long wall of ticket windows. Figure out which is right for you before you wait in line (all are labeled in English). Generally, windows 1-10 (on the left) are for local trains, such as to Sitges; windows 11-21 handle advance tickets for long-distance trains; the information windows are 23-26—go here first if you're not sure which window you want; windows 27-31 sell tickets for long-distance trains leaving today. The two information booths by windows 1 and 21 can help you find the right line and can provide some train schedules. If you know what you want, there are also automated train-ticket vending machines for mid-distance trains *(media distancia)*, just beyond window 1. If you made online reservations in advance and have a confirmation code for long-distance trains, you can print your tickets at the purple ATM-like machines, but you can't buy tickets from them.

To get into downtown Barcelona from Sants Station, simply follow signs for the Metro. The L3 (green) line zips you directly to a number of useful points in town, including all of my recommended hotels. Alternatively, local trains leave from track 8 for Plaça de Catalunya (catch *cercanías* lines C1, C3, C4, or C7). Purchase tickets for the trains or Metro (€1.45) at touch-screen machines near the tracks (where you can also buy the cost-saving T10 Card, explained on page 1187).

If departing from the downtown **Passeig de Gràcia Station,** where three Metro lines converge with the rail line, you might find the underground tunnels confusing. You can't access the RENFE Station directly from some of the entrances. Use the northern entrances to this station (rather than the southern "Consell de Cent" entrance, which is closest to Plaça de Catalunya).

By Plane

Barcelona's **El Prat de Llobregat Airport,** eight miles southwest of

BARCELONA

town, has two large terminals: 1 and 2. Terminal 2 is divided into sections A, B, and C. Terminal 1 and the bigger sections of terminal 2 (A and B) each have a post office, a pharmacy, a left-luggage office, plenty of good cafeterias in the gate areas, and ATMs (avoid the gimmicky machines before the baggage carousels; instead, use the bank-affiliated ATMs at the far-left end of the arrivals hall as you face the street). Airport info tel. 913-211-000, www.aena.es.

You have two options for getting downtown cheaply and quickly: The **Aerobus** (#A1 and #A2, corresponding with terminals 1 and 2) stops immediately outside the arrivals lobby of both terminals (and in each section of terminal 2). In about 30 minutes, it takes you to downtown, where it makes several stops, including Plaça d'Espanya and Plaça de Catalunya—near many of my recommended hotels (departs every 6 minutes, from airport 6:00-1:00 in the morning, from downtown 5:30-24:15, €5.30 one-way, €9.15 round-trip, buy ticket from machine or from driver, tel. 934-156-020). The line to board the bus can be very long, but—thanks to the high frequency of buses—it moves fast.

The second option from terminal 2 is the RENFE *cercanías* **train,** which involves more walking. Head down the long orange-roofed overpass between sections A and B to reach the station (2/hour at about :08 and :38 past the hour, 20 minutes to Sants Station, 25 minutes to Passeig de Gràcia Station—near Plaça de Catalunya and many recommended hotels, 30 minutes to França Station; €3 or covered by T10 Card, which you can purchase at automated machines at the airport train station). Long-term plans call for the RENFE *cercanías* train and eventually the AVE to be extended to terminal 1, and for the Metro's L9 (orange) line to be extended to both terminals 1 and 2. Stay tuned.

A **taxi** between the airport and downtown costs about €30—about €25 on the meter plus a €3.10 airport supplement and fee of €1 per bag. For good service, add an additional 10 percent tip (or €33 total).

Some budget airlines, including Ryanair, use **Girona–Costa Brava Airport,** located 60 miles north of Barcelona near Girona. Sagalés buses link to Barcelona (departures timed to meet flights, 1.25 hours, €12, tel. 935-931-300 or 902-361-550, www.sagales .com). You can also go to Girona on a Sagalés bus (hourly, 25 minutes, €3) or a taxi (€25), then catch a train to Barcelona (at least hourly, 1.25 hours, €15-20). A taxi between the Girona airport and Barcelona costs at least €120. Airport info tel. 972-186-600.

By Car

Barcelona's parking fees are outrageously expensive (the lot behind La Boquería market charges upward of €25/day). You won't need a car in Barcelona, because the taxis and public transportation are so good.

By Cruise Ship

Cruise ships arrive in Barcelona at seven different terminals, spread among three different ports (all just southwest of the Old City, beneath Montjuïc).

Most American cruise lines put in at **Moll Adossat/Muelle Adosado,** a long two miles from the bottom of the Ramblas. This port has four modern, airport-like terminals (lettered A through D); most have a café and shops; some have Internet access and other services). Another terminal, **Moll de la Costa,** is tucked just beneath Montjuïc. The **World Trade Center,** just off the southern end of the Ramblas, has two terminals: Terminal N (north) and Terminal S (south).

From any of the cruise terminals, it's easy to reach the Ramblas.

Taxis meet each arriving ship and are waiting as you exit any of the terminal buildings. The short trip into town (i.e., to the bottom of the Ramblas) runs about €10. During high season, a ride into town can take longer and cost €10 more. For a one-way journey to other parts of town, expect to pay these fares: to the Picasso Museum or Plaça de Catalunya—€15; to the Sagrada Família—€20; and to the airport—€35-40.

Getting to the sights via **public transportation** requires heading to the Columbus Monument at the bottom of the Ramblas. From Moll Adossat/Muelle Adosado take the shuttle bus (*lanzadera,* #T3, a.k.a. Portbús, departs from parking lot in front of terminal—follow *Public Bus* signs, €3 round-trip, €2 one-way, buses leave every 20-30 minutes, timed to cruise ship arrival, tel. 932-986-000). The shuttle drops you right at the Columbus Monument; pay careful attention to where they drop you off if you want to catch the return bus later.

If you arrive at Moll de la Costa, you're not allowed to walk through the port area. You'll ride a free, private shuttle bus to the World Trade Center. From the World Trade Center, you can easily walk into town: Head straight up the wide pier for about five minutes, bear right along the waterfront (walking alongside the long sandstone building), and you'll pop out at the Columbus Monument. From there you can connect—by foot, Metro, or bus—to wherever you're going in town (see "Getting Around Barcelona," later).

Barcelona attracts more than one million cruise passengers every year. If your trip includes cruising beyond Barcelona, consider my new guidebook, *Rick Steves' Mediterranean Cruise Ports.*

BARCELONA

Helpful Hints

Theft Alert: You're more likely to be pickpocketed here—especially on the Ramblas—than about anywhere else in Europe. Most of the crime is nonviolent, but muggings do occur. Leave valuables in your hotel and wear a money belt.

Street scams are easy to avoid if you recognize them. Most common is the too-friendly local who tries to engage you in conversation by asking for the time, talking sports, asking whether you speak English, and so on. Beware of thieves posing as lost tourists who ask for your help. A typical street gambling scam is the pea-and-carrot game, a variation on the shell game. The people winning are all ringers, and you can be sure that you'll lose if you play. Also beware of groups of women aggressively selling carnations, people offering to clean off a stain from your shirt, and people picking things up in front of you on escalators. If you stop for any commotion or show on the Ramblas, put your hands in your pockets before someone else does. Assume any scuffle is simply a distraction by a team of thieves. Crooks are inventive, so keep your guard up. Don't be intimidated...just be smart.

Some areas feel seedy and can be unsafe after dark; I'd avoid the southern part of the Barri Gòtic (basically the two or three blocks directly south and east of Plaça Reial—though the strip near the Carrer de la Mercè tapas bars is better), and I wouldn't venture too deep into the Raval (just west of the Ramblas). One block can separate a comfy tourist zone from the junkies and prostitutes.

US Consulate: It's at Passeig Reina Elisenda 23 (passport services Mon-Fri 9:00-13:00, closed Sat-Sun, tel. 932-802-227, after-hours emergency tel. 915-872-200).

Emergency Phone Numbers: General emergencies—112, police—092, ambulance—061 or 112.

Sight Reservations: To avoid standing in long lines, call or go online to book ahead for the Picasso Museum (see page 1209), Sagrada Família (see page 1217), Casa Batlló (see page 1216), and Casa Milà (see page 1214). An Articket Card (described earlier) allows you to skip the lines at the Picasso Museum and Casa Milà, but not at Sagrada Família or Casa Batlló. To tour the Catalan Concert Hall, you'll need to reserve at least two days in advance (see page 1210).

Internet Access: Navega Web has hundreds of computers for accessing the Internet and burning pictures onto a disk. It's conveniently located across from La Boquería market, downstairs in the bright Centre Comercial New Park (daily 10:00-24:00, Ramblas 88-94, tel. 933-179-193).

Pharmacy: A 24-hour pharmacy is near La Boquería market at

#98 on the Ramblas.

Laundry: Several self-service launderettes are located around the Old City. **Wash 'n Dry** is on the edge of the tourist zone, near a seedy neighborhood just down the street past the Palau Güell (self-service: wash-€5/load, dry-€2/load, daily 7:00-22:00; full-service: €15/load, daily 9:00-14:00 & 16:00-22:00; Carrer Nou de la Rambla 19, tel. 934-121-953).

Getting Around Barcelona

By Metro: Barcelona's Metro, among Europe's best, connects just about every place you'll visit. Rides cost €1.45. The T10 Card is a great deal—€8.25 gives you 10 rides (cutting the per-ride cost nearly in half), and the card is shareable. It's good on all Metro and local bus lines as well as the RENFE train lines (including rides to the airport and train station) and the suburban FGC lines (with service to Montserrat). Full- and multi-day passes are also available (€6.20/1 day, €11.50/2 days, €16.50/3 days, €21/4 days, €25/5 days, www.tmb.cat). Automated machines at the Metro entrance have English instructions and sell all types of tickets (these can be temperamental about accepting bills, so try to have change on hand).

Pick up the free Metro map (at any TI) and study it to get familiar with the system. There are several color-coded lines, but most useful for tourists is the **L3 (green)** line. Handy city-center stops on this line include (in order):

Sants Estació—Main train station

Espanya—Plaça d'Espanya, with access to the lower part of Montjuïc and trains to Montserrat

Paral-lel—Funicular to top of Montjuïc

Drassanes—Bottom of the Ramblas, near Maritime Museum, Maremagnum mall, and the cable car up to Montjuïc

Liceu—Middle of the Ramblas, near the heart of the Barri Gòtic and cathedral

Plaça de Catalunya—Top of the Ramblas and main square with TI, airport bus, and lots of transportation connections

Passeig de Gràcia—Classy Eixample street at the Block of Discord; also connection to L2 (purple) line to Sagrada Família and L4 (yellow) line (described below)

Diagonal—Gaudí's Casa Milà

The **L4 (yellow)** line, which crosses the L3 (green) line at Passeig de Gràcia, is also useful. Helpful stops include **Joanic** (bus #116 to Parc Güell), **Jaume I** (between the Barri Gòtic/cathedral and La Ribera/Picasso Museum), and **Barceloneta** (at the south end of the Ribera, near the harbor action).

When you enter the Metro, first look for your line number and color, then follow signs to take that line in the direction you're

Barcelona's Metro

going. The names of the end stops are used to indicate directions. Insert your ticket into the turnstile (with the arrow pointing in), then reclaim it. On board, most trains have handy Metro-line diagrams with dots that light up next to upcoming destinations. Because the lines cross one another multiple times, there can be several ways to make any one journey. (It's a good idea to keep a general map with you—especially if you're transferring.) Watch your valuables. If I were a pickpocket, I'd set up shop along the made-for-tourists L3 (green) line.

By Public Bus: Given the excellent Metro service, it's unlikely you'll take a local bus (also €1.45 or covered by T10 Card, insert ticket in machine behind driver), although I've noted places where the bus makes sense. In particular, bus #50 is good for a tour of Gràcia and Montjuïc (see page 1191).

By Tourist Bus: The handy hop-on, hop-off Tourist Bus (Bus Turístic) offers three multi-stop circuits in colorful double-decker buses that go topless in sunny weather. The two-hour blue route covers north Barcelona (most Gaudí sights); the two-hour red route covers south Barcelona (Barri Gòtic, Montjuïc); and the shorter, 40-minute green route covers the beaches and modern Fòrum complex. All have headphone commentary (44 stops, daily 9:00-22:00 in summer, 9:00-21:00 in winter, buses run every 5-25 minutes, most frequent in summer, no green route Oct-March). Ask for a brochure (includes city map) at the TI or at a pick-up point. One-day (€23) and two-day (€30) tickets, which you can buy on the bus or at the TI, offer 10-20 percent discounts on the city's major sights and walking tours, which will likely save you about the equivalent of half the cost of the Tourist Bus. From Plaça de Catalunya, the blue northern route leaves from El Corte Inglés; the red southern route leaves from the west—Ramblas—side of the square (www.barcelonabusturistic.cat).

By Taxi: Barcelona is one of Europe's best taxi towns. Taxis are plentiful (there are more than 10,000) and honest (whether they like it or not—the light on top shows which tariff they're charging). They're also reasonable (€2 drop charge, €1/kilometer, these *"Tarif 2"* rates are in effect 7:00-21:00, pay higher *"Tarif 1"* rates off-hours, luggage-€1/piece, other fees posted in window). Save time by hopping a cab (figure €10 from Ramblas to Sants Station).

Tours in Barcelona

Walking Tours—The TI at Plaça de Sant Jaume offers great guided walks through the **Barri Gòtic** in English only (€13, daily at 10:00, 2 hours, groups limited to 35, buy your ticket 15 minutes early at the TI desk—not from the guide, in summer call ahead to reserve, tel. 932-853-832, www.barcelonaturisme.cat). A local guide will explain the medieval story of the city as you walk from Plaça de Sant Jaume through the cathedral neighborhood.

The TI at Plaça de Catalunya offers a **Picasso** walk, taking you through the streets of his youth and early career and finishing in the Picasso Museum (€19.50, includes museum admission; Tue, Thu, and Sat at 16:00; 2 hours plus museum visit). There are also **gourmet** walks (€19.50, Fri and Sat at 10:00, 2 hours) and **Modernisme** walks (€13, Fri and Sat June-Sept at 18:00, Oct-May at 15:00, 2 hours). These tours depart from the TI at Plaça de Catalunya.

Guided Bus Tours—The Barcelona Guide Bureau offers several sightseeing tours leaving from Plaça de Catalunya. Departure times can vary—confirm locally. The **Gaudí** tour visits the facades of Casa Batlló and Casa Milà, as well as Parc Güell and the Sagrada Família (€45, includes Sagrada Família admission, daily at 9:00, also mid-April-Oct Mon-Sat at 15:15, 3 hours). Other tours offered year-round include the **Montjuïc** tour (€33, includes Spanish Village admission, daily at 12:00, 3 hours) and the **All Barcelona Highlights** tour (€60, includes Sagrada Família and Spanish Village admissions, daily at 9:00, 6 hours). During the high season, there's also the **Gaudí Plus** tour, which combines the Gaudí tour with some "off-the-beaten-path masterpieces" (€52, mid-April-Oct Mon-Sat at 9:00, 4 hours). You can get detailed information and book tickets at a TI, on their website, or simply by showing up at their departure point on Plaça de Catalunya in front of the Hard Rock Café—look for the guides holding orange umbrellas. Buying tickets online can save you a few euros—usually about 10 percent. You can also buy tickets at many hotels for no extra charge (tel. 933-152-261, www.barcelonaguidebureau.com).

Bus #50 Self-Guided Tour—Taking bus #50 (€1.45 or use T10 card) gives you an inexpensive, 45-minute tour through Gràcia and Montjuïc. You can catch bus #50 at the Sagrada Família along Carrer de Mallorca (around the right from the church's ticket entrance). Grab a seat on the right side of the bus. You'll wind through Gràcia's streets down to the Gran Via de les Corts Catalanes, crossing the Passeig de Gràcia (a block away from Plaça de Catalunya). Enjoy the long blocks of Gràcia until you reach Plaça d'Espanya, where on the right you'll see Barcelona's bullring (which is being turned into a mall). You'll go through the two towers of Plaça d'Espanya, with the Catalan Art Museum on the hill in front of you. Then you'll loop through the hills of Montjuïc, passing the Spanish Village, the site of the '92 Olympics (with the communications tower and stadium), the Fundació Joan Miró, and the funicular and cable car up to the Castle of Montjuïc. The end of the line is about a block away from the funicular. From here you can walk back to the Joan Miró or Catalan Art museums; or

BARCELONA

continue in the direction of the bus route down the hill to a different cable car, which takes you to the Barceloneta area.

Bike Tours—Several companies run bike tours around Barcelona.
Un Cotxe Menys ("One Car Less") organizes three-hour English-
only bike tours daily at 11:00 (April-mid-Sept also Fri-Mon at
16:30). Your guide leads you from sight to sight, mostly on bike
paths and through parks, with a stop-and-go commentary (€22
includes bike rental and drink, no reservations needed, just show
up at Plaça de Sant Jaume, next to TI, tel. 932-682-105, www.bike
toursbarcelona.com).

Local Guides—The Barcelona Guide Bureau is a co-op with
about 20 local guides who give personalized four-hour tours (week-
days-€216, per-person price drops as group gets bigger; weekends
and holidays-€256, no price break with size of group); **Joana
Wilhelm** and **Carles Picazo** are excellent (Via Laietana 54, tel.
932-682-422 or 933-107-778, www.bgb.es). **Jose Soler** is a great and
fun-to-be-with local guide who enjoys tailoring a walk through his
hometown to your interests (€195/half-day per group, mobile 615-
059-326, www.pepitotours.com, info@pepitotours.com).

Self-Guided Walks

These walks through the atmospheric Old City introduce you to
places you may want to explore further. They're easy to follow, pass
by some major sights, and provide background to this complex
metropolis. The first begins at Barcelona's main square and leads
you down the city's main drag: the Ramblas. The second walk
guides you into the heart of the Barri Gòtic, the neighborhood
around Barcelona's impressive cathedral.

▲▲▲The Ramblas Ramble: From Plaça de Catalunya to the Waterfront

For over a century, this walk down Barcelona's main boulevard
has drawn locals and visitors alike. While its former elegance has
been tackified somewhat by tourist shops and fast-food joints, this
is still the best place to see the city in action. Walk the Ramblas
at least once to get the lay of the land, then venture farther afield.
It's a one-hour, downhill stroll, with an easy way to get back by
Metro.

This pedestrian-only Champs-Elysées takes you from rich (at
the top) to rough (at the port). You'll raft the river of Barcelonese
life past a grand opera house, elegant cafés, flower stands, retread
prostitutes, brazen pickpockets, power-dressing con men, artists,
street mimes, an outdoor bird market, great shopping, and people
looking to charge more for a shoeshine than what you paid for the
shoes.

The Ramblas Ramble

Ramblas
Ramblas walk
Ⓜ Metro Station
Ⓑ Bus Stop

BERGARA

RONDA

PLAÇA DE CATALUNYA

TO BLOCK OF DISCORD + CASA MILÀ

FNAC

FGC TRAIN INFO

EL CORTE INGLÉS DEP'T. STORE

Ⓑ

START

Ⓜ Catalunya

BUS TO AIRPORT (+ TAXIS)

BONSUCCES

SANTA ANNA

PINTOR

CLOCK

C. XUCLÀ

FORT.

ROMAN NECRO-POLIS

CAFÉ GRANJA VIADER

CARME

CULTURAL INFO PALAU DE LA VIRREINA

PORTAFERRISSA

PORTAL DE L'ANGEL

CANUDA

DUC. VIU.

ARCS

PL. NOVA

Ⓜ Liceu

CIGARS

LA BOQUERÍA MARKET

HOSP.

MIRO MOSAIC

EROTIC

C. DEL PI

PALLA

TO CATHEDRAL

EL RAVAL

Liceu Ⓜ

DRAGON

BOQUERÍA

CARD.

PL. PI

NOUS

BANYS

S. MARIA DEL PI

CAFÉ DE OPERA

SANT PAU

LICEU OPERA HOUSE

CARRER FERRAN

AVINYO

TO PLAÇA S. JAUME

NOU RAMBLA

PLAÇA REIAL

200 YARDS

200 METERS

PALAU GÜELL

HERB. FERRAN

PL. ORWELL

ESCUDELLERS

AV. DRASS.

L'ARC TEATRE

SKY-SCRAPER

PROST. MARKS

NOU

SAN FRAN.

CODOLS

MARITIME MUSEUM

Ⓜ Drassanes

MUSEU DE CERA

CLAVE

PL. MED.

PASSEIG DE COLÓM

COLUMBUS MONUMENT

FINISH

MOLL DE BOSCH

SHUTTLE BUS FOR MOLL D'ADOSSAT

Ⓑ

GOLONDRINAS CRUISES

HARBOR

RAMBLA DE MAR

TO MAREMAGNUM

1 Plaça de Catalunya
2 Fountain of Canaletes
3 Rambla of the Little Birds
4 Betlem Church
5 Rambla of Flowers
6 La Boquería
7 Liceu—Heart of the Ramblas
8 Plaça Reial
9 To Raval Neighborhood
10 Columbus Monument & Waterfront

BARCELONA

The word "Ramblas" is plural, and the street is actually a succession of five separately named segments. But street signs and addresses treat it as a single long street—"La Rambla," singular. *Rambla* means "stream" in Arabic, and it used to be a drainage ditch along the medieval wall of the Barri Gòtic (Gothic Quarter). Today that "stream" has become a river of humanity.

• *Start your ramble at the top of the Ramblas, where it connects with Plaça de Catalunya.*

❶ **Plaça de Catalunya:** Dotted with fountains, statues, and pigeons, and ringed by grand Art Deco buildings, this plaza is Barcelona's center. It's the hub for the Metro, bus, airport shuttle, and Tourist Bus. It's where Barcelona congregates to watch soccer matches on the big screen, to demonstrate, to celebrate, and to enjoy outdoor concerts and festivals. It's the center of the world for seven million Catalan people.

Geographically, the 12-acre square links old Barcelona (the narrow streets to the south) with the new (the broad boulevards to the north). Four great thoroughfares radiate from here. The Ramblas is the popular pedestrian promenade. Passeig de Gràcia has fashionable shops and cafés (and noisy traffic). Rambla de Catalunya is equally fashionable but cozier and more pedestrian-friendly. Avinguda Portal de l'Angel (shopper-friendly and traffic-free) leads to the Barri Gòtic.

Historically, Plaça de Catalunya links the modern city with its past. In the 1850s, when Barcelona tore down its medieval walls to expand the city, this square on the edge of the walls was one of the first places to be developed.

Overlooking the square, the huge **El Corte Inglés** department store offers everything from bonsai trees to a travel agency, haircuts, and cheap souvenirs—get the complete list by picking up an English directory at their info desk. There's a supermarket in the basement and a ninth-floor view café (Mon-Sat 10:00-22:00, closed Sun). Across the square is **FNAC,** a French department store popular for electronics, music, and books. It also sells tickets for major concerts and events (Mon-Sat 10:00-22:00, closed Sun).

In case you're wondering, the odd, inverted-staircase statue in the square honors a former president of Catalunya. It was designed by the sculptor Josep María Subirachs, whose work you'll see at the Sagrada Família (see page 1220). The venerable Café Zürich, at the corner of the square near the Ramblas, is a popular downtown rendezvous spot for locals. Homesick Americans might prefer the nearby Hard Rock Café.

• *Start heading down the Ramblas, and pause 20 yards down at the ornate lamppost with a fountain as its base (near #129).*

❷ **Fountain of Canaletes:** This black-and-gold drinking fountain has been a local favorite for over a century. When Barcelona tore down its medieval wall and transformed the Ramblas from a drainage ditch into an elegant promenade, this fountain was one of its early attractions. Legend says that a drink from the fountain ensures that you'll return to Barcelona one day.

It's still a popular let's-meet-at-the-fountain rendezvous spot and a gathering place for celebrations and demonstrations. Fans of the Barcelona soccer team rally here before a big match—some touch their hand to their lips, then "kiss" the fountain with their hand for good luck.

Continue downhill. All along the Ramblas, you'll see newspaper stands (open 24 hours, selling phone cards). Among their souvenirs, you'll see soccer paraphernalia, especially the scarlet-and-blue of FC Barcelona (known as "Barça"). You'll also pass ONCE booths. All over town, these sell lottery tickets that support Spain's organization of the blind, a powerful advocate for the needs of people with disabilities.

Got some change? As you wander downhill, drop coins into the cans of the human statues (the money often kicks them into entertaining gear). If you take a photo, it's considered good etiquette to drop in a coin. Warning: Wherever people stop to gawk, pickpockets are at work.

• *Walk 100 yards downhill to #115 and the...*

❸ **Rambla of the Little Birds:** Traditionally, kids bring their parents here to buy pets, especially on Sundays. Apartment-dwellers find birds, turtles, fish, hamsters, and rabbits easier to handle than dogs and cats. If you're walking by at night, you'll hear the sad sounds of little tweety birds locked up in their collapsed kiosks.

The Academy of Science's clock (at #115) marks official Barcelona time—synchronize. The Carrefour Express supermarket has cheap groceries (at #113, Mon-Sat 10:00-22:00, closed Sun, shorter checkout lines in back of store).

At #122 (the big, modern Citadines Hotel), a 100-yard detour through the passageway leads to a recently discovered **Roman necropolis.** Here you can look down and imagine the tomb-lined road leading into the Roman city of Barcino 2,000 years ago.

• *Backtrack to the Ramblas and continue down another 100 yards. At Carrer del Carme (at #105), look over your right shoulder at the main entrance to the...*

❹ **Betlem Church:** This 17th-century church is Baroque; check out its sloping roofline, ball-topped pinnacles, corkscrew columns, and scrolls above the entrance. Baroque is unusual in Barcelona; the city's heyday was during the medieval period. After 1500, the city's importance dropped when New World discoveries shifted lucrative trade to ports on the Atlantic. The church is dedicated to Bethlehem, and for centuries locals have flocked here at Christmastime to see Nativity scenes.

For a sweet treat, head down the narrow lane behind the church (going uphill parallel to the Ramblas about 30 yards) to the recommended **Café Granja Viader,** which has specialized in baked and dairy delights since 1870. (For more sugary treats nearby, follow "A Short, Sweet Walk" on page 1247.)

• *Continue down the boulevard, through the stretch called the. . .*

❺ **Rambla of Flowers:** This colorful block, lined with flower stands, is the "Rambla" of the Flowers. Check out the balconies of the buildings. Elegant ironwork is found all over the city. Generally speaking, buildings with balconies adorned with plants and flowers are living spaces; balconies with air-conditioners generally indicate offices. The plane trees that line the Ramblas (called sycamores in America) are known for their peeling bark and hardiness in urban settings.

• *Continue to the Metro stop marked by the red M. At #91 (on the right) you'll find the arcaded entrance to...*

❻ **La Boquería:** This lively produce market is an explosion of chicken legs, bags of live snails, stiff fish, delicious oranges, odd odors, and sleeping dogs (Mon-Sat 8:00-20:00, best mornings after 9:00, closed Sun). Since as far back as 1200, Barcelonans have bought their animal parts here. Originally located by the walled city's entrance (as many medieval markets were), it expanded into the colonnaded courtyard of a now-gone monastery before being topped with a colorful arcade in 1850. Wander around—as local architect Antoni Gaudí used to—and gain inspiration.

The Graus Conserves shop (straight in, near the back) sells 25 kinds of olives. Full legs of ham abound. Of the many varieties of *jamón serrano*, the best are *Paleta Ibérica de Bellota*, costing about €140 each. Beware: *Huevos del toro* are bull testicles—surprisingly inexpensive...and oh so good.

Drop by a café for an *espresso con leche* or breakfast *tortilla española* (potato omelet). Try the recommended **Pinotxo Bar**—it's just inside the market, under the sign—and snap a photo of Juan. Animated Juan and his family are always busy feeding shoppers. Getting Juan to crack a huge smile and a thumbs-up for your camera makes a great shot...and he loves it. The stools nearby are a fine perch for enjoying both your coffee and the people-watching. The market and lanes nearby are busy with tempting little eateries (several are listed on page 1238).

Across the boulevard at #96, the **Museum of Erotica** is your standard European sex museum (€9, daily 10:00-20:00).

To the left, at #100, **Gimeno** sells cigars. Step inside and appreciate the dying art of cigar boxes. Go ahead, do something forbidden in America but perfectly legal here...buy a Cuban (little singles for €1). Tobacco shops sell stamps and phone cards, plus bongs and marijuana gear—the Spanish approach to pot is very casual.

• *Continue down the Ramblas, glancing to the left through a modern archway for a glimpse of the medieval church tower of Santa Maria del Pi. It's clear that, as you walk the Ramblas, you're skirting along the west boundary of the old Barri Gòtic neighborhood. After 100 yards, you reach the Liceu Metro station, marking the...*

❼ **Liceu—Heart of the Ramblas:** At the Liceu Metro station, the Ramblas widens a bit into a small, lively square (Plaça de la Boquería). Liceu marks the midpoint of the Ramblas, halfway between Plaça de Catalunya and the waterfront.

Underfoot in the center of the Ramblas, find the much-trodden-upon red-yellow-and-blue **mosaic** by homegrown abstract artist Joan Miró. The mosaic's black arrows represent anchors, a reminder of the city's attachment to the sea. Miró's childlike designs are found all over the city, from murals to mobiles to the La Caixa bank logo.

The surrounding buildings have playful ornamentation typical of the city. The Chinese dragon holding a lantern (at #82) decorates a former umbrella shop still adorned with umbrellas. Hungry? The recommended **Taverna Basca Irati** tapas bar is a block up Carrer del Cardenal Casenas.

A few steps down is the **Liceu Opera House,** which hosts world-class opera, dance, and theater. Opposite the opera house is Café de l'Opera (#74), an elegant stop for a beverage. This bustling café, with Modernista decor and a historic atmosphere, boasts that it's been open since 1929, even during the Spanish Civil War.

• *To cut this walk short, you could catch the Metro back to Plaça de Catalunya. Otherwise, continue down the Ramblas another 30 yards. The wide, straight street that crosses the Ramblas at this point (Carrer de Ferran) leads to Plaça de San Jaume, the government center.*

Continue down the Ramblas another 50 yards (to #46), and turn left down an arcaded lane (Correr de Colom) to a square filled with palm trees.

❽ **Plaça Reial:** Dotted with palm trees, surrounded by an arcade, and ringed by yellow buildings with white Neoclassical trim, this elegant square has a colonial ambience. It comes complete with old-fashioned taverns, modern bars with patio seating, and a Sunday coin-and-stamp market (10:00-14:00). Completing the picture are Gaudí's first public works (the two colorful helmeted lampposts) and characters who don't need the palm trees to be shady. **Herbolari Ferran** is a fine and aromatic shop of herbs, with fun souvenirs such as top-quality saffron, or *safra* (Mon-Fri 9:30-14:00 & 16:30-20:00, closed Sat-Sun, downstairs at Plaça Reial 18—to the right as you enter the square). The small streets stretching toward the water from the square are intriguing, but less safe.

Back on the other side of the Ramblas, a half-block detour to Carrer Nou de la Rambla 3-5 brings you to the **Palau Güell**, designed by Antoni Gaudí (1886-90). Even from the outside, you get a sense of this innovative apartment, the first of Gaudí's Modernist buildings. The two parabolic-arch doorways and elaborate wrought-iron work signal his emerging nonrectangular style. Recently renovated, the Palau Güell offers an informative look at a Gaudí interior (for cost and hours, see page 1217). Pablo Picasso had a studio at #10 (though there's nothing to see there today).

• *Continue downhill on the Ramblas.*

❾ The Raval Neighborhood (Barri Xines): The neighborhood on the right-hand side of this stretch of the Ramblas is El Raval. Its nickname was Barri Xines—the world's only Chinatown with nothing even remotely Chinese in or near it. Named for the prejudiced notion that Chinese immigrants go hand-in-hand with poverty, prostitution, and drug dealing, the neighborhood's actual inhabitants were poor Spanish, North African, and Roma (Gypsy) people. At night, the Barri Xines was frequented by prostitutes, many of them transvestites, who catered to sailors wandering up from the port. Today, it's becoming gentrified, but it's still a pretty rough neighborhood. Prostitution is nothing new here. Check out the thresholds at #22 and #24 (along the left side of the Ramblas)—with holes worn in long ago by the heels of anxious ladies.

Take note of the Drassanes Metro stop (near the Museo de Cera, or wax museum), which can take you back to Plaça de Catalunya when this walk is over. The skyscraper to the right of the Ramblas is the Edificio Colón. When it was built in 1970, the 28-story structure was Barcelona's first high-rise. Near the skyscraper is the Maritime Museum, housed in what were the city's giant medieval shipyards (see page 1205).

• *Up ahead is the...*

❿ Columbus Monument and Waterfront: The 200-foot column marks the spot where Christopher Columbus debarked after returning from America (see page 1207 for more).

Continue ahead to the waterfront. Barcelona is one of Europe's top-10 ports, though this stretch of the harbor is a pleasant marina with sailboats.

Stand here and survey some of your sightseeing options: At your feet are the *golondrinas* harbor cruise boats (page 1207). Across the harbor (though not really visible from here) is the spit of land called Barceloneta, home to some nice restaurants and sandy beaches (see page 1240). To the right of the harbor rises the majestic, 570-foot bluff of Montjuïc, a park-like setting dotted with a number of sights and museums (see page 1225).

The pedestrian bridge jutting into the harbor is a modern

extension of the Ramblas called La Rambla del Mar ("Rambla of the Sea"). This popular wooden bridge—with waves like the sea—leads to Maremagnum, a shopping mall with a cinema, a huge aquarium, restaurants, and piles of people. Late at night, it's a rollicking youth hangout.

• *Your ramble is over. The easiest way home is to backtrack to the Drassanes Metro stop or catch buses #14 or #59 to Plaça de Catalunya.*

▲▲The Barri Gòtic: From Plaça de Catalunya to the Cathedral

Barcelona's Barri Gòtic, or Gothic Quarter, is a bustling world of shops, bars, and nightlife packed into narrow, winding lanes and undiscovered courtyards. This is Barcelona's birthplace—where the ancient Romans built a city, where medieval Christians built their cathedral, and where Barcelonans lived within a ring of protective walls until the 1850s, when the city expanded.

Today, it's Barcelona's most historic, atmospheric, characteristic, and colorful neighborhood. Concentrate on the area around the cathedral (since the section near the port is somewhat dull and seedy). The Barri Gòtic is a tangled-yet-inviting grab bag of grand squares, schoolyards, Art Nouveau storefronts, baby flea markets (on Thu, closed Aug), musty junk shops, classy antiques shops (on Carrer de la Palla), street musicians strumming Catalan folk songs, and balconies with domestic jungles behind wrought-iron bars. Go on a cultural scavenger hunt. Write a poem. Take artsy pictures. This self-guided walk gives you a structure, covering the main sights and offering a historical overview before you get lost.

• *Start on Barcelona's bustling main square, Plaça de Catalunya (described on page 1194). From the southeast corner (near El Corte Inglés), head downhill along the broad pedestrian boulevard called...*

❶ Avinguda Portal de l'Angel: For much of Barcelona's history, this was one of the main boulevards leading into town. A medieval wall enclosed the city, and there was an entrance here—the "Gate of the Angel" that gives the street its name. An angel statue atop the gate kept the city safe from plagues, and bid voyagers safe journey as they left the security of the city. Imagine the fascinating scene here at the Gate of the Angel, where Barcelona stopped and the wilds began.

Today's street is pretty globalized and sanitized, full of international chain stores. Pause at Carrer de Santa Anna to admire the Art Nouveau awning at (another) El Corte Inglés store.

• *A half-block detour down Carrer de Santa Anna (at #32) leads to a pleasant, flower-fragrant courtyard with the...*

❷ Eglesia de Santa Anna: This 12th-century gem was one of those *extra muro* churches, with its marker cross still standing outside. As part of a convent, the church has a fine cloister, an arcaded

Barri Gòtic: Cathedral Neighborhood

TO SANTA ANNA ②,
AVINGUDA DE PORTAL L'ANGEL ①
& PLAÇA DE CATALUNYA

—— BARRI GOTIC WALK

→ ENTRY / EXIT
POINT TO SIGHTS

NOT TO SCALE

③ FOUNTAIN

ARCS

ARCHITECTS' HOUSE

SARDANA DANCERS

BOTERS   PLAÇA   A V I N G U D A   C A T E D R A L

TO RAMBLAS

LA PALLA

④ PLAÇA NOVA

BARCINO

DEACON'S HOUSE

⑥

PLAÇA DE LA SEU

⑤

MUSEU DIOCESÀ

PLAÇA SANT FELIP NERI

①

⑧ MONT DE BISBE

SHOE MUSEUM

⑦

SANT SEVER

TO RAMBLAS

IRURITA

CLOISTERS

GEESE   WC

SHOP

DEL   BISBE

MARÈS MUSEUM

COMTES

CHOIR

CATHEDRAL

ROYAL PALACE

FRENERIA

PLAÇA DEL REI

⑫

⑨ BRIDGE OVER STREET

PALAU DE LA GENERALITAT (CATALAN GOV'T.)

CARRER   DEL

⑪

C. DEL PARIDÍS

"MONT" TÀBER ROMAN TEMPLE

CITY HISTORY MUSEUM

PLAÇA DE

⑩

SANT JAUME

LLIBRETERIA

CARRER   DE   JAUME I

TO PICASSO MUSEUM & LA RIBERA

DCH

TO RAMBLAS

① Avinguda Portal de l'Angel
② Eglesia de Santa Anna
③ Fountain
④ Plaça Nova
⑤ Cathedral
⑥ Casa de l'Ardiaca
⑦ Martyrs Statue
⑧ Plaça Sant Felip Neri
⑨ Carrer del Bisbe Bridge
⑩ Plaça de Sant Jaume
⑪ Roman Temple of Augustus
⑫ Plaça del Rei

BARCELONA

walkway around a leafy courtyard (viewable through the gate to the left of the church). Climb the modern stairs for views of the bell tower.

If the church is open, you'll see a bare Romanesque interior and Greek-cross floor plan, topped with an octagonal wooden roof. The recumbent-knight tomb is of Miguel de Boera, renowned admiral of Charles V. The door at the far end of the nave leads to the cloister (church hours vary but usually daily 9:00-13:00 and 18:00-20:00).

• *Continue down Avinguda Portal de l'Angel until you run into a building at a fork in the road, with a...*

❸ **Fountain:** The fountain's blue-and-yellow tilework depicts ladies carrying jugs of water. In the 17th century, this was the last watering stop for horses before leaving town. As recently as 1940, one in nine Barcelonans got their water from fountains like this. It's still used today.

• *Take the left fork, passing by the Royal Art Circle Museum (temporary exhibits). Enter the large square called the...*

❹ **Plaça Nova:** Two bold **Roman towers** flank the main street. These once guarded the entrance gate of the ancient Roman city of Barcino. The big stones that make up the base of the (reconstructed) towers are actually Roman. At the base, find the **modern bronze letters** spelling out "BARCINO." The city's name may have come from Barca, one of Hannibal's generals, who is said to have passed through during Hannibal's roundabout invasion of Italy. At Barcino's peak, the **Roman wall** (see the section stretching to the left of the towers) was 25 feet high and a mile around, with 74 towers. It enclosed an area of 30 acres—population 4,000.

One of the towers has a section of **Roman aqueduct** (a modern reconstruction). These bridges of stone carried fresh water from the distant hillsides into the walled city. Here the water supply split into two channels, one to feed Roman industry, the other for the general populace. The Roman aqueducts would be the best water system Barcelona would have until the 20th century.

Opposite the towers is the modern College of Architects building with a **frieze designed by Picasso** (1960). In Picasso's distinctive childlike style, it shows branch-waving kings and children celebrating a local festival. Picasso spent his formative years (1895-1904, ages 14-23) in the Barri Gòtic. He had a studio a block east of here (where the big Caixa Catalunya building stands today). He drank with fellow bohemians at the "Four Cats," two blocks north (where a touristy incarnation stands today), and frequented brothels a few blocks south of here on Carrer d'Avinyo ("Avignon"), which inspired his seminal Cubist painting *Les Demoiselles d'Avignon*. Picasso's Barri Gòtic was a hotbed of trendsetting art, propelling Picasso forward just before he moved to

BARCELONA

Paris and remade modern art.

• *Now head to the left and take in the mighty facade of the...*

❺ Cathedral of Barcelona (Catedral de Barcelona): This location has been the center of Christian worship since the fourth century, and this particular building dates (mainly) from the 14th century. The facade is a virtual catalog of Gothic motifs: a pointed arch over the entrance, robed statues, tracery in windows, gargoyles, and bell towers with winged angels. The style is French Flamboyant (meaning "flame-like"), and the roofline sports the prickly spires meant to give the impressions of a church flickering with spiritual fires. The facade is typically Gothic...but not medieval. It's a Neo-Gothic work from the 19th century. The area in front of the cathedral is where they dance the *sardana*.

The cathedral's interior—with its vast size, peaceful cloister, and many ornate chapels—is worth a visit (see "Sights in Barcelona," later).

• *The Frederic Marès Museum (see page 1209 for details) is just to the left of the cathedral. But for now, return to the Roman towers. Pass between the towers up Carrer del Bisbe, and take an immediate left, to the staircase entrance of the...*

❻ Casa de l'Ardiaca *(Archivo)*: It's free to enter this mansion, which was once the archdeacon's house and today functions as the city archives. The elaborately carved doorway is Renaissance. To the right of the doorway is a carved mail slot by 19th-century Modernist architect Lluís Domènech i Muntaner. Enter into a small courtyard with a fountain. Notice how the century-old palm tree seems to be held captive by urban man. Next, step inside the lobby of the city archives. You can't tour the archives, but there are often temporary exhibits in the lobby. At the left end of the lobby, step through the archway and look down into the stairwell—this is the back side of the ancient Roman wall. Back in the courtyard, head up to the balcony for views of the cathedral steeple and gargoyles.

• *Return to Carrer del Bisbe and turn left. After a few steps you reach a small square with a bronze statue ensemble.*

❼ Martyrs Statue: Five Barcelona patriots calmly receive their last rites before being garroted (strangled) for resisting Napoleon's 1809 invasion of Spain. They'd been outraged by French atrocities in Madrid (depicted in Goya's "Third of May" painting in Madrid's Prado Museum). The plaque marking their mortal remains says these martyrs to independence gave their lives *"por Dios, por la Patria, y por el Rey"*—for God, country, and king.

The plaza offers interesting views of the cathedral's towers. The doorway here is the (not-always-open) "back door" entrance to the cathedral (at the cloister), letting you avoid the long lines at the cathedral's main entrance.

• *Exit the square down tiny Carrer de Montjuïc del Bisbe. This leads to the cute...*

❽ **Plaça Sant Felip Neri:** This square serves as the playground of an elementary school and is often bursting with youthful energy. The Church of Sant Felip Neri, which Gaudí attended, is still pocked with bomb damage from the Civil War. As a stronghold of democratic, anti-Franco forces, Barcelona saw a lot of fighting. The shrapnel that damaged this church was meant for the nearby Catalan government building (Palau de la Generalitat, described below).

Study the carved reliefs on nearby buildings, paid for by the guilds that powered the local economy. It's clear that the building on the far right must have housed the shoemakers. In fact, just next door is the fun little Shoe Museum (described on page 1208).

• *Exit the square down Carrer de Saint Felip Neri, turn left, and return to the square with the Martyrs Statue. Then turn right, walking along Carrer del Bisbe. Up ahead is the...*

❾ **Carrer del Bisbe Bridge:** This Bridge-of-Sighs-like structure connects the Catalan government building on the right with the Catalan president's residence (ceremonial, not actual). Though the bridge looks medieval, it was constructed in the 1920s by Joan Rubió, who also did the carved ornamentation on the buildings.

It's a photographer's delight. Check out the jutting angels on the bridge, the basket-carrying maidens on the president's house, the gargoyle-like faces on the government building. Zoom in even closer. Find monsters, skulls, goddesses, old men with beards, climbing vines, and coats of arms—a Gothic museum in stone.

• *Continue along Carrer del Bisbe to...*

❿ **Plaça de Sant Jaume** (jow-mah): This stately central square of the Barri Gòtic, once the Roman forum, has been the seat of city government for 2,000 years. Today the two top governmental buildings in Catalunya face each other.

For more than six centuries, the **Palau de la Generalitat** has housed the autonomous government of Catalunya. It always flies the Catalan flag (red and yellow stripes) next to the obligatory Spanish one. Above the doorway is Catalunya's patron saint— St. Jordi (George), slaying the dragon. From these balconies, the nation's leaders (and soccer heroes) greet the people on momentous days. The square is often the site of demonstrations, from a single aggrieved citizen with a megaphone to riotous thousands.

The **Barcelona City Hall** (Casa de la Ciutat) sports a statue of "Jaume el Conqueridor," for whom this plaza is named (free, open Sun 10:00-13:30). King Jaume I (1208-1276, also called "the Just") is credited with freeing Barcelona from French control, granting self-government, and setting it on a course to become a major city. He was the driving force behind construction of the Royal Palace

BARCELONA

(which we'll see shortly).

Locals treasure the independence these two government buildings represent. In the 20th century, Barcelona opposed the dictator Francisco Franco (who ruled from 1939 to 1975) and Franco retaliated. He abolished the regional government and (effectively) outlawed the Catalunyan language and customs. Two years after Franco's death, joyous citizens packed this square to celebrate the return of self-rule.

Look left and right down the main streets branching off the square. Carrer de Ferran (which leads to the Ramblas) is classic Barcelona—lined with ironwork streetlamps and balconies draped with plants.

In ancient Roman days, Plaça de Sant Jaume was the town's forum or central square, located at the intersection of the two main streets—the *decumanus* (Carrer del Bisbe) and the *cardus* (Carrer de la Llibreteria). The forum's biggest building was a massive temple of Augustus, which we'll see next.

• *Facing the Generalitat, exit the square to the right, heading uphill on tiny Carrer del Paradís. Follow this street as it turns right. When it swings left, pause at #10, the entrance to the...*

⓫ Roman Temple of Augustus: You're standing at the summit of Mont Tàber. A plaque on the wall says it all: "Mont Tàber, 16.9 meters"—elevation 55 feet. The Barri Gòtic's highest spot is also marked with a millstone inlaid in the pavement at the doorstep of #10. It was here, atop this lofty summit, that the ancient Romans founded the town of Barcino around 15 B.C. They built a *castrum* (fort) on the hilltop, protecting the harbor.

Step inside for a peek at the imposing Roman temple (Temple Roma d'August). These four huge columns, from around A.D. 1, are as old as Barcelona itself. They were part of the ancient town's biggest structure, a temple dedicated to the Emperor Augustus, worshipped as a god. These Corinthian columns (with deep fluting and topped with leafy capitals) were the back corner of a 120-foot-long temple that extended from here to the Fòrum (free, good English info; April-Sept Tue-Sun 10:00-20:00; Oct-March Tue-Sat 10:00-14:00 & 16:00-19:00, Sun 10:00-20:00; closed Mon year-round).

• *Continue down Carrer del Paridís one block. When you bump into the back end of the cathedral, take a right, and go downhill a block (down Baixada de Santa Clara) until it emerges into a square called...*

⓬ Plaça del Rei: The buildings that enclose this square once housed Spain's kings and queens. The central section (topped by a six-story addition) was the core of the Royal Palace. It has a vast hall on the ground floor that served as the throne room and reception room. From the 13th to the 15th centuries, the Royal Palace housed Catalunya's counts as well as resident Spanish kings. In 1493, a triumphant Christopher Columbus, accompanied by six

New World natives (whom he called "Indians") and several pure-gold statues, entered the Royal Palace. King Ferdinand and Queen Isabel rose to welcome him home, and honored him with the title "Admiral of the Oceans."

To the right is the palace's church, the Chapel of Saint Agatha. It sits atop the foundations of the Roman wall.

To the left is the Viceroy's Palace (for the ruler's right-hand man), which also served as the archives of the Kingdom of Aragon. After Catalunya became part of Spain in the 15th century, the Royal Palace became a small regional residence, and the Viceroy's Palace became the headquarters of the local Inquisition. Today the Viceroy's Palace is once again home to the archives. Step inside the courtyard. It has an impressive Renaissance courtyard, a staircase with coffered wood ceilings, and a temporary exhibit space. Among the archive's treasures (though it's rarely on display) is the 1491 Santa Fe Capitulations, a contract between Columbus and the monarchs about his upcoming voyage.

Ironically, Columbus and the Kingdom of Aragon played a role in Barcelona's decline as an independent kingdom. When Ferdinand of Aragon married Isabel of Castile, Catalunya got swallowed up in greater Spain. Columbus' discovery of new trade routes made Barcelona's port less important, and soon the royals moved elsewhere.

The City History Museum's entrance is at the near end of Plaça del Rei. This museum (see details on page 1209) is the only way to see the interior of the Royal Palace and Chapel of Saint Agatha. It's a fine way to retrace all the history we've seen on this walk—from modern to medieval to the Roman foundations of Barcino.

• *Your tour is over. It's easy to get your bearings by backtracking to either Plaça de Sant Jaume or the cathedral. The Jaume I Metro stop is two blocks away (head downhill and turn left). Or simply wander and enjoy Barcelona at its Gothic best.*

Sights in Barcelona

Barcelona's Old City

I've divided Barcelona's Old City sights into three neighborhoods: near the harbor, at the bottom of the Ramblas; the cathedral and nearby (Barri Gòtic); and the Picasso Museum and nearby (La Ribera).

On the Harborfront, at the Bottom of the Ramblas

▲**Maritime Museum (Museu Marítim)**—Barcelona's medieval shipyard, the best preserved in the entire Mediterranean, has an impressive collection covering the salty history of ships and

Barcelona's Barri Gòtic

THE EIXAMPLE

GRAN VIA DE LES CORTS CATALANES

PLAÇA UNIV.

Ⓜ Univ.

CARRER PELAI

VALLDON.

MACBA CONTEMP. ART MUSEUM

ELIS.   BONSUCCES

PINTOR

CARME

Cultural Info PALAU DE LA VIRREINA

Liceu Ⓜ

LA BOQUERÍA MARKET

HOSP.

SANT PAU

LICEU OPERA HOUSE

NOU RAMBLA

PALAU GÜELL

L'ARC TEATRE

MARITIME MUSEUM

Ⓜ Drassanes

RONDA UNIVERSITAT

BERGARA

FNAC

FGC TRAIN INFO

Ⓜ Catalunya

SANTA ANNA

BONSUCCES

L

BANS

BERT.

CANUDA

DUC. VIU.

PORTAFERRISSA

PETRITXOL

C. DEL PI

CARD.

BANYS NOUS

BOQUERIA

Liceu

FERRAN

D'AVINYO

PLAÇA REIAL

PL. ORWELL

ESCUDELLERS

NOU

SAN FRAN.

CODOLS

CLAVE

PL. MED.

RONDA

PLAÇA DE CATALUNYA

START Ⓑ

ⓘ

SANT

Catalunya ✚

PORTAL DE L'ANGEL

ARCS

PL. NOVA

AV. CATEDRAL MAURA

PALLA

PAL. GEN.

PLAÇA S. JAUME

ⓘ

CITY HALL

UTAT

SOBRE

D'AVINYO

GIGNAS

AMPLE

MERCE

Ramblas
Ⓜ Metro Station
Ⓑ Bus Stop
Barri Gotic Walk

TO BLOCK OF DISCORD + CASA MILÀ

PASSEIG DE GRACIA

El Corte Inglés Dept. Store

FONTANELLA

BUS TO AIRPORT (+ TAXIS)

COMTAL

MONTSIO

CATALAN CONCERT HALL

S. P. ALT

S. P. BAIX

MARÈS MUSEUM

✚ CATHEDRAL

FINISH

PLAÇA DE L'ANGEL   PRINCESA

Jaume I Ⓜ

ARGENTERIA

CAN NOUS

POST

CONS. MAR.

TO BARCELONETA

TO PICASSO Mus.

TO S. MARIA D. MAR

PERE

ZV

L A

R I B E R A

L U T I R I A

PL. DE L'ANGEL

COLUMBUS MONUMENT

SHUTTLE BUS FOR MOLL ADOSSAT Ⓑ

GOLONDRINAS CRUISES

PASSEIG DE COLÓM

MOLL DE BOSCH / ALSINA / LA FUSTA

HARBOR

← RAMBLA DE MAR

↓ TO MAREMAGNUM ↓

200 YARDS

200 METERS

EL RAVAL

RAMBLAS

BARCELONA

navigation from the 13th to the 20th centuries. Riveting for nautical types, and interesting for anyone, its modern and beautifully presented exhibits will put you in a seafaring mood. The museum is undergoing a major renovation, closing off large sections one at a time through 2013, so what you see will depend on when you visit. The museum's cavernous halls evoke the 14th-century days when Catalunya was a naval and shipbuilding power, cranking out 30 huge galleys a winter. As in the US today, military and commercial ventures mixed and mingled as Catalunya built its trading empire. The excellent included audioguide tells the story and explains the various seafaring vessels displayed—including an impressively huge and richly decorated royal galley. Your ticket also includes entrance to the Santa Eulàlia, an early 20th-century sailing vessel docked just a short walk from the Columbus Monument.

Cost and Hours: €2.50, prices may change as more exhibits reopen, museum—open daily 10:00-20:00, last entry 30 minutes before closing; Santa Eulàlia—generally open Mon-Sat 12:00-17:30, Sun 10:00-17:30, but hours vary with seasons; breezy courtyard café, Avinguda de la Drassanes, Metro: Drassanes, tel. 933-429-920, www.mmb.cat.

▲**Columbus Monument (Monument a Colóm)**—Marking the point where the Ramblas hits the harbor, this 200-foot-tall monument was built for an 1888 exposition. The tight four-person elevator takes you to the glassed-in observation area at the top for congested but sweeping views. There is also a small TI inside. It was here in Barcelona that Ferdinand and Isabel welcomed Columbus home after his first trip to America. It's ironic that Barcelona would so honor the man whose discoveries ultimately led to its downfall as a great trading power.

Cost and Hours: €4, daily May-Oct 9:00-20:30, Nov-April 10:00-18:30.

Golondrinas **Cruises**—At the harbor near the foot of the Columbus Monument, tourist boats called *golondrinas* offer two different unguided trips. The shorter version goes around the harbor in 35 minutes (€6.80, daily on the hour 11:30-19:00, every 30 minutes mid-June-mid-Sept, may not run Nov-April—call ahead, tel. 934-423-106). The longer 1.5-hour trip goes up the coast to the Fòrum complex and back (€14, can disembark at Fòrum in summer only, about 7/day, daily 11:30-19:30, shorter hours in winter).

▲**Cathedral of Barcelona**

This has been Barcelona's holiest spot for 2,000 years. The Romans built their Temple of Jupiter here. In A.D. 343, the pagan temple was replaced with a Christian cathedral. That building was supplanted by a Romanesque-style church (11th century). The current Gothic structure was built in the 14th century (1298-1450), during the glory days of the Catalan nation. The facade was humble, so in the 19th century the proud local bourgeoisie redid it in a more ornate, Neo-Gothic style. Construction was capped in 1913 with the central spire, 230 feet tall.

The church is worth visiting for its vast nave, rich chapels, tomb of St. Eulàlia, and the oasis-like setting of the cloister. Other sights inside (sometimes requiring separate admission charges) are the elaborately carved choir, the elevator up to the view terrace, and the altarpiece museum.

The spacious church is 300 feet long and 130 feet wide. Tall pillars made of stone blocks support the crisscross vaults. Each round keystone where the arches cross features a different saint. Typical of many Spanish churches, there's a choir—an enclosed area of wooden seats in the middle of the nave. The Gothic church also has fine stained glass, ironwork chandeliers, a 16th-century organ (left transept), tombstones in the pavement, and an ambulatory floor plan, allowing worshippers to amble around to the chapel of their choice.

Cost: Until 14:00, the cathedral is free to enter, but you must pay to visit several sights inside: the choir (€2.50), terrace (€2.50), and museum (€2). The cathedral is closed in the afternoon; starting at 17:15, you pay €6 to enter, which also covers admission to the three special sights (tel. 933-151-554, www.catedralbcn.org). The dress code is strictly enforced; don't wear tank tops, shorts, or skirts above the knee.

Hours: Cathedral—Mon-Fri 8:00-12:45 & 17:15-19:30, Sat 8:00-12:45 & 17:15-20:00, Sun 8:00-13:45 & 17:15-20:00; choir—Mon-Sat 9:00-12:45 & 17:15-19:00, Sun 9:00-12:45; terrace—Mon-Sat 9:00-12:30 & 17:15-18:00, closed Sun; museum—daily 10:00-12:30 & 17:15-19:00.

Avoiding Lines: Mornings are most crowded. You can sometimes avoid lines at the main entrance by entering through the cloister (around the right side of the church, on Carrer del Bisbe), although this entrance isn't always open. The elevator to the view terrace often has lines, which you can't avoid.

WCs: Tiny, semi-private WC in the center of the cloister.

Getting There: The huge can't-miss-it cathedral is in the center of the Barri Gòtic, on Plaça de la Seu, Metro: Jaume I. For an interesting way to reach the cathedral from Plaça de Catalunya, and some commentary on the surrounding neighborhood, see my self-guided walk of the Barri Gòtic, described earlier.

In the Barri Gòtic, near the Cathedral

Shoe Museum (Museu del Calçat)—Shoe-lovers enjoy this small museum of footwear in glass display cases, watched over by an earnest attendant. You'll see shoes from the 1700s to today:

fancy ladies' boots, Tibetan moccasins, big clown shoes, and shoes of minor celebrities such as the president of Catalunya. The huge shoes at the entry are designed to fit the foot of the Columbus Monument at the bottom of the Ramblas.

Cost and Hours: €2.50, Tue-Sun 11:00-14:00, closed Mon, one block beyond outside door of cathedral cloister, behind Plaça de G. Bachs on Plaça Sant Felip Neri, Metro: Jaume I, see "Plaça Sant Felip Neri" on page 1203 for directions, tel. 933-014-533.

▲▲**City History Museum (Museu d'Història de la Ciutat)**— Walk through the history of the city with the help of an included audioguide. First watch the nine-minute introductory video in the small theater (playing alternately in Catalan, Spanish, and English)—it's worth viewing in any language. Then take an elevator down 65 feet (and 2,000 years—see the date spin back while you descend) to stroll the streets of Roman Barcelona. You'll see sewers, models of domestic life, and bits of an early-Christian church. Finally, an exhibit in the 11th-century count's palace shows you Barcelona through the Middle Ages.

Cost and Hours: €7, free all day first Sun of month and other Sun from 15:00 in summer, no audioguide during free times; Tue-Sat April-Oct 10:00-19:00, Nov-March 10:00-17:00; Sun 10:00-20:00, closed Mon, last entry 30 minutes before closing; Plaça del Rei, enter on Vageur street, Metro: Jaume I, tel. 932-562-122.

Frederic Marès Museum (Museu Frederic Marès)—This museum has an eclectic collection of local artist (and packrat) Frederic Marès, and sprawls around a peaceful courtyard through several old Barri Gòtic buildings. The biggest part of the collection is sculpture, hailing from ancient times to the early 20th century. But even more interesting is Marès' vast collection of items he found representative of everyday life in the 19th century—rooms upon rooms of fans, stamps, pipes, and other bric-a-brac, all lovingly displayed. There are also several sculptures by Frederic Marès himself, and temporary exhibits. The delightfully tranquil courtyard café offers a nice break, even when the museum is closed.

Cost and Hours: €4.20, free Sun from 15:00; open Tue-Sat 10:00-19:00, Sun 11:00-20:00, closed Mon; Plaça de Sant Iu 5-6, Metro: Jaume I, tel. 932-563-500, www.museumares.bcn.cat.

▲▲▲**Picasso Museum (Museu Picasso)**
This is the best collection in the country of the work of Spaniard Pablo Picasso (1881-1973), and—since he spent his formative years (age 14-23) in Barcelona—it's the best collection of his early works anywhere. By seeing his youthful, realistic art, you can more fully appreciate the artist's genius and better understand his later, more challenging art. The collection is scattered through several connected Gothic palaces, six blocks from the cathedral in the Ribera

BARCELONA

district (for more on this area, see below).

Cost and Hours: €10, free all day first Sun of month and other Sun from 15:00; open Tue-Sun 10:00-20:00, closed Mon, last entry 30 minutes before closing; Montcada 15-23, ticket office at #21, Metro: Jaume I, tel. 932-563-000, www.museupicasso.bcn.cat.

Crowd-Beating Tips: There's almost always a line, sometimes with waits of more than an hour. Mornings until 13:00 and all day Tuesday are busiest. If you have an Articket Card (see page 1182), skip the line by going to the "Meeting Point" entrance. You can also skip the line by buying your ticket online at www.museupicasso.bcn.cat (no additional booking fee). Stuck in line without a ticket? Figure that about 25 people are admitted every 10 minutes.

Services: The ground floor has a required bag check, as well as a handy array of other services (bookshop, WC, and cafeteria).

Cuisine Art: The museum itself has a good **café** (€8 sandwiches and salads). Across the street, the **Dhub Café** hides in a pleasant courtyard next door to the Textile Museum (Montcada 12-14, tel. 932-954-657). And just down the street is a neighborhood favorite for tapas, the recommended **El Xampanyet** (closed Mon).

In La Ribera, near the Picasso Museum

There's more to the Ribera neighborhood than just the Picasso Museum. While the nearby waterfront Barceloneta district was for the working-class sailors, La Ribera housed the wealthier shippers and merchants. Its streets are lined with their grand mansions—which, like the much-appreciated Church of Santa Maria del Mar, were built with shipping wealth.

La Ribera (also known as "El Born") is separated from the Barri Gòtic by Via Laietana, a four-lane highway built through the Old City in the early 1900s to alleviate growing traffic problems. From the Plaça de l'Angel (Metro: Jaume I), cross this busy street to enter an up-and-coming zone of lively and creative restaurants and nightlife. The Carrer de l'Argenteria ("Goldsmiths Street"—streets in La Ribera are named after the workshops that used to occupy them) runs diagonally from the Plaça de l'Angel straight down to the Church of Santa Maria del Mar. The Catalan Concert Hall is to the north.

▲▲Catalan Concert Hall (Palau de la Música Catalana)—This concert hall, finished in 1908, features my favorite Modernista interior in town (by Lluís Domènech i Muntaner). Inviting arches lead you into the 2,138-seat hall. A kaleidoscopic skylight features a choir singing around the sun, while playful carvings and mosaics celebrate music and Catalan culture. You can only get in by tour, which starts with a relaxing 12-minute video.

Barcelona's La Ribera

TO CATALAN CONCERT HALL

TO CATHEDRAL + RAMBLAS

Ⓜ METRO STATION

CHOCOLATE MUSEUM

PL. PONS I CLERCH

CARDERS

BOUGER

ASSAONADORS

PLAÇA DE L'ANGEL

C. DE LA BORIA

CARRER DE COTONERS

LA PRINCESA

Ⓜ Jaume I

BARRA DE FERRO

CARRER

PICASSO MUSEUM

COMERÇ

❶ VIGATANS

C. DE'N GRUNYÍ

BROSOLÍ

❺

FLASSADERS

C. DEL REC

FUSINA

DEL

CARRER DE L'ARGENTERIA

MANRESA

❸

ROSIC

C. D'EN MIRALLERS

C. DE BANYS VELLS

❹

MONTCADA

MOSQUES

BORN MARKET

VIA LAIETANA

❷

C. DE LA NAU

ABAIX.

SOMBRERERS

PASSEIG DEL BORN

ANT.

SANTA MARIA DEL MAR

RIBERA

CANVIS NOUS

AGULLERS

CANVIS VELLS

PL. STA. MARIA

MALCUINAT

❻ STA. MARIA

L'ESPASERIA

ASES

VIDRIERA

❼

PL. OLLES

RERA PAL.

PESCATERIA

SANT JOAN

CARRER

CONSOLAT DE MAR

LA LLOTJA

PLAÇA DEL PALAU

MARQUÈS DE L'ARGENTERIA

FRANÇA TRAIN STN.

POST

PLAÇA ANTONI LOPEZ

AVINGUDA DEL

TO MAREMAGNUM + BARCELONETA

TO Ⓜ Barceloneta

❶ Gothic Point Hostel
❷ Sagardi Euskal Taberna Rest. & Bar
❸ Taller de Tapas
❹ El Xampanyet Bar
❺ Dhub Café
❻ 1714 Massacre Monument
❼ Un Cotxe Menys Bike Rental

Cost and Hours: €12, 50-minute tours in English run daily every hour 10:00-15:00, may have longer hours on weekends and holidays, tour times may change based on performance schedule, about 6 blocks northeast of cathedral, Metro: Urquinaona, tel. 932-957-200, www.palaumusica.org.

The Catch: You must buy your ticket in advance to get a spot on an English guided tour (tickets available up to 7 days in advance—ideally buy yours at least 2 days before, though they're sometimes available the same day or day before). You can buy the ticket in person at the concert hall box office (open daily 9:30-15:30); by phone with your credit card (toll tel. 902-485-475); or online at the concert hall website (€1 fee, www.palaumusica.org).

Concerts: It might be easier to get tickets for a concert (300 per year, tickets for some performances as cheap as €7, see website for details).

▲**Church of Santa Maria del Mar**—This church is the proud centerpiece of La Ribera. "Del Mar" means "of the sea," and that's where the money came from. The proud shippers built this church in only 55 years, so it has a harmonious style that is considered pure Catalan Gothic. As you step in, notice the figures of workers carved into the big front doors. During the Spanish Civil War (1936-1939), the Church sided with the conservative forces of Franco against the people. In retaliation, the working class took their anger out on this church, burning all of its wood furnishings and decor (carbon still blackens the ceiling). Today it's stripped down—naked in all its Gothic glory. The tree-like columns inspired Gaudí (their influence on the columns inside his Sagrada Família church is obvious). Sixteenth-century sailors left models of their ships at the foot of the altar for Mary's protection. Even today there remains a classic old Catalan ship at Mary's feet. As within Barcelona's cathedral, here you can see the characteristic Catalan Gothic buttresses flying inward, defining the chapels that ring the nave.

Cost and Hours: Free entry, daily 9:00-13:30 & 16:30-20:00, Plaça Santa Maria, Metro: Jaume I, tel. 933-102-390.

Nearby: Exit the church from the side, and you arrive at a square with a modern **monument** to a 300-year-old massacre that's still part of the Catalan consciousness. On September 11, 1714, the Bourbon king ruling from Madrid massacred Catalan patriots, who were buried in a mass grave on this square. From that day on, the king outlawed Catalan culture and its institutions (no speaking the language, no folk dances, no university, and so on). The eternal flame burns atop this monument, and 9/11 is still a sobering anniversary for the Catalans.

To the Picasso Museum: From behind the church, the Carrer de Montcada leads two blocks to the Picasso Museum (described earlier). The street's mansions—built by rich shippers centuries ago—now house galleries, shops, and even museums. The Picasso Museum itself consists of five such mansions laced together.

Passeig del Born—Just behind the church, this long square was formerly a jousting square (as its shape indicates). This is the neighborhood center and a popular springboard for exploring tapas bars, fun restaurants, and nightspots in the narrow streets all around. Wandering around here at night, you'll find piles of inviting and intriguing little restaurants (I've listed my favorites on page 1241).

Enjoy a glass of wine on the square facing the church, or consider renting a bike here for a pedal down the beach promenade.

Chocolate Museum (Museu de la Xocolata)—This museum, only a couple of blocks from the Picasso Museum, is a delight for chocolate-lovers. Operated by the local confectioners' guild, it tells the story of chocolate from Aztecs to Europeans via the port of Barcelona, where it was first unloaded and processed. But the history lesson is just an excuse to show off a series of remarkably ornate candy sculptures. These works of edible art—which change every year but often include such Spanish themes as Don Quixote or bullfighting—begin as store-window displays for Easter or Christmas. Once the holiday passes, the confectioners bring the sculptures here to be enjoyed.

Cost and Hours: €4.30, Mon-Sat 10:00-19:00, Sun 10:00-15:00, Carrer Comerç 36, Metro: Jaume I, tel. 932-687-878, www.museuxocolata.com.

The Eixample: Modernisme and Antoni Gaudí

Wide sidewalks, hardy shade trees, chic shops, and plenty of Art Nouveau fun make the Eixample a refreshing break from the Old City. For the best Eixample example, ramble Rambla de Catalunya (unrelated to the more famous Ramblas) and pass through Passeig de Gràcia (Metro for Block of Discord: Passeig de Gràcia, or Metro for Casa Milà: Diagonal).

The 19th century was a boom time for Barcelona. By 1850 the city was busting out of its medieval walls. A new town was planned to follow a grid-like layout. The intersection of three major thoroughfares—Gran Via, Diagonal, and Meridiana—would shift the city's focus uptown. But uptown Barcelona is a unique variation on the common grid-plan city: Barcelona snipped off the building corners to create light and spacious eight-sided squares at every intersection.

The Eixample, or "Expansion," was a progressive plan in which everything was made accessible to everyone. Each 20-block-square district would have its own hospital and large park, each 10-block-square area would have its own market and general services, and each five-block-square grid would house its own schools and day-care centers. The hollow space found inside each "block" of apartments would form a neighborhood park.

Although much of that vision never quite panned out, the Eixample was an urban success. Rich and artsy big shots bought plots along the grid. The richest landowners built as close to the center as possible. For this reason, the best buildings are near the Passeig de Gràcia. While adhering to the height, width, and depth limitations, they built as they pleased—often in the trendy new Modernista style.

BARCELONA

For many visitors, Modernista architecture is Barcelona's main draw. (The TI even has a special desk set aside just for Modernisme-seekers.) And one name tops them all: **Antoni Gaudí** (1852-1926). Barcelona is an architectural scrapbook of Gaudí's galloping gables and organic curves. A devoted Catalan and Catholic, he immersed himself in each project, often living on-site. At various times, he called Parc Güell, Casa Milà, and the Sagrada Família home.

First I've covered the main Gaudí attractions close to the Old City. The Sagrada Família and Parc Güell are farther afield, but worth the trip.

Gaudí Sights near the Old City

▲▲**Casa Milà (La Pedrera)**—This Gaudí exterior laughs down on the crowds filling Passeig de Gràcia. Casa Milà, also called La Pedrera ("The Quarry"), has a much-photographed roller coaster of melting-ice-cream eaves. This is Barcelona's quintessential Modernista building and was Gaudí's last major work (1906-1910) before dedicating his final years to the Sagrada Família.

You'll visit three sections of Casa Milà: the apartment, the attic, and the rooftop. It's best to reserve ahead—sometimes there's a 1.5-hour wait to get in.

Cost and Hours: €14, good audioguide-€4, daily March-Oct 9:00-20:00, Nov-Feb 9:00-18:30, last entry 30 minutes before closing, Passeig de Gràcia 92, Metro: Diagonal, info toll tel. 902-400-973, advance tickets toll tel. 902-101-212, www.lapedrera educacio.org.

Visiting the Casa Milà: Enter and head upstairs to the apartment. If it's near closing time, continue up to see the attic and rooftop first, to make sure you have enough time to enjoy Gaudí's works and the views.

The typical fourth-floor **apartment** is decorated as it might have been when the building was first occupied by middle-class urbanites (a seven-minute video explains Barcelona society at the time). Notice Gaudí's clever use of the atrium to maximize daylight in all of the apartments.

The **attic** houses a sprawling multimedia exhibit tracing the history of the architect's career with models, photos, and videos of his work. It's all displayed under distinctive parabola-shaped arches. While evocative of Gaudí's style in themselves, the arches are formed this way partly to support the multilevel roof above. This area was also used for ventilation, helping to keep things cool in summer and warm in winter. Tenants had storage spaces and did their laundry up here.

From the attic, a stairway leads to the fanciful, undulating, jaw-dropping **rooftop,** where 30 chimneys play volleyball with the clouds.

Modernista Sights

ⓑ Bus Stop　Ⓜ Metro Station

N

RONDA DE DALT

TORRE DE BELLESGUARD

GAUDÍ HOUSE & MUSEUM

PARC GÜELL

#24, #92 + TOURIST BUS

FINCA GÜELL

FINCA MIRALLES

COL·LEGI DE LAS TERESIANES

LESSEPS

#116 ⓑ

TERRACE + FRONT ENTRANCE

GIRONA

DIAGONAL

SANTS TRAIN STN.

TRAV. GRACIA

CASA VICENS

Ⓜ ⓑ #116

FONTANA

TRAV. DALT

HOSPITAL DE LA SANTA CREU I SANT PAU (BY MUNTANER)

CASA MILÀ

ⓑ #92

DIAGONAL

PROVENÇA

AV. GAUDÍ

Ⓜ ⓑ #19 + #50

BLOCK OF DISCORD
• CASA BATLLÓ - BY GAUDÍ
• CASA AMATLLER BY CADAFALCH
• CASA LLEÓ MORERA BY MUNTANER
• FUNDACIÓ ANTONI TÀPIES BY MUNTANER

PASSEIG DE GRÀCIA

SAGRADA FAMÍLIA

GRAN VIA

CASA CALVET

PLAÇA D'ESPANYA

PLAÇA DE CATALUNYA & ⓑ #24

PARAL·LEL

RAMBLAS

CATALAN CONCERT HALL (BY MUNTANER)

MONTJUÏC

LICEU

BARRI GÒTIC

OLYMPIC PORT + "FISH" (BY GEHRY)

PALAU GÜELL

DRASS.

FRANÇA TRAIN STN.

NOT TO SCALE

HARBOR

DCH

BARCELONA

Back at the **ground level** of Casa Milà, poke into the dreamily painted original entrance courtyard. The first floor hosts free art exhibits.

Concerts: On summer weekends, Casa Milà has an evening rooftop concert series, "La Pedrera by Night," featuring live jazz. In addition to the music, it gives you the chance to see the rooftop illuminated (€25, mid-June-Aug Fri-Sat 20:30-23:00, advance tickets toll tel. 902-101-212, http://obrasocial.caixacatalunya.com).

Eating: Try the recommended **La Bodegueta,** a long block away (daily lunch special).

▲**Block of Discord**—Several colorful Modernista facades compete for your attention along this single stretch of Passeig de Gràcia. All were built by well-known architects at the end of the 19th century. Because the mansions look as though they are trying to outdo each other in creative twists, locals nicknamed the noisy block the "Block of Discord."

It's on Passeig de Gràcia between Consell de Cent and Aragó streets. It's three blocks north of Plaça de Catalunya (and four blocks south of Casa Milà), right by the Passeig de Gràcia Metro stop.

Casa Batlló (#43): First and most famous is the green-blue ceramic-speckled facade of Casa Batlló, designed by Antoni Gaudí. It has tibia-like pillars and shell-like balconies, inspired by the time-tested natural forms that Gaudí knew made the best structural supports. The tiled roof has a soft-ice-cream-cone turret topped with a cross. The humpback roofline suggests a cresting dragon's back. Gaudí based the work on the popular legend of St. Jordi (George) slaying the dragon. By the way, if you're tempted to snap photos from the middle of the street, be careful—Gaudí died after being struck by a streetcar.

You can tour the interior. You'll see the main floor (with a funky mushroom-shaped fireplace nook), the blue-and-white-ceramic-slathered atrium, the attic (more parabolic arches), and the rooftop, all with the help of the good audioguide. Because preservation of the place is privately funded, the entrance fee is steep—but the interior is even more fanciful and over-the-top than Casa Milà's. There's barely a straight line in the house (€18.15, includes audioguide, daily 9:00-20:00, may close early for special events—closings posted in advance at entrance, tel. 932-160-306, www.casabatllo.cat). Avoid lines (especially in the morning) by calling 932-853-832 or buying online at http://bcnshop.barcelona turisme.com.

Casa Amatller (#41): Next door is Josep Puig i Cadafalch's creative mix, combining three of Spain's historical traditions. There are Moorish-style pentagram-and-vine designs; Gothic-style tracery, gargoyles, and bay windows; and the step-gable roof from Spain's Habsburg connection to the Low Countries. Look through the bay window to see the corkscrew column inside. Pop inside for more peeks at the elaborate entrance hall.

Casa Lleó Morera (#35): A few doors to the left, the corner building offers another paella-like mix of styles. The lower floors have classical columns and a Greek-temple-like bay window. Farther up are Gothic balconies of rosettes and tracery, while the upper part has faux Moorish stucco work. The whole thing is ornamented with fantastic griffins, angels, and fish. Unfortunately, the wonderful interior is closed to the public. The architect, Lluís Domènech i Muntaner, also designed the Catalan Concert Hall (you'll notice similarities).

More Discord: While these three buildings were done by famous, ground-breaking architects, the whole block is a jumble of delightful architectural whimsy. Reliefs, coats of arms, ironwork, gables, and bay windows adorn otherwise ordinary buildings.

A half-block from Casa Batlló is the **Fundacio Antoni Tapies,** a museum dedicated to Tapies, a 20th-century abstract artist from Barcelona. The Muntaner-designed building sums up the Modernist credo: constructed of modern brick, iron, and glass; decorated with playful motifs; and spacious, functional, and full of light inside. Inside, you can see Tapies' distinct mud-caked canvases (there's a new array every few months). Tapies (b. 1923) lays the canvas on the floor; covers it with wet varnish; sprinkles in dust, dirt, and paint; then draws simple designs in the still-wet goop. He tries to capture the primitive power of cavemen tracing the first art in mud with a stick (€7 includes audioguide, Tue-Sun 10:00-20:00, closed Mon, tel. 934-870-315, www.fundaciotapies.org).

The recommended **La Rita** restaurant, just around the corner from the Block of Discord on Carrer Aragó, serves a fine three-course lunch for a great price (Mon-Fri from 13:00).

▲**Palau Güell**—Just as the Picasso Museum reveals a young genius on the verge of a breakthrough, this early Gaudí building (completed in 1890) shows the architect taking his first tentative steps toward what would become his trademark curvy style. The parabolic-arch doorways, viewable from the outside, are the first clue that this is not a typical townhouse. The Neo-Gothic cellar was used as a stable—notice the big carriage doors in the back and the rings on some of the posts used to tie up the horses. But the most dramatic space is its rooftop; Gaudí slathered the 20 chimneys with bits of stained glass, ceramic tile, and marble. Despite the fanciful roof (visible from the street if you crane your neck), I'd skip the Palau Güell if you plan to see the more interesting Casa Milà (€10, Tue-Sun April-Sept 10:00-20:00, Oct-March 10:00-17:00, closed Mon, a half-block off the Ramblas at Carrer Nou de la Rambla 3-5, Metro: Liceu or Drassanes, tel. 934-725-775, www.palauguell.cat).

▲▲▲Sagrada Família (Holy Family Church)

There's something powerful about a community of committed people with a vision, working on a church that won't be finished in their lifetime—as was standard in the Gothic age.

Antoni Gaudí's most famous and persistent work is this unfinished, super-sized church. Gaudí labored on the Sagrada Família for 43 years, from 1883 until his death in 1926. Since then, construction has moved forward in fits and starts. Even today, the half-finished church is not expected to be completed for years. But over 30 years of visits, I've seen considerable progress. It's a testament to the generations of architects, sculptors, stonecutters, fundraisers, and donors who've been caught up in the audacity of Gaudí's astonishing vision.

Sagrada Família

To Hospital de la Santa Creu i Sant Pau

POND

PLAÇA DE GAUDI

Sagrada Familia Ⓜ

CARRER DE LA MARINA

Ⓜ Sagrada Familia

CARRER DE PROVENÇA

NATIVITY FACADE

❻

❼

GLORY FACADE

❹

❺

Ⓑ #50

DE MALLORCA

❸

❷

PASSION FACADE

❽

FINISH

La Caixa Bank

ENTRANCE

CARRER DE SARDENYA

CARRER

❶

START

PLAÇA DE SAGRADA FAMILIA

100 YARDS

100 METERS

DCH

Ⓜ METRO STATION

Ⓑ BUS STOP

↗ VIEW

BARCELONA

❶ View of the Exterior
❷ Passion Facade
❸ Atrium
❹ Interior

❺ Nave & Glory Facade
❻ Nativity Facade
❼ To Museum & Crypt
❽ School

Cost and Hours: €12.50 (cash only), daily April-Sept 9:00-20:00, Oct-March 9:00-18:00, tel. 932-073-031, www.sagrada familia.cat.

Getting There: The Sagrada Família Metro stop puts you right on the doorstep: Exit toward Plaça de la Sagrada Família. The entrance for individuals (not groups) is on the west side of the church.

Crowd-Beating Tips: Waits in the ticket line can be up to 45 minutes at peak times. It's most crowded in the morning, and less crowded 14:00-15:00 and after 18:30.

Advance Tickets: To skip the ticket-buying line, you can reserve an entry time and buy tickets (with a €1.30 booking fee) from ATMs at many La Caixa bank branches throughout the city—including the branch just to the left of the Passion Facade. If tickets are available, you can buy them for the same day, even for immediate entry. However, not every La Caixa ATM sells tickets (use their larger ServiCaixa machines), and the instructions may be in Spanish (though English-only users can figure it out). Start the transaction by selecting "Event Tickets/Entrada Espectáculos" at the top of the screen. You can also reserve tickets and an entry time online at www.servicaixa.com—you'll pick your tickets up at the ServiCaixa machine outside the Passion Facade (instructions may be in Spanish). With your La Caixa–bought ticket in hand, you'll enter through an immediate-entry gate at the Passion Facade.

Tours: The 45-minute English tours (€4) run June-Oct daily at 11:00, 12:00, and 13:00; Nov-May Mon-Fri at 11:00 and 13:00, Sat-Sun at 11:00, 12:00, and 13:00. Or rent the good 70-minute audioguide (€4).

Elevators: Two different elevators (€2.50 each, pay at main ticket office) take you partway up the towers for a great view of the city and a gargoyle's-eye perspective of the loopy church. The Passion Facade elevator takes you 215 feet up, where you can climb higher if you want; then an elevator takes you back down. The Nativity Facade elevator is similar, but you can also cross the dizzying bridge between the towers—and you must walk all the way down. If you plan to climb higher, expect the spiral stairs to be tight, hot, and congested. Lines can be up to two hours long. For the shortest lines, arrive right when the church opens and go directly to the elevators. The Nativity Facade elevator generally has a shorter line.

➲ Self-Guided Tour: Start at the ticket entrance (at the Passion Facade) on the western side of the church. The view is best from the park across the street.

❶ View of the Exterior: Stand and imagine how grand this church will be when completed. The four 330-foot spires topped with crosses are just a fraction of this mega-church. When finished, the church will have 18 spires. Four will stand at each of the three entrances. Rising above those will be four taller towers, dedicated to the four Evangelists. A tower dedicated to Mary will rise still higher—400 feet. And in the very center of the complex will stand the grand 560-foot Jesus tower, topped with a cross that will shine like a spiritual lighthouse, visible even from out at sea.

The Passion Facade that tourists enter today is only a side entrance to the church. The grand main entrance will be around to the right. That means that the nine-story apartment building will eventually have to be torn down to accommodate it. The three facades—Passion, Nativity, and Glory—will chronicle Christ's life from birth to death to resurrection.

When Gaudí died in 1926, only one spire (on the Nativity Facade) had been completed. The rest of the church has been inspired by Gaudí's vision but designed and executed by others. This artistic freedom was amplified in 1936, when Civil War shelling burned many of Gaudí's blueprints. Gaudí knew he wouldn't live to complete the church and recognized that later architects and artists would rely on their own muses for inspiration. It's a long-range vision. If there's any building on earth I'd like to see, it's the Sagrada Família...finished.

• Pass through the ticket entrance into the complex, approaching closer to the...

❷ **Passion Facade:** Judge for yourself how well Gaudí's original vision has been carried out by later artists. The Passion Facade's four spires were designed by Gaudí and completed (quite faithfully) in 1976. But the lower part was only inspired by Gaudí's designs. The stark sculptures were interpreted freely (and controversially) by Josep María Subirachs (b. 1927), who completed the work in 2005.

Subirachs tells the story of Christ's torture and execution. The various scenes—Last Supper, betrayal, whipping, and so on—zigzag up from bottom to top, culminating in Christ's crucifixion over the doorway. The style is severe and unadorned, quite different from Gaudí's signature playfulness. But the bone-like archways are very much in the Gaudí style. And Gaudí had made it clear that this facade should be grim and terrifying.

The facade is full of symbolism: there's a stylized Alpha-and-Omega over the door. Jesus, hanging on the cross, has hair made of an open book, symbolizing the word of God. To the left of the door, there's a grid of numbers, always adding up to 33—Jesus' age at the time of his death. The distinct face of the man below and just left of Christ is a memorial to Gaudí. Now look high above: The two-ton figure suspended between the towers is the soul of Jesus, ascending to heaven.

• Enter the church. As you pass through the ❸ **Atrium**, look down at the fine porphyry floor (with scenes of Jesus' entry into Jerusalem) and look right to see one of the elevators up to the towers. For now, continue into the...

❹ **Interior:** Walk through a forest of 56 massive columns to the center of the church. Part of Gaudí's religious vision was a love for nature. He said, "Nothing is invented; it's written in nature."

Like the trunks of trees, these columns blossom with life, complete with branches, leaves, and knot-like capitals. Little windows let light filter in like the canopy of a rain forest, giving both privacy and an intimate connection with God.

The columns are a variety of colors—brown clay, gray granite, dark-gray basalt. The taller columns are 72 feet tall—the shorter ones are exactly half that.

At the center of the church, find the four red porphyry columns. These support a ceiling vault that's 200 feet high. Eventually, these columns will support the central steeple, the 560-foot Jesus tower with the shining cross. The steeple will be further supported by four underground support pylons, each consisting of 8,000 tons of cement. It will be the tallest church steeple in the world.

• *Stroll (to the right) down the nave, to what will eventually be the main entrance.*

❺ **The Nave and Glory Facade:** The church floor-plan is in the shape of a Latin cross, 300 feet long and 200 feet wide. Ultimately, the church will encompass 48,000 square feet, accommodating 8,000 worshippers. The U-shaped choir, suspended above the nave, can seat 1,000. The singers will eventually be backed by four organs (there's one now).

The nave's roof is 150 feet high. The crisscross arches of the ceiling (the vaults) show off Gaudí's distinctive engineering. You'll see both parabolas (u-shaped) and hyperbolas (flatter, elliptical shapes). Gaudí's starting point was the Gothic pointed arch used in medieval churches. But he tweaked it after meticulous study of which arches are best at bearing weight.

The church's roof and flooring were only completed in 2010—just in time for Pope Benedict XVI to arrive and consecrate the church. Sagrada Família is a Catholic church and is used regularly for services. Future construction is focused on a few major tasks. They need to stabilize the existing nave, which has been rattled by vibrations from Metro and AVE train lines passing underground. They're also replacing the temporary clear windows with stained glass. Gaudí envisioned a semi-dark church for a contemplative mood.

The largest remaining construction project is the third, biggest entry—the Glory Facade. When completed, the Glory Facade will have a grand staircase leading up to the doors. Four towers will rise up. The facade's sculpture will represent how the soul passes through death, faces the Last Judgment, avoids the pitfalls of Hell, and finds its way to eternal glory with God. Gaudí purposely left the facade's design open for later architects—stay tuned. Above the Glory doorway (inside the church) stands Subirachs' statue of one of Barcelona's patron saints, St. Jordi (George of dragon-slaying fame).

• *Backtrack up the nave and exit out the right transept. Once outside, back up as far as you can to take in the...*

❻ **Nativity Facade:** The four spires decorated with Gaudí's unmistakable cake-in-the-rain sculpture mark this facade as part of his original design. It's the only part of the church essentially finished in his lifetime.

The theme is Christ's birth. A statue above the doorway shows Mary, Joseph, and Baby Jesus in the manger, while curious cows peek in. It's the Holy Family—or "Sagrada Família"—for whom this church is dedicated. Flanking the doorway are the three Magi and adoring shepherds. Other statues show Jesus as a young carpenter and angels playing musical instruments. Higher up on the facade, in the arched niche, God crowns Mary triumphantly.

The facade is all about birth and new life, from the dove-covered Tree of Life on top to the turtles at the base of the columns flanking the entrance. It's as playful as the Passion Facade is grim. Gaudí's plans were for this facade to be painted. Cleverly, this attractive facade was built and finished first to attract financial support for the project.

The four spires are dedicated to Apostles, and they bear the word "Sanctus," or holy. Their colorful ceramic caps symbolize the miters (formal hats) of bishops. Mixing Gothic-style symbolism, images from nature, and Modernista asymmetry, the Nativity Facade is the best example of Gaudí's original vision, and it established the template for future architects.

To the left of the facade is one section of the cloister. Whereas most medieval churches have their cloisters (or arcaded walkways) inside the church, surrounding a courtyard, the Sagrada Família's cloister will wrap around the building, more than 400 yards long.

• *Notice the second elevator up to the towers. But for now, head down the ramp to the left of the facade, which leads to the...*

❼ **Museum:** Housed in what will someday be the church's crypt, the museum displays Gaudí's original models and drawings, and chronicles the progress of construction over the last 130 years.

Wander among the plaster models used for the church's construction, including a model of the nave so big you walk beneath it. You'll notice that the models don't always match the finished product—these are ideas, not blueprints set in stone. The Passion Facade model shows Gaudí's original vision, with which Subirachs tinkered (very freely). The models make clear that the church's design is a fusion of nature, architecture, and religion. The columns seem light, with branches springing forth and capitals that look like palm trees.

The most intriguing display is the hanging "Funicular Model." It illustrates how Gaudí used gravity to calculate the arches that support the church. Wires dangle like suspended chains, forming perfect hyperbolic arches. Attached to these are bags, representing the weight the arches must support. Flip these arches over, and they can bear the heavy weight of the roof. The mirror above the model shows how the right-side-up church is derived from this.

Nearby, you'll find some original Gaudí architectural sketches in a dimly lit room, and a worthwhile 20-minute movie (generally shown in English at :50 past each hour). You can peek into a busy workshop still used for making the same kind of plaster models Gaudí used to envision the final product in 3-D.

You'll see photos of Gaudí himself. Look for the replicas of the pulpit and confessional that Gaudí, the micro-manager, designed for his church. Photos and a timeline illustrate how construction work has progressed from Gaudí's day to now.

❽ **School and Rest of Visit:** Outside the Passion Facade stands a small building—a school Gaudí erected for the children of the workers building the church. Along with temporary exhibits, you'll see a classroom and a replica of Gaudí's desk as it was the day he died.

Gaudí is buried in the crypt beneath the apse. Gaudí lived on the site for more than a decade, and is buried in a Neo-Gothic 19th-century crypt (which is where the church began). His tomb is viewable for free from the small church around the corner from the main ticket entrance (during Mass—Mon-Sat 8:30-10:00 & 18:30-21:00, longer hours on Sun). There's a move afoot to make Gaudí a saint. Perhaps someday his tomb will be a place of pilgrimage. Gaudí—a faithful Catholic whose medieval-style mysticism belied his Modernista architecture career—was certainly driven to greatness by his passion for God. When undertaking a lengthy project, he said, "My client"—meaning God—"is in no hurry."

▲Parc Güell

Gaudí fans enjoy the artist's magic in this colorful park. Gaudí intended this 30-acre garden to be a 60-residence housing project—a kind of gated community. As a high-income housing development, it flopped; but as a park, it's a delight, offering another peek into Gaudí's eccentric genius. Notice the mosaic medallions that say "park" in English, reminding folks that this is modeled on an English garden.

Cost and Hours: Free, daily 10:00-20:00, tel. 932-130-488.

Getting There: From Plaça de Catalunya, the blue Tourist Bus or bus #24 will leave you at the park's side entrance, or an €8 taxi will drop you off at the main entrance. From elsewhere in the city, do a Metro-plus-bus combination: Go by Metro to the Joanic stop and look for the Carrer de l'Escorial exit. Walk up Carrer de l'Escorial to the bus stop in front of #20. Take bus #116 directly to the park's main entrance; you'll see gingerbread-gate houses and a grand stairway. To get back to the city center after your visit, catch bus #116 going in the same direction; get off at Plaça de Lesseps and take the Metro from there.

⊘ Self-Guided Tour: This tour assumes you're arriving at the front/main entrance (by taxi or bus #116). If you instead arrive at the side entrance, walk straight ahead through the gate to find the terrace with colorful mosaic benches, then walk down to the stairway and front entrance.

As you wander the park, imagine living here a century ago—if this gated community had succeeded and was filled with Barcelona's wealthy.

Front Entrance: Entering the park, you walk by Gaudí's wrought-iron gas lamps (1900-1914). His dad was a blacksmith, and he always enjoyed this medium. Two gate houses made of gingerbread flank the entrance. One houses a good bookshop; the other is home to the skippable Center for Interpretation of Parc Güell (Centre d'Interpretació), which shows Gaudí's building methods plus maps, photos, and models of the park (€2.30, daily 11:00-15:00, tel. 933-190-222). The Gaudí House and Museum, described later, is better.

Stairway and Columns: Climb the grand stairway, past the famous ceramic dragon fountain. At the top, dip into the "Hall of 100 Columns," designed to house a produce market for the neighborhood's 60 mansions. The fun columns—each different, made from concrete and rebar, topped with colorful ceramic, and studded with broken bottles and bric-a-brac—add to the market's vitality.

As you continue up (on the left-hand staircase), look left, down the playful "pathway of columns" that supports a long arcade. Gaudí drew his inspiration from nature, and this arcade is like a surfer's perfect tube.

Terrace: Once up top, sit on a colorful bench—designed to fit your body ergonomically—and enjoy one of Barcelona's best views. Look for the Sagrada Família church in the distance. Gaudí was an engineer as well. He designed a water-catchment system by which rain hitting this plaza would flow into and through the columns from the market below, and power the park's fountains.

When considering the failure of Parc Güell as a community development, also consider that it was an idea a hundred years ahead of its time. Back then, high-society ladies didn't want to live so far from the cultural action. Today, the surrounding neighborhoods are some of the wealthiest in town, and a gated community here would be a big hit.

Gaudí House and Museum: This pink house with a steeple, standing in the middle of the park (near the side entrance), was actually Gaudí's home for 20 years, until his father died. His humble artifacts are mostly gone, but the house is now a museum with some quirky Gaudí furniture and a chance to wander through a model home used to sell the others. Though small, it offers a good taste of what could have been (€5.50, daily April-Sept 10:00-20:00, Oct-March 10:00-18:00).

Montjuïc

Montjuïc ("Mount of the Jews"), overlooking Barcelona's hazy port, has always been a show-off. Ages ago it had an impressive fortress. In 1929 it hosted an international fair, from which most of today's sights originated. And in 1992 the Summer Olympics directed the world's attention to this pincushion of attractions once again.

I've listed these sights by altitude, from highest to lowest; if you're visiting all of them, do them in this order so that most of your walking is downhill (for selective sightseers, the Fundació Joan Miró and Catalan Art Museum are the most worthwhile). Note that if you want to visit only the Catalan Art Museum, you can just take the Metro to Plaça d'Espanya and ride the escalators up (with some stair-climbing as well) to the museum.

Getting to Montjuïc: You have several options. The simplest is to take a **taxi** directly to your destination (about €7 from downtown).

Buses from various points in the city take you up to Montjuïc, including bus #50 (from the corner of Gran Via and Passeig de Gràcia, or from the Sagrada Família), bus #55 (from Plaça de Catalunya, next to Caja de Madrid building), and the red Tourist Bus.

A **funicular** takes visitors from the Paral-lel Metro stop up to Montjuïc (covered by a Metro ticket, every 10 minutes, 9:00-22:00). To reach the funicular, take the **Metro** to the Paral-lel stop, then follow signs for *Parc Montjuïc* and the little funicular icon—you can enter the funicular directly without using another ticket (number of minutes until next departure posted at start of entry tunnel). From the top of the funicular, turn left and walk two minutes to the Joan Miró museum, six minutes to the Olympic Stadium, or ten minutes to the Catalan Art Museum.

From the port, the most scenic way to Montjuïc is on the **cable car,** called the 1929 Transbordador Aereo (€9.50 one-way, €13 round-trip, 3/hour, daily 10:45-19:00, until 20:00 in June-Sept, closed in high wind, tel. 932-252-718).

Getting Around Montjuïc: Up top, the bus marked *Parc de Montjuïc* (#PM) loops between the sights. This circular line starts at Plaça d'Espanya and goes to the Catalan Art Museum, the Joan Miró museum, the funicular, and the Castle of Montjuïc. Public bus #50 and the red Tourist Bus also do circuits around the top of Montjuïc.

Montjuïc

M METRO STATION
♦ VIEW

¼ MILE
400 METERS

GRAN VIA DE LES CORTS CATALANES

FORMER BULLRING

PLAÇA D'ESPANYA M

AVINGUDA DE

VAN DER ROHE PAVILLION

SPANISH VILLAGE

MAGIC FOUNTAINS

AVINGUDA

CALATRAVA TOWER

CATALAN ART MUSEUM

OLYMPIC + SPORTS MUSEUM

POBLE SEC M

AVINGUDA DEL PARAL-LEL

FUNDACIÓ JOAN MIRÓ

PARAL-LEL M

TO OLD CITY

CARRER NOU DE LA RAMBLA

L'ESTADI

FUNICULAR

OLYMPIC STADIUM

POOL

SARDANA SCULPTURE

CABLE CAR TO PORT

MONTJUÏC CASTLE

CABLE CAR

MIRAMAR

CARNER

PASSEIG JOSEP

DCH

Castle of Montjuïc—The castle offers great city views from its fortress. The castle itself has a fascist past rife with repression. It was built in the 18th century by the central Spanish government to keep an eye on Barcelona and stifle citizen revolt. When the 20th-century dictator Franco was in power, the castle was the site of hundreds of political executions.

Cost and Hours: Free, daily April-Sept 9:00-21:00, Oct-March 9:00-19:00, tel. 932-564-445, www.bcn.cat/castellde montjuic.

Getting There: To spare yourself the hike up to the castle, and to catch some great views of the city, take the **cable car** from just above the upper station of the Montjuïc funicular (€6.50 one-way, €9.30 round-trip, June-Sept daily 10:00-21:00, until 19:00 March-May and Oct, until 18:00 Nov-Feb).

▲Fundació Joan Miró—Showcasing the talents of yet another Catalan artist, this museum has the best collection of Joan Miró art anywhere. You'll also see works by other Modern artists (such as *Mercury Fountain* by American sculptor Alexander Calder). If you don't like abstract art, you'll leave here scratching your head. But those who love this place are not faking it...they understand the genius of Miró and the fun of abstract art.

As you wander, consider this: Miró believed that everything in the cosmos is linked—colors, sky, stars, love, time, music, dogs, men, women, dirt, and the void. He mixed childlike symbols of these things creatively, as a poet uses words. It's as liberating for the visual artist to be abstract as it is for the poet: Both can use metaphors rather than being confined to concrete explanations. Miró would listen to music and paint. It's interactive, free interpretation. He said, "For me, simplicity is freedom."

Here are some tips to help you enjoy and appreciate Miró's art: First meditate on it, then read the title (for example, *The Smile of a Tear*), then meditate on it again. Repeat the process until you have an epiphany. There's no correct answer—it's pure poetry. Devotees of Miró say they fly with him and don't even need drugs. You're definitely much less likely to need drugs if you take advantage of the wonderful audioguide, well worth the €4 extra charge.

Cost and Hours: €9; Tue-Sat July-Sept 10:00-20:00, Oct-June 10:00-19:00, Thu until 21:30; Sun 10:00-14:30, closed Mon, 200 yards from top of funicular, Parc de Montjuïc, tel. 934-439-470, www.bcn.fjmiro.es. The museum has a cafeteria, a café, and a bookshop.

Olympic and Sports Museum (Museu Olímpic i de l'Esport)—This museum, opened in 2007, rides the coattails of the stadium across the street (see next listing). You'll twist down a timeline-ramp that traces the history of the Olympic Games, interspersed with random exhibits about various sports. Downstairs you'll find exhibits designed to test your athleticism, a play-by-play rehash of the '92 Barcelona Olympiad, a commemoration of Spaniard Juan Antonio Samaranch (the influential president of the IOC for two decades), a sports media exhibit, and a schmaltzy movie collage. High-tech but hokey, the museum is worth the time and money only for those nostalgic for the '92 Games.

Cost and Hours: €4.50; Tue-Sat April-Sept 10:00-20:00, Oct-March 10:00-18:00; Sun 10:00-14:30, closed Mon, Avinguda de l'Estadi 60, tel. 932-925-379, www.fundaciobarcelona olimpica.es.

Olympic Stadium (Estadi Olímpic)—For two weeks in the summer of 1992, the world turned its attention to this stadium (between the Catalan Art Museum and the Fundació Joan Miró at Passeig Olímpic 17). Redesigned from an earlier 1929 version, the stadium was updated, expanded, and officially named for Catalan patriot Lluís Companys i Jover.

The XXV Olympiad kicked off here on July 25, when an archer dramatically lit the Olympic torch—which still stands high at the end of the stadium overlooking the city skyline—with a flaming arrow. Over the next two weeks, Barcelona played host to the thrill of victory (most memorably at the hands of Michael Jordan, Magic Johnson, Larry Bird, and the rest of the US basketball "Dream Team") and the agony of defeat (i.e., the nightmares of the Dream Team's opponents).

Hovering over the stadium is the futuristic Montjuïc Communications Tower, designed by Santiago Calatrava and used to transmit Olympic highlights and lowlights around the world. Aside from the memories of the medals, Olympic Stadium offers little to see today.

Spanish Village (Poble Espanyol)—This tacky five-acre model village uses fake traditional architecture from all over Spain as a shell to contain gift shops. Craftspeople do their clichéd thing only in the morning (not worth your time or €8.90, www.poble -espanyol.com). After hours, it's a popular local nightspot.

▲▲Catalan Art Museum (Museu Nacional d'Art de Catalunya)—The big vision for this wonderful museum is to showcase Catalan art from the 10th century through about 1930. Often called "the Prado of Romanesque art" (and "MNAC" for short), it holds Europe's best collection of Romanesque frescoes.

Cost and Hours: €8.50, ticket valid for two days within one month, free first Sun of month; audioguide-€3.10; open Tue-Sat 10:00-19:00, Sun 10:00-14:30, closed Mon, last entry 30 minutes before closing; in massive National Palace building above Magic Fountains, near Plaça d'Espanya—take escalators up; tel. 936-220-376, www.mnac.es.

➲ **Self-Guided Tour:** As you enter, pick up a map (helpful for such a big and confusing building). The left wing is Romanesque, and the right wing is Gothic, exquisite Renaissance, and Baroque. Upstairs is more Baroque, plus modern art, photography, coins, and more.

The MNAC's rare, world-class collection of **Romanesque** art came mostly from remote Catalan village churches in the Pyrenees (saved from unscrupulous art dealers, including many Americans). The Romanesque wing features frescoes, painted wooden altar fronts, and ornate statuary. This classic Romanesque art—with flat 2-D scenes, each saint holding his symbol, and Jesus (easy to identify by the cross in his halo)—is impressively displayed on replicas of the original church ceilings and apses.

Across the way, in the **Gothic** wing, fresco murals give way to vivid 14th-century wood-panel paintings of Bible stories. A roomful of paintings (Room 34) by the Catalan master Jaume Huguet (1412-1492) deserves a look, particularly his altarpiece of one of Barcelona's patron saints, Jordi.

For a break, glide under the huge dome (which once housed an ice-skating rink) over to the air-conditioned cafeteria. This was the prime ceremony room and dance hall for the 1929 International

Exposition. Then, from the big ballroom, ride the glass elevator upstairs, where the **Modern** section takes you on a delightful walk from the late 1800s to about 1930. It's kind of a Catalan Musée d'Orsay, offering a big chronological clockwise circle covering Spain's Golden Age (Zurbarán, heavy religious scenes, Spanish royals with their endearing underbites), Symbolism and Modernisme (furniture complements the empty spaces you likely saw in Gaudí's buildings), Impressionists, *fin de siècle* fun, and Art Deco.

Upstairs you'll also find photography, seductive sofas, and the chic Oleum restaurant, with vast city views (and €27 fixed-price lunches).

▲**Magic Fountains (Font Màgica)**—Music, colored lights, and huge amounts of water make an artistic and coordinated splash on summer nights at Plaça d'Espanya (20-minute shows start on the half-hour; almost always May-Sept Thu-Sun 21:00-23:30, no shows Mon-Wed; Oct-April Fri-Sat 19:00-21:00, no shows Sun-Thu; from the Espanya Metro stop, walk toward the towering National Palace).

Sleeping in Barcelona

Book ahead. Barcelona is Spain's most expensive city. Still, it has reasonably priced rooms. Cheap places are more crowded in summer; fancier business-class hotels fill up in winter and offer discounts on weekends and in summer. When considering relative hotel values, in summer and on weekends you can often get modern comfort in business-class hotels for about the same price (€100) as you'll pay for ramshackle charm (and only a few minutes' walk from the Old City action). Some TI branches (including those at Plaça de Catalunya, Plaça de Sant Jaume, and the airport) offer a room-finding service, though it's cheaper to go direct.

While many of my recommendations are on pedestrian streets, night noise can be a problem (especially in cheap places, which have single-pane windows). For a quiet night, ask for "*tranquilo*" rather than "*con vista*."

Business-Class Comfort near Plaça de Catalunya

These hotels have sliding-glass doors leading to plush reception areas, air-conditioning, and perfectly sterile modern bedrooms. Most are on big streets within two blocks of Barcelona's exuberant central square. As business-class hotels, they have hard-to-pin-down prices that fluctuate wildly. I've listed the average rate you'll pay. But in summer and on weekends, supply often far exceeds the demand, and many of these places cut prices to around

Sleep Code

(€1 = about $1.40, country code: 34)
S = Single, **D** = Double/Twin, **T** = Triple, **Q** = Quad, **b** = bathroom, **s** = shower only. Unless otherwise noted, credit cards are accepted, English is spoken, and prices listed generally include the 7-8 percent tax. Hotel breakfasts can range from free to simple €6 spreads to €21 buffets.

To help you easily sort through these listings, I've divided the accommodations into three categories, based on the price for a standard double room with bath (during high season):

$$$ Higher Priced—Most rooms €150 or more.
 $$ Moderately Priced—Most rooms between €100-150.
  $ Lower Priced—Most rooms €100 or less.

Prices can change without notice; verify the hotel's current rates online or by email. For other updates, see www.ricksteves.com/update.

€100—always ask for a deal.

$$$ Hotel Catalonia Duques de Bergara has four stars, an elegant old entryway, splashy public spaces, slick marble and hardwood floors, 150 comfortable but simple rooms, and a garden courtyard with a pool a world away from the big-city noise (Db-€200 but can drop to as low as €100, extra bed-€35, breakfast-€16, air-con, elevator, free Internet access and Wi-Fi, a half-block off Plaça de Catalunya at Carrer de Bergara 11, tel. 933-015-151, fax 933-173-442, www.hoteles-catalonia.com, duques@hoteles-catalonia.es).

$$$ Nouvel Hotel, in an elegant, Victorian-style building on a handy pedestrian street, is less business-oriented and offers more character than the others listed here. It boasts royal lounges and 78 comfy rooms (Sb-€110, Db-€192, includes breakfast; ask about discount with this book—you must reserve direct by email, not their website; extra bed-€35, deposit for TV remote-€20, air-con, elevator, pay Wi-Fi, Carrer de Santa Anna 20, tel. 933-018-274, fax 933-018-370, www.hotelnouvel.com, info@hotelnouvel.com, Roberto).

$$ Hotel Reding, on a quiet street a five-minute walk west of the Ramblas and Plaça de Catalunya action, is a slick and sleek place renting 44 mod rooms at a good price (Db-€120—ask about free breakfast with this book but only if you book direct, prices go up during trade fairs, extra bed-€38, breakfast-€14, online deals don't include breakfast, air-con, elevator, free Internet access and Wi-Fi, near Metro: Universitat, Gravina 5-7, tel. 934-121-097, fax

932-683-482, www.hotelreding.com, recepcion@hotelreding.com).

$$ Hotel Denit is a small hotel with contemporary decor on a pedestrian street two blocks off the Plaça de Catalunya (Sb-€99, Db-€119, superior Db-€139, includes breakfast when you book direct—otherwise pay €6, air-con, elevator, free Wi-Fi, Metro: Plaça de Catalunya, Estruc 24-26, tel. 935-454-001, fax 935-454-001, www.denit.com, info@denit.com).

$$ Hotel Inglaterra, on the other side of Plaça de Catalunya, is owned by the same people as Hotel Denit and has a similar style for a tad more (Sb-€119-149, Db-€129-159, higher rates are for bigger and exterior rooms, pay Internet and Wi-Fi, Metro: Plaça de Catalunya, Pelai 14, tel. 935-051-100, www.hotel-inglaterra.com, recepcion@hotel-inglaterra.com).

$$ Hotel Duc de la Victoria, with 156 rooms, is professional yet friendly, buried in the Barri Gòtic just three blocks off the Ramblas (Db-€140, rates fluctuate with demand, bigger "superior" rooms on a corner with windows on 2 sides-€25 extra, breakfast-€15, air-con, elevator, Internet access, free Wi-Fi in lobby—30-minute limit, Duc 15, tel. 932-703-410, fax 934-127-747, www.nh-hotels.com, nhducdelavictoria@nh-hotels.com).

$$ Hotel Lleó (YEH-oh) is well-run, with 89 big, bright, and comfortable rooms; a great breakfast room; and a generous lounge (Db-€130 but flexes way up with demand, can be cheaper in summer, extra bed-about €30, breakfast-€13, air-con, elevator, small rooftop pool, free Internet access and Wi-Fi, 2 blocks west of Plaça de Catalunya at Carrer de Pelai 22, tel. 933-181-312, fax 934-122-657, www.hotel-lleo.com, info@hotel-lleo.com).

$$ Hotel Atlantis is solid, with 50 big, homey-yet-mod rooms and great prices for the location (Sb-€92, Db-€108, Tb-€125, check for deals on website, breakfast-€9, air-con, elevator, free Internet access and Wi-Fi, older windows let in a bit more street noise than other hotels in this category—request a room with double-paned windows or a quieter room in back, Carrer de Pelai 20, tel. 933-189-012, fax 934-120-914, www.hotelatlantis-bcn.com, inf@hotel atlantis-bcn.com).

Hotels with "Personality" on or near the Ramblas

These recommended places are generally family-run, with ad-lib furnishings, more character, and lower prices. Only the Jardí offers a quaint square buried in the Barri Gòtic ambience—but you're definitely paying for the location.

$ Hostería Grau is homey, family-run, and almost alpine. Its 25 cheery, garden-pastel rooms are a few blocks off the Ramblas in the colorful university district. The first two floors have seven-foot-high ceilings, then things get tall again (S-€35, D-€65, Db-€90,

Hotels near the Ramblas

THE EIXAMPLE

GRAN   VIA   DE   LES
PLAÇA
UNIV.
Univ.
CARRER   PELAI
CARRER
BERGARA   ①
PLAÇA DE CATALUNYA
FGC TRAIN INFO

③
⑤
⑦
VALLDON.
RAMBLA DE CATALUNYA
PASSEIG DE GRACIA

to BLOCK OF DISCORD
& CASA MILÀ

CORTS   CATALANES

Ramblas
Ⓜ METRO STATION
Ⓑ BUS STOP

SANT
El Corte Inglés Dep't. Store
FONTANELLA
④
BUS TO AIRPORT

PERE
Catalan Concert Hall

MACBA CONTEMP. ART MUSEUM
⑧
ELIS.   BONSUCCES
PINTOR
C. XUCLA   FORT.
CARME
EL   RAVAL

Catalunya
⑩
SANTA ANNA
②
⑭
CANUDA
⑥
DUC. VIC.
PORTAFERRISSA
⑮
⑨ C. DEL P.
PETRIXOL
Liceu
LA BOQUERIA MARKET
MIRO
CARD.
BOQUERIA
Liceu
FERRAN
PLAÇA REIAL
PL. ORWELL
ESCUDELLERS

Cultural Info PALAU DE LA VIRREINA →

⑪
SANT PAU
LICEU OPERA HOUSE
NOU RAMBLA
⑰ PALAU GÜELL
L'ARC TEATRE
MARITIME MUSEUM

Ⓜ Drassanes

R A M B L A S

PORTAL DE L'ANGEL
COMTAL
MONTSIO
ARCS
PL. NOVA
AV. CATEDRAL MAURA
BANYS NOUS
PALLA
⑫
PAL GEN
PLAÇA S. JAUME
CITY HALL
D'AVINYO
CIUTAT
LLEDO
PL. MED.
CLAVE
COLODS
SAN FRAN.
GIGNAS
AMPLE
MERCE

S. P. ALT
S. P. BAIX
⑬
MARÈS MUSEUM
CATHEDRAL
TO PICASSO MUS.
PLAÇA DE L'ANGEL   PRINCESA
Ⓜ Jaume I
ARGENTERIA
TO S. MARIA D. MAR
CAN. NOUS
POST
CONS. MAR.
TO BARCELONETA
⑯

LA RIBERA

COLUMBUS MONUMENT
GOLONDRINAS CRUISES
PL. MED.
PASSEIG   DE   COLÓM
MOLL DE BOSCH / ALSINA / LA FUSTA
RAMBLA DE MAR
to MAREMAGNUM

HARBOR

200 YARDS
200 METERS

Hotels Key

1. Hotel Catalonia Duques de Bergara
2. Nouvel Hotel
3. Hotel Reding
4. Hotel Denit
5. Hotel Inglaterra
6. Hotel Duc de la Victoria
7. Hotels Lleó & Atlantis
8. Hostería Grau & Barcelona Rent-A-Bike
9. Hostal el Jardí
10. Hotel Continental Barcelona
11. Hostal Opera
12. Hotel Neri
13. Hotel Regencia Colón
14. Hostal Campi
15. Hostal Maldá
16. To Sea Point Hostel
17. Launderette

extra bed-€15; 2-bedroom family suites: Db-€95, Tb-€130, Qb-€160; slippery prices jump during fairs and big events, prices include breakfast, ask about discount when you book direct and show this book, air-con, elevator, free Internet access and Wi-Fi, 200 yards up Carrer dels Tallers from the Ramblas at Ramelleres 27, tel. 933-018-135, fax 933-176-825, www.hostalgrau.com, reservas@hostalgrau.com, Monica). Before booking, confirm the hotel's strict cancellation policy—generally if canceling a room less than 48 hours in advance (or a suite less than five days in advance), you'll pay for the first night.

$ Hostal el Jardí offers 40 clean, remodeled rooms on a breezy square in the Barri Gòtic. Many of the tight, plain, comfy rooms come with petite balconies (for an extra charge) and enjoy an almost Parisian ambience. It's a good deal only if you value the cute square location. Book well in advance, as this family-run place has an avid following (small basic interior Db-€75, nicer interior Db-€90, outer Db with balcony or twin with window-€95, large outer Db with balcony or square-view terrace-€110, extra bed-€12, breakfast-€6, air-con, elevator, some stairs, free Wi-Fi in lobby, halfway between Ramblas and cathedral at Plaça Sant Josep Oriol 1, tel. 933-015-900, fax 933-425-733, www.eljardi-barcelona.com, reservations@eljardi-barcelona.com).

$ Hotel Continental Barcelona, in a building overlooking the top of the Ramblas, offers classic, tiny-view balcony opportunities if you don't mind the noise. Its comfortable rooms come with double-thick mattresses, wildly clashing carpets and wallpaper, and perhaps one too many clever ideas (they're laden with microwaves, fridges, a "command center" of light switches, and Tupperware drawers). Choose between your own little Ramblas-view balcony (where you can eat your breakfast) or a quieter back room (Sb-€90, Db-€100, twin Db-€110, Db with Ramblas balcony-€120, extra bed-€40, mention this book for best prices, prices

BARCELONA

include breakfast, air-con, elevator, free Internet access and Wi-Fi, Ramblas 138, tel. 933-012-570, fax 933-027-360, www.hotel continental.com, barcelona@hotelcontinental.com). J. M.'s (José María's) free breakfast and all-day snack-and-drink bar are a plus.

$ Hostal Opera, with 70 stark rooms 20 yards off the Ramblas, is clean, institutional, and modern. The street can feel seedy at night, but it's safe, and the hotel is very secure (Sb-€43-60, Db-€63-90, no breakfast, air-con only in summer, elevator, pay Internet access, free Wi-Fi in lobby, Carrer Sant Pau 20, tel. 933-188-201, www.operaramblas.com, info@operaramblas.com).

Deep in the Barri Gòtic

$$$ Hotel Neri is chic, posh, and sophisticated, with 22 rooms spliced into the ancient stones of the Barri Gòtic, overlooking an overlooked square (Plaça Sant Felip Neri) a block from the cathedral. It has big plasma-screen TVs, pricey modern art on the bedroom walls, and dressed-up people in its gourmet restaurant (Db-€300, suites-€365-450, generally cheaper on weekdays, breakfast-€21, air-con, elevator, free Wi-Fi, rooftop tanning deck, St. Sever 5, tel. 933-040-655, fax 933-040-337, www.hotelneri .com, info@hotelneri.com).

$$ Hotel Regencia Colón, one block in front of the cathedral square, offers 50 solid, well-priced rooms in a handy location (Db-€110, more on weekends, breakfast-€12, air-con, elevator, Carrer Sagristans 13-17, tel. 933-189-858, fax 933-172-822, www .hotelregenciacolon.com, info@hotelregenciacolon.com).

Humble, Cheaper Places Buried in the Old City

$ Hostal Campi is big, subdued, and ramshackle, but offers simple class. This easygoing old-school spot rents 24 rooms a few doors off the top of the Ramblas (S-€33, D-€56, Db-€65, T-€75, Tb-€85, no breakfast, lots of stairs with no elevator, pay Internet access, free Wi-Fi in some rooms, Canuda 4, tel. & fax 933-013-545, www.hostalcampi.com, reservas@hostalcampi.com, friendly Margarita and Nando).

$ Hostal Maldá rents the best cheap beds I've found in the old center. With 25 rooms above a small shopping mall near the cathedral, it's a time-warp—quiet and actually charming. It generally remains full through the summer, but it's worth a shot (S-€15, D-€30, T-€45, cash only, free Wi-Fi, lots of stairs with no elevator, 100 yards up Carrer del Pi from delightful Plaça Sant Josep Oriol, Carrer del Pi 5, tel. 933-173-002, www.hostalmalda.com). Good-natured Aurora doesn't speak English, but Delfi, who works only half the year, does.

Hostels in the Center of Town

Barcelona has a wonderful chain of well-run and centrally located hostels (www.equity-point.com), providing €21-29 dorm beds in 4- to 14-bed coed rooms with €2 sheets and towels, free Internet access, Wi-Fi, breakfast, lockers (B.Y.O. lock, or buy one there), and plenty of opportunities to meet other backpackers. They're open 24 hours but aren't party hostels, so they enforce quiet after 23:00. There are three locations to choose from: Eixample, Barri Gòtic, or near the beach.

$ Centric Point Hostel is a huge place renting 430 cheap beds at what must be the best address in Barcelona (bar, kitchen, Passeig de Gràcia 33, see map on page 1236, tel. 932-151-796, fax 932-461-552, www.centricpointhostel.com).

$ Gothic Point Hostel rents 150 beds a block from the Picasso Museum (roof terrace, Carrer Vigatans 5, see map on page 1211, tel. 932-687-808, www.gothicpoint.com).

$ Sea Point Hostel has 70 beds on the beach nearby (Plaça del Mar 4, tel. 932-247-075, www.seapointhostel.com).

In the Eixample

For an uptown, boulevard-like neighborhood, sleep in the Eixample, a 10-minute walk from the Ramblas action (see map on page 1236).

$$ Hotel Granvía, filling a palatial 1870s mansion, offers Botticelli and chandeliers in the public areas; a sprawling, peaceful sun patio; and 54 spacious, comfy rooms. Its salon is plush and royal, making the hotel an excellent value for romantics. To reduce street noise, ask for a quiet interior room or a room overlooking the courtyard in the back of the building (Sb-€60-114, Db-€76-162, Tb-€103-200, can be cheaper in slow times, ask for Rick Steves rates when you book direct, prices include breakfast, air-con, elevator, free Internet access and Wi-Fi, Gran Via de les Corts Catalanes 642, tel. 933-181-900, fax 933-189-997, www.hotelgranvia .com, hgranvia@nnhotels.com, Asun works the morning shift).

$$ Hotel Continental Palacete, with 19 rooms, fills a 100-year-old chandeliered mansion. With flowery wallpaper and ornately gilded stucco, it's gaudy in the city of Gaudí, but it's also friendly, clean, quiet, and well-located. Most of the rooms have been recently updated, there's an outdoor terrace, and guests have unlimited access to the "cruise-inspired" fruit, veggie, and drink buffet—worth factoring into your comparison-shopping (Sb-€103, Db-€138, €35-45 more for bigger and brighter view rooms, extra bed-€55, ask about discount with this book, prices include breakfast, air-con, free Internet access and Wi-Fi, 2 blocks north of Plaça de Catalunya at corner of Carrer Diputació, Rambla

Hotels & Restaurants in Barcelona's Eixample

BARCELONA

M METRO STATION

200 YARDS

200 METERS

TO ⑪

TO GRÀCIA & PARK GÜELL

AVINGUDA

CORSEGA

ROSSELLO

RAMBLA DE CATALUNYA

Diagonal **M**

DIAGONAL

TO SANTS TRAIN STN.

M Provença

⑧

GRANADOS

BALMES

D'ARIBAU

PASSEIG DE CATALUNYA DE

⑦

CASA MILÀ

PROVENÇA

MALLORCA

VALÈNCIA

D'ARAGÓ

Verdaguer **M**

TO SAGRADA FAMÍLIA

⑩

BLOCK OF DISCORD →

⑨

④   ②   ⑤

GRÀCIA

⑥

M Passeig de Gràcia

CONSELL

DE CENT

DIPUTACIÓ

Girona **M**

TO PLAÇA D'ESPANYA

GRAN VIA DE LES

PL. UNIV

M Universitat

⑬

⑭

CASP

③

PLAÇA DE CATALUNYA

PELAI

M

⑫

CORTS CATALANES

①

CLARIS

PAU

LLÚRIA

ROGER

BRUC

GIRONA

DCH

RAMBLAS

UNIVERSITAT

i

L'ANGEL

PORTAL DE

RONDA

FONT.

EL CORTE INGLÉS

LAIETANA

DE

SANT PERE

M Urquinaona

OLD CITY

EL RAVAL

GOTHIC QUARTER

LA RIBERA

① Hotel Granvía
② Hotel Continental Palacete
③ Hotel Ginebra
④ Somnio Hostel
⑤ Centric Point Hostel
⑥ La Rita Restaurant
⑦ La Bodegueta

⑧ Restaurante la Palmera
⑨ Restaurant Flauta
⑩ Cinc Sentits
⑪ To Hofmann Restaurant
⑫ "Qu Qu" Quasi Queviures
⑬ Ciudad Condal Cerveceria
⑭ La Tramoia

de Catalunya 30, tel. 934-457-657, fax 934-450-050, www.hotel continental.com, palacete@hotelcontinental.com).

$ Hotel Ginebra is minimal, clean, and quiet considering its central location. The Herrera family rents 12 rooms in a dated apartment building overlooking the main square (Db-€75-80, extra bed-€15, air-con, elevator, free Wi-Fi, Rambla de Catalunya 1/3, third floor, tel. 933-171-063, www.hotelginebra.net, info @hotelginebra.net, Juan speaks English).

$ Somnio Hostel, an innovative newer place run by a pair of American expats, has both dorm beds and private rooms (dorm bed-€26, S-€44, D-€78, Db-€87; prices include sheets, towels, and lockers; air-con, elevator, free Internet access and Wi-Fi, Carrer de la Diputació 251, second floor, tel. 932-725-308, www.somnio hostels.com, info@somniohostels.com).

Apartments in Barceloneta

$$ 1001 Nights Barcelona, run by American Frederick and his Spanish wife, rents 40 renovated apartments with kitchens near the beach in the lively Barceloneta neighborhood, the former fishermen's quarter that's become increasingly gentrified (2 people-€100 April-Oct, €80 Nov-March; first child to age 10 years old pays, second kid free; prices vary with size—see photos and videos on website, €40 cleaning fee, 3-night minimum stay, 10 percent less for 7-night stay, 20 percent deposit required to reserve online, pay balance in cash when you arrive, no breakfast, Frederick or an associate will meet you to check in—arrange when you reserve, mobile 620-585-594, www.1001nights.es, info@1001nights.es). They also have 12 units in the somewhat seedy Barri Gòtic near Las Ramblas.

Eating in Barcelona

Barcelona, the capital of Catalan cuisine—featuring seafood—offers a tremendous variety of colorful eateries, ranging from basic and filling to chic and trendy. Because of their common struggles, Catalans seem to have an affinity for Basque culture, so you'll find a lot of Basque tapas places here, too. Most of my listings are lively spots with a busy tapas scene at the bar, along with restaurant tables for *raciones*. A regional specialty is *pa amb tomaquet* (pah ahm too-MAH-kaht), bread topped with a mix of crushed tomato and olive oil.

I've listed mostly practical, characteristic, colorful, and affordable restaurants. My recommendations are grouped by neighborhood—along the Ramblas; in Barceloneta; in the Barri Gòtic; in the Ribera neighborhood (best for foodies); and in the Eixample—followed by some budget options scattered throughout the city.

Note that many restaurants close in August (or July), when the owners take a vacation.

Restaurants generally serve lunch from 13:00 to 16:00 and dinner from 20:00 until very late (Spaniards don't start dinner until about 21:00). It's deadly to your Barcelona experience to eat too early—if a place feels touristy, come back later and it may be a thriving local favorite. For an afternoon sweet treat, I've suggested "A Short, Sweet Walk" (see page 1247).

Along the Ramblas

Within a few steps of the Ramblas you'll find handy lunch places, an inviting market hall, and a slew of vegetarian options.

Lunching Simply yet Memorably near the Ramblas

Although these places are enjoyable for a lunch break during your Ramblas sightseeing, many are also open for dinner. For locations, see the map on page 1242.

Taverna Basca Irati serves 40 kinds of hot and cold Basque *pintxos* for €1.80 each. These are small open-faced sandwiches—like sushi on bread. Muscle in through the hungry local crowd, get an empty plate from the waiter, and then help yourself. Every few minutes, waiters prance proudly by with a platter of new, still-warm munchies. Grab one as they pass by...it's addictive. You pay on the honor system: You're charged by the number of toothpicks left on your plate when you're done. Wash it down with €2-3 glasses of Rioja (full-bodied red wine), Txakolí (sprightly Basque white wine) or *sidra* (apple wine) poured from on high to add oxygen and bring out the flavor (daily 11:00-24:00, a block off the Ramblas, behind arcade at Carrer Cardenal Casanyes 15, Metro: Liceu, tel. 933-023-084).

Restaurant Elisabets is a happy little neighborhood eatery packed with antique radios; it's popular with locals for its €11 "home-cooked" three-course lunch special. Stop by for lunch, survey what those around you are enjoying, and order what looks best (Mon-Sat 7:30-23:00, closed Sun and Aug, lunch special served 13:00-16:00, otherwise only €3 tapas—not full meals except for Friday night's fixed-price dinner, 2 blocks west of Ramblas on far corner of Plaça Bonsucces at Carrer Elisabets 2, tel. 933-175-826, run by Pilar).

Café Granja Viader is a quaint time capsule, family-run since 1870. They boast about being the first dairy business to bottle and distribute milk in Spain. This feminine-feeling place—specializing in baked and dairy delights, toasted sandwiches, and light meals—is ideal for a traditional breakfast. Or indulge your sweet tooth: Try a glass of *orxata* (or *horchata*—*chufa*-nut milk, summer only), *llet mallorquina* (Majorca-style milk with cinnamon, lemon, and sugar), *crema catalana* (crème brûlée, their specialty), or *suis* ("Swiss"—hot chocolate with a snowcap of whipped cream). *Mel y mató* is fresh cheese with honey...very Catalan (Tue-Sat 9:00-13:30 & 17:00-20:30, Mon 17:00-20:30 only, closed Sun, a block off the Ramblas behind El Carme church at Xucla 4, tel. 933-183-486).

Picnics: Shoestring tourists buy groceries at **El Corte Inglés** (Mon-Sat 10:00-22:00, closed Sun, supermarket in basement, Plaça de Catalunya) and **Carrefour Market** (Mon-Sat 10:00-22:00, closed Sun, Ramblas 113).

In and near La Boquería Market

Try eating at La Boquería market at least once (#91 on the Ramblas). Like all farmers' markets in Europe, this place is ringed by colorful, good-value eateries. Lots of stalls sell fun take-away food—especially fruit salads and fresh-squeezed fruit juices. There are several good bars around the market busy with shoppers munching at the counter (breakfast, tapas all day, coffee). The market, and most of the eateries listed here (unless noted), are open Monday through Saturday from 8:00 until 20:00 (though things get very quiet after about 16:00) and are closed on Sunday.

Pinotxo Bar is just to the right as you enter the market. It's a great spot for coffee, breakfast (spinach *tortillas,* or whatever's cooking with toast), or tapas. Fun-loving Juan and his family are La Boquería fixtures. Grab a stool across the way to sip your drink with people-watching views. Have a Chucho?

Kiosko Universal is popular for its great prices on wonderful fish dishes. As you enter the market from the Ramblas, it's all the way to the left in the first alley. If you see people waiting, ask who's last in line *("¿El último?").* You'll eat immersed in the spirit of the market (€14 fixed-price lunches with different fresh-fish options 12:00-16:00, always packed but better before 12:30, tel. 933-178-286).

Restaurant la Gardunya, at the back of the market, offers tasty meat and seafood meals made with fresh ingredients bought directly from the market (€13 fixed-price lunch includes wine and bread, €16 three-course dinner specials don't include wine, €10-20 à la carte dishes, Mon-Sat 13:00-16:00 & 20:00-24:00, closed Sun, mod seating indoors or outside watching the market action, Carrer Jerusalem 18, tel. 933-024-323).

Vegetarian Eateries near Plaça de Catalunya and the Ramblas

Biocenter, a Catalan soup-and-salad restaurant popular with local vegetarians, takes its cooking very seriously and feels a bit more like a real restaurant than most (€7-10 weekday lunch specials include soup or salad and plate of the day, €15 dinner specials, Mon-Sat

13:00-23:00, Sun 13:00-16:00, 2 blocks off the Ramblas at Pintor Fortuny 25, Metro: Plaça de Catalunya, tel. 933-014-583).

Juicy Jones is a tutti-frutti vegan/vegetarian eatery with colorful graffiti decor, a hip veggie menu (served downstairs), groovy laid-back staff, and a stunning array of fresh-squeezed juices served at the bar. Pop in for a quick €3 "juice of the day." For lunch you can get the Indian-inspired €6 *thali* plate, the €6.25 plate of the day, or an €8.50 meal including one of the two plates plus soup or salad and dessert (daily 13:00-23:30, also tapas and salads, Carrer Cardenal Casanyes 7, tel. 933-024-330). There's another location on the other side of the Ramblas (Carrer Hospital 74).

In Barceloneta

La Mar Salada is a traditional seafood restaurant with a slight modern twist, located on the strip leading to the Barceloneta beach. Their à la carte menu includes seafood-and-rice dishes, fresh fish, and homemade desserts. A nice meal will run you about €30-35 per person (€15 fixed-price weekday meal, Wed-Mon 13:00-16:00 & 20:00-23:00, Sat-Sun 13:00-23:00, closed Tue, indoor and outdoor seating, Passeig Joan de Borbó 59, tel. 932-212-127).

In the Barri Gòtic

These eateries populate Barcelona's atmospheric Gothic Quarter, near the cathedral. Choose between a sit-down meal at a restaurant or a string of tapas bars.

Restaurants in the Barri Gòtic

Café de l'Academia is a delightful place on a pretty square tucked away in the heart of the Barri Gòtic—but patronized mainly by the neighbors. They serve "honest cuisine" from the market with Catalan roots. The candlelit, air-conditioned interior is rustic yet elegant, with soft jazz, flowers, and modern art. And if you want to eat outdoors on a convivial, mellow square...this is the place. Reserve for Friday nights (€10-13 first courses, €12-16 second courses, fixed-price lunch for €10 at the bar or €14 at a table, Mon-Fri 13:30-16:00 & 20:30-23:30, closed Sat-Sun, near the City Hall square, off Carrer de Jaume I up Carrer Dagueria at Carrer Lledo 1, tel. 933-198-253).

Popular Chain Restaurants: Barcelona enjoys a chain of several bright, modern restaurants. These five are a hit for their modern, artfully presented Spanish and Mediterranean cuisine, crisp ambience, and unbeatable prices. Because of their three-course €10 lunches and €16-20 dinners (both with wine), all are crowded with locals and in-the-know tourists (all open daily 13:00-15:45 & 20:30-23:30, unless otherwise noted). My favorite of the bunch is **La Crema Canela,** which feels cozier than the others and is the only one that takes reservations (opens at 20:00 for dinner, 30 yards north of Plaça Reial at Passatge de Madoz 6, tel. 933-182-744). The rest are notorious for long lines at the door—arrive 30 minutes before opening, or be prepared to wait. Like La Crema Canela, the next two are also within a block of the Plaça Reial: **La Fonda** (opens at 19:30 for dinner, Carrer dels Escudellers 10, very close to a seedy stretch of street—approach it from the Ramblas rather than from Plaça Reial, tel. 933-017-515) and **Les Quinze Nits** (on Plaça Reial at #6—you'll see the line, tel. 933-173-075). The fourth place, **La Dolça Herminia,** is near the Catalan Concert Hall (2 blocks toward Ramblas from Catalan Concert Hall at Carrer de les Magdalenes 27, tel. 933-170-676). The fifth restaurant in the chain, **La Rita,** is described later, under "Restaurants in the Eixample."

Tapas on Carrer de la Mercè in the Barri Gòtic

Barcelona boasts great *tascas*—colorful local tapas bars. Get small plates (for maximum sampling) by asking for "tapas," not the bigger *"raciones."* Glasses of *vino tinto* go for about €1. And though trendy uptown restaurants are safer, better-lit, and come with English menus and less grease, these places will stain your journal. The neighborhood's dark, the regulars are rough-edged, and you'll get a glimpse of a crusty Barcelona from before the affluence hit. Nowadays some new, mod restaurants are popping up in this area, but don't be seduced—you came here for something different. Try *pimientos de padrón*—Russian roulette with peppers that are lightly fried in oil and salted...only a few are jalapeño-spicy. At the cider bars, it's traditional to order *queso de cabrales* (a traditional, very moldy bleu cheese) and spicy chorizo (sausage), ideally prepared *al diablo* ("devil-style")—soaked in wine, then flambéed at your table. Several places serve *leche de pantera* (panther milk)—liquor mixed with milk.

From the bottom of the Ramblas (near the Columbus Monument), hike east along Carrer Clave. Then follow the small street that runs along the right side of the church (Carrer de la Mercè), stopping at the *tascas* that look fun. For a montage of edible memories, wander Carrer de la Mercè west to east and consider these spots, stopping wherever looks most inviting. I've listed ye olde dives, but there are many trendy places here as well. Most of these places close down around 23:00.

La Pulpería (at #16) has a bit less character than the others, but eases you into the scene with fried fish, octopus, and *patatas bravas,* all with Galician Ribeiro wine. Farther down at the corner (#28), **La Plata** keeps things wonderfully simple, serving extremely cheap plates of sardines (€1.70), little salads (€1.50), and small glasses of keg wine (less than €1). **Tasca el Corral** (#17) serves mountain favorites from northern Spain by the half-*ración* (see

Barcelona's Barri Gòtic Restaurants

Restaurants Key

1. Taverna Basca Irati
2. Restaurant Elisabets
3. Café Granja Viader
4. Supermarket
5. La Boquería Market Eateries
6. Biocenter Veggie Rest.
7. Juicy Jones
8. To La Mar Salada
9. Café de l'Academia
10. La Crema Canela
11. La Fonda
12. Les Quinze Nits
13. La Dolça Herminia
14. Carrer de la Mercè Tapas Bars
15. Casa Colomina
16. Granja La Pallaresa
17. Fargas Chocolate Shop

their list), such as *queso de cabrales* and chorizo *al diablo* with *sidra* (hard cider sold by the bottle—€5.50). **Sidrería Tasca La Socarrena** (#21) offers hard cider from Asturias in €6.50 bottles with *queso de cabrales* and chorizo. At the end of Carrer de la Mercè, **Cerveceria Vendimia** slings tasty clams and mussels (hearty *raciones* for €4-6 a plate—they don't do smaller portions, so order sparingly). Sit at the bar and point to what looks good. Their *pulpo* (octopus) is more expensive and is the house specialty. Carrer Ample and Carrer Gignas, the streets parallel to Carrer de la Mercè inland, have more refined bar-hopping possibilities.

In the Ribera District, near the Picasso Museum

La Ribera, the hottest neighborhood in town, sparkles with eclectic and trendy as well as subdued and classy little restaurants hidden in the small lanes surrounding the Church of Santa Maria del Mar. While I've listed a few well-established tapas bars that are great for light meals, to really dine, simply wander around for 15 minutes and pick the place that tickles your gastronomic fancy. I think those who say they know what's best in this area are kidding themselves—it's changing too fast and the choices are too personal. One thing's for sure: There are a lot of talented and hardworking restaurateurs with plenty to offer. Consider starting your evening off with a glass of fine wine at one of the *enotecas* on the square facing the Church of Santa Maria del Mar. Sit back and admire the pure Catalan Gothic architecture. My first three listings are all on the main drag, Carrer de l'Argenteria. For locations, see the map on page 1211.

Sagardi offers a wonderful array of Basque goodies—tempting *pinchos* and *montaditos* at €1.80 each—along its huge bar. Ask for a plate and graze (just take whatever looks good). You can sit on the square with your plunder for 20 percent extra. Wash it down with Txakolí, a Basque white wine poured from the spout of a huge wooden barrel into a glass as you watch. When you're done, they'll count your toothpicks to tally your bill (daily 12:00-24:00, Carrer de l'Argenteria 62-64, tel. 933-199-993).

Sagardi Euskal Taberna, hiding behind the thriving Sagardi tapas bar (described above), is a mod, rustic, and minimalist woody restaurant committed to serving Basque T-bone steaks and grilled specialties with only the best ingredients. Crisp, friendly service and a big open kitchen with sizzling grills contribute to the ambience. Reservations are smart (€10-20 first courses, €20-30 second courses, plan on €45 for dinner, daily 13:00-16:00 & 20:00-24:00, Carrer de l'Argenteria 62, tel. 933-199-993).

Taller de Tapas ("Tapas Workshop") is an upscale, trendier tapas bar and restaurant that dishes up well-presented, sophisticated morsels and light meals in a medieval-stone-yet-mod setting. Pay 10 percent more to sit on the square. Elegant, but a bit stuffy, it's favored by local office workers who aren't into the Old World Gothic stuff. Four plates will fill a hungry diner for about €20 (daily 8:30-24:00, Carrer de l'Argenteria 51, tel. 932-688-559).

El Xampanyet, a colorful family-run bar with a fun-loving staff (Juan Carlos, his mom, and the man who may be his father), specializes in tapas and anchovies. Don't be put off by the seafood from a tin: Catalans like it this way. A *sortido* (assorted plate) of *carne* (meat) or *pescado* (fish) with *pa amb tomaquet* (bread with crushed-tomato spread) makes for a fun meal. It's filled with tourists during the sightseeing day, but this is a local favorite after dark. The scene is great but—especially during busy times—it's tough without Spanish skills. When I asked about the price, Juan Carlos said, "Who cares? The ATM is just across the street." Plan on spending €20 for a meal with wine (same price at bar or table, Tue-Sat 12:00-15:30 & 19:00-23:00, Sun 12:00-16:00 only, closed Mon, a half-block beyond the Picasso Museum at Montcada 22, tel. 933-197-003).

In the Eixample

The people-packed boulevards of the Eixample (Passeig de Gràcia and Rambla de Catalunya) are lined with appetizing eateries featuring breezy outdoor seating. Choose between a real restaurant or an upscale tapas bar. For locations, see the map on page 1236.

Restaurants in the Eixample

La Rita is a fresh and dressy little restaurant serving Catalan cuisine near the Block of Discord. Their lunches (three courses with wine for €10, Mon-Fri 13:00-15:45) and dinners (€10 plates, Sun-Thu 20:00-23:30, Fri-Sat from 21:00) are a great value. Like most of its sister restaurants—described under "Dining in the Barri Gòtic," earlier—it takes no reservations and its prices attract long lines, so arrive just before the doors open...or wait (a block from Metro: Passeig de Gràcia, near corner of Carrer de Pau Claris and Carrer Aragó at Aragó 279, tel. 934-872-376).

La Bodegueta is an atmospheric below-street-level bodega serving hearty wines, homemade vermouth, *anchoas* (anchovies), tapas, and *flautas*—sandwiches made with flute-thin baguettes. Its daily €12 lunch special of three courses with wine is served 13:00-16:00. A long block from Gaudí's Casa Milà, this makes a fine sightseeing break (Mon-Sat 8:00-24:00, Sun 19:00-24:00, at intersection with Provença, Rambla de Catalunya 100, Metro: Provença, tel. 932-154-894).

Restaurante la Palmera serves a mix of Catalan, Mediterranean, and French cuisine in an elegant room with bottle-lined walls. This place offers great food, service, and value—for me, a very special meal in Barcelona. They have three zones: the classic main room, a more forgettable adjacent room, and a few outdoor tables. I like the classic room. Reservations are smart (€12-16 plates, creative €17 six-plate *degustation* lunch, Tue-Sat 13:00-15:45 & 20:30-23:15, closed Sun-Mon, Enric Granados 57, at the corner with Mallorca, tel. 934-532-338).

Restaurant Flauta fills two floors with enthusiastic eaters (I prefer the ground floor). It's fresh and modern, with a fun, no-stress menu featuring €5 small plates, creative €4 *flauta* sandwiches, and a €12.50 three-course lunch deal including a drink. Good €2.30 wines by the glass are listed on the blackboard. This is a place to order high on the menu for a satisfying, moderately priced meal (Mon-Sat 13:00-24:00, closed Sun, fun-loving and helpful staff recommends the fried vegetables, no reservations, just off Via Diputació at d'Aribau 23, tel. 933-237-038).

Cinc Sentits ("Five Senses"), with only about 30 seats, is my gourmet recommendation. It's a chic, minimalist, smoke-free, but slightly snooty place where all the attention goes to the fine service and elegantly presented dishes. It's run by Catalans who lived in Canada (so there's absolutely no language barrier) and serve avant-garde cuisine inspired by Catalan traditions and ingredients. Their €49 and €69 *degustation menus* are unforgettable extravaganzas. Reservations are required (Tue-Sat 13:30-15:00 & 20:30-23:00, closed Sun-Mon, near Carrer d'Aragó at d'Aribau 58, tel. 933-239-490).

A Bit Farther Out: **Hofmann** is a renowned cooking school with an excellent if pricey restaurant serving modern Mediterranean market cuisine. Dress up and dine in intimate rooms papered with photos of famous patrons. The four-course €40 lunches are made up of just what the students are working on that day—so there's no choice (watch the students as they cook). Dinners can easily cost twice as much (à la carte). Save room (and euros) for the incredible desserts. Reserve long in advance, because locals love this place (Mon-Fri 13:30-15:15 & 21:00-23:15, closed Sat-Sun and Aug, 4 blocks northwest of Casa Milà at La Granada del Penedès 14-16, tel. 932-187-165, www.hofmann-bcn.com).

Tapas Bars in the Eixample

Many trendy and touristic tapas bars in the Eixample offer a cheery welcome and slam out the appetizers. These three are my favorites.

Quasi Queviures (**"Qu Qu"** for short) serves upscale tapas, sandwiches, or the whole nine yards—classic food served fast from a fun menu with modern decor and a high-energy sports-bar ambience. It's bright, clean, and not too crowded. Walk through their enticing kitchen to get to the tables in back. Committed to developing a loyal following, they claim, "We fertilize our local customers with daily specialties" (€2-5 tapas, €5 dinner salads, €8 plates, prices 17 percent higher on the terrace, daily 8:00-24:00, between Gran Via and Via Diputació at Passeig de Gràcia 24, tel. 933-174-512).

Ciudad Condal Cerveceria brags that it serves the best *montaditos* (€2-3 little open-faced sandwiches) and beers in Barcelona. It's an Eixample favorite, with an elegant bar and tables plus good seating out on the Rambla de Catalunya for all that people-watching action. It's classier than Qu Qu and packed after 21:00, when you'll likely need to put your name on a list and wait. While it has no restaurant-type menu, the list of tapas and *montaditos* is easy, fun, and comes with a great variety (including daily specials). This place is a cut above your normal tapas bar, but with reasonable prices (most tapas around €4-10, daily until 24:00, facing the intersection of Gran Via and Rambla de Catalunya at Rambla de Catalunya 18, tel. 933-181-997).

La Tramoia, at the opposite corner from Ciudad Condal Cerveceria, serves piles of *montaditos* and tapas at its ground-floor bar and at nice tables inside and out. If Ciudad Condal Cerveceria is jammed, you're more likely to find a seat here. The brasserie-style restaurant upstairs bustles with happy local eaters enjoying grilled meats (€8-20 plates), but I'd stay downstairs for the €4-10 tapas (open daily, also facing the intersection of Gran Via and Rambla de Catalunya at Rambla de Catalunya 15, tel. 934-123-634).

Budget Options Around Town

Bright, clean, and inexpensive sandwich shops proudly hold the cultural line against the fast-food invasion hamburgerizing the rest of Europe. Catalan sandwiches are made to order with crunchy French bread. Rather than butter, locals prefer *tomaquet* (a spread of crushed tomatoes). You'll see two big local chains (Pans &

Company and Bocatta) everywhere, but these serve mass-produced McBaguettes ordered from a multilingual menu. I've had better luck with hole-in-the-wall sandwich shops—virtually as numerous as the chains—where you can see exactly what you're getting. Kebab places are another good, super-cheap standby.

A Short, Sweet Walk

Let me propose this three-stop dessert (or, since these places close well before the traditional Barcelona dinnertime, a late-afternoon snack). You'll try a refreshing glass of *orxata*, munch some *churros con chocolate,* and visit a fine *xocolateria,* all within a three-minute walk of one another in the Barri Gòtic just off the Ramblas. Start at the corner of Carrer Portaferrissa midway down the Ramblas. For the best atmosphere, begin your walk at about 18:00 (note that the last place is closed on Sun). For locations, see the map on page 1242.

Turrón at **Casa Colomina:** Walk down Carrer Portaferrissa to #8 (on the right). Casa Colomina, founded in 1908, specializes in homemade *turróns*—a variation of nougat made with almond, honey, and sugar, brought to Spain by the Moors 1,200 years ago. Three different kinds are sold in €8-12 slabs: *blando, duro,* and *yema*—soft, hard, and yolk (€2 smaller chunks also available). In the summer, the shop also sells ice cream and the refreshing *orxata* (or *horchata*—a drink made from the *chufa* nut). Order a glass and ask to see and eat a *chufa* nut (a.k.a. earth almond or tiger nut; Mon-Sat 10:00-20:30, Sun 12:30-20:30, tel. 933-122-511).

Churros con Chocolate at **Granja La Pallaresa:** Continue down Carrer Portaferrissa, taking a right at Carrer Petritxol to this fun-loving *xocolateria.* Older, elegant ladies gather here for the Spanish equivalent of tea time—dipping their greasy *churros* into pudding-thick cups of hot chocolate (€4.25 for five *churros con chocolate,* Mon-Fri 9:00-13:00 & 16:00-21:00, Sat-Sun 9:00-13:00 & 17:00-21:00, Carrer Petritxol 11, tel. 933-022-036).

Homemade Chocolate at Fargas: For your last stop, head for the ornate Fargas chocolate shop. Continue down Carrer Petritxol to the square, hook left through the two-part square, and then left up Carrer del Pi—it's on the corner of Portaferrissa and Carrer del Pi. Since the 19th century, gentlemen with walking canes have dropped by here for their chocolate fix. Founded in 1827, this is one of the oldest and most traditional chocolate shops in Barcelona. If they're not too busy, ask to see the old chocolate mill *("¿Puedo ver el molino?")* to the right of the counter. They sell even tiny quantities (one little morsel) by the weight, so don't be shy. A delicious chunk of the crumbly semi-sweet house specialty costs €0.45 (tray by the mill). The tempting bonbons in the window cost about €1 each (Mon-Fri 9:30-13:30 & 16:00-20:00, Sat 10:00-14:00 & 16:00-20:00, closed Sun, tel. 933-020-342).

Barcelona Connections

By Train

Unless otherwise noted, all of these trains depart from the Sants Station; however, some trains also stop at other stations more convenient to the downtown tourist zone: França Station, Passeig de Gràcia, or Plaça de Catalunya. Figure out if your train stops at these stations (and board there) to save yourself the trip to Sants.

The **AVE train to Madrid** has shaved hours off that journey, making it faster than flying (when you consider that you're zipping from downtown to downtown). The train departs almost hourly. The nonstop train is a little more expensive (€140, 2.5-3 hours) than the slightly slower train that makes a few stops and adds about a half-hour (€120, 3.5 hours). Regular reserved AVE tickets can be prepurchased at www.renfe.com and picked up at the station. If you have a railpass, you'll pay only a reservation fee of €25 for first class, which includes a meal (€15 second class, buy at any train station in Spain). Passholders can't reserve online through RENFE but can make the reservation at www.raileurope.com for delivery before leaving the US ($17 in second class, $40 in first class).

From Barcelona by Train to: Sevilla (3/day—two fast, 5.5 hours, €145; one slow, 12 hours, €62), **Granada** (1/day Wed, Fri, and Sun only, 11.5 hours, €61; also 1 night train/day, 12 hours, €63), **Lisbon** (no direct trains, head to Madrid and then catch night train to Lisbon, 17 hours, about €100), **Nice** (1/day via Montpelier, about €100; cheaper connections possible with multiple changes including Cerbère), **Paris** (2/day, 7.5 hours, change in Figueres, more connections possible with multiple changes; 1 night train/day, 13.5 hours, about €200, or €50 with railpass, reservation mandatory). Train info: toll tel. 902-320-320, www.renfe.com.

By Bus

Destinations include **Madrid** (nearly hourly, 8 hours, €29—a fraction of the AVE train price), departs from Nord bus station at Metro: Arc de Triomf, bus info toll tel. 902-260-606, Alsa bus company toll tel. 902-422-242. For bus schedules, see www.barcelonanord.com.

By Plane

Check the reasonable flights from Barcelona to Sevilla or Madrid. Vueling is Iberia's most popular discount airline (e.g., Barcelona–Madrid flights as low as €40 if booked in advance, toll tel. 902-333-933, www.vueling.com). Iberia (toll tel. 902-400-500, www.iberia.com) and Air Europa (toll tel. 902-401-501 or 932-983-907, www.aireuropa.com) offer €80 flights to Madrid. Also, for flights to other parts of Europe, consider British Airways (toll tel. 902-

111-333, www.britishairways.com), easyJet (toll tel. 902-299-992, www.easyjet.com), and Ryanair (www.ryanair.com).

Most flights use Barcelona's **El Prat de Llobregat Airport** (tel. 913-211-000). Its two terminals serve both domestic and international flights and are linked by shuttle buses. Air France, Air Europa, American, British, Continental, Delta, Iberia, Lufthansa, Spanair, US Airways, Vueling, and others use the newer terminal 1. EasyJet and minor airlines use terminal 2. Ryanair uses a smaller airstrip 60 miles away, called **Girona–Costa Brava Airport** (tel. 972-186-600). Information on both airports can be found on the official Spanish airport website, www.aena.es.

For details on getting between either airport and downtown Barcelona, see "Arrival in Barcelona—By Plane" on page 1183.

BARCELONA

SWITZERLAND

GIMMELWALD
and the Berner Oberland

Interlaken • Lauterbrunnen • Gimmelwald •
Mürren • Wengen

Frolic and hike high above the stress and clouds of the real world. Take a vacation from your busy vacation. Recharge your touristic batteries high in the Alps, where distant avalanches, cowbells, the fluff of a down comforter, the whistle of marmots, and the crunchy footsteps of happy hikers are the dominant sounds. If the weather's good (and your budget's healthy), ride a cable car from the traffic-free village of Gimmelwald to a hearty breakfast at the revolving Piz Gloria restaurant, 10,000 feet up on the Schilthorn. Linger among alpine whitecaps before riding, hiking, or paragliding down 5,000 feet to Mürren and home to Gimmelwald.

Your gateway to the rugged Berner Oberland is the grand old resort town of Interlaken. Near Interlaken is Switzerland's open-air folk museum, Ballenberg, where you can climb through original traditional houses gathered from every corner of this diverse country.

Ah, but the weather's fine and the Alps beckon. Head deep into the heart of the Alps, and ride the cable car to the stop just this side of heaven—Gimmelwald.

Planning Your Time

Rather than tackle a checklist of famous Swiss mountains and resorts, choose one region to savor: the Berner Oberland.

Interlaken is the region's administrative headquarters and transportation hub. Use it for business—banking, post office, laundry, shopping—and as a springboard for alpine thrills.

If the weather's decent, explore the two areas that tower above either side of the Lauterbrunnen Valley, south of Interlaken:

On one side is the Jungfrau (and beneath it, the town of Kleine Scheidegg), and on the other is the Schilthorn (overlooking the villages of Gimmelwald and Mürren).

Ideally, spend three nights in the region, with a day exploring each side of the valley. For accommodations without the expense and headache of mountain lifts, consider the valley-floor village of Lauterbrunnen. But for the best overnight options, I'd stay on the scenic ridge high above the valley, in the rustic hamlet of Gimmelwald or the resort town of Mürren. I've also listed a few high-altitude options in the resort of Wengen and several other mountain towns.

For a summary of the wildly scenic activities this region has to offer (from panoramic train rides and lifts to spectacular hikes and mountain biking), see "Activities in the Berner Oberland" on page 1293.

If time is limited, consider a night in Gimmelwald, breakfast at the Schilthorn, an afternoon doing the Männlichen-Wengen hike, and an evening or night train out. What? A nature-lover not spending the night high in the Alps? Alpus interruptus.

Getting Around the Berner Oberland

For more than a century, this region has been the target of nature-worshipping pilgrims. And Swiss engineers and visionaries have made the most exciting alpine perches accessible.

By Lifts and Trains

Part of the fun—and most of the expense—here is riding the many mountain trains and lifts (gondolas and cable cars).

Trains connect Interlaken to Wilderswil, Grindelwald, Lauterbrunnen, Wengen, Kleine Scheidegg, and the Jungfraujoch. Lifts connect Wengen to Männlichen and Grund (near Grindelwald); Grindelwald to First; Lauterbrunnen to Grütschalp (where a train connects to Mürren); and the cable-car station near Stechelberg to Gimmelwald, Mürren, and the Schilthorn.

For an overview of your many options, study the "Alpine Lifts in the Berner Oberland" map on page 1255. Lifts generally go at least twice hourly, from about 7:00 until about 20:00 (sneak preview: www.jungfraubahn.ch or www.schilthorn.ch).

Beyond Interlaken, trains and lifts into the Jungfrau region are only 25 percent covered by Eurail Passes, without using a travel day; with the Swiss Pass, they're free up to Wengen or Mürren (uphill from there, Swiss Pass-holders pay half-price). Ask about discounts for early-morning and late-afternoon trips, youths, seniors, families, groups (assemble a party of 10 and you'll save about 25 percent), and those staying awhile. Generally, round-trips are double the one-way cost, though some high-up trains and lifts

Berner Oberland

Note: This bird's-eye view looks **south**

Jungfraujoch 11,300'

Mönch 13,449'   Jungfrau 13,642'

Eiger 13,026'

Schilthorn 9,748'

TUNNEL

BIRG 8,784'

Kleine Scheidegg 6,762'

GIMMEL-WALD 4,593'

3,025'
STECHEL-BERG

MÜRREN 5,381'

GREAT HIKE   WENG.-ALP

LIFT STN.

NICE WALK

GRINDEL-WALD 3,393'

Männlichen 7,317'

GRUND

GRÜTSCHALP 4,879'

To First

WENGEN 4,180'

BUS

LAUTERBRUNNEN 2,612'

ISENFLUH

Schynige Platte 6,454'

ZWEILÜTSCHINEN

WILDERSWIL 1,916'

To Luzern

OST STN.

ISELTWALD

To Bern

BRIENZ

Lake Brienz

Aare River

WEST STN.

Lake Thun

SPIEZ

BALLENBERG OPEN-AIR MUSEUM

INTERLAKEN 1,860'

ST. BEATUS CAVES

GIMMELWALD

are 10-20 percent cheaper. It's possible to buy your entire package of lifts at once, but then you don't have the flexibility to change with the weather.

Popular Passes: The **Junior Card,** for families traveling with children, is a great deal, and pays for itself in the first hour of trains and lifts (30 SF/one child, 60 SF/two or more children, lets children under 16 travel free with at least one parent, buy at Swiss train stations).

The **Berner Oberland Regional Pass** is a good idea for those staying a week and exploring the region extensively (7-day version-233 SF, discount with Swiss Pass, includes 3 days of unlimited travel and 4 days of half-price fares on all trains, buses, and lifts—even all the way south to Gstaad and Brig, valid May-Oct, 15-day version-290 SF, www.regiopass-berneroberland.ch).

The **Jungfraubahnen Pass** is more limited in scope, covering six consecutive days of unlimited transportation in just the Jungfrau region. This pass covers all the trains, lifts, buses, and funiculars, with one exception: You pay half-price for the train between Kleine Scheidegg and the Jungfraujoch (210 SF, 160

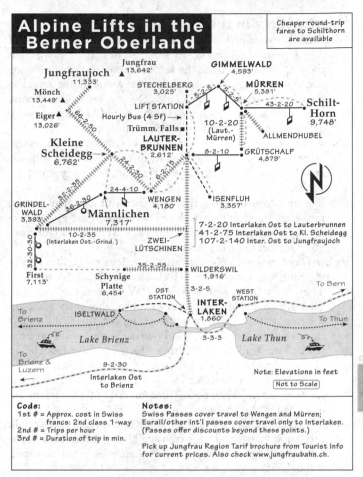

Alpine Lifts in the Berner Oberland

Cheaper round-trip fares to Schilthorn are available

GIMMELWALD 4,593'

Jungfrau 13,642'

Jungfraujoch 11,333'

STECHELBERG 3,025'

MÜRREN 5,381'

Mönch 13,449'

LIFT STATION

Schilt-Horn 9,748'

43-2-20

Eiger 13,026'

Hourly Bus (4 Sf)

5-2-5

5-2-5

Trümm. Falls

10-2-20 (Laut.-Mürren)

ALLMENDHUBEL

LAUTER-BRUNNEN 2,612'

Kleine Scheidegg 6,762'

8-2-10

GRÜTSCHALP 4,879'

6-2-15

66-2-50

24-2-30

ISENFLUH 3,357'

36-2-35

24-4-10

WENGEN 4,180'

GRINDEL-WALD 3,393'

36-2-30

Männlichen 7,317'

7-2-20 Interlaken Ost to Lauterbrunnen
41-2-75 Interlaken Ost to Kl. Scheidegg
107-2-140 Inter. Ost to Jungfraujoch

10-2-35 (Interlaken Ost.-Grind.)

ZWEI-LÜTSCHINEN

32-30-30

35-2-55

WILDERSWIL 1,916'

First 7,113'

Schynige Platte 6,454'

OST STATION

3-2-5

WEST STATION

To Bern

To Brienz

ISELTWALD

INTER-LAKEN 1,860'

To Thun

Lake Brienz

3-3-3

Lake Thun

To Brienz & Luzern

9-2-30
Interlaken Ost to Brienz

Note: Elevations in feet

Not to Scale

Code:
1st # = Approx. cost in Swiss francs: 2nd class 1-way
2nd # = Trips per hour
3rd # = Duration of trip in min.

Notes:
Swiss Passes cover travel to Wengen and Mürren; Eurail/other int'l passes cover travel only to Interlaken. (Passes offer discounts beyond these points.)

Pick up Jungfrau Region Tarif brochure from Tourist Info for current prices. Also check www.jungfraubahn.ch.

GIMMELWALD

SF with Swiss Pass, valid May-Oct, tel. 033-828-7233, www .jungfraubahn.ch).

By Car

Interlaken, Lauterbrunnen, Isenfluh, and Stechelberg are all accessible by car. You can't drive to Gimmelwald, Mürren, Wengen, or Kleine Scheidegg, but don't let that stop you from staying up in the mountains; park the car and zip up on a lift. To catch the lift to Gimmelwald, Mürren, and the Schilthorn, park at the cable-car station near Stechelberg (2 SF/2 hours, 6 SF/day, cash only; see page 1276 for more information). To catch the train to Wengen or Kleine Scheidegg, park at the train station in Lauterbrunnen (2 SF/2 hours, 10 SF/9-24 hours).

Helpful Hints in the Berner Oberland

Weather: Let your plans flex with the weather. If it's good—go! Ask at your hotel or the TI for the latest info. A webcam showing live video from the famous (and most expensive-to-reach) peaks plays just about wherever you go in the area. For the current weather, you can also check www.swisspanorama .com (entire area), www.jungfraubahn.ch (for Jungfraujoch), or www.schilthorn.ch (for Schilthorn peak).

Closed Days: On Sundays and holidays (including the lesser-known religious holidays), small-town Switzerland is quiet. Hotels are open and lifts and trains run, but many stores are closed.

Off-Season Closures: Note that at higher altitudes many hotels, restaurants, and shops are closed between the skiing and hiking seasons: from late April until late May, and again from mid-October to early December.

Rainy-Day Options: When it rains here, locals joke that they're washing the mountains. If clouds roll in, don't despair. They can roll out just as quickly. With good rain gear and the right choice of trail, you can thoroughly enjoy a hike in the rain, with surprise views popping out all around you as the clouds break. Some good bad-weather options are the North Face Trail, the walk from Mürren or Allmendhubel to Grütschalp, the Sefinen Valley hike, and the Lauterbrunnen Valley walk. Also consider a visit to Trümmelbach Falls or the Lauterbrunnen Valley Folk Museum. All of these options are described in this chapter.

Local Guidebook: For an in-depth look at the area's history, folk life, flora, fauna, and for extensive hiking information, consider Don Chmura's *Exploring the Lauterbrunnen Valley* (sold throughout the valley, 8 SF).

Visitors Cards *(Gästekarten)*: The hotels in various towns issue free Visitors Cards that include small discounts on some sights. Though these cards won't save you much, you can ask at your hotel for the details.

Skiing and Snowboarding: The Berner Oberland is a great winter-sports destination, with good snow on its higher runs, incredible variety, relatively reasonable prices, and a sense of character that's missing in many swankier resort areas. You can even swish with the Swiss down the world's longest sledding run (9 miles long, out of Grindelwald, only open when snow's good). Three ski areas cluster around the Lauterbrunnen Valley: Mürren-Schilthorn (best for experts), Kleine Scheidegg-Männlichen (busiest, best variety of runs), and Grindelwald-First (best for beginners and intermediates, but lower elevation can make for iffier snowpack). Lift tickets cost around 70 SF a day, or you can buy the two-day Sportspass Jungfrau, which covers all three areas, for about 130 SF (see www.jungfrauwinter.ch for prices and info).

Interlaken

When the 19th-century Romantics redefined mountains as something more than cold and troublesome obstacles, Interlaken became the original alpine resort. Ever since, tourists have flocked to the Alps "because they're there." Interlaken's glory days are long gone, its elegant old hotels eclipsed by the newer, more swanky alpine resorts. Today, its shops are filled with chocolate bars, Swiss Army knives, and sunburned backpackers.

While European jet-setters are elsewhere, Interlaken is cashing in on a huge interest from India and the Arab world. Indians come to escape their monsoon season—especially in April and May—and to visit places they've seen in their movies. (The Alps often stand in for Kashmir, which is less accessible to film crews.) There's even a restaurant called "Bollywood" atop the Jungfraujoch. People from the hot and dry Arabian Peninsula come here just to photograph their children frolicking in the mist and fog.

Orientation to Interlaken

Efficient Interlaken (pop. 5,500) is a good administrative and shopping center. Take care of business, give the town a quick look, and view the webcam coverage of the weather higher up (at the TI)... then head for the hills.

Tourist Information

The TI, with good information on the region, is located under the 18-story skyscraper on the main street between the two train stations, a 10-minute stroll from either (May-June Mon-Fri 8:00-18:00, Sat 8:00-16:00, closed Sun; July-Aug Mon-Fri 8:00-19:00, Sat 8:00-17:00, Sun 10:00-12:00 & 17:00-19:00; Sept Mon-Fri 8:00-18:00, Sat 9:00-13:00, closed Sun; shorter hours Oct-April, Höheweg 37, tel. 033-826-5300, www.interlaken.ch). The *You Want It All* booklet is an almanac covering everything you need in Interlaken (except for some events, which are covered more thoroughly in the monthly entertainment guide). There's no point in buying a regional map, as good mini-versions of the map are included in various free transportation and hiking brochures.

GIMMELWALD

Arrival in Interlaken

Interlaken has two train stations: Ost (East) and West. All trains coming from western Switzerland stop at both stations. If heading for higher-altitude villages, get off at Ost Station. For hotels in Interlaken, get off at West Station, which has a helpful and friendly information center for in-depth rail questions (Mon-Fri 9:00-12:00 & 13:30-18:20, Sat until 17:00, closed Sun, tel. 058-327-4750, www.bls.ch; ticket windows open daily 6:40-19:00). Ask about discount passes, special fares, railpass discounts, and schedules for the scenic mountain trains. There's an exchange booth next to the ticket windows and a very pricey Internet-access computer. A post office with a cluster of phone booths is a few blocks away.

It's a pleasant 20-minute walk between the West and Ost train stations; an easy, frequent train connection (2-3/hour, 3.40 SF); or a quick trip on the bus (2/hour, 10 minutes, 3.40 SF). From Ost Station, private trains take you deep into the mountainous Jungfrau region (see "Interlaken Connections," on page 1269).

Helpful Hints

Baggage Storage: Both stations have lockers (small locker-4 SF, large-5 SF) as well as left-luggage counters (5 SF, West Station—daily 9:00-12:00 & 13:30-18:00, Ost Station—daily 7:00-18:30).

Laundry: Friendly Helen Schmocker's **Wäscherei** has a change machine, soap, English instructions, and a delightful riverside location (self-service daily 7:00-22:00—wash-6 SF/load, dry-about 5 SF/load; full service Mon-Fri 8:00-12:00 & 13:30-18:00, Sat until 16:00, closed Sun, drop off in the morning and pick up that afternoon—12 SF/load; from the main street take Marktgasse over two bridges to Beatenbergstrasse 5, tel. 033-822-1566).

Bike Rental: You can rent bikes (both regular and electric) at West Station (11.50 SF/2 hours, 25 SF/half-day, 33 SF/day, 5 SF less with Eurail Pass or Swiss Pass, daily 9:00-18:00, www.rentabike.ch).

Flying Wheels, a short walk from Ost Station, is a hip, well-organized, family-friendly outfit that specializes in electric bikes and guided bike tours of the area. Its amiable English-speaking staff can help you pick the right bike and give tips on where to go (electric or hard-core mountain bikes—35 SF/half-day, 50 SF/day; normal mountain bikes—25 SF/half-day, 33 SF/day; 5 SF cheaper with Swiss Pass, no discount with Eurail Pass, tandem electric bikes available, daily 9:00-19:00, across street from the northeast corner of Höhematte Park at Höheweg 133, tel. 033-511-2161, www.flyingwheels.ch). For info on their tours, see "Adventure Sports," later.

A short walk from West Station, **Eiger Sport** rents bikes for a little less than Flying Wheels (8 SF/hour, 10 SF/2 hours, 15 SF/3 hours, 20 SF/half-day, 30 SF/day, Mon-Fri 8:30-12:00 & 13:30-18:30, Sat 8:30-16:00; from West Station, cross river—it's on the right at Bahnhofstrasse 2, tel. 033-823-2043).

Self-Guided Walk

Welcome to Interlaken

Most visitors use Interlaken as a springboard for high-altitude thrills (and rightly so). But the town itself has history and scenic charm and is worth a short walk. This 45-minute stroll circles from the West train station, down the main drag to the big meadow, past the casino, along the river to the oldest part of town (historically a neighboring town called Unterseen), and back to the station.

• *From the West train station, walk along...*

Bahnhofstrasse: This main drag, which turns into Höheweg as it continues east, cuts straight through the town center from the West train station to the Ost train station. The best Swiss souvenir shopping is along this stretch (finer shops are on the Höheweg stretch, near the fancy hotels). At the roundabout is the handy post office (with free public WCs). At Höheweg 2, the TV in the window of the Schilthornbahn office shows the weather up top.

The 18-story **Metropole Hotel** (a.k.a. the "concrete shame of Interlaken") is by far the town's tallest building. Step right into the main lobby (through the second set of doors) and ride the elevator to the top for a commanding view of the "inter-laken" area, and gaze deep into the Jungfrau region to the scenic south. A meal or drink here costs no more than one back on earth. Consider sipping a drink on its outdoor view terrace (or come back tonight—it's open very late).

• *On your right is...*

Höhematte Park: This "high meadow," or Höhematte (but generally referred to simply as "the park"), marks the beginning of Interlaken's fancy hotel row. Hotels like the Victoria-Jungfrau hearken back to the days when Interlaken was *the* top alpine resort (late 19th century). The first grand hotels were built here to enjoy the views of the Jungfrau in the distance. (Today, the *jung Frau*s getting the most attention are next door, at Hooters.)

The park originated as farmland of the monastery that pre-dated the town (marked today by the steeples of both the Catholic and Protestant churches—neither are of any sightseeing interest). The actual **monastery site** is now home to the courthouse and county administration building. With the Reformation in 1528, the monastery was shut down, and its land was taken by

GIMMELWALD

Interlaken

Woods

UNTERSEEN

BEATEN

Funicular to
Harderkulm

To Brienz
& Luzern

BOAT
DOCK

Aare River

POOL

OST
(EAST)
STATION

Private Trains
to Jungfrau
Region

CASINO
KURSAAL

BIG, RITZY
HOTELS

HÖHEWEG

Höhe-
matte
Park

LINDENALLEE

POST

WEST
STATION

BOAT
DOCK

BAHNHOFSTRASSE

MARKTSTRASSE

AARMÜHLESTR.

NIESENSTR.

CENTRAL

ROSENSTR.

GUISANSTR.

BERNSTR.

RUGENPARKSTRASSE

WALDEGGSTRASSE

Ship Canal

Aare River

JUNGFRAUSTR.

Alpenstrasse

PARKSTR.

KLOSTERSTR.

UNTERDORFSTR.

WYCHELSTRASSE

HAUPTSTRASSE

TELLWEG

TELL
OPEN-AIR
THEATER

MATTEN

GSTEIGSTRASSE

OELESTR.

ALLMENDSTR.

FREIESTRASSE

Woods

To N18
Autobahn
(Bern &
Luzern)

DARLINGENSTRASSE

SEILPARK

200 meters

200 yards

To N18 Autobahn
(Bern & Luzern) &
Lauterbrunnen
Valley

1 Hotel Lötschberg, Guest House Susi's B&B & Sirinya's Thai Rest.	**9** Happy Inn Lodge
2 Sunny Days B&B	**10** Restaurant Bären
3 Hotel Aarburg & Launderette	**11** Goldener Anker
4 Katy's Lodge B&B	**12** Rist. West End & Migros Grocery
5 Villa Margaretha	**13** Città Vecchia
6 Backpackers' Villa (Sonnenhof)	**14** Metropole Hotel's "Top O'Met"
7 Balmer's Herberge & Metro Bar	**15** Restaurant Schuh
8 Interlaken Hostel	**16** Funny Farm Bar
	17 Co-op Supermarket/Cafeteria
	18 Town History Mus./Mus. of Tourism
	19 Vertical Sport & K4 Climbing
	20 Flying Wheels Bike Rental

the state. Later, when the land was being eyed by developers, the town's leading hotels and business families bought it and established that it would never be used for commercial buildings (a very early example of smart town planning). There was talk of building a parking lot under it, but the water table here, between the two lakes, is too high. (That's why the town cemetery is up on the hillside.) Today, this is a fine place to stroll, hang out on the park benches or at Restaurant Schuh, and watch the paragliders gracefully land.

Across the street from the park, right where the path that bisects the park hits Höheweg, turn left onto the grounds of the **Casino Kursaal,** where, at the top of each hour, dwarves ring the toadstools on the flower clock. The Kursaal, originally a kind of 19th-century fat farm, is now both a casino (passport but no tie required to enter) and a convention center.

• *Follow the path left of the Kursaal to the river (huge public swimming pool just over the river). Walk downstream under the train track and cross the pedestrian bridge, stopping in the middle to enjoy the view.*

Aare River: The Aare River is Switzerland's longest. It connects Lake Brienz and Lake Thun (with an 18-foot altitude difference—this short stretch has quite a flow). Then it tumbles out of Lake Thun, heading for Bern and ultimately into the Rhine. Its level is controlled by several sluices. In the distance, a church bell tower marks a different parish and the neighborhood of Unterseen, which shares the town's name, but in German: Like the word *Interlaken, Unterseen* means "between the lakes." Behind the spire is the pointy summit of the Niesen (like so many Swiss peaks, capped with a restaurant and accessible by a lift). Stroll downstream along the far side of the river to the church spire. The delightful riverside walk is lined by fine residences. Notice that your Jungfrau view now includes the Jungfraujoch observation deck (the little brown bump in the ridge just left of the peak).

• *At the next bridge, turn right to the town square lined with 17th-century houses on one side and a modern strip on the other.*

Unterseen: This was a town when Interlaken was only a monastery. The church is not worth touring. A block away to the left, the (generally empty) **Town History Museum/Museum of Tourism** shows off classic posters, fascinating photos of the construction of the Jungfraujoch, and exhibits on folk life, crafts, and winter sports—all well-described in English (5 SF, covered by Swiss Pass, May-mid-Oct Tue-Sun 14:00-17:00, closed Mon and mid-Oct-April, Obere Gasse 26).

Return to Station: From Unterseen, cross the river on Spielmatte, and you're a few minutes' walk from your starting point. On the second bridge, notice the border between the two towns/parishes, marked by their respective heraldic emblems (each with an ibex, a wild mountain goat). A block or so later, on the left, is the Marktplatz. The river originally ran through this square. The town used to be called "Aaremühle" ("Aare mill") for the mill that was here. But in the 19th century, town fathers made a key marketing decision: Since "Aaremühle" was too difficult to pronounce for English tourists who flocked here, they changed the name to "Interlaken." Judging from the throngs of tourists on the main drag, it worked.

Sights near Interlaken

▲▲Swiss Open-Air Folk Museum at Ballenberg

Across Lake Brienz from Interlaken, the Swiss Open-Air Museum of Vernacular Architecture, Country Life, and Crafts in the Berner Oberland is a rich collection of more than 100 traditional and historic buildings brought here from every region of the country. All the houses are carefully furnished, and many feature traditional craftspeople at work. The sprawling 50-acre park, laid out roughly as a huge Swiss map (Italian Swiss in the south, Appenzell in the east, and so on), is a natural preserve providing a wonderful setting for this culture-on-a-lazy-Susan look at Switzerland.

The Thurgau house (#621) has an interesting wattle-and-daub (half-timbered construction) display, and house #331 has a fun bread museum and farmers' shop. There are daily events and demonstrations (near the east entry), hundreds of traditional farm animals (like very furry-legged roosters, near the merry-go-round in the center), and a chocolate shop (under the restaurant on the east side).

An outdoor cafeteria with reasonable prices is inside the west entrance, and fresh bread, sausage, mountain cheese, and other goodies are on sale in several houses. Picnic tables and grills with free firewood are scattered throughout the park.

The little wooden village of Brienzwiler (near the east entrance) is a museum in itself, with a lovely pint-size church.

Cost and Hours: 20 SF, covered by Swiss Pass; RailAway combo-ticket includes transportation to and from Ballenberg—41 SF from West Station, 38 SF from Ost Station, add 15 SF to return by boat instead, ticket available at both Interlaken stations; houses open daily mid-April-Oct 10:00-17:00, grounds and restaurants stay open until 18:00.

Information: Pick up a daily craft demonstration schedule at the entry, and buy the 2-SF map/guide so you'll know where you are. The more expensive picture book is a better souvenir than guide; tel. 033-952-1030, www.ballenberg.ch.

Getting There: From Interlaken, take the train from either station to Brienz (2/hour, 30 minutes, 9.20 SF one-way from West Station or get the RailAway combo-ticket—described earlier). From the Brienz train station, catch a bus to Ballenberg (10 minutes, 4.20 SF one-way). The bus back to Brienz leaves Ballenberg's east entrance on the hour, then picks up at the west entrance at :07 after the hour (after 18:00, buses leave only from the west entrance). Consider returning from Brienz by boat (boat dock next to train station, one-way to Interlaken's Ost Station-28 SF). Parking is free outside both entrances to the park.

Boat Trips

"Interlaken" is literally "between the lakes" of Thun and Brienz. You can explore these lakes on a lazy boat trip, hopping on and off as the schedule allows (free with Swiss Pass or Eurail Pass but uses a travel day, schedules at TI or at travel center in West Station). The boats on Lake Thun (5/day in summer, 2/day spring and fall, 5-hour round-trip, 68 SF) stop at the St. Beatus caves (30 minutes away, described next) and two visit-worthy towns: Spiez and Thun. The boats on Lake Brienz (5/day July-Aug, 2-4/day off-season, 3-hour round-trip, 48 SF) stop at the super-cute village of Iseltwald and at Brienz (near Ballenberg Open-Air Folk Museum; easy bus and train connections back to Interlaken from Brienz).

The **St. Beatus caves** on Lake Thun can be visited with a one-hour guided tour (18 SF, 2/hour, April-mid-Oct daily 9:30-17:00, closed mid-Oct-March, tel. 033-841-1643, www.beatushoehlen .ch). The best excursion plan: Ride bus #21 from Interlaken (1-2/hour, 25 minutes, 5 SF, departs West Station at :17 and :47 past the hour, direction: Thun); tour the caves; take the short, steep hike down to the lake; and return to Interlaken by boat (30 minutes, 13 SF one-way).

Adventure Sports

High-Adrenaline Trips—For the thrill-seeker with money, several companies offer trips such as rafting, canyoning (rappelling down watery gorges), bungee jumping, and paragliding. Costs range from roughly 150 SF to 200 SF—higher for skydiving and hot-air balloon rides. Interlaken's two dominant companies are **Alpin Raft** (tel. 033-823-4100, www.alpinraft.com) and **Outdoor Interlaken** (tel. 033-826-7719, www.outdoor-interlaken.ch). Other companies are generally just booking agents for these two outfits. For an overview of your options, visit www.interlakenadventure .com or study the racks of brochures at most TIs and hotels (everyone's getting a cut of this lucrative industry).

Several years ago, two fatal accidents jolted the adventure-sport business in the Berner Oberland, leading to a more professional respect for the risks involved. Companies have very high standards of safety. Statistically, the most dangerous sport is mountain biking. Enjoying nature up close comes with risks. Adventure sports increase those risks dramatically. Use good judgment.

Indoor Climbing—K44 is a breathtaking indoor climbing facility where you can snack or enjoy a nice cup of hot chocolate while watching hotshots practice their gravity-defying skills.

Cost and Hours: Free entry for viewing, 39 SF for one hour of climbing; open longer hours in bad weather: Mon 16:00-22:00, Tue-Fri 9:00-22:00, Sat 9:00-20:00, Sun 9:00-18:00; in good weather: Tue-Fri 9:00-18:00, Sat 9:00-16:00, closed Sun-Mon;

next to—and run by—**Vertical Sport**, at the back of the park across from Hotel Savoy at Jungfraustrasse 44, tel. 033-821-2821, www.k44.ch.

Rope Courses—**Outdoor Interlaken's Seilpark** offers five rope courses of varying difficulty and height in a forest, giving you a tree-top adventure through a maze of rope bridges and zip lines.

Cost and Hours: 37 SF, family deals, must weigh between 44 and 264 pounds; June-Aug daily 10:00-18:00; April-May and Sept-Oct Mon-Fri 13:00-18:00, Sat-Sun 10:00-18:00; closed Nov-March; from Interlaken's West Station, it's a 15-minute walk—head right up Rugenparkstrasse and into the park, then look for signs; tel. 033-826-7719, www.outdoor-interlaken.ch.

Bike Tours—**Flying Wheels** offers bike tours of varying length and difficulty around the area. They also offer an interesting "bike and fly" deal: Ride your electric bike up the hill and paraglide back into Interlaken (around 200 SF). If it rains the day you're booked to go, they'll take you on a bus tour instead to a nearby indoor destination.

Cost and Hours: Interlaken-only tour—60 SF, 3 hours; Lauterbrunnen Valley up to Stechelberg—100-110 SF, 6 hours, includes picnic and Trümmelbach Falls visit; around Lake Brienz—90-100 SF, 6 hours, includes picnic; shorter tours start at 9:45, longer tours at 8:30; for contact info, see page 1258.

Castles

A few impressively well-kept and welcoming old castles in the Interlaken area are worth considering for day trips by boat, bus, or car.

Thun Castle (Schloss Thun)—Built between 1180 and 1190 by the Dukes of Zähringen, the castle houses a five-floor historical museum offering insights into the cultural development of the region over a period of some 4,000 years. From the corner turrets of the castle, you are rewarded with a spectacular view of the city of Thun, the lake, and the Alps.

Cost and Hours: 8 SF, April-Oct daily 10:00-17:00, Nov-Jan Sun only 13:00-16:00, Feb-March daily 13:00-16:00, tel. 033-223-2001, www.schlossthun.ch.

Hünegg Castle (Schloss Hünegg)—Located in Hilterfingen (farther along Lake Thun, toward Interlaken), this castle contains a museum exhibiting furnished rooms from the second half of the 19th century. The castle is situated in a beautiful wooded park.

Cost and Hours: 9 SF, mid-May-mid-Oct Mon-Sat 14:00-17:00, Sun 11:00-17:00, closed off-season, tel. 033-243-1982, www.schlosshuenegg.ch.

Oberhofen Castle (Schloss Oberhofen)—Also on Lake Thun, this place is ideal for those interested in gardens. Its beautifully

GIMMELWALD

landscaped park with exotic trees is a delight. The museum in the castle depicts domestic life in the 16th-19th centuries, including a Turkish smoking room and a medieval chapel.

Cost and Hours: Gardens-free, mid-May-mid-Oct daily 10:00-dusk; museum-10 SF, mid-May-mid-Oct Mon 14:00-17:00, Tue-Sun 11:00-17:00; both closed off-season, 40 minutes from Interlaken on bus #21, tel. 033-243-1235, www.schlossober hofen.ch.

Nightlife in Interlaken

Youthful Night Scenes—For counterculture with a reggae beat, check out **Funny Farm** (past the recommended Balmer's Herberge hostel, in Matten). The young frat-party dance scene rages at the **Metro Bar** at Balmer's (bomb-shelter disco bar, with cheap drinks and a friendly if loud atmosphere). And if you're into **Hooters,** you won't have a hard time finding it.

Mellower After-Dark Hangouts—To nurse a drink with a view of the park, the outdoor tables at **Restaurant Schuh** are convenient if you don't mind the schlocky music. The **"Top O'Met"** bar and café has great indoor and outdoor view seating with reasonable prices, 18 floors above everything else in town (in the Metropole Hotel skyscraper, open nightly until late, see "Eating in Interlaken," later). **Hotel Oberland** (near the post office) has live alpine music in its restaurant (Tue at 19:00 or 20:00).

Sleeping in Interlaken

I'd sleep in Gimmelwald, or at least Lauterbrunnen (20 minutes by train or car). In ski season, however, prices go down in Interlaken, while they shoot up at most hotels in the mountains. Interlaken is not the Alps. But if you must stay here...

$$$ Hotel Lötschberg, with a sun terrace and 21 rooms, is run with lots of thoughtful touches by English-speaking Susi (Sb-135 SF, Db-178 SF, big Db-198 SF, extra bed-35 SF, family deals, closed Nov-mid-April, elevator, pay Internet access, free Wi-Fi, free laundry machines, free loaner bikes; lounge with microwave, fridge, and free tea and coffee; 3-minute walk from West Station: leaving station, turn right, after Migros at the circle go left to General-Guisan-Strasse 31; tel. 033-822-2545, fax 033-822-2579, www.lotschberg.ch, hotel@lotschberg.ch).

$$$ Guest House Susi's B&B is Hotel Lötschberg's no-frills, cash-only annex, offering three nicely furnished, cozy rooms and four apartments with kitchenettes (Sb-119 SF, Db-151 SF; apartment-140 SF/2 people, 250 SF/4-5 people; free Wi-Fi, hotel closed Nov-mid-April but apartments available with 5-night stay,

Sleep Code

(1 SF = about $1.10, country code: 41)
S = Single, **D** = Double/Twin, **T** = Triple, **Q** = Quad, **b** = bathroom,
s = shower only. Unless otherwise noted, credit cards are
accepted, English is spoken, and breakfast is included.

To help you sort easily through these listings, I've divided
the accommodations into three categories, based on the price
for a standard double room with bath during high season:

$$$ Higher Priced—Most rooms 150 SF or more.
$$ Moderately Priced—Most rooms between 90–150 SF.
$ Lower Priced—Most rooms 90 SF or less.

Prices can change without notice; verify the hotel's
current rates online or by email. For other updates, see www
.ricksteves.com/update.

same contact info as Hotel Lötschberg, above).

$$ Sunny Days B&B, run by Dave from Britain, is a homey,
nine-room place in a quiet residential neighborhood (Sb-108-140
SF, Db-120-158 SF, prices vary with size of room and view, less
in winter, 1-night stay-20 SF extra, discount for 4 or more nights,
extra bed-about 40 SF, pay Wi-Fi, patio; from West Station: exit
left out of station and take first bridge to your left, after crossing
two bridges turn left on Helvetiastrasse and go 3 blocks to #29; tel.
033-822-8343, www.sunnydays.ch, mail@sunnydays.ch).

$$ Hotel Aarburg offers nine plain, peaceful rooms over
a restaurant in a beautifully located but run-down old building
in Unterseen, a 10-minute walk from West Station (Sb-70 SF,
Db-140-150 SF, 10 SF more in July-Aug, 2 doors from launderette
at Beatenbergstrasse 1, tel. 033-822-2615, hotel-aarburg@quick
net.ch).

$$ Katy's Lodge B&B is a funky old house in a quiet, handy
location. It's not cozy, but it rents seven basic rooms at a good price.
All the beds are twins—no double beds here (D-90-108 SF, T-114-
126 SF, Q-140-160 SF, 6-bed room-160-180 SF, lowest prices in
winter, reception open 7:00-12:00 & 14:00-20:00, garden, play-
ground, 3-minute walk from West Station, around the corner from
Hotel Lötschberg at Bernastrasse 7, mobile 078-604-6507, www
.katys-lodge.ch, katyslodge@hotmail.com).

$$ Backpackers' Villa (Sonnenhof) Interlaken is a creative guest house run by a Methodist church group. Renovated in
2009, it's fun, youthful, and great for families, without the frat-
party scene of Balmer's Herberge (listed later). Travelers of any
age feel comfortable here (dorm bed in 2- to 7-bed room with free

locker, sheets, and towel-37-47 SF, S-69 SF, view S-74 SF, Sb-79 SF, D-98-106 SF, view D-110-114 SF, Db-138 SF, T-135-141 SF, view T-153-159 SF, Tb-165-171 SF, Q-164-172 SF, view Q-180-188 SF, Qb-196-204 SF, view rooms have balconies and WCs, lowest prices in winter, kitchen, garden, movies, small game room, pay Internet access, free Wi-Fi, laundry, free admission to public swimming pool/spa, no curfew, no membership required, open all day, reception open 7:00-23:00, free use of public buses—bus #102 runs from hostel to either of Interlaken's stations, 10-15-minute walk from stations, across the park from the TI at Alpenstrasse 16, tel. 033-826-7171, fax 033-826-7172, www.villa.ch, mail@villa.ch).

$ **Villa Margaretha,** run by English-speaking Frau Kunz-Joerin, offers the best cheap beds in town. It's like Grandma's big Victorian house on a residential street. Keep your room tidy, and you'll have a friend for life (D-90 SF, T-135 SF, Q-180 SF, the three rooms share one big bathroom, 2-night minimum, apartment for 2-3 people-1,000 SF/week, closed Oct-April, cash only, no breakfast served but dishes and kitchenette available, lots of rules to abide by, go up small street directly in front of West Station to Aarmühlestrasse 13, tel. 033-822-1813, www.villa-margaretha.com, info@villa-margaretha.com).

$ **Balmer's Herberge** is many people's idea of backpacker heaven. This Interlaken institution comes with movies, table tennis, a launderette, bar, restaurant, tiny grocery, kitchen, bike rental, swapping library, excursions, bus pass, shuttle-bus service (which meets important arriving trains), and friendly, hardworking staff. This hive of youthful fun and activities is home for those who miss their fraternity. It can be a mob scene, especially on summer weekends (bunk in 6- to 12-bed dorm-27 SF, S-45 SF, D-74 SF, T-99 SF, Q-132 SF, these are walk-in prices—booking online costs 1-2 SF more, includes sheets and breakfast, open year-round, emailed reservations recommended at least 5 days in advance for private rooms, free Wi-Fi, pay Internet access, Hauptstrasse 23, in Matten, 15-minute walk from either train station, tel. 033-822-1961, fax 033-823-3261, www.balmers.com, mail@balmers.ch). They also have private rooms in an adjacent guest house (Db-130 SF, Tb-165 SF, Qb-220 SF).

$ **Interlaken Hostel,** opened in 2012, isn't your cheapest option, but it's convenient (right next to the Ost train station), huge (with 220 beds), thoroughly modern, and full of daylight. It also offers plenty of amenities (bed in 6-bed dorm-39 SF, bed in 4-bed dorm-43 SF, Sb-121 SF, Db-134-138 SF, includes sheets, all rooms have sinks, restaurant, swimming pool, game room, lockers, Internet access and Wi-Fi, check-in 15:00-24:00, Untere Bönigstrasse 3, tel. 033-826-1090, www.youthhostel.ch/interlaken, interlaken@youthhostel.ch).

$ **Happy Inn Lodge,** above the lively, noisy Brasserie 17 restaurant, has 16 cheap backpacker rooms and two doubles with private baths; come here as a last resort only if you belong to the young-and-scrappy set (bed with bedding in 4- to 8-bed dorm-22-24 SF, S-32-60 SF, D-52-80 SF, Db-84-104 SF, breakfast-8-9 SF, no membership required, no curfew, pay Internet access, free Wi-Fi, bus pass, 5-minute walk from West Station at Rosenstrasse 17, tel. 033-822-3225, fax 033-822-3268, www.brasserie17.ch, info @happyinn.com).

Eating in Interlaken

In Unterseen, the Old Town Across the River

Restaurant Bären, in a classic low-ceilinged building with cozy indoor and fine outdoor seating, is a great value for *Rösti*, fondue, raclette, fish, traditional sausage, and salads (20-30-SF plates including fondue for one, Cordon Bleu is popular; open Tue-Thu 16:30-23:30, Fri-Sun 10:30-23:30 or later—but may close 14:00-17:30 in off-season, closed Mon; from West Station, turn left on Bahnhofstrasse, cross the river, and go several blocks to Seestrasse 2; tel. 033-822-7526).

Goldener Anker is *the* local hangout—with smokers lingering outside, a pool table inside, and a few unsavory types. If you think Interlaken is sterile, you haven't been to the "Golden Anchor." Jeannette serves and René cooks, just as they have for 25 years. This place, with its "melody rock and blues" ambience, sometimes hosts small concerts and has actually launched some of Switzerland's top bands (hearty 15-25-SF salads, fresh vegetables, 3 courses for 15-20 SF, daily from 16:00, Marktgasse 57, tel. 033-822-1672).

Ristorante West End is a reliable Italian place and a local favorite for *cucina casalinga* (20-SF pasta, 25-SF plates, no pizza, Mon-Sat 17:30-22:30, closed Sun, next to West Station and across the street from Migros at Rugenparkstrasse 2, tel. 033-822-1744).

Città Vecchia serves decent Italian with seating indoors or out, on a leafy square (16-22-SF pizzas, 20-28-SF pastas, 30-40-SF plates, daily 10:30-14:00 & 18:00-23:00, closed during the day Tue-Wed Oct-May, on main square in Unterseen at Untere Gasse 5, tel. 033-822-1754, Rinaldo).

On or near Höheweg

Interlaken's main drag, Höheweg, is lined with eateries. Tourists dampen the local ambience, but you have plenty of options.

Sirinya's Thai Restaurant is run by charming Sirinya, who serves great Thai dishes and popular spring rolls at reasonable prices (20-25-SF plates, Tue-Sat 16:00-23:30, Sun 16:00-22:00, closed Mon, at the recommended Hotel Lötschberg, General-Guisan-Strasse 31, tel. 033-821-6535).

Metropole Hotel's "Top O'Met," capping Interlaken's 18-story aesthetic nightmare, is actually a decent café/restaurant serving traditional and modern food at down-to-earth prices. For just 6 SF, you can enjoy a glass of wine and awesome views from an indoor or outdoor table (25-SF lunch deals Mon-Sat include two courses and coffee, 25-35-SF dinner plates, daily 11:30-24:00, no hot food 14:00-18:00 or after 22:00, Höheweg 37, just step into the Metropole Hotel and go up the elevator as far as you can, tel. 033-828-6666).

Supermarkets

Interlaken's two big supermarkets sell picnic supplies and also have reasonable self-service restaurants: **Migros** is across the street from West Station (Mon-Thu 8:00-18:30, Fri 8:00-21:00, Sat 7:30-17:00, closed Sun), while the **Co-op** is across the river from West Station, on your right (same hours as Migros except Mon-Thu until 19:00). The only grocery store open late at night is **Co-op Pronto** (daily 6:00-22:30, 30 yards west of TI on Höheweg).

Interlaken Connections

There are a few long-distance trains from Interlaken—you'll generally transfer in **Bern.** Train info: toll tel. 0900-300-300 or www.rail.ch.

From Interlaken Ost by Train to: Bern (2/hour, 55 minutes, some with change in Spiez), **Spiez** (3/hour, 25 minutes), **Brienz** (2/hour, 20 minutes), **Zürich** and **Zürich Airport** (2/hour, 2-2.5 hours, most with transfer in Bern or Spiez), **Luzern** (2/hour, 2 hours direct, 2.5 hours with 1-2 changes), **Lugano** (hourly, 4.75 hours, 1-2 changes), **Zermatt** (hourly, 2.25 hours, transfer in Spiez and Visp), **Florence** (5/day, 5.5-6 hours, 2-3 changes), **Venice** (6/day, 6-8.5 hours, 2-4 changes), **Nice** (4/day, 8.5-10 hours, 2-4 changes), **Paris** (9/day, 5-6 hours, 1-2 changes).

From Interlaken to the Lauterbrunnen Valley: To reach the heart of the valley, drive or take the train to **Lauterbrunnen** (train leaves hourly from Interlaken's Ost Station, 20 minutes). You cannot drive to Gimmelwald (park at the cable-car station near Stechelberg and ride up on the lift; see page 1277) or to Mürren or Kleine Scheidegg (park in Lauterbrunnen and take the cable car to Mürren or the train to Kleine Scheidegg). For more details, see "Lauterbrunnen Valley Connections" on page 1276.

Lauterbrunnen

Lauterbrunnen is the valley's commercial center and transportation hub. In addition to its train station and cable car, the one-street town is just big enough to have all the essential services (bank, post office, bike rental, launderette, and so on)—plus several hotels and hostels. It's idyllic, in spite of the busy road that slices it in two. Sitting under sheer cliffs at the base of the valley, with its signature waterfall spurting mightily out from the cliff (floodlit at night), Lauterbrunnen is a fine springboard for Jungfrau and Schilthorn adventures. But for spending the night, I still prefer Gimmelwald or Mürren, perched on the ledge above the valley.

Orientation to Lauterbrunnen

Tourist Information: Stop by the friendly TI to check the weather forecast, find out about guided walks and events, and buy hiking maps or any regional train or lift tickets you need (June-mid-Sept daily 9:00-12:00 & 13:30-18:00, off-season Mon-Fri 9:00-12:00 & 13:30-17:00, closed Sat-Sun, located on the main street a block up from the train station, tel. 033-856-8568, www.mylauterbrunnen .com).

    Arrival in Lauterbrunnen: The slick, modern train station has lockers and is across the main street from the cable-car station. Go left as you exit the station to find the TI. Drivers can find parking in the large multistory pay lot behind the station (2 SF/2 hours, 10 SF/9-24 hours, www.jungfraubahn.ch).

Helpful Hints

Medical Help: Dr. Bruno Durrer, who has a clinic (with pharmacy) near the Jungfrau Hotel (look for *Arzt* sign), is good and very busy. He splits his time between seeing patients at his main office here, spending a couple of days a week up in Mürren, and buzzing around the region in helicopters to rescue injured adventure-seekers. He and his associate both speak English (tel. 033-856-2626, answered 24/7).

Money: Several ATMs are along the main street, including one immediately across from the train station.

Internet and Laundry: Two places are within a short walk of each other in the town center: The **Valley Hostel** is automated (Internet access-2.50 SF/15 minutes, launderette-5 SF/load, includes soap, May-Oct daily 9:00-22:00, shorter hours Nov-April, don't open dryer door until machine is finished or you'll have to pay another 5 SF to start it again, tel. 033-855-2008); **Airtime** is fully staffed (Internet access-5 minutes

Lauterbrunnen

To Trümmelbach Falls, Schilthorn Cable Car (to Gimmelwald & Mürren) & Stechelberg Village via Trail

Staubbach Waterfall

To Trümmelbach Falls, Schilthorn Cable Car (to Gimmelwald & Mürren) & Stechelberg Village via Road

Weisse

FOLK MUSEUM

To Wengen, Kleine Scheidegg & Jungfraujoch

Lütschine

MAIN DRAG

To Wengen

To Grütschalp & Train to Mürren

POST

To Grütschalp & Train to Mürren

TRAIN STATION

CABLE-CAR STATION

River

To Isenfluh

Not to Scale

Note: Train station to church is a 5 min. walk

To Interlaken & Grindelwald

GIMMELWALD

❶ Hotel Restaurant Silberhorn
❷ Hotel Staubbach
❸ Valley Hostel/ Laundry/Internet
❹ Chalet im Rohr
❺ Matratzenlager Stocki
❻ Mountain Holiday Park-Camping Jungfrau
❼ Schützenbach Retreat
❽ Hotel Restaurant Oberland
❾ Hotel Restaurant Jungfrau
❿ Airtime Café/ Laundry/Internet
⓫ Pub Horner
⓬ Co-op Grocery
⓭ Bike Rental
⓮ Alpia Sports Shop

free, 2 SF/15 minutes, pay Wi-Fi, self-service laundry-10 SF/
load, full-service laundry-25 SF/load, daily 9:00-19:00, closed
Nov).

Grocery Store: The **Co-op** is on the main street across from the
station (Mon-Sat 9:00-19:00, closed Sun).

Bike Rental: You can rent mountain bikes at **Imboden Bike** on the
main street (25 SF/half-day, 35 SF/day; full-suspension—35
SF/half-day, 55 SF/day; daily July-Aug 8:30-20:00, Sept-June
9:00-18:30 except closed for lunch 12:00-13:00 Oct-May, tel.
033-855-2114, www.imboden-bike.ch). They work with the
bike-rental shop in Mürren, allowing you to pick up a bike
here and drop it off there—or vice versa (8 SF supplement).

Sports Gear: You can rent hiking boots, skis, and snowboards
at the **Alpia Sports** shop (daily 8:00-12:30 & 13:30-19:00,
shorter hours on weekends and in fall, closed in May, at Hotel
Crystal, tel. 033-855-3292, www.alpiasport.ch).

Activities in and near Lauterbrunnen

Hikers' Loop from Lauterbrunnen—If you're staying in
Lauterbrunnen, consider this ambitious but great day plan: Ride
the cable car to Grütschalp, walk along the ridge to Mürren, take
the cable car up to the Schilthorn and back down to Mürren, ride
the funicular up to Allmendhubel, hike the North Face Trail to
Gimmelwald, take the lift down to the Schilthornbahn station
near Stechelberg, catch the PostBus to Trümmelbach Falls, and
walk through the valley back into Lauterbrunnen. Make it more
or less strenuous or time-consuming by swapping lifts and hikes
(all described later in this chapter). Or rent a mountain bike and do
a wheeled variation on this (parking your bike in Mürren for the
Schilthorn trip).

▲**Trümmelbach Falls**—If all the waterfalls have you intrigued,
sneak a behind-the-scenes look at the valley's most powerful, Trümmelbach Falls. You'll ride an elevator up through the
mountain and climb through several caves (wet, with lots of stairs,
and—for some—claustrophobic) to see the melt from the Eiger,
Mönch, and Jungfrau grinding like God's bandsaw through the
mountain at the rate of up to 5,200 gallons a second (that's 20,000
liters—nearly double the beer consumption at Oktoberfest). The
upper area is the best; if your legs ache, skip the lower falls and
ride down on the elevator.

Cost and Hours: 11 SF, daily July-Aug 8:30-18:00, April-June
and Sept-mid-Nov 9:00-17:00, closed mid-Nov-March, tel. 033-
855-3232, www.truemmelbach.ch.

Getting There: It's about halfway between Lauterbrunnen
and the Schilthornbahn cable-car station; from either, it's a short

ride on the PostBus or a 45-minute walk.

▲▲**Cloudy-Day Lauterbrunnen Valley Walks**—Try the easy trails and pleasant walks along the floor of the Lauterbrunnen Valley. For a smell-the-cows-and-flowers lowland walk—ideal for a cloudy day, weary body, or tight budget—take the PostBus from Lauterbrunnen town to the Schilthornbahn cable-car station near Stechelberg (left of river), and follow the riverside trail back for three basically level miles to Staubbach Falls, near the town church (you can reverse the route, but it's a very gradual uphill to Stechelberg). A trail was cut into the cliff to take visitors up "behind" Staubbach Falls (at the uphill end of Lauterbrunnen town). But, depending on the wind, the trail may be closed short of the actual falls.

You don't ever need to walk along the road. A fine, paved, car-free riverside path goes all the way along the valley (popular with bikers). Detour to Trümmelbach Falls (described earlier) en route (it's a 45-minute walk from the Schilthornbahn station to Trümmelbach Falls, and another 45 minutes to Lauterbrunnen). In this "Valley of Many Waterfalls" (literally), you'll see cone-like mounds piled against the sides of the cliffs, formed by centuries of rocks hurled by tumbling rivers. Look up to see BASE jumpers between Trümmelbach Falls and Lauterbrunnen.

If you're staying in Gimmelwald, try this plan: Take the Schilthornbahn lift down to the station near Stechelberg (5 minutes), then walk 1.5 hours along the river to Lauterbrunnen (side-tripping to Trümmelbach Falls after 45 minutes). To return to Gimmelwald from Lauterbrunnen, take the cable car up to Grütschalp (10 minutes), then either walk to Gimmelwald (1.5 hours) or take the train to Mürren (10 minutes). From Mürren, it's a downhill walk (30 minutes) to Gimmelwald. (This loop trip can be reversed or started at any point along the way—such as Lauterbrunnen or Mürren.)

Hang Out with BASE Jumpers—In recent years, the Lauterbrunnen Valley has become an El Dorado of BASE jumping (parachuting off cliffs), and each season thrill-seekers hike to the top of a cliff, leap off—falling as long as they can (this provides the rush)—and then pull the ripcord to release a tiny parachute, hoping it will break their fall and a gust won't dash them against the walls of the valley. (For a fascinating look at this sport, search for "BASE jumping Lauterbrunnen" at www.youtube.com.)

Some Swiss consider BASE jumpers reckless and don't respect them. But, like other adventure sports, it is getting safer and more accepted. To learn more, talk with the jumpers themselves, who congregate at the **Pub Horner,** at the upper end of town (near the waterfall). This is the grittiest place in Lauterbrunnen, providing cheap beds and meals for BASE jumpers and the only real after-dark scene in town. Locals, jumpers, and stray tourists gather here in the pub each evening (9 rooms, bunks-32 SF, D-86 SF, cheaper apartments, no breakfast, free Wi-Fi and Internet access for customers, dancing nightly from 22:00 upstairs, tel. 033-855-1673, www.hornerpub.ch, mail@hornerpub.ch, run by Gertsch Ferdinand). Their kitchen sells cheap pastas and raclette, and puts out a nightly salad bar (8-14-SF meals, BBQ dinner-15 SF in summer).

Lauterbrunnen Valley Folk Museum (Talmuseum Lauterbrunnen)—This interesting museum shows off the region's folk culture and two centuries of mountaineering from all the towns of this valley. You'll see lots of lace, exhibits on cheese and woodworking, cowbells, and classic old photos.

Cost and Hours: 3 SF, free with Visitors Card given by local hotels, mid-June–mid-Oct Tue and Thu-Sun 14:00-17:30; closed Mon, Wed, and off-season; English handout, just over bridge and below church at the far end of Lauterbrunnen town, tel. 033-855-3586, www.talmuseumlauterbrunnen.ch.

Sleeping in Lauterbrunnen

(2,612 feet, 1 SF = about $1.10, country code: 41)

$$$ Hotel Silberhorn is a big, formal, 32-room, three-star hotel that still manages to feel family-run. It has generous public spaces and a recommended, elegant-for-Lauterbrunnen restaurant just above the quiet lift station across from the train station. Almost every double room comes with a fine view and balcony (Sb-89-109 SF, Db-159-179 SF, bigger "superior" Db-180-209 SF, Internet access, Wi-Fi, tel. 033-856-2210, www.silberhorn.com, info@silberhorn.com).

$$$ Hotel Staubbach, a big, Old World place, is one of the oldest hotels in the valley (1890). The staff is friendly, and the hotel has the casual feel of a national park lodge, with 30 simple and comfortable rooms. It's family-friendly and has a kids' play area. Rooms that face up the valley have incredible views, though you may hear the happy crowd across the meadow at Pub Horner or the church bells chiming on the hour. If the weather's bad, you can watch a DVD of my Switzerland TV show in the lounge (S-100 SF, Sb-120 SF, D-120 SF, Db-150-170 SF, Tb-210-240 SF, Qb-240 SF, closed Nov–mid-April, elevator, free Wi-Fi, 4 blocks up from station on the left, tel. 033-855-5454, fax 033-855-5484, www.staubbach.com, hotel@staubbach.com, run by American Craig and his Swiss wife, Corinne).

$ Valley Hostel is practical and comfortable, offering 70 inexpensive beds for quieter travelers of all ages, with a pleasant garden and the welcoming Abegglen family: Martha, Alfred, Stefan, and

*(vertical margin text)* GIMMELWALD

Fränzi (D with bunk beds-66 SF, twin D-66 SF, beds in larger family-friendly rooms-28 SF/person, breakfast-6 SF, rooms have no sinks, free kitchen, Internet access, Wi-Fi, coin-op laundry, reception open 8:00-12:00 & 15:00-22:00, 2 blocks up from train station, tel. & fax 033-855-2008, www.valleyhostel.ch, info@valley hostel.ch).

$ Chalet im Rohr—a creaky, old, woody firetrap of a place— has oodles of character (and lots of Asian groups, paragliders, and BASE jumpers). It offers 50 beds in big one- to four-bed rooms that share six showers (28 SF/person, no breakfast, cash only, common kitchen, free Wi-Fi, across from church on main drag, tel. & fax 033-855-2182, www.chaletimrohr.ch, bookings@chaletimrohr .ch, Elsbeth von Allmen-Müller).

$ Matratzenlager Stocki is rustic and humble, with the cheapest beds in town (15 SF with sheets in easygoing little 25-bed co-ed dorm with kitchen, closed Nov-Dec, across river from station, tel. 033-855-1754, run by elderly Frau Graf, who often ignores the phone).

$ *Camping:* Two campgrounds just south of town provide beds in dorms and 2- and 4-bed bungalows (rentable sheets, kitchen facilities, cash only, big English-speaking tour groups). **Mountain Holiday Park-Camping Jungfrau,** romantically situated beyond Staubbach Falls, is huge and well-organized by Hans. It also has fancy cabins and mobile homes you can rent by the week (30-35-SF beds, tel. 033-856-2010, www.camping-jungfrau .ch). **Schützenbach Retreat,** on the left just past Lauterbrunnen toward Stechelberg, is a simpler campground (bed in 6- and 12-bed rooms-17 SF, often full with groups, tel. 033-855-1268, www .schuetzenbach.ch).

Eating in Lauterbrunnen

At **Hotel Restaurant Oberland,** Mark (Aussie) and Ursula (Swiss) Nolan take pride in serving tasty, good-value meals from a fun menu. It's a high-energy place with lots of tourists and a huge front porch good for lingering into the evening (17-SF pizzas, 20-25-SF main courses, traditional Swiss dishes, daily 11:30-21:00, tel. 033-855-1241).

Hotel Restaurant Jungfrau, along the main street, offers a wide range of specialties, including fondue and *Rösti,* served by a friendly staff. Their terrace has a great valley view (daily 12:00-14:00 & 18:00-21:00, tel. 033-855-3434, run by Brigitte Melliger).

Hotel Restaurant Silberhorn is the local choice for a fancy meal out. Call to reserve a view table (18-SF salad plate, 23-35-SF main dishes, daily from 18:00, classy indoor and outdoor seating, above the cable-car station, tel. 033-856-2210).

GIMMELWALD

Airtime Café feels like an alpine Starbucks with hot drinks, homemade treats, breakfast, simple lunches, and light early dinners (7.50-SF sandwiches made to order, 6-SF meat pies). Besides food, they offer other services, including laundry, Internet access, Wi-Fi, and an English-language swap library. They can also help you book adventure-sport activities (May-Oct daily 9:00-19:00, shorter hours off-season, closed Nov, tel. 033-855-1515, www.air time.ch, Daniela and Beni).

Lauterbrunnen Valley Connections

The valley-floor towns of Lauterbrunnen and Stechelberg have connections by mountain train, bus, and cable car to the traffic-free villages, peaks, and hikes high above. Prices and trip durations given are per leg unless otherwise noted.

From Lauterbrunnen by Train to: Interlaken (hourly, 20 minutes, 7.20 SF), **Wengen** (1-2/hour, 15 minutes, 6.40 SF), continues to **Kleine Scheidegg** (hourly, 30 minutes, 30 SF), where you change to a different train to reach the **Jungfraujoch** (2/hour, 50 minutes, 66 SF) or **Grindelwald** (2/hour, 30 minutes, 32 SF).

By Cable Car to: Grütschalp (2/hour, 10 minutes), where you can catch a train to **Mürren** (2/hour, 10 minutes); total trip time 30 minutes, total cost 10.40 SF.

By PostBus to: Schilthornbahn cable-car station (buses depart with the arrival of trains in Lauterbrunnen, 15-minute ride, 4 SF, covered by Swiss Pass), continues to **Stechelberg town.**

By Car to: Schilthornbahn cable-car station (10-minute drive, parking lot: 2 SF/2 hours, 6 SF/day, cash only).

From Schilthornbahn cable-car station near Stechelberg to: Gimmelwald (2/hour, 5 minutes, 5.80 SF), continues to **Mürren** (2/hour, 10 minutes, 10.40 SF) and the **Schilthorn** (2/hour, 20 minutes, 55.20 SF). The cable car runs up from the valley station—and down from Mürren—at :25 and :55 past the hour (5:55-19:55; after 19:55, runs only once an hour until 23:45 Sun-Thu, until 24:55 Fri-Sat). From Gimmelwald to both Mürren and the valley station, the cable car runs at :00 and :30 (6:00-20:00; after 20:00 runs only once an hour).

Gimmelwald

Saved from developers by its "avalanche zone" classification, Gimmelwald was (before modern tourism) one of the poorest places in Switzerland. Its traditional economy was stuck in the hay, and its farmers—unable to make it in their disadvantaged trade—survived only on a trickle of visitors and on Swiss government subsidies (and working the ski lifts in the winter). For some travelers, there's little to see in the village. Others (like me) enjoy a fascinating day sitting on a bench and learning why they say, "If heaven isn't what it's cracked up to be, send me back to Gimmelwald."

Take a walk through the town. The huge, sheer cliff face that dominates your mountain views is the Schwarzmönch ("Black Monk"). The three peaks above (or behind) it are, left to right, Eiger, Mönch, and Jungfrau. While Gimmelwald's population dropped in the last century from 300 to about 120 residents, traditions survive. Most Gimmelwalders have one of two last names: von Allmen or Feuz. They are tough and proud. Raising hay in this rugged terrain is labor-intensive. One family harvests enough to feed only about 15 cows. But they'd have it no other way, and, unlike the absentee-landlord town of Mürren, Gimmelwald is locally owned. (When word got out that urban planners wanted to develop Gimmelwald into a town of 1,000, locals pulled some strings to secure the town's bogus avalanche-zone building code. Today, unlike nearby resort towns, Gimmelwald's population is the same all year.) Those same folks are happy the masses go to touristy and commercialized Grindelwald, just over the Kleine Scheidegg ridge. Don't confuse Gimmelwald and Grindelwald—they couldn't be more different.

Thanks to the leadership of schoolteachers Olle and Maria, and their son Sven, Gimmelwald has a helpful little website (www.gimmelwald.ch), where you can check out photos of the town in different seasons, get directions for 11 of the best hikes out of town, and see all the latest on activities and rooms for rent.

Getting to Gimmelwald

To get from Lauterbrunnen to Gimmelwald, you have two options:

1. Schilthornbahn Cable Car: The faster, easier way—best in bad weather or at the end of a long day with lots of luggage—is to drive. It's 10 minutes from Lauterbrunnen (or 30 minutes from Interlaken) to the Schilthornbahn cable-car station near Stechelberg (parking lot: 2 SF/2 hours, 6 SF/day, cash only).

If you don't have a car, ride the PostBus from Lauterbrunnen to the Schilthornbahn cable-car station (buses depart with the

GIMMELWALD

Gimmelwald

To Gimmeln & Mürren

To Mürren (30-min. Uphill Hike)

To Sprutz Waterfall, Spielbodenalp, Brünli, Rotstockhütte & Schilthorn

WALTER'S HOTEL MITTAGHORN

PAVED ROAD

BENCHES

To Mürren (5 min) & on to Schilthorn (30 min) via lift

FORMER SCHOOL

FIRE STN.

VIA FERRATA SUSPENSION BRIDGE

BENCHES

CABLE-CAR STATION

Cliffs

To Sefinen Valley

Cliffs

Not to Scale

Note: Cable-car station to Walter's = 10-min. walk

To Stechelberg (1 Hour Hike)

To Schilthornbahn Valley Station, Bus Stop & Car Park

1. Olle & Maria's B&B
2. Esther's Guest House
3. Pension Gimmelwald & Honesty Shop
4. Hotel Mittaghorn
5. Liesi's Heart Place
6. Mountain Hostel/Restaurant
7. Erika's Cheese Hut

GIMMELWALD

arrival of trains in Lauterbrunnen, 15-minute ride, 4 SF, www.postauto.ch).

From Schilthornbahn, the cable car whisks you in five thrilling minutes up to Gimmelwald (2/hour at :25 and :55 past the hour 5:55-19:55; after 19:55, runs only once an hour until 23:45 Sun-Thu, until 24:55 Fri-Sat; 5.80 SF, Gimmelwald is the first stop). Note that the Schilthornbahn cable car is closed for servicing for a week in early May and also from mid-November through early December. If you're here during this time, you'll ride the cargo cable car directly from the valley floor up to Mürren, where a small bus shuttles you down to Gimmelwald.

2. Grütschalp Cable-Car and Mürren Train: This is the more scenic route. Catch the cable car from Lauterbrunnen to Grütschalp. As you glide from Lauterbrunnen upward, notice the bed of the 100-year-old funicular train track that the new cable-car recently replaced. At Grütschalp, a special vintage train will roll you along the incredibly scenic cliffside to Mürren (total trip from Lauterbrunnen to Mürren: 30 minutes, 10.40 SF, www.jungfraubahn.ch). From there, either walk to the middle of Mürren and take a left down a moderately steep paved path 30 minutes to Gimmelwald, or walk 10 minutes across Mürren to catch the cable car down to Gimmelwald (5.80 SF).

Self-Guided Walk

Welcome to Gimmelwald

Gimmelwald, though tiny, with one zigzag street, offers a fine look at a traditional Swiss mountain community.

• *Start this quick walking tour at the...*

Cable-Car Station: When the lift came in the 1960s, the village's back end became its front door. Gimmelwald was, and still is, a farm village. Stepping off the cable car and starting up the path, you see a sweet little hut. Set on stilts to keep out mice, the hut was used for storing cheese (the rocks on the rooftop here and throughout the town are not decorative—they keep the shingles on through wild storms). Behind the cheese hut stands the village schoolhouse, long the largest structure in town (in Catholic Swiss towns, the biggest building is the church; in Protestant towns, it's the school). But in 2010, classes ceased. Gimmelwald's students now go to school in Lauterbrunnen, and the building is being used as a chapel when the Protestant pastor makes his monthly visit. Up and across from the station, just beyond the little playground, is the recommended Mountain Hostel and Restaurant.

• *Walk up the lane 50 yards, past the town's Dalí-esque art gallery (Who's showing in the phone booth?), to Gimmelwald's...*

"Times Square": The yellow alpine "street sign" shows where you are, the altitude (1,370 meters, or 4,470 feet), how many hours *(Std.)* and minutes it takes to walk to nearby points, and which tracks are serious hiking paths (marked with red and white, and further indicated along the way with red and white patches of paint on stones). You're surrounded by buildings that were built as duplexes, divided vertically right down the middle to house two separate families. Look for the Honesty Shop at Pension Gimmelwald, which features local crafts and little edibles for sale.

The writing on the post office building is a folksy blessing: "Summer brings green, winter brings snow. The sun greets the day, the stars greet the night. This house will protect you from rain, cold, and wind. May God give us his blessings." Small as Gimmelwald is, it still has daily mail service. The postman comes down from Mürren each day (by golf cart in summer, sled in winter) to deliver mail and pick up letters at the communal mailbox. The date on this building indicates when it was built or rebuilt (1911). Gimmelwald has a strict building code: for instance, shutters can only be painted certain colors.

• *From this tiny intersection, walk away from the cable-car station and follow the town's...*

Main Street: Walk up the road past the gnome greeting committee on the right. Notice the announcement board: one side for tourist news, the other for local news (e.g., deals on chainsaw sharpening, upcoming shooting competitions). Cross the street and peek into the big barn, dated 1995. To the left of the door is a cow-scratcher. Swiss cows have legal rights (e.g., in the winter, they must be taken out for exercise at least three times a week). This big barn is built in a modern style. Traditionally, barns were small (like those on the hillside high above) and closer to the hay. But with trucks and paved roads, hay can be moved more easily, and farm businesses need more cows to be viable. Still, even a well-run big farm hopes just to break even. The industry survives only with government subsidies. As you wander, notice private garden patches. Until recently, most locals grew their own vegetables—often enough to provide most of their family's needs.

• *Go just beyond the next barn. On your right is the...*

Water Fountain/Trough: This is the site of the town's historic water supply—still perfectly drinkable. Village kids love to bathe and wage water wars here when the cows aren't drinking from it. Detour left down a lane about 50 yards (along a wooden fence), passing the lovingly tended pea-patch gardens of the woman with the best green thumb in the village (on your left). Go to the next trough and the oldest building in town, Husmättli, from 1658. (Most of the town's 17th-century buildings are on the road zig-zagging below town.) Study the log-cabin construction. Many are built without nails. The wood was logged up the valley and cut on the water-powered village mill (also below town). Gimmelwald heats with wood, and since the wood needs to age a couple of years to burn well, it's stacked everywhere.

From here (at the water trough), look up at the solar panels on the house of Olle and Maria. A Swiss building code requires that new structures provide 30 percent of their own power, part of a green energy policy. Switzerland is gradually moving away from nuclear power; its last reactor is supposed to close in 2034.

• *Return to the main paved road and continue uphill.*

Twenty yards along, on the left, the first house has a bunch of scythes hanging above the sharpening stone. Farmers pound, rather than grind, the blade to get it razor-sharp for efficient cutting. Feel a blade...carefully.

A few steps farther, notice the cute **cheese hut** on the right. This is Erika's hut, and she loves to sell her alpine cheese to visitors (an arrow points to her house). Its front is an alpine art gallery with nail shoes for flower pots. Nail shoes grip the steep, wet fields—this is critical for safety, especially if you're carrying a sharp scythe. Even today, farmers buy metal tacks and fasten them to boots. The hut is full of strong cheese—up to three years old.

Look up. In the summer, a few goats are kept here (rather than in the high alp) to provide families with fresh milk (about a half-gallon per day per goat). The farmers fence off the fields, letting the goats eat only the grass that's most difficult to harvest.

On the left (at the *B&B* sign) is Olle and Maria's home. Maria runs the **Lilliput shop** (the "smallest shop with the greatest gifts"—handmade delights from the town and region; just ring the bell and meet Maria). She does a booming trade in sugar-coated almonds.

• *Fifty yards farther along is the...*

Alpenrose: At the old schoolhouse, you might see big ceremonial cowbells hanging under the uphill eave. These swing from the necks of cows during the procession from the town to the high Alps (mid-June) and back down (mid-Sept).

• *At the end of town, pause where a lane branches off to the left, leading into the dramatic...*

Sefinen Valley: All the old homes in town are made from wood cut from the left-hand side of this valley (shady side, slow-growing, better timber) and milled at a water-powered sawmill on the valley floor.

• *A few steps ahead, the road switches back at the...*

Gimmelwald Fire Station: The *Föhnwacht Reglement* sheet, posted on the fire-station building, explains rules to keep the village from burning down during the fierce dry wind of the Föhn season. During this time, there's a 24-hour fire watch, and even smoking cigarettes outdoors is forbidden. Mürren was devastated by a Föhn-caused fire in the 1920s. Because villagers in Gimmelwald—mindful of the quality of their volunteer fire department—are particularly careful with fire, the town has not had a terrible fire in its history (a rare feat among alpine villages).

Check out the other posted notices. This year's Swiss Army calendar tells reservists when and where to go (in all four official Swiss languages). Every Swiss male does a 22-week stint in the military, then a few days a year in the reserves until about age 30. The *Schiessübungen* poster details the shooting exercises required this year. In keeping with the William Tell heritage, each Swiss man does shooting practice annually for the military (or spends three days in jail).

• *Take the...*

High Road to Hotel Mittaghorn: The resort town of Mürren hovers in the distance. And high on the left, notice the hay field with terraces. These are from WWII days, when Switzerland, wanting self-sufficiency, required all farmers to grow potatoes. Today, this field is a festival of alpine flowers in season (best at this altitude in May and June).

• *Our walk is over. A peaceful set of benches, just off the lane on the downhill side, lets you savor the view. From Hotel Mittaghorn, you can return to Gimmelwald's "Times Square" via the path with the steps cutting downhill.*

Nightlife in Gimmelwald

These two places provide after-dark entertainment in Gimmelwald. The **Mountain Hostel and Restaurant**, where Petra and her staff serve drinks nightly, is lively with locals and backpackers alike. It's easy to make friends here and share travel experiences. There's a pool table and lots of youthful impromptu fun. **Pension Gimmelwald** (which is next door on the uphill side) offers a mellower scene with an old-time bar, cozy lounge, and view terrace. And from almost anywhere in Gimmelwald, you can watch the sun tuck the mountaintops into bed as the moon rises over the Jungfrau. If that's not enough nightlife, stay in Interlaken.

Sleeping in Gimmelwald

(4,593 feet, 1 SF = about \$1.10, country code: 41)
Gimmelwald is my home base in the Berner Oberland. To inhale the Alps and really hold them in, you'll want to sleep high in Gimmelwald, too. Poor and pleasantly stuck in the past, the village has only a few accommodations options—all of them quirky and memorable. Rates include entry to the public swimming pool in nearby Mürren (at the Sportzentrum—see page 1285).

Be warned: You'll meet a lot of my readers in this town. This is a disappointment to some; others enjoy the chance to be part of a fun extended family.

$$ At Olle and Maria's B&B, the Eggimanns rent two rooms—Gimmelwald's most comfortable—in their quirky but alpine-sleek chalet. Having raised three kids of their own here, Maria and Olle offer visitors a rare and intimate peek at this community (D-130 SF, Db with kitchenette-190 SF for 2 or 200 SF for 3 people, optional breakfast-20 SF, 3-night minimum, cash only, guarantee your reservation with PayPal, free Wi-Fi, laundry service; from cable car, continue straight for 200 yards along the town's only road, B&B on left; tel. 033-855-3575, oeggimann @bluewin.ch).

$$ Esther's Guest House, overlooking the village's main intersection, rents seven clean, basic, and comfortable rooms, three of which have private bathrooms and share a generous lounge and kitchen (S-55-75 SF, big D-130 SF, Db-130 SF, big T-150 SF, Tb-180-190 SF, Q-180 SF, Qb-200-210 SF, family room with private bath for up to 5 people-230 SF, cash preferred, breakfast-15 SF, 2-night minimum, pay Internet access, free Wi-Fi, low ceilings, tel. 033-855-5488, fax 033-855-5492, www.esthersguesthouse.ch, info@esthersguesthouse.ch). Esther, a bundle of entrepreneurial energy, also rents two four-person **apartments** with kitchenettes next door (3-night minimum, see website for details).

$$ Pension Gimmelwald is an old, low-ceilinged farmhouse converted into a family-style inn, with 12 simple rooms, a restaurant, and a cozy bar. Its six-bed dorm attracts more mature guests than your usual hostel. Its terrace, overlooking the Mountain Hostel, has gorgeous views across the valley (bed in 6-bed dorm-25 SF, S-60 SF, D-100 SF, T-150 SF, Q-185 SF, less in winter, 10 percent discount for 3 nights with this book, breakfast-12 SF, Wi-Fi, open June-mid-Oct and mid-Dec-mid-April, 2-minute walk up from cable-car station, tel. 033-855-1730, www.pension gimmelwald.com, tsnewark@yahoo.com, Englishman David).

$$ At Liesi's Heart Place, friendly owner Liesi rents a little suite in her home with a view and terrace (Db-120 SF, Tb-150 SF, Qb-170 SF, minimum 2-night stay, at the town's water fountain find the little house about 100 feet to the left, tel. 033-841-0880, www.liesisheartplace.ch).

$ Hotel Mittaghorn is a classic creaky, thin-walled, alpine-style place with superb views. It's run by Walter Mittler, an elderly Swiss gentleman, with help from trusty Tim. The hotel has three rooms with private showers (first-come, first-served) and four rooms that share a coin-operated shower. Walter's guests-only dinner is the cheapest hot meal in the valley (S-54 SF, D-86 SF, T-129 SF, 6-SF surcharge per person for 1-night stays, cash only, simple but hearty 15-SF dinner at 19:30 by reservation only, free Internet access, open April-Oct, a five-minute climb up the path from the village center, tel. 033-855-1658, www.ricksteves.com/mittaghorn, mittaghorn@gmail.com—email answered May-Sept only). It's necessary to reconfirm by phone the day before your arrival. If no one's there when you arrive, look for a card in the hallway directing you to your room.

$ Mountain Hostel is a beehive of activity, as clean as its guests, cheap, and friendly. The hostel has low ceilings, a self-service kitchen, a mini-grocery, a bar, a free pool table, and healthy plumbing. It's mostly a college-age crowd; families and older travelers will probably feel more comfortable elsewhere. Petra Brunner, who lines the porch with flowers, runs this relaxed hostel with the help of its guests. Read the signs, respect Petra's rules, and leave it tidier than you found it. This is one of those rare spots where a congenial atmosphere spontaneously combusts as the piano plays, and spaghetti becomes communal as it cooks (28 SF/bed in 6- to 15-bed rooms, includes sheets, no breakfast, showers-1 SF, laundry-5 SF, pay Internet access and Wi-Fi, open mid-April-mid-Nov, 20 yards up the trail from lift station, reserve with credit card through website or by phone, tel. 033-855-1704, www .mountainhostel.com, info@mountainhostel.com). The hostel has a full-menu restaurant, described next.

Eating in Gimmelwald

Gimmelwald has two good eating options.

Mountain Hostel Restaurant is open for lunch and dinner and comes with fun, mountain-high energy and a youthful spirit (15-SF plates, popular 17-SF pizzas, daily 12:00-21:00). You can eat inside or with breathtaking views on the terrace.

Pension Gimmelwald Restaurant has a good, simple menu featuring local produce served in a rustic indoor dining room or on a jaw-dropping-view terrace. The atmosphere here is a little more jazz-and-blues mellow (13-22-SF main dishes, daily in summer 12:00-15:00 & 18:00-21:00, bar open until 23:00).

Picnic: Consider packing in a picnic meal from the larger towns. Mürren, a five-minute cable-car ride or a 30-minute hike up the hill, has good restaurants and a grocery (see "Eating in Mürren," later). If you need a few groceries and want to skip the hike to Mürren, you can buy the essentials—noodles, spaghetti sauce, and candy bars—at the Mountain Hostel's reception desk or the little Honesty Shop at Pension Gimmelwald. Farmers post signs to sell their produce. Farmer Erika sells meat, cheese, and eggs—and sometimes bread and milk—from her picturesque hut on the town's main lane (see "Self-Guided Walk," earlier).

Mürren

Pleasant as an alpine resort can be, Mürren is traffic-free and filled with cafés, souvenirs, old-timers with walking sticks, employees enjoying incentive trips, and snap-happy tourists. Its chalets are prefab-rustic. With help from a cliffside train, a funicular, and a cable car, hiking options are endless from Mürren. Sitting on a ledge 2,000 feet above the Lauterbrunnen Valley, surrounded by a fortissimo chorus of mountains, the town has all the comforts of home (for a price) without the pretentiousness of more famous resorts.

Historic Mürren, which dates from 1384, has been over-whelmed by development. Still, it's a peaceful town. There's no full-time doctor, no police officer (they call Lauterbrunnen if there's a problem), and no resident priest or pastor. (The Protestant church—up by the TI—posts a sign showing where the region's roving pastor preaches each Sunday.) There's not even enough business to keep a bakery open year-round (bread is baked down in Lauterbrunnen and shipped up to the "bakery," which is open in-season only)—a clear indication that this town is either lively or completely dead, depending on the time of year. (Holiday population: 4,000. Permanent residents: 400.) Keep an eye open for the "Milch Express," a tiny cart that delivers fresh milk and eggs to hotels and homes throughout town.

Getting to Mürren

There are two ways to get to Mürren: on the train from Grütschalp (10 minutes, connects by 10-minute cable car to Lauterbrunnen, 30-minute total trip) or on the Schilthornbahn cable car from near Stechelberg (in the valley), which stops at Gimmelwald, Mürren, and continues up to the Schilthorn. The train and cable-car stations (which both have WCs and lockers) are at opposite ends of town.

Orientation to Mürren

Mürren perches high on a ledge, overlooking the Lauterbrunnen Valley. You can walk from one end of town to the other in about 10 minutes.

Tourist Information: Mürren's TI can help you find a room and gives hiking advice (July-mid-Sept daily 8:30-19:00, Thu until 20:00, shorter hours off-season, above the village, follow signs to *Sportzentrum*, tel. 033-856-8686, www.mymuerren.ch).

Helpful Hints

Money: An ATM is by the **Co-op** grocery in the middle of town. You can change money at the TI.

Internet Access: Connect at the **TI** (5 SF/15 minutes), at the **cable-car station** inside an old gondola (5 SF/15 minutes), or at the **Eiger Guesthouse** (4 SF/20 minutes, daily 8:00-23:00, across from the train station).

Laundry: Hotel Bellevue has a slick and modern little self-service launderette in its basement (5 SF/wash, 5 SF/dry, open 24/7).

Bike Rental: You can rent mountain bikes at **Stäger Sport** (25 SF/ half-day, 35 SF/day, includes helmet, daily 9:00-18:00, closed late Oct-mid-May, in middle of town, tel. 033-855-2355, www.staegersport.ch). There's a bigger bike-rental place in Lauterbrunnen (Imboden Bike, described on page 1272).

R & R: The slick **Sportzentrum** (sports center) that houses the TI offers a world of indoor activities. The pool is free with the regional Visitors Card given by area hotels (July-mid-Sept daily 8:30-19:00, Thu until 20:00, Sun until 18:00; pool and sauna generally opens at 10:00 Tue-Wed and Fri, otherwise at 13:00; shorter hours off-season, closed May and Nov-mid-Dec, www.muerren.ch/sportzentrum). In season, they offer squash, mini-golf, table tennis, and a fitness room.

Yoga: Denise offers weekly yoga lessons in summer (off Chalet

Mürren

To Birg & Schilthorn

To Birg & Schilthorn

To Gimmeln

UPPER NORTH FACE TRAIL

SUPPENALP

SONNENBERG

LOWER NORTH FACE TRAIL

SCHILTHORNBAHN

CABLE-CAR STATION

OLD HUTS & GARDENS

Service Road Down to Gimmelwald

PAVED ROAD

SCHILTHORNBAHN

OLD SCHOOLHOUSE

5 **6** **3**

8

7 POST

To Gimmelwald & Schilthornbahn Valley Station

"VIA FERRATA"

Cliffs

LIFT FOR SUPPLIES (NOT PEOPLE)

GIMMELWALD

Fontana, mobile 078-642-3485).

Skiing and Snowboarding: The Mürren-Schilthorn ski area is the Berner Oberland's best place for experts, especially those eager to tackle the famous, nearly 10-mile-long Inferno run. The runs on top, especially the Kanonenrohr, are quite steep and have predictably good snow; lower areas cater to all levels, but can be icier. For rental gear, try the friendly, convenient **Ed Abegglen** shop (best prices, next to recommended Chalet Fontana, tel. 033-855-1245), **Alfred's Sporthaus** (good selection and decent prices, between ski school and Sportzentrum, tel. 033-855-3030), or **Stäger Sport** (one shop in Sportzentrum and another on the lower road near cable-car station, tel. 033-855-2330).

Self-Guided Walk

Welcome to Mürren

Mürren has long been a top ski resort, but a walk across town offers a glimpse into a time before ski lifts. This stroll takes you through town on the main drag, from the train station (where you'll arrive if coming from Lauterbrunnen) to the cable-car station, then back

- 1 Hotel Eiger & Eiger Guesthouse
- 2 Hotel Edelweiss & Cafeteria
- 3 Hotel/Restaurant Bellevue & Launderette
- 4 Hotel Jungfrau
- 5 Hotel/ Restaurant Blumental
- 6 Chalet Fontana
- 7 Stägerstübli Restaurant
- 8 Co-op Grocery

To Birg & Schilthorn

ALLMENDHUBEL

To Grütschalp

FUNICULAR

SPORT-ZENTRUM

To Grütschalp & Lift Down to Lauterbrunnen

TENNIS COURTS

TRAIN STATION

Cliffs

Note:
Cable-car station to train station = 10-min. walk

Not to Scale

GIMMELWALD

up to the Allmendhubel funicular station.

• *Start at the...*

Train Station: The first trains pulled into Mürren in 1891. (A circa-1911 car is permanently parked at Grütschalp's station.) A display case inside the station displays an original car from the narrow-gauge, horse-powered line that rolled fancy visitors from here into town. The current station, built in 1964, comes with impressive engineering for heavy cargo. Look out back, where a small truck can be loaded up, attached to the train, and driven away.

• *Wander into town along the main road (take the lower, left fork) for a stroll under the...*

Alpin Palace Hotel: This towering place was the "Grand Palace Hotel" until it burned in 1928. Today it's closed, and no one knows its future. The small wooden platform on the left—looking like a suicide springboard—is the place where snow-removal trucks dump their loads over the cliff in the winter. Look back at the meadow below the station: This is a favorite grazing spot for chamois (the animals, not the rags). Ahead, at Edelweiss Hotel, step to the far corner of the restaurant terrace for a breathtaking view stretching from the big three (Eiger, Mönch, and Jungfrau) on the left to the lonely cattle farm in the high alp on the right. Then look down.

• *Continue toward an empty lot with a grand view.*

Viewpoints: There are plans for a big apartment-hotel to be built here, but the project is waiting for investment money. Detour from the main street around the cliff-hanging tennis court. Stop at one of the little romantic shelters built into the far wall. Directly below, at the base of the modern wall, is the start of a one-mile "trail" with a steel cable *(via ferrata),* which mountaineers use to venture safely along the cliff all the way to Gimmelwald (described later). You can see the Gimmelwald lift station in the distance.

• *Return to the main street and continue to...*

"Downtown" Mürren: This main intersection (where the small service road leads down to Gimmelwald) has the only grocery store in town (Co-op). A bit farther on, the tiny fire barn (labeled *Feuerwehr*) has a list showing the leaders of the volunteer force and their responsibilities. The old barn behind it on the right evokes the time, not so long ago, when the town's barns housed cows. Imagine Mürren with more cows than people, rather than with more visitors than residents.

About 65 feet beyond the fire barn (across the street from the old schoolhouse—Altes Schulhaus), detour right uphill a few steps into the oldest part of town. Explore the windy little lanes, admiring the ancient woodwork on the houses and the cute little pea patches.

• *Back on the main drag, continue to the far end of Mürren, where you come to the...*

Cable-Car Station: The first cable car (goes directly to the valley floor) is for cargo, garbage, and the (reputedly) longest bungee jump in the world. The other takes hikers and skiers up to the Schilthorn and down to the valley via Gimmelwald.

• *Hiking back into town along the high road, you'll enter...*

Upper Mürren: You'll pass Mürren's two churches, the Allmendhubel funicular station, and the Sportzentrum (with swimming pool and TI).

• *Our walk is finished. Enjoy the town and the views.*

Activities in Mürren

During ski season and the height of summer, the Mürren area offers plenty of activities for those willing to seek them out. In spring and fall, Mürren is pretty dead.

Allmendhubelbahn—A quaint-looking but surprisingly rewarding funicular (from 1912, renovated in 1999) carries nature-lovers from Mürren up to Allmendhubel, a perch offering a Jungfrau view that, though much lower, rivals the Schilthorn. At the station, notice the 1920s bobsled. Consider mixing a mountain lift, grand views, and a hike with your meal by eating at the restaurant on Allmendhubel (good chef, open daily until 18:00).

Allmendhubel is particularly good for families. The entertaining Adventure Trail children's hike—with rough and thrilling kid-friendly alpine rides along the way—starts from here. This is also the departure point for the North Face hike and walks to Grütschalp (see page 1299). While at Allmendhubel, consider its Flower Trail, a 20-minute loop with nice mountain views and (from June through Sept) a chance to see more than 150 different alpine flowers blooming.

Cost and Hours: 7.40 SF one-way, 12 SF round-trip, 6 SF round-trip with Swiss Pass, mid-June–mid-Oct daily 9:00–17:00, runs every 20 minutes, tel. 033-855-2042 or 033-856-2141, www .schilthorn.ch.

Mürren Via Ferrata (Klettersteig Mürren)—Mountaineers and thrill-seekers can test their nerves on this one-mile trail along the cliff running from Mürren to Gimmelwald. A *via ferrata* ("way of iron" in Italian) or *Klettersteig* ("climbing path" in German) is a cliffside trail made of metal steps drilled into the mountainside with a cable running at shoulder length above it. Equipped with a helmet, harness, and two carabiners, you are clipped to the cable the entire way. Experienced mountaineers can rent gear (25 SF from the Gimmelwald hostel or Mürren's Intersport) and do it independently; others should hire a licensed mountain guide. For a peek at what you're getting yourself into, search "*via ferrata* Switzerland Murren" at www.youtube.com.

The journey takes about three hours. While half of the route is easily walked, several hundred yards are literally hanging over a 3,000-foot drop. I did it, and through the most dangerous sections, I was too scared to look down or take pictures. Along with ladders and steps, the trip comes with three thrilling canyon crossings—one by zip line (possible with guide only), another on a single high wire (with steadying wires for each hand), and a final stint on a terrifying suspension bridge (which you can see from the Gimmelwald-Mürren cable-car—look for it just above Gimmelwald).

Cost and Hours: 95 SF, includes gear and donation to the Mürren Via Ferrata Association, guided tours in small groups of 4-8, tel. 033-821-6100, www.klettersteig-muerren.ch.

Nightlife in Mürren

These are all good places for a drink after dinner: **Eiger Guesthouse** (a popular sports bar-type hangout with pool tables, games, and Internet terminals), **Stägerstübli** (where old-timers nurse a drink

GIMMELWALD

and gossip), **Hotel Blumental** (with a characteristic cellar—lively when open), and **Hotel Bellevue** (with its elegant alpine-lounge ambience). All of these places are further described under "Sleeping in Mürren" or "Eating in Mürren." In July and August, you can enjoy occasional folkloric evenings (some Wednesdays, at the Sportzentrum—listed earlier, under "Helpful Hints").

Sleeping in Mürren

(5,381 feet, 1 SF = about $1.10, country code: 41)
Prices for accommodations are often higher during the ski season. Many hotels and restaurants close in spring, roughly from Easter to early June, and may also shut down any time between late September and mid-December.

$$$ Hotel Eiger, a four-star hotel dramatically and conveniently situated just across from the tiny train station, is a good bet. Family-run for four generations, Adrian and Susanna Stahli offer all the service you'd expect in a big city hotel (plush lounge, indoor swimming pool, and sauna) while maintaining a creaky, Old World, woody elegance in its 50 rooms. Their family suites, while pricey, include two double rooms and can be a good value for groups of four or five (Db-275-315 SF with grand breakfast, view rooms-about 20 SF extra, discounts for stays of three nights or more, email for best deals, Wi-Fi, tel. 033-856-5454, fax 033-856-5456, www.hoteleiger.com, info@hoteleiger.com). If you opt for their five-course dinner with your reservation, it'll cost you about 50 SF extra per person.

$$$ At **Hotel Edelweiss,** it's all about the location—convenient and literally hanging on the cliff with devastating views. It's a big, modern building with 30 basic rooms and a busy, recommended restaurant well-run by hard-working Sandra and Daniel Kuster von Allmen (Db-145-180 SF depending on view and balcony, 10 percent discount for 2 nights, Wi-Fi, piano in lounge, tel. 033-856-5600, fax 033-856-5609, www.edelweiss-muerren.ch, edelweiss@muerren.ch).

$$$ Hotel Bellevue has a homey lounge, solid woodsy furniture, a great view terrace, the hunter-themed Jägerstübli restaurant, and 19 great rooms at fair rates—most with balconies and views (Sb-105-145 SF, viewless Db-140 SF, view Db-170-190 SF—150 SF if staying 2 nights or more in June or Sept-Oct, free Internet access and Wi-Fi, closed May and Nov, tel. 033-855-1401, fax 033-855-1490, www.muerren.ch/bellevue, bellevue-crystal@bluewin.ch, Ruth and Othmar Suter). In summer, Othmar offers a morning flowers and wildlife tour of Allmendhubel (10 SF includes funicular ride up, Sun at 9:00, 1.5 hours, meet at Allmendhubel funicular station, tel. 078-604-1401).

$$$ Hotel Jungfrau offers 29 modern and comfortable rooms and an apartment for up to 6 people (Sb-95-120 SF, Db-140-200 SF, lower prices are for viewless rooms, email for best deals, elevator, laundry service-15 SF, Wi-Fi, downhill from TI/Sportzentrum, tel. 033-856-6464, fax 033-856-6465, www.hoteljungfrau.ch, mail@hoteljungfrau.ch, Alan and Véronique).

$$$ Hotel Blumental has 16 older but nicely furnished rooms, a fun game/TV lounge, and a recommended restaurant (Sb-75-80 SF, Db-150-170 SF, 10 percent cheaper in Sept-Oct, higher prices are for July-Aug, outside of July-Aug book direct and ask for a 10 percent Rick Steves discount, pay cable Internet and Wi-Fi, tel. 033-855-1826, fax 033-855-3686, www.muerren.ch/blumental, blumental@muerren.ch; Ralph and Heidi, fourth generation in the von Allmen family). Their modern little chalet out back rents six rooms (Db-140-155 SF, includes breakfast in the hotel).

$$ Eiger Guesthouse offers 12 good budget rooms. This friendly, creaky, easygoing home away from home was renovated in 2009 (S-75 SF, Sb-80-95 SF, D-100-120 SF, Db-130-160 SF, bunk Q-180-200 SF, Qb-200-240 SF, special with this book: D-95 SF with a 2-night minimum year-round—making this a great deal for cheap beds in July-Aug; Wi-Fi, game room, terrace, across from train station, tel. 033-856-5460, fax 033-856-5461, www.eigerguesthouse.com, info@eigerguesthouse.com, Ema and Robert).

$ Chalet Fontana, run by charming Englishwoman Denise Fussell, is a rare budget option in Mürren, with simple, crispy-clean, and comfortable rooms (S-45-55 SF, D-75-85 SF, large D-95 SF, T-130 SF, price varies with size of room, cash only, closed Nov-April, fridge in common kitchen, across street from Stägerstübli restaurant in town center, mobile 078-642-3485, www.chaletfontana.ch, chaletfontana@gmail.com). If no one's home, check at the Ed Abegglen shop next door (tel. 033-855-1245, off-season only). Denise also rents a family apartment with kitchen, bathroom, and breakfast (two bedrooms with 3 beds each, 140 SF/2 people, 160 SF/3 people, 200 SF/4 people, 260 SF/6 people).

Eating in Mürren

Many of these restaurants are in or near my recommended hotels. Outside of summer and ski season, it can be hard to find any place that's open (ask around).

Stägerstübli is everyone's favorite Mürren diner. It's the only real restaurant not associated with a hotel. Located in the town center, this 1902 building was once a tearoom for rich tourists, while locals were limited to the room in the back—which is now the nicer area to eat. Sitting on its terrace, you know just who's out and about in town (18-35-SF lunches and dinners, big portions, lovely lamb, daily 11:30-21:00, closed first week of Sept, Lydia).

Hotel Blumental specializes in typical Swiss cuisine, but also serves fish, international, and vegetarian dishes in a stony and woody dining area. It's one of Mürren's most elegant, romantic settings (18-30-SF specials, 21-31-SF fondue served for one or more, 15-SF pastas, daily from 17:00, tel. 033-855-1826).

Edelweiss cafeteria offers lunches and restaurant dinners with the most cliff-hanging dining in town—the views are incredible (pizzas, hearty salads, sandwiches; daily specials around 20 SF, family-friendly, tel. 033-856-5600).

Hotel Bellevue's restaurant is atmospheric, with three dining zones: a spectacular view terrace, a sophisticated indoor area, and the Jägerstübli—a cozy, well-antlered hunters' room guaranteed to disgust vegetarians. This is a good bet for game, as they buy chamois and deer direct from local hunters (lamb or game-34-44 SF, cheaper options as low as 15 SF, mid-June-Oct daily 11:30-14:00 & 18:00-21:00, closed off-season, tel. 033-855-1401).

Supermarket: The **Co-op** is the only grocery store in town, with good picnic fixings and sandwiches (Mon-Fri 8:00-12:00 & 13:45-18:30, Sat until 17:00, closed Sun). Given restaurant prices, this place is a godsend for those on a tight budget.

Wengen

Wengen—a bigger, fancier Mürren on the east side of the valley—has plenty of grand hotels, restaurants, shops, diversions, and terrific views. This traffic-free resort is an easy train ride above Lauterbrunnen and halfway up to Kleine Scheidegg and Männlichen. From Wengen, you can catch the Männlichen lift up to the ridge and take the rewarding, view-filled, nearly downhill "Männlichen-Kleine Scheidegg" hike, rated ▲▲▲ and described on page 1300.

Wengen's **TI** is two blocks from the station: Go up to the main drag, turn left, and it's on the left. They have info on hiking and sell hiking maps (tel. 033-855-1414, www.mywengen.ch).

The **Co-op grocery**, across the square from the train station, is great for picnic fixings, and is larger than most groceries in the area (Mon-Sat 8:00-18:30, closed Sun).

For an overnight stay, consider **Hotel Falken** (www.hotel falken.com), **Hotel Berghaus** (www.berghaus-wengen.ch), **Hotel Schönegg** (www.hotel-schoenegg.ch), or the cheaper **Bären Hotel** (www.baeren-wengen.ch).

Activities in the Berner Oberland

Scenic Lifts and Trains

Enjoying at least one of the two high-altitude thrill rides described here is an essential Berner Oberland experience.

▲▲▲The Schilthorn and a 10,000-Foot Breakfast

The Schilthornbahn cable car carries skiers, hikers, and sightseers effortlessly to the 10,000-foot summit of the Schilthorn, where the Piz Gloria cable-car station awaits, with its solar-powered revolving restaurant, shop, and panorama terrace. At the top, you have a spectacular panoramic view of the Eiger, Mönch, and Jungfrau mountains, lined up on the horizon.

Ascending the Schilthorn: You can ride to the Schilthorn and back from several points—the cable-car station near Stechelberg on the valley floor (95 SF), Gimmelwald (85 SF), or Mürren (74 SF). Snare a 25 percent discount for early and late rides (roughly before 9:00 and after 15:30) and in spring and fall (roughly May and Oct). If you have a Swiss Pass (50 percent discount) or Eurail Pass (25 percent off), you might as well go whenever you like, because you can't double up discounts. Lifts go twice hourly, and the ride from Gimmelwald (including two transfers) to the Schilthorn takes 30 minutes. You can park your car at the valley station near Stechelberg (2 SF/2 hours, 6 SF/day, cash only). For more information, including current weather conditions, see www.schilthorn.ch or call 033-826-0007.

As the cable car floats between Gimmelwald and Mürren you'll see the metal bridge that marks the end of the *via ferrata*. You'll also see fields of wooden tripods, which serve two purposes: They stop avalanches and shelter newly planted trees. Made of wood, they're designed to eventually rot when the tree they protect is strong enough to survive the winter snowpack. From Mürren to Birg, keep an eye on the altitude meter.

At the Top: Head out to the terrace, where information boards identify each peak. The names of the hard-to-miss big three hint at local folklore: The cowled Mönch (monk—note the shape of its peak) fends off the Eiger (ogre) to protect the Jungfrau (maiden—though she hardly seems to need the help). Directional signs point hikers toward some seriously steep downhill climbs. Watch paragliders set up, psych up, and take off, flying

45 minutes with the birds to distant Interlaken. Walk along the ridge out back. This is a great place for a photo of the mountain-climber you. Youth hostelers—not realizing that rocks may hide just under the snow—scream down the ice fields on plastic-bag sleds from the mountaintop. (There's an English-speaking doctor in Lauterbrunnen—see page 1270.)

Inside, Piz Gloria has a free "touristorama" **film** room. The 20-minute video shows the natural wonders of the area, highlights a few activities—including racing down the famous Inferno ski run, briefly shares the story of the Schilthornbahn lift itself, and shows a substantial clip from the 1969 James Bond movie, *On Her Majesty's Secret Service.* That movie used the newly completed station as one of its major film sets.

You can ride up to the Schilthorn and hike down, but it's tough. (Hiking *up* from Gimmelwald or Mürren is easier on your knees...if you don't mind a 5,000-foot altitude gain.) For information on **hikes** from lift stations along the Schilthorn cable-car line, see "Hiking and Biking," later. My favorite "hike" from the Schilthorn is simply along the ridge out back, to get away from the station and be all alone on top of an Alp.

Breakfast at 10,000 Feet: The huge 28-SF "007 Breakfast Buffet" is served 8:00-11:00. The restaurant also serves hot dishes all day at prices that don't rise with the altitude (around 24 SF).

▲▲▲Jungfraujoch

The literal high point of any trip to the Swiss Alps is a train ride through the Eiger to the Jungfraujoch (the saddle between the Mönch and Jungfrau mountains). At 11,300 feet, it's Europe's highest train station. (If you have a heart or lung condition, you may want to check with your doctor before making this ascent.)

Ascending to the Jungfraujoch: Train runs all year to the Jungfraujoch from Lauterbrunnen (166 SF round-trip) and from Kleine Scheidegg (112 SF round-trip). The first trip of the day to the Jungfraujoch is discounted—ask for a Good Morning Ticket and leave the top by 12:30 (first train from Lauterbrunnen—130 SF, leaves about 7:00; from Kleine Scheidegg—90 SF, leaves about 8:00; Nov-April you can get Good Morning rates for the first or second train and return any time that day; confirm all times and prices, 25 percent discount with Swiss Pass and Eurail Pass, railpass holders get a better deal than Good Morning Ticket and can't combine discounts). Pick up a leaflet on the lifts at a local TI (www.jungfraubahn.ch). If it's cloudy, skip the trip; for a terse trilingual weather forecast from the Jungfraujoch, call 033-828-7931.

The ride from Kleine Scheidegg takes about an hour (sit on the right side for better views), including two five-minute stops at stations actually halfway up the notorious North Face of the Eiger.

You have time to look out windows and marvel at how people could climb the Eiger—and how the Swiss built this train track more than a hundred years ago. The second half of the ride takes you through a tunnel inside the Eiger (some newer train cars run multilingual videos about the history of the train line).

At the Top: Once you reach the top, study the Jungfraujoch chart to see your options (many of them are weather-dependent). There's a restaurant, a history exhibit, an "ice palace" (a cavern with a gallery of ice statues), and a 20-minute video that plays continuously. A tunnel leads outside, where you can summer ski (33 SF for gear and lift ticket), sled (free loaner discs with a 5-SF deposit), or hike an hour across the ice to Mönchsjochhütte (a mountain hut with a small restaurant). An elevator leads to the Sphinx observatory for the highest viewing point, from which you can see the Aletsch Glacier—Europe's longest, at nearly 11 miles—stretch to the south. Remember that your body isn't used to such high altitudes. Signs posted at the top remind you to take it easy.

You can combine one of the best hikes in the region—from Männlichen to Kleine Scheidegg—with your trip up to the Jungfraujoch (see page 1300).

Hiking and Biking

This area offers days of possible hikes. Many are a fun combination of trails, mountain trains, and cable-car rides. I've listed them based on which side of the Lauterbrunnen Valley they're on: west (the Gimmelwald/Mürren/Schilthorn side) or east (the Jungfrau side).

On the Gimmelwald (West) Side of the Lauterbrunnen Valley
Hikes from the Schilthorn
Several tough trails lead down from the Schilthorn, but most visitors take the cable car round-trip simply for the views (see "Lifts and Trains," earlier). If you're a serious hiker, consider walking all the way down (first hike) or part of the way down (second hike) back into Gimmelwald. Don't attempt to hike down from the Schilthorn unless the trail is clear of snow. Adequate shoes and clothing (weather can change quickly) and good knees are required. You can visit the Sprutz Waterfall on your way to Gimmelwald.

From the Top of the Schilthorn (very difficult)—To hike downhill from the Piz Gloria revolving restaurant at the peak, start at the steps to the right of the cable, which lead along a ridge between a cliff and the bowl. As you pass huge rocks and shale fields, keep an eye out for the painted rocks that mark the scant trail. Eventually, you'll hit the service road (a ski run in the

Gimmelwald Area Hikes

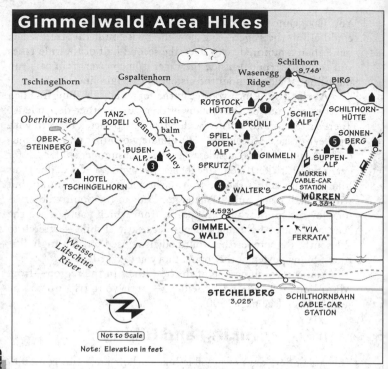

Not to Scale

Note: Elevation in feet

GIMMELWALD

winter), which is steep and not very pleasant. Passing a memorial to a woman killed by lightning in 1865, you come to the small lake called Grauseeli. Leave the gravel road and hike along the lake. From there, follow the trail (with the help of cables when necessary) to scamper along the shale in the direction of Rotstockhütte (to Gimmelwald, see next hike) or Schilttal (the valley leading directly to Mürren; follow *Mürren/Rotstockhütte* sign painted on the rock at the junction).

▲▲**Birg to Gimmelwald via Brünli (moderately difficult)**— Rather than doing the very long hike all the way back down into Gimmelwald, I prefer walking the easier (but still strenuous) hike from the intermediate cable-car station at Birg. This is efficiently combined with a visit to the Schilthorn (from Schilthorn summit, ride cable car halfway down, get off at Birg, and hike down from there; buy the round-trip excursion early-bird fare, which is cheaper than the Gimmelwald-Schilthorn-Birg ticket, and decide at Birg whether you want to hike or ride down).

The most interesting trail from Birg to Gimmelwald is the high one via Grauseeli lake and Wasenegg Ridge to Brünli, then down to Spielbodenalp and the Sprutz Waterfall. Warning: This trail is quite steep and slippery in places, and can take four hours.

Bietenhorn

ALLMENDHUBEL

6

7 WINTEREGG

MÜRREN
TRAIN
STATION

GRÜTSCHALP
4,879'

*Staubbach
Falls*

CAMPING
JUNGFRAU

CAMPING
SCHÜTZENBACH

*Trümmelbach
Falls*

LAUTER-
BRUNNEN
2,612'

To
Interlaken

To Wengen &
Kleine Scheidegg

1 Birg to Gimmelwald
via Brünli

2 Up Sefinen Valley
to Kilchbalm

3 Gimmelwald-
Tanzbodeli-
Obersteinberg-
Stechelberg/
Gimmelwald

4 Sprutz Waterfall

5 North Face Trail
from Allmendhubel

6 Allmendhubel/
Mürren to
Grütschalp

7 Allmendhubel to
Grütschalp via
Winteregg

GIMMELWALD

Locals take their kindergartners on this hike, but it can seem dangerous to Americans unused to alpine hikes. Do not attempt this hike in snow, which you might find at this altitude even in the peak of summer. (Get local advice.)

From the Birg lift station, hike toward the Schilthorn, taking your first left down and passing along the left side of the little Grauseeli lake. From the lake, a gravelly trail leads down rough switchbacks (including a stretch where the path narrows and you can hang onto a guide cable against the cliff face) until it levels out. When you see a rock painted with arrows pointing to Mürren and Rotstockhütte, follow the path to Rotstockhütte (traditional old farm with light meals and drinks, mattress loft with cheap beds), traversing the cow-grazed mountainside.

For a thrill, follow Wasenegg Ridge. It's more scary than dangerous if you're sure-footed and can handle the 50-foot-long "tightrope-with-handrail" section along an extremely narrow ledge with a thousand-foot drop. This trail gets you to Brünli with the least altitude drop. (The safer, well-signposted approach to Brünli is to drop down to Rotstockhütte, then climb back up to Brünli.) The barbed-wire fence leads you to the knobby little summit, where you'll enjoy an incredible 360-degree view and a chance to sign your name on the register stored in the little wooden box.

A steep trail winds directly down from Brünli toward Gimmelwald and soon hits a bigger, easier trail. The trail bends right (just before the farm/restaurant at Spielbodenalp), leading to Sprutz. Walk under the Sprutz Waterfall, then follow a steep, wooded trail that deposits you in a meadow of flowers at the top side of Gimmelwald.

Hikes from Gimmelwald

▲**Up Sefinen Valley to Kilchbalm (easy)**—The trail from Gimmelwald up the Sefinen Valley (Sefinental) is a good rainy-weather hike, as you can go as far as you like. After two hours and a gain of only 800 feet, you hit the end of the trail and Kilchbalm, a dramatic bowl of glacier fields. Snow can make this trail unsafe, even into the summer (ask locally for information), and there's no food or drink along the way.

From the Gimmelwald fire station, walk about 100 yards down the paved Stechelberg road. Leave it on the dirt Sefinental road, which becomes a lane, then a trail. You'll cross a raging river and pass a firing range where locals practice their marksmanship (Fri and Sat evenings; the *danger of fire* sign refers to live bullets). Follow signs to Kilchbalm into a forest, along a river, and finally to the glacier fields.

▲**Gimmelwald-Tanzbodeli-Obersteinberg-Stechelberg/ Gimmelwald (more difficult, for good hikers)**—This eight-hour, 11-mile hike is extremely rewarding, offering perfect peace, very few people, traditional alpine culture, and spectacular views. (There's no food or drink for five hours, so pack accordingly.) The trail can be a bit confusing, so this is best done with a good, locally purchased map.

About 100 yards below the Gimmelwald firehouse, take the Sefinental dirt road (described in previous listing). As the dirt road switches back after about 30 minutes, take the right turn across the river and start your ascent, following signs to *Obersteinberg*. After 1.5 hours of hard climbing, you have the option of a side-trip to Busenalp. This is fun if the goat-and-cow herder is there, as you can watch traditional cheesemaking in action. (He appreciates a bottle of wine from hikers.) Trail markers are painted onto rocks— watch carefully. After visiting Busenalp, return to the main path.

At the *Obersteinberg 50 Min/Tanzbodeli 20 Min* signpost, head for Tanzbodeli ("Dancing Floor"). This is everyone's favorite alpine perch—great for a little romance or a picnic with breathtaking views of the Obersteinberg valley. From here, you enter a natural reserve, so you're likely to see chamois and other alpine critters. From Tanzbodeli, you return to the main trail (there's no other way out) and continue to Obersteinberg. You'll eventually hit the

Mountain Hotel Obersteinberg (see "Sleeping in Obersteinberg," later; American expat Vickie will serve you a meal or drink).

From there, the trail leads to Mountain Hotel Tschingelhorn (see "Sleeping in Obersteinberg," later). About an hour later, you hit a fork in the trail and choose where you'd like your hike to end: back to Gimmelwald (2 hours total) or Stechelberg (near the bottom of the Schilthornbahn cable car, 1.5 hours total).

▲**Sprutz Waterfall (moderately difficult)**—The forest above Gimmelwald hides a powerful waterfall with a trail snaking behind it, offering a fun gorge experience. While the waterfall itself is not well-signed, it's on the Gimmelwald-Spielbodenalp trail. It's steep, through a forest, and can be very slippery when wet, but the actual crossing under the waterfall is just misty.

The hike up to Sprutz from Gimmelwald isn't worth the trip in itself, but it's handy when combined with the hike down from Birg and Brünli (described earlier) or the North Face Trail (see next listing). As you descend on either of these two hikes, the trail down to Gimmelwald splits at Spielbodenalp—to the right for the forest and the waterfall; to the left for more meadows, the hamlet of Gimmeln, and more gracefully back into Gimmelwald.

Hikes from Mürren/Allmendhubel

▲▲**North Face Trail from Allmendhubel (easy and family-friendly)**—For a pleasant two-hour hike, head out along this four-mile trail, starting at 6,385 feet and finishing at 5,375 feet (some stretches can be challenging if you're not in shape). To reach the trail, ride the Allmendhubel funicular up from Mürren (much cheaper than Schilthorn, good restaurant at top, see page 1288). From there, follow the well-signed route, which loops counterclockwise around to Mürren (or cut off at Spielbodenalp, near the end, and descend into Gimmelwald via the Sprutz Waterfall). As this trail doesn't technically begin at Allmendhubel, you'll start by following signs to *Sonnenberg*. Then just follow the blue signs. You'll enjoy great views, flowery meadows, mountain huts, and a dozen information boards along the way, describing the fascinating climbing history of the great peaks around you.

Along the trail, you'll pass four farms (technically "alps," as they are only open in the summer) that serve meals and drinks. Sonnenberg was allowed to break the all-wood building code with concrete for protection against avalanches. Suppenalp is quainter. Lean against the house with a salad, soup, or sandwich and enjoy the view. Just below Suppenalp is a little adventure park with zip lines and other kid-pleasing activities.

Notice how older huts are built into the protected side of rocks and outcroppings, in anticipation of avalanches. Above Suppenalp, Blumental ("Flower Valley") is hopping with marmots. Because

GIMMELWALD

hunters are not allowed near lifts, animals have learned that these are safe places to hang out—giving tourists a better chance of spotting them.

The trail leads up and over to a group of huts called Schiltalp (good food, drink, and service, and a romantic farm setting). If the poles under the eaves have bells, the cows are up here. If not, the cows are still at the lower farms. Half the cows in Gimmelwald (about 100) spend their summers here. In July, August, and September, you can watch cheese being made and have a snack or drink. Thirty years ago, each family had its own hut. Labor was cheap and available. Today, it's a communal thing, with several families sharing the expense of a single cow herder. Cow herders are master cheesemakers and have veterinary skills, too.

From Schiltalp, the trail winds gracefully down toward Spielbodenalp. From there you can finish the North Face Trail (continuing down and left through meadows and the hamlet of Gimmeln, then back to Mürren, with more historic signposts), or cut off right (descending steeply through a thick forest and under the dramatic Sprutz Waterfall into Gimmelwald—see Sprutz Waterfall, previous page, for details).

▲**Allmendhubel/Mürren to Grütschalp (fairly easy)**— For a not-too-tough two-hour walk with great Jungfrau views, ride the funicular from Mürren to Allmendhubel and walk to Grütschalp (a drop of about 1,500 feet), where you can catch the train back to Mürren. An easier version is the lower Bergweg from Allmendhubel to Grütschalp via Winteregg and its cheese farm. For a super-easy family stroll with grand views, walk from Mürren just above the train tracks either to Winteregg (40 minutes, restaurant, playground, train station) or through even better scenery on to Grütschalp (1 hour, train station), then catch the train back to Mürren.

Hikes on the Jungfrau (East) Side of the Lauterbrunnen Valley

▲▲▲**Männlichen-Kleine Scheidegg (easy and with dramatic views)**—This is my favorite easy alpine hike (2.5 miles, 1-1.5 hours, 900-foot altitude drop to Kleine Scheidegg). It's entertaining all the way, with glorious mountain views. If you missed the plot, it's the Young Maiden (Jungfrau), being protected from the Ogre (Eiger) by the Monk (Mönch). Trails may be snowbound into June; ask about conditions at the lift stations or at TIs (see "Jungfraujoch" listing on page 1294).

If the weather's good, start off bright and early. From the Lauterbrunnen train station, take the little mountain train up to Wengen. Sit on the right side of the train for great valley and waterfall views. In Wengen, buy a picnic at the Co-op grocery across from the station, walk across town, and catch the lift to Männlichen, located on the top of the ridge high above you. The lift can be open even if the trail is closed; if the weather is questionable, confirm that the Männlichen-Kleine Scheidegg trail is open before ascending. Don't waste time in Wengen if it's sunny—you can linger back here after your hike.

Riding the gondola from Wengen to Männlichen, you'll go over the old lift station (inundated by a 1978 avalanche that buried a good part of Wengen—notice there's no development in the "red zone" above the tennis courts). Farms are built with earthen ramps on the uphill side in anticipation of the next slide. The forest of avalanche fences near the top was built after that 1978 avalanche. As you ascend you can also survey Wengen—the bright red roofs mark new vacation condos, mostly English-owned and used only a few weeks a year.

For a detour that'll give you an easy king- or queen-of-the-mountain feeling, turn left from the top of the Wengen-Männlichen lift station, and hike uphill 10 minutes to the little peak (Männlichen Gipfel, 7,500 feet).

Then go back to the lift station (which has a great kids' area) and enjoy the walk—facing spectacular alpine panorama views—to Kleine Scheidegg for a picnic or restaurant lunch. To start the hike, leave the Wengen-Männlichen lift station to the right. Walk past the second Männlichen lift station (this one leads to Grindelwald, the touristy town in the valley to your left). Ahead of you in the distance, left to right, are the north faces of the Eiger, Mönch, and Jungfrau; in the foreground is the Tschuggen peak, and just behind it, the Lauberhorn. This hike takes you around the left (east) side of this ridge. Simply follow the signs for Kleine Scheidegg, and you'll be there in about an hour—a little more for gawkers, picnickers, and photographers. You might have to tiptoe through streams of melted snow—or some small snow banks, even well into the summer—but the path is well-marked, well-maintained, and mostly level all the way to Kleine Scheidegg.

About 35 minutes into the hike, you'll reach a bunch of benches and a shelter with incredible unobstructed views of all three peaks—the perfect picnic spot. Fifteen minutes later, on the left, you'll see the first sign of civilization: Restaurant Grindelwaldblick (the best lunch stop up here, open daily, closed Dec and May, described on page 1304). Hike to the restaurant's fun mountain lookout to survey the Eiger and look down on the Kleine Scheidegg action. After 10 more minutes, you'll be at the Kleine Scheidegg train station, with plenty of lesser lunch options (including Restaurant Bahnhof, described on page 1304).

From Kleine Scheidegg, you can catch the train up to "the top of Europe" (see Jungfraujoch listing, earlier), take the train back down to Wengen, or hike downhill (gorgeous 30-minute hike to Wengernalp Station, a little farther to the Allmend stop; 60 more steep minutes from there into Wengen). The alpine views might be accompanied by the valley-filling mellow sound of alphorns and distant avalanches. If the weather turns bad or you run out of steam, catch the train at any of the stations along the way. After Wengernalp, the trail to Wengen is steep and, though not danger-ous, requires a good set of knees. The boring final descent from Wengen to Lauterbrunnen is knee-killer steep—catch the train instead.

▲▲**Schynige Platte to First (more difficult)**—The best day I've had hiking in the Berner Oberland was when I made this demanding six-hour ridge walk, with Lake Brienz on one side and all that Jungfrau beauty on the other. Start at the Wilderswil train station (just outside Interlaken), and catch the little train up to Schynige Platte (6,560 feet; 2/hour, 55 minutes, 35 SF). The high point is Faulhorn (8,790 feet, with its famous mountaintop hotel). Hike to a small mini-gondola called "First" (7,110 feet), then ride down to Grindelwald and catch a train back to your starting point, Wilderswil. Or, if you have a regional train pass (or no car but end-less money), take the long, scenic return trip: From Grindelwald, take the lift up to Männlichen (2/hour, 30 minutes, 36 SF), do the hike to Kleine Scheidegg and down to Wengen (described earlier), then head down into Lauterbrunnen.

For a shorter (3-hour) ridge walk, consider the well-signposted Panoramaweg, a loop from Schynige Platte to Daub Peak.

The alpine flower park at Schynige Platte Station offers a delightful stroll through several hundred alpine flowers (free, June-Sept daily 8:30-18:00, www.alpengarten.ch), including a chance to see edelweiss growing in the wild.

Lowa, a leading local manufacturer of top-end hiking boots, has a promotional booth at Schynige Platte Station that provides free loaners to hikers who'd like to give their boots a try. They're already broken in, but bring thick socks (or buy them there).

If hiking here, be mindful of the last lifts (which can be as early as 16:30). Hiking from First (7,113 feet) to Schynige Platte (6,454 feet) gives you a later departure down and less climbing. The TI produces a great Schynige Platte map/guide narrating the train ride up and describing various hiking options from there (available at Wilderswil Station).

Mountain Biking

Mountain biking is popular and accepted, as long as you stay on the clearly marked mountain-bike paths. You can rent bikes in Mürren (Stäger Sport, see page 1285) or in Lauterbrunnen (Imboden Bike, see page 1272). The Lauterbrunnen shop is bigger, has a wider selection of bikes, and is likely to be open when the Mürren one isn't. The two shops work together: For an 8-SF surcharge, you can pick up your bike at one location and leave it at the other. On trains and cable cars, bikes require a separate ticket.

The most popular bike rides include the following:

Lauterbrunnen to Interlaken: This is a gentle downhill ride on a peaceful bike path across the river from the road (don't bike on the road itself). You can return to Lauterbrunnen by train (13 SF total for bike and you). Or rent a bike at either Interlaken station, take the train to Lauterbrunnen, and ride back.

Lauterbrunnen Valley (between Stechelberg and Lauterbrunnen town): This delightful, easy bike path features plenty of diversions along the way (several listed under "Activities in and near Lauterbrunnen" on page 1272).

Mürren to Winteregg to Grütschalp and Back: This fairly level route takes you through high country, with awesome mountain views.

Mürren to Winteregg to Lauterbrunnen: This scenic descent, on a service road with loose gravel, takes you to the Lauterbrunnen Valley floor.

Mürren-Gimmelwald-Sefinen Valley-Stechelberg-Lauterbrunnen-Grütschalp-Mürren: This is the best ride, but it's demanding—with one very difficult stretch where you'll likely walk your bike down a steep gulley for 500 yards. While you'll be on your bike most of the time, to complete the loop take the cable car from Lauterbrunnen up to Grütschalp and then bike back to Mürren.

More in the Berner Oberland

I'd sleep in Gimmelwald, Mürren, or Lauterbrunnen. But you could also consider the following places.

Sleeping and Eating at or near Kleine Scheidegg
(6,762 feet)

This high settlement above the timberline is where you catch the train up to the Jungfraujoch. All of these places serve meals. Confirm prices and availability before ascending. Note that the last train down to Wengen leaves Kleine Scheidegg at 18:30.

$$$ Hotel Bellevue des Alpes, lovingly maintaining a 1930s elegance, is a worthwhile splurge. Since the 1840s, five generations of von Allmens have run this classic old alpine hotel (subsidized by the family income from Trümmelbach Falls). The hallway is like a museum, with old photos (Sb-220-260 SF, Db-370-540 SF, includes breakfast and sumptuous four-course dinner, open only mid-June–mid-Sept, tel. 033-855-1212, fax 033-855-1294, www .scheidegg-hotels.ch, welcome@scheidegg-hotels.ch).

$$ Restaurant Bahnhof invites you to sleep face-to-face with the Eiger (dorm bed-53 SF with breakfast, 73 SF also includes dinner; D-135 SF with breakfast, D-170 SF with breakfast and dinner; in the train station building, tel. 033-828-7828, www.bahnhof -scheidegg.ch, info@bahnhof-scheidegg.ch).

$ Restaurant Grindelwaldblick, a 10-minute hike from the train station, is more charming, romantic, and remote than Restaurant Bahnhof (40 SF/bed in 6- to 20-bed rooms, includes sheets and breakfast, closed Nov and May, tel. 033-855-1374, fax 033-855-4205, www.grindelwaldblick.ch). The restaurant, with a great sun terrace and a cozy interior, sells good three-course lunches (15-25 SF) and 25-SF dinners.

Sleeping in Stechelberg
(3,025 feet)

Stechelberg is the hamlet at the end of the road up the Lauterbrunnen Valley; it's about a mile beyond the Schilthornbahn lift that goes up to Gimmelwald, Mürren, and the Schilthorn (it's a five-minute PostBus ride or a 20-minute trail walk between the lift station and the village). Beyond Stechelberg lies the rugged Rear Lauterbrunnen Valley, the edge of the Jungfrau-Aletsch-Bietschhorn nature reserve—the most glaciated part of the Alps.

$$ Hotel Stechelberg, at road's end, is surrounded by waterfalls and vertical rock, with a garden terrace, a good restaurant, and 16 quiet rooms—half in a creaky old building, half in a concrete, no-character new building (D-90-120 SF, Db-138, Db with balcony-170 SF, T-165 SF, Tb-210 SF, Q-210 SF, bus stops here 1-2/hour, free Wi-Fi, tel. 033-855-2921, fax 033-855-4438, www .hotel-stechelberg.ch, hotel@stechelberg.ch, Marianne and Otto).

$ The Alpenhof fills a former "Nature Friends' Hut" with cheap beds. Creaking like a wooden chalet built in 1926 should, and surrounded by a broad lawn, it provides a good, inexpensive base for drivers and families (28 SF/bed in 2- to 6-bed rooms, each group gets a private room, breakfast-12 SF, tel. 033-855-1202, www.alpenhof-stechelberg.ch, alpenhof@stechelberg.ch, Diane and Marc). From the Hotel Stechelberg, go up the paved path, go right at the fork, and cross the river; it's on your left.

Sleeping in Obersteinberg
(5,900 feet)

Here's a wild idea: **$$ Mountain Hotel Obersteinberg** is a working alpine farm with cheese, cows, a mule shuttling up food once a day, and an American (Vickie) who fell in love with a mountain man. It's a 2.5-hour hike from either Stechelberg or Gimmelwald. They rent 12 primitive rooms and a bunch of loft beds. There's no shower, no hot water, and only meager solar-panel electricity. Candles light up the night, and you can take a hot-water bottle to bed if necessary (S-85 SF, D-170 SF, includes linen, sheetless dorm beds-68 SF; these prices include breakfast and dinner, without meals S-37 SF, D-74 SF, dorm beds-20 SF; closed Oct-May, tel. 033-855-2033). The place is filled with locals and Germans on weekends, but it's all yours on weekdays. Why not hike here from Gimmelwald and leave the Alps a day later?

APPENDIX

Embassies and Consulates

Austria: US Embassy, Boltzmanngasse 16, Vienna, tel. 01/313-390, embassy@usembassy.at; consular services at Parkring 12a, Mon-Fri 8:00-11:30 by appointment only, after-hours emergency tel. 01/31339, online appointments possible, tel. 01/313-397-535, http://austria.usembassy.gov, consulatevienna@state.gov

  Belgium: US Embassy, 27 Boulevard du Régent/Regentlaan, Brussels, tel. 02-811-4300, Mon-Fri 9:00-18:00, closed Sat-Sun, after-hours emergency call and ask to be connected to the duty officer, http://belgium.usembassy.gov; US Consulate, next door to embassy at 25 Boulevard du Régent/Regentlaan, passport services Mon-Thu 13:30-15:30, Fri 9:00-11:00, closed Sat-Sun

  France: US Embassy, 4 avenue Gabriel, to the left as you face Hôtel Crillon, Paris, Mo: Concorde, tel. 01 43 12 22 22, passport services open Mon-Fri 9:00-11:00, closed Sat-Sun; after-hours emergency call, dial 0, and ask to be connected to the duty officer; online appointments possible, http://france.usembassy.gov

  Germany: US Embassy, Pariser Platz 2, Berlin, tel. 030/83050; consular services at Clayallee 170, Mon-Fri 8:30-12:00 by appointment only, closed Sat-Sun, tel. 030/8305-1200—calls answered Mon-Fri 14:00-16:00 only, after-hours emergency call and ask to be connected to the duty officer, online appointments possible, http://germany.usembassy.gov, acsberlin@state.gov

  Great Britain: US Embassy, 24 Grosvenor Square, London, Tube: Bond Street, tel. 020/7499-9000, passport services available Mon-Fri 8:30-12:00 & 14:00-16:00 by appointment only, http://london.usembassy.gov, SCSLondon@state.gov

  Italy: US Embassy, Via Vittorio Veneto 119/A, Rome, 24-hour

European Calling Chart

Just smile and dial, using this key:
AC = Area Code, LN = Local Number.

European Country	Calling long distance within...	Calling from the US or Canada to...	Calling from a European country to...
Austria	AC + LN	011 + 43 + AC (without the initial zero) + LN	00 + 43 + AC (without the initial zero) + LN
Belgium	LN	011 + 32 + LN (without initial zero)	00 + 32 + LN (without initial zero)
Bosnia-Herzegovina	AC + LN	011 + 387 + AC (without initial zero) + LN	00 + 387 + AC (without initial zero) + LN
Britain	AC + LN	011 + 44 + AC (without initial zero) + LN	00 + 44 + AC (without initial zero) + LN
Croatia	AC + LN	011 + 385 + AC (without initial zero) + LN	00 + 385 + AC (without initial zero) + LN
Czech Republic	LN	011 + 420 + LN	00 + 420 + LN
Denmark	LN	011 + 45 + LN	00 + 45 + LN
Estonia	LN	011 + 372 + LN	00 + 372 + LN
Finland	AC + LN	011 + 358 + AC (without initial zero) + LN	999 (or other 900 number) + 358 + AC (without initial zero) + LN
France	LN	011 + 33 + LN (without initial zero)	00 + 33 + LN (without initial zero)
Germany	AC + LN	011 + 49 + AC (without initial zero) + LN	00 + 49 + AC (without initial zero) + LN
Gibraltar	LN	011 + 350 + LN	00 + 350 + LN
Greece	LN	011 + 30 + LN	00 + 30 + LN
Hungary	06 + AC + LN	011 + 36 + AC + LN	00 + 36 + AC + LN
Ireland	AC + LN	011 + 353 + AC (without initial zero) + LN	00 + 353 + AC (without initial zero) + LN

European Country	Calling long distance within ...	Calling from the US or Canada to ...	Calling from a European country to ...
Italy	LN	011 + 39 + LN	00 + 39 + LN
Montenegro	AC + LN	011 + 382 + AC (without initial zero) + LN	00 + 382 + AC (without initial zero) + LN
Morocco	LN	011 + 212 + LN (without initial zero)	00 + 212 + LN (without initial zero)
Netherlands	AC + LN	011 + 31 + AC (without initial zero) + LN	00 + 31 + AC (without initial zero) + LN
Norway	LN	011 + 47 + LN	00 + 47 + LN
Poland	LN	011 + 48 + LN	00 + 48 + LN
Portugal	LN	011 + 351 + LN	00 + 351 + LN
Slovakia	AC + LN	011 + 421 + AC (without initial zero) + LN	00 + 421 + AC (without initial zero) + LN
Slovenia	AC + LN	011 + 386 + AC (without initial zero) + LN	00 + 386 + AC (without initial zero) + LN
Spain	LN	011 + 34 + LN	00 + 34 + LN
Sweden	AC + LN	011 + 46 + AC (without initial zero) + LN	00 + 46 + AC (without initial zero) + LN
Switzerland	LN	011 + 41 + LN (without initial zero)	00 + 41 + LN (without initial zero)
Turkey	AC (if there's no initial zero, add one) + LN	011 + 90 + AC (without initial zero) + LN	00 + 90 + AC (without initial zero) + LN

- The instructions above apply whether you're calling a land line or mobile phone.

- The international access code (the first numbers you dial when making an international call) is 011 if you're calling from the US or Canada. It's 00 if you're calling from virtually anywhere in Europe (except Finland, where it's 999 or another 900 number, depending on the phone service you're using).

- To call the US or Canada from Europe, dial 00, then 1 (the country code for the US and Canada), then the area code and number. In short, 00 + 1 + AC + LN = Hi, Mom!

emergency line—tel. 06-46741, non-emergency—tel. 06-4674-2420, Mon-Fri 8:30-12:00, closed Sat-Sun, http://italy.usembassy .gov, uscitizensrome@state.gov; US Consulate, Lungarno Vespucci 38, Florence, tel. 055-266-951, http://florence.usconsulate.gov

The Netherlands: US Embassy, Lange Voorhout 102, The Hague, tel. 070/310-2209, visits by appointment only, http://nether lands.usembassy.gov; US Consulate, Museumplein 19, Amsterdam, Mon-Fri 8:30-11:30 by online appointment only, closed Sat-Sun; tel. 020/575-5309 during office hours: Mon-Fri 13:30-16:30, after-hours emergency call officer at tel. 070/310-2209, http: //amsterdam.usconsulate.gov, USCitizenServicesAms@state.gov

Spain: US Embassy, Calle Serrano 75, Madrid, tel. 915-872-240, Mon-Fri 8:30-13:00, emergency tel. 915-872-200, http: //madrid.usembassy.gov

Switzerland: US Embassy, Sulgeneckstrasse 19, Bern, tel. 031-357-7011, Mon-Fri 9:00-11:30 by appointment only, closed Sat-Sun, emergency tel. 031-357-7777, online appointments possible, http://bern.usembassy.gov, bernacs@state.gov

Transportation

This section contains basic information on trains, driving, and flights.

By Car or Public Transportation?

If you're debating between public transportation and car rental, consider these factors: Trains, buses, and boats are best for an ambitious, multi-country itinerary, and especially so for solo travelers, blitz tourists, and city-to-city travelers, and those who don't want to drive in Europe. A car is worth considering for three or more people traveling together (especially families with small kids), or if you're packing heavy, or planning on scouring the countryside. But while a car gives you more freedom—enabling you to search for hotels more easily and carrying your bags for you—trains, buses, and boats zip you effortlessly and scenically from city to city, usually dropping you in the center, often near a tourist office. Cars are great in the countryside, but a worthless headache in places like Rome and Paris.

Trains

A major mistake Americans make is relating public transportation in Europe to the pathetic public transportation they're used to at home. By rail, you'll have Europe by the tail. While many people simply buy tickets as they go ("point to point"), the various train passes give you the simplicity of ticket-free, nearly unlimited

POINT-TO-POINT RAIL TICKETS: COST & TIME

This chart shows the cost of second-class train tickets. Connect the dots of your itinerary, add up the cost, compare it with a railpass, and see what is better for your trip.

— RAIL   --- BUS   ••• BOAT
● CITY COVERED BY EURAIL GLOBAL   ○ CITY NOT COVERED BY EURAIL GLOBAL

First number between cities = Approximate cost in US dollars for a one-way, second class ticket. **Second number** = Number of hours the trip takes.

Important: These fares and times are based on European web sources. Actual prices may vary due to currency fluctuations and local promotions. Local competition can cut the actual price of some boat crossings (from Italy to Greece, for example) by 50 percent or more. For approximate first-class rail prices, add 50 percent. Travel times and fares are for express trains where applicable.

travel, and depending on how many trips you do, often offer a savings over regular point-to-point tickets. Fast, long-distance, international, or overnight trains are more likely to require reservations at some point before boarding; you can make your more critical reservations from home.

For a summary of railpass deals and point-to-point ticket options (available in the US and in Europe), check out our free, annually updated *Guide to Eurail Passes* at www.ricksteves.com /rail. If you decide to get a railpass, this guide will help you know you're getting the right one for your trip. To study ahead on the Web, check www.bahn.com (Germany's excellent Europe-wide timetable).

Eurail Global Pass and Eurail Select Pass

Eurail Global passes offer you nearly unlimited travel on all public railways in 23 European countries. These popular passes give you most of Europe (except Great Britain and some of Eastern Europe) by the tail. Choose between the consecutive-day pass (ranging from 15 days to three months) or the cheaper flexipass (any 10 or 15 individual days in two months). Travel partners (2-5 people traveling together) save 15 percent with Saverpasses, available in consecutive-day and flexipass versions. Youths under 26 travel cheaper with second-class passes (for the rest of us, this pass is only available for first-class travel). Kids under 12 pay half the adult rate.

Eurail Select Passes give you a selected number of travel days in your choice of three, four, or five adjoining Eurail countries, whether connected by rail or ferry (e.g., a three-country Select Pass could cover France, Italy, and Switzerland). Select Passes are fine for a focused trip, but to see the Best of Europe, you'd do best with a Eurail Global pass. These passes also give a 15 percent Saverpass discount to two or more companions traveling together.

Eurail Analysis

For an at-a-glance break-even point, remember that a one-month Eurail Global pass is a good value if, for example, your route is Amsterdam-Rome-Madrid-Paris. Passes pay for themselves quicker in the north, where the cost per mile is higher. Check the Rail Tickets map in this chapter to see if your planned travels merit purchasing a train pass. If it's about even, go with the pass for the convenience of not having to wait in line to buy tickets (on trains that don't require paid reservations) and for the fun and freedom to travel "free." Even if second-class tickets work out a bit cheaper than a first-class pass for travelers over 26, consider the added value of a first-class pass: On a crowded train, your chances of getting a seat are much better if your pass allows you to sit anywhere on the train.

Rail-and-drive passes are popular varieties of many of these passes. Along with a railpass (Eurail Pass, Eurail Select Pass, or individual country), you get vouchers for a few Hertz or Avis car-rental days. These allow travelers to do long trips by train and enjoy a car where they need the freedom to explore. Great areas for a day of joyriding include Germany's Rhine Valley or Bavaria, France's Provence, and the Alps (for "car hiking"). When comparing prices, remember that each day of car rental comes with about $50 of extra expenses (CDW insurance, gas, parking), which you can divide among the people in your party.

Renting a Car

If you're renting a car, bring your driver's license. In some countries (including Austria, Italy, and Spain), you're also technically required to have an International Driving Permit—a translation of your driver's license (sold at your local AAA office for $15 plus the cost of two passport-type photos; see www.aaa.com). While that's the letter of the law in those countries, I've rented many cars in Europe in without ever having—or being asked to show—this permit.

As Europe's internal borders fade, your car comes with the paperwork you need to drive wherever you like in Western and most of Eastern Europe (always check when booking). But if you're heading to a country in far-eastern or southeastern Europe that still has closed borders, state your travel plans up front to the rental company when making your reservation. Some companies have limits on eastward excursions (for example, you can only take cheaper cars, and you may have to pay extra insurance fees). When you cross these borders, you may be asked to show proof of insurance (called a "green card"). Ask your car-rental company if you need any other documentation for crossing the borders on your itinerary.

For trips of at least three weeks, leasing—which includes taxes and insurance—is the best way to go (for more information, see www.ricksteves.com/driving).

Car Insurance Options

When you rent a car, you are liable for a very high deductible, sometimes equal to the entire value of the car. Limit your financial risk by choosing one of these three options: Buy Collision Damage Waiver (CDW) coverage from the car-rental company, get coverage through your credit card (free, if your card automatically includes zero-deductible coverage), or buy coverage through Travel Guard.

Buying CDW insurance is the easiest but priciest option. Using the coverage that comes with your credit card is cheaper, but can involve more hassle. If you're taking a short trip, the cheapest solution is to buy CDW insurance from Travel Guard (tel. 800-826-4919, www.travelguard.com). It's valid everywhere in Europe except the Republic of Ireland, and some Italian car-rental companies refuse to honor it. Various US states differ on which products and policies are available to their residents. For more information, see www.ricksteves.com/cdw.

Theft insurance (separate from CDW insurance) is mandatory in Italy. The insurance usually costs about $15-20 a day, payable when you pick up the car.

Driving

I use the freeways whenever possible. They're free in the Netherlands and Germany; you'll pay about $4-9 per hour in Italy, France, and Spain; roughly $40 for the toll sticker as you enter Switzerland; and about $10 for a toll sticker in Austria. It costs about $20 a day to park safely in big cities, and there's a $16 "congestion charge" to drive in downtown London.

Be warned that driving is restricted in many Italian city centers. If you drive in an area marked *Zona Traffico Limitato* (ZTL, often shown above a red circle), your license plate can be photographed and a hefty (€100-plus) fine mailed to your home without your ever being stopped by a cop.

Cheap Flights

If you're considering a train ride that's more than five hours long, a flight may save you both time and money. When comparing your options, factor in the time it takes to get to the airport and how early you'll need to arrive to check in.

Good comparison search engines for international flights include www.kayak.com and www.hipmunk.com. For comparing inexpensive flights within Europe, try www.skyscanner.com. If you're not sure who flies to your destination, check its airport's website for a list of carriers. Well-known cheapo airlines include easyJet (www.easyjet.com) and Ryanair (www.ryanair.com).

Be aware of the potential drawbacks of flying on the cheap: nonrefundable and nonchangeable tickets, minimal or nonexistent customer service, treks to airports far outside town, and stingy baggage allowances with steep overage fees. If you're traveling with lots of luggage, a cheap flight can quickly become a bad deal. To avoid unpleasant surprises, read the small print before you book.

Resources

Resources from Rick Steves

Rick Steves' Best of Europe 2013 is one of many books in my series on European travel, which includes country guidebooks, city

guidebooks (Rome, Florence, Paris, London, etc.), Snapshot guides (excerpted chapters from my country guides), Pocket Guides (full-color little books on big cities), and my budget-travel skills handbook, *Rick Steves' Europe Through the Back Door*. Most of my titles are available as ebooks. My phrase books—for Italian, French, German, Spanish, and Portuguese—are practical and budget-oriented. My other books include *Europe 101* (a crash course on art and history), *Mediterranean Cruise Ports* (how to make the most of your time in port), and *Travel as a Political Act* (a travelogue sprinkled with tips for bringing home a global perspective). A more complete list of my titles appears near the end of this book.

Video: My public television series, *Rick Steves' Europe,* covers European destinations in 100 shows. To watch episodes, visit www.hulu.com/rick-steves-europe; for scripts and other details, see www.ricksteves.com/tv.

Audio: My weekly public radio show, *Travel with Rick Steves,* features interviews with travel experts from around the world. I've also produced free, self-guided audio tours of the top sights in London, Paris, Florence, Rome, and Venice. All of this audio content is available for free at Rick Steves Audio Europe, an extensive

APPENDIX

Begin Your Trip at www.ricksteves.com

At ricksteves.com, you'll discover a wealth of free information on European destinations, including fresh monthly news and helpful tips from thousands of fellow travelers. You'll find my latest guidebook updates (www.ricksteves.com/update), a monthly travel e-newsletter (easy and free to sign up), my personal travel blog, and my free Rick Steves Audio Europe smartphone app (if you don't have a smartphone, you can access the same content via podcasts). You can even follow me on Facebook and Twitter.

Our **online Travel Store** offers travel bags and accessories that I've specifically designed to help you travel smarter and lighter. These include my popular carry-on bags (roll-aboard and backpack versions), money belts, totes, toiletries kits, adapters, other accessories, and a wide selection of guidebooks, planning maps, and DVDs.

Choosing the right **railpass** for your trip—amidst hundreds of options—can drive you nutty. We'll help you choose the best pass for your needs and ship it to you for free, plus give you a bunch of free extras.

Rick Steves' Europe Through the Back Door travel company offers **tours** with more than three dozen itineraries and 450 departures reaching the best destinations in this book... and beyond. You'll enjoy great guides, a fun bunch of travel partners (with small groups of generally around 24-28), and plenty of room to spread out in a big, comfy bus. You'll find European adventures to fit every vacation length. For all the details, and to get our Tour Catalog and a free Rick Steves Tour Experience DVD (filmed on location during an actual tour), visit www.ricksteves.com or call us at 425/608-4217.

online library organized by destination. Choose whatever interests you, and download it for free at www.ricksteves.com/audioeurope, iTunes, or the Rick Steves Audio Europe smartphone app.

Conversions

Numbers and Stumblers

- Europeans write a few of their numbers differently than we do: 1 = 1, 4 = 4, 7 = 7.
- In Europe, dates appear as day/month/year, so Christmas is 25/12/13.
- Except in Great Britain, commas are decimal points, and decimals commas. A dollar and a half is 1,50, one thousand is 1.000, and there are 5.280 feet in a mile.
- When pointing, use your whole hand, palm down.
- When counting with fingers, start with your thumb. If you hold up your first finger to request one item, you'll probably get two.
- What we Americans call the second floor of a building is the first floor in Europe.
- Europeans keep the left "lane" open for passing on escalators and moving sidewalks. Keep to the right.

Metric Conversions (approximate)

A kilogram is 2.2 pounds, and 1 liter is about a quart, or almost four to a gallon. A kilometer is six-tenths of a mile. I figure kilometers to miles by cutting them in half and adding back 10 percent of the original (120 km: 60 + 12 = 72 miles, 300 km: 150 + 30 = 180 miles).

1 foot = 0.3 meter	1 square yard = 0.8 square meter
1 yard = 0.9 meter	1 square mile = 2.6 square kilometers
1 mile = 1.6 kilometers	1 ounce = 28 grams
1 centimeter = 0.4 inch	1 quart = 0.95 liter
1 meter = 39.4 inches	1 kilogram = 2.2 pounds
1 kilometer = 0.62 mile	32°F = 0°C

APPENDIX

Temperature Conversion:
Fahrenheit and Celsius

For Weather   For Health

Europe takes its temperature using the Celsius scale, while we opt for Fahrenheit. For a rough conversion from Celsius to Fahrenheit, double the number and add 30. For weather, remember that 28°C is 82°F—perfect. For health, 37°C is just right.

Packing Checklist

Whether you're traveling for five days or five weeks, here's what you'll need to bring. Pack light to enjoy the sweet freedom of true mobility. Happy travels!

- ❑ 5 shirts: long- and short-sleeve
- ❑ 1 sweater or lightweight fleece
- ❑ 2 pairs pants
- ❑ 1 pair shorts
- ❑ 1 swimsuit
- ❑ 5 pairs underwear and socks
- ❑ 1 pair shoes
- ❑ 1 rainproof jacket with hood
- ❑ Tie or scarf
- ❑ Money belt
- ❑ Money—your mix of:
  - ❑ Debit card (for ATM withdrawals)
  - ❑ Credit card
  - ❑ Hard cash (in easy-to-exchange $20 bills)
- ❑ Documents plus photocopies:
  - ❑ Passport
  - ❑ Printout of airline eticket
  - ❑ Driver's license
  - ❑ Student ID and hostel card
  - ❑ Railpass/car rental voucher
  - ❑ Insurance details
- ❑ Daypack
- ❑ Electronics—your choice of:
  - ❑ Camera (and related gear)
  - ❑ Computer/mobile devices (phone, MP3 player, ereader, etc.)
  - ❑ Chargers for each of the above
  - ❑ Plug adapter
- ❑ Empty water bottle

- ❑ Wristwatch and alarm clock
- ❑ Earplugs
- ❑ Toiletries kit
  - ❑ Toiletries
  - ❑ Medicines and vitamins
  - ❑ First-aid kit
  - ❑ Glasses/contacts/sunglasses (with prescriptions)
- ❑ Sealable plastic baggies
- ❑ Laundry soap
- ❑ Clothesline
- ❑ Small towel
- ❑ Sewing kit
- ❑ Travel information (guidebooks and maps)
- ❑ Address list (for sending postcards)
- ❑ Postcards and photos from home
- ❑ Notepad and pen
- ❑ Journal

If you plan to carry on your luggage, note that all liquids must be in 3.4-ounce or smaller containers and fit within a single quart-size sealable baggie. For details, see www.tsa.gov/travelers.

Hotel Reservation

To: _____   _____
          hotel   *email or fax*

From: _____   _____
          name   *email or fax*

Today's date: _____ / _____ / _____
                    day   *month*   *year*

Dear Hotel _____ ,
Please make this reservation for me:

Name: _____

Total # of people: _____   # of rooms: _____   # of nights: _____

Arriving: _____ /_____/ _____   My time of arrival (24-hr clock): _____
              day   *month*   *year*   (I will telephone if I will be late)

Departing: ____ /____ /_____
                day   *month*   *year*

Room(s): Single____   Double ____   Twin ____   Triple ____   Quad____

With: Toilet _____   Shower_____   Bath _____   Sink only ____

Special needs: View____   Quiet____   Cheapest ____   Ground Floor____

Please email or fax confirmation of my reservation, along with the type of
room reserved and the price. Please also inform me of your cancellation
policy. After I hear from you, I will quickly send my credit-card information
as a deposit to hold the room. Thank you.

_____
Name

_____
Address

_____
City   *State*   *Zip Code*   *Country*

*Before hoteliers can make your reservation, they want to know the informa-
tion listed above. You can use this form as the basis for your email, or you can
photocopy this page, fill in the information, and send it as a fax (also available
online at www.ricksteves.com/reservation).*

INDEX

D

INDEX

INDEX

INDEX

INDEX

MAP INDEX

Audio Europe

Rick's Free Travel App

Get your FREE **Rick Steves Audio Europe**™ app to enjoy…

- Dozens of self-guided tours of Europe's top museums, sights and historic walks
- Hundreds of tracks filled with cultural insights and sightseeing tips from Rick's radio interviews
- All organized into handy geographic playlists
- For iPhone, iPad, iPod Touch, Android

With Rick whispering in your ear, Europe gets even better.

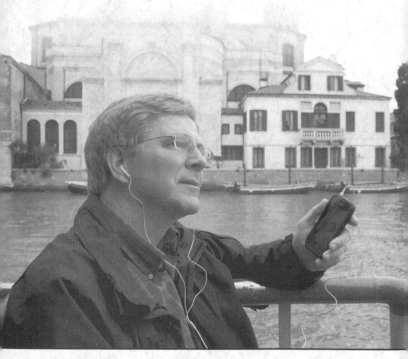

Find out more at ricksteves.com

Start your trip at

Free information and great gear to

▸ Plan Your Trip

Browse thousands of articles and a wealth of money-saving tips for planning your dream trip. You'll find up-to-date information on Europe's best destinations, packing smart, getting around, finding rooms, staying healthy, avoiding scams and more.

▸ Eurail Passes

Find out, step-by-step, if a railpass makes sense for your trip—and how to avoid buying more than you need. Get free shipping on online orders

▸ Graffiti Wall & Travelers Helpline

Learn, ask, share—our online community of savvy travelers is a great resource for first-time travelers to Europe, as well as seasoned pros.

Rick Steves' Europe Through the Back Door, Inc

Rick Steves®

www.ricksteves.com

EUROPE GUIDES

Best of Europe
Eastern Europe
Europe Through the Back Door
Mediterranean Cruise Ports

COUNTRY GUIDES

Croatia & Slovenia
England
France
Germany
Great Britain
Ireland
Italy
Portugal
Scandinavia
Spain
Switzerland

CITY & REGIONAL GUIDES

Amsterdam, Bruges & Brussels
Barcelona
Budapest
Florence & Tuscany
Athens & the Peloponnese
Istanbul
London
Paris
Prague & the Czech Republic
Provence & the French Riviera
Rome
Venice
Vienna, Salzburg & Tirol

SNAPSHOT GUIDES

Barcelona
Berlin
Bruges & Brussels
Copenhagen & the Best of
    Denmark
Dublin
Dubrovnik
Hill Towns of Central Italy
Italy's Cinque Terre
Krakow, Warsaw & Gdansk
Lisbon
Madrid & Toledo
Munich, Bavaria & Salzburg
Naples & the Amalfi Coast
Northern Ireland
Norway
Scotland
Sevilla, Granada & Southern Spain
Stockholm

POCKET GUIDES

Athens
London
Paris
Rome

TRAVEL CULTURE

Europe 101
European Christmas
Postcards from Europe
Travel as a Political Act

NOW AVAILABLE:
eBOOKS, DVD & BLU-RAY

eBOOKS

Most guides are available as eBooks from Amazon, Barnes & Noble, Borders, Apple, and Sony. Free apps for eBook reading are available in the Apple App Store and Android Market, and eBook readers such as Kindle, Nook, and Kobo all have free apps that work on smartphones.

RICK STEVES' EUROPE DVDs

10 New Shows 2011–2012
Austria & the Alps
Eastern Europe
England & Wales
European Christmas
European Travel Skills & Specials
France
Germany, BeNeLux & More
Greece & Turkey
Iran
Ireland & Scotland
Italy's Cities
Italy's Countryside
Scandinavia
Spain
Travel Extras

BLU-RAY

Celtic Charms
Eastern Europe Favorites
European Christmas
Italy Through the Back Door
Mediterranean Mosaic
Surprising Cities of Europe

PHRASE BOOKS & DICTIONARIES

French
French, Italian & German
German
Italian
Portuguese
Spanish

JOURNALS

Rick Steves' Pocket Travel Journal
Rick Steves' Travel Journal

PLANNING MAPS

Britain, Ireland & London
Europe
France & Paris
Germany, Austria & Switzerland
Ireland
Italy
Spain & Portugal

Rick Steves books and DVDs are available at bookstores and through online booksellers.

Credits

Contributors
Gene Openshaw

Gene is a writer, composer, and lecturer on art and history. Specializing in writing walking tours of Europe's cultural sights, Gene has co-authored 10 of Rick's books. When not traveling, Gene enjoys composing music, recovering from his 1973 trip to Europe with Rick, and living everyday life with his daughter.

Steve Smith

Steve manages tour planning for Rick Steves' Europe Through the Back Door and co-authors the France guidebooks with Rick. Fluent in French, he's lived in France on several occasions, starting when he was seven, and has traveled there annually since 1986.

Researchers
Amanda Buttinger

Amanda moved to Madrid in 1998, thinking she'd be there a year. Since then she's found many reasons to stay, from learning more Spanish to guiding and travel writing to the best of all—sunny city walks with her dog and her boys.

Ben Cameron

Ben experienced his first taste of European travel when he was three, exploring medieval castles with his parents. Returning after graduation, he was hooked and has spent much of his time since exploring Europe independently and leading tours for Rick Steves. When not living out of his backpack, Ben splits his time between Rome and Seattle.

Cameron Hewitt

Cameron writes and edits guidebooks for Rick Steves, specializing in Eastern Europe. For this book, Cameron updated the chapters on Vienna and London. He lives in Seattle with his wife Shawna.

Karin Kibby

Having lived in Italy for more than 10 years, Karin guides Rick Steves tours, researches guidebooks, and helps private travelers get in touch with the real Tuscany. When she's not working, you'll find her with her husband skiing in the Alps, exploring Italian islands by boat, and hanging out with friends and family in Tuscany.

Marijan Kriškovič

Born and raised in Slovenia and Croatia, Marijan got hooked on *Kaffee und Kuchen* (coffee and dessert) while visiting German relatives. He lives in Ljubljana with his wife, Barbara, and cat, John Travolta III. Whether leading a Rick Steves tour or at home, Marijan is probably drinking *Kaffee* and eating *Kuchen* right now.

Kristen Kusnic Michel

Kristen, a native of Seattle, first came to Europe as an exchange student, studying theater. Years later, she is fluent in French, German, red wine, and dark chocolate. For the last decade, she's been leading tours and researching guidebooks for Rick Steves. She lives in Paris with her husband, Sylvain.

Sarah Murdoch

Sarah developed a fascination for Britain over tea and games of whist with her English grandmother. London—full of bookshops, museums, markets, and delicious British accents—is Sarah's idea of heaven. When not tracking down the perfect scone or leading tours for Rick Steves, she lives in Seattle with her understanding husband Patrick and their sons Lucca and Nicola.

Gretchen Strauch

Before Gretchen became a guidebook editor for Rick Steves, she lived in Europe for four years: studying in Scotland, teaching in Germany, and traveling constantly. She gladly attempts Dutch pronunciation in return for the tulips, pancakes, and canals, and she'd do just about anything for a fresh Liège waffle.

Ian Watson

Ian has worked with Rick's guidebooks since 1993, after starting out with Let's Go and Frommer's guides. Originally from upstate New York, Ian speaks several European languages and makes his home in Reykjavík, Iceland.

Chapter Images

Location	Photographer
Introduction	
Gondolas in Venice	Dominic Bonuccelli
Austria	
Full-page image:	
Vienna—St. Peter's Church	Cameron Hewitt
Vienna—Belvedere Palace Grounds	Cameron Hewitt
Salzburg	Gretchen Strauch
Hallstatt	Gretchen Strauch
Belgium	
Full-page image: Bruges Market Square	Cameron Hewitt
Bruges Canal	Dominic Bonuccelli
France	
Full-page image: Paris—	
Venus de Milo, Louvre Museum	Rob Unck
Paris—The Seine	Ben Cameron
Provence—Pont du Gard	Rick Steves
The French Riviera—Nice	Cameron Hewitt
Germany	
Full-page image: Munich—Marienplatz	Cameron Hewitt
Bavaria—Neuschwanstein Castle	Dominic Bonuccelli
Rothenburg	Ben Cameron
Rhine River	Dominic Bonuccelli
Berlin—Gendarmenmarkt	Cameron Hewitt
Great Britain	
Full-page image:	
London's British Museum	Rick Steves
London—Houses of Parliament	Rick Steves
Italy	
Full-page image: Florence—	
Michelangelo's David	Rick Steves
Rome—Forum	Ben Cameron
Venice—Gondolier	Dominic Bonuccelli
Florence—Ponte Vecchio	Ben Cameron
The Cinque Terre—Vernazza	Dominic Bonuccelli
Netherlands	
Full-page image: Amsterdam	Rick Steves
Amsterdam—Canal	Rick Steves
Haarlem—Canal	Gretchen Strauch

Spain
Full-page image: Casa Mila, Barcelona
Barcelona—Catalan Art Museum

Cameron Hewitt
Cameron Hewitt

Switzerland
Full-page image: Gimmelwald
Gimmelwald

Dominic Bonuccelli
Cameron Hewitt

Avalon Travel
a member of the Perseus Books Group
1700 Fourth Street
Berkeley, CA 94710, USA

Maps © 2012, 2011, 2010, 2009, 2008, 2007 by Europe Through the Back Door
Printed in Canada by Friesens
First printing September 2012

For the latest on Rick's lectures, guidebooks, tours, public radio show, and public television
series, contact Europe Through the Back Door, Box 2009, Edmonds, WA 98020, 425/771-
8303, fax 425/771-0833, www.ricksteves.com, rick@ricksteves.com.

ISBN: 978-1-61238-371-2
ISSN: 1096-7702

Europe Through the Back Door

Managing Editor: Risa Laib
Editors and Researchers: Gretchen Strauch, Tom Griffin, Suzanne Kotz, Cameron
    Hewitt, Cathy MacDonald, Cathy Lu, Sheridan Smalley
Graphic Content Director: Laura VanDeventer
Maps and Graphics: David C. Hoerlein, Laura VanDeventer, Lauren Mills, Twozdai
    Hulse, Barb Geisler

Avalon Travel

Senior Editor and Series Manager: Madhu Prasher
Associate Editor: Jamie Andrade
Assistant Editor: Nikki Ioakimedes
Editorial Intern: Jessica Garcia
Proofreader: Rebecca Freed
Indexer: Stephen Callahan
Production and Typesetting: McGuire Barber Design
Cover Design: Kimberly Glyder Design
Maps and Graphics: Mike Morgenfeld, Brice Ticen, Kat Bennett, Chris Markiewicz
Front Matter Color Photos: Page i: Reichstag Dome, Berlin © Laura VanDeventer
Front Cover Photo: Bruges, Belgium © Gretchen Strauch

ABOUT THE AUTHOR

RICK STEVES

 Since 1973, Rick Steves has spent 100 days every year exploring Europe. Along with writing a bestselling series of guidebooks, Rick produces a public television series (*Rick Steves' Europe*), a public radio show (*Travel with Rick Steves*), and a podcast (*Rick Steves Audio Europe*); writes a nationally syndicated newspaper column; organizes guided tours that take thousands of travelers to Europe annually; and offers an information-packed website (www.ricksteves.com). With the help of his hardworking staff of 80 at Europe Through the Back Door—in Edmonds, Washington, just north of Seattle—Rick's mission is to make European travel fun, affordable, and culturally enlightening for Americans.

You can connect with Rick at:

f facebook.com/RickSteves

twitter: @RickSteves